THE OXFORD HAND

MEDIEVAL
PHILOSOPHY

THE OXFORD HANDBOOK OF

MEDIEVAL PHILOSOPHY

Edited By

JOHN MARENBON

OXFORD
UNIVERSITY PRESS

OXFORD
UNIVERSITY PRESS

Oxford University Press is a department of the University of Oxford.
It furthers the University's objective of excellence in research, scholarship,
and education by publishing worldwide.

Oxford   New York
Auckland   Cape Town   Dar es Salaam   Hong Kong   Karachi
Kuala Lumpur   Madrid   Melbourne   Mexico City   Nairobi
New Delhi   Shanghai   Taipei   Toronto

With offices in
Argentina   Austria   Brazil   Chile   Czech Republic   France   Greece
Guatemala   Hungary   Italy   Japan   Poland   Portugal   Singapore
South Korea   Switzerland   Thailand   Turkey   Ukraine   Vietnam

Oxford is a registered trade mark of Oxford University Press
in the UK and certain other countries.

Published in the United States of America by
Oxford University Press
198 Madison Avenue, New York, NY 10016

Library of Congress Cataloging-in-Publication Data
The Oxford handbook of medieval philosophy / edited by John Marenbon.
    p.   cm.—(Oxford handbooks)
ISBN 978-0-19-537948-8 (hardcover : alk. paper); 978-0-19-024697-6 (paperback : alk. paper)
1. Philosophy, Medieval. I. Marenbon, John.
B721.O94   2012
189—dc23   2011022383

1 3 5 7 9 8 6 4 2

Contents

....

Contributors

....

PETER ADAMSON is Professor of Late Ancient and Arabic Philosophy at the Ludwig-Maximilians-Universität, Munich. He is the author of the monographs *The Arabic Plotinus* and *Al-Kindi*, and has edited numerous books on Arabic philosophy. He is currently at work on a monograph devoted to Abu Bakr al-Razi.

ANDREW ARLIG is Associate Professor of Philosophy at Brooklyn College, The City University of New York. He works primarily on medieval metaphysics, especially at present on medieval theories of parts and wholes.

BÖRJE BYDÉN is a Research Fellow at the University of Gothenburg. His main interests lie in the history and reception of Greek thought and learning. He has published a monograph on Theodore Metochites and a number of articles on various aspects of Byzantine philosophy. He is currently preparing the *editio princeps* of Metochites's commentary on Aristotle's *De anima*.

MARGARET CAMERON is Canada Research Council Chair in philosophy and Associate Professor at the University of Victoria. Her primary research interests are the history of the philosophy of language and the medieval Aristotelian tradition. She has published on Boethius's philosophy of language in the *Cambridge Companion to Boethius*, and co-edited *Methods and Methodologies in Aristotelian Medieval Logic*. Currently she is co-editing *Linguistic Meaning: Essays in the History of the Philosophy of Language*.

LAURENT CESALLI is Professor of Medieval Philosophy at the University of Geneva. He works on semantics, philosophy of mind and ontology in medieval philosophy (twelfth–fourteenth centuries) as well as in the Austro-German tradition (late nineteenth–early twentieth century).

RICHARD CROSS is John A. O'Brien Professor of Philosophy at the University of Notre Dame. He is the author of *Duns Scotus on God* (Ashgate, 2005).

MATTEO DI GIOVANNI is Assistant to the Chair of Late Ancient and Arabic Philosophy at the Ludwig-Maximilians-Universität, Munich. He works on the Aristotelian tradition in Arabic philosophy. Among his publications are 'Averroes and the Logical Status of Metaphysics' (2011) and 'The Commentator: Averroes's Reading of the Metaphysics' (2014).

CHRISTOPHE ERISMANN is SNF Professor of Medieval Philosophy at the University of Lausanne, Switzerland. He has published articles on the problems of essence, universals and individuation during Late Antiquity and the Early Middle Ages.

RUSSELL L. FRIEDMAN is professor at the Institute of Philosophy, Katholieke Universiteit Leuven. His publications include *Medieval Trinitarian Thought from Aquinas to Ockham* (2010). His main academic interests are medieval Trinitarian theology and philosophical psychology, and genres of medieval philosophical discourse.

NADJA GERMANN is Junior Professor of Arabic Philosophy at the Albert-Ludwigs-Universität, Freiburg. She works on metaphysics, epistemology and semantics in medieval Arabic philosophy (9th–12th centuries) as well as on natural philosophy in early Latin thought (11th–12th centuries).

STEVEN HARVEY is Professor of Philosophy at Bar-Ilan University. He has published extensively on the medieval Jewish and Islamic philosophers, with special focus on Averroes's commentaries on Aristotle and on the influence of the Islamic philosophers on Jewish thought. He is the author of *Falaquera's* Epistle of the Debate: *An Introduction to Jewish Philosophy* (1987) and editor of *The Medieval Hebrew Encyclopedias of Science and Philosophy* (2000) and *Anthology of the Writings of Avicenna* (2009, in Hebrew).

KATERINA IERODIAKONOU is Associate Professor of Ancient Philosophy at the University of Athens and at the University of Geneva. She has published extensively on ancient and Byzantine philosophy, especially in the areas of epistemology and logic. She is currently working on a book about ancient theories of colour.

TERENCE IRWIN is Professor of Ancient Philosophy at the University of Oxford and a Fellow of Keble College. He is the author of: *Plato's Gorgias (translation and notes)* (1979); *Aristotle's Nicomachean Ethics* (translation and notes), (1999, 2nd edn); *Aristotle's First Principles* (1988); *Classical Thought* (1989); *Plato's Ethics* (1995); *The Development of Ethics,* 3 vols. (2007–9).

PETER KING is Professor of Philosophy and of Mediaeval Studies at the University of Toronto (since 2003). After a Ph.D. at Princeton (1982), he taught at Fordham University (1981–1982), the University of Pittsburgh (1982–1989), and The Ohio State University (1989–2002). Most recently he has published *Augustine: On the Free Choice of the Will, On Grace and Free Choice, and Other Writings* (2010), and he is currently working on editions of Peter Abelard.

GYULA KLIMA is Professor of Philosophy at Fordham University in New York, N.Y. He specialises in medieval logic and metaphysics and their bearing on understanding present-day philosophical problems. His books include *John Buridan* (2009), *Medieval Philosophy: Essential Readings with Commentary* (2007), *John Buridan: Summulae de Dialectica: An Annotated Translation with a Philosophical Introduction* (2001), and *ARS ARTIUM: Essays in Philosophical Semantics, Medieval and Modern* (1988).

SIMO KNUUTTILA is Professor of Thelogical Ethics and the Philosophy of Religion at the University of Helsinki. His publications include *Modalities in Medieval Philosphy* (1993) and *Emotions in Ancient and Medieval Philosophy* (2006).

TANELI KUKKONEN is Senior Lecturer in Religious Studies at the University of Otago. He has published widely on topics in Arabic philosophy and the Aristotelian commentary tradition.

HENRIK LAGERLUND is an Associate Professor and the Chair of Philosophy at the University of Western Ontario. He has published numerous articles in medieval philosophy, and his books include: *Modal Syllogistics in the Middle Ages* (2000), *Representation and Objects of Thought in Medieval Philosophy* (2007), and *Rethinking the History of Skepticism* (2010). He is also the editor-in-chief of the *Encyclopedia of Medieval Philosophy* (2010).

MARTIN LENZ is Associate Professor of Philosophy at the University of Groningen. He works on the philosophy of language and mind, and on epistemology; his historical research is on medieval and modern philosophy. After obtaining his Ph.D. (Bochum 2001), he was Visiting Scholar at the University of Cambridge (2002–2004). From 2004, he was Research Associate at the Free University Berlin, and from 2006 at Humboldt University (Habilitation in 2009). From 2009 to 2010 he was Visiting Professor at Tübingen University. His publications include: 'Peculiar Perfection: Peter Abelard on Propositional Attitudes' (2005), 'Why Is Thought Linguistic? Ockham's Two Conceptions of the Intellect' (2008) and *Lockes Sprachkonzeption* (2010).

ANTHONY J. LISSKA is Maria Theresa Barney Professor of Philosophy at Denison University, and was the 1994 Carnegie Foundation United States Baccalaureate Colleges Professor of the Year and the 2006 President of the American Catholic Philosophical Association. His *Aquinas's Theory of Natural Law* was published in 1996; recent essays have appeared in *The Routledge Companion to Ethics*, *Semiotica*, and *A History of the Philosophy of Law from the Ancient Greeks to the Scholastics*.

CHARLES H. MANEKIN Professor of Philosophy, and the Director of the Joseph and Rebecca Meyerhoff Center for Jewish Studies, at the University of Maryland, where he specializes in the history of medieval Jewish philosophy. He is the author of *The Logic of Gersonides*, *On Maimonides*, *Medieval Jewish Philosophical Texts*, and numerous studies.

JOHN MARENBON is Senior Research Fellow, Trinity College, Cambridge, and Honorary Professor of Medieval Philosophy at the University of Cambridge. He has recently published *Medieval Philosophy: An Historical and Philosophical Introduction* (2007) and, as editor, *The Cambridge Companion to Boethius* (2009).

CHRISTOPHER J. MARTIN teaches philosophy at the University of Auckland and has published widely on ancient and medieval logic.

CARY J. NEDERMAN is Professor of Political Science at Texas A&M University and the author or editor of more than twenty books, including, most recently, *Mind Matters: Medieval and Early Modern Essays in Honour of Marcia Colish* (2010), *Lineages of European Political Thought: Explorations along the Medieval/Modern Divide* (2009), and *Machiavelli* (2009).

GRAHAM OPPY is Professor of Philosophy at Monash University. He is author of *Ontological Arguments and Belief in God* (1996), *Arguing about Gods* (2006), *Reading Philosophy of Religion* (2010, with Michael Scott), *The Best Argument against God* (2013), *Reinventing Philosophy of Religion* (2014), and *Describing Gods: An Investigation of Divine Attributes* (2014). He has edited *The History of Western Philosophy of Religion* (OUP, 2009, five volumes, with Nick Trakakis).

CLAUDE PANACCIO holds the Canada Research Chair in the Theory of Knowledge at the University of Quebec at Montreal and is a fellow of the Canadian Royal Society. He is the author of several books and articles, among which are *Le discours intérieur. De Platon à Guillaume d'Ockham* (1999) and *Ockham on Concepts* (2004).

ROBERT PASNAU is Professor of Philosophy at the University of Colorado. He is the author of *Metaphysical Themes 1274–1671* (Clarendon Press, 2011).

DOMINIK PERLER is Professor of Philosophy at Humboldt-Universität, Berlin. He works on medieval as well as early modern epistemology and philosophy of mind. His books include *Theorien der Intentionalität im Mittelalter* (2002) and *Zweifel und Gewissheit. Skeptische Debatten im Mittelalter* (2006).

THOMAS PINK is Professor of Philosophy at King's College London. He is the author of *Free Will: A Very Short Introduction* and the forthcoming *The Ethics of Action* for Oxford University Press, and has published numerous articles on ethics and the history of philosophy. He is editing *The Questions Concerning Liberty, Necessity and Chance* for the Clarendon edition of the works of Thomas Hobbes, and a collection of Francisco Suarez's moral and political writings for Liberty Fund.

JACOB SCHMUTZ is Assistant Professor of Philosophy and currently serves as Head of the Department of Philosophy and Sociology at Paris-Sorbonne University Abu Dhabi (United Arab Emirates). He was educated in Brussels, Cambridge, Madrid and Paris, and wrote his dissertation on the development of early modern Jesuit metaphysics (1540–1767). He has published widely on the early modern reception of medieval philosophical ideas, on early modern school formation, and on the historical development of possible worlds semantics. He currently works on medieval theories of belief in a comparative perspective.

ANDREAS SPEER is Professor of Philosophy and Director of the Thomas-Institut at the University of Cologne. He has written books and many articles concerning the history of medieval philosophy and theology, and on natural philosophy, epistemology and aesthetics. He is the editor of the writings of Abbot Suger and is working on the *Schedula diversarum artium*. He directs various major research projects (the *Averroes Latinus*, the edition of the commentary on *Sentences* by Durandus of St Pourçain, etc.) and is the General Editor of the series *Miscellanea Mediaevalia* and *Studien und Texte zur Geistesgeschichte des Mittelalters*.

PAUL THOM is an Honorary Professor in Philosophy at the University of Sydney. His latest book, *The Logic of the Trinity: Augustine to Ockham*, is forthcoming with Fordham University Press.

IAN WILKS is Associate Professor, Department of Philosophy, Acadia University. His research speciality is the philosophy of Peter Abelard. He is the author of 'Peter Abelard and his Contemporaries' in *Handbook of the History of Logic*.

ACKNOWLEDGMENTS

Two colloquia were organised to allow contributors to discuss their own and others' chapters, one in Cambridge, the other in Toronto. The Cambridge colloquium was made possible by the generosity of the Raymond and Beverly Sackler fund; additional funding was given by Oxford University Press, New York, and Trinity College, Cambridge, and the philosophy faculty here kindly allowed the use of its building. The Toronto colloquium was funded by the Centre for Medieval Studies of the University of Toronto and also supported by the Pontifical Institute of Mediaeval Studies, Toronto. I am very grateful to all these institutions, and also to the individual authors, who contributed by financing their own travel. I would also like to thank especially, for their support and participation, Arif Ahmed, Tim Crane, Nick Denyer, Imogen Dickie, Lloyd Gerson, Brad Inwood, Philip Kremer, John Magee, and Alex Oliver. Peter Ohlin has been an encouraging, wise and tolerant editor at OUP, and I am grateful to him and his friendly and efficient assistant, Emily Sacharin.

THE OXFORD HANDBOOK OF

MEDIEVAL
PHILOSOPHY

INTRODUCTION

JOHN MARENBON

1. AIMS

Oxford Handbooks are designed to show the state of the art in a specialised field. This volume presents the state of the art in medieval philosophy as studied in connection with contemporary analytical philosophy. The second and larger section ('Issues in Medieval Philosophy') consists of chapters that explore, topic by topic, the relationship between medieval thinking and the ideas and methods of contemporary philosophers in the broadly analytical tradition. The aim is not to give a complete coverage of every area of what is usually called 'medieval philosophy'—something that several recent publications have done well[1]—but to concentrate on themes which offer the best opportunities for this sort of treatment and to give authors the space to develop important and original analyses. Contributors have been chosen who combine expertise in medieval material with an interest and training in contemporary philosophy. They have been encouraged to explore particular ideas and arguments in detail, using the scope that the size and sophisticated audience of an *Oxford Handbook* afford. Each chapter of the 'Issues' section does not, then, survey a field but provides an introduction to thinking philosophically about a topic discussed in the Middle Ages. No party line has been set about the character of the relationships between medieval questions and arguments and those of philosophers today, and the various contributors have a whole variety of different views and approaches.

The first section is a 'Survey of Medieval Philosophy'. One of its aims is to provide a wider context for the detailed studies of issues (and, since recent general books have been topic-based, it provides the fullest up-to-date chronological-geographical account of medieval philosophy written by specialist authors now available). A second aim is to show that the scope offered by medieval thinking for interested philosophers is much wider than it would appear from the 'Issues' section alone. Most of the writers in the 'Issues' section chose to concentrate on philosophers writing in Latin in the hundred years from 1250 to 1350, and in particular on Aquinas, Duns Scotus, Ockham and Buridan. There are occasional glances back to

Augustine, Boethius and Abelard, and a few forward, and only a very little on the Arabic, Hebrew and Greek traditions. This relative narrowness is no accident, but an accurate reflection of the state of the art among the medieval specialists who have the strongest links with contemporary philosophy. There is, however, a different side to recent work on medieval philosophy—a parallel state of the art—which has opened up the field both chronologically and geographically. It has shown that, from the beginning to the end of the Middle Ages, philosophy was practised at a high level, and that the traditions of thinking in Greek, Arabic and Hebrew should be considered together, as the branches of a single, broad tradition of medieval philosophy.[2] The chapters in the 'Survey' explore this whole, wide tradition; one result is to show that the range of medieval philosophy that remains to be brought into relation with contemporary concerns is still enormous.

The 'Survey' section has a third aim, too—the most important of the three. It is to show that studying the philosophy of the past is a type of history: the study of thinking that went on in particular places and times, in a certain order and with certain internal relations. This objective might seem, at first sight, to be at odds with the declared intention of the *Handbook* to consider medieval texts in their relation to contemporary philosophy. It is worth pausing, before looking over the contents of each section, to explain why it is not. And the best way to do so is by raising an apparent objection to the special emphasis of this whole project.

Aiming to bring philosophy of the distant past into relation with contemporary work has a rather old-fashioned air about it. Fifty years ago the idea might have seemed bold. Now, and for some time already, it has been the normal way of studying texts of the past in philosophy departments, and it is how 'historians' within such departments distinguish their work from that of historians of ideas or intellectual historians in history departments. What is more, the tendency over the last two decades among those philosophers who are historians has been—whilst accepting the value of analytical techniques and an engagement with contemporary work—to stress the importance of recognising the differences between the present and the past, of paying attention to the varying contexts of the texts we now describe as philosophy and of studying their relations to what we distinguish as other disciplines, such as natural science.[3] So, by setting out explicitly to look at medieval philosophy in connection with contemporary analytical philosophy, this *Handbook* might seem to be making a special feature of what should be taken for granted and, far worse, insisting on a narrowness of approach that recent research has rightly rejected. But this line of attack rests on two mistakes, one about the special conditions of work on *medieval* philosophy, the other about the nature of the objectives of this book.

Thirty years ago, when ancient and modern philosophy was already widely studied in a way that linked it to contemporary work in analytical philosophy, such work was rare in medieval philosophy. Norman Kretzmann and the other editors of the *Cambridge History of Later Medieval Philosophy* (1982) hoped to end the era when medieval philosophy 'was studied in a philosophical ghetto', with specialists ignorant of contemporary philosophy and contemporary philosophers ignorant of medieval achievements.[4] Their hope has been fulfilled to a considerable extent. Articles and monographs have been written that bring medieval philosophers out of the ghetto, and there is now a group of specialists worldwide who are at home at once in the worlds of medieval and contemporary analytical philosophy—as the 'Issues' section here shows very clearly. Yet much remains as it was when Kretzmann wrote. On the one hand, medieval philosophy is still on the sidelines so far as most analytical philosophers are concerned: most departments—especially the most highly rated—lack a medieval specialist, and many students will still be expected to jump from Aristotle to Descartes. On the other hand, most work on medieval philosophy still goes on in at least partial ignorance of the techniques and discussions of contemporary analytical philosophy, undertaken by scholars with a mainly philological, historical and literary training.[5] For these reasons, it cannot at all be taken for granted either that analytical philosophers will think that there are discussions by medieval thinkers they will find interesting or important (or, indeed, comprehensible), or that even learned and highly intelligent medievalists will have tried to make connections between their texts and contemporary discussions. Originally, this Introduction was entitled 'Making the Case for Medieval Philosophy'. Such a declaration seemed, on reflection, too strident, but there is certainly a case that still needs to be made: to mainstream philosophers that medieval thinking has as much or more of value for them as that of any other period of the past, and to medievalists that knowing about current concerns in philosophy will deepen their understanding of texts from the Middle Ages and enable them to communicate the interest of what they study.

It is, however, no part of making this case to argue for the type of simple-minded analytical approach to philosophy of the past that flourished half a century ago, in which arguments from historical texts are treated in isolation, and as if they had been written yesterday. Contributors to the 'Issues' section were asked, rather, to consider an aspect of medieval thinking in its relation to contemporary analytical thinking. Some have taken the opportunity to explain how, once account is taken of context, very close links can be made (e.g., Chapters 13—logical consequence, 16—mental language & 19—states of affairs), even to the extent that lines of argument developed in the Middle Ages can contribute directly to present-day discussions (e.g., Chapter 17—universals). Others argue for a looser relationship, and a more indirect contribution (e.g., Chapters 22—mind and hylomorphism & 23—body and soul), or concentrate on showing how contemporary techniques and questionings can illuminate the medieval material (e.g., Chapters 14—modality & 20—parts and wholes). Others devote their chapters to showing the difficulties of making links and the ways in which the formulation of problems have changed (e.g., Chapters 12—logical form, 15—meaning & 26—freedom of the will).

From these two responses, it will be clear why there is no contradiction between the emphasis placed in the 'Issues' section on considering the links between contemporary and medieval philosophy, and insisting that the historical character of the subject, as brought out by the 'Survey' section, should not be forgotten. Medieval philosophy still needs the case to be made for it to the wider philosophical community, but philosophical acumen should not exclude historical understanding. The two sections of the *Handbook* contribute to a common goal. Nonetheless, there is certainly not a contradiction, but a gap in approach between the 'Survey' chapters and at least some of those in the 'Issues' section. How to bridge the division it epitomises remains a fundamental problem not just for medievalists, but for all historians of philosophy.[6]

2. THE 'SURVEY'

The 'Survey' section divides its material into the four main traditions of medieval philosophy: Greek, Arabic, Jewish (in Arabic and Hebrew) and Latin.[7] Although by far the majority of specialists work on the Latin tradition, most would now accept that all four traditions are integral parts of the subject. They are not different plants of the same species (as might be said of the various 'world philosophies'), but intertwined branches from the same trunk. All of them—as explained in Chapter 1—have the same point of departure, the late-ancient Greek tradition, to which they constantly look back. Moreover, they are intricately interlinked. Greek Christian philosophy influenced Latin thinking at least up until the thirteenth century, through translations made in antiquity and later. There was further, strong influence from the Greek tradition, both through the transmission of ancient texts and of current thinking, in the fifteenth century.[8] In the opposite direction, from the later thirteenth to the fifteenth century a considerable variety of Latin philosophical material was translated into Greek.[9] Although there were earlier translations of some scientific texts, the movement to translate Arabic philosophy (including works by Jewish writers) into Latin began in the twelfth century and continued into the fourteenth; further material was translated via Hebrew in the following two hundred years.[10] Jewish philosophy in Hebrew was inaugurated by a movement to translate material from Arabic, and later on considerable amounts of Latin scholastic writing were put into Hebrew.[11]

The division of material between chapters dealing with each tradition is straightforward, except with regard to the relationship between 'Arabic Philosophy' and 'Jewish Philosophy in Arabic'. In the early centuries of Islam, Muslims, Christians and Jews all engaged in the study of philosophy in Arabic, so that arguably there should not be a special chapter on 'Jewish Philosophy in Arabic'. But there are some very particular considerations that set Jewish philosophers apart, and leading Jewish thinkers such as Solomon ibn Gabirol and Maimonides wrote both in Hebrew and Arabic. In order, therefore, to capture the multi-religious character of early philosophy in Arabic, the Jewish thinker, Sa'ādia, is discussed in Chapter 3.3, on Arabic philosophy, along with the Christian, Yahya ibn 'Adî, but the other Arabic-writing Jewish philosophers are treated in Chapter 7, which is specially dedicated to them.

In the Arabic world (Muslim, Jewish and Christian), the earliest philosophising in the eighth century conveniently marks the beginning of the medieval tradition (though the label is strange in the context). But when does medieval philosophy

begin—and ancient philosophy end—in the Greek and Latin worlds? The usual solution is to begin medieval philosophy somewhere around the beginning of the
ninth century, but to add a look back, as major influences and sources, to some of
the Christian thinkers of earlier centuries. My own view is that this periodisation is
muddled, and that a better understanding of philosophical developments would be
gained by starting from the time of Plotinus (third century) and including both
pagan and Christian philosophers.[12] A *Handbook*, however, should be designed to
meet usual expectations about the scope of its subject, and so c. 800 has been made
the general starting point (slightly earlier for some work in Arabic), and a short first
chapter (Chapter 1) in the 'Survey' section sketches some outlines of late-ancient
thought and goes into a little more detail about Augustine and Boethius.[13]

Determining the end of medieval philosophy is even harder than finding its
beginning. Philosophy in Greece, at least, did not flourish long after the Fall of Constantinople in 1453. Arabic philosophy, it used to be thought, died with Averroes just
before the turn of the thirteenth century, but scholars now are increasingly aware
(cf. Chapter 4.6) of the vigour of philosophy in the East in the thirteenth century
and continuing even into the eighteenth century. Historians of Latin philosophy
(and Jewish philosophy in Latin Europe) usually think of the medieval period as
ending sometime around 1500, although they often do not stick to this or any other
date in a straightforward chronological manner. Some philosophers, such as Ficino
and Pico, although they worked before 1500, are held to be, not of the Middle Ages,
but the Renaissance (see Chapter 10.1). Yet the medieval tradition is also sometimes
stretched forward to include later philosophers working within a scholastic tradition, up to Suárez, who died as late as 1617. My own view is that, even more than in
the case of the starting point of medieval philosophy, it would be good to abandon
these traditional demarcations and, whilst recognising different currents of thought,
study together the material up to c. 1700.[14] Again, however, usual expectations have
been allowed to prevail in the *Handbook*, though with two small exceptions. First,
Chapter 10 on 1350 to 1550 attempts to treat all the philosophical material from these
years, rather than sectioning off the Renaissance authors. Second, Chapter 11 on
'Medieval Philosophy after the Middle Ages' makes it clear that the strand of six-
teenth- to eighteenth-century philosophy that is continuous with medieval thinking
was not a hangover from a well-forgotten past but an important aspect of thought
in the period, which was deeply influential on the shape of what is now described as
'modern philosophy'.

3. The 'Issues'

The 'Issues' section, as was made clear at the beginning of this Introduction, does
not aim to be comprehensive. Even some topics where excellent work linking medieval and contemporary thinking has been done recently had to be omitted, from

shortage of space or failure to find suitable authors.[15] The areas considered do, however, range broadly, from logic and philosophy of language, to metaphysics, to
ethics, aesthetics and philosophy of religion.

A thorough training in logic was considered the foundation for the education
of a philosopher, in the Middle Ages just as in analytical departments today. Logic
was developed in the Latin world from the twelfth to fourteenth centuries to a level
of sophistication that was reached again only in the twentieth century, and, as with
contemporary analytical work, every area of philosophy was marked by this logical
training. Although they also introduce important branches of the subject (syllogistic [Chapter 12], *consequentiae* [Chapter 13], and Obligations [Chapter 14.2]) in
the Middle Ages, the main aim of the chapters on logic is to explore three questions
about the relationship between medieval and contemporary approaches to it. How
formal was medieval logic? Paul Thom (Chapter 12) argues that, although various
notions of form in logic were widely discussed, and parts of some medieval systems
functioned in a way we would judge as formal, it was never self-consciously formal,
in the manner of much contemporary logic. But he also shows that the notion of
logical form is not itself simple in meaning, nor is it fixed. Chris Martin (Chapter 13)
is concerned with the relation of logical consequence. In classic contemporary logic,
neither material nor strict implication includes any relevance conditions—hence
the paradoxes of implication. Martin charts how the brilliant twelfth-century logician Peter Abelard, who succeeded in grasping the concept of propositional operation, absent in Boethius, his main source, created a system of relevantistic logic,
akin to ones devised in twentieth-century non-classical logic. Abelard's system,
however, was internally inconsistent, and Martin goes on to show how, gradually,
considerations of relevance were dropped by medieval logicians. Simo Knuuttila
has been a pioneer in the study of medieval conceptions of modality and their relation to contemporary ideas. Thirty years ago, he suggested (Knuuttila 1981) that a
conception akin to the idea of possible worlds, and different from any of the Aristotelian approaches to possibility, first emerged at the turn of the fourteenth century
in the work of Duns Scotus. In his chapter here (Chapter 14), he preserves this
original insight, much nuanced and qualified by his own and others' work in the
intervening period.

The two chapters on the philosophy of language tell contrasting stories. According to the 'new theorists' of the 1970s, especially Putnam, most previous theorists,
including the whole ancient and medieval tradition, explained the way in which
names and kind terms have meaning by concepts in the minds of speakers and lis-
teners. They insisted, by contrast, that meaning is not 'in the head': names and kind
terms are linked to objects in the world by an initial baptism and then by a continuing tradition of social practice. Medieval specialists, however, have argued that
Putnam's historical judgement was awry, since some philosophers in the twelfth and
fourteenth centuries seem to have developed their own versions of the new, direct
reference theory. Margaret Cameron (Chapter 15) gives a wide-ranging review of
the positions from the Middle Ages and today, which suggests that, despite many
interesting parallels, the framework of today's discussion of meaning does not fit the

medieval texts as closely as has been thought. Martin Lenz (Chapter 16) investigates the medieval debate over the 'structure problem'. Are the sentences of mental language structured like those of conventional spoken language or not? He draws the conclusion that there are indeed important parallels between this discussion and the contemporary dispute over whether mental language is internalised conventional language or not, especially in the way that participants in both medieval and contemporary debates see that the best answers rise above the apparent opposition between the two views.

Writers in the medieval universities had a precisely circumscribed, though far-from-settled, conception of metaphysics, derived from Aristotle's *Metaphysics* and the differing views of its subject matter proposed by the two great Arabic commentators, Avicenna and Averroes. One of Aristotle's definitions held it to be the study of being as being, and so there was much medieval discussion about the notion of being. Anthony Kenny expressed, though more forthrightly, a view that many contemporary philosophers share, when he argued that Aquinas—in other areas, he believes, one of the greatest philosophers—was confused in his account of being. Gyula Klima (Chapter 18) tackles Kenny by providing a semantic analysis—using the logical tools commonly employed by philosophers today—that shows Aquinas to have a subtle and coherent account of being. Although this chapter's focus is narrow, its implications are wide, not only with regard to other medieval theories of being, but also because Klima champions the idea that Aquinas is thinking in a different 'conceptual idiom' from ours, but one that we can learn to understand.

Medieval metaphysics is far wider than the topics linked to Aristotle's text studied under that name in the medieval universities. There are treatments from all periods of the Middle Ages of the various different themes that are nowadays loosely gathered under the label 'Metaphysics'. One (strongly linked to logic, especially then, since it was frequently examined in connection with a passage at the beginning of Porphyry's *Isagoge*, the first work in the logical curriculum) is the Problem of Universals. As Claude Panaccio (Chapter 17) observes, this problem is very much alive among analytical philosophers today, even though their predecessors, a half-century ago, were confident that it was dead. But is our Problem of Universals the same as the medieval Problem of Universals? Panaccio argues, against the views of some recent writers, for a moderate continuist view and looks in some detail at William of Ockham's theory, which he considers to remain philosophically appealing today. Another metaphysical problem closely linked to logic concerns the semantics of propositions. A simple proposition refers to some positive or negative state of affairs, but *what* is a state of affairs? Laurent Cesalli (Chapter 19) distinguishes five different types of solutions, ranging from 'reism', which constructs states of affairs from things in the world, to 'eliminativism', which does away with them entirely. He argues that each of the five sorts of medieval theory can be found also in some late-nineteenth-, twentieth-, and twenty-first-century philosophers.

An area of medieval metaphysics that has only recently begun to be explored in detail is mereology. Andrew Arlig (Chapter 20) uses the distinctions established by contemporary theorists to investigate how Abelard, Ockham and Buridan tackle the puzzles generated by their view that the whole is nothing other than the sum of its parts. This position is also at the centre of Henrik Lagerlund's chapter (Chapter 21), but he is concerned with what might be called the metaphysical parts of a natural substance. Whereas thinkers such as Aquinas or Duns Scotus saw such substances as persisting thanks to either a single substantial form or a multiplicity of them, Ockham and Buridan, Lagerlund suggests, provided a mereological account of substances, in which the whole is simply the sum of its parts, form and matter, with none specially privileged. This analysis led away from an Aristotelian view towards the corpuscularianism that became prominent in the seventeenth century. The differences between the Aristotelian framework and the one prevalent since then make it hard to compare medieval discussions about substance with contemporary ones, but careful study of medieval developments throws light on the origins of the modern theories.

In thirteenth- to sixteenth-century Latin philosophy, considerations of this sort about the metaphysical structure of particulars belonging to natural kinds is intimately connected to what, for us now, is a quite different topic in metaphysics: the relation of mind and body. Robert Pasnau (Chapter 22) explains how, following Aristotle's *On the Soul,* the idea of substantial form, which provides a general explanation for the unity and persistence of (natural) particulars, was used to explain the unity of human beings, their ability to think and the immortality of their thinking part, the intellective soul. His account brings to light the aspects of this Aristotelian picture that thinkers today would find unacceptable, while making clear the philosophical interest of a theory that uses a single item to explain both the substantial unity of humans and the fact that they think. Peter King (Chapter 23) also discusses theories about mind and body, concentrating on the distinctions between them rather than their metaphysical background. Platonic dualism, he argues, was very unusual in the Middle Ages. A materialist account of the mind was developed, especially in the Late Middle Ages, but the dominant theory (which goes back to Augustine, a thinker whom many consider wrongly to have been a Platonic dualist) is a property dualism, which was developed using the Aristotelian theory of matter and form. King shows why this hylomorphic theory is of value to philosophers by analysing in detail the sophisticated version of it developed by Duns Scotus.

Taneli Kukkonen's discussion of eternity (Chapter 24) is deliberately placed at the end of this group of chapters on metaphysics. Although time and eternity are discussed by contemporary metaphysicians in ways that seem to link with the intricate treatments of the theme in the Middle Ages, for the medieval philosophers the topic is always linked with questions in what is now called the philosophy of religion. How is God to be described, in a way that respects his otherness and yet allows him to be a provident creator? A particular aspect of this concern, the Problem of Prescience (if God foreknows everything, how can humans be free to act one way or another?), is very frequently the occasion for medieval analyses of eternity. Kukkonen, who ranges widely over Latin and Arabic material, examines how philosophers today have tried to capture these debates in our contemporary terms but also shows how the character and variety of the positions have limited their success.

The single chapter on epistemology (Chapter 25) addresses an immediate question raised by the medieval discussions. We are used, from Descartes, to thinking of epistemological scepticism as a fundamental philosophical problem—one, some would say, that must be tackled before any progress towards solid knowledge can be made. There is an obvious absence of this sort of fundamental, Cartesian scepticism in the Middle Ages. Dominik Perler shows that it is missing, neither because of ignorance of the ancient sceptical tradition, nor because of the pressure of Christian belief or dogmatic Aristotelianism. Indeed, writers such as Aquinas and Buridan were willing to explore sceptical epistemological arguments, but from their hierarchical or teleological view of nature they derived a reliabilism that ruled out the possibility of being deceived about everything in the way Descartes would canvass. The moral Perler draws—which links this chapter with those preceding—is that differences between medieval and modern thinkers in their approach to scepticism depend on differences in their wider metaphysical framework.

Today, as in the Middle Ages, it is usually accepted that, for an action to be morally good or evil, it must be, in some relevant sense, free. Thomas Pink (Chapter 26) argues that this sense has not, however, remained at all the same. In the Middle Ages, an idea of freedom as a metaphysical power of the will underlay ethical discussion. By the time of Hobbes, freedom came to be conceived rather, as it is now, as a lack of constraint from exercising other powers. Instead of requiring a multi-way power of the will, we consider that an ethical action need just be voluntary. Ian Wilks, by contrast, argues (Chapter 27) for a continuity between medieval ethical theory and more recent, Kantian approaches, by looking at two intention-based theories of morals—those of Abelard and Ockham—and the background to them in the work of Augustine and Anselm. But the 'staples' of medieval ethics, as Wilks says, are virtue theory and natural law. They are discussed in the two following chapters. Terence Irwin points out (Chapter 28) that these two staples do not, in fact, combine together, since a theory of natural law would lay down certain sorts of actions as being obligatory, whereas virtue theory looks on actions as being good only because they are performed by virtuous agents. Irwin restricts his analysis to Aquinas and argues that he is not a virtue theorist, although he gives virtues an important role in his theory, which can be categorised neither as deontological nor consequentialist. The implication of Irwin's discussion is that, in evading the main contemporary categories of moral theory, Aquinas's may be all the stronger and worthy of the attention of moralists today. Aquinas's theory of natural law is an area of his thought that lives on in contemporary theorising by a group of thinkers who are perhaps less troubled than Irwin by the tensions between virtue theory and natural law but concur in valuing an approach that avoids consequentialism and Kantian deontology. Anthony Lisska (Chapter 29) surveys this contemporary revival of a medieval approach.

The area of medieval political philosophy that has the closest links with contemporary questions is the theory of rights. There was, of course, plenty of discussion about *legal* rights, but did medieval thinkers anticipate, in their treatment of *natural* rights, modern political theories based on subjective rights? And was there any conception of *human* rights in the Middle Ages. Cary Nederman (Chapter 30) addresses these two questions, suggesting that the answer to the first is probably negative but that Marsilius of Padua and Bartolomé de las Casas do indeed have an idea of what we now call 'human rights'.

Of all the branches of contemporary philosophy, none poses questions about the relationship with medieval thinking more sharply than aesthetics. On the one hand, there are a number of studies of 'medieval aesthetics' by distinguished scholars; on the other hand, there are good reasons to think that medieval authors never discussed the matters conceived as aesthetics since the eighteenth century. Andreas Speer (Chapter 31) addresses this question, showing that aesthetic theory is often discerned in medieval texts only by misreading them, and by pointing to the real characteristics of medieval theorising about beauty and the arts.

The field in which the connections with medieval philosophy have already been drawn most often and distinctly by contemporary analytical writers is the philosophy of religion. Just as, in epistemology and many other areas, the classic texts to which philosophers now look back, not as authorities but as points of departure for their debates, are from the early modern period, so in philosophy of religion the foundational ideas are provided by the thinkers of the Middle Ages (Augustine, Boethius, Anselm, Aquinas, Scotus). For example, most types of argument intended to demonstrate the existence of God are medieval formulations (in some cases, developing suggestions in ancient authors). Contemporary debate is couched in terms of whether, for example, some much adapted version of the ontological argument, or one of Aquinas's cosmological arguments, is valid and what premises it asks to be accepted. Graham Oppy (Chapter 32) takes a variety of such medieval arguments, and their adaptations by philosophers today, and he argues that all of them are flawed.

Richard Cross's chapter (Chapter 33) on philosophical analyses of the Trinity explores a more intricate relation between medieval and contemporary thinking, which links his discussion back to those on metaphysics. As mentioned above, much of the best medieval philosophising is done by theologians in the course of tackling problems that are ultimately theological ones. It might seem, then, from the point of view of the interested philosopher now, that the doctrinal subject matter is a mere distraction. It is a good thing that so many logically trained and brilliant minds were made to tackle difficult metaphysical questions in the course of examining dogma such as the Trinity, the hypostatic union or the Eucharist, but a pity—for anyone without an interest in Christian doctrine itself—that they could not have confined their speculations to the world. Cross, however, argues that for thinkers such as Duns Scotus, on whom he concentrates, the need to explain supernatural things, such as divine triunity, was a stimulus to developing theories about sameness and difference and other metaphysical matters to the highest degree of generality: the theological subject matter thus makes them better as philosophers.

NOTES

....

1. See Pasnau (2010), and the topics chapters in Lagerlund (2011); and, for a broader, more introductory treatment, McGrade (2003).

2. De Libera (1993) pioneered this approach, which I followed and tried to develop in Marenbon (2007). The approach is implicit in Lagerlund (2011).

3. An outstanding and influential example of this tendency is provided by the work of Dan Garber—for example, Garber (1992).

4. Kenny, Kretzmann and Pinborg (1982, 3).

5. Most work on medieval philosophy continues to be done in France, Germany and Italy, where the training, even in philosophy departments, is traditionally far more philological and historical than in the Anglophone world; important work in the field is also done by historians and other medievalists in English-speaking countries. This generalisation should not obscure the appearance of a new generation of specialists from Continental Europe, many of whose names figure among the contributors to this *Handbook,* who combine philological skill and historical sensibility with analytical training and ability.

6. This is not the place for me to develop my own views about methodology in the history of philosophy: for a sketch of them, see Marenbon (2011).

7. This list is not exhaustive. Were space available, discussion of the Syriac tradition should have been included. Syriac was the language of many Eastern Christians, and as well as playing a very important role as intermediaries in translating Greek texts into Arabic, Syriac scholars had their own tradition of Aristotelian logical commentary, most stretching back to the sixth century (Sergius of Resh'ainâ, d. 536; Paul the Persian), but stretching on until Bar Hebraeus in the thirteenth (cf. Brock 1993; Hugonnard-Roche 2004). It was also planned to have a chapter on philosophy in the Western European vernaculars. Much of it is of interest mainly because it shows the dissemination of ideas to a broader public, but some thinkers—almost always ones who wrote in Latin, too—arguably did produce strikingly original ideas, which should qualify as philosophy in a broad sense, in their vernacular works: especially Ramon Llull (in, for instance, his *Dialogue of the Gentile*), Meister Eckhart (in his German sermons) and Dante (in the *Convivio* and the *Commedia*) in the years after 1300, and Boccaccio (in the *Decameron*) a little later in that century (cf. Bray and Sturlese 2003; Imbach 1989; and, for Dante and Boccaccio, Chapter 10.2.3 below).

8. See below, Chapter 10.

9. See below, Chapter 2 and Pasnau (2010, 822–6).

10. See below, Chapter 9 and Pasnau (2010, 814–22; by Charles Burnett), which should be supplemented by his list and discussion in Burnett (2005), for further information and for the fifteenth- and sixteenth-century material. The most important of all Jewish philosophical writings in Arabic, Maimonides's *Guide of the Perplexed*, was in fact put into Latin via a Hebrew translation, in the early thirteenth century—see Kluxen (1954).

11. See below, Chapter 7.

12. See Marenbon (2011, 71–2).

13. Chapter 2.1.2 looks back at the late-ancient Greek Christian tradition.

14. I have suggested this idea in Marenbon (2007, 349–51, and 2011, 71–72). Although they do not propose anything quite so wild, strong support for the idea that, at least, *study* of the history of philosophy should ignore the usual divisions and treat the whole period from the fourteenth to the seventeenth century as an area for research comes from Pasnau (2011) and Perler (2011), both of which range widely between 1270 and 1670, with impressive results.

15. Two obvious examples are theories of intentionality and mental representation (see Lagerlund 2007; Perler 2002) and theories of emotion (see Knuuttila 2004; Perler 2011).

BIBLIOGRAPHY

Bray, Nadia and Loris Sturlese, eds. 2003. *Filosofia in volgare nel medioevo*. Louvain-La-Neuve, Belgium: Fédération Internationale des Instituts d'Études Médiévales (Textes et études du moyen âge 21).

Brock, Sebastian. 1993. 'The Syriac Commentary Tradition'. In *Glosses and Commentaries on Aristotelian Logical Texts. The Syriac, Arabic and Medieval Latin traditions*, ed. Charles Burnett, 3–15. London: the Warburg Institute (Warburg Institute Surveys and Texts 23).

Burnett, Charles. 2005. 'Arabic into Latin: the Reception of Arabic Philosophy into Western Europe'. In *The Cambridge Companion to Arabic Philosophy*, ed. Peter Adamson and Richard Taylor, 370–404. Cambridge: Cambridge University Press.

Garber, Daniel. 1992. *Descartes' Metaphysical Physics*. Chicago and London: Chicago University Press.

Hugonnard-Roche, Henri. 2004. *La logique d'Aristote du grec au syriaque. Études sur la transmission des textes de l'Organon et leur interprétation philosophique*. Paris: Vrin.

Imbach, Ruedi. 1989. *Laien in der Philosophie des Mittelalters. Hinweise und Anregungen zu einem vernachlässigten Thema*. Amsterdam: Grüner (Bochumer Studien zur Philosophie 14).

Kluxen, Wolfgang. 1954. Literargeschichtliches zum lateinischem Moses Maimonides. *Recherches de théologie ancienne et médiévale* 21:23–50.

Knuuttila, Simo. 1981. 'Time and Modality in Scholasticism'. In *Reforging the Great Chain of Being: Studies of the History of Modal Theories*, ed. Simo Knuuttila, 163–257. Synthese Historical Library, 20. Dordrecht, The Netherlands: Reidel.

Lagerlund, Henrik, ed. 2007. *Representation and Objects of Thought in Medieval Philosophy*. Aldershot and Burlington, UK: Ashgate.

———, ed. 2011. *Encyclopedia of Medieval Philosophy*. Dordrecht, The Netherlands: Springer.

de Libera, Alain. 1991. *Penser au moyen âge*. Paris: Seuil.

———. 1993. *La Philosophie médiévale*. Paris: Presses Universitaires de France.

Marenbon, John. 2007. *Medieval Philosophy: An Historical and Philosophical Introduction*. London and New York: Routledge.

———. 2011. 'Why Study Medieval Philosophy?' In *Warum noch Philosophie? Historische, systematische und gesellschaftliche Positionen*, ed. Marcel van Ackeren, Theo Kobusch and Jörn Müller, 60–73. Berlin and Boston: de Gruyter.

Pasnau, Robert, ed. 2010. *The Cambridge History of Medieval Philosophy*. Cambridge: Cambridge University Press.

———. 2011. *Metaphysical Themes, 1274–1671*. New York: Oxford University Press.

Perler, Dominik. 2002. *Theorien der Intentionalität im Mittelalter*. Frankfurt, Germany: Klostermann (Philosophische Abhandlungen 82).

———. 2011. *Transformationen der Gefühle, Philosophische Emotionstheorien 1270–1670*. Frankfurt, Germany: Fischer.

PART I

A Survey of Medieval Philosophy

CHAPTER 1

....

THE LATE ANCIENT BACKGROUND TO MEDIEVAL PHILOSOPHY

....

JOHN MARENBON

THE following chapters survey philosophy in four traditions—Greek, Arabic, Hebrew and Latin. All of them have their origin in the philosophy of Late Antiquity. Arguably, the historian would do better to begin any survey from then, ignoring the usual division between the ancient and medieval periods. A poor second best is, as here, to sketch out that background, placing particular emphasis on the aspects of it that most influenced the medieval centuries. The Greek tradition depends directly, and the Arabic (and so, ultimately the Hebrew) through translations, on the Platonic schools of the fourth to sixth centuries: their masters, curriculum and teaching are the focus of the first part of the chapter. The Greek heritage of the Medieval Latin tradition was mediated, and to some extent transformed, by the tradition of Latin philosophy, pagan and Christian, from Cicero to Cassiodorus. It is the subject of the second part, in which Augustine and Boethius—two figures whoare discussed frequently in the 'Issues' section of the *Handbook*—receive special attention.[1]

1. The Greek Tradition

1.1 Plotinus, Porphyry and the Origins of the Platonic Schools

Plato died in 347 or 348 BC, Aristotle in 322. Although in most periods and places medieval philosophers would have access to many of Aristotle's texts themselves, and perhaps a little by Plato, the ancient thought they received was the product of the near millennium of intellectual work that had taken place between the days of these two founding giants of philosophy and the closing of the School of Alexandria after the Arab conquest in 640 AD. In the centuries immediately following them, both Plato and Aristotle had their schools. After his immediate successors, Plato's school became sceptical in outlook (the New Academy); then, from the first century AD, philosophers such as Plutarch, Alcinous and Numenius developed a systematic view of Platonic teaching known, in its various versions, as Middle Platonism.[2] After Aristotle's own pupils, the leading Aristotelian was Alexander of Aphrodisias, at the turn of the third century AD, though an independent Aristotelian school lasted up until the time of Themistius, in the fourth century. Throughout this period, however, it was the other schools that tended to flourish most: Pyrrhonian sceptics, Epicureans and, above all, the Stoics. Stoicism was the dominant philosophy at the time of Cicero (106–43 BC) and remained so for the first two centuries of the Roman Empire. Its moral teaching, according to which virtue alone is of value, appealed to aristocratic Roman sentiments and profoundly influenced the ethics of future generations of philosophers who rejected most other aspects of Stoic thought, especially its materialism.[3]

These Hellenistic schools dwindled, however, eclipsed by the popularity of Platonism in the formulation by Plotinus (c. 204/5–270). He is often branded the first 'Neoplatonist', but the 'Neo-' belies both his wish to present Plato's own thinking as he best understood it (cf. Gerson 2010, 3) and the continuities between his thought and that of his Platonic predecessors in the previous two or three centuries. Plato's *Timaeus* presents a divine demiurge, using the Ideas as the model according to which a World Soul forms matter, and the Middle Platonic tradition had transformed the demiurge into something nearer to Aristotle's God, Intellect, and made the Ideas into its thoughts. Plotinus changes and develops this reading of Plato by positing an unknowable, absolutely unitary first principle, the One or the Good, from which derives Intellect, identical to the Ideas; from Intellect derives Soul, which enters into and animates bodies. This process of derivation is explained by a distinction between primary acts—for instance, fire being fire, burning intransitively—and secondary transitive acts—fire making something else hot. The secondary act of the One is to produce an act of Intellect, which is given its form by making the One its object. Soul derives from Intellect in a similar manner. Matter, Plotinus holds (according at least to some interpreters), does not exist independently, but also derives ultimately from the One, though it lacks the ability to turn back and consider its origin—hence its lack of definition and so its evil nature. If this reading is correct, Plotinus is suggesting that evil is just the cost of the Good's self-diffusion. Plotinus was much more, however, than a powerful and original systematiser. His philosophical manner is as exploratory in its own way as Plato's; argumentative reasoning is the philosopher's task, and it (as opposed to religious practices) is the method by which the sage can free himself from the body and rise even to the level of the One.

Porphyry (234–345) has a significant place in the history of ancient philosophy both as the pupil of Plotinus who edited his work into the form of the six *Enneads* in which it has been preserved, and as a prolific writer of commentaries on Plato and metaphysical works, many of them lost, which draw both on Plotinus and the Platonic tradition before him. Looking back from the perspective of medieval philosophy, and its origins in the Platonic schools, a different aspect of his work is of outstanding, indeed fundamental importance. Plotinus had been critical of Aristotelian logic, especially the *Categories*, which asserts that unless primary substances— that is to say, particular members of natural kinds—exist, nothing else can do. By contrast, Porphyry was an enthusiastic student of the *Categories* and Aristotelian logic in general. He reconciled Aristotle's views with Plato's by arguing that Aristotelian logic is concerned primarily with language, not as a formal system, but as words as signifying things. What they signify are the particular substances and their attributes that we perceive with our senses, rather than the intelligible reality investigated by Platonic metaphysics. The claim that the two philosophers were writing about different subject matter could be used more generally to promote the idea of their harmony—Porphyry wrote a treatise, now lost, on the topic. Aristotle's works came to be incorporated into the curriculum of the Platonic schools: pupils began by studying them, before moving on to Plato's dialogues. And, at the start, there was logic, introduced by Aristotle's *Categories* and, appropriately, as a preface to them, a work by Porphyry, his *Eisagôgê* (*Isagoge*) or 'Introduction', which became for the later ancient and medieval traditions as much a text of the Aristotelian logical Organon as any by Aristotle himself. Porphyry can be seen, though this is an oversimplification, as trying to be thoroughly Aristotelian, following the example of Alexander of Aphrodisias, in his writing on logic.[4] This side of his work—reinforced by the predilections of the School of Alexandria (see below)—provides at least part of the explanation of how the logic-loving, Aristotelian traditions of medieval philosophy derived from the Platonic schools.

1.2 The Schools of Athens and Alexandria

The two philosophers who did most to shape the Platonic tradition after Porphyry were Iamblichus (d. early 320s) and Proclus (412–485). Little by Iamblichus survives, but it is clear that he contributed to the process of elaborating Plotinus's scheme of hypostases with sub-divisions. His attitude to religion was different from that of his predecessors. Although, unlike Plotinus, Porphyry respected traditional religion and oracular texts (and was an outspoken critic of Christianity), he did not think that theurgy—a ritual in which the gods manifested themselves in statues and other physical things—was useful for philosophers, who should aim to cut themselves off so far as possible from the physical world in order to ascend to the intelligible. Iamblichus rejected this philosophical disdain for the world of nature and believed that theurgy and worship of the gods—he esteemed especially the ancient gods of Egypt—were valuable tools for re-sacralising the world of nature.

The strong connection forged by Iamblichus between Platonism and pagan religion influenced the School of Athens, especially after Syrianus became its head in 432. Proclus, his pupil, presided over the school for almost fifty years. His religious aims are particularly evident in his *Platonic Theology* where, in a universe of triads that divide and sub-divide the three hypostases, at each level there are henads, deriving from the unparticipated One, each identified with a member of the pagan pantheon. Although such a system can have the air of metaphysico-theological fantasy, Proclus wanted to reach his conclusions in the most rigorous way. The *Elements of Theology* is organised as a series of propositions followed by proofs, and it tries to show that the whole complex structure of the intelligible universe can be demonstrated from a small number of supposedly self-evident principles. Although the *Elements* was influential in the Arabic and especially the Latin traditions,[5] it was, ironically, in Christian guise that Proclus would have his widest readership in later centuries. Sometime in the late fifth or early sixth century, a set of writings, probably by a Syrian monk, were issued under the name of Dionysius, the Athenian philosopher converted by St Paul. Soon accepted as authentic, these works carried special authority by their presumed near apostolic origin. They were translated into Syriac almost immediately, and into Latin in the ninth century; Thomas Aquinas and Albert the Great, among many others, wrote commentaries on them. Pseudo-Dionysius, as he is known, adapted Proclus's hierarchies, replacing the ancient gods with the orders of angels and the hierarchy of the Church, and from the tradition of commentary on Plato's *Parmenides,* as developed by Proclus, brought to Christian thought a radically negative theology.[6]

Proclus's pious paganism was already an anachronism in an increasingly intolerant Christian Empire, and in 529, the Emperor Justinian decreed the closure of the School of Athens. The School of Alexandria, however, endured until the city fell to the Arabs in 641. It had gained its prestige and its characteristic orientation only in the fifth century, when Ammonius (c.435/45–517/26) was master. Ammonius was an Aristotelian specialist, with a particular interest in logic, and this emphasis is also found to an extent in his successor, Olympiodorus, and in his successors, Elias, David and Stephanus, the last representatives of the ancient tradition. Whether or not Ammonius made some sort of compact with the Christian authorities to enable pagan philosophy to continue being taught is still debated, but he and the other Alexandrian masters were certainly less openly and aggressively opposed to the new religion than their Athenian counterparts. Elias and David may have been Christians, and Stephanus certainly was.[7]

2. THE LATIN TRADITION

2.1 Roman Philosophy

Greek was the normal language of philosophy throughout the Empire, even in Rome itself—where, for example, Plotinus worked. But there was also a tradition of philosophising in Latin, going back to Cicero (106–43 BC), whose wide range of philosophical work intended for a general, educated audience is marked both by the then dominant Stoicism, but also its author's eclecticism and interest in comparing the teachings of the different schools. His *Topics* inaugurated a Roman tradition of logic, closely linked to oratory, which would have an important role in the early Middle Ages.[8] His treatises on ethics and law helped to ensure that Stoic moral philosophy survived, whilst a brief classification of the virtues near the end of a treatise about rhetoric, *On Invention*, formed the basis for twelfth-century discussion of the virtues. The letters of Seneca (d. 65 AD) provided a more consistent guide to Stoic moral views and, at least for a few writers, a much better account of Epicureanism than the caricatures which circulated among its enemies, pagan and Christian.[9] A masterly presentation of this philosophy could be found in Lucretius (mid-first century BC), but, despite a few ninth-century manuscripts, his poem was not studied until the fifteenth century.

Thus the Latin heritage gave medieval readers in the West at least a glimpse of the varied types of philosophy that had flourished in the Hellenistic period. It also provided Platonic material of various sorts. Apuleius's *On Plato*, from the second century AD, belongs to the world of Middle Platonism. Macrobius's *Commentary* on Cicero's *Dream of Scipio* (c. 430) presents some of Plotinus's thoughts in a popularised form. More ambitiously, Calcidius (most probably early fourth century) translated more than half of the *Timaeus* (Cicero had previously made a partial, but much shorter, translation) and added a long commentary, reflecting Middle Platonic views and, perhaps, a personal stance of a Christian who, nonetheless, wishes to reach an authentic understanding of Plato (Dronke 2008).[10] Two other Christian writers, Augustine and Boethius, did more than anyone to transmit late ancient philosophy to the Middle Ages.

2.2 Augustine[11]

But how wrong to cast Augustine as the transmitter of existing traditions! Certainly, themes from Augustine's reading of some Plotinus and Porphyry in Latin translation are evident especially in his *On the Trinity* and parts of the *Confessions,* and a broadly Platonic orientation guides most of his earlier works. *Against the Academicians*, though written to refute the academic sceptics, became the most important medieval source for ancient scepticism, whilst the *Literal Commentary on Genesis* draws on the Stoics in its notion of 'seminal reasons' that allow the features of God's creation to develop over time. Augustine's two greatest legacies to his medieval readers, however, were the critical distance he took with regard to pagan thought, despite his admiration for it, and the example he set of thinking through specifically Christian ideas rigorously and philosophically.

The circumstances of Augustine's life helped him to reach this position. Son of a Christian mother and pagan father, he devoted his life to Christianity only after a long search for the truth, during which for a time he followed the dualist beliefs of the Manichees and was rescued from them by his reading of the Platonists. Whether or not in the earliest period after his conversion (386) Augustine treated Platonic and Christian thinking as hardly distinct from one another, by the time of the *Confessions* (397–401) he was very clear that, although the Platonists had an understanding of God, they did not know how to reach him. In *The City of God* (413–26/7), Augustine thought further and more radically about the relationship of Christianity to Greek and Roman civilisation. The work was occasioned by reactions to the sack of Rome in 410 by Alaric and his Gothic troops: the pagans, a small but educated and influential group of whom still remained, put the catastrophe down to a ban that had been imposed on public worship of the traditional gods. From discrediting the various attempts to explain and rationalise the pagan pantheon, and showing that these supposed gods had never offered Rome any protection, Augustine moves on to attack the heroic version of ancient history, which many Christians had been willing to accept, once their religion became the official creed of the Empire. The story of Rome is, rather, Augustine insisted, one of violence and bloodshed, and the growth of its power was not a reflection of divine favour. God has placed his imprint more clearly on a different, parallel history, narrated in the Bible, from the creation, the Fall, through the story of God's chosen people, the Jews, to the Incarnation; yet Augustine also stresses that the membership of the city of God is hidden and by no means to be identified with the Church as a visible, human institution. Although Augustine gives Platonism the highest place among pagan achievements, the context is one in which the virtues of pagans are mere shams, and their limited wisdom not an example to be followed.

Long before he had reached so critical a view of ancient culture, Augustine's method, in his more speculative works, was to start from a philosophical perplexity that arose within Christian teaching (though perhaps, in a different form, elsewhere, too), and reason about it, within the framework of faith but obedient to the demands of reason. So, for example, in *On Free Choice of the Will* (388–95), he considers problems such as how there can be evil when God is good and omnipotent, and, more precisely, how God can have created Adam free to sin without being responsible for his sinning, and how God's foreknowledge is compatible with human freedom. The autobiographical and meditative *Confessions* end with an exegesis of the opening of Genesis, which contains a sophisticated and original discussion of the nature of time. *On the Trinity* uses Aristotle's *Categories* in order to explore how far God and his triune nature can be described using the metaphysical distinctions that apply to the world around us.

These are just a few examples; the list could be made longer and longer—and the diversity and quantity of what Augustine wrote (more survives written by him than by any other single ancient author) added an extra element of value for medieval readers.

Augustine wrote prolifically but not systematically. He returned to the same subjects at different times in his life, and his ideas about them changed. Moreover, his intellectual energies were often directed towards controversy or what he considered to be heresy. He spent much of his time at the end of his life fighting Pelagianism, the view that humans who try enough can, without freely given assistance from God, merit at least some divine reward. The struggle made him strengthen and develop his own views on the gratuity of grace and God as predestiner. These factors made Augustine's works, not into the source of a system for medieval thinkers, but into a resource that could be used to bolster diverse and often opposing positions, and into a stimulus for debate. So, for instance, Abelard used the *City of God* as a main source for material to support a golden view of pagan antiquity quite at odds with Augustine's own attitude. Both in the ninth century and again in the sixteenth and seventeenth, controversy over predestination was centred on Augustine's varied texts on this subject, with both sides claiming his backing. The respect for authority in medieval culture is often exaggerated by historians who fail to take proper account of the great latitude offered for interpretation. In the case of Augustine, the changing, open and sometimes conflicted nature of his thinking made such interpreting a necessity and so set readers who took different views of his meaning on to the path of argumentative dissension.

2.3 Boethius[12]

Unlike Augustine, Boethius is often seen precisely as a transmitter of knowledge, particularly from the late ancient Platonic schools—a conduit through which a quantity of Greek texts and ideas reached the Middle Ages, a little muddied but otherwise unaltered. His work in logic is presented as little more than translation, and the *Theological Tractates* and even the *Consolation of Philosophy* are held to depend largely on Greek sources for their arguments.[13] But a different view can be justified: the choices Boethius made *for* and *in* logic moulded the whole medieval philosophical tradition; in theological method he provided both a development of Augustine's and a complement to it; in the *Consolation* he both opened a whole way for Christian authors to relate to ancient philosophy and elaborated an argument about a major theological problem, divine prescience and human freedom, to which thinkers returned throughout the Middle Ages.

Although his birth (475–7) coincided with the deposition of the last Roman Emperor, and he lived his life under Ostrogothic rule in Italy, Boethius belonged more closely to the ancient world than Augustine had done a century before. Born and then adopted into the highest Roman aristocracy, his education gave him fluency in Greek and the knowledge of Greek philosophy that a student at Athens or Alexandria might have gained. For most of his life, he lived in Rome and enjoyed exercising the trappings of power that the Ostrogothic ruler Theodoric allowed the senatorial elite, while devoting most of his time to making Greek learning available in Latin.

After writing treatises on arithmetic and music, closely based on Greek originals, Boethius turned to logic. He wrote (c. 504–9) a commentary on Porphyry's *Isagoge*, making use of an existing Latin version by Marius Victorinus. But he was dissatisfied with Victorinus's, and he made his own translations of all Aristotle's logic except the *Posterior Analytics*. These translations were, ostensibly, part of a larger project: in about 516 he announced his intention to put into Latin all the works of Aristotle he could and all of Plato's dialogues, to comment on them and to show that Plato and Aristotle are essentially in agreement with each other. Although, in the event, Boethius's life was cut short, it is hard to see how he could have expected to complete this task. Rather than rush to do so, he chose to give logic all the attention that it needed, not only providing double commentaries (to the *Isagoge* and *On Interpretation*, and perhaps also to the *Categories*) but also by writing a series of logical textbooks and turning his attention to the post-Aristotelian elaboration of a whole new area, the logical of topical inference.[14]

Not only did Boethius single out logic for special attention; he also chose a very particular approach to it. His commentaries are not very original works. Like the Greek commentators of his time, Boethius was mainly concerned to pass on an established tradition of exegesis—though there is no reason to consider him, as some scholars have done, a cipher, mindlessly putting Greek scholia into Latin. But he chose, in the main, to follow not his contemporaries but the commentaries of Porphyry. Porphyry (see above) had introduced Aristotelian logic into the Platonic curriculum, explaining that its subject matter was not intelligible reality, which Plato's dialogues explored. Usually, he explored Aristotelian logic in Aristotelian terms, making considerable use of the greatest Aristotelian exegete, Alexander of Aphrodisias. Later Athenian and Alexandrian commentators tended, however, to try to introduce Platonic themes into their logical commentaries. By sticking so closely to Porphyry, Boethius gave the Middle Ages not just a genuinely Aristotelian logic, but an Aristotelian approach to the various other branches of philosophy that earlier medieval philosophers developed in the course of discussing logical texts—metaphysics, philosophy of language and philosophy of mind. The implications of Boethius's choice are vividly illustrated by the most famous passage of his commentaries, his discussion of the Problem of Universals in his second commentary on the *Isagoge*. Here he draws explicitly on Alexander of Aphrodisias for an argument to show that there are no universals, and he responds to it also with ideas going back to Alexander; twelfth-century discussions were thereby set on a track sharply divergent from any version of Platonism.

Boethius lived in an entirely Christian milieu. Though not a priest, he decided to use his training and talents in logic and philosophy to help resolve the doctrinal disputes about Christology and the Trinity that divided Catholics like himself in Italy from the Church in Greece. The method he uses in his three *Theological Treatises* on these subjects (I and II on the Trinity; V on the union of divine and human nature in Christ)[15] develops the one pioneered by Augustine at one point in *On the Trinity*. Usually, Augustine made his arguments from within Christian doctrine, but in Book 5 of this work (see above) he first turns to Aristotle's division of things in the world into ten Categories and then explores how far such a classification can be applied to God. With this passage in mind, Boethius engages in a more elaborate discussion of Aristotle's *Categories* in Treatise II and then attempts to mark out in exactly what ways the account of relation there needs to be adapted so as to provide the clue to understanding—though not a complete grasp of—God as three and one. In the earlier Treatise V, the Aristotelian physics of mixture is similarly employed to help make the hypostatic union comprehensible and show that two views he rejects are not merely heretical but also go against reason. This way of going from the outside in, tackling theological questions by developing philosophical analyses in their own terms and applying them analogically to Christian teaching, would be the main methodological model for medieval speculative theologians, alongside Augustine's usual method of working from inside the doctrine of the faith.

The setting for the *Consolation of Philosophy* is the cell of a man condemned to die: Boethius, the prisoner, argues with Philosophia or 'Lady Philosophy'. She, of course, is a personification, but the rest is far from a poetic fiction. Having accepted the post of Theodoric's chief minister, Boethius quickly fell victim to court intrigue and was sentenced to death on a trumped-up charge of treason. The first four of the five books of the *Consolation* are strongly influenced by the tradition of the *protrepticus*—an introduction to philosophy. Boethius represents himself as having forgotten, under the stress of his sudden fall from power, almost all he had learned in his philosophical education. Philosophia's job is to argue him back into understanding that, despite appearances, the world is providentially ordained, the wicked do not prosper and the good are not oppressed. She draws on common Stoic, and then Platonic, ideas for this task, though arguably Boethius the author deliberately complicates the picture by juxtaposing a partial and a total rejection of worldly values, and a scheme in which the Highest Good, which is God, acts only as a final cause, with one in which he organises human affairs more directly. The most dramatic feature of the *Consolation* lies, however, in something unmentioned. Boethius is a Christian, but it is not a representative of the Christian heaven who comes to console him as he awaits execution, but the personification of the ancient, pagan tradition of philosophy. Recent explanations have ranged from the unlikely suggestion that, faced by death, Boethius abandoned Christianity, to the idea, equally unlikely, that his intention is to satirise the inadequacy of philosophy and assert the need for faith, but the majority of historians accept that it is not incongruous with his Christian faith for Boethius to have set this final work in terms of the ancient culture and way of thought to which he had devoted his life.[16] Medieval readers were, for the most part, quick to find an implicit Christian meaning in this text, and their doing so had two important effects. On the one hand, it drew the other genuinely pagan works with which the *Consolation* had thematic links, especially Plato's *Timaeus*, into the ambit of Christianising interpretation; on the other hand, it suggested the possibility of following through pagan philosophical ideas to reach an ultimate truth that would be acceptable to Christians, too.

The greater part of Book 5 of the *Consolation* is devoted to a problem that is much more technically and intricately discussed than anything in the preceding books: how God's prescience is compatible with future contingent events, such as the actions we freely choose to perform.[17] If God already knows what I shall do later this afternoon, then no one doubts, intuitively, that there is a problem about maintaining that I shall still have the power to choose between different alternative courses of action. But formulating this intuition is not easy. Philosophers from the twelfth century onwards have been quick to point out that is not enough to say that, if God knows something, then what he knows is necessarily the case, because here 'necessarily' has to be understood as applying just to the link between the knowledge and the event in question, not to the event itself. Necessarily, if God knows that I shall finish this chapter in 30 minutes' time, I shall finish it then; but my finishing it then is not, unfortunately, itself a necessity.

Although Boethius lacked the grasp of propositional logic to make this distinction, he found a different way of expressing it in his analysis of the intuitive problem. If *A* is not the cause of a contingent event *B* (in the strong sense, that it is in no way causally related to *B*), then *B* will be the same whether or not *A* obtains. Divine prescience is not the cause of a future event *B*, and so if *B* is considered to be contingent were it not for divine prescience, then it will not be changed and must remain contingent, even if God foreknows it. The problem is, rather, how, if it is contingent and therefore uncertain until it happens, it can be known before it takes place. If God believes that *B* is certain (which Boethius takes to be entailed by his foreknowing *B*), then he believes *B* to be other than it is—it is contingent and so uncertain; but how can a belief that something is otherwise than it is be knowledge?

Boethius explains that, contrary to what is usually thought, the way something is known depends not on itself but on the cognitive level of the knower. Just as an object such as a human being is grasped differently by the senses, as a remembered image, as a universal by the reason, and differently again by God's single act of intelligence, so a future event, which is uncertain and contingent from the perspective of human reason (and so cannot be known), is certain and necessary from God's point of view because God knows everything, past, present and future, in just the way we know the present. But this necessity, from God's point of view, does not constrain human freedom of choice, just as the necessity of what is the case, when it is the case (a view of modality Boethius takes from Aristotle) does not mean that it is not the result of free choice.

Boethius found many of the elements of this reasoning in other writers, but he put them together in his own way, and his argument loomed over medieval discussions long after philosophers learned to make the distinctions in propositional logic that escaped him. It is not merely Aquinas who follows him closely;[18] even Ockham ends up by proposing, in his own terms, a solution to the problem along surprisingly Boethian lines.[19]

NOTES

1. Since these pages sketch a very large background to the detailed historical and topic-based chapters that follow, the bibliography is mainly restricted to references to fuller introductions, themselves with fuller bibliographies. For a quick guide to further reading, see Marenbon (2007, 354–57).

2. See the chapters by Tarrant (63–99: sceptical about label 'Middle Platonism') and Edwards ('On Numenius', 115–25) in Gerson (2010).

3. For an authoritative recent survey, see Algra et al. (2005).

4. See Ebbesen (1981), Evangeliou (1988) and (for qualifications) Chiaradonna (2007).

5. Adapted material from *The Elements of Theology* was put into Arabic, in the circle of al-Kindî, as the *Book of the Pure Good*.

6. See Perl (767–87) in Gerson (2010).

7. See below, Chapter 2, p. 32; and for the most distinguished Christian pupil of Ammonius, John Philoponus, p. 32.

8. See Marenbon (2008).

9. Strange and Zupko (2004).

10. An important study of the transmission of Platonic material to the Latin world is Gersh (1986).

11. The bibliography on Augustine is vast. An invaluable list of editions of his texts, and an up-to-date, but uncritical listing of secondary works is given in Gerson (2010, 1105–14). Kirwan (1989) gives a clear and critical account of some philosophical topics; Rist (1994) and especially Flasch (2003) provide a fuller view of his thought, as do the contributions to Stump and Kretzmann (2001).

12. Marenbon (2003) provides a quick survey, and Marenbon (2009) brings together a group of specialists to give a more sophisticated and nuanced view; for details of Boethius's works and their editions, see 303–10. Chadwick (1981) remains the best study of the historical and theological background.

13. Courcelle (1967) takes this approach to an extreme for the *Consolation*.

14. Boethius translated Aristotle's own *Topics* and wrote a commentary to it, now lost. But he also wrote a very extensive commentary on Cicero's *Topics* and a monograph *On Topical Differentiae*.

15. Treatise III is a discussion about divine and creaturely goodness, which contains nothing specifically Christian; Treatise IV is a straightforward confession of Christian faith.

16. A sophisticated exponent of the view that Boethius has a satirical intention is Joel Relihan (see Relihan 2006); for a critique, see Danuta Shanzer ('Interpreting the *Consolation*') in Marenbon (2009, 228–54).

17. Sharples ('Fate, prescience and free will') in Marenbon (2009, 207–27), provides a very balanced discussion of this complicated topic and gives full reference to past treatments. Note also Marenbon (forthcoming).

18. See Marenbon (2005) for the tradition up to the time of Aquinas, and Hoenen (1993) for a longer survey.

19. See his *Treatise on Predestination, God's Knowledge and Future Contingents*, Assumption 6.

BIBLIOGRAPHY

Algra, Kempe et al., eds. 2005. *The Cambridge History of Hellenistic Philosophy*. Cambridge: Cambridge University Press.

Chadwick, Henry. 1981. *Boethius. The Consolations of Music, Logic, Theology, and Philosophy*. Oxford: Oxford University Press.

Chiaradonna, Riccardo. 2007. Porphyry and Iamblichus on Universals and Synonymous Predication. *Documenti e studi sulla tradizione filosofica medievale* 18:123–40.

Courcelle, Pierre. 1967. *La Consolation de Philosophie dans la tradition littéraire.* Paris: Études Augustiniennes.

Dronke, Peter. 2008. *The Spell of Calcidius. Platonic Concepts and Images on the Medieval West.* Florence: Galluzzo.

Ebbesen, Sten. 1981. *Commentators and Commentaries on Aristotle's* Sophistici Elenchi. Leiden, the Netherlands: Brill (Corpus Latinum Commentariorum in Aristotelem Graecorum 7).

Evangeliou, Christos. 1988 *Aristotle's Categories and Porphyry.* Leiden, the Netherlands: Brill (Philosophia antique 48).

Flasch, Kurt. 2003. *Augustin. Einführung in sein Denken.* Stuttgart, Germany: Reclam, 3rd ed.

Gersh, Stephen. 1986. *Middle Platonism and Neoplatonism: The Latin Tradition.* Notre Dame: University of Notre Dame Press (Publications in Mediaeval Studies 23).

Gerson, Lloyd P., ed. 2010. *The Cambridge History of Philosophy in Late Antiquity.* Cambridge: Cambridge University Press.

Hoenen, Maarten J. F. M. 1993. *Marsilius of Inghen. Divine Knowledge in Late Medieval Thought.* Leiden, the Netherlands: Brill (Studies in the History of Christian Thought 50).

Kirwan, Christopher. 1989. *Augustine.* London and New York: Routledge.

Marenbon, John. 2003. *Boethius.* New York: Oxford University Press.

Marenbon, John. 2005. *Le temps, l'éternité et la prescience de Boèce à Thomas d'Aquin.* Paris: Vrin.

Marenbon, John. 2007. *Medieval Philosophy: an Historical and Philosophical Introduction.* London and New York: Routledge.

Marenbon, John. 2008. 'The Latin tradition of logic'. In *Handbook of the History of Logic.* 2. *Mediaeval and Renaissance Logic*, ed. Dov. M. Gabbay and John Woods, 1–63. Amsterdam: Elsevier.

Marenbon, John, ed. 2009. *The Cambridge Companion to Boethius.* Cambridge: Cambridge University Press.

Marenbon, John. Forthcoming. Divine Prescience and Contingency in Boethius's *Consolation of Philosophy. Rivista di storia della filosofia* (2012).

Relihan, Joel C. 2006. *The Prisoner's Philosophy: Life and Death in Boethius's Consolation.* Notre Dame, IN: University of Notre Dame Press.

Rist, John. 1994. *Augustine.* Cambridge: Cambridge University Press.

Strange, Stephen K. and Jack Zupko, eds. 2004. *Stoicism. Traditions and Transformations.* Cambridge: Cambridge University Press.

Stump, Eleonore and Norman Kretzmann, eds. 2001. *The Cambridge Companion to Augustine.* Cambridge: Cambridge University Press.

CHAPTER 2

GREEK PHILOSOPHY

BÖRJE BYDÉN
& KATERINA IERODIAKONOU

1. Historical Overview

1.1. Prolegomena

Which medieval Greek texts and authors should be counted as philosophical is not as immediately clear as, for instance, which ancient Greek texts and authors should (which is not to deny that there may also be room for debate about the canon of ancient Greek philosophy). Thus, some recent works on Byzantine philosophy focus entirely on authors who are at best background figures in others.[1] Part of the explanation for this is that Byzantine philosophy is not a well-established academic discipline. Since, in addition, the word 'philosophy' is used by Byzantine authors in different senses, some (or possibly all) of which are very different from its modern academic use, individual scholars have felt free to define 'Byzantine philosophy' in accordance with their own scholarly interests and convictions.

Our conviction is that 'philosophy' is the name not of a well-defined species of human activity but of a tradition that constantly redefines itself and, consequently, resists universal definition. Philosophy is, ultimately, whatever philosophers think it is. This leads us to consider that the most reasonable way of dealing with the vagueness of the term 'Byzantine philosophy' is to focus on those Byzantine texts and authors that most closely relate, consciously or otherwise, to the concerns of other, more generally recognised, philosophical texts and authors. From a historical point of view, ancient Greek philosophical texts and authors constitute an obvious frame of reference since they are practically the only ones known in Byzantium. From a philosophical point of view, it would perhaps be more rewarding to highlight ideas in Byzantine authors that somehow tie in with preoccupations of the modern analytical or Continental tradition. And for readers of this volume, no doubt, any themes and problems shared by the Byzantines with contemporary medieval philosophers will be of particular interest. We shall try in this chapter to discuss Byzantine philosophy in a way that will be illuminating and interesting to modern students, but of necessity the historical point of view will dominate. More specifically, we will start by sketching a historical overview of Greek philosophy in the Middle Ages, and then present some philosophical issues on logic, epistemology, metaphysics and natural philosophy in which Byzantine philosophers engaged. It should perhaps be pointed out that epistemology was not regarded as a separate division of philosophy by these philosophers, whereas the four mathematical disciplines, and likewise ethics, economics and politics, were. Our account is understandably not comprehensive but merely aims to give a representative sample of Byzantine philosophical production.

1.2. The Background: Neoplatonism and Christianity

It has become something of a commonplace to say that philosophy in Antiquity was not an academic subject but a way of life. If we look specifically at philosophy in Late Antiquity, it is easy to see that this commonplace has much to recommend it. There were no longer any competing schools of philosophy. Practically all known pagan philosophers from the mid–third century onwards seem to have identified themselves as members of a single philosophical community—notwithstanding significant local and individual differences—which they thought had overcome the disagreements of the previous periods and now continued in the spirit of the ancient masters.[2]

It is the theory and practice of this community that we call Neoplatonism. The theory was a systematic framework based on the interpretation of Plato's dialogues, which integrated elements of Pythagorean, Aristotelian and, to a lesser extent, Stoic thought. The practice aimed at identification, so far as possible, with God, through submission to the rule of reason and hence the development first of political, then of theoretical, virtues. Even though many Neoplatonists insisted that this development had to be supported by theurgic ritual, it is important to realise that philosophy in Late Antiquity was not any old way of life; its practitioners conceived of it as a life according to reason.

In this respect philosophy differs subtly, but crucially, from other ways of life that developed in parallel in the world of Late Antiquity. The practitioners of a Christian way of life, for instance, have usually considered it more important to live in faith than according to reason, whether or not they think that these two principles ultimately coincide. This is obviously not to say that Christianity does not have a significant theoretical dimension.

This dimension came to the fore in the second and third centuries, when polemics against Gnosticism and Judaism helped shape the orthodox Christian body

of doctrines. Many fundamental philosophical notions, mostly of Platonic provenance, were tacitly adopted and integrated; others were vehemently repudiated as
being in conflict with the revealed truth. But it was especially the internal Christian
controversies, first (in the fourth century) over the relation between Christ and the
Father, and later over the relation between the divine and human natures of Christ,
that pressed upon the parties the need to resort to Aristotelian logic (as taught in
the Neoplatonist schools) in order to clarify their concepts and refine their arguments. Those Christian authors who took integration furthest were initially on the
losing side and thus branded as heretics (Arius, Eunomius and others), but from the
mid–fifth century onwards philosophical concepts and arguments came to occupy
a more central space in the works of Chalcedonian, Nestorian and Monophysite
authors (see Frede 2005).

An extreme example of orthodox Christian assimilation of Neoplatonic philosophy (including theurgy) is provided by the late-fifth or early-sixth-century author
who presented himself as Dionysius the Areopagite. His doctrines were accepted as
apostolic by the Church partly thanks to the interpretative efforts of his commentators John of Scythopolis (early to mid-sixth) and Maximus the Confessor (580–
662).[3] Maximus exploited Platonic and Aristotelian concepts, at least partly drawn
directly from philosophical sources, to develop not only a highly sophisticated
Christology but also a comprehensive Christian cosmology and anthropology,
which have attracted much scholarly attention in recent years.[4] The role of Aristotelian logic as a propaedeutic to Christian theology was further strengthened by the
inclusion of fifty 'philosophical chapters' (sixty-eight in a later redaction), elucidating basic concepts mainly from Porphyry's *Isagoge* and Aristotle's *Categories*, in
John of Damascus's (c. 675–749) *Fountainhead of Knowledge*, which enjoyed immense authority and wide circulation throughout the Greek Middle Ages.[5]

These authors (and others before and after them) sometimes set up a contrast
between Christian and pagan philosophy. The former is often qualified as 'true'.
According to Maximus the Confessor (*Capita de caritate* 4.47), for instance, Christian philosophy (in other texts divided into 'practical', 'natural' and 'theological philosophy') is concerned with three things: the commandments, the dogmas and the
faith (see Tollefsen 2008, 6–8 and 183–89). This explains how '(true) philosophy' can
be used as a synonym for Christian piety, especially that exhibited by monks. It is
precisely the conscious replacement of the traditional rule of reason with that of
faith that persuades us to leave '(true) philosophy', so understood, out of account in
this chapter. '(True) philosophy' is intended to supplant, not to be a continuation of,
'pagan philosophy'.[6]

Greek Christian philosophy in the sense that concerns us here can be said to
have been brought to maturity in the late fifth and early sixth centuries. If we think
of ancient (or Late Antique) philosophy as characteristically involving rational argument, or more specifically, valid arguments from premises that are either true
and primary or more or less universally acceptable, then it is natural that the first
attempts by Greek Christians to pursue philosophy on a large and systematic scale
should have been made in the context of competition with pagan philosophers.

Such a context was provided in Alexandria, where Christian students frequently attended the courses of Ammonius and his successors. To get the better of the philosophers and set the students' minds at rest, it was not enough, in these circumstances, to argue from Scriptural authority. The challenge was to prove by rational argument that the Christian revelation was true.

This challenge was taken up by John Philoponus (c. 490–c. 570) in a series of three voluminous works on the question of the eternity of the world, designed to show, first, that the arguments of Aristotle and Proclus in favour of eternity were inconclusive; and second, that there were conclusive arguments against it. Many of Philoponus's arguments went on to have a spectacular career in the Islamic and Jewish as well as the Latin Christian traditions.[7] Some examples of their use by later Greek authors will be mentioned in the section on natural philosophy. But perhaps an even more important legacy was Philoponus's rationalist approach to the Christian revelation. Many later philosophers shared his assumption that it was possible to demonstrate the truth of the biblical account of creation—some of them, no doubt, because they found his arguments compelling.

Philoponus's works should probably be seen as the crowning achievement of a long-term campaign to defend Christian doctrine against the Neoplatonists' arguments. They were preceded, notably, by two surviving dialogues in the style of Plato: Aeneas of Gaza's *Theophrastus* (c. 485), which deals extensively with the question of the pre-existence of the soul,[8] and Zacharias Scholasticus's *Ammonius* (probably after 512), which focuses on the question of the eternity of the world.[9] Not much is known about the direct effects of the campaign. But some of Ammonius's successors to the chair at Alexandria bear Christian names. Men like David, Elias and Stephanus in the mid to late sixth century carried on the tradition of expounding Aristotle's *Organon*, hardly ever revealing their religious persuasion.[10] The same studied disinterest may be noticed in many later commentators and paraphrasts. The fact that practical philosophy was replaced with piety—and reason, as a guiding principle, with faith—may go some way towards explaining why theoretical philosophy was to a large extent reduced to an element of classical education in Byzantium.

1.3. The Recovery of Ancient Philosophy

The disintegration of the ancient city culture set in a little later in Byzantium than in the Latin West. It was also less thorough and sooner interrupted. No philosophy schools survived the political and economic crises of the seventh century (including, crucially, the capture of Alexandria by the Arabs in 641), but when higher education was restored after the end of iconoclasm (in 843),[11] teachers and scholars very much picked up where their Alexandrian colleagues had left off.

There were never any autonomous universities in the Byzantine Empire.[12] During periods of cultural revival, higher education was available at the imperial or patriarchal schools of Constantinople; apart from that, it was offered by private teachers. The emphasis was on rhetoric. The modest philosophical curriculum would normally include elementary Aristotelian logic and natural philosophy combined with elementary mathematics (based on Nicomachus's *Introductio arithmetica* and the first six books of Euclid's *Elements*). A standard logic course would cover the subject matter of Porphyry's *Isagoge* and Aristotle's *Categories, On Interpretation, Prior Analytics* 1.1–7 and *Sophistical Refutations* 1–7, supplemented by a brief sketch of the hypothetical syllogisms in the Peripatetic or in the Stoic tradition. The original texts would be studied with the aid of Late Antique or Byzantine commentaries. In many cases, however, they would be replaced with paraphrases or compendia (for instance, the short synopsis from the beginning of the eleventh century by the so-called 'Anonymus Heiberg'). This applies even more to natural philosophy, for which the earliest more substantial evidence is provided by a few eleventh-century compendia (Michael Psellos, *De omnifaria doctrina*; Anonymus Baroccianus; Symeon Seth, *Conspectus rerum naturalium*). The attribution to Michael Psellos of a full-length commentary on Aristotle's *Physics* has recently been disputed.[13]

The first period of cultural revival (ninth–early tenth centuries) was of critical importance for the survival of ancient Greek philosophy as well as other literature. The vast majority of extant texts other than the Bible and the Church Fathers go back to one or two minuscule copies prepared in this period. Some of these manuscripts, notably Arethas's annotated copy of Aristotle's *Organon* (MS Vaticanus Urbinas graecus 35), also testify to scholarly efforts to collect and preserve ancient traditions of commentary.[14] Photios's essays on topics from the *Isagoge* and the *Categories* (mid–ninth century) will be briefly discussed in the section on metaphysics.

The second period of cultural revival (mid–eleventh to mid–twelfth centuries) produced a relatively large number of works of interest for the history of philosophy. The famous historian and polymath Michael Psellos (1018–c. 1078) had a strong partiality for the Late Antique Neoplatonists—especially Proclus—so much so that it has been doubted whether he really was a sincere Christian.[15] His philosophical works display vast erudition but are, for the most part, derivative.[16] An example of his ability to bring his scholarly experience to bear on traditional philosophical topics is found in his essay on homonymy and synonymy, which will be discussed in the section on logic. Usually, however, his notes on theological authors, especially Gregory of Nazianzus, show more originality, not least by virtue of the fact that they draw freely on philosophical sources.

Many of Psellos's works seem related to his teaching activities, for instance, his paraphrases of the *On Interpretation* and the *Prior Analytics*. The same is true of the works of his student and successor in the office of Consul of the Philosophers, John Italos (c. 1025–c. 1083). Italos was put on trial (and finally condemned) by the Orthodox Church in 1077 and 1082, on the charge of having advocated the systematic use of logical reasoning in trying to resolve central theological issues, such as the incarnation of Christ or the relation of Christ's two natures. The collection of ninety-three answers to philosophical questions posed by his students, known as the *Quaestiones quodlibetales*, includes treatments of philosophical issues like the theory of universals, which will be briefly discussed in the section on metaphysics.

In 1117, history repeated itself, as Italos's student Eustratios (c. 1050–c. 1120), Bishop of Nicaea, was suspended on charges similar to those brought against his teacher. Shortly thereafter, he was commissioned by the disenfranchised princess Anna Komnene to write commentaries on Books 1 and 6 of the *Nicomachean Ethics*;[17] his commentary on Book 2 of the *Posterior Analytics* may also have been requested by Anna. Other commentaries were composed by Michael of Ephesus (fl. c. 1125): on Books 5, 9 and 10 of the *Nicomachean Ethics*, on the *Politics* (fragmentarily preserved; see O'Meara 2008), on *Metaphysics* 6–14 (see Luna 2001), on the *Sophistical Refutations* (see Ebbesen 1981, I, 262–85), on the *Parva naturalia*, and on Aristotle's zoological treatises (see Arabatzis 2006). Around the same time, two commentaries on the *Rhetoric*, one by a certain Stephanus and one by an unknown author, possibly Michael of Ephesus, were also produced (see Conley 1994). By and large, these commentaries are the oldest extant on the respective Aristotelian works, a fact that in itself suggests that they were written as part of a coordinated project.[18] Having said that, it is perfectly clear that the twelfth-century commentators based their works on pre-existing material, often of ancient origin. Their own contribution may for all that have been of no small significance. Sometimes they defended views that betray their Christian faith. Such an example from Eustratios's comments will be briefly discussed in the section on epistemology.

The commentary project was an exceptional enterprise, which left few traces in the learned activities of the immediately following decades, at least in Byzantium. But Michael of Ephesus's commentary on the *Sophistical Refutations*, which was almost immediately rendered into Latin by James of Venice, contributed (as the work of 'Alexander') towards the establishment of the New Logic in the West.[19] It has been suggested (Ebbesen 2008, 121–22) that James may have been personally acquainted with Michael. Similarly, Robert Grosseteste's translations of the *Ethics* commentaries by Michael, Eustratios and an anonymous twelfth- or thirteenth-century author on Book 7 came to play a role in the rediscovery of Aristotelian ethics in the latter half of the thirteenth century.

The Neoplatonic influence on some of these *Ethics* commentaries is pervasive (see, e.g., Trizio 2009). That especially Proclus's popularity continued to soar in twelfth-century Byzantium is evidenced by such items as Isaac Komnenos Sebastokrator's (1093–1152) Christianising paraphrases of the *Three Treatises on Providence* (otherwise only extant in Latin translation) and Nicholas of Methone's (d. c. 1160/66) detailed refutation of the *Elements of Theology*.[20]

Another commentary on Book 2 of the *Posterior Analytics* was composed by Theodore Prodromos (c. 1100–c. 1170).[21] Prodromos was an astonishingly versatile author, from whose pen also flowed the *Xenedemus* (1836), a short Plato-style elenctic dialogue on themes from Porphyry's *Isagoge*, as well as a small essay, *On 'Great' and 'Small'* (1887), in which he attacks Aristotle's claims in the *Categories* that these terms are neither quantities (but relatives) nor contraries.

1.4. The Palaiologan Renaissance

In 1204 Constantinople fell into the hands of the Crusaders. Devastating as this event may have been to the infrastructure of education and scholarship, it was also the beginning of a period of intensified contact with Western European culture.

Debates with Dominicans and Franciscans over the conditions for a reunion of the Churches are likely to have stimulated renewed interest in the application of logic to theology, but more importantly, the awareness of the Westerners' reverence especially for Aristotle had the effect of raising the prestige of philosophical studies in general. The Byzantine Empire was now reduced to a small, ethnically homogeneous state. Ancient philosophy became national heritage.[22]

Yet Greeks were also curious to learn about the peculiarities of the Western tradition. In the years after the reconquest of Constantinople in 1261, the first translations of Latin philosophical and theological works appeared. Boethius's *De topicis differentiis* and *De hypotheticis syllogismis* were done by Manuel Holobolos, who also back-translated the pseudo-Aristotelian *De plantis* from Alfred of Sareshel's Latin rendering of the Arabic text.[23] Maximus Planoudes (b. c. 1255/60) translated Cicero's *Somnium Scipionis* with Macrobius's commentary, as well as Augustine's *De trinitate* and Boethius's *De consolatione philosophiae*. A second wave of translations came in the 1350s–60s, when the brothers Demetrios and Prochoros Kydones produced Greek versions of central works of Thomas Aquinas and others.

A seminal figure in the revival of learning in the mid–thirteenth to mid–fourteenth century (the so-called 'Palaiologan renaissance') was Nikephoros Blemmydes (1197–c. 1269), the most celebrated teacher of his day. His two compendia, *Epitome logica* (1885a) and *Epitome physica* (1885b), which combine the basics of Aristotelian logic and natural philosophy with elements from other sources (such as John of Damascus and the Stoic cosmologist Cleomedes), enjoyed very wide circulation.[24] Besides these, Blemmydes composed two anthropological works, *De anima* and *De corpore* (still not available in critical editions), and two short treatises on a much-discussed question of both theological and philosophical import, *Against the Predetermination of the Terminus of Life*, in which he defends the causal connection between an individual's moral choices and his or her life span.[25]

Blemmydes's efforts were continued by a number of his students and admirers. Recent studies have shed light on the role of the historian George Pachymeres (1242–c. 1310) not only as a textbook author but also as a philosophical editor and commentator. His *Philosophia* is a huge paraphrase-compendium covering not only Aristotle's logic and natural philosophy but also his metaphysics and ethics. His *Quadrivium* bears witness to improved standards of knowledge in the mathematical disciplines. But Pachymeres is now also recognised as the author of proper, so-called 'exegetical' commentaries: his supplement to Proclus's incompletely transmitted commentary on the *Parmenides* was the first Greek Plato commentary since the sixth century, and comprehensive 'exegetical' commentaries on Aristotle's *Organon*, *Physics*, *Metaphysics* and *Nicomachean Ethics* have also been more or less securely attributed to him.[26] Around the same time, the monk Sophonias composed a series of 'mixed' paraphrases of Aristotelian works, which incorporate portions both of the original text and of earlier 'exegetical' commentaries: the one of the *De anima* preserves parts of John Philoponus's commentary on Book 3, which is lost in the Greek original.

While encouraging a more profound study of ancient philosophy in general, the 'Palaiologan renaissance' also fostered a more independent attitude towards the individual philosophers, especially Aristotle. This is exemplified in the works of Nikephoros Choumnos (c. 1250/55–1327) and Theodore Metochites (1270–1332), both high officials at the court of Andronikos II around the turn of the fourteenth century. Choumnos is the author of a small collection of philosophical essays, mainly on elemental theory, cosmology and psychology, which have been very little studied; most of them are still not available in critical editions. It is typical of his approach that he seeks to argue philosophically, that is, by valid inference from principles and definitions that are universally accepted, for views that are already theologically established.

His rival Theodore Metochites wrote a handbook to Ptolemy's *Almagest* (the *Stoicheiosis astronomike*) and commentaries on all of Aristotle's writings on natural philosophy. In addition, he gathered inspiration from Plutarch and Synesius to create a new philosophical genre, embodied in the *Semeioseis gnomikai*, a collection of 120 essays on subjects as diverse as the reasons for Aristotle's obscurity and for Plato's use of the dialogue form, the interrelations between different faculties of soul and the pros and cons of different political constitutions. A leitmotif running through most of this work as well as Metochites's numerous speeches and poems is the sentiment that there is nothing stable in the world of sense perception. The epistemological pessimism that results from this sentiment will be briefly discussed in the epistemology section. Of particular interest in this connection is that Metochites criticises Aristotle for having promised scientific knowledge in fields where it is not to be had, out of intellectual vanity.

This criticism was taken one step further by Metochites's student Nikephoros Gregoras (c. 1293/94–1360/61), especially in the dialogue *Florentius*, which constitutes a highly dramatised account of one of the author's debates with Barlaam of Calabria (c. 1290–1348). Gregoras's attacks on Aristotle's (and by extension all Latin Aristotelians') views are so apparently random and arbitrary that one cannot help but wonder what his own position is. The answer is to be sought in his criticism of Aristotle's theory of science, which makes it clear that he takes an even more radically pessimistic view concerning knowledge of the natural world than his teacher did. It is an intriguing fact that Gregoras is the exact contemporary of Nicholas of Autrecourt.[27]

Gregoras was also engaged in the great theological struggle of the fourteenth century, the one related to the claims of the Hesychast monks of Mount Athos to be able to attain direct spiritual and bodily experience of the uncreated light of God by employing certain techniques of prayer. Their claims were disputed by the above-mentioned Barlaam, who understood them to imply that the Hesychast monks could have bodily experience of God's inscrutable essence (*ousia*). In their defence Gregory Palamas (1296–1359) developed the Patristic notion of divine activities (*energeiai*) in such a way as to allow for these to be uncreated (see Bradshaw 2004, 234–42 and 268–75; Podskalsky 1977, 124–73). When accusations of polytheism were levelled by Gregoras and others, he replied by stressing the ontological dependence of the divine activities on God's inscrutable essence. In the end, Palamism carried the day; many of its opponents converted to Catholicism.

1.5. The Great Controversy

Metochites's and Gregoras's criticism of Aristotle was counterpointed by praise for Plato. This trend was carried over into the fifteenth century, culminating in 1439 when George Gemistos Plethon (c. 1355/60–1452) published his *De differentiis*, in which he tried to show that Aristotle's philosophy was much inferior to Plato's, in spite of being more admired, especially in the Latin West. This sparked a controversy that lasted for thirty years, engaging many of the best minds of Byzantium in the years immediately before and after the fall of Constantinople; most of them already lived in Italian exile.[28]

Plethon's criticism was more systematic and substantial than Metochites's and Gregoras's, and even if his arguments are often specious, he clearly has a knack for pinpointing features of Aristotelian doctrine that may be likely to cause worry, not least to Christian followers. In theology he found fault with Aristotle's God for being only a final, not a productive cause, and thus not of the existence but merely the movement of the world; in ontology he discarded the homonymy of being and the hierarchy of substances asserted in the *Categories*; in logic he objected to the claim in *De interpretatione* 7 that pairs of 'indefinite statements' constitute an exception to the law of non-contradiction, as well as to that in *Prior Analytics* 1.9 that a syllogism with an apodeictic major premise and an assertoric minor premise yields an apodeictic conclusion; in psychology he criticised Aristotle's description of the soul as changeless (and not merely incapable of locomotion) and pointed out inconsistencies in his noetics; in ethics he inveighed against the definition of virtue as a mean between extremes and the conception of contemplative pleasure as the goal of life; in cosmology he attacked the theory of a fifth element; in general physics he questioned the possibility of teleology without rational agency and, especially, he accused Aristotle of sacrificing the principle that everything has a cause in order to evade determinism while saving the principle that 'every cause produces its effect in a necessary way'. More than a third of the treatise was taken up by a rebuttal of Aristotle's criticism of the theory of Forms.

Of the several replies to Plethon's arguments, the weightiest was that of George Scholarios (c. 1405—after 1472), whose *Contra Plethonem* bears testimony to a philosophical education that was clearly more Latinate than Greek. Scholarios was filled with indignation at Plethon's suggestion that Aristotle's philosophy was incompatible with the Christian faith, and he took particular care to repudiate the claim that Aristotle's God is not creator of the world, which he did by resorting to the thesis of creation *ab aeterno*.

Plethon took the opportunity to develop and expand his criticism in a second treatise, *Contra Scholarii obiectiones*. Others rose to speak on Aristotle's behalf, among them Theodore of Gaza and, most zealously, George of Trebizond. The latter wrote in Latin, and so did another native of Trebizond, Cardinal Bessarion, whose relatively balanced refutation of the frantic anti-Platonism of his former compatriot, *In calumniatorem Platonis*, was printed in 1469 in more than seventy copies. Bessarion and his coauthors sought to give a fair hearing to both philosophers; their full-scale systematic account of Platonism contributed significantly to its dissemination in early-modern Western Europe.[29]

A few years after his appointment as patriarch in 1454 (thus after the fall of Constantinople), Scholarios gave orders for all existing copies of Plethon's *Book of Laws* to be destroyed. It is clear from the remaining fragments that this work set out Plethon's proposals for the improvement of human life, advocating an ethics and a politics inspired by Plato himself as well as by Middle Platonic, Neoplatonic and Stoic writers, and propagating a philosophically refined form of the old Olympian religion. One surviving chapter (*De fato*) argues, both from the nature of causation and from the assumption that the gods have foreknowledge, that all events are determined by fate. According to Plethon, this is compatible with freedom, not in the sense that human beings are not ruled by anything, but in the sense that they are ruled by their own intellect: being free is simply submitting to the decree of Zeus. Divine punishment is justified as a means for teaching human beings to be free. A combination of Platonic and Stoic influences is also manifest in another short treatise by Plethon, *On Virtues* (on which see, most recently, Tambrun-Krasker 2009).

2. LOGIC

2.1. Byzantine Logic?

There is no doubt that Byzantine logical writings rely heavily on Neoplatonic sources. Their authors knew well the ancient Aristotelian commentaries, either directly or from previous compilations, and drew extensively from them. Moreover, some of these authors incorporated elements from the works of the Greek Fathers into their texts, thereby showing that they considered the ancient logical theories to be perfectly compatible with Christian doctrine. For instance, there are many cases in which they showed a preference for using Christian names and phrases as examples illustrating Aristotle's logical doctrines. Finally, during the last century of the Byzantine Empire, and in particular in George Scholarios's logical commentaries, we encounter for the first time in Byzantine logic the influence of Western scholasticism. Scholarios explicitly said that the Latin logical works had been very instructive to him both in terms of their content and in terms of their method, and he stressed that it was exactly this dependence that added extra value to his commentaries, as compared with the works of previous Byzantine authors (see Ebbesen and Pinborg 1981–82; Ierodiakonou 2011).

Given all these influences, it is reasonable to question whether there is anything original in Byzantine logic, anything that may be treated on a par with the developments in the late-medieval West. The reply is, regrettably, that Byzantine philosophers seem to have been interested in reading and interpreting Aristotle's logic simply as the preliminary stage of the philosophical curriculum, that is to say, as

something to learn and use as an instrument without any ambition to develop it further. There are at least two factors that can be adduced to explain this phenomenon:
first, since there was no university in Byzantium and the learned community was
quite small, the old encyclopedic attitude to education was never abandoned, and
logic was not perceived as an area of specialised philosophical research (see Ebbesen
1996, 77; Bydén 2003, 23–24); second, Byzantine theology never acquired the systematic character it came to have in the West and, consequently, never required the ser-
vices of any cutting-edge logic. Still, the careful study of Byzantine logical texts proves
rewarding for two reasons: first, because they sometimes constitute sources for
ancient logical doctrines; and second, because they may be interesting as attempts to
apply logic on theological issues.

2.2. Psellos on Homonymy and Synonymy

An example of such a Byzantine text is the small essay by Michael Psellos on the
issue of homonymy and synonymy (*Philosophica minora* 1 [1992], opusc. 6). This is
actually a letter that Psellos sent to the *logothetēs tou dromou*, the equivalent of a
foreign minister, who had asked him whether the two Basils and the two Gregories
are homonyms or synonyms (quite a surprising question to come from an administrator, at least for our modern ears, but this clearly suggests that at the time some
knowledge of Aristotle's logic was a prerequisite for anyone who wanted to make a
career in the Byzantine bureaucracy). The account given by Psellos is on the whole
in close agreement with what the Neoplatonist commentators have to say about the
first lines of Aristotle's *Categories* (see especially Ammonius, *In Categorias* 19.17–
20.12; 22.12–19). That is to say, homonyms are things that have a name in common,
but the definition of being that corresponds to the name is different; whereas synonyms not only have a name in common, but in their case the definition of being that
corresponds to the name is also the same. Furthermore, things can be both homonyms and synonyms in relation to different names; for instance, the two Ajaxes,
namely Ajax from Salamis and Ajax from Locri, are said to be homonyms with
respect to the proper name 'Ajax', which they share in spite of not having exactly the
same description—after all, the one is the son of Telamon and the other the son of
Oileus—but with respect to the specific name 'man' they are said to be synonyms
since the same definition of 'man' applies in both cases.

Most Byzantine commentators follow the ancient commentators on this subject
and their discussion ends here.[30] Psellos's essay, however, also reveals influences from
other sources. For instance, he explicitly refers to Plato, who calls the two Socrateses
homonyms (*Theaetetus* 147d1; *Sophist* 218b3), and to Gregory of Nazianzus (*Oration*
29.14), who similarly treats the two Gregories as homonyms. And this is the position
Psellos himself wants to defend, that is, that the two Gregories should be regarded
only as homonyms and not as synonyms. Briefly stated, Psellos's reasoning is the
following: to each of the two Gregories, for instance, Gregory of Nyssa and Gregory
of Nazianzus, at least three definitions may apply: namely, one as animal, one as man
and one as the particular individual with the proper name 'Gregory'. Strictly speaking,

of course, as Psellos rightly points out, individuals and highest genera cannot be defined in the standard Aristotelian sense since there are no further essential differentiae or higher genera available; hence, an individual can only be described in terms of its individual characteristics. But leaving this difficulty aside, Psellos argues that the two Gregories share the first two definitions, namely, the definition of animal and the definition of man, but they cannot possibly share the third; for it is impossible that they are exactly the same, that is, that they share exactly the same features, country, parents, age and education. Psellos, therefore, claims that the two Gregories share the definitions of their common species and genera, but not the definitions 'of their being' (*tōn huparxeōn*), which consist of enumerations of the accidental properties that jointly distinguish the individuals.

Psellos's insistence here on regarding the two Gregories only as homonyms and not as synonyms, and thus on deviating from the accounts given by the ancient commentators and by other Byzantine scholars, is interesting for two reasons: (a) it reveals the influence, most probably indirect rather than direct, of another ancient philosophical tradition, namely the Stoic one; and (b) it seems that the issue of homonymy was not only discussed in the narrow milieu of people interested in logic for logic's sake, but had significant implications in central theological disputes.

The central point of Psellos's thesis that the two Gregories are homonyms rather than synonyms relies on the assumption that individuals as such also have a definition of sorts, an account of what it is to be that individual. That is to say, on Psellos's view, when we ask whether the two Gregories are homonyms or synonyms, what we are interested in is whether the two Gregories as individuals are homonyms or synonyms in relation to their name. So, we need to check whether the appropriate descriptions of the two Gregories are identical or not; and since, of course, they are not—for it is impossible for two individuals to be perfectly identical—the two Gregories are homonyms. Now, the description of an individual, being the enumeration of the jointly distinctive accidental properties of this individual, provides us with an understanding of what Psellos calls the 'peculiar being' (*idia huparxis*) and the 'peculiarity' (*idiotēs*) of this individual. He also claims that the description of an individual determines what the Byzantines call the 'hypostasis' (subsistence) of this individual. Also, in what follows, Psellos stresses that the task of the true philosopher is not just to grasp the species and the genus to which an individual belongs; rather, the true philosopher tries to acquire knowledge of the peculiar being, the peculiarity and the subsistence of individuals.

But it is not only the term 'subsistence' that is not to be found in Aristotle and his ancient commentators; the terms 'peculiar being' and 'peculiarity' are also foreign to the Aristotelian discussion about homonymy and synonymy. And there clearly is a connection between these terms and a Stoic doctrine, the so-called Stoic doctrine of the four categories. According to the Stoics (as reported by, e.g., Simplicius, *In Categorias* 66.32–67.2), either we characterise an object (a) as a certain matter, that is, a substance (*hupokeimenon*); or (b) as a certain matter being qualified in a certain way (*poion*)—either 'commonly' (*koinōs*), for instance as a human being, or 'peculiarly' (*idiōs*), for instance as Socrates; or (c) as a certain matter being somehow disposed (*pōs echon*), for instance as running; or (d) as a certain matter being somehow disposed relative to something (*pros ti pōs echon*), for instance, as being the man on the right or the son of somebody. It is clear that the category of the peculiarly qualified is the relevant one when drawing the connection between the Stoic categories and Psellos's discussion on homonymy. For in his attempt to under-line the importance of knowing the particular individual, rather than the genera and the species of the individual, Psellos moves in the direction of the Stoic category of the peculiarly qualified. Needless to say, Psellos does not explicitly refer to the Stoics here, and there is no indication that the influence is direct. However, it seems clear that when it comes to the knowledge of individuals, Psellos feels the need to supple-ment the Aristotelian doctrine with elements of other ancient philosophical tradi-tions, which have been transmitted through the centuries and appropriated or assimilated by generations of philosophers in one way or another, for instance, by Porphyry and John of Damascus.

To turn next to the other interesting aspect of Psellos's account of homonymy, let me introduce what Gregory of Nazianzus has to say on the subject. The issue discussed here is the divine nature of Christ, and in particular the thesis ascribed to Gregory's opponents, most probably Nestorius and his followers, that Christ may be called God but is not really God. Apparently, these people maintained that the no-tion of Christ's divinity was based on a homonymy: in the same way that a dog and the dog-star share the same name 'dog', though its definition is different in the two cases, the Father and Christ share the same name, but they are essentially different. John of Damascus, too, mentions Nestorius's reference to homonymy, before he himself stresses that the two natures of Christ are indivisible and form the unity of his subsistence (*Dialectica* 48 65.121–3; *Fragmenta philosophica* 6.21–3; *Expositio fidei* 47.53–66). It thus becomes obvious how important it was, for theological rea-sons, to understand homonymy. Of course there are no clear traces of this discus-sion in Psellos's letter about homonymy and synonymy, but the reference to the views of Gregory of Nazianzus suggests that what he has in mind there may well be the Christological and Trinitarian problems.

3. EPISTEMOLOGY

Neoplatonic influence as well as the Christian appropriation of ancient philosoph-ical theories leave their mark on the Byzantines' views regarding not only logical matters but also the nature, scope and sources of human knowledge. For although there are no writings from the Byzantine period devoted exclusively to epistemolog-ical issues, still such issues are addressed, sometimes cursorily, sometimes in greater detail, in the context of discussions, for instance, about the soul's cognitive faculties and states, or in the Byzantine comments on Aristotle's theory of demonstration in the *Posterior Analytics*.

3.1. Knowledge of First Principles

One notable example is Eustratios's discussion of *Posterior Analytics* 2.19 (257.33–258.27), which seems to introduce a Christian alternative to both Plato's theory of recollection and Aristotle's doctrine of the knowledge of first principles: an alternative that allows for innate knowledge without necessitating the assumption of the pre-existence of the soul (see Ierodiakonou 2010). According to Eustratios, both Plato and Aristotle denied that human beings are born with full knowledge of first principles; in Plato's view such knowledge is forgotten at birth, while Aristotle held that we are born with only potential, not actual knowledge of first principles. Eustratios's own opinion, in contrast, is that we do have full knowledge of first principles from birth, but this knowledge is obscured by our bodily impulses, and it is only when our soul is guided either by our sense perceptions or by appropriate instruction that the first principles come forth, so that we can assent to them. It seems that, in defending this position, Eustratios makes an effort to be in line with Christian doctrine. For the soul, according to Christian doctrine, when created by God, is created perfect, that is, with all the knowledge it needs. Consequently, if human beings lose sight of the knowledge and understanding that their soul actually possesses, it is because they are susceptible to being led astray by their bodily impulses.

That Eustratios did have this Christian doctrine in mind is borne out by a passage in his commentary on *Nicomachean Ethics* 6.3 (297.15–298.6). Here Eustratios explicitly states that the fact that man is created perfect from the beginning entails not only that he is capable of discursive thought, but also that he comprehends the intelligibles immediately by simple intuition. But he can only do this insofar as he retains the position allotted to him by the Creator and directs his desire towards the intellectual realm; since he inclines towards a sensual life, his intellectual eye is clouded. This is why he has recourse to sense perception; through the immediate cognition of particulars, sense perception provides the intellect with material for constructing universal concepts on which human knowledge can securely rest. In this way man is healed from his affliction and can again turn his attention towards the intellectual realm and his Creator. A similar position was defended by Nikephoros Choumnos in his essay *Adversus Plotinum* (1887, PG 140: 1420–28).

3.2. Possibility of Knowledge

Nevertheless, a certain distrust of the senses as sources of knowledge was also expressed by many Byzantine thinkers, owing to the direct or indirect influence of Platonism. In his *Semeioseis gnomikai*, Theodore Metochites expresses sympathy with a view that he ascribes to the ancient Sceptics and traces back to the aporetic dialogues of Plato, namely, that knowledge is impossible, at least in the domains of natural philosophy, ethics and the arts (*technai*), where the objects studied are in constant flux. As for mathematics, Metochites argued that it is superior to natural philosophy, in that it alone studies objects that are in the strict and proper sense knowable. Theology was, according to him, a different kettle of fish: the truth about divine matters can be attained, but only through inspiration from above (Bydén 2002; Demetrakopoulos 1999).

The idea that human reason is incapable of fully comprehending things divine has been present from the very beginning of Greek philosophical thought. The Christian Fathers endorsed this idea in a radical version, claiming that God's essence (*ousia*) is, in principle, indescribable and incomprehensible and thus the object of faith alone, whereas, on the other hand, his attributes, including existence, unity and being the creator of the world, are susceptible of proof. In the Late Byzantine period, both Gregory Palamas and Barlaam of Calabria stressed that neither demonstrative nor dialectical syllogisms can yield any knowledge of God's essence, but they debated fiercely over the question as to whether God's attributes can be the subject of demonstrative or only of dialectical syllogisms, the former alternative being defended by Palamas (Ierodiakonou 2002b; Sinkewicz 1980, 1982).

4. METAPHYSICS

A recurrent feature in Byzantine philosophical texts is the attempt to bring fundamental Aristotelian or Platonic terms into harmony with the usage of the Church Fathers. This could be interpreted more ambitiously as part of an endeavour to coordinate philosophy and theology, but it is, in fact, very rarely pursued beyond a purely negative criticism of the philosophers' definitions.

4.1. Photios on Substance

A first example is Photios's *Amphilochia* 138, where Aristotle's account of substance in the *Categories* is criticised for bringing together two entirely different things. The two entirely different things are not, as in Plotinus's famous criticism in *Ennead* 6.1, sensible and intelligible substance, but what Aristotle himself calls primary and secondary substance: individuals and universals. Photios assumes that Aristotle's categories are highest genera in the strict sense. Genera in the strict sense are always predicated synonymously—according to the same name and definition—of all the species, sub-species and individuals they subsume. But primary and secondary substance do not seem to be substances according to the same name and definition—in fact, of the six characteristics of substance given by Aristotle, only two are both necessary and sufficient conditions for being a substance. The others are either shared with other categories or exclusive to either primary or secondary substance. Of the first-mentioned two characteristics, namely, 'to be numerically one and still be able to receive contraries' and 'not to admit of a more and a less', Photios interprets the latter in such a way as to suggest that only one of the two sets of substance can be properly called 'substance'. For if they were both properly so called, the very distinction between primary and secondary would indicate (as Aristotle would readily admit) a difference in degree of substantiality between the two sets, but if the characteristic of 'not to admit of a more and a less' holds true of substance itself (as Photios insists, contrary to Aristotle, *Categories* 3b33–36; cf. 2b7–8), then this is impossible.

It seems as though Photios's solution is to restrict the category of substance properly so called to the most specific species. This has obvious disadvantages: what to do, for instance, with all the other universal substances? The advantage in Photios's view would be a better correspondence with the definition of the Fathers, who (according to John of Damascus, *Dialectica* 31) used the words 'substance', 'nature' and 'form' (*morphē*) interchangeably for infimae species, while reserving the word 'hypostasis' for individuals.[31]

4.2. Photios and Others on Universals

'Hypostasis' is indeed the word used by Photios for individuals in another discussion (*Amphilochia* 77), concerned with a question familiar from the introduction to Porphyry's *Isagoge*, namely, whether genera and species are bodies or incorporeal. According to Photios, genera and species are parts of 'accounts' (*logoi*), and these have nothing in common with bodies. Therefore, we may expect them to be incorporeal. Now, there is nothing to prevent this being true of genera and species of incorporeal individuals, but in the case of genera and species of bodies a difficulty arises. For how can 'the incorporeal' (*to asōmaton*) be predicated of a body? If the universal predicate 'man' is incorporeal, and Socrates is a man, it will follow that Socrates is incorporeal. The ensuing discussion makes it clear that Photios does not suspect that the middle term could be ambiguous. Instead, he proposes the solution that genera and species of bodies are neither bodies (*sōmata*), in the sense of having mass and extension, nor incorporeal, but corporeal (*sōmatika*), in the sense of being indicative of bodies.

Photios was only the first of a series of Byzantine writers who showed an interest in the problems of universals.[32] Their discussions were cast in terms introduced by the Late Antique commentators on Porphyry's *Isagoge* and Aristotle's *Categories*. It seems to have been Ammonius who—following the lead of Proclus (*In Euclidis Elementa* 50.16–51.13)—first formulated a distinction between (1) the genera and species *before* the particulars (*pro tōn pollōn* or *ante res*), that is to say, the Platonic Ideas, being separate (intelligible) substances present to the mind of the Demiurge; (2) the genera and species *in* the particulars (*en tois pollois* or *in rebus*); and (3) the genera and species *based upon* the particulars (*epi tois pollois* or *post res*), which are universal concepts, existing only in individual human souls.[33] It is the genera and species *post res* that are predicable of all the individuals falling under them.

According to Proclus and many of his followers (see especially Simplicius, *In Categorias* 5), the genera and species *ante res* are the transcendent formal causes of the generic and specific character of individuals, which are not themselves covered

by the definitions that apply to the individuals. They are not, therefore, the correlates of universal concepts. This role is played by their products, the genera and
species *in rebus*. These, however, are in themselves inseparable from the differentiae, distinctive qualities and matter of the individuals in which they inhere. They
have generic or specific, but not numerical unity. In order to be predicable of all the
individuals falling under them, the genera and species will have to be completely
abstracted from all the particular properties with which they are bound up in
nature. This abstraction, which results in universal concepts, is carried out by individual human souls.

This standard position might be described, then, as non-realism concerning
universal predicates, insofar as and to the extent that realism is the view that any
universal predicate has a correlate in nature that is numerically one. It does, however, state that universal predicates have correlates in nature that are only specifically one. (It is also realist in the sense that it assumes the existence outside
nature of Forms that are numerically one and that are causes of the universals in
the world, but, as we have seen, this is not relevant to the question of predication.) Thus, it has been labelled both as 'moderate realism' and as 'conceptualism'
or 'broad nominalism', depending on whether or not 'realism' was considered to
involve the assumption of actually existing universals in nature.

A. C. Lloyd (1990, 70–75), who emphasised the non-realist features of the standard position, pointed out that the Byzantines had a theological reason for drifting
towards realism. For if it is applied to a theological context, a non-realist position
may seem to entail that the Divine Nature shared by the Father, the Son and the
Holy Spirit is dependent on individual human souls. And even if the Divine Nature
in each of the three hypostases is specifically one, this will not be enough to save the
numerical unity of the Godhead. John Philoponus seems to have actually drawn
this conclusion and defended it, in his lost work *On the Trinity*. His view was condemned as the tritheist heresy.[34]

Proclus and his followers were, of course, not committed to any conclusions
that seemed to follow from the application of their non-realism to a realm above
nature. That John Italos and Eustratios insisted, in spite of this and notwithstanding
the cautionary example of Philoponus, on discussing theological matters from a
non-realist position was taken by Lloyd (1990, 74–75) as a clear sign of their
antirealist predilections.

4.3 John Italos on Universals

It is true that there are passages in Italos's *Quaestiones* that lend support to Lloyd's
statement that he 'perfectly understood' (1990, 71) and espoused Alexander's and
Porphyry's non-realist interpretation of Aristotle.[35] Writing several decades before
the celebrated debates between William of Champeaux and Abelard, Italos showed
keen interest in the problems of universals.[36] In *QQ* 5 he draws a basic distinction
between non-predicable genera *ante res* and predicates. He then goes on to consider the latter both in relation to the soul as separate entities, predicable of each

and every thing that falls under them, and in relation to the things themselves, in which case they are naturally inseparable from these and incapable of being predicated of a plurality. In fact, he suggests that they *are* genera only insofar as they are abstracted.

It may be noted that Italos invokes the two-sided character of the predicates also in reply to the Porphyrian question that had occupied Photios, namely, whether genera and species are bodies or incorporeal. Considered as inherent in particulars, they are bodies, he says, but as abstracted by the soul they are incorporeal.[37] When he later maintains that the genera *in rebus* (which, as we have seen, amount only to particular forms) are as such predicable of the single individuals 'by which each of them is participated', it seems likely that this inconsistency is caused by the double wish to, on the one hand, save the genera's and species' predicability of individuals and, on the other hand, remove the transitivity assumption on which the fallacy of incorporeal Socrates depends.

Italos also takes on the first of the questions posed by Porphyry at the beginning of his *Isagoge*: Do genera and species exist? They have to exist, he says, since their destruction (and introduction) entails that of the particulars, which exist. He tries to corroborate this by an elimination argument. There are four senses of non-being: by excess, by default, by privation and absolute non-being. Genera and species cannot be non-being by privation since in that case they could not be predicated of individuals. Nor can they be absolutely non-being, for then they could not even be spoken of. But if they are non-being by excess or default, they are still being something. More precisely, they are *en-upostata*, that is, entities inhering in hypostases (or individuals). The term is Christian and suggests the influence of John of Damascus.

However, in QQ 67, which is a systematically arranged series of thirty-one brief questions and answers on the predicables, Italos argues that considered in relation to particulars, genera and species both are and are not, although neither in the strict sense. Viewed in themselves, on the other hand, they are actually non-being. The same conclusion seems to be reached in QQ 52, where it is said of the genera *in rebus* that their existence is necessarily bound up with the things in which they inhere, so that they are particular (and even 'individual', but this must be understood in the adjectival sense of 'being characteristic of an individual'), whereas the genera *post res*, being neither intelligibles nor sensibles, can only be commonalities; commonalities, however, do not exist in themselves but, again, only in the things in which they inhere.

Some of these passages seem to confirm Lloyd's later admission that 'their often ambiguous pronouncements' indicate that 'Byzantine authors had not sufficiently focused the question what exactly the *fundamentum in re* amounted to. Consequently it is in a sense anachronistic to expect in each case to assess their commitment to nominalism' (1990, 73–74). Both these tendencies, to ambiguity as well as to broad non-realism, are clearly present in the early-fourteenth-century essay by Nikephoros Choumnos, *On Matter and Forms* (ed. Benakis 1973). This will be discussed in a later section.

5. Natural Philosophy

Byzantine writers on natural philosophy normally adhered to the Neoplatonic Aristotelianism of their Late Antique predecessors, so long as it was not perceived as contradictory to Christian doctrine. In the following, we will focus on some of the deviations from the norm. One of the most important points of conflict, in Middle and Late Byzantium as in the fifth and sixth centuries, was the question as to whether or not the world had had a beginning (and would come to an end). We shall return to this question, but let us first look at some examples of critical discussions of the traditional conceptual framework of general physics.

5.1. Nature, Matter and Forms

Aristotle's concept of nature, like that of substance, was sometimes declared to be in need of a redefinition in accordance with the usage of the Fathers. In spite of Joannou (1956, 79–80) and Benakis (1963), there is no clear evidence for any such concern in Michael Psellos, who seems to have been content with promulgating the Neoplatonic interpretation of Aristotle ('nature is the proximate cause of movement and rest in bodies, ultimately dependent on God') as valid for the sensible world, while insisting that 'nature' as applied to soul, intellect or God can only signify the mere fact of existence (*Theol.* 69).

The case is different with John Italos. In two rather curious texts, printed by Joannou as QQ 4β′ (92) and 4γ′ (93), he sets himself the task of refuting the ancient philosophers' conceptions of matter and nature. The Middle Platonist notion that the world was fashioned out of pre-existent matter was a favourite target of Christian attacks since the early third century. Italos, too, in QQ 92, initially promises to deal especially with pre-existent matter, but in the end he leaves us not so much with a series of arguments against any specific views of the ancient philosophers as with an assorted list of real and (mostly) apparent contradictions inherent in the concept of matter as such. Similarly, his arguments in QQ 93 against the purported Aristotelian, Platonic and Stoic definitions of 'nature' are at times so glaringly fallacious that one cannot help but wonder whether he really wants his readers to draw a different conclusion than the one stated. The stated conclusion is that nature, since all the definitions under review have proved inaccurate, can only be the same thing as the substance, the form (*morphē*) and the infima species, as the Fathers tell us, namely, the container of the individuals. Italos probably has one particular Father in mind: namely, again, John of Damascus, who in his *Institutio elementaris* (ch. 7) describes the most specific species of the divine hypostases, the angels and human beings alike as 'containers of the individuals'.[38] Joannou (1956, 84–85) suggested that both QQ 92 and QQ 93 should be dated after the trial in 1077. It is certainly tempting to see them as evidence of a forced, and perhaps not very sincere, recantation.

There is, however, no reason to doubt the sincerity of Nikephoros Choumnos's opposition to what he understood to be the doctrines of Plato and Aristotle both on matter and on forms. The learned courtier of Andronikos II devoted his philosoph-ical essay *On Matter and Forms* to showing that matter cannot be ungenerated, cannot have been generated by anything else than God and cannot ever have existed in separation from forms, while forms cannot exist in separation from matter.

As regards forms, it is principally the Platonic (separate and causative) ones with which Choumnos is occupied (182–316). He argues that if they do not allow self-predication, they cannot be participated in by individuals; whereas if they do, they cannot be universal and eternal, but must be particular and perishable. But they must be participated in by individuals. Therefore, he suggests, we would do better to think of the first created man as the Idea of Man. Adam was really a mortal rational animal, and he was designed to beget offspring that corresponded to the same definition (and similarly with every other natural entity). Forms, then, are really particular and perishable, but the new ones that are constantly generated give rise to an appearance of eternality and an opportunity for forming a concept and a definition, which applies equally to the actual man and the form. It is not always easy to follow Choumnos's reasoning, but for the most part he appears to be taking an even more decidedly antirealist stance than was usual in Byzantium. Some of his statements strongly suggest that he wished to deny the existence not only of forms *ante res* but also of universal forms *in rebus*. Obviously, this does not necessarily mean that he had a well-considered theory of universals. Some of his statements may also suggest that he was a traducianist: that he believed that the souls of human beings are generated by the parents, not created by God. But what he says about the perishability of the forms of man will not apply to the rational soul since he evi-dently believed in its immortality.

5.2. Place, Time and Eternity

Some Byzantine authors were loath to accept Aristotle's definition of place as 'the limit of the containing body', partly, it seems, because it entailed the non-existence of extra-cosmic void. They might draw support from the Stoic Cleomedes's *Caeles-tia*, which enjoyed considerable popularity in the Middle and Late Byzantine period (see Todd 1992). So did, for instance, Nikephoros Blemmydes, in his *Epitome physica* 31 (Bydén 2003, 163–68). Blemmydes also praised the greater accuracy of the defini-tion provided by Damascius apud Simplicium (*In Physica* 4), who says that place is the measure of the position of things in a position. Most likely, his reason for prefer-ring Damascius's definition to Aristotle's was that the former takes the places of in-corporeal entities into account.

The Aristotelian definition of time as 'the measure of movement with respect to before and after' seems to have been generally accepted in Byzantium, with the ob-vious proviso—in compliance with Plato's *Timaeus* 38b—that it had to have been cre-ated, since before creation there was no movement. So, for instance, argued Michael Psellos (1989b, *Theologica* 88). But as against a conception of eternity as circular move-ment, ascribed by him to Aristotle as well as to Plato, and the Plotinian account of it as involving neither movement nor extension, Psellos championed that of Gregory of

Nazianzus (*Oration* 38.8), according to which eternity and time are different because eternity is immeasurable, but analogous since eternity is also coextensive with the eternal beings, like a kind of temporal movement and extension (see also Benakis 1980–81). This notion of an extended eternity, similar to that defended in Late Antiquity by John Philoponus, was also favoured by Blemmydes (although it looks like a concession to Plotinus's account that he qualifies the relevant kind of extension as 'concentrated' [*Epitome physica* 24.21]). Neither he nor Psellos made any distinction in this context between 'transcendent' and 'angelic' eternity, but Choumnos (*De natura mundi*) was careful to point out that sensible time and intelligible eternity are both created (and thus both, in a sense, time), whereas the Creator transcends even the everlastingness of eternity (see Bydén 2003, 129–30).

5.3 Arguments for a Beginning

Without a doubt, the doctrine that the world is eternal was the one item of Aristotelian natural philosophy that most provoked the antagonism of Byzantine writers. They tended to resolve the tension between this doctrine and (Platonic or Christian) creationism not by recourse to a definition of creation that allowed for the world's being eternal, but by rejection of the Aristotelian doctrine. The example was set by John Philoponus, who attempted to prove through philosophical argument, in his *Contra Proclum*, *Contra Aristotelem* and *De contingentia mundi*, that it is both possible and necessary for the world to have had a beginning, before he proceeded to show by scriptural exegesis that the biblical account of creation does not contradict the findings of natural philosophy (*De opificio mundi*). Some of Philoponus's arguments appear fairly regularly in Byzantine texts at least from the eleventh century onwards. For instance, John Italos (*QQ* 61), Symeon Seth (*Conspectus rerum naturalium* 30), Nikephoros Blemmydes (*Epitome physica* 24.20–25) and Nikephoros Choumnos (*De natura mundi*) all make use of (more or less garbled versions of) the famous argument that states that if the world is a finite body (as Aristotle proves in *De caelo* 1.5–7) and all finite bodies have a finite power (as Aristotle proves in *Physics* 8.10), then, assuming that a finite power is by definition one whose effects will eventually cease, the world will come to an end. And if the world must come to an end, it must also have had a beginning, according to the rule laid down in Aristotle's *De caelo* 1.12.[39] Byzantine writers also draw on Philoponus for arguments against Aristotle's theory of a fifth element (see Bydén 2003, 178–99).

NOTES

1. Compare, for example, Kapriev (2005) with more traditional accounts like Hunger (1978, 3–62); de Libera (1993, 9–51); Eleuteri (1995, 437–64) or the present one. For some reflections on the historiography of Byzantine philosophy, see Trizio (2007).

2. See Section 1.1 of Chapter 1.

3. On the Neoplatonism of Ps.-Dionysius, see Klitenic Wear and Dillon (2007). On his reception in Byzantium, see Rorem and Lamoreaux (1998); Louth (2008a, 2008b). On his importance in the Latin tradition, see above, Chapter 1, p. 20.

4. On Maximus's philosophical sources, see Mueller-Jourdan (2005, 44–48); Törönen (2007, 13–43); Tollefsen (2008, 6–16). For a general account of Maximus, see also Louth (1996).

5. The original redaction of the philosophical chapters aka the *Dialectica* seems to have been intended as an introduction only to Book 3 of the *Fountainhead of Knowledge*, namely, 'On the Orthodox Faith'. John depends heavily on an earlier tradition of Christian logical textbooks, in which the commentators on Porphyry and Aristotle were excerpted and summarised. On this tradition, see Roueché (1974, 1980). For a general account of John of Damascus, see Louth (2002).

6. The semantics of 'philosophy' and its cognates in Antiquity was studied by Malingrey (1961). Her conclusion that 'philosophy' was an ambiguous term in Antiquity was called into question by Barnes (2002). For Byzantine examples supporting Malingrey's conclusion, see Podskalsky (1977, 19–22).

7. See Sorabji (1983); Davidson (1987).

8. See Krausmüller (2009, 54–58), who questions Aeneas's seriousness. See also S. Gertz, J. Dillon, D. Russell (trans.), *Aeneas of Gaza, Theophrastus, with Zacharias of Mytilene, Ammonius* (London: Bristol Classical Press, 2012); M. W. Champion, *Explaining the Cosmos: Creation and Cultural Interaction in Late-Antique Gaza* (Oxford: OUP, 2014).

9. See Bydén (2012). See also Minniti Colonna (1973); Watts (2005).

10. On David and Elias, see Wildberg (2003a, 2003b). On Stephanus, see Searby (forthcoming). On the occasional surfacing of what seem like distinctively Christian views, see Westerink (1990, 338–41).

11. The imperial school at Magnaura was probably established sometime after 843. An interest in classical education, including philosophy, is noticeable already in the late eighth century, but Leon the Mathematician complains that he was still unable to get beyond grammar school in Constantinople in the 820s. See Lemerle (1971); Louth (2007).

12. On the universities of Western Europe, see below, Chapter 9, Section 1.2. On Byzantine education in general, see, most recently, Markopoulos (2008), with bibliography.

13. By Golitsis (2007). The largely codicological evidence presented by Golitsis is compelling, if not conclusive. See also Benakis's reply (Psellos 2008, 5*–10*) with Bloch's review (2009).

14. On Arethas as a bookman and an Aristotelian scholar, see the introduction by Share in his edition of Arethas's scholia. On the transmission of Aristotle, see Harlfinger (1971, 46–50).

15. Most radically, perhaps, by Kaldellis (2007, 191–224).

16. A more benevolent view of Psellos as a philosopher is taken by O'Meara (1998), Duffy (2002) and Ierodiakonou (2002b).

17. On the twelfth-century *Ethics* commentaries, see, most recently, the papers in Barber and Jenkins (2009) with Ebbesen's review (2010). See also Mercken (1990).

18. On the 'circle of Anna Komnene', see Browning (1962), and, more recently, Frankopan (2009).

19. Only fragments of James's translation are preserved. See Ebbesen (1981, vol. 1, 286–89; vol. 2, 331–555; vol. 3, 4–7).

20. Isaac Komnenos Sebastokrator (1977, 1979, 1982); Nicholas of Methone (1984). On the study of Proclus in Byzantium, see, Parry (2006). On the study of Proclus in Byzantium, see Parry (2006), and, most recently, the papers by D.J. O'Meara, M. Trizio and S. Gersh in S. Gersh (ed.), *Interpreting Proclus: From Antiquity to the Renaissance* (Cambridge: CUP, 2014).

21. On this commentary, which is still unedited, see Cacouros (1994–95).

22. On Greek-Latin philosophical interaction, see Ebbesen (1992, 1996, 2002).

23. For the anonymously transmitted *De plantis* translation, see Drossaart, Lulofs and Poortman (1989). On Holobolos as a translator, see also Bydén (2004); Fisher (2006).

24. Blemmydes's two compendia are still not available in critical editions. Wegelin's editions of 1605 were reprinted in *Patrologia graeca*, vol. 142.

25. On these and similar texts, see Lackner's introduction in his edition of 1985.

26. On Pachymeres's Aristotelian commentaries, see Golitsis (2008). They are unedited, with the exception of the *Physics* commentary, which was edited by Benakis as the work of Michael Psellos (2008).

27. See below pp. 214, 480–1.

28. On Plethon's life and works, see Woodhouse (1986). On the controversy, see also Karamanolis (2002).

29. On George of Trebizond's *Comparatio* and Bessarion's *In calumniatorem Platonis*, see Monfasani (2007); see also below, Chapter 10, 227.

30. For example, Photios, *Epistulae et Amphilochia* 5, q. 137.62–65; Arethas, *In Categorias* 139.30–140.13; 144.22–33; Scholarios, *In Categorias* 122.22–27.

31. For a more detailed analysis of *Amphilochia* 138, see Bydén (2013). For Photios's criticism of Aristotle's treatment of other categories, see Schamp (1996a, 1996b); Ierodiakonou (2005a).

32. A terse but incisive discussion of the problem of universals in Late Antiquity and Byzantium generally will be found in Lloyd (1990, 36–75); see also Benakis (1982).

33. Ammonius, *In Isagogen* 39.8–42.26; 68.25–69.11; 104.27–105.14.

34. On the other hand, as John of Damascus also saw (*Dialectica*, ἕτερον κεφάλαιον 39–44), if the Divine Nature is endowed with separate existence, there will be four substances in the Trinity. For a study, and a comparison with the Latin writer Roscelin, see Erismann (2008).

35. For a more detailed exposition of Italos's views on universals, see Ierodiakonou (2007). On Eustratios's theory of universals, see Lloyd (1987); Ierodiakonou (2005b).

36. On twelfth-century Latin debates on universals, see below, Chapter 8, pp. 173–8.

37. *Quaestiones quodlibetales* 4.8–10; 4.33–38; cf. ibid. 3.16–26; 19; 67.18–27.

38. As we have already seen, John regarded nature, substance, form and infima species as synonymous terms. His way of talking about the infimae species as 'containers of the individuals' is evidently inspired by Porphyry's *Isagoge* 5.12–16 and 7.27–8.3. On the *Institutio elementaris*, see Louth (2002, 38–40).

39. Symeon Seth (fl. c. 1080) also quotes a passage of Philoponus's criticism of Aristotle's theory of aether, which was edited by Wildberg as fr. 1/2, on the assumption that it is quoted independently from Simplicius, who reports the same argument. Since Symeon was probably a native Syriac speaker and is known as a translator of Arabic texts, it seems not impossible that he was familiar with some of the Philoponean arguments from one or other of these traditions. On Symeon Seth, see Magdalino (2002, 46–50).

BIBLIOGRAPHY

Anonymus Barroccianus. 1992. *Anonymi Miscellanea Philosophica: A Miscellany in the Tradition of Michael Psellos (Cod. Barrocianus Gr. 131)*, ed. I. N. Pontikos. Athens: The Academy of Athens (Corpus Philosophorum Medii Aevi: Philosophi Byzantini 6).

Anonymus Heiberg. 1929. *Anonymi Logica et Quadrivium*, ed. J. L. Heiberg. Copenhagen: Andr. Fred. Høst & Søn.

Arabatzis, Georgios. 2006. *Παιδεία καὶ Ἐπιστήμη στον Μιχαὴλ Ἐφέσιο. Εἰς Περὶ ζώων μορίων Α 1,3–2,10*. Athens: The Academy of Athens.

Arethas of Caesarea. 1994. *Scholia on Porphyry's Isagoge and Aristotle's Categories (Codex Vaticanus Urbinas Graecus 35)*, ed. M. Share. Athens: The Academy of Athens (Corpus Philosophorum Medii Aevi: Commentaria in Aristotelem Byzantina 1).

Barber, Charles and David Jenkins. 2009. *Medieval Greek Commentaries on the Nicomachean Ethics*, Leiden, the Netherlands: Brill.

Barlaam of Calabria. 1981. Solutions, ed. R. E. Sinkewicz. *Medieval Studies* 43:200–17.

Barnes, Jonathan. 2002. 'Ancient philosophers'. In *Philosophy and Power in the Graeco-Roman World*, ed. Gillian Clark and Tessa Rajak, 293–306. Oxford: Oxford University Press.

Benakis, Linos G. 1963. 'Michael Psellos' Kritik an Aristoteles und seine eigene Lehre zur "Physis" und "Materie-Form"-Problematik'. *Byzantinische Zeitschrift* 56:213–27 (reprint: 2002, 395–410).

———. 1980–81. '*Χρόνος καὶ αἰών. Ἀντιπαράθεση ἑλληνικῆς καὶ χριστιανικῆς διδασκαλίας στὸ ἀνέκδοτο ἔργο τοῦ Μιχαὴλ Ψελλοῦ*'. *Φιλοσοφία* 10–11: 398–421 (reprint: 2002, 463–86).

———. 1982. 'The problem of general concepts in Neoplatonism and Byzantine thought'. In Dominic J. O'Meara, *Neoplatonism and Christian Thought*. Albany, NY: SUNY Press.

———. 2002. *Texts and Studies on Byzantine Philosophy*. Athens: Parousia.

Blemmydes, Nikephoros. 1885a. 'Epitome logica'. In *Patrologia graeca*, ed. J. Wegelin, vol. 142, 685–1004. Paris: Garnier Fratres.

———. 1885b. 'Epitome physica'. In *Patrologia graeca*, ed. J. Wegelin, vol. 142:1004–320. Paris: Garnier Fratres.

———. 1985. *Gegen die Vorherbestimmung der Todesstunde*, ed. W. Lackner. Athens: The Academy of Athens (Corpus Philosophorum Medii Aevi: Philosophi Byzantini 2).

Bloch, David. 2009. Review of Psellos 2008. *Aestimatio* 6:180–87.

Bradshaw, David. 2004. *Aristotle East and West*. Cambridge: Cambridge University Press.

Browning, Robert. 1962. 'An unpublished funeral oration on Anna Comnena'. *Proceedings of the Cambridge Philological Society* n.s. 8:1–12 (reprint: 1990, in Richard Sorabji, ed., *Aristotle Transformed*. London: Duckworth, 393–406).

Bydén, Börje. 2002. '"To Every Argument There Is a Counter-Argument": Theodore Metochites' defence of scepticism (*Semeiosis* 61)'. In Ierodiakonou, 2002a, 183–217.

———. 2003. *Theodore Metochites' Stoicheiosis astronomike and the Study of Natural Philosophy and Mathematics in Early Palaiologan Byzantium*. Gothenburg: Acta Universitatis Gothoburgensis (Studia Graeca et Latina Gothoburgensia 66).

———. 2004. '"Strangle Them with These Meshes of Syllogisms": Latin philosophy in Greek translations of the thirteenth century'. In *Interaction and Isolation in Late Byzantine Culture*, ed. Jan Olof Rosenqvist, 133–57. Stockholm: Almqvist & Wiksell Tryckeri.

———. 2013. 'Photios and the Byzantine reception of the *Categories*'. In *The Reception of Aristotle's Categories in the Byzantine, Latin and Arabic Traditions*, ed. Sten Ebbesen, John Marenbon and Paul Thom. Copenhagen: Royal Danish Academy of Science and Letters.

———. 2012. 'A case for creationism: Christian cosmology in the 5th and 6th centuries'. In *The Many Faces of Byzantine Philosophy*, ed. Börje Bydén and Katerina Ierodiakonou. Papers from the Norwegian Institute at Athens.

Cacouros, Michel. 1994–95. 'La tradition du commentaire de Théodore Prodrome au deuxième livre de *Seconds Analytiques* d'Aristote: quelques étapes dans l'enseignement de la logique à Byzance'. *Δίπτυχα* 6:329–54.

Choumnos, Nikephoros. 1887. 'Adversus Plotinum'. In *Patrologia graeca*, ed. F. Creuzer, vol. 140, 1404–38. Paris: Garnier Fratres.

———, 1973. Περὶ τῆς ὕλης καὶ τῶν ἰδεῶν, ed. L. G. Benakis. Φιλοσοφία 3:360–79 (reprint: Benakis, 2002, 554–73).

Conley, Thomas M. 1994. 'Notes on the Byzantine reception of the peripatetic tradition in Rhetoric'. In *Peripatetic Rhetoric after Aristotle*, ed. William W. Fortenbaugh and David C. Mirhady, 217–42. New Brunswick and London: Transaction Publishers.

Davidson, Herbert A. 1987. *Proofs for Eternity, Creation and the Existence of God in Medieval Islamic and Jewish Philosophy*. Oxford: Oxford University Press.

De Libera, Alain. 1993. 'La philosophie à Byzance'. In *La philosophie médiévale*. Paris: Presses Universitaires de France.

Demetrakopoulos, Giannis A. 1999. Νικολάου Καβάσιλα Κατὰ Πύρρωνος. Πλατωνικὸς Φιλοσκεπτικισμὸς καὶ Ἀριστοτελικὸς Ἀντισκεπτικισμὸς στὴ Βυζαντινὴ Διανόηση του 14ου αἰώνα. Athens: Parousia.

Drossaart Lulofs, H. J. and E. L. J. Poortman, eds. 1989. *Nicolaus Damascenus, De Plantis: Five Translations*. Amsterdam: North-Holland.

Duffy, John. 2002. 'Hellenic philosophy in Byzantium and the lonely mission of Michael Psellos'. In Ierodiakonou, 2002a, 139–56.

Ebbesen, Sten. 1981. *Commentators and Commentaries on Aristotle's Sophistici Elenchi: A Study of Post-Aristotelian Ancient and Medieval Writings on Fallacies*, 3 vols. Leiden, the Netherlands: Brill.

———. 1992. Western and Byzantine Approaches to Logic. *Cahiers de l'Institut du Moyen-Age Grec et Latin* 62:167–78.

———. 1996. Greek and Latin Medieval Logic. *Cahiers de l'Institut du Moyen-Age Grec et Latin* 66:67–95.

———. 2002. 'Greek and Latin philosophical interaction'. In Ierodiakonou 2002a, 15–30.

———. 2008. 'Jacques de Venise'. In *L'Islam médiéval en terres chrétiennes: Science et idéologie*, ed. Max Lejbowicz, 115–32. Lille, France: Septentrion.

———. 2010. Review of Barber and Jenkins (2009). *The Medieval Review* 10.11.07.

Ebbesen, Sten and Jan Pinborg. 1981–82. Gennadios and Western Scholasticism: Radulphus Brito's *Ars vetus* in Greek Translation. *Classica et Medievalia* 33:263–319.

Eleuteri, Paolo. 1995. 'La filosofia'. In *Lo spazio letterario della Grecia antica*, vol. 2: *La ricezione e l'attualizzazione del testo*, ed. Giuseppe Cambiano, Luciano Canfora and Diego Lanza, 437–64. Rome: Salerno.

Erismann, Christophe. 2008. The Trinity, Universals, and Particular Substances: Philoponus and Roscelin. *Traditio* 53:277–305.

Eustratios of Nicaea. 1892. *In ethica Nicomachea commentaria*, ed. G. Heylbut. Berlin: Reimer (Commentaria in Aristotelem Graeca 20).

———. 1907. *In Analyticorum posteriorum librum secundum commentarium*, ed. M. Hayduck. Berlin: Reimer (Commentaria in Aristotelem Graeca 21.1).

Fisher, Elizabeth A. 2006. Manuel Holobolos, Alfred of Sareshal, and the Greek Translator of Ps.-Aristotle's *De Plantis*. *Classica et Mediaevalia* 57:189–213.

Frankopan, Peter. 2009. 'The literary, cultural and political context for the twelfth-century commentary on the *Nicomachean Ethics*'. In Barber and Jenkins, 2009, 45–62.

Frede, Michael. 2005. 'Les Catégories d'Aristote et les Pères de l'Église Grecs'. In *Les Catégories et leur histoire*, ed. Otto Bruun and Lorenzo Corti, 135–73. Paris: Vrin.

Golitsis, Pantelis. 2007. Un commentaire perpétuel de Georges Pachymère à la *Physique* d'Aristote, faussement attribué à Michel Psellos. *Byzantinische Zeitschrift* 100(2): 637–76.

———. 2008. *Georges Pachymère comme didascale*. *Jahrbuch der Österreichischen Byzantinistik* 58:53–68.

Gregoras, Nikephoros. 1975. *Fiorenzo o Intorno alla sapienza*, ed. P. L. M. Leone. Naples: University of Naples.

Harlfinger, Dieter. 1971. *Die Textgeschichte der pseudo-aristotelischen Schrift Περὶ ἀτόμων γραμμῶν: Ein kodikologisch-kulturgeschichtlicher Beitrag zur Klärung der Überlieferungsverhältnisse im Corpus Aristotelicum*. Amsterdam: Hakkert.

Holobolos, Manuel. 1982. *Eine byzantinische Übersetzung von Boethius' De hypotheticis syllogismis*, ed. D. Z. Nikitas. Göttingen, Germany: Vandenhoeck & Ruprecht (*Hypomnemata* 69).

———. 1990. *Boethius, De topicis differentiis καὶ οἱ μεταφράσεις τῶν Μανουὴλ Ὁλοβώλου καὶ Προχόρου Κυδώνη*, ed. D. Z. Nikitas. Athens: The Academy of Athens (Corpus Philosophorum Medii Aevi: Philosophi Byzantini 5).

Hunger, Herbert. 1978. *Die hochsprachliche profane Literatur der Byzantiner*, vol. 1. Munich: C.H. Beck'sche Verlagsbuchhandlung.

Ierodiakonou, Katerina. ed. 2002a. *Byzantine Philosophy and Its Ancient Sources*. Oxford: Oxford University Press.

———. 2002b. 'Psellos' paraphrasis on Aristotle's *De interpretatione*'. In Ierodiakonou 2002a, 157–81.

———. 2002c. 'The anti-logical movement in the fourteenth century'. In Ierodiakonou 2002a, 219–36.

———. 2005a. The Byzantine Reception of Aristotle's *Categories*. *Synthesis Philosophica* 39:7–31.

———. 2005b. Metaphysics in the Byzantine Tradition: Eustratios of Nicaea on Universals. *Quaestio* 5:67–82.

———. 2007. John Italos on Universals. *Documenti e studi sulla tradizione filosofica medievale* 18:231–48.

———. 2010. 'Eustratios' comments on *Posterior Analytics* B19'. In *Interpretations of Aristotle's Posterior Analytics*, ed. Frans de Haas, 55–71. Leiden, the Netherlands: Brill.

———. 2011. 'The Western influence on Late Byzantine Aristotelian commentaries'. In *Greeks, Latins, and Intellectual History* 1204–1500, ed. Martin Hinterberger and Chris Schabel, 373-83. Leuven: Peeters.

Isaac Komnenos Sebastokrator. 1977, 1979, 1982. 'On the substance of evils'. In *Proclus, Trois études sur la providence*, ed. D. Isaac, vol. 1, 153–223; vol. 2: 99–169; vol. 3, 127–200. Paris: Les Belles Lettres.

Italos, John. 1956. *Quaestiones Quodlibetales (Ἀπορίαι καὶ λύσεις)*, ed. P. Joannou. Ettal, Germany: Buch-Kunstverlag (Studia Patristica et Byzantina 4).

Joannou, Perikles. 1956. *Christliche Metaphysik in Byzanz. I. Die Illuminationlehre des Michael Psellos und Joannes Italos*. Ettal, Germany: Buch-Kunstverlag (Studia Patristica et Byzantina 3).

John of Damascus. 1969 and 1973. *Die Schriften des Johannes von Damaskos*, vols. 1 and 2, ed. B. Kotter. Berlin: De Gruyter.

Kaldellis, Anthony. 2007. *Hellenism in Byzantium. The Transformations of Greek Identity and the Reception of the Classical Tradition*. Cambridge: Cambridge University Press.

Kapriev, Georgi. 2005. *Philosophie in Byzanz*. Würzburg, Germany: Königshausen & Neumann.

Karamanolis, George E. 2002. 'Plethon and Scholarios on Aristotle'. In Ierodiakonou, 2002a, 253–82.

Klitenic Wear, Sarah and John M. Dillon. 2007. *Dionysius the Areopagite and the Neoplatonist Tradition: Despoiling the Hellenes*. Aldershot, UK: Ashgate.

Krausmüller, Dirk. 2009. 'Faith and reason in Late Antiquity: The perishability axiom and its impact on Christian views about the origin and nature of the soul'. In *The Afterlife of the Platonic Soul*, ed. Maha Elkaisy-Friemuth and John M. Dillon, 47–76. Leiden, the Netherlands: Brill.

Lemerle, Paul. 1971. *Le premier humanisme byzantin*. Paris: Presses Universitaires de France.

Lloyd, Anthony C. 1987. 'The Aristotelianism of Eustratius of Nicaea'. In *Aristoteles, Werk und Werkung*, ed. Jürgen Wiesner, vol. 2: 341–51. Berlin and New York: De Gruyter.

———. 1990. *The Anatomy of Neoplatonism*. Oxford: Oxford University Press.

Louth, Andrew. 1996. *Maximus the Confessor*. London: Routledge.

———. 2002. *St. John Damascene. Tradition and Originality in Byzantine Theology*. Oxford: Oxford University Press.

———. 2007. *Greek East and Latin West. The Church AD 681–1071*. New York: St Vladimir's Seminary Press.

———. 2008a. The Reception of Dionysius up to Maximus the Confessor. *Modern Theology* 24(4):573–83.

———. 2008b. The Reception of Dionysius in the Byzantine World: Maximus to Palamas. *Modern Theology* 24(4):585–89.

Luna, Concetta. 2001. *Trois études sur la tradition des commentaires anciens à la Métaphysique d'Aristote*. Leiden, the Netherlands: Brill.

Magdalino, Paul. 2002. 'The Byzantine reception of classical astrology'. In *Literacy, Education and Manuscript Transmission in Byzantium and Beyond*, ed. Catherine Holmes and Judith Waring, 33–58. Leiden, the Netherlands: Brill.

Malingrey, Anne Marie. 1961.'Philosophia': Étude d'un groupe de mots dans la littérature grecque des présocratiques au IVe siècle après J.-C. Paris: Klincksieck.

Markopoulos, Athanasios. 2008. 'Education'. In *The Oxford Handbook of Byzantine Studies*, ed. Elizabeth Jeffreys, John Haldon and Robin Cormack, 785–95. Oxford: Oxford University Press.

Maximus the Confessor. 1963. *Capita de caritate*, ed. A. Ceresa-Gastaldo. Rome: Editrice Studium.

Mercken, H. P. F. 1990. 'The Greek commentators on Aristotle's *Ethics*'. In *Aristotle Transformed*, ed. Richard Sorabji, 407–43. London: Duckworth.

Metochites, Theodoros. 2002. *Semeioseis gnomikai 1–26 & 71*, ed. K. Hult. Gothenburg, Sweden: Acta Universitatis Gothoburgensis (Studia Graeca et Latina Gothoburgensia 65).

Michael of Ephesus. 1898. *Alexandri quod fertur in Aristotelis Sophisticos elenchus commentarium*, ed. M. Wallies. Berlin: Reimer (Commentaria in Aristotelem Graeca 2.3).

Minniti Colonna, Maria. 1973. *Zaccaria Scolastico: Ammonio*. Introduzione, testo critico, traduzione, commentario. Naples.

Monfasani, John. 2007. A Tale of Two Books: Bessarion's *In calumniatorem Platonis* and George of Trebizond's *Comparatio Philosophorum Platonis et Aristotelis*. *Renaissance Studies* 22(1): 1–15.

Mueller-Jourdan, Pascal. 2005. *Typologie spatio-temporelle de l'ecclesia Byzantine: La mystagogie de Maxime le Confesseur dans la culture philosophique de l'antiquité tardive*. Leiden, the Netherlands: Brill.

Nicholas of Methone. 1984. *Refutation of Proclus' Elements of Theology*, ed. A.A. Angelou. Athens: The Academy of Athens (Corpus Philosophorum Medii Aevi: Philosophi Byzantini 1).

O'Meara, Dominic. 2008. 'Spätantike und Byzanz: Neuplatonische Rezeption—Michael von Ephesos'. In *Politischer Aristotelismus. Die Rezeption der aristotelischen Politik von der Antike bis zum 19. Jahrhundert*, ed. Christoph Horn and Ada Neschke-Hentschke, 42–52. Stuttgart, Germany: Metzler.

Pachymeres, George. 1989. *Commentary on Plato's Parmenides (Anonymous Sequel to Proclus' Commentary)*, ed. L. G. Westerink et al. Athens: The Academy of Athens (Corpus Philosophorum Medii Aevi: Philosophi Byzantini 4).

Palamas, Gregory. 1988. *The One Hundred and Fifty Chapters*, ed. R. E. Sinkewicz. Toronto: Pontifical Institute of Mediaeval Studies.

Parry, Ken. 2006. 'Reading Proclus Diadochus in Byzantium'. In *Reading Plato in Antiquity*, ed. Harold Tarrant and Dirk Baltzly, 223–35. London: Duckworth.

Photios. 1986. *Epistulae et Amphilochia*, ed. L. G. Westerink, vol. 5. Leipzig, Germany: Teubner.

Plethon, George (Gemistos). 1973. Le *De Differentiis* de Pléthon d'après l'autographe de la Marcienne, ed. B. Lagarde. *Byzantion* 43:312–43.

———. 1987. *Traité des vertus*, ed. B. Tambrun-Krasker. Athens: The Academy of Athens (Corpus Philosophorum Medii Aevi: Philosophi Byzantini 3).

———. 1988. *Contra Scholarii pro Aristotele obiectiones*, ed. E. V. Maltese. Leipzig, Germany: Teubner.

Podskalsky, Gerhard. 1977. *Theologie und Philosophie in Byzanz: Der Streit um die theologische Methodik in der spätbyzantinischen Geistesgeschichte (14./15. Jh.)*. Munich: C.H. Beck'sche Verlagsbuchhandlung (Byzantinisches Archiv 15).

Prodromos, Theodore. 1836. 'Ξενέδημος ἢ φωναί'. In *Anecdota graeca e codicibus manuscriptis Bibliothecarum Oxoniensium*, ed. J. A. Cramer, vol. 3, 204–15. Oxford.

———. 1887. Théodore Prodrome sur le grand et le petit, ed. P. Tannery. *Annuaire de l'Association pour l'encouragement des études grecques en France* 21:104–9.

Psellos, Michael. 1948. *De omnifaria doctrina*, ed. L. G. Westerink. Utrecht, the Netherlands: J.L. Beijers.

———. 1989a. *Philosophica minora*, vol. 2, ed. D. O'Meara. Leipzig: Teubner.

———. 1989b. *Theologica*, ed. P. Gautier. Leipzig: Teubner.

———. 1992. *Philosophica minora*, vol. 1, ed. J. Duffy. Stuttgart and Leipzig, Germany: Teubner.

———. 2008. *Kommentar zur Physik des Aristoteles*, ed. L.G. Benakis. Athens: The Academy of Athens (Corpus Philosophorum Medii Aevi. Commentaria in Aristotelem Byzantina 5).

Rorem, Paul and John C. Lamoreaux, eds, 1998. *John of Scythopolis and the Dionysian Corpus: Annotating the Areopagite*. Oxford: Clarendon Press.

Rouéché, Mossman. 1974. Byzantine Philosophical Texts of the Seventh Century. *Jahrbuch der Österreichischen Byzantinistik* 23:61–76.

———. 1980. A Middle Byzantine Handbook of Logic Terminology. *Jahrbuch der Österreichischen Byzantinistik* 29:71–98.

Schamp, Jacques. 1996a. 'Photios aristotélisant? Remarques critiques'. In Καινοτομία. *Le renouvellement de la tradition hellénique*, ed. Margarethe Billerbeck and Jacques Schamp, 1–17. Fribourg, Switzerland: Éditions universitaires.

———. 1996b. 'La "localisation" chez Photios. Traduction commentée de *Questions à Amphilochios* 145'. In *Aristotelica Secunda. Mélanges offerts à Christian Rutten*, ed. André Motte and Joseph Denooz, 265–79. Liège, Belgium: C.I.P.L.

Scholarios, George (Gennadios). 1936. *Œuvres complètes*, ed. L. Petit, X. A. Sideridès and M. Jugie, vol. 7. Paris: Maison de la bonne presse.

Searby, Denis. Forthcoming. 'Stéphanos d'Alexandrie'. In *Dictionnaire des philosophes antiques* 5, ed. Richard Goulet. Paris: CNRS.

Ševčenko, Ihor. 1962. *Études sur la polémique entre Théodore Métochite et Nicéphore Choumnos*. Brussels.

Sinkewicz, Robert E. 1980. A New Interpretation for the First Episode in the Controversy Between Barlaam the Calabrian and Gregory Palamas. *Journal of Theological Studies* 31:489–500.

———. 1982. The Doctrine of the Knowledge of God in the Early Writings of Barlaam the Calabrian. *Mediaeval Studies* 44:181–242.

Sophonias. 1883. *In libros Aristotelis De anima paraphrasis*, ed. M. Hayduck. Berlin: Reimer (Commentaria in Aristotelem Graeca 23.1).

Sorabji, Richard. 1983. *Time, Creation and the Continuum: Theories in Antiquity and the Early Middle Ages*. London: Duckworth.

Symeon Seth. 1939. *Anecdota Atheniensia et alia, v*ol. 2: *Textes grecs relatifs à l'histoire des sciences*, ed. A. Delatte. Liège, Belgium: Faculté de philosophie et lettres.

Tambrun-Krasker, Brigitte. 2005. 'Plethons Abhandlung *Über die Tugenden'*. In Georgios Gemistos Plethon (1355–1452) *Reformpolitiker, Philosoph, Verehrer der alten Götter*, ed. Wilhelm Blum and Walter Seitter, 101–17. Zürich & Berlin: Diaphanes.

Todd, Robert B. 1992. 'Cleomedes" In *Catalogus Translationum et Commentariorum: Mediaeval and Renaissance Latin Translations and Commentaries. Annotated Lists and Guides*, ed. Virginia Brown, vol. 7, 1–11. Washington, DC: Catholic University of America Press.

Tollefsen, Torstein T. 2008. *The Christocentric Cosmology of St Maximus the Confessor*. Oxford: Oxford University Press.

Törönen, Melchisedec. 2007. *Union and Distinction in the Thought of St Maximus the Confessor*. Oxford: Oxford University Press.

Trizio, Michele. 2007. Byzantine Philosophy as a Contemporary Historiographical Project. *Recherches de Théologie et Philosophie Médiévales* 74(1):247–94.

———. 2009. Neoplatonic Source-Material in Eustratios of Nicaea's Commentary on book VI of the *Nicomachean Ethics*. In Barber and Jenkins, 2009, 71–109.

Watts, Edward. 2005. 'An Alexandrian Christian response to fifth-century Neoplatonic influence'. In *The Philosopher and Society in Late Antiquity. Essays in Honour of Peter Brown*, ed. Andrew Smith, 215–29. Swansea, UK: The Classical Press of Wales.

Westerink, Leendert G. 1990. 'The Alexandrian commentators and the introductions to their commentaries'. In *Aristotle Transformed*, ed. Richard Sorabji, 325–48. London: Duckworth.

Wildberg, Christian. 2003a. 'David'. In the *Stanford Encyclopedia of Philosophy*. http://plato.stanford.edu/entries/david/

———. 2003b. 'Elias'. In the *Stanford Encyclopedia of Philosophy*. http://plato.stanford.edu/entries/elias/

Woodhouse, Christopher Montague. 1986. *Gemistos Plethon. The Last of Hellenes*. Oxford: Oxford University Press.

CHAPTER 3

ARABIC PHILOSOPHY AND THEOLOGY BEFORE AVICENNA

PETER ADAMSON

In the year 833 CE, year 218 of the Islamic calendar, the caliph al-Maʾmūn (r. 813–33) wrote a letter laying down a point of Islamic doctrine. According to the caliph, the Qurʾān is created, and not eternal as held by some theologians of the time. Judges and scholars were to be interrogated as to whether or not they accepted this doctrine of the Qurʾān's createdness. Thus began the infamous *miḥna*, a 'test', or more sinisterly, 'inquisition', during which the political authority of the ʿAbbāsid caliphs would lend support to what seems to be a rather abstruse question in Islamic theology. The policy was abandoned by the later ʿAbbāsid caliph al-Mutawakkil (r. 847–61), and thereafter it became orthodox to hold that the Qurʾān is co-eternal with God. The *miḥna* was an atypical event in the history of Islam. Thereafter, theological orthodoxy in sunnī Islam was normally settled by the consensus of scholars and the community, rather than by the unilateral decision of any political ruler.[1]

This may seem to have little to do with philosophy. Yet it was under the same caliph, al-Maʾmūn, that the political elite sponsored the massive translation movement that rendered works of Greek philosophy and science into Arabic. Later sources, influenced by al-Maʾmūn's propaganda, tend to give him credit for initiating this translation movement. In fact, the second ʿAbbāsid caliph, al-Manṣūr (r. 754–75), already began to put serious resources behind the translations.[2] Still, there is no doubting that philosophy and theology flourished under al-Maʾmūn. During his reign al-Kindī (d. after 866), usually recognised as the first philosopher of Islam, began his career. Al-Maʾmūn's policy of support for the translation movement was continued by his successor al-Muʿtaṣim (r. 833–42). He does not seem to have had much of an intellectual bent himself, but al-Kindī served as tutor to his son Aḥmad, and the caliph was the addressee of al-Kindī's most important work, *On First Philosophy*. Whether he appreciated its intricate metaphysical arguments is, to put it mildly, doubtful.

Al-Muʿtaṣim also continued the *miḥna*, albeit somewhat half-heartedly, and it was imposed with enthusiasm by his son and successor al-Wāthiq (r. 842–47) before al-Mutawakkil put a stop to the policy in 848–49. Of course, it was not the caliphs who came up with the idea that the Qurʾān was created rather than eternal. It was a thesis held by a range of theologians, especially those we call the Muʿtazila. These were rationalist thinkers who seem to have been influenced by Greek philosophical ideas. The ninth century was their heyday, as part of a more general cultural flowering under the ʿAbbāsids.[3] After its brief period of influence, Muʿtazilism would never again have the kind of backing it received from these ʿAbbāsid caliphs. In the later history of Islam, we never find such a confluence of centralised political power, Greek-inspired philosophy and rationalist theology as occurred in the ninth century. Yet into the tenth century and beyond, philosophers and theologians were in intellectual competition. They often reached similar conclusions on the same topics, albeit by following different paths. This chapter will sketch some prominent issues in both traditions, looking especially at cases where philosophers of the ninth to tenth centuries responded directly to theological discussions.

First, a word about this contrast between 'philosophy' and 'theology'. I use the word 'philosophy' narrowly, as a translation of the Arabic *falsafa*. As you might guess by looking at this term, it is itself a loan word from the Greek *philosophia*. The etymology is not misleading: *falsafa* means direct engagement with the Greek works translated into Arabic under the ʿAbbāsids. Of course, one could instead use the word 'philosophy' more broadly, as including all texts and authors that strike us as having philosophical interest. In this broad sense, much of the theological material of our period is 'philosophical'. Theologians of the period argued about atomism, free will, morality, divine attributes and so on.[4] The narrower sense, though, is faithful to the outlook of the medieval authors themselves, who distinguish between theologians and 'philosophers (*falāsifa*)'. The Arabic expression I render as 'theology' is *ʿilm al-kalām* (or just *kalām*, with theologians referred to as *mutakallimūn*). Literally this means 'science of the word', which may be an allusion to the debate over the status of the Qurʾān as God's word, though the exact origins of the term are obscure.[5]

To some extent the boundary between *falsafa* and *kalām* is easy to mark: the *falāsifa* explicate Greek sources and use these as the basis of their doctrines, whereas the *mutakallimūn* explicate and use the Qurʾān and *ḥadīth* (reports about the sayings and deeds of the Prophet). But the line is often blurry. Some figures seem not quite to belong to either camp, for instance, one of the thinkers we will examine below, Abū Bakr al-Rāzī (d. 925). Other authors used philosophical materials to defend distinctive theological positions within Islam, especially a branch of shīʿī Islam called Ismāʿīlism.[6] Furthermore, 'philosophical' authors like al-Kindī do cite and explicate the Qur'ān, while Greek influence is often detected in *kalām*. Admittedly, in *kalām* this influence is subtle, whereas Greek ideas animate the entire output of philosophers like al-Kindī or al-Fārābī. More fundamental than this question of sources, but also more controversial, is the question of how philosophical discourse relates to theological discourse, especially when the two traditions address themselves to the same topics. As we will see, the Aristotelian thinker al-Fārābī (d. 950) draws a strong contrast between *falsafa* and *kalām*, identifying the latter as 'dialectical' and hence inferior to the 'demonstrative' discipline of *falsafa*. Yet in the wake of Avicenna on the *falsafa* side and al-Ash'arī (d.935) on the *kalām* side, it becomes increasingly common to see authors combining *falsafa* and *kalām* into a hybrid discipline that, for lack of any better expression, we may as well call 'philosophical theology'.

1. THE MUʿTAZILA AND THE ASHʿARITE CRITIQUE

The Muʿtazila were known as 'the upholders of justice and oneness'. In this slogan, 'justice ('*adl*)' stands for their claim that God does no wrong, and 'oneness (*tawḥīd*)' for their claim that God is one. Of course, no Muslim would reject either claim, when put this baldly; what is distinctive about the Muʿtazila is the way they interpret justice and oneness. To begin with justice, the Muʿtazila hold that human reason is capable of discriminating good from evil. For instance, even without revelation we can know that we should acknowledge and show gratitude to God.[7] This still sounds rather innocuous. The position becomes more controversial when the Muʿtazila point out that if moral strictures are knowable by reason, then even God is bound by them. Some Muʿtazilite thinkers held that God cannot do what is unjust, others that he can do so but never does. Opposing views were held on this question by the two greatest exponents of Muʿtazilism in the first half of the ninth century, Abū l-Hudhayl (d. 841?) holding the latter view and his student and nephew al-Naẓẓām (d. 836) holding the former.[8] Either way, it is not up to God to decide what will constitute justice. Rather, God performs justice *because* it is just. To put this in the language of contemporary philosophy of religion, this means that the Muʿtazila reject a divine command theory of ethics.

The Muʿtazila highlight one particular moral requirement that God must observe. It would, they say, be unjust for him to punish creatures for sinning, if they lacked the ability (*qudra*) to refrain from sin. Thus, their position on justice leads directly to another signature doctrine, their endorsement of human free will. The Muʿtazilites anticipate modern libertarian conceptions of freedom to a striking degree, even insisting that moral responsibility requires the presence of alternative possibilities. Thus, we find al-Naẓẓām saying that a genuine choice (*ikhtiyār*) requires the presence of two inclinations (*khāṭirāni*), one that would lead the agent to perform the action, the other leading the agent to refrain from it.[9] His point would seem to be that, if the agent has only a motivation to act, he will inevitably act, and this inevitability will eliminate freedom of choice.[10] Yet alongside these resonances with contemporary philosophical debates about free will, we find a preoccupation with distinctively theological concerns. A great deal of attention was directed, for instance, to the question of whether or not human actions are 'created' by God. If so, then God would wind up creating evil actions; but if not, then humans would seem to be usurping God's unique status as Creator. The Mu'tazila avoid the first horn of this dilemma but, as their opponents pointed out, risk being impaled on the second.[11]

The Mu'tazilite position on God's oneness was no less contentious. As with divine justice, divine oneness or *tawḥīd* is a common commitment of all Muslims. The *shahāda* itself, the affirmation of Muslim belief, asserts that 'there is no God but God.' God's uniqueness rules out the existence of other entities that have a divine status. God can have no 'partners,' and it is unbelief to recognise such partners (hence the term *shirk*, for polytheism, from the verb *sharaka* meaning to share or associate with). From this fundamental teaching of Islam, the Mu'tazila inferred that there can be no multiplicity within God. Here Christianity was a clear target. Trinitarian doctrine was seen as an obvious violation of *tawḥīd*, and Muslim theologians of all persuasions delighted in comparing their opponents' positions to the doctrine of the Trinity. The Mu'tazila and some other theologians of the period argued that accepting multiple divine attributes (*ṣifāt*), such as justice, knowledge or power, would violate *tawḥīd* just as much as belief in the Trinity.

There was a further reason for the Mu'tazila to be suspicious of real divine attributes: it says in the Qur'ān (42:9) that God 'has no like' among created things. Obviously a man may be just, knowing and so on. To avoid saying that a just, knowing man is 'like' God, it seems we must say either that God is not just and knowing, or that if he is just and knowing, it is in a quite different way from what we find in humans, so different, indeed, that there is no 'likeness.' Some *mutakallimūn*, such as Ḍirār ibn 'Amr, Mu'ammar, and al-Naẓẓām, adopted a version of the former solution. Anticipating the 'negative theology' of the great Jewish thinker Maimonides, they explained that apparently positive divine predications are, in fact, concealed negations: to say that God is knowing is to deny that he is ignorant, for example.[12] Obviously this doctrine tends to make God unknowable since even positive statements about him are unmasked as mere denials. This consequence was highlighted by opponents of the Mu'tazila, who accused them of going so far in avoiding *tashbīh* (the 'assimilation' of God to creatures) that they fell into *ta'ṭīl* ('voiding' God's attributes).[13]

But Mu'tazilite authors adopted a variety of ways to strike a balance between *ta'ṭīl* and *tashbīh*, to affirm divine attributes without violating *tawḥīd*. Here the most prominent view is that of Abū l-Hudhayl, who held that God's attributes are identical with God Himself. He said that God 'is knowing through a knowledge which is He (*huwa ʿālim bi-ʿilm huwa huwa*),'[14] and likewise for the other attributes.[15] This may seem to be a merely verbal solution—a suspicion that arises not infrequently when looking at *kalām* doctrines. That is, it seems Abū l-Hudhayl wants to preserve words like 'just' and 'knowing' because of their usage in the Qur'ān, and he simply asserts that God is the same as his attributes to prevent any multiplicity from arising. But there is more to the doctrine than meets the eye. Consider, for example, the implications of Abū l-Hudhayl's view for divine justice. If God's justice is identical to God, then it will not be contingent, chosen from among various possibilities. Rather, divine justice will be nothing other than God. This helps explain why Abū l-Hudhayl rejected the divine command theory. The point also shows that Abū l-Hudhayl is not vulnerable to a criticism often made of the Muʿtazilite theory of justice, namely, that if the laws of justice are discoverable by reason, they must be something independent of God that He must obey.[16]

The Muʿtazilite doctrines of justice and oneness were, then, closely related. Taken together, they undergird further doctrines on a wide range of theological issues, including the one that was at stake in the *miḥna*: the createdness of the Qurʾān. Again, the connection may not be immediately obvious. The origins of the controversy seem to lie in the eighth century, when some theologians designated the Qurʾān as God's word or 'speech'. As such, the Qurʾān belongs intimately to God. Certain other theologians, forerunners of the Muʿtazila, detected a violation of *tawḥīd*. If God's word is distinct from God, and yet uncreated, then it will be a second divine thing alongside God himself—which is polytheism. It was only at this point that the debate was put in the terms we find in al-Maʾmūn's letter, namely, that the Qurʾān is not 'eternal (*qadīm*)'.[17] The point here is to assert the absolute contrast between God and everything other than God, by preserving 'eternity' as the prerogative of the divine and calling all other things 'created'. Muʿtazilite thinkers would also have seen the issue of human freedom as relevant. This is because some of Muḥammad's opponents and detractors are singled out by name in the Qurʾān as sinners who will be punished in hell. If the Qurʾān were eternal, then it would seem to follow that these individuals did not sin freely but were determined from eternity to sin. In that case, punishing them would violate God's justice.

Of course, not all theologians in the ninth and tenth centuries subscribed to these doctrines. For one thing, the Muʿtazila were only one group of theologians and were bitterly opposed by other factions even before the searching criticism of the lapsed Muʿtazilite theologian al-Ashʿarī. In particular, their rather negative approach to divine simplicity was diametrically opposed to the 'traditionalist' view, represented most prominently by Ibn Ḥanbal, who ran afoul of the *miḥna* when he refused to accept the Qurʾān's createdness.[18] Traditionalists not only accepted the standard divine attributes, but they also took more or less at face value anthropomorphic passages in the Qurʾān that talk of God's having a face or sitting upon a throne. Muʿtazilite interpretations of such passages, of course, were less literal. Furthermore, different theologians who are retrospectively grouped under the rubric of 'Muʿtazilism', in fact, disagreed on a range of issues. Theological controversy was as likely to take place between opposed Muʿtazilites as between Muʿtazilites and traditionalists. Finally, it was common for theologians to adopt some 'Muʿtazilite' views while rejecting others.[19]

It actually took several generations for a group of rationalist *mutakallimūn* to group themselves together around the banner of 'justice and oneness.' Muʿtazilism is usually said to begin with a stance adopted by a man named Wāṣil ibn ʿAṭāʾ (d. 748). The question at issue was whether a 'grave sinner' should be considered to be a 'believer' or a 'hypocrite'. Wāṣil adopted the conciliatory view that such a sinner is in an 'intermediary position', that is, neither a believer nor a hypocrite. The name 'Muʿtazila', meaning 'those who withdraw', is traced to a supposed event where Wāṣil asserted this doctrine and hence 'withdrew' from those gathered around al-Ḥasan al-Baṣrī (d. 728).[20] Wāṣil's 'intermediate position' was named by Abū l-Hudhayl as one of the five chief doctrines of the Muʿtazila, along with the commitments to God's oneness and justice, the 'promise and the threat' (i.e., of divine reward and punishment) and the command to do good and avoid evil. But this belies the complexity of the subsequent tradition. Even leaving aside the spread of Muʿtazilite doctrines beyond the heart of the ʿAbbāsid empire in Iraq,[21] the ninth century saw the development of two Muʿtazilite 'schools', one in Baghdad and one in Basra, which differed on numerous points despite their agreement to the basic doctrines described above. We are better informed about the tradition in Basra. After the early theorists Abū l-Hudhayl and al-Naẓẓām, who may take much of the credit for the development of Muʿtazilism into a sophisticated theology, we have something more like a Basran 'school' initiated by the father and son Abū ʿAlī (d. 915) and Abū Hāshim ibn al-Jubbāʾī (d. 933). His followers included the Qāḍī ʿAbd al-Jabbār (d. 1024), whose voluminous *Mughnī fī abwāb al-tawḥīd wa-l-ʿadl* (*Comprehensive Work on Topics of Oneness and Justice*) displays mature Muʿtazilism in all its scholastic glory.[22]

A few Muʿtazilite authors from the earlier period have left extant works.[23] But unfortunately, most of the authors just mentioned are known to us chiefly through the reports of later more or less hostile heresiographers. Among these hostile authors, the most important is al-Ashʿarī.[24] He began his theological career as a student of Abū ʿAlī al-Jubbāʾī but then turned against Muʿtazilism. He and his followers, the Ashʿarites, accepted the existence of divine attributes that are really distinct from God. These attributes are eternal but, because they are in some sense dependent on God, the doctrine leaves room for contingency. In fact, for Ashʿarite *mutakallimūn* God's actions are wholly unrestricted, and the nature of justice is determined by His choices rather than vice versa. This Ashʿarite tendency to make all things dependent on God's unconstrained will has consequences for human freedom. The Ashʿarites were uncomfortable with making humans effectively the 'creators' of their own actions. They instead developed a doctrine of 'acquisition (*kasb*)', according to which God creates our actions but we 'acquire' them and thus take upon ourselves the responsibility for those actions.[25]

It is tempting to understand Ashʿarism as little more than reverse Muʿtazilism, an acceptance of everything al-Ashʿarī's masters had rejected and vice versa. But on several points, we can find continuity between the two schools. For example, both sorts of *kalām* had a tendency towards irenicism. As we saw, the very name 'Muʿtazila' may refer to a conciliatory position taken on a politicised theological issue. For all the controversy that raged around various Muʿtazilite views, most members of the school sought to resolve intellectual conflict rather than to stoke it.[26] (An exception should probably be made for al-Naẓẓām, who is noted for his bold and provocative theses.) Consider the most sensitive issue of the ninth century, namely, the claim of unique political and religious authority made by the descendants of ʿAlī, the cousin of the Prophet. Like the caliph al-Ma'mūn, Mu'tazilites tended to make conciliatory gestures towards 'Alid sympathies, without actually endorsing the doctrine of the *shī'a*, or 'party' of 'Alī.[27] Another example is the Mu'tazilite habit of giving merely 'verbal' answers to theological dilemmas. Such answers may annoy philosophically minded readers, but they need to be seen in context. These careful formulations were, arguably, designed to satisfy as many people as possible, much as the studied ambiguity of a political manifesto enables it to represent the diverse views of party members. We find a similar tendency among Ash'arites, who sought a broad consensus among the sunnī community on theological issues, often by leaving questions open rather than insisting on any particular solution. It is in this light that we might understand their use of the slogan *bi-lā kayf*: 'without [saying] how', which was applied, for instance, to the way in which descriptions of God in the Qur'ān hold true.[28]

Another manifestation of this irenic sensibility is the emphasis both schools placed upon reason (*'aql*). Of course, the Qur'ān and *ḥadīth* were common ground for all Muslim scholars, even if there was controversy about which *ḥadīth* were genuine. *Kalām*, like the Islamic jurisprudential tradition with which it was intertwined, rarely strayed far from expounding these sources. But the interpretation of religious texts lay at the heart of various disputes, and reason offered an independent means of finding a resolution. The Mu'tazilites duly placed great trust in reason, regarding it as a gift from God that empowers humans to discern many things even without the aid of revelation. They held that humans grasp good and evil through reason alone, as we've seen, and on other issues, too, they appealed to universal intuitions as well as revealed sources.[29] They devoted considerable attention to the rules of reasoning, engaging in detailed technical disputes that one can only describe as logical in character.[30] With their tactic of *bi-lā kayf* and their conviction that good and evil are determined only by God's will, the Ash'arites seem to have been more impressed by reason's limits than by its powers. But Ash'arism has its own rationalist commitments, as shown by its most famous exponent, al-Ghazālī (d. 1111). Al-Ghazālī's famous corrective to philosophy consisted in a careful delineation of what reason can achieve, not in a rejection of rationality. One sign of this is his disdain for those who reject the utility of Aristotelian logic.[31]

Mu'tazilite and Ash'arite *kalām* is also unified by similar ideas about the metaphysics of created objects. As usual, the details differ from thinker to thinker, but for almost all the *mutakallimūn* mentioned above, created things consist of 'substances (*jawāhir*)' that have 'attributes (*ṣifāt*)', often called 'accidents (*a'rāḍ*)'. Despite the Aristotelian terminology, this was a distinctly un-Aristotelian theory, according to which created substances are atoms ('indivisible parts') to which God joins accidental properties. Substances are preserved in existence moment-to-moment by divine power, so that God's creative activity continues at all times rather than being limited to an initial act that brings the world into existence. This general framework was broadly agreed, but the Basran Mu'tazilite school in particular engaged in refined analysis of the different sorts of attributes that can inhere in substances.[32] The Ash'arites, meanwhile, used the atom/attribute ontology to emphasise once again the complete freedom and power of God. For them, God may join attributes to substances however he wishes, so long as he does not violate the law of non-contradiction (he cannot make something both alive and dead). As made clear in al-Ghazālī's famous discussion of miracles in his *Incoherence of the Philosophers*, on this view the stability of the created world depends on the fact that God's habits never change, not on the intrinsic features of created beings.[33]

2. THE MUSLIM *FALĀSIFA*

Given the political resonance, intellectual sophistication and central geographical location of the *kalām* activities just surveyed, it is hardly surprising that the philosophers of ninth- to tenth-century Islam felt obliged to respond to the *mutakallimūn*. One could multiply examples, but I will concentrate on the three most famous Muslim *falāsifa* before Avicenna, namely, al-Kindī, al-Fārābī and al-Rāzī. (Some might hesitate to call al-Rāzī a 'Muslim' *faylasūf*; I will argue that one should instead hesitate to call him a Muslim '*faylasūf*.') In Section 3, I will discuss how two philosophers from other faiths, but within the same cultural milieu, engaged with Islamic *kalām*.

As already mentioned, al-Kindī's career peaked under the very caliphs who imposed the Muʿtazilite doctrine of the Qurʾān's createdness upon their subjects.[34] Al-Kindī never explicitly alludes to the doctrine in his extant writings. Nor, in fact, does he speak directly about *kalām* as an intellectual phenomenon.[35] Nonetheless, al-Kindī's work was implicitly engaged with the Muʿtazila.[36] A particularly clear case is the topic of divine simplicity. Al-Kindī is best known for coordinating a circle of (mostly Christian) translators who rendered texts such as Aristotle's *Metaphysics*, Plotinus's *Enneads* and Proclus's *Elements of Theology* into Arabic.[37] Already in the Kindī circle version of the *Enneads*, we find a preoccupation with the problem of God's 'attributes (*ṣifāt*)'. Plotinus's stress on the ineffability of the One naturally lent itself to the Kindī circle project of making Greek philosophy relevant to contemporary theological concerns. In the Arabic Plotinus, numerous passages recast Plotinus's doctrine of ineffability as a denial of attributes. Using terminology that has attracted much discussion, the translator identifies the Plotinian One—now called 'the Creator'— as 'nothing but being (*anniyya faqaṭ*)', with no attributes superadded to divine being or essence.[38]

God's unity is a central issue in al-Kindī's own works, too, especially the aforementioned *On First Philosophy*.[39] Sections 3 and 4 of the extant first part deal with God as the 'true One', by first proving the existence of a principle of unity, and then showing that this principle is not subject to any form of predication.[40] This understanding of God is strikingly similar to the Muʿtazilite conception, on which God's unity (*tawḥīd*) rules out the application of attributes to the divine essence. Al-Kindī's refutation of the world's eternity in the previous section of *On First Philosophy* should be understood in the same context.[41] The Mu'tazila distinguished God from all other things (including the Qur'ān) by saying that whereas the latter are created, God alone is eternal. Al-Kindī follows their lead, even at the price of disagreeing with Aristotle on the topic of the world's eternity.[42]

However, al-Kindī's procedure throughout *On First Philosophy* is self-consciously philosophical, with no recourse to revealed texts.[43] Only at the end of Section 4 does al-Kindī reveal, with a flourish of Qur'ānic epithets, that the true One is to be identified with the almighty Creator of Islam. Prior to that, he mostly employs ideas and terminology drawn from basic works of Aristotelian logic, especially Porphyry's *Isagoge*. He uses the same materials elsewhere to refute the Christian doctrine of the Trinity.[44] An even more striking deployment of Aristotelian materials in a 'theological' context is al-Kindī's epistle *On the Prostration of the Outermost Sphere*.[45] Taking as his text the Qur'ānic statement (55:6) that the stars 'prostrate' themselves before God, al-Kindī offers something new in the burgeoning literature of Qur'ānic commentary (*tafsīr*): he explains a revealed text purely in terms of *falsafa*.[46]

Even though philosophy establishes the same truths that are contained in revelation, the Qur'ān delivers these truths in a more powerful way. This point is made in another treatise, when al-Kindī rather surprisingly digresses from enumerating Aristotle's works to explain a Qur'ānic passage (36:79–82) about God's power to create and resurrect the dead. He states that an expert philosopher will provide the same answer as was provided by the Prophet on this topic.[47] He then goes on to use materials drawn from the Christian philosopher John Philoponus, as he expounds the Qur'ānic idea that God creates by saying to a thing, 'be!'.[48] In another digression, this time in a work on meteorology, he explains the superiority of prophets to philosophers by explaining that the former are spared the need to exert effort and long study since God reveals the truth to them directly.[49] There is no suggestion here that prophets know things that philosophers cannot.

Al-Kindī wanted to show that Greek sources could provide a foundation for understanding Islamic texts and doctrines. Though the doctrines he supported in this way were frequently reminiscent of Mu'tazilism, his sources and methods were quite different. Still, al-Kindī was not necessarily trying to replace *kalām* with *falsafa*. More likely, he sought simply to show the power and usefulness of the Greek inheritance. A work like *On First Philosophy* aimed to show al-Kindī's contemporaries (including the caliph!) what could be achieved by supporting the translation movement. His motivation is made clear in *On First Philosophy*, in an impassioned criticism of those who reject wisdom just because it comes from a foreign culture.[50] This need not be taken, as has been suggested, as a broadside aimed at the Mu'tazila. Rather, the targets were unnamed theologians (they engage in 'speculation' and 'traffic in religion'), perhaps traditionalists, who opposed ideas imported from the Greeks.[51] First- and second-generation students of al-Kindī's were also quite open to *kalām*. This further undermines the notion that *falsafa*, as al-Kindī understood it, involved hostility towards the whole enterprise of rationalist theology.[52] Our admittedly incomplete evidence never shows him distinguishing *falsafa* from *kalām* or arguing that the former is superior to the latter.

Before long, though, philosophers did seek to differentiate themselves more explicitly from the *mutakallimūn*. One reason for this was, no doubt, the increasing specialism of *falsafa* as more texts entered into the Arabic milieu. The members of the so-called 'Baghdad school' of peripatetic philosophers in the tenth century were 'professionals' in a much narrower sense than al-Kindī, with his immense breadth of interests, had ever been. They were experts in logic and the exegesis of Aristotelian texts, who saw *falsafa* as a separate and legitimate enterprise of its own. To some extent they were also on the defensive. Clearly, al-Kindī's programme of integrating Greek wisdom into the Arabic-speaking world had its detractors, such as the theologians he rails against in *On First Philosophy*. But a man can afford to be confident when he is in a position to address a treatise to the caliph personally. The members of the Baghdad school wrote in a less advantageous context. They were mostly Christians, and their founder, the logician and translator Abū Bishr Mattā, had been embarrassed in a famous clash with the grammarian al-Sīrāfī. He heaped scorn on the *falāsifa* for resorting to pretentious foreign learning in place of indigenous Arabic disciplines like grammar.[53]

It was in this rather more fraught atmosphere that al-Fārābī, a Muslim student of Abū Bishr's and the most famous member of the Baghdad school, decided to put *kalām* and other non-philosophical disciplines firmly in their place. He discusses *kalām* in several passages, including the conclusion of his *Enumeration of the Sciences (Iḥṣāʾ al-ʿulūm)*.[54] This was not a case of saving the best for last. Al-Fārābī's treatment of *kalām* is designed to show that even when done well, theology is a second-rate discipline. He does recognise a legitimate, but limited, purpose for theology, namely, defending religion from its detractors. Unfortunately, the *mutakallimūn* of al-Fārābī's day do not, according to him, stay within this apologetic remit. They try instead to build up positive theories, and they engage in heated disputes with one another as to which of these theories is correct. Some theologians, observes a horrified al-Fārābī, even resort to threats when their argumentative skills are insufficient.

Al-Fārābī's stance is grounded in his understanding of the types of argumentative discourse set forth in Aristotle's logical works. The best type is demonstration, as described in the *Posterior Analytics*.[55] Demonstration provides genuine knowledge (*ʿilm*, here translating the Greek *epistêmê*) and certainty, by proceeding from absolutely certain first principles and restricting itself to that which is necessary and universal.[56] Other forms of discourse differ from demonstration chiefly in the sorts of premises they use. Poetic discourse uses symbolic images; rhetoric chooses its premises on the basis of what is persuasive rather than what is certain; and dialectic begins from whatever premises command assent in a given context. These premises may be widely accepted or taken from esteemed authorities (what Aristotle calls *endoxa*), or alternatively, they may simply be agreed on by the parties to the discussion at hand.

With these distinctions in hand, al-Fārābī explains how religion (*milla* or *dīn*) and *kalām* relate to philosophy. Philosophy is demonstrative. Proceeding from indubitable first principles, it generates knowledge through syllogistic proof. Religious discourse, by contrast, is rhetorical or dialectical. A text like the Qur'ān conveys the truth non-demonstratively, aiming at mere conviction.[57] *Kalām*, meanwhile, is purely dialectical. Hence, al-Fārābī's claim that its proper purpose is apologetic: the aim of dialectic is to refute one's opponent, not to demonstrate the truth from first principles. The mistake made by the *mutakallimūn* is that they begin from the rhetorical and poetical basis of the Qur'ān, occasionally adding dialectical premises of their own. Yet they think their discipline is certain and systematic, as if they were philosophers.[58] Here one can draw an analogy to the contrast between logic and grammar. Grammarians think that by studying the expressions of one language, such as Arabic, they can establish the rules for correct speech. But it is actually logic, the universal science of truth and meaning, that shows which statements are certainly true, and which are merely 'correct' by convention.[59]

This condescending attitude towards *kalām*, which is taken over and amplified by Averroes in his famous *Decisive Treatise*,[60] suggests that al-Fārābī would have spent little energy keeping up with the theological disputes of his day. Yet he shows a reasonable knowledge of contemporary *kalām*, and especially of the Mu'tazilites.[61] He alludes to such details as their definition of knowledge, their non-literal interpretation of the Qur'ān, and their conviction that some things are known immediately by human reason. The latter example shows how theology operates dialectically. Instead of seeking indubitable first principles, the *mutakallimūn* proceed from what is 'acknowledged at first glance'.[62] Another example is al-Fārābī's discussion of the problem of logical determinism in his commentary on Aristotle's *On Interpretation*.[63] Not only does al-Fārābī assert that if determinism were true, God would be unjust in meting out reward and punishment, but he raises the problem of whether God can do evil.[64] He sees that this involves the question of whether a thing can be possible, yet never occur—something that we would now take for granted but is arguably excluded by Aristotle's modal notions.[65]

These glancing references to al-Fārābī's contemporaries among the *mutakallimūn* show that he was well aware of intellectual debates beyond the confines of *falsafa*, and that he recognised the philosophical interest of such debates. This is entirely consistent with his criticism of *kalām*. His complaint is not that theologians never raise issues of philosophical significance, but—to the contrary—that they stray into philosophical territory, overstepping their proper apologetic role, and thus sow discord and confusion. Where al-Kindī sought merely to show the relevance of philosophy for Islamic theological problems, al-Fārābī adopted a more aggressive posture, claiming that key theological questions can only be answered definitively by the philosopher. Consider what may be his best-known work, *The Principles of the Opinions of the Inhabitants of the Perfect City*.[66] Al-Fārābī would have us believe that, insofar as his discussion is 'philosophical', it rests upon indubitable first principles. But he tackles themes also prevalent in contemporary *kalām*—this, it has been argued, is key to understanding the purpose of the *Principles*.[67] Its structure and subject matter are strikingly parallel to works on the 'principles of religion (*uṣūl al-dīn*)' written by theologians like al-Ash'arī. Of course, al-Fārābī was not engaging in *kalām*. He hoped, rather, to supplant *kalām*, with demonstrative philosophical knowledge of such matters as the afterlife, the soul and God's relation to the created universe.

Despite the influence of al-Fārābī's stance on Averroes, his position on these matters was very unusual for the period we are considering (or any period of Islamic thought, for that matter). Few, if any, other thinkers of the time were so condescending towards revealed religion, and so disdainful of *kalām* attempts to explicate that religion. For some readers, one name may leap to mind: the great medical clinician and controversial philosopher Abū Bakr al-Rāzī. Al-Rāzī is known principally for two things, apart from his influential and sophisticated work in medicine. First is his theory of the 'five eternals', according to which the world is produced not solely by God, but out of an interaction between God and four other eternal principles (soul, matter, time and place). Second is his scathing critique of revealed religion. We learn about this especially from al-Rāzī's contemporary, the Ismāʿīlī philosopher Abū Ḥātim al-Rāzī (no relation: 'Rāzī' means someone from Rayy, a city in Northern Persia). Abū Ḥātim tells us of a debate between himself and al-Rāzī and quotes from a book in which al-Rāzī purportedly denied the validity of prophecy, rejected prophetic miracles and sneered at revealed religion.[68]

This portrayal of al-Rāzī has occasioned both dismay and fascination. Whereas Abū Ḥātim refers to him simply as 'the heretic', in recent times scholars have admired him as a 'free thinker' who boldly departed from his religious and philosophical context.[69] I would contend, however, that al-Rāzī's engagement with religion was more subtle and less scandalous than it may seem. Abū Ḥātim's evidence is thrown into doubt by testimony from a less hostile witness, the great theologian Fakhr al-Dīn al-Rāzī (also from Rayy!).[70] Fakhr al-Dīn quotes al-Rāzī as citing the Qurʾān and other prophets in support of his own views, and he gives us a detailed account of his dispute with the Muʿtazilite theologian Abū l-Qāsim al-Balkhī (known as al-Kaʿbī) over the correct reading of certain passages in the Qurʾān. This dispute concerned theodicy—the question of why God allows evil in the world. Pain and suffering clearly weighed heavily in al-Rāzī's philosophical considerations, perhaps because of his experiences as a doctor. This seems to have been a primary motivation for his theory of the 'five eternals', which allowed him to explain evil in terms of the soul's foolish choice to become associated with matter, rather than by admitting that a perfectly wise God chose to create an imperfect world.

It seems difficult to reconcile this al-Rāzī with the heretic portrayed by Abū Ḥātim. I suspect that Abū Ḥātim deliberately misdescribed al-Rāzī's position as a thoroughgoing rejection of Islam, indeed of all revealed religion. The target was, in fact, narrower: he took issue with groups who relied on miracles to validate Muḥammad's prophecy, who accepted anthropomorphic descriptions of God, and above all whose religious beliefs rested on uncritical acceptance of authority (*taqlīd*) rather than rational enquiry (*naẓar*).[71] 'Traditionalists' like Ibn Ḥanbal and his followers would have been among the offenders. Also under attack were the Ismāʿīlīs, who were certainly not guilty of anthropomorphism, but whose theological system could be taken as the ultimate endorsement of *taqlīd*.[72] Their teaching was built around the need for infallible *imāms*, whose religious teaching is authoritative. This helps to explain why Abū Ḥātim and other Ismāʿīlīs are such rich sources of (hostile) testimony about al-Rāzī. Stung by his criticism, they set about refuting him with great vigour. In this context they summarised his views, not without the occasional strategic distortion.

Al-Rāzī's relationship to the Muʿtazila was more nuanced. The report of Abū Ḥātim indicates numerous points of possible agreement between al-Rāzī and the Muʿtazila. These include his suspicion of anthropomorphism and *taqlīd*, and to some extent his rejection of miracles. In the more reliable context of his own authentic works, al-Rāzī also extols reason (*ʿaql*) as God's greatest gift to mankind and the basis for all correct ethical teaching.[73] Rationalism was common ground between him and the Muʿtazila, something he exploited in the debate about theodicy. His solution to the problem of evil emphasises that a wise Creator would not permit pointless evil and suffering. Some theologians of medieval Islam, and some philosophers of religion nowadays, would simply reply that God's ways are unknowable for mankind. But against a Muʿtazilite opponent like al-Kaʿbī, al-Rāzī's argument had considerable force. For the Muʿtazila likewise emphasised God's perfect wisdom and justice and assumed that human reason is capable of discerning the requirements of this justice. In fact, al-Rāzī's thought on these issues seems to have developed precisely through his dialectical engagement with Muʿtazilite *kalām*.[74]

Al-Rāzī also reacted to the *falāsifa* of his day and their Greek sources. In one area where he at first seems to adopt a *kalām* view, he turns out to be more dependent on the Hellenic tradition. He differs from the *falāsifa* in accepting an atomic view of bodies, as did the theologians. But his version of atomism has more to do with the pre-Socratic type of atomism attacked by Aristotle than with the more mathematical version of atomism we find in *kalām*, where atoms are akin to geometrical points.[75] As should be clear from this example and the theory of the five eternals, al-Rāzī was no Aristotelian. Among the Greeks, his main authorities were Plato and the medical writers, especially Galen. In keeping with his disdain for *taqlīd*, he criticised even these favourite Greek authorities—one Razian work has the self-explanatory title *Doubts About Galen*. But he was entirely unimpressed by the Aristotelians, especially when it came to matters of physics.[76] For this reason, al-Rāzī cannot neatly be classified as a *faylasūf*, and still less was he a *mutakallim*. His primary vocation was medicine, not philosophy or theology. The delight he took in disputing with both philosophers and the theologians no doubt says as much about his personality as about his intellectual formation: al-Rāzī was above all a man who loved a good argument.

3. JEWISH AND CHRISTIAN *FALSAFA*

For a more harmonious marriage of *falsafa* and *kalām*, we may turn to a contemporary Jewish thinker, Saʿādia Gaon (882–942). Saʿādia hailed from Egypt but moved to Iraq where he headed a rabbinical school near Baghdad. He integrated Graeco-Arabic philosophical ideas and Muslim *kalām* into Judaism, adopting a number of doctrines directly from Mu'tazilism; he is sometimes described as a 'Jewish Mu'tazilite'.[77] A particularly clear example is his embrace of free will as a pre-condition for moral responsibility, so that God cannot punish us justly if we are unfree.[78] He also assumes that reason is able to discover the necessity for God's commanding and prohibiting as he does,[79] going so far as to claim that it is rationally necessary for God to supply humankind with guidance from prophets, a position we also find in contemporary Mu'tazilism.[80]

Sa'ādia's most extensive development of a Mu'tazilite theme is his treatment of divine attributes. This dominates the second treatise of his *Book of Doctrines and Beliefs*. Sa'ādia has already laid out a qualified empiricist epistemology that recognises various paths to knowledge but insists that all methods are grounded in sensation.[81] When he comes to discuss divine attributes, he sticks to his empiricist guns and argues that God transcends the limits of what we can grasp because the progress of our knowledge ends with the most 'subtle' (*laṭīf*) of sensible things.[82] Since God is not a body, but rather the maker (*ṣāniʿ*) of all bodies, and since all human knowledge is based ultimately on our experience of bodies, God is beyond human knowledge. Those who speak as if God can be known, or described in human language, are in effect implying that he is a body: 'those who seek to give Him motion, rest, wrath, delight, or anything of the sort, have in truth sought to make Him a body, in terms of meaning if not in terms of expression'.[83] We are thus forced to adopt a negative theology, in which God's attributes are apparently denied, so as to avoid *tajsīm*: speaking as if God were corporeal (from *jism*, 'body'). To the extent that Scripture seems to engage in *tajsīm*, this is to be understood as providing believers with 'an approximation and image (*taqrīb wa tamthīl*)' of God. Scripture must use such metaphorical language because we could say essentially nothing about God if we restricted ourselves to literal truth: 'if we kept ourselves to His attributes according to strictly true expression, then we would have to deny that He is hearing, seeing, merciful, and willing, so that we would be restricted to His being alone (*anniyya faqaṭ*)'.[84]

Yet there is a tension in Sa'ādia between a general ban on divine attributes and a commitment to certain privileged attributes.[85] Scholars disagree even about how many attributes Sa'ādia recognises (if any). Sa'ādia says that revelation teaches us five things about God: He is one, living, powerful, knowing and unlike any of his creatures.[86] The last of these is not really an attribute, and the attribute 'one' could also be understood in a negative way, as indicating that God lacks the multiplicity characteristic of bodies.[87] So perhaps we have only three positive attributes. Unfortunately, this still seems to be three attributes too many, given the wholly negative theology set out by Sa'ādia in close proximity to these passages. Sa'ādia tries to solve the difficulty by emphasising that the three attributes simply spell out the implications of God's being a maker. It is only the exigencies of language that prevent us from using a single word to express the notion that a maker must be living, powerful and knowing; in the mind, they are grasped 'all at once'. Furthermore, these attributes imply no multiplicity in the divine essence (*dhāt*) but merely explicate the fact that things are made by Him.

It has thus been suggested that Sa'ādia is aligning himself with Mu'tazilites who accepted 'attributes of action' but rejected 'attributes of essence'.[88] Attributes of essence express what God is. Attributes of action express what God does and are far less troublesome because they can be taken as referring indirectly to created things. In favour of this interpretation is the fact that Sa'ādia thinks we know of God's existence only because the physical world requires an external cause: 'there is no means of proof that is not on the basis of creation'.[89] On the other hand, Sa'ādia elsewhere speaks of attributes of essence (*ma'ānī dhātiyya*), which include the three just mentioned.[90] For clarification we may turn to Sa'ādia's lengthy discussion of biblical names and statements about God. The material considered so far looks indebted to Mu'tazilite *kalām* rather than Aristotelian philosophy. But here Sa'ādia shows the *falsafa* side of his thought, classifying Scriptural language in accordance with Aristotle's ten categories. It has been suggested that the categories simply give Sa'ādia a convenient way of organising his material.[91] More likely, he chooses this strategy precisely because the categories analyse language as it applies to physical objects.[92] Of particular interest for the question regarding attributes of essence and attributes of action is Sa'ādia's treatment of the category of action. He stresses that divine agency is very different from physical agency, for instance, in needing no time, place, instrument or motion. Still, we can say that God acts in *some* sense, however disanalogous divine action might be to the actions we normally experience. For instance, when Scripture speaks of God being vengeful, this refers obliquely to his actions in the created world. Sa'ādia adds, 'all these names that function in this way go back to the things that are made. This is the difference between the names of essence and the names of actions'.[93]

Sa'ādia's theory of divine attribution is, then, more complex and more positive than it at first appears. Most terms are to be denied of God because they would immediately imply His corporeality and fall into the trap of *tajsīm*. A second type of term seems to apply to God but, in fact, applies to his works in the created world. These are names or attributes of action. Finally, a third type of term expresses the divine essence itself. There are only a few such 'essential attributes': 'knowing', 'powerful' and 'living'—perhaps also 'one' and 'inimitable', to the extent that these have a positive content. But these terms introduce no multiplicity, and hence no corporealisation. For we grasp them all simultaneously, upon grasping that God is a Creator. This would seem to be the limit of what we can know about God: that he must have these features, if he created the world we see.

Sa'ādia was not the only Jewish philosopher to write in Arabic in the ninth and tenth centuries. For instance, there was Isaac Israeli (d. 955), whose extant works show pervasive influence from al-Kindī.[94] But in this early period, Christian thinkers were even more central to the *falsafa* tradition. They played a crucial role as translators of philosophical and scientific works from Greek into Arabic (sometimes by way of Syriac), and also as philosophers in their own right. We have already met al-Fārābī's teacher, the founder of the 'Baghdad school', Abū Bishr Mattā. Little of his thought is preserved for us, unfortunately. We are much better informed about a thinker who reportedly studied with both Abū Bishr and al-Fārābī: Yaḥyā ibn 'Adī

(d. 974).[95] Ibn ʿAdī was nicknamed 'the logician (*al-manṭiqī*)' for his expertise in Aristotelian logic. He wrote extensively on this and other aspects of *falsafa*. As a Christian, he also used Aristotelian ideas in apologetic works defending the doctrine of the Trinity.[96]

Unlike Saʿādia, Ibn ʿAdī was not deeply influenced by *kalām*. His interest in Islamic theology was that of a mildly interested outsider, which is perhaps unsurprising. *Mutakallimūn* rarely found common cause with Christians and excoriated the doctrines of the Trinity and Incarnation. Yet we do find Ibn ʿAdī addressing distinctively *kalām* themes.[97] In one short epistle, he criticises the recently developed *kalām* theory of 'acquisition',[98] the idea that God creates human actions that are appropriated or acquired by human agents. This text is evidently the exception that proves the rule, given that Ibn ʿAdī begins by remarking that he takes up the subject only at the behest of the epistle's addressee. Accordingly, he gives the theory rather short shrift in the subsequent discussion. A more nuanced engagement with 'theological' issues—again in the form of the problem of divine attributes—can be found in his little-studied treatise *On Unity*.[99] The treatise explores the sense in which 'oneness (*tawḥīd*)' applies to God; he does not say explicitly that *On Unity* is meant to support a Christian understanding of divine unity, but this is clearly his intention. He proceeds by proposing and then refuting, in considerable detail, a whole series of possible ways to understand God's oneness.

For instance, he considers the claim that God is one in the sense that nothing is like him. Ibn ʿAdī says that this must mean either that God is not like anything else in *any* respect, or that God is not like anything else in *every* respect. But the first is impossible: if A and B are distinct, they will always have at least something in common. For one thing, they will, ironically, both have in common that they are dissimilar to the other. Furthermore, God must have something in common with, say, man, in that neither God nor man is a horse.[100] As for the second suggestion, Ibn ʿAdī points out that equally, nothing is like anything else in every respect. If A is distinct from B, A must have some feature or other that B lacks (so he endorses the principle now called the 'identity of indiscernibles').[101] Another position considered by Ibn ʿAdī is that God is 'one' in virtue of a unity (*waḥda*) that belongs to God. This is ruled out through a complex treatment of the relationship between the supposed 'property (*maʿnā*)' of unity and God's essence or self (*dhāt*). For instance, Ibn ʿAdī considers whether the unity would be identical to the essence, or created by God and hence posterior to the essence.[102]

This highly scholastic discussion of divine unity has obvious resonances with *kalām* discussions of the problem of attributes, and in style and content it is also reminiscent of al-Kindī's *On First Philosophy*.[103] But when Ibn ʿAdī sets out his own view, he argues for a conclusion that al-Kindī would reject: God must be in a sense one, and in a sense many, as neither pure unity nor pure multiplicity are possible.[104] Even so, most of the ways in which a thing can be one or many are inapplicable to God.[105] By process of elimination, Ibn ʿAdī concludes that God will be 'one' only in respect of definition. However, this does not rule out God's being multiple. In fact, we know that he is multiple because our experience of created things proves that

God possesses the attributes (*ṣifāt*) of generosity, wisdom and power.[106] This is strikingly similar to what we have seen in Saʿādia, albeit that Ibn ʿAdī has the attribute of 'generosity (*jūd*)' instead of Saʿādia's 'living'. However, Saʿādia was at pains to deny that the three attributes constitute a genuine multiplicity and, in fact, criticises Christians precisely for believing that the three attributes constitute a genuine multiplicity. Saʿādia explains that the doctrine of the Trinity arose from a misunderstanding of this point on the part of the more sophisticated Christians, who understood that God is not a body but still believed that his multiple attributes mean that he is three as well as one.[107] Saʿādia could almost have written this with Ibn ʿAdī in mind. It was clearly the latter's intention to leave room for a genuine, and triune, multiplicity in God.

The materials surveyed here would still allow us to divide the thinkers who wrote in Arabic prior to Avicenna into two camps, the *falāsifa* and the *mutakallimūn*. It is legitimate, as well as useful, to say that al-Kindī and al-Fārābī were 'philosophers' whereas Abū l-Hudhayl and al-Ashʿarī were 'theologians'. But this should not blind us to the complex and productive exchanges between the two groups, or to the variety of attitudes that philosophers adopted towards *kalām*. The picture is complicated still further by the activity of Jewish and Christian thinkers who pursued theological concerns of their own, sometimes drawing on Islamic *kalām*. Matters are equally complex once we get to Avicenna. Recent attempts to emphasise the *kalām* influence on Avicenna himself remain controversial but seem plausible in light of the considerable importance of *kalām* for philosophers in previous generations.[108] In the Eastern Islamic heartlands, the criticism of Avicenna by al-Ghazālī and others did not lead to an abandonment of *falsafa*.[109] We instead find, alongside other developments, a fusion of Avicennian (rather than Aristotelian) philosophy with sunnī *kalām*. This later tradition stands as a living rebuke to al-Fārābī. For many centuries, authors would try their hand at developing systems that were clearly theological, and admittedly dialectical—yet also philosophical.[110]

NOTES

1. On the *miḥna* see Patton 1965. On the broader issues, see Crone and Hinds (2003). I speak here of sunnī, as opposed to shīʿī Islam—the shīʿa being those who believed that political authority is passed down through the family of the Prophet and in particular through his cousin ʿAlī. Theological groups could cross this divide; many later Muʿtazilite authors were shīʿī.

2. As shown by Gutas (1998). On the translations see also Endress (1987–92) and Gutas's appendix in Pasnau (2010). For translations of Aristotle, still useful is Peters (1968).

3. For a lively account of the period, see Kennedy (2005). See also Young et al. (1990).

4. Thus, Marenbon (2007, 60) rightly designates *kalām* as a type of 'Islamic philosophy'.

5. The most important study of theology in this period is the monumental van Ess (1991–95); see, more briefly, van Ess (2006). Also important are numerous publications by

R. M. Frank, including Frank (1978), as well as Nader (1984); Watt (1998). For a briefer survey, see Blankinship (2008).

6. On Ismāʿīlī philosophers, see De Smet (1995), Walker (1993, 1999); for Ismāʿilism more generally, Daftary (1996).

7. al-Sharastānī (1984, 42). See also Frank (1971, 7).

8. For al-Naẓẓām, God must do what is beneficial for his creatures, and he cannot, for instance, increase or decrease the suffering of the damned. See Nader (1984, 77–78). Against the possibility that God could perform evil, he argues that even the possibility (*tajwīz*) of evil is evil, so this possibility is incompatible with God's justice (report by al-Sharastānī 1984, 49). Abū l-Hudhayl admits that it is 'inconceivable' that God do evil, because of his good nature but insists that he does have the power to do so. See van Ess (1991–95), vol. 5, 401–2 (texts XXI.79–80). Cf. Daiber (1975, 233) on the question of whether God must create, if creation is good.

9. Report by al-Sharastānī (1984, 52).

10. See further Frank (1982).

11. Abū l-Hudhayl, for instance, firmly denies that God has power over the actions performed by humans. See van Ess (1991–5), vol.5, 402–4 (texts XXI.82–86).

12. See Daiber (1975), 132–36

13. For instance, al-Shahrastānī's overview of Muʿtazilite views on divine predication by remarking that they 'entirely (*aṣalan*) reject the eternal attributes' (al-Sharastānī 1984, 41).

14. van Ess (1991–95), vol. 5, 392 (text XXI.56).

15. See further Frank (1969). See Frank (1978, 53); Frank (1979, 74–75).

16. More problematic is the apparent result that God's justice will be identical to his power and his knowledge since all of these are identical to God. In another seemingly 'verbal' solution, he claims that the attributes are 'neither identical nor not-identical' to one another. See van Ess (1967, 112).

17. For all this see Madelung (1974).

18. See van Ess (1967, 103), and more generally Melchert (2006).

19. A prominent example would be Ḍirār ibn ʿAmr (d. 815) who is normally classified as a Muʿtazilite, but who accepted that God creates human actions—view shared with the 'determinist' Jahm ibn Ṣafwān (d. 745)—while insisting that humans are *also* the agents of their actions.

20. For a summary and critical discussion of this account, see Watt (1998, 209ff).

21. Nader (1984; 45–46).

22. For studies see Heemskerk (2000); Hourani (1971); Peters (1976); Reynolds (2004).

23. Particularly al-Khayyāt, author of *al-Intiṣār*, and the multi-faceted literary genius al-Jāḥiẓ (d. 869), a student of al-Naẓẓām. Other important early witnesses include al-Nāshiʾ, for whom see van Ess (1971).

24. Despite his rejection of Muʿtazilite doctrines, he summarises them in his invaluable *Maqālāt*, a major source for early theological teachings. Other key sources include al-Sharastānī (1984), al-Baghdādī (1919–35).

25. See further Allard (1964); Gimaret (1990); McCarthy (1953).

26. The fifth 'principle' to command good and evil is usually taken as a call to political activism, but it was honoured more in the breach than in the observance. See 'Muʿtazila', *Encyclopedia of Islam*, new ed., 12 vols (Leiden, the Netherlands: Brill, 1960–2004).

27. The *miḥna* itself is often seen in this context. For Muʿtazilite views on the question of the *imām* (political and religious leader), see el-Omari (2007).

28. Not dissimilar is the approach of al-Maturīdī, founder of the other main post-Muʿtazilite school of Sunnī *kalām*, which spread in Central Asia. See further Rudolph (1997).

29. For instance, our freedom of action is known to us innately and also confirmed by revelation, as remarked by al-Sharastānī (1984, 44).

30. Schöck (2005).

31. See his autobiography, the *Deliverer from Error* (trans. Watt 1994), and further Griffel (2009); Shihadeh (2005).

32. On which see Frank (1978); Dhanani (1994).

33. See M. Marmura, 'Al-Ghazālī,' in Adamson and Taylor (2005, 137–54). His occasionalist interpretation, which I follow here, challenges the reading of Frank (1992).

34. For a comprehensive translation of his works, see Adamson and Pormann (2011).

35. He uses the word *mutakallimūn* at least once, but not for theologians. The term appears, of all places, in his treatise explaining why air is colder at higher altitudes (al-Kindī 1950–53, vol. 2, 100). The word *mutakallimūn* here refers simply to people who have expressed views on such scientific phenomena.

36. Adamson (2003). The topic was previously discussed by Ivry (1974, 22–34).

37. For the Arabic version of Proclus, called in Arabic *Book on the Pure Good*, and in the Latin translation of this Arabic version, the *Book of Causes*, see D'Ancona (1995); Endress (1973). On the Kindī circle more generally, see Endress (1997).

38. See Adamson (2002, 165–70), and further D'Ancona (2000); Frank (1956); Taylor (1998).

39. Ed. al-Kindī (1950–3, 97–162); Rashed and Jolivet (1998, 9–99); English translations Ivry (1974)(, Adamson and Pormann (2011).

40. See Adamson (2007a, 47–57).

41. Or so I have argued in Adamson (2007a, 98–105).

42. For the topic more generally, see Davidson (1987).

43. Al-Kindī wrote a work, now lost, called *On Oneness by way of Commentaries* (*Fī l-tawḥīd bi-tafsīrāt*); Ivry (1974, 30) suggests that this might have grounded the same theory in religious texts. Information about al-Kindī's many lost treatises is found in Ibn al-Nadīm's *Fihrist* (translation in Dodge 1970). For lists of al-Kindī's writings, see McCarthy (1962); Adamson and Pormann (2011).

44. For the work see Rashed and Jolivet (1998, 122–27); Adamson and Pormann (2011).

45. Ed. al-Kindī (1950–53, vol. 1, 244–61); Rashed and Jolivet (1998, 177–99); English translation Adamson and Pormann (2011).

46. Janssens (2007).

47. Al-Kindī (1950–53, vol. 1, 373).

48. Adamson (2003, 57–66); Adamson (2007a, 43–44 and 63–66). Al-Kindī may not have known that Philoponus was a Christian but did know he was a fierce critic of Aristotle.

49. Al-Kindī (1950–53, vol. 2, 93).

50. Al-Kindī (1950–53, vol. 1, 103–4).

51. Adamson (2007a, 23–24), against Ivry (1974, 33).

52. See Adamson (2007b).

53. See Endress (1986); Margoliouth (1905).

54. Al-Fārābī (1931, 131–38).

55. This work was simply called *The Demonstration* (*al-Burhān*), and al-Fārābī wrote a paraphrase of the work with the same title. See Fakhry (1987). English translation by Fakhry in Nasr and Aminrazavi (1999, 93–110).

56. See Black (2006); Adamson (2007c).

57. He makes this point in several works, but especially the *Book of Religion* (*Kitāb al-Milla*), in al-Fārābī (1968, 41–66). French translation by Mallet (1989, 117–45). English translation by Butterworth (2001, 93–113).

58. See Mahdi (1972); Reisman (2005, 65–69).

59. For the parallel see N. Lahoud and E. Gannagé in *Mélanges de l'Université Saint-Joseph* 57 (2004), following a suggestion by F. W. Zimmermann.

60. Averroes (1997). English translations include Averroes (1961).

61. See Rudolph (2007).

62. *Letter on the Intellect*, ed. al-Fārābī (1938, 7–8). English translation in McGinnis and Reisman (2007, 68–78). See Rudolph (2007, 70), which is my source for the other allusions to Muʿtazilite doctrines just mentioned.

63. Ed. al-Fārābī (1960), English translation in Zimmermann (1981). See Adamson (2006).

64. Al-Fārābī (1960, 98–100).

65. See further Wisnovsky (2003, 219–25); and Knuuttila's paper in this volume.

66. Ed. and trans. al-Fārābī (1985).

67. Rudolph (2008).

68. In his work *The Tokens of Prophecy* (ed. Abū Ḥātim al-Rāzī 1977).

69. See Stroumsa (1999); Urvoy (1996, 142–52). On him see further Druart (1996, 1997).

70. As discussed in two important articles, Rashed (2000, 2008).

71. See Abū Ḥātim al-Rāzī (1977), 191 (on miracles), 114 (on anthropomorphism, *tashbīh*), 13 (on *taqlīd*).

72. The same criticism is levelled at the Ismāʿīlīs by al-Ghazālī. See Watt (1994, 45–56), and further Frank (1991–92).

73. See the opening of his *Spiritual Medicine*, ed. Abū Bakr al-Rāzī (1939), 15–96, trans. Arberry (1950).

74. Here I agree with the conclusions of Rashed (2000).

75. See Baffioni (1982, ch. 2).

76. Even more so if we accept the authenticity of *On Metaphysics*: see Abū Bakr al-Rāzī (1939, 116–34); studied in Lucchetta (1987).

77. For example, by Alexander (1984, 22).

78. Arabic and Hebrew (ed. Saadia Gaon 1880, 150–51). English translation by Saadia Gaon (1948). See further Efros (1974, ch.6); Adamson (2010a).

79. Saadia Gaon (1880, 114).

80. Saadia Gaon (1880, 118); cf. El-Omari (2007, 51).

81. Saadia Gaon (1880, 12–14); cf. Efros (1942).

82. Saadia Gaon (1880, 73ff).

83. Saadia Gaon (1880, 78, cf. 92–93).

84. Saadia Gaon (1880, 97). Note his use of the phrase *anniyya faqaṭ*, which has been mentioned above as appearing in texts from al-Kindī's circle.

85. Efros (1974, 50–60); Kaufmann (1967); Neumark (1928); Rawidowicz (1943).

86. Saadia Gaon (1880, 79).

87. This is how it is taken by Kaufmann (1967, 16–17).

88. Efros (1974, 52–53).

89. Saadia Gaon (1880, 80–81). Cf. Efros (1974, 49).

90. Saadia Gaon (1880, 110).

91. Kaufmann (1967, 55).

92. So also Neumark (1928, 184).

93. Saadia Gaon (1880, 106). Cf. Kaufmann (1967, 68–69, n. 127).

94. Altmann and Stern (1958).

95. See Endress (1977); Platti (1983). Though there is evidence for his having studied with al-Fārābī, recent studies have suggested that intellectually he may be closer to al-Kindī than al-Fārābī on some points. See Rashed (2009); Adamson (2010b).

96. Périer (1920).

97. This was already pointed out by Endress (1986, 204–5).

98. Pines and Schwarz (1979). Cf. Adamson (2010a, 405–6).

99. Ed. Ibn ʿAdī (1988, 375–404).

100. Ibn ʿAdī (1988, 377–78).

101. Ibn ʿAdī (1988, 379).

102. Ibn ʿAdī (1988, 381–83).

103. For instance, the last argument is comparable to al-Kindī's argument that nothing can cause itself (*dhātuhu*) to exist (al-Kindī 1950–3, 123–24).

104. Ibn ʿAdī (1988, 390–92). But compare al-Kindī (1950–53, 132–41) for a demonstration that created things must be both one and many.

105. He rules out unity with respect to genus, species, relation, continuity and undividedness (Ibn ʿAdī 1988, 394).

106. Ibn ʿAdī (1988, 404).

107. Saadia Gaon (1880, 86). See further Wolfson (1977).

108. See especially R. Wisnovsky (2003); Rudolph (1996).

109. Important recent studies include Eichner (2007); Gutas (2002); Michot (1993); Shihadeh (2005).

110. I would like to thank Nadja Germann for her helpful comments on a previous draft, and the Leverhulme Trust for their support as the chapter was completed.

BIBLIOGRAPHY

Adamson, P. 2002. *The Arabic Plotinus: A Philosophical Study of the 'Theology of Aristotle'.* London: Duckworth.

———. 2003. Al-Kindī and the Muʿtazila: Divine Attributes, Creation and Freedom. *Arabic Sciences and Philosophy* 13:45–77.

———. 2006. The Arabic Sea Battle: Al-Fārābī on the Problem of Future Contingents. *Archiv für Geschichte der Philosophie* 88:163–8.

———. 2007a. *Al-Kindī.* New York: Oxford University Press.

———. 2007b. 'The Kindian tradition: The structure of philosophy in Arabic Neoplatonism'. In *Libraries of the Neoplatonists*, ed. C. D'Ancona, 351–70. Leiden, the Netherlands: Brill.

———. 2007c. Knowledge of Universals and Particulars in the Baghdad School. *Documenti e Studi sulla Tradizione Filosofica Medievale* 18:141–64.

———. 2010a. 'Freedom and determinism'. In Pasnau 2010, vol. 1, 399–413.

———. 2010b. Yahyā Ibn ʿAdī and Averroes on *Metaphysics* Alpha Elatton. *Documenti e Studi sulla Tradizione Filosofica Medievale* 21:343–74.

Adamson, P. and P. E. Pormann. 2011. *The Philosophical Works of al-Kindī.* Karachi: Oxford University Press.

Adamson, P. and R. C. Taylor, eds. 2005. *The Cambridge Companion to Arabic Philosophy.* Cambridge: Cambridge University Press.

Alexander, P. S. 1984. *Textual Sources for the Study of Judaism.* Chicago: University of Chicago Press.

Allard, M. 1964. *Le problème des attributs divins dans la doctrine d' al-Ashʿarī et de ses premiers grands disciples.* Beirut: Imprimerie Catholique.

Altmann, A. and S. M. Stern. 1958. *Isaac Israeli: A Neoplatonic Philosopher of the Early Tenth Century.* Oxford: Oxford University Press.

Arberry, A. J. 1950. *The Spiritual Physick of Rhazes.* London: John Murray.

Averroes. 1961. *On the Harmony of Religion and Philosophy*, trans. G. F. Hourani. London: E.J.W. Gibb.

————. 1997. *Faṣl al-Maqāl*, ed. M. A. Jābarī. Beirut: Markaz Dirāsāt al-Waḥda al-'arabiyya.

Baffioni, C. 1982. *Atomismo e antiatomismo nel pensiero islamico.* Naples: Instituto Universitario Orientale.

al-Baghdādī. 1919–35. *Moslem Schisms and Sects.* 2 vols. New York: Columbia University Press.

Black, D. L. 2006. Knowledge ('*Ilm*) and Certainty (*Yaqīn*) in al-Fārābī's Epistemology. *Arabic Sciences and Philosophy* 16:11–45.

Blankinship, K. 2008. 'The Early Creed'. In *The Cambridge Companion to Classical Islamic Theology*, ed. T. Winter, 33–54. Cambridge: Cambridge University Press.

Butterworth, C. 2001. *Alfarabi. The Political Writings. Selected Aphorisms and Other Texts.* Ithaca, NY: Cornell University Press.

Crone, P. and M. Hinds. 2003. *God's Caliph: Religious Authority in the First Centuries of Islam.* Cambridge: Cambridge University Press.

Daftary, F. 1996. *Mediaeval Isma'ili History and Thought.* Cambridge: Cambridge University Press.

Daiber, H. 1975. *Das theologisch-philosophische System des Mu'ammar Ibn 'Abbād as-Sulamī.* Beirut: Franz Steiner.

D'Ancona, C. 1995. *Recherches sur le Liber de Causis.* Paris: J. Vrin.

———— 2000. 'L'influence du vocabulaire arabe: *causa prima est esse tantum*'. In *L'élaboration du vocabulaire philosophique au Moyen Âge*, ed. J. Hamesse and C. Steel, 51–97. Turnhout, Belgium: Brepols.

Davidson, H. A. 1987. *Proofs for Eternity, Creation and the Existence of God in Medieval Islamic and Jewish Philosophy.* New York: Oxford University Press.

De Smet, D. 1995. *La quiétude de l'intellect: néoplatonisme et gnose ismaélienne dans l'œuvre de Ḥamîd ad-Dîn al-Kirmâni (Xe/XIe s.).* Leuven, Belgium: Peeters.

Dhanani, A. 1994. *The Physical Theory of the Kalām.* Leiden, the Netherlands: Brill.

Dodge, B. 1970. *The Fihrist of al-Nadīm.* New York: Columbia University Press.

Druart, T.-A. 1996. Al-Razi's Conception of the Soul: Psychological Background to his Ethics. *Medieval Philosophy and Theology* 5:245–63.

————. 1997. The Ethics of al-Razi. *Medieval Philosophy and Theology* 6:47–71.

Efros, I. 1942. Saadia's Theory of Knowledge. *The Jewish Quarterly Review* 33:133–70.

————. 1974. *Studies in Medieval Jewish Philosophy.* New York: Columbia University Press.

Eichner, H. 2007. Dissolving the Unity of Metaphysics: from Faḫr al-Din al-Rāzī to Mullā Ṣadrā al-Šīrāzī. *Medioevo* 32:139–98.

el-Omari, R. 2007. 'Abu l-Qāsim al-Balkhī al-Ka'bī's doctrine of the *Imāma*'. In *A Common Rationality: Mu'tazilism in Islam and Judaism*, ed. C. Adang, S. Schmidt, and D. Sklar, 39–57. Würzburg, Germany: Ergon.

Endress, G. 1973. *Proclus Arabus: Zwanzig Abschnitte aus der Institutio Theologica in arabischer Übersetzung.* Beirut: Steiner.

————. 1977. *The Works of Yaḥyā Ibn 'Adī. An Analytical Inventory.* Weisbaden, Germany: Ludwig Reichert.

————. 1986. 'Grammatik und Logik. Arabische Philologie und griechische Philosophie im Widerstreit'. In *Sprachphilosophie in Antike und Mittelalter*, ed. B. Mojsisch, 163–299. Amsterdam: B.R. Grüner.

———. 1987 and 1992. 'Die wissenschaftliche Literatur'. In *Grundriss der arabischen Philologie*, ed. H. Gätje, vol. 2, 400–506, and vol. 3 (supplement), 3–152. Wiesbaden, Germany: Ludwig Reichert.

———. 1997. 'The circle of al-Kindī'. In *The Ancient Tradition in Christian and Islamic Hellenism*, ed. G. Endress and R. Kruk, 43–76. Leiden, the Netherlands: Research School CNWS.

Fakhry, 1987. *Manṭiq 'inda 'l-Fārābī: Kitāb al-Burhān wa-Kitāb Sharā'it al-Yaqīn*. Beirut: Dar el-Machreq.

al-Fārābī. 1931. *Iḥṣā' al-'ulūm*, ed. U. Amīn. Cairo: Maṭba'a al-Sa'āda.

———. 1938. *Risāla fī l-'aql*, ed. M. Bouyges. Beirut: Imprimerie Catholique.

———. 1960. *Commentary on Aristotle's Peri Hermêneias*, ed. W. Kutsch and S. Marrow. Beirut: Catholic University Press.

———. 1968. *Kitāb al-Milla wa-nuṣūṣ ukhrā*, ed. M. Mahdi. Beirut: Dār al-Mashriq.

———. 1985. *On the Perfect State*, ed. and trans. R. Walzer. Oxford: Oxford University Press.

Frank, R. M. 1956. The Origin of the Arabic Philosophical Term *Anniyya*. *Cahiers de Byrsa* 6:181–201.

———. 1969. The Divine Attributes According to the Teaching of Abū 'l-Hudhayl al-Allāf. *Le Muséon* 82:451–506.

———. 1971. Several Fundamental Assumptions of the Baṣra School of the Mu'tazila. *Studia Islamica* 33:5–18.

———. 1978. *Beings and Their Attributes: The Teachings of the Basrian School of the Mu'tazila in the Classical Period*. Albany: SUNY Press.

———. 1979. 'Kalām and Philosophy, A Perspective from One Problem'. In *Islamic Philosophical Theology*, ed. P. Morewedge, 71–95. Albany: SUNY Press.

———. 1982. The Autonomy of the Human Agent in the Teaching of 'Abd al-Jabbār. *Le Muséon* 95:323–55.

———. 1991–92. Al-Ghazālī on Taqlīd. *Zeitschrift für die Geschichte der arabisch-islamischen Wissenschaften* 7:207–52.

———. 1992. *Creation and the Cosmic System*. Heidelberg, Germany: Carl Winter.

Gimaret, D. 1990. *La doctrine de al-Ash'arī*. Paris: Cerf.

Griffel, F. 2009. *Al-Ghazālī's Philosophical Theology*. New York: Oxford University Press.

Gutas, D. 1998. *Greek Thought, Arabic Culture: the Graeco-Arabic Translation Movement in Baghdad and Early Society (2nd–4th /8th–10th Centuries)*. London: Routledge.

———. 2002. 'The heritage of Avicenna: The golden age of Arabic philosophy, 1000–ca. 1350'. In *Avicenna and His Heritage*, ed. J. Janssens and D. De Smet, 81–97. Leuven, Belgium: Leuven University Press.

Heemskerk, M. T. 2000. *Suffering in the Mu'tazilite Theology: 'Abd al-Jabbār's Teaching on Pain and Divine Justice*. Leiden, the Netherlands: Brill.

Hourani, G. F. 1971. *Islamic Rationalism: The Ethics of 'Abd al-Jabbār*. Oxford: Clarendon Press.

Ibn 'Adī, Yaḥyā. 1988. *Philosophical Treatises*, ed. S. Khalifat. Amman, Jordan: University Press of Amman.

Ivry, A. L. 1974. *Al-Kindi's Metaphysics*. Albany: SUNY Press.

Janssens, J. 2007. Al-Kindī: The Founder of Philosophical Exegesis of the Qur'ān. *Journal of Qur'anic Studies* 9:1–21.

Kaufmann, D. 1967. *Geschichte der Attributenlehre in der jüdischen Religionsphilosophie des Mittelalters von Saadja bis Maimuni*. Amsterdam: Philo.

Kennedy, H. 2005. *The Court of the Caliphs: When Baghdad Ruled the World*. London: Phoenix.

al-Kindī. 1950–53. *Rasā'il al-Kindī al-falsafiyya*, ed. M. Abū Rīda, 2 vols. Cairo: Dār al-Fikr al-ʿArabī.

Lucchetta, G. A. 1987. *La natura e la sfera: la scienza antica e le sue metafore nella critica di Rāzī*. Bari, Italy: Milella.

Madelung, W. 1974. 'The origins of the controversy concerning the creation of the Koran'. In *Orientalia Hispanica,* vol. 1, ed. J. M. Barral, 504–25. Leiden, the Netherlands: Brill.

Mahdi, M. 1972. Alfarabi on Philosophy and Religion. *Philosophical Forum* 4:5–25.

Mallet, D. 1989. *Farabi. Deux traités philosophiques.* Damascus, Syria: Institute Francais de Damas.

Marenbon, J. 2007. *Medieval Philosophy: An Historical and Philosophical Introduction.* London: Routledge.

Margoliouth, D. S. 1905. The Discussion between Abu Bishr Matta and Abu Saʿid al-Sirafi on the Merits of Logic and Grammar. *Journal of the Royal Asiatic Society:* 79–129.

McCarthy, J. 1953. *The Theology of al-Ashʿarī.* Beirut: Imprimerie Catholique.

McCarthy, R. J. 1962. *Al-Taṣānīf al-Mansuba ilā Faylasūf al-ʿarab.* Baghdad: Matbaʾa al-ʾani.

McGinnis, J. and D. C. Reisman, ed. and trans. 2007. *Classical Arabic Philosophy: An Anthology of Sources.* Indianapolis, IN: Hackett.

Melchert, C. 2006. *Aḥmad ibn Ḥanbal.* Oxford: Oneworld.

Michot, Y. J. 1993. La pandémie avicennienne au VIᵉ /XIIᵉ siècle. *Arabica* 40:287–344.

Nader, A. 1984. *Le système philosophique des Muʿtazila.* Beirut: Dar El-Machreq Sarl.

Nasr, S. H. and M. Aminrazavi 1999. *An Anthology of Philosophy in Persia,* vol. 1. Oxford: Oxford University Press.

Neumark, D. 1928. *Geschichte der jüdischen Philosophie des Mittelalters* II.2. Berlin: Walter de Gruyter.

Pasnau, R., ed. 2010. *The Cambridge History of Medieval Philosophy.* 2 vols. Cambridge: Cambridge University Press.

Patton, W. M. 1965. *Aḥmed ibn Ḥanbal and the Miḥna.* Leiden, the Netherlands: Brill.

Périer, A. 1920. *Petits traités apologétiques de Yaḥyā ben ʿAdī.* Paris: J. Gabalda.

Peters, F. E. 1968. *Aristoteles Arabus.* Leiden, the Netherlands: Brill.

Peters, J. R. T. M. 1976. *God's Created Speech.* Leiden, the Netherlands: Brill.

Pines, S. and M. Schwarz. 1979. 'Yaḥyā Ibn ʿAdī's refutation of the doctrine of acquisition (Iktisāb)'. In *Studia Orientalia Memoriae D.H. Baneth Dedicata,* ed. J. Blau, S. Pines, M. J. Kister and S. Shaked, 49–94. Jerusalem: Magnes.

Platti, E. 1983. *Yaḥyā Ibn ʿAdī: Théologien chrétien et philosophe arabe.* Leuven, Belgium: Departement Oriëntalistiek.

Rashed, M. 2000. Abū Bakr al-Rāzī et la kalām. *Mélanges de l'institut dominicain détudes orientales du Caire* 24:39–54.

———. 2008. Abū Bakr al-Rāzī et la prophétie. *Mélanges de l'institut dominicain détudes orientales du Caire* 27:169–82.

———. 2009. On the Authorship of the *Treatise on the Harmonization of the Opinions of the Two Sages* Attributed to Al-Fārābī. *Arabic Sciences and Philosophy* 19:43–82.

Rashed R. and J. Jolivet, ed. and trans. 1998. *Oeuvres Philosophiques & Scientifiques d'al-Kindī. Volume 2, Métaphysique et cosmologie.* Leiden, the Netherlands: Brill.

Rawidowicz, S. 1943. 'Saadya's purification of the idea of God'. In Rosenthal 1943, 139–65.

al-Rāzī, Abū Bakr. 1939. *Rasā'il falsafiyya (Opera philosophica),* ed. P. Kraus. Cairo: Paul Barbey.

al-Rāzī, Abū Ḥātim. 1977. *Kitāb Aʿlām al-nubuwwa,* ed. Ṣ al-Sāwī. Tehran: Imperial Iranian Academy of Philosophy.

Reisman, D. C. 2005. 'Al-Fārābī and the philosophical curriculum'. In Adamson and Taylor
   2005, 52–71.

Reynolds, G. S. 2004. *A Muslim Theologian in a Sectarian Milieu: 'Abd al-Jabbār and the
   Critique of Christian Origins.* Leiden, the Netherlands: Brill.

Rosenthal, E. I. J., ed. 1943. *Saadya Studies.* Manchester, UK: Manchester University Press.

Rudolph, U. 1996. Ibn Sīnā et le Kalām. *Bulletin d'Études Orientales* 98:131–36.

———. 1997. *Al-Māturīdī und die sunnitische Theologie in Samarkand.* Leiden, the Netherlands: Brill.

———. 2007. 'Al-Fārābī und die Mu'tazila'. In Adang et al. 2007, 59–80.

———. 2008. 'Reflections on al-Fārābī's *Mabādi' ārā' ahl al-madīna al-fāḍila*'. In *In the Age
   of al-Fārābī: Arabic Philosophy in the Fourth/Tenth Century*, ed. P. Adamson, 1–14.
   London: Warburg Institute.

Saadia Gaon. 1880. *Kitāb al-Amānāt wa 'l-I'tiqādāt*, ed. S. Landauer. Leiden, the Netherlands: Brill.

———. 1948. *The Book of Beliefs and Opinion*, trans. S. Rosenblatt. New Haven, CT: Yale
   University Press.

Schöck, C. 2005. *Koranexegese, Grammatik und Logik: Zum Verhältnis von arabischer und
   aristotelischer Urteils-, Konsequenz-und Schlusslehre.* Leiden, the Netherlands: Brill.

al-Sharastānī. 1984. *Muslim Sects and Divisions*, trans. A. K. Kazi and J. G. Flynn. London:
   Kegan Paul.

Shihadeh, A. 2005. From al-Ghazālī to al-Rāzī: 6th/12th Century Developments in Muslim
   Philosophical Theology. *Arabic Sciences and Philosophy* 15:141–79.

Stroumsa, S. 1999. *Freethinkers of Medieval Islam.* Leiden, the Netherlands: Brill.

Taylor, R. C. 1998. Aquinas, the *Plotiniana Arabica* and the Metaphysics of Being and
   Actuality. *Journal of the History of Ideas* 59:241–64.

Urvoy, D. 1996. *Les penseurs libres dans l'Islam classique.* Paris: Albin Michel.

van Ess, J. 1967. Ibn Kullāb und die Miḥna. *Oriens* 18–19:92–142.

———. 1971. *Frühe Mu'tazilitische Häresiographie.* Beirut: Orient-Institut der Deutschen
   Morgenländischen Gesellschaft.

———. 1991–95. *Theologie und Gesellschaft im 2. und 3. Jahrhundert Hidschra: Eine
   Geschichte des religiösen Denkens im frühen Islam.* Berlin: Walter de Gruyter.

———. 2006. *The Flowering of Muslim Theology.* Cambridge, MA: Harvard University
   Press.

Walker, P. 1993. *Early Philosophical Shiism: The Ismaili Neoplatonism of Abū Ya'qūb
   al-Sijistānī.* Cambridge: Cambridge University Press.

———. 1999. *Ḥamīd al-Dīn al-Kirmānī: Ismaili Thought in the Age of al-Ḥākim.* London: I.B.
   Tauris.

Watt, W. M. 1994. *The Faith and Practice of al-Ghazālī*, 2nd edition. Oxford: Oneworld.

———. 1998. *The Formative Period of Islamic Thought*, 2nd edition. Oxford: Oneworld.

Wisnovsky, R. 2003. *Avicenna's Metaphysics in Context.* London: Duckworth.

Wolfson, H. A. 1977. 'Saadia on the Trinity and Incarnation'. In Wolfson, *Studies in the
   History of Philosophy and Religion*, vol. 2, 394–414. Cambridge, MA: Harvard University
   Press.

Young, M. J. L., J. D. Latham and R. B. Serjeant, eds. 1990. *Religion, Learning and Science in
   the 'Abbāsid Period.* Cambridge: Cambridge University Press.

Zimmermann, F. W. 1981. *Al-Farabi's Commentary and Short Treatise on Aristotle's De
   Interpretatione.* Oxford: Oxford University Press.

CHAPTER 4

AVICENNA AND AFTERWARDS

NADJA GERMANN

1. AVICENNA'S BACKGROUND

> Every essence or quiddity can be understood without anything being understood
> about its existence. For I can understand what a man is, or what a phoenix is,
> without knowing anything about their existence. It is clear, therefore, that
> existence is other than essence or quiddity, unless perhaps there exists a thing
> whose quiddity is its existence.[1]

This assertion, made by Thomas Aquinas, is one of the most influential references in
the Latin West to Avicenna's famous distinction between essence and existence. It can
be interpreted as the forerunner of a fierce debate concerning nothing less than the
fundamentals of Western metaphysics, a debate that had its peak around the verge of
the thirteenth and fourteenth centuries and set the framework for discussions on
being far into modernity.[2] Yet the significance of Avicenna's philosophy was not limited
to the field of metaphysics; his innovations in logic and natural philosophy, including
psychology, had a comparable impact on subsequent intellectual history. Moreover,
his writings were not only studied in his immediate context, the Islamic world, but also
in Jewish philosophy and—as the quotation above shows—in the Latin-Christian
West. Who was this outstanding figure, and what are the characteristics of his thought?

Avicenna (Abū ʿAlī l-Ḥusayn ibn Sīnā, c. 980–1037) was born in the vicinity of
Bukhārā, the centre of the Sāmānids who ruled the district of Khurāsān.[3] He therefore lived and wrote at a time when all Greek philosophical texts translated into
Arabic were largely accessible and at least one generation of scholars had worked on
them. Furthermore, owing to his upbringing and precocity, he acquired a broad and
thorough education in the various branches of science (both religious and 'secular')

already in his early years. This, in turn, not only earned him a position as physician (and later on also as political administrator) for the Amīr Nuḥibn Manṣūr at the age of approximately seventeen but, additionally, furnished him with access to the excellent Sāmānid library in Bukhārā where the translations from Greek and the most recent scholarship were available.[4] Philosophy was now in a considerably different situation from that of the period stretching from its first introduction into Arabic-Islamic culture up to Abū Bishr Mattā and the emergence of the Baghdād peripatetics. Whereas the first philosophers to write in Arabic, such as al-Kindī, felt the need to justify their occupation with philosophy and employment of philosophical methods, in the age of Avicenna, philosophy was much more accepted. Accordingly, mutual influence across the boundaries of the disciplines as well as cross-fertilization in terms of topics and methods, particularly between theology (*kalām*) and philosophy, can be observed.[5]

Avicenna, unlike any other philosopher or theologian in the Arabic-Islamic world before, inextricably merged the various intellectual traditions of his time and thus created a unique blend that was to shape the framework of philosophical as well as theological (both Sunni and Shī'ite) reasoning for centuries to come.[6] For one, this is obvious in light of the numerous commentaries (and supercommentaries) on his grand philosophical summas, particularly his *Ishārāt wa-Tanbīhāt* (*Pointers and Reminders*), a tradition that began shortly after his lifetime and continued to exist even in modernity. His trend-setting influence is further evident in the emergence of a theological type of encyclopedia that incorporates Avicennian concepts and theory of science.[7]

2. AVICENNA'S PHILOSOPHY

Avicenna's writings consist mainly of comprehensive philosophical summas, covering all branches of the sciences and logic as their propaedeutic tool, but also of smaller writings on selected topics.[8] In view of their structure and range of objects, these summas belong to the Neoplatonic-Aristotelian tradition with its specific curriculum that emerged within the context of the late ancient schools.[9] In what follows, I will focus on treatises belonging to one of his grand summas, the *Kitāb al-Shifā'* (*Book of the Healing*), which embraces logic, natural philosophy (including psychology), mathematical sciences and metaphysics. It is the only Avicennian oeuvre of which substantial parts were translated into Latin. According to Gutas's chronology (see note 8), it belongs to Avicenna's middle period and is the most detailed elaboration of his philosophy. Even though his later summa, the *Ishārāt wa-Tanbīhāt*, was more influential in the Arabic-Islamic East (see above), the *Kitāb al-Shifā'* is often much more explicit than the *Ishārāt* and gives more detailed discussions of the topics under consideration. I shall concentrate on just three areas: abstraction and intellection, essence and existence, and bridging physical and mental existence. All three are much debated in Avicenna scholarship today and give a vivid impression of the way Avicenna subtly interrelated the various fields of scientific enquiry to create one coherent and comprehensive philosophical system.[10]

3. ABSTRACTION AND INTELLECTION

In psychology, Avicenna's chief point of reference, inherited from Aristotle, is the idea that there are essentially three kinds of animate beings and accordingly three types of souls. The most basic animate beings are plants, which possess, according to this theory, a vegetative soul. This kind of soul serves the elementary functions of animate beings: it simply keeps them alive.[11] Animals, by contrast, are more complex animate beings, and this is due to their having a more powerful kind of soul, the so-called sensible soul. This type of soul enables them not only to live and propagate, but also to move locally and have sense perception.[12] The most sublime kind of soul, finally, is the rational soul, which is the distinctive feature of human beings and provides them with the additional means to think and understand.[13] While most scholars in the Aristotelian tradition basically accepted this model, they encountered a number of problems linked with it, owing to the vagueness and obscurity of several passages in Aristotle's De anima. Thus, for example, Aristotle explains (III, 8, 431b20–432a14) that in order to acquire knowledge we must start with sense perception and, through a process of analysis (what we call 'abstraction' in modern terminology), reveal the unchangeable forms and principles of reality; however, he does not give a detailed account of the steps involved. The situation is even more complicated with regard to the proper act of understanding, as laid out in the third book of De anima (430a14–18): here, in the notoriously difficult chapter 5, Aristotle introduces the distinction between mind 'in a passive sense', which 'becomes all things', and in another, active sense 'in that it makes all things' and hence 'is separable, impassive and unmixed'. This passage already puzzled the late ancient commentators who faced the problem of whether Aristotle meant to say that there are two distinct minds or rather one single mind with, however, two aspects. Either answer raises yet further questions; for example, if the solution is that Aristotle conceived of two distinct minds, it remains unclear how they are related: whether they are in one and the same person, or whether one of them (typically the active mind) is an external principle instead.[14]

Avicenna's contribution to the doctrine of the soul consists primarily in his attempt to deal with these problematic issues. The cornerstones of his theory are his concept of interior senses and, on the part of mind, his notion of intellection. Whereas intellection is required in order to grasp universal notions (intelligibles), the interior senses play a pivotal role in bridging the gap between sense perception and intellection. What Avicenna has in mind is the following. Human souls have the three 'layers' mentioned above: the vegetative, sensible and rational powers.[15] While the functions of the vegetative 'layer' are of no further interest for the present purpose, the sensible 'layer' plays an important role because Avicenna locates the interior senses here—which, of course, also means that animals possess interior senses. According to Avicenna there are five interior senses: common sense, estimation, the image-storing faculty, memory, and the image-forming faculty.[16] Within this group, the image-forming faculty plays a peculiar role: basically, it is the power by means of which images, 'particular' forms of perceived extra-mental objects, can be composed and divided. However, for humans this image-forming faculty has the further function of serving as the cogitative power. The task of this power, says Avicenna, consists in nothing less than preparing the 'particular' forms in a way that enables the human mind (intellect) to abstract the corresponding universal forms. A glance at Avicenna's theory of knowledge will help to explain what this means.

Just like Aristotle, Avicenna is convinced that the acquisition of knowledge ultimately starts from sense perception. What one sees, hears, smells, however, is in itself not yet knowledge, as knowledge can only be *about* something seen, heard, smelled. Consequently, the simplest form of knowledge one can acquire is the knowledge of *what* a certain perceived thing *is*; in short, it consists in the formation of a simple but universal concept (e.g., tree, noise, sweetness, which can be applied to any instantiation of tree, noise and sweetness).[17] This, however, raises the question of how to get from single sense perceptions to corresponding universal concepts. Avicenna's reply rests on a further presupposition: universal concepts can only be thought by the intellect, the rational 'layer' of the human soul; otherwise, animals would be capable of knowledge—which according to him and the Aristotelian tradition is absurd. Therefore, if cognition indeed starts from sense perception, Avicenna faces the problem of explaining how the image of a perceived thing can not only be transformed into a universal concept but also 'move' from the interior senses into the intellect.

At this stage, Avicenna's theory of intellection comes into play. This theory is meant to explain how humans grasp intelligibles, and it represents Avicenna's reply to Aristotle's puzzling distinction of two intellects, one active, the other passive. In accordance with his immediate predecessor, al-Fārābī, he considers both intellects to be really distinct: the human mind is the passive intellect mentioned by Aristotle, while the active mind is identified with the agent intellect, an external entity that can best be described as a cosmological intellect.[18] Hence, there is just one single agent intellect, whereas the passive intellect is a species with as many individuals as there are human beings. The agent intellect always actually thinks the intelligibles, in contrast to the passive human intellects, which somehow must be actualised. In this connection, Avicenna introduces his theory of the four stages of human intellect, echoing Aristotle's distinction between first and second actuality (*entelecheia*). Accordingly, the human's intellect at first (directly after birth) is in the stage of mere potentiality, like a blank sheet. Shortly after, it acquires what Avicenna calls the 'primary intelligibles' (*al-maqūlāt al-ūlā*). As will be discussed below, these are self-evident first principles of conceptualization and judgement like 'the whole is bigger than its part'.[19] The third stage is reached when the human intellect has acquired some of the so-called 'secondary intelligibles', which are universal concepts (such as tree, noise or sweetness); the fourth stage, finally, consists in the intellect actually thinking universal concepts, forming propositions and composing syllogisms.[20] While Avicenna leaves it open how the human intellect acquires the primary intelligibles and thus the second stage, the last two stages are brought about by the external agent intellect.

This, quite naturally, raises the question of how, in Avicenna's view, the agent intellect performs its actualising activity. The short answer is that the human intellect must put itself in contact with the agent intellect and track down the intelligibles. When it ceases to think, it does not retain the intelligibles it has just thought. Rather, they remain 'in' the external agent intellect (or better: continue to be thought by it), which means that the human intellect does not have its own memory for universals but, instead, must again tap the agent intellect.[21] This contact between the agent and the human intellect and human's resultant thinking of a universal concept is what I refer to as intellection.[22] While this is the standard process through which humans form new concepts, it is also at the core of Avicenna's theories of intuition and prophecy. A prophet, according to him, is simply someone who either 'intelligises' the intelligibles all at once or in a very short time. Prophets therefore differ from ordinary human beings in that they intuit as if out of themselves, do not need learning and teachers and know things far beyond the usual, due to their ease in coming into contact with the agent intellect and staying in this state.[23]

Avicenna's language with regard to intellection is surprisingly metaphorical. Moreover, he employs clearly Neoplatonist vocabulary when he characterises the acquisition of universal concepts as an 'emanation' from the agent intellect and an 'influx' into the human mind.[24] The most striking example might be his explanation of how an actual intelligible is brought about in the mind. The agent intellect is the cause of the universal form because it 'contains' the principles of the abstracted intelligible forms.[25] Its role, now, in comparison to our souls is similar to the role the sun has in relation to vision. For whenever humans by means of their rational power (the cogitative faculty) consider particular forms stored in the image-storing faculty, these particular forms become completely abstracted and impressed in the rational 'layer'. This however, Avicenna emphasises, takes place if and only if the particular forms at this very moment are illuminated by the agent intellect—just as sunlight is required in addition to vision to make colour visible.[26]

But how, one would like to ask, can this condition be fulfilled? As if anticipating this question, Avicenna continues by considering the role of the cogitative faculty. Abstracting and reflecting on particular forms plays a crucial role in preparing the soul for the reception of the intelligibles from the agent intellect.[27] Avicenna compares this preparatory activity performed by the cogitative faculty to the function of the middle terms in syllogisms, which, to him, pave the way to *receive* the conclusions *by necessity*.[28] Since the attainment of conclusions in syllogisms is described as a 'reception' and as 'necessary', it follows that what is being compared, the 'reception' of the intelligibles, also comes about *by necessity*. Further, the parallel to syllogistic reasoning suggests that just as conclusions follow from antecedents only if the syllogisms are constructed correctly, so the intelligibles are brought about by means of abstracting and considering particular forms only if this cogitative activity is performed correctly.

This point is further substantiated by another passage where Avicenna argues that just as particular forms, which resemble the visible forms of the things, occur in the common sense if these things are *rightly exposed* to the light, so the intellect needs to be prepared in order for the universal forms to come about.[29] Visible things must not merely be exposed to the light but exposed *in a certain way*. This implies, according to the comparison, that intelligibles are brought about only if the particular forms have been prepared *in a certain way* by the cogitative power. Only then will the corresponding universal concepts occur in the intellect, however, with the same necessity as a conclusion follows from a correctly constructed syllogism.[30]

There are, then, two requirements for acquiring a 'new' universal concept (such as tree, noise or sweetness). On the part of the cogitative faculty, the particular forms must be abstracted and analysed correctly so that, on the part of the intellect, there can be an influx of the corresponding universal concepts that are always actually thought by the external agent intellect. If and only if the preparation of the particular form is appropriate—and the comparison with the construction of a well-formed syllogism gives some idea of what Avicenna has in mind here—the contact with the agent intellect and the influx of the universal concept occur. But they do so necessarily. Even though Avicenna's theory of the soul entails several problems, particularly for a Muslim audience,[31] it became highly influential, especially the doctrine of the interior senses, and his accounts of abstraction, intellection and prophecy.

4. ESSENCE AND EXISTENCE

In metaphysics, as in psychology, Avicenna's chief point of reference is Aristotle, but his discussions also display the impact of Islamic theological concerns.[32] Historically speaking, his metaphysical thought constitutes a turning point in Arabic-Islamic intellectual culture to an extent that has only recently been fully appreciated. One of his core contributions to the field consists in his reflections on the concept of metaphysics and the sciences.[33] Ultimately, his considerations are driven by the problem of the subject matter of metaphysics—a puzzle primarily provoked by the ambiguities of the fourteen books transmitted as Aristotle's *Metaphysics*. For a reader in the age of Avicenna, it was unclear whether Aristotle understood the science 'he was looking for' to be dealing with first causes and principles, with separate and hence the most sublime entities, including God, or simply with being in the most general sense.[34] The solution Avicenna suggests, is an attempt to safeguard as much as possible of the diverging conceptions found in Aristotle without sacrificing coherence. According to him, the subject matter of metaphysics is 'the existent as existent' (*al-mawjūd bi-mā huwa mawjūd*).[35] However, it also deals with the separate substances—the supreme kind of beings (including God)—and the first causes and principles.

In order to explain how all these three former candidates for the position of subject matter are interrelated, Avicenna applies Aristotle's theory of science as developed in the *Posterior Analytics*. Consequently, he distinguishes between the subject matter proper and 'things sought after' in this discipline, its objects (*maṭlūbāt*).[36] Whereas existence is the subject matter, both the first causes and principles and the separate entities (including God) are 'things sought after' in metaphysics.[37] Avicenna obviously has a very precise structure in mind. Metaphysics has a general subject matter, namely, existence, which, in turn, embraces several 'species' (*anwāʿ*) and 'properties' (*ʿawāriḍ khāṣṣa*). These 'species' and 'properties' represent the main division of existence and hence two (of the three) main branches of metaphysics. So, for example, the various 'species' of existence correspond to the ten categories, while certain notions like priority/posteriority, universality/particularity and actuality/potentiality are considered as 'properties' of existence.[38] Whereas these 'properties' obviously spell out the range of predicates applicable to existence (*wujūd*) or the modes in which it can occur, the 'species' are the various kinds of existents (*mawjūdāt*) that can be distinguished. The third branch of metaphysics, finally, is dedicated to the causes and principles and bridges the gap between metaphysics and the remaining philosophical disciplines.[39] Since, according to Avicenna, metaphysics ascertains the first causes and principles of any of the particular sciences (mathematics, natural philosophy), these are subordinate to metaphysics. They rely on the causes and principles established by metaphysics (e.g., physics relies on the four causes) in order to derive conclusions, which can serve in their turn as principles for the applied sciences, such as medicine and engineering. But there then arises the question: from where does metaphysics itself obtain its principles?

Avicenna's reflections on the principles of metaphysics are probably one of the most fascinating chapters of the history of philosophy. He presents them immediately following his discussion of the subject matter and structure of metaphysics.[40] He begins by characterising his discussion as an 'indication' (*dalāla*)—a technical term intimating that the following discourse is not scientific by Avicenna's standards: it will not, therefore, prove the truth of a certain proposition or show the existence of something demonstratively. The proposition (or notion) under discussion will not (and in this case: cannot) be demonstrated but only pointed at, alluded to. Why the following issues are only treated 'indicatively' and not demonstratively becomes clear right away, as Avicenna introduces some of the notions he has in mind, namely, 'the existent' (*al-mawjūd*), 'the thing' (*al-shayʾ*) and 'the necessary' (*al-ḍarūrī*), and maintains that they 'are impressed in the soul in a primary way' and do not need 'better known things to bring [them] about'.[41]

The thing and the necessary, to which Avicenna later adds 'the one' (*al-wāḥid*), are 'primary intelligibles' since they are so fundamental that they underlie any further knowledge: they are, according to him, *principles* of conceptualization (*mabādiʾ li-l-taṣawwur*). In whatever way one tries to refer to them, one must already presuppose them;[42] moreover, they are primary in that they are 'common to all things' (*al-ashyā' al-'āmma li-l-umūr kullihā*).[43] Consequently, one can only point at them (give an indication, *dalāla*) and never provide an essential definition nor deduce them from more basic notions. With this background, Avicenna launches a discussion of these primary intelligibles in the course of which he introduces his distinction between essence and existence alluded to at the beginning of this chapter. He takes his starting point from the notion of 'thing'.[44] After having explained that 'the thing' cannot be defined properly because it also belongs to the primary intelligibles, his attention shifts to the meaning (*ma'nan*) of 'thing' in contrast to 'existent'.[45] Although these two concepts are co-extensive, he says, they have different intensions. Thus, 'thing' basically serves as a placeholder, as it points at any other meaning whatsoever ('*alā ma'nan akhar*). The term 'existent', in turn, has a slightly different meaning. To Avicenna it can, first, signify 'proper existence' (*al-wujūd al-khāṣṣ*), which is a synonym for 'essence' (*māhiyya*) or 'true nature' (*ḥaqīqa*) by virtue of which a thing is what it is; second, it can denote 'affirmative existence' (*al-wujūd al-ithbātī*).[46] In this case, it addresses a thing's existence (*that* it is, not: *what* it is),[47] which corresponds to how Avicenna himself usually employs this term.

If, however, 'thing' can denote *any* meaning (*ma'nan*), we must conclude that it can refer not only to a certain something (an existent), but also to anything's essence, properties or further accidents (i.e., 'parts' of the 'whole').[48] Hence, the scope of 'thing' seems to be the broadest one can possibly think of: literally anything can be called a 'thing'. This, however, raises certain problems, once the term 'thing' itself occurs in the context of existential predications, such as the proposition p_1, 'The thing may be absolutely non-existent'.[49] Given that Avicenna's notion of 'the thing' can refer to virtually anything, including, one must infer, also non-existent things, it seems that for him the proposition p_1 could be true. This problem was far more than an issue of philosophical terminology. It was linked to an ongoing debate in the *kalām* tradition: there, the question concerning the ontic status of things was very controversial since, according to the Qur'ān, God created every thing by saying 'Be!' to it. This, however, raised the problem of what kind of entities God addressed, given that nothing existed before creation. If God gave his command to something, it must have 'been there' somehow, but that seems to contradict the very concept of creation.

Avicenna's analysis of this problem is based on three elements: the distinction between essence and existence, his theory of two modes of existence and his cosmology. His cosmology will be discussed in the next section, and so in what follows I will examine how Avicenna prepares the ground for his final solution by a careful semantic examination of the concepts involved. The two modes of existence are physical and mental existence, which is to say that according to Avicenna not only physical entities (substances and their properties), but also mental objects (concepts) exist. In the *Isagoge* (*Madkhal*) of his *Kitāb al-Shifā'*, Avicenna introduced this peculiarity by means of his essence–existence distinction: 'The essences (*māhiyyāt*) of things may exist in reality (*fī a'yān al-ashyā'*) or in conception (*fī l-taṣawwur*)'.[50] While these essences are the same with regard to definition, they differ in that different sets of accidents are attached to them.[51] Applied to the problem of non-existing things, Avicenna can thus argue that, so far as human cognition is concerned, p_1 must be rejected as false: once the subject term ('the thing') is uttered, which presupposes that its corresponding concept is thought, it is absurd to deny its, and the underlying concept's, existence. For while it may well be possible that the thing (essence) referred to by the subject term of the predication does not exist in *physical* reality (e.g., the phoenix), it must exist *in the mind*. Otherwise, it would not be possible even to form a proposition about it.[52]

It is with this background that Avicenna can defend a necessary connection between 'the thing' and 'existence': 'thing' necessarily implies existence, at least in the mind.[53] With regard to the theologians and their quarrel concerning the ontic status of things before creation, Avicenna here anticipates the solution his cosmology will provide: all the things did indeed exist—as mental concepts. The distinction between essence and existence is, then, fundamental in two ways. First, these notions (along with 'the one', 'the necessary', 'the possible') are impressed in our souls in a primary way and not acquired by abstraction and intellection.[54] They are themselves not concepts strictly speaking but, rather, *principles* for conceptualisation (*taṣawwur*); hence, they are required in order to grasp any universal concept whatsoever. Second, these notions are fundamental because they are 'common to all things' (*al-ashyāʾ al-ʿāmma li-l-umūr kullihā*); whatever exists (regardless of whether physically or mentally), is *something* (essence), does *exist* (existence), is some *one* thing (oneness). In short, Avicenna is convinced that the mental framework by means of which we understand *what* a thing is, *that* it is, that it is some *one* thing, neatly represents the metaphysical structure of reality (both physical and mental). According to him, not only epistemologically but also metaphysically speaking, things have an essence, do exist, and are some one thing.[55] In this regard, Avicenna has appropriately been described as a realist, as will be further corroborated by the findings of our final section on cosmology and the relation of reality and cognition.

5. BRIDGING PHYSICAL AND MENTAL EXISTENCE

As stated above, the distinction of essence and existence is a core element in Avicenna's reply to the problem concerning the ontic status of the things that God, according to the Qurʾān, had brought into existence by saying 'Be!' to them. His theory, basically, is that the essences of all the things already existed mentally and acquired physical existence only additionally. However, one might object, is this to say that *God* had all these essences in his mind before he created them? If so, would not this interpretation violate a principal Islamic dogma, namely the *tawḥīd*, the doctrine of the absolute oneness and uniqueness of God? Would it not imply multiplicity and change in God? Avicenna believes that he can avoid this consequence. Though it may seem, from a contemporary per-spective, to arise from an extra-philosophical consideration, Avicenna's rea-soning here goes beyond providing a solution to this particular problem. It is central to Avicenna's philosophy in general because it bridges the gap between metaphysics, psychology and epistemology. It clarifies Avicenna's concept of coming into being as well as the connection between reality and human cogni-tion of it.

Creation, according to Avicenna, is a complex process, taking its starting point from God. God however, if well (i.e., philosophically) understood, has a unique nature: he is the only existent (*mawjūd*) whose essence *is* its existence. Furthermore, he is the only existent that is *necessary* by virtue of itself (*min nafsihī*), whereas everything else exists by virtue of another (*min ghayrihī*); everything else is only *possible* by virtue of itself. Therefore, Avicenna refers to God as the Necessary Exis-tent who is the ultimate cause of everything. That something else actually exists is, therefore, contingent on one or more causes external to the thing itself. As this de-scription shows, Avicenna employs modality in a very peculiar way: it indicates causal relations grounded in the very essences of things. Due to his unique essence, God is the only existent that is uncaused and therefore necessary by virtue of itself, while everything else that exists exists only in a way that is necessary because of something else.[56]

Even though the Necessary Existent is the ultimate cause of everything, he does not directly bring about multiplicity. According to Avicenna (in harmony with the Islamic doctrine of *tawḥīd*), this would be a contradiction: it is absurd to assume that he intends 'the existence of the whole (that proceeds) from Him, [since] this would lead to a multiplicity in His essence'.[57] Rather, the Necessary Existent must be a true intellect whose 'first and essential act . . . is to intellectually apprehend His (own) essence, which in itself is the principle of the order of the good in existence'.[58] This act of intellection is the cause of existence for everything else that comes into being in accordance with this principle. Its coming into being is by necessity—due to his necessity—however, it occurs in a gradual progression. For, given the sim-plicity of the origin, the very first 'effect' must also be one in number and pure intel-lect in nature. However, this first 'separate intellect' slightly differs from the Necessary Existent in that it is in itself only *possible* of existence. Consequently, its mental activity varies from that of the Necessary Existent, as it has three different objects of apprehension: first, it understands itself as necessary (by virtue of the Necessary Existent); second, it contemplates itself as possible (by virtue of itself); and third, it apprehends the Necessary Existent. Not only is this mental activity the way multiplicity first occurs in the process of coming into being, but also, these three cognitive acts are the blueprint for how everything else is brought about. Con-sequently, already at this stage we can note that it is not God who has all the things in his mind; he thinks whatever follows him only insofar as he is the one *principle* of everything.

As far as the further process of coming into being is concerned, each of the mental acts of the first separate intellect has its own effect. By contemplating the

Necessary Existent, a further separate intellect comes into existence; through considering itself as possible, the outermost sphere is brought about;[59] and through apprehending itself as necessary, there emerges the form of the outermost sphere, that is to say, its soul. According to Avicenna, '[t]his is the state of affairs in each successive intellect and each successive sphere, until it [this progression] terminates with the agent intellect that governs our selves'.[60] The corresponding last sphere is the sphere of the moon, which already in ancient Greek cosmology separates the immaterial supra-lunar from the material sub-lunar world. Creation, on Avicenna's account, is thus something considerably different from the common Islamic view. His theory turns out to be a peculiar blend of Neoplatonic emanation theory and ancient cosmology, heavily inspired by the writings of al-Fārābī. In Avicenna's account, there is no place for individual voluntary acts on the part of God: instead, 'creation' evolves by necessity. God is the one principle of everything; whatever is not 'enclosed' in or 'implied' by this principle does not fall within the range of possible existents. In turn, this means that God's knowledge of his 'creation' is the knowledge of its principle, which is its ultimate cause.[61]

Having explained the supra-lunar coming into being of the separate intellects, souls and celestial spheres, Avicenna is now in a position to elucidate the coming into being of the sub-lunar world. This account will finally solve the problem of who actually thought all the things (at least, those belonging to the sub-lunar realm) before they came into existence. While the Necessary Existent is the first principle of everything and as such 'only' the remote cause of everything except the first separate intellect, coming into being in the sub-lunar world can be explained as the interaction of the celestial spheres—notably their circular motion, which influences the mixture of the elements, that is, of matter—and the separate intellects, or 'rather, the last of them, which is close to us' and 'from which there [emanate], in participation with the celestial movements', the forms 'of the lower world'.[62] Owing to this function, the last separate intellect, the agent intellect, is also referred to as the 'giver of forms' (wāhib al-ṣuwar)[63] which provides the appropriate form once matter in the sub-lunar realm is prepared for its reception. Hence, the Qur'ānic account of creation, Avicenna appears to think, is just metaphorical shorthand for this complex process. It is not *God* who has all the things in his mind; rather, it is the agent intellect who always actually thinks the immaterial forms. Consequently, with regard to the sub-lunar sphere, Avicenna can maintain that all the essences mentally exist even before they are instantiated, without at the same time implying that there is multiplicity in God.

As is, moreover, clear from his cosmology, according to Avicenna there is a neat isomorphism between physical reality and cognition. The forms that the agent intellect provides to inform the sub-lunar physical reality are identical with the intelligibles the human mind tracks down when it learns the corresponding universal concepts; they are one and the same in terms of their essence. The agent intellect thus guarantees both the unity of science—my concepts, syllogisms, conclusions, and so forth, are exactly the same as yours—and the objectivity (and accuracy) of knowledge.[64]

6. AVICENNA'S LEGACY

The history of Avicenna's impact differs with respect to geographical region, culture and time. Roughly speaking, we can distinguish between his reception in the (Latin) Christian, the Jewish and—within the Islamic culture—the Eastern and Western traditions. Since the Christian, Jewish and Western Islamic spheres will be explored in more detail in other chapters of this book,[65] I will limit my remarks to the Islamic East.

It was once believed that, at Averroes's death, philosophy vanished altogether from Islamic lands, but it is now clear that this is not true, at least for the East. First of all, the mass of manuscripts in various libraries, hardly yet investigated, testifies to the existence of a lively intellectual exchange over philosophical topics throughout centuries.[66] Moreover, as current studies in the post-classical period of Islamic thought have revealed, philosophy merged with theology and became an integral part of the curriculum for higher education.[67] The framework for this amalgamation was distilled from Avicenna's concept of philosophy as fleshed out, most explicitly, in the first book of the *Metaphysics* of the *Shifā'*. A key role in this process of adapting Avicennian thought was played by Fakhr al-Dīn al-Rāzī (d. 1209) and, in particular, his *Mulakhkhaṣ fī l-ḥikma* (*Abridgment of Philosophy*).[68] Just like Avicenna's summas, this work belongs to the genre of encyclopedic writings and served as a model for the emerging teaching tradition at the *madrasa*.

The *Mulakhkhaṣ* has several structural peculiarities. First, it consists of four parts with the first part, on logic, serving as a propaedeutic. Next, Avicenna's theory of science and his fundamental considerations of the primary concepts (Book I of his *Metaphysics*) have moved into Part 2 of the *Mulakhkhaṣ* where they now form a separate discipline whose subject matter is 'the common things' (*al-ashyā' al-'āmma*).[69] Part 3 of the *Mulakhkhaṣ* discusses possible being, which, in turn, is divided into substances (body, soul, intellect) and accidents and hence represents categorial being. The resulting 'new' discipline, dedicated to whatever falls under the ten categories, connects metaphysical reflections on possible being with natural philosophy based on these considerations.[70] The only kind of being, finally, that is also 'natural' but not subject to the categories is necessary being, which is, accordingly, studied in the last part of the *Mulakhkhaṣ* and constitutes a further discipline, called 'pure divine sciences' (*ilāhiyyāt maḥḍa*) and dedicated to God's essence (*dhāt*), his attributes (*ṣifāt*), and operations (*af'āl*). With their clear-cut focus on God's essence, attributes and operations, now, the *ilāhiyyāt al-maḥḍa* offer an excellent model for integrating properly theological thinking into the frame of philosophical disciplines.[71] It remains clear, however, that this new curriculum is based on philosophical principles and topics, even in the realm of *ilāhiyyāt maḥḍa*.

Amongst the chief figures who initiated this fusion of philosophy and theology is, of all scholars, al-Ghazālī (d. 1111).[72] While it has long been acknowledged that al-Ghazālī expressly promoted the study of syllogistic reasoning and the integration of logic into a theological education, both his autobiographical *Deliverance from Error* (*Munqidh min al-ḍalāl*) and *Incoherence of the Philosophers* (*Tahāfut al-falāsifa*) seemed to be unequivocal in their rejection of the Aristotelian metaphysical tradition. As recent research, however, has shown, al-Ghazālī's own positions on topics such as prophecy, theory of the soul, and even ontology, are highly indebted to philosophy and most notably, to Avicenna.[73] Moreover, al-Ghazālī's survey of the *Intentions of the Philosophers* (*Maqāṣid al-falāsifa*) turns out to be a close paraphrase (if not translation) of Avicenna's *Book of Science for 'Alā' al-Dawla* (*Daneshname-ye 'Ala'i*), an abridged version of his philosophy that Avicenna had written in Persian. Similarly, in the attacks launched against 'the philosophers' in his *Incoherence*, al-Ghazālī argues against one specific target: Avicenna, in particular, this latter's defence of the eternity of the world, his denial of *bodily* resurrection, and his theory of God's universal way of knowing particulars.

As these few indications already reveal, Avicenna's posterity is unanimous in concentrating primarily on Avicenna's thought as if it were the paradigm of philosophy. There is, however, a wide range of individual stances towards his teachings. Writings such as those of al-Ghazālī bring to the fore how heterogeneous the position of even one and the same scholar towards his predecessor can be, oscillating between downright adoption and categorical rejection. However diverse the reactions might seem, they attest that Avicenna's writings struck a nerve of the time, in terms of both the topics he raised and the methods applied. As can be seen from the examples of al-Ghazālī and al-Rāzī, they attracted forceful and far-reaching reactions on the part of chief Ash'arite theologians.[74] However, they also provoked vivid discussions amongst philosophers, more properly speaking. In this connection, one can distinguish between three 'major lines of development': one embodied by the 'reactionaries', a second, by the 'reformists' and a third, by the 'supporters'.[75]

The most representative 'reactionary' of the Islamic East is 'Abd al-Laṭīf al-Baghdādī (d. 1232). He is 'reactionary' in that he adheres to a strictly traditional approach to philosophy and hence rejects Avicenna's innovations. According to him, the only task of philosophy after Plato and Aristotle consists in elucidating their writings, since they had already discovered everything philosophy could possibly detect.[76] As such, his notion of philosophy is inspired by the late ancient commentators. It contrasts with the position developed by the so-called 'reformers', the most famous of whom are Abū l-Barakāt al-Baghdādī (d. 1165)[77] and al-Suhrawardī (d. 1191). The latter, who is usually considered as the founder of illuminationism, is of particular interest for this survey, as he exemplifies how some of the most original Avicennian ideas were received and further developed. Al-Suhrawardī is particularly well known for his defence of the 'primacy of essence' (*aṣāla l-māhiyya*)—in contrast to the 'primacy of existence' (*aṣāla l-wujūd*), held by Mullā Ṣadrā (d. 1640) some four centuries later.[78] While Avicenna, as discussed above, was convinced that the essence–existence distinction (as well as the other primary intelligibles) has a foundation in reality, al-Suhrawardī argued that existence is a metaphysical construct that is purely mental (*iʿtibārī*). The only things that *really* are there in physical reality are the particulars; all additional distinctions made in metaphysics are products of mental activities—in this regard, al-Suhrawardī has aptly been described as a nominalist.[79]

The last group of philosophers in the legacy of Avicenna, his 'supporters', are the most difficult to capture; they are still hardly studied. On the one hand, there are his immediate disciples—al-Jūzjānī, Bahmanyār, Ibn Zayla and al-Maʿṣūmī—who seem to have played a key role in collecting Avicennian material and writing the first commentaries.[80] Except for Bahmanyār's *Kitāb al-Taḥṣīl* (*Studybook*), none of their own philosophical writings appear to have had significant impact on the later tradition. While the *Kitāb al-Taḥṣīl* used also to be described as a mere abridgement of Avicenna's philosophy, we now know that in this case the situation is different. Despite its own focus on philosophy proper, the *Kitāb* plays a significant role in the formation of Ashʿarite mainstream theology, insofar as it profoundly inspired Fakhr al-Dīn al-Rāzī whose reshaping of the philosophical (or rather: theologico-philosophical) sciences was mentioned at the beginning of this section.[81]

Two further scholars, who are usually also quoted among Avicenna's immediate disciples, are al-Lawkarī and al-Īlāqī. Very little is known about their lives; however, it is most likely that al-Lawkarī died during the first quarter of the twelfth century and al-Īlāqī around 1141.[82] Accordingly, both are second- or third-generation followers rather than direct students. While al-Īlāqī seems to be particularly important for the transmission of Avicenna's chief medical text, the *Qānūn fī l-ṭibb* (*Rule of Medicine*), al-Lawkarī had some influence on the formation of the new theologico-philosophical tradition. Just like Bahmanyār, al-Lawkarī did not simply summarise Avicenna but, rather, continued this latter's effort towards developing an appropriate structure for philosophy. Nonetheless, his *Bayān al-Ḥaqq* apparently did not have the same success as Bahmanyār's *Kitāb al-Taḥṣīl*.

The last two philosophers I wish to mention in the line of Avicenna's 'supporters' lead us already into the thirteenth century—a generation or two after Fakhr al-Dīn al-Rāzī and al-Suhrawardī. The first is Athīr al-Dīn al-Abharī, the second his student Najm al-Dīn al-Kātibī. They are noteworthy in the present context insofar as each of them contributed two textbooks with which 'Avicenna's philosophy finds its classical scholastic formulation'.[83] These are, respectively, al-Abharī's *Hidāya fī l-ḥikma*; his *Īsāghūjī*; al-Kātibī's work on logic, the *Risāla al-Shamsiyya*; and this latter's *Ḥikma l-ʿAyn*, which may even surpass al-Abharī's *Hidāya* in terms of impact.[84] These books became extraordinarily popular as can be seen from both the numerous commentaries and the fact that they were used in higher education until recently. It is because of phenomena like these that scholarship on Avicenna can point to his long-lasting and deep influence on intellectual history in the Islamic East. It seems, indeed, as if it were close to impossible 'to overestimate the impact of Avicenna's system of thought'[85]—and this not only for the East, but also for the West, as a number of contributions in this volume will corroborate.

NOTES

1. Thomas Aquinas, *De ente et essentia* III. I wish to thank Peter Adamson, Laurent Cesalli, Steven Harvey and Maarten Hoenen for their careful reading of and valuable comments on earlier versions of this chapter.

2. Cf. the old but still helpful study Gilson (1952); on modern and contemporary developments, see Esposito (2009).

3. For his life, see the numerous encyclopedia entries and handbook articles on Avicenna, for example, in the *Encyclopaedia of Islam*, *Encyclopaedia Iranica*, *Encyclopedia of Medieval Philosophy*, *The Cambridge Companion to Arabic Philosophy*; for a general study of Avicenna's philosophy, see still Gutas (1988); most recently, McGinnis (2010).

4. Regarding Avicenna's biography, we are in the fortunate position of possessing an autobiography that he had dictated to his student al-Jūzjānī, who after his master's death finished it on his own. However, this autobiography, and particularly Avicenna's report on his own youth and education, has a highly programmatic character and therefore must be interpreted with caution; this was first observed and studied by Gutas (1988, 149–98).

5. For this gradual approximation between philosophy and Arabic-Islamic sciences, particularly theology (*kalām*), see Chapter 3 above.

6. The first study to programmatically underscore Avicenna's pivotal role with regard to both his context and legacy was Gutas (2002).

7. For further indications regarding the afterlife of Avicenna's thought, see Section 6, 'Avicenna's Legacy', of this chapter.

8. An authoritative bibliography of Avicenna's works still remains to be established. For a list and discussion of Avicenna's major philosophical works, see Gutas (1988, 79–145). Although Gutas's chronology did not remain undisputed, it usually serves as reference point for current research.

9. See Chapter 1 above.

10. Avicenna also wrote important works on logic that had an enormous impact on subsequent Arabic-Islamic thought: primarily due to al-Ghazālī, logic became absorbed by theology and was taught in schools of higher education as an indispensable tool for religious studies. For a general survey of Avicenna's logic, see Street (2002, 129–60); rather technical in its nature is Thom (2003, 65–80). Another field that has attracted increasing attention in the more recent past is physics, in particular Avicenna's innovative treatment of motion, including, for example, his unprecedented theory of motion at an instant. For a general introduction to Avicenna's natural philosophy, see McGinnis (2010, 53–88).

11. Thus, the functions of this soul are limited to growth, nourishment, procreation and the like. For Aristotle's account see his *De anima* (II, 3, 414a29–415a14).

12. It is important to underscore the spatial aspect of motion here since any kind of change (including, e.g., growth and aging) is considered as motion in the Aristotelian tradition. Consequently, while plants partake in this general kind of motion (they grow and age), they are not able to move locally—contrary to most animals.

13. The relation between these types of souls is unidirectional, according to the Aristotelian tradition: while plants possess only a vegetative soul and hence this latter's functions, animals' souls include both the basic vegetative faculties and the above-mentioned specific sensible powers; humans, finally, possess all these plus reason. Sometimes it is therefore difficult to tell whether medieval authors, when they speak, for example, about the human soul, refer to the specific faculty of the human soul or to the human soul in general, that is, including all the other faculties.

14. A discussion of the various problems posed by Aristotle's text and the struggles of the commentators with his account can be found in the introduction to Averroes (2009, particularly xix–xxviii).

15. Cf. n. 13 above. In what follows, I will refer to different 'layers' rather than actual 'souls'. For a discussion of the problem of soul's unity in Avicenna, see Adamson (2004); for some problems Avicenna's account involves with regard to his own doctrine of the afterlife, see Druart (2000).

16. Note that there are two senses with very similar names, the image-storing and the image-forming faculties; however, their function is quite different. While the image-storing faculty is a storage place for images (particular forms), the image-forming faculty combines and divides these images and thus produces new ones (which, again, can be stored in the image-storing faculty). Regarding the remaining senses, common sense is responsible for displaying the form of a perceived extra-mental object; estimation, for perceiving connotational attributes of extra-mental objects (e.g., the famous 'danger' of the wolf perceived by the sheep); memory (just like the image-storing faculty) is a storage place for these 'particular' forms. More on the image-forming faculty in what follows. For an overview over the five interior senses and their function, see Avicenna (*On the Soul* I, 5, 1959, particularly pp. 44–45; 1972, 87:10–90:60). *On the Soul* has not yet been translated into English, which is why I refer not only to the Arabic original but also to the medieval Latin translation throughout.

17. With regard to knowledge, Avicenna—again closely related to Aristotle (cf. *De anima* III, 6, 430a26–29)—distinguishes between the formation of a simple concept (*taṣawwur*; e.g., 'tree') and of a judgement, that is, of an assent connected with a (simple or complex) concept (*taṣdīq*; e.g., 'this is a tree'). It is only at the level of *taṣdīq* that the truth or falsity of knowledge (or pseudo-knowledge) can be pondered. For Avicenna's general idea of *taṣawwur* and *taṣdīq*, see his *Isagoge* (*Madkhal*) of the *Kitāb al-Shifā'*, chapter 3 (Avicenna 1952, 17).

18. On Avicenna's cosmology see below, Section 5, 'Bridging Physical and Mental Existence' of this chapter.

19. *On the Soul* I, 5 (1959, 48–49; 1972, 96:37–97:55). That Avicenna here thinks of both primary metaphysical notions (i.e., transcendentals) and first principles (like the example above) is obvious in the light of his *Metaphysics* I, 5, (2) (2005, 23), concerning 'conceptual matters' (being, thing, etc., constituting the mental grid required in order to form a simple concept at all), and ibid. I, 5, (1) (2005, 22), regarding the 'category of assent' (i.e., 'primary principles, found to be true in themselves'). For a discussion of the primary metaphysical notions, see below, Section 4, 'Essence and Existence'.

20. The last two stages are described in *On the Soul* I, 5 (1959, 49–50; 1972, 97:56–99:78). On Avicenna's distinction of the four stages of human intellect and its reception in the Latin West, see Hasse (1999; on Avicenna particularly, 28–40).

21. For this process see in particular *On the Soul* (V, 5–6, 1959, 234–50; 1968, 126–53).

22. For this see particularly *On the Soul* (V, 6, 1959, 248–50; 1968, 151:75–153:18). Regarding intellection, see, for instance, ibid. (I, 5, 1959, 50; 1972, 99:70–73), where Avicenna underscores, '. . . that the intellect in potency [sc. on stage three] is actualized through that intellect which is always in act [sc. the agent intellect] . . . through some kind of conjunction' [my translation].

23. Intellection in general cannot be confused with Avicenna's more specific notion of intuition (*ḥads*), which usually refers to the just described particularly fast and/or comprehensive form of intellection; also, Avicenna often explicitly relates it to the acquisition of middle terms of syllogisms. For Avicenna's theory of intuition, see Gutas (2001). For

Avicenna's theory of prophecy, see, in addition to the above passage of *On the Soul*, his *Metaphysics* (X, 1–2, 2005, 358–66).

24. Current research is split between a group who emphasise the role of emanation and another one who underscore the significance of abstraction. For the former see Black (1997, for instance, 445) and Davidson (1992, for instance, 93–94). On the significance of abstraction, by contrast, see Hasse (2001) and McGinnis (2006).

25. *On the Soul* V, 5 (1959, 234; 1968, 126:29–127:35).

26. *On the Soul* V, 5 (1959, 235; 1968, 127:36–47). The light metaphor as such is, of course, already present in Aristotle's *De anima* (III, 5).

27. *On the Soul* V, 5 (1959, 235; 1968, 127:48–49) [my translation]: 'For cogitations and considerations are movements that make the soul ready to receive an emanation [sc. from the agent intellect]'.

28. *On the Soul* V, 5 (1959, 235; 1968, 127:49–50) [my translation]: '[. . .] just like middle terms prepare the reception of the conclusion by necessity'; cf. Aristotle, *Prior Analytics* (I, 1, 24b19–20).

29. *On the Soul* V, 5 (1959, 235–36; 1968, 128:58–63) [my translation]: '[. . .] for just as the operation [regarding sensible forms, NG] [. . .] takes place by means of the light if the receivable [thing] is *right opposite* [*muqābil*], thus the rational soul [. . .] is made ready that by means of the light of the agent intellect a form stripped off of all mixture [with matter] occurs in it [my emphasis]'.

30. Already Jon McGinnis (2006) has drawn attention to the parallel between Avicenna's reflections on sight (and the role of light) and intellection.

31. Among the major concerns in the Arabic-Islamic culture were the implications of Avicenna's psychology with regard to the concept of human's afterlife: accordingly, the soul survives the body after death; however, not only does Avicenna reject the idea of a bodily resurrection, but also the afterlife is quite 'immaterial' and hence in contrast with Qur'ān's descriptions of the paradise. To Avicenna, 'paradise' consists in the human (rational) soul's constantly intelligising the intelligibles. Since, however, the soul no longer has a body, it can no longer abstract particular forms (for lack of the exterior senses) and by this means cognise 'new' universal concepts, which is also why it is humanity's supreme good to acquire knowledge during a lifetime (as Aristotle had already stated), for after death the soul can only fall back on those intelligibles it has already acquired. For Avicenna's idea of the afterlife, see Michot (1986).

32. For *kalām* influences on Avicenna's metaphysics, see Jolivet (1984) and Wisnovsky (2003).

33. On this see Bertolacci (2006).

34. As Bertolacci (2006, 3–103) has shown, this uncertainty was due, on the one hand, to the various contradicting accounts that can be found in Aristotle's *Metaphysics*; on the other hand, however, it can be connected with the historical process of the reception of these books in the Arabic-Islamic world (e.g., that for a long time, only Books II and XII were available, which rather favour the view that the subject matter of metaphysics is the separate substances).

35. It should be noted that the Arabic term *wujūd* can mean both 'existence' and 'being'. For the sake of clarity (i.e., in order to capture the distinction between the present participle and the verbal noun), I will translate 'existent'/'existence' throughout, even though more often than not the term 'being' would sound more natural.

36. According to Avicenna, each science has its own subject matter (*mawḍū'*), searches after certain things (*maṭlūbāt*) and is based on a number of principles that serve as premises for demonstrations. This doctrine is fleshed out in his *Burhān* (1956, here II, 6),

a logical treatise that parallels Aristotle's *Posterior Analytics* (here I, 10, 76b11–22). For a discussion of these issues, see Bertolacci (2006, 134–35, with translation of the relevant Avicenna and Aristotle passages, and 149–211).

37. Which is also the reason why for Avicenna, the proof of the existence of God must (and can) be performed in metaphysics: God (and his existence) is one of the 'things sought after' and not the subject matter of metaphysics. While, however, according to Aristotle's theory of science, the subject matter must be posited, the objects and their existence can (and must) be subject to scrutiny. On Avicenna's metaphysical proof of God's existence see Bertolacci (2007).

38. The chief feature of these notions is that, according to Avicenna, they are common to all the sciences.

39. It is this branch that also deals with the separate substances and hence the most sublime existents (including God).

40. Together, these sections form the first part of metaphysics as conceived by Avicenna; the 'new' structure of this discipline, hence, is roughly: I. theory of science and primary metaphysical notions/common things (Book I); II. species of being (Books II and III); III. properties of being (Books IV–VI); IV. causes and principles (Books VIII–X, 3); V. practical philosophy (this last section on practical philosophy has sometimes been described as an appendix to metaphysics; however, it seems to be a plausible addition, given that to the Neoplatonic tradition cosmology not only consists of emanation but also of the corresponding return. Yet in human affairs this necessarily involves the question of 'what to do' in order to accomplish the desired return).

41. *Metaphysics* I, 5, (1) (2005, 22:19–21). In what follows, I quote the English translation of Michael Marmura. On several occasions, however, I have slightly modified his wording in order to safeguard coherence with the terminology applied in this chapter. The key notion in the quotes above is 'impressed in a primary way', which refers back to Avicenna's theory of the soul, more precisely, to the second stage of the human intellect. At this stage, as was mentioned above, the human mind receives the primary intelligibles, that is, the principles of cognition.

42. Avicenna is very unambiguous that such a reference does not impart new knowledge but only makes one *aware* of these notions; see, for example, *Metaphysics* I, 5, (2)–(3) (2005, 23:2–11).

43. *Metaphysics* I, 5, (5) (2005, 23:16); 'all things' instead of Marmura's 'all matters'— *amr*, pl. *umūr*, just like *shay'*, pl. *ashyā'*, means 'thing', not necessarily 'matter' as translated by Marmura.

44. Cf. Wisnovsky (2003); for a shorter discussion, see Wisnovsky (2005); cf. also Wisnovsky (2000).

45. *Metaphysics* V, 1, (8) (2005, 24:11–15).

46. *Metaphysics* V, 1, (9) (2005, 24:16–28).

47. Although Avicenna does not offer any further explanations for this second meaning of 'existence', the logical term *ithbāt* supports the suggested interpretation, as it primarily means 'to affirm *that* [x is the case]'.

48. Cf., for example, *Metaphysics* I, 5, (5) (2005, 24:34–36).

49. *Metaphysics* I, 5, (12) (2005, 25:17).

50. *Madkhal* 2 (1952, 15; 1980, 247).

51. While essences in (physical) reality have accidents like corporeality, motion or further qualities (e.g., colour) and quantities (e.g., weight), accidents for mental existence would be being a subject, universality, particularity, etc. cf. *Madkhal* 2 (1952, 15; 1980, 247); for a detailed metaphysical discussion of this topic, see particularly *Metaphysics* V, 1, where Avicenna introduces his famous 'pure horseness' (*farasiyya faqaṭ*).

52. Cf., for example, *Metaphysics* I, 5, (18) (2005, 27:11–12): 'Predication, in truth, is about what exists in the soul and [only] accidentally about what exists extra-mentally' (I translate 'predication' and 'extra-mentally' instead of Marmura's 'information' and 'externally'). For Avicenna's concept regarding the relation of words, objects and concepts, see his *On Interpretation* ('*Ibāra*) of the *Kitāb al-Shifā*', I, 1 (1970, 5:10–13).

53. Cf. *Metaphysics* I, 5, (19) (2005, 27:13–16): 'Hence, you have now understood [. . .] that [. . .] the two [that is, 'the thing' and 'the existent'] are necessary concomitants'.

54. Cf. above, Section 3, 'Abstraction and Intellection'.

55. It is worth noting that despite his insistence on *two* modes of existence, Avicenna emphasises that we can additionally *consider* things just as such—horse as horse, phoenix as phoenix, existence as existence, essence as essence—independent from either mode of existence. For the three different modes of consideration applied in the sciences according to Avicenna, see again his *Madkhal* 2 (1952, 15; 1980, 247). On the question of the ontic status of these 'pure' essences, see particularly Porro (2002); further de Libera (1996, 177–206; 1999, 499–607); Marmura (2005, 61–70).

56. For a succinct discussion of the modalities, see Wisnovsky (2003, 197–263).

57. *Metaphysics* IX, 4, (2) (2005, 326:28–29).

58. *Metaphysics* IX, 4, (4) (2005, 327:18–20). See Chapter 1, pp. 18–9, for the Neoplatonic background to this process.

59. The 'outermost sphere' is the sphere of night and day in the Ptolemaic worldview. According to this worldview, the Earth is at the centre of the universe and surrounded by several spheres (the most common number is ten). These spheres are identified with the spheres of the single planets (including moon and sun) and the fixed stars; the innermost sphere is the sphere of the moon. Already al-Kindī and al-Fārābī had translated emanation theory into Ptolemaic cosmology.

60. *Metaphysics* IX, 4, (12) (2005, 331:20–22); 'agent intellect' instead of 'active intellect' as translated by Marmura.

61. Even though this is knowledge in the strict sense of the Aristotelian tradition, it is in sharp contrast to what the Qur'ān has to say about God's concern for each thing individually. This was one of the reasons Avicenna's cosmology was rejected in the Arabic-Islamic East. On God's knowledge, see particularly *Metaphysics* VIII, 6, (6)–(22) (2005, 284–90); Avicenna refers to this as knowledge of the particulars in a universal way. This topic is vividly discussed in research; see, for example, Adamson (2005), Marmura (1962) and Zghal (2004).

62. *Metaphyics* IX, 5, (3) (2005, 335:12–15).

63. *Metaphysics* IX, 5, (10) (2005, 337:26).

64. For this, see in particular de Libera (as above, n. 56).

65. For Jewish philosophy, see Chapters 6, and 7; for Averroes and Spain, Chapter 5; the (Latin) Christian thought of the relevant period is fathomed in the majority of chapters belonging to Part II of this book.

66. Cf., in this connection, the Post-classical Islamic Philosophy Database Initiative (PIPDI), located at McGill University (Montreal) and dedicated to creating the infrastructure required in order to study the bulk of Islamic philosophical texts from approximately 1100 to 1900 (see http://islamsci.mcgill.ca/RASI/pipdi.html).

67. The currently most important study on Avicenna's posterity in this field is Eichner (2007). In what follows, I rely on this article and Eichner's (to date) unpublished *Habilitationsschrift* of which she generously gave me a copy. For the teaching at the *madrasa* and in particular the role of Avicenna's thought in this context, see Endress (2006).

68. Unfortunately, the *Mulakhkhaṣ* has neither been edited nor translated so far, which may be why it has attracted considerably less scholarly attention than al-Rāzī's other

encyclopedia, the *Mabāḥith al-mashriqiyya* (edited by Muḥammad al-Muʿtaṣim bi-llāh al-Baghdādī in 1990). However, it was primarily the *Mulakhkhaṣ* that had tremendous impact on Islamic theology and teaching.

69. The list of 'common things', notably, consists of the following five items: existence (*wujūd*), essence (*māhiyya*), unity–multiplicity (*waḥda wa-kathra*), necessary–possible (*wājib wa-mumkin*) and eternality–origination (*qidam wa-ḥudūth*). Hence, compared with Avicenna's primary intelligibles, only eternality–origination is new; it is, however, a pair that already played an important role in earlier *kalām*, particularly in the proofs for the existence of God; cf. Wisnovsky (2003, 227–43).

70. In short, al-Rāzī spells out Avicenna's claim that metaphysics provides the principles of the subordinate (particular) sciences. The science of possible being, therefore, takes the categories for granted and studies all those beings that fall under one of these predicaments.

71. In this connection, it is striking that theology (proper) is henceforth called *ilāhiyyāt* ('divine sciences'), a term used by Avicenna to denote metaphysics. Metaphysics, by contrast, is now called (and reduced to) the 'common things'. It is thus identified with the ontological and epistemological considerations of the first book of Avicenna's *Metaphysics*. While metaphysics consequently clarifies the (transcendental) ground for any scientific activity, the remaining (two) sciences, that is, natural philosophy and theology, deal with the two main kinds of existents, namely, (1) categorial, contingent or caused being, and (2) transcategorial, necessary or uncaused being.

72. Traditionally, al-Ghazālī is considered to be the theologian whose *Incoherence of the Philosophers* (*Tahāfut al-falāsifa*) sounded the death knell for philosophy.

73. In the meanwhile, there is a quite recent monographical study available that carefully examines al-Ghazālī's philosophical positions; see Griffel (2009), and for a more succinct survey, Griffel (2007).

74. Further important theologians who controversially discussed Avicenna were, for example, al-Shahrastānī (d. 1153), Abū Ḥafs ʿUmar al-Suhrawardī (d. 1234) and Ibn Taymiyya (d. 1328).

75. For this, see Gutas (2002, here 90). This is currently the most succinct general survey of Avicenna's posterity; for a broader (and more diverse, because multi-authored) treatment of this period of Arabic philosophy, see Langermann (2009); see also Janssens (2006).

76. The most important 'school' of reactionaries to this taxonomy is, of course, the Andalusian tradition (Ibn Bājja, Ibn Ṭufayl and Averroes); cf. Gutas (2002, 90–91).

77. On al-Baghdādī, see Pines (1979) (which contains several of his articles on al-Baghdādī).

78. On Mullā Ṣadrā, see Rahman (1975).

79. For a survey of al-Suhrawardī's philosophy, see Walbridge (2005); still helpful is Corbin (1971).

80. See al-Rahim (2009, here 1). According to al-Rahim, '[a] detailed study of [these disciples'] lives and works remains a major desideratum' (ibid.).

81. For this and the following remarks on al-Lawkarī, see particularly the studies by Heidrun Eichner, mentioned above in n. 67.

82. In this connection, compare al-Rahim's (2009, 18–25) careful discussion of the available bio-bibliographical tradition (and scholarship thereof).

83. Gutas (2002, 94).

84. On the role of the *Risāla al-Shamsiyya*, see Street (2005, 247–65).

85. McGinnis (2010, 244).

BIBLIOGRAPHY

Adamson, Peter. 2004. 'Correcting Plotinus: Soul's relationship to body in Avicenna's commentary on the *Theology of Aristotle*'. In *Philosophy, Science and Exegesis in Greek, Arabic and Latin Commentaries*, ed. Peter Adamson et al., vol. 2, 59–75. London: Institute of Classical Studies, School of Advanced Study, University of London.

———. 2005. On Knowledge of Particulars. *Proceedings of the Aristotelian Society* 105:273–294.

Averroes (Ibn Rushd) of Cordoba. 2009. *Long Commentary on the 'De Anima' of Aristotle*, trans. with introduction and notes by Richard C. Taylor with Thérèse-Anne Druart. New Haven, CT, and London: Yale University Press.

Avicenna. 1952. *Al-Shifā'. Al-Manṭiq. Al-Madkhal*, ed. Maḥmūd al-Khuḍayrī et al. Cairo: Al-Maṭbaʿa al-amīriyya. [An English translation of chapter 2 is available in Marmura, Michael E. 1980. 'Avicenna on the Division of the Sciences in the Isagoge of His Shifā'. *Journal for the History of Arabic Science* 4:239–51].

———. 1956. *Al-Shifā'. Al-Manṭiq. Al-Burhān*, ed. 'Abū l-'Alā 'Afīfī. Cairo: Al-Maṭbaʿa al-amīriyya.

———. 1959. *Avicenna's De Anima* [Arabic Text], *Being the Psychological Part of the Kitāb al-Shifā'*, ed. Fazlur Rahman. London, New York and Toronto: Oxford University Press.

———. 1970. *Al-Shifā'. Al-Manṭiq. Al-'Ibāra*, ed. Maḥmūd al-Khuḍayrī. Cairo: Dār al-Kātib al-'arabī.

———. 2005. *The Metaphysics of the Healing. A Parallel English-Arabic Text*, ed. and trans. Michael E. Marmura. Provo, UT: Brigham Young University Press.

Avicenna Latinus. 1968. *Liber de anima seu sextus de naturalibus, iv–v*, ed. Simone Van Riet. Louvain, Belgium: Peeters; Leiden: Brill.

———. 1972. *Liber de anima seu sextus de naturalibus, i–iii*, ed. Simone Van Riet. Louvain, Belgium: Peeters; Leiden: Brill.

Bertolacci, Amos. 2006. *The Reception of Aristotle's Metaphysics in Avicenna's Kitāb al-Šifā': A Milestone of Western Metaphysical Thought*. Leiden, the Netherlands: Brill.

———. 2007. Avicenna and Averroes on the Proof of God's Existence and the Subject-Matter of Metaphysics. *Medioevo* 32:61–97.

Black, Deborah. 1997. Avicenna on the Ontological and Epistemic Status of Fictional Beings. *Documenti e studi sulla tradizione filosofica medievale* 8:425–53.

Corbin, Henri. 1971. *En Islam iranien: aspects spirituels et philosophiques. Vol. 2: Sohrawardī et les platoniciens de Perse*. Paris: Gallimard.

Davidson, Herbert A. 1992. *Alfarabi, Avicenna, and Averroes on Intellect*. New York and Oxford: Oxford University Press.

de Libera, Alain. 1996. *La querelle des universaux: de Platon à la fin du Moyen Âge*. Paris: Seuil.

———. 1999. *L'Art des généralités: théories de l'abstraction*. Paris: Aubier.

Druart, Thérèse-Anne. 2000. The Human Soul's Individuation and its Survival After the Body's Death: Avicenna on the Causal Relation Between Body and Soul. *Arabic Sciences and Philosophy* 10:259–73.

Eichner, Heidrun. 2007. Dissolving the Unity of Metaphysics: From Fakhr al-Dīn al-Rāzī to Mullā Ṣadrā al-Shīrāzī. *Medioevo* 32:139–97.

Endress, Gerhard. 2006. 'Reading Avicenna in the *Madrasa*: intellectual genealogies and chains of transmission of philosophy and the sciences in the Islamic East'. In *Arabic Theology, Arabic Philosophy: From the One to the Many. Essays in Celebration of Richard M. Frank*, ed. James E. Montgomery, 371–422. Leuven, Belgium: Peeters.

Esposito, Costantino, ed. 2009. *Origins and Developments of Ontology 16th–21st Century.* Turnhout, Belgium: Brepols.—Bari: Pagina (= *Quaestio* 9).

Gilson, Étienne. 1952. *Being and Some Philosophers*, 2nd edition. Toronto: Pontifical Institute of Mediaeval Studies.

Griffel, Frank. 2007. 'Al-Ghazālī'. In *Stanford Encyclopedia of Philosophy.* http://plato. stanford.edu/entries/al-ghazali/ (Fall 2008 edition).

———. 2009. *Al-Ghazālī's Philosophical Theology.* Oxford and New York: Oxford University Press.

Gutas, Dimitri. 1988. *Avicenna and the Aristotelian Tradition: Introduction to Reading Avicenna's Philosophical Works.* Leiden, the Netherlands: Brill.

———. 2001. 'Intuition and thinking. The evolving structure of Avicenna's epistemology'. In *Aspects of Avicenna*, ed. Robert Wisnovsky, 1–38. Princeton, NJ: Wiener.

———. 2002. 'The heritage of Avicenna: the golden age of Arabic philosophy, 1000–ca. 1350'. In *Avicenna and His Heritage. Acts of the International Colloquium, Leuven–Louvain-la-Neuve September 8–September 11, 1999*, ed. Jules Janssens and Daniel De Smet, 81–97. Leuven, the Netherlands: Leuven University Press.

Hasse, Dag N. 1999. Das Lehrstück von den vier Intellekten in der Scholastik: Von den arabischen Quellen bis zu Albertus Magnus. *Recherches de théologie et philosophie médiévales* 66:21–77.

———. 2001. 'Avicenna on Abstraction'. In *Aspects of Avicenna*, ed. Robert Wisnovsky, 39–72. Princeton, NJ: Wiener.

Janssens, Jules. 2006. 'Ibn Sīnā, and his heritage in the Islamic world and in the Latin West'. In *Ibn Sīnā and His Influence on the Arabic and Latin World*, ed. Jules Janssens, study I, 1–14. Aldershot, UK, and Burlington, VT: Ashgate (Variorum collected studies series, 843).

Jolivet, Jean. 1984. 'Aux origines de l'ontologie d'Ibn Sina'. In *Études sur Avicenne*, ed. Jean Jolivet and Roshdi Rashed, 11–28. Paris: Les Belles Lettres.

Langermann, Y. Tzvi, ed. 2009. *Avicenna and His Legacy: A Golden Age of Science and Philosophy.* Turnhout, Belgium: Brepols.

Marmura, Michael E. 1962. Some Aspects of Avicenna's Theory of God's Knowledge of Particulars. *Journal of the American Oriental Society* 82:299–312.

———. 2005. 'Quiddity and universality in Avicenna'. In *Probing in Islamic Philosophy: Studies in the History of Ibn Sīnā, al-Ghazālī and Other Major Muslim Thinkers*, ed. Michael E. Marmura, 61–70. Binghamton, NY: Global Academic Publishing.

McGinnis, Jon. 2006. Making Abstraction Less Abstract: The Logical, Psychological, and Metaphysical Dimensions of Avicenna's Theory of Abstraction. *Proceedings of the American Catholic Philosophical Association* 80:169–83.

———. 2010. *Avicenna.* Oxford and New York: Oxford University Press.

Michot, Jean R. [Yahya M.] 1986. *La destinée de l'homme selon Avicenne: le retour à Dieu (ma'ād) et l'imagination.* Louvain, Belgium: Peeters.

Pines, Shlomo. 1979. *The Collected Works of Shlomo Pines, vol. I: Studies in Abu l-Barakāt al-Baghdādī: Physics and Metaphysics.* Jerusalem: Magnes Press.—Leiden: Brill.

Porro, Pasquale. 2002. Universaux et *esse essentiae*: Avicenne, Henri de Gand et le 'Troisième Reich'. In *Cahiers de philosophie de l'Université de Caen* (Le réalisme des universaux) 38–39:9–51.

al-Rahim, Ahmed H. 2009. 'Avicenna's immediate disciples: their lives and works'. In *Avicenna and His Legacy. A Golden Age of Science and Philosophy*, ed. Y. Tzvi Langermann, 1–25. Turnhout, Belgium: Brepols.

Rahman, Fazlur. 1975. *The Philosophy of Mullā Ṣadrā (Ṣadr al-Dīn al-Shīrāzī).* Albany, NY: State University of New York Press.

Street, Tony. 2002. An Outline of Avicenna's Syllogistic. *Archiv für Geschichte der Philosophie* 84:129–60.

———. 2005. 'Logic'. In *The Cambridge Companion to Arabic Philosophy*, ed. Peter Adamson and Richard C. Taylor, 247–65. Cambridge: Cambridge University Press.

Thom, Paul. 2003. *Medieval Modal Systems: Problems and Concepts*. Aldershot, UK, and Burlington, VT: Ashgate.

Walbridge, John. 2005. 'Suhrawardī and Illuminationism'. In *The Cambridge Companion to Arabic Philosophy*, ed. Peter Adamson and Richard C. Taylor, 201–23. Cambridge: Cambridge University Press.

Wisnovsky, Robert. 2000. Notes on Avicenna's Concept of Thingness (*Shay'iyya*). *Arabic Sciences and Philosophy* 10:181–221.

———. 2003. *Avicenna's Metaphysics in Context*. Ithaca, NY: Cornell University Press.

———. 2005. 'Avicenna and the Avicennian Tradition'. In *The Cambridge Companion to Arabic Philosophy*, ed. Peter Adamson and Richard C. Taylor, 92–136. Cambridge: Cambridge University Press.

Zghal, Hatem. 2004. 'La connaissance des singuliers chez Avicenne'. In *De Zénon d'Élée à Poincaré: recueil d'études en hommage à Roshdi Rashed*, ed. Régis Morelon and Ahmad Hasnawi, 685–718. Leuven, Belgium: Peeters.

CHAPTER 5

AVERROES AND PHILOSOPHY IN ISLAMIC SPAIN

MATTEO DI GIOVANNI

1. THE CONTEXT AND UNITY OF ANDALUSIAN PHILOSOPHY

Averroes and philosophy in Islamic Spain constitute a unitary chapter in the history of philosophy. Averroes makes up a unity with philosophy in Islamic Spain or, as it is called, Andalusian philosophy. In turn, the latter displays a fundamental unity of its own. The first point should be evident. Averroes is 'one' with Andalusian philosophy because he is part of it. He is its principal representative. The second is true in two ways. On the historical level, Andalusian philosophy is the expression of one well-defined society. On the doctrinal level, it is 'one' because it is singular in its focus on a definite set of philosophical questions.

The society that produced Andalusian philosophy was shaped by the advent of Islam in the Iberian Peninsula as early as 711 AD. The region had been inhabited by the Vandals since the twilight of the Roman Empire (409). Muslims called it 'al-Andalus', which in Arabic seems to mean 'land of the Vandals'.[1] In 1147 al-Andalus was taken over by combatants of Berber origin known as Almohads (al-Muwaḥḥidūn). The new rulers championed a rationalistic cult based on two principles. First, God is essentially known through the use of reason alone. Second, revelation is obscured by legal scholasticism, whereas the dictates of Islamic law are accessible through a rightly guided use of independent judgement (ijtihād). In this connection the Almohads endorsed the teaching of al-Ghazālī (d. 1111), who had begun an intellectualistic strand of theology imbued with philosophical notions. Their founder, Muḥammad Ibn Tūmart (d. 1130), portrayed himself as a zealous student of al-Ghazālī and is credited with introducing his work into the Islamic West.

Almohad ideology created a positive climate for philosophy and intellectual endeavour (*nazar*). But it did so at a price. The new creed unsettled religious conservatives, who encouraged submission to authority (*taqlīd*) and opposed independent judgement (*ijtihād*) and speculation (*nazar*). Furthermore, the regime's endorsement of al-Ghazālī posed a challenge to philosophers themselves. For al-Ghazālī was not only a refined theologian but also a fierce critic of the independence of philosophy. In his *Tahāfut al-falāsifa* ('The Incoherence of the Philosophers'), he rejected a number of philosophical theses as incompatible with Islamic doctrine and argued that metaphysics cannot produce valid conclusions independent of revelation.

These socio-cultural dynamics are reflected in the main concerns of Andalusian philosophy. First, the attack of traditionalists on supporters of rational sciences prompted a reflection on the role of philosophers in society. Should philosophers engage in public debate or, rather, withdraw into solitary contemplation? Second, the kind of rationalism implicit in Almohad theology ushered in a naturalistic account of religion. By this account philosophers can know the sphere of the divine independent of revelation. This is typically achieved through a conjunction (*ittiṣāl*) between human intellect and the divine intelligence from which revelation emanates. Finally, there is a third view that is not directly connected with social history but is nevertheless typical of Andalusian philosophy. This is the view of concrete substances as constituted by a plurality of substantial forms.

All these issues are remarkable in various respects. First, the plurality thesis is prima facie at odds with a principle of Aristotelian philosophy, namely, that a substantial form is what brings unity to the composite substance.[2] For if a substance has many forms, and each of them is what imparts unity to it, this implies that none of the others does so by itself. That is, none is truly a substantial form. Second, the naturalistic conception of religion is noteworthy for the way in which Andalusian philosophers depart from the common notion of revelation as transcending natural reason. Finally, the issue of the role of philosophy is an interesting case in which Andalusians disagree with their major authority, Abū Naṣr al-Fārābī (d. 950). Al-Fārābī was inspired by Plato's ideal of the philosopher-king and argued that philosophers should participate in the government of the city. By contrast, Andalusian philosophers generally conceived of the pursuit of wisdom as a rather solitary undertaking.

The structure of substances, the position of philosophy with regard to revelation and its function in society represent, then, the main focuses of Andalusian philosophy in metaphysics, rational theology, and political philosophy. Not all of these questions receive consistent answers from all thinkers, nor are they unique to the Andalusian tradition. Still, they all run through Averroes's predecessors and culminate in Averroes, thus making the philosophical debate fundamentally one and coherent. Major figures in this debate are Ibn Bājja (Avempace,

d. 1139), Ibn Ṭufayl (Abubacer, d. 1185) and Ibn Rushd (Averroes, d. 1198). The issues discussed, however, emerge a century earlier with Ibn Gabirol (Avicebron, d. after 1050) and Ibn Ḥazm (d. 1064). Neither was an Arabic philosopher in the full sense of the term. Ibn Ḥazm was primarily a jurist and theologian. Ibn Gabirol was ethnically and religiously Jewish, although he used Arabic for his philosophical works. Ibn Ḥazm is especially renowned as the codifier of Ẓāhirism, a strand of Islamic jurisprudence based on the literal sense (*ẓāhir*) of Scriptures. His output ranges from love stories to moral, theological and legal treatises, and it includes the *Ṭawq al-ḥamāma* ('The Dove's Neckring'), the *K. al-Akhlāq wa-al-siyar* ('Character and Conduct'), the *K. al-Muḥallā* ('The Embellished Book'), the *Taqrīb li-ḥadd al-manṭiq* ('Approach to the Definition of Logic'), and the monumental *K. al-Fiṣal fī al-milal wa-al-ahwāʾ wa-al-niḥal* ('Opinions on Religions, Sects, and Heresies'). Ibn Gabirol, likewise, composed literary and philosophical works such as the *K. Iṣlāḥ al-akhlāq* ('Improvement of Moral Qualities'), the *K. Mukhtār al-jawāhir* ('Choice Pearls'), and his masterpiece, the *K. Yanbūʿ al-ḥayāt* ('The Fountain of Life').

Ibn Gabirol and Ibn Ḥazm are forerunners of some of the main trends of philosophy in Islamic Spain. Ibn Gabirol set forth the first organic pluralistic theory. He argued that natural substances have forms composed of several layers, which correspond to as many forms in their turn. In line with his Neoplatonic sources, he posited that the cosmos unfolds through distinct levels of reality. Higher levels correspond to simpler forms: these are, in descending order, the form of intelligence, soul, nature, substance, body, figures and colours, elements, plants and animals. As he claims in a passage from the *K. Yanbūʿ al-ḥayāt*, preserved in Latin, 'The first form that combines with the first matter is spiritual and simple (*simplex*), while the last form is corporeal and compound (*composita*). Between these extremes are intermediates that link and unite them.'[3] The *K. Yanbūʿ al-ḥayāt* was translated into Latin around 1150 under the title of *Fons Vitae*. In Christian Europe it soon enjoyed great popularity because it appeared to validate the pluralistic thesis of many Latin authors, particularly in the Franciscan tradition.

For his part, Ibn Ḥazm put forward an insightful view of the relationship between reason and revelation. As a theologian he was faced with a fundamental dilemma. On the one hand, revelation is necessary for salvation, and salvation is, in principle, available to everyone. On the other hand, revelation will not be universal if it can only be accessed through acquaintance with a determinate religion. Ibn Ḥazm's solution revolves around the Quranic notion of inborn nature (*fiṭra*). By this account the essence of revelation is encoded in the nature of man. As such it does not depend exclusively on prophetic instruction or any historical circumstances; neither, however, is it reducible to a product of human intellectual acumen. Rather, the essence of revelation consists of an inborn faith (*īmān*) common to all men just like reason but distinct from it. In this way Ibn Ḥazm avoids thoroughgoing rationalism, namely, the reduction of revelation to a set of rational truths. Nevertheless, his position displays a naturalistic tinge that will appear in all Andalusian philosophers: revelation is inscribed in the nature of man. Islam is what best interprets his natural religion.

2. Abū Bakr Muḥammad Ibn Bājja (Avempace)

With Abū Bakr Muḥammad Ibn Bājja, Andalusian thought reaches its full maturity. The first to comment on Aristotle's natural philosophy, he made remarkable contributions especially in physics and psychology. His teachings inspired Averroes, who nevertheless questioned some of their assumptions or rejected their implications.[4] Through Averroes's critiques, moreover, Ibn Bājja became known to Latin philosophers, who embraced his views, for example, on the possibility of motion in the void.

Ibn Bājja and Averroes differ remarkably in the breadth and depth of their accomplishments. Averroes was committed to organising the philosophical corpus in a demonstrative way. Ibn Bājja contented himself with providing an indication (*dalāla*) of what a logically rigorous discourse would be.[5] This is partly due to the social and political contexts in which each lived. Averroes worked for, and was long supported by, the Almohad regime. Ibn Bājja lived in the troubled times following the downfall of the Umayyad Caliphate of Cordoba (1031). In Saragozza, where he was born, Ibn Bājja benefitted from a stimulating intellectual environment. When the city was conquered by the Almoravids (1109), he served as a vizier for them and eventually retired to a solitary life of study. His work can be divided into three parts corresponding to the successive phases of his reflection and centring on: music, astronomy and logic; natural philosophy and medicine; the composition of his original treatises, that is, the *Tadbīr al-mutawaḥḥid* ('Rule of the Solitary'), the *Risāla al-Wadā'* ('Letter of Farewell') and the *Risāla Ittiṣāl al-'aql bi-l-insān* ('Epistle on the Conjunction of the Intellect with Man').[6] Among the principal achievements of Ibn Bājja is his analysis of movement, in which he innovated on Aristotle's physics and anticipated the principles of Newtonian dynamics. Ibn Bājja questioned Aristotle's assumption that natural movements require a medium, such as air or water, through which they take place. He observed that celestial spheres do not move through a medium and took this to imply that the medium is not necessary but, rather, as he saw it, merely a retarding factor for movement. Similarly, he elaborated on the notion of resistance (*muqāwama*) beyond Aristotle's treatment of the subject. Aristotle assumed that violent movements depend precisely on the force exerted by the mover. Ibn Bājja took them to result from the difference between the force exerted by the mover and the force of resistance opposed by the thing moved.[7]

Movement, as change in place, is naturally related to generation, which is change in substance. Now generation is a phenomenon in which a portion of matter acquires a given form. Thus, matter and form become a secondary focus of Ibn Bājja's reflection. His analysis pertains to the domain of metaphysics as much as physics. For matter and form are principles of being as well as of change. That is, they explain not only generation and corruption but also the structure and unity of composite substances. These have composite forms (*al-ṣuwar al-murakkaba*) resulting from simple forms (*al-ṣuwar al-basā'iṭ*). Ibn Bājja gives the example of a jar, whose form is a complex entity made of several layers or degrees (*marātib*).[8] More elaborate layers contain simpler ones. Thus, the form of the jar consists of that of copper and of more elementary materials down to the forms of the elements. Ibn Bājja is clearly committed to a pluralistic view similar to Ibn Gabirol's. As already noted, this thesis seems to clash with the notion of form as a principle of unity. At the same time, it is possible that the many layers combine in such a way as to make up a substantial form that is essentially one. If this is the case, Ibn Bājja can maintain that the final form, though analysable into simpler constituents, is in reality one and a source of unity for the compound. Unfortunately, Ibn Bājja is sparing with details, and it is not clear whether in his view layers of form remain in the compound as really or only logically distinct from one another.

Ibn Bājja's metaphysics is consistent with his epistemology. Knowledge is explained as a two-step process. First, (i) the human intellect analyses concrete substances and separates forms from matter. Second, (ii) it analyses forms themselves into their constituents. This explanation accords with his pluralistic assumption according to which forms are compounded. For, by this assumption, forms can be analysed in much the same way as compounds of matter and form. In fact, Ibn Bājja speaks not so much of 'forms' as of 'intentions' (*maʿnā*), which are, in turn, rendered as 'quiddities' (*quidditas*) in the Latin translation of Averroes's *Long Commentary* on the *De anima*.[9] Such details apart, however, the gist of his theory is clear. Initially (i) forms are abstracted from matter and in this way become intelligible. Intelligibles are first produced by the agent intellect and then received by the potential intellect. 'Agent intellect' designates the active power involved in conceptualisation, which resides in a self-subsistent form separate from matter. 'Potential intellect' is the potentiality to receive intelligible notions, and it is located in man's soul or, more precisely, in his imagination. It is the disposition of mental images for receiving abstracted forms. Or, put differently, it is a property of mental images that allows them to sustain intelligible notions in a way similar to the way that matter sustains substantial forms in nature. Intelligible notions are like forms that have as their matter the forms of imagination.[10] When all intelligibles are acquired, the potential intellect turns into an 'acquired intellect' (*al-ʿaql al-mustafād*). At this point (ii), the agent intellect processes these abstracted forms themselves and frees them from any residual link with matter. The end product is the most immaterial entity, which corresponds to the most abstract notion: the mere notion of form. Ibn Bājja suggests that the two phases of conceptualisation, corresponding to (i) and (ii) above, yield distinct objects of knowledge. Material forms, due to their link with matter, constitute the content of physical sciences (*al-maʿrifa al-naẓariyya*). They are the concepts used to classify and explain the phenomena of the natural world. In contrast, the notion of form that is extracted from them is the notion of what it means to be a form separately from matter. This is what the agent intellect is, namely, a separate form. In this sense, the knowledge of concrete substances culminates in the knowledge of the agent intellect and the separate substances.

This theory has two implications. First, man is able to know separate substances through his rational faculty. This means that he is able to know the transcendental or the divine independently of revelation. The function of revelation is, accordingly, not so much to supply some knowledge that is not accessible to humans as to stimulate the human pursuit of knowledge itself. Religion is an exhortation to know (*al-khaḍḍ 'alā al-'ilm*).[11] In this way, the naturalistic line that surfaces in Ibn Ḥazm reappears clearly in Ibn Bājja. Second, Ibn Bājja assumes that when someone attains knowledge of the divine he thereby divinises himself. In theological terms, salvation like revelation is naturally available to man. The argument of Ibn Bājja is ultimately inspired by Aristotle's psychology. According to Aristotle the knowledge of a thing entails some assimilation to it.[12] For the knower is potentially the thing known in the same way that an empty tablet is potentially a tablet that is written on. When it knows in actuality and acquires its mental contents, the knower actualises this potentiality and becomes one with the things that it knows. This may be taken to suggest that man becomes one with the agent intellect that forms the object of his knowledge. In this condition man is indistinguishable from the agent intellect: since the agent intellect is eternal, man is eternal, too. Since it is one for all men, all men are one. That is, men lose their personal identity. Thus, the kind of immortality that is available by conjunction (*ittiṣāl*) with the agent intellect is entirely impersonal.[13] Admittedly, it is not clear how a thorough identification with the agent intellect can be attained. For men have bodies, whereas the agent intellect is immaterial. Perhaps Ibn Bājja assumes that man can become, if not unqualifiedly, at least essentially one with the agent intellect. After all, what becomes identical with it is man's intellect, and man is essentially his own intellect. For being a man means essentially being so constituted as to be able to perform certain intellectual activities.

Ibn Bājja proposed his epistemology in response to two major concerns. On the one hand, he endorsed Aristotle's teaching that theoretical activity makes man similar to the divine. On the other hand, he interpreted this assimilation along Neoplatonic lines as a full identification with God. In this vein, he viewed philosophical endeavour as a nearly mystical ascent (*ṣu'ūd*) and, concomitant to this, a withdrawal from the external world.[14] Philosophers should occupy themselves with the things that are above and not with earthly matters. In this respect Ibn Bājja upheld a definite view of the relationship between politics and philosophy. His position anticipated the ideal of philosophical solitude in Ibn Ṭufayl. At the same time, he adopted an intuition of al-Fārābī, who, in contrast, advocated philosophers' engagement in the life of the city. This he did by discriminating between the ends and the means of social life. The former bear on the intellectual progress of the individual, the latter on the external circumstances that prepare and sustain it. Philosophers seek the former but disregard the latter, especially when these are perverted by a corrupt regime. The conclusions of Ibn Bājja's reflection are expounded in his significantly titled work *Rule of the Solitary*. 'Rule' (*tadbīr*) is said in many ways: of the management of the city, of household affairs, and of the individual. A solitary man (*al-mutawaḥḥid*), the philosopher will focus on the last of these. His intellectual life is the supreme good to which the good of society itself is subordinated.

3. Abū Bakr Muḥammad Ibn Ṭufayl (Abubacer)

The takeover by the Almohads in 1147 began an age of intellectual flowering in al-Andalus. First secretary in Ceuta and Tangier to a son of the first Almohad ruler ('Abd al-Mu'min, d. 1163), and later confidant and court physician of the succeeding Caliph (Abū Ya'qūb Yūsuf, d. 1184), Ibn Ṭufayl vividly embodied the cultural policy of the new regime. He organised the intellectual life of al-Andalus under the auspices of the enlightened Caliph Abū Ya'qūb Yūsuf. For the Caliph, presumably, he composed his philosophical masterwork. And he introduced to him the young Averroes, who would succeed Ibn Ṭufayl as court physician in 1182. The prominence of Ibn Ṭufayl in the different fields of Western Islamic education is attested by the diversity of his literary output, which ranges from poetic and historical compositions to works on natural philosophy and medicine, as well as a correspondence with Averroes on the latter's medical summa, the *Kulliyyāt* or *Colliget* ('Book of Generalities'). But it is largely due to his philosophical novel, the *Risāla Ḥayy b. Yaqẓān fī asrār al-ḥikma al-mashriqiyya* ('Alive, Son of the Awake. On the Secrets of Eastern Philosophy') that Ibn Ṭufayl was to achieve his enduring reputation in the centuries to come.

The *R. Ḥayy b. Yaqẓān* was commissioned by a noble friend who had asked Ibn Ṭufayl to disclose the secrets of 'oriental philosophy' (*al-ḥikma al-mashriqiyya*). Ibn Ṭufayl declined to provide anything more than a 'brief glimpse of the road that lies ahead',[15] convinced as he was that the summits of philosophy are achieved by long endeavour and personal effort. On the way to the attainment of wisdom, however, he installed signposts to guide the steps of his reader. This he did by narrating the story of Ḥayy b. Yaqẓān, a solitary man on a deserted island who arrives at the loftiest truths about God by relying exclusively on his reasoning and personal observations. What unfolds throughout the tale is a refined example of literary prose where the author, through the persona of Ḥayy b. Yaqẓān, popularises the teachings of philosophers. A similar task was undertaken during the same period, at the request of the same Abū Ya'qūb Yūsuf, by Averroes, the then protégé of Ibn Ṭufayl, who composed for the prince his explanatory paraphrase (*talkhīṣ*) of Aristotle's works.

The novel describes the adventures and intellectual quest of Ḥayy, a man of exceptional mind. How Ḥayy appeared on the uninhabited island off the coast of India where he would spend his life is not clear, the author says. Some say that he was carried by the flood current in a chest where he was put by his mother after his birth. Others relate that he was born on the island by spontaneous generation from a mass of fermenting clay. What is certain is that, when he was still a child, Ḥayy was rescued and suckled by a gazelle who adopted him until she died. The death of the gazelle grieved and puzzled Ḥayy, who made his first scientific observations in a vain attempt to heal her. He dissects her body, and so he realises that the principle of life must be located in the heart. This prompts him to undertake a thorough exploration of the natural world. His discoveries reflect and correspond to the major teachings of philosophy, while at the same time preparing his mystical union with God. Ḥayy observes that things are composed of matter and form, that they are generated and, as such, require an agent. At the age of twenty-eight, he moves from the contemplation of the sub-lunary to that of the supra-lunary world. He finds that the heavens have bodies, that heavenly bodies have a spherical shape and need a First Cause that sustains them in being or in motion. The First Cause is incorporeal and can be known, accordingly, through annihilation of the body and, ultimately, of the self. For this reason Ḥayy begins to lead an ascetic life and eventually achieves a mystical elevation in which he can contemplate the heavens, their order and perfection. At the age of fifty he encounters and becomes the friend of Asāl, a devout man from a near island, who symbolises religion and theology. Asāl realises that the conclusions reached by Ḥayy are a scientific and philosophical interpretation of his same beliefs. So he arranges for Ḥayy to share his knowledge with his fellow believers on his home island, but the project fails. At this point Ḥayy and Asāl understand and recommend that common believers should keep to the religious custom of their ancestors, whilst they leave and return to their contemplative life.

The *Ḥayy b. Yaqẓān* does not stand out for the originality of its doctrines. For example, the theory of forms is taken over by Ibn Ṭufayl from the philosophical koine of al-Andalus. Like Ibn Bājja and Ibn Gabirol, Ḥayy b. Yaqẓān believes that generally composite substances contain many forms: 'Composed with just one form are the four elements, occupying the lowest ontic rungs in the world of generation and decay. From these are compounded things with more than one form'.[16] However, Ibn Ṭufayl's work is remarkable for the peculiar way in which the indigenous tradition is reinterpreted in at least three respects: (i) the naturalistic conception of the relationship between reason and revelation; (ii) the reflection on the social role of the philosopher; (iii) the interpretation and appreciation of mysticism.

The joyful encounter between Ḥayy and Asāl is supposed to suggest that reason and revelation are not incompatible with one another. This may represent a natural assumption for believers of all religions, but the specific way in which Ibn Ṭufayl interprets this concordance is far from obvious. If revelation agrees with reason, it is because (i) revelation adds nothing to the results of rational investigation and the positive contents of science. In the words of Edward Pocock, the author of the first Latin translation of the *Ḥayy b. Yaqẓān*, natural reason unaided by revelation is able to ascend to the highest objects of contemplation (*ex inferiorum contemplatione ad superiorum notitiam*).[17] Indeed, revelation expresses the truths of reason 'in symbols, providing concrete images of things and impressing their outlines on the people's souls, just as orators do when addressing a multitude'.[18] It is through men's natural capacity, however, that such truths are accessed in the first place. In Ibn Ṭufayl as in Ibn Ḥazm, a key epistemic role is played by the notion of inborn nature (*fiṭra*). Thanks to his *fiṭra*, Ḥayy b. Yaqẓān discovers the true nature of the heavens; due to their deficient *fiṭra*, likewise, the companions who join Ḥayy b. Yaqẓān are unable to understand his metaphysical teachings and eventually leave him.[19]

The dramatic failure of Ḥayy's attempt to build a society informed by philosophy represents (ii) a secondary motif in Ibn Ṭufayl's tale: 'Ḥayy b. Yaqẓān began to teach this group and explain some of his profound wisdom to them. But the moment he rose the slightest bit above the literal or began to portray things against which they were prejudiced, they recoiled in horror from his ideas and closed their minds'.[20] The discouraging ending of Ḥayy's story is calculated to convey a definite message, but its meaning is not obvious. One possibility is that Ḥayy's failure symbolises the incompatibility between the theoretical dimension of truth and the pragmatic exigencies of its outward communication. On this reading, Ḥayy b. Yaqẓān has been taken as embodying the elitist image of the Neoplatonic philosopher, who should be imitated as a final cause rather than engage with the external world as an efficient cause.[21] Be that as it may, the theme of the philosopher's solitude establishes a clear connection between Ibn Ṭufayl and Ibn Bājja. The solitary man celebrated by Ibn Bājja abandons the city and thereby frees himself to pursue the three goals related to his corporeal, particular spiritual and universal spiritual forms. Analogously, on his deserted island Ḥayy b. Yaqẓān sets himself three duties that 'fall under three heads, those in which he would resemble an inarticulate animal, those in which he would resemble a celestial body, and those in which he would resemble the Necessarily Existent Being'.[22]

It is, however, on another level that Ibn Ṭufayl's vision in the *Ḥayy b. Yaqẓān* finds its ultimate meaning: namely (iii), its championing of mysticism and visionary experience. The contemplation of Ḥayy b. Yaqẓān culminates in a direct vision (*mushāhada*), an intuitive perception or taste (*dhawq*), of the One; dianoetic reasoning gives way to noetic apperception, ratiocination (*naẓar*) to love (*wilāya*), and dying to oneself or annihilation (*fanā'*) paves the way to the self-disclosure of the Divine. Ibn Ṭufayl insists that the content of this ecstatic experience transcends ordinary language or logic, although it can be alluded to by symbols (*mithāl*) and hints (*ishāra*).[23] At the same time, he asserts the critical function of rational inquiry. If he blames Ibn Bājja for his failure to experience an ecstatic state that invests more than the theoretical part of the soul,[24] it is because he maintains that the study of theoretical sciences is indeed preliminary to the attainment of mystical vision. The work of the mind and the intuition of the heart are different roads to the same truth. Their difference consists in the degree of clarity and the emotional overtones accompanying them. For 'the difference between the rationalist and those who enjoy intimacy is that, while both are concerned with the self-same things, the latter enjoy a clearer view and far greater delight'.[25]

In this way Ibn Ṭufayl reconciles the two strands that constitute the cultural texture of Almohad Spain: on one side the legacy of Arabic philosophy, on the other the mystical tradition. Both are acknowledged and embraced as ultimately convergent. At the same time, they represent autonomous methods and distinct modes or degrees (*rutba*) of discovery. Cultural traditions have their heroes, and Ibn Ṭufayl names them in his introduction to the *Ḥayy b. Yaqẓān*: 'I myself would have not garnered what truth I have attained, the culmination of my intellectual efforts, without pursuing the arguments of Ghazālī and Avicenna'.[26] On one side there is al-Ghazālī, the master interpreter of Islam, who advocates an experiential approach to religion as represented by Islamic mysticism. On the other side, Avicenna incarnates the tradition of philosophical rationalism and the crowning glory of the Islamic intellectual sciences. As he brings together al-Ghazālī and Avicenna and merges mysticism with philosophy, Ibn Ṭufayl pursues a sophisticated strategy that has been magisterially investigated by Dimitri Gutas.[27] Ibn Ṭufayl creatively reworks materials from Avicenna's *K. al-Shifāʾ* ('The Cure'), his *K. al-Ishārāt wa-al-tanbīhāt* ('Pointers and Reminders') and his *Qiṣṣa Ḥayy b. Yaqẓān* ('Story of Ḥayy b. Yaqẓān'), and he clothes Avicenna in the raiment of an esotericism that corresponds to al-Ghazālī's stance on mysticism, prophecy and suprarational knowledge. In the final analysis, the doctrine that Ibn Ṭufayl presents is highly innovative. While he assumes from Avicenna that discursive reason is epistemically sufficient for a thorough exploration of reality, he agrees with al-Ghazālī that the work of reason is but a preparation for the experience of a knowledge different in kind, if not in substance. Moreover, Ibn Ṭufayl projects the same view onto Avicenna himself. In so doing he exploits a distinction in the *Shifāʾ* between different ways of communicating philosophical doctrines, and he interprets it as a distinction between different doctrines themselves. By this account, Avicenna adheres to mainstream Aristotelianism in the *Shifāʾ*, where he sets forth his exoteric teaching, while at the same time entrusting his personal views to his esoteric work on Eastern philosophy. The latter is portrayed as valuing mysticism over and above theoretical philosophy, and this finally brings Avicenna, or at least Ibn Ṭufayl's simulacrum of Avicenna, into perfect alignment with the doctrine of al-Ghazālī.

This fictional representation exerted an enormous, if quite misleading, impact on later scholarship. Yet, what it reflects of its own socio-cultural background characterises Ibn Ṭufayl's philosophy according to its own principles and Andalusian philosophy at the turn of the Almohad era. The Almohads advocated an intellectualistic creed based on the principle that 'it is by the necessity of reason that the existence of God is known'.[28] They championed al-Ghazālī as the icon of a sophisticated approach to religion. At the same time, their attempts at reform were countered by religious leaders, who embraced the values of tradition as opposed to theoretical speculation. All these aspects of Andalusian history are reflected in Ibn Ṭufayl's novel. First, the naturalistic stance implied in Ḥayy's ascent to God gives literary flesh to the Almohad dogma, so that Ḥayy incarnates 'a rough description of the official theology of the Almohad movement expounded in the creed (*ʿAqīda*) of Ibn Tūmart'.[29] Similarly, the appropriation of the Ghazālian view of mysticism and its projection onto Avicenna reflect the regime's endorsement of al-Ghazālī and his accommodation within a rationalistic ideology. Finally, Ḥayy's ill-fated attempt to reform society appears to be a living record of the difficulties of Almohadism in the face of the religious establishment and its steadfast resistance.[30] In the end Ibn Ṭufayl provides a rich tapestry of Almohad society and its cohesive ideology. His work anticipates the later developments of Andalusian philosophy. His same concerns will inform Averroes's reflection.

4. Abū al-Walīd Muḥammad Ibn Rushd (Averroes)

Abū al-Walīd Muḥammad Ibn Rushd (Averroes) epitomises the richness and complexity of philosophical debate as it was pursued up to the threshold of the modern era. At once a continuator of the Greek tradition, an apex of the Arabic and an authority in the Latin, Averroes transcends the immediate context of al-Andalus. Indeed, he surpasses all of his predecessors in the breadth of his work, the depth of his doctrine, and his impact on later philosophy. Yet his project cannot be understood apart from the context of Islamic Spain. His philosophy expresses the typical concerns of the Almohad age as broadly anticipated by Ibn Ṭufayl. The questions asked are in essence the same, but his answers differ significantly and show the uniqueness of Averroes's thought. Contrary to Ibn Ṭufayl with respect to the role of philosophers, that is, point (ii) above, Averroes believed that the intellectual flowering fostered by the Almohads should be upheld through active engagement in the public arena. His career stands in opposition to the celebration of the solitary philosopher in Ibn Bājja and Ibn Ṭufayl. While serving as judge in Seville (1169) and chief judge of Cordoba (1182),[31] Averroes launched himself into the heart of the cultural debate with an influential treatise of comparative jurisprudence (*ikhtilāf*). The *Bidāya al-mujtahid wa-nihāya al-muqtaṣid* ('Starting-Point of the Studious and End-Point of the Contentable') was conceived as a blueprint for a large-scale reform at the hands of the Caliph and reflects a project to rebuild the juridical foundations of Andalusian society.[32] Similarly, in another tract of theology known as *Kashf 'an manāhij al-adilla fī 'aqā'id al-milla* ('The Exposition of the Methods of Proof on the Principles of Religion'), he presented an interpretation of Islam that does away with the tradition of *kalām* and advocates a drastic alternative to the canonical doctrine. The goal of Averroes was to innovate within the context of Islamic doctrine so as to bring it into full accordance with the results of philosophical investigation. He assumed that (i) reason and revelation are two paths leading to the same truth, based on the principle that 'truth does not oppose truth; rather it agrees with and bears witness to it' (*al-ḥaqq lā yuḍāddu al-ḥaqq bal yuwāfiquhū wa-yashhadu lahū*).[33] In this synthesis the predominant role is, again, assigned to philosophy. Philosophers, not the experts in religious sciences, are the heirs of prophets (*waratha al-anbiyā'*).[34] It is their responsibility to determine the true sense of Scripture whenever the latter is either wanting in inner coherence or does not conform to the evidence of apodictic knowledge. Revelation is confined to the ancillary role of divulging the conclusions of philosophy through images and signs that can be understood by all believers. For 'what is intended by the Law is, indeed, to teach everyone' (*ta'līm al-jamī'*).[35]

In full accord with the spirit of Almohadism, Averroes maintained that 'the Qur'ān in its entirety is but a call to theoretical investigation'.[36] What is more, he assumed that the content of revelation is not only available to rational investigation but also enriched, made coherent and perfected by the work of philosophy and the use of demonstrative reason (*burhān*). In this way he continued the naturalistic thread that runs all through Andalusian philosophy and finds in Ibn Ṭufayl one of its highest expressions. At the same time, (iii) just like Ibn Ṭufayl, Averroes was faced with the doctrine of al-Ghazālī, according to which philosophy is unable to afford valid conclusions in metaphysics and should yield the ground to the unadulterated letter of revelation. After an initial attempt to accommodate al-Ghazālī along the lines followed by his predecessor, Averroes despaired of reaching a satisfactory compromise. In the mature phase of his career, he resolved the conflict by sacrificing all allegiance to al-Ghazālī.[37] Around 1180 he composed his famous refutation of al-Ghazālī's *Tahāfut al-falāsifa*, the *Tahāfut al-tahāfut* ('The Incoherence of the Incoherence'), where he rejected all claims against the supposed inconclusiveness of philosophy and argued that metaphysics is a solid, demonstrative science. An echo of this project can be found in the *Long Commentary* on the *De anima*, roughly contemporary with the *Tahāfut al-tahāfut*, where metaphysics is placed at the summit of the Aristotelian system of sciences by virtue of the 'confirmation associated with demonstration' (*confirmatio demonstrationis*) and the 'nobility of subject' (*nobilitas subiecti*).[38]

It is, however, in a different context that this defence of metaphysics as a science stands out most clearly: in the *Long Commentary* (*Tafsīr*) on Aristotle's *Metaphysics*, probably the last composed by Averroes (1192–94), the structure of Aristotle's *Metaphysics* is reinterpreted as a coherent deductive system. Aristotle describes his method as an analysis that ascends from effects to causes, and hence in reverse order to the pattern of deductive reasoning codified in the *Posterior Analytics*. Nevertheless, Averroes maintains that metaphysics proceeds essentially in a demonstrative manner. The arguments that are used in this science (*'ilm*), he claims, are 'logical demonstrations' (*barāhīn manṭiqiyya*), by which he means demonstrations based on premises that belong to logic.[39]

Upon reflection, this interpretation poses a problem. For a science must use only appropriate (οἰκεῖος) premises, as Aristotle argues in the *Organon* (*Post Anal.* A 2). And according to *Post. Anal.* A 7 and 9, appropriate premises bear on the same subject matter of the science in which they are used. Now the premises of logic do not seem to be appropriate to metaphysics inasmuch as they bear on a subject matter different from that of metaphysics. Logic is the study of concepts and their properties, usually termed mental being. Metaphysics, by contrast, is the study of what exists in the outside world, such as substances and their properties, which is extra-mental being. If this is so, the premises of logic cannot be used in metaphysics without violating the Aristotelian principle laid down in *Post. Anal.* A 7 that forbids transitions from a different subject matter (μετάβασις ἐξ ἄλλου γένους).

Averroes resolves this problem by rejecting the assumption according to which logic and metaphysics have different subject matters. To his mind, in fact, both logic and metaphysics are about neither mental nor extra-mental but 'absolute' being (*al-mawjūd al-muṭlaq*).[40] This view plays a crucial role,[41] but its import is not obvious. What does it mean for logic and metaphysics to be concerned with absolute being? More fundamentally, what is absolute being? Clearly it is not indeterminate being, namely, being as not in any way specified or qualified. This is, indeed, how Aristotle uses the expression 'absolute being' or 'being simply' ($\check{o}\nu\ \dot{\alpha}\pi\lambda\hat{\omega}s$) in *Met.* E 1, where he explains that metaphysics does not mark off any particular kind of being. In *Met.* Z 1, however, a different conception emerges, and this is the conception that Averroes takes up. In this second sense, absolute being is indeed a determinate kind of being, which is called 'absolute' because it is spoken of in the full, or primary, sense of the word. It is the kind of being that is prior to all other beings. Such is substance with respect to accidents. For a substance can exist apart from an accident, but no accidents can exist apart from a substance. Furthermore, among substances form is prior to both matter and the compound. For matter cannot exist separately from form, whereas form can exist separately from matter. The compound, finally, is secondary to both because it results from a combination of matter and form.

From this Averroes concludes that absolute being means essentially substantial form. This equivalence presupposes a definite ontology, namely, an analysis of certain beings as dependent on and explained by other more basic entities. Most remarkably, it explains why metaphysics, as a study of absolute being, is primarily focused on form. But what should be said about logic? According to Averroes logic has the same subject matter as metaphysics. As such it should be likewise focused on the notion of substantial form. This view is problematic, however. For Averroes defines logic as a study of second intentions or, as he says, 'second intelligibles' (*al-ma'qūlāt al-thawānī*) such as genera and species.[42] These are not entities that exist in nature like substantial forms. Rather, they exist in the mind and are considered precisely insofar as they exist in the mind. In this sense second intentions are distinct from substantial forms. So logic seems to have a subject matter different from that of metaphysics.

Averroes's solution consists roughly in saying that second intentions, though logically distinct from substantial forms, are really identical with them. His strategy is not explicit but may be reconstructed as follows. First, Averroes establishes that logic is to species what metaphysics is to substantial form. He applies to logic a strategy similar to that which he applies to metaphysics. Just as other beings depend ultimately on substantial form, so logical notions presuppose the notion of species. Species is the most basic content of thought. As such it is presupposed by more abstract concepts (genera) and, through the latter, logical relations and operations. Therefore, logic is primarily focused on species in the same way that metaphysics is focused on substantial form. Second, Averroes assumes that species is really identical with substantial form. Indeed, one may think of the substantial form of a man and his species, for example, as distinct entities. For one may consider them as a metaphysical principle and its conceptual representation. What exists in reality, however, are not two entities (the principle and its representation) but a single entity, man's essence, with different instantiations: in matter and in the mind.[43] Insofar as man's essence is present in the mind, one speaks of it in terms of mental being and calls it 'species'. Insofar as it is located in matter, one speaks of it as extramental being and calls it 'substantial form'. This distinction has to do with the way in which one looks at things rather than with things as they are in themselves. Of course, depending on whether it exists in the mind or in matter, an essence acquires different properties. Insofar as it is in the mind, it can be predicated, classified and combined with other concepts in assertions and deductions. Insofar as it is in matter, it can bring potentiality into actuality, unify the compound, produce physical transformations and orient teleological processes. These different properties are brought into focus, respectively, in logic and in metaphysics. Yet they are all properties of a single entity or subject, which is the subject matter shared by logic and metaphysics.

The real identity of form and species is a distinctive view of Averroes. Thomas Aquinas, an attentive reader of Averroes, described it with reference to the case of man. *Humanity* is the species of man or, in Aquinas's terminology, his 'form of the whole'. Analogously, the soul of man is his substantial form or 'form of the part'. Aquinas observes that the two notions may be considered identical. As a matter of fact, some say that 'in reality the form of the whole, which is signified by the word humanity, is the same (*eadem secundum rem*) as the form of the part, which is signified by the word soul, but that they differ only in definition (*differunt solum secundum rationem*) [. . .]. This appears to be the opinion of Averroes and of certain of his followers'.[44] Most importantly, the identity between form and species explains why Averroes maintains that logic and metaphysics have the same subject matter. For logic investigates all that is related to species, so that the subject matter of logic is primarily species. Likewise, metaphysics explores what is related to substantial form, and its subject matter is substantial form. Now species is really identical with substantial form. In this sense, then, the subject matter of logic can be said to be identical with the subject matter of metaphysics.

This doctrine has two important implications. First, substantial form must be a composite entity. For if form and species are identical, they will be identical also in structure. Now species has a structure composed of many predicates that designate, from the generic (*'āmm*) to the specific (*khāṣṣ*), the nature of the thing defined. Man, for example, is generically designated as animal and specifically as rational. Accordingly, form will be constituted by several layers that run parallel to the predicates of the species, beginning with the generic form (*al-ṣūra al-'āmma*) up to the specific one (*al-ṣūra al-khāṣṣa*). This means that form is not distinct from matter in the way that it is usually thought to be. Rather, form encompasses all that is specifically or essentially constitutive of man, including the different materials of which he is made: elemental (e.g., earth and water), lower (e.g., flesh and bones) and functional (i.e., organic). In the end, Averroes upholds what can be called a *holistic* conception of substantial form. To his mind, substantial form embraces all essential properties that belong to a thing, whether acknowledgedly formal or supposedly material.[45]

Each of these properties corresponds to a distinct layer of form. In line with Ibn Gabirol, Ibn Bājja and Ibn Ṭufayl, Averroes assumes that composite substances have 'forms composed of proximate and perfective forms and these forms', that is, the forms of the four elements (*al-ṣuwar al-murakkaba min al-ṣuwar al-qarība wa-al-tamāmiyya* wa-hādhihi al-ṣuwar).[46] By the same token, prime matter is said to receive 'first the generic form and then, through the generic form, all the other forms up to the particular ones' (innamā taqbalu awwalan al-sūra al-'āmma thumma taqbalu bi-tawassut al-sūra al-'āmma sā'ir al-suwar hattā al-suwar al-shakhsiyya).[47] In Latin scholasticism the thesis of the plurality of forms would be frequently associated with Averroes. Indeed, it became the hallmark of Averroean as opposed to Avicennian metaphysics.

Second, the identity between species and form entails a distinct view of individuation. Since species is one for all the individuals within the same kind, form must be likewise one. As the species of man is a single concept predicated of all individual subjects, so his form is a single principle common to all concrete men. Consequently, substantial form is not unique to each individual but universal. It is the same form replicated in multiple instances. These instances are made numerically many by matter. For each portion of matter is distinct from all others and so it individuates the concrete substance to which it belongs. In other words, the structure of substances results from a combination of matter, which makes substances many in number, and form, which is one in species and one with species itself. As a result 'everything that is one and many in number, that is one in species and many in number, has matter'.[48] For it is only by virtue of matter that concrete things are made individual (innamā tashakhkhaṣat li-kawnihā fī 'unṣur).[49]

In the mature phase of his thought, Averroes drew from this principle important consequences for his theory of the intellect. He started by observing that the object appropriate to the human intellect is the universal since apprehending means receiving the universal forms embedded in sensory images. In consistency with his theory of individuation, he concluded that the intellect must be free from matter. For otherwise its material substratum would turn the universals into individuals and apprehension would become impossible. As he states in the *Long Commentary* on Aristotle's *De anima*, 'it is evident that this substance which is called the material intellect is neither a body nor a form in the body; it is, therefore, altogether unmixed with matter'.[50] Averroes refers here to the 'material intellect' (al-'aql al-hayūlānī, Lat. *intellectus materialis*). This is the part of the intellect for which apprehending means precisely receiving universal forms in a way similar to how corporeal matter receives particular forms. Complementary to the material intellect is the 'agent intellect' (al-'aql al-fa''āl, Lat. *intellectus agens*), which actualises the universal forms potentially contained in senses and imagination. Averroes assumes that the material intellect must be free from matter in order to receive universals precisely as universals. On these grounds he argues that the material intellect must be a 'fourth kind of being' (quartum genus esse) that is neither matter, nor a form in matter, nor a composite of these. Moreover, being removed from the source of plurality in number, this intellect must be one for all men, a distinctly Averroean thesis that will be highly debated in Latin scholasticism.[51] On this view each man performs his acts of thinking by connecting in a peculiar way with the unique material intellect. That is, each man refines his imagined intentions through cogitation (fikr, Lat. *cogitatio*), an individual faculty that processes images and passes them on to the material intellect subsequent to the actualisation produced by the agent intellect. In this way intelligible notions become located in two different subjects: first, in the material intellect common to all men and, second, in the soul (that is to say, the imagination) of each thinking agent. On one side, the material intellect, being identical for all men, ensures the objectivity of intelligible notions. On the other side, imagination, being particular to each man, accounts for the various degrees of intellectual engagement and proficiency among different individuals.[52]

This theory constitutes the mature stage of a long reflection as expounded in Averroes's *Long Commentary* on the *De anima* (ca. 1186). The initial and the intermediate phases are represented, respectively, by the *Short* (1158–1160) and the *Middle Commentary* (1181) and testify to Averroes's progression from a materialistic to a dualistic conception of the relationship between intellect and body.[53] In the *Short Commentary*, as well as the *Epistle on the Possibility of Conjunction* and the earlier *Epistle on Conjunction with the Agent Intellect*, Averroes came close to an intuition of Alexander of Aphrodisias. According to Alexander the material intellect is just a property or a disposition of the body. Averroes slightly corrected Alexander's view with reference to that of Ibn Bājja and described the intellect as a disposition not of the body but of certain bodily functions, particularly imagination. Mental images can be actualised by the agent intellect and become intelligible notions. The material intellect was still seen as the potentiality in mental images to become actually one with intelligible notions in a way similar to that in which matter becomes actually one with substantial forms. Later Averroes recanted this view and criticised Ibn Bājja.[54] He realised that the intellect could not perform its function if it were mixed with any pre-existing forms that either limit or distort reception. Therefore, in the *Middle Commentary* he reconsidered his previous position and inclined towards what he took to be Themistius's theory. In his view Themistius had assumed the material intellect to be a separate, independently existent, substance. Averroes did not follow him to the point of dismissing his own notion of the material intellect as dependent upon the existence of the human soul. But he started to conceive at least a kind of relative separation, and, contrary to his early view in the *Short Commentary*, he described the material intellect as a disposition unmixed with material forms. Finally, Averroes perfected and made coherent his interpretation by linking together the logical and the ontological sides of separation. In the *Long Commentary*, he concluded that, just as the material intellect can logically be described without any reference to matter or material forms, so it is able to exist as ontologically independent from them.[55]

The development of Averrocan noetics is indeed remarkable. At the same time, there is one aspect that remained relatively unchanged across the different stages of Averroes's reflection. This is the defence of the possibility of conjunction (*ittiṣāl*) between man and the agent intellect.[56] In line with Ibn Bājja, Averroes maintained that full conjunction can be realised by a few exceptional individuals, this representing the perfection of human nature and the essence of happiness. It corresponds to the final stage of intellection, when the intellect has acquired all intelligibles and become an 'acquired intellect' (*al-'aql al-mustafād*, Lat. *intellectus adeptus*). The acquired intellect is able to perform its activity, thinking, simply by reactivating the intelligible notions that it has progressively stored up. Now, it is a general assumption 'that in virtue of which something carries out its proper activity is the form', and the acquired intellect has become able to think 'in virtue of the agent intellect'; from this it follows that 'the agent intellect be form in us'.[57] In the state of full conjunction, in other words, the human intellect is joined to the agent intellect as its final form. Furthermore, this intellect is able to know not only the intelligibles but also itself, which is formally identical with the agent intellect. Thus, man will be capable of knowing the separate substances in addition to the world of experience. For the agent intellect, which is known by the conjoined intellect through an act of self-intellection, is itself a separate substance, and through it the other separate substances can be known.[58]

This doctrine of conjunction allows Averroes to explain the capacity of natural reason for acquiring knowledge of the transcendent through the exercise of philosophy and speculative sciences. In this way the naturalistic stance that is characteristic of Ibn Ṭufayl and to some degree of Ibn Ḥazm is combined with a theory of the soul that may be credited to Ibn Bājja. The study of the soul is a clear example of the vital connection between Averroes and the Andalusian tradition, and, through the latter, with the Greco-Arabic intellectual heritage. It is this fertile dialogue together with the sophistication of its doctrinal elaborations that distinguishes the philosophical culture of the Islamic West and made for its rich afterlife throughout the course of Latin Middle Ages.

NOTES

1. The origin of the word is controversial. The traditional account has been questioned, most influentially, by Halm (1989), who interprets 'al-Andalus' as an Arabised form of the Gothic toponym *landahlauts* (lit. 'lot land'). My warmest thanks to Peter Adamson, John Marenbon, and Richard C. Taylor for their precious feedback and advice. I am solely responsible for any mistake.

2. *Metaphysics* Z 17, 1041 b 11–33.

3. Ibn Gabirol (1987), 264 (modified). Latin text in Ibn Gabirol (1895, 295:3–6).

4. Particularly representative are the doctrines on material intellect and movement in the void, which Ibn Rushd initially, in his *Short Commentaries*, respectively, on the *De anima* and the *Physics*, assumed from Ibn Bājja and later rejected.

5. As already noticed by Ibn Ṭufayl (2009, 99). Arabic text in Ibn Ṭufayl (1936, 13).

6. This classification is proposed by Jamāl al-Dīn al-'Alawī in Ibn Bājja (1983a, 156–66). The two initial phases are represented, respectively, by Ibn Bājja's *Ta'alīq* ('Annotations') on al-Fārābī's commentaries on the *Organon*; and several commentaries on Aristotle's works including the *Physics*, the *Metereology, On Generation and Corruption, On the Soul,* the so-called *Book of Animals* and the pseudo-Aristotelian treatise *On Plants.*

7. On the import of Ibn Bājja's physics, see Lettinck (1994); Moody (1951); Pines (1964); Puig Montada (1993).

8. Ibn Bājja (1983b, 103–5); *Fī al-ṣūra al-ūlā wa-al-madda al-ūlā.* Spanish translation in Ibn Bājja (2003).

9. Ibn Bājja's psychology was probably expounded in a lost section of his commentary on the *De anima*, and it is now largely reconstructed through Averroes's critiques. See Altmann (1965); Wirmer (2006).

10. Ibn Bājja (1942, 13); *R. Ittiṣāl.* Spanish trans. (ibid., 30). The *Risāla Ittiṣāl* has been published recently, together with the *Tadbīr al-mutawaḥḥid* and the *Risāla al-Wadāʿ,* in Ibn Bājja (2010). I was not able to get hold of this new edition while I was writing the present chapter.

11. Ibn Bājja (1943, 38–39); *R. al-Wadāʿ.* Spanish trans. (ibid., 84).

12. *De anima* Γ 4, 429 b 30–430 a 5; Γ 7, 431 b 17. Black (1999a) shows that this principle is also crucial to Averroes's theory of conjunction.

13. See Ibn Bājja (1942, 21). English translation in Altmann (1965, 79): 'This [ultimate stage of the intellect], and it alone, is *one* in every respect, imperishable and incorruptible. At it alone all those who went before and those who will come after are numerically one'.

14. For the Neoplatonic aspects and mystical tinge of Ibn Bājja's account, see Altmann (1965) and Ibn Bājja (1997, 52–55). In essence Ibn Bājja's position is incompatible with the anti-intellectualistic stance of Islamic mysticism as described by Ibn Bājja (1946, 27). Spanish translation (ibid., 59).

15. Ibn Ṭufayl (2009, 103). Arabic text in Ibn Ṭufayl (1936, 20). On the sources of the novel see A.-M. Goichon (1986).

16. Ibn Ṭufayl (2009, 140). Arabic text in Ibn Ṭufayl (1936, 101). Cp. Ibn Ṭufayl (2009, 139–40, 124). Arabic text in Ibn Ṭufayl (1936, 100, 66).

17. Ibn Ṭufayl (1671).

18. Ibn Ṭufayl (2009, 156). Arabic text in Ibn Ṭufayl (1936, 136).

19. Ibn Ṭufayl (2009, 128–29, 162). Arabic text in Ibn Ṭufayl (1936, 75–78, 148).

20. Ibn Ṭufayl (2009, 163). Arabic text in Ibn Ṭufayl (1936, 150).

21. Kukkonen (2008). See also Kukkonen (2009).

22. Ibn Ṭufayl (2009, 142). Arabic text in Ibn Ṭufayl (1936, 107).

23. Ibn Ṭufayl (2009, 95–103, 148–55). Arabic text in Ibn Ṭufayl (1936, 4–20, 120–34).

24. Ibn Ṭufayl (2009, 96). Arabic text in Ibn Ṭufayl (1936, 5–6).

25. Ibn Ṭufayl (2009, 98). Arabic text in Ibn Ṭufayl (1936, 9).

26. Ibn Ṭufayl (2009, 102). Arabic text in Ibn Ṭufayl (1936, 18).

27. Gutas (1994).

28. Fletcher (1997, 192).

29. Montgomery Watt (1964, 48). The doctrine of Ibn Tūmart is expounded in his *ʿAqīda* ('Creed') and in the two *Murshidas* ('Spiritual Guides') that summarise the teachings in the *ʿAqīda.* First edition of the Arabic text in Ibn Tūmart (1903; for further notice on manuscripts and other editions, see Griffel 2005, 766–70). French translation in Ibn Tūmart (1928); partial English translation in Fletcher (1997).

30. On the relationship between Almohadism and religious conservativism in al-Andalus, see Fierro (1999); Urvoy (1992).

31. Before 1169 Averroes composed the first of the three categories of Aristotelian commentaries that constitute the main body of his philosophical work. These are generally referred to as *Short, Middle* and *Long Commentaries.* After the *Short Commentaries,* Averroes around 1169 started the *Middle Commentaries* and finally around 1182 the *Long Commentaries.* For some complications on this chronology and the *status quaestionis,* see Averroes (2009, xv–xvii, xxviii–xxxiii).

32. Fierro (1999); Urvoy (1992).

33. Averroes (2001b, 9). The source of this famous dictum has been identified with Aristotle's *Prior Analytics*, I, 32, 47 a 8-9 by Taylor (2000). For Averroes, apparently, the unity of truth is itself a philosophical, not religious, doctrine.

34. Averroes (2001a, 48–49). Arabic text in Ibn Rushd (1964, 163).

35. Averroes (2001b, 24). The social implications of this view are clarified by Endress (1997, 41): 'Averroès conçoit son projet à long terme: fonder la communauté—religieuse, scientifique, intellectuelle—sur la seule et irréfutable vérité atteinte par ἀπόδειξις, la méthode démonstrative'.

36. Averroes (2001a, 32). Arabic text in Ibn Rushd (1964, 149). Averroes is credited with a commentary on the *'Aqīda* of Ibn Tūmart; moreover, he may be responsible for the form given to the *'Aqīda* at the time when the text was set down, under the Caliph Abū Ya'qūb Yūsuf. See Fletcher (1992, 244, 1997, 190).

37. On the development of Averroes's attitude towards al-Ghazālī, from accommodating to severely critical, see Griffel (2002).

38. Averroes (2009, 1–2). Latin text in Averroes (1953, 3–4). The integral text of Averroes's *Long Commentary* on the *De anima* is preserved in Latin.

39. Averroes (1938–48, vol. 2, 749:1–9). Latin text in Averroes (1562–74, 153vB). Accordingly, the kernel of the *Metaphysics* following the preliminaries in Book B unfolds 'demonstratively' (*min qibal al-burhān*): '[Aristotle] thought that the best didactic procedure was to devote a special inquiry to the problems of this science and their investigation together with the dialectical arguments that raise doubts concerning each one of its aims in a separate book. Then, in the remaining books of this treatise, he sets out to solve the problems arising in this science' (Averroes 1938–48, vol. 3, 1398:11–15. Eng. trans. in Ibn Rushd 1986, 61. Latin text in Averroes 1562–74, 287v); for 'the perfect way in which the science of a thing occurs, I mean the demonstrative science, requires that one determine in the first place the opposed arguments concerning that thing and then their solution by means of the demonstration (*min qibal al-burhān*) that is [given] about that thing' (Averroes 1938–48, vol. 1, 166:14–167:1; not in the Latin). The English translations of Averroes's *Long Commentary* on the *Metaphysics* are mine except for the commentary on Book Λ, which is quoted from Ibn Rushd (1986). On the Averroean 'logicisation' of Aristotle's physics and metaphysics, see Elamrani-Jamal (2000) (on physics) and Di Giovanni (2009) (on metaphysics).

40. Averroes (1938–48, vol. 2, 749:6–9): 'Now, when [the logical premises] are employed in this science, they are something close to the appropriate premises, because this discipline [i.e., metaphysics] studies absolute being (*al-mawjūd al-muṭlaq*) and it is for absolute being that the logical premises, such as definitions, descriptions and so on, are laid down'. Cp. Averroes (2010, 21–22): 'Furthermore, it has been mentioned in the *Book of Demonstration* that there are two sorts of theoretical disciplines: universal and departmental. Universal [disciplines] are those which take into consideration being as such (*al-mawjūd bi-iṭlāq*) and its essential concomitants. There are three such [disciplines]: dialectic, sophistics, and this science [of metaphysics]. The departmental [disciplines], on the other hand, take into consideration being in a certain disposition'.

41. See Di Giovanni (2011a).

42. Averroes (1938–48, vol. 1, 306:16–17). Latin text in Averroes (1562–74, 65vB).

43. A similar view on the relationship between mental and extra-mental being is credited to Avicenna by Black (1999b).

44. Thomas Aquinas (1961, vol. 2, 556). Latin text in Thomas Aquinas (1950, 358; *In Metaphysicorum*, Lib. VII, l. 9, n. 1467).

45. See Di Giovanni (2011b); Maurer (1951). The identity of form and essence, or quiddity, is stated in Averroes (1938–48, vol. 2, 834:9) (Latin text in Averroes 1562–74, 171rB): 'If there were a definition for every name, there would be a definition for the quiddity of the thing, I mean its form'; ibid., 836:11–13 (Latin text in Averroes 1562–74, 171vA): 'The quiddity of man in one sense is man and in another sense is not man. It is the form of man and not the man composed of form and matter'. For the composition of forms in terms of layers that are referred to as generic and specific forms, see ibid. (953:13–14) (Latin text in Averroes 1562–74, 196rA): 'There is no difference between genus and differentia for [Aristotle] except that the genus is for him a generic form (*ṣūra 'āmma*) and the differentia a specific form (*ṣūra khāṣṣa*)'; (ibid., 919:16–17) (Latin text in Averroes 1562–74, 189rA): 'Definition is of the universal entity and of the form, that is of the generic form and of the specific one (*li-al-ṣūra al-'āmma wa-al-khāṣṣa*), not of the entity composed of matter and form'.

46. Averroes (1938–48, vol. 3, 1520:12–13). English translation in Ibn Rushd (1986, 119) slightly modified. Latin text in Averroes (1562–74, 308rA).

47. Averroes (1938–48, vol. 1, 97:18–20). Latin text in Averroes (1562–74, 14vB).

48. Averroes (1938–48, vol. 3, 1685:4–5). English translation in Ibn Rushd (1986, 187). Latin text in Averroes (1562–74, 333vA).

49. Averroes (1938–48, vol. 2, 933:4). Latin text in Averroes (1562–74, 191vB).

50. Averroes (2009, 302). Latin text in Averroes (1953, 385–86).

51. On material intellect as a fourth kind of being, see Averroes (2009, 326); Latin text in Averroes (1953, 409). The connection between individuation by matter and the unity of intellect appears in Averroes (2009, 317–20). Latin text in Averroes (1953, 401–6). See also below, Chapter 9, pp. 212–13, and Chapter 10, pp. 231–32.

52. Averroes (2009, 315–17). Latin text in Averroes (1953, 399–402).

53. The chronology of Averroes's commentaries on the *De anima* is highly controversial. In several studies Alfred Ivry has argued that the *Long Commentary* dates prior to, not later than, the *Middle Commentary* based on various passages in the *Middle Commentary* that appear to be literal borrowings from the *Long Commentary* and are hardly intelligible without the latter. On the other hand, scholars generally agree that the doctrine expounded in the *Long Commentary* represents a refinement and, naturally enough, a later development of the doctrine contained in the *Middle Commentary*. To date the dominant opinion is that an earlier version of the *Long Commentary* may have been executed, though not also published, prior to the composition of the *Middle Commentary*, whereas a final version of the *Long Commentary* characterised by textual insertions with major doctrinal innovations was completed after the *Middle Commentary* and formed the basis of Michael Scot's Arabic-Latin translation. The most recent and compact presentation of Averroes's psychology and related issues is Averroes (2009, xv–cix). See also Ivry (1995) and the reply by Herbert A. Davidson (1997). On Averroean treatises of noetics other than Averroes's commentaries on the *De anima*, see Geoffroy and Steel (2001).

54. Averroes (2009, 321). See also ibid. (314–15).

55. A transitional phase between the middle and the final positions is represented by Averroes's *Chapter on the Conjunction of the Separate Intellect with Man*. This is characterised by an inchoate anticipation of the thesis of the unity of material intellect. See Averroes (2009, xlii–xlix).

56. See Black (1999a); Geoffroy (2007); Ivry (2007); Taylor (2009).

57. Averroes (2009, 399). Latin text in Averroes (1953, 499–500).

58. Averroes (2009, 327–28). Latin text in Averroes (1953, 410–11). Averroes (2009, 387). Latin text in Averroes (1953, 485).

BIBLIOGRAPHY

Altmann, Alexander. 1965. 'Ibn Bājja on man's ultimate felicity'. In *Harry Austryn Wolfson Jubilee Volume*, English Section, vol. 1, 47–87. Jerusalem: American Academy for Jewish Research.

Aristotle. 1997. *Metaphysics*, ed. William D. Ross. 2 vols. Oxford: Clarendon Press.

Averroes. 1562–1574. *Aristotelis Metaphysicorum libri XIIII cum Averrois Cordubensis in eosdem Commentariis et Epitome*. Vol. 8 of *Aristotelis Opera cum Averrois Commentariis*. 11 vols. Venetiis apud Junctas.

———. 1938–48. *Tafsīr Mā baʿd aṭ-ṭabīʿa*, ed. Maurice Bouyges. 3 vols. Beyrouth, Lebanon: Imprimerie Catholique (Bibliotheca Arabica Scholasticorum, Série Arabe).

———. 1953. *Commentarium magnum in Aristotelis De anima libros*, ed. F. Stuart Crawford. Cambridge, MA: The Medieval Academy of America (Corpus Commentariorum Averrois in Aristotelem).

———. 2001a. *Faith and Reason. Averroes' Exposition of Religious Arguments*, trans. Ibrahim Y. Najjar. Oxford: Oneworld Publications.

———. 2001b. *The Book of the Decisive Treatise Determining the Connection Between the Law and Wisdom & Epistle Dedicatory*, trans. Charles E. Butterworth. Provo, UT: Brigham Young University Press.

——— (Ibn Rushd) of Cordoba. 2009. *Long Commentary on the De Anima of Aristotle*, trans. Richard C. Taylor. New Haven, CT, and London: Yale University Press.

———. 2010. *On Aristotle's 'Metaphysics'*, trans. Rüdiger Arnzen. Berlin and New York: De Gruyter.

Black, Deborah. 1999a. Conjunction and the Identity of Knower and Known in Averroes. *American Catholic Philosophical Quarterly* 73:159–84.

———. 1999b. Mental Existence in Thomas Aquinas and Avicenna. *Medieval Studies* 61:45–79.

Davidson, Herbert A. 1997. The Relationship Between Averroes' Middle and Long Commentaries on the *De Anima*. *Arabic Sciences and Philosophy* 7:139–51.

Di Giovanni, Matteo. 2009. Demonstration and First Philosophy. Averroes on Met. Zeta as a Demonstrative Examination (al-faḥs al-burhānī). *Documenti e studi sulla tradizione filosofica medievale* 20:95–125.

———. 2011a. 'Averroes and the logical status of metaphysics'. In *Methods and Methodologies. Aristotelian Logic East and West, 500–1500*, ed. Margaret Cameron and John Marenbon, 53–74. Leiden, the Netherlands, and Boston: E.J. Brill.

———. 2011b. 'Substantial form in Averroes's Long Commentary on the Metaphysics'. In *In the Age of Averroes: Arabic Philosophy in the 6th/12th Century*, ed. Peter Adamson, 175–94. Warburg Institute Colloquia. London: Warburg Institute.

Elamrani-Jamal, Abdelali. 2000. La démonstration du signe (burhān al-dalīl) selon Ibn Rushd (Averroès). *Documenti e studi sulla tradizione filosofica medievale* 11:113–31.

Endress, Gerhard. 1997. L'Aristote arabe. Réception, autorité et transformation du premier Maître. *Medioevo. Rivista di storia della filosofia medievale* 23:3–42.

Fierro, Maribel. 1999. The Legal Policies of the Almohad Caliphs and Ibn Rushd's Bidāyat al-Mujtahid. *Journal of Islamic Studies* 10(3):226–48.

Fletcher, Madeleine. 1992. 'Al-Andalus and North Africa in the Almohad ideology'. In *The Legacy of Muslim Spain*, ed. Salma Khadra Jayyusi, 235–58. Leiden, the Netherlands, New York and Cologne, Germany: E.J. Brill.

———. 1997. 'The Almohad creed (1183)'. In *Medieval Iberia. Readings from Christian, Muslim, and Jewish Sources*, ed. Olivia Remie Constable, 190–97. Philadelphia: University of Pennsylvania Press.

Geoffroy, Marc. 2007. 'Averroès sur l'intellect comme cause agente et cause formelle et la question de la "Jonction"'. In *Averroès et les Averroïsmes juif et latin. Acted du colloque international (Paris, 16–18 juin 2005)*, ed. Jean-Baptiste Brenet, 77–110. Turnhout, Belgium: Brepols.

Geoffroy, Marc and Carlos Steel, eds. 2001. *La Béatitude de l'âme. Editions, traductions annotées, études doctrinales et historiques d'un traité d' Averroès*. Paris: Librarie Philsophique J. Vrin.

Goichon, Anne-Marie. 1986. 'Ḥayy b. Yaqẓān'. In *Encyclopaedia of Islam, Second Edition*, ed. B. Lewis, V. L. Ménage, C. Pellat and J. Schacht, vol. 3, 330–34. Leiden, the Netherlands and London: E.J. Brill-Luzac & Co.

Griffel, Frank. 2002. 'The relationship between Averroes and al-Ghazālī as it presents itself in Averroes' early writings, especially in his commentary on al-Ghazālī's al-Mustaṣfā'. In *Medieval Philosophy and the Classical Tradition in Islam, Judaism, and Christianity*, ed. John Inglis, 51–63. Richmond, UK: Curzon.

———. 2005. 'Ibn Tūmart's rational proof for God's existence and unity, and his connection to the Niẓāmiyya Madrasa in Baghdad'. In *Los Almohades: Problemas y perspectivas*, ed. Patrice Cressier, Maribel Fierro and Luis Molina. 2 vols, vol. 2, 753–813. Madrid: Consejo Superior de Investigaciones Científicas.

Gutas, Dimitri. 1994. Ibn Ṭufayl on Ibn Sīnā's Eastern Philosophy. *Oriens* 34:222–41.

Halm, Heinz. 1989. Al-Andalus und Gothica Sors. *Islam*, 66:252–63.

Ibn Bājja. 1942. *Tratado de Avempace sobre la unión del intelecto con el hombre*, ed. and trans. Miguel Asín Palacios. *Al-Andalus* 7(1):1–47.

———. 1943. *La «Carta de Adiós» de Avempace*, ed. and trans. Miguel Asín Palacios. *Al-Andalus* 8(1):1–87.

———. 1946. *El regimen del solitario*, ed. and trans. Miguel Asín Palacios. Madrid and Granada: Imprentas de la Escuela de Estudios Árabes de Granada y Francisco Román Camacho.

———. 1983a. *Mu'allafāt Ibn Bājja*, ed. Jamāl al-Dīn al-'Alawī. Beirut and Casablanca: Dār al-thaqāfa, Dār al-nashr al-maghribiyya.

———. 1983b. *Rasā'il falsafiyya li-Abī Bakr ibn Bājja. Nuṣūṣ falsafiyya ġayr manšūra*, ed. Jamāl al-Dīn al-'Alawī. Beirut and Casablanca: Dār al-thaqāfa, Dār al-nashr al-maghribiyya.

———. 1997. *El regimen del solitario [Tadbīr al-mutawaḥḥid]*, trans. Joaquín Lomba. Madrid: Editorial Trotta.

———. 2003. *Sobre la forma primera y la materia primera*, trans. Charif Dandachli Zohbi-Pilar Zaldívar Bouthelier. *Revista Española de Filosofía Medieval* 10:107–10.

Ibn Bājja (Avempace). 2010. *La conduite de l'isolé et deux autres épîtres*. Introduction, édition critique du texte arabe, traduction et commentaire par Charles Genequand. Paris: J. Vrin.

Ibn Gabirol. 1895. *Fons vitae*, ed. Clemens Baeumker. Münster, Germany: Aschendorff (Beiträge zur Geschichte der Philosophie und Theologie des Mittelalters, 1/2–4).

———. 1987. *The Fountain of Life (Fons Vitae) by Solomon Ben Judah Ibn Gabirol (Avicebron)*, trans. Alfred B. Jacob. Stanwood, WA: Sabian Publishing Society.

Ibn Rushd. 1964. *Kashf 'an manāhij al-adilla fī 'aqā id al-milla*, ed. Maḥtmūd Qāsim. Cairo: Maktaba al-Anjilū al-Miṣriyya.

———. 1986. *Ibn Rushd's Metaphysics. A Translation with Introduction of Ibn Rushd's Commentary on Aristotle's Metaphysics, Book Lām*, trans. Charles Genequand. Leiden, the Netherlands: E.J. Brill.

Ibn Ṭufayl. 1671. *Philosophus autodidactus, sive Epistola Abi Jaafar Ebn Tophail de Hai Ebn Yoqdhan, in qua ostenditur quomodo ex Inferiorum contemplatione ad Superiorum notitiam Ratio humana ascendere possit*, trans. Edward Pocock. Oxford: H. Hall.

———. 1936. *Hayy Ben Yaqdhān. Roman philosophique d'Ibn Thofaïl*, ed. Léon Gauthier. Beirut, Lebanon: Imprimerie Catholique.

———. 2009. *Hayy Ibn Yaqzān. A Philosophical Tale*, trans. Lenn E. Goodman. Chicago: University of Chicago Press.

Ibn Tūmart. 1903. *Le livre de Mohammed Ibn Toumert Mahdi des Almohades. Texte arabe accompagné de notices biographiques et d'une introduction par I. Goldziher*, ed. Jean Dominique Luciani. Alger: Imprimerie Orientale Pierre Fontana.

———. 1928. 'La profession de foi ('aqīda) et les guides spirituels (morchida) du Mahdi Ibn Toumart', trans. Henri Massé. In *Mémorial Henri Basset. Nouvelles etudes nord-africaine et orientales publiées par l'institut des hautes-études marocaines*. 2 vols, vol. 2, 105–21. Paris: Librarie Orientaliste Paul Geuthner.

Ivry, Alfred L. 1995. Averroes' Middle and Long Commentaries on the De Anima. *Arabic Sciences and Philosophy* 5:75–92.

———. 2007. 'Conjunction in and of Maimonides and Averroes'. In *Averroès et les Averroïsmes juif et latin. Actes du colloque international (Paris, 16–18 juin 2005)*, ed. Jean-Baptiste Brenet, 231–47. Turnhout, Belgium: Brepols.

Kukkonen, Taneli. 2008. No Man Is an Island: Nature and Neo-Platonic Ethics in Ḥayy Ibn Yaqzān. *Journal of the History of Philosophy* 46(2):187–204.

———. 2009. 'Ibn Ṭufayl and the wisdom of the East: On apprehending the divine'. In *Late Antique Epistemology. Other Ways to Truth*, ed. Panayiota Vassilopoulou and Stephen R. L. Clark, 87–102. New York: Palgrave Macmillan.

Lettinck, Paul. 1994. *Aristotle's Physics and Its Reception in the Arabic World. With an Edition of the Unpublished Parts of Ibn Bāǧǧa's Commentary on the Physics*. Leiden, the Netherlands, New York and Cologne, Germany: E.J. Brill.

Maurer, Armand. 1951. Form and Essence in the Philosophy of St. Thomas. *Mediaeval Studies* 13:165–76.

Montada, Josep Puig. 1993. Un aspecto de la influencia de Avempace en Averroes. *Anaquel de Estudios Árabes* 4:149–59.

Montgomery Watt, William. 1964. Philosophy and Social Structure in Almohad Spain. *The Islamic Quarterly. A Review of Islamic Culture* 8(1–2): 46–51.

Moody, Ernest A. 1951. Galileo and Avempace. The Dynamics of the Leaning Tower Experiment. *Journal of the History of Ideas* 12:163–93, 375–422.

Pines, Shlomo. 1964. La dynamique d'Ibn Bajja. In *Mélanges Alexandre Koyré: L'Aventure de la science*, 442–68. Paris: Hermann.

Taylor, Richard C. 2000. "Truth Does Not Contradict Truth". Averroes and the Unity of Truth. *Topoi* 19:3-16.

———. 2009. 'Intellect as intrinsic formal cause in the soul according to Aquinas and Averroes'. In *The Afterlife of the Platonic Soul. Reflections on Platonic Psychology in the Monotheistic Religions*, ed. Maha El-Kaisy Friemut and John M. Dillon, 187–220. Leiden, the Netherlands: E.J. Brill.

Thomas Aquinas. 1950. *In duodecim libros Metaphysicorum Aristotelis expositio*, ed. M. R. Cathala-Raimondo Spiazzi. Turin and Rome: Marietti.

————. 1961. *Commentary on the Metaphysics of Aristotle*, trans. John P. Rowan. 2 vols. Chicago: H. Regnery Co.

Urvoy, Dominique. 1992. 'The 'Ulamā' of al-Andalus'. In *The Legacy of Muslim Spain*, ed. Salma Khadra Jayyusi, 849–77. Leiden, the Netherlands, New York and Cologne, Germany: E.J. Brill.

Wirmer, David. 2006. 'Avempace—'ratio de quiditate'. Thomas Aquinas's Critique of an Argument for the Natural Knowability of Separate Substances'. In *Wissen über Grenzen. Arabisches Wissen und lateinisches Mittelalter*, ed. Andreas Speer and Lydia Wegener, 569–590. Berlin and New York 2006: De Gruyter (Miscellanea Mediaevalia 33).

CHAPTER 6

MEDIEVAL JEWISH PHILOSOPHY IN ARABIC

CHARLES MANEKIN

1. Introduction: Context and Historiography

In his *Exposition of the Generations of Nations*, the Muslim historian of science Ṣā'id al-Andalusī wrote:

> The eighth nation [to have cultivated science] is Banū Israel. They were not known for their interest in philosophy, as they were occupied in the study of law and the biographies of prophets . . . Among the Jewish scholars, there were a few who showed some interest in certain branches of philosophy. . . . (Al-Andalusī 1991, 79–81)

Although Ṣā'id made this comment in the mid–eleventh century, it is a fairly accurate characterisation of Jewish intellectual activity in the world of Islam. Science and philosophy constituted a small part of that activity, albeit a significant one. Just how significant is difficult to say, for not everyone who pursued science and philosophy composed books, and not all books survived—and some that did survive have not yet been properly identified, much less studied. Jewish savants, unlike their Christian and Muslim counterparts, could not count on institutional support or governmental patronage. Many were physicians, and some were literary figures who were supported by private patrons. Still, although the Jewish savants who actually composed books that are extant today number only a few dozen, we find them wherever we find Jewish centres of learning, especially in the towns of al-Andalus, Northern Africa, Iraq and Yemen.

Nineteenth-century scholars of Jewish philosophy initially focused their attention on works of this tradition that were extant in European Hebrew and Latin translations. That focus was broadened in the nineteenth century as Jewish orientalists like Solomon Munk, Moritz Steinschneider and Adolph Neubauer began examining and cataloguing manuscripts written in Judeo-Arabic (a form of post-classical Arabic prevalent among the Jews, written in Hebrew characters). Still, in the standard histories of Jewish philosophy before Sirat (1985) the common historiographical premise was that Jewish philosophy in Arabic began in the ninth century with the Jewish Kalām, continued in the tenth and eleventh centuries with Jewish Neoplatonism and more or less peaked in the twelfth century with the Jewish Aristotelian philosopher, Moses Maimonides—at which point the torch of enlightenment was transmitted to the Jewish intellectuals of Christian Europe (Munk 1859; Guttmann 1964; Husik 1916). That premise paralleled the assumption that Arabic philosophy began with the Neoplatonic circle of al-Kindī (some, like Boer, began with Kalām), continued with the Neoplatonised Aristotelianism of Al-Fārābī and Avicenna and reached its peak in the twelfth century with Averroes, after which it survived in Europe and declined in the world of Islam. Both assumptions were aided by the preliminary state of scholarly research of Arabic and Judeo-Arabic manuscripts, where many works had not yet been identified, much less studied.

Around a decade ago, Dimitri Gutas sketched a new outline of Arabic philosophy and classification of Arabic philosophers from the ninth to the eighteenth centuries (Gutas 2002).[1] Gutas divided Arabic philosophers into pre-and post-Avicennian, and, significantly for our purposes, he included within his new classification six Arabic-writing Jewish philosophers, including two whose writings were unknown in medieval Europe.[2] In this chapter I have commented on his characterisations of the Jewish philosophers and suggested where other Jewish philosophers may be placed according to his scheme. At the very least, the new classification underscores not only that Jewish philosophers continued to write in the world of Islam after the twelfth century but also that they were cognizant of the ongoing developments in Arabic philosophy. As more texts of medieval Arabic philosophy are identified and studied, our picture of Jewish philosophy written in Arabic will continue to be modified.

This chapter, then, covers some of the prominent philosophers who wrote in Judeo-Arabic or Arabic, and who were Jewish, at least for a considerable part of their lives.[3] Unlike most of their counterparts in Christian lands, who were either ignorant of Latin or had little access to Latin texts, Jewish intellectuals under Muslim rule were familiar with Arabic culture and read Arabic works in Arabic characters, and, occasionally, Hebrew characters (Langermann 1996a). This meant that, again unlike their European coreligionists, Jewish intellectuals felt no need to create a separate corpus of philosophical and scientific texts translated from another language. Still, those intellectuals, when they chose to write in Judeo-Arabic, wrote for a minority group with its own cultural codes, tradition, and autonomy, and hence appropriated and occasionally modified the external philosophical material.

2. Jews and the 'Arabic Plotinus' in North Africa and al-Andalus

The first Arabic-writing philosopher among the Jews—if by 'philosopher' we mean an adherent of the Greek tradition of philosophy—was Isaac Israeli (c. 855–955). Israeli was best known in the Middle Ages for his medical treatises, but his philosophical treatises were also translated into Hebrew and Latin and widely cited. His main philosophical sources derive, perhaps entirely, from the writings composed by the Baghdad circle of al-Kindī, who, in addition to composing his own works, commissioned adaptations of the main tenets of Greek philosophy. This circle was responsible inter alia for creating the main texts of the 'Arabic Plotinus', such as the *Theology of Aristotle* (a free adaptation of parts of books IV–VI of Plotinus's *Enneads*), the *Book of Pure Good* (the *Liber de Causis* of the West) and minor texts such as the *Book of the Five Chapters of the Pseudo-Empedocles* (see Adamson 2002). The al-Kindī circle was known for its near strict adherent to Hellenism against the commitments of the Muslim theologians (mutakallimūn), whom the philosophers tended to belittle. Isaac shows some evidence of Kalām in his writings, but from an anecdote of his student, Dūnaš b. Tāmīm, it may be inferred that he didn't think much of the philosophical calibre of his contemporary Saʿadia Gaon, a Jewish mutakallim, who also appears to have been influenced by some concepts of the philosophers (Dūnaš ben Tāmīm 2002, 39).[4]

Isaac's philosophy is expounded in a handful of treatises that are collections and compilations of material mostly from the al-Kindī circle texts. There is little that is identifiably 'Jewish' in these works, although Isaac appears to have written at least one work of philosophical scriptural exegesis, and another work uses verses from scriptures as prooftexts. As for his system, it is thoroughly Neoplatonist, with religious modifications that he either inherited from the al-Kindī circle, or that he himself added. God is the Creator, the cause of causes, who acts perpetually out of goodness and love, through power and will. Israeli distinguishes between 'origination', 'creation' and 'generation.' Origination is the act of making existing things exist from the non-existent; creation is the bringing into being existences from the existing; generation is the passing of corporeal substances from privation to existence (Israeli 1958a, §§ 41–44, 66–67). Only God originates, and only the 'spherical power' or 'nature' causes the cycle of corporeal generation and corruption in the sub-lunary world, so 'creation' refers to the mediated process of emanation that God's activity originates with the origination of the first two substances, First Matter and First Form. Although God's activity is eternal, the world has a beginning, for it can only pass from potentiality to actuality at the time when it does pass (Israeli 1958c, frag. II, p. 82), due to God's power and will. The phrase 'power and will,' which appears in the Arabic Plotinus, should not be given an interpretation of the sort that we shall find in Maimonides, that is, the ability to will or not to will (*Guide* II, 18, 301, in Maimonides 1963). There is no evidence in Isaac's writing that the world is the non-necessary product of a freely choosing deity.[5]

There are some distinctive features of Isaac's account of the 'descent from the Creator' that differ from the extant works of the al-Kindī circle. The first substance that is created by God without mediation is not First Intellect but First Matter, which, together with another substance, First Form, produces First Intellect. Isaac's interposition of First Matter and First Form between the Creator and Intellect may be due to Isaac's interpretation of a passage in the *Long Version* of the *Theology of Aristotle*, popular in Jewish circles (Fenton 1986), in which First Intellect is said to combine two aspects, a 'material' substratum and a formal principle (Zimmermann 1986, 193).[6] First Intellect in the *Long Version* is said to unite with the divine Word in bringing forth other beings, but Isaac, perhaps because of Jewish scruples, omits mention of the divine Word. A doctrine that appears both in Isaac and in the *Long Version* is the tripartite division of the Soul that emanates from Intellect into rational, animal and vegetative, mirroring the souls in the sub-lunar world. The last of the 'simple substances' is the Sphere or Nature, which though corporeal, is sufficiently different from sub-lunar bodies to warrant its inclusion within the supernal realm. The motion of the sphere causes the four sub-lunar elements to come into being and regulates the cycle of generation and corruption. United with the sphere is the Soul, and through this union it is joined to the bodies and acts upon them.

Although the second half of the Neoplatonic journey, the return trip of the soul to its source, is not described in much detail by Isaac, the gist is clear. Once the rational soul is separated from the 'husks and darkness' of its lower desires, it receives 'light and splendor from Intellect, which informs it of properties, and forms, and spiritual things' and instructs it concerning the soul's virtues and its spiritual forms. Such a soul will be able to interpret dreams correctly by disengaging the spiritual forms from its corporeal husks. After illumination comes the final stage, which is conjunction or union, not with God, but with Intellect (Israeli 1958c, cf. Altmann and Stern, 1958, 188–89).

The writings of the al-Kindī circle had an impact on the *Long Version* of the *Theology of Aristotle*, Isaac Israeli's writings[7] and the tenth-century *Encyclopedia of the Sincere Brethren of Piety*, and these in turn had a decisive impact on Jewish philosophy until the early twelfth century. In al-Andalus, moralists like Baḥya Ibn Pakuda, a poet-exegete like Moses Ibn Ezra and jurists like Joseph Ibn Ṣaddik expounded doctrines closely related to those of the al-Kindī circle. Unquestionably the greatest philosophical product of Arabic Neoplatonism was Solomon Ibn Gabirol, the poet-philosopher who was known to the Latin West as Avicebron. Unlike Israeli, who was content to make relatively small modifications to the doctrines he found, Ibn Gabirol created out of those materials an original system whose claims he defended tirelessly with proofs and arguments—a practice that was mocked a century later by the Jewish Aristotelian, Abraham Ibn Daud (Ibn Daud 1852, Introduction, 2–3). Ibn Gabirol was fond of logic, according to Ṣāʿid Andalusī (Al-Andalusī 1991, 81), and that fondness is on display in his philosophical masterpiece, *The Source of Life*.

According to Ibn Gabirol, since things exist, there must be a cause for their existence, and a mediator between cause and effect. So reality is reducible to three fundamental principles: First Essence (cause), divine will (mediator) and matter and form (effect) (I, 7). The highest knowledge is knowledge of the First Essence, but only its existence, which is described through its activities, can be known (I, 4–5). So the road to knowledge begins not with a 'top-down' deduction of the procession of the hierarchy of being from the First Essence, as in many Neoplatonic schemes, but rather a 'bottom-up' deduction that proceeds from the notion of matter and form in sub-lunar corporeal existence to the limits of what is knowable about First Essence. Not coincidentally, this bottom-up deduction corresponds to the liberation of the soul from nature's prison through self-knowledge (knowledge of one's own soul, since the First Essence encompasses and penetrates all things) and action (the return of the soul in imitation of will, which stands for divine activity) (I, 2; V, 43). Apparently, Ibn Gabirol intended to treat the irreducible elements of reality in a trilogy of books, moving from matter and form, to divine will, and finally to the First Essence. As it is, he only completed the first work, which shows how the soul ascends to the science of universal matter and universal form; other fundamental questions, such as his cosmology, are found in his philosophical poem, the *Kingly Crown* (Ibn Gabirol 2003).

The most famous feature of the *Source of Life* is Ibn Gabirol's universal hylomorphism, the claim that every created substance and accident possesses matter and form, not only corporeal substances, but also incorporeal, simple substances, such as intellect and soul. In fact, the terms 'matter' and 'form,' insofar as they conjure up common associations, are misleading; taken as ontological principles, matter is understood as whatever supports and underlies, and form as whatever specifies and particularises (*Fons Vitae*, I, 10, 13–14, in Ibn Gabirol 1895). Neither is static; due to will, form permeates and penetrates, and matter moves to receive the form out of love and desire for the source of the form, the divine will. (In one account form comes from will and matter from the First Essence (*FV* V, 41, 330); in another, universal matter and universal form are created by God (*FV* II, 13, 47).)

It may be thought that Gabirol's emphasis on the divine will contains an implicit critique of the notion of a necessary emanation associated with pagan Neoplatonism, as does his adherence to creation ex nihilo. But, as we noted with respect to Isaac Israeli, there is no good reason to believe that the Jewish philosophers within the tradition of the al-Kindī circle felt that God's creation of the world was incompatible with God's eternal origination of the world ex nihilo. In this regard, they did not differ from Avicenna, whose doctrines were destined to be well known to Jewish philosophers. Once this compatibilism was subjected to the critiques of al-Ghazālī and Maimonides, both of whom posited a more robust notion of will, comprising the ability to choose otherwise, subsequent Jewish philosophers had at least to respond it. At this point, however, any such incompatibilist scruples were associated with Kalām, whose metaphysical speculations were not highly valued by those within the circle, as was noted above. Thus, although Joseph Ibn Ṣaddiq, for example, insists that the world was not originated *in* time (time does not exist *before* God's creation), he refers his students to the Muslim philosophers for the proper understanding of origination, and to pseudo-Empedocles for the proper explanation of how God wills with his eternal will the origination of the world without a change in his essence (Haberman 2003, 116–18).

3. Jews and the 'Arabic Aristotle' in al-Andalus

As the philosophical doctrines of the Arabic Aristotle spread, they made their mark on the Jewish intellectuals of al-Andalus. (By 'Arabic Aristotle' I mean not only the writings of Aristotle translated into Arabic but also the commentorial and interpretative tradition, of which Al-Fārābī and Avicenna were the outstanding representatives.) Maimonides writes in his *Guide of the Perplexed*,

> As for the Andalusians among the people of our nation, all of them cling to the affirmations of the philosophers (*falāsifa*) and incline to them in so far as these do not ruin a foundation of the religious Law (*Shari'a*). You will not find them in any way taking the paths of the mutakallimūn. (*Guide* I, 71, 177)

Maimonides may be including in this remark the Andalusian Jewish intellectuals influenced by the Arabic Plotinus mentioned above. But more probably he limits it to more Aristotlelian thinkers like Abraham Ibn Daud of Toledo and Joseph b. Judah Ibn Aknin of Fez, whose families, like his, had left al-Andalus as a result of the Almohad conquest in 1148. In any event, the remark points to two important features of Andalusian Jewish philosophy of this period: first, principles of Jewish religion are interpreted to conform with the philosophical doctrines of the Arabic Aristotle, and second, limits are placed on this reinterpretation when there appears to be irresolvable conflict with those principles. Indeed, the very project of placing 'the foundations of religious Law' at the heart of the philosophical enterprise is one of the many similarities between Maimonides and his older contemporary, Ibn Daud. Although there is no evidence directly linking the two, they were both products of a Cordoban education in science and philosophy in the late Almoravid period, and it is hardly surprising that there are many points of contact. This can be seen in their respective treatment of the problem of divine attributes, and in their attempt to naturalise phenomena such as divine providence and prophecy.

The problem of divine attributes in its Andalusian Jewish context is twofold: how to reconcile the unity of God with the ontology of attribution, since the subject–predicate distinction implies multiplicity, and how to interpret true statements about God that appear to predicate essential attributes. (Accidental attributes—properties that God may or may not have—are incompatible with God's immutability.) To a philosopher, Andalusian Jewish thinkers reject the predication of essential attributes of God; for example, they deny that a sentence like 'God is knowing' should be interpreted as predicating an attribute of God. Instead, such sentences should be interpreted negatively, as denying the privation (in this case, 'ignorance') of God. Both Ibn Daud and Maimonides consider negative descriptions of God to be the most correct descriptions (*Emunah Ramah* II.2.3, 51, *Guide* I, 58, 134), and Maimonides goes so far as to say that there is no other way to describe his essence. Both also claim that attributes that imply a relation between God and his creatures do not imply multiplicity in the divine essence, that God is incomparable to his creatures, and that he can be described as cause of the world, which Ibn Daud recognises as an attribute of relation, although Maimonides apparently does not.

Even Maimonides's famous doctrine that the term 'existence' is predicated of God and his creatures with pure equivocation has its precedents and parallels within the Andalusian philosophical tradition. Like Maimonides, Ibn Daud claims that the term 'existent' is not univocal with respect to God and other existing things, that existence is neither an essential attribute, nor is it a genus comprising God and other existing things (*ER* II.2.3, 53). To be sure, he does not claim with Maimonides that 'existent' is purely equivocal with respect to God and other existing things, a claim that was criticised by Aquinas and Gersonides on the grounds that if the term 'existent' has no shared meaning when applied of God and other existents, how can we justify applying it to God? These later philosophers claimed that the term applies to God and other existents analogously (Aquinas), or by primary and posterior signification (Gersonides). But since that sort of signification, although found occasionally in the Arabic Aristotelian tradition, does not appear in the Andalusian Jewish tradition, it is not clear that Ibn Daud and Maimonides were aware of it, much less that they deliberately rejected it. Nor is it clear that pure equivocation, as was understood by the Aristotelians, is incompatible with analogous predication. The Andalusian philosopher Averroes, Maimonides's contemporary, claims both that the term 'knower' is said of God and of other knowers 'with pure equivocation' *and* that 'intellect' is said of God and other intellects 'by primary and posterior signification' (see Druart 1994). Moreover, when Maimonides discusses the signification of 'purely equivocal' terms in non-theological contexts, he does not rule out such terms sharing meaning in some way (see Manekin 2002). So there does not seem to be much difference between Ibn Daud and Maimonides, or for that matter, between both of them and Averroes on this issue.

I have emphasised some of the many points of contact between Ibn Daud and Maimonides not only because the latter is by far better known, but also because Gutas, in his aforementioned outline of Arabic philosophy, labels Ibn Daud a 'mainstream Avicennian' and Maimonides an 'anti-Avicennian Peripatetic'. Yet, while Ibn Daud was indeed greatly influenced by Avicennian arguments and doctrines (Fontaine 1990), his divergences from Avicenna on key doctrines are substantial and, once again, anticipate Maimonides. Thus, while he tends to accept Avicenna's picture of the heavens, he questions the explanation of how the spheres and celestial intellects proceed from the Necessary of Existence: 'We still do not understand how [the philosophers'] statements [concerning the heavens] are demonstrations, in the way that we understand their statements concerning the causes of living and vegetative things. Maybe someone besides us understands this'. By attempting to explain how many things proceed from the Necessary of Existence, the philosophers fell into other absurdities—all because they imagined that humans are capable of knowing everything about reality (*ER* III, 1, 67). Ibn Daud also does not adopt Avicenna's view that God knows future possibles in a universal manner (as instantiations of universal patterns), nor does he embrace the deterministic implications of emanationism. For Avicennians, all particulars are necessitated by virtue of their causes, and this is how God knows them. But for Ibn Daud at least some particulars are possible because God created them as such; they 'just happen to be', and these cannot be known even by God (II, 6.2, 96). Such future possibles are often the project of human choice, which also is not necessitated. Ibn Daud's discussion of choice and possibility falls squarely within the Aristotelian tradition, with all its peculiarities (see Sorabji 1980) and should not be mistaken for a strongly libertarian notion of free will. But it certainly diverges from Avicennism, and his view of God's knowledge of future possibles is not only unprecedented but arguably more libertarian than that of Gersonides, with whose solution it is usually compared.

The view of Maimonides as an 'anti-Avicennian Peripatetic' is no less problematic. For one thing, Maimonides appears to be much less acquainted with Avicennian doctrines than is Ibn Daud; his own version of Avicenna's proof for the existence of God rests on some un-Avicennian premises (Guide II, 1, 247–8; see Davidson, 1987, 378–85), and his critique of emanationism does not rest on peripatetic premises. True, he occasionally arrives at conclusions that are reminiscent of Averroes's peripatetic critique of Avicenna—such as the claim, shared with Averroes, that 'knowing' and 'willing' are said of God and of other knowers with pure equivocation. Maimonides, also like Averroes, tends to eschew Avicennian reconciliations of apparent contradictions between philosophy and religion (e.g., the view of creation as the eternally willed origination of the world, or that God knows particulars in their universal aspect). But his criticism of these Avicennian doctrines palls besides his criticism of peripatetic doctrines when they are seen by him to conflict with the foundations of the Torah.

Where Maimonides diverges most from the Arabic Aristotelians, including Ibn Daud, is in his emphasis on creation as a product of a Divine will that could have been other than it was. Thus, he explicitly rejects the compatibilist move of the 'latter day philosophers' to give emanation a voluntarist spin, while retaining its necessitarianism. 'These people have altered the word "necessity", but have let its meaning remain' (*Guide* II, 21, 314–15). But more than that, he explicitly rejects the Aristotelian commitment to an eternal world and invariant nature because it implies the 'disgraceful consequence . . . that the deity, whom everyone who is intelligent recognises to be perfect in every kind of perfection could as far as all the beings are concerned produce nothing new in them; if He wished to lengthen a fly's wing or to shorten a worm's foot, He would not be able to do it' (*Guide* II: 22, 319; cf. II, 19, 302; II, 22, 320). At times Maimonides appeals to the words of Aristotle and his commentators to criticise the more recent Arabic Peripatetics like Al-Fārābī, as when he praises Aristotle for having conceded that he lacks a demonstration for the eternity of the world or when he cites Alexander of Aphrodisias, who holds that in cases where demonstration is not possible, one chooses the opinion that is the 'best and fittest to be regarded as sound of all opinions about God Most High'. The Arabic Peripatetics themselves argued for the eternity of the world by appealing to the disgraceful implications for divine action where the world originated at a certain time; Maimonides, citing Aristotle and Alexander, repays them in their own coin.

To argue for a more robust notion of divine will and purpose, one in which God can will to create the world differently from the way it is, or not to create it at all, Maimonides argues that certain celestial phenomena are best explained as the result of divine 'particularisation', rather than natural necessity, as posited by the Arabic Peripatetics. To do this he raises doubts as to the adequacy of Aristotle's explanations, although like Ibn Daud, he accepts the Aristotelian picture of the heavens and their movements (including the view that the celestial orbs are living, and that they are moved by incorporeal intelligences); indeed, he holds that much of this picture has been demonstrated. Once one has allowed for celestial phenomena that defy Aristotelian explanation, but are better attributed to God's will, 'consequent upon His wisdom', all of creation is indicative of divine purpose, including the sub-lunar phenomena that occur because of a fathomable nature. In the sub-lunar realm, Aristotle's explanations are convincing and adequate.

Maimonides applies a robust notion of divine will and purpose to other doctrines, notably prophecy and miracles. Prophecy consists of an overflow of intelligence from God, through the intermediation of the Active Intellect, towards first the intellect and then the imagination (*Guide* II, 36, 369). According to the *falāsifa*, prophecy is an entirely natural phenomenon. An individual who has the right native disposition, and who perfects his or her faculties of intellect and imagination, must inevitably prophesy. Because this sounds too necessitarian for Maimonides (based on his understanding of the clear intent of scripture), he adds the rider that God can miraculously prevent prophetic inspiration from one naturally ready to prophesy; a God who wills the world to behave according to certain natures can change how that world behaves for his own purposes. Yet although God could do so, Maimonides holds that he would not want to diverge permanently from the natures that he himself implanted in things. Like the Aristotelians, Maimonides views those natures as the vehicles of God's providence over the various species of beings. But he also allows for individual providence, again following what he considers to be the clear intent of scripture. His reconciliation of Aristotelianism and scripture consists in claiming that humans differ in their individual measure of providence according to the perfection of their intellects.

In short, although some of Maimonides's divergences from the Arabic Aristotelian tradition fall squarely within the Andalusian Jewish tradition exemplified by Ibn Daud, his emphasis on a robust notion of divine will is unprecedented in that tradition. Something akin to it may be found in the *Kuzari*, the defence of Judaism by the Andalusian poet Judah Halevi, where miracles are said to prove that 'the Creator of the world is able to accomplish what He wills and whenever He wills'

(*Kuzari* I, 67, cf. I.83; I, 89, V, 4; in Halevi 1964). Yet as always with Halevi, matters are not that simple. Although his language suggests divine voluntarism or even spontaneity (Silman 1995, 216ff.), Halevi considers divine action to be regulated by the divine thing (*al-'amr al-ilāhī*), which, though above nature, is lawlike. Moreover, Halevi himself does not consider the eternity of the world or matter to be anathema to Jewish belief (*Kuzari* I, 67, 54), as does Maimonides. Maimonides's turn to voluntarism, which occurs later in his literary career, owes more to the claims and arguments of al-Ghazālī than to Halevi (who himself may have been indebted to al-Ghazālī, see Baneth 1981 and Kogan 2002; for possible influence of Halevi on Maimonides, see Kreisel 1991).

Because of the difficulty of reconciling Maimonides's views on divine will with his Aristotelianism, some readers have doubted his sincerity. Even before he wrote the *Guide of the Perplexed*, he was read by some as having offered a figurative interpretation of the resurrection of the dead, an interpretation he vehemently denied in the *Treatise on Resurrection*. In fourteenth-century Europe, Jewish Averroists like Moses of Narbonne suggested that while exoterically he appeared to diverge from Aristotle, esoterically he was often in concordance with him. The view of Maimonides as a secret adherent of Aristotelian doctrines such as the eternity of the world was revived in the twentieth century by students of Leo Strauss, and it still has its followers today. Another interpretation views him as denying the possibility of obtaining the metaphysical knowledge for the survival of the human intellect; one scholar sees him as a proto-Kantian (Pines 1979a), another as a sceptic (Stern 2005). Common to all these interpretation is the assumption that the *Guide* contains an esoteric doctrine that differs considerably from the exoteric. As far as we know, this assumption was not shared by Maimonides's readers in the Arabic world.

Although it is still not possible to give a satisfactory picture of the legacy of Maimonides in that world, given the state of the field, some remarks can be made. The Arabic original of the *Guide* is extant in a few dozen manuscripts, and some of these are in Arabic rather than Hebrew characters. A commentary on the twenty-five propositions of Aristotelian physics and metaphysics at the outset of *Guide* II was made by al-Tabrizi, a Persian Muslim, probably in the second half of the thirteenth century, and translated into Hebrew twice. As we shall see, the *Guide* was well known to the Baghdad philosopher, Sa'd Ibn Kammūna. Maimonides's greatest influence appears to have been in Yemen, where he was referred to as the 'Moses of [our] time' or simply, 'our master'. This did not mean that the Yemenite Jews faithfully followed Maimonides's Aristotelian lead; on the contrary, they combined some of his ideas with Neoplatonic and Muslim religious thought, notably al-Ghazālī (Langermann 1996b). Maimonides's works were studied in Yemen in manuscript until the mid–twentieth century, when virtually the entire Yemenite Jewish community migrated to the State of Israel. The last traditional Yemenite scholar of Maimonides, Rabbi Joseph Kafiḥ, the author of editions, translations and commentaries on Maimonides's works, died in 2007. His grandfather, Rabbi Yiḥyeh Kafiḥ, led a movement among Yemenite Jews back to the philosophical rationalism of Maimonides.

Most interesting is the reception of Maimonides's philosophy among his own descendants, who were the undisputed leaders of Egyptian Jewry for around two centuries after his death. While Maimonides was a proud heir of the Andalusian Jewish tradition, his son Abraham was born in 1186 in Egypt, where the dominant intellectual current was Sufi. Abraham went on to compose a huge work entitled *A Compendium for Devotees*, only sections of which are known to be extant. These deal with Jewish law, ethics and liturgy, but no philosophy. To be sure, the *Guide* itself had ended with chapters instructing its reader how to worship and serve God once one has achieved wisdom, and there is, at least arguably, a certain continuity between the contemplative strategies of these chapters and the way of life advocated in Abraham's *Compendium*. But on the whole, the soil of Egypt was not fertile in the twelfth century for the continuation of the Andalusian tradition. Towards the end of his life, Maimonides would write to Rabbi Jonathan ha-Cohen in Provence that 'while you study the Talmud, you also cultivate the other sciences, whereas here in the East, men of wisdom diminish and disappear. Thus salvation will only come to us through you' (cited in Fenton 2009).

4. JEWISH PHILOSOPHY IN ARABIC IN THE WEST AFTER MAIMONIDES

Jews continued to study Arabic philosophy in Southern Spain well into the thirteenth century and to compose works in Arabic that combined the traditions of the Arabic Plotinus and the Arabic Aristotle with the traditions of Kabbalah and, occasionally, astrology. Thus, Judah ben Solomon ha-Cohen wrote an 'encyclopedia' of science called the *Investigation of Wisdom*, which begins with a section on logic, physics and metaphysics adapted mostly from Averroes, then criticises the pretensions of Aristotelian science and ends with a section on divine science, that is, revelation in the Torah and *kabbalah*. If Maimonides had identified the esoteric lore of the rabbis with Aristotelian physics and metaphysics, Judah ben Solomon finds it in revelation and tradition, that is, *kabbalah* (Fontaine 2000). Two other thirteenth-century Southern Spanish philosophers writing in Arabic who combined Neoplatonic and kabbalistic ideas were Judah ben Nissim ibn Malkah and Isaac ben Abraham Ibn Latif; unlike some of the kabbalists in Northern Spain, they know quite well the Aristotelian science they criticise. By contrast, the last Spanish Jewish thinker writing in Arabic, Joseph ibn Waqar, attempts to offer a reconciliation between philosophy, astrology and kabbalah in his voluminous *Treatise on the Reconciliation of Kabbalah, Astrology and Philosophy*, written in Toledo in the early fourteenth century.

Ibn Waqar's treatise includes the *Metaphorical Aphorisms* by Moses ben Joseph Halawi of Seville, a thirteenth-century thinker who was considered an important philosopher and mathematician by Spanish Jews in the late thirteenth and fourteenth centuries. Ḥasdai Crescas ranked him alongside al-Fārābī, Avicenna and al-Ghazālī, and he is cited by several fourteenth-century Spanish Jewish philosophers. Moses was best known for his defence of Avicenna's view that the Prime Mover (i.e., the mover of the outermost celestial sphere) is not God but the First Intelligence that emanates from Him. In the *Metaphysical Aphorisms*, Moses defends Avicenna's view that God knows particulars 'in their universal aspect'.

According to Moses, God knows particulars, and he rewards and punishes people according to their deserts. But God does not know particulars in their particular aspect, that is, as concrete particulars located in space and time, for this would entail that his knowledge change whenever new particulars are generated and destroyed. Moreover, it would be beneath God to have corporeal individuals as the object of his knowledge. Hence, God knows particulars in a general or universal fashion, that is, as universal types rather than as concrete particulars. This characteristically Avicennian view appears briefly in Abraham Ibn Ezra and later in Abner of Burgos and Gersonides. Because Halawi appears to embrace Avicenna's metaphysical determinism, he may be considered an important antecedent for Abner of Burgos and Ḥasdai Crescas.[8]

To explain how God can reward and punish individuals who are known only as types, Moses invites the reader to conduct the following thought experiment: Suppose that you have been appointed governor of a city. Your knowledge includes all the sort of actions that the inhabitants can perform, and you arrange matters such that the various actions bring about the appropriate consequences. Although you are not acquainted directly with individual citizens, you know, for example, that a certain type of individual will behave wickedly under certain types of circumstance, and you create laws and institutions so that this type of behaviour carries with it the appropriate punishment. If Zaid commits a crime, he will be punished because the system you have set up punishes individuals for crimes automatically. The fact that you do not know whether Zaid actually committed a crime does not imply a deficiency in your knowledge. In a similar fashion, God governs the world, and the fact that he is not directly acquainted with individuals qua individuals does not constitute a deficiency in his knowledge or his providence.

How then does God know that there are individuals who act in accordance with this plan if he is not directly acquainted with them? Moses's answer is that God implants within the nature of most people 'the love of goods and the fear of evils' so that they are determined to act according to their divinely bestowed natures; reward and punishment in this world are nothing more than the natural consequences of their actions. This veiled reference to Avicenna's determinism is reinforced when, in the parable of the city, the inhabitants are said to obey the laws by virtue of the 'general charge' that proceeds from the leader. Moses calls this subject 'a gate of knowledge upon which the multitude are not allowed to knock'—perhaps because they would confuse causal determinism with the fatalistic claim that they will be rewarded and punished no matter what they do. The Avicennian notion that causal determinism is a secret of divine recompense to be hidden from the multitude appears later in Abner and Crescas.

5. JEWISH PHILOSOPHY IN THE EAST

Baghdad in the tenth century was a centre of philosophy and science, and it was also the centre of the rabbinic Jewish world. The rabbinical academy of Pumpeditha had been transferred to Baghdad at the end of the ninth century, and the rabbinical academy of Sura at the end of the tenth. Two heads (*geonim*) of the Sura yeshiva, Saʿadia Gaon (d. 942) and Samuel ben Ḥofni (d. 1013), lived and wrote in Baghdad at around the time that Muʿtazilite Kalām was the dominant theology (Brody 1998). Prior to them, Dāwūd al Muqammiṣ, who lived in Syria and Northern Iraq, wrote a Kalāmic work entitled *The Twenty Chapters* (Stroumsa 1989). What these works share in common with each other, and with Kalām works in general, is the eclectic and polemical employment of philosophical principles in the service of theology. Kalām was also quite popular among Karaite Jews in the tenth and eleventh centuries (Ben Shammai 2003).

With the passage of time, however, Jews in the East were exposed to Arabic philosophical works that depended largely on Avicenna's philosophy. Thus, at the height of the controversy over Maimonides's views on physical resurrection, Maimonides accused his rival in Baghdad, Samuel ben Ali, of confusing mutakallimūn for philosophers, and of relying on two works whose contents he mistook to be purely philosophical: the treatise on the afterlife (*al-Maʿad*) by Avicenna,[9] and the *Muʿtabar*, 'which one of theirs in Baghdad wrote' (*Essay on Resurrection*, Halkin, p. 218). The *Kitāb al-Muʿtabar* (according to the translation of Shlomo Pines: 'the Book of What Has Been Established Through Personal Reflection') was written by Abu'l Barakāt al Baghdādī (fl. first half of the twelfth century), who converted to Islam later in life. Whether Maimonides deliberately omitted mentioning the author's name because of his conversion to Islam is a matter of speculation. What is clear, however, is that Samuel ben Ali had no problem utilising passages from the book, and a manuscript of Abu'l Barakāt's commentary on Ecclesiastes was copied in 1335. (See also Langermann 1996c for further evidence of influence.)

Al-Muʿtabar is based on a collection of notes on logic, physics and metaphysics that Abu'l Barakāt composed for himself; some of those notes were copied verbatim from works of other philosophers, notably Avicenna. Although he subjects his philosophical sources to detailed argument and counterargument, Abu'l Barakāt relies on what he considers to be self-evident and self-validating propositions procured by the immediate awareness of self. This allows him to jettison the Aristotelian doctrine of the various parts or faculties of the soul because of the unity of apperception, a position that could certainly annoy Maimonides, for whom the distinction of intellect from other faculties of the soul is crucial. Abu'l Barakāt also argues for time and space as a priori concepts of awareness and views time as a measure of being rather than a measure of motion, and hence a subject for metaphysics rather than physics. He proposes as a thought experiment the case of men sitting in an utter dark cave, who, although they perceive no motion, experience the passage of time. There is only one sort of time, and it is experienced by all conscious beings, including God. Similarly, space can be conceived without bodies. As for his theology, Abu'l Barakāt takes aim at the Peripatetics' rejection of essential attributes. As Pines points out, Abu'l Barakāt may have been influenced by similar doctrines in the Asharite Kalām (which also may help explain Samuel b. Ali's endorsement and Maimonides's dismissal of *Muʿtabar* as 'not purely philosophical'). As for God's knowledge, Abu'l Barakāt criticises Avicenna's view that God knows particulars in their universal aspect. Instead, he starts from the human experience of direct, certain knowledge of particulars within consciousness (strictly speaking, sense knowledge is not tied to the senses but to our unitary awareness) and claims that God has this direct awareness of particulars including incorporeal particulars (Pines 1979b, 259–338, esp. 312).

Abu'l-Barakāt's emphasis on self-awareness and self-validating knowledge proved congenial to the Illuminationist school of Arabic philosophy, associated with al-Suhrawardī, a Persian philosopher of the twelfth century. Some of his criticisms of Avicenna were mentioned by Fakhr al-Dīn al-Rāzī and answered in Naṣīr al-Dīn al-Ṭūsī. The degree of influence on Suhrawardī, who refers to him disparagingly as 'one of the so-called philosophers among the Jews' (cited in Pourjavady and Schmidtke 2006, p. 24), has yet to be studied.

One philosopher upon whom Abu'l-Barakāt had a major impact was Ibn Kammūna, the last, and arguably the most, influential Jewish philosopher in the Arabic world after the twelfth century, if one may judge from the number of extant manuscripts of his work and later references. Indeed, he has recently been called 'one of the most popular and influential philosophers of the Eastern lands of Islam both during his lifetime and in the decades following his death' (Pourjavady and Schmidtke 2006, 28). Until recently, Ibn Kammūna was known among scholars of Judaism mostly for his *Examination of Three Faiths*, a comparison of the truth claims of Christianity, Judaism and Islam (Perlmann 1971), which showed a decided bias towards rabbinic Judaism. Although isolated scholars looked at some of his philosophical works, many of which are still in manuscript, throughout the twentieth century, more of his philosophical and pietistic writings have only begun to be studied in the last decades (for an inventory, see Pourjavady and Schmidtke 2006, 59–138). Philosophically, he was a follower, albeit a critical one, of Avicenna, borrowing from him his cosmology, his distinction between the Necessary of Existence (God) and other contingent existents and aspects of his psychology, especially the primacy of the awareness of soul/self, which he may have received both from Avicenna and Abu'l Barakāt; yet he argued in favour of the pre-eternality of the soul. One of Ibn Kammūna's claims to fame was a commentary he wrote on the *Talwīḥāt* of Suhrawardī, the founder of the Illuminationist school, which was highly popular; over fifty manuscripts are extant. Later philosophers wrongly ascribed to Ibn Kammūna a set of paradoxes, or *insolubilia*, including the famous liar's paradox, although he does discuss some of them. Recently, Tzvi Langermann has drawn attention to some aspects of his pietistic writings (first published in Pourjavady and Schmidtke 2006), which appear to be directed to a Muslim audience (Langermann 2005).

Conclusion

This short survey of medieval Jewish philosophy in Arabic began with Isaac Israeli, who wrote works of pure philosophy in Judeo-Arabic presumably for a Jewish audience and ended with Ibn Kammūna, who wrote works of pure philosophy in Arabic, presumably for a Muslim audience. While much of the Arabic (and Judeo-Arabic) tradition of philosophy among the Jews of al-Andalus dealt with works of religious philosophy and theology, some Jewish intellectuals in the East in the twelfth and thirteenth centuries participated in current trends in Arabic philosophy, and in the fourteenth century a descendant of Maimonides quotes from philosophical writings of Ibn Kammūna in his Judeo-Arabic commentary on his ancestor's famous code of law (Pourjavady and Schmidtke 2006, 56 n. 251). It is still too early to provide a new outline of medieval Jewish philosophy in Arabic, but not to early to reach the conclusion that Arabic-writing Jewish intellectuals were influenced by, and participated in, the shifting currents of the dominant culture, and this continued throughout much of the medieval period.

NOTES

1. See above, Chapter 4, pp. 94–97.

2. Isaac Israeli, Solomon Ibn Gabirol, Abraham Ibn Daūd, Maimonides, Abu'l Barakāt, Ibn Kammūna.

3. This chapter will not deal with Jewish intellectuals influenced by *Kalām*, such as Saʿadia Gaon. This is in accord with conventional historiography of Arabic philosophy, which no longer includes the *mutakallimūn*.

4. On Saʿadia, see above, Chapter 3, pp. 70–74. Y. Tzvi Langermann (Langermann, forthcoming) has discovered in manuscript a defence of creationism, which he attributes to a contemporary of Saʿadia and Isaac, and which appears to draw eclectically from *Kalām* and from *falsafa*.

5. This is admittedly an argument *ex silentio*, but Altmann offers a similar one for the contrary view (Altmann and Stern 1958, 155). Surely in the absence of strong textual evidence one way or the other, the default position should be that of the Arabic Plotinus, concerning which Adamson writes, 'There are strong indications in the Arabic Plotinus that the Adaptor follows Plotinus in holding that creation is necessary' (Adamson 2002, 146).

6. This follows Zimmermann's suggestion that the source of Isaac's hypostasis of First Matter and First Form is the *Long Version* rather than a lost Neoplatonist text that survived in a thirteenth-century Hebrew translation, as Stern maintained. That text, according to Zimmermann, is probably a lost work of Isaac (Zimmermann 1986).

7. Al-Kindī's own writings were less influential, although traces have been found in the Karaite thinker, al-Qirkisānī, and as late as Shem Tov b. Joseph Falaquera in the thirteenth century (Zonta 2011).

8. See below, Chapter 7, pp. 159–61.

9. It is not clear to what work Maimonides refers, or why he refers to it, since in our copy of Samuel b. Ali's letter, there is no reference to Avicenna (Langermann 2000, 59, n. 60)

BIBLIOGRAPHY

Adamson, Peter. 2002. *The Arabic Plotinus: A Philosophical Study of the Theology of Aristotle*. London: Duckworth.

Al-Andalusī, Ṣāʿid. 1991. *Science in the Medieval World: 'Book of the Categories of Nations'*, ed. and trans. Semaʾan I. Salem and Alok Kumar. Austin: University of Texas Press.

Altmann, A. and S. M. Stern, eds. 1958. *Isaac Israeli, a Neoplatonic Philosopher of the Early Tenth Century*. Oxford: Clarendon Press.

Baneth, D. H. 1981. 'Judah Halevi and al-Ghazali'. In *Studies in Jewish Thought: An Anthology of German-Jewish Scholarship*, ed. A. Jospe, 181–99. Detroit, MI: Wayne State University Press.

Ben-Shammai, Haggai. 2003. 'Major trends in Karaite philosophy and polemics in the tenth and eleventh centuries'. In *Karaite Judaism. A Guide to Its History and Literary Sources*, ed. Meira Polliack, 339–62. Leiden, the Netherlands, and Boston: Brill.

Brody, Robert. 1998. *The Geonim of Babylonia and the Shaping of Medieval Jewish Culture*. New Haven, CT: Yale University Press.

Davidson, Herbert A. 1987. *Proofs for Eternity, Creation, and the Existence of God in Medieval Islamic and Jewish Philosophy*. New York: Oxford University Press.

Druart, Thérèse-Anne. 1994. Averroes on God's Knowledge of Being Qua Being. *Anaquel de estudios árabes* 5:39–57. Reprinted in *Studies in Thomistic Theology*, ed. Paul Lockey, 175–205. Houston, TX: Center for Thomistic Studies, University of St. Thomas.

Dūnaš ben Tāmīm. 2002. *Le commentaire sur le Livre de création de la Dūnaš ben Tāmīm de Kairouan: (Xe siècle)*, ed. Georges Vajda. Nouvelle édition revue et augmentée par Paul B. Fenton. Paris-Louvain: Peeters.

Fenton, Paul B. 1986. 'The Arabic and Hebrew versions of the *Theology of Aristotle*'. In *Pseudo-Aristotle in the Middle Ages: The Theology and Other Texts*, ed. Jill Kraye, Charles B. Schmitt and W. F. Ryan, 241–64. London: Warburg Institute, University of London.

———. 2009. A Re-Discovered Description of Maimonides by a Contemporary. *Maimonidean Studies* 5: 267–93.

Fontaine, T. A. M. 1990. *In Defence of Judaism: Abraham Ibn Daud: Sources and Structures of ha-Emunah ha-Ramah*. Assen/Maastricht, the Netherlands: Van Gorcum.

———. 2000. 'Judah ben Solomon ha-Cohen's *Midrash ha-Hokhmah*: Its sources and use of sources'. In *The Medieval Hebrew Encyclopedias of Science and Philosophy*, ed. S. Harvey, 191–210. Dordrecht, the Netherlands, Boston and London: Kluwer.

Gutas, Dimitri. 2002. The Study of Arabic Philosophy in the Twentieth Century: An Essay on the Historiography of Arabic Philosophy. *British Journal of Middle Eastern Studies*. 29(1):5–25.

Guttmann, Julius. 1964. *Philosophies of Judaism: The History of Jewish Philosophy from Biblical Times to Franz Rosenzweig*. New York: Holt, Rinehart and Winston.

Haberman, Jacob. 2003. *The Microcosm of Joseph ibn Ṣaddiq*. Madison, NJ Fairleigh Dickinson University Press.

Halevi, Judah. 1964. *The Kuzari (Kitab al Khazari)*, trans. Hartwig Hirschfeld. New York: Schocken Books.

Halkin, Abraham, trans. 1985. 'The Essay on Resurrection'. In *Crisis and Leadership: Epistles of Maimonides*, 211–45. Philadelphia: Jewish Publication Society of America.

Husik, Isaac. 1916. *A History of Mediaeval Jewish Philosophy*. New York: Macmillan

Ibn Daud, Abraham. 1852. *Das Buch Emunah ramah, oder: Der erhabene Glaube*. Frankfurt, Germany: Typographischen Anhalt.

Ibn Gabirol, Solomon. 1892–5. *Fons vitae: ex Arabico in Latinum Translatus ab Iohanne hispano et dominico Gundissalino*, trans. Johannes Hispanus and Dominicus Gundusalvi. ed. Clemens Baeumker. Münster, Germany: Aschendorff.

Ibn Gabirol, Solomon and Andrew Lee Gluck. 2003. *The Kingly Crown = Keter Malkhut*, ed. and trans. Bernard Lewis. Essay by Andrew Lee Gluck. Notre Dame, IN: University of Notre Dame.

Israeli, Isaac. 1958a. 'Book of Definitions'. In Altmann and Stern, 1958.

———. 1958b. 'Book of Elements'. In Altmann and Stern, 1958.

———. 1958c. 'Book of Substances'. In Altmann and Stern, 1958.

Kogan, Barry S. 2002. 'Al-Ghazali and Halevi on philosophy and the philosophers'. In *Medieval Philosophy and the Classical Tradition*, ed. John Inglis, 64–80. Richmond, UK: Curzon.

Kreisel, Howard. 1991. Judah Halevi's Influence on Maimonides: A Preliminary Appraisal. *Maimonidean Studies* 2:95–121.

Langermann, Y. Tzvi. 1996a. Arabic Writings in Hebrew Manuscripts: A Preliminary Relisting. *Arabic Sciences and Philosophy* 6:137–60.

———. 1996b. *Yemenite Midrash: Philosophical Commentaries on the Torah*. San Francisco, CA: Harper.

———. 1996c. 'Fragment from the *Al-Muʿtabar* of Abu l-Barakat al-Baghdadi'. In *Mi-ginzei ha-makhon le-tazlumei kitvei ha-yad ha-ivriyim*, ed. A. David. 50–51. Jerusalem: Jewish and National University Library.

———. 2000. The Letter of R. Shmuel ben Eli on Resurrection. *Kovetz al Yad* 15:41–92 (Hebrew).

———. 2005. Ibn Kammūna and the New Wisdom of the Thirteenth Century. *Arabic Sciences and Philosophy* 15:277–327.

———. Forthcoming. 'An Early Jewish Defense of Creationism'. In *Exchange and Transmission Across Cultural Boundaries: Philosophy and Science in the Mediterranean World. Proceedings of a Workshop in Memory of Professor Shlomo Pines, Jerusalem 28 February – 2 March 2005*, eds. S. Stroumsa, H. Ben Shammai and Sh. Shaked. Jerusalem: The Israel Academy of Sciences.

Malpas, J., 'Donald Davidson'. In *The Stanford Encyclopedia of Philosophy* (Winter 2003 edition), ed. Edward N. Zalta. http://plato.stanford.edu/archives/win2003/entries/davidson/

Manekin, Charles H. 2002. Maimonides on Divine Knowledge—Moses of Narbonne's Averroist Reading. *American Catholic Philosophical Quarterly* 76:51–74.

Moses Maimonides. 1963. *The Guide of the Perplexed*, trans. Shlomo Pines. Chicago: University of Chicago Press.

Munk, Salomon. 1859. *Mélanges de philosophie juive et arabe, renfermant des extraits méthodiques de la Source de vie de Salomon ibn-Gebirol (dit Avicebron)*. Paris: A. Franck.

Perlmann, Moshe. 1971. *Ibn Kammūna's Examination of the Three Faiths: A Thirteenth Century Essay in Comparative Study of Religion*. Berkeley-Los Angeles: University of California.

Pines, Shlomo. 1979a. 'The limitations of human knowledge according to Al-Farabi, Ibn Bajja, and Maimonides'. In *Studies in Medieval Jewish History and Literature*, ed. Isadore Twersky 82–109. Cambridge, MA: Harvard University Press.

———. 1979b. *Studies in Abu'l-Barakāt al-Baghdādī Physics and Metaphysics*. Jerusalem: Magnes Press.

Pourjavady, Reza and Sabine Schmidtke. 2006. *A Jewish Philosopher of Baghdad: 'Izz al-Dawla Ibn Kammuna (d. 683/1284) and His Writings*. Leiden, the Netherlands: Brill.

Silman, Yochanan. 1995. *Philosopher and Prophet Judah Halevi, the Kuzari, and the Evolution of His Thought*. Albany: State University of New York Press.

Sirat, Colette. 1985. *A History of Jewish Philosophy in the Middle Ages*. Cambridge: Cambridge University Press.

Sorabji, Richard. 1980. *Necessity, Cause, and Blame: Perspectives on Aristotle's Theory*. London: Duckworth.

Stern, Josef. 2005. 'Maimonides' epistemology'. In *The Cambridge Companion to Maimonides*, ed. K. M. Seeskin, 105–33. Cambridge: Cambridge University Press.

Stroumsa, Sarah. 1989. *Dāwūd ibn Marwān al-Muqammiṣ's 'Twenty Chapters' ('Ishrūn Maqāla)*. Leiden, the Netherlands / New York / København / Köln, Germany: E. J. Brill.

Zimmermann, F. W. 1986. 'The origins of the so-called *Theology* of Aristotle'. In *Pseudo-Aristotle in the Middle Ages: The Theology and Other Texts*, ed. Jill Kraye, Charles B. Schmitt and W. F. Ryan, 110–240. London: Warburg Institute, University of London.

Zonta, Mauro. 2011. 'Influence of Arabic and Islamic philosophy on Judaic thought'. In *The Stanford Encyclopedia of Philosophy* (Spring 2011 edition), ed. Edward N. Zalta. http://plato.stanford.edu/archives/spr2011/entries/arabic-islamic-judaic

CHAPTER 7

JEWISH PHILOSOPHY IN HEBREW

STEVEN HARVEY

1. INTRODUCTION: CONTEXT AND BACKGROUND

The present chapter is a continuation of the previous chapter on medieval Jewish philosophy in Arabic. Although medieval philosophy in Hebrew begins in earnest with two Jewish Spaniards, Abraham ibn Ezra and Abraham bar Ḥiyya, writing in the first half of the twelfth century (see Sela 2003), and although the study of philosophy continues in some form among the Jews in the East in Arabic till the end of the Middle Ages (Fenton 2009), we will not be too amiss if we begin our account with the death of Maimonides in 1204, and with the emergence of Hebrew at about that time as the language of philosophy among the Jews.

It is useful for appreciating the concerns and development of our subject to consider briefly that by the first decades of the fourteenth century one could write a fairly accurate account of medieval Islamic philosophy under the parallel title, 'Medieval Islamic Philosophy in Hebrew'. The reference is, of course, to the medieval word-for-word Hebrew translations of Arabic works of Islamic philosophy. Indeed, one is in a far better position today for presenting the philosophy and science of Averroes on the basis of these Hebrew translations than on the basis of extant Arabic and Judeo-Arabic manuscripts of Averroes's writings.[1] Although the same cannot be said regarding the other Islamic *falāsifa*, the medieval Hebrew translations made it possible for medieval Jewish philosophers, who did not read Arabic, to be informed and discriminating students of all the leading Islamic *falāsifa*, including especially al-Fārābī, Avicenna and Ibn Bājja, in addition to Averroes. The heyday of this translation movement was the century extending approximately from 1230 to 1330, although certain of al-Fārābī's writings are thought to have been translated already in the twelfth century, and al-Ghazālī's *Incoherence of the Philosophers* was not translated till the early fifteenth century. In contrast, a chapter on medieval Christian philosophy in Hebrew would be far less helpful, although still of great interest. The writings of the Church Fathers as well as those of the Jewish philosopher, Philo of Alexandria, were virtually unknown to the Jews until the Renaissance and even then only to a small number of intellectuals in Italy who read them in Latin. While Hebrew versions of the first chapter of Thomas Aquinas's *Tractatus de unitate intellectus contra Averroistas* and of sections of Dominicus Gundisalvi's *Liber de anima* were imbedded by Hillel of Verona in 1291 in his *Tagmulei ha-Nefesh* (*Rewards of the Soul*)—in the case of the work by Thomas, anonymously—it is not until the translation activity of Judah Romano in the second and third decades of the fourteenth century that the Hebrew reader began to learn something of scholastic methodology and thought through direct translations from the Latin. Judah translated several works by Albertus Magnus, including Book III, Treatises 1–2 of his *De anima* and part of his *Summa creaturis*; by Thomas Aquinas, including *De esse and essentia* and the section of the *Summa theologica* on ideas; by Giles of Rome, including his *Theoremata de esse et essentia* I–VIII, *De plurificatione intellectus possibilis*, and sections of his commentaries on Aristotle's *Physica* and *De anima*; as well as selected writings by other scholastics. Not much more was available until the anonymous Hebrew translations of the mid–fifteenth century of Thomas's commentary on the *De anima* and Robert Grosseteste's *Summa of Aristotle's Physica*. In the 1470s in Spain, Eli Ḥabillo translated additional writings by Thomas and Pseudo-Thomas and several writings by Johannes Versor (Jean Letourneur), especially his *Questions* on Aristotle's various writings. The picture of Jewish awareness of scholastic thought and its influence on Hebrew authors has recently been updated and surveyed anew by Mauro Zonta in his introduction to his *Hebrew Scholasticism in the Fifteenth Century*. He concludes that 'a fully fledged "Hebrew Scholasticism"—characterised by the production of Hebrew philosophical works that use Latin scholastic texts, doctrines and techniques in a way that is direct and clearly identifiable, systematic and mostly explicit—does not come into being before the late fifteenth century' (Zonta 2006, 13). Indeed, while this late-fifteenth-century Hebrew scholasticism looms today as one of the most promising and intriguing areas of research in medieval Jewish philosophy, the fact that for nearly three centuries Hebrew-reading Jews studied philosophy and science (although not medicine and logic) through the single lens of the Islamic *falāsifa* characterises and colours the methods and discussions of those engaged in medieval Jewish philosophy in Hebrew. Notwithstanding, as we shall see, there were significant and fascinating exceptions to this uniform picture.

Pre-Maimonidean Jewish philosophy—that is, the philosophy that was written in Judeo-Arabic as well as the Hebrew writings of Ibn Ezra and Bar Ḥiyya—was, with the sole exception of Maimonides's immediate predecessor, the Avicennian philosopher, Abraham ibn Daud, either rooted in the teachings and methods of the *Mutakallimûn* or those of the Neoplatonists or was an eclectic blend of traditions, including some Platonism and Aristotelianism. For Maimonides, such philosophies were not true philosophy, and studying them was a waste of valuable time. In a famous letter to Samuel ibn Tibbon, the Hebrew translator of the *Guide of the Perplexed*, written about five years before his death, Maimonides patiently explained which philosophers are worth reading and which not. His advice is telling and, as has been argued elsewhere, determined to a great extent which philosophers would be translated into Hebrew and thus influence the course of Jewish philosophy (Harvey 1992). He made clear that Aristotle is the foremost philosopher, but that he can only be understood with the commentaries of Alexander of Aphrodisias, Themistius and Averroes. Al-Fārābī, Ibn Bājja and, to a lesser extent, Avicenna (perhaps because of his tendency to stray from the path of Aristotle) are all important philosophers and should be studied. Significantly, not a single Jewish thinker is recommended, nor are any of the many Neoplatonic treatises written in or translated into Arabic. As a consequence, in contrast to pre-Maimonidean Jewish philosophy, post-Maimonidean philosophy is markedly Aristotelian in the tradition of the Islamic Aristotelianism founded by al-Fārābī. This tradition features an emphasis on mastering Aristotelian formal logic as a required propaedeutic for the study of science and philosophy. It also emphasises the need for the proper orderly study of the sciences according to the arrangement of the Aristotelian corpus. Practically speaking, this meant that young Jewish would-be philosophers began their studies with logic and then turned to the careful reading of Aristotle's books on natural science in their proper order. Insofar as Maimonides cautioned that Aristotle needed to be studied with the commentaries, these Jews learned Aristotelian science through the accurate Hebrew translations of the commentaries of Averroes on Aristotle's books. Naturally enough, the first such commentaries to be translated into Hebrew were Averroes's middle commentaries on the first four books of the *Organon* (along with his middle commentary on Porphyry's *Isagoge*), which were translated by Jacob Anatoli in Naples in 1232 (Robinson 2005, 216–20), in the same city and at the same time that William of Luna was working on Latin translations of the very same Averroean commentaries.[2]

Although one may speak of the systematic effort to translate all of Averroes's thirty-six Aristotelian commentaries into Hebrew, these translations did not take place overnight and, indeed, took over a century. Thirteenth-century Jews longed desperately for the needed texts—unlike their pre-Maimonidean coreligionists, who for the most part did not seem so concerned with formal logic or the careful study of books of Aristotelian science—and pleaded for their translation. At stake was not only the knowledge of true science, but also the ability to read and understand philosophico-theological works such as Maimonides's *Guide of the Perplexed*. Maimonides had explicitly written in the introduction to the *Guide* that that work was written for those who have studied the 'sciences of the philosophers and come to know what they signify' (*Guide of the Perplexed*, intro., 5; cf. 3–4, 10). Without knowledge of Aristotelian natural science, the *Guide* could not be properly understood. How then did they study science when the requisite texts were not yet translated? It is at this time that the thirteenth-century encyclopedias of science and philosophy emerged to fill the void. Levi ben Abraham of Villefranche wrote his rhymed encyclopedia, *Battei ha-Nefesh ve-ha-Leḥashim*, in 1276 explicitly in order to make available the scientific knowledge needed for understanding the *Guide*, and the same seems to have been his motivation for writing his later and lengthier prose encyclopedia, *Livyat Ḥen* (W. Harvey 2000a, 172, 179). This also seems to have been the concern of the author of the anonymous *Ruaḥ Ḥen*, a very popular encyclopedia in a nutshell from the first half of the thirteenth century.[3] But, of greater interest for understanding the programme of study of post-Maimonidean Jewish students of philosophy and science are the Hebrew encyclopedias of Judah ben Solomon ha-Kohen of Toledo and Shem-Ṭov ben Joseph Falaquera. Judah's *Midrash ha-Ḥokhmah* was compiled in Hebrew in Italy in 1247 and constituted the first Hebrew systematic attempt to put forward Aristotelian science in a single volume. Falaquera's *De'ot ha-Filosofim*, written several decades later, was the second such attempt. Both authors based their encyclopedias primarily on Averroes's middle commentaries on Aristotle's books, following, for the most part, the traditional order of the Aristotelian corpus. Judah's treatment is much briefer and more concise, contenting himself with the main points of the sciences. Resianne Fontaine, who has written several important studies on the *Midrash ha-Ḥokhmah*, has concluded that it 'remains doubtful to what extent the epitomised pieces of information could actually have enabled a reader without previous scientific knowledge to get a clear picture of Aristotelian philosophy' (Fontaine 2000, 201). In contrast, Falaquera's *De'ot* presented a full treatment of Aristotelian science through translation and effective blending of Averroes's commentaries (Harvey 2000b, 213, 216–7, 237). For the first time, the full range of Aristotelian science became available to Hebrew readers, and this made it possible for them to learn and even master it. With the many translations of Averroes's commentaries by Qalonimos ben Qalonimos and his colleagues in Provence in the second decade of the fourteenth century, which virtually completed the Averroean translation project, study of the Aristotelian encyclopedias was soon replaced by the careful reading of Averroes's commentaries (already begun to the extent possible in the previous century) and the new genre, inaugurated by Gersonides in the early 1320s, of writing super-commentaries on Averroes's commentaries with the aim of explicating and, at times, even correcting those authoritative texts (Glasner 1995).

The pre-Maimonidean Jewish thinkers were not bookish students of Aristotelian philosophy. None of them wrote commentaries on Aristotle's books or, for that matter, on any Greek philosophic book. For the most part, they turned to the philosophers for rational support for strengthening the theological principles of their religion. They did not seek to write works of natural science. Indeed, Maimonides said the same thing about his *Guide* (II, 2, 253):

> My purpose in this treatise of mine is not to compose something on natural science, or to make an epitome of notions pertaining to divine science according to some doctrines, or to demonstrate what has been demonstrated in them.... For the books composed concerning these matters are adequate.

The post-Maimonideans spent most of their time trying to understand, interpret and make known the teachings of Plato, Aristotle and the Islamic *falāsifa*. In
any case, lofty philosophico-theological discussions of the metaphysical principles
of religion could not be undertaken until one had first mastered logic and all of
natural science. The weighty discussions of these principles that accentuated post-
Maimonidean Jewish philosophy were premised upon a sound and sophisticated
knowledge of Greek and Islamic philosophy. These discussions were often moder-
ated by a method of writing dictated by Platonic political philosophy, as adopted by
al-Fārābī and his followers, that sought to conceal certain truths from the multitude. Many of these post-Maimonidean Jewish philosophers were the true inheri-
tors of the tradition of Aristotelian *falsafa*, which was inaugurated by al-Fārābī at
the beginning of the tenth century and which for all intents and purposes came to
an abrupt end in Islam with the death of Averroes in 1198.[4]

2. PHILOSOPHICAL AND THEOLOGICAL DISCUSSIONS

2.1 Creation

I begin with the unusual and the not so influential. Scholars disagree which Latin
schoolmen—if any—indeed maintained the doctrine of the *double vérité*, that is,
that two contradictory teachings, one learned from philosophy and the other from
revelation, may be simultaneously true (Bianchi 2008). Was it Siger of Brabant,
Boethius of Dacia, John of Jandun or someone else? Within medieval Jewry there
seems to have been one controversial thinker whose major work puts forward such
a doctrine. The philosopher is Isaac Albalag, and his book is *Tiqqun ha-Deʿot (Correction of Opinions)*. Not coincidentally, he wrote it at the very end of the thirteenth
century. *Tiqqun ha-Deʿot* is a commentary on al-Ghazālī's *Intentions of the Philosophers*, which was translated for the first time into Hebrew by Albalag himself.[5]
Albalag emerges, already in the introduction to his book, as firmly planted in the
tradition of the Islamic *falāsifa*. He explains that all revealed religions—and philosophy as well—share in common four fundamental beliefs: reward and punishment,
immortality of the soul, the existence of a God who rewards and punishes, and the
existence of divine providence to give to each according to his merit. The Torah
teaches these things to the many via narrative; philosophy teaches them to the few
via demonstration. The ultimate intention of the Torah is the happiness of the many,
keeping them far from evil and teaching them the truth to the extent their mind can
bear it, for they cannot grasp the truth of things as they are, so the Torah teaches
them through corporeal representations and similitudes. Philosophy, on the other
hand, teaches through demonstration (Albalag 2000, 247–50). Albalag's statements

immediately bring to mind al-Fārābī's teachings in the *Attainment of Happiness* on the relation between philosophy and religion. For al-Fārābī, both treat the same subjects, both 'supply knowledge about the first principle and cause of the beings, and both give an account of the ultimate end for the sake of which man is made— that is, his supreme happiness. . . . In everything of which philosophy gives an account that is demonstrative and certain, religion gives an account based on persuasive arguments.'[6] Like al-Fārābī, Albalag distinguished between the few (that is, the philosophers) and the multitude. But what is the difference between the ways in which religion and philosophy perceive the truths of the world? Let us consider Albalag's views on creation.

Virtually all post-Maimonidean Jewish discussions of creation are rooted in Maimonides's discussion of creation in the second part of the *Guide*. For Maimonides, believers in God are divided on this subject: some hold the world is created in time out of nothing (that is, not from any thing), some hold it is created from eternal matter and some hold it is eternal. Maimonides states that his opinion and the opinion of all Jews is creation out of nothing (*Guide* II, 13, 281–85). This is Maimonides's explicit teaching, but he counts creation as one of the secrets of the Torah that ought not to be taught publicly (I, 33, 80–81), and his own discussions on the subject are brimming with intentional contradictions.[7] As a result, modern scholars are still today in vehement disagreement as to which of the three views was in truth Maimonides's own. This uncertainty is already reflected in Albalag's discussion. 'Who knows', he wrote, 'why Maimonides did not reveal this own thoughts on this matter [viz., the eternal creation of the world], at times speaking with cunning, and hinting and indicating that this is his belief, . . . and at times responding to the philosophers with counterfeit theoretical arguments and trying to refute their opinion'. Albalag adds that perhaps Maimonides in his discretion did not see fit to reveal what the Torah had concealed from the multitude, and then he proceeds to list several reasons why he himself did not do likewise. His most curious reason is that his readers, the Jews of his time, are already acclimatised to the view of the eternity of the world, whereas in Maimonides's day (a century earlier), such a view was totally foreign to the extent that the multitude 'imagined that whoever acknowledges the eternity of the world is as if he denies the entire Torah'. Albalag tells us he accepts the opinion of the philosophers on eternal creation because theoretical research does not allow him to deny it, and so 'I accept it by way of human knowledge, not by way of faith'. He sums up that the opinion of the philosophers on eternity is indeed his opinion, while the opposing belief of the Torah is his belief, 'the one by way of nature, the other by way of miracle'. He concludes: 'If you understand all my words, you will know that my opinion [on this matter] is true and my belief is true' (Albalag 1973, 50–52).

While Albalag fully adopted and openly taught in his own name al-Fārābī's teachings on the relation between philosophy and religion, Shem-Ṭov Falaquera, one of the most philosophically learned and sophisticated of the medieval Jewish thinkers, could not bring himself even to allude to them, not even in the course of paraphrasing al-Fārābī's *Attainment of Happiness*. Indeed, the same short section of

the *Attainment*, to which we have already referred (above, n. 6), is completely
omitted by Falaquera in his paraphrase of this book, even though he translates from
the previous and following sections (see Harvey 2002). Falaquera, it seems, had no
interest in publicising al-Fārābī's account of philosophic religion, where 'philosophy
is prior to religion in time' and 'religion an imitation of philosophy'.

Falaquera's own views on creation, written a few decades before Albalag wrote
his, are quite different. In his early popular introductory works, Falaquera explicitly
counts creation from nothing as a root and true opinion of the Torah. However, in
his commentary on Maimonides's *Guide, Moreh ha-Moreh*, he, like Maimonides,
calls creation one of the divine secrets (Falaquera 2001, intro., 116). Here he reveals
his own opinion that the world is not created from nothing, but from eternal matter,
the view that Maimonides had ascribed to Plato. Falaquera writes (Falaquera 2001,
261 [on *Guide* II, 13]):

> It appears to me that there is no need to say that the Creator, may He be exalted,
> brought into existence the existent from non-existence [*me-ha-he'der*], but rather
> that he brought it into existence *after* complete non-existence, for this is possible
> according to our faith. Therefore, those that say that He, may He be exalted,
> brought [the world] into existence from nothing [do] not [express] a precise
> belief; rather, He brought it into existence after nothing, that is, He brought it into
> existence after the thing did not exist.

In other words, for Falaquera, the true interpretation of the teaching of the Torah
is indeed creation, but creation, not ex nihilo, but rather, *after* non-existence, that
is, after privation of form. Creation, for him, is thus creation through informing
prime matter.

The first post-Maimonidean to struggle at length with the question of creation
was the translator of the *Guide*, Samuel ibn Tibbon. Ibn Tibbon was the first of the
radical Maimonideans, whose readings of the *Guide* fleshed out concealed and often
heterodox theological teachings, which they themselves held in one form or another. Carlos Fraenkel, who has recently written a book on Ibn Tibbon's glosses on
the *Guide*, calls him the 'first student of the Arabic *falāsifa* in Christian Europe'.
Fraenkel speaks of Ibn Tibbon's 'intellectual independence as a philosopher in his
own right' and explains that among the teachings of the *falāsifa*, 'he adopted those
he thought valid on the basis of philosophical considerations' with no regard to
whether they were in agreement with those found in the *Guide*.[8] Not surprisingly,
Ibn Tibbon put forth a naturalistic interpretation of creation, but his desire to
understand philosophically how the world came to be led him, following the advice
of Maimonides, to many years of painstaking study of Aristotle's *Meteorology* and
the Greek and Arabic commentaries on it.[9] Recently Gad Freudenthal has suggested
how precisely Ibn Tibbon in his exegetical work, *Ma'amar Yiqqawu ha-Mayim*
(*Treatise on 'Let the waters be gathered'* [Gen. 1:9]), understood eternity. The separate forms (the deity and the intelligences) are eternal, as are the material heavenly
bodies. The creation story in Genesis thus applies only to the sub-lunar world and
is seen as an entirely natural process. Ibn Tibbon's understanding of this process,
which is marked by the emergence of dry land from under the water that at first

covered the globe, derives from his reading of Avicenna's section on meteorology in the *Shifāẽ*, where Avicenna maintains eternity, while rejecting that dry land is preserved permanently, and instead gives a naturalistic account of how dry land emerges from beneath the water (Freudenthal 2008).

We thus have seen three different unorthodox accounts of creation in the thirteenth century, one from a commentary on a book by al-Ghazālī, one from a commentary on Maimonides's *Guide* and one from a book of biblical exegesis. Post-Maimonideans often put forward their philosophico-theological views in commentaries rather than in independent treatises. Although they found some safety in locating their views in commentaries, it is worth noting that all three of these thinkers were castigated and denounced by later Jewish thinkers for their views on creation/eternity. The last thinker we shall mention on this topic is Gersonides, and he did put forward his views on creation in a systematic fashion in a treatise, the *Wars of the Lord*.

Gersonides (d. 1344) makes clear in the introduction to the *Wars* that he believes his predecessors did not really put forward philosophical arguments for the creation or eternity of the world, and accordingly, none of them has hit upon the truth of the matter (*Wars*, intro., vol. 1, 94–96). He promises he will do so in the last book of the *Wars*. There he undertakes an exhaustive and multi-layered philosophical discussion of the origin of the world (*Wars* VI, 1, vol. 3, 217–409). In the course of the discussion, he puts forward his doctrine of creation from eternal matter: 'The world is created from something insofar as it is generated from [some kind] of body; it is created from nothing insofar as this body is devoid of form' (*Wars* VI, 1, 17, vol. 3, 330). For Gersonides, God produces the forms eternally through thinking himself, and he bestows them at an instant in this formless matter. This is the creation.

Thus in the *Wars*, Gersonides rejects the opinion that prime matter was generated out of nothing. Surprisingly, he propounds this view in his earlier super-commentary on Averroes's *Middle Commentary on Aristotle's Physics*. Averroes, following Aristotle, had argued near the end of Book 1 that prime matter cannot be generated and is not corruptible.[10] Gersonides writes in his commentary on this passage (Gersonides MS, fol. 19v):

> O reader, do not deceive yourself into thinking that this is a decisive demonstration for the pre-eternity of the world, for the generation one means by creation [*ḥiddush*] is different from the generation mentioned here. This generation is natural, while one who speaks of creation does not say that the world is created naturally. Thus the generation about which those who hold creation speak is not the informing of matter, but *the absolute generation of the substratum*.

Here it is clear that Gersonides includes himself among those who hold creation, and that by the phrase 'the absolute generation of the substratum,' he means the supra-natural generation of prime matter out of nothing.

Gersonides's comments in his super-commentary are in the context of a rare theological digression, wherein he reassures the reader that the Aristotelian proof that prime matter was not generated is not a decisive proof for the pre-eternity of the world. In support of this claim, he argues that prime matter was generated supra-naturally, and that its generation is thus outside the purview of natural science. It is hard to know why he contradicts his own position here, and it may be that he changed his mind at some point. It is quite likely that in his formulation in the super-commentary, Gersonides was influenced by a statement by Thomas Aquinas in his commentary on this passage in the *Physics*. After concluding that it is impossible for prime matter to be generated or corrupted, he adds: 'But by this we do not deny that it comes into existence through creation' (Aquinas 1963, 66).

2.2 Free Will, Determinism, and God's Knowledge of Particulars

For the medieval Jewish philosophers, the philosophical quagmire of a world in which man is free to choose his own actions or a world in which there is no choice and everything is determined was perhaps the most challenging and perplexing of the philosophico-theological issues they sought to resolve. For some the determinism they confronted was that of a strict causality, for others it was an astral determinism and for others it was a result of God's unchanging knowledge of all things. The philosophers, whose views on this subject will be discussed, all present creative attempts to resolve the problem.[11]

Among the medieval Jewish philosophers, some posed the problem of free will versus determinism primarily in theological terms and some in purely philosophical terms. The pre-Maimonideans tended to focus on the theological dilemma: man must have free will (as Scripture teaches) or there is no purpose to the divine commandments and there can be no justification for reward and punishment, but how can man have free will if God is all knowing (as Scripture also teaches)? If God knows what one will do, which possibility one will choose, then how can one be free to make this choice? Various solutions were put forward, and some even held that the human intellect is incapable of resolving this problem (Altmann 1974). Most creative among the pre-Maimonideans on this topic was Abraham ibn Daʾud (1110–80) who was the first Jewish thinker willing to limit God's knowledge in order to guarantee freedom of choice (Pines 1967, 90–92). The post-Maimonideans we will consider were more concerned with the challenges to free will posed by causal necessity and astral determinism.

Albalag discusses the possibility of knowledge of future contingents and its consequences for free will in his comments on al-Ghazālī's discussion in the Metaphysics of the *Intentions of the Philosophers* of the extent to which God and humans can know future contingents. Albalag divides the causes of the possible into efficient and material and, following several Jewish authors—most notably, Maimonides (*Guide* II, 48, 410–11), divides the efficient causes into natural, volitional and accidental. While natural causes bring about an order that may be known, volitional and accidental causes can interfere with that knowable order. The eclipse of the sun is an example of an effect from natural causes that is necessary and thus may be known, and that volitional and accidental causes cannot prevent. On the other hand, a person poking his eye with his finger is an example of an accidental cause that can't really be known before it happens. The same is true for the person who stumbles on a stone that just fell from a roof as a result of the movement of a mouse who imagines bread before him or a cat lurking behind him. Albalag's claim is that there is no cause that necessitates these images in the mouse. The effects of the stone falling and the person tripping on it can thus not be known with certainty on the basis of the causes. On the other hand, where the causes follow each other naturally without external hindrance, then certain knowledge of the possible may be attained. Following Averroes's teaching in his dialectical writings, Albalag claims he does not deny God's knowledge of future contingents, but only that God knows them—as al-Ghazālī claims—in the same way that humans do. According to Albalag, al-Ghazālī's understanding leaves no room for human free choice and for the existence of the possible, for all man's actions would be compelled by necessitating causes. Such opinions, Albalag concludes, 'not only constitute repudiations of philosophy, but also heresy with respect to the Torah' (Manekin 2007, 140–42).

Gersonides does not seem to have known Albalag's commentary on al-Ghazālī and, in any case, was not influenced by it. Yet, like Albalag, Gersonides maintained freedom of choice even at the expense of God's knowledge. In Book 2 of the *Wars of the Lord*, Gersonides puts forward a theory in which human affairs are determined and ordered by the heavenly bodies. Indeed, he writes that all human actions and thoughts are ordered by the heavenly bodies. Thus, if one had sufficient knowledge of the heavenly bodies, one could correctly predict what a person will do and think. However, this astral determinism does not deny the possible, for '[intellect and choice] have the power to move us contrary to that which is determined by the heavenly bodies'. In other words, our future is determined by the position of the heavenly bodies, but we have the intellectual ability to choose to act otherwise and pursue a path other than that which was determined for us (Gersonides 1984–99, *Wars* II, 2, 32–36).

If we can part from our pre-determined destiny, can God know our actions? Gersonides devotes the third of the six treatises of his *Wars of the Lord* to the problem of God's knowledge of particulars. The discussions of the medieval Aristotelians on this subject took as their starting point Aristotle's teaching in *Metaphysics* Λ, chapter 9, that the Intellect [or God] intellects only Itself eternally and nothing else. The Arabic and Hebrew tradition knew that Alexander of Aphrodisias interpreted this passage to mean exactly what it says: God knows only Himself and nothing else. But they also knew that Themistius understood it otherwise: God, 'in intellecting His own Self, intellects, all the intelligibles together'. In other words, 'God is the First *Arché* . . . He intellects together His own Self and all the things of which He is the *Arché*' (Pines 1987, esp. 179–89). Avicenna identifies with Themistius's teaching and cites it almost verbally. In contrast, Averroes in his *Long Commentary on the Metaphysics* mocks this interpretation of Themistius as that of 'one who does not understand the proofs of Aristotle here' and basically identifies with Alexander's interpretation (Pines 1987, 191–95). Unfortunately, Gersonides's super-commentary on the *Metaphysics* is no longer extant. Nonetheless, his position is clearly stated in the *Wars*. Gersonides begins Book 3 by explaining that there are two main views to the question regarding God's knowledge, that of Aristotle and that of the Jewish sages. He then recounts the two different interpretations of Aristotle's teaching on the subject in the *Metaphysics*. Here his source is certainly the medieval Hebrew translation of Themistius's paraphrase of *Metaphysics* Λ, a work he had in his own personal library, and likely also Averroes's *Long Commentary* on this passage in the *Metaphysics*. As an example of the Jewish sages, he cites a passage from Maimonides's *Guide of the Perplexed* III, 20, that states that God knows particular contingent things before they take place in an eternal unchanging knowledge. He then considers the philosophic merit of these various opposing views.

He begins by bringing eight known arguments in support of the Aristotelian position that God does not know particulars. One such argument—the first that he brings—runs as follows: God has no material faculty, every thing that apprehends particulars has a material faculty, and so, God does not apprehend particulars. Surprisingly, the argument he considers the strongest of those who deny God's knowledge of particulars is actually a variation of an Epicurean argument, cited by Maimonides in the name of the philosophers and debunked by him (*Guide* III, 16, 461–62). The argument is based on the disorder and evil in the world, which a knowing God would not have caused. Gersonides does not mention Maimonides's arguments against this proof (Gersonides 1984–99, *Wars* III, 2, 92–96). He does, however, bring arguments, which he explicitly takes from Maimonides (*Guide* III, 20–21), in support of the view of the sages that God does know particulars and against the view of the philosophers that He does not. Most notably he rehearses the details of Maimonides's emphasis on the great difference between human and divine cognition and that the term 'knowledge' is absolutely equivocal when applied to God and man. He then devotes the following chapter of the *Wars* (III, 3) to showing the inadequacy of Maimonides's arguments against the philosophers' position that God does not know particulars and, in particular, against his claim that the term 'knowledge' is applied absolutely equivocally when applied to God and man. Gersonides holds that it is predicated of God primarily and of man secondarily. Gersonides then suggests some other arguments for God's knowledge of particulars. He thus reaches the conclusion that God must know particulars in one respect but does not know them in another respect. He knows them in the sense that they are ordered and determined; He does not know them in the sense that they are not ordered, that is, in the sense that they are contingent and may be altered by human choice. He then shows that none of the eight arguments of the philosophers is valid against his own theory regarding God's knowledge.

Gersonides takes pains to show that his theory concerning God's knowledge of particulars is arrived at through theoretical speculation and differs in crucial respects from that of many philosophers and from that of the Jewish sages. For Gersonides, God has knowledge of particulars only insofar as human affairs are ordered and determined, which they are by the positions of the heavenly bodies, but also by God's eternal unchanging knowledge and by a causal determinism. Yet God does not know particulars insofar as this order may be altered or broken by human choice. God's knowledge does not change when an event happens or when one of two possibilities comes to be. Gersonides explains: 'God's knowledge of these events is based upon the intelligible order in His intellect, and since this order is immutable, His knowledge does not change when one of these events is realised, for His knowledge is not based upon them. . . . He knows them in a common, general way' (*Wars* III, 5, vol. 2, 134). Through this theory of causality, Gersonides is able to uphold man's absolute freedom of choice. Yet he does not really explain if the heavenly bodies, indeed, determine one's thoughts as well as one's activities, how it is that they do not determine one's choice. Gersonides concludes this discussion with a chapter (III, 6) in which he tries to show that his rather unorthodox position, arrived at through philosophical reasoning, is the same as that of the Torah.[12]

Moses Narboni (d. 1361) was a faithful and profound follower of Averroes and one of the most learned of the medieval Jews in the Greco-Arabic philosophical tradition. He is best known for his commentaries on Maimonides's *Guide* and al-Ghazālī's *Intentions of the Philosophers*, but he also wrote commentaries on numerous writings of the *falāsifa*, including a super-commentary on Averroes's *Middle Commentary on Aristotle's Physics*. His little *Treatise on Choice* was written shortly before his death. In this treatise he argues against determinism and for freedom of choice.

Narboni wrote the *Treatise on Choice* in response to a treatise by the apostate, Abner of Burgos, who had died some fifteen years earlier. Abner maintained a strict determinism and held that 'everything is predestined by divine decree.' Narboni, who considered Abner 'quite sagacious' and 'one of the distinguished of his generation', could not believe that such a philosopher could really hold such preposterous views, and he questioned his motives in doing so. Apparently Abner also maintained that even though all is necessitated, endeavour is necessary in order to achieve the desired result. Narboni did not accept determinism and claimed that Aristotle had already refuted it in *On Interpretation*, the *Physics*, and *Metaphysics*, Book 6. Yet for one who does hold determinism, he felt it absurd to claim that endeavour is needed to attain the predestined result. If an event is pre-determined, it must take place, and no lack of effort to bring it about or effort to prevent it will make a difference. In any case, if the outcome requires endeavour, then that endeavour is itself compelled (Narboni 2007, 144–45).

For Narboni, one may not argue that since all movements go back to the first movement, everything is determined causally, for 'what is subsequent does not follow of necessity from the antecedent' (Narboni 2007, 147). For example, an accidental cause may intervene. As for God's knowledge determining all, Narboni argues that this cannot be true. God 'is the most perfect existent and the most separate and most excellent form. He is intellect *per se* and independent of any other' (Narboni 2007, 148). He thinks Himself and in so doing thinks all existing things in an excellent manner, but not in the manner in which they actually exist, for then they would be prior in knowledge to Him. By knowing Himself, He, in a sense, knows all things in a single unchanging knowledge, yet His knowledge cannot be said to apply to particulars or to universals. Man thus has free choice, and God's knowledge does not determine which of two possibles will occur, for His knowledge does not apply to possible particulars. Yet in some way—which is not specified—'everything that obtains does so from His knowledge, and every good proceeds from Him; the possible is known to Him without being compelled' (Narboni 2007, 150–51). Narboni's God here may not be very different from Aristotle's Intellect of *Metaphysics* Λ. What is certain is that his discussion is premised on the Averroean-Maimonidean emphasis on the vast difference in kind between human and divine knowledge.

The last thinker we will discuss is Ḥasdai Crescas (1340–1410/1), pious rabbi of Barcelona and Saragossa, leader of Aragonese Jewry and learned critic of Averroean-Aristotelian physics, known for his bold pioneering concepts of time, space, actual infinity and the void, which helped pave the way for the overthrow of Aristotelian natural science. Crescas's radical deterministic views influenced Spinoza in his own rejection of free will. These teachings may all be found in his *Light of the Lord*.

Crescas held that there are six fundaments of Judaism, among which he counted God's knowledge of particulars and man's freedom of choice. In his discussion of God's knowledge of particulars, he, too, claims to rely on theoretical speculation. For Crescas, God knows particulars and He knows the infinite, the non-existent and the future, and He knows which of two possibilities will come to be. In the course of his discussion, he carefully considers and rebuts various claims and arguments on this topic by Maimonides and Gersonides (Crescas 2007; *Light of the Lord* II, 1).

While Crescas's view on God's knowledge of particulars is traditional, his opinion on free will is startling and unexpected and, as has been shown, developed during different stages of his life, at first under the influence of the Arabic-Hebrew Aristotelian tradition, and later in light of 'developments in contemporary Latin philosophy, particularly the theories of voluntarism which were advanced by Duns Scotus and his followers' (Harvey 1998, 137–38). Crescas's discussion of choice is well organised and takes place in the *Light of the Lord* II, 5, and is divided into six chapters. The first chapter brings arguments for the existence of the possible, the second for the antithesis that the possible does not exist, and the third counters all the arguments from the first two chapters. Crescas's conclusion is that the possible must exist in one sense, but not in another, and, in the fourth chapter, he brings biblical and rabbinic support for this conclusion. The fifth chapter, under the influence of the Christian voluntarists, treats the problem of morality in a strictly deterministic world. In what sense are we responsible for our pre-determined actions? The sixth chapter provides rabbinic support for the teachings of chapter 5. In the third chapter, Crescas shows that all the arguments for the existence of the possible prove only that the possible exists in itself, and all the arguments for its non-existence are only from the point of view of its causes. Crescas concludes in Avicennian fashion: 'Thus the complete truth implied by the Torah and by theoretical speculation is that the nature of the possible exists in things with respect to themselves, but not with respect to their causes'. No doubt aware that not all readers would appreciate or benefit from his deterministic picture of the world, Crescas immediately added: 'However, publicizing this is dangerous to the masses, for they will consider this an excuse to do evil' (Crescas 2007; *Light of the Lord* II, 5, 3, 224). According to Crescas's view, one may still justify reward and punishment in this deterministic world, but 'only when the agent does not feel coerced or compelled' (*Light* II, 5, 3, 224). As Warren Z. Harvey has explained, although for Crescas 'strict causal determinism prevails in nature, there is still a meaningful sense in which a thing may be said to be possible' (Harvey 1998, 142–43). This sense is from the agent's perspective when the 'agent does not feel coerced or compelled, which is the foundation of choice and will'. It is only for such an act—necessitated by the causes but still voluntary for Crescas—that divine punishment may be justified. Such an act, Crescas adds, is in accord with the appetitive faculty and the imaginative faculty, and thus 'an act of one's soul'.[13]

Crescas thus maintains a deterministic view of the world where everything is caused including human choice. Yet it is a world in which Crescas can still speak of choice as a fundament of the Law, through which one can justify divine reward and punishment. In the *Light* II (5, 5), under the influence of current scholastic discussions, Crescas addresses anew the problem of divine reward and punishment in a deterministic world, in particular with regard to one's beliefs. After all, if punishments are the effects of our acts—as Crescas had explained in chapter 3, one who comes close to a fire will be burned, whether his approach is voluntary or not—then what does it matter whether the act is voluntary or not? The punishment, which is the effect, will be the same. Nonetheless, Crescas argues that punishment should properly be for voluntary acts. He explains here that all beliefs are involuntary, for the believer feels compelled in his beliefs: 'Beliefs are not subject to human choice, and will has no influence on them'. Crescas's solution is that reward and punishment for beliefs are not for the beliefs themselves—for example, whether one believes that God exists or not—for beliefs are involuntary and not subject to the will. Reward and punishment are, rather, for the desire and joy that one has from these beliefs and the diligence and effort in acquiring them. Desire and joy are 'nothing other than the pleasure of will doing good' (*Light* II, 5, 5, 229–34). Of course, this desire and joy are also necessitated by the causes, but they are not accompanied by a feeling of coercion and thus voluntary. In short, they arise from the personality of the individual, from that individual's own soul.

3. CONCLUSION

Sir David Ross, the well-known Oxford ethicist and editor of Aristotle's writings, made virtually no use of Averroes's commentaries on the Aristotelian corpus in his commentaries on these texts. It seems his justification for this omission was that Averroes incorporated 'elements which belong to Muslim theology rather than to Aristotle' (Aristotle 1961, 44). We have seen that with regard to important theological principles such as creation and God's knowledge of particulars, Averroes's opinions

were hardly coloured by Muslim theology, and indeed, he put forward rather heterodox views in his commentaries. Curiously, the same charge of one's philosophy being
prejudiced by one's theology was leveled against Maimonides by certain post-Maimonidean Jewish philosophers. Albalag, for example, coupled Maimonides with the
great Islamic theologian al-Ghazālī, both of whom 'inclined from the path of Aristotle' and erred. According to Albalag, Maimonides, at least with regard to the problem
of creation, 'wanted to uphold the literal meaning of the Torah and refute the opinion of the philosophers' (Albalag 1973, 5, 50–51). Similarly, Gersonides claimed that
Maimonides's view on divine cognition 'is not implied by any philosophical principles', but it seems rather that 'theological considerations have forced him to this view'
(Gersonides 1984–99, vol. 2, 107). It is quite possible that both Albalag and Gersonides read Maimonides too literally. Regardless, the above discussions of the philosophical views of the medieval Jewish philosophers who wrote in Hebrew paint a
very different picture of the extent to which Jewish theology determined or influenced the philosophical teachings of many of them. Virtually all of them held that
philosophical demonstration leads to truth that is certain and cannot be denied.
Gersonides wrote that the 'Torah is not a *nomos* that compels us to believe false
things [that is, things that go against philosophical demonstration]' (Gersonides
1984–99, intro., vol. 1, 98). It should thus not be surprising that the views of the post-
Maimonidean Jewish philosophers on central topics such as creation and free will
are not at all monolithic. The wide spectrum of opinions on such basic philosophico-
theological subjects evidences a respect and appreciation for the powers of reason
and an unequivocal awareness of the certainty to which valid demonstration can
lead.

NOTES

1. There were medieval Arabic-to-Hebrew translations of all of Averroes's thirty-six
commentaries on Aristotle's writings, with the exception of the *Long Commentary on the
De anima* and the possible exception of the *Long Commentary on the De caelo*. The
former commentary is extant in a late-fifteenth-century Latin-to-Hebrew translation.
Five of Averroes's commentaries are extant in Hebrew translation, but not in the original
Arabic.

2. Hasse (forthcoming) has shown that William of Luna translated Averroes's middle
commentaries on *On Interpretation*, *Prior Analytics* and *Posterior Analytics* as well as those
on the *Categories* and Porphyry's *Isagoge*. These are precisely the five middle commentaries
translated into Hebrew by Anatoli.

3. See *Ruah Hen*, critical ed. in Elior (2011, intro. 237). On the author's aim to provide
an introduction or scientific background for understanding Maimonides's *Guide*, see Elior
(2011, 16–17, 52–58). Elior (59–72, 265–75) brings arguments for attributing *Ruah Hen* to
Jacob Anatoli.

4. This is not, of course, to say that philosophy died out in Islam. We are, for
example, learning more and more about the rich and scholarly study of Avicenna's writings
in the East for many centuries after his death, but this philosophic tradition was quite

different from the one established by al-Fārābī. See Wisnovsky (2004), and essays collected in the recent collections, Janssens (and De Smet 2002) and Langermann (2009). See also Nadja Germann's section on Avicenna's legacy in her chapter (Chapter 4) on Avicenna in the present volume.

    5. Albalag did not finish the translation. Isaac Pulgar, a contemporary and somewhat like-minded thinker, completed the third and final section on natural science.

    6. Al-Fārābī (1969, sec. 55, pp. 44–45): 'Now when one acquires knowledge of the beings or receives instruction in them, if he perceives their ideas themselves with his intellect, and his assent to them is by means of certain demonstration, then the science that comprises these cognitions is *philosophy*. But if they are known by imagining them through similitudes that imitate them, and assent to what is imagined of them is caused by persuasive methods, then the ancients call what comprises these cognitions *religion*. . . . In everything of which philosophy gives an account that is demonstrative and certain, religion gives an account based on persuasive arguments'.

    7. Cf., for example, *Guide* II (13) and II (25). Maimonides famously explains the seven causes for contradictions in books in his introduction to the *Guide*, 17–20. He explicitly states at the conclusion of this discussion that 'Divergences that are to be found in this Treatise are due to the fifth cause and the seventh'.

    8. Fraenkel (2007, xii). Fraenkel discusses Ibn Tibbon's interpretation of Maimonides's views on creation in chap. 3, 162–76.

    9. *Guide* II (30, 353). For Maimonides here, Aristotle's *Meteorology* is the key for unlocking the secrets of creation. Ibn Tibbon's ensuing great interest in the *Meteorology* led him to translate that work from Arabic into Hebrew in 1210, the first book of Aristotle to be translated into Hebrew.

    10. Aristotle (*Physics* I, 9 192a 26–34); Averroes (MS, I.3.5, fol. 11v).

    11. Cf. the approaches to this subject by the Christian thinkers discussed by Thomas Pink and John Marenbon in their chapters (Chapters 26 and Chapter 1.2.3) in the present volume.

    12. Charles Manekin, in several learned articles over the past two decades, has propounded a far more conservative or religious interpretation of Gersonides's opinion regarding God's knowledge of particulars. For Manekin's Gersonides, it is not true that God does not know particulars insofar as the astral order may be altered or broken by human choice. Rather, Manekin explains, the human mind 'contains, in a certain manner, part of the intelligible plan of the universe, and, in a certain manner, the human individual becomes (part of) that plan. Now God, in knowing Himself, knows the intelligible plan of the universe, and in so far as humans acquire knowledge from the agent intellect, and act according to it, they are known by God' (Manekin 1998, 152). In other words, God knows when human choice based on reason chooses a different path than that ordered by the celestial bodies because this choice is ordered by God's intelligible plan, even when it goes against the astrally determined plan. See, for example, Manekin (1998).

    13. *Light* (II, 5, 224). Cf. Spinoza (*Ethics* I, definition 7).

BIBLIOGRAPHY

Albalag, Isaac. 1973. *Sefer Tiqqun ha-De'ot*, ed. Georges Vajda. Jerusalem: Israel Academy of Sciences and Humanities.

———. 2000. *The Emendation of the Opinions*, introduction, trans. Charles H. Manekin. In *The Jewish Philosophy Reader*, ed. Oliver Leaman, Daniel H. Frank and Charles H. Manekin, 247–50. London: Routledge.

Al-Fārābī. 1969. *The Attainment of Happiness*, trans. Muhsin Mahdi. In his *Alfarabi's Philosophy of Plato and Aristotle*, rev. ed. Ithaca, NY: Cornell University Press.

Altmann, Alexander. 1974. 'The religion of the thinkers: Free will and predestination in Saadia, Bahya, and Maimonides'. In *Religion in a Religious Age*, ed. S. D. Goitein, 25–52. Cambridge, MA: Association for Jewish Studies.

Aquinas, Thomas. 1963. *Commentary on Aristotle's Physics*, ed. Richard J. Spath and W. Edmund Thirlkel. New Haven, CT: Yale University Press.

Aristotle. 1961. *De anima*, ed. David Ross. Oxford: Oxford University Press.

Averroes. MS. *Middle Commentary on Aristotle's Physics*. Hamburg, Germany: Staatsbibliothek (MS Hebr. 20).

Bianchi, Luca. 2008. *Pour une histoire de la 'double vérité'*. Paris: Librairie Philosophique J. Vrin.

Crescas, Hasdai. 2007. *Light of the Lord*, II, 1, and II, 5, trans. Charles Manekin. In Manekin 2007.

Elior, Ofer. 2011. *Ruaḥ Ḥen as a Looking Glass: The Study of Science in Different Jewish Cultures as Reflected in a Medieval Introduction to Aristotelian Science and in its Later History* [Hebrew; abstract in English]. Ph.D. diss., Ben Gurion University of the Negev, Israel.

Falaquera, Shem-Ṭov ben Joseph. 2001. *Moreh ha-Moreh*, ed. Yair Shiffman. Jerusalem: World Union of Jewish Studies.

Fenton, Paul B. 2009. 'Maimonides—Father and son: Continuity and change'. In *Traditions of Maimonideanism*, ed. Carlos Fraenkel, 103–37. Leiden, the Netherlands: Brill.

Fontaine, Resianne. 2000. 'Judah ben Solomon ha-Cohen's *Midrash ha-Ḥokhmah*: Its sources and use of sources'. In Harvey, 2000a, 191–210.

Fraenkel, Carlos. 2007. *From Maimonides to Samuel ibn Tibbon: The Transformation of the Dalâlat al-ḥâ'irîn into the Moreh ha-Nevukhim* [Hebrew; abstract in English]. Jerusalem: Magnes Press.

Freudenthal, Gad. 2008. Samuel Ibn Tibbon's Avicennian Theory of an Eternal World. *Aleph* 8:41–129.

Gersonides. MS. Commentary on Averroes' Middle Commentary on *Aristotle's Physics*. MS Paris, BNF Hebr. 964.

———. 1984–99. *The Wars of the Lord*, trans. Seymour Feldman. 3 vols. Philadelphia: Jewish Publication Society.

Glasner, Ruth. 1995. Levi ben Gershom and the Study of Ibn Rushd in the Fourteenth Century. *Jewish Quarterly Review* 86:51–90.

Harvey, Steven. 1992. Did Maimonides' Letter to Samuel ibn Tibbon Determine Which Philosophers Would Be Studied by Later Jewish Thinkers? *Jewish Quarterly Review* 83:51–70.

———, ed. 2000a. *The Medieval Hebrew Encyclopedias of Science and Philosophy*. Dordrecht, the Netherlands: Kluwer Academic Publishers.

———. 2000b. 'Shem-Ṭov ibn Falaquera's *De'ot ha-Filosofim*: Its sources and use of sources'. In Harvey 2000, 211–37.

———. 2002. Falaquera's Alfarabi: An Example of the Judaization of the Islamic *falāsifah*. *Trumah: Zeitschrift der Hochschule für Jüdische Studien Heidelberg* 12:97–112.

Harvey, Warren Zev. 1998. *Physics and Metaphysics in Ḥasdai Crescas*. Amsterdam: J.C. Gieben.

———. 2000. 'Levi ben Abraham of Villefranche's controversial encyclopedia'. In Harvey 2000a, 171–88.

Hasse, Dag N. Forthcoming. 'Latin Averroes translations of the first half of the thirteenth century'. In *Proceedings of the XII International Congress of Medieval Philosophy, Palermo, 16– 22 September 2007*.

Janssens, Jules and Daniel De Smet, eds. 2002. *Avicenna and His Heritage*. Louvain, Belgium: Leuven University Press.

Langermann, Y. Tzvi, ed. 2009. *Avicenna and His Legacy: A Golden Age of Science and Philosophy*. Turnhout, Belgium: Brepols.

Maimonides. 1963. *The Guide of the Perplexed*, trans. Shlomo Pines. Chicago: University of Chicago Press.

Manekin, Charles. 1998. 'On the limited-omniscience interpretation of Gersonides' theory of divine knowledge'. In *Perspectives on Jewish Thought and Mysticism*, ed. Alfred L. Ivry, Elliot R. Wolfson and Allan Arkush, 135–70. Amsterdam: Harwood Academic Publishers.

———, ed. 2007. *Medieval Jewish Philosophical Writings*. Cambridge: Cambridge University Press.

Narboni, Moses. 2007. *The Treatise on Choice*, trans. Charles Manekin. In Manekin 2007, 143–52.

Pines, Shlomo. 1967. *Scholasticism after Thomas Aquinas and the Teachings of Ḥasdai Crescas and his Predecessors*. Jerusalem: Israel Academy of Sciences and Humanities.

———. 1987. 'Some distinctive metaphysical conceptions in Themistius' commentary on Book Lambda and their place in the history of philosophy'. In *Aristoteles Werk und Wirkung Paul Moraux Gewidmet*, ed. Jürgen Wiesner, vol. 2, 177–204. Berlin: Walter De Gruyter.

Robinson, James T. 2005. 'The Ibn Tibbon family: A dynasty of translators in medieval Provence'. In *Be'erot Yitzhak: Studies in Memory of Isadore Twersky*, ed. Jay M. Harris, 193–224. Cambridge, MA: Harvard University Press.

Sela, Shlomo. 2003. *Abraham Ibn Ezra and the Rise of Medieval Hebrew Science*. Leiden, the Netherlands: Brill.

Shiffman, Yair. 1992–3. Shem Ṭob Ibn Falqerah as Interpreter of Maimonides' *Guide of the Perplexed*—Outlines of His Thought [Hebrew; abstract in English]. *Maimonidean Studies* 3:1–29.

Wisnovsky, Robert. 2004. 'The nature and scope of Arabic philosophic commentary in post-classical (ca. 1100–1900 AD) Islamic intellectual history: Some preliminary observations'. In *Philosophy, Science and Exegesis in Greek, Arabic and Latin Commentaries*, ed. Peter Adamson, Han Baltussen and M. W. F. Stone, vol. 2, 149–91. London: Institute of Classical Studies.

Zonta, Mauro. 2006. *Hebrew Scholasticism in the Fifteenth Century: A History and Sourcebook*. Dordrecht, the Netherlands: Springer.

CHAPTER 8

LATIN PHILOSOPHY TO 1200

CHRISTOPHE ERISMANN

THE first centuries of the Middle Ages can be identified as a distinct period in the history of medieval philosophy. Its most obvious characteristic is the fact that texts central to Aristotle's thought, such as the *Metaphysics*, the *Physics* and *On the Soul* were not available to Latin readers. By contrast, during this period, the logical treatises of Aristotle—first and foremost the *Categories* and the *De interpretatione* (*On Interpretation*)—supplemented by Porphyry's *Isagoge* (*Introduction*), were often read, commented upon and used as a basis for philosophical reasoning. The content of these texts set most of the philosophical agenda. The main feature of this period—the Early Middle Ages—which ends with the foundation of the first universities, is a concentration on logic and its possible ontological implications, with special focus on issues such as essence, the status of genera and species (problem of universals) and individuality. Much thought was given to the relation between language and reality, ranging from the naïve theory of Fredegisus of Tours early in the ninth century, who held that since there are names of negative things, the negative things to which these names refer must exist, to much more technical debates during the twelfth century on the reference of common names. The other main aspect of early-medieval philosophical enquiry—which probably stems from the lack of a clear distinction between the fields of application of logic and ontology—is the question of whether logical tools such as Aristotle's ten categories and Porphyry's Tree[1] can also be used to understand sensible reality. This is formulated in the following question: Are the categories ten genera of being, or are they only a means of classifying predicates? In its realist form, this reflection tends to hold to a logic of being, in the sense that logical structures are supposed to map the structure of reality itself. One of the central fields of enquiry of philosophical thought in this period is categorical ontology. Aristotle's ontological square—the distinction between particular substances, universal substances, particular accidents and universal accidents—provides the terms of the problem: which among these four types of entities must be admitted into one's ontology?

Early-medieval philosophy was not only concerned with logic; it also gave rise to such interesting theories in other areas of philosophy as Anselm of Canterbury's ontological proof of the existence of God and Peter Abelard's intentionalist ethics. Before moving to the main philosophical discussions of this time, three preliminary comments must be made on (1) the chronological limits of the period, (2) the available texts and (3) the places of learning and the great figures. We shall then go on to examine the contribution of early-medieval philosophy to categorical ontology, logic and semantics, ethics and philosophical theology.

1. CONTEXT AND FIGURES

1.1. Chronological Limits

To use a 'philosophical' chronology, early-medieval philosophy is the historical space between two waves of translation of Aristotle's works into Latin: that of Aristotle's logical texts (*Categories, De interpretatione, Prior Analytics, Topics, Sophistical Refutations*) and of Porphyry's *Isagoge* by Boethius between 510 and 522 and the translation, from Greek or Arabic, of the so-called 'natural writings' of Aristotle during the second half of the twelfth century, but entering widespread use only in the period from about 1200. The period finishes with the entry of Arabic thought (mainly Avicenna) and the rediscovery of all Aristotle's works. This second wave includes Latin translations by James of Venice,[2] Burgundio of Pisa[3] and Gerard of Cremona.[4] Gerard also translated the *Liber de causis*—an influential summary of the philosophy of Plotinus and Proclus, of which traces can be found in Alan of Lille.

Translations allow us to define the period; they also provide many of the questions that were discussed (this is obvious in the case of texts of Aristotelian logic). The reason for this is the nature of philosophical enquiry during the Early Middle Ages: a large part of philosophy was exegesis, that is, rational presentation and discussion of texts. Leaving aside Boethius, who followed the Neoplatonic habit of writing commentaries, early-medieval exegesis began with the practice of writing glosses in the margins and between lines of texts and evolved towards a more sophisticated form of commentary that follows the text, and later a form of commentary that reorganises its matter. Commentaries were often the place in which philosophical theories were expounded—these theories being sometimes quite distant from the position defended in the text with which the commentary deals. Boethius set out his abstractionism in his second commentary to Porphyry's *Isagoge*; Abelard, his semantics in his commentary to the *De interpretatione*; Bernard of Chartres—if Dutton's attribution is correct—his philosophy of nature in his commentary to the *Timaeus*; Gilbert of Poitiers, his innovative particularist ontology in his commentary to Boethius's *Opuscula sacra*. Other examples could be given. Obviously, not all texts are commentaries—think, for example, of John Scottus Eriugena's *Periphyseon* and Anselm of Canterbury's *Monologion*; however, the proportion of commentaries in the philosophical production of the period is very high and can be compared to the intense exegetical practice that took place among Neoplatonic authors in Athens and Alexandria, or to the central role of discussions of the *Sentences* of Peter Lombard in the last centuries of the Middle Ages.

The first Latin author to practise philosophical exegesis, Boethius was a translator and commentator of Peripatetic logic, but he was also a philosopher in his own right. He opened a long tradition that was to reach its climax in the dozens of commentaries that were written on the logical corpus during the twelfth century.[5]

1.2. Early Medieval Libraries and Readings

Which philosophical texts could an early-medieval Latin author read? Aristotle, indeed, but only his logical texts; very little of Plato[6] (the part of the *Timaeus* translated by Calcidius); and texts whose main intention was theological, but which had much philosophical content—mainly Boethius's *Opuscula sacra*, the writings of pseudo-Dionysius in Eriugena's translation, and Augustine. Logic held a central role; it 'represented' philosophy in the educational scheme of the time, that of the seven 'liberal arts' (the linguistic arts of the *trivium*, including grammar, logic, rhetoric; and the mathematical arts of the *quadrivium*, including arithmetic, geometry, astronomy and music).

Knowledge of Aristotle's texts was limited to the logical treatises included in the set of texts called the *logica vetus*. These were first and foremost the *Categories* (which were known at first only through a paraphrase, probably of Neoplatonic origin, that circulated under the title *Categoriae decem* [*The Ten Categories*] and was falsely attributed to Augustine; in fact, it probably originated in the circle of Themistius in the fourth century), *On Interpretation* and, to a lesser degree and mainly during the twelfth century, the *Topics*. Some knowledge of the *Prior Analytics* is attested before the end of the twelfth century, and the *Sophistical Refutations* were intensively studied from the 1130s. Authors from Alcuin to the tenth century knew logic mainly through encyclopedias by Cassiodorus, Isidore of Seville and Martianus Capella, and also through Apuleius's *Periermenias* and the above-mentioned *Categoriae decem*. By the eleventh century, the textual basis of the logical curriculum broadened and was organised around the translations and commentaries Boethius had given of Aristotle's *Categories* and of the text supposed to introduce them, Porphyry's *Isagoge* (early-medieval authors kept the Neoplatonic habit of reading the *Isagoge* in parallel with—or even before—the *Categories*); this was completed by Boethius's textbooks on categorical and hypothetical syllogisms and topical arguments. Regarding the only text of the *Organon* not to have been translated by Boethius, the *Posterior Analytics*, commentaries appeared in the 1230s only.

Given the available texts and the fact that the doctrine of the *Categories* was the principal and most useful philosophical tool available, it is hardly surprising that the issue of the object of logic arose and that we find reflections on its field of validity (the order of words or the order of being) and its possible application to God. This last question had particular weight due to the fact that both Augustine and Boethius considered it in their respective *De trinitates* (Augustine, *De trinitate* V.1.2–V.2.3; Boethius, *De trinitate*, ch. IV).

1.3. Centres of Learning

Early-medieval philosophy[7] developed in several different types of settings. For the most part, it followed the more general evolution of scholarly institutions devoted to the teaching of theology and of the seven liberal arts, in particular the move from monasteries to cathedral schools. It was particularly marked, however, by the development in twelfth-century Paris of many competing schools dedicated to the teaching of logic. This review of institutions will give us the opportunity to introduce some of the main figures of thought during the first centuries of the Middle Ages.[8]

Properly medieval philosophy in Latin began three centuries after Boethius, at the royal court of the Carolingian king, during the period of cultural revival called the Carolingian Renaissance. Alcuin of York[9] revived the study of arts and theology at the court of Charlemagne, whose personal involvement in this intellectual project was remarkable, in particular in approving of logic as a tool for understanding Christian doctrine and as a weapon in religious controversy.

Philosophy continued to be present at the court of Charles the Bald—Charlemagne's grandson—where John Scottus Eriugena[10] held a central place. Here again, the support given by the king to philosophy was important, in particular to the programme of translations from the Greek of Church Fathers (pseudo-Dionysius, Maximus the Confessor, Gregory of Nyssa), which Eriugena set out to provide.

At the end of the ninth century, thought developed in large monasteries in what is now France (St Amand, Corbie, Fleury and Tours), Germany (Reichenau, Fulda), Italy (Bobbio), and Switzerland (St Gallen). Discussions stemming in these intellectual milieus often originated in theological questions of the time (predestination, the Eucharist).[11] Monastic activity was pursued during the two following centuries.[12] It culminated with one of the most brilliant early-medieval thinkers, Anselm of Canterbury.[13] During the eleventh century, debates emerged on the philosophical rationalisation of theological discourse and on the role of dialectic in this process.[14]

From the end of the tenth century, and during the eleventh, urban cathedral schools became particularly important—the best known being Notre Dame in Paris; this phenomenon is illustrated by thinkers such as Gerbert in Rheims, Fulbert in Chartres and Anselm (not to be confused with Anselm of Canterbury) in Laon.[15]

The beginning of the twelfth century gave rise to intense debates about logic;[16] these became even more frequent with the flourishing of competing and self-consciously different schools of liberal arts, mainly logic, all based in Paris and its surroundings— Paris underwent at the time a period of very rapid growth. This multiplication can be explained by a historical process, which Richard Southern called the deinstitutionalisa- tion of the *schola*, that is, the fact that teaching became detached from the corporate schools of the past and attached to an individual master who taught wherever he could find a place to teach. While cathedral schools only allowed one master, in Paris it was possible to buy a *licentia docenti* (licence to teach) by paying a fee to the cathedral authorities and to open a school and settle as a master.

The success of this new type of teaching was such that there were at least 25 well-known schools within a hundred miles of Paris. From the point of view of the history of philosophy, the most important were concentrated in Paris and on the Mont Ste Geneviève. These schools, also called *sectae*, varied in size, structure and, most importantly, doctrinal position. The main ones are the fol- lowing: the *Nominales* (the followers of Peter Abelard), the *Porretani* (Gilbert of Poitiers or Porreta[17] had a posterity and influence unequalled in the twelfth cen- tury[18]), the *Parvipontani or Adamitae* (the sectators of Adam of Balsham,[19] also known as Parvipontanus, because his school was to be found at the Petit Pont in Paris), the *Melidunenses* or *Robertini* (the disciples of Robert of Melun (d. 1167), whose teaching is known to us through the *Ars Meliduna*) and the *Albricani* or *Montani* (the disciples of Alberic[20] on the Mont Ste Geneviève).[21] This multipli- cation of schools and the need to defend the one to which one belonged against the attacks of rival schools had as a consequence increased technicality of phi- losophy and a higher degree of determination of positions. John of Salisbury (d. 1180), who studied with Peter Abelard and William of Conches, gives in the *Metalogicon* a vivid testimony of the milieu of the schools of logic (John of Salisbury 1991).

Although the schools of logic—through their novelty, their vitality and the quality of their philosophical productions—held a central role, they do not account for all institutions during the twelfth century, nor for the width of philosophical interests of the period. Aristotelianism dominated in milieus interested in the study of logic, but there was also a Platonic trend, characterised by strong interest in nat- ural philosophy[22] in a theoretical approach, by the practice of exegesis of Plato's *Timaeus*[23] and by a taste for literary or even allegorical writings. This sort of specu- lation is often associated with the School of Chartres; however, the institutional reality of this school has been questioned.[24]

The field of theology, never absent from the schools of logic that were often theologico-logical schools, was particularly considered in the one founded by Wil- liam of Champeaux, the School of St Victor[25] and by some of the notable figures of the century, from the conservative theologian Bernard of Clairvaux (d. 1153) to Peter Lombard (d. 1160).[26]

In 1200, Philip Augustus issued the privilege to the schools in Paris, which marks, at least symbolically, the beginning of the University of Paris. The founding of universities is the starting point of a new era in medieval philosophy, that of the great masters of scholasticism.

2. Areas, Problems and Theses

Philosophical speculation during the Early Middle Ages, although often under-estimated nowadays, was rich and diverse. It touched many fields of philosophy: logic, the ontology of the sensible world, semantics, the metaphysics of divine being and ethics were the most discussed; topics in psychology and natural philosophy were also considered. In what follows, we shall attempt to present some of the most original and philosophically interesting aspects of this thought. The classification into fields that is used here refers to the nature of the debated issues such as it is understood today and not to the division of the sciences[27] at the time, and this for several reasons. We cannot speak of *a* division of philosophy accepted by all early medieval thinkers; two competing models of division, the one Platonic, the other Peripatetic, were upheld. Both models were outlined by Isidore of Seville in the chapter of his *Etymologiae* (II.24.3–16) he dedicates to *dialectica*. The so-called Platonic model divides philosophy into *physica* (*naturalis*), *ethica* (*moralis*) and *logica* (*rationalis*). The model attributed to Aristotle divides philosophy into *inspectiva* (which is itself subdivided into *naturalis*, *doctrinalis* and *divina*) and *actualis* (which subdivides into *moralis*, *dispensativa* and *civilis*).

2.1. Categorical Ontology

The central issue of ontological thought during the Early Middle Ages can be summarised as a questioning on the types of entities that make up the furniture of the sensible world. This questioning is based on the ontological square of Aristotle's *Categories*: the division of beings into primary and secondary substances, and into particular and universal accidents,[28] as well as the relations these entities have to each other. This square—an exhaustive division of everything there is—is obtained through the combination of a purely ontological criterion—inherence or not in another entity— which allows the distinction between substance and accident, and of a predicative and ontological criterion—that of being said or predicated of another entity—which allows to distinguish between particular and universal items see table 8.1. The ontological aspect of this criterion is emphasised if we postulate that 'being said of' is the linguistic expression of the ontological fact 'being instantiated or exemplified by'.

The nature of each of the types of entities that compose this ontological square has been discussed. Two of them were particularly debated during the Early Latin Middle Ages: universal substances and particular accidents—in contemporary

Table 8.1. Aristotle's Ontological Square

	Inherent in something else (in a subject)	Not inherent in something else (not in a subject)
Predicated of something else (said of a subject)	Universal accidents (e.g., white, knowledge)	Universal substances (e.g., man, horse)
Not predicated of something else (not said of a subject)	Individual accidents (e.g., this white, this knowledge)	Individual substances (e.g., this man, this horse)

language, universals and tropes. The early-medieval debate on secondary substances covers the field of the contemporary debate on essence, universals and natural kinds; it is one of the debates in which early-medieval inventiveness was strongest. The Latin Early Middle Ages provided the first medieval formulation of the main alternatives: universalism, which was defended in the form of immanent realism, and ontological particularism. The strictly Platonic position, which postulates separate universals, was not defended during the Early Middle Ages (although its Christianised *ersatz*, the theory of divine ideas—that is, *ante rem* universals in the mind of God—was generally accepted). Before considering in more detail these competing positions, note that there was a general agreement on some ontological theses originating in the *Categories*:

    1. An individual is constituted of a substance and of accidental properties.

The scheme in use was that of substance-accidents, in which substance is a subject of inherence for accidents, and not the hylemorphic model, in which an individual is defined as a composite of matter and form. The acceptance of this thesis also means holding a constituent ontology and not a relational ontology. Early-medieval philosophers believed that an individual is constituted of both essential and accidental properties.

    2. The world is made up of members of natural kinds.

This belief, which can be qualified as naturalist or essentialist, originates in Aristotle's *Categories*; it states that any given individual is necessarily a member of a species: for each individual, x, there is one specific universal, U, such that x is U. This thesis has an epistemological dimension: we know unproblematically to which kind any given particular substance belongs. A correlated thesis was made explicit by Peter Abelard: only the particulars belonging to natural kinds are substances, artefacts are not. He states (Abelard 1970, 417: 23–37; Abelard 1919–27, 298: 33–36) that human artificers do not produce new substances but merely make new accidental alterations to already existing substances. Since Porphyry's Tree was a universally accepted conceptual structure, we can extend this thesis to say that every member of a given natural kind has the same underlying ontological structure that can be analysed in terms of genera, species and differentiae. This thesis, however, does not imply anything as to the ontological status of the specific universal in question.

Here the agreement ceases because the mode of being of these genera and species is debated. So the structure of Porphyry's Tree is understood either as a hierarchy of universals, or, following Peter Abelard, as an 'analysis of the structure of particular substances of different kinds from particular differentiae' (Marenbon 1997a, 118). The alternative that structures early-medieval questioning[29] is given in the following interrogation:[30]

> Do *in re* universals (that is, entities which are neither separate Platonic forms, nor divine ideas, nor concepts, nor, obviously, concrete individuals) exist? In contemporary terms, do repeatable entities instantiated by many spatio-temporally distinct individuals exist?

Authors who answer 'yes' to this question defend realism; authors who answer 'no' believe that everything that exists is particular. However, this commitment to particularism is only a partial answer that has to be completed by an explanation of the resemblance that exists among co-specific individuals and of the reference of common names. Let us consider these alternatives more closely.

a. An Endorsement of Universalism: Immanent Realism

Immanent realism[31] was widely accepted during the Early Middle Ages until the potent criticism Peter Abelard gave of the version of this theory defended by William of Champeaux—William's first theory of universals, known as material essence realism. It can be argued that immanent realism was held by three authors in addition to William: John Scottus Eriugena, Anselm of Canterbury and Odo of Cambrai (see Erismann 2007). In a nutshell, this theory states that universal entities exist in individuals, and not as separate entities. This theory is truly realist insofar as it states the real existence of the universal as a universal. Universals do not exist separately but are immanent to individuals; they are just as real as individuals. The universal cat is completely realised in each particular cat and causes its catness. This theory does not consider universality to be restricted to predication—being said of several—but as the capacity of existing simultaneously in several spatio-temporally distinct individuals.

Early-medieval immanent realism can be summarised in six theses. This metaphysical theory states: (1) the real existence of universals, that is, of the natural kinds to which particulars belong; (2) that universals do not exist separately from particulars (universals and particulars are in a relation of ontological interdependence); (3) that universals constitute the substantial being of the particulars that are subordinate to them; (4) that a genus or species is entirely and simultaneously present in each of its subdivisions (no degrees of instantiation); (5) that the specific substance is common to all members of a species (the species expresses all the essential being of its members—substantially Plato is nothing more than man); and (6) that individuals of the same species are individuated by a unique bundle of accidents (no essential individuation).[32] In this theory the universal man is taken to exist simultaneously in each of its particulars and to be fully realised in them. Socrates is composed of the universal man—which constitutes his essence, common to all the members of the species—and of a bundle of accidents, the *collectio proprietatum* in Anselm's words (e.g., *De processione Spiritus Sancti* XVI, 217: 17–20, see Erismann 2003). There is no essential individuation of particulars (the specific essence is all the individual's substantial being, and this essence is common to all the members of the species); individuality is explained through the possession of a unique bundle of accidental properties, following the pattern of the *bundle of properties* that was given by Porphyry (*Isagoge* 7: 9–27) and endorsed by Boethius in the *De trinitate* (167: 46–168: 63). This particular collection cannot be found in another individual, in particular, because of the properties of place and time.

This theory is a reinterpretation of the ontology of the *Categories* with the help of Porphyry's *Isagoge*, which often provides textual authority for taking some distance with Aristotle's text. This doctrine is clearly of Aristotelian inspiration as it admits kind essentialism and rejects uninstantiated universals by assuming a clear commitment to instantiation (there is no such thing as a universal essence that is not instantiated by at least one individual). The thesis of the complete realisation of the universal in each individual follows from Aristotle's statement that substances do not admit of more or less (*Categories* 2b23–28, 3b33, 4a7). Eriugena makes use of this idea when he emphasises the omnipresence of the universal in the following formula: *nullus homo alio homine humanior est* (*Periphyseon* 943 A).

This theory questions some of Aristotle's positions—an example of this is the rejection of the ontological priority of primary substances (on the basis of a passage from the *Isagoge* in which essences are said to be prior to that of which they are predicated, 23: 21–22). This is completed by the claim that the species is a substantially complete entity, and the passage to the inferior level—that of the individuals—does not bring any additional substantiality since no substantial element, but only accidental ones, is added. In this version of realism, if U is a specific universal (e.g., the human species) and x is a member of the species (e.g., Paul), then U just is, and so exhausts, the essence of x. This position also states, still on the basis of the *Isagoge*, strong substantial unity of the species. From the point of view of substance, all men are one man.

b. A Commitment to Ontological Particularism

As such, ontological particularism is a general metaphysical concern; it is an essential part of non-realist theories. Its tenet can be expressed as follows:

> Every thing that exists is essentially particular.

This principle was not invented during the Middle Ages—it can be found in Late Antiquity, for example, in the ontology of John Philoponus—but it was stated particularly clearly during the twelfth century. It can be understood in terms of separateness. According to this position, there is a basic and unanalysable fact that every thing, whether a substance or a property (a *form* in the vocabulary of the twelfth century), whether it is essential, such as the differentiae, or accidental, is separate from every other thing. The principle of ontological particularism implies the principle of the essential individuality of the particular: this individual is such by its own essence, or, to use Abelard's expression, 'personally discrete in its essence'.

This position does not state that nothing can exist unless it is individuated; it rejects the whole idea of individuation (for it involves entities that are universal before individuation) in favour of the idea that individuality is a primitive fact and not the product of a process of individuation.

On the basis of this particularist thesis, different ontologies were developed. Three of them deserve particular attention.

According to the testimony of Anselm in his *Epistola de incarnatione Verbi*, Roscelin[33] defended particularism and strict ontological economy. His position was based on two principles:

1. Universality is a property of terms only; universals have no real existence and are only words—more precisely, Roscelin states that universal substances—that is, genera and species—are only words;
2. Qualities exist only in a particular state in individual subjects (application of (1) to the case of qualities).

Taken literally, the first thesis, according to which the universal is just a *flatus vocis* (an 'emission of sound'; a universal name is a *flatus vocis* insofar as it does not refer to anything; in particular it does not refer to any existing universal essence), involves the rejection, not only of strong ontological realism (this is obvious), but also of a strong version of conceptualism, upholding that universals are conceptual beings. Roscelin's theory, as we can attempt to reconstruct it from Anselm's testimony, appears to depend upon a transfer of the problem to language. First, Roscelin clearly rejects reified universals—nothing that exists can be universal. Second, Roscelin does not appear to emphasise the importance of concepts in the way Aristotle did. Third, Roscelin introduces his own solution: the unity of the members of a species is neither ontological nor conceptual, but it can be explained through predication. Roscelin interprets specific unity as being one of name. Belonging to a species does not depend upon having a common specific essence, but on the fact that the name of the species can be correctly attributed to the different individuals, in other words, that the same name can be predicated univocally of those individuals, and only of them. Socrates belongs to the species man because it is correct to predicate 'man' of his particular substance. Unfortunately we have no information as to what might be the criterion of correctness of predication.

Peter Abelard combines particularist theses with a semantic account of universality.[34] Abelard's solution is interesting in that it avoids attributing the being of a thing (*res*) to universals (he only ascribes universality to words). He does this by introducing two notions into his ontology: that of 'condition', 'state' (*status*), and that of 'what a statement says' (*dictum propositionis*). None of these notions refer to a thing, but they are not nothing (*nihil*) either; they have being in thought (which is not the being of things—Abelard denies the existence of propositions—nor that of names); they are non-thing items. These two notions allow Abelard to provide an answer to the two main questions of his ontological particularism: (1) What underlies the resemblance between two individuals of the same species or possessing the same property? And (2) what grounds the predication of the common name 'man' as to its subjects? The answer holds in the following position. Socrates and Plato are alike in being men. Abelard holds that Socrates and Plato come together in this, that they are men (*in esse hominem*); they agree in the status of man. This '*esse hominem*' expresses the status, the fact that Socrates and Plato are both men (its closest contemporary philosophical equivalent is the notion of a state of affairs). This status grounds both resemblance and predication. The common causes of the imposition of universal words are status.

Another possible combination of ontological particularism is with an exemplarist theory, or even with Platonism: the form or model is particular, and all its copies or imitations, realised or not in matter, are also particular. Gilbert of Poitiers seems to be an example of this. He is an ontological particularist[35] but seems to endorse some Platonic claims.

Gilbert states his ontology on the basis of two couples of concepts: *quod est* and *quo est* on the one hand, *subsistens* and *subsistentia* on the other. Following Boethius, he distinguishes between 'that which is' (*quod est*) and 'that through which a particular thing is' (*quo est*). A *quod est*, also called *subsistens*, is an individual, a concrete object, whereas the *quo est* is the property by which the individual is and is what it is. For Gilbert, anything that subsists is a particular thing. This is true of individuals (*subsistents* in Gilbert's terminology), but also of every subsistence (that is, every essential property), every quality and quantity, every accident. Every human being is a human being through his or her own humanity; every white thing is white through its own whiteness. There are as many humanities as there are men,[36] as many whitenesses as there are white things. The number of subsistences is the same as that of the subsistents of which they are the being. The central principle of Gilbert's ontology is: 'That which is in one thing cannot at the same time be in another' ('nihil quod sit in uno est in alio'). This principle is drawn from Boethius (*everything that is in a singular is itself singular*, 'quicquid in singulari est, singulare est') and precludes the notion of sharing or commonness. Considered in the *subsistens–subsistentiae* framework that underlies Porretan ontology, the plurality of individuals—which can be easily and undeniably observed—presupposes an equivalent plurality of subsistences. A subsistence can be the cause of the being of only one subsistent (*una singularis subsistentia nonnisi unum numero facit subsistentem*; Gilbert of Poitiers 1966, 58: 42–45). No subsistence can be common to two or more subsistents, for that would make them common entities.[37] Forms, or *subsistentiae*, *must* be particular properties—that is to say, contemporary philosophers' tropes (or 'abstract particulars').

Gilbert's theory of universals is first and foremost anti-realist. Universals are 'gatherings' or groups of particular properties on the basis of resemblance. Gilbert's theory is based upon the notion of *conformitas*. Conformity is the exact resemblance between two (or more) particular properties of two (or more) given individuals, such as the exact resemblance—the natural conformity (*conformitas*)—that holds between the humanities of two men through the conformity of these humanities. This thesis is stated in the *Summa Zwettlensis* (1977), an anonymous text by a disciple of Gilbert that reproduces accurately his thought: 'The conformity of singular natures is the full resemblance which brings it about that Socrates and Plato are said to be naturally similar to each other through the singular humanities which make them conform to each other'.

According to the testimony of John of Salisbury's *Metalogicon* (II, 17),[38] Gilbert added to his ontological particularism some degree of Platonism: the particular *subsistentiae* that are conform to each other (those of individuals of the same species or genus, or which possess the same type of accidental properties) are so because they are copies or reflections of the same divine idea. Plato's and Socrates's particular rationalities are conform because they are copies of the divine idea of rationality. The exemplarity of ideas is taken to be the cause of the conformity of particular essential or accidental *subsistentiae*.

The second section of the ontological square of special interest is that of particular accidents. Some authors consider particular accidents as primitive; in this case, they can be identified as what today we would call tropes. Others see them as individuated by the substance in which they inhere. There were some clear defenders of the theory of tropes during the Early Middle Ages: Chris Martin and John Marenbon have shown Abelard to be one of them;[39] the same demonstration can be made for Gilbert of Poitiers, as a consequence of his ontological particularism. However, particular accidents are not necessarily tropes. An earlier author, Berengar of Tours, discussed the issue of the transferability of particular accidents because of its theological implications in relation to the Eucharist.[40] In his 'Reply against Lanfranc', Berengar reformulates his opponent's position in the language of Aristotle. Lanfranc believed in the real Eucharistic presence of Christ, that is to say, that the bread and wine really turn into Christ's body and blood, although they continue to look, feel and taste like bread and wine. In Aristotelian terms, as follows from Berengar's rephrasing, this position must involve a change of substance and a continuity of accidents since it continues to appear that there is wine and bread on the altar. In his reply, Berengar uses two ontological principles: the existence of particular accidents and their non-transferability. This bread's whiteness w_1 is distinguished from other particular whitenesses w_2, w_3, w_4, and so on, by the fact of belonging to this precise loaf of bread. It is impossible for this whiteness w_1—this precise white—to be transferred to another substance. So it is impossible for the same accidents—that is, the accidents of the bread—to move to another substance to be the accidents of the flesh of Christ. If the substance flesh of Christ is white, it is so by another particular whiteness, w_2, which is numerically different from w_1, though it may be exactly similar to it. The permanence of accidents implies the permanence of substance (Berengar 1988, 159: 2138–40). If the bread and the wine were to disappear, nothing that was in them as in a subject, that is, their accidents, could survive. The fact that the same accidents remain after the consecration means that the bread and the wine continue to exist. Therefore, the mode of presence of Christ is to be understood as symbolic; he is present *intellectualiter* but not *sensualiter*.

While Berengar rejects the transferability of particular accidents, Abelard seems more open to the possibility of transferable tropes. According to him, forms are particular properties. Contrary to Berengar, who believes that accidents are individuated by the substance to which they belong, Abelard holds that 'the forms themselves are in themselves diverse from one another' (Abelard 1919–27, 13: 25–26). This allows Abelard to state the following: 'For it seems that the whiteness of this body, when it is innate in this body, might in the same way have come to other bodies . . . It might perhaps happen that, although it came to this subject, it came to another subject and thus was always in the other subject, because it had never happened to this subject' (Abelard 1919–27, 129: 34–36; 130: 6–7, trans. by J. Marenbon). It seems that for Abelard this white thing T1 is white by the particular whiteness w1 in the actual world. But there are possible worlds in which T1 is informed or made white by the particular whiteness w2 or w3.

2.2. Semantics

One of the most philosophically rich notions under discussion is that of *appellatio*, which can be translated as 'appellation', 'appellative function' or 'naming' (this term is synonymous with *nominatio*). It can be contrasted with the notion of signification. Anselm's *De grammatico*[41] offers the first detailed discussion of this notion. Anselm seeks to complete Aristotle, who, according to him, considers only signification and not appellation. What is more, he only considers direct signification (*per se*) and not signification 'through something else' (*per aliud*). According to Aristotle, 'white' signifies only the quality, whereas according to Anselm, 'white' also signifies indirectly the white thing. Anselm treats this case with the more complex example of *grammaticus*; *grammaticus* is a paronym, that is to say, it is something picked out, not because of what it is as a substance, but because of an accident—in this case, knowledge of grammar. Aristotle says that paronyms are qualities, but anything that is a grammarian is a man, that is to say, a substance. Anselm explains that the name 'man' both signifies and appellates the same thing: this substance. '*Grammaticus*' signifies directly or in itself the qualitative accident, that is, grammatical knowledge, then through this accident, that is, through something else (*per aliud*), it signifies the subject, man. Concrete accidental terms signify directly the quality, but, according to Anselm, they do not appellate it. However, they do appellate the subject but do not signify it directly. So '*grammaticus*' does not signify 'man who knows grammar', but just 'knowledge of grammar' and appellates—or refers in an indeterminate manner to—the individual man who knows grammar. To the causal semantic relation between words and thoughts that is signification, Anselm adds appellation, which is the capacity for a word, used in a determinate context, to point to an object. '*Grammaticus*' and 'white thing' signify a quality, but, according to appellation, they refer to substances. This allows us to see that the objects picked out by paronymic words, like the man who knows grammar and the white thing, are substances. This theory seeks to express an ontological fact: the *grammaticus* according to its being a man (*secundum hominem*) is a substance and according to its having knowledge of grammar (*secundum grammaticam*) is a quality.

2.3. Ethics and Moral Agency

Debate on ethical issues was omnipresent during the Early Middle Ages. By contrast with ontological and logical discussions, it did not originate in the philosophical exegesis of Aristotle, but in debates internal to the Christian tradition. Beside

Anselm's ethical thought,[42] two contributions are particularly notable: the Carolingian debate on predestination and Abelard's moral thought.

The debate on predestination occupied the mind of ninth-century thinkers to an unequalled extent (see Ganz 1990). It was initiated by a monk from Fulda, Gottschalk, who defended a theory of twin predestination (*gemina praedestinatio*), reminiscent of that of the late Augustine, which can be summarised in the following thesis:

> Every human being is either predestined to be saved or else predestined to be damned.

His opponents took this to mean that the personal merit of individuals plays no role in causing salvation or damnation. The actions of a person, good or bad, cannot change her destiny after death. This amounts to theological fatalism. Individual responsibility is impossible, and there is no reason to act in a good or evil way since nothing we do will change our eternal destiny.

Understood in this way, the theory precludes an ethical system that attempts to explain the moral values of actions in terms of their conduciveness to a good ultimate end. Man cannot want to act well; his will can only be put in him through the action of grace and thus be the sign of his election. The adversaries of Gottschalk, Hincmar of Rheims and Hrabanus Maurus, also saw in his theory the danger that God is made responsible for sin. They proposed an alternative theory of single predestination, which states that just a few men are predestined, and that this predestination is to salvation. All the other men are not predestined at all.

John Scottus Eriugena was required to take a position and to provide a refutation of Gottschalk's thesis in order to back up Hincmar's criticisms (see Marenbon 1990). In his treatise *De praedestinatione*, in which he defends the use of logic in order to respond to a theological question, he argues on the basis of the following demonstrations: (1) that God is not responsible for evil, (2) that human beings have free will, and (3) that God is just in his judgements of individuals. The decisive argument he uses for the first claim has two stages: God cannot predestine to damnation, as eternal punishment is an evil. Also, evil is not a thing but a deficiency. Deficiencies have no efficient cause, so they are caused neither by God, nor by anything else. Second, free will (*libera voluntas*) is a part of human nature. Man would not be man without a 'rational will', and God, according to Eriugena, would not make a rational will that is not free. But Eriugena limits the power (*potestas*) of free will. Contrary to what was the case for Adam before he sinned, men cannot completely fulfil God's commandments without the help of grace, even if they would like to do so. Fallen man needs grace in order to use his free will rightly. How then can (3) be explained? Eriugena says that it is not God who judges and punishes sinners. Sinners will be punished by an eternal punishment, but they are themselves the authors of their punishment: 'his own wickedness will punish each man'. The sin punishes the sinner. For in every sinner, the original emergence of the sin and the punishment of it are simultaneous. So God does not punish human nature, but he allows that which he did not make—the evil will of the wicked—to be punished. The punishment is self-inflicted, which has the advantage of not making God a judge or, worse, a tormentor, but a referee, a legislator. He is just the maker of the laws from which no creature can escape. Freedom of man is thus respected. The theses John defended were strongly criticised and condemned, and it appears that he was not able to provide a definitive rejection of the thesis of double predestination.

Another original contribution to ethics was given by Peter Abelard. Abelard's ethical system can be understood as a morality of intention.[43] It centres on the following thesis:

> The moral worth of an action is determined by the agent's intention.

This has as a consequence that acts are not sinful or meritorious, but the intentions with which they are committed are. So there is moral agency only if there is an intentional activity (a tsunami is not morally evil). With the help of counterexamples, Abelard rejects three criteria (the desires of the agent, the agent's character and the deed itself) that could be chosen in order to determine the moral worth of an action and offers a fourth (the agent's intention): (1) Desires are rejected on the basis of a distinction between the desire to do something *simpliciter* and the desire to do something for the sake of something else (Abelard 2001, 8: 21–26). Abelard takes the example of an innocent man whose cruel lord is so furious at him that he pursues him with his sword in order to kill him. The man tries to flee and finally, unwillingly, kills his lord in order to avoid being killed by him (Abelard 2001, 6: 24–29). Abelard emphasises that no evil desire is present in this example. The innocent man had no desire to kill his lord, but merely to preserve his life. This desire to survive is praiseworthy, as it is a moral imperative to preserve one's own life. Actions that we consider to be evil, such as killing another person, can be committed without any evil desire. (2) Character traits are rejected on the basis of the previous argument, as they are just mental dispositions-to-desire. (3) The last rejected criterion is the idea that moral worth comes from the deed itself. Abelard takes the example of the same deed, the hanging of a convict, committed by two different agents, the one seeking the action of justice, the other seeking to take revenge of an old enemy. The act of hanging is the same, and both agents do what is good to do and what justice requires; nevertheless, the difference in the intentions of both agents causes the fact that the hanging is done meritoriously by the one, and sinfully by the other. The difference in intentions means that we have to give a different moral judgement in both cases. According to Abelard, the performance of deeds is in no way relevant to the increase of sin and adds nothing to alter the moral value (Abelard 2001, 22: 31–34; 14: 20–21). Deeds are, following a claim inherited from Stoicism, in themselves indifferent. A passage of the *Ethics* (Abelard 2001, 44: 30–32) is particularly clear: deeds are common to good and evil men alike. In themselves they are indifferent and should only be called 'good' or 'evil' on account of the agent's intention. An intention should be called 'good' if and only if it is believed to conform to God's will. If someone mistakenly believes that intending to do a certain action would displease God and nonetheless has this intention, then, even if his belief was mistaken and, in fact, God approves of this intention, his intention was still evil.

2.4. Philosophical Theology

Medieval philosophical theology is the product of the application and use—and of reflection on the limits of this use—of Aristotelian logic in connection with issues of dogmatic Christian theology. Boethius initiated the method in his *Opuscula sacra*. He was certainly influenced in this direction by his Greek patristic readings. His theological project is similar to that of several Byzantine theologians contemporary to him (see Daley 1984), that is, the deliberate use of the Aristotelian logical tradition as it had developed within Neoplatonism to solve theological problems and to tackle heresy.

The use of logical tools in theological thought was not an obvious step to take. One of the most debated issues in early-medieval philosophy was that of the application of the categories to God. This question was extensively treated by John Scottus Eriugena, who dedicates a large part of the first book of the *Periphyseon* to the demonstration of the fact that God is beyond categorical predication, including in difficult cases, such as essence or relation (see O'Meara 1983). We cannot state anything positive about God because no statement can be appropriate to such a transcendent being.

During the eleventh century, there developed a movement of rationalisation of discourse on issues relating to faith. Disputes do not oppose theologians and philosophers; both sides are made up of monks educated in logic who disagree on problems that often stem from patristics.

Even defenders of a limited use of logic in theology have good knowledge of its content; for example, Peter Damian and Lanfranc of Pavia used logic in order to limit its application in theology. Some chose to take the use of logic further—such as Berengar in the case of the Eucharist—thus contributing in an important way to the logicisation of theology. Berengar's argument against the real sensible presence of Christ in the consecrated host is an example of the twofold nature of the logic that is used, both logico-linguistic and ontological. The ontological aspect of his argument, as we have seen, rejects the permanence of accidents if the substance (bread) has ceased to exist; the logico-linguistic part of his argument states that, if Lanfranc's theory were true, the consecratory statement 'hoc est enim corpus meum' would be impossible to complete, as it would change reference during the time of its utterance. The subject of the sentence at the beginning of the utterance (bread) would not be the same at the end (the body of Christ). Berengar argues that a statement cannot change subjects in the course of its utterance without ceasing to exist.

Another example of overlapping problems is the reflections on original sin developed by Anselm of Canterbury and Odo of Cambrai. The issue of the transmission of original sin is solved with a logico-ontological doctrine, realism about universals, in the version of immanent realism explained above. The principle of Odo's solution 'when Adam sinned, man [the universal] sinned' ('cum Adam peccavit, homo peccavit') can be fully understood only in the framework of a realist ontology (see Erismann 2011c).

Beside these debates a more fundamental reflection on God emerges, considering his existence and attributes, the most obvious example being Anselm, both in his *Monologion* and in his *Proslogion*. A little before Anselm appears the first example of a debate that was to become central in the fourteenth century, that on divine omnipotence.

This problem stems from the discussion of a passage of a letter of Jerome in which he states that 'God can do everything, but he cannot restore the virginity of a girl who has lost it'. For the first time during the Middle Ages, Peter Damian[44] uses a dialectical approach to ask the following question: Can God make what has happened not to have happened? Can he undo what has been done? The problem is obviously that answering 'no' to this question removes from God what is supposed to be one of his essential attributes, omnipotence, but answering 'yes' removes the foundations of everything we think we know, and makes truth, both in rational thought and in faith, uncertain. The arguments used to defend both positions are philosophical; natural law, said to be universal, and the Aristotelian principles of non-contradiction and bivalence are invoked to state that it is impossible for what is not to be. Boethius and the scope of the principle of non-contradiction are called upon in favour of the positive answer. The first argument uses Boethius's conception of eternity, which states that what is past for us is present for God. God can do at time *t* what we think at *t* that he could do at *t-1*, since our past, present and future are all simultaneously present to God. The second argument reconsiders the extension of the validity of the principle of non-contradiction. This principle is valid in the domain of natural necessity but cannot constrain God, who is the creator of nature. The argument goes as follows: that which is legal in nature is wanted by God. The legality of what is legal is nothing other than the omnipotent will of God. God cannot be constrained by an exterior law because he is the source of all legality, and his will is the substance of what is legal in nature. As the author of nature and of its laws, God has the power to change the laws of nature following his free choice. God is capable of restoring virginity if he wants to do so.

Anselm's reflection on God can be qualified as a 'perfect-being theology'. This theology is rational or philosophical in that it proceeds 'by reason alone' and not by the use of authorities. Anselm seeks to describe the nature of an omniperfect being, to prove its existence and to describe its attributes understood as perfections. The idea of perfection is central since Anselm's argument relies on what can be called, following John Marenbon, the 'Principle of God's necessary perfection'. This principle, which can be gathered from *Monologion* 15 and *Proslogion* 5, works as follows:

> If F is a nonrelative attribute, and it is better to be F, all other things remaining the same, than not to be F, then F is a perfection; and if F is a perfection, God is F.

The most famous aspect of Anselm's thought, although it had little influence on his contemporaries and on twelfth-century thought, is his so-called ontological argument, which allows him, on the basis of his first premise, 'God is that than which nothing greater can be thought', to conclude that God exists in reality.

Thought in the field of physics was first and foremost philosophy of nature. It was not founded on the natural writings of Aristotle but, on the one hand, on the

Timaeus and the complements brought by Calcidius and Macrobius and, on the other hand, on the patristic tradition of commentaries on *Genesis* (most importantly, Augustine's *De Genesi ad litteram*). Early-medieval thought on nature precedes both the era of Aristotelian science and the era of the science of 'calculation' and the mathematization of the world. It is mostly cosmogonical in nature and takes the form either of a philosophical interpretation of *Genesis*, sometimes completed by reflection on the four elements, or of a reading of the *Timaeus*.

Despite the existence of several Carolingian treatises named *De anima*, early-medieval psychological reflection has only little in common with what we take today to be philosophical psychology, which includes, for example, theories of cognition, the status of mental acts and intentionality. The early-medieval investigation is closer to that about universals and discusses the existence of a universal soul, which is taken to be the species of particular souls.

NOTES

1. The schematic representation, in the form of an inverted tree, of the subdivision of essence into the two highest genera (corporeal and incorporeal essence) and then into lower genera and species, such as man, dog, horse.

2. In particular, the *Metaphysics* (Books I–IV.4; this translation is called 'the oldest', *vetustissima*), *Physics*, *On the Soul*, *Posterior Analytics*, *Sophistical Refutations*.

3. *Nicomachean Ethics*, *On Generation and Corruption*.

4. *Physics*, *On the Heavens*, *On Generation and Corruption*, *Meteorology* (Books I–III), *Posterior Analytics*.

5. See Marenbon (1993), updated in Marenbon (2000).

6. See McKitterick (1992) and Gibson (1969).

7. Very useful for the understanding of the period are Marenbon (1981, 1983, 2000, 2008), d'Onofrio (1986, 1996), and Gregory (1958) and, for the twelfth century, Dronke (1988) and Chenu (1957). For logic, see Gabbay and Woods (2008).

8. Updated entries on particular authors can be found in Lagerlund (2011) and Pasnau (2010).

9. Alcuin (d. 804) contributed to the *trivium* an important *De dialectica*, the first medieval Latin logical textbook. On the basis of the *Categoriae decem*, he developed an understanding of logic centred on the categories. See Marenbon (1981, 1994 and 1997b).

   Another literary production related to logic is the *Libri Carolini* ('Caroline books'), by Theodulf of Orléans (d. 821), the response in Charlemagne's name to the Greek defence of image worship (cf. Freeman 2003, Mitalaïté 2007). A student of Alcuin, Fredegisus of Tours (fl. 800–30) wrote a letter *De substantia nihili et tenebrarum* ('On the Substance of Nothing and Shadows'), arguing for the reality of nothingness on the basis of rather naïve semantics (or on grammatical Platonism), according to which if a given name has a meaning, then what is referred to by the name exists. See Mignucci (1979).

10. The Irishman Eriugena (d. c. 877) was master at the court of Charles the Bald, teaching the liberal arts, as testified by his glosses to Martianus Capella's *De nuptiis Philologiae et Mercurii* (see von Perger 2005). He dedicated his first treatise to predestination

(*De divina praedestinatione*). He translated from the Greek the writings of pseudo-Dionysius (whose *Celestial Hierarchy* he also commented upon), the *Questions to Thalassius* and
the *Ambigua* of Maximus the Confessor, and Gregory of Nyssa's *On the Making of Man* (*De
hominis opificio*). The *Periphyseon* ('On Nature', also known as *De divisione naturae*) is a
systematic analysis of the world, starting with its creation by God and finishing with its
return to its creator, according to the Neoplatonic scheme of procession and return.
Eriugena is also the author of a commentary to the *Gospel of John* and of a homily on the
prologue of this Gospel. See Beierwaltes (1994), Cappuyns (1969), Moran (1989) and
Schrimpf (1982). Although we cannot really speak of an Eriugenian *school*, John's thought
was echoed to some degree in the School of Auxerre, in particular by Heiric of Auxerre (d.
876/7), the author of glosses to the *Categoriae decem* and to Boethius's *Opuscula sacra*, and
Remigius of Auxerre (d. 908), the author of a commentary on Martianus Capella. Honorius
of Autun (d. ca. 1157) gave in his *Clavis physicae* a compendium of Eriugena's *Periphyseon*.

11. A disagreement about predestination initiated by Gottschalk of Orbais (d. 868, see
Jolivet 1958) challenged several ninth-century thinkers, in particular Hincmar of Rheims
(d. 882), Hrabanus Maurus (d. 856, the author of an encyclopedia *De rerum naturis*) and
Ratramnus of Corbie (d. after 868). Ratramnus wrote a Eucharistic treatise *De corpore et
sanguine Domini* and the *Liber de anima ad Odonem Bellovacensem* in which he argues
against the position of Macarius, who held that all men are one man in substance just as all
souls are one soul in substance; see Delhaye (1950). On the ninth-century debate on the
Eucharist, see Cristiani (1968); on theological method, see Bisogno (2008) and d'Onofrio
(1991).

A second phase of the Eucharistic debate can be identified during the 1060s and 1070s
with the opposition of Berengar of Tours (d. 1088) and Lanfranc of Pavia (d. 1089), whose
De corpore et sanguine Domini (ca. 1066) is an attack on the Eucharistic theology of
Berengar, who replies in his *Rescriptum contra Lanfrannum*. See de Montclos (1971) and
Rosier-Catach (2004).

12. During the tenth and eleventh centuries, some remarkable intellectual figures
worked in monasteries: Notker Labeo (d. 1022), a monk at St Gallen who translated
Boethius's *Consolation of Philosophy* and Aristotle's *Categories* and *De interpretatione* into
German; Gerbert of Aurillac (became Pope Sylvester II, d. 1003), who wrote a *De rationali
et ratione uti* and Abbo of Fleury (d. 1004), who demonstrated great interest for science,
grammar and logic, in particular for syllogisms.

13. Anselm of Canterbury (d. 1109) is the author of important and diverse works. In his
Monologion and *Proslogion*, he reflects on divine attributes, this second work also containing
his famous ontological argument on the existence of God. He is also the author of three
philosophical dialogues, the first dedicated to truth (*De veritate*), in which he develops his
thought about rightness (*rectitudo*), the second to free will (*De libero arbitrio*), and the third,
to the pursuit of themes present in the second, by analysing the moral psychology of Lucifer
(*De casu diaboli*). In his *De grammatico*, he develops semantic considerations. His letter *On
the Incarnation of the Word* is a forceful reflection on the application of dialectic to theology
and the opportunity of criticising the nominalist theory of universals of Roscelin of Compiègne (d. 1120/25). On Anselm, see Davies and Leftow (2005), Mazzarella (1962), Southern
(1990) and Visser and Williams (2008). Odo of Cambrai (d. 1113), whose thought is close to
that of Anselm on many points, discusses in his *De peccato originali* the notion of natural sin
and provides thereby a treatise of realist ontology.

14. Discussions appear on God's omnipotence. Peter Damian (d. 1072) was the first to
deal with the subject in his *De divina omnipotentia*, in which he provides an interesting
reflexion about modalities. See Holopainen (1996) and Resnick (1992).

15. See Giraud (2010).

16. Discussions develop about the interpretation to be given of the texts of the *logica vetus*, the *Categories* and the *Isagoge*: are they about words (*in voce*) or about things (*in re*)? Beside Roscelin, Garland of Besançon (fl. 1075/1130?), the author of a *Dialectica*, argues that the categories deal with words only. The clearest advocate of the opposite answer is William of Champeaux (d. 1122), who supported successively two different realist theories of universals. The debate was deeply modified by the contribution of Peter Abelard (d. 1142). He is the author of a *Dialectica*, of a *Logica 'Ingredientibus'*, an opinionated reading of the philosophical content of the *Isagoge*, the *Categories* and the *De interpretatione* and of a *Logica 'Nostrorum petitioni sociorum'*. He also wrote a *Scito teipsum* ('Know yourself', also known as the *Ethics*) and the *Collationes*, a dialogue between a Christian, a Jew and a philosopher, as well as a work of theology, the *Theologia summi boni*, which was expanded into the *Theologia Christiana* and then revised to become the *Theologia scholarium*. See Brower and Guilfoy (2004), Jolivet (1982, 1997), Marenbon (1997a) and Mews (2005).

17. The Chancellor of Chartres, Gilbert of Poitiers (d. 1154), gave one of the most innovative metaphysical systems of the Middle Ages in his commentaries to the *Opuscula sacra*. A very sophisticated logician and theologian, he originated one of the most successful theological and logical schools of the twelfth century.

18. Many authors were to feel 'Porretani'—disciples of Gilbert—and to defend their master from the criticisms that the Council of Rheims had formulated against him. Among these Porretans, we can mention Alan of Lille (d.1203), a theologian, philosopher and poet, the author of, among other works, the *De planctu naturae*, the *De regulae caelestis juris* and a *Summa 'Quoniam homines'*, which states the main lines of Porretan ontology; Simon of Tournai (d. 1201); Nicholas of Amiens (d. after 1203); and William of Lucca (d. 1178), the author of a commentary on pseudo-Dionysius's *De divinis nominibus* and of a *Summa dialectice artis*, also influenced by Abelard. Among the most interesting attempts to promote and defend the thought of Gilbert of Poitiers, note that of Everard of Ypres (d. after 1191), the author of a *Dialogus Ratii et Everardi*; that of Peter of Vienna (d. 1183), the supposed author of the *Summa Zwettlensis*; and that of Porretans who sought to defend Gilbert's thought by reference to Greek patristic authorities. In this last group, note Hugh of Honau (d. after 1180), the author of a *Liber de diversitate naturae et personae* and Adhemar of St Ruf (d. 1184), a Porretan theologian and the author of a *De trinitate* and of a collection of patristic texts. See Catalani (2008), Marenbon (1988) and Valente (2008).

19. Adam of Balsham (d. 1157/69), the author of an *Ars disserendi*.

20. Alberic of Paris (fl. 1130s–40s), an opponent of nominalism who replaced Abelard at the School of the Mont Ste Geneviève.

21. Another important master was Walter of Mortagne (d. 1174), the author of a *Tractatus de generali*.

22. Natural philosophy was explored by Adelard of Bath (d. ca. 1152), the author of *Quaestiones naturales* and of a work of metaphysics, *De eodem et diverso*.

23. This exegetical path was chosen first and foremost by thinkers who have been associated with the so-called School of Chartres, in particular Bernard of Chartres (d. ca. 1130), the author of a commentary to the *Timaeus*, on which William of Conches (d. ca. 1154) also commented. William also composed a treatise on natural science, the *Philosophia mundi* (the content of which he reworked into a dialogue form in his *Dragmaticon*), a commentary to Boethius's *Consolation* and one to Cicero's *The dream of Scipio*. Bernardus Silvestris (d. ca. 1160) is the author of a prosimetrum on creation, the *Cosmographia*. Another Chartrian interested in natural philosophy is Thierry of Chartres (d. after 1156),

who gave a commentary to Boethius's *Opuscula sacra*. Among Thierry's students were Clarembald of Arras (d. ca. 1187), also the author of a commentary on the *Opuscula sacra*, and Hermann of Carinthia (d. after 1143), who wrote a treatise on the origins of the world and human nature, the *De essentiis*. See Gregory (1955), Lemoine (1998), Maccagnolo (1976, 1980), and Wetherbee (1972).

24. On this debate see Jeauneau (1973), Häring (1974) and Southern (1970).

25. Notable members of the School were Hugh of St Victor (d. 1141), the author of a work on the creation, *De tribus diebus*, and of a *Didascalicon de studio legendi*, which gives a classification of the fields of knowledge (see Rorem 2009), Richard of St Victor (d. 1173) and Achard of St Victor (d. 1171), the author of *De unitate divinae essentiae et pluralitate creaturarum*.

26. Lombard's *Sentences*—a compilation of patristic authorities—were to become the textbook of the later Middle Ages. These *Sententiae* are divided into four books: the first deals with God, the second with creatures, the third with Christ and the fourth with sacraments. See Rosemann (2004).

27. On the early-medieval division of sciences and philosophy, see Iwakuma (1999).

28. See Aristotle, *Categories* 1a20–b5 (Latin version by Boethius, ed. L. Minio-Paluello, 5:22–6:13).

29. The most remarkable Latin contribution to this issue before the ninth century is that of Boethius. He seems to defend various opinions about universals. However, his most clearly stated and most developed theory may be found in his second commentary to Porphyry's *Isagoge* and can be called, following John Marenbon, 'realist abstractionism' (see de Libera 1999, 159–280; Marenbon 2003). This position is the result of reading Porphyry's text in the light of Alexander of Aphrodisias (see de Libera 1999, 25–157; Rashed 2004, 2007; Sharples 2005; Tweedale 1984). According to Boethius, genera and species do not exist as such (Boethius's argument is that an entity that would be wholly instantiated by several distinct individuals would not reach the unity needed to exist outside the mind; see King 2011), but only as particularised. They can, however, be thought as universals, through the process of abstraction. Each individual of a given species has a nature or, as Boethius calls it here, a 'similarity' (*similitudo*), which resembles exactly the nature of any other individual of the same species. The thought that gathers these similarities constitutes the species. '*Similitudo*', here, is not to be understood as the relation, but as the foundation of the relation. Each individual has a [particular] similarity, that is, one of the foundations of the relation of resemblance. This similarity becomes universal when it is thought; it is both particular (when it is perceived in things) and universal (when it is thought).

30. I will not give an exhaustive list of all positions that were defended. However, let us mention the collection theory according to which a universal is an integral whole consisting of particular things. The semantic aspect of this theory holds that the sentence 'Adam is a human being' is true because Adam is a part of the integral whole Human; see Freddoso (1978).

31. See Erismann (2011a, 2011b).

32. This thesis is described as the 'standard theory of individuality' and analysed in Gracia (1984).

33. On Roscelin's ontology, see Erismann (2008), Jolivet (1992) and Kluge (1976).

34. See Jacobi (2004), Marenbon (1997a, 174–209) and Tweedale (1976).

35. See Maioli (1979), Nielsen (1982), Van Elswijk (1966) and Westley (1960).

36. According to the expression used in an anonymous handbook of Porretan logic, the *Compendium logicae Porretanum*: 'Quot ergo homines, tot humanitates'. (Ed. Ebbesen-Fredborg-Nielsen, 41: 67–68) See Martin (1983).

37. Gilbert of Poitiers (1966, 146: 14–16).

38. 'Still another, in his attempt to explain Aristotle, attributes universality to the "native forms", as does Gilbert, Bishop of Poitiers, who seeks to prove their conformity (*in earum conformitate laborat*). A "native form" is an example of an original [exemplar]. It [the native form, unlike the original] inheres in created things, instead of subsisting in the divine mind' (trans. in MacGarry, 1982, 115).

39. See de Libera (2002), Marenbon (1997a, 119–30, 2008) and Martin (1992).

40. Thinking about the theological question of the Eucharist involves discussing the possibility of accidents that do not inhere in any substance and that of the separability of accidents.

41. On this text see Boschung (2006), Henry (1964, 1974) and McCord Adams (2000).

42. See Briancesco (1982), Brower (2004), Goebel (2001) and Trego (2010).

43. See Blomme (1958), King (1995), Marenbon (1997a, 251–65) and Saarinen (1994).

44. See Holopainen (1996), Moonan (1980), Remnant (1978) and Resnick (1992).

BIBLIOGRAPHY

Abelard. 1919–27. 'Logica "*ingredientibus*"', ed. Bernhard Geyer. In *Peter Abaelards Philosophische Schriften*. Münster, Germany: Aschendorff (Beiträge zur Geschichte der Philosophie und Theologie des Mittelalters, vol. 21, Heft 1–3).

———. 1970. *Dialectica*, ed. L.M. De Rijk. Assen, the Netherlands: Van Gorkum.

———. 2001. *Petri Abaelardi opera theologica*. 4, 'Scito te ipsum', ed. Rainer M. Ilgner. Turnhout, Belgium: Brepols (Corpus Christianorum Continuatio Mediaevalis 190).

Beierwaltes, Werner. 1994. *Eriugena. Grundzüge seines Denkens*. Frankfurt: V. Klostermann.

Berengar of Tours. 1988. *Rescriptum contra Lanfrannum*, ed. R.B.C. Huygens. Turnhout, Belgium: Brepols (Corpus Christianorum Continuatio Mediaevalis 84).

Bisogno, Armando. 2008. *Il metodo carolingio. Identità culturale e dibattito teologico nel secolo nono*. Turnhout, Belgium: Brepols.

Blomme, Robert. 1958. *La doctrine du péché dans les écoles théologiques de la première moitié du XIIe siècle*. Louvain, Belgium: Publications universitaires de Louvain.

Boschung, Peter. 2006. *From a Topical Point of View. Dialectic in Anselm of Canterbury's De grammatico*. Leiden, the Netherlands: Brill.

Briancesco, Edouard. 1982. *Un triptyque sur la liberté. La doctrine morale de saint Anselme*: De veritate, De libertate arbitrii, De casu diaboli. Paris: Desclée de Brouwer.

Brower, Jeffrey E. 2004. 'Trinity', in Brower and Guilfoy, 2004, 223–57.

Brower, Jeffrey E. and Kevin Guilfoy, eds. 2004. *The Cambridge Companion to Abelard*. Cambridge: Cambridge University Press.

Cappuyns, Maïeul. 1969. *Jean Scot Erigène, sa vie, son œuvre, sa pensée*. Brussels: Culture et civilisation.

Catalani, Luigi. 2008. *I Porretani. Una scuola di pensiero tra alto e basso Medioevo*. Turnhout, Belgium: Brepols.

Chenu, Marie-Dominique. 1957. *La théologie au douzième siècle*. Paris: Vrin.

Cristiani, Marta. 1968. La controversia eucaristica nella cultura del secolo IX. *Studi Medievali* 9:167–233.

Daley, Brian E. 1984. Boethius' Theological Tracts and Early Byzantine Scholasticism. *Mediaeval Studies* 46:158–91.

Davies, Brian and Brian Leftow, eds. 2005. *The Cambridge Companion to Anselm*. Cambridge: Cambridge University Press.

Delhaye, Philippe. 1950. *Une controverse sur l'âme universelle au IXe siècle*. Lille: Giard.

Dronke, Peter, ed. 1988. *A History of Twelfth-Century Western Philosophy*. Cambridge: Cambridge University Press.

Erismann, Christophe. 2003. *Collectio proprietatum*. Anselme de Canterbury et le problème de l'individuation. *Mediaevalia. Textos e estudos* 22:55–71.

———. 2007. Immanent Realism. A Reconstruction of an Early Medieval Solution to the Problem of Universals. *Documenti e studi sulla tradizione filosofica medievale* 18:211–29.

———. 2008. The Trinity, Universals and Particular Substances: Philoponus and Roscelin. *Traditio* 63:277–305.

———. 2011a. *L'homme commun. La genèse du réalisme ontologique durant le haut Moyen Âge*. Paris: Vrin.

———. 2011b. 'Penser le commun. Le problème de l'universalité métaphysique aux XIe et XIIe siècles'. In *Arts du langage et théologie aux confins des XIe /XIIe siècles*, ed. I. Rosier-Catach, 373–92. Turnhout, Belgium: Brepols.

———. 2011c. 'Un péché de nature. Péché originel et réalisme des universaux selon Odon de Cambrai'. In *The Medieval Paradigm: Religious Thought and Philosophy*, ed. G. d'Onofrio, 289–307. Turnhout, Belgium: Brepols.

Freddoso, Alfred J. 1978. Abailard on Collective Realism. *The Journal of Philosophy* 75:527–38.

Freeman, Ann. 2003. *Theodulf of Orléans: Charlemagne's Spokesman against the Second Council of Nicaea*. Aldershot, UK: Ashgate.

Gabbay, Dov M. and John Woods, eds. 2008. *Handbook of the History of Logic. Volume 2: Mediaeval and Renaissance Logic*. Amsterdam: Elsevier.

Ganz, David. 1990. 'The debate on predestination'. In *Charles the Bald, Court and Kingdom*, 2nd edition, ed. M. Gibson, J. Nelson, 283–302. Aldershot, UK: Ashgate.

Gibson, Margaret T. 1969. The Study of the *Timaeus* in the Eleventh and Twelfth Centuries. *Pensiamento* 25:183–94.

Gilbert of Poitiers. 1966. *The Commentaries on Boethius by Gilbert of Poitiers*, ed. Nikolaus M. Häring. Toronto: Pontifical Institute of Mediaeval Studies.

Giraud, Cédric. 2010. *Per verba magistri. Anselme de Laon et son École au XIIe siècle*. Turnhout, Belgium: Brepols.

Goebel, Berndt. 2001. *Rectitudo. Wahrheit und Freiheit bei Anselm von Canterbury: Eine philosophische Untersuchung seines Denkansatzes*. Münster, Germany: Aschendorff.

Gracia, Jorge J. E. 1984. *Introduction to the Problem of Individuation in the Early Middle Ages*. Munich: Philosophia.

Gregory, Tullio. 1955. *Anima mundi: la filosofia di Guglielmo di Conches e la scuola di Chartres*. Florence: G. C. Sansoni.

———. 1958. *Platonismo medievale. Studi e ricerche*. Rome: Istituto Storico Italiano per il Medio Evo.

Häring, Nikolaus. 1974. 'Chartres and Paris revisited'. In *Essays in Honour of Anton Charles Pegis*, ed. James R. O'Donnell, 268–329. Toronto: Pontifical Institute of Mediaeval Studies.

Henry, Desmond P. 1964. *The De grammatico of Saint Anselm. The Theory of Paronymy*. Notre Dame: The University of Notre Dame Press.

———. 1974. *Commentary on De grammatico. The Historical-Logical Dimensions of a Dialogue of St. Anselm's*. Dordrecht, the Netherlands, and Boston: D. Reidel.

Holopainen, Toivo J. 1996. *Dialectic and Theology in the Eleventh Century*. Leiden, the Netherlands, New York, and Cologne: Brill.

Iwakuma, Yukio. 1999. 'The division of philosophy and the place of the Trivium from the 9th to the mid-12th centuries'. In *Medieval analyses in language and cognition*, ed. S. Ebbesen, 165–89. Copenhagen: The Royal Danish Academy of Sciences and Letters.

Jacobi, Klaus. 2004. 'Philosophy of language'. In Brower and Guilfoy 2004, 126–57.

Jeauneau, Edouard. 1973. *Lectio philosophorum: Recherches sur l'Ecole de Chartres*. Amsterdam: A. M. Hakkert.

Jolivet, Jean. 1958. *Godescalc d'Orbais et la Trinité: La méthode de la théologie à l'époque carolingienne*. Paris: Vrin.

———. 1982. *Arts du langage et théologie chez Abélard*, 2nd ed. Paris: Vrin.

———. 1992. Trois variations médiévales sur l'universel et l'individu: Roscelin, Abélard, Gilbert de la Porée. *Revue de métaphysique et de morale* 97:111–55.

———. 1997. *La théologie d'Abélard*. Paris: Cerf.

King, Peter. 1995. Abelard's Intentionalist Ethics. *The Modern Schoolman* 72:213–31.

———. 2011. Boethius's Anti-Realist Arguments. *Oxford Studies in Ancient Philosophy* 40.

Kluge, Eike-Henner W. 1976. Roscelin and the Medieval Problem of Universals. *Journal of the History of Philosophy* 14:405–14.

Lagerlund, Henrik, ed. 2011. *Encyclopedia of Medieval Philosophy. Philosophy between 500 and 1500*. Berlin: Springer.

Lemoine, Michel. 1998. *Théologie et platonisme au XIIe siècle*. Paris: Cerf.

de Libera, Alain. 1999. *L'Art des généralités. Théories de l'abstraction*. Paris: Aubier.

———. 2002. Des accidents aux tropes: Pierre Abélard. *Revue de métaphysique et de morale* 36:509–30.

Maccagnolo, Enzo. 1976. *Rerum universitas: Saggio sulla filosofia di Teodorico di Chartres*. Florence: F. Le Monnier.

———. 1980. *Il divino e il megacosmo: Testi filosofici e scientifici della scuola di Chartres*. Milan: Rusconi.

McCord Adams, Marilyn. 2000. Re-reading *De grammatico* or Anselm's Introduction to Aristotle's *Categories*. *Documenti e studi sulla tradizione filosofica medievale* 11:83–112.

MacGarry, Daniel D. 1982. *The Metalogicon of John of Salisbury: A Twelfth-Century Defence of the Verbal and Logical Arts of the Trivium*. Westport, CT: Greenwood Press.

Maioli, Bruno. 1979. *Gilberto Porretano. Dalla grammatica speculativa alla metafisica del concreto*. Rome: Bulzoni.

Marenbon, John. 1981. *From the Circle of Alcuin to the School of Auxerre: Logic, Theology and Philosophy in the Early Middle Ages*. Cambridge: Cambridge University Press.

———. 1983. *Early Medieval Philosophy, 480–1150*. London: Routledge & Kegan Paul.

———. 1988. *A Note on the Porretani. In* Dronke, 1988, 353–57.

———. 1990. 'John Scottus and Carolingian theology: From the *De praedestinatione*, its background and its critics, to the *Periphyseon*'. In *Charles the Bald, Court and Kingdom*, 2nd edition, ed. M. Gibson and J. Nelson, 303–25. Aldershot, UK: Ashgate.

———. 1993. 'Medieval Latin commentaries and glosses on Aristotelian logical texts before c. 1150 AD'. In *Glosses and Commentaries on Aristotelian Logical Texts*, ed. C. Burnett, 77–127. London: The Warburg Institute (Warburg Institute surveys and texts 23).

———. 1994. 'Carolingian thought'. In *Carolingian Culture: Emulation and Innovation*, ed. R. McKitterick, 171–92. Cambridge: Cambridge University Press.

———. 1997a. *The Philosophy of Peter Abelard*. Cambridge: Cambridge University Press.

———. 1997b. 'Alcuin, the Council of Frankfurt and the beginnings of medieval philosophy'.
    In *Das Frankfurter Konzil von 794: Kristallisationspunkt karolingischer Kultur*, ed.
    R. Berndt, 603–15. Mainz, Germany: Selbstverl. der Gesellschaft für Mittelrheinische
    Kirchengeschichte.

———. 2000. *Aristotelian Logic, Platonism, and the Context of Early Medieval Philosophy in
    the West*. Aldershot, UK: Ashgate (Variorum Collected Studies series 696).

———. 2003. *Boethius*. Oxford: Oxford University Press.

———. 2008. 'Logic before 1100: the Latin Tradition'. In Gabbay and Woods, 2008, 1–64.

Martin, Christopher J. 1983. The *Compendium logicae Porretanum*: A Survey of Philosophi-
    cal Logic from the School of Gilbert of Poitiers. *Cahiers de l'Institut du Moyen Âge grec
    et latin* 46:xviii–xlvi.

———. 1992. The Logic of the *Nominales*, or, the Rise and Fall of Impossible Position.
    Vivarium 30:110–26.

Mazzarella, Pasquale. 1962. *Il pensiero speculativo di S. Anselmo d'Aosta*. Padua: CEDAM.

McKitterick, Rosamond. 1992. 'Knowledge of Plato's *Timaeus* in the ninth century: The
    Implications of Valenciennes, Bibl. municipale MS 293'. In *From Athens to Chartres.
    Neoplatonism and Medieval Thought. Studies in Honour of Édouard Jeauneau*, ed. H. J.
    Westra, 85–95. Leyden, the Netherlands, New York, and Cologne: Brill.

Mews, Constant J. 2005. *Abelard and Heloise*. Oxford: Oxford University Press.

Mignucci, Mario. 1979. 'Tradizioni logiche e grammaticali in Fredegiso di Tours'. In *Actas del
    V congreso internacional de filosofia medieval*, vol. II, 1005–15. Madrid: Editora Nacional.

Mitalaïté, Kristina. 2007. *Philosophie et théologie de l'image dans les Libri Carolini*. Paris:
    Institut d'études augustiniennes.

de Montclos, Jean. 1971. *Lanfranc et Béranger. La controverse eucharistique du XIe siècle*.
    Leuven, Belgium: Spicilegium sacrum Lovaniense.

Moonan, Lawrence. 1980. Impossibility and Peter Damian. *Archiv für Geschichte der
    Philosophie* 62:146–63.

Moran, Dermot. 1989. *The Philosophy of John Scottus Eriugena. A Study of Idealism in the
    Middle Ages*. Cambridge: Cambridge University Press.

Nielsen, Lauge O. 1982. *Theology and Philosophy in the Twelfth Century: A Study of Gilbert
    Porreta's Thinking and the Theological Expositions of the Doctrine of the Incarnation
    during the Period 1130–80*. Leiden, the Netherlands: Brill.

O'Meara, Dominic J. 1983. 'The problem of speaking about God in John Scottus Eriugena'.
    In *Carolingian Essays*, ed. U.-R. Blumenthal, 151–67. Washington, DC: The Catholic
    University of America Press.

d'Onofrio, Giulio. 1986. '*Fons scientiae*'. *La dialettica nell'Occidente tardo-antico*. Naples:
    Liguori.

———. 1991. Theological Ideas and the Idea of Theology in the Early Middle Ages. *Freiburger
    Zeitschrift für Philosophie und Theologie*, 38:273–97.

———. 1996. *Storia della teologia nel medioevo*, Vol. I: *I princìpi*. Casale Monferrato, Italy:
    Piemme.

Pasnau, Robert, ed. 2010. *The Cambridge History of Medieval Philosophy*, 2 vols. Cambridge:
    Cambridge University Press.

von Perger, Mischa. 2005. 'Eriugenas Adaptation der aristotelischen Kategorienlehre'. In
    Logik und Theologie. Das Organon im arabischen und im lateinischen Mittelalter, ed. D.
    Perler, U. Rudolph, 239–303. Leiden, the Netherlands, and Boston: Brill.

Rashed, Marwan. 2004. Priorité de l'*eidos* ou du *genos* entre Andronicos et Alexandre:
    Vestiges arabes et grecs inédits. *Arabic Sciences and Philosophy*, 14:9–63.

———. 2007. *Essentialisme. Alexandre d'Aphrodise entre logique, physique et cosmologie.* Berlin and New York: Walter de Gruyter.

Remnant, Peter. 1978. Peter Damian: Could God Change the Past? *Canadian Journal of Philosophy* 8:259–68.

Resnick, Irven M. 1992. *Divine Power and Possibility in St. Peter Damian's* De divina omnipotentia. Leiden, the Netherlands: Brill.

Rorem, Paul. 2009. *Hugh of Saint Victor.* Oxford: Oxford University Press.

Rosemann, Philip W. 2004. *Peter Lombard.* Oxford: Oxford University Press.

Rosier-Catach, Irène. 2004. *La parole efficace: signe, rituel, sacré.* Paris: Seuil.

Saarinen, Risto. 1994. *Weakness of the Will in Medieval Thought: From Augustine to Buridan.* Leiden, the Netherlands: Brill.

Schrimpf, Gangolf. 1982. *Das Werk des Johannes Scottus Eriugena im Rahmen des Wissenschaftsverständnisses seiner Zeit: Eine Hinführung zu* Periphyseon. Münster, Germany: Aschendorff (Beiträge zur Geschichte der Philosophie und Theologie des Mittelalters: Texte und Untersuchungen. N. F. Bd. 23).

Sharples, Richard W. 2005. Alexander of Aphrodisias on Universals: Two Problematic Texts. *Phronesis* 50:43–55.

Southern, Richard W. 1970. 'Humanism and the school of Chartres'. In *Medieval Humanism and Other Studies*, ed. R. Southern, 61–85. Oxford: Blackwell.

———. 1990. *Saint Anselm: A Portrait in a Landscape.* Cambridge: Cambridge University Press.

Summa Zwettlensis. 1977. *Die Zwettler Summe*, ed. N. M. Häring. Münster, Germany: Aschendorff (Beiträge zur Geschichte der Philosophie und Theologie des Mittelalters N. F. 15).

Trego, Kristell. 2010. *L'essence de la liberté. La refondation de l'éthique dans l'œuvre de saint Anselme de Cantorbéry.* Paris: Vrin.

Tweedale, Martin. 1976. *Abailard on Universals.* Amsterdam: North Holland.

———. 1984. Alexander of Aphrodisias' Views on Universals. *Phronesis* 29:279–303.

Valente, Luisa. 2008. *Logique et théologie: Les écoles parisiennes entre 1150 et 1220.* Paris: Vrin.

Van Elswijk, H. C. 1966. *Gilbert Porreta: sa vie, son œuvre, sa pensée.* Leuven, Belgium: Spicilegium sacrum Lovaniense.

Visser, Sandra and Thomas Williams. 2008. *Anselm.* Oxford: Oxford University Press.

Westley, Richard J. 1960. A Philosophy of the Concreted and the Concrete. *The Modern Schoolman* 37:257–86.

Wetherbee, Winthrop. 1972. *Platonism and Poetry in the Twelfth Century: The Literary Influence of the School of Chartres.* Princeton NJ: Princeton University Press.

CHAPTER 9

LATIN PHILOSOPHY,
1200–1350

RUSSELL L. FRIEDMAN

INTRODUCTION

The period under discussion here, 1200–1350, is on any account a watershed in the history of Western philosophy. To see this, one has only to consider that the three giants of later medieval philosophy, Thomas Aquinas (d. 1274), John Duns Scotus (d. 1308) and William of Ockham (d. 1347), lived their entire lives in this time span. If the period boasted exclusively these three thinkers, it would be worthy of a great deal of attention. Yet these 150 years also saw the philosophical activity of, among others, Robert Grosseteste (d. 1253), Bonaventure (d. 1274), Siger of Brabant (d. ca. 1284), Henry of Ghent (d. 1293), Peter John Olivi (d. 1298), Radulphus Brito (d. ca. 1320), Peter Auriol (d. 1322), John Buridan (d. ca. 1361), Adam Wodeham (d. 1358) and Gregory of Rimini (d. 1358), each of whom in his own way is first rate in terms of the originality, quality and influence of his ideas. What is more, this was the era in which the university system was consolidated in Western Europe, when Paris and Oxford came into their own, bringing together the best minds of Europe in close debate and in a regulated educational system that gave the thought produced a continuity and a coherence not seen before. Further, the Aristotelian intellectual heritage was largely recovered and digested in these 150 years, giving the era's philosophers the intellectual resources and the specialised vocabulary to deal with issues that Aristotle himself could never have foreseen. Finally, the mendicant orders, especially the Dominicans and the Franciscans, established their hierarchical educational systems in these years, systems that would train many of the most important thinkers for the next four centuries. Thus, this period saw a sea change in the institutions that nurtured philosophy, and correspondingly, it witnessed the development of solutions and models in physics and natural philosophy, metaphysics, epistemology, philosophy of mind, ethics, and philosophical theology that would remain influential well into the early-modern period, and, in some cases, until today.

The chapter comprises two main parts. The first part describes the cultural and institutional developments that conditioned in one way or another nearly all of the philosophical thought produced in the period: the translation into Latin of Aristotle's works, along with further Greek, Arabic and Hebrew philosophical texts (§1.1); the universities (§1.2); the mendicant orders and their educational system (§1.3); and finally the major genres of philosophical writing (§1.4). The second part is a short, highly selective sketch of major trends, figures and lines of influence in the period. Throughout the chapter, my aim is to bring to the reader's attention not only the recognised major figures, but also some of the lesser-known ones, not only those who gave the classic statements of and compelling arguments for philosophical positions, but also those who nuanced, extended, or popularised those positions and arguments—bearing in mind that we are far from having a full picture of the period's philosophy, in large part because so little of the basic primary source material is yet available in a modern critical edition.

A methodological remark at the outset: I think that in approaching 150 years of intense philosophical activity, with literally dozens of distinctive philosophical minds and positions on a wide range of issues, our point of departure must be the recognition that a century and a half is a very long time. The 150 years between 1200 and 1350 was the same amount of time as that between 1850 and 2000, and this has consequences. In 150 years, philosophical topics that were all the rage at one time are passé thirty years later; new vocabulary, arguments and conceptual breakthroughs ensure that there is a constant turnover in the focus of the philosophical debate. In short, there is no reason to think that what seemed a pressing issue in 1230 was still topical (or perhaps: still topical in the same way) in 1330. In my view, then, it is best to look at the entire period as an evolution, not only in *solutions* to philosophical problems but also in the very *problems* themselves. Philosophical 'highpoints' or 'main issues' change over time, and to talk about one philosopher (say, Thomas Aquinas) as being the zenith of philosophical development in this period is to turn a blind eye to dozens of topics that that philosopher might not have considered to be central to his own philosophical project. This certainly does not mean that some philosophical solutions are not more elegant or persuasive than others, and when we are convinced that authors are talking about the same thing, we can certainly compare and contrast to see the upsides and downsides of their views. But it does mean that we should be careful not to compare apples with oranges, and not to dictate to the medieval authors what they 'should' have been interested in.

1. Institutional and Intellectual Context

Latin philosophy of the period 1200–1350 is conditioned in large part by three interrelated developments in the period: the translations into Latin of a good deal of the Greek thought from antiquity, along with much of the Muslim and the Jewish thought that took its own point of departure in the Hellenistic thought; the rise of the universities; and the formation of the mendicant orders, above all the Dominicans and the Franciscans. These three developments were by no means limited to the period under discussion here—the translations and the universities had their roots in the twelfth century, and the universities and mendicant orders would maintain their importance in intellectual matters into the early-modern period and beyond—but their confluence in the thirteenth and the early fourteenth centuries had much to do with making the period into one of the most creative in the history of philosophy. In this section, I examine each of these developments in turn: translations, universities, mendicant orders. Thereafter, I offer a description of some major genres of scholastic philosophical writing, showing in general how they fit into the medieval educational curriculum and what type of philosophical thought they might contain.

1.1. The Translations[1]

Boethius (d. 525) translated a number of Aristotle's logical works from Greek into Latin: the *Categories, De Interpretatione, Prior Analytics, Topics* and *Sophistici Elenchi*, as well as Porphyry's *Isagoge*. Part of this collection, specifically the *Categories, De Interpretatione* and *Isagoge*, was used throughout the Middle Ages and for this reason was collectively referred to in the later Middle Ages as the *logica vetus* ('the old logic'). In the early twelfth century, when Western European intellectuals began to actively seek out material from the Greek, Arabic and Hebrew philosophical traditions, Boethius's translations of the *Prior Analytics, Topics*, and *Sophistici Elenchi* were recovered and, along with James of Venice's translation of the *Posterior Analytics*, formed what was known as the *logica nova* ('the new logic'). James, whom we know to have been in Constantinople in 1136, was the most important of several twelfth-century translators of Aristotelian works from Greek into Latin; just how widely James's translations were used is indicated by the fact that five of his translations of Aristotelian works exist today in more than a hundred manuscript copies, specifically the *Posterior Analytics* (275 copies), the *Physics* (139), the *De anima* (144), the *De memoria* (115) and the *De longitudine* (101). James translated several other works directly from Greek into Latin, as did a number of other twelfth-century translators, both named and anonymous. Their efforts to translate directly from the Greek were supplemented by those of several translators of Aristotelian works in Arabic, most significantly Gerard of Cremona (d. 1187), whose translations of Aristotle's *De caelo* and *Meteorologica* (books I–III) as well as the pseudo-Aristotelian

De causis, were included around 1230 in a standard collection of Aristotelian natural philosophical works that modern researchers have titled the *corpus vetustius* ('the older collection'). Notable about the twelfth-century translations is that they were by no means a systematic project: many works were translated more than once, and many works were translated from both Greek and Arabic, although the version that had the widest circulation and the greatest impact was, with few exceptions, the one translated from the Greek.[2]

By the beginning of the thirteenth century, translations of the largest number of Aristotle's works existed, and by around 1230 the *corpus vetustius* was assembled. Nevertheless, there was lively interest in translating Aristotle in the thirteenth century, with, for example, Robert Grosseteste, the Bishop of Lincoln, translating the *Nicomachean Ethics* and several other works, and Bartholomew of Messina translating a series of pseudo-Aristotelian works including the *Problemata physica* and the *Magna moralia*. But the translations of Aristotle were put on a new footing with the work of the Flemish Dominican William of Moerbeke (d. 1286). Moerbeke translated four of Aristotle's works for the first time into Latin (including the *Politics* and the *Poetics*) and made fresh translations or revised older translations of about a dozen more. It is a testimony to the respect in which Moerbeke's translation work was held that, in the later thirteenth century, many of his Latin translations of Aristotle's works formed the core of a newly assembled standard collection, known to modern researchers as the *corpus recentius* ('the newer collection'), and this remained in widespread use into the Renaissance. Thomas Aquinas was one of the first to use Moerbeke's Aristotle translations, most of which became standard, existing in more than 150 manuscripts each; the great exception to this rule is the logical works, where Boethius's and James of Venice's translations remained the norm. Moreover, William translated directly from Greek many other works by such authors as Alexander of Aphrodisias, Archimedes, Galen, Proclus and Themistius.

Along with these translations of Aristotle primarily from the Greek came a great number of translations of works from the Arabic traditions. From the mid–twelfth century and into the fourteenth, works by, among others, al-Kindi, al-Farabi and al-Ghazali were translated into Latin. But most significant from a philosophical point of view was the translation of works by Avicenna (d. 1037) and Averroes (d. 1198), both of whom had an impact on Latin philosophy that would be difficult to exaggerate. Avicenna's *al-Shifa* (*The Healing*), his most influential work, was translated in stages into Latin as the *Sufficientia*; the earliest translations—those of, for example, the sections on the soul and on metaphysics, and a portion of the logic—were made in Toledo in the mid–twelfth century. Averroes, who had sought to comment on all of Aristotle's works in short (epitome), middle and long commentaries, was becoming available already by the 1230s and 1240s, probably mostly through the efforts of Michael Scot (d. 1234/1236) and Herman the German (d. 1272). Since Averroes's long commentaries contained the entire text of the relevant work of Aristotle, Latin translations of these commentaries were one way in which the Arabic Aristotle had an impact in the Latin West; moreover, through Averroes later medieval scholastics gained some knowledge of other untranslated Arabic and Greek thinkers, like Ibn-Bajja (Avempace; d. 1139).

Two works translated into Latin from the Jewish philosophical tradition had widespread influence in our period: the *Fons vitae* of Avicebron (Ibn Gabirol, d. ca. 1057), which was translated in the twelfth century from the (no longer extant) Arabic original, and which inspired thirteenth-century Latin universal hylomorphism (the theory that all created beings without exception consist of both form *and* matter), and Maimonides's (d. 1204) *Guide of the Perplexed*, translated around 1220 from a Hebrew translation of the original Arabic and cited frequently throughout the Middle Ages.

Mention should be made of 'florilegia', collections of sayings taken from philosophical and theological writings and used often by scholastics as a way of having at their fingertips the most important passages from their 'authorities', that is to say, from the authors whose works and words had enough weight to warrant citation in various contexts. The most famous of the florilegia is the *Auctoritates Aristotelis*, a work compiled sometime between 1267 and 1325 and listing the most important and well-known quotations, especially from the works of Aristotle and some of his commentators (particularly *the* Commentator, Averroes).[3]

Aristotle was known in the Middle Ages as 'the Philosopher', and in that connection it is important to note that the history of scholastic thought in our period could without great anachronism be written as the history of Aristotelian thought (including Greek, Arabic and Hebrew Aristotelianism). Although there were translations of nearly all of Aristotle in the twelfth century, it is in the first fifty years of the thirteenth century that his thought begins to be utilised, as the assembly of the *corpus vetustius* as well as an increasing number of commentaries and constructive uses of the Aristotelian corpus in the period shows. But with the translations of works from the Aristotelian tradition, and especially Averroes, there is a quantum leap in engagement with Aristotle in the second half of the thirteenth century, as is witnessed both by the incorporation of Aristotle into the mandated course of studies in the arts at Paris (by 1255) as well as William of Moerbeke's translation work and the *corpus recentius*. This is a period of digestion of Aristotle, determining how to understand his philosophy and how to use it in conjunction with the Christian faith. And finally, to continue the history of scholasticism as a history of Aristotelian thought, the fourteenth century saw an expansion of Aristotelian philosophy, sometimes along Aristotelian lines but in ways untested or little tested in the foregoing Aristotelian tradition, sometimes in ways that Aristotle never could have imagined.

1.2. The Universities[4]

In medieval Latin, the word *universitas* designated a guild, and in their origins universities were just that: guilds, groups of workers who bound themselves together in order to have greater influence on their working and living conditions. As such, the earliest universities do not have a foundation date but, rather, coalesced over time into a recognisable corporate body. A basic division in any guild's membership was between, on the one hand, 'masters' (*magistri*), who were full members of the guild and able to practise their craft without direct supervision, and, on the other, apprentices of various levels, progressing from being mere beginners in the craft to being 'bachelors' (*baccalarii*), who were able to take on more and more complicated and independent work as they matured, until finally themselves joining the guild as full members through becoming masters. This terminology was preserved in the medieval (and modern) world of higher education, where (a) the beginning apprentices were students (*scholares*) learning from masters and from more advanced students, where (b) there were various levels of bachelors, indicating the realisation of certain educational goals, and where (c) masters were also known as 'doctors' (*doctores*), that is, teachers. In Southern Europe, the earliest universities, like Bologna or Padua, were student guilds, while in the northern European universities, like Paris, Oxford and Cambridge, they were masters' guilds; the southern universities were best known for law and medicine, the northern for theology. Medieval universities were also known as *studia generalia* (singular: *studium generale*), or 'general places of study', and this is probably due to the fact that students would come from all over Europe, and, if they received their master's degree there, they would be entitled, in principle (not always in practice), to teach anywhere (they received the *ius ubique docendi*).

To get an idea of how a medieval university looked, we can focus on the University of Paris. The educational guild there coalesced towards the end of the twelfth century and is referred to as a type of corporate entity in letters from kings and popes in the early thirteenth century. The formation of the guild appears to have been set in motion by struggles between the masters in Paris, who were actually doing the teaching, and the Chancellor of Notre Dame, who on behalf of the Bishop of Paris had the power to grant licences to teach in the diocese: the masters sought to win influence by banding together. Eventually the university comprised four separate guilds, known as faculties: arts, medicine, canon law (civil law was banned by papal decree) and theology. The Faculty of Arts had by far the greatest number of students, and the arts degree was generally required to continue study in one of the three higher faculties (mendicants formed an exception, see §1.3). Although work of philosophical importance was certainly written by scholars primarily associated with faculties of law (especially political or ethical thought, for example, just war theory) or of medicine (Peter of Abano [d. 1316] with his *Conciliator* and Marsilius of Padua [d. 1342], who later wrote *Defensor Pacis*, come to mind), the present chapter concentrates on arts and theology. In all the coursework, Latin was the language of instruction, and indeed it was the language of international Western academia to a far greater extent than English is today. Students in arts were usually between 15 and 21 years old, progressing from passively observing lectures, disputations and other educational exercises (see §1.4) to participating in them actively, and becoming, upon successfully completing set educational requirements, a bachelor; upon fulfilling all university requirements, and at a minimum age of 21, a student in arts might be admitted to the guild of masters and as 'regent master' (*magister actu regens*) take on his own students. The progression of studies involved in the arts curriculum was also content determined: moving from the foundational logical works of Aristotle, Boethius and Porphyry, to more advanced physics and metaphysics, and eventually to ethics. The theological programme was a good deal more time consuming than the arts, involving seven years as a basic student, and thereafter various duties as a bachelor—lecturing on (also known as 'commenting on' or 'reading') the Bible and Peter Lombard's *Sentences*—until fulfilling all statutory requirements and being able to take a chair in theology as regent master; a statutory minimum age for someone to be master in theology was 35, although this was reduced in the fourteenth century to 30. The age difference between art students and theological students gives an indication as to why much study of later medieval philosophy focuses upon theologians: they were in general more mature thinkers and have left us more mature work. On the other hand, the difference between artists and theologians can be exaggerated: masters in arts often went on to take theology degrees, and theologians frequently lectured on 'philosophical' works, like those of Aristotle, and the philosophical content in more strictly 'theological' works is often extremely rich (see §1.4).

All students at the medieval university had some form of clerical status, and this indicates that universities, and especially the University of Paris, were heavily influenced by ecclesiastical considerations. Perhaps this is nowhere better seen than in the reception of Aristotle and a number of condemnations that had as their background the fear that Aristotelian ideas were to one extent or another incompatible with Christianity. Indeed, in 1210, 1215 and 1231, Church authorities, in the form of bishops, papal legates and the Pope himself, prohibited the teaching of Aristotle's works of natural philosophy (but not works of logic) in the Faculty of Arts in Paris. We can surmise, however, from, among other sources, a 'Guide for Students' written around 1240 and reflecting earlier practice, that Aristotle's philosophical works were taught.[5] If we were in any doubt about the point, just a look at the works of philosophy and theology being produced in the period would serve to show that Aristotle was in fact being studied (see §2.1). Indeed, by 1255 the Parisian arts faculty mandated lectures on all of Aristotle's works. This was by no means the end of the story of the controversy over the reception of Aristotle: Aristotelian philosophy, its teaching and its interpretation, showed up in a condemnation in 1270 at Paris and especially in the mammoth condemnation by the Bishop of Paris, Etienne Tempier, of 219 articles in 1277. Modern historians are in basic agreement that the condemnation of 1277, taking up a range of issues in physics, metaphysics and ethics, was aimed in part at certain masters in the Arts faculty, among them Siger of Brabant and Boethius of Dacia (i.e., Denmark; d. after 1277), whom the committee of theological masters appointed by Tempier to draw up the condemned articles saw as accepting Aristotelian doctrines that were not compatible with the Christian faith; the Condemnation appears also to have touched on views of Thomas Aquinas as well.[6] The Parisian Condemnation of 1277 is the most famous condemnation of the Middle Ages, but it represents just one instance in which limits were imposed upon free debate of the issues, imposed by a university faculty, by a bishop or pope or by a religious order. It should be stressed that later medieval thinkers were, in general, given very wide berth, but at all times there were boundaries beyond which a condemnation and a recantation might follow.[7]

Finally, a word should be said about book production for the higher educational market in this period. Books were expensive: laboriously copied by hand on costly materials like parchment and (more rarely and only in the later part of the period) paper. The scribes (or students) would use a system of highly abbreviated script that takes training and practice to read and can at times be ambiguous, leading to reading errors. In the later thirteenth century, a system was developed at some universities that made the copying of entire works less time consuming. Known as the *pecia* (or 'piece') system, this involved a master copy of a work being divided into several physically distinct parts of roughly equal length and made available for hire, part by part, to scribes and students by booksellers selected for the task by the university. This would allow several scribes to be working on parts of the book simultaneously, speeding up the process of copying it.[8] This was one way in which philosophical works could be quickly propagated.

1.3. The Mendicant Orders

With their beginnings in the first two decades of the thirteenth century, the Franciscans and the Dominicans came to play an immense role in the medieval world in general, and in the medieval philosophical endeavour in particular. The Dominicans (also known as Black Friars, and the Order of Preachers or O.P.), founded by the Spaniard Dominic Guzmán as a group to combat the Albigensian heresy, were dedicated from their beginning to argument and preaching, and hence to education; indeed, their educational system took as its point of departure that every convent was to be a school. From their early headquarters in Toulouse, the Dominicans received papal approval in 1216, and very soon thereafter they were in Paris and in Oxford. The Franciscans (also known as Grey Friars, and the Order of Friars Minor or O.F.M.) were conceived by their founder, Francis of Assisi, as devoting themselves to leading a simple life of preaching and begging (Latin: *mendicare*), but Franciscan efforts to attain theological education for members of the order came very soon after the foundation of the order itself. By 1219 Franciscans had reached Paris, and soon thereafter they began theological studies there; by 1224 they were in Oxford.

The convents erected by the Dominicans and Franciscans in the two great centres of theological training became in time the apex of large systems of education, running parallel to the normal university training that a non-mendicant arts and theology student would receive. These educational systems were pyramidal in structure, consisting of several levels of regional schools, each level having fewer schools and fewer students than the one beneath it. The base of the pyramid consisted of nearly every convent in the order, each offering the Latin grammar training and basic theological instruction that any friar would need to fulfil his preaching and confessional duties. Young Dominicans and Franciscans, however, who showed signs of academic talent would be sent for further training to one of the regional *studia grammaticalia*, specialising in Latin grammatical studies. The most gifted of those students would progress to a *studium logicale* (also known as a *studium artium*), where that most central of medieval philosophical disciplines, logic, was taught. Some of the students who successfully completed their logic training would advance to a *studium philosophiae* (also known as *studium naturale*), where they would learn philosophy in the broad sense, including physics, metaphysics and ethics. Finally, there were regional *studia theologica* at which more advanced theological training would be offered. Only the most successful of students would be sent to one of the degree-granting *studia generalia* for high-level training in theology, and of those students most would return to a provincial school, teaching philosophy or theology. All of these *studia* were located at convents of the order, often with several levels of *studia* at one and the same convent. The students who actually progressed to take a theology degree at Paris or Oxford were indeed considered to be the top achievers. Note that this parallel system of education gave members of the mendicant orders exemption from taking the arts curriculum at the universities.[9] Two other mendicant orders, the Augustinian Hermits and the Carmelites, set up corresponding educational systems and were extremely influential in the later thirteenth and fourteenth centuries; famous Augustinian Hermits from our period include Giles of Rome, James of Viterbo (d. 1308) and Gregory of Rimini, and among the Carmelites were numbered Gerard of Bologna (d. 1317) and John Baconthorpe (d. ca. 1348).[10]

Mendicant orders were important to medieval philosophy for many reasons. Many of the most important philosophers were mendicants, from Alexander of Hales (d. 1245) and Albert the Great (d. 1280), through Aquinas, Scotus and Ockham, and up to Gregory of Rimini. Just as importantly, the mendicant educational system was one of the major modes of transmission for high-level philosophical thought. A mendicant scholar, both before and after any possible doctorate in theology, might be sent by his order to one of the order's schools to offer instruction there. Examples abound of theologians spending time in lesser *studia* of their order: Thomas Aquinas in Cologne (with Albert the Great) before his regency in Paris, and in Orvieto and Rome after it; John Duns Scotus in Oxford and then Paris and finally in Cologne, where he died; Peter Auriol in Bologna and Toulouse, before advancing to Paris to read the *Sentences* and become regent master; and Gregory of Rimini at Bologna, Padua, Perugia and Rimini, both before and after obtaining his doctorate in Paris around 1346. Some well-known scholars did most of their teaching and writing away from the universities, for example, Peter John Olivi, who taught in Franciscan convents in Southern France and in Florence for much of his career and never became a master. Through all this moving around of teaching personnel, the mendicant orders became a prime conduit for the spreading of books and ideas. And in contrast to the mendicant tendency to move frequently from place to place, seculars (i.e., priests who did not belong to one of the religious orders) might remain master at the University of Paris for decades, witness Henry of Ghent (master ca. 1276–1293) and Godfrey of Fontaines (master ca. 1285–1298, and again from around 1303) in theology and John Buridan (master ca. 1325–ca. 1361) in arts.

Two interrelated disputes involving mendicants deserve special mention for the material of philosophical relevance they have left us, treating as they do political and legal issues like the nature of and relationship between church and state, the relation between individual and society, and the theory of rights (especially property rights) and dominion. The first is a dispute in the later thirteenth to early fourteenth century between the mendicants at the University of Paris and the seculars there. While behind this dispute lay a competition between the two groups for students and for privileges, the writings that issued from it dealt with some of the most important aspects of religious and economic life and involved a good deal of what we would today consider political thought. Moreover, some of the most important thinkers at the late-thirteenth-century University of Paris took part in the dispute, among others, Thomas Aquinas, Bonaventure, John Pecham (d. 1292), Gerard of Abbeville (d. 1272), Henry of Ghent and into the fourteenth century with John of Pouilly (d. after 1328) at Paris and Richard FitzRalph (d. 1360) on the British Isles.[11] The second dispute is the controversy over 'apostolic poverty', an ideal of absolute poverty inherited by the Franciscan order from its founder. A group of Franciscans in the late thirteenth and early fourteenth centuries (the 'Spiritual Franciscans') held that the Franciscan order and its members should be absolutely poor. In the 1320s this led to a clash with the papacy over the extent to which absolute poverty could and should be practised. Fleeing from Pope John XXII in 1328, Franciscan thinkers like William of Ockham and Francis of Marchia (d. after 1344) joined the Master of Arts and Medicine (and political philosopher) Marsilius of Padua at the court of Emperor Ludwig of Bavaria. Ockham penned his extensive political writings as a consequence of this dispute.

1.4. Major Genres of Philosophical Writing, 1200–1350

Some of the works that survive from our period appear to have been in conception and execution *written* works, with no immediate relation to the author's teaching duties as such. Examples of this type of work are Peter of Spain's *Summulae logicales*, Albert the Great's *Tractatus de homine*, Thomas Aquinas's *Summa contra Gentiles* and *Summa theologica*, William of Ockham's *Summa logicae* and Thomas Bradwardine's *Summa de causa Dei*. Moreover, some works were penned as broadsides, contributions to debates then raging, like the heated discussions over the eternity of the world or the unicity of the human intellect that stretched from the mid–thirteenth into the fourteenth century, or the secular-mendicant dispute or the controversy over apostolic poverty; each of these controversies generated an extensive literature usually unconnected with the authors' teaching obligations. But with that acknowledged, the fact remains that the largest amount of surviving philosophical literature from the period had its origins in the classroom, related in one way or another to one of the teaching exercises that masters or advanced students were required to perform.

In fact, the works that we possess from this period might stem from any of a number of stages in the process of an author's revision of his own lectures or disputations. Normally in a medieval classroom, several students would be designated 'reporters' (*reportatores*), who would take detailed notes of the proceedings.

An issue of great importance for the study of medieval scholastic literature in general is the path taken from a work's oral delivery to its written form since how much weight we can give to a text as a reliable witness to the author's thought will be in part contingent upon the way the text came into being. We tend to classify medieval texts on the basis of their place in an idealised 'composition process': student reports of lectures, untouched by the 'author's' hand, are called *reportationes*; student reports that have been moderately reworked by the 'author', *reportationes examinatae* or *reportationes editae*; and works that have been thoroughly revised by their author, *ordinationes*. We have quite a few examples of pure *reportationes*, and these must in general be read with caution since the extent to which the text reflects the thought of the author depends on the talent and the diligence of the student reporter. We also have many *ordinationes* that have been thoroughly revised by their author and can be considered definitive statements; when available these are to be preferred to all forms of *reportationes*, which, however, can always be used as supplemental evidence. There has been a good deal of recent secondary literature on the process by which medieval authors would revise their text, sometimes to completion but sometimes only partially.[12]

The later medieval philosopher or theologian was expected to teach in two major ways: through disputations and through lectures. In addition there were a variety of other exercises, most importantly 'recitations' with corresponding 'collations', as well as *sophismata* and obligational disputations, which led to a variety of logical treatises and profoundly influenced both philosophical and theological literature, especially in the fourteenth century.[13]

As they developed in the course of the thirteenth century, disputations were set academic exercises, presided over by a master (of arts or theology) but involving in an active way at least two advanced students; other less advanced students would observe the proceedings as part of their education. Although the structure varied, in an 'ordinary' disputation, a disputation arranged by the master as part of his regular teaching duties, the master himself would pose an issue to be addressed along with a solution; one or more advanced students would act as 'opponent', arguing against the solution; another student would act as 'respondent', attempting to reply to the arguments put forward by the opponent(s). These disputations would take place over two days: the first day, the disputation proper, would comprise the dialectical argumentation of opponent and respondent; on a later day the master would give his 'determination' of the question, including his response to arguments raised during the first day that went against his considered view.[14] Among many thirteenth-century examples of this genre could be mentioned Alexander of Hales's disputed questions from 'before he became a friar' (*Antequam esset frater*); Thomas Aquinas's *On truth*, *On the soul* and *On power*; and Henry of Ghent's *Summa of Ordinary Questions*.

A special form of disputation was the 'quodlibet'. The disputation itself was organised in the same way as ordinary disputed questions, taking place over two days and involving an opponent, a respondent and a presiding master. Quodlibetal questions were different, however, inasmuch as they were held only twice a year, just before Christmas and just before Easter, and, when they were held, all other university activities were suspended so that as many persons could attend as possible; most importantly, the questions addressed were posed *a quolibet de quolibet*: by anyone in the audience concerning any topic. There are many *quodlibeta* (i.e., sets of quodlibetal questions) from the thirteenth and early fourteenth century (after 1330 they become very rare), and for some major thinkers from the era like Godfrey of Fontaines and Gerard of Abbeville they are basically the only works we have. Quodlibetal questions often touch on a very wide range of topics, from metaphysics and physics to philosophical psychology and philosophical theology to economics and ecclesiology (including church–state relations). They are for this reason an extremely rich source for the student of medieval philosophy.[15]

There were several exercises for students that could lead to written works by the supervising master or bachelor. To strengthen their grasp of the material, students were expected, for example, to recite lectures they had heard earlier, and this recitation might be joined to a *collatio*, in which students were supposed to come up with objections or questions that the presiding master or advanced student would seek to address; we have famous examples of written *collationes* in those of Bonaventure and of Duns Scotus. In order to train the students in logic, various exercises were held, and again some of them were eventually passed on in written form. Thus, a popular logical exercise was the *sophisma* (pl.: *sophismata*), in which ambiguous terms create problems for the correct understanding of a sentence, and the student (or master) would have to disambiguate it. For example: 'All the apostles are twelve' is true if the 'all' is taken collectively as applying to all twelve apostles, but it is false if taken distributively, as applying to this apostle and to that apostle. Ambiguities like this, focusing on grammatical, logical and physical issues, would be tackled in the *sophismata* in the classroom and in writing. We have many examples of written *sophismata* from throughout our period, and important authors of the genre are Richard the Sophister (fl. 1230s or 1240s), Siger of Brabant, Radulphus Brito, John of Jandun (d. 1328), Walter Burley (d. after 1344) and John Buridan. Around 1335, the English author William Heytesbury (d. 1372/73) wrote an extremely popular treatise on *Rules for solving sophisms* (*Regulae solvendi sophismata*), and we also have from him many written sophisms, as we do from many of his English colleagues from the mid–fourteenth century. Closely linked to *sophismata* were the medieval treatises on 'insolubles' or paradoxical self-referential sentences like 'this proposition is false' ('the liar's paradox'); many treatments of insolubles are found in *sophisma* literature (e.g., Heytesbury's treatise), although entire works were also dedicated to the genre, like the *Insolubilia* of Thomas Bradwardine (d. 1349).[16] Finally, mention should be made of obligational disputations, in which the disputants were bound by strict rules (hence the 'obligation'), the opponent attempting to make the respondent contradict himself within a limited amount of time. There are several treatises expounding on the rules governing obligations, and particular elements in this disputation—for example, 'impossible position', a type of counterfactual reasoning—were already absorbed into several theological contexts in the thirteenth century. All of these exercises had the purpose of training students in their required logical, philosophical and theological knowledge, and all of them have left important traces in the period's philosophical literature available to us today.

Lectures would be held on the major textbooks in the various areas of intellectual endeavour in philosophy, primarily various works of Aristotle (but also, for example, those of Boethius, Priscian and Donatus), while in theology, Peter Lombard's *Sentences* and the Bible. Aristotle commentaries from the Middle Ages are extraordinarily plentiful, having been written by both artists and theologians.[17] These commentaries come in two basic varieties, exposition commentaries and question commentaries, with some examples of mixed versions.[18] Thomas Aquinas wrote exposition commentaries: these stay quite close to Aristotle's text, expounding the words of the Philosopher, while injecting into that explanation a great deal of insight original to the commentator. Question commentaries, on the other hand, are more loosely connected to Aristotle's text, perhaps reproducing short passages from it as a prelude to focusing on an issue that the commentator would then investigate at length. Important in this regard is that 'questions' (*quaestiones*) have a rather fixed form that mirrors the dialectical structure of a classroom disputation. Take the example of one question from the commentary on *De caelo* by one of the most important later medieval Aristotle commentators, Peter of Auvergne (d. 1304):

> *De caelo*, book 2, q. 25[19]
>   (a) topic: Do the stars generate heat through their light?
>   (b) two arguments for the negative position (*videtur quod non . . .*): these are preliminary or initial arguments
>   (c) an argument for the positive position (*oppositum apparet*)
>   (d) a treatment of the question, including description of other views on the topic as well as Peter's definitive solution
>   (e) replies to the two preliminary arguments for the negative position (= ~b)

Thus, in a question, the author usually presents some preliminary arguments against the view that he will support, some preliminary arguments in favour of that view, then gives his own view, and finally responds to the preliminary arguments that seemed to speak against him. Although the size and specific composition of *quaestiones* vary greatly and develop over time, this basic structure remains relatively stable throughout our period. Question commentaries (as opposed to exposition commentaries) became more and more predominant as the thirteenth century wore on. Siger of Brabant's commentary on III *De anima*, Boethius of Dacia's on the *Topics*, John Duns Scotus's commentaries on the *De anima* and the *Metaphysics* and John of Jandun's on the *Parva naturalia* are all good examples of question commentaries. Moreover, in general as the fourteenth century progresses, the Aristotelian material is treated in fewer questions, but on the other hand, the questions became longer and more complex. Take as an example the difference between Peter of Auvergne's late-thirteenth-century commentary on *De memoria et reminiscentia* and John Buridan's commentary on the same work from the first half of the fourteenth century: Peter asks sixteen questions versus John's five, and John's five questions are both more comprehensive than Peter's and tend to focus on the single issue of the definition of memory while Peter tried to deal with many issues that arise from Aristotle's text.[20]

In the theological faculty, bachelors normally held lectures on Peter Lombard's *Sentences* and on the Bible. Lectures on the Bible survive in literally hundreds of commentaries on all parts of the Old and New Testament.[21] Some commentaries are clear sources for philosophical thought and have been used as such. For example, the commentaries on the *Hexameron*, or seven days of creation, like that by Robert Grosseteste, often dealt with metaphysical and physical/scientific issues (matter, form, light, seminal reasons, the plant and animal world, anthropology, etc.); the beginning of John's Gospel lent itself to a discussion of mental words (i.e., concepts); finally, commentaries on Paul's letter to the Romans often contained discussions of predestination, free will, and the nature of willing. Commentaries on other parts of the Bible have been examined for the way the scholastic theologian, trained in systematic theology, brings his craft to commenting on the Bible and what the commentaries tell us about a theologian's philosophy.[22]

A better-known and better-explored theological context for the study of later medieval philosophy is found in the period's many commentaries on the *Sentences* of Peter Lombard. Lombard's work, finished by 1155, was divided into four books, and each of them had ample material for philosophical speculation:

> Book I: God as three and one, including our knowledge of God, whether theology is a scientific discipline, divine attributes, trinitarian theology, divine names, God's knowledge (including foreknowledge), power and will
>
> Book II: creation, including the divine act of creation, the eternity of the world, angelology, matter and the elements, the heavens, philosophical anthropology (free will, intellect and sin)
>
> Book III: Christ, including the hypostatic union and Mary's motherhood, and the virtues (in general, individually and as connected)
>
> Book IV: the sacraments and last things, including a treatment of each of the sacraments (often involving aspects of what we would call social and political philosophy), the separated soul and the beatific vision

Lombard himself subdivided each book into 'chapters', but in his glosses on the *Sentences* written at the University of Paris sometime between 1223 and 1227, Alexander of Hales organised the books of the *Sentences* according to the 'distinctions' best known to those studying *Sentences* commentaries today. Alexander's use of the *Sentences* as a textbook in his ordinary lectures seems to have been emulated by several masters of theology who have left us written commentaries, first at Paris with Hugh of St Cher (d. 1263), and later at Oxford by Richard Fishacre (d. 1248). Although lecturing on the *Sentences* (as opposed to the Bible) was not universally favoured— Roger Bacon (d. 1293), for instance, thought that Alexander had contributed to the ruin of theology by introducing this novelty, and Robert Grosseteste rebuked Fishacre for doing just this—nevertheless it soon became a traditional part of the requirements for advanced theological students to gain their master's degree. It is for this reason that we have *Sentences* commentaries from nearly every major theologian of the period 1250–1350, and especially in the fourteenth century the *Sentences* commentary is often the only piece of scholastic writing we have from many authors. Moreover, in much the same way as the Aristotelian question commentaries, the

Sentences commentaries underwent a strong development in their organisation. In the second half of the thirteenth century, the commentaries (e.g., those of Aquinas and Bonaventure from around 1250) are extremely comprehensive in the topics discussed and hold fairly close to Lombard's overall organisational scheme; indeed, they often include a number of individual questions in each of the 'distinctions' that Alexander of Hales had introduced. In the early fourteenth century, theologians begin to become much more selective in the topics they take up for discussion, and one can see this already in the commentaries of, for example, John Duns Scotus, Peter Auriol and William of Ockham. Here there are most often no more than one or two questions per distinction, and some distinctions are ignored altogether. This trend towards selectivity becomes extremely marked, especially in English commentaries from the period after 1320, where they begin to lose contact with Lombard completely.[23]

2. Trends, Figures and Lines of Influence: The Ebb and Flow of the Philosophical Discussion, 1200–1350

A convenient way to get an overview of the main philosophical figures and currents between 1200 and 1350 is to divide the period into three unequal parts. These are: 1200–1250 (§2.1), 1250–1320 (§2.2) and 1320–1350 at Oxford and at Paris (§2.3). Although they are not entirely arbitrary, these divisions represent a convenient way to survey a very long time span full with philosophical activity.

2.1. 1200–1250

The first division coincides with the beginnings of three major developments that were traced in part one of this chapter. Thus, this early period saw the firm establishment of the universities at both Oxford and Paris, along with the beginnings of a relatively standardised curriculum. At this point in time, Oxford was definitely the more minor seat of learning, and nearly all important philosophers of the day received a good deal of their education in Paris. The period also witnessed the founding of the two largest mendicant orders, the Dominicans and the Franciscans, and their entrance into the university context. And this was the time of the first reception of much of the newly translated Aristotelian works. These fifty years are also as yet extremely poorly researched, with many of the fundamental texts remaining in manuscript, which in turn masks the lines of influence and truly major figures.

With that said, we can certainly point out some major figures and developments. Thus, Stephen Langton (d. 1228), a leading figure of late-twelfth-century thought, contributed decisively to the philosophical and theological education in the new century by producing the first known full-fledged question commentary on Peter Lombard's *Sentences*, utilizing the freedom that separate questions could provide to investigate at length issues on all four books. This is also the period in which Alexander of Hales introduced the *Sentences* into regular university teaching and entered the Franciscan Order in 1236/37, thus giving the Franciscans their first chair of theology at Paris. This was roughly simultaneous with the Dominicans gaining their first chair of theology when Roland of Cremona (d. 1259) entered the order in 1229; a second chair came to the order in 1230 with John of St Giles (d. after 1258).

Four theologians of particular significance in this era are Philip the Chancellor (d. 1236), William of Auxerre (d. 1231), William of Auvergne (d. 1249) and Robert Grosseteste. Philip's importance and that of his major work, the *Summo de bono* (1225–28), is becoming increasingly recognised; Philip shows the influence of, among others, Aristotle and Avicenna, and his own influence can be traced on such subjects as the rational soul, the eternity of the world, the virtues and the transcendentals. William of Auxerre's claim to fame is his *Summa aurea*, an early theological *summa* that had immense impact, although it is somewhat traditional in content. William of Auvergne, Bishop of Paris from 1228 until his death, shows a strong engagement with the new Aristotelian and especially Avicennean ideas on a spectrum of issues in his massive, multi-part work, the *Magisterium divinale et sapientiale*. Finally, the Englishman Grosseteste, who translated the *Nicomachean Ethics* from Greek into Latin and was the first Latin author to comment on the *Posterior Analytics*, was a philosopher and theologian of stature who wrote on many subjects and showed early influence from Avicenna and Averroes. As the Bishop of Lincoln, in whose diocese Oxford lay, Grosseteste was a seminal figure, especially in English university thought, and he had a special bond with Oxford Franciscans, among them Roger Bacon and Richard Rufus of Cornwall, but he also influenced such Dominicans from this early period as Richard Fishacre and Robert Kilwardby.

Aristotle's use in the thought of this period is witnessed not only by the appearance of the *corpus vetustius* (§1.1), but also by important commentary work on the newly appeared Aristotelian texts by such thinkers as, in England, Adam of Buckfield (fl. 1230–1250) and Geoffrey of Aspall (d. 1287), and, at Paris, John the Page (fl. 1225–1245), Robert Kilwardby and Albert the Great (who in this respect was influenced by Kilwardby). In addition, Peter of Spain's *Tractatus* or *Summulae logicales* was composed in this period, and this work remained a standard logical textbook for centuries, even commented upon by John Buridan. All in all, these fifty years saw the coalescing of the institutional and philosophical foundation upon which the remainder of our period would build.

2.2. 1250–1320

The second division in our period is temporally the largest and by far the best studied. Reasons for this are not difficult to find, and the most obvious of them is that most of the figures mentioned at the beginning of this chapter as being of recognised significance were active in this time frame. The time span also straddles the thirteenth-/fourteenth-century divide, so it is best to say something immediately about the relation between the thought of the two centuries. Often in more general secondary literature, thirteenth-century thought is presented as something very different from fourteenth-century thought, with some type of implicit break at around 1300. Usually there is appeal to differing characteristics of each century: for example, the thirteenth century being metaphysical and speculative, and realist on the issue of universals, the fourteenth century being logical and empiricist, and nominalist on universals. While acknowledging that there is some truth to this view, I want to resist the comfort of easy labels and claim that there was far more continuity between thirteenth- and fourteenth-century thought than is sometimes acknowledged. Continuity was to a large extent guaranteed by the fact that, as we will see, fourteenth-century theologians, especially Dominicans, often took the thought of Thomas Aquinas as their point of departure. Something similar can be said about John Duns Scotus, especially for Franciscan authors: Scotus was the heir of a great deal of late-thirteenth-century ideas developed by Bonaventure (and the group surrounding him), by Peter John Olivi and by Henry of Ghent, and Scotus passed on their general views in a heavily altered form to many fourteenth-century thinkers who appear to have seen their task as building upon the foundation that Scotus laid. Another way in which there is more resemblance than difference between the two centuries can be seen in the very question of universals. While it is true that nominalism re-emerged in the fourteenth century in a way not seen in the thirteenth, with such thinkers as Durand of St Pourçain (d. 1334), Peter Auriol and especially William of Ockham, John Buridan, Adam Wodeham and Gregory of Rimini, nevertheless one has to acknowledge that there were many major fourteenth-century thinkers who were realists when it came to universals, beginning with many of those who can be looked at as 'Scotists' or 'Thomists' but also including such major thinkers as Walter Burley and Walter Chatton (d. 1343), who developed coherent defences of realism in the face of the new nominalist thought. Thus, although it cannot be denied that between the two centuries there are significant differences in tendencies or leanings, nevertheless this should not be allowed to mask the great deal of continuity between them. It is for this reason that I find it best to look at the period stretching from Bonaventure and Aquinas, around 1250, to Peter Auriol and William of Ockham, around 1320, as a unit. A more significant change happens after around 1320, when the two major universities considered here, Oxford and Paris, begin to develop rather different intellectual profiles (see §2.3).

   With a good deal of justification, Thomas Aquinas is the best-known medieval philosopher today. Nevertheless, to understand his place in medieval philosophy, several things need to be borne in mind about him. First, it was only with the Counter-Reformation and Neo-Thomism that Aquinas became the medieval philosopher par excellence. Although, as we will see, Aquinas had a large following, especially in the Dominican Order, during the Middle Ages, nevertheless his philosophical and theological ideas were routinely (and sometimes bitterly) challenged (even after his canonisation in 1323), and in terms of influence in the period to 1350 and even beyond, John Duns Scotus may well exceed Aquinas. Second,

Aquinas is a product of his time, and this can be seen in the fact that, on some of the few issues on which we have actually done the research, his views have clear relation to the views found in the first half of the thirteenth century, as well as in the fact that in his works Aquinas is often in discussion with contemporaries, like Bonaventure, John Pecham, Gerard of Abbeville (on mendicant privileges) and Siger of Brabant.[24]

With that said, Aquinas was a rare philosophical genius, whose works display an unparalleled architectonic vision, with a generally transparent rationale for the placing of topics, divisions and subdivisions, and even individual arguments exactly where they are within the context of the work as a whole. This architectonic vision is just one facet of the impressive systematic coherency that one finds throughout Aquinas's thought. His works also display a profound and extensive knowledge of the intellectual tradition available to him, and most particularly, a fresh reading of Aristotle, eventually in the new translations of Moerbeke. Thus, already in Aquinas's *Sentences* commentary, his earliest major work (mid-1250s), there is an explosion in the explicit use of Aristotle as compared with Aquinas's predecessors: there are two thousand quotations there from Aristotle, nearly twice as many as there are from Augustine![25] This desire to utilize Aristotle in all aspects of philosophy and theology can be seen in Aquinas's eleven commentaries on Aristotelian works and in his deep interest in important test cases in the process of adopting Aristotelianism in the Christian university context, test cases such as the eternity of the world and the Averroist thesis that all humankind share one intellect ('monopsychism'). Moreover, for all that Aquinas was a product of his time, he certainly did not shy away from taking radical views for his day, for example, his thesis that every created being has one and only one substantial form, the so-called unicity of substantial form thesis, which appears to have been unprecedented in thirteenth-century scholasticism. Finally, on issue after issue—the scientific nature of theology, concepts and their formation, the distinction between being and essence, the analogy of being between God and creatures, divine foreknowledge, the will's freedom, the nature of matter, and so on— Aquinas's view was one of the standard points of departure throughout our period.

Aquinas taught for some twenty years for the Dominican Order, both in Italy and in Paris, and he was heavily involved in important Dominican educational initiatives; moreover, he wrote works on a very broad spectrum of topics from systematic theology to Aristotelian commentaries. For these reasons, as well as the power and coherency of his thought, Aquinas became a central figure in the scholastic discussion from the time of his death in 1274, and this can be seen in a number of concrete ways. First, it is widely held that some of Aquinas's views were targeted in the Condemnations of 1277, although without explicit attribution to Aquinas; it is indisputable that 51 articles taken from the works of Giles of Rome, intellectually aligned with Aquinas but a formidable and creative thinker in his own right and from 1287 the teaching doctor of the Augustinian Hermits, were censured in an independent condemnation in 1277, and it has even been suggested that there was an abortive attempt to directly censure Aquinas at the same time. Perhaps as a result of the negative attention lavished on Aquinas in 1277, Thomas became *the* major thinker of the Dominican Order very quickly. Already in 1279, in the wake of the Condemnations of 1277, there was Dominican legislation on Thomas; in 1286, just twelve years after Aquinas's death, all those occupying teaching positions in the order were required to uphold his thought.

This legislative activity paralleled a major effort by individual members of the Dominican Order to defend Thomas's ideas from attack, usually attack from Franciscans. Thus, when in 1282 the Franciscan Order officially endorsed William de la Mare's (d. after 1282) *Correctorium fratris Thomae*, a 'correction' to some 118 views taken from a variety of Aquinas's theological works, no fewer than four replies to de la Mare's work were penned by Dominicans—within about two years! Dominicans also wrote Thomistic responses to other authors' works: for example, the important English Dominican Thomas of Sutton (d. after 1315) wrote a work answering many of the points in John Duns Scotus's *Quodlibet*, and Hervaeus Natalis (d. 1323), future master general of the Dominican Order and a major force in Aquinas's 1323 canonisation, wrote several treatises against Henry of Ghent from a Thomistic perspective.[26] With Hervaeus, indeed, we enter another phase of the earliest battles over Thomas since he attacked in writing also Dominican writers, most spectacularly Durand of St Pourçain. Durand was hounded by Hervaeus and other Dominicans for allegedly contradicting Thomas's theology and philosophy: Durand's works were investigated by the order and were replied to by several Dominicans in the period up to 1330, and probably on account of Durand, legislation on Thomas and his place in the order was enacted in 1309 and 1313 (and again in 1329). Interesting in this regard is that, while on some issues Durand clearly did contradict Thomas Aquinas, on others there seems to have been a genuine interpretational disagreement between him and other Dominican Thomists, each being able to find support in Thomas's many works for their views. It is worth remarking that a more nuanced view has emerged recently of two other Dominicans from this period who have traditionally been considered anti-Thomistic in spirit: Dietrich of Freiburg (d. 1318/1320) and Meister Eckhart (d. 1328). These two thinkers are increasingly recognised to have been complex when it came to their relation to Thomas, in some cases anti-Thomistic, in others simply adhering to an intellectual tradition more closely tied to Albert the Great than to Thomas.[27] Important in all this is that, through its promotion of Aquinas, the Dominican Order was defining itself intellectually, setting up a clear contrast to especially the Franciscan thinkers of the day. With that said, it should be noted that in defending what they understood to be Thomistic doctrine against contemporary attacks, Dominicans of the time necessarily reacted to new challenges to and attacks on their views, and for this reason early Thomism is a lively affair, continually renewing itself.

Franciscan philosophical and theological tendencies, descended from Alexander of Hales, were woven into a compelling system by Hales's student, Bonaventure, whose role in the order's thought is just one facet of his immense impact on the Franciscan Order as a whole: with Bonaventure Franciscan thought was set upon firm ground. This is not to say that the order's philosophy and theology had no room to grow: in the later thirteenth century it was developed considerably—and increasingly in opposition to Dominican views—by, among others, John Pecham (d. 1292, and a determined critic of Aquinas's thought), Matthew of Aquasparta (d. 1302), Peter John Olivi and William of Ware (d. after 1305?). Many of these Franciscan thinkers used to be characterised as 'neo-Augustinians', wary of or even inimical to the use of Aristotle in theology and philosophy, but more recent research has nuanced this picture considerably by showing how these thinkers used Aristotle in substantial and highly innovative ways. That the Franciscan intellectual current was not limited to members of the order is shown most clearly by the Parisian secular theologian Henry of Ghent, whose positions and dispositions on many issues fit neatly into the Franciscan intellectual tradition and who made significant contributions to the tradition in his own right.

Much of John Duns Scotus's thought is, in fact, a reaction to or a development of Henry of Ghent's. Scotus came from Scotland and studied first at the Franciscan convent in Oxford and later at Paris, where he became a master of theology in 1305. Scotus's immense philosophical imagination and acuity of mind can be seen in his treatments of many issues; nevertheless, most of his views have clear roots in the Franciscan tradition of the second half of the thirteenth century. One example of this can be seen in Scotus's theory of divine foreknowledge and future contingents, which shows the strong influence of Henry of Ghent, as well as his postulation that 'synchronic contingency' is crucial to the will's freedom, a view related to that of Peter John Olivi. Further, Scotus's detailed argumentation for his view that human knowledge is entirely natural, requiring no immediate divine aid, is a direct reaction to Henry of Ghent's theory of divine illumination. Finally, and perhaps most famously, Scotus's 'formal distinction' builds on ideas of earlier Franciscan writers. In short, on many matters Scotus acted as something of a filter, taking in a (mostly) Franciscan intellectual tradition that he inherited, and passing it on to those coming after him in a terminologically and conceptually modified form that would exercise immense influence into the early-modern period. There is, however, at least one issue on which Scotus seems to have introduced a radically new position into the scholastic theological discussion: the univocity of the concept of being, that when we say 'being' of substances and accidents, and of God and creatures, the word 'being' in each case has the same meaning and is not being used analogically or equivocally. But even here he appears to have been employing a view held commonly by logicians of the late thirteenth century: that there is no midpoint between equivocity and univocity. Above all, it should be stressed that Scotus fashioned a sophisticated and highly elaborate theological and philosophical *system*.

Scotus's impact was immediate and wide ranging: it would be difficult to find a medieval scholastic after him who does not show his influence in some way, and this influence can be seen in nearly every facet of philosophy and theology. Although his influence on Dominican theologians in certain areas has been demonstrated, generally Dominicans criticised his views. Franciscans reacted to him in a variety of ways. These ranged from the rare uncritical endorsement of Scotus's theology (e.g., Peter of Aquila [d. 1361]) to attempts to defend the main lines of Scotus's thought and develop his ideas in creative directions (e.g., the secular theologian Henry of Harclay [d. 1317], and the Franciscans William of Alnwick [d. 1333],

Landulph Caracciolo [d. 1351] and Francis of Meyronnes [d. ca. 1328]) to a critical reception of Scotus's views by highly independent scholars who became influential in their own right. Included among the latter group are two of the most creative and significant Franciscan theologians of the fourteenth century: the Frenchman Peter Auriol and the Englishman William of Ockham. Although today Auriol is not as well known as Ockham, in his own day he probably had more impact, with his provocative views—on such issues as cognition, Trinitarian theology, the univocity of the concept of being and divine foreknowledge and future contingents—being heatedly discussed on both sides of the English Channel. Auriol's slightly younger contemporary, Ockham, completed all the requirements for the doctorate in theology but never received it, probably because he ran into trouble first with the English province of the Franciscan Order and then with Pope John XXII. His scholastic works were never condemned, but he spent the last twenty years of his life writing pamphlets against the Pope on issues having to do with apostolic poverty. His philosophy is nominalist not only in the sense that he rejects any extra-mental existence for universals but also in the sense that he has a strong tendency towards ontological reductionism, recognising just two of the Aristotelian categories: substance and quality. He effects this ontological reduction by means of the semantic distinction between absolute and connotative terms, a distinction related to perhaps his most famous developments: an elaborate theory of mental language undergirded by a use of the distinction between intuitive and abstractive cognition. In ethics he defended a strong voluntarism while rejecting Scotus's synchronic contingency, and he developed a highly nuanced virtue ethics; his political thought is marked by careful discussions of rights and dominion. The reading of Ockham's works was actually banned by the arts faculty at Paris in 1339–40, but the reason behind the prohibition is difficult to pinpoint, and Ockham's influence in the period, especially at Paris, appears to have been limited.[28]

Although the philosophy produced by Dominicans and Franciscans dominates our understanding of the period, there were, of course, other extremely important philosophical currents at the time, originating mainly in the arts faculties but influencing also the theologians. One of these currents is 'modism', a theory of 'speculative' grammar, grammar meant to answer to the requirements of strict Aristotelian science (especially universal application). The modists developed a theory of language in which things and the ways in which they exist (*modi essendi*) are strongly correlated with the ways they can be understood (*modi intelligendi*), which in turn are strongly correlated with the ways they can be signified (*modi significandi*), for example, as nouns or verbs. Important modist thinkers include Boethius of Dacia and Radulphus Brito, and echoes of the doctrine can be found in theologians like Scotus and Auriol; two major modistic textbooks were Martin of Dacia's (d. 1304) *De modis significandi*, and Thomas of Erfurt's *Grammatica speculativa* (ca. 1300). Critical reaction to modist theory came from, among others, John of Jandun and John Buridan.

A second current that deserves mention is Averroism. Averroes was an important philosophical source on many issues, but the view that is perhaps most specifically 'Averroist' is the unicity of the intellect, the view that there is one and only one intellect separate from and shared by all human beings. A small but important group of thinkers subscribed in one form or another to this view, including Siger of Brabant, Walter Burley's teacher Thomas Wylton (d. before 1327), John Baconthorpe and John of Jandun; against it were ranged a tremendous number of (especially) theologians, from Aquinas, Bonaventure and Albert the Great through Auriol and Ockham and further to Gregory of Rimini, although the controversy was at its height in the late thirteenth century.

2.3. 1320–1350 at Oxford and at Paris[29]

Philosophical work was written in many places in the period 1200–1350. Over and above the medicine and law faculties (also in southern universities like Bologna, Montpellier and Orleans), there were many mendicant *studia* where talented friars taught and wrote, in Florence, Barcelona, Toulouse, Cologne, Norfolk and at the papal palace, to name just a few. But Paris and Oxford universities were the major sources both of high-level philosophical education and of the largest amount of high-level philosophical work. Throughout the period 1200–1320, Oxford and Paris certainly had some divergent philosophical interests and inclinations,[30] yet the two universities can be considered one 'research zone'. This is seen just in the fact that nearly every English author who wrote before 1320 spent at least some of his career in Paris: take the examples of John Duns Scotus, Thomas Wylton, Henry of Harclay, William of Alnwick and Walter Burley. This began to change in the first part of the fourteenth century with scholars like Thomas of Sutton and William of Ockham, who spent their entire career in England. But in the period 1320–1350, the two universities truly went their separate ways.

In the period after William of Ockham's English career, Oxford experienced a 'Golden Age', basically divorced from Paris (due in part to the Hundred Years War), and boasting such important scholars as Walter Chatton, Richard Fitz-Ralph, Robert Holcot (d. 1349), Adam Wodeham and Thomas of Buckingham. It should be pointed out that, although Ockham's ideas figure in the English thought of the era, nevertheless he was by no means an overwhelming influence and was on many issues sharply contested or simply ignored. English thinkers of this period explored new and extremely fruitful lines of enquiry, much influenced by innovative logical and mathematical concepts and reflecting a strong interest in natural philosophy. Thus, the second quarter of the fourteenth century was the time of so-called 'Oxford Calculators', including thinkers like Thomas Bradwardine, Richard Kilvington (d. 1361), William Heytesbury, Richard Swineshead (d. 1355), and John Dumbleton (d. ca. 1348), who produced a string of logical and physical treatises. Perhaps the most famous development from the school was the 'mean speed theorem', postulating a mathematical equivalence between the distance moved by a body for a certain time at a constant speed and the distance moved by the same body in the same time under a constant acceleration.[31] This interest in logic and mathematics also strongly coloured the many (mostly unedited) theological works of the era, nearly all of which are *Sentences* commentaries, and in which the focus is on a small number of problems with logical and psychological ramifications, for example, will and willing, sin, future contingents and Trinitarian logic, and in which 'obligations' logic (§1.4) was used to new ends in the theological discourse.[32]

In the same period, roughly 1320–50, Paris was well represented by John Buridan, a thinker of enormous impact throughout the remainder of the medieval period and considered today one of the greatest medieval thinkers. Buridan pursued in his many Aristotle commentaries as well as in separate treatises, like his *Summulae*, a programme of ontological reductionism, employing in it, as had Ockham, semantic analysis related to the use of mental language; Buridan also had innovative ideas in psychology and ethics. While Buridan's interest in logic and natural philosophy might be considered compatible with English thought contemporary with him, much of the material from this era at Paris comes in the form of *Sentences* commentaries, in which the Parisian authors of the period show little or no cognizance of contemporary English thought, being more consumed with replying to especially Peter Auriol's views on many issues, for example, human cognition and free will. Indeed, such thinkers from the 1320s as Francis of Marchia, Francis of Meyronnes, Gerard Odo (d. 1349) and Nicholas Bonet (d. 1343), all of them Franciscans, made original contributions to the scholastic debate and were known into the early-modern period. Perhaps the most notorious figure of the time at Paris was the secular theologian Nicholas of Autrecourt (d. 1369), who in 1346 was forced to recant a number of suspect theses related to his stringent criteria for metaphysical or theological certitude. Although scholastic production continued in the 1330s at Paris, there appears nevertheless, to have been something of a slump around then. But Paris returns to full glory with the commentary on I–II *Sentences* of the Augustinian Hermit Gregory of Rimini from the mid-1340s. Gregory had a wide and deep familiarity with the fruits of English thought of the preceding twenty years, and he integrated that thought into the Parisian theological tradition he inherited. Gregory was the first serious conveyer of the new English thought, initially to a Parisian audience and then to the rest of Continental Europe; his work was still being printed in the sixteenth century.

NOTES

For comments and suggestions, thanks to William J. Courtenay, Pieter De Leemans, John Marenbon and Chris Schabel. The bibliography is highly selective and meant to lead readers on to further literature. Indispensable to research on this period's philosophy is the repertory of editions of Latin philosophical texts found in Schönberger (2011). For a very inclusive bibliographic treatment of medieval scholastics (not exclusively arts masters), see the ongoing multi-volume Weijers (1994–2010); for works by British and Irish authors in the period, see Sharpe (2001); still useful is Glorieux (1933–34). See also the many relevant articles in the on-line *Stanford Encyclopedia of Philosophy* (ed. E. N. Zalta) or the *Encyclopedia of Medieval Philosophy* (ed. Henrik Lagerlund; Springer, 2011).

1. Dod (1982) gives a brief but excellent survey of the translating of Aristotelian works into Latin (with 'A Table of Medieval Latin Translations of Aristotle's Works and of Greek and Arabic Commentaries' on pp. 74–79, which is updated in Bloch and Ebbesen [2010, 12–16]). D'Alverny (1991) focuses on the eleventh- and twelfth-century translations, and Lindberg's contribution on the translations in Lindberg (1978) is good on scientific works. Brams (2003) offers sketches of the major translators, along with a description of the Aristoteles Latinus, the ongoing project to edit the medieval Latin translations of Aristotle's works. On William of Moerbeke in particular, see Brams and Vanhamel (1989). For translations of Arabic philosophical works into Latin, see Burnett (2005) (with a table of 'Arabic philosophical works translated into Latin before ca. 1600' on pp. 391–404). I do not deal here with translations of Greek Church Fathers, such as Gregory of Nyssa, Gregory of Nazianzen, the Ps.-Dionysius, Maximus Confessor, John Damascene and Nemisius of Emesa, whose works were, however, used extensively in philosophical writings in this period, as were important Latin Church Fathers, particularly Augustine, Boethius and Anselm.

2. Notable exceptions being the three translations by Gerard of Cremona, mentioned above, and Michael Scot's early-thirteenth-century translation of the *Metaphysics* from the Arabic.

3. See for the *Auctoritates Aristotelis*, Hamesse (1974).

4. For general history of the medieval university movement, see Cobban (1975), Ridder-Symoens (1992) and Verger (1997), and for a brief but excellent introduction focusing on natural philosophical education, Kibre and Siraisi's contribution to Lindberg (1978). For Oxford, see Catto (1984) and Catto and Evans (1993); for Cambridge, Leader (1988). More generally on English education, Courtenay (1987); there is no corresponding work for Paris, but see Courtenay (2007).

5. On this particular Student Guide, see the articles collected in Lafleur and Carrier (1997), especially that of Bianchi for the interdiction of Aristotle's works.

6. On the Parisian condemnations, see Bianchi (2009) and note that there was a less comprehensive condemnation on 18 March 1277 promulgated by Robert Kilwardby, Archbishop of Canterbury, although there is no completely decisive evidence for a connection between the two condemnations.

7. On medieval academic censure in general, see Thijssen (1998) and Bianchi (1999), which also deals with the diffusion of Aristotle at the University of Paris in the thirteenth century.

8. See on books and their production, for example, Rouse and Rouse (2000).

9. On the Dominican educational system, see Mulchahey (1998); on the Franciscan, see Roest (2000). For an inventory of Dominican writings, listed alphabetically by author, see Kaeppeli (1978–93; vol. 4 [1993], edited with E. Panella O. P., contains a supplement to the first three volumes).

10. On Augustinian Hermits, see the contributions by Pini in Schabel (2006) and by Schabel and Courtenay in Schabel (2007). On the Carmelites, see Xiberta (1931) and Schabel's article on Carmelite *Quodlibeta* in Schabel (2007).

11. For the early part of the dispute, see Douie (1954); for more recent literature, Torrell (1996, 75–95).

12. For an excellent example of this type of recent work, see Nielsen's chapter in Evans (2002).

13. In addition, many medieval thinkers held sermons (which rarely contain philosophical material), and many of them were consulted by secular rulers or Church prelates for advice on various issues (and these *consilia* might indeed have philosophical importance).

14. On disputations, see, for example, Bazán (1985) and Weijers (2009).

15. See the nearly exhaustive discussions found in Schabel (2006) and Schabel (2007); for lists of questions addressed in the *quodlibeta* that he knew, see Glorieux (1925–35).

16. For a catalogue of sophismata, see Ebbesen and Goubier (2010); for their place in the medieval educational scheme, see Maierù (1994, esp. 117–41); for the example of the twelve apostles, see Spade (2010, 192). For a catalogue of the insoluble literature, see Spade (1975).

17. See for a list, Lohr (1967–74), updated by Lohr (2005). See also Newton (2008) for a collection of articles on medieval *Categories* commentaries; and Zimmermann (1971) for unpublished *Physics* and *Metaphysics* commentaries.

18. For a more nuanced view of the types of Aristotle commentaries found in the period, see Weijers's article in Honnefelder et al. (2005).

19. For the Latin text, see Galle (2003, 224–30).

20. My exposition and examples are inspired by Bloch and Ebbesen (2010, 60–100), with the comparison between Peter of Auvergne's and John Buridan's commentaries on *On Memory* found on pp. 97–98 there.

21. See for a catalogue of these commentaries, Stegmüller (1950–80). Of course, some of these biblical commentaries are clearly unrelated to lectures as such.

22. See, for an example, Stump (1993).

23. For the surviving *Sentences* commentaries, see Stegmüller (1947) and Doucet (1954); an update of Stegmüller is planned under the direction of William J. Courtenay (see *Bulletin de philosophie médiévale* 51 [2009], 29–31). For more information on the *Sentences* commentaries of this era, see articles in Evans (2002) and in Rosemann (2010), and see Rosemann (2007). 'Principial' lectures were an official part of a bachelor's *Sentences* lectures and, beginning in the fourteenth century, often contain rich philosophical material; see on this Courtenay (2007, 29–36).

24. For Aquinas and Bonaventure, see, for example, Wéber (1974); for his dispute with Gerard of Abbeville on mendicant privileges, John Pecham on numerous issues and Siger of Brabant on the human intellect, see Torrell (1996).

25. The figures can be found in Torrell (1996, 41); recent research by, among others, Richard C. Taylor has revealed that in his *Sentences Commentary*, Aquinas was also heavily influenced by Averroes.

26. On these types of Thomist works, see Friedman's contribution to Evans (2002, esp. §IV) and Friedman's chapter in Schabel (2007).

27. See on these two thinkers most recently the 'Introduction' to the articles collected in *Freiburger Zeitschrift für Philosophie und Theologie* 57(2) (2010, esp. pp. 228–34).

28. On the prohibition of Ockham's works, see Bianchi (1999, 129–62).

29. On Oxford thought in the period, see Courtenay (1987) and Gelber (2004), as well as relevant articles in Catto (1984) and Catto and Evans (1993). On Paris, as well as Paris and Oxford, see the relevant articles in Evans (2002).

30. See, for example, Libera (1982) and Wood's chapter in Evans (2002).

31. On the Oxford Calculators, see, for example, Sylla (1982).

32. See Courtenay (1987, esp. 255–58, 276–80); on obligations in theology, see Gelber (2004, esp. 151–90). One effect of this focusing of attention upon these issues is that schools of thought, Thomism or Scotism, are basically non-existent at Oxford in this period.

BIBLIOGRAPHY

Bazán, Bernardo C. 1985. 'Les questions disputées, principalement dans les facultés de théologie'. In B. C. Bazán, et al., *Les questions disputées et les questions quodlibétiques dans les facultés de théologie, de droit, et de médecine*, 13–149. Turnhout, Belgium: Brepols.

Bianchi, Luca. 1999. *Censure et liberté intellectuelle à l'université de Paris (XIIIe–XIVe siècles)*. Paris: Les Belles Lettres.

———. 2009. Students, Masters, and 'Heterodox' Doctrines at the Parisian Faculty of Arts in the 1270's. *Recherches de théologie et philosophie médiévales* 76(1):75–109.

Bloch, David and Sten Ebbesen. 2010. *Videnssamfundet i det 12. og 13. århundrede. Forskning og formidling*. Copenhagen: The Royal Danish Academy of Science and Letters.

Brams, J. and W. Vanhamel, eds. 1989. *Guillaume de Moerbeke: recueil d'études à l'occasion du 700e anniversaire de sa mort (1286)*. Leuven, Belgium: Leuven University Press (Ancient and Medieval Philosophy, 7).

Brams, Jozef. 2003. *La riscoperta di Aristotele in Occidente*, trans. Antonio Tombolino. Milan: Jaca Books.

Burnett, Charles. 2005. 'Arabic into Latin: the reception of Arabic philosophy into Western Europe'. In *The Cambridge Companion to Arabic Philosophy*, ed. Peter Adamson and Richard C. Taylor, 370–404. Cambridge: Cambridge University Press.

Catto, J. I., ed. 1984. *The History of the University of Oxford, Vol. 1: The Early Oxford Schools*. Oxford: Oxford University Press.

Catto, J. I. and Ralph Evans, eds. 1993. *The History of the University of Oxford, vol. 2: The Late Middle Ages*. Oxford: Oxford University Press.

Cobban, A. B. 1975. *The Medieval Universities: Their Development and Organization*. London: Methuen & Co Ltd.

Courtenay, William J. 1987. *Schools and Scholars in Fourteenth-Century England*. Princeton, NJ: Princeton University Press.

———. 2007. *Changing Approaches to Fourteenth-Century Thought*. Toronto: Pontifical Institute of Mediaeval Studies (The Etienne Gilson Series 29).

D'Alverny, Marie-Thérèse. 1991. 'Translations and Translators'. In *Renaissance and Renewal in the Twelfth Century*, eds. Robert L. Benson and Giles Constable, 421–62. Toronto: University of Toronto Press (first printing, Cambridge: Harvard University Press, 1982).

Dod, Bernard G. 1982. 'Aristoteles latinus'. In Kretzmann et al. 1982, 45–79.

Doucet, Victorin. 1954. *Commentaires sur les Sentences: supplément au répertoire de M. Frédéric Stegmueller*. Florence: Typographia Collegii S. Bonaventurae.

Douie, Decima L. 1954. *The Conflict between the Seculars and the Mendicants at the University of Paris in the Thirteenth Century*. London: Blackfriars (The Aquinas Papers, 23).

Ebbesen, Sten and Frédéric Goubier. 2010. *A Catalogue of 13th-Century Sophismata*. 2 vols. Paris: Vrin (Sic et non).

Evans, G. R. 2002. *Mediaeval Commentaries on the Sentences of Peter Lombard*, vol. 1. Leiden, the Netherlands: Brill.

Galle, Griet. 2003. *Peter of Auvergne, Questions on Aristotle's De caelo. A Critical Edition with an Interpretative Essay*. Leuven, Belgium: Leuven University Press (Ancient and Medieval Philosophy, 29).

Gelber, Hester Goodenough. 2004. *It Could Have Been Otherwise: Contingency and Necessity in Dominican Theology at Oxford, 1300–1350*. Leiden, the Netherlands, and Boston: Brill (Studien und Texte zur Geistesgeschichte des Mittelalters, 81).

Glorieux, Palémon. 1925–35. *La littérature quodlibétique de 1260 à 1320.* 2 vols. Paris: Vrin.

———. 1933–34. *Répertoire des maîtres en théologie de Paris au XIIIe siècle.* 2 vols. Paris: Vrin.

Hamesse, Jacqueline. 1974. *Les Auctoritates Aristotelis: une florilège médiéval. Étude historique et édition critique.* Louvain, Belgium: Publications universitaires (Philosophes médiévaux, 17).

Honnefelder, Ludger, et al. 2005. *Albertus Magnus und die Anfänge der Aristoteles-Rezeption im lateinischen Mittelalter. Von Richardus Rufus bis zu Franciscus de Mayronis.* Münster, Germany: Aschendorff.

Kaeppeli, Th. O. P., ed. 1978–93. *Scriptores Ordinis Praedicatorum Medii Aevi.* 4 vols. Rome: Ex curia generalitia o.p. ad S. Sabinam.

Kretzmann, Norman, Anthony Kenny and Jan Pinborg, eds. 1982. *The Cambridge History of Later Medieval Philosophy.* Cambridge: Cambridge University Press.

Lafleur, Claude and Joanne Carrier eds. 1997. *L'enseignement de la philosophie au XIIIe siècle. Autour du Guide de l'étudiant' du ms. Ripoll 109.* Turnhout, Belgium: Brepols (Studia Artistarum 5).

Leader, D. R. 1988. *A History of The University of Cambridge: Vol. 1: The University to 1546.* Cambridge: Cambridge University Press.

Libera, Alain de. 1982. 'The Oxford and Paris Traditions in Logic'. In Kretzmann et al. 1982, 174–87.

Lindberg, David C., ed. 1978. *Science in the Middle Ages.* Chicago: University of Chicago Press, 1978.

Lohr, Charles H. 1967–74. Medieval Latin Aristotle Commentaries. *Traditio* 23–4, 26–30.

———. 2005. *Latin Aristotle Commentaries, V: Bibliography of Secondary Literature.* Florence: SISMEL, Edizioni del Galluzzo.

Maierù, Alfonso. 1994. *University Training in Medieval Europe.* Trans. D. N. Pryds. Leiden, the Netherlands: Brill.

Mulchahey, M. Michèle. 1998. *First the Bow Is Bent in Study. Dominican Education before 1350.* Toronto: Pontifical Institute of Mediaeval Studies.

Newton, Lloyd A., ed. 2008. *Medieval Commentaries on Aristotle's Categories.* Leiden, the Netherlands: Brill (Brill's Companions to the Christian Tradition, 10).

Ridder-Symoens, Hilde de, ed. 1992. *A History of the University in Europe, Vol. 1: Universities in the Middle Ages.* Cambridge: Cambridge University Press.

Roest, Bert. 2000. *A History of Franciscan Education (c. 1210–1517).* Leiden, the Netherlands: Brill.

Rosemann, Philipp W. 2007. *The Story of a Great Medieval Book: Peter Lombard's Sentences.* Peterborough, Ontario, Canada: Broadview.

———, ed. 2010. *Mediaeval Commentaries on the Sentences of Peter Lombard*, vol. 2. Leiden, the Netherlands: Brill.

Rouse, Richard H. and Mary A. Rouse. 2000. *Manuscripts and Their Makers: Commercial Book Producers in Medieval Paris 1200–1500.* Turnhout, Belgium: Brepols.

Schabel, Christopher, ed. 2006. *Theological Quodlibeta in the Middle Ages. The Thirteenth Century* (vol. 1). Leiden, the Netherlands: Brill (*Brill's Companions to the Christian Tradition*, 1).

———, ed. 2007. *Theological Quodlibeta in the Middle Ages. The Fourteenth Century* (vol. 2). Leiden, the Netherlands: Brill (*Brill's Companions to the Christian Tradition*, 7).

Schönberger, Rolf et al. 2011. *Repertorium edierter Texte des Mittelalters aus dem Bereich der Philosophie und angrenzender Gebiete*, 2nd ed. Berlin: Akademie Verlag.

Sharpe, Richard. 2001. *A Handlist of the Latin Writers of Great Britain and Ireland before 1540*, 2nd ed. Turnhout, Belgium: Brepols.

Spade, Paul Vincent. 1975. *The Mediaeval Liar: A Catalogue of the Insolubilia-Literature.* Toronto: Pontifical Institute of Mediaeval Studies (Subsidia Mediaevalia, 5).

———. 2010. 'Sophismata'. In *The Cambridge History of Medieval Philosophy*, ed. Robert Pasnau, 185–95. Cambridge: Cambridge University Press.

Stegmüller, Friedrich. 1947. *Repertorium Commentariorum in Sententias Petri Lombardi.* 2 vols. Würzburg, Germany: Ferdinand Schöningh.

———. 1950–1980. *Repertorium Biblicum Medii Aevi.* 11 vols. Madrid: Consejo superior de investigacionis cientificas. Instituto Francisco Suárez.

Stump, Eleonore. 1993. 'Biblical commentary and philosophy'. In *The Cambridge Companion to Aquinas*, ed. Norman Kretzmann and Eleonore Stump, 252–68. Cambridge: Cambridge University Press.

Sylla, Edith Dudley. 1982. 'The Oxford Calculators'. In Kretzmann et al., 1982, 540–63.

Thijssen, J. M. M. H. 1998. *Censure and Heresy at the University of Paris, 1200–1400.* Philadelphia: University of Pennsylvania Press.

Torrell, Jean-Pierre. 1996. *Saint Thomas Aquinas. The Person and His Work*, trans. Robert Royal. Washington DC: Catholic University of America Press.

Verger, Jacques. 1997. *L'essor des universités au XIIIe siècle.* Paris: Cerf (Initiations au Moyen-Âge).

Wéber, Edouard-Henri. 1974. *Dialogue et dissensions entre Saint Bonaventure et Saint Thomas d'Aquin á Paris (1252–1273).* Paris: Vrin.

Weijers, Olga. 1994–2010. *Le travail intellectuel à la Faculté des arts de Paris: textes et maîtres (ca. 1200–1500). I–VIII.* Turnhout, Belgium: Brepols (Studia Artistarum).

———. 2009. *Queritur utrum: recherches sur la disputatio dans les universités médiévales.* Turnhout, Belgium: Brepols (Studia Artistarum, 20).

Xiberta, Bartholomaeus Maria. 1931. *De scriptoribus scholasticis saeculi XIV ex ordine Carmelitarum.* Louvain, Belgium (Bibliothèque de la Revue d'histoire ecclésiastique, 6).

Zimmermann, Albert. 1971. *Verzeichnis ungedruckter Kommentare zur Metaphysik und Physik des Aristoteles.* Leiden, the Netherlands: Brill.

CHAPTER 10

LATIN PHILOSOPHY,

1350–1550

JOHN MARENBON

1. LATE MEDIEVAL PHILOSOPHY? RENAISSANCE PHILOSOPHY?

The two centuries beginning in 1350 lead a double life in the history of philosophy.[1] They—or more often their first hundred or hundred and fifty years—provide an epilogue to *Histories* of medieval philosophy, usually a short chapter by comparison with the preceding section, and one that tells a story of decline.[2] The same period, sometimes extended to 1600, forms the entire subject for what is called 'Renaissance philosophy' and has its own *Histories*, conferences and professors.[3] Although Nicholas of Cusa and sometimes other philosophers appear in both sorts of *History*—and although much use is made (see below, 2.3) of the concept of humanism, by contrast with scholasticism, in distinguishing Renaissance from medieval philosophy, in practice, logic apart, the criterion is often brutally geographical: Italians (and Greeks who came to Italy) belong to the Renaissance, their contemporaries elsewhere in Europe to the Middle Ages.[4] Specialists in Renaissance philosophers have plenty, then, to say about Italian scholastics, but they rarely show much interest in their 'late medieval' coevals. Medievalists sometimes eye Renaissance thought with longing, but more often, their attitude is contempt, usually silent, but eloquently voiced by Robert Pasnau, when he directs readers of his magnificent study of metaphysics from 1274–1671 to look for another guide if they are 'aficionados of humanism or the wild and wooly ideas of Renaissance Platonism'.[5] Pasnau's frankness points to where the most striking difference of all between medieval and Renaissance philosophy lies: in the distinct ways in which they are discussed today. Medieval philosophy is, at least to some extent, discussed philosophically. Renaissance philosophy tends rather to be the preserve of scholars with a strong interest in the history of ideas, religion, culture and the transmission of ancient sources, and less in the detailed arguments and their analysis. Perhaps both late medieval and Renaissance philosophy will be better understood and more fairly valued if they are not divided in the usual way, and the philosophy of the Latin world from 1350–1550 is treated as one. This chapter is an attempt at such a discussion, but in the space it cannot even offer a guidebook, but merely a map. First, however, a very brief look at the landscape—the institutional and historical context in which philosophising took place.

Although the structure of university courses and the types of writing associated with university teaching remained much the same as in the preceding century (see above, Chapter 9.1.2 and 9.1.4),[6] four important changes took place. First, new universities began to be founded throughout Europe, starting with Prague (1347–8), Cracow (1364) and Vienna (1365) and continuing with many others (including Heidelberg 1386; Cologne 1389; St Andrew's 1413; Louvain 1425; Basel 1460; Uppsala 1477; Tübingen 1477; Alcalá 1499).[7] By driving German students and masters out of Paris, the Great Schism (1378–1417) succoured the new Central European universities: the second change was a geographical shift. Paris never entirely lost its prestige, but much of the most interesting university philosophy began to be done in the lands of the Empire, Louvain, Italy and, by the end of the period, Spain, finally entirely free from Muslim rule in 1492 and made rich and powerful, in the sixteenth century, by its American colonies. Third, in Italy above all, exciting philosophical developments also took place, more than previously, outside the universities, especially in Florence under the Medicis; and the influx of Greek scholars before and after the Fall of Constantinople in 1453 reinforced an interest in reading original Greek texts. Fourth, heresy and schism began to impinge more directly than before on philosophers and philosophical theologians. John Hus and Jerome of Prague, masters at Prague University, burned as heretics at the Council of Constance (1414–18), saw themselves as followers of the Oxford theologian John Wyclif. The Reformation—its beginning marked by Luther's final break with Rome at the Diet of Worms (1521)—would divide Christian universities and philosophers on confessional grounds.

2. A MAP

2.1. Paris and Oxford, 1350–c. 1400

In 1350, the Universities of Paris and Oxford were still the two great centres for philosophy and theology. The greatest influence on philosophy in Paris in the mid-fourteenth century was John Buridan, who died c. 1360 after a life spent teaching in the Arts Faculty there.[8] His nominalism, a broad reworking of logic so as to make realist commitments unnecessary,[9] was followed by the leading Paris masters of the next generation, Nicholas Oresme (c. 1320–82),[10] Albert of Saxony (d. 1390)[11] and

Marsilius of Inghen (d. 1396),[12] though none was his pupil, and Albert was, in some respects, a critic of his views (Thijssen 2004). Like Buridan, Albert and Marsilius were both important writers on logic and Aristotelian commentators.[13] Oresme combined Aristotelian exegesis with a special interest in natural science and was also a pioneering translator of Aristotle into French. Helped by royal patronage, Oresme ended his life as a bishop; in 1365 Albert became rector of the newly established University of Vienna, whilst Marsilius became the first rector of Heidelberg University in 1386. There he finished the theological studies he had begun in Paris and wrote an influential, though unoriginal, commentary on the *Sentences,* which reflected the intellectual milieu of his Paris days.[14] Nicholas Oresme and Albert of Saxony played an important role, following Buridan, in developing a 'mereological' conception of material substance (see below, Chapter 21.3), which is taken on by the Aristotelian tradition and leads to aspects of seventeenth-century physics (cf. Pasnau 2011). They also follow Buridan in the view that, so far as natural reason and the best interpretation of Aristotle are concerned, it is most plausible to consider that human souls do not survive the death of the body—although this view is shown to be wrong by Christian teaching (Pluta 1986; and see below, Chapter 23.3).

Peter of Ailly, an influential figure at University of Paris and Chancellor there from 1389–95, worked in a similar mould, adding a vigorous opposition to Thomism.[15] Even in a culture where unacknowledged borrowing from early writers was accepted, Peter has a reputation for the extent of his plagiarisms. Yet in, for instance, his commentary on Boethius's *Consolation,* he moulds his borrowings into something new—an account, very much in line with Boethius's own thought, of the ability of human reason to grasp true happiness.[16] His pupil and successor as Chancellor, John Gerson (1363–1429), had different intellectual priorities.[17] He was an ecclesiastical and educational reformer, leaning to mysticism and the study of pseudo-Dionysius, but also deeply committed to pastoral theology (and so writing frequently in the vernacular). Although he accepted the need for a training in logic and metaphysics, he opposed the way theologians of his time allowed these 'hand-maidens' to dominate theology itself (cf. Jean Gerson 1960–67, 3, 240). His especial vitriol was reserved for the Scotists (who seem, in fact, to have belonged to a previous generation): the *formalizantes,* whose teachings, he thought, suggested that there are Ideas co-eternal and not identical with God. But he also condemned more generally those so occupied 'with useless argumentation and I know not what little questions' that they forgot their own mortality (ibid., 247) and, in condemning theological innovation and praising the 'well-worn way', he pointed to one of the directions for theology in the following decades.[18] A more direct polemic against nominalist domination at Paris was made in the same period by John of Maisonneuve (de Nova Domo). John, an arts master, looked back to Albert the Great, whose thinking he adopted directly and often unchanged, as the sure guide to Aristotle and to philosophy in general, and he reintroduced Albert's identification of nominalists as belonging to the School of Epicurus.[19]

Oxford philosophy and theology in the second half of the fourteenth century is usually seen as being in decline, after the glory days of Ockham, Chatton,

Wodeham and Bradwardine, though the blame is now placed on changing professional aspirations rather than the Black Death.[20] Yet, at least for the years from 1350 to 1380, such judgements may turn out to be premature, as the texts become better known. The style of logic practised by masters such as Richard Brinkley (fl. 1350–73),[21] Henry Hopton (fl. 1350s–60s),[22] Richard Ferrybridge (fl. 1350s–60s),[23] Ralph Strode[24] (wrote c. 1360) and John Huntman (1370s–80s)[25] was like that of their Oxford predecessors, with its concentration on the areas newly developed in the Middle Ages (*logica modernorum*), such as the theory of the properties of terms, entailments and the game of Obligations. The difference, besides a tendency to write for beginners, is their realist view of universals.[26] Brinkley was also a theologian whose thought was much discussed in Paris.[27] As well as developing positions opposed to Scotus and Ockham, he engaged in controversy with his fellow Englishman, Nicholas of Aston, arguing against his view that 'God does not exist' is a self-contradiction.[28]

The outstanding figure in Oxford during this period was, of course, John Wyclif (c. 1330–84).[29] Long celebrated for his unorthodox doctrinal and political views, he is slowly coming to be recognised as an original and powerful philosopher. Not merely was he—in line with other Oxford thinkers of his time—a realist about universals. His programme was almost the diametrical opposite of Buridan's: rather than use distinctions in language as a way to reduce the ontological variety that needs be supposed in the world, Wyclif thought that the certainty of knowledge required an isomorphism between mental language and the nature of things.[30] So, although he does not hold that universals are really distinct from particulars, he argues that, on the nominalist view that there are no universal things at all, the whole basis for division into species and genera would be destroyed. Earlier Oxford thinkers, including Brinkley, had developed new ideas about the semantics of propositions (Cesalli 2007). Wyclif took this line of thought further, arguing that everything has a propositional structure.[31] Other aspects of his thought were also bold. He developed an atomistic theory of matter (see Chapter 21.4) and, tackling the perennial problem of reconciling divine providence with human freedom, elaborated a theory involving reciprocal relation between divine volitions and human acts.[32]

Wyclif was an outspoken critic of what he considered the ecclesiastical abuses of his time: he wanted the Church to concentrate on its spiritual mission, under the protection of strong Christian princes. These views put him at odds with the Church authorities, whilst his attack on the doctrine of transubstantiation alienated almost everyone. But it was only posthumously that Wyclif was condemned and excoriated as a heretic (in 1428 his bones were dug up and burned), partly because of the association of the Hussites with his thought (see below, 2.2). Earlier, he had exercised a strong influence on the logic, philosophy of language and metaphysics of a generation of Oxford thinkers, such as the German, Johannes Sharpe (d. after 1415),[33] Robert Alyngton (d. before 1398)[34] and William Penbygull (d. 1420)[35]—as well as Paul of Venice (see below, 2.4), especially by inspiring the development of sophisticated realist theories of universals (cf. De Libera 1996, 402–42).

2.2. The New Universities and Philosophy in Northern Europe, 1400–1550

It is not surprising that the University of Vienna, which had Albert of Saxony as its first rector, should have followed his nominalism, and similarly at Heidelberg, under the influence of Marsilius of Inghen. Other new universities, such as Cologne, Erfurt (founded 1392), Leipzig (1409), and even later foundations, including Freiburg (1456) and Basel, also began by adopting nominalism. So did Cracow and Prague, but by 1400 Prague was strongly influenced by Wyclif in philosophy and theology, and this brand of realism became associated with the condemnation of John Hus and Jerome of Prague.[36] But opposition to nominalism, along the lines opened by John of Maisonneuve and partly implied by Gerson's attitude to novelties, became widespread from the 1420s onwards.

The result was, in the universities of German-speaking lands, the *Wegestreit*: the clash between the defenders of nominalism (the *via moderna*) and the upholders of realism (the *via antiqua*), which is already vividly evoked in a Cologne document of 1425.[37] Some universities devoted themselves almost entirely to one *via*, such as Cologne, where, in the document just mentioned, the masters reject the call for nominalist teaching, though without outlawing it, or Erfurt and Vienna (until 1490s), where the *via moderna* dominated. In other universities (for instance, Tübingen, Freiburg and Basel after an initial nominalist period), both ways were followed. Students would choose between nominalist or realist masters and be housed in different *bursae* accordingly. The realists looked back to Aquinas, Albert, Scotus and Giles of Rome, claiming that these writers provided the correct understanding of Aristotle and thereby the best way to defend Christian faith. There were also differences between the supporters of each of these older authorities. The nominalists also looked back to earlier—though slightly more recent—writers, yoking together Ockham, Buridan, Wodeham, Holcot, Gregory of Rimini and Marsilius of Inghen into a single school to which they had never, in reality, belonged. The nominalists did not usually attack the thirteenth-century realist authorities but argued (cf. Ehrle 1925, 282) that they were too hard for beginners to understand. As a result students might be led into heresy—and the nominalists were quick to point to the connection between Hus and realism (cf. Kaluza 1995a, 299–306). Despite the titles 'nominalist' and 'realist', the *Wegestreit* was not, then, a philosophical debate about the problem of universals. The ideological difference, which took on life as institutional conflict, was rather about the relationship of philosophy and theology (Hoenen 2004, 140–44). Should they be rigorously separated, and the limitations of Aristotle and natural reason emphasised, as the *moderni* wished? Or did Aristotle, as understood by the great thirteenth-century thinkers, the *antiqui*, provide a philosophical defence of Catholic truth? In Paris, too, there was a similar conflict. A resurgence of nominalism in the 1460s led its opponents to persuade the King, Louis XI, to issue a decree in 1474, in his capacity of defender of the faith, banning nominalism. The nominalists defended their position, and in 1481 this decree and any others against them were revoked.[38]

The fifteenth century was a golden period for Poland and for philosophy there.[39, 40] With the development of the University of Cracow in particular (established already in 1364, it was refounded in 1400 by King Władysław Jagiełło), the Western *Wegestreit* moved eastwards. During a first period, nominalism flourished, as in Vienna, under the influence of John Buridan; during a second period, Cologne Albertism and Thomism became increasingly popular; during a third period, these trends were consolidated, and a Scotist Franciscan tradition also grew up (Goddu 2010, 72). Moreover, the influence of the Viennese mathematical school explains the remarkable development of Cracow's astronomical and astrological tradition. The Silesian John of Glogovia (c. 1445–1507; *Glogau* in its German spelling or *Głogów* in Polish) was a particularly important author of numerous commentaries on Aristotle, in which he re-enacts the controversy between Albertist and Thomists. Like many other Polish scholars, he was innovative in logic and devoted much attention to astronomy. He is believed to have been one of the teachers of Cracow's most talented astronomer, the famous Nicholas Copernicus, who matriculated at the university in 1491.[41]

The period of the *Wegestreit* may seem to be a philosophical desert, where thinkers differed, not over new ideas, but over which older model to follow. Yet even thinkers who are professedly imitative can be interesting. Consider the Dominican, John Capreolus (c.1380–1444).[42] A herald of the *via antiqua*, in his life's work, the *Defensiones theologiae Divi Thomae Aquinatis*, Capreolus aims to set out and vindicate Aquinas's positions against the attacks of later thirteenth- and fourteenth-century theologians. Apparently, an entirely unoriginal endeavour—except that, in adapting Aquinas's ideas to meet objections he had not foreseen, Capreolus changes and develops them in ways that would greatly influence future Thomists. Other thinkers were less keen to follow a given model. John Versor (d. after 1482), master in Paris and one of the most widely read commentators on Aristotle and on Peter of Spain's logical textbook, has been described variously as a Thomist and an Albertist, but further study shows that he took up his own philosophical positions (Rutte 2005). Heymeric of Campo (or Van de Velde; c. 1395–1460), who taught at Cologne and then Leuven, had been John of Maisonneuve's pupil in Paris and developed his Albertism in an original way.[43] Much of his work is still unedited, but what is available shows its distinctive character. Heymeric sees Aristotelian metaphysics, as understood by Albert, as the path to universal truth; he lays great emphasis on the principle of non-contradiction as a foundation for argument, and he is more inclined to present his views as a close-knit, self-sustaining system, than to expound arguments for and against a position.

This manner also characterises the work of Heymeric's far more famous friend, Nicholas of Cusa (1401–64).[44] Although Nicholas studied at Heidelberg, he went to Padua as a law student, and he came to know many of the leading Italian intellectuals and the new translations of writings by Plato and Platonists (see 2.3 below). His career was outside the universities, first as a proponent of Conciliarism, and then, by contrast, as a papal representative and minister, Cardinal and Prince-Bishop. Nicholas draws together an assortment of influences—Albertism, Platonic speculation on the One, as found both in Proclus and Pseudo-Dionysius, the Hermetic writings, Llull,[45] Eckhart, early-medieval authors (John Scottus Eriugena, Alan of Lille, Thierry of Chartres)—into self-contained treatises, written in a highly individual, often paradoxical language, that aim to teach how we can think about an infinite, unknowable God.[46] Like Heymeric, he focuses on the principle of non-contradiction—but so as to contradict it, insisting that in God, who is the maximum but also the minimum, there is a 'coincidence of opposites', an idea which he uses mathematical examples to explain and make vivid. He sees humans as endowed with a Godlike ability to create mentally, and the universe as so created that it can be understood by them, so that (*De beryllo* 6) man is, as Protagoras said, the 'measure of all things'. On a more practical level, Nicholas was horrified by the conflicts and suffering occasioned by religious differences. His response to the Fall of Constantinople was a dream vision, *De pace Fidei* (Nicholas of Cusa 1932–, VII), in which the Word of God shows representatives of different faiths and sects the underlying (Catholic) unity of their views.

John Mair (or Major; 1467/9–1550), the Scottish master, who, with his pupils, dominated Paris logic and theology at the beginning of the sixteenth century, was in a more traditional mould, a nominalist logician and theologian, able to draw widely on the whole later medieval tradition, though often developing original arguments.[47] Yet Mair had learned Greek; he was abreast of current events and trends, referring to the natives of the lands recently discovered by the Spaniards (Commentary on *Sentences* II, d. 44, q. 3),[48] and he prefaced the edition of his *Sentences* commentary with an imaginary dialogue in which his friend, Gavin Douglas, the Scottish humanist and translator of Virgil, criticises his manner of doing philosophy and theology, and his pupil, David Cranston, defends him and attacks the treatise on free will by the leading humanist, Lorenzo Valla. Mair's other pupils included fellow Scotsmen Robert Caubraith, author of an important logical treatise, the *Quadrupertitum*, and George Lokert, another logician, as well as the Thomist, Pierre Crockaert, and Domingo de Soto.[49]

Although, in this period, there were celebrated North European humanists, such as Erasmus and Thomas More, their writings are on the edges of philosophy, and it is, rather, in logic that a distinctively humanist strand appears outside Italy before 1550. Logic in the broad tradition of Buridan continued to be studied, and even developed, until the 1530s, but a new approach to the subject was popularised by Rudolph Agricola's *De inventione rhetorica*, written c. 1479 but not published until 1515. Whereas logicians had concentrated on *judging* arguments—investigating ways to discern valid from invalid ones—Agricola devotes himself (as the title announces) to showing readers how to *find* arguments. Finding arguments was, indeed, part—but, in the late Middle Ages, a marginal part—of the Aristotelian tradition, the concern of the *Topics*. Agricola breaks the connection between the Aristotelian topics and argumentation, reorganises them and writes avoiding medieval logical jargon and giving plenty of literary examples. Students continued, however, to study the other parts of Aristotelian logic, and the popular logical textbooks of Philip Melanchthon (1497–1560) return to a more faithful presentation of

Aristotle. But the characteristically medieval contributions to logic, such as the theory of supposition and the study of *sophismata*, were rapidly consigned to obsolescence.[50]

2.3. Non-University Philosophy in Italy

That humanism—the movement which made the study of ancient texts and the imitation of classical Latin style a central goal for scholars—touched philosophy north of the Alps before 1550 only at the edges is not surprising, since it originated in Italy.[51] But even in Italy, humanism did not have its most distinctive influence on philosophy as studied in universities. What marked out Italy in the period was a combination of humanism with philosophy *outside* the university, and this tradition had roots going back to a figure whom few would describe as a humanist. Dante (1265–1321) anticipated the humanists' reverence for Roman civilisation but was happy to write his Latin in scholastic style and to use Averroes, Albert the Great, Siger of Brabant and Aquinas as the launching pads for his own thought.[52] Another great Italian writer of the period, lover of Antiquity and an early commentator of the *Commedia*, Boccaccio, can also be considered as a philosopher.[53] It is, however, the third great figure of early Italian literature, Petrarch (1304–74), who is usually considered the first distinctively humanist philosophical thinker. Unlike Dante and Boccaccio, he consciously sought classical elegance in his Latin prose, and he tried to learn Greek and read Homer. More strikingly, unlike them, he was an outspoken opponent of Aristotle and scholastic ways of thought and writing. Among ancient philosophers, he far preferred Cicero and, even more, Plato. By far the most powerful influence on him, however, was Augustine, and one of his achievements was to find (though inspired by monastic tradition) a new, more intimate way of reading his works—especially evident in his *Secretum*. In his late *De sui ipsius et multorum ignorantia*, Petrarch presents scholastic philosophy, with its reliance on Aristotle and Averroes, as the enemy of Christianity.[54] Indeed, Petrarch could never see value in logic or metaphysics; the one branch of philosophy he thought worth cultivating was ethics.[55]

Petrarch's efforts at Greek were not very successful, but early in the fifteenth century, the Byzantine diplomat, Manuel Chrysoloras, and his Latin-educated pupils produced translations of Plato's *Republic*, *Laws*, *Gorgias* and *Phaedrus*. Among these pupils was Leonardo Bruni (1370–1444), Chancellor of Florence, whose dislike of what he found in Plato made him turn to putting Aristotle (the *Ethics*, *Politics* and the pseudo-Aristotelian *Economics*) into classicising Latin. The range of new Aristotle translations was expanded by John Argyropulos (c. 1410–87), a Byzantine working in Florence, and a controversy developed about how Aristotle should be put in Latin. Theodore of Gaza (c. 1400–75), translator of the zoological works, valued good Latinity. His near-contemporary and fellow Byzantine, George of Trebizond, put accuracy in first place and acknowledged the value of the accepted medieval translations.[56] At the same time, Hellenistic philosophy (not as ignored in the preceding centuries as often represented) became better known through Poggio

Bracciolini's discovery in 1417 of a complete manuscript of Lucretius's *De rerum natura,* a principal source for Epicureanism, Ambrogio Traversari's translation in 1424–33 of Diogenes Laertius's *Lives* and Niccolò Perotti's translation (1451) of Epictetus's Stoic *Enchiridion.*[57]

Lorenzo Valla (1406–57) organised his early *De voluptate* (1431) around the clash between Stoic and Epicurean points of view, though he did not, in fact, know Lucretius's poem. He contrasts, as Petrarch had done, the truth of Christianity with the errors of the different kinds of pagan philosophy. But he takes the unusual step of suggesting that Stoicism, often held to be close in its morality to Christianity, is much more distant than Epicureanism, and, while trying to distinguish between earthly and heavenly pleasure, he gives a decidedly Epicurean tinge to Christian teaching.[58] A formidable philologist—it was he who first showed that the Donation of Constantine is a forgery—Valla followed Petrarch also in his demonstrative hostility to scholasticism and, especially, the sophisticated technicality of late medieval logic. In his *Repastinatio dialectice et philosophie,* as well as rejecting in their usual form some main tenets of scholastic Aristotelianism—the division into ten categories,[59] the transcendentals, Porphyry's Tree—he sets out an approach to logic that favours persuasion, and so the topics, over syllogistic.[60] Despite the similarity between aspects of Valla's approach and that of the Northern humanist logicians (see above, 2.2), the *Repastinatio* appears not to have been much known, whereas Valla's short *De libero arbitrio* was widely read. In it, he criticises Boethius's attempt to reconcile divine prescience and human freedom (see Chapter 1.2.3 above). Despite the tendency to abandon argument for fideism, Valla grasps at what Leibniz, an admirer of this dialogue, would develop into the complete concept theory of substance.

A different relationship between humanistic interests and philosophy emerges in the second half of the fifteenth century. Marsilio Ficino (1433–99) was supported in Florence by the Medici to translate all of Plato (finished by 1469), the Hermetic writings, Plotinus's *Enneads* (published 1492) and other writings by the late ancient Platonists. He also wrote commentaries on Plotinus and various Platonic dialogues—the most celebrated is on the *Symposium*—and (1469–74) a long treatise, its title *Theologia Platonica* consciously recalling one of his philosophical heroes, Proclus.[61] Although his work as translator and commentator made him, in part, a philologist, he was unconcerned with the niceties of Latin style. Rather, he succeeded in becoming a Platonist philosopher in his own right, using and, where he wished, adapting, the metaphysics elaborated by the late ancient followers of Plotinus. Yet Ficino considered himself, as Petrarch and Valla had done, as a defender of Christianity. The *Theologia Platonica* is concerned to demonstrate the immortality of the soul, using Platonic arguments (which are, of course, far better for this purpose than anything provided by Aristotle) but also taking account of the medieval debates and the positions of Averroes and Aquinas. Ficino removed the possible tension between his Platonism and his Christian faith by the idea that there was a *prisca theologia,* an ancient theology, divinely inspired, on which Plato had drawn and because of which he was able to anticipate some of the truths of Christianity; hence the importance to him of Hermes Trismegistus, Orpheus and Zoroaster.[62]

An even wider syncretism was the guiding principle of the work that Giovanni
Pico della Mirandola produced during his short life (1463–94).[63] His brief *De ente et
uno* attempts to harmonise Aristotelian and Platonic views about being (though in
an Aristotelian way, opposed to Ficino's Platonism). His most remarkable work are
the *Conclusiones*: a set of nine hundred theses, some his own, others drawn from
every tradition of philosophy and theology—the scholastic (such as Albert the
Great, Aquinas, Scotus, Henry of Ghent), Islamic and Jewish Aristotelianism (including al-Farabi, Avicenna, Averroes, and Maimonides and Moses of Narbonne),
the ancient Greek tradition (such as Pythagoras, Plato, Plotinus, Proclus, Ammonius and Simplicius), Zoroaster and the Chaldaeans, magic and the Kabbala. Two
aspects of this list are especially striking: the inclusion of the scholastics, and the use
of the Kabbala. Pico had studied in Paris and shared nothing of earlier humanist
contempt for the scholastic tradition, even defending its language in a correspondence with the Venetian humanist Ermolao Barbaro.[64] Pico was the first Christian
to exploit the Kabbala, which he saw as a source of ancient wisdom; he had first
learned about it from the Jewish philosopher Elijah Delmedigo (c. 1458–93)—
though Elijah himself disapproved of it thoroughly.[65] Pico had intended these nine
hundred theses to be the subject of a public disputation, but papal suspicions about
the orthodoxy of some of them stopped the event. The introductory oration Pico
had planned for it was published later. The second half confirms the syncretic purpose of the theses; the first, which earned for the whole piece the title *De hominis
dignitate* ('On the Dignity of Man'), has become the most famous work of 'Renaissance' philosophy. The central idea, that humans have no fixed nature but are able to
decline to be like beasts or rise to a God-like level, is certainly not new, but the
striking manner in which it is expressed has led to a myriad of different interpretations, of which those that go furthest from its context within sixteenth-century philosophy are the least plausible.[66] Pico's works were edited by his nephew, Gianfranceso
Pico della Mirandola (1469–1533), who was also an important thinker in his own
right, interested in pagan philosophy but, by contrast with his uncle, so as to show
its emptiness compared with Christian truth. To this end his *Examen vanitatis doctrinae gentium* (1520) makes use of Sextus Empiricus's scepticism, long before the
full of texts of his works became available.

2.4. University Philosophy in Italy

By 1350, there were already eight universities in Italy (Bologna, the oldest; Padua,
Siena, Naples and Rome, thirteenth-century foundations; Perugia, Pisa and Florence,
fourteenth-century foundations), and universities would soon open in Parma,
Pavia, Turin and Catania. The most striking difference between them and the
institutions north of the Alps was theology's lack of prominence, even after the
subject began to be taught in some universities in the fourteenth century.
Whereas many Parisian arts masters went on to study and teach theology, Italian arts masters tended to make their careers as salaried professors, dedicated to
the exposition of the Aristotelian curriculum.[67] Although their work followed

different channels from the non-university philosophy examined above, they were not isolated from it—indeed, Valla taught at university for a time, though his subject was eloquence rather than philosophy. The university Aristotelians used the new translations of ancient Greek commentators, and some (such as Nifo) learned Greek so as to gain a better understanding of the authoritative texts. At the same time, they studied intensely the Aristotelian commentaries of Averroes, the writer so intensely disliked by Petrarch and many other human- ists—even writing super-commentaries on them.[68] The 1550–52 edition of Aris- totle published in Venice by Giunta brings together both aspects of this approach to Aristotle, using humanist translations of the texts but adding the most com- plete collection of Averroes's commentaries (many translated from the Hebrew) yet assembled.

This survey must restrict itself to six outstanding Italian university philosophers, briefly positioning their lives and their work and then comparing their different ap- proaches to a problem that was central for them all: the immortality of the soul. The earliest of them, Biagio Pelacani of Parma (d. 1416), taught at Bologna, Padua, Pavia and Florence. Influenced by Buridan and Albert of Saxony, he went far further than they—and indeed than Aristotle himself—to a materialist naturalism, which he combined with an astrological determinism.[69] Paul of Venice (Paolo Nicoletti; 1368/9–1429), who belonged to the Order of Augustinian hermits, was sent to study in Oxford, where he was deeply influenced by Wyclif and the Oxford realists, and his metaphysics reflects and develops their views, though it carefully avoids any heret- ical implications of Wyclif's thought.[70] He greatly contributed to the already strong influence of fourteenth-century Oxford logic in Italy by his handbooks, the *Logica parva* (c. 1393–5) and in the enormous *Logica magna* (c. 1396–9), a real compendium of later medieval thinking in the area.[71] Another religious, the Dominican Thomas de Vio (Cajetan; 1468–1534), taught at Padua and Pavia, before becoming a leading administrator of his order, a Cardinal (1510) and a papal legate involved in coun- tering Protestantism.[72] Cajetan, like many Dominicans, was a devoted follower of Aquinas, and his major work is the first ever complete commentary on the *Summa Theologiae* (published 1508–23). But his Thomism, often influenced by Capreolus (see above 2.2), sometimes involves views very different from Aquinas's, as in his widely read treatise on analogy.

The lives and work of the remaining three thinkers intersect. Nicoletto Vernia (1420–99) taught at Padua for over thirty years and had Pomponazzi and Nifo as his pupils.[73] Pietro Pomponazzi (1462–1525) taught principally at Padua and Bologna.[74] Besides commentaries on Aristotle and his work on the soul, he wrote late in life but did not publish two treatises, *De naturalium effectuum causis sive de incantationibus* and *Libri quinque de fato, de libero arbitrio et de praedestinatione*. The first gives naturalistic explanations of supposed miracles, in terms of the workings of an Aris- totelian God and the Intelligences, and without the intervention of angels or demons; the miracles of the New Testament, however, are excepted. The second is an intricate treatment of the problem of how to reconcile divine foreknowledge and predestina- tion with human freedom, which examines with remarkable critical detachment and acuity all the different arguments proposed both by ancient philosophers and thirteenth- and fourteenth-century theologians. Pomponazzi finds powerful philosophical reasons to accept a Stoic determinism, although he also presents theological arguments that would preserve some human freedom.[75] Relations between him and Agostino Nifo seem never to have been good. Nifo (c. 1470–1538) had a broken career, teaching at Padua, Pisa, Salerno and Naples, practising as a doctor and writing prolifically: commentaries on Aristotle and Averroes (his *Incoherence of the Incoherence*), and treatises on logic, metaphysics, beauty, political theory and the soul.[76]

By the late fourteenth century, the immortality of the soul was already a much-debated debated question, with four main lines of approach open to thinkers.[77] At the root of the problem was the difficulty of remaining faithful to Aristotle's *On the Soul*—the authoritative text on psychology—without contradicting the Church doctrine that, in the period between death and the Last Judgement, disembodied souls survive. Nonetheless, many thinkers, including Aquinas, devised Aristotelian-like theories that not only did not contradict, but rather claimed to vindicate the Christian view. Some philosophers, however, were convinced by Averroes's interpretation in his Great Commentary on *On the Soul*. Averroes asserted the immortality of the human intellect, but only by conceiving it as one in number and detached from particular human beings. Since this position denies individual immortality and so goes against Christian teaching, those who accepted it (for instance, Siger of Brabant and John of Jandun) had to qualify their views by saying that they were simply giving the best interpretation of Aristotle, and/or the best account available to reason unaided by revelation. Another position that needed similar qualification was Alexander of Aphrodisias's reading, according to which the human soul is a material form like that of other animals and is not immortal. John Buridan was followed by a line of later fourteenth-century thinkers in holding that this view would be the most convincing, except that the teaching of the faith shows it to be wrong (cf. Pluta 1986). Finally, Aristotle could be rejected as an authority in favour of Plato, who clearly argued for the soul's immortality. This alternative was not popular in the thirteenth or fourteenth centuries but was followed enthusiastically by some (notably Ficino), especially outside the universities, in the fifteenth.

Although Averroism is often said to have been a powerful force in the fifteenth- and sixteenth-century Italian universities, none of the six university philosophers considered here remained a straightforward Averroist. Biagio of Parma followed Alexander's reading, treating the human soul as mortal. In the earlier version of his question commentary on *On the Soul* (1385), he states this view without qualification, although in the later one (1397), written after the intervention of the Bishop of Parma, he adds a set of different conclusions given 'as a Christian'.[78] Paul of Venice seems, by contrast, to be a classic Averroist, since he accepts that, according to natural reason, there is a single intellect for all humans, though he rejects the view according to the faith. But his position turns out to be far more complicated: on the one hand, he disagrees with Averroes's reading on a number of important points; on the other hand, the view he develops in accord with the faith is not a mere assertion of doctrine, but is argued using a mixture of revelation and natural reasoning (Kuksewicz 1983). As an enthusiastic Thomist and a leading churchman, Cajetan might have been expected to endorse Aquinas's view of the immortality of the soul, especially since he attended the Fifth Lateran Council of 1512–17, when it was ordered that philosophers should find arguments to show that the soul is immortal and to refute the positions contrary to Christian doctrine. In fact, Cajetan voted against this injunction, and he maintained that the soul's immortality cannot be rationally demonstrated.

Vernia began by accepting Averroes's reading of Aristotle as the correct one, but by 1492 he had come to interpret *On the Soul* as upholding individual immortality. Although there is evidence of ecclesiastical pressure behind the change of view, Vernia was able to justify his new stance by reference to a wider reading of newly translated Greek philosophers and commentators, which enabled him to take a critical distance from Averroes. Nifo, too, began as an Averroist, but he soon became a critic of his interpretation of Aristotle and drew on a wide range of ancient philosophers, and contemporaries such as Ficino, to argue for individual immortality. Pomponazzi also began his career by following Averroes's interpretation of Aristotle's position. But by the time of his *On the Immortality of the Soul* (1516), he had moved—despite the decision of the Lateran Council—to defending a position near to Alexander's as that in accord with natural reason, although he also emphasised that the truth of the matter is what Christian doctrine teaches. He finds Aquinas's arguments against Averroes convincing, and he accepts, with Aquinas, that the human soul is in some way immortal. But whereas for Aquinas the essence of the soul is unqualifiedly immortal, but in a qualified way mortal, Pomponazzi holds that it is unqualifiedly mortal and immortal only in a qualified sense, which seems to amount just to its ability to cognise eternal things. The clinching argument against Aquinas's position, he believes, is that human thinking always *requires* sense images, and so a corporeal organ, even if intellectual thought is itself not a corporeal process. When Pomponazzi considers the wider arguments that have been made against those who claim the soul is mortal (Chapters 13–14), he is even bolder. Experiences that supposedly prove the immortality of the soul are explained away naturalistically or as impostures, and the consensus of religions in its favour is seen as the result of political manipulation, to ensure good behaviour of the multitude. But, for a good person, he argues, the acceptance of mortality merely emphasises that virtue is its own reward; positing post-mortem reward and punishment undermines true virtue by making good behaviour self-serving. Pomponazzi's treatise was widely attacked, and Nifo was among its severest critics. But Pomponazzi did not suffer professionally, despite having flouted the Lateran Council's requirement.

2.5. University Philosophy in Spain

Spanish scholasticism is often considered as a rather anachronistic survival of 'medieval' philosophy into the early modern period. This characterisation is, however, doubly wrong. First, even before the final expulsion of Muslims from Southern Spain in

1492, there was a specifically Spanish late medieval tradition of philosophy and theology, which echoed the debates of Northern European universities. Second, from the perspective taken here, the developments in Spain after 1500, though linked in ways to the earlier Spanish tradition, look forward to the period considered in the next chapter, since the most important philosophers of this school worked after 1550.[79]

There had been intense intellectual activity in Salamanca since the thirteenth century: its status as a university was confirmed by Alfonso X el Sabio in 1254–55, but there was scholarly activity there since at least 1226. Valladolid and Lerida were for a long time the only other important university-type institutions in the country. Spanish universities differed from North European ones by having added theology faculties only at a late stage: 1381 for Salamanca and 1417 for Valladolid. Spaniards who wanted a theological career often, therefore, chose to go abroad, as did the important Augustinian Alfonso Vargas of Toledo (d. 1366), who became a respected master in Paris. With universities dominated by faculties of arts and law, theology had long remained the preserve of the monastic *studia*, a situation that explains the prestige of some convents, such as the Dominicans' Convento de San Esteban in Salamanca, as well as the rich Franciscan tradition outside the universities. There were several influential and original Franciscans, including Francesc Eiximenis (ca. 1330–1409), a Catalan church and political reformer, educated in Valencia, Cologne, Paris, Oxford and Toulouse. An important spiritual writer with eschatological ideas, he became famous for his angelology and his vernacular writings on political issues, such as his *El Regiment de la cosa pública*.[80]

With the establishment of the faculty of theology of Salamanca and in close connection with the Dominican convent of the city, a specifically Spanish Thomist school emerged during the fifteenth century, with figures such as Juan de Torquemada (1388–1468), educated in Salamanca, Valladolid and Paris, mainly famous for his ecclesiology (*Summa ecclesiastica*) and commentaries on Gratian, and Alonso Fernández de Madrigal (c. 1410–55), known as 'el Tostado', who taught moral philosophy and then Sacred Scripture.[81] His huge biblical commentaries abound with long scholastic discussions mainly inspired by Aquinas. Towards the end of the century, the most remarkable writer was perhaps Pedro Martínez de Osma (c. 1420–80), who taught philosophy and then theology in Salamanca. Integrating humanist ideals with Thomism, he attacked the hair-splitting of the Scotists and nominalists. His commentaries on ethics and metaphysics are now being discovered.[82] From the sixteenth century, ethics lost its independence in the Spanish tradition and was completely absorbed into moral theology (see below, Chapter 11).

The great Spanish academic renaissance of the turn of the sixteenth century was symbolised by the foundation of the University of Alcalá in 1499 (the historical ancestor of the present-day Complutense in Madrid) by the powerful Archbishop Francisco Jiménez de Cisneros (1436–1517),[83] and by the progressive reorganisation of the Salamanca faculties. Both were strongly indebted to foreign influences. On the one hand, Italian humanism became popular (especially since the foundation of the Spanish College in Bologna by Cardinal Albornoz had provided a regular hub for the transmission of Italian humanist ideals); on the other hand, most first-generation masters at Alcalá as well as numerous masters of

Salamanca were Paris-educated, as were many of the Portuguese in the same years.[84] This massive migration imported to Spain the North European and Parisian *Wegestreit*, and the system of chairs in Spanish universities was organised according to the labels of 'Thomism', 'Scotism' and 'Nominalism' (more exactly 'Durandism', referring to Durandus of Saint-Pourçain). Nonetheless, Thomism displayed exceptional resilience, perhaps as a result of the domestic tradition of the fifteenth century.

Most of the prominent figures of the sixteenth-century scholastic 'revival' all, then, had their roots in the Paris of the late fifteenth and early sixteenth century. They include important and original first-generation masters at Alcalá such as Pedro Sánchez Ciruelo (1470–1548), famous for his logic and mathematics, and the humanist Martín Pérez de Ayala (1504–66), who are less known than their Salamancan counterparts, mainly because most documentation has been lost.[85] In the Salamanca tradition, Domingo de Soto (1494–60)[86] had studied under John Mair; Francisco Vitoria (c. 1486–1546),[87] already a Dominican, was probably taught, not by Mair himself, but by his pupils, including Peter Crockaert (García Villoslada 1938, 95–96). Crockaert made the innovation of using Aquinas's *Summa Theologiae* as a text on which to lecture.[88] When Vitoria became professor at Salamanca, he copied this practice, not without some opposition, and so established one of the characteristic practices of the school. In commenting on the *Summa*, Vitoria used both Capreolus's *Defensiones* and Cajetan's commentary: although he was a disciple of Aquinas, he viewed his theories through the prism of later medieval criticisms and conflicting positions, and he often took a line of thought far beyond its original formulation. As well as his lectures on the *Summa*, Vitoria gave a number of *relecciones*, in which he was able to explore a particular theme in depth. His best-known work is his *Releccio de Indis* (1539), where Vitoria dismisses most of the grounds that might legitimate Spanish activities in America. His examination of what is permissible to the Spaniards, and why, laid foundations for international law (as did the *releccio* he attached to this one, on the just war).[89] Just as important, though, Vitoria starts to rethink the relationship between Christianity and paganism, on Thomist principles, but in light of the fact that it was no longer possible confidently to believe that the Gospel had been preached almost everywhere.[90] De Soto, too. worked on the application of Aquinas's ideas to current practical and legal problems (in his *De iustitia et iure*, 1559). At the same time, he retained the interest in logic he had developed in Paris, before he became a Dominican, publishing in 1539 a revised edition of his commentary on Peter of Spain.[91]

3. Conclusion

During the two centuries from 1350 to 1550 in Latin Europe, there were, as might be expected, different styles of philosophising, inside and outside the universities. But, as the map above should indicate, there is no justification for the traditional bisection of the subject into 'late medieval philosophy' on the one hand and 'Renaissance philosophy' on the other: the material is both more homogeneous and more subtly and multiply varied. One question, especially, that cuts across the usual categories concerns the relationship between Christian doctrine and the tradition of philosophy. The *Wegestreit*, although superficially about realism and nominalism, was really a dispute about whether autonomous philosophical thinking should be tolerated and cultivated, or whether speculation should be guided by an aspiration towards a unified philosophical and theological teaching. A similar contrast can be seen at the same period elsewhere in Europe, between syncretists of different varieties (Nicholas of Cusa, and Ficino and Pico, and, in a different way, Vitoria) and the writers (ranging from Biagio of Parma to Paul of Venice and Cajetan, and including, at some time of their careers, Vernia, Nifo and Pomponazzi) who held that the conclusions of philosophy might be very different from the teaching of the faith. Such general themes provide a pathway into the period unobstructed by arbitrary historiographical barriers; the final goal, however, should be to bring to the thinkers of this time, as has already been done with their early fourteenth-century predecessors and early-modern successors, the rigorous analysis that alone can reveal which of them are outstanding as philosophers and why.

NOTES

This chapter, written at short notice to fill an unexpected gap, is less ambitious than the others in the *Survey* section since it offers just a map of the area, without starting to engage in philosophical discussion. I am enormously grateful to Jacob Schmutz, who read through the chapter and gave me some paragraphs full of important information and bibliography, mainly about philosophy in Poland and in Spain before 1500. I have adapted his material and shortened it, but it displays *his* extraordinary learning, and not anything of mine. I have indicated in the notes which paragraphs are from him. Laurent Cesalli also kindly read the chapter and made a number of suggestions and corrections, which I have followed.

1. Given space constraints, bibliographies will be concise. 'B:' means 'For further bibliography, see:'; *E* stands for the *Encyclopedia of Medieval Philosophy* (Lagerlund 2011); *P* for Pasnau (2010) and *S* for Schmitt and Skinner (1988); *SE* for the *Stanford Encyclopedia of Philosophy* (on-line).

2. An important exception is Flasch (2000), whose approach to the philosophy of this period, though different from that in this chapter, was one of its inspirations.

3. For example: Schmitt and Skinner (1988) provide a very thorough introduction to the area, organised by topic; Copenhaver and Schmitt (1992) give an excellent guide, organised by author; a more recent survey is Hankins (2007).

4. Spanish scholasticism from c. 1500 onwards tends to be treated as an extension of medieval philosophy, but so far as *Histories* of philosophy are concerned, it is more often in those of Renaissance philosophy that a chapter is given to it. Logicians aside, non-Italian 'Renaissance philosophers' are mostly from the period after 1550 or humanist thinkers like Erasmus and More, whose work is at the edge of philosophy.

5. Pasnau (2011, 4).

6. There was, of course, an important change in the technology of their publication—the introduction of printing in the mid–fifteenth century: see *S* 25–53.

7. See Seibt (1973).

8. For the institutional background, see Courtenay (2004).

9. Klima (2011).

10. See Quillet (1990); B: *E* 88–89.

11. See Biard (1991); B: *E* 40–41.

12. See Braakhuis and Hoenen (1992); Hoenen and Bakker (2002); B: *E* 711–17.

13. On logic in Paris at this time, see Dutilh Novaes (2008, esp. 445–48) (and detailed thematic discussions later in the article). Note also John Dorp's 1393 commentary on Buridan's *Summulae* (effectively a shortening of it), which became a set text in Paris.

14. Courtenay (1992); Hoenen (2002).

15. B: *E* 953–57.

16. See Chappuis (1993).

17. On Gerson generally, see McGuire (2006), Vial (2006); B: *E* 621–63.

18. See Kaluza (1988, 35–86).

19. Kaluza (1988, 87–120; 1995b); B: *P* 910.

20. See Courtenay (1987, 327–74) for a full and nuanced account of Oxford academic life in this period, and for general background see Catto and Evans (1992).

21. On all these logicians, see Ashworth and Spade (1992). Brinkley—B: *E* 1120–23.

22. B: *P* 882.

23. B: De Libera (2002).

24. B: *E* 1101–3.

25. B: *P* 906.

26. On the tendency to simplify, see Ashworth and Spade (1992, 48) and Maierù (*E* 1103, on Strode). Brinkley's *Summa logicae* hardly fits this description, however. See also Dutilh Novaes (2008, 440–43) and thematic discussions later in her chapter.

27. See Kaluza (1989).

28. Kaluza (1978; 1989, 230–34; 1998, 431–33).

29. See Kenny (1985); Levy (2006); Lahey (2009); B: *S*.

30. See Conti (2006), an excellent philosophical introduction to Wyclif.

31. See Chapter 19.3.1 below.

32. The same problem was also tackled in the same period on the Continent, though less originally: see Hoenen (1993).

33. See John Sharpe (1990); Conti (2005) and (B) his article in *SE*.

34. See John Sharpe (1990, 211–336) and (B) Conti's article 'Robert Alyngton' in *SE*.

35. See Conti, article in *SE* (B).

36. On Prague: see essays in Šmahel (2007) [I owe this note to Jacob Schmutz].

37. Ehrle (1925, 282–85); cf. Gabriel (1974, 465–66). On the *Wegestreit*, see Gabriel (1974); Hoenen (2003, 2004).

38. Kaluza (1995a); for the generally realist tenor of early- and mid-fourteenth-century Paris, see Kaluza (1995b). On fifteenth-century Oxford theology, see Catto (1992).

39. This paragraph is the work of Jacob Schmutz.

40. For this reason, we owe the most impressive history of fifteenth-century European philosophy to a Polish scholar, Stefan Swieżawski (1907–2004). Swieżawski's eight-volume *Dzieje Filozofii europejskiej w XV wieku* has never been translated into any Western language, apart from a rather anecdotical French *abrégé* (Swieżawski 1990).

41. On the development of Polish Thomism and Albertism, see Kuksewicz (1962, 1973, 1989); Markowski (1981). On natural philosophy, see Markowski (1973, 1978). On this whole pre-Copernican context in Kraków, see the monograph by Goddu (2010).

42. B: *E* 606–8.

43. B: *E* 473–77, and add Calma and Imbach (2008). Imbach and Ladner (2001) give editions of selected works.

44. B: *P* 931–32. Flasch (1998) is a fine, historical and philosophical study; Flasch (2004) a briefer introduction; Hopkins (1978) provides a more detached assessment of Nicholas as a philosopher, along with a text and translation of the *Trialogus de possest.*

45. See Charles Lohr in *S*, 538–56.

46. The best known is *De docta ignorantia*, but the treatise written by Nicholas himself to introduce his thinking is *De beryllo* (Nicholas of Cusa 1932– XI, 1,2). For translations, see Nicholas of Cusa (2001).

47. See, for example, the analysis of his discussion of future contingents in Martin (2004).

48. See Pagden (1982, 38–40), but note that his emphasis on the reference to the theory of natural slavery somewhat distorts the balance of Mair's whole discussion.

49. B: *S* 825. See Broadie (1983, 1985) and (for a brief summary) (2010, 69–86), and for more general discussion of masters in Paris García Villoslada (1938) and Élie (1950–51).

50. See Ashworth (2008, 624–28), the outlines of whose account I have followed. On Agricola, see Mack (1993, 117–374). On Melanchthon, Risse (1964, 79–121).

51. Cf. Kristeller's concise and lucid discussion in *S* 113–37.

52. For Dante as a philosopher, see Dante (1996–2004, an edition with commentary of the *Convivio*), Dante (2010), Gentili (2005) and Imbach (1996).

53. Gagliardi (1999, to be read with caution); Flasch (2003).

54. On this work, see Imbach (2004). It is translated into English in Cassirer, Kristeller and Randall (1948), a valuable collection that also includes translations of Valla's dialogue on free will, Pico's oration on the dignity of man and Pomponazzi's treatise on the immortality of the soul.

55. B: *S* 831.

56. A complicated dispute among these writers, and others from Greece, arose over the respective merits of Plato and Aristotle, and it became entangled with Gemisthos Plethon's exaggerated admiration for Greek Antiquity: for a short summary, see Kraye (1993, 28–33).

57. See Kraye (2007), though the contrast drawn with the medieval period is arguably too sharp.

58. B: *S* 838. On his attitude to philosophy and religion, see Fois (1969). In the later *Repastinatio*, the position remains similar, and similarly unclear: see Nauta (2009, 152–71).

59. He accepts just three categories: substance, quality and action. See Nauta (2009, 82–125), especially for why this move is not like Ockham's reduction of the categories.

60. On the *Repastinatio* see Mack (1993, 22–116) and Nauta (2009).

61. B: *S* 817; Allen and Rees (2002).

62. An important discussion of the type of multi-linear syncretism Ficino employs is given in Idel (2002).

63. B: *S* 832; Dougherty (2008).

64. He says at the beginning of the *Conclusiones* (Pico della Mirandola 1973, 27) that in setting them out he will follow 'not the lustre of the Roman tongue but the manner of speaking of the very famous Parisian disputers.'

65. Restrictions of space make it impossible to pursue here the fascinating theme of how Jewish elements (and the tradition of Averroes) mixed with Latin culture in the work of Delmedigo and that of his contemporary, Leo the Jew (c. 1460–1523): cf. Sirat (1985, 405–10) and, for Delmedigo, the entry in *SE*.

66. Cf. Craven (1981).

67. On the universities, their structure and curricula, see Grendler (2002).

68. See Hasse (2007).

69. B: *P* 858. See Federici Vescovini (1979).

70. B: *E* 925–31. See Conti (1996).

71. See Paul of Venice (1978–91); Maierù (1982).

72. B: *E* 1295–30.

73. B: *S* 839. See Mahoney (2000) (Essay 1 = Mahoney 1983 provides a useful survey of the development of Vernia's and Nifo's thought, and the remaining articles more specialised studies).

74. B: *SE* (Stefano Perfetti). See Pine (1986); Sorge (2010, 7–25) gives a useful review of scholarship and different interpretations; Sgarbi (2010).

75. See *S* 653–60 (Antonino Poppi).

76. B: *S* 828. See Mahoney (1983 and 2000).

77. For a much more sophisticated analysis of the problem, see Peter King's discussion below, Chapter 23.

78. Biagio of Parma (1974, ch. 8, Section 9).

79. This paragraph is partly the work of Jacob Schmutz, and the next three and a half paragraphs, up to note 86 are wholly his (slightly adapted) work.

80. On Eiximenis's political thought, see, for instance Brines y García (2004).

81. On Madrigal, see Belloso Martín (1989). For a good summary on the fifteenth-century theological movement in Salamanca, see Vázquez Janeiro (2006); on the Thomist school, see a summary in Belda Plans (2000, 58–73 in particular).

82. On Pedro de Osma's philosophical commentaries, see García y García and Muñoz Delgado (1981) (politics); Labajos Alonso (1992) (metaphysics); Labajos Alonso (1996) (ethics); on his theological method, see Santiago-Otero and Reinhardt (1987).

83. The philosophical impact of Alcalá is largely underrated in international scholarship, which has over-concentrated on Salamanca. Many documents have been lost. See Jiménez Moreno (1996).

84. This story has often been told: see the classical survey on Spanish theology by Andrés Martín (1976); more specifically on the different 'ways' of dealing with logic, see Muñoz Delgado (1964, 1970, 1986).

85. The section by Jacob Schmutz ends here.

86. B: *S* 836. See Hamilton (1963) and (for his logic) Risse (1964, 329–36).

87. B: *E* 367–71.

88. On Vitoria's time in Paris, see García Villoslada (1938).

89. See especially Pagden (1982, 64–108) for an introduction to these discussions.

90. Translations of these two *relecciones* and other political writing by Vitoria in Francisco Vitoria (1991); cf. Hamilton (1963) and Pagden (1982, 57–108).

91. Commentaries on Peter of Spain continued to be published in the Spanish-speaking world, but not elsewhere, to the end of the sixteenth century: see Ashworth (2008, 625).

BIBLIOGRAPHY

Aertsen, Jan A. and Martin Pickavé, eds. 2004. *'Herbst des Mittelalters'? Fragen zur Bewertung des 14. und 15. Jahrhunderts.* Berlin and New York: De Gruyter (Miscellanea Mediaevalia 31).

Allen, Michael J. B. and Valery Rees, eds. 2002. *Marsilio Ficino: His Theology, His Philosophy, His Legacy.* Leiden, the Netherlands, Boston and Cologne, Germany: Brill (Brill's Studies in Intellectual History 108).

Andrés Martín, Melquíades. 1976. *La teología española en el siglo XVI,* Madrid: BAC.

Ashworth, E. Jennifer. 2008. *Developments in the Fifteenth and Sixteenth Centuries.* In Gabbay and Woods, 2008, 609–43.

Ashworth, E. Jennifer and Paul V. Spade. 1992. 'Logic in Late Medieval Oxford'. In Catto and Evans, 1992, 35–64.

Belda Plans, Juan. 2000. *La Escuela de Salamanca y la renovación de la teología en el siglo XVI.* Madrid: BAC Maior.

Belloso Martín, Nuria. 1989. *Política y humanismo en el siglo XV. El maestro Alfonso de Madrigal el Tostado.* Valladolid, Spain: Universidad de Valladolid.

Biagio of Parma. 1974. *Le Quaestiones de anima,* ed. Graziella Federico Vescovini. Florence: Olschki (Academia toscana di scienze e lettere 'La Colombaria', Studi 30).

Biard, Joël, ed. 1991. *Itinéraires d'Albert de Saxe. Paris-Vienne au XIVe siècle.* Paris: Vrin.

Braakhuis, Henk A. G. and Maarten Hoenen, eds. 1992. *Marsilius of Inghen,* Nijmegen, the Netherlands: Ingenium.

Brines i García, Lluís. 2004. *La filosofia social i política de Francesc Eiximenis.* Sevilla, Spain: Nova edició.

Broadie, Alexander. 1983. *George Lokert. Late-Scholastic Logician.* Edinburgh: Edinburgh University Press.

———. 1985. *The Circle of John Mair: Logic and Logicians in Pre-Reformation Scotland.* Oxford: Oxford University Press.

Calma, Dragos and Ruedi Imbach. 2008. A Fifteenth-Century Metaphysical Treatise: Preliminary Remarks on the *Colliget principiorum* of Heymericus de Campo. *Przeglad Tomistyczny* 14:231–78.

Cassirer, Ernst, Paul O. Kristeller and John H. Randall, Jr., eds. 1948. *The Renaissance Philosophy of Man,* Chicago and London: University of Chicago Press.

Catto, Jeremy I. 1992. 'Theology after Wycliffism'. In Catto and Evans, 1992, 263–80.

Catto, Jeremy I. and Ralph Evans. 1992. *The History of the University of Oxford. II. Late Medieval Oxford.* Oxford: Oxford University Press.

Cesalli, Laurent. 2007. *Le réalisme propositionnel. Sémantique et ontologie des propositions chez Jean Duns Scot, Gauthier Burley, Richard Brinkley et Jean Wyclif.* Paris: Vrin.

Chappuis, Marguerite. 1993. *Le Traité de Pierre d'Ailly sur la Consolation de Boèce, Qu. 1.* Amsterdam and Philadelphia: Grüner (Bochumer Studien zur Philosophie 20).

Conti, Alessandro D. 1996. *Esistenza et verità. Forme e strutture del reale in Paolo Veneto e nel pensiero filosofico del tardo medioevo.* Rome: Edizioni dell'Istituto Storico Italiano per il Medio Evo.

———. 2005. Johannes Sharpe's Ontology and Semantics: Oxford Realism Revisited. *Vivarium* 43: 156–86.

———. 2006. 'Wyclif's logic and metaphysics'. In Levy 2006, 67–126.

Copenhaver, Brian P. and Charles B. Schmitt, eds. 1992. *Renaissance Philosophy.* Oxford and New York: Oxford University Press.

Courtenay, William J. 1987. *Schools and Scholars in Fourteenth-Century England*. Princeton, NJ: Princeton University Press.

———. 1992. 'Marsilius of Inghen as a Theologian'. In Braakhius and Hoenen, 1992, 39–57.

———. 2004. The University of Paris at the Time of John Buridan and Nicole Oresme. *Vivarium* 42:3–17.

Craven, William G. 1981. *Giovanni Pico della Mirandola, Symbol of his Age. Modern Interpretations of a Renaissance Philosopher*. Geneva: Droz.

Dante Alighieri. 1996–2004. *Das Gastmahl*. Commentary by Thomas Ricklin and others. Hamburg, Germany: Meiner (Philosophische Bibliothek 466a–d).

———. 2010. *De l'éloquence en vulgaire*. Traduction et commentaire sous la direction d'Irène Rosier-Catach, Paris: Fayard.

Dougherty, Michael V., ed. 2008. *Pico della Mirandola. New Essays*. Cambridge: Cambridge University Press.

Dutilh Novaes, Catarina. 1988. 'Logic in the 14th century after Ockham'. In Gabbay and Woods 2008, 433–504.

Ehrle, Franz. 1925. *Der Sentenzenkommentar Peters von Candia, des pisaner Papstes Alexanders V.* Münster, Germany: Aschendorff (Franziskanische Studien, Beiheft 9).

Élie, Hubert. 1950–51. Quelques maitres de l'université de Paris vers l'an 1500. *Archives d'histoire doctrinale et littéraire du moyen âge* 18:193–243.

Federici Vescovini, Graziella. 1979. *Astrologia e scienza: La crisi dell'aristotelismo sul cadere del Trecento e Biagio Pelacani da Parma*. Florence: Vallecchi.

Flasch, Kurt. 1998. *Nicholas von Kues. Geschichte einer Entwicklung. Vorlesungen zur Einführung in seine Philosophie*. Frankfurt, Germany: Klostermann.

———. 2000. *Das philosophische Denken im Mittelalter. Von Augustin zu Macchiavelli*, 2nd edition. Stuttgart, Germany: Reclam.

———. 2003. *Lobrede auf Boccaccio*. Basel, Switzerland: Schwabe.

———. 2004. *Nikolaus von Kues in seiner Zeit. Ein Essay*. Stuttgart, Germany: Reclam. French transl. (2008), *Initiation à Nicolas de Cues*, Fribourg, Switzerland, and Paris, Academic Press and Éditions du Cerf (Vesitigia 36).

Fois, Mario. 1969. *Il pensiero cristiano di Lorenzo Valla nel quadro storico-culturale del suo ambiente*. Rome: Gregoriana (Analecta Gregoriana 174).

Francisco de Vitoria. 1991. *Political Writings*, ed. Anthony Pagden and Jeremy Lawrance. Cambridge: Cambridge University Press.

Gabbay, Dov M. and John Woods. 2008. *Handbook of the History of Logic. 2. Mediaeval and Renaissance Logic*. Amsterdam: Elsevier.

Gabriel, Astrik L. 1974. '"Via Antiqua" and "Via Moderna" and the migration of Paris students and masters to the German universities in the fifteenth century'. In Zimmermann, 1974, 439–83.

Gagliardi, Antonio. 1999. *Giovanni Boccaccio: poeta, filosofo, averroista*. Soveria Mannelli: Rubbetino.

García Villoslada, Ricardo. 1938. *La Universidad de Paris durante los estudios de Francisco de Vitoria O.P. (1507–1522)*. Rome: Gregoriana (Analecta Gregoriana 14).

García y García, Antonio and Vicente Muñoz Delgado. 1981. La 'Suma' de Pedro de Osmasobre la «Política» de Aristóteles. *Celtiberia* (Soria) 31:87–110.

Gentili, Sonia. 2005. *L'Uomo aristotelico alle origini della letteratura italiana*. Rome: Carocci and Università La Sapienza (La ricerca letteraria. Studi 2).

Goddu, André. 2010. *Copernicus and the Aristotelian Tradition: Education, Reading, and Philosophy in Copernicus's Path to Heliocentrism*. Leiden, the Netherlands: Brill.

Grendler, Paul F. 2002. *The Universities of the Italian Renaissance*. Baltimore and London: Johns Hopkins University Press.

Hamilton, Bernice. 1963. *Political Thought in Sixteenth-Century Spain: A Study of the Political Ideas of Vitoria, De Soto, Suarez, and Molina*. Oxford: Oxford University Press.

Hankins, James, ed. 2007. *The Cambridge Companion to Renaissance Philosophy*. Cambridge: Cambridge University Press.

Hasse, Dag N. 2007. 'Arabic philosophy and Averroism'. In Hankins 2007, 113–33.

Hoenen, Maarten J. F. M. 1993. *Marsilius of Inghen. Divine Knowledge in Late Medieval Thought*. Leiden, the Netherlands: Brill (Studies in the History of Christian Thought 50).

———. 2002. 'The Commentary on the Sentences of Marsilius of Inghen'. In *Mediaeval Commentaries on the Sentences of Peter the Lombard*, ed. Gillian R. Evans, 465–506. Leiden, the Netherlands: Brill.

———. 2003. '*Via antiqua* and *via moderna* in the fifteenth century: Doctrinal, institutional, and church political factors in the *Wegestreit*'. In *The Medieval Heritage in early Modern Metaphysics and Modal Theory, 1400–1700*, ed. Russell L. Friedman and Lauge O. Nielsen, 9036. Dordrecht, the Netherlands, Boston and London: Kluwer (The New Synthese Historical Library 53).

———. 2004. 'Zurück zu Autorität und Tradition. Geistesgeschichtliche Hintergründe des Traditionalismus an den spätmittelalterlichen Universitäten'. In Aertsen and Pickavé, 2004, 133–46.

Hoenen, Maarten J. F. M. and Paul J. J. M. Bakker, eds. 2002. *Theologie und Philosophie des ausgehenden Mittelalters. Marsilius von Inghen und das Denken seiner Zeit*. Leiden, the Netherlands: Brill.

Hopkins, Jasper. 1978. *A Concise Introduction to the Philosophy of Nicholas of Cusa*. Minneapolis: University of Minnesota Press.

Idel, Moshe. 2002. '*Prisca Theologia* in Marsilio Ficino and in some Jewish treatments'. In Allen and Rees 2002, 137–58.

Imbach, Ruedi. 1996. *Dante, la philosophie et les laïcs*, Paris and Fribourg, Switzerland: Cerf and Éditions universitaires de Fribourg.

———. '*Virtus illiterata*. Zur philosophische Bedeutung der Scholastikkritik in Petrarcas Schrift "De sui ipsius et multorum ignorantia"' in Aertsen and Pickavé 2004, 84–104.

Jean Gerson. 1963–73. *Oeuvres complètes*, ed. P. Glorieux. Paris, Tournai (Belgium), Rome and New York: Desclée et cie.

Jiménez Moreno, Luis, ed. 1996. 'La Universidad Complutense Cisneriana'. *Impulso filosófico, científico y literario. Siglos XVI y XVII*, Madrid: Universidad Complutense.

John Sharpe. 1990. *Quaestio super universalia*, ed. Alessandro D. Conti. Florence: Olschki (Testi e studi per il 'Corpus Philosophorum Medii Aevi' 9; Fonti per la storia della logica 1).

Kaluza, Zénon. 1978. L'oeuvre théologique de Nicolas Aston. *Archives d'histoire doctrinale et littéraire du moyen âge* 45: 45–82.

———. 1988. *Les Querelles doctrinales à Paris. Nominalistes et realistes aux confins du XIVe et du XV siècles*. Bergamo, Italy: Lubrina.

———. 1990. L'oeuvre théologique de Richard Brinkley. *Archives d'histoire doctrinale et littéraire du moyen âge* 56: 169–273.

———. 1995a. 'La Crise des années 1474–82: l'interdiction du nominalisme par Louis XI'. In *Philosophy and Learning. Universities in the Middle Ages*, ed. Maarten J. F. M. Hoenen, J. H. Josef Schneider and Georg Wieland, 293–327. Leiden, the Netherlands, New York, and Cologne, Germany: Brill: (Education and Society in the Middle Ages and Renaissance 6).

———. 1995b. 'Les débuts de l'albertisme tardif (Paris et Cologne)'. In *Albertus Magnus und der Albertismus. Deutsche philosophische Kultur des Mittelalters*, 207–95. Leiden, the Netherlands, New York, and Cologne, Germany: Brill.

———. 1998. 'Late medieval philosophy, 1350–1500'. In *Medieval Philosophy*, ed. John Marenbon, 426–51. London and New York: Routledge (Routledge History of Philosophy 4).

Kenny, Anthony. 1985. *Wyclif*. Oxford and New York: Oxford University Press.

Klima, Gyula. 2011. 'Two summulae, two ways of doing logic: Peter of Spain's "realism" and John Buridan's "nominalism"'. In *Methods and Methodologies. Aristotelian Logic East and West, 500–1500*, ed. Margaret Cameron and John Marenbon, 109–26. Leiden, the Netherlands: Brill (Investigating Medieval Philosophy 2).

Kraye, Jill. 1993. 'The philosophy of the Italian Renaissance'. In *The Renaissance and Seventeenth-century Rationalism*, ed. G. H. R. Parkinson, 16–69. London and New York: Routledge (Routledge History of Philosophy 4).

———. 'The revival of Hellenistic philosophies'. In Hankins 2007, 97–112.

Kuksewicz, Zdzislaw. 1962. Le prolongement des polémiques entre les albertistes et les thomistes vu à travers le commentaire du *De anima* de Jean de Glogów. *Archiv für Geschichte der Philosophie* 44:151–71.

———. 1973. *Albertyzm i tomizm w XV wieku w Krakowie i Kolonii* [Albertism and Thomism in Kraków and Cologne]. Wroclaw, Poland: Ossolineum.

———. 1989. 'Die Einflüsse der Kölner Philosophie auf die Krakauer Universität im 15. Jahrhundert'. In *Die Kölner Universität im Mittelalter*, ed. Albert Zimmermann, 287–98. Berlin and New York: de Gruyter.

Labajos Alonso, José. 1992. *Pedro de Osma y su Comentario a la Metafísica de Aristóteles*. Salamanca, Spain: Editorial San Esteban.

———. 1996. *Pedro de Osma. Comentario a la Etica de Aristóteles*. Salamanca, Spain: Publicaciones Universidad Pontificia.

Lagerlund, Henrik, ed. 2011. *Encyclopedia of Medieval Philosophy*. Dordrecht, the Netherlands: Springer.

Lahey, Stephen E. 2009. *John Wyclif*. New York: Oxford University Press.

Levy, Ian C. 2006. *A Companion to John Wyclif: Late Medieval Theologian*. Leiden, the Netherlands: Brill (Brill's Companions to the Christian Tradition 4).

de Libera, Alain. 1996. *La Querelle des universaux. De Platon à la fin du Moyen Age*. Paris: Seuil.

———. 2002. 'Richard Ferrybridge'. In *Dictionnaire du Moyen Âge*, ed. Claude Gauvard, Alain de Libera and Michel Zink, 1216. Paris: Quadrige and Presses universitaires de France.

Mack, Peter. 1993. *Renaissance Argument. Valla and Agricola in the Traditions of Rhetoric and Dialectic*. Leiden, the Netherlands, New York, and Cologne, Germany: Brill (Brill's Studies in Intellectual History 43).

Mahoney, Edward P. 1983. 'Philosophy and science in Nicoletto Vernia and Agostino Nifo'. In *Scienza e filosofia all'Università di Padova nel Quattrocento*, ed. Antonio Poppi, 135–203. Padua and Trieste, Italy: LINT (Contributi alla storia dell'università di Padova 15).

———. 2000. *Two Aristotelians of the Italian Renaissance: Nicoletto Vernia and Agostino Nifo*. Aldershot: Ashgate (Varorium Collected Studies 697).

Maierù, Alfonso, ed. 1982. *English Logic in Italy in the 14th and 15th Centuries*, Naples: Bibliopolis (History of Logic 1).

Markowski, Mieczyslaw. 1973. 'Die neue Physik an der Krakauer Universität im XV. Jahrhundert'. In Zimmermann, 1974, 501–8.

———. 1978. 'Astronomie an der Krakauer Universität im XV. Jahrhundert'. In *The Universities in the Late Middle Ages*, 256–75. Leuven, Belgium: Leuven University Press.

———. 1981. 'Albert und der Albertismus in Krakau'. In *Albert der Grosse. Seine Zeit, sein Werk, seine Wirkung*, 177–92. Berlin and New York: De Gruyter.

Martin, Christopher J. 2004. 'John Mair on future contingency'. In *John Buridan and Beyond. Topics in the Language Sciences 1300–1700*, ed. Russell L. Friedman and Sten Ebbesen, 183–201. Copenhagen: Reitsel (Det Kongelige Danske Videnskabernes Selskab. Historisk-filosofiske Meddelelser 89).

McGuire, Brian P. 2006. *A Companion to Jean Gerson*. Leiden, the Netherlands: Brill.

Muñoz Delgado, Vicente. 1964. *La lógica nominalista en la Universidad de Salamanca (1510–1530)*. Madrid, Spain: Revista Estudios.

———. 1970. La obra lógica de los españoles en París (1500–1525). *Estudios* 26:209–80.

———. 1986. 'Nominalismo, lógica y humanismo'. In *El erasmismo en España*, 109–74. Santander, Spain: Sociedad Menéndez Pelayo.

Nauta, Lodi. 2009. *In Defence of Common Sense. Lorenzo Valla's Humanist Critique of Scholastic Philosophy*. Cambridge, MA, and London: Harvard University Press.

Nicholas of Cusa. 1932–. *Opera omnia*, ed. Ernst Hoffmann et al., Leipzig, Germany: Meiner.

———. 2001. *Complete Philosophical and Theological Treatises*, trans. Jasper Hopkins. Loveland, CO: Banning.

Pagden, Anthony. 1982. *The Fall of Natural Man. The American Indian and the Origins of Comparative Ethnology*. Cambridge: Cambridge University Press.

Pasnau, Robert, ed. 2010. *The Cambridge History of Medieval Philosophy*. Cambridge: Cambridge University Press.

———. 2011. *Metaphysical Themes, 1274–1671*. New York: Oxford University Press.

Paul of Venice. 1978–91. *Logica Magna*, various editors [incomplete edition]. Oxford: British Academy (Classical and Medieval Logical Texts 1–8).

Pine, Martin L. 1986. *Pietro Pomponazzi: Radical Philosopher of the Renaissance*. Padua: Antenore (Centro per la storia della tradizione aristotelica nel Veneto, Saggi e testi 21).

Pluta, Olaf. 1986. *Kritik der Unsterblichkeitsdoktrin im Mittelalter und Renaissance*. Amsterdam: Grüner (Bochumer Studien zur Philosophie 7).

Quillet, Jeannine, ed. 1990. *Autour de Nicole Oresme: Actes du Colloque Oresme*, Paris: Vrin.

Risse, Wilhelm. 1964. *Die Logik der Neuzeit* 1 (1500–1640). Stuttgart and Bad Cannstatt, Germany: Frommann.

Rummell, Erika. 1995. *The Humanist-Scholastic Debate in the Renaissance and Reformation*, Cambridge, MA, and London: Harvard University Press.

Rutte, Pepijn. 2005. 'Secundum processum et mentem Versoris.' John Versor and His Relation to the Schools of Thought Reconsidered. *Vivarium* 43:292–329.

Santiago-Otero, Horacio and Klaus Reinhardt. 1987. *Pedro Martínez de Osma y el método teológico. Edición de algunos escritos inéditos*, Madrid: CSIC.

Schmitt, Charles B. and Quentin Skinner, eds. 1988. *The Cambridge History of Renaissance Philosophy*. Cambridge: Cambridge University Press.

Seibt, Ferdinand. 1973. 'Von Prag bis Rostock. Zur Gründung der Universitäten in Mitteleuropa'. In *Festschrift für Walter Schlesinger*, ed. Helmut Beumann, 406–26. Cologne, Germany, and Vienna: Böhlau (Mitteldeutsche Forschungen 74,1).

Sgarbi, Marco, ed. 2010. *Pietro Pomponazzi: Tradizione e dissenso*, Florence: Olschki.

Sirat, Colette. 1985. *A History of Jewish Philosophy in the Middle Ages*. Cambridge and Paris: Cambridge University Press and Éditions de la Maison des Sciences de l'Homme.

Šmahel, František. 2007. 'Die Prager Universität'. in *Gesammelte Aufsätze*. Leiden, the Netherlands: Brill.

Sorge, Valeria. 2010. *Tra Contingenza e necessità. L'ordine delle cause in Pietro Pomponazzi.* Milan and Udine, Italy: Mimesis.

Swieżawski, Stefan. 1990. *Histoire de la philosophie européenne au XVe siècle*, adapted by M. Prokopowicz. Paris: Beauchesne.

Thijssen, J. M. M. H. 2004. The Buridan School Reassessed. John Buridan and Albert of Saxony. *Vivarium* 42(1):3–17.

Vázquez Janeiro, Isaac. 2006. 'La teología en el siglo XV'. In *Historia de la Universidad de Salamanca*, 3.1, *Saberes y confluencias*, ed. Luis E. Rodríguez San Pedro-Bezares, 171–201. Salamanca, Spain: Ediciones Universidad de Salamanca.

Vial, Marc. 2006. *Jean Gerson, théoricien de la théologie mystique.* Paris: Vrin.

Zimmermann, Albert, ed. 1974. *Antiqui und Moderni*, ed. Albert Zimmerman. Berlin and New York: De Gruyter. (Miscellanea Mediaevalia 9).

CHAPTER 11

MEDIEVAL PHILOSOPHY AFTER THE MIDDLE AGES

JACOB SCHMUTZ

'HASN'T Amerigo Vespucci discovered lands unknown to Ptolemy, Pliny and other geographers up to the present? Why shouldn't the same be the case in other matters?', asked the acclaimed Parisian professor of theology John Mair (1467–1550) in the first decade of the sixteenth century (Mair 1509, 1v). His judgement could well appear prophetic for all admirers of modern novelties in science, philosophy and religion, if only his name wasn't the symbol of that very tradition that has usually been seen as the major obstacle to discoveries, namely, medieval-rooted scholasticism. From Erasmus, Rabelais and Luther down to Voltaire, passing through Puritan pulpits or Parisian ladies'*salons*, his name and that of his contemporaries used to stand for the idle and obscure debates of academic philosophy: 'to me, a *Cursus philosophicus* is but an Impertinency in *Folio*; and the studying of them a laborious idleness' wrote, for instance, Joseph Glanvill (1636–80) in his attempt to break scholastic dogmatism by the introduction of experimental method (Glanvill 1661, 151, quoted by Knebel 2000, 3). But whereas enlightened minds knew to express their disgust with wit, modern scholars satisfy themselves with a simply dismissive tone. Among historians of logic, for instance, it is commonly held that the creativity of scholasticism came to a certain form of standstill somewhere between the sixteenth and seventeenth century, and that there was something like a 'big void', filled only by the birth of analytical philosophy in the nineteenth century.[1] This standing prejudice against the intellectual value of post-medieval scholasticism is due to a peculiar nineteenth-century blend of anti-clerical positivism and romantic fascination for the Middle Ages. But the empirical reality of the evolution of philosophy is different: during the early-modern period, the medieval scholastic heritage was progressively transformed into a powerful and continuous tradition of academic philosophy that would be projected, thanks to the discoveries mentioned by John Mair, on the entire planet. It is well known that all major philosophers of the seventeenth century were educated by scholastics, such as Descartes, Leibniz, Spinoza or Locke.[2] But the influence of academic philosophy also reached later authors, such as Kant, Hamilton, De Morgan, Bolzano and even Cantor. Even numerous fields we study today were actually inventions of post-medieval scholasticism: it was, for instance, during the sixteenth century that Aristotelian metaphysics became, properly speaking, *ontology*, that the doctrine of the operations of the soul was for the first time dubbed *psychology* and promising new fields such as *meta-ethics*[3] were invented. In this contribution, we shall defend three historical theses: (1) medieval sources remained a living material for early-modern readers, although some selections were made; (2) early-modern readers were eager not to repeat, but to expand the medieval doctrines; (3) a close historical study of early-modern scholasticism can explain numerous and important features of contemporary philosophy, such as, for instance, the opposition between realism and idealism or even the famous 'Continental-analytical' divide.

1. Material History

Early-modern scholasticism starts when the medieval authors were labelled as *antiqui* and submitted to a process of continuous interpretation.[4] There isn't a line of Thomas Aquinas, wrote the imaginative Basque Jesuit Juan Bautista Poza (1588–1659), that may not be explained and defended in an optimal fashion.[5] But not all medieval authors enjoyed that enviable fate of being the subject of continuous and charitable interpretation, which in the Gutenberg Galaxy was closely linked to the commercial and material dimension of printing as well as to institutional commissions, prohibitions and political command.[6] Later Protestant historians liked to ridicule Catholic scholasticism as *philosophia in servitutem theologiae papae* (Heumann 1719, XXII), but most reformed universities, in particular in Germany, had also strongly insisted on the need to submit philosophical teaching to the creed: in Herborn, for instance, Johann Heinrich Alsted asked that professors of philosophy refute any philosophical doctrine in conflict with Scripture. New libraries were set up everywhere, manuscripts were classified and separated from printed works and a new map of the past slowly emerged: only those medieval authors who were printed turned out to be massively read, and those left in manuscripts were definitively forgotten until twentieth-century medievalists uncovered them again. Those authors were printed whose work the universities or specific religious orders wanted to use as textbooks: this benefited some medieval authors and very often only some of their works. Conversely, due to a lack of patronage or insufficient printing presses, other traditions were doomed to remain totally unknown up to present. Besides a few later figures such as Versor or Almain, fifteenth-century authors would almost entirely be neglected.

A striking feature of this printing movement is that most medieval authors printed and commented on in the early-modern period were actually *theological* authorities, and their *theological* texts were at the centre of enquiry. So it was the case for Thomas Aquinas (for the Dominicans, Jesuits, reformed Carmelites and progressively the entire secular clergy),[7] whose *Summa* was progressively adopted as a standard text in most universities for the teaching of theology, replacing Peter Lombard's *Sentences*. It was also the case for John Duns Scotus (for the Franciscans),[8] Bonaventure (for the Capuchins), Giles of Rome and Gregory of Rimini (for the Augustinians), Henry of Ghent (whom the Servites believed was of theirs), John Baconthorpe (for non-reformed Carmelites) and, of course, Anselm of Canterbury (for some Benedictines[9]) and Bernard of Clairvaux (for some Cistercians). Thanks to the work of some sharpshooters, Peter Auriol was re-edited and became a 'source of inspiration for the moderns' (Mastri 1727, 33, calls him a *promptuarium Neotericorum*), Durandus of Saint-Pourçain remained a reference because of his adoption by Spanish universities in the early sixteenth century, Peter of Tarentaise had some admirers and Guillaume de Saint-Amour remained a political hero for French Gallicans. Some late medieval authorities such as Peter of Ailly or Jacques Almain made it even into Protestant circles as authorities for theologians eager to defend divine command ethics. But only rare birds kept reading the texts of William of Ockham, and the alleged 'nominalism' of Descartes or Hobbes remains largely a historiographical myth.[10] Hereby the medieval canon was progressively set: after the seventeenth century, nobody would read the manuscripts of authors who became the heroes of twentieth-century medievalism, such as Peter John Olivi, Matthew of Acquasparta or Francis of Marchia, nor would medieval manuscripts benefit from the interest in the Church Fathers and biblical philology of the second half of the seventeenth century, as, for instance, promoted by the Maurists in France.[11] The only exception is perhaps the splendid Paris edition of William of Auvergne's *Opera Omnia* (1674), but that happened precisely because its editor, the Sorbonne-scholar Blaise Le Féron, saw in him the last Church Father.

The status of, strictly speaking, medieval *philosophical* texts was different. The only medieval 'philosopher' who was continuously read and reprinted in the West was actually the Arab Averroes.[12] Still among philosophers, Raymond Lull enjoyed a vivid tradition and inspired numerous original encyclopedic projects, in the Catholic just as in the Protestant world.[13] Important new Renaissance translations of Aristotle himself, the 'eternal philosophical dictator' (Heumann 1719, XIX), such as those by John Argyropoulos (1415–87), Joachim Périon (ca. 1499–1559) or the Jesuit commentators of Coimbra (1592–1606), would overshadow the medieval Aristotelian commentators and translations. The reason is that during the sixteenth century, universities and religious orders were eager to commission rapidly new introductory textbooks that would replace them: in logic, for instance, the *Summulae* by the Spanish Dominican Domingo de Soto (1494–1560, cf. Soto 1529) or by Gaspar Cardillo de Villalpando (1527–81) would soon become European bestsellers, and nobody would have a direct access to Peter of Spain's medieval original anymore. The same can be said about other disciplines. Some commentaries on

Metaphysics were still read in the sixteenth century, such as those of Antonio Andrés, John Buridan or Dominic of Flanders, but most of their material would be quickly integrated into new synthetic and widely used commentaries such as those produced by the Italian Dominicans Paolo Barbo 'Soncinas' (d.1494) and Crisostomo Iavelli (ca. 1470–1538). First-hand knowledge of all these medieval philosophical commentaries progressively died out with the strong rise of the philosophical textbook, the famous *Cursus philosophicus*, of which hundreds were produced over the decades. Each order, each province, each university would start commissioning textbooks for its own use.[14] Francisco Suárez's (1548–1617) famous *Disputationes metaphysicae* (1597) were also the result of such an institutional commission to produce a prolegomena to theology.

It was also during the early-modern age that medieval philosophy and theology became a truly 'global' heritage, in no way restricted to a few Western European Catholic monasteries and universities. The Protestant reception of the (mainly) sixteenth-century and Spanish scholastic production has been well documented, at least for the German and Dutch lands, and this explains why philosophers such as Leibniz and Spinoza were still arguing with so many medieval ideas.[15] But regardless of confessional barriers, the modern age saw the rapid expansion of the European network of universities and the projection of its ideas on the rest of the world through colonisation and missionary activity. Medieval authors and ideas rapidly became solidly rooted in the New World: the Portuguese-born Jesuit António Vieira (1608–97) imagined the fate of Aquinas's doctrine of ignorance among the Gentiles of the Brazilian jungle, and the Puritan Samuel Willard (1640–1707), pastor of South Church in Boston and one of the first vice presidents of Harvard College, still echoed late medieval theologians when he claimed that the equity of God's law is founded on the goodwill and pleasure of God. The role of Portugal and Spain was, of course, important in this expansion. The nation of seafarers and the huge empire of the Habsburgs brought the thought of the *Illustri Hispani* to remote places where scholasticism was already well established, such as Flanders or Bavaria, to places where it had to be restored, such as the Czech lands, but also to totally new places, such as Lithuania, Croatia, Hungary and Transylvania, Greece and even remote Armenia and Ukraine, where the metropolitan and prince Peter Mohyla (1597–1647) imported German and Polish professors to educate new generations of Ukrainians in Latin scholasticism in an Academy still existing today.[16] Academic mobility was sometimes also imposed, as for highly creative recusant English, Scottish and Irish scholars who wandered all over Continental Europe during two centuries. If men did not travel, then their books did: some textbooks such as the logical *Manuductio* of Philippe Du Trieu (1580–1645)[17] or the *Medulla* by Hermann Busembaum (1600–68) were on the best-seller list for more than a century; the rather clumsy textbooks by the French Dominican Antoine Goudin (1639–95, Goudin 1670–71) were used in the mountains of Armenia, and those of the Sorbonne philosopher Edmond Pourchot (1651–1734) became popular in Italy but also, more surprisingly, in Ottoman Greece.[18] Some South American colleges and universities, such as those of Mexico and Peru in particular, would quickly rise to the top tier of the world's academic institutions.[19] Even the lands of Africa and Asia were not untouched by those doctrines: Francisco Furtado (1589–1653) translated the logic manual of the famous Conimbricenses (the Jesuit commentators from the Portuguese College of Coimbra) under the title *Ming li t'an* into Mandarin Chinese (Hangzhou, 1631).[20]

2. THE ORDER OF KNOWLEDGE

The medieval philosophical curriculum usually followed an order based upon the Arabic classification of the works of Aristotle, starting with logic, continuing with physics (including general and 'special' or 'particular' physics, i.e., the science of the heaven, the world, generation and corruption, etc.) and finishing with metaphysics and in some cases including a section dedicated to ethics. This order (Type I below) remained common in European universities during the 1350–1500 period, and it can be still found, for instance, in the Aristotelian commentaries of Pierre Tartaret (e.g., Tartaretus 1581) or of an Italian secular university tradition such as Padua. It was also adopted by most of the first-generation Jesuit colleges as well as in the universities of Reformation Germany, under the action of Philipp Melanchthon (1497–1560), the *Praeceptor Germaniae*. Some authors chose to modify it slightly, by introducing *ethics* before *metaphysics* (Type I modified), using as criterion the fact that beyond logic, the sciences had to proceed from the most sensible (physics) to the most abstract (metaphysics), and that ethics dealing with the soul's affection was still including a sensible dimension (e.g., Goudin 1670, Praef.).

This order had, however, a couple of problematic issues, and the differential treatment given to them explains the progressive modification in structure that affected the classical teaching of philosophy. Although the local variations are almost infinite,[21] two general trends can be observed: Type II shifted directly the place of ethics to the second place of the curriculum. But it kept untouched, from the classical model, the idea that the objects of physics and metaphysics were actually per se mind independent, whereas logic and ethics were dealing with human mental and physical acts. Type III, on the contrary, modified the classical structure very substantially, by bringing together logic and metaphysics at the beginning of the course, and by relegating physics (now independent) to the end of the whole curriculum. In this last model, there were also some variations about the respective place of ethics, when included: usually treated briefly, many colleges dealt with it before getting to the exposition of physics.

The shifting place of physics is probably the easiest to be explained. According to the classical Aristotelian curriculum, physics, mathematics and metaphysics were sciences dealing with extra-mental objects, of which the first kind was defined as being in matter and in movement. This abstract and very formal characterisation of the object of physics and its classical principles (such as matter and form) would progressively give way to the development of experimental physics,

Table 11.1 Ideal-Types of Early-Modern Scholastic Philosophy Courses

Classical Type Ia & Ib	Modern Type II	Modern Type IIIa & IIIb
Logic	Logic	Logic
Physics (general and special), Psychology	Ethics	Metaphysics (including Psychology)
Metaphysics Ethics	Physics	[Ethics] Physics
[Ethics] Metaphysics	Metaphysics	Physics Ethics
Noteworthy examples:		
Most *cursus philosophicus* produced by religious orders, such as, for the Jesuits, Arriaga 1632; Compton Carleton 1649; Hurtado de Mendoza 1615; Losada 1724–35, Lourenço 1688; Mayr 1739; Oviedo 1640; etc.; for the Dominicans, Poinsot 1631–34; all without ethics; some courses inverted the order between ethics and metaphysics (Ib): e.g., Goudin 1670.	Some French Catholic courses, such as Abra de Raconis 1617; Eustachius a Sancto Paulo 1609; numerous Protestant textbooks also follow this order, e.g., Piccart 1655, 159–67 (who argues that this order goes back to Simplicius); Rabe 1703; Stier 1652.	Already Bouju 1614 (IIIb),[22] and most French courses after Descartes: for instance, Frassen 1657 (IIIb), Pourchot 1695 (IIIb); numerous Central European Jesuit courses in the eighteenth century, but often without ethics: e.g., Gremner 1748; Horváth 1767; Mangold 1755, etc. In Italy, the model was followed by the influential Genovesi 1743–45. Among Protestants, see Scheibler 1623 (IIIb); Walch 1730 (IIIb), pp. 41–48 explains also its epistemological foundation.

accomplishing in a certain way Descartes's aspiration for a more 'practical' science of nature (Descartes 1637, p. 62). The relationship between the 'old' and the 'new' physics gave rise to numerous censorships and complex debates about specifically theological issues, such as the compatibility of a revised physics with the Christian doctrine of the Eucharist. There was no uniformity in the development of experimental science: it was slow in some regions and traditions and much more rapid in others. But eventually, laboratories measuring the trajectories of canon bullets or air pressure would be set up even in the most remote colleges of the Andes.[23] Even where physics remained conservative, the classical Aristotelian doctrines of matter and space, and place and time, would actually be transformed into something quite different, such as, for instance, an atomistic theory of matter or the replacement of the Aristotelian doctrine of space by the notion of a three-dimensional space.[24] Equally, the epistemology of Aristotle's *Posterior Analytics* would keep inspiring the new theories of scientific demonstration and scientific discovery. Creativity in physics could go hand in hand with conservatism in logic or ethics: John T. Needham (1713–81), famous for his theory of spontaneous generation and first Catholic fellow of the Royal Society, came from a rather classical scholastic curriculum in the recusant colleges of Douai and Lisbon. In Paris, Pierre Lemonnier (1676–1757) satisfied himself with teaching a quite uninspiring logic and metaphysics course but devoted all his attention to chemistry, physical optics, magnetism, natural history and mathematics. Laplace and Diderot were educated by progressive physics teachers. It should be clear that neither the Spanish expulsion of Jesuits nor the French revolution was about scientific progress, nor was the Enlightenment as 'radical' as sometimes claimed.

The second critical issue was the status of the classical Aristotelian 'science of the soul', which had already enjoyed a wide range of positions in the medieval tradition. Naturalist Aristotelianism considered it as a simple appendix to physics qua biology, whereas a more powerful tradition rooted in the Arabic tradition made it the queen of the sciences, defining philosophy as the correct ordering of the soul. This ultimately Neoplatonic heritage would enjoy a form of revival through the process of secession of psychology from physics. In the Catholic tradition, the focus was set on the soul's immateriality and immortality, especially since the Lateran decree of 1513, which echoed the massive debates at the University of Padua.[25] The question of the soul would from then be treated as a special part of metaphysics, dedicated to the species of spiritual being or substance, often labelled *pneumatologia*. In reformed territories, due to the lasting influence of Marburg professors Rudolf Goclenius (1547–1628) and Otto Cassmann (1526–1607; see Casmann 1594), the question of the soul became part of an encompassing new science called *anthropologia*, divided into *somatologia* (body) and *psychologia* (soul),[26] still practised by Wolff and Kant and whose name has survived to this day. Other more ambitious attempts to look at the soul from the point of view of its intellectual capacity of apprehending simple principles (*gnostologia*) or complex propositions (*noologia*), as it had been promoted by the Königsberg philosopher Abraham Calov (1612–82; cf. Calov 1651), did not survive as a consecrated field of study.

The third transformation affected the status and place of metaphysics. Considered as the highest of the speculative sciences in the Aristotelian classification, it was now increasingly taught together with logic at the beginning of a philosophy course. The early-modern commentators resolved the medieval tension between the definition of metaphysics as science of being qua being, and the definition of metaphysics as science of the highest being by a clear-cut division between both perspectives, which can be found, for instance, in the works of Benet Perera (Pererius, ca. 1535–1610, cf. Perera 1576) and Suárez and in some reformed authors such as Goclenius or Johannes Micraelius (1597–1658).[27] It began from the consideration that metaphysics is the most 'abstract' science. Two different ways of envisaging abstraction entail two different types of objects: either metaphysics makes an 'abstract' consideration of everything there is, including God and creatures, in which case it becomes the science of the first fundamental objective concepts of the soul. Metaphysics in this most 'general' sense would thus consider being and its fundamental attributes, such as the classical transcendentals (unity, goodness, truth), categories and post-predicaments and also its modal divisions into possible, impossible, necessary and contingent. In some specific cases, the entire field of metaphysics was actually presented as a 'modal' metaphysics, starting with the distinction between possible and impossible being. According to the second understanding, abstraction should not be referred to the speculative power of the thought but to the abstract (i.e., immaterial) nature of the objects of thought themselves, and metaphysics in this sense deals primarily with God, angels and the soul, considered as abstract entities. This is why the French Jesuit Honoré Fabri (1607–88) could reasonably claim that there 'was little metaphysics to be found in Descartes', and that his work actually belongs to theology.[28] Numerous new names were given to that new division of metaphysics: the standard distinctions ran between *metaphysica generalis* and *metaphysica specialis*, or between *ontologia* on one side[29] and *theologia* and *pneumatologia* on the other side. In the eighteenth-century French tradition, general metaphysics would become the so-called *philosophie générale* (see, for instance, the course by Béguin 1782), still taught today as an introductory course to philosophy in the standard curriculum.

The last problematic issue was the status of ethics. More than in other fields, the reception of medieval ethics was highly conditioned by the humanist-scholastic alternative. 'Lay' or 'secular' ethics followed Platonic and literary sources from the Renaissance, whereas more strictly 'theological' ethics used medieval authorities to construct a new discipline called *theologia moralis*.[30] Some scholastic traditions, notably in Spain and Portugal, actually managed completely to exclude ethics from the philosophy course and reduced it to a part of theology. But the apparent subsistence of a strictly philosophical ethics in other Catholic lands should not be mistaken for its independence from theology: just as metaphysics included natural theology and angelology, most ethics were basically constructed as commentaries of Aquinas's *Prima-Secundae* with sections on human acts, freedom and will, and passions of the soul. The most fascinating ethical and legal issues were then treated in specifically dedicated treatises of moral theology and in confession manuals, as can be appreciated by the lasting influence of the *Enchiridion* or *Manual for Confessors and Confessants* (1552) by Martín de Azpilcueta (1492–1586).[31] The discussion about the right action to undertake in unclear circumstances was at the basis of the emergence of the huge literature today often described as casuistry or 'probabilism'. The scholastics developed a fantastic framework of philosophy of action and *Tiefenpsychologie* in order to explain why we choose to act in certain ways. They did so by reviving numerous Late Antique or medieval questions, such as the doctrine of the first movements of sensibility and their moral characterisation.[32] The treatment of theological virtues and sacraments included important discussions on the relationship between belief and action. 'Business ethics' about just price and just employment was developed in the tradition of *De iustitia* treatises,[33] and sexual ethics was treated in theological treatises on marriage, such as the famous *De matrimonio* by the Andalucian Jesuit Tomás Sánchez (1550–1610).[34] In all ethical and also legal discussions, medieval authorities were still held in particularly high esteem. The early-modern scholastics produced sometimes huge commentaries on the responses given, for instance, by Duns Scotus or Gregory of Rimini to the classical Euthyphro-dilemma: is something good because God wills it, or does God will because it is good in itself? One tradition would favour a classical account in terms of natural law and advocate positions closely akin to today's moral realism.[35] Others harked back to the Augustinian distinction between *natura* and *voluntas* and developed an autonomous *scientia moralis*, claiming that moral principles could in no way be simply deduced from nature or reality: *Oportet de moralibus moraliter philosophari, sicut de realibus realiter.*[36] This distinction can be seen as the true scholastic ancestor of Giambattista Vico's pragmatic redefinition of human sciences as well as the Neo-Kantian distinction between *Naturwissenschaft*, ruled by causes to be explained, and *Kulturwissenschaft*, ruled by norms and beliefs to be understood.

3. The Scholastic Matrix of Contemporary Philosophy

As this short presentation shows, numerous contemporary issues appear actually to be inherited from the early-modern transformation of medieval philosophy. In this last part, I shall go one step further and argue more generally that our various conceptions of 'what there is' and of the functions of philosophical discourse are largely inherited from these early-modern debates. The opposition between the three ideal-types identified above is in no way just a matter of organisation of teaching: they say a lot about how we should look at reality. Type I and Type II kept from the old Aristotelian heritage the idea that sciences are divided according to the nature of things, as expressed by the medieval axiom *scientiae secantur ut res*. Logic treats human second intentions, whereas physics and metaphysics (including theology) treat extra-mental and thought-independent objects. But even within those more classical structures, one can observe a clearly 'mentalistic turn' (Knebel 2009, 424): both the logician and the metaphysician, wrote the Spanish Thomist Domingo Báñez (1528–1604), look at reality 'from the point of view of our concepts of it',[37] whereas the physician considers extra-mental objects directly in themselves. This turn would then definitely be accomplished with the massive adoption of Type III, especially in a post-Cartesian context. The authors following Type III justified the integration of logics and metaphysics by the fact that *both* sciences (and not only logic) were dealing with the mind and its operations or, as Edmond Pourchot put it, 'ideas of the mind and first notions of things'.[38] Logic is not seen as a formal classification of terms and analysis of the structure of propositions, but as 'facultative',[39] that is, as an analysis of the cognitive faculties of the mind: 'The newer logics (. . .) both on the continent and in Britain, concentrated more upon the nature and operation of the faculties than upon arguments and valid inference forms' (Yolton 1984, 105). In Britain, it took the form of the famous 'way of ideas', claiming that science was primarily concerned with our ideas of things rather than with the things themselves.

In France, it was consecrated by the influence of Cartesian 'metaphysics' and the acclaimed Port-Royal Logic. The slow Cartesian reception within the German Catholic tradition would explain, in the middle of the eighteenth century, the rejection of Type I (still followed by Mayr 1739) and adoption of Type III (e.g., Mangold 1755). In Protestant Germany, the integration of logic and metaphysics was already eased by the very idealist interpretation of the object of metaphysics as 'intelligible being' or 'supertranscendental'[40] and would then also be generalised with the reception of Cartesian logic and metaphysics as exemplified by the work of Johannes Clauberg (1622–65).[41] The integration between logic and metaphysics would survive until the Kantian aftermath: this is how his disciple Karl Ludwig Poerschke (1752–1812) would start teaching the *Critique of Pure Reason* (Pozzo 1998).

The transmission and filtering of the medieval heritage thus followed two paths: Path I has been widely studied since it crosses the classical European philosophical heartland (French Cartesianism, English and German idealism, Wolffian-Leibnizian rationalism, etc.), whereas Path II remains largely untravelled by historians.[42] Ironically, it corresponds to the division between the culturally dominant ancestors of the 1957 EEC and its 'new' Southern and Eastern enlargement:

Table 11.2 Early Modern Paths of Transmission of Scholastic Ideas

	Path I The Idealistic Main Road	Path II The Realistic By-Pass
Logic deals with	The activity of the mind: formal truth as dependent on the mind and its cognitive faculties ('facultative' logic)	Mind-independent objects and structures: objective propositions and truths, formal modes of reasoning
Metaphysics deals with	Objective (i.e., mind-dependent) concepts, first ideas or notions of things	Mind- and God-independent objects and states of affairs (*status rerum*)
God	Philosophically significant as warrant of theoretical or moral truths.	Philosophically insignificant: no divine warranty for theoretical or moral truths.
Traditions	*Idealist interpretation of medieval metaphysics* France, Protestant Germany (Leibniz-Wolff), Holland, Britain and all Cartesian-influenced traditions (e.g., Pourchot, Genovesi and Italian idealism, etc.)	*Realist interpretation of medieval metaphysics* *Mitteleuropa*: some authors from Poland, Czech lands, Bavaria, Austria, Hungary, etc.; some Catholic colleges such Colegio Imperial (Madrid), Collegium Romanum
Aftermath	Kant German and British Idealism	Bolzano Frege Neo-Aristotelianism

Kant's Copernican revolution was not, however, the only possible way to read the medieval heritage. According to the principle of interpretation mentioned above, Duns Scotus's doctrine of *esse obiectivum* (the fact that all beings are objects of thought), for instance, could equally be seen as a form of proto-idealism but also as a form of radical realism. This largely explains the long debates among seventeenth-century Scotists about the true teaching of Scotus and more generally of medieval authors on the question of whether 'formalities' or 'possibilia' were, for instance, mind dependent or not.[43] Those who considered God as the ultimate source of ideas and possibles would eventually embrace the idealist road. But those who took seriously the claim that truths remain truths (*circumscripto omni actu intellectus*) or that moral truth would remain moral (*etiamsi fingamus Deum non esse in rerum natura*) (Bellarmino) engaged themselves on a new realistic road in which the object of philosophical discourse was considered as ultimately independent of human thought. Just like the idealist road, this interpretation can be traced back to a number of Spanish colleges, whose teaching then spread over a variety of European academic institutions. Its paragon author was the very creative and idiosyncratic Jesuit Sebastián Izquierdo (1606–81), who had tried to develop an innovative doctrine of mind-independent states of affairs (*status rerum*), which science would have progressively to discover.[44] The concept of state of affairs was a generic way to designate all the possible (but not actual) objects of the human mind: essential or existential, future or present, disjunctive or vague, and so on. Following this realist premise, other early-modern authors did not hesitate to enrich our ontological vocabulary and developed, for instance, an ontology of events (*eventus*), a doctrine of mind-independent truth-makers (*verificativa*) or an complex ontology of 'moral beings' (*entia moralia* or *moralitates*). The conception of science is transformed: it is not considered as the result of the correct use of the cognitive faculties, but rather as the sum of the mind-independent facts and truths that are slowly discovered by enquiring human thought.

In conclusion, one can say that medieval philosophy had a paradoxical fate after the Middle Ages. Its conceptual tools finally led not only the famous *novatores* but also the more orthodox scholastics to embrace new world views that are quite far from the medieval one. It is therefore no surprise that the late-nineteenth-century revival of interest in medieval philosophy in confessional Catholic circles would often go hand in hand with a strong rejection of early-modern philosophy at large, including its scholastic background. On the one hand, the idealistic or mentalistic tradition, including the doctrine of Suárez and numerous Jesuits, is accused of being too proto-idealistic or 'nominalistic' and is presented as an unhappy parenthesis in the history of thought. On the other, the more realistic tradition is seen as guilty of having lost sight of the foundational character of divine power and knowledge in the constitution of the world and in the orientation of morality. The early-modern scholastic transformations of late medieval thought therefore even reached the status of new heresies, called *ontologismus* and *philosophismus*, another interesting seventeenth-century scholastic neologism later used by the German theologian Joseph Anton Sambuga (1752–1815) to attack rationalism in all its forms.[45] Medieval philosophy would then become a safe haven for anti-moderns or simply the object of antiquarian and aesthetic fascination. It would not be a living material anymore—what precisely it had been for so long from the sixteenth to the eighteenth century. In the last decades, the analytical revival has helped to change this situation, by inviting us to look at the medievals from the point of view of the coherence of their arguments and the pertinence of their concepts. It is to be hoped that this revival will also finally reach the early-modern scholastic tradition and help us to write a more varied history of philosophy without gaps.

NOTES

1. See, for instance, Ashworth (1982, 787); De Libera (2002, 33). For the development of early-modern logic, the major tool remains Risse (1964–70). For an example of its creativity, see, for instance, Roncaglia (1996); Redmond (2002); Friedman and Nielsen (2003); on the relationship with semantics, the best synthesis is Meier-Oeser (1997).

2. There is an important literature on each individual figure. See, for instance, Ariew (2011) for Descartes. More generally, on the French context, see Brockliss (1987).

3. Cf. Caramuel (1682): just as there are metaphysics, conceived as a science of the first concepts and first rules of the understanding, there must be a meta-ethics, defined as a science of the first principles of morality.

4. Suárez (1655, 326b): 'Sub Scholasticis antiquis comprehendimus omnes qui ante nostra tempora et ante Calvini errorem scripserunt . . .'. On the early-modern conceptions of scholasticism, see Quinto (2001), and on the historiographical names ('second scholasticism', 'late aristotelianism', 'academic philosophy', etc.), see Forlivesi (2006).

5. Poza (1627, 1211): 'Nulla est propositio Doctoris Sancti quae non optime explicari et defendi queat'.

6. For a synthesis on the prohibitions and commissions in the Catholic tradition, see Schmutz (2010).

7. It was also during the seventeenth century that the first vernacular translations of the *Summa* were published. The bibliography on this early-modern Thomism is huge: on the Renaissance Thomism, see the classical monograph by Kristeller (1970); on the Spanish school of Salamanca and its sources, see Belda Plans (2000); on the varieties of attitudes towards Thomism, and a more extensive bibliography, see Schmutz (2008a); De Franceschi (2010).

8. For a survey, see Porro and Schmutz (2008) (including an extensive bibliography); Schmutz (2002).

9. The French Jesuit Théophile Raynaud produced also a beautiful new edition of Anselm's works, including his prayers, in 1630.

10. This myth should at least have been dismantled since Hübener (1983). Authentic nominalists were rare, such as the Frenchman Jean Salabert (cf. Salabert 1651) or the Englishman Obadiah Walker (cf. Walker 1673). Among the members of the Society of Jesus, the most 'nominalistic' course was that of Hurtado de Mendoza (1615), who influenced several of his pupils (R. de Arriaga, A. Pérez).

11. On the revival of Church Fathers, which in some circles would be seen as an alternative to medieval theology, see contributions in Backus (1996), as well as the monographs of Quantin (1999, for France) and Quantin (2009, for England).

12. On this Italian Aristotelianism and the reading of Averroes in particular, such as in the Padua school, see Hasse (2004); Poppi (1970). More generally, on the specific issues of early-modern Aristotelianism, see Bianchi (2003); Frank and Speer (2007); Piaia (2002); Pozzo (2003); Schmitt (1983a); Tucker (2000).

13. See the classical survey by Rossi (2000).

14. On this tradition of textbooks, see Blum (1998); Freedman (1993, 1999); Thorndike (1951).

15. On the German Protestant reception within the Schulmetaphysik, see the ground-breaking works of Eschweiler (1928) and Lewalter (1935). On the further development in the German lands, see Freedman (1984, 1988); Leinsle (1985, 1988); Petersen (1921); Trueman and Clark (1999); Wundt (1939). For a case study on Dutch reformed scholasticism, see Goudriaan (1999). For Britain, see Costello (1958); Howell (1961); Schmitt (1983b); Yolton (1986). There were also minor and little studied scholastic traditions in reformed Denmark and Finland.

16. Cf. Symchych (2009). More generally, there has been a renewed interest, since the fall of communism, in the national traditions of scholasticism in Eastern Europe. Other important contributions include Darowski (2008) (Lithuania); Darowski (1994, 1998) (Poland); Ibrulj (2009) (Croatia and Bosnia-Herzegovina); Sousedík (2007) (Bohemia).

17. One of the sources of John Locke: Milton (1984).

18. Cf. Demetracopoulos (2010).

19. The study of South American colonial scholasticism has made considerable progress in the last decades. The best starting point remains the precious sources inventory by Redmond (1972). Important case studies include Beuchot (1997); Beuchot and Marquínez Argote (1996); Hampe Martínez (1999).

20. Cf. Wardy (2000).

21. A general overview can be found in Brockliss (1996).

22. Note that Bouju's title page actually claims following the traditional order (Ia), but effectively he starts with logics followed by 'universal metaphysics' and physics, and finishes with ethics. On the relationship between Descartes's order of science and the scholastic order, see Ariew (2011, 55–64).

23. Some good recent case studies on scientific traditions are Baldini (1992) (for the Roman Jesuits); Brockliss (2004) (on the end of Aristotelian physics at the University of Paris colleges); Des Chene (1996); Dollo (1979; 1984) (on Sicily); Feingold (2003) (on the Jesuits in general); Hellyer (2005) (for the German Jesuits); Kusukawa (1995) (on German reformation); Leijenhorst (2003) (pre-Hobbesian context in England). The literature dedicated to specific figures is huge, and there are numerous overviews on the universities: see Feingold and Navarro-Brotóns (2006). For an example of the scientific culture in South American colleges, see, for instance, the excellent case study by Keeding (1983) (Ecuador).

24. See, for example, the case study by Leijenhorst and Lüthy (2002).

25. There is a vast bibliography on this decree. See Grendler (2002) for its reception in Italian universities, and a full bibliography in Schmutz (2010). On the problematic of the immortality of the soul, the standard synthesis remains Di Napoli (1963).

26. On the epistemological status of the *De anima*, see Wels (2007, 201–2) in particular; more generally, on the background, still useful, the general presentation by Kessler (1982). On the emergence of psychology as an independent scientific discipline, see the important and erudite monographs by Salatowsky (2006) and Vidal (2006), quoting most of the older bibliography on the subject. Des Chene (2000) has a more limited textual basis.

27. This story has often been told, since Vollrath (1961). See general presentations in Courtine (1990); Darge (2003); Honnefelder (1990); Leinsle (1985, 1988). Recent collections of essays in Forlivesi (2009) and Esposito (2009) have added considerable new material.

28. Fabri (1674, 13), quoted by Knebel (2009, 400): 'Ad Metaphysicam venio, de qua ille [sc. Cartesius] pauca scripsit; nec enim meditationes illae de Deo et anima, quas "metaphysicas" vocat, ad Metaphysicam pertinent, sed ad Theologiam. Aliam ego Metaphysicam agnosco, nimirum rationum universalium scientiam, cuius ille numquam meminit (. . .)'.

29. As recently discovered (2002), the first author to have used the expression *ontologia* seems to have been the Swiss Calvinist theologian Jakob Lorhard in 1606, and not Rudolf Goclenius as commonly acknowledged. On the historiography on this term, most older literature is inaccurate: see Devaux and Lamanna (2009).

30. On the development of the teaching of moral philosophy in a more secular context, see Kraye (1982); Lines (2003, 2007); and on the Renaissance sources, Ebbersmeyer (2010). On the opposite, on the development of moral theology into an autonomous discipline, see Theiner (1970). A good sketch of the development of moral theology remains Vereecke (1986). On the history of probabilism, see Kantola (1994); Schüssler (2003); Schüssler (2006). Knebel (2000) uncovers the metaphysical foundations of the doctrine of probabilism.

31. On the complex relationship between legal discipline and confessional issues in post-Tridentine Catholicism, see the excellent work by Lavenia (2004) and a good survey article by Decock (2011).

32. See, for instance, the monograph by Couture (1962).

33. See, for instance, the classical De Roover (1971); more recently, Gómez Camacho (1998); Decock (2009).

34. See the excellent reconstruction by Alfieri (2010).

35. Natural law theory (as well as international law, *ius gentium*) is one of the aspects in which historiography has always acknowledged the originality of second scholasticism. The bibliography on specific authors such as Vitoria, Suárez or the scholastic sources of Grotius is intimidating and often very repetitive. Todescan (2007) gives an excellent bibliographical overview. Important recent contributions include Grunert & Seelman (2001); Kaufmann & Schnepf (2007); Scattola (1999); Todescan (1973); on the history of 'subjective' rights, see Brett (1997); Guzmán Brito (2009).

36. Caramuel (1645, 17). For a critical assessment of this scholastic distinction between 'nature' and 'culture', see Schmutz (2008b).

37. Báñez (1584, 289a), quoted by Knebel (2009, 421): 'Logicus vero et metaphysicus considerat res per ordinem ad conceptum mentis'.

38. Pourchot (1695, 218): '. . . Deinde tanta est illius, tamque arcta cum logica connexio, ut prima pars Logicae eadem ac prima Metaphysicae pars esse videatur: utraque enim circa mentis ideas, primasve rerum notiones aut perceptiones esse occupata'.

39. The expression was coined by a seminal article by Buickerood (1985); for a convincing argument on its development down to eighteenth-century German *Vernunftlehre* and Kant, see Tonelli (1994), with new materials in Sgarbi (2008, 2010).

40. See Doyle (1997, 1998).

41. Clauberg (1691, II, 592): 'Quibus de rebus tractat Metaphysica sive prima Philosophia, illa inprimis quae a Renato Cartesio publice data? Resp.: tractat de principiis cognitionis humanae, sive de primis initiis et fundamentis omnis nostrae scientiae, quam ex naturae lumine possumus haurire'. For a contextual analysis of Descartes' metaphysical project, see the classic work by Marion (1986); Savini (2009).

42. For a first sketch, see Schmutz (2009).

43. On this well-studied debate, see Hoffmann (2002); Sousedík (1996).

44. See Izquierdo (1659). For an attempt in interpretation, see Schmutz (2009).

45. Cf. Sambuga (1805). The expression goes back to the seventeenth century and was used to describe a position in ethics claiming that there were strictly 'philosophical' sins, and that directedness towards God was not a criterion for moral acts.

BIBLIOGRAPHY

Abra de Raconis, Charles-François d'. 1617. *Totius philosophiae, hoc est Logicae, Moralis, Physicae et Metaphysicae brevis et accurata, facilique et clara methodo disposita Tractatio*. Paris: Denys de la Noue.

Alfieri, Fernanda. 2010. *Nella camera degli sposi. Tomás Sánchez, il matrimonio, la sessualità (secoli XVI–XVII)*. Bologna, Italy: Il Mulino.

Ariew, Roger. 2011. *Descartes among the Scholastics*. Leiden, the Netherlands: Brill.

Arriaga, Rodrigo de. 1632. *Cursus philosophicus*. Antwerp, Belgium: B. Moretus (Plantin).

Ashworth, E. J. 1982. 'The eclipse of medieval logic'. In Kretzmann, Kenny and Pinborg, 1982, 787–96.

Backus, Irena, ed. 1996. *The Reception of the Church Fathers in the West: From the Carolingians to the Maurists*. 2 vols. Leiden, the Netherlands: Brill.

Baldini, Ugo. 1992. *Legem impone subactis. Studi su filosofia e scienza dei Gesuiti in Italia, 1540–632*. Rome: Bulzoni.

Báñez, Domingo. 1584. *Scholastica commentaria in primam partem Angelici Doctoris D. Thomae*, Rome: G. Ruffinelli.

Béguin, Nicolas. 1782. *Principes de philosophie générale, de physique, de Chimie et de géométrie transcendante*. 2 vols. Paris: Nyon.

Belda Plans, Juan. 2000. *La Escuela de Salamanca y la renovación de la teología en el siglo XVI*. Madrid: BAC Maior.

Beuchot, Maurício. 1997. *Historia de la filosofía en el México colonial*. Barcelona: Herder.

Beuchot, Maurício and Germán Marquínez Argote, eds. 1996. *La filosofía en la América colonial. Siglos XVI, XVII y XVIII*. Santa Fé de Bogotá: El Buho.

Bianchi, Luca. 2003. *Studi sull'aristotelismo del Rinascimento*. Padua, Italy: Il Poligrafo.

Blum, Paul Richard. 1998. *Philosophenphilosophie und Schulphilosophie. Typen des philosophierens in der Neuzeit*. Stuttgart, Germany: Franz Steiner Verlag.

Bouju, Théophraste. 1614. *Corps de toute la philosophie divisé en deux parties*. Paris: Denys de la Noue.

Brett, Annabel S. 1997. *Liberty, Right and Nature. Individual Rights in Later Scholastic Thought*. Cambridge: Cambridge University Press.

Brockliss, L. W. B. 1987. *French Higher Education in the Seventeenth and Eighteenth Centuries. A Cultural History*. Oxford: Clarendon Press.

———. 1996. 'Curricula'. In *A History of the University in Europe, vol. 2: Universities in Early-Modern Europe*, ed. Hilde de Ridder-Symoens, 563–620. Cambridge: Cambridge University Press.

———. 2004. The Moment of No Return. The University of Paris and the Death of Aristotelianism, *Science and Education* 15(2–4): 1–20.

Buickerood, James G. 1985. The Natural History of the Understanding: Locke and the Rise of Facultative Logic in the Eighteenth Century. *History and Philosophy of Logic* 6:157–90.

Calov, Abraham. 1651. *Scripta philosophica*. Rostock and Lübeck, Germany: Wild and Hakelmann.

Caramuel Lobkowitz, Juan. 1645. *Theologia moralis ad prima eaque clarissima principia reducta*. Louvain, Belgium: P. Zangrius.

———. 1682. *Met-ethica*. Vigevano, Italy: C. Corrado.

Cardillo de Villapando, Gaspar. 1567. *Summa summularum*. Alcalá, Spain: Juan de Villanueva.

Casmann, Otto. 1594. *Psychologia anthropologica, sive animae humanae doctrina*. Hanau, Germany: G. Antonius.

Clauberg, Johannes. 1691. *Opera omnia philosophica*, ed. J. Th. Schalbruch, 2 vols. Amsterdam: P. and I. Blaeu.

Compton Carleton, Thomas. 1649. *Philosophia universa*. Antwerp, Belgium: Meursius.

Costello, William T. 1958. *The Scholastic Curriculum at Early Seventeenth-Century Cambridge*. Cambridge, MA: Harvard University Press.

Courtine, Jean-François. 1990. *Suárez et le système de la métaphysique*, Paris: PUF.

Couture, Roger A. 1962. *L'imputabilité morale des premiers mouvements de la sensualité de saint Thomas aux Salmanticenses*. Rome: Gregorian University Press.

Darge, Rolf. 2003. *Suárez' transzendentale Seinsauslegung und die Metaphysiktradition*. Leiden, the Netherlands: Brill.

Darowski, Roman. 1994. *Filozofia w szkolach jezuickich w Polsce w XVI wieku*. Kraków: Fakultet Filozoficzny TJ.

———. 1998. *Studia z filozofii jezuitów w Polsce w XVII i XVIII wieku*, Wydz. Filozoficzny Tow. Jezusowego: Kraków.

———. 2008. Philosophy of Jesuits in Lithuania since the Sixteenth until the Eighteenth Century. *Problemos* 73: 18–24.

Decock, Wim. 2009. Lessius and the Breakdown of the Scholastic Paradigm. *Journal of the History of Economic Thought* 31(3): 57–78.

———. 2011. From Law to Paradise: Confessional Catholicism and Legal Scholarship. *Rechtsgeschichte* 18:12–34.

De Franceschi, Sylvio H. 2010. L'empire thomiste dans les querelles doctrinales de l'âge classique. Le statut théologique de Thomas d'Aquin au XVIIᵉ siècle. *XVIIe siècle* 62(2):313–34.

De Libera, Alain. 2002. *La référence vide. Théories de la proposition*. Paris: PUF.

Demetracopoulos, John. 2010. Purchotius Graecus I: Vikentios Damodos' *Concise Ethics*, *Verbum*. *Analecta Neolatina* 12(1):41–67

De Roover, Raymond. 1971. *La pensée économique des scolastiques*. Paris and Montréal: Vrin.

Des Chene, Dennis. 1996. *Physiologia. Natural Philosophy in Late Aristotelian and Cartesian Thought*. Ithaca, NY: Cornell University Press.

———. 2000. *Life's Form. Late Aristotelian Conceptions of the Soul*. Ithaca, NY: Cornell University Press.

Descartes, René. 1637. *Discours de la méthode*. In *Œuvres*, vol. 6, ed. Ch. Adam and P. Tannery. Paris: L. Cerf, 1902.

Devaux, Michaël and Marco Lamanna. 2009. The Rise and Early History of the Term Ontology. 1606–1730. *Quaestio* 9: 173–208.

Di Napoli, Giovanni. 1963. *L'immortalità dell'anima nel Rinascimento*. Torino: S.E.I.

Dollo, Corrado. 1979. *Filosofia e scienze in Sicilia*. Padua: CEDAM.

———. 1984. *Modelli scientifici e filosofici nella Sicilia spagnola*. Naples: Guida.

Doyle, John P. 1997. Between Transcendental and Transcendental: The Missing Link? *Review of Metaphysics* 50: 783–815.

——. 1998. 'Supertranscendental being: On the verge of modern philosophy'. In *Meeting of the Minds. The Relations Between Medieval and Classical Modern Philosophy*, ed. Stephen F. Brown, 297–315. Turnhout, Belgium: Brepols.

Ebbersmeyer, Sabine. 2010. *Homo agens. Studien zur Genese und Struktur frühhumanistischer Moralphilosophie*. Berlin and New York: de Gruyter.

Eschweiler, Karl. 1928. 'Die Philosophie der spanischen Spätscholastik auf den deutschen Universitäten des 17. Jahrhunderts'. In *Spanische Forschungen der Görres-Gesellschaft* 1: 251–325.

Esposito, Costantino, ed. 2009. *Origini e sviluppi dell'ontologia. Secoli XVI–XXI*. Turnhout, Belgium, and Bari, Italy: Brepols and Pagina (Quaestio, 9).

Eustachius a Sancto Paulo. 1609. *Summa philosophiae quadripartita, de rebus dialecticis, moralibus, physicis et metaphysicis*, Paris: Ch. Chastellain.

Fabri, Honoré. 1674. *Epistolae tres de sua hypothesi philosophica*. Mainz, Germany: P. Zubrodt.

Feingold, Mordechai, ed. 2003. *The New Science and Jesuit Science. Seventeenth Century Perspectives*. Dordrecht, the Netherlands, and Boston: Kluwer.

Feingold, Mordechai and Víctor Navarro Brotóns, eds. 2006. *Universities and Science in the Early-Modern Period*. Dordrecht, the Netherlands: Springer.

Forlivesi, Marco. 2006. 'A Man, an age, a book'. In *Rem in seipsa cernere. Saggi sul pensiero filosofico di Bartolomeo Mastri (1602–673)*, ed. M. Forlivesi, 24–144. Padua: Il Poligrafo.

——, ed. 2009. *I dibattiti sull'oggetto della metafisica dal tardo medioevo alla prima età moderna*. Padua: Il Poligrafo (Medioevo, 34).

Frank, Günter and Andreas Speer, eds. 2007. *Der Aristotelismus in der frühen Neuzeit— Kontinuität oder Wiederaneignung?* Wiesbaden, Germany: Harrassowitz.

Frassen, Claude. 1657. *Philosophia academica*. Paris: D. Thierry.

Freedman, Joseph S. 1984. *Deutsche Schulphilosophie im Reformationszeitalter (1500–650). Ein Handbuch für den Hochschulunterricht*. Münster, Germany: MAKS.

——. 1988. *European Academic Philosophy in the Late Sixteenth and Early Seventeenth Centuries: The Life, Significance and Philosophy of Clemens Timpler*. 2 vols. Hildesheim, Germany: G. Olms.

——. 1993. Aristotle and the Content of Philosophy Instruction at Central European Schools and Universities during the Reformation Era (1500–1600). *Proceedings of the American Philosophical Society* 2:213–53.

——. 1999. *Philosophy and Arts in Central Europe, 1500–700: Teaching and Texts at European Schools and Universities*. Aldershot, UK: Ashgate.

Friedman, Russell L. and Lauge O. Nielsen, eds. 2003. *The Medieval Heritage in Early Modern Metaphysics and Modal Theory, 1400–700*. Dordrecht, the Netherlands: Kluwer.

Genovesi, Antonio. 1743. *Elementa metaphysicae*. Naples: B. Gessari.

——. 1745. *Elementorum artis logico-criticae libri V*. Naples: P. Palumbo.

Glanvill, Joseph. 1661. *The Vanity of Dogmatizing*. London: Henry Eversden.

Gómez Camacho, Francisco. 1998. *Economía y filosofía moral. La formación del pensamiento económico europeo en la escolástica española*. Madrid: Síntesis.

Goudin, Antoine. 1670–71. *Philosophia iuxta inconcussa tutissimaque D. Thomae dogmata*. 4 vols. Lyons, France: A. Jullieron.

Goudriaan, Aza. 1999. *Philosophische Gotteserkenntnis bei Suárez und Descartes, im Zusammenhang mit der niederländischen reformierten Theologie und Philosophie des 17. Jahrhunderts*. Leiden, the Netherlands: Brill.

Gremner, Johann. 1748. *Philosophia vetus et nova*. Prague: J. Schweiger.

Grendler, Paul F. 2002. *The Universities of the Italian Renaissance*. Baltimore: The Johns Hopkins University Press.

Grunert, Frank and Kurt Seelman, eds. 2001. *Die Ordnung der Praxis. Neue Studien zur spanischen Spätscholastik*. Tübingen, Germany: Mohr.

Guzmán Brito, Alejandro. 2009. *El derecho como facultad en la neoescolástica española del siglo XVI*. Madrid: Iustel.

Hampe Martínez, Teodoro, ed. 1999. *La tradición clásica en el Perú virreinal*. Lima: Fondo Editorial de la Universidad Nacional Mayor de San Marcos.

Hasse, Dag Nikolaus. 2004. 'The attraction of Averroism in the Renaissance: Vernia, Achillini, Prassico'. In *Philosophy, Science and Exegesis in Greek, Arabic and Latin Commentaries*, ed. P. Adamson, H. Balthussen and M. W. F. Stone, 131–47. London: Institute of Classical Studies.

Hellyer, Marcus. 2005. *Catholic Physics. Jesuit Natural Philosophy in Early Modern Germany*. Notre Dame, IN: Notre Dame University Press.

Heumann, Christoph August. 1719. *Praefatio, in qua de appellatione, natura atque ἀσοφία theologiae et philosophiae scholasticae disputatur*. In Adam Tribbechow, *De doctoris scholasticis et corrupta per eos divinarum humanarumque rerum scientia liber singularis*, 2nd edition. Jena, Germany: J. F. Bielckius.

Hoffmann, Tobias. 2002. *Creatura intellecta. Die Ideen und Possibilien bei Duns Scotus mit Ausblick auf Franz von Mayronis, Poncius und Mastrius*. Münster, Germany: Aschendorff.

Honnefelder, Ludger. 1990. *Scientia transcendens. Die formale Bestimmtheit der Seiendheit und Realität in der Metaphysik des Mittelalters und der Neuzeit (Duns Scotus, Suárez, Wolff, Kant, Peirce)*. Hamburg: Meiner.

Horváth, János. 1767. *Institutiones logicae et metaphysicae*. Trnava, Slovakia.

Howell, Samuel W. 1961. *Logic and Rhetoric in England, 1500–700*. New York: Russell and Russell.

Hübener, Wolfgang. 1983. 'Die Nominalismus-Legende. Über das Mißverhältnis zwischen Dichtung und Wahrheit in der Deutung der Wirkungsgeschichte des Ockhamismus'. In *Spiegel und Gleichnis. Festschrift für Jacob Taubes*, ed. N. W. Bolz and W. Hübener, 87–111. Würzburg, Germany: Königshausen and Neumann.

Hurtado de Mendoza, Pedro. 1615. *Disputationes a summulis ad metaphysicam*, Valladolid, Spain: Juan Godínez de Millis.

Ibrulj, Nijaz. 2009. Bosnia Porphyriana. An Outline of the Development of Logic in Bosnia and Herzegovina. *Survey. Periodical for Social Studies* 2 (Sarajevo):109–66.

Izquierdo, Sebastián. 1659. *Pharus Scientiarum*, Lyons, France: Cl. Bourgeat and M. Lietard.

Kantola, Ilka. 1994. *Probability and Moral Uncertainty in Late Medieval and Early Modern Times*. Helsinki: Luther-Agricola Society.

Kaufmann, Matthias and Schnepf, Robert, eds. 2007. *Politische Metaphysik. Die Entstehung moderner Rechtskonzeptionen in der Spanischen Scholastik*. Frankfurt, Germany: Peter Lang.

Keeding, Ekkehard. 1983. *Das Zeitalter der Aufklärung in der Provinz Quito*. Cologne, Germany, and Vienna: Böhlau Verlag.

Kessler, Eckhart. 1982. 'The intellective soul'. In Kretzmann, Kenny and Pinborg 1982, 484–584.

Knebel, Sven K. 2000. *Wille, Würfel und Wahrscheinlichkeit. Das System der moralischen Notwendigkeit in der Jesuitenscholastik 1550–700*. Hamburg, Germany: Meiner.

———. 2009. 'Metaphysikkritik'? Historisches zur Abgrenzung von Logik und Metaphysik. *Medioevo* 34:399–424.

Kraye, Jill. 1982. 'Moral philosophy'. In Kretzmann, Kenny and Pinborg, 1982, 303–86.

Kretzmann, Norman, Anthony Kenny and January Pinborg, eds. 1982. *The Cambridge History of Later Medieval Philosophy*. Cambridge: Cambridge University Press.

Kristeller, Paul Oskar. 1967. *Le thomisme et la pensée italienne de la Renaissance.* Montréal and Paris: Institut d'Etudes Médiévales and Vrin.

Kusukawa, Sachiko. 1995. *The Transformation of Natural Philosophy: The Case of Philip Melanchthon.* Cambridge: Cambridge University Press.

Lavenia, Vincenzo. 2004. *L'infamia e il perdono. Tributi, pene e confessione nella teologia morale della prima età moderna.* Bologna: Il Mulino.

Leijenhorst, Cees. 2003. *The Mechanisation of Aristotelianism. The Late Setting of Thomas Hobbes' Natural Philosophy.* Leiden, the Netherlands: Brill.

Leijenhorst, Cees and Christoph Lüthy. 2002. 'The erosion of Aristotelianism: confessional physics in early-modern Germany and the Dutch Republic'. In *The Dynamics of Aristotelian Natural Philosophy from Antiquity to the Seventeenth Century,* ed. C. Leijenhorst, Chr. Lüthy and J. M. M. H. Thijssen, 375–441. Leiden, the Netherlands: Brill.

Leinsle, Ulrich Gottfried. 1985. *Das Ding und die Methode. Methodische Konstitution und Gegenstand der frühen protestantischen Metaphysik,* Augsburg, Germany: Maro Verlag.

———. 1988. *Reformversuche protestantischer Metaphysik im Zeitalter des Rationalismus.* Augsburg, Germany: Maro Verlag.

Lewalter, Ernst. 1935. *Spanisch-Jesuitische und Deutsch-Lutherische Metaphysik des 17. Jahrhunderts. Ein Beitrag zur Geschichte der iberisch-deutschen Kulturbeziehungen und zur Vorgeschichte des deutschen Idealismus.* Hamburg, Germany: 1935 (Ibero-Amerikanische Studien, 4).

Lines, David A. 2003. *Aristotle's 'Ethics' in the Italian Renaissance (ca. 1300–650): The Universities and the Problem of Moral Education.* Leiden, the Netherlands: Brill.

———. 2007. 'Humanistic and scholastic ethics'. In *The Cambridge Companion to Renaissance Philosophy,* ed. James Hankins, Cambridge: Cambridge University Press, 304-318.

Losada, Luis de. 1724–35. *Cursus philosophicus Regalis Collegii Salmanticensis Societatis Iesu in tres partes divisi.* Salamanca, Spain: E. García de Honorato y San Miguel.

Lourenço (Laurentius), Agostinho. 1688. *De triplici ente cursus philosophicus tripartitus.* Liège, Belgium: G. H. Streel.

Mair, John. 1509. *In quartum Sententiarum.* Paris: P. Pigouchet and J. Granion.

Mangold, Josef. 1755. *Philosophia rationalis et experimentalis hodiernis.* Munich and Ingolstadt, Germany: J. F. -X. Craetz and Th. Summer.

Marion, Jean-Luc. 1986. *Sur le prisme métaphysique de Descartes.* Paris: PUF.

Mastri, Bartolomeo. 1727. 'Metaphysica'. In *Cursus philosophicus ad mentem Scoti,* 4th edition. Venice: N. Pezzana.

Mayr, Anton. 1739. *Philosophia peripatetica antiquorum principiis et recentiorum experimentis conformata.* 4 vols. Ingolstadt, Germany: J. A. de La Haye.

Meier-Oeser, Stephan. 1997. *Die Spur des Zeichens. Das Zeichen und seine Funktion in der Philosophie des Mittelalters und der frühen Neuzeit.* New York and Berlin: de Gruyter.

Milton, J.R. 1984. The Scholastic Background to Locke's Thought. *Locke Newsletter* 15 (1984), 25–34.

Oviedo, Francisco de. 1640. *Integer cursus philosophicus ad unum corpus redactus.* Lyons, France: P. Prost.

Perera (Pererius), Benet. 1576. *De communibus omnium rerum naturalium principiis et affectionibus libri quindecim,* Rome: Tramezini.

Petersen, Peter. 1921. *Geschichte der aristotelischen Philosophie im protestantischen Deutschland.* Leipzig, Germany: Meiner, 1921.

Piaia, Gregorio, ed. 2002. *La presenza dell'aristotelismo padovano nella filosofia della prima modernità.* Padua: Antenore.

Piccart, Michael. 1655. *Isagoge in lectionem Aristotelis, hoc est, Hypotyposis totius Philosophiae Aristotelis*, ed. J. C. Dürr. Altdorf, Germany: G. Hagen.

Poinsot, João (John of Saint Thomas). 1631–4. *Cursus philosophicus thomisticus*. 5 vols. Alcalá, Spain: A. Vázquez.

Poppi, Antonino. 1970. *Introduzione all'aristotelismo padovano*. Padua: Antenore.

Porro, Pasquale and Jacob Schmutz, eds. 2008. *La posterità di Giovanni Duns Scoto*. Turnhout, Belgium, and Bari, Italy: Brepols and Pagina *(Quaestio, 8)*.

Pourchot, Edmond. 1695. *Institutiones philosophicae ad faciliorem veterum et recentiorum Philosophorum intelligentiam*. 4 vols. Paris: J.-B. Coignard.

Poza, Juan Bautista. 1627. *Elucidarium Deiparae*. 2nd edition. Lyons: Rouillé.

Pozzo, Riccardo. 1998. Kant within the Tradition of Modern Logic: The Role of the 'Introduction Idea of a Transcendental Logic'. *Review of Metaphysics* 52: 295–310.

——, ed. 2003. *The Impact of Aristotelianism on Modern Philosophy*. Washington DC: The Catholic University of America Press.

Quantin, Jean-Louis. 1999. *Le Catholicisme classique et les Pères de l'Eglise. Un retour aux sources (1669–713)*. Paris: Institut d'Etudes Augustiniennes.

——. 2009. *The Church of England and Christian Antiquity. The Construction of a Confessional Identity in the Seventeenth Century*. Oxford: Oxford University Press.

Quinto, Riccardo. 2001. *Scholastica. Storia di un concetto*. Padua: Il Poligrafo.

Rabe, Paul. 1703. *Cursus philosophicus, sive compendium praecipuarum scientiarium philosophicarum*. Königsberg, Germany: Boye.

Redmond, Walter B. 1972. *Bibliography of the Philosophy in the Iberian Colonies of America*. The Hague, the Netherlands: Nijhoff.

——. 2002. *La lógica del Siglo de oro. Una introducción a la historia de la lógica*. Pamplona, Spain: EUNSA.

Risse, Wilhelm. 1964–70. *Die Logik der Neuzeit*. 2 vols. Stuttgart and Bad Cannstatt, Germany: Frommann and Holzboog.

Roncaglia, Gino. 1996. *Palaestra rationis. Discussioni su natura della copula e modalità nelle filosofia 'scolastica' tedesca del XVII secolo*. Florence: Olschki.

Rossi, Paolo. 2000. *Logic and the Art of Memory. The Quest for a Universal Language*, trans. Steven Clucas, London: Athlone Press (1st Italian edition 1960).

Salabert, Jean. 1651. *Philosophia nominalium vindicata*. Paris: S. and G. Cramoisy.

Salatowsky, Sascha. 2006. *De Anima. Die Rezeption der aristotelischen Psychologie im 16. und 17. Jahrhundert*. Amsterdam and Philadelphia: B.R. Grüner.

Sambuga, Joseph Anton. 1805. *Über den Philosophismus, welcher unser Zeitalter bedroht*. Munich: J. Lentner.

Savini, Massimiliano. 2009. Johannes Clauberg e l'esito cartesiano dell'ontologia. *Quaestio* 9:153–72.

Scattola, Merio. 1999. *Das Naturrecht vor dem Naturrecht. Zur Geschichte des 'ius naturae' im 16. Jahrhundert*. Tübingen, Germany: Niemeyer.

Scheibler, Christoph. 1623. *Philosophia compendiosa*. Giessen, Germany: Chemlinus.

Schmitt, Charles B. 1983a. *Aristotle and the Renaissance*. Cambridge, MA: Harvard University Press.

——. 1983b. *John Case and Aristotelianism in Renaissance England*. Montreal and Kingston, Ontario, Canada: McGill and Queen's University Press.

Schmutz, Jacob. 2002. L'héritage des Subtils. Cartographie du scotisme du XVIIe siècle. *Les Etudes philosophiques* (1):51–81.

——. 2008a. Bellum scholasticum. Thomisme et antithomisme dans les débats doctrinaux modernes. *Revue thomiste* 108(1):131–82.

———. 2008b. 'Juan Caramuel on naturalistic fallacy'. In *Juan Caramuel Lobkowitz, The Last Scholastic Polymath*, ed. P. Dvorak and J. Schmutz, 45–69. Prague: Filosofia.

———. 2009. 'Quand le langage a-t-il cessé d'être mental? Remarques sur les sources scolastiques de Bolzano'. In *Le langage mental du Moyen Age à l'âge classique*, ed. J. Biard, 306–37. Louvain-la-Neuve, Belgium: Editions de l'ISP.

———. 2010. 'Les normes théologiques de l'enseignement philosophique dans le catholicisme romain moderne (1500–1650)'. In *Philosophie et théologie à l'époque moderne*, ed. J.-C. Bardout, 129–50. Paris: Ed. du Cerf.

Schüssler, Rudolf. 2003. *Moral im Zweifel*, vol. I: *Die scholastische Theorie des Entscheidens unter moralischer Unsicherheit*. Paderborn, Germany: Mentis Verlag.

———. 2006. *Moral im Zweifel*, vol. II: *Die Herausforderung des Probabilismus*. Paderborn, Germany: Mentis Verlag.

Sgarbi, Marco. 2008. 'Aristotle, Kant and the rise of facultative logic'. In *Aristotle and the Aristotelian Tradition*, ed. E. De Bellis, 97–108. Soveria Mannelli: Rubbettino.

———. 2010. *La Kritik der reinen Vernunft nel contesto della tradizione logica aristotelica*. Hildesheim, Germany: G. Olms.

Soto, Domingo de. 1529. *Summulae*. Burgos, Spain: J. Junte.

Sousedík, Stanislav. 1996. 'Der Streit um den wahren Sinn der scotischen Possibilienlehre'. In *John Duns Scotus, Metaphysics and Ethics*, ed. Ludger Honnefelder, Rega Wood and Mechthild Dreyer, 191–204. Leiden, the Netherlands: Brill.

———. 2007. *Filosofie v českých zemích mezi středověkema osvícenstvím*, Prague: Višehrad.

Stier, Johann. 1652. *Praecepta doctrinae logicae, ethicae, physicae, metaphysicae, sphaericaeque*, 4th edition. London: R. Daniel.

Suárez, Francisco. 1597. *Disputationes metaphysicae*. Salamanca, Spain: J. and A. Renaut.

———. 1655. *Tractatus theologicus de vera intelligentia auxilii efficacis eiusque concordia cum libero arbitrio. Opus Posthumum*. Lyons, France: Borde, Arnaud and Rigaud.

Symchych, Mykola. 2009. *Philosophia rationalis у Києво-Могилянській академії: компаративний аналіз могилянських курсів логіки кінця XVII-першої половини XVIII ст.* Vinnitsa, Ukraine: O. Vlasiuk.

Tartaretus, Petrus. 1581. *In Aristotelis philosophiam naturalem, divinam et moralem exactissima commentaria*. Venice: Melchiorre Sessa, 1581.

Theiner, Johann. 1970. *Die Entwicklung der Moraltheologie zur eigenständigen Disziplin*. Regensburg, Germany: Pustet.

Thorndike, Lynn. 1951. The Cursus philosophicus before Descartes. *Archives internationales d'histoire de la science* 4:16–24.

Todescan, Franco. 1973. *Lex, natura, beatitudo. Il problema della legge nella scolastica spagnola del secolo XVI*. Padua: Cedam.

———. 2007. 'Il problema del diritto naturale fra Seconda scolastica e giusnaturalismo laico secentesco. Una introduzione bibliografica'. In *Iustus ordo e ordine della natura. Sacra doctrina e saperi politici fra XVI e XVIII secolo*, ed. F. Arici and F. Todescan, 1–61. Padua: Cedam.

Tonelli, Giorgio. 1994. *Kant's Critique of Pure Reason Within the Tradition of Modern Logic. A Commentary on Its History*, ed. David H. Chandler. Hildesheim, Germany: G. Olms.

Trueman, Carl R. and R. Scott Clark, eds. 1999. *Protestant Scholasticism. Essays in Reassessment*. Carlisle, UK: Paternoster Press.

Tucker, George H., ed. 2000. *Forms of the 'Medieval' in the 'Renaissance'. A Multidisciplinary Exploration of a Cultural Continuum*. Charlottesville, VA: Rookwood Press.

Vereecke, Louis. 1986. *De Guillaume d'Ockham à saint Alphonse de Liguori. Etudes d'histoire de la théologie morale moderne, 1300–787.* Rome: Collegium S. Alfonsi de Urbe.

Vidal, Fernando. 2006. *Les sciences de l'âme, XVIe–XVIIIe siècle*, Paris: Champion.

Vollrath, Ernst. 1961. Die Gliederung der Metaphysik in eine metaphysica specialis und eine metaphysica generalis, *Zeitschrift für philosophische Forschung* 16(2):258–84.

Walch, Johannes Georg. 1730. *Introductio in philosophiam*. Leipzig, Germany: J.F. Gleditsch.

Walker, Obadiah. 1673. *Artis rationis maxime ad mentem Nominalium libri tres*. Oxford: Sheldon.

Wardy, Robert. 2000. *Aristotle in China: Language, Categories and Translation*. Cambridge: Cambridge University Press.

Wels, Henrik. 2007. 'Die Unsterblichkeit der Seele und der epistemologische Status der Psychologie im Aristotelismus des 16. Jahrhundert'. In Frank and Speer, 2007, 191–214.

Wundt, Max. 1939. *Die deutsche Schulmetaphysik des 17. Jahrhunderts*. Tübingen, Germany: Mohr.

Yolton, John W. 1984. *Perceptual Acquaintance from Descartes to Reid*. Minneapolis: University of Minnesota Press.

———. 1986. 'Schoolmen, Logic and Philosophy'. In *The History of the University of Oxford*, vol. V: *The Eighteenth Century*, ed. L. S. Sutherland and L. G. Mitchel, 565–90. Oxford: Oxford University Press.

PART II

Issues in Medieval Philosophy

Logic and Philosophy
of Language

CHAPTER 12

....

LOGICAL FORM

....

PAUL THOM

'MEDIEVAL logic cannot have been very formal. Its content is not very similar to that of modern formal logic; at best it can only be considered a remote ancestor of the discipline that is practised by logicians today.' This perception is shared by historians of medieval thought and modern logicians alike. On the one hand, if we look honestly at the texts, we find there none of the apparatus of modern mathematical logic—no artificial symbolic languages, no formal semantics. On the other hand, the relation between medieval and modern logic might be compared to that between an outdated scientific theory such as the theory of the four humours and its modern counterpart.

It is true that much of medieval logic is not formal in anything like the sense in which modern logic is formal. Medieval logic is not a single thing. It spreads out over a thousand years, and its content, always multifarious, alters greatly over that time span. Thus, rather than talking in an undifferentiated way about medieval logic, it is better to talk about medieval logics as advanced by individual logicians. The variety displayed by these logics is considerable. Some give only a rudimentary coverage of Aristotle's *Categories* and *Peri Hermeneias*, others comment in depth on the entire *Organon* (including, in the Arabic-speaking world, the *Rhetoric* and *Poetics*), and yet others offer specialised treatments of logical disciplines unknown to Aristotle, such as the theories of *suppositio*, *consequentia* and *obligatio*. Among this wealth of material, some seems to us not to be logic at all. Other parts (for example, the material related to Aristotle's *Categories*) may seem to us to be close to logic but to belong, properly speaking, to metaphysics. Some of the traditional books (the *Topics* and *Sophistical Refutations*) seem to be informal rather than formal logic.

That medieval logics should be partly non-formal is a necessary consequence of the fact that for much of the time their central concern was with the theory of argumentation. The theory of argumentation is more specific than the theory of consequences, since the conditions on good argumentation are more numerous than those on a good consequence. Now, it can be argued that some of these extra conditions can be given a formal representation.[1] But not all of them can, and these non-formal conditions of good argumentation (including conditions specific to rhetorical, dialectical or demonstrative argumentation, and the avoidance of fallacy) were much studied in the Middle Ages.

All the same, at least some aspects of what constitutes good argumentation were seen as deriving from formal considerations. These aspects were treated by the medievals as falling under a concept of logical form, but there were at least two notions of logical form. In one sense, form is contrasted with matter in the context of Aristotelian hylomorphic theory. In another sense, form contrasts with matter, not in the sense of that from which a thing is generated (*id ex quo*) but that which it is about (*id de quo*). In this second sense, the matter that is opposed to form is *subject matter*, or content (in a broad sense that includes both subject and predicate). Both these notions of form can be traced back to Aristotle, the hylomorphic concept to his physical and metaphysical works, the notion of form as opposed to content to some of his logical works.

1. Hylomorphic Conceptions

Some medieval logicians thought that the form of a proposition or an argument could be understood through concepts of matter and form that they found in Aristotle's *Physics* and *Metaphysics*. When, in answer to the question 'What does the copula signify?', the fourteenth-century master John Buridan (d. c. 1358) applies the matter/form distinction to mental propositions, he explicitly takes this distinction in a hylomorphic sense. The subject and predicate are the matter of the mental proposition, and its form is an affirmative or negative structuring concept [*conceptus complexiuus*], which the mind adds to that matter. These structuring concepts are signified by the verbs 'is' and 'is not'. Buridan compares the process whereby a mental proposition is generated by adding a complexive concept to a pair of simple concepts, to the process whereby a physical thing is generated by the addition of a substantial form to pre-existing matter. As is the case with physical things, the form of a mental proposition cannot exist in the absence of all matter.[2]

According to the hylomorphic concept of form, a subject can acquire a form. Indeed, it is the concept of form and its correlative concept of matter that Aristotle invokes in the *Physics* to explain the very possibility of change. So we must assume that Buridan thinks that the subject and predicate of a mental proposition acquire a propositional form at the moment when the mind relates them in a predicative structure.

About a hundred years before Buridan, Robert Kilwardby (d. 1279) had adopted a hylomorphic view of the form of a syllogism. Commenting on *Prior Analytics*, Book I, Chapter 32, Kilwardby uses the expression 'to-be-syllogised' (*syllogizanda*) to describe inferences prior to their reduction to syllogistic form, and the expression 'syllogised' (*syllogizata*) to describe them after that reduction.[3] The reduction itself therefore marks the imposition of form on relatively unformed material (just as Aristotle had thought of form in the *Physics*). Kilwardby shows that this is a temporal process when he notes that in reality [*secundum rem*] the yet-to-be-syllogised precedes the syllogised. Thus, his conception of syllogistic form differs from the modern notion of logical form, in that he thinks of it as a state that is acquired through a temporal process.

Kilwardby holds that a given syllogism is characterised by *two* forms, corresponding, respectively, to its Figure and its Mood. This leads him to the view that, in the process of acquiring its full form, a syllogism may be incompletely formed, and this is a second way in which his conception of logical form differs from modern notions. Kilwardby's doctrine of the plurality of forms (and matters) for the syllogism is a special case of a doctrine of the plurality of forms, which he applied more generally. Indeed, the proposition that there is just a single substantial form of Man was one of those that Kilwardby condemned in 1277.

Kilwardby views the terms and premises of a syllogism as its matter—the premises being the proximate, arranged, completing or ultimate matter, while the terms are the remote, unarranged, incomplete matter in potentiality. Corresponding to these, he sees the mood and figure as the syllogism's form—the mood being the proximate form whereby the premises are organised according to their quality and quantity, the figure being the remote form that organised the terms according to the position of the middle term in the two premises.[4] His application of the matter/form dichotomy to the syllogism is summarised in Table 12.1.

The expressions 'incomplete' and 'completing' make it clear that in his view the proximate and completing form pre-supposes the remote and incomplete form, so that an argument possessing the completing form must also possess the incomplete form. But the converse is not true. Kilwardby believes that an argument can possess an incomplete form without possessing a corresponding completing form. He states in general that 'two propositions, made with three terms, necessarily determine a Figure through the placing of the terms, but don't necessarily determine a mood'.[5] He gives two examples. First, commenting on the Aristotelian rule that a syllogism must have a universal premise, he states that a third Figure inference from two singular premises is incompletely formed because it is not 'competently related and arranged according to mood'.[6] Such inferences may be valid and may be in the third

Table 12.1. Robert Kilwardby's Classification of Syllogistic Matter and Form

	Matter	Form
Proximate / arranged / completing / ultimate	Premises	Mood
Remote / unarranged / incomplete / in potentiality	Terms	Figure

Figure, but he denies that they are syllogisms properly arranged in a Mood. Kilward-by's approach to singular propositions is complex. He says that a singular proposi-tion 'is nothing but a contracted particular [*particulare contractum*]',[7] and he treats the conversion of singular propositions, insofar as it falls under the syllogistic art, as being included under that of particulars.[8] But he doesn't treat singulars as particu-lars in the third Figure syllogism under consideration: to do so would be to regard that syllogism as invalid. It seems, then, that in some contexts singular propositions fall within the scope of the categorical syllogism, and in other contexts they fall outside its scope. Kilwardby's second example of a partly formed argument con-cerns arguments containing prosleptic propositions, such as Aristotle's inference (*Prior Analytics* B5, 58a26–32).

A is in none of C   What A is in none of, B is in all of

                  B is in all of C

Figure 12.1. Prosleptic syllogism.

Kilwardby says that this seems not to be a syllogism since it appears to conflict with the two principles governing first Figure syllogisms, namely that the Major must be universal and that the Minor must be affirmative. His answer is that this inference is in the first Figure but is not in any Mood. In fact he thinks it should be construed as a hypothetical syllogism along the following lines:

A is in none of C   If A is in none of C then B is in all of C

                  B is in all of C

Figure 12.2. Kilwardby's analysis of the prosleptic syllogism.

This syllogism he takes to be in the first Figure, but not in any Mood.[9]

On modern accounts, it is possible to separate an argument's form from all matter so that we have a pure form devoid of matter. But on a hylomorphic concep-tion of form, the complete separation of form from all matter is impossible. In a syllogistic form, there is still matter—what Kilwardby calls transcendental matter, in the shape of the schematic letters. In the *De Ortu Scientiarum*, he notes that syllogistic form, while abstract, doesn't abstract from *all* matter (because that can't be done) but possesses 'intelligible matter', just as in mathematics, and this matter consists of 'three terms, two extremes and a middle, from which two propositions are connected'.[10]

Kilwardby's application of the notion of form to the syllogism is part of a com-prehensive application of the Aristotelian doctrine of the four causes to the subject matter of logic. Thus, for example, he sees the syllogism's final cause as being to show something about something.[11] Henrik Lagerlund reminds us that the idea of applying Aristotle's physical/metaphysical notions of cause to the syllogism is also found, before Kilwardby, in al-Ghazali, who compares the syllogism with a coin:

> The matter of the coin is the gold it is made of and its form is its roundness. If the form is destroyed or falsified in some way, we will not call it a coin anymore. Sometimes the matter of the coin is also changed, that is, a coin, he notes, might be made from iron or silver. It is then not worth as much, but it is still a coin.[12]

By implication, a syllogism whose form is deficient is not a syllogism, but one that is deficient in matter is still a syllogism, though a defective one. Kilwardby offers a qualified defence of this position. He considers the opposing view that a syllogism from false premises is not a syllogism, since it is deficient in matter. In his *Prior Analytics* commentary, he solves the puzzle by distinguishing the matter of the syllogism *simpliciter* from the matter of various special syllogisms, such as the ostensive syllogism.[13] And in his *De Ortu Scientiarum*, he states that a syllogism from false premises doesn't offend against the syllogism *simpliciter*, but against demonstration (which has to have true premises).[14]

2. Modern Conceptions

The hylomorphic notion of form is quite foreign to modern logics, where the concern is not with the coming into being of the propositions and arguments. On the contrary, propositions and arguments, as they are studied by modern logics, are generally assumed to be timeless entities, so the question of their coming into being does not arise. Modern logics, however, do need a concept of form that is opposed to content, precisely so that they can ignore the content of propositions and arguments.

Such a concept of propositional and argument form is taught very early on in modern logic courses. And often enough, it is just such a concept that a reader finds when for the first time opening the pages of a medieval logic text. The sense of recognition experienced by such a reader points to a significant element of continuity between medieval and modern logic.

Some modern writers explain logical form by reference to something with blanks or gaps in it,[15] like a school report form.[16] Such a thing can exist before it is filled in with specific content. According to this modern conception, the form of a categorical proposition is not (as Buridan would have it) something signified by a copula but is a 'propositional framework expressed by the formula "S is P"'.[17] Form in this sense is sometimes contrasted with matter; however, the proper antonym of 'form' in this sense is 'content'. Insofar as logical form in the modern sense is contrasted with matter, it is matter in the sense of *subject* matter, not the matter from which something comes into existence. The subject matter of the school report is Johnny's academic performance; the matter from which it is generated is a tree.[18]

A concept of propositional form as opposed to content can already be seen in the *Peri Hermeneias* account of the relations of contradiction, contrariety and subalternation. These relations—all of them definable in terms of a relation of logical consequence—are portrayed in that text as holding among propositions by virtue of the form that propositions have, as specified by their quantity, quality and modality. This concept of propositional form became part of the stock-in-trade of the medievals. It is susceptible of formalisation in several different ways.[19]

Also in Aristotle is a concept of syllogistic form as opposed to content. John Corcoran argues that there is a distinction between Aristotle's general theory of deduction and his special theory of the categorical syllogism.[20] The distinction manifests itself, inter alia, in the fact that Aristotle's general definition of deduction (*sullogismos*) requires that a deduction exhibit necessity but does not require that it hold by virtue of its form,[21] whereas the special theory of the categorical syllogism is presented as a formal theory in which the validity of an inference is shown by its form.

This is clear from the way he presents his theory of the syllogism. By expressing syllogistic laws in schematic letters that function as placeholders for an indefinite array of concrete terms, he shows that he understands these laws as holding irrespective of specific content. And by formulating counter-examples to pseudo-laws, he shows that he knows that a single instance where the putative law fails to hold is sufficient to demolish its claim to formal status. But there is no *explicit* definition of logical form in Aristotle. That would only come with the medievals.

An explicit formulation of a concept of logical form can be found in Abelard's distinction between perfect and imperfect inferences. A perfect inference is one where the truth of consequent is clear from the structure of the antecedent (*ex ipsius antecedentis complexione*) because the construction of the antecedent is arranged in such a way as to contain the construction of the consequent—as happens in syllogisms.[22] An imperfect inference lacks this kind of structural integrity, even if it is necessary—as is the inference 'If every man is an animal, every man is animate' or the inference 'If every man is an animal, no man is a stone'.[23] Our knowledge of imperfect inferences comes from our knowledge of the *things* that the inference is about (men, animals and stones in the above examples), not just our knowledge of the inference's structure.[24] But knowledge of a perfect inference depends on no such knowledge since the inference holds for all terms similarly arranged, whether the premises relating them are true of false.[25] Imperfect inferences, by contrast, do not hold for all terms similarly arranged: if we replace 'man' by 'stone' in 'If it's a man it's an animal', the resulting inference is false. Perfect inferences don't depend on the nature of things, and their structure (*complexio*) preserves a necessary consequence equally in all things, no matter how they are related.[26]

Abelard is here articulating what Catarina Dutilh Novaes calls a 'variational' concept of logical form, according to which form is invariant with respect to variations in content.[27] Abelard seems to identify inferences whose validity is formal in this sense with those whose validity flows from their structure. His account aligns three concepts: structure [*complexio*], invariance over content, and syllogistic form.[28] These alignments seem reasonable. To pair the concept of structure with that of invariance over varied content seems no more than to embrace a concept of form defined by invariance over varied content. And to align this concept with that of syllogistic form, while not reasonable from a modern standpoint, is perfectly understandable from the perspective of a logical theory that places the syllogism at the centre of inferential theory. (Abelard has a relatively fixed idea of what must be taken as invariant in logical form and what may be varied, but in some modern logics this fixity is relaxed so that any element at all in a proposition can be regarded as variable.)

Kilwardby, alongside his hylomorphic concept of form, also employs a variational concept. In discussing the sophism 'All bronze is natural, every statue is bronze, so every statue is natural', he states that we must say that either the conclusion is true (albeit per accidens) or else that the first premise is false. We must never say that this inference is invalid. Its syllogistic form (which is in the most general matter, abstracting from what is probable or necessary or apparent) is good because its necessity is merely structural (*complexionalis tantum*).[29] Like Abelard, he aligns structural validity with syllogistic form. He knew that the hylomorphic form of the syllogism was also a structural form that would hold for all possible content. But unlike Abelard, he explicitly rejected the converse of this principle, by drawing attention to the fact that some inferences that hold for all possible content are not syllogistic.

In the course of his analysis of modal syllogisms, he mentions that there are valid inferences having a Figure and Mood but not satisfying Aristotle's requirement that syllogisms in the second figure must have a negative premise. For convenience let's call these 'non-Aristotelian syllogisms'. One of them takes the following form:

It's contingent that no C is A   It's necessary that all B is A
———
It's possible that no C is B

Figure 12.3. Camestres LQM.

The inference has no negative premise. Obviously the necessity premise is affirmative. But so is the contingency premise according to Aristotle, who holds that all contingency propositions are affirmative.[30] The validity of Camestres LQM can be shown *per impossibile*: Suppose it's not possible that no C is B. Then it's necessary that some C is B. But we have as a premise that it's necessary that all B is A. Therefore, by a perfect first figure syllogism, it follows that it's necessary that some C is A:

It's necessary that some C is B   It's necessary that all B is A
———
It's necessary that some C is A

Figure 12.4. Darii LLL.

But we supposed that it was contingent that no C is A, so it can't be necessary that some C is A. Kilwardby therefore recognises that Camestres LQM and a number of other non-Aristotelian syllogisms are valid in the sense that they hold for all content and no counter-example can be found in which the premises are true and the conclusion false; but he denies them the status of Aristotelian syllogisms because they lack 'the property of the second figure', namely, to have a negative premise.[31]

The inferences identified by Kilwardby do indeed have characteristics that set them apart from Aristotelian syllogisms.[32] In recognising this distinction, Kilwardby makes an advance on Abelard's contrast by loosening the association between two of the concepts that Abelard had aligned—syllogistic form and the variational notion of formal validity. At the same time, Kilwardby's own *description* of these inferences reads strangely. Taking up Abelardian terminology, he says that the inferences hold by virtue of a relationship among the things (*sequitur secundum habitudinem et consequentiam rerum*), not by virtue of syllogistic form (*ex formam syllogizandi*). Having distinguished those syllogisms that are approved by Aristotle from those that are not, he reserves the concept of syllogistic form for the former and then (confusingly) subsumes the latter under Abelard's concept of inferences that hold by virtue of the consequences of the things, while also treating them as variationally valid.

3. VARIATIONAL CONCEPTIONS

The variational concept of logical consequence—which has also come to be known as the 'Continental' concept—was given a definitive formulation by John Buridan:

> A consequence may be said to be formal when it is valid for all terms (a similar form being retained). Or if you want to speak expressly about the force of the words, a consequence is formal when any proposition that is formally like it would be a good consequence were it to be formed, e.g. 'What is A is B, so what is B is A'.[33]

Catarina Dutilh Novaes argues that the modern notion of formal validity is, in fact, a hybrid that combines his modal notion of validity (as the impossibility of the consequent being false while the antecedent is true) with the substitutional notion of the truth of all instances of a given form.[34] In the terminology of John Etchemendy, these are two different conceptions of validity—the former being a representational one, the latter interpretational.[35] Etchemendy's distinction can be brought to bear on the duality we saw in Aristotle's treatment of deduction, where a general conception of a deduction as modal (representational) is contrasted with a specific conception of syllogistic deduction as both modal and formal (interpretational).

A variant of the variational conception of formal validity combines elements of this conception with the hylomorphic approach. It is found in what some scholars call the 'British' tradition of thinking about formal consequences. The opposition between the formal and what holds solely because of the terms is given a new twist by William Ockham (d. 1347). For him, a formal consequence is one that can be validated by a proposition that either does or does not contain the terms that occur in the consequence, whereas a material consequence cannot be validated in any such way but holds solely because of the terms that occur in it. In the case of formal consequences whose validating proposition contains terms that occur in the validated consequence, Ockham says there is an 'intrinsic middle'; where the validating proposition contains terms that do not occur to the validated consequence, he says there is an 'extrinsic middle'. Syllogisms are formal by virtue of extrinsic middles, and to this extent his notion of a formal consequence owes something to the variational conception of form. The inference 'A man is running, so an animal is running' is formal by virtue of an intrinsic middle, and to this extent Ockham's formal validity is not consistent with the variational conception. Ockham takes the inference of a necessary consequent from an arbitrary antecedent to be a material consequence.[36]

A similar distinction (but without the apparatus of internal and external middles) can be found in the *De Puritate Artis Logicae Tractatus Longior* of Walter Burleigh (d. 1344):

> It is to be said that there are two types of formal consequence. There are some that hold by reason of the form of the whole structure (and to this type belong conversion, and the syllogism, and other consequences that hold by reason of the whole structure). And some formal consequences hold by reason of the form of things that are unstructured (e.g. in the way that a consequence from an inferior to a superior by way of affirmation is formal, and yet it holds by reason of the terms). Hence, there are two ways in which a consequence can hold by reason of the terms—either because it holds materially by reason of the terms, or because it holds formally by reason of the terms (i.e. from the formal account of the terms). I say then that a consequence can be formal by reason of the terms (and this is if it holds *per se* by reason of the terms). If however it holds by reason of the terms *per accidens* then it is not formal.[37]

Here he combines consideration of form as opposed to content, with consideration of a thing's defining form as exhibited by its superiors in a category tree. The latter depends on hylomorphic considerations, albeit ones that concern the forms of the things that the inference is about, rather than the form of the syllogism (as with the use of hylomorphism in Kilwardby's logical theory). As a consequence, Burleigh's notion of logical form seems to be lacking in conceptual homogeneity.

Such a combined conception of a formal consequence is found again in the later *Consequentiae* of Ralph Strode (d. 1387). Here, a formal consequence is one whose consequent is *de formali intellectu* of the antecedent:

> A consequence is said to be formally valid when it is such that if <things> are understood to be as is adequately signified by the antecedent, they are understood as is adequately signified by the consequent. For if someone understands that you are a man they understand that you are an animal. And so in such a consequence the consequent is said to be of the formal understanding of the antecedent.[38]

The inference from an inferior to its superior is thus given as the paradigm example of a formally valid consequence. But Strode's concept of a formal consequence also makes use of the variational (Continental) account:

> For a consequence is called formal when every similar one (i.e. in which individual terms stand in entirely the same relations to one another) is said to be formally valid.[39]

In summary, we can say that of the two main conceptions of logical form that were given explicit expression by medieval logicians, the conception of the hylomorphic form of a proposition or a syllogism is metaphysical rather than purely logical, even if it implicitly contains the variational concept. The variational conception most closely matches modern conceptions of logical consequence. The British conception of formal validity is heterogeneous.

4. FORM AND FORMALISATION

One indicator of the degree to which medieval logicians were concerned with formality is evident in the extent to which they were concerned to show that what appears not to be formal is implicitly governed by formal considerations. This concern is evident in what they say about the applicability of formal theories to informal material. The application of a theory of logical form to unformed material can be considered as a kind of formalisation of that material. The programme of demonstrating the applicability of logical theory to informal material is one that Aristotle had started in the section of the *Prior Analytics* starting at I.32, where he shows that his formal theory of the syllogism can be applied to ordinary language reasoning on whose surface there are no marks of universality and particularity, or of figure and mood. Indeed the name 'analytics' derives from the practice of putting unformed linguistic material into the forms that the *Analytics* recognises.

Formal analysis may be applied not only to the everyday propositions and arguments that constitute the principal subject matter of logic, but also to the arguments that logicians themselves use. Aristotle had not shown much interest in this sort of self-reflexive analysis. For example, when he presented Cesare ('If M belongs to no N and M belongs to all X, then N belongs to no X'), he argued that it is reducible to Celarent ('If N belongs to no M and M belongs to all X, then N belongs to no X'):

> For let M be predicated of no N and of all X. Now since the privative premiss converts, N will belong to no M; but it was assumed that M belongs to all X, so that N will belong to no X—this was proved before.[40]

But his argument to the effect that the validity of Celarent implies that of Cesare is not a formal one. Ebert and Nortmann point out that Aristotle's argument rests on an application of a principle that is not explicitly stated,[41] namely:

> From the validity of a syllogistic mood it is permitted to generate the validity of further syllogistic moods by strengthening the premises or weakening the conclusion.[42]

Only when some such principle is made explicit do we have a formal deduction of the validity of Cesare from that of Celarent.[43] Now, there is no doubt that Aristotle implicitly accepted such a principle. However, because he does not include it in his reduction of Cesare to Celarent, we cannot say that his reduction is presented as a formal deduction. In general, we may observe that if a body of logical insights is presented as a theory, the deductive links binding its elements together may or not be presented as holding formally. If the deductive links between different elements in the theory are presented as holding formally—if their formal connectedness is displayed—then the body of insights is presented as *formal* theory. This is what Aristotle did *not* do in showing that Cesare reduces to Celarent.

It is also what the medievals did not do, most of the time. Granted, it is not uncommon for medieval authors when arguing for a point of logical theory to present the argument in a formal manner, even citing the formal principle on which it relies—'from the first to the last', or 'by the second [mood] of the second [figure]', or 'by the destruction of the consequent' and so forth. Much less common is the presentation of a whole body of logical theory as formally valid deductions.

Walter Burleigh clearly had such a project in mind in presenting his theory of consequences in his *De Puritate Artis Logicae Tractatus Longior*. He there presents a theory of consequences based on five principal rules with corollaries derived from them. Catarina Dutilh Novaes shows how Burleigh derives some of these corollaries from the principal rules in formally valid deductions. For example, from the principal rule 'What follows from the consequent follows from the antecedent', together with the rule 'Every proposition implies itself together with its consequent', he deduces the corollary that what follows from a consequent together with its antecedent follows from the antecedent by itself.[44] This is indeed a beautiful example of logical procedures being rigorously applied to the presentation of a logical theory. However, Burleigh's execution of his project is not without flaws. The deductions he uses in deriving the corollaries are not always formally valid. Here, for example, is his first principal rule:

> In every valid simple consequence (where a 'simple' consequence is contrasted with an *ut nunc* consequence) the antecedent can never be true without the consequent.[45]

And here is his deduction of the first corollary of the first rule:

> The first is that the impossible does not follow from the contingent in a simple consequence. . . . And the reason . . . is that the contingent can be true without the impossible . . . And because of this, the impossible does not follow from the contingent. . . .[46]

The deduction is not formal. In order to be formal, it would have to include an explicit statement of the first rule, and it does not do this (because it's obvious in the context). An interest in presenting logical theory in the form of deductions that are themselves formally valid is therefore not characteristic of the medieval period, as it is of the modern. This is one way in which we would have to say that medieval logics are generally not very formal at all when compared to modern logics.

In other respects, however, there is a high degree of formality in many medieval logics. Apart from the accounts of propositional and inferential form already cited, one could mention medieval theories of supposition and of *obligationes*, which have been argued to be implicitly formal, to the extent that they can readily be rendered in modern formal terms with a minimum of modern formal apparatus.[47] But, even when it is reasonable to speak of understandings of formality being shared between us and the medievals, it remains true that medieval logic never became self-consciously formal in the modern manner.

It is also worth remarking that our question about the formality of medieval logic cannot be properly considered without taking into account the point in time from which it is posed. There was a time when modality was thought to belong to the matter, not the form of propositions and arguments; then logicians became aware, once again, that there could be a formal logic of modality. There was a time when logicians were not aware of the possibility of a formal logic of tenses; then A. N. Prior demonstrated this possibility—or rather, reminded the intellectual world of it, and of the fact that the medievals knew about it. So, if we wish to consider medieval logics in relation to modern conceptions of formality, we need to be careful about which modern conceptions we are talking about because they change over time. Indeed, we cannot rule out the possibility that there are parts of medieval logic not presently considered formal that may come to be regarded as formal in the future, as a result of further developments in our modern logic—developments of which we have as yet no inkling.[48]

NOTES

1. See Thom (2010).

2. *Summulae de Dialectica* I.3.2; (John Buridan 2001, 24). See Maierù (2004, 41–42): 'Ad primum dubitationem dicendum est quod propositio uocalis debet significare mentalem propositionem, sicut ante dictum est, propositio autem mentalis consistit in complexione conceptuum; ideo presupponit conceptus simplices in mente et super hos addit conceptum complexiuum, quo intellectus affirmat uel negat unum istorum conceptuum de reliquo. Illi ergo conceptus presuppositi sunt subiectum et predicatum in propositione mentali, et vocantur materia propositionis mentalis, quia presupponuntur formationi propositionis, sicud materia in generatione substantiali presupponitur formae; ille autem conceptus complexiuus dicitur copula et tanquam formale in propositione mentali. Et tunc apparet quod subiectum et predicatum propositionis vocalis significant in mente predicatum et subiectum mentalis; hec autem copula "est" significat conceptum complexiuum affirmati- uam, et hec copula "non est" significat conceptum complexiuum negatiuum. Et intellectus non potest formare illum conceptum complexiuum nisi formatis illis que sunt subiectum et predicatum, quia non est possibilis complexio predicati ad subiectum sine predicato et subiecto'.

3. *Notule libri Priorum* A32–3 *dub.*2, in Robert Kilwardby (1516/1968, henceforth *Notule*, f. 44rb): 'Sed tunc dubitatur, potentia enim est ante actum, quare oratio syllogiçan- da prior est quam oratio actu syllogiçata, quare cum hic determinet reductionem orationis syllogiçande, superius autem determinavit reductionem orationis syllogiçate. Patet quod non bene procedit, debet enim hec reduction precedere illam que in precedentibus determinata est. . . .

Et dicendum at primam quod si oratio que solum in potentia syllogiçata est debeat in formam syllogisticam reduci, necesse est illam formam syllogisticam prius cognosci. Sed illa non cogniscitur nisi per syllogismorum generationem, quare oportet precognoscere syllogismorum generationem si debeat fieri reductio orationis inordinate ad syllogismum. Sed generationi syllogismorum connexa est duplex reductio, scilicet que est aliarum figurarum in primam, et que est omnium syllogismorum aliorum in universales prime, sicut patet ex predictis. Quare ante istam reductionem que fit hic, necesse fuit illam duplicem reductionem prius determinare. Quamvis ergo secundum rem precedat oratione syllogiçanda orationem syllogiçatam, tamen necessitas ipsius artis exigit prius determinari reductionem orationis syllogiçate quam syllogiçande'.

4. *Notule* A4 Part 2 dub.4, f.10va: 'Sed tunc dubitatur quomodo hoc sit cum unius rei una sit forma et non multe.

Et dicendum quod sicut ordo est in materiis (quidam enim est remota et indisposita, quidam autem propinqua et disposita), sic est in formis. Quidam est forma materialis et in potentia ad formam ulteriorem, quidam autem est ultima et completiva. Et sic invenimus in syllogismo ordinem in materia et formi: in materiis quia termini est materia eius remota et indisposita, propositio vero est materia propinqua et disposita, in formis etiam quia figura est forma incompleta et in potentia ad ulteriorem formam, modus autem est forma ultima syllogismi completiva, et respondet incompletum in formis incompleto in materiis, scilicet figura termino, et completum in formis completo in materiis ut modum propositioni'.

5. *Notule* A28 Part 2 dub.2, f.40vb: 'Consequenter queritur cum duplex sit dispositio formalis in syllogismo, scilicet modus et figura, et sunt inutiles inspectiones contra modum, quare non sunt alie inutiles peccantes contra figuram.
Et dicendum quod hoc est quia due propositiones facte in tribus terminis per situm terminorum ex necessitate determinant figuram sed non ex necessitate determinant modum; et si abesset figura non esset dispositio ad syllogismum, et ideo quantum ad figuram nulla inspectio'.

6. *Notule libri* A24 dub.2, f.35va–b: 'Consequenter forte dubitabit de sua probatione, videtur enim opposita dicet. Intendit enim probare quod sine universali non fit syllogis-mus. In sua autem probatione supponit quod sine universali possit esse syllogismus, sed non ad propositum, et ita supponit opposita probanda.

Et dicendum quod non est intentio Aristotelis quod sine universali nullo modo fit syllogismus, quia ex singularibus in tertia figura concludit necessario, sed quod syllogis-mus competenter se habens et secundum modum dispositus non fiat sine universalibus'.

7. *Notule* A1 Part 2 *dub*.6, f.4rb.

8. *Notule* A2 *dub*.6, f.6ra.

9. *Notule* B5 *dub*.9, f.61va: 'Et dicendum quod iste syllogismus est in prima figura non tamen in aliquo modo quia non insunt per virtutem quod est dici de omni et de nullo sed per virtutem maioris propositionis in qua implicatur talis causa ut uno remoto ab alio eidem insit reliquum et habet illa maior quasi virtutem conditionalis. Unde totus syllogis-mus hypotheticus est inferens a positione antecedentis.

. . . nec est etiam inconveniens inferre per syllogismum hypotheticum a positione antecedentis ex minore negativa quia negatio non cadit super totum medium immo quasi eius pars est nec etiam est inconveniens sic inferre affirmativam ex negativam'.

10. *De Ortu Scientiarum* §501, in Robert Kilwardby (1976): 'Nota tamen quod non ita abstrahitur haec forma quod determinetur de ipsa sine omnimoda materia, quia hoc esse non posset. Sed sicut mathematica abstrahuntur a materia physica tantum et nihilominus ipsa habent suam materiam intelligibilem, ut in praecedentibus ostendimus, sic forma

syllogistica et omnino ratiocinativa abstrahitur a materia communi et propria, id est probabili et necessaria. Habet tamen secum quandam materiam simpliciorem quae est intra
utramque dictam, scilicet tres terminos, duo extrema et medium unum ex quibus connec-
tuntur duae propositiones'.

11. *Notule* A23 *dub.*1, f.34vb. 'Causa enim finalis syllogismi est ostendere aliquid de
aliquo'.

12. Lagerlund (2008, 292–3); Lohr, 1965. 'Maniera quarta (495–505). Materia
syllogismi sunt propositiones. Quae si fuerint credibiles et verae, erunt conclusiones
credibiles et verae. Si vero fuerint falsae, non concludentur credibiles. Si autem fuerint
opinabiles, non concludentur verae. Sicut enim aurum est materia nummi et rotunditas
forma eius, sed falsificatur nummus aliquando inflexione formae vel privatione rotundi-
tatis, eo quod sit obliqua—et tunc non vocabitur nummus; aliquando vitio materiae,
scilicet cum fuerit ex ferro vel aere. Similiter, syllogismus est vitiosus aliquando vitio
formae, scilicet cum non fuerit secundum aliquam figurarum praemissarum; aliquando
vitio materiae, quamvis forma sit recta, scilicet cum propositio fuerit opinabilis vel
falsidica'.

13. *Notule* B2 Part 2 dub.2, f.57rb: 'Ad dictorum evidentiam consequens est questio
utrum syllogismus ex falsis sit syllogismus vel non. Et hoc est utrum inferat ex necessitate.
Et primo videtur quod non sic. Syllogismus cum sit quodam compositum debetur compositio a materia et forma, quarum si deficiat altera non syllogismus erit. Si ergo peccat in
materia syllogismi non erit syllogismus. Sed dicitur quod syllogismus ex falsis peccat in
materia, ex hoc est verum, quare non est syllogismus.

Ad primum autem obiectionem dicendum quod syllogismo simpliciter sunt principia
materialia que sunt due propositiones et si hic sit defectus non erit syllogismus, syllogismi
autem ostensivi sunt due propositiones vere. Quamvis ergo syllogismus ex falsis deficiat in
materia non deficit in materia syllogismi simpliciter sed in materia syllogismi ostensivi. Et
immo quamvis ex falsis sit, non tamen sequitur quod non sit syllogismus, sed quod non
ostensivus simpliciter'.

14. *De Ortu Scientiarum* §509, in Robert Kilwardby (1976): ' . . . ex utraque vel altera
praemissa falsa concludit, sed ex propriis et in propriis terminis ratiocinatur et concludit ex
necessitate, quia non peccat contra formam syllogisticam, sed contra rationem demonstrationis, quae debet esse semper ex veris'.

15. Faris (1962, 5).

16. Mitchell (1962, 12–13).

17. Mitchell (1962, 15).

18. Mitchell (1962): 'What in propositions is formal and what material may most
readily be distinguished if we consider examples' (14); 'the inconsistency of the two
propositions is to be explained by reference not to their content but to their forms' (15).

19. See, for example, Parsons (2008, 158–64); Kilma (2008, 427–31).

20. Corcoran (2009, 2).

21. Parsons (2008, 173).

22. *Dialectica*, in Peter Abelard (1956), henceforth *Dial.*, 253:31–254:1: 'Haec autem
inferentia alias perfecta est, alias imperfecta. Perfecta quidem est inferentia, cum ex ipsius
antecedentis complexione consequentis veritas manifesta est et antecedentis constructio ita
est disposita, ut in se consequentis quoque constructionem contineat, veluti in syllogismis
aut in his hypotheticis quae formas habent syllogismorum'.

23. *Dial.*, 255:1–6.

24. *Dial.*, 255:13–17.

25. *Dial.*, 255:31–37.

26. *Dial.*: 'Istae ergo consequentiae recte ex natura rerum verae dicuntur quarum veritas una cum rerum natura variatur; illae vero veritatem ex complexione, non ex rerum natura, tenent quarum complexio necessitatem in quibuslibet rebus, cuiuscumque sint habitudinis, aeque custodit, sicut in syllogismo vel in consequentiis quae formas eorum tenent, ostenditur'.

27. Dutilh Novaes (2007, 228–30).

28. Martin (1986, 566). See also Kneale and Kneale (1962, 216) and Wilks (2008, 126).

29. *Notule* A4 *dub*.6, f.10va–b: 'omne es est naturale, omnis statua est es, sit ita, et tamen nulla statua est naturalis. Et dicendum quod instancia nulla est. Hic enim determinatur forma syllogistica in communissima materia que abstrahit a materia probabili et necessaria et apparenti. Unde forma hic determinata non tantum inueniri potest in dialeticis et demonstratiuis sed etiam in sophisticis. Unde dicendum quod sequitur conclusio, scilicet "Omnis statua est naturalis", secundum artificem huius libri, uel si non, neganda est prima secundum ipsam. Forma enim bona est secundum ipsam et non excluditur a forma syllogistica hic determinata. Et ad evidenciam huius sciendum quod duplex est syllogismus, scilicet ille cuius necessitas est localis, ut ex maiore uel minore necessario sequitur conclusio, et talis est syllogismus dialecticus uel demonstratiuus. Alius est cuius necessitas est complexionalis tantum, hoc est tanta ex debita complexione terminorum ad inuicem et propositionum, et talis communis est syllogismo dialectico, demonstratiuo et sophistico; et talis syllogismi necessitas et forma hic determinatur. Artifex ergo libri *Priorum* abstrahit syllogismum, et similiter esse predicatum in propositionibus syllogisticis. Unde abstrahit illud esse ab esse per se et per accidens et ita concedit predicationes accidentales. Unde cum sic arguitur, "Omne es est naturale, omnis statua est es", diceret uel quod conclusio est uera, quamuis per accidens, uel quod prima est falsa, quamuis per accidens. Numquam autem formam argumentandi negaret.'

30. *Notule* A3 Part 2, 25b19, f.7vb: 'Similiter se habet "esse" in propositionibus de inesse et "contingere" in illis de contingenti. Sed "esse" affirmato in propositionibus de inesse semper fit affirmatio. Ergo "contingere" affirmato in propositionibus de contingenti erit in illis affirmatio, et ita cum in propositionibus de contingenti prius habitis affirmetur "contingere", patet quod ipse secundum formam et speciem affirmatiue sunt.'

31. *Notule* A19 *dub*.10, f.31ra–b: 'Uidetur enim quod maiore existente affirmatiua de necessario sit utilis coniugatio, respectu conclusionis negatiua de contingenti pro possibili. . . . sic: de necessitate omne B est A, contingit nullum C esse A, ergo contingit nullum C esse B. Si non sequitur detur oppositum, scilicet "Non contingit nullum C esse B", quod equipollet isti "Necesse est aliquod C esse B", cum sit de contingent pro possibili. Ex hac autem et maiore sequitur oppositum minoris ex utraque de necessario in prima figura sic: de necessitate omne B est A, necesse est aliquod C esse B, ergo necesse est aliquod C esse A, quod non stat cum minori. . . . Ad omnia his dici potest quod negatiua de contingenti pro possibili sequitur secundum habitudinem et consequentiam rerum, sicut iam ostensum est. Et sic dicitur in conuertibilibus sequi conclusionem uniuersalem in tertia figura et affirmatiuam in secunda. Hoc enim non est nisi gratia terminorum et non gratia forme. Non tamen sequitur talis conclusio uirtute premissarum sic dispositarum in dictis coniugationibus et sub tali figura ex quo utraque secundum rem affirmatiua est, quod repugnat proprietati secunde figure. Aristoteles igitur respiciens dispositionem premissarum et formam cum proprietate figure ponit tales coniugationes inutiles esse. Numquam enim gratia forma ex affirmatiuis immediate sequitur negatiua. Unde attendendum quod per terminos quos ponit Aristoteles ad

instantiam non excludit quin sequatur negatiua de contingenti pro possibili, quia respiciendo ad consequentiam rerum sequitur. Ponit tamen coniugationes inutiles esse quia ex formam syllogizandi et proprietate figure non possunt in talem conclusionem. Et sic considerat ubique in hiis mixtionibus'.

32. All of these inferences have two-way contingency propositions as premises. Now, such a contingency proposition is semantically equivalent to the conjunction of two propositions: a one-way affirmative possibility proposition and a negated necessity proposition. ('It's contingent that a horse is running' is equivalent to the conjunction of 'It's possible that a horse is running' and 'It's not necessary that a horse is running'.) The Aristotelian syllogisms having a contingency premise depend, for their validity, on the affirmative possibility proposition; the non-Aristotelian syllogisms identified by Kilwardby depend, for their validity, on the negated necessity proposition.

33. John Buridan (1985, 22/23, 5–9): 'Consequentia formalis vocatur quae in omnibus terminis valet retenta forma consimili. Vel si vis expresse loqui de vi sermonis, consequentia formalis est cui omnis propositio similis in forma quae formaretur esset bona consequentia, ut "quod est A est B; ergo quod est B est A"'.

34. Dutilh Novaes (2007, 79–124).

35. Etchemendy (1990, 63–64).

36. Dutilh Novaes (2008, 474–77).

37. *De Puritate Artis Logicae Tractatus*, in Walter Burley (1955, 86:9–21): 'Dicendum, quod consequentia formalis est duplex: quaedam, quae tenet ratione formae totius complexionis, et huismodi consequentia est conversio, syllogismus et sic de aliis consequentiis, quae tenent ratione totius complexionis. Et quaedam est consequentia formalis tenens ratione formae incomplexorum, sicut consequentia ab inferiori ad superius affirmando est formalis, et tamen tenet ratione terminorum. Unde aliquam consequentiam tenere ratione terminorum potest esse dupliciter, vel quia tenet materialiter ratione terminorum, vel quia tenet formaliter ratione terminorum, hoc est ex ratione formali terminorum. Dico tunc, quod consequentia potest esse formalis ratione terminorum, et hoc si per se teneat ratione terminorum. Si vero teneat ratione terminorum per accidens tunc non est formalis'.

38. Strode (1507, f.1va): 'Consequentia bona de forma dicitur esse illa cuius si sic esse sicut adequate significatur per antecedens intelligitur sic esse sicut adequate significatur per consequens intelligitur. Si quis enim intelligat te esse hominem tunc intelligit te esse animal. Et ideo dicitur in tali consequentia consequens esse de formali intellectu antecedentis'.

39. Strode (1507, f.14rb-va): 'Consequentia namque formalis dicitur illa cui quaelibet similis, id est in qua singuli termini consimiles habent respectus omnino ad invicem, dicitur esse bona de forma'.

40. Aristotle, *Prior Analytics*, A5, 27a5–8. Translation in Aristotle (2009).

41. Aristoteles (2007, 314).

42. Aristoteles (2007, 308).

43. The principle enunciated by Ebert and Nortmann is not the same as Buridan's suggestion that the proof of Cesare rests on the principle that what follows from the consequent follows from the antecedent: John Buridan (2001, 323). The following in question has to be syllogistic following.

44. Dutilh Novaes 2008 (479–82).

45. Walter Burleigh (1955, 61:30–32): 'Prima talis: In omni consequentia bona simplici, ut consequentia simplex distinguitur contra consequentiam ut nunc, antecedens numquam potest esse verum sine consequente'.

46. Walter Burleigh (1955, 62:1–7): 'Prima est, quod ex contingenti non sequitur impossibile in consequentia simplici. . . . Et ratio . . . est, quia contingens potest esse verum sine impossibile. . . . Et propter hoc ex contingenti non sequitur impossibile . . .'

47. See Dutilh Novaes (2007).

48. I thank Laurent Cesalli and Phillip Kremer for their comments on earlier versions of this paper.

BIBLIOGRAPHY

Aristoteles. 2007. *Analytica Priora Buch I, übersetzt und erläutert von Theodor Ebert und Ulrich Nortmann*. Berlin: Akademie.

Aristotle. 2009. *Prior Analytics Book I*, translated with an introduction and commentary by Gisela Striker. Oxford: Clarendon.

Corcoran, John. 2009. Aristotle's Demonstrative Logic. *History and Philosophy of Logic* 30:1–20.

Dutilh Novaes, Catarina. 2007. *Formalizing Medieval Logical Theories: Suppositio, Consequentiae and Obligationes*. Dordrecht, the Netherlands: Springer.

———. Catarina. 2008. 'Logic in the 14th century after Ockham'. In Gabbay and Woods 2008, 433–504.

Etchemendy, J. 1990. *The Concept of Logical Consequence*. Cambridge, MA: Harvard University Press.

Faris, J. A. 1962. *Truth-Functional Logic*. London: Routledge & Kegan Paul.

Gabbay, Dov M. and John Woods, eds. 2008. *Handbook of the History of Logic, Vol. 2: Medieval and Renaissance Logic*. Dordrecht, the Netherlands: Springer.

John Buridan. 1985. *Jean Buridan's Logic: The Treatise on Supposition, the Treatise on Consequences*, translated with a philosophical introduction by Peter King. Dordrecht, the Netherlands: Reidel.

———. 2001. *Summulae de Dialectica*, an annotated translation, with a philosophical introduction by Gyula Klima. New Haven, CT: Yale University Press.

Kilwardby, Robert. 1516/1968. *Notule libri Priorum = Reverendi Magisti Egidii Romani In Libros Priorum Analeticorum Aristotelis Expositio*. Reprint, Frankfurt: Minerva.

———. 1976. *De Ortu Scientiarum*, ed. Albert G. Judy. London: British Academy.

Klima, Gyula. 2008. 'The nominalist semantics of Ockham and Buridan: A "rational reconstruction"'. In Gabbay and Woods 2008, 389–432.

Kneale, William and Martha Kneale. 1962. *The Development of Logic*. Oxford: Clarendon Press.

Lagerlund, Henrik. 2008. 'The assimilation of Aristotelian and Arabic logic up to the later thirteenth century'. In Gabbay and Woods 2008, 281–346.

Lohr, C. 1965. Logica Algazelis: Introduction and Critical Text. *Traditio* 21:223–90.

Maierù, Alfonso. 2004. 'Mental language and Italian scholasticism in the fourteenth and fifteenth centuries'. In *John Buridan and Beyond: Topics in the Language Sciences 1300–1700*, ed. R. L. Friedman and S. Ebbesen, 33–68. Copenhagen: The Royal Danish Academy of Sciences and Letters.

Martin, Christopher J. 1986. William's Machine. *The Journal of Philosophy* 83:564–72.

McCall, Storrs. 1966. Connexive Implication. *Journal of Symbolic Logic* 31:415–33.

Mitchell, David. 1962. *An Introduction to Logic*. London: Hutchinson.

Parsons, Terence. 2008. 'The development of supposition theory in the later 12th through 14th centuries'. In Gabbay and Woods 2008, 157–280.

Peter Abelard. 1956. *Dialectica, first complete edition of the Parisian manuscript by L.M. De Rijk*. Assen, the Netherlands: Van Gorcum.

Ralph Strode. 1507. *Consequentiae*. In *Consequentie Strodi cum Commento Alexandri Sermonete, Declarationes Gaetani in eadem Consequentias, Dubia Magistri Pauli Pergulensis, Obligationes eiusdem Strodi, Consequentie Ricardi de Ferabrich, Expositio Gaetani super easdem*. Venice.

Thom, Paul. 2010. Three Conceptions of Formal Logic. *Vivarium* 48:228–42.

Walter Burleigh. 1955. *De Puritate Artis Logicae Tractatus Longior, with a Revised Edition of the Tractatus Brevior*, ed. Philotheus Boehner. St Bonaventure, NY: The Franciscan Institute.

Wilks, Ian. 2008. 'Peter Abelard and his contemporaries'. In Gabbay and Woods 2008, 83–156.

CHAPTER 13

LOGICAL CONSEQUENCE

CHRISTOPHER J. MARTIN

1. INTRODUCTION

One of the main concerns of philosophical logic is the investigation of the relation of logical consequence. In modern times this project has its origin in the work of Kant and Bolzano and receives its first formal expression in the work of Frege. It culminates in Tarski's paper *Logical Consequence* of 1936 in which, in response to the difficulty of characterising consequence syntactically, he proposes the semantical definition that we now formulate in terms of truth in models, or, in the case of modal logic, in possible worlds.[1] Tarski provides a definition of what we might call classical logical consequence, which has as corollaries that everything follows from a formal impossibility and that a formal necessity follows from everything. The classical notion of consequence with these so-called 'paradoxes of implication' has been the standard one employed in the development of logic in the twentieth century, but it has not gone unchallenged. When Tarski wrote, alternatives to classical logic were already available that tried to capture the conviction that in order for an inference to be good there must be a relevant connection between what is inferred and what it is inferred from. The intuition that relevance has a role to play in inference has been of considerable importance in the development of formal and philosophical logic over the past forty or so years, as the adequacy of Tarski's definition has been challenged, and new systems of relevant logic have been developed.[2] The results, however, still remain rather on the periphery of contemporary thinking about logic.

Although medieval logicians had no interest in general in formalisation or in the development of deductive systems, they were deeply concerned with the notion of logical consequence, and the history of their thinking about it has striking parallels with the contemporary developments just sketched. In the present chapter, I will give an outline of this history with each section corresponding to what I take to be an important phase in it. In the first I consider the material transmitted to the Early Middle Ages from Antiquity in order to show how thinking about consequence and, in particular, about the conditional proposition became the central project of early-twelfth-century logic. In the second I try to summarise the extraordinary development by Abelard of a unified relevantistic theory of the conditional and argument on the basis of Boethius's confused accounts of the hypothetical syllogism and topical inference. This phase of my history ends with the collapse of Abelard's project when it was discovered that his proposed logic was inconsistent. It is followed by a period of crisis, discussed in the third section, and its resolution late in the twelfth century in favour of the medieval version of the classical account of logical consequence, which became the standard one for the following century. This account is supplemented, however, with a relevantistic version of the consequence relation for use in special circumstances. The third phase ends, as does the chapter, with William of Ockham's rejection of this pair of consequence relations in favour of a contrast between what he calls material and formal consequences in which relevance as a semantical requirement no longer has a place.

2. FRAGMENTS OF CLASSICAL LOGIC

The moods of the categorical syllogism provided logicians of the Middle Ages with a paradigm of logical consequence, and in one version of Boethius's translation of Aristotle's *Prior Analytics*, which first became fully available around around 1140, the relation between the premises and conclusion is characterised in precisely this way:[3]

> A syllogism is an expression in which from certain things being posited something other than what is posited follows (*consequitur*) of necessity from these being so. By 'from these being so' I mean comes about through these <and by 'comes about through these',> that no extrinsic term is required in order that the conclusion come about necessarily. (24b19–23)

Aristotle provides no explicit account of the strength of the connection required for consequence. From his appeal to counter-examples in rejecting putative syllogisms and of reduction to impossibility in proving the moods of the second and third figures from the first, we may infer, however, that he believed that it was necessary in order for this connection to hold that it not be possible for the premises of an argument of the appropriate form to be true and the conclusion false at the same time. Aristotle's use of reduction does not show that he thought that the *inseparability* of the truth of the premise from that of the conclusion is alone sufficient for validity since the moods of the secondary figures are required to satisfy the principles of construction characteristic of each figure.[4]

The developers of relevantistic accounts of consequences in the twelfth century did not draw directly upon Aristotle but, rather, before the *Prior Analytics*[5] became available, found the material on which to base their accounts in Boethius's various commentaries on Porphyry and Aristotle, his epitome *Prior Analytics* I.1–6, *De Syllogismo Categorico*,[6] his account of topical inference, *de Topicis Differentiis*[7] (TD) and of hypothetical syllogisms, *de Hypotheticis Syllogismis*[8] (DHS).

From Boethius, twelfth-century philosophy took the claim that a true categorical proposition signifies what Abelard at least would understand to be a state of affairs (*existentia rei*) while a true conditional proposition signifies a consequence (*consequentia*). In order thus to prove that a given conditional is not true according to Boethius, we must show that it does not signify an 'immutable consequence', and to do this we must show that it is possible for what the antecedent signifies to be so when what the consequent signifies is not so. That is, a necessary condition for the truth of a conditional and so for a consequence is that the truth of the antecedent is *inseparable* from the truth of the consequent.[9]

Boethius goes on to note that this inseparability requirement can be met in two ways. Of the first he provides an example but not an explanation. The conditional 'if fire is hot, then the heavens are spherical' holds, he says, accidentally (*secundum accidens*), and so, presumably, simply because both antecedent and consequent are necessarily true. In contrast, conditionals that express a consequence of nature (*consequentia naturae*) satisfy the inseparability requirement, and in addition there is an explanatory connection between their antecedents and consequents. Either the antecedent is explained by consequent 'if something is human, then it is an animal', or the consequent by the antecedent 'if the Earth stands between the sun and the moon, an eclipse follows'.

Nothing that Boethius says indicates that he might have been aware that a corollary of his inseparability requirement is that every conditional with an impossible antecedent or a necessary consequent holds accidentally. The corresponding 'paradoxes' are not stated anywhere in the remains of ancient logic that have come down to us[10] but, as we will see below, appear as logicians' slogans for the first time in the second half of the twelfth century.

Boethius's characterisation of both the inseparability condition and of the additional connection required for there to be a consequence of nature are very general, and one of the main goals of Peter Abelard's work in philosophical logic will be to make them more precise. To do this, with his contemporaries, he draws upon ideas developed by Boethius in works other than *DHS*, connecting them together with the theory of the conditional in an entirely novel and revolutionary way. In particular, for further information on the nature of inseparability, the interested early-twelfth-century reader turned to Boethius's remarks on inseparable accidents in his longer commentary on Porphyry's *Isagoge*.[11]

In his comments on Porphyry's remarks on *differentiae*, Boethius contrasts those predicables that are involved in the constitution of a species, that is, its genus and *differentiae* and that belong to it *per se*, with the other predicables, property and accident, that belong *per accidens*. Those features that belong *per se* to their subjects 'cannot be separated from the subject without the destruction of the nature of the subject'.[12] The crucial problem here is to understand how something may be accidental to its subject but not separable from it, as required by Aristotle's definition of an accident as a feature that is able to come and go from its subject. In particular, since properties—those feature, such as being able to laugh in the case of humans, that belong to all and only the members of a species—are not part of the definition of the substances of which they are the properties; they are accidents. It seems, however, that they cannot be separated from their subjects without destroying them.

The solution proposed by Porphyry and endorsed by Boethius is to distinguish between what we may call physical, or real, and conceptual separability. Accidents such as the states of being asleep and being awake are really separable from their subjects—they are present at one time and absent at another. There is no physical way, however, to remove the blackness from a raven or an Ethiopian. These features may, nevertheless, be separated according to Boethius because: 'if we separate in imagination the colour black from a raven, it remains nevertheless a bird, and the species is not destroyed. Therefore that an accident is said to be present or absent is to be understood not with respect to things but with respect to the mind.'[13] The conceivable thus includes both the possible and the impossible. To connect this account of accidents with Boethius's account of conditionals, a twelfth-century reader could appeal to the examples of consequence that he gives in his commentary on Cicero's *Topics*.[14] There the relationship of consequence that holds between species and genus and between cause and effect is contrasted as substantial with that which holds where being black follows on being a raven, which involves an accident.

Boethius, as I noted, does not seem aware of the principle that everything follows from an impossibility. He does, however, allow that one may reason constructively about impossibilities and so requires an account of consequence for which this principle does not hold. Both in *DHS* and in his *Theological Treatise* III, on divine goodness, *Quomodo Substantiae* (*QS*),[15] he claims that we may legitimately take an impossibility as an hypothesis in our reasoning in order, as he says in *DHS*, to discover what follows from it.[16] In *QS*, in a remark that a medieval reader could not fail to associate with his claims about the separability of accidents, he observes that 'There are many things which, although they cannot be separated in act, are separated in the mind and by cogitation',[17] and then he proposes that we consider the nature of created things apart from their dependence on God in order to establish the truth of the counter-possible conditional 'if creatures did not depend on God for their existence, they would not be good'.

The purpose of this kind of argument is quite different from that of reduction to impossibility where, starting from what we take, perhaps only for the sake of argument, to be a possibility, we end up with an impossibility and conclude that our original hypothesis was itself impossible. In what I have called elsewhere Eudemian procedures,[18] in contrast, we start with an acknowledged impossibility and end with an impossibility, having thus discovered something interesting about the relationship between them.

With *TD*, Boethius, drawing upon Cicero's *Topica* and work by Themistius that no longer exists,[19] provided medieval philosophers with a catalogue of the varieties of non-syllogistic arguments and an account, he claimed, of how such arguments may be discovered to answer any given question. The catalogue remained in use throughout the Middle Ages but was especially important in the twelfth century, providing commentators with instruments with which they could dissect the structure of authoritative texts. Much more importantly, the theory of topical arguments that he inherited from Boethius gave Abelard the foundations for his theory of hypothetical propositions and the technical terminology with which to formulate it.

TD is concerned with dialectical questions, that is, with questions in disjunctive form and the problem of how they are to be resolved in favour of one of the disjuncts. Such questions may, according to Boethius, be either categorical, 'Is *S P* or not?', or conditional, 'Is it the case that if *P*, then *Q*, or not?' The work thus promises, though it provides only by implication, an account of how we may argue in favour of the truth or falsity of a conditional. To settle a dialectical question, according to Boethius, following Cicero, we must find an *argumentum*, that is a 'reason (*ratio*) bringing conviction where something is in doubt'.[20] The resolution appears as the conclusion of an argument (*argumentatio*), and a *locus*, or topic, is where we must go to find the *argumentum*, which Boethius characterises as the *sense* of the argument, to support it. At the beginning of *TD*, he claims that the work will show which *loci* are suited to which syllogisms, and later after classifying arguments as either syllogisms, inductions, enthymemes or examples, he gives a definition of a syllogism differing from that of Aristotle quoted above only in requiring that in addition to being posited, the premises are '*conceded*'[21]—a very small difference in wording that will take on great theoretical significance for Abelard. None of the arguments given as examples in *TD* are, in fact, instances of the canonical moods of categorical and hypothetical syllogisms, though, importantly, two may easily be reconstructed as such.

The arguments drawn from the various *loci* in *TD* are all invoked to answer categorical questions. Often, however, the answer does not take the form of a premise or premises supporting a conclusion but, rather, is given as a conditional with the appropriate disjunct of the question as its consequent. The connection between the premises and the conclusion or between the antecedent and consequent is guaranteed by what we would now call an 'inference warrant', which Boethius characterises as a *maximal proposition*. Such propositions are universal, indemonstrable and self-evident (*per se notae*). They are themselves *loci*, the source of *argumenta*, and those maximal propositions that express different properties of the same topical relationships are said to have the same *locus differentia*.

So, for example, in answer to the question of whether human affairs are ruled by providence, Boethius replies, 'if the world is ruled by providence and human affairs are part of the world, then human affairs are ruled by providence'. He supports this inference with the maximal proposition 'whatever holds of an (integral) whole, holds of an (integral) part'. The *locus differentia* in this case is 'from an integral whole'.[22] We thus prove the conditional by appealing to the properties of integral wholes as expressed in the maximal proposition, which according to Boethius *contains* the consequence of the conclusion (*consequentia conclusionis*).

TD provides two different classifications of *loci differentiae*, one from Themistius and the other from Cicero. They agree in that what both offer as maximal propositions are for the most part general claims about the world as it is understood by Aristotelian essentialism: as consisting, that is, of substances belonging to strictly demarcated natural kinds, each definable by qualifying a genus with *differentiae*, possessing both separable and inseparable accidents, subject to the four kinds of cause recognised by Aristotle and so on. Though most of the maximal propositions express what we may think of as putative metaphysical principles, not all have this status. In particular, both catalogues include a *locus* in which an appeal is made to authority, the maximal propositions of which Boethius distinguishes from others as not necessary but only probable (*probabilis*), in the technical sense of appearing to be so to 'everyone, to many, or to the wise'.

Perhaps because he uses the word '*propositio*', which we naturally translate as 'proposition', and he left us with a book on the hypothetical syllogism, Boethius has generally been supposed to have something interesting to say about propositional logics.[23] This is a serious mistake since he has nothing like our contemporary understanding of propositionality and so no logic that we might characterise as 'propositional', if we intend thereby to suggest some connection with contemporary propositional logics. Such logics are the logics of particular propositional operations. While Boethius recognises two kinds of connectives, conditional and disjunctive, which may be used to form compound 'propositions', however, he has no notion that what is compounded is what we now call a propositional content and that the compounding of propositional contents may be repeated without limit.

The crucial distinction between force and content necessary for the contemporary account of propositional operations and their logic was famously christened by Peter Geach as the *Frege Point*,[24] but we will see below that it was misnamed. The point is that to properly account for the properties of propositional operations we must distinguish between the content of a speech act and the character of the act in which that content is deployed. The same content appears, for example, in an assertion, a wish and a question. Propositional content is transformed into new propositional content by propositional operations. For example, with the operation of propositional negation we form the contradictory of a given content, defined to be true if the original is false and false if it is true. Such operations may be iterated without limit.

Boethius, on the other hand, develops Aristotle's psychologistic account of propositional meaning in which an affirmation signifies, that is to say, causes, an act of understanding in a listener in which the concepts signified by the subject and predicate terms are conjoined while the corresponding negation causes a mental act in which they are separated. Affirmation and negation are thus defined only for categorical propositions, and that a given negation divides truth and falsity with the corresponding affirmation is a claim which has to be argued for. Boethius has no procedure for forming the negation of a compound proposition and, indeed, rejects, clearly without understanding it, what he reports as the Stoic proposal that negation can be preposed to the subject of proposition on the grounds that one would not then be able to tell whether the proposition had an infinite or a finite subject.[25] He does, however, stipulate that, whatever the quality of its antecedents, a conditional proposition is affirmative if its consequent is affirmative and negative if it is negative.

More importantly, Boethius denies that a copulative conjunction forms a single proposition from the two propositions conjoined:[26]

> Another is that composed either from terms or propositions coupled by a conjunction but multiple and signifying many. . . . Conjoined from propositions but signifying many, for example if someone says: both Apollo is a prophet and Jupiter thunders.

Although he formulates his paradigms for the moods of the categorical syllogism as conditionals with copulative antecedents, however, he offers no account of this construction.[27]

Boethius's treatment of hypothetical syllogisms clearly reveals his lack of anything corresponding to our concepts of propositionality and propositional compounding. To a modern reader, it is a rather tedious and seemingly bizarre exercise,[28] in which we are introduced first to simple and then compound conditionals, but in which the most complex form allowed has a simple conditional for both antecedent and consequent. Boethius then considers all the possible variations of quality for the simple propositions that make up the various kinds of conditionals and the two hypothetical syllogisms available for each. The oddness of this procedure is explained when one realises that Boethius is not thinking at all in terms of propositional operations and propositional substitution. In his formulation of the members of various classes of conditionals that he recognises he uses letters to stand for general terms exactly as he does in formulating the figures and moods of the categorical syllogism: 'for the sake of brevity', he tells us and 'in order to indicate that the argument holds universally'.[29] Thus, just as (a) 'if every B is C and every A is B, then every A is C' and (b) 'if no B is C and every A is B, then no A is C' are different forms, or complexions, according to Boethius, of categorical syllogism, so (c) 'if it's A, then it's B, it's A; therefore it's B' and (d) 'if it's A, then it's not B, it's A; therefore it's not B' are different forms of hypothetical syllogism.[30] Every uniform substitution of *terms* for these letters yields in each case a syllogism, but nowhere does Boethius even hint that (c) and (d) might be conceived of as instances of the same propositional form, 'if P, then Q, P; therefore Q'. Quite the contrary. His goal in dealing with the hypothetical syllogism as he conceives it is the same as that of his treatment of the categorical syllogism, to list all the various forms of argument constructed from propositions of a certain kind that hold for all substitutions of general terms.

Two features of Boethius's treatment of the hypothetical syllogism have attracted modern commentators and played a role in the development of what are known as connexive logics.[31] The first is that he appears to commit himself to the so-called principle of conditional excluded middle (*CEM*) by giving as schemata, for example, 'if it's A, (then if it's B, then it's not C), if it's B, then it's C; therefore it's not A', and 'if (if it's A, then it's B), it's C, it's not C; therefore if it's A, then it's not B'. In fact, he was certainly not committed to this principle and in this respect was better understood in the twelfth century than in the twentieth. The schemata reflect, rather, the fact that his negation is not propositional and his account of compound conditionals imposes restrictions on the relations between the terms that must be met if such propositions are to be true.[32]

The second feature is a claim about the conditional that was crucial in the development of medieval propositional logic. Having told us at the beginning of *DHS* that Aristotle wrote nothing on hypothetical propositions, Boethius takes from him a principle for the logic of conditionals. In discussing the properties of syllogisms in *Prior Analytics* II.5, Aristotle argues that we cannot have a pair of syllogisms with the same conclusion but in which the premises of one are the negations of those of the other. To prove this he treats the syllogism as if it had only a single premise and so appears to argue that 'if it's *A*, then it's *B*' and if 'it's not *A* then it's *B*' cannot both be true.[33] This is what Boethius claims on Aristotle's authority, offering in support a rather confused argument to the effect that if such a pair of conditionals were true, then both 'not B' and 'B' might be true together. He thus indicates again that he is not aware of the principle that anything follows from an impossibility.[34]

3. Abelard's Project

At some time towards the end of the eleventh century in the schools of Northern France, revolutionary changes in thinking about logic began to take place. They are marked by the appearance alongside the traditional glosses on Aristotle and Porphyry of self-contained textbooks and in both kinds of work of innovations, in particular the invention of new topical principles and the use of new forms of argumentation. In the earliest of the textbooks, the *Dialectica* of Garlandus Compotista,[35] we have the first clear characterisation of the propositional negation of a conditional as formed by preposing the negative particle to the whole to form a proposition that divides truth and falsity with the original.[36]

Garland notices propositional negation only briefly and only to argue that the propositional negation of a conditional with an affirmative antecedent and consequent differs in truth value from the conditional formed by negating its consequent. He is thus aware, at least, that the Boethian negative of a conditional is different from its propositional negation, which, he observes, is not a hypothetical proposition.

Even if we cannot claim for Peter Abelard the invention of propositional negation, it is in his works, however, that we find the first general discussion of negation and other connectives as propositional operations. These ideas are already present in the *Dialectica*,[37] written probably around 1113, in which Abelard sets out the 'novelties' that he had been criticised for introducing into the teaching of logic in the previous decade.[38] The semantical foundations for these theories are developed in his commentary on the *logica vetus* known as the *Logica 'Ingredientibus'*,[39] which was written perhaps five or more years later.[40]

Abelard is clearly aware of the distinction between propositional content and the force with which that content is deployed, and he relies on the distinction in developing his account of propositional operations. He thus deserves at least some

of the credit that has gone to Frege for the discovery of the famous point. In particular, in his account of the various kinds of speech act, Abelard notes that exactly the
same content is presented with different force in the wish 'would that the King
should come', and in the assertion 'I hope that the King comes',[41] and when he is
speaking precisely he characterises assertive utterance as the act of 'proposing with
assertion what is true or false.'[42]

Abelard accepts Boethius's account of the semantics of what he calls *separa-
tive*, or *remotive*, negation, formed by applying the negative adverb to the verb
phrase of an affirmative categorical proposition. This negation does not divide
truth and falsity with the corresponding affirmation since for the truth of either
proposition it is necessary that subject term not be empty.[43] Furthermore, it cannot,
according to Abelard, be iterated since it functions solely to separate terms. Presumably, like Frege, he does not see how the mental operation of separation in a
second application can sew together what in the first it tore apart.[44] Like Frege, too,
in order to form the contradictory of any given proposition Abelard introduces an
operation whose application produces a proposition defined to be false if the original is true and true if it is false, which he calls *destructive*, or *extinctive* negation;
it 'totally cancels what the other proposes'.[45] Extinctive negation is indicated by
preposing the negative particle to the whole of a proposition, it may apply to any
kind of proposition whether simple or compound, affirmative or separatively negative, it does not require for its truth that that the subject term not be empty and it
may be iterated, presumably without limit, though Abelard mentions only the case
of double negation.[46]

In the *Dialectica*, indeed, we find the first reference to double propositional negation in the Latin tradition and the first observation on its logic anywhere in the West:[47]

> Destructive and proper negations may be applied not only to separative negations
> but also perhaps to those which are destructive and which extinguish and falsify
> the whole of the sense. So to assert 'not not every human is an animal', . . . is to
> assert that what the negative 'not every human is animal' says is not so. But since
> a negation of this kind is equipollent to the universal affirmation 'every human is
> an animal', it seems to be affirmative in sense . . . Granted, however, that it is
> equipollent in a certain way to the other, they are very different in sense since the
> latter proposes an affirmation and the former a negation. And although they seem
> always to agree with one another (*sese comitari*), they do not entail one another
> (*inferentiam custodiunt*). Every proposition is thus seen to have its proper
> negation <formed> with a preposed negation <sign> which simply destroys and
> extinguishes its sense. So to 'every human is white' there is opposed the negation
> 'not every human is white' . . .

We will come back to the difference between accompaniment and entailment
below.

The clearest, and most remarkable, indication of Abelard's understanding of
propositionality and propositional operations is found in his rejection of
Boethius's claim, quoted above, that the copulative conjunction does not combine the propositions it couples into a single propositional unit. In an observation

that marks a fundamental turning point in the history of logic, Abelard complains that:[48]

> Since <Boethius> concedes that 'if it's day, then it's light' is a single proposition in which different propositions are reduced to the sense of one proposition by the preposed conjunction, I do not see why 'both Apollo is a prophet and Jupiter thunders', cannot be said to be a single proposition, just as 'when Apollo is a prophet, Jupiter thunders.' Whence each may have a single dividing opposite, so that just as we say 'not (if it's day, then it's light)', so also we should say 'not (both Apollo is a prophet and Jupiter thunders).'

Abelard now has all the material needed for a properly propositional logic. In particular, he can explain the properties of conditionals with copulative antecedents, and he invokes his account of propositional negation to do just this in his discussion of Boethius's account of hypothetical syllogisms involving compound conditionals.

In formulating such conditionals, Boethius always uses '*si*' as the major and '*cum*' as the embedded connective, having claimed earlier in *DHS* that they may have the same meaning and not hinting that there might be a difference when both appear in a compound.[49] While acknowledging that '*cum*' may indeed function just as '*si*' does to form a conditional, Abelard, however, notes that it also has the sense of '*whenever*' and gives Boethius's example of a conditional holding accidentally, which he had formulated using '*cum*', as his own example of such a *temporal* proposition.[50] Abelard insists that when it is employed as a propositional connective and is embedded in a conditional '*cum*', it is always temporal and that the resulting proposition is true at a time if and only if each conjunct is true then, and there is no time at which one is true and the other false.[51]

Adopting this account of compound conditionals, Abelard claims that no sense can be made of the argument schemata, such as those noted above, which appear to modern commentators to commit Boethius to *CEM*. He thus proposes to emend Boethius's account so that in such schemata the opposite of what we must construe to be a temporal proposition is its propositional negation.[52] Furthermore, in discussing the truth conditions of such compound conditionals Abelard formulates for the first time a version of a principle familiar from modern propositional logic: 'if an antecedent holds with something, then each consequent of it holds', what is now known as conditional simplification.[53]

Abelard likewise corrects what he takes to be Boethius's account of disjunction. He agrees that a simple disjunction is equipollent to the simple conditional that has the negation of the first disjunct as its antecedent and the second disjunct as its consequent and so is exhaustive, and he therefore accepts disjunctive syllogism. Abelard disagrees, however, that disjunction is also exclusive, pointing to the truth of the propositional disjunction 'either not every human is white or some human is white'.[54]

Abelard sets out his account of the semantics of conditional propositions in the treatise on the topics in his *Dialectica* and begins it with a new definition of a *locus* that seems to be entirely his own. Making explicit what was only implicit in Boethius, he tells us that, generally speaking, a locus is an entailment warrant (*vis inferentiae*).[55] 'Entailment' is an appropriate translation since Abelard holds that the connection warranted is that which holds between the antecedent and consequent in a true conditional and that for this more is required than a guarantee of the mere inseparability of the truth of the antecedent from that of the consequent:[56]

> Entailment consists in the necessity of consecution (*consecutio*), that is that the sense of the consequent is required by the sense of the antecedent.

Later he notes, again for the first time in the Latin tradition, the explosive consequences of holding that inseparability is sufficient for the truth. If it were, then all conditionals with impossible antecedents such as 'if Socrates is a stone, then Socrates is an ass' would be true.[57] But Abelard holds, though without ever explicitly saying so, that it is false that everything *follows* from an impossibility since for there to be a relation of consecution, there must be a relevant connection. That connection exists when the antecedent *requires* the consequent in that the sense, or 'understanding' of the antecedent *contains* that of the consequent.[58] However, although Abelard claims that in the act of understanding the antecedent of a true conditional such as 'if Socrates is a human, then Socrates is an animal' we in a sense understand the consequent, he does not suppose that someone who understands the term 'human' will thereby be able to provide the definition. Being able to use a natural kind term correctly certainly does not require being able to give a complete account of what it means. That is something that is discovered by the investigations of natural science, the job of which it is to explore the natures of things and thereby to establish the laws of nature, which, according to Abelard, are what are expressed in true, topically warranted, conditionals. Such conditionals are thus what we would now call analytic *a posteriori* truths.[59]

The central problem for Abelard's philosophical logic is to establish just when this relation of containment holds. He distinguishes among entailments between those that require a topical warrant, and which are thus, he says, *imperfect*, and those that hold in virtue of the complexion, or form, of their constituents alone, and so are *perfect*. The latter satisfy the condition now sometimes characterised as the Bolzano-Quine definition of logical truth, that is to say, for Abelard, that uniform substitution for term-variables preserves consecution. This holds in the case of the conditionalisations of the canonical moods and figures of both the categorical and hypothetical syllogism. Note that the substitution is for the categorematic terms not, in the case of the hypothetical syllogism, for the propositional contents. 'If (if Socrates is human, then Socrates is an animal) and Socrates is human, then Socrates is an animal' is thus a perfect entailment because every uniform substitution for the terms yields a conditional that can be seen to be true, according to Abelard, because the formal structure (*complexio*) of the antecedent contains the consequent. In addition to requiring that uniform substitution preserves consecution, however, Abelard restricts perfection to the conditionalised canonical syllogisms, claiming in particular that the conditional 'if it's animate, then it's animate' is not a perfect entailment.[60] Although he formulates the principles governing the hypothetical syllogism, affirming the antecedent and denying the consequent, completely generally in terms of the relation between antecedent and consequent propositional contents, neither Abelard nor any other medieval that I know of employs propositional variables to construct the corresponding argument schemata. Rather, he accepts and rehearses Boethius's classification of hypothetical syllogisms by form and figure depending on the quality of the antecedent and consequent.[61]

The general formulation of a given form of perfect entailment is what Abelard calls a *rule*, for example, 'if something is predicated of something universally and something else is predicated of the predicate universally, the same is predicated of the subject universally'.[62] These rules, he insists, must be distinguished from the maximal propositions such as 'of whatever a species is predicated, the genus is predicated' (*M*), which warrant true conditionals. Such conditionals do not hold for all uniform substitutions for their terms but only for those that preserve the topical relationship (*habitudo*) between them in virtue of which the conditional is true. The topical relationship that determines the relevant substitution class for imperfect entailments is the *locus differentia* that appears in the maximal proposition, warranting, for example, in the case of (*M*), both 'if Socrates is a human, then Socrates is an an animal' and 'if Socrates is as pearl, then Socrates is a stone'. The rules for syllogisms, on the other hand, contain no topical difference, and so, contrary to Boethius, a syllogism does not require a *locus*—a claim that was taken by their contemporaries to be a characteristic and peculiar doctrine of Abelard and his followers the *Nominales*.

The relationship between the antecedent and consequent of perfect and imperfect entailments is precisely the same, that of containment of sense, and they play precisely the same role in Abelardian logic. They instantiate the strongest consequence relation that he recognises but it is not the only one. The relationship of 'accompaniment' (*comitatio*) referred to in an earlier quotation is weaker and guarantees only the inseparability of truth. This Abelard maintains is all that is needed for a good argument since it always takes us from true premises to a true conclusion. Arguments are in this respect, he insists, different from conditional propositions. Appealing to both the Boethian formulation of the definition of the syllogism quoted above and the definition of an *argumentum,* he requires that the premises of an argument be conceded and, much more importantly, for what we would call validity, only that it not be possible for the premises to be true when the conclusion is false.[63] We thus cannot conditionalise every enthymeme to produce a true conditional, and so the deduction theorem does not hold for Abelardian logic.

The challenge for Abelard is to distinguish among maximal propositions those that warrant entailments, those that support only the weaker connection required for a valid enthymeme, and those that he acknowledges have some plausibility but do not support any kind of necessary connection. His most important strategy invokes a rejection rule that relies upon what he takes from Boethius to be the most fundamental principles governing the logic of the conditional, the connexive theses, that no proposition may entail or be entailed by its own negation.[64] Where Boethius had no notion of propositionality, however, Abelard takes these principles as the foundation for his propositional logic, proving that it follows from them that no proposition may entail both another proposition and its negation or be entailed both by another proposition and its negation. It follows, and this became another characteristic thesis of the *Nominales,* that no true conditional has an antecedent and consequent of different quality. Although Abelard himself never proves it, we can show now why conditionalised double negation fails in his logic.

1. $(P\&\sim P) \rightarrow P$ Simplification
2. $(P\&\sim P) \rightarrow \sim P$ Simplification
3. $P \rightarrow \sim\sim P$ Hypothesis
4. $\sim\sim P \rightarrow \sim(P\&\sim P)$ 2, Contraposition
5. $(P\&\sim P) \rightarrow \sim(P\&\sim P)$ 1, 3, 4, Transitivity

Contrary to a connexive thesis, and likewise that '$\sim\sim P \rightarrow P$' is false, using only principles which Abelard explicitly accepts: the double propositional negation of a given proposition, as Abelard says, accompanies it but is not entailed by it.

Abelard's construction of a relevantistic theory of the conditional is quite extraordinary and deserves to be recognised as a very great achievement in the history of logic. Tragically, he failed to see that, while the connexive principles are perhaps plausible for term logic, his reliance on them for his propositional logic is incompatible with his acceptance of conditional simplification. In contemporary terms simplification is a form of monotonicity and connexive logic is nonmonotonic. The fatal flaw was realised, apparently in the 1130s, by Alberic of Paris, who stands to Abelard with his discovery of the following devastating argument in the twelfth century as Russell does to Frege in the twentieth:

1. If Socrates is a human and not an animal, then Socrates is a human.
2. If Socrates is a human, then Socrates is an animal.
3. If Socrates is an animal, it is not the case that Socrates is a human and not an animal.
4. Therefore if Socrates is human and not an animal, then it is not the case that Socrates is a human and not an animal.

According to Abelard's logic, each of 1, 2, and 3, are entailments, so his theory has been shown to contravene its own most fundamental principle.[65]

4. THE DECLINE OF RELEVANCE

In Paris in the 1130s, Abelard and the *Nominales* were only one of a number of outstanding schools of logicians whose discussions of the conditional recalls that which excited even the crows in Antiquity[66] and about which we have considerably more information, though sadly much of it remains unpublished. In particular, the followers of Gilbert of Poitiers, the *Porretani*, correctly proposed to save connexivity by denying simplification, while the followers of Robert of Melun, the *Melidunenses*, maintained the extraordinary thesis that nothing follows from the false, the latter agreeing with Abelard that all conditionals with negative antecedents and affirmative consequents are all false, but unlike him allowing some with affirmative antecedent and negative consequent to be true.[67]

In the end, however, it was the position of the school known as the *Parvipontani*, the followers of Adam of the Petit-Pont, which provided the solution. According to it, inseparability is both necessary and sufficient for the truth of a conditional and so, as orthodox logicians have declaimed ever since, *ex impossibili sequitur quodlibet!*[68] The famous Lewis argument is another example of misnaming since it was apparently discovered by William of Soissons in the 1150s and is reported as being entirely obvious, for the first time by Alexander Neckham—something that he learnt as a student at the school of the *Parvipontani* in the 1170s.[69] To show that everything follows from a contradiction, Neckham argues:[70]

1. If Socrates is a human and Socrates is not a human, then Socrates is a human.
2. If Socrates is a human, then Socrates is a human or a stone.
3. If Socrates is a human and Socrates is not a human, then Socrates is a human or a stone.
4. If Socrates is a human and Socrates is not a human, then Socrates is not a human.
5. Therefore if Socrates is a human and Socrates is not a human, then Socrates is a stone.

Where for 'Socrates is a stone' occurs, we may substitute any proposition we wish. The argument relies upon transitivity, simplification in 1 and 4, and two claims about the logic of disjunction. The second, disjunctive syllogism, was, as we have seen, introduced by Boethius as a basic principle for the logic of the connective and was accepted by Abelard for whom, like Boethius, a simple disjunction is equipollent to a simple conditional. The first principle, on the other hand, is entirely new in the history of logic; it is the conditionalised version of what is now called *addition*, which permits one to infer the truth of any disjunction from the truth of one or both disjuncts without requiring any connection between them. Nothing by way of justification has survived for this shift from an intensional, in Abelard's case hyperintensional, to a purely extensional account of disjunction, but this is how it was understood for the rest of the Middle Ages.

Following Boethius, philosophers in the twelfth century held that one may reason constructively about impossibilities and did so in dealing with certain theological problems.[71] With the acceptance of the *Parvipontanian* principle, however, impossible hypotheses had to be insulated from the explosion of consequences that follow from them according to it. What seems to be the earliest proposal for achieving this is found in an account of an entirely new practice known as *obligatio*. Treatises on *obligatio* set down rules for disputation conducted under various forms of hypothesis (*positio*), in which a respondent is required to uphold the original hypothesis (*positum*) and everything that follows from it in answering questions put to him by the opponent. The hypothesis may be possible or impossible, and in the latter case, as the *Tractaus Emmeranus*[72] notes, in order to avoid the *Parvipontanian* principle, one must concede at any point in the *obligatio* only what follows in the sense of being 'included in the understanding' of that to which one is already committed. Abelard's relevantistic requirement for entailment thus survives to distinguish a special class of conditionals, and what is more, according the *Tractatus*, they have the feature that no conditional with an affirmative antecedent and a negative consequent is true. Unlike the denial that affirmation may follow from negation, this thesis seems only to have been advocated by the *Nominales* and, if they are responsible for this account of impossible *positio*, it must date from well before the end of the twelfth century.[73]

Unfortunately only very few accounts of impossible *positio* have survived though, as we will see, one if its applications has a central place in the history of logic. To discover more about the role of relevance in thinking about the conditional, we have to turn to yet another new genre in logic, the treatises devoted to the discussion of syncategorematic terms. The two best-known authors of introductory logic books from the thirteenth century, William of Sherwood and Peter of Spain, both also wrote *Syncategoremata*, and in both cases the accounts of the conditional in the two kinds of works are curiously different. In William's *Introductiones* and Peter's *Tractatus*,[74] hypothetical propositions are barely mentioned, and there is no discussion at all of the hypothetical syllogism. Indeed, perhaps as a result of Abelard's despair of understanding it, Boethius's *De Syllogismis Hypotheticis* was not included in the *logic vetus* studied as part of the Arts curriculum at Paris and, although the work is mentioned by later writers, it seems that no one was prepared to try to make sense of its logic for compound conditionals.

All that a beginning student would have learnt from William's *Introductiones* is that, in order for a conditional to be true, the consequent must follow from the antecedent.[75] In Peter's *Tractatus* he would have discovered that, for this, it is necessary that the inseparability requirement is satisfied[76] and that there are two sorts of consequences, one holding in virtue of a topical relationship (*habitudo localis*), the other by reason of circumstances, and studied in rhetoric[77]—a half sentence is all Peter has to say about the subject that occupied Abelard for hundreds of pages in his *Dialectica*.

Turning to William's *Syncategoremata*, our student would have found a much more sophisticated treatment of the conditional, though again no account of its logic.[78] According to William, a true conditional may indicate either a natural or a nonnatural consequence, where a natural consequence holds in virtue of a relationship (*habitudo*) between antecedent and consequent. A nonnatural consequence, however, holds solely in virtue of the impossibility of the antecedent or the necessity of the consequent.[79] William thus completely obliterates the distinction made by Abelard between topical relationships that warrant imperfect entailments, expressing laws of nature, and those that guarantee mere inseparability connecting, for example, being a human with being able to laugh, or being a human with not being an ass. Curiously, however, William claims in the discussion of a sophism that the conditional 'if it is not day, then it is night' is false and goes on to observe, without further explanation, that 'an affirmative never follows from a negative'. Abelard, as we have seen, would have enthusiastically endorsed this claim. Not, however, because he thought that there was no necessary connection between the antecedent and the consequent but, rather, because the connection is not appropriately relevant, thus making a distinction for which there is no place in William's account of conditionals.

If our student also had access to Peter's *Syncategoremata*, he would have found there a discussion of just the sophism that prompts William to deny that an affirmation may follow from a negation, but also he would have seen that Peter raises no such objection.[80] Reading on, he would have come upon, in Peter's discussion of the proof that *ex impossibili quodlibet*, the earliest, and perhaps the only, anticipation of Anderson and Belnap's location in it of a fallacy of relevance.[81] Peter accepts his own version of Neckham's argument up to the final move, from 'if Socrates is a human and not a human, then Socrates is either a human or an ass, and Socrates is not a human' to 'if Socrates is a human and is not a human, Socrates is an ass', putatively warranted by an appeal to the *locus* from division, that is, disjunctive syllogism.

Modern-day dialetheists hold that this principle fails to be universally applicable because there are real contradictions in the world.[82] Peter certainly does not believe this, but like them and for precisely the same reason—the failure of truth preservation where a contradiction is hypothesised—he insists that the application of the *locus* from division, which appears as a perfectly respectable topic in the *Tractatus*,[83] must be restricted:[84]

> the ... inference does not hold because it does not destroy 'Socrates is a human' which is required if 'Socrates is an ass' is to follow when 'Socrates is a human or an ass' is true. This is because the aforementioned contradiction, that is 'Socrates is a human and not a human' equally destroys and posits 'Socrates is a human'. So it no more destroys it than posits it. And for this reason it does not destroy one part of the disjunction. So the *locus* from division cannot be appealed to here.

Peter is, as far as I know, the only medieval logician to challenge the proof of *ex impossibili quodlibet* in this way. Anyone, however, who wished to reason constructively about impossibility needed an account of which principles of inference are acceptable under such hypotheses. At the beginning of the fourteenth century, John Duns Scotus invoked the procedure of impossible *positio* to answer the particularly difficult but important theological question of whether if the Holy Spirit were not to proceed from the Son, it would be distinct from the Son.[85] If this conditional with an impossible antecedent could be shown to be true, then the Western Church would have an argument with which to challenge the Greek refusal to accept the *Filioque*.

Arguing that the impossible hypothesis that the Holy Spirit does not proceed from the Son may be posited, Scotus notes that in the resulting impossible *positio* one is required to concede only what follows from the *positum* in a *natural consequence*, that is to say, only what is 'understood *per se* in the antecedent'. He contrasts this with what follows in an *accidental consequence*, which holds only in virtue of an extrinsic *locus*, guaranteeing no more than the inseparability of the truth of the antecedent from that of the consequent. Thus, he notes, if we posit that a human being is not able to laugh, we are not required to concede the conditional 'if Socrates is a human being, then Socrates is able to laugh' since this holds only accidentally and positing, *per impossibile*, the opposite of the antecedent destroys the consequence in virtue of which it is true. Scotus thus partitions the class of consequences into natural or accidental, relying on the semantical property that Abelard used to distinguish true conditionals from those that merely satisfy the inseparability requirement. Unfortunately, he seems nowhere to indicate the extension of these two classes, so we cannot tell whether his natural consequences coincide with Abelard's entailments.

Scotus goes on to argue that if we apply the proper rules for reasoning about impossibility to the question of the procession of the Holy Spirit, we can reason constructively to an answer. His is that:[86]

> ... *it does not follow formally* that if the Holy Spirit is not from the Son, it is not distinguished from Him, but it does follow *concomitantly* ...

Here where Scotus speaks of following 'formally', he is referring to what he elsewhere characterises as following 'naturally' or 'essentially' and using 'concomitantly' for 'accidentally'. Though he does not mention his theory of the formal distinction in dealing with the problem of procession, he could now argue that the property of proceeding from the Son is formally distinct from the Holy Spirit. His treatment of the question shows that, in his terminology, a necessary and sufficient condition for *A* to be formally distinct from *B* is that *A* and *B* are numerically the same, but being *B* does not *follow formally* from being *A*. The great change that Ockham makes to the theory of consequences can, and should, it seems to me, be understood as his response to the possibility available to Scotus of employing the distinction between natural or, as Scotus has it, 'formal', and accidental consequence in this way for his own ontological ends.

Contrary to Scotus, Ockham holds that the consequent of the problematic conditional does indeed follow formally from the antecedent:[87]

> ... *this follows formally and necessarily*: the Holy Spirit does not proceed from the Son, therefore it is not distinguished from the Son ...

He insists, however, that it does not do so evidently.

Just as Ockham allows no distinctions in the world except real distinctions, he allows no relation of logical consequence other than inseparability. He is able to classify the problematic conditional as formal because he has an account of formal consequence radically different from that employed by Scotus. Whereas Scotus's formal consequence is what others called natural consequence, the distinction between natural and accidental consequences has no place in Ockham's logic. It is replaced with one that divides consequences into the *material* and the *formal*, where all consequences are formal apart from the merely trivial ones, which hold in virtue of the principles that anything follows from an impossibility and a necessity follows from anything. Ockham's formal consequence thus includes many consequences that Scotus would hold to be merely accidental. Indeed, the only accidental consequences that are not included are the merely trivial ones classified as *material*. Ockham thus finds a formal consequence where Scotus found only an interesting concomitance.

To characterise formal consequences, Ockham appeals to the notion of a middle. 'If *A*, then *B*' is a formal consequence true in virtue of an *extrinsic middle* according to Ockham, if it is an instance of a general rule 'which makes no reference to the particular terms occurring in the antecedent and consequent', for example: 'an exclusive and the corresponding universal proposition with the terms transposed signify the same and convert with one another.'[88] 'If *A*, then *B*', is a formal consequence holding in virtue of an *intrinsic middle,* however, just in case it is possible for '*A*' to be true and '*B*' false but there is a proposition '*R*' formed from the particular terms appearing in '*A*' and '*B*' such that it is not possible for '*A*' and '*R*' both to be true and '*B*' false. Here '*R*' is the intrinsic middle. So, for example, 'if Socrates is not running, then a human being is not running' holds according to Ockham in virtue of the intrinsic middle 'Socrates is a human being'.

Ockham's strategy is thus to treat all conditionals as either (a) holding for all uniform substitutions of terms and so as instances of general rules in the way Abelard understood perfect entailment, but including conditionals that Abelard would certainly not have classified as perfect; or (b) as conditionalisations of enthymemes that fall under one of the general rules when the appropriate intrinsic middle is provided. There is no place here for the topical warrants required by Abelard and the theory of natural and accidental consequences. Although in practice Ockham sometimes relies on such warrants and on relations between antecedent and consequent that cannot be reconstructed in terms of his account of extrinsic and intrinsic middles, it was his theory of consequence that defined the project of the next phase in the history of thinking about the conditional, the investigation of formal and material consequences and their logic.

NOTES

1. Tarski (1956, 409–20).
2. See Etchemendy (1990).
3. Aristotle (1962, 143–44).
4. See Thom (1981, 127–30).
5. On the ancient material available in the twelfth century, see Martin (2006).
6. Boethius (2008).
7. Boethius (1990).
8. Boethius (1969).
9. Boethius (1969, 1.9.6).

10. See Martin (1999).

11. Boethius (1906, 280–83).

12. Boethius (1906, 250).

13. Boethius (1906, 282).

14. Boethius (1833, 384).

15. Boethius (2000, 190–93, 44–49).

16. Boethius (1969, 1.2.5–6).

17. Boethius (2000, 190).

18. Martin (1999, 282).

19. See Cicero (2003, 29–35).

20. Boethius (1990, 3).

21. The same definition is given in Boethius (2008). See Martin (2010, 163 n. 13).

22. Boethius (1990, 32–33).

23. Barnes 1981; Dürr 1951; Pinzani 2003.

24. 'Assertion' in Geach (1972, 254–69).

25. Boethius (1880, 261–62).

26. Boethius (1880, 109–10).

27. Aristotle does the same leading (Thom 1981, 23), to treat 'if . . . and . . . then necessarily . . . ' as 'single implicative connective'.

28. Kneale (1962, 190).

29. Boethius (2008), II.20.

30. I have regimented these expressions for clarity but given them in the form that Boethius's does—conditionals for the categorical syllogism and inference schemata for the hypothetical syllogism. See Boethius (2008), II.86, 89, and Boethius (1969), II.2.1, II.2.2.

31. Beginning with McCall (1966). For a recent bibliography, see Wansing (2010).

32. See Martin (1991).

33. See 'Aristotle on Conjunctive Propositions' in Geach (1972, 13–27).

34. Some sense can be made of these arguments. See Martin (1991, 298–301).

35. There has been some debate about the dating of this work, but it is clear that it belongs with the anti-realist school associated with Abelard's master Roscelin and was most likely produced around 1100 and certainly before Abelard's *Dialectica*. See Iwakuma (1992, 47–55) and Marenbon (2011, 194–95).

36. Garlandus (1959, 133.) See Martin (2011a, 226).

37. Abelard (1970).

38. See Martin (2011b).

39. Published in Abelard (1919–31). References to the commentary on *de Interpretatione* are to page numbers of the new edition (Abelard 2010), followed by the page number in Geyer's edition.

40. For the dating of Abelard's works on logic, see Marenbon (1997, ch. 2).

41. Abelard 2010, 150 (374).

42. Abelard 2010, 153 (375).

43. Abelard (1970, 177).

44. See Frege (1960).

45. Abelard (1970, 173).

46. For the distinction between the two kinds of negation and examples of all of these features of extinctive negation, see Abelard (1970, 173–84) and Abelard (2010, 203–34) (401–14) (*glossing de Interpretatione*, 7).

47. Abelard (1970, 179). The Stoics recognised double negation, and we have examples from them of statements in which it occurs but not of arguments to illustrate its logic. See

Frede (1974, esp. 71–73). In the Arab tradition, Ibn Sina, like Garland, invokes propositional negation to negate conditionals and also disjunctions but seems not to offer a general account of such negation or note the possibility that it might be iterated. See Ibn Sina (1984, 78–79). Abelard knew nothing of the Arab discussion, and of Stoic negation only through Boethius's comments on Cicero's report on the indemonstrables, where negation is treated as applying to terms, not to propositions. See Martin (1991).

48. Abelard 2010, 160 (380).
49. Boethius (1969, 1.3.6).
50. Abelard (1970, 483).
51. Abelard (1970, 485).
52. Abelard (1970, 488).
53. Abelard (1970, 482).
54. Abelard (1970, 491).
55. Abelard (1970, 253).
56. Abelard (1970, 253).
57. Abelard (1970, 285).
58. Abelard (1970, 285).
59. See Martin (2009).
60. Abelard (1970, 255).
61. Abelard (1970, 530–32).
62. Abelard (1970, 261).
63. Abelard (Abelard 1969, 309; 1970, 455).
64. For Abelard's use of this strategy see Martin (1987).
65. See Martin (1987).
66. *Sextus Empiricus* (1949, I.309).
67. For the responses of these and the other schools to Alberic's argument, see Martin (1987).
68. See Martin (1987).
69. See Martin (1986).
70. Neckham (1863, 288–89).
71. See Martin (1998).
72. De Rijk (1974).
73. See Martin (2001).
74. Peter of Spain (1972).
75. William of Sherwood (1983, 229).
76. Peter of Spain (1972, 9).
77. Peter of Spain (1972, 170).
78. William of Sherwood (1941).
79. William of Sherwood (1941, 80).
80. Peter of Spain (1992, 232–36).
81. See Anderson and Belnap (1975, 165): 'The validity of this form of inference is something Lewis never doubts . . . and is something which has perhaps never been seriously questioned before . . . '
82. Priest (2006, 110–22).
83. Peter of Spain (1972, 77).
84. Peter of Spain (1992, 236).
85. The discussion of this question in Scotus, Ockham and others is exceedingly complex. For an extended study, see Martin (2004).
86. Scotus (1966, d. 11, q. 2, 145–46).

87. Ockham (1977, d. 11, q. 2, 369).
88. Ockham (1974, 587–90).

BIBLIOGRAPHY

Alexander Neckham. 1863. *De Naturis Rerum*, ed. Thomas Wright. London: Longman.

Anderson, Alan R. and Nuel Belnap. 1975. *Entailment, the Logic of Relevance and Necessity*. Princeton, NJ: Princeton University Press.

Aristotle. 1962. *Prior Analytics*, trans. Boethius, recensio Carnutensis. Leiden, the Netherlands: Brill (Aristoteles Latinus, III.1–4).

Barnes, Jonathan. 1981. 'Boethius and the study of logic'. In *Boethius: His Life, Thought and Influence*, ed. Margaret Gibson, 73–89. Oxford: Blackwell.

Boethius. 1833. *In Topica Ciceronis commentaria in Cicero: Opera Omnia*, V.1, ed. J. Orelli. Turin: Orelli, Fuesslini & Co.

———. 1880. *In Librum Aristotelis* ΠΕΡΙ ΕΡΜΕΝΙΑΣ, Part 2, ed. Karl Meiser. Leipzig, Germany: Teubner.

———. 1906. *In Isagogen Psorphyrii commenta*, ed. Samuel Brandt. Vienna and Leipzig, Germany: Tempsky and Freitag.

———. 1969. *De hypotheticis syllogismis*, ed. Luca Obertello. Brescia, Italy: Paideia.

———. 1990. *De topicis differentiis kai hoi buzantines metafraseis ton Manouel Holobolou kai Prochorou Kudone*, ed. Dimitri Z. Nikitas. Athens: Academy of Athens.

———. 2000. *De Consolatione Philosophiae, Opuscula Theologica*, ed. Claudio Moreschini. Munich and Leipzig, Germany: Saur.

———. 2008. *De Syllogismo categorico*, ed. and trans. Christina Thomsen Thörnqvist. Göteborg, Sweden: University of Göteborg.

Cicero. 2003. *Topica*, ed. and trans. Tobias Reinhardt. Oxford: Oxford University Press.

De Rijk, Lambertus M. 1974. Some Thirteenth Century Tracts on the Game of Obligation. *Vivarium* 12: 94–123.

Dürr, Karl. 1951. *The Propositional Logic of Boethius*. Amsterdam: North-Holland.

Etchemendy, John. 1990. *The Concept of Logical Consequence*, Cambridge, MA: Harvard University Press.

Frede, Michael. 1974. *Die Stoische Logik*. Göttingen, Germany: Vandenhoek and Ruprecht.

Frege, Gottlob. 1960. *Translations from the Philosophical Writings of Gottlob Frege*, ed. Peter Geach and Max Black. Oxford: Basil Blackwell.

Garlandus Compotista. 1959. *Dialectica*, ed. Lambertus M. de Rijk. Assen, the Netherlands: Van Gorcum.

Geach, Peter. 1972. *Logic Matters*. Oxford: Blackwell.

Ibn Sina. 1984. *Remarks and Admonitions, Part One: Logic*, trans. S.H. Inati.Toronto: Pontifical Institute of Mediaeval Studies.

Iwakuma, Yukio. 1992. 'Vocales', or Early Nominalists. *Traditio* 47:37–111.

John Duns Scotus. 1966. *Lectura* I in Opera Omnia 17. Vatican City: Typis Polyglottis Vaticanis.

Kneale, William and Martha Kneale. 1962. *The Development of Logic*. Oxford: Clarendon Press.

Marenbon, John. 1997. *The Philosophy of Peter Abelard*. Cambridge: Cambridge University Press.

———, John. 2011. 'Logic at the Turn of the Twelfth Century: A Synthesis. In Rosier-Catach, 2011, 181–217.

Martin, Christopher J. 1986. William's Machine. *Journal of Philosophy* 83:564–72.

———. 1987. 'Embarrassing arguments and surprising conclusions in the development of theories of the conditional in the twelfth century'. In *Gilbert de Poitiers et ses contemporains,* ed. Jean Jolivet and Alain de Libera, 377–401. Naples: Bibliopolis.

———. 1991. The Logic of Negation in Boethius. *Phronesis* 36:277–301.

———. 1998. The Logic of Growth: Twelfth-Century Nominalists and the Development of Theories of the Incarnation. *Medieval Philosophy and Theology* 7:1–14.

———. 1999. Non-reductive Arguments from Impossible Hypotheses in Boethius and Philoponus. *Oxford Studies in Ancient Philosophy* 17:279–302.

———. 2001. 'Obligations and liars'. In *Medieval Formal Logic,* ed. Mikko Yrjönsuuri, 63–94. Dordrecht, the Netherlands: Kluwer.

———. 2004. 'Formal consequence in Scotus and Ockham'. In *Duns Scot à Paris, 1302–2002,* ed. Olivier Boulnois, Elisabeth Karger et al., 117–50. Turnhout, Belgium: Brepols.

———. 2006. 'Medieval (European) logic'. In *The Encyclopedia of Philosophy* 5, 421–437. Detroit, MI: Macmillan Reference.

———. 2009. 'Imposition and essence: Peter Abaelard and the new theory of reference'. In *The Word in Mediaeval Philosophy,* ed. Charles Burnett, 56–84. Turnhout, Belgium: Brepols.

———. 2010. 'They had added not a single tiny proposition': The Reception of the Prior Analytics in the First Half of the Twelfth Century. *Vivarium* 48:159–92.

———. 2011a. '*De Interpretatione* 5–8: Aristotle, Boethius, and Abaelard on propositionality, negation, and the foundations of logic'. In *Methods and Methodologies: Aristotelian Logic East and West, 500–1500,* ed. Margaret Cameron and John Marenbon, 207–28. Leiden, the Netherlands: Brill.

———. 2011b. 'A Note on the Attribution of the Literal Glosses in Paris, BnF, lat. 13368 to Peter Abaelard'. In Rosier-Catach 2011, 605–46.

McCall, Storrs. 1966. Connexive Implication. *Journal of Symbolic Logic* 31:415–33.

Peter Abelard. 1919–31. *Peter Abaelards philosophische Schriften,* ed. Bernhard Geyer. Münster: Aschendorff (Beiträge zur Geschichte der Philosophie des Mittelalters 21).

———. 1969. *Super topica glossae.* In *Pietro Abelardo, Scritti di logica,* ed. Mario dal Pra, 205–330. Florence: La nuova Italia.

———. 1970. *Dialectica,* ed. Lambertus M. de Rijk. 2nd edition. Assen, the Netherlands: Van Gorcum.

———. 2010. *Petri Abaelardi Glossae Super Peri Hermenias,* ed. Klaus Jacobi and Christian Strub. Turnhout, Belgium: Brepols (Corpus Christianorum continuatio mediaeualis 206).

Peter of Spain. 1972. *Tractatus,* ed. Lambertus M. de Rijk. Assen, the Netherlands: Van Gorcum.

———. 1992. *Syncategoreumata,* ed. Lambertus M. de Rijk. Leiden, the Netherlands: Brill.

Pinzani, Roberto. 2003. *La Logica di Boezio.* Milan: Franco Angeli.

Priest, Graham. 2006. *In Contradiction.* Oxford: Oxford University Press.

Rosier-Catach, Irène, ed. 2011. *Arts du langage et théologie aux confins des XIe et XIIe siècles. Textes, maîtres, débats.* Turnhout, Belgium: Brepols (Studia Artistarum 26).

Sextus Empiricus. 1949. *Against the Professors,* ed. Richard G. Bury. Cambridge, MA: Harvard University Press.

Tarski, Alfred. 1956. *Logic, Semantics, Metamathematics.* Oxford: Clarendon Press.

Thom, Paul. 1981. *The Syllogism.* Munich: Philosophia Verlag.

Wansing, Heinrich. 2010. 'Connexive logic'. In *The Stanford Encyclopedia of Philosophy.* http://plato.stanford.edu/archives/fall2010/entries/logic-connexive/

William of Ockham. 1974. *Summa Logicae*, ed. Philotheus Boehner, Gedeon Gàl, Stephen Brown. St Bonaventure, NY: St Bonaventure University (Opera Philosophica I).

———. 1977. *Scriptum in Librum Primum Sententiarum: Ordinatio, Distinctiones IV–XVII*, ed. Girard I. Etzkorn, 361–73. St Bonaventure, NY: St Bonaventure University (Opera Theologica III).

William of Sherwood. 1941. *Syncategoremata*, ed. James R. O'Donnell. *Mediaeval Studies* 3:46–93.

———. 1983. *Introductiones in Logicam*, ed. Charles Lohr. *Traditio* 39:218–99.

CHAPTER 14

MODALITY

SIMO KNUUTTILA

MANY thinkers of the Late Middle Ages distanced themselves from the traditional patterns of interpreting Aristotle's modal syllogistic and other received views of necessity and possibility. While the modal paradigms being criticised were derived from ancient philosophy, the new conceptions associated with the alternativeness relation were for the most part medieval. Since the eighteenth century, some elements of late medieval insights have been known through Leibniz's philosophy of possible worlds, which was partially based on late medieval theories, but otherwise these developments were hardly mentioned in philosophical works until the middle of the last century. (For the historical background of Leibniz's theory, see Schmutz 2006.) Things then changed when many scholars began to investigate medieval logic and semantics, including modal logic and modal theories. Philosophically oriented historians of philosophy became interested in medieval modal theories, partly because of the lively discussion of modalities in the 60s and 70s and partly because they thought that, as distinct from ancient theories, there were similarities between some systematic assumptions of medieval theories and possible worlds semantics (PWS), which was the most influential philosophical modal paradigm of the last century.[1] One point of similarity was the association of the meaning of modal terms with the idea of simultaneous alternatives at the level of logical modalities. Whereas this aspect of modality was largely absent from ancient philosophy, it came to play an increasing role in late medieval theories, thus making them more similar to PWS than to ancient modal paradigms in this respect. On the other side, the more traditional potency model was also widely used as a theoretical framework (King 2001; Normore 2006).

I shall first summarise some key points of PWS in Section 1. In Section 2, I describe the main lines of the medieval uses of traditional extensional modalities, particularly in obligations logic and indirect proofs. Section 3 offers a brief account of early-medieval deviations from ancient modal theories. Section 4 deals with

Scotus's intentional modal semantics and its applications. The influence of new modal semantics on modal logic is discussed in Section 5.

1. Modalities in Possible Worlds Semantics

In the last fifty years, PWS has been a much-used theory in formal logic, the philosophical analysis of intensional phenomena, and some other areas of research, such as linguistics, cognitive science and the philosophy of art. In a narrow sense, 'possible worlds semantics' refers to the model theoretical semantics for modal logic that was developed in the late 50s and early 60s by many logicians, particularly Jaakko Hintikka, Stig Kanger, Arnould Bayart, Saul Kripke and Richard Montague (Copeland 2002; Lindström and Segerberg 2006, 1159–74). The basic ideas of this logical theory are conveniently summarised in Kripke's 1963 paper 'Semantical Considerations on Modal Logic'. Kripke introduces a set theoretical model structure that could be intuitively understood, as Kripke says, to involve the real world, the set of all possible worlds and relative possibilities between the worlds; for example, when every proposition that is true in one world is possible in another world, the former is possible relative to the latter. Each propositional variable has a truth value of 'true' or 'false' in each world. A proposition is necessarily true in a world iff it is true in all worlds that are possible relative to that world. For quantified modal logic, Kripke adds the sets of individuals in each world to this model structure. The corresponding quantificational model provides the truth values of various predications with respect to individuals in various worlds.

Describing the set-theoretical frame for modal logic in terms of possible worlds and their ingredients, as suggested by Kripke for truth-concerning 'alethic' modalities, is an attempt to add to the formal set-theoretical approach an applied possible worlds semantics that serves as a link between the formal model and philosophical or natural language ideas of necessity and possibility (Divers 2006; Plantinga 1974, 124–26). The modern possible worlds vocabulary was introduced by Rudolf Carnap, with a reference to Leibniz, although Carnap did not operate with the idea of alternative sets, which is crucial in PWS (Hintikka 1975, 220). The relation that Kripke called 'relative possibility' was later usually called the 'accessibility relation'. An important systematic result of the early formal studies was to show how various combinations of the properties of the accessibility relation—reflexivity, transitivity and symmetry—determined the formal semantics of the axiomatic systems of propositional modal logic that were developed in the first half of the twentieth century. The model theoretical interpretation of modal predicate logic is a more complicated matter involving questions of the structure of quantified modal propositions and the nature of quantification over possible things. A much-debated question concerning the relationship between modal

propositions *de dicto* and *de re* is often understood in terms of the so-called Barcan formula, particularly in the form

$$(1) \quad \forall x \Box \phi x \rightarrow \Box \forall x \phi x.$$

Other variants of the Barcan formula also deal with the relationship between forms
with a different order of quantifiers and modal operations $\Box$ (necessity) and $\Diamond$ (possibility), for example

$$(2) \quad \Diamond \exists x \phi x \rightarrow \exists x \Diamond \phi x.$$

Referring to (1), one can ask whether modalities *de re* can be reduced to modalities
de dicto and how the answer depends on whether the quantifiers are taken to range
over individuals of the actual world or possible worlds and whether the individuals
of alternative worlds are the same or not (Kripke 1963, 87–88; Hughes and Cresswell
1996, 238–41, 252–55; Parsons 1995).

The applied PWS associates the meaning of modal terms with multiple reference in possible worlds, necessarily true propositions being regarded as true in
all worlds independently of what the other truths might be, and possibly true
propositions being true at least in one world. The individual members of alternative worlds have properties that are invariant (necessary) or variant (contingent)
with respect to the worlds in which they exist. Many writers refer to broadly logical necessities and possibilities or metaphysical modalities in this context, and
much of the philosophical discussion of the applied PWS is, consequently, concentrated on the realism and non-realism of the possible worlds and the nature of
possible beings.[2] While there has been considerable criticism of these approaches
to modal truth (Hintikka 1982), more restricted applications of PWS for epistemic logic, deontic logic and temporal logic are found less problematic because
of the relative definiteness of the relevant alternative scenarios (Hilpinen 2005;
Hintikka 2006, 23–30).

The original formal basis of PWS represents the model theoretical methods of
its time and is as such not relevant in dealing with historical theories of modality,
except in comparative studies, but the philosophical discussions and applications of
PWS include interconnected ways of understanding modal ideas that may help interpreters to see what is or is not included in historical texts. The hallmark of the
methods based on PWS is the conception of alternative scenarios with respect to
which modal or other intensional terms are defined and modal assertions are evaluated. The idea of combining modality with simultaneous alternatives had a long
history before PWS, although not as long as the extensional view, the basic assumption of which was famously called the 'principle of plenitude' by Arthur A. Lovejoy
(1936, 52): 'No genuine potentiality of being can remain unfulfilled'. This is one of the
ideas the history of which Lovejoy traces from ancient philosophy to the nineteenth
century—without too much sophistication, to be sure. (For various criticisms, see
Knuuttila 1981.) The extensional view of possibility expressed by the principle of
plenitude is quite different from the intensional view typical of PWS. It is of some

interest that in 1957 Jaakko Hintikka published two papers in which he explained his view of modality as multiplicity of reference with respect to simultaneous alternative states of affairs and compared this basis of modal logic with Aristotle's logic where universality and omnitemporality were equated with necessity, and the principle of plenitude was taken to hold of the kinds of possibilities.[3] He argues that Aristotle treated possibilities from the point of view of their realisation in time without a conception of alternative possibilities, which is found, for example, in Leibniz's theory of possible worlds. Hintikka also mentions the separation of temporal syllogisms and modal syllogisms in William Ockham and John Buridan and refers to Arthur Prior (1957), whose works aroused interest in historical and systematic questions of tense logic and the relationship between time and modality.

The philosophical discussion of modal logic and modal theories that was incited by PWS was one of the factors that directly or indirectly influenced the study of medieval modalities since the 70s. In his article 'The Medieval Contribution to Logic' from 1969, Ernest A. Moody had not much to say about medieval modal logic.[4] The same largely holds of the history of logic by William and Martha Kneale from 1962. Now, fifty years later, there are several monographs and numerous articles on medieval modal logic and semantics, many of these concentrating on those late medieval views that abandoned the principle of plenitude for any philosophically significant kinds of modality.

2. Extensional Modalities in Obligations Logic and Indirect Proofs

My aim in this section is to delineate some influential applications of extensional modalities in medieval philosophy. Special attention is paid to their role in obligations logic and indirect proofs, which was criticised by later medieval logicians—I shall return to these developments in Section 4. Logical treatises on obligations (*De obligationibus*) deal with rules for disputations in which various statements are put forward by an opponent and evaluated by a respondent. The term 'obligation' refers to the respondent's being obliged to grant an initial statement and then to evaluate whether the opponent's new statements could be accepted in a consistent way. While disputations of this kind may have been practised in logic teaching, obligations treatises increasingly tackled various theoretical issues of coherence and consistency. (For medieval obligations logic, see Dutilh Novaes 2007; Keffer 2001; Yrjönsuuri 1994; Yrjönsuuri, ed., 2001.) In an obligational *positio* disputation, a usually false and contingent statement was first put forward and accepted. The rules of consistency defined how new statements were to be evaluated with respect to the initial statement (*positum*) and other correctly evaluated statements by answering 'I grant it', 'I deny it' or 'I don't know'.

The *positio* rules were associated with modal questions because the initial state-ment was typically said to be false but not impossible. An anonymous thirteenth-century treatise, putatively attributed to William of Sherwood, included a rule pertaining to time and possibility as follows:

> (3) When a contingently false statement referring to a present instant is posited, one must deny that it is [now]. (Anonymous 1963, 8:32–33)

When the *positum* is, say, 'You are in Rome', which is false but not impossible, treat-ing it as true demands that one should deny that the time at which the *positum* is assumed to be true is the present time of the disputation. The time rule (3), which is based on the principle of the necessity of the present, is also found in other thirteenth-century obligations treatises (Anonymous 1974a, 112–13; 1975, 32). In Anonymous 1963, the rule (3) is proved as follows:

> Let A be the name of the present instant. I call it a discrete name and not a common name. When it is false that you are in Rome, it is impossible that it is true then or in A. It can be made true only by movement or by change. It cannot be made true by movement in A, because there is no movement in an instant. Neither can it be made true by change, since if there were a change into truth in A, the truth would be in A, since whenever there is a change, there is the term of that change. Therefore it is impossible that this which is false is made true in A. Therefore, if it is true, [the time] is not A. (8:33–9:8)

The background of this proof is Aristotelian. For one thing, 'that you are in Rome' is treated as a temporally indefinite sayable that is true or false depending on how things are at various moments at which it is uttered. (See, for example, Aristotle, *Categories* 5, 4a23–2; Hintikka 1973, 150–52; Prior 1957, appendix A.) Second, it is assumed that when such a statement is true/false, it is necessarily true/false at that time. This principle of the necessity of the present, which is formulated in Chapter 9 of Aristotle's *De interpretatione*, is explained by referring to the impossibility of change at an instant of time.

In his *De libero arbitrio* (c. 1230), Robert Grosseteste describes and criticises an argument that is similar to the one just quoted:

> If it is true that Socrates is white at the instant of time A, this cannot be false at A. If, namely, that which is true at A could be false at A and this possibility were realise, the same statement would be both true and false at the same indivisible instant of time. This is impossible. But if this possibility cannot be realise, it is in vain. However, God does not create any possibility in vain. (Grosseteste 1991, 53:580–85)

The necessity of the present is defended here by arguing that the hypothesis of an unrealised possibility with respect to the actual instant is impossible because the assumption of the actuality of such a possibility leads to contradiction. This is what Aristotle maintained in *De caelo*:

> A man has at once the capacity of sitting and standing, in the sense that when he has the one he also has the other; but it does not follow that he can sit and stand simultaneously, but only at another time. But if a thing has more than

one capacity for infinite time, there is no other time and these coincide. Thus if anything which exists for an infinite time is destructible, it will have the capacity of not being. Now if it exists for infinite time, let this capacity be actualise, and it will be and not be in actuality at once. (*De caelo* I.12, 281b15–22)

In defining the notion of contingency in the *Prior Analytics* (I.13, 32a18–20), Aristotle states that if something is possible, it can be assumed to be actual without anything impossible following from this assumption. Since he thinks that this assuming is to locate a possibility in the one and only real history, it follows, as in *De caelo*, that an assumption is impossible if its opposite is always actual. This makes the truth of a now true statement necessary, as it is explained in the argument discussed by Grosseteste. Similarly the statements that are true at all times are necessary. The same ideas follow from the equation of contingency with change in the anonymous obligations treatise quoted above.

These conceptions were known to early-medieval thinkers through Boethius's two commentaries on Aristotle's *De interpretatione* (Boethius 1877–80). In explaining Aristotle's thesis of the necessity of the present (19a23–27), Boethius argues that when Socrates is seated, it is not possible that he is not seated at that time, which is in agreement with the Aristotelian assumption that possibilities refer to one and the same history. This seems to be the common view of ancient thinkers who made use of the conception of modality as alternativeness only in the context of singular prospective options.[5] The necessity of the present to which Boethius refers can be expressed as follows:

$$(4) \quad \forall x(\phi_t x \to \Box_t \phi_t x).$$

Even though things and statements about them at the present are temporally necessary, these statements as such, without a temporal specification, are contingently true or false when they are about changing things. This was one of Boethius's explanations of what Aristotle meant when he wrote that what is necessarily is when it is, although is not necessary *simpliciter* (Boethius 1877, 121:20–122:15; Boethius 1880, 241:1–242:15).[6] Aristotle applied the frequency view of necessity and contingency to the truth and falsity of temporally indefinite statements and to things in general in many places. (See, for example, *Metaphysics* IX.10 [1051b10–17].) According to this paradigm, what always is, is by necessity, and what never is, is impossible. Possibility is interpreted as expressing what is at least sometimes actual. (See Boethius 1877, 124:30–125:14; 200:20–201:3; Boethius 1880, 237:1–5.) Correspondingly, a property that belongs to all members of a group is necessary with respect to that group. An impossible property does not belong to any members, and a possible property belongs to at least one member (Boethius 1877, 120:24–121:16; for this modal conception in Aristotle and medieval authors, see Knuuttila 1993, 51–54, 101–6, 113–14, 119–21, 130–33; Knuuttila 2008, 507–15).

The quasi-statistical frequency model was often applied to types of things and statements until late medieval times. For example, in dealing with the traditional square of opposition between universal and particular statements, many authors classified statements on the basis of their modal matter: whether they are about necessary, contingent or impossible states of affairs. According to Aquinas, in contingent matter the opposite universal affirmative and negative statements are both false, and the opposite particular affirmative and negative statements are both true. This is said to apply to the pairs of statements, whether in the past, present or future tense (Thomas Aquinas 1964, *In Aristotelis libros Peri Hermeneias expositio* I, lect. 13, n. 168).[7] The same extensional interpretation of modality with respect to universal and particular statements was often associated with doctrine of the threefold modal matter before Aquinas. It was derived from Boethius but was also found in Ammonius's commentary on the *Perihermenias*, the Latin translation of which was available to Aquinas (Knuuttila 2008, 508–9).

A well-known example of the medieval temporal view of contingency is found in Aquinas's third proof of God's existence, which is based on the premise that things which may not-be at some time are not (*Summa theologiae* I, q. 2, a. 3). This is in agreement with what Aristotle says in Chapter 9 of the first book of his *De caelo*, an often-quoted source in Aquinas's time. Following Averroes, John of Jandun explicates Aristotle's view as follows:

> Such a thing cannot be destroyed from the assumed extinction of which something impossible follows since nothing impossible follows from assuming that a possibility is actual, although something false may follow from it. But if an omnitemporal thing were destroyed, an impossibility follows, namely that the same thing simultaneously is and is not . . . It follows from these that whatever can be destroyed will be destroyed by necessity, and if this is a demonstrative argument, we can deduce by it that what can be generated will be generated by necessity.

He adds that the principle that what can be generated will be generated and what can be destroyed will be destroyed applies to all sorts of entities: simple and composite substances and real or intentional accidents (*In libros Aristotelis De caelo et mundo quae extant quaestiones*, I, q. 34; John of Jandun 1552, f. 21vb).[8] This sounds deterministic, but others, following Boethius, added that free choices as well as some contingencies of nature are not predetermined, being antecedently associated with alternatives.[9]

Extensional modal ideas were also interwoven with the popular Aristotelian doctrine of active and passive potencies, which provided a model for explaining various kinds of changes: a passive potency becomes a source of change when it is activated by a contact with a corresponding active potency and there is no external hindrance. The potencies could be separately referred to as non-actualised partial possibilities, although it was thought that all types of natural possibilities built of these components were sometimes actualised. Medieval Aristotelians treated active potencies as efficient causes and divided them into necessary contingent causes. Necessary causes are always effective when they are in contact with passive powers. Contingent causes produce their effect in most cases (*in pluribus*), being prevented by chance in a few cases, or are not determined more to acting than not-acting (*ad utrumlibet*), some acts of the free will being examples. Singular caused events are considered necessary or contingent, depending on how the causes or objects of the same kind behave in other situations.[10]

Let us take a look at how the extensional view of modalities figured in indirect proofs and other arguments operating with impossible premises. Aristotle's theory of indirect proof was based on the idea that a refutable position can be shown to have impossible consequences and hence to be impossible itself: 'The impossible only follows from the impossible' (*De caelo* I.12, 281b15–16). In his reductive proofs, Aristotle often adds auxiliary premises that he himself elsewhere regards as impossibilities. This method is explained in *Topics* VII.1, 152b17–24. Galen argued that Aristotle derived impossible conclusions from other people's opinions by mixing them with impossible premises of his own. Alexander of Aphrodisias did not accept Galen's criticism. He wrote that Aristotle's impossible premises were weaker than strict impossibilities but did not explain what this meant. The same discussion continued in the sixth-century commentaries by Simplicius and Philoponus on Aristotle's *Physics* and in Arabic philosophy (Kukkonen 2002, 65–76). Apart from criticising existing theories, Aristotle also employed impossible premises in other contexts, for example, in considering things that were not separable in actuality but 'separated in thought' (*Metaphysics* VII.3). These ideas were developed by late ancient commentators into what was sometimes called the Eudemian procedure, a method of 'assuming something impossible in order to see what follows'. It has been argued that these discussions of counter-possible premises form the historical background of the branch of obligations logic that was called *positio impossibilis* (Martin 1997, 1999, 2001a).

An anonymous twelfth-century obligations treatise on impossible position (1974b) concentrated on the question of what follows when the impossible *positum* is 'Socrates is a donkey'. The content of this statement is said to be understandable, although it is incompatible with the natural course of things because it is understandable that Jesus Christ is a human being and a divine being simultaneously even though the divinity and humanity differ from each other more than humanity and donkeyhood. This sounds like a very fideist defence of the intelligibility of a position. It is added that when the *positum* is 'Socrates is a donkey', one should deny the conditional: 'If he is a donkey, he is not a man'. Following Abelard's logic, the author thinks that the meaning of the consequent is entailed by the meaning of the antecedent in a good consequence, this not being the case with various topical rules in which the consequent includes a negation (Anonymous 1974b, 118–19; for Abelard's theory of conditionals, see Martin 1987, 388–97). The two types of non-natural union on which *positio impossibilis* disputations are meant to shed light are as follows: the union of essences without the union of persons and the union of persons without the union of essences (Anonymous 1974b, 120–21). The examples are not directly theological, but their logical analysis was thought to be relevant to theology. Obligations treatises with an impossible position were also later concentrated on doctrinal impossibilities. (Examples from Henry of Ghent, John Duns Scotus and William Ockham are discussed in Knuuttila 1997.)

More elaborated discussions of the nature of impossible premises are found in the interpretations of Aristotle's reduction arguments. Averroes dealt with these in various places in his commentaries and questions on Aristotle's *Physics*. In answering the Galenic criticism mentioned above, Averroes explains that the impossible premises that Aristotle adds to the arguments are not simply impossible, but accidentally (per accidens) impossible and essentially (per se) possible. When an essentially impossible conclusion is derived from a thesis that is criticised and an auxiliary premisee that is accidentally impossible, the thesis criticised must be essentially impossible:

> It is evident that in the case of a syllogism in which both premises are possible, no impossible conclusion whatever can be inferred. If there is, however, only one possible premise in the syllogism, an impossible conclusion cannot, indeed, be inferred from that possible premise. Rather, if such a conclusion is inferred, it must follow from the impossible premise in the syllogism. It makes no difference whether the possible premise is possible essentially, but impossible accidentally (e.g., in a certain place), or whether it is possible and in no sense impossible. By this I mean to say that an absolutely impossible conclusion cannot be inferred from the premise which is essentially possible and accidentally impossible. (*Questions in Physics*, trans. Goldstein, VIII.8; Averroes 1991, 31)

Averroes explains the distinction between essential and accidental modalities when he discusses Aristotle's modal syllogistic. The syllogistic necessity premises are per se necessity statements, the necessity of which corresponds to the essential relations between things. The terms of these statements, such as 'horse' or 'animal', are also necessary, standing for invariant aspects of the things to which they refer. The statements that are impossible per accidens and possible per se are false and impossible in the sense that they are always false, although this is not based on essential relations between the terms as such (*Quaesita octo in librum Priorum*, IV.3.83–84; Averroes 1562–74, vol. I, 2b; Thom 2003, 81–85).

Averroes says that when Aristotle adds an accidentally impossible premise into an argument, it is supposed to be true 'in so far as it is possible, not in so far as it is impossible' (*Epitome of the Physics*, trans. Goldstein; Averroes 1991, 135, 139; *Commentary on the Physics*, 307vb–308ra; Averroes 1562–74, vol. IV; Kukkonen 2005). For example, when Aristotle assumes that there is a body larger than the heavens, this is possible with reference to a body qua body, but accidentally impossible with reference to the universe (*Questions in Physics*, trans. Goldstein VIII.10–12; Averroes 1991, 32). These possibilities and impossibilities do not belong to the same level of analysis. Counter-possible possibilities refer to abstract entities, such as a body *qua* body or motion *qua* motion, which do not exist as such and have no realizable possibilities (Knuuttila and Kukkonen 2011).

Thomas Aquinas also explained Aristotelian impossible hypotheses with the help of abstract possibilities. Something that is possible for a member of a genus as such may be impossible for it as a member of a species, and similarly with a thing as a member of a species and a singular being. Accidental impossibilities are irrelevant in arguments that proceed *per abstractionem* (Thomas Aquinas 1952, *In Aristotelis libros De caelo et mundo expositio* III, lect. 3, n. 560–61; cf. Thomas Aquinas, *Summa theologiae* I, q.85, a.1, ad 1). According to Aquinas, in speaking of humans as animals one can state that it is contingent that they are winged because this is not incompatible with being an animal, although humans qua humans cannot be winged. Similarly, Aristotle is said to assume that it is possible that all moving things are continuous with each other, although 'this is impossible if moving things are considered according to their determinate natures' (Thomas Aquinas 1965, *In octo libros Physicorum Aristotelis expositio*, VII, lect. 2, n. 896). Aquinas comments here on Aristotle's reduction argument against the theory of self-movers at the beginning of *Physics* VII. He refers to abstract possibilities in order to explain how Aristotle could use the impossible assumption that movers from different spheres form a continuous whole. In his commentary on *Physics* VII, Averroes gives a similar answer to the question of how anything in motion can be at rest, even though it is impossible that what is eternally moved is at rest (Averroes 1562–74, vol. IV, 307vb). This solution is also found in the commentaries on the *Physics* of Albert the Great (1890a, 488; VII, tract. 1, c. 2) and Giles of Rome (1502, f. 164vb; VII, lect. 2).

Aquinas refers to a criticism of this argument by Avicenna: if a predicate is repugnant to a subject because of the subject's specific difference, it is simply repugnant to that subject and, consequently, cannot be assumed in an argument (Thomas Aquinas 1965, *Phys.* VII, lect. 1, n. 888). He suggests that one could reformulate Aristotle's arguments without positing impossible things by proceeding with conditional statements, such as Averroes's formulation of the indirect argument against self-movers: 'If it is true that the body of the heavens stands, if one part of it stands, then it is moved by something else'. These conditionals are true, but the antecedent conditional is denied by the assumption that the heavenly body is in motion by itself (Averroes 1562–74, vol. IV, f. 308ra). Averroes and Aquinas apparently thought that the antecedent of the first conditional was, in fact, possible in an abstract sense. Aquinas does not discuss this; he was interested in conditionalising as an answer to those who found positing abstract possibilities problematic (Thomas Aquinas 1965, *Phys.* VII, lect. 1, n. 889).

In his questions in Aristotle's *Physics*, John of Jandun criticised the abstract possibilities of Averroes and Aquinas. Following the frequency interpretation of modalities, he asks how such possibilities could be treated as possibilities when they remain eternally frustrated (John of Jandun 1488, 109va, 110ra–b). His own interpretation of the indirect proofs with impossible premises in *Physics* VII is that Aristotle may have thought that the impossibilities were implied in the opponent's position or that he wanted to keep the discussion at the level of conditionals.[11]

3. EARLY-MEDIEVAL DEVIATIONS FROM THE EXTENSIONAL THEORY

Augustine's idea of God's free choice involved an intuitive idea of simultaneous alternatives from which the actual providential history is chosen; it is one of the scenarios of what could be (Knuuttila 2001, 108–9). Augustine's works were very influential in the Middle Ages and, although he did not develop any detailed theistic modal meta-physics, his conception of divine choice was probably the most influential single factor that led to theories of simultaneous alternatives as an intensional basis of mo-dalities. Some authors regarded divine possibilities as a special theological matter that did not affect the use of traditional modal ideas in other disciplines, an attitude sup-ported by the general reception of Aristotle in the thirteenth century, but there were others who found Augustine's theological modalities philosophically significant.

According to Thomas Aquinas, the active and passive natural potencies of the members of a species are among their essential properties. Therefore, miraculous events, which take place against the common course of nature, require a special supernatural active cause and a corresponding passive power, *potentia oboe-dientialis*, in created things (Knuuttila 1993, 131–32). This was a metaphysical expla-nation for the often-repeated early-medieval theological notion that things which are impossible according to lower natural causes may be possible for the higher supernatural causes. Referring to unrealised divine possibilities was part of the orthodox Augustinian view that the scope of divine omnipotence is more extensive than what takes place in the world, whether naturally or supra-naturally. John of Jandun typically writes, after having presented the main lines of what he regarded as the Aristotelian view of necessity and possibility:

> However, it should be said, according to the faith and truth, that something can be generated even though it will be never generated and cannot be generated and that one can will what one never can will and do what one never can do. One must believe this which Aristotle could not understand because it cannot be demonstrated on the basis of sensory things: it is our principle because it is above nature and based on God's power, which can do everything. To believe this is a merit, for as Augustine says, the merit ceases where the human reason offers experience. (*In libros Aristotelis De caelo et mundo Quaestiones*, I, q. 34; Jandun 1552, 22rb)

Supernatural possibilities are treated as mysterious and contrary to reason here. By statements like 'one can do what one never can do', Jandun apparently means that the possibilities of faith may be naturally impossible. A great deal of the extensive discussion of divine power was more religious than philosophical, stressing the sov-ereignty of God, but there were also attempts to reconsider the meaning of modal concepts in this context. (For divine omnipotence, see Courtenay 1990; Gelber 2004, 309–49; Holopainen 1996, 6–43; Moonan 1994; Normore 1985.)

Before the intensional modal semantics of John Duns Scotus, various new modal ideas were developed in the twelfth century. According to Abelard, what nature demands or allows and what is repugnant to it is the same for all members of a species, and what is possible in this sense for one member of a species can be derived from what is actualised in other members of the same species (Abelard 1956, *Dialectica*, 193:36–194:3; 385:1–8). This is in agreement with the traditional idea of partial potencies, but Abelard also developed some aspects of the model of simul-taneous alternatives. In his *City of God* (V.9), Augustine argued that the possibility of events having happened otherwise than divine providence had foreseen did not imply the possibility of error in God. In discussing the same example, Abelard applies a distinction that he drew elsewhere between *de sensu* and *de re* reading of modal propositions.[12] While the *de sensu* reading of 'A thing can be otherwise than God knows it to be' is false (it is possible that God knows that A is B and A is not B), the *de re* is true (God knows that A is B and A can be not B); if things were otherwise, God would possess different knowledge of them (Abelard 1919–27, *Logica* 'Ingredientibus', 429.26–430.36; Abelard 1956, *Dialectica*, 217.27–219.24). Following Abelard, Peter Lombard argued that 'Things cannot be other than as God foreknows them' is true in the compound sense and false in the divided sense. This influential formulation implies that when something is actual, its opposite could be actual at that very instant of time (Peter Lombard 1971, *Sententiae*, I, d. 38, a. 2).

In discussing future contingent propositions, Abelard retained the principle of bivalence for all assertoric statements but rejected the stronger principle that all of these are determinately true or determinately false. The notions of 'determinate' or 'definite' apply primarily to the truth-makers of statements and only secondarily to the truth of statements.[13] Abelard assumes that what is actual is temporally necessary as no longer avoidable, but he denies the unqualified necessity of the present, arguing that mutually exclusive alternatives are possible at the same time in the sense that one or another of them could have happened at that time.[14] These possibilities are compared with what are called 'broadly metaphysical possibilities' in contemporary discussion (Martin 2003, 239; for a possible worlds interpretation, see Pinzani 2003, 189–92). Abelard thinks that one might analyse the example 'A standing man can sit' as

$$(8) \quad \exists x(-\phi_t x \,\&\, \Diamond \phi_t x),$$

which denies the traditional reading of the necessity of the present (4). He seems to accept that what is actual is temporally necessary but its opposite may be simultaneously possible in a non-temporal sense. Marenbon (2006, 338–40) argues that Abelard usually thinks of possibilities as diachronic potencies.

Similar ideas are found in other twelfth-century authors. Gilbert of Poitiers argued in an Augustinian manner that God could have created a world with individuals and natural necessities other than those of the actual world. Because of the divine power, things that do not exist or will not exist can exist, and those that have not existed may have existed, and those that have existed may have been non-existent (Gilbert of Poitiers 1966, 129:25–28).

Some commentators have taken Gilbert to think that God could change the past, but he apparently means that temporal necessities, such as the necessity of the past, are based on God's free choice and do not imply any lack of divine power, similarly to Anselm of Canterbury, who says about God that 'all necessity and impossibility are subject to His will, but His will is not subject to any necessity or impossibility' (Anselm of Canterbury 1946b, 2.17; 1946c, 86:60–62). Gilbert states that Plato's 'Platonitas' is constituted by everything that in actuality or by nature (without actualisation) has belonged or belongs or will belong to Plato. Even though he does not explain why there is a modal element in the individual concept, it was probably needed in order to speak about Plato in alternative providential scenarios (Gilbert of Poitiers 1966, 144:77–78; 274:75–76; Marenbon 2007, 158–59). While many twelfth-century writers were interested in the same person's being included in alternative histories, for example, Peter as predestined to heaven or not (for example, Peter of Poitiers 1961, 128–43; *Sententiae* I c. 14), Gilbert seems to have been the first to formulate an individual concept in this way.

Peter of Poitiers was one of the authors to make use of the doctrines of the twelfth-century group called *nominales*, who argued that singular declarative statements should be primarily treated as temporally definite and as having an unchanging truth value. One of their theses was that 'What is once true is always true' (Iwakuma and Ebbesen 1992, 194, 196, 199–201, 205–6). According to Peter of Poitiers, the unchanging truth value of singular statements about contingent things could be otherwise, although they are unchangeably true or false because of God's eternal choice. The equation of necessity and immutability is here denied on the basis of simultaneous alternatives. Similarly, possibilities corresponding to divine power are immutably what they are, although things in history may begin to be temporally necessary or impossible (*Sententiae* I, c. 7, 133–43; I, c. 12, 172–82, 199–223; I, c. 14, 328–53; Peter of Poitiers 1961, 53, 114–16, 141–42). Similar ideas were developed by Robert Grosseteste, who taught that things are primarily called necessary or possible 'from eternity and without beginning' with respect to God's eternal cognition. In addition to these simple modalities, there are necessities and impossibilities with a beginning in God's unchangeable providence that are eternal contingencies in the sense that God could have chosen their opposites (Robert Grosseteste 1912, 168.26–170.33, 178.24–29; Grosseteste's views are compared with those of Duns Scotus in Lewis 1996).

4. SCOTUS'S MODAL METAPHYSICS AND OTHER FOURTEENTH-CENTURY INNOVATIONS

An influential revision of obligations logic was the change in the time rule (3) suggested by John Duns Scotus. In his *Lectura on the Sentences*, written in Oxford in the 1290s, Scotus argues that this rule may be omitted from obligations logic without changing anything else (*Lectura* I, d. 39, q. 1–5, n. 59; John Duns Scotus 1960b, 499). The background of Scotus's proposal is his refutation of the necessity of the present as a logical or metaphysical principle. In explaining the contingency of an individual state of affairs in the created order of things in a later work, Scotus defines the notion of contingency as follows:

> I do not call something contingent because it is not always or necessarily the case, but because the opposite of it could be actual at the very moment when it occurs. (*Ordinatio* I, d. 2, p. 1, q. 1–2, n. 86; John Duns Scotus 1950, 178; *Tractatus de primo principio*, IV, concl. 4; John Duns Scotus 1974, 56)

He first distances himself from the frequency division between necessity and contingency and then characterises the meaning of contingency by referring to simultaneous alternatives. Referring to the passage from the anonymous obligations treatise quoted above (Anonymous 1963), Scotus states that the rule and its proof are false since, even if 'You are in Rome' is false now, it can be true now (*Lectura* I, d. 39, q. 1–5, n. 56; John Duns Scotus 1960b, 498). Because of his interpretation of possibility, Scotus qualifies Aristotle's principle that nothing impossible will follow if a possibility is assumed to be actual—this is true, except for assuming that a counterfactual possibility is actual, where an incompossibility with respect to what is actual follows (*Lectura* I, d. 39, q. 1–5, n. 72; John Duns Scotus 1960b, 504).

Thomas Aquinas describes divine omnipotence as being determined by absolute possibilities that are expressed by statements in which the predicate is not repugnant to the subject (*Summa theologiae*, I. q. 25, a. 3c; Aquinas 1977, *In duodecim libros Metaphysicorum Aristotelis expositio* V, lect. 14, n. 971). This had become a common view in his time. What is new in Scotus is his applying the notion of 'logical possibility' (*possibile logicum*) to what Aquinas calls absolute possibilities and providing logical possibilities with a systematic role in his theistic metaphysics. Scotus was first to use the term *possibile logicum*, which is applicable to anything that can be posed as actual without incoherence; logically impossible is the same as contradictory. The notion of logical possibility is conceptually prior to that of metaphysical possibility (*potentia metaphysica*), which is associated with active and passive potencies, whether divine or created (see Honnefelder 1991, 45–74).

In order to explain the status of logical possibilities, Scotus states that if it is assumed that neither God nor the world existed and that the proposition 'The world will be' then existed in some intellect, this would be possibly true; similarly, 'The world is possible' would be true. Independently of which intellect formulates these propositions, they are logically possible or true (*Ordinatio* I, d. 7, q. 1, n. 27; John Duns Scotus 1956, 118; *Lectura* I, d. 7, n. 32; John Duns Scotus 1960a, 484; *Lectura* I, d. 39, q. 1–5, n. 49; John Duns Scotus 1960b, 494; *Quaestiones super libros Metaphysicorum Aristotelis* IX, q. 1–2, n. 18; John Duns Scotus 1997, 514). Logically possible predications about non-existent subjects, as in these examples, are about beings in the sense that they pertain to something to which existence is not repugnant. To be a being at this logical level is to have a concept that is not contradictory or, which amounts to the same, to be thinkable as existent. Scotus describes the difference between a never-actualised human being, the concept of which is not contradictory, and a never actualised chimera, the concept of which is contradictory, as follows:

> Why it is repugnant to the human being and why it is repugnant to the chimera is only because this is this and that is that, as is realise by any intellect . . . The human being is possible by logical potency, because it is not repugnant to it to be a thing, and the chimera is impossible by the opposed impossibility because it is repugnant to it to be a thing . . . this logical possibility, taken as such, could stand in its own right even though, *per impossibile*, there were no omnipotence to regard it. (*Ordinatio* I, d. 36, n. 60–61; John Duns Scotus 1963, 296)

Scotus stresses that logical possibilities have no kind of existence by themselves. However, they differ by their thinkable actuality from the absolute nothingness of impossible things, and they are objective in the sense that their intelligibility is the same for any intellect (*Ordinatio* II, d. 1, q. 2, n. 81–84; John Duns Scotus 1973, 43–44).

Scotus thinks that logical modalities determine the content of the infinite act about everything that is intelligible in God's intellect which, as distinct from divine will, is a necessarily acting power without liberty. This act of the divine intellect provides logical possibilities with 'intelligible being' in God's intellect, and they are said to have 'possible being' as the intentional correlates of God's power. A stone produced in an intelligible being by the divine intellect has this status formally of itself and principiatively, as it were, through the divine intellect (*Tractatus de primo principio* IV, concl. 9; John Duns Scotus 1974, 68; *Ordinatio* I, d. 35, n. 32; I, d. 38, n. 9; d. 43, n. 14–16; I, d. 45, n. 4; John Duns Scotus 1963, 258, 306, 354, 372).

Although possibilities in themselves are necessary presuppositions of anything that is or might be, the actualisation of the finite world is contingent, depending ultimately on the free choice of the first cause. Actual states of affairs consist of compossibilities that form a subset of alternative possibilities with respect to the same time. All alternatives are logical possibilities, though not compossible: they belong to alternative sets of compatible possibilities. Incompossibilities remain outside the combinations that divine intellect presents to divine will, which reacts with liking (*complacentia*) to everything that can be understood as good and with an efficacious act to the much more limited group of those combinations that will be true (*Ordinatio* I, d. 38, n. 10; d. 43, n. 14; John Duns Scotus 1963, 307; 358–61; *Lectura* I, d. 39, q. 1–5, n. 62–65; John Duns Scotus 1960b, 5001; *Quodlibet* q. 16, n. 7; John Duns Scotus 1895, 190. For Scotus's modal theory, see also Hoffmann 2009; Honnefelder 1991; Knuuttila 1996; Langston 2010; Normore 2003.)

Scotus's theory of modality is characterised by the theoretical ideas of logical possibility, possible beings without existence, alternativeness and compossibility. Logical possibilities are distinguished from metaphysical or real possibilities, which are associated with powers. These are the elements that show similarities to some tenets of PWS. Needless to say, he did not operate with model-theoretical concepts or other logical tools of the twentieth century, as is stressed by Wyatt (2000) and Vos (2006, 271–72). It may be added he did not use the term 'possible world'.

After Scotus's revision, the time rule of obligations logic (3) was still used in Walter Burley's obligations treatise in 1304, but after this it is seldom mentioned (Yrjönsuuri 1994, 74). Dropping (3) had consequences for interpreting the *positio* game. According to the old rules, all answers were taken to refer to the time of the truth of the *positum* (Anonymous 1963, 10:17–20; Walter Burley 1963, 61:22–23). While this time was different from the present in the case of a false *positum*, the statements that were logically independent of the *positum* and other accepted and denied statements were evaluated by attending to their present truth or falsity. Obligational answers could remain consistent on these lines, to be sure, but there was no sensible interpretation of the set of answers that, in fact, were formed with respect to different moments of time. In Scotus's approach the answers could be regarded as descriptions of possible states of affairs that differed from the actual one because of the counterfactual *positum* and its implications. The Scotist version of obligations logic was employed in some Oxford discussions of divine omniscience and future contingent statements. In dealing with the question of whether things can be otherwise than God eternally knows them to be, Arnold of Strelley and Robert Holcot put forward a counterfactual *positum*, arguing that God's foreknowledge of its opposite can be denied. This counterfactual of the past was said to be only accidentally impossible, that is, impossible relative to a contingent future fact. The truths about future contingent events in God's knowledge are eternally true, but they could have been eternally false (Gelber 2004, 158–78). These were reformulations of twelfth-century ideas mentioned above.

Another interpretation of counterfactual obligational statements was developed by Richard Kilvington, who argued that impertinent propositions should be given the responses that would be reasonable if the counterfactual *positum* were true and things would otherwise differ from the actual world as little as possible. For example, if the false *positum* in the disputation taking place in Oxford is 'You are in Rome', and the opponent then proposes: '"You are in Rome" and "You are a bishop" are alike', one should deny this if one is not a bishop (Richard Kilvington 1990, 47q). The statements are alike as such, both being false and contingent, but if this is conceded, then one should concede the problematic conclusion 'You are a bishop' and, it seems, any false contingent proposition could be proved when a false and contingent *positum* has been accepted. (For this example in Anonymous 1963, see 5:29–6:6.) Kilvington's approach shows some similarities to the theories of subjunctive conditionals that are based on PWS.[15] A different fourteenth-century innovation was Richard Swyneshed's revision of obligations logic to the effect that relevant and irrelevant statements should be evaluated separately. This theory of two-column bookkeeping could be understood as an attempt to deal separately with the domains of actuality and possibility (Yrjönsuuri 1994, 89–101; Yrjönsuuri 1998).

The question of impossible assumptions in indirect proofs was also re-evaluated in the light of the new modal semantics. As mentioned above, John of Jandun criticised the abstract possibilities in Averroes and Aquinas from the point of view of his frequency interpretation of modality. In his quite different criticism of abstract possibilities, John Buridan summarises its main lines as follows: even though various moving bodies cannot be continuous, this is not impossible with respect to the common concept of a moving body. When the assumption of this possibility, together with the position that is criticised, results in an impossible consequent, it is the position criticised that is responsible for the impossibility (*Quaestiones super octo Physicorum libros Aristotelis* VII, q. 3; John Buridan 1509, f. 105ra). Buridan's comments on this:

> Were this a good solution, one could say as well: every body is at rest, but some bodies are in motion, namely the heavenly bodies; therefore that which is at rest is in motion. This conclusion is repugnant to the concepts of motion, rest and bodies, but the second premise is true and the first premise is not repugnant to the concepts of motion, rest and body. Therefore this mode of argument is totally invalid. (*Phys.* VII, q. 3; Buridan 1509, f. 105rb)

Buridan thought that operating with abstract possibilities (*rationes communes*), as Averroes and Aquinas did, was a seriously mistaken idea. John of Jandun refuted abstract possibilities because they were never realised, but this was not Buridan's point because he thought that most possibilities remain unrealised. However, every possibility could be actual, and this is not the case with abstract counterfactuals, the assumed actuality of which leads to contradictories. This cannot be what Aristotle had in mind, Buridan concludes; therefore, Aristotle in fact made use of the idea of absolute or simple possibilities, that is, alternative physical systems that are false but not contradictory and that might have been realised by a divine power. (For Buridan's discussions of how various possibility propositions are assumed to be true without contradiction, see, e.g., *Phys.* III, q.15; Buridan 1509, f. 57rb–58rb; Sylla 2001.) Buridan reasons that since Aristotle's counterfactual assumptions do not make sense without the distinction between simple and natural modalities, he must have made use of it. Buridan's interpretation makes Aristotle an adherent of the Scotist conception of possibilities as alternative scenarios, one of which is the actual world. He writes that he feels great joy in having noticed that Aristotle 'to a great extent agreed with our true faith and firmly believed that many things are impossible with respect to natural possibilities and simply possible through supernatural potency' (*Phys.* VII, q. 3; Buridan 1509, f. 105rb).

Apart from Buridan's considerations about Aristotle, his interpretation of counterfactual arguments in physics supported an increasing interest in cosmological thought experiments with a reference to divine omnipotence and alternative scenarios, such as Nicolas Oresme's *On the Heavens and Earth* (Kukkonen 2005, 461–63). Treating possibilities as thinkable ways of being actual separated this trend from conceptualising thought experiments with the help of abstract possibilities of Averroes, Aquinas and others. Buridan criticised the abstractive approach for operating with possibilities that cannot be actualised, but they were not even meant to be thought of as actualised, being embedded in a different conceptual model (see also Knuuttila and Kukkonen 2011).

5. THE NEW MODAL SEMANTICS AND MODAL SYLLOGISTICS

In the second part of the thirteenth century, the study of modal logic was furthered by several new commentaries on Aristotle's *Prior Analytics*, which are not yet edited. This literature was influenced by Robert Kilwardby's commentary (c. 1240, printed in 1516). Also printed is Albert the Great's mid-thirteenth-century commentary, which is closely based on Kilwardby's work (Lagerlund 2000, 59–60). Kilwardby regarded Aristotle's modal syllogistics as a correct theory of reality, the explication of which often demanded special philosophical considerations.

One of the traditional problems of Aristotle's theory was how to understand the conversions of syllogistic modal statements, which Kilwardby read *de re* rather than *de dicto*:

(9) 'Every (some) A is necessarily B' to 'Some B is necessarily A'.
   (10) 'Every (some) A is contingently B' to 'Some B is contingently A'.

As for (9), Kilwardby argues, like Averroes, that Aristotle restricted syllogistic necessity premises to necessity propositions per se. These are convertible because the
terms are essential and signify necessary constituents of things. Convertibility does
not apply to accidentally necessary statements, such as 'Every awake being is necessarily an animal', which are taken to be necessary in the sense of being always true
when the subjects exist (Kilwardby 1516, 7ra–b; 45rb; for the nature of the terms in
per se predications, see also 8va; 21ra; 22ra; 25rb).

   Following Aristotle, Kilwardby taught that a two-edged negative contingency
statement (neither necessary nor impossible) implies an affirmative contingency
statement of the same quantity, that is, universal or particular, and all contingency statements are converted by the conversion of terms into particular contingency statements (10) (Kilwardby 1516, 7vb–8rb). Referring to Aristotle's remark
that 'A contingently belongs to B' may mean either 'to that to which B belongs' or
'to that to which B contingently belongs' (*An. pr.* I.13, 32b23–32), Kilwardby argues
that the subject terms in contingency syllogisms are 'ampliated' in the latter way,
if syllogistic relations do not demand restriction. As for the necessity propositions, he thinks that since the terms in per se necessity propositions are essential,
'Every A is necessarily B' and 'Whatever is necessarily A is necessarily B' mean
the same. Ampliated and non-ampliated contingency premises do not mean the
same, although both are convertible. The conversion of non-ampliated contingency premises *de re* is in agreement with a frequency interpretation of universal
and particular contingency propositions (Kilwardby 1516, 19vb; 21ra–b; 22ra–b;
see also Thom 2003, 102–3; 2007, 23–40, 88–99).

   In dealing with Aristotle's mixed first-figure syllogisms with a major necessity
premise and a minor assertoric premise, Kilwardby argues that the non-modalised
premise is, in fact, necessary per se. He calls this a simply assertoric premise. The
valid first-figure syllogisms with contingent and assertoric premises are also said to
require simply assertoric premises, but this time the predicate of such a premise is
said to belong to the subject essentially, invariably or by natural contingency
(Kilwardby 1516, 16va–17ra; 18vb; 21rb; 24vb; 25rb). Kilwardby explains the various
readings of assertoric premises by stating that a first-figure major necessity premise
'appropriates' to itself a minor premise of a certain kind. There are analogous appropriation rules for mixed second-figure and third-figure moods and mixed necessity–contingency and contingency–assertoric moods (Kilwardby 1516, 16vb; 17va–b;
18vb; 24vb; 25ra; 27va–b; see also Thom 2007, 160–61, 165–66, 172–74, 219–20).

   The subject term of the first premise is ampliated in uniform contingency syllogisms, but not in mixed contingency syllogisms (Kilwardby 1516, 19vb; 21ra–b). The
ampliated major contingency premise is always false when the subject is an accidental term and the predicate a substantial term, but the minor contingency premise
may be true even when the predicate is a substantial term, if the subject term is not
ampliated (Kilwardby 1516, 22ra). There are further metaphysical assumptions of

this kind, which in Kilwardby's view are required for a right interpretation of
Aristotle's theory. In this approach, modal terms are interpreted in an essential or
extensional way. These conceptions played an important role in Richard Campsall's
early-fourteenth-century *Questions on Aristotle's Prior Analytics*. He argued that *de
re* necessity with respect to actual things equates to unchanging predication and
contingency to changing predication.[16]

William Ockham, John Buridan and many other fourteenth-century logicians
took the notion of possibility as non-contradictoriness with respect to actual and
possible beings as the starting point of their modal logic, which largely dropped the
thirteenth-century essentialist assumptions. Possibility does not entail actuality and
immutable actuality does not entail necessity. In treatises on modal logic based on
these principles, modal statements were discussed separately with respect to compound *(de dicto)* and divided *(de re)* senses. In the former case, a modal term was
taken to qualify the *dictum* that was the content of the corresponding assertoric
statement, for example, the *dictum* that all human beings are mortal. In the latter
case, a modal term was taken to qualify the copula. The distinction between these
senses can be exemplified as follows:

(9) It is possible that some A is B
or
(10) Some A is-possibly B.

Divided modals were divided into two groups depending on whether the subject
term was taken to stand for actual beings or unrestrictedly for possible beings. It was
thought that logicians should analyse the relationships between all readings of modal
statements and, furthermore, the conversions, syllogisms and other inferences with
respect to these. Against this background, Aristotle's modal syllogistics was seen as
incomplete. It was thought that reconstructing Aristotle's theory as a uniform system
without distinguishing between the fine structures of modal premises was not possible (Knuuttila 2008, 551–59; Lagerlund 2000, 91–201; Thom 2003, 141–91).

Ockham and Buridan state that the truth of 'A white thing can be black'
demands the truth of 'This can be black' and that 'This can be black' and '"This is
black" is possible' mean the same (William Ockham 1974, 276–79; 448; 632–34;
Summa logicae II, c. 10; III-1, c. 32, III-3, c. 10; John Buridan 1976, 75–76; Buridan,
Tractatus de consequentiis II, c. 7, concl. 16). The latter statement exemplifies a compound reading and the former a divided reading. In Ockham and Buridan, these
are equated at the basic level with demonstrative pronouns, but are separated in the
discussion of quantified universal and particular statements. Ockham discusses divided possibility statements with actual and merely possible subjects, but divided
necessity statements with actual subjects only, which makes his theory less systematic than that of Buridan, who took the subject terms of all quantified divided modal
statements to stand for possible beings if they are not said to be restricted to actual
ones (see Lagerlund 112–15). The truth of quantified divided modals demands the
truth of all or some relevant singular statements of the type just mentioned; the
demonstrative pronoun is then apparently imagined to refer to a possible being

(*Summa logicae* I, c. 72; III-3, c. 10; William Ockham 1974, 215–16, 634; *Tractatus de consequentiis* II, c. 6, concl. 5; John Buridan 1976, 66–67). While Ockham and Buridan employ the Scotist view of alternative logical possibilities in dealing with modal syllogistic, they treated real possibilities diachronically. Ockham stresses that what is temporally present is necessary (Normore 1982, 370–73; for the difficulties in combining these view, see Normore 2006). Ockham was interested in syllogistic tense logic, like Richard of Campsall (1968, q. 4, 11); see Broadie 1993, 177–90. (For thirteenth-century tense logic, see Goris 2001, Uckelman 2009, 85–102.)

Buridan seems to think that the possible truth of 'This is an X' means that it is true in at least one of the possible states of affairs in which the possible being referred to by 'this' occurs; for example, in describing his identity theory of predication, Buridan suggests that 'An A was B' means that a past thing had the (past) predicates A and B, and that 'An A is possibly B' means that a possible thing has the (possible) predicates A and B:

> Furthermore, it is also clear that if we say 'A is B', then provided that the terms are
> not ampliated to the past or future, it follows that 'A is B' is equivalent to 'A is the
> same as B' . . . in the sense that some A should be posited to be the same as some
> B. And the same goes for the past and the future. For there is no difference in
> saying 'Aristotle was someone disputing' and 'Aristotle was the same as someone
> disputing' . . . not because Aristotle and someone disputing are the same, but
> because they were the same, and the case is similar with the future and the
> possible. (*Sophismata* 2, concl. 10; John Buridan 2001, 855–56)

The necessary truth of 'This is an X' would mean that it is true in all possible states of affairs in which the thing referred to by 'this' occurs (Knuuttila 2009; for the relative or conditional notion of necessity, see *Tractatus de consequenciis* IV; John Buridan 1976, 112). If a counterfactual state of affairs is possible, it can be coherently imagined as actual. This was Buridan's criticism of the interpretation of Aristotle's indirect proofs as impossible hypotheses by Averroes and Thomas Aquinas (Section 2 above). Buridan typically writes that the matter of water can take the form of air that does not now exist, although not the non-existing form of air (Buridan 1976, 76; *Tractatus de consequentiis*, II, c. 7, concl. 16). This matter could be informed by the form of air instead of the form of water; there can be the same being in alternative situations, as in the Scotist obligational example of being in Rome instead of Oxford. Buridan's interest in this question is shown in his discussions of the reference of definite descriptions and proper names, some similarities of which to contemporary discussions are mentioned in Ashworth (2004).

Many scholars have found Buridan's modal logic congenial with the philosophical assumptions of PWS. George Hughes (1989, 97) writes: 'It seems to me, in fact, that in his modal logic he is implicitly working with a kind of possible worlds semantics throughout'. He ends his paper stating that one could give a Kripke-style semantics for Buridan's modal systems and an axiomatic basis for it, 'but it would take us well into the twentieth century' (108). Other commentators have referred to usefulness of the PWS perspective but also to historical differences (Dutilh Novaes 2007, 90–102; Knuuttila 1993, 171; Lagerlund 2000, 163; see also Klima 2001, 72, 78,

82–83). One theory that is mentioned in this context is Buridan's octagon of oppo-sition for divided modal statements (Hughes 1989, 109–10; Klima 2001, 82–83). The equivalent formulations of modals with the different order of quantifying terms (every, some), negation and modal terms, which are treated like operators over possible situations, are combined into eight groups of nine equivalent formulae. These are presented in a diagram that shows the relations of contradiction, contra-riety, sub-contrariety and sub-alternation between them (see also Karger 2003.) The new modal semantics also influenced late medieval theories of epistemic logic and deontic logic (Knuuttila 2008, 559–67).

NOTES

1. For various references to PWS in studies of medieval logic and semantics, see Knuuttila (1981, 232); Knuuttila (1982, 335); Spade (1982, 3, 11); Goddu (1984, 59–78); King (1985, 81); Hughes (1989, 97); Martin (1990, 578–79); Vos et al. (1994, 30–32); Knuuttila (1996, 141–43); Lagerlund (2000, 163–64); Klima (2001, 72, 78, 82–83); Pinzani (2003, 186–92); Vos (2006); Dutilh Novaes (2007, 90–102); Uckelman (2009, 80–81, 93).

2. Kripke (1972) explained that proper names are rigid designators the invariant reference of which in alternative possible worlds exemplifies metaphysical necessity. Putnam applied Kripke's theory to natural kinds (1973, 1975, 215–71). These works gave rise to an extensive discussion of modality, meaning and reference. For Putnam's later view, see Putnam (1990, 54–79). According to Plantinga, broadly logical necessity is 'wider than that captured in first order logic' and 'narrower than that of causal or natural necessity' (1974, 2). For realism and non-realism of possible worlds, see Chihara (1998); Divers (2002); Stalnaker (2003). For logical and metaphysical modalities in general, see Hale and Hoffmann (2010).

3. Hintikka (1957a) (Modality as Referential Multiplicity) and Hintikka (1957b) (Necessity, Universality and Time in Aristotle). He has discussed similar questions in many studies of the history of modal theories (1973, 1981, 1988, and, with Heikki Kannisto, 1981).

4. Moody (1975, 371–92). Referring to the extension of contemporary logical studies into the fields of semantics, modal logic and philosophy of language, Moody writes that these 'turn out to be the areas in which the medieval logicians made their most interesting contributions' (372).

5. See Knuuttila (2008, 516–17). The idea of prospective possibilities with respect to future alternatives was mentioned by Aristotle and was developed further in later discus-sions between peripatetic and Stoic thinkers. Boethius assumed that there were alternative future possibilities, of which those that would remain unrealised disappear. Boethius and his followers did not mean that the idea of diachronic alternatives could refute the necessity of the present; they thought that prospective alternatives made it compatible with a non-deterministic view of action.

6. Boethius argues that ϕ_t (a) is compatible with the temporally indefinite

$$(5)\ \Diamond - \phi(a),$$

which is true if it is not determined that $\phi(a)$ is always true when a exists. Boethius also refers to antecedent prospective alternatives, arguing that

$$(6) \; \Box_t \, \phi_t \, (a)$$

is compatible with

$$(7) \; \Diamond_{\text{earlier than } t} \, \text{-}\phi_t \, (a).$$

See Boethius (1880, 245:4–246:19). These approaches, which, in fact, did not undermine the necessity of the present, were often repeated in medieval discussions (Knuuttila 2008, 512, 517, 536).

7. See also Thomas Aquinas (1977), *In duodecim libros Metaphysicorum Aristotelis expositio* IX, lect. 11, n. 1900.

8. For a similar equation of modal and temporal notions in Avicenna and Averroes, see Street (2005, 99–116); Kukkonen (2000, 329–47).

9. For Boethius, see Kretzmann (1985, 47–51). For qualifying the necessity of the present by antecedent alternatives, see Boethius (1880, 235:4–246:19); Anselm of Canterbury (1946a, 250.113–16; 251.20–28; *De concordia* I.3); Albert the Great (1890b, 421; *Liber I Perihermeneias* I, tract. 5, c. 5); Thomas Aquinas (1964; *In Peri Hermeneias expositio* I, lect. 15, n. 201); Siger of Brabant (1954, 32.4–118).

10. See Maier (1949, 219–50); Knuuttila (1993, 131–36). The temporal frequency qualification of the necessity of the present causation was analogous to the shift from present applications of token reflexive statements about changeable things to their behaviour as temporally indefinite statements (see note 6 above). Many authors referred to the distinction between unchangeably true per se necessary statements and accidentally necessary past tense statements that had begun to be true (Knuuttila 1993, 114–18).

11. John of Jandun (1488, 110vb). John of Jandun criticises the conditional version of Aquinas, but his own conditionalising of the argument does not differ formally from that of Averroes and Aquinas—a refutable thesis is now an antecedent and a false conditional a consequent.

12. See Abelard (1958, *Super Periermenias XII–XIV*, 3–47). Later authors usually spoke about a distinction between modalities *de dicto* and *de sensu* or the compound and divided sense. For this terminology and Abelard's detailed discussions of the relationship between modal and temporal terms in statements, see Knuuttila (2008, 533–38). For the historical background of Abelard's argument, see Marenbon (1997, 226–28).

13. Lewis (1987). After Abelard, medieval authors usually regarded future contingent statements as either true or false. Abelard thought that this was Aristotle's view as well, but later authors mostly believed that Aristotle gave up bivalence with respect to these statements; Knuuttila (2010, 75–95).

14. 'Whence we concede that all men are able to see, even those who are blind, but nevertheless there may be no reversion from privation to habit. For it might have fallen out, that he who has been made blind, would have seen even at this time at which he remains blind, in such a way, that is, that he never would have been blind . . . and we concede that a standing man might sit at the present moment, but not that he is able to sit, while he stands, in such a way, that is, that he is able to be both sitting and standing'; Abelard (1919–27, 273:39–274:19); translated in Martin (2003, 238–39). See the discussion of this and some other texts in Martin (2001, 2003).

15. See Spade (1982, 19–28). For some discussions of Spade's attempt to interpret obligations logic in general as a theory of counterfactual conditionals, see Yrjönsuuri (1994, 158–74); Martin (2001, 69–70).

16. Richard Campsall (1968, 5.38; 5.43–5; 6.25; 9.19; 12.31). He says that an affirmative *de re* possibility statement with terms standing for actual things implies the corresponding assertoric statement (5.40) and a negative *de re* possibility statement about the present

implies the corresponding *de re* necessity statement (5.50). All possibilities are actualised, and things cannot be otherwise because all present-tense negative statements are necessarily true. An affirmative assertoric statement about the present does not imply the corresponding *de re* necessity statement because of the definition a *de re* contingency statement as a conjunction of an affirmative and corresponding negative possibility proper statement (7.34–36). For the same reason, a negative *de re* possibility statement does not imply the corresponding assertoric statement. For a different interpretation of Campsall's confusing formulations, see Lagerlund (2000, 87–90).

BIBLIOGRAPHY

Albert the Great. 1890a. *Physicorum libri VIII*. Opera omnia, vol. 3, ed. August Borgnet. Paris: Vivès.

———. 1890b. *Liber I Perihermeneias*, Opera omnia, vol. 1, ed. August Borgnet. Paris: Vivès.

Anonymous. 1963. *De obligationibus*, ed. Romuald Green in *The Logical Treatise 'De obligationibus': An Introduction with Critical Texts of William of Sherwood (?) and Walter Burley*. Ph.D. diss., University of Louvain, Belgium.

———. 1974a. *Tractatus Emmeranus de falsi positione*. An edition in L. M. de Rijk, Some Thirteenth Century Tracts on the Game of Obligation I. *Vivarium* 12:94–123, translated by Mikko Yrjönsuuri in Yrjönsuuri, ed. 2001, 199–215.

———. 1974b. *Tractatus Emmeranus de impossibili positione*. An edition in L. M. de Rijk, Some Thirteenth Century Tracts on the Game of Obligation I. *Vivarium* 12:94–123, translated by Mikko Yrjönsuuri in Yrjönsuuri, ed. 2001, 217–23.

———. 1975. *Obligationes Parisienses*. An edition in L. M. de Rijk, Some Thirteenth Century Tracts on the Game of Obligation II. *Vivarium* 13:22–54.

Anselm of Canterbury. 1946a. *De concordia praescientiae et praedestinationis et gratiae Dei cum libero arbitrio*, Opera omnia, 2, ed. Franciscus Salesius Schmitt. Edinburgh: Nelson.

———. 1946b. *Cur Deus homo*, Opera omnia, 2, ed. Franciscus Salesius Schmitt. Edinburgh: Nelson.

———. 1946c. *Meditatio Redemptionis Humanae*, Opera omnia, 3, ed. Franciscus Salesius Schmitt. Edinburgh: Nelson.

Ashworth, E. Jennifer. 2004. 'Singular terms and singular concepts: From Buridan to the early sixteenth century'. In *John Buridan and Beyond: Topics in the Language Sciences, 1300–1700*, ed. Russell L. Friedman and Sten Ebbesen, 121–51. Copenhagen: The Royal Danish Academy of Sciences and Letters.

Averroes. 1991. *Averroes' Questions in Physics from the Unpublished Sêfer ha-derûšîm ha-tib'îyîm*, translated and edited by Helen Tunik Goldstein. Dordrecht: Kluwer (The New Synthese Historical Library, 39).

———. 1562–74. *Aristotelis Opera cum Averrois Commentariis*. Venice; reprint Frankfurt am Main, Germany: Minerva, 1962.

Boethius. 1877–80. *Commentarii in librum Aristotelis* Perihermeneias *I–II*, ed. C. Meiser. Leipzig, Germany: Teubner.

Broadie, Alexander. 1993. *Introduction to Medieval Logic*. Oxford: Clarendon Press.

Chihara, Charles S. 1998. *The Worlds of Possibility: Modal Realism and the Semantics of Modal Logic*. Oxford: Clarendon Press.

Copeland, B. Jack. 2002. The Genesis of Possible Worlds Semantics. *Journal of Philosophical Logic* 31:99–137.

Courtenay, William J. 1990. *Capacity and Volition: A History of the Distinction of Absolute and Ordained Power*. Bergamo, Italy: Pierluigi Lubrina Editore.

Divers, John. 2002. *Possible Worlds*. London: Routledge.

———. 2006. Possible-Worlds Semantics without Possible Worlds: The Agnostic Approach. *Mind* 115:187–225.

Dutilh Novaes, Catarina. 2007. *Formalizing Medieval Logical Theories: Suppositio, Obligationes and Consequentia. Logic, Epistemology, and the Unity of Science, 7*. Dordrecht, the Netherlands: Springer.

Gelber, Hester Goodenough. 2004. *It Could Have Been Otherwise: Contingency and Necessity in Dominican Theology at Oxford, 1300–1350*. Leiden, the Netherlands, and Boston: Brill (Studien und Texte zur Geistesgeschichte des Mittelalters, 81).

Gilbert of Poitiers. 1966. *The Commentaries on Boethius*, ed. Nicholas M. Häring. Toronto: Pontifical Institute of Mediaeval Studies.

Giles of Rome. 1502. *Commentaria in octo libros Phisicorum Aristotelis*. Venice: Andra de Toresanis de Asula.

Goddu, André. 1984. *The Physics of William of Ockham*. Leiden, the Netherlands: Brill. (Studien und Texte zur Geistesgeschichte des Mittelalters 16).

Goris, Harm. 2001. Tense Logic in 13th-Century Theology. *Vivarium* 39:161–84.

Hale, Bob and Aviv Hoffmann, eds. 2010. *Modality: Metaphysics, Logic, and Epistemology*. Oxford: Oxford University Press.

Hilpinen, Risto. 2005. 'Deontic, epistemic, and temporal modal logics'. In *A Companion to Philosophical Logic*, ed. Dale Jacquette, 491–509. Oxford: Blackwell

Hintikka, Jaakko. 1957a. Modality as Referential Multiplicity. *Ajatus* 20:49–64.

———. 1957b. Necessity, Universality, and Time in Aristotle. *Ajatus* 20:65–90.

———. 1973. *Time and Necessity: Studies in Aristotle's Theory of Modality*. Oxford: Clarendon Press.

———. 1975. 'Carnap's heritage in logical semantics'. In Rudolf Carnap, *Logical Empiricist*, ed. Jaakko Hintikka, 217–42. Dordrecht: Reidel (Synthese Library, 73).

———. 1981. 'Leibniz on plenitude, relations, and the "Reign of Law"'. In Knuuttila, ed., 1981, 259–86.

———. 1982. 'Is alethic modal logic possible?' In *Intensional Logic: Theory and Applications*, ed. Ilkka Niiniluoto and Esa Saarinen. Helsinki: The Philosophical Society of Finland (Acta Philosophica Fennica 35: 89–105); also published in Jaakko and Merrill Hintikka, *The Logic of Epistemology and the Epistemology of Logic*, 1–15. Dordrecht, the Netherlands: Kluwer (Synthese Library, 200).

———. 1988. 'Was Leibniz's deity an *Akrates*?' In *Modern Modalities: Studies of the History of Modal Theories from Medieval Nominalism to Logical Positivism*, ed. Simo Knuuttila, 85–108. Dordrecht, the Netherlands: Kluwer (Synthese Historical Library, 33).

———. 2006. 'Intellectual autobiography'. In *The Philosophy of Jaakko Hintikka*, ed. Randall E. Auxier and Lewis Edwin Hahn, 3–84. Chicago and La Salle, IL: Open Court (Library of Living Philosophers, 30).

Hintikka, Jaakko and Heikki Kannisto. 1981. 'Kant on "The Great Chain of Being" or on the eventual realization of all possibilities: A comparative study'. In Knuuttila, ed., 1981, 287–308.

Hoffmann, Tobias. 2009. 'Duns Scotus on the origin of the possibles in the divine intellect'. In *Philosophical Debates at Paris in the Early Fourteenth Century*, ed. Stephen F. Brown, Thomas Dewender and Theo Kobusch, 359–79. Leiden, the Netherlands: Brill.

Holopainen, Toivo. 1996. *Dialectic and Theology in the Eleventh Century*. Leiden, the
    Netherlands: Brill.

Honnefelder, Ludger. 1991. *Scientia transcendens. Die formale Bestimmung der Seiendheit
    und Realität in der Metaphysik des Mittelalters und der Neuzeit*. Hamburg, Germany:
    Felix Meiner.

Hughes, George E. 1989. 'Modal logic of John Buridan'. In *Atti del convegno Internazionale
    di Storia della Logica. Le Teorie della Modalità*, ed. Giovanna Corsi, Corrado
    Mangione and Massimo Mugnai, 93–111 Bologna: CLUEB.

Hughes, George H. and Maxwell J. Cresswell. 1996. *A New Introduction to Modal Logic*.
    London: Routledge.

Iwakuma, Yukio and Sten Ebbesen. 1992. Logico-Theological Schools from the Second Half
    of the 12th Century: A List of Sources. *Vivarium* 30:173–210.

John Buridan. 1509. *Quaestiones super octo Physicorum libros Aristotelis*. Paris. Reprint,
    Franfurt am Main, Germany: Minerva, 1964.

——. 1976. *Tractatus de consequentiis*, ed. Hubert Hubien. Louvain, Belgium: Publications
    universitaires; Paris: Vander-Oyez (Philosophes médiévaux, 16).

——. 2001. *Summulae de Dialectica*, an annotated translation with a philosophical
    introduction by G. Klima. New Haven, CT, and London: Yale University Press.

John Duns Scotus, 1895. *Quodlibet*. Opera omnia, 25 (Paris: Vives).

——. 1950. *Ordinatio* I, d. 1–2. Opera omnia, 2. Vatican City: Typis Polyglottis Vaticanis.

——. 1956. *Ordinatio* I, d. 4–10. Opera omnia, 4. Vatican City: Typis Polyglottis Vaticanis.

——. 1960a. *Lectura* I, Prologus, d. 1–7. Opera omnia, 16. Vatican City: Typis Polyglottis
    Vaticanis.

——. 1960b. *Lectura* I, d. 8–45. Opera omnia, 17. Vatican City: Typis Polyglottis Vaticanis.

——. 1963. *Ordinatio* I, d. 26–48. Opera omnia, 6. Vatican City: Typis Polyglottis
    Vaticanis.

——. 1973. *Ordinatio* II, d. 1–3. Opera omnia, 7. Vatican City: Typis Polyglottis Vaticanis.

——. 1974. *Tractatus de primo principio/Abhandlung über das erste Prinzip*, edited with a
    translation and notes by Wolfgang Kluxen. Darmstadt, Germany: Wissenschaftliche
    Buchgesellschaft, 1974.

——. 1997. *Quaestiones super libros Metaphysicorum Aristotelis libri VI–IX,* ed. Robert
    Andrews et al. St Bonaventure, NY: The Franciscan Institute, St Bonaventure Univer-
    sity.

John of Jandun. 1488. *Quaestiones in libros Physicorum Aristotelis*. Venice: Hieronymus de
    Sanctis and Johannes Lucilius Santritter, for Petrus Benzon and Petrus de Plasiis.
    Reprint of the 1551 edition, Frankfurt am Main: Minerva, 1969.

——. 1552. *In libros Aristotelis De caelo et mundo quae extant quaestiones*. Venice: Apud
    Iuntas.

Karger, Elizabeth. 2003. 'John Buridan's Theory of the Logical Relations between General
    Modal Formulae'. In *Aristotle's* Peri Hermeneias *in the Latin Middle Ages: Essays on
    the Commentary Tradition*, ed. Henk Braakhuis and C. H. Kneepkens, 429–44.
    Groningen/Haren, the Netherlands: Ingenium Publihers (Artistarium supplementa, 10).

Keffer, Hajo. 2001. *De obligationibus: Rekonstruktion einer spätmittelalterlichen Disputation-
    stheorie*. Leiden, the Netherlands: Brill.

King, Peter. 1985. *Jean Buridan's Logic: The Treatise on Supposition, The Treatise on Conse-
    quences*, translated, with a philosophical introduction. Dordrecht, the Netherlands:
    Reidel (Synthese Historical Library, 27).

——. 2001. 'Duns Scotus on possibilities, powers, and the possible'. In *Potentialität und
    Possibilität: Modalaussagen in der Geschichte der Metaphysik*, ed. Thomas Buchheim,

Corneille H. Kneepkens and Kuno Lorenz, 275–99. Stuttgart, Germany: Frommann-Holzbook.

Klima, Guyla, 2001. See John Buridan 2001.

Kneale, William and Martha Kneale. 1962. *The Development of Logic*. Oxford: Oxford University Press.

Knuuttila, Simo. 1981. 'Time and modality in Scholasticism'. In *Reforging the Great Chain of Being: Studies of the History of Modal Theories*, ed. S. Knuuttila, 163–257. Dordrecht, the Netherlands: Reidel (Synthese Historical Library, 20).

———. 1982. 'Modal logic'. In *The Cambridge History of Later Medieval Philosophy*, ed. Norman Kretzmann, Anthony Kenny, and Jan Pinborg, 342–57. Cambridge: Cambridge University Press.

———. 1993. *Modalities in Medieval Philosophy*. London: Routledge.

———. 1996. 'Duns Scotus and the foundations of logical modalities'. In *John Duns Scotus: Metaphysics and Ethics*, ed. Ludger Honnefelder, Rega Wood and Mechthild Dreyer, 127–43. Leiden, the Netherlands: Brill (Studien und Texte zur Geistesgeschichte des Mittelalters, 53).

———. 1997. 'Positio impossibilis in medieval discussion of the Trinity'. In *Vestigia, imagines, verba: Semiotics and Logic in Medieval Theological Texts (XIIth–XIVth Century)*, ed. Costantino Marmo, 277–88. Turnhout, Belgium: Brepols (Semiotic and Cognitive Studies, 4).

———. 2001. 'Augustine on time and creation'. In *The Cambridge Companion to Augustine*, ed. Norman Kretzmann and Eleonore Stump, 103–15. Cambridge: Cambridge University Press.

———. 2008. 'Medieval modal theories and modal logic'. In *Handbook of the History of Logic 2: Mediaeval and Renaissance Logic*, ed. Dov M. Gabbay and John Woods, 505–78. Amsterdam: the Netherlands: Elsevier.

———. 2009. 'New ideas on subject and identity in medieval logic'. In *Unity and Time in Metaphysics*, ed. Ludger Honnefelder, Edmund Runggaldier and Benedikt Schich, 183–97. Berlin: de Gruyter.

———. 2010. Medieval Commentators on Future Contingents in *De Interpretatione 9*. *Vivarium* 48:75–95.

Knuuttila, Simo and Taneli Kukkonen. 2011. 'Thought experiment and indirect proof in Averroes, Aquinas, and Buridan'. In *Thought Experiments: Methodological and Historical Perspectives*, ed. Katerina Ierodiakonou and Sophie Roux, 83–99. Leiden, the Netherlands: Brill.

Kretzmann, Norman. 1985. '*Nos ipsi principia sumus*: Boethius and the Basis of Contingency'. In *Divine Omniscience and Omnipotence in Medieval Philosophy*, ed. Tamar Rudavsky, 23–50. Dordrecht, the Netherlands: Reidel (Synthese Historical Library, 25).

Kripke, Saul. 1963. 'Semantical considerations on modal logic'. In *Proceedings of a Colloquium on Modal and Many-valued Logics*, Helsinki 23–26 August 1962. Helsinki: The Philosophical Society of Finland, 83–94. (Acta Philosophica Fennica); reprinted in *Reference and Modality*, ed. Leonard Linsky, 63–72. Oxford: Oxford University Press, 1972.

———. 1972. 'Naming and necessity'. In *Semantics of Natural Language*, ed. Donald Davidson and Gilbert Harman, 253–355, 763–69. Dordrecht: Reidel (Synthese Library, 40); a revised and enlarged edition in 1980, *Naming and Necessity*. Cambridge, MA: Harvard University Press.

Kukkonen, Taneli. 2000. 'Possible Worlds in the *Tahâfut al-Tahâfut*: Averroes on Plenitude and Possibility'. *Journal of the History of Philosophy* 38:329–47.

———. 2002. Alternatives to Alternatives: Approaches to Aristotle's Arguments *per impossibile*. *Vivarium* 40:65–76.

———. 2005. "'The impossible insofar as it is possible": Ibn Rushd and Jean Buridan on logic and natural theology'. In *Logic und Theologie. Das Organon im arabischen and lateinischen Mittelalter*, ed. Dominik Perler and Ulrich Rudolph, 447–67. Leiden, the Netherlands: Brill (Studien und Texte zur Geistesgeschichte des Mittelalters, 84).

Lagerlund, Henrik. 2000. *Modal Syllogistics in the Middle Ages*. Leiden, the Netherlands: Brill (Studien und Texte zur Geistesgeschichte des Mittelalters, 70).

Langston, Douglas. 2010. God's Willing Knowledge. *Redux. Recherches de Théologie et Philosophie médiévales* 77, 235–82.

Lewis, Neil. 1987. Determinate Truth in Abelard. *Vivarium* 25:81–109.

———. 1996. 'Power and contingency in Robert Grosseteste and Duns Scotus'. In *John Duns Scotus: Metaphysics and Ethics*, ed. Ludger Honnefelder, Rega Wood and Mechthild Dreyer, 205–25. Leiden, the Netherlands: Brill (Studien und Texte zur Geistesgeschichte des Mittelalters, 53).

Lindström, Sten and Krister Segerberg. 2006. 'Modal logic and philosophy'. *Handbook of Modal Logic*, ed. Patrick Blackburn, Johan van Benthem and Frank Wolter, 1149–214. Amsterdam, the Netherlands: Elsevier (Studies in Logic and Practical Reasoning, 3).

Lovejoy, Arthur. O. 1936. *The Great Chain of Being: A Study of the History of an Idea*. Cambridge, MA: Harvard University Press.

Maier, Anneliese. 1949. *Die Vorläufer Galileis im 14. Jahrhundert*. Rome: Edizioni di Storia e Letteratura.

Marenbon, John. 1997. *The Philosophy of Peter Abelard*. Cambridge: Cambridge University Press.

———. 2006. The Rediscovery of Peter Abelard's Philosophy. *Journal of the History of Philosophy* 44:331–51.

———. 2007. *Medieval Philosophy: An Historical and Philosophical Introduction*. London: Routledge.

Martin, Christopher J. 1987. 'Embarrassing arguments and surprising conclusions in the development of theories of the conditional in the twelfth century'. In *Gilbert of Poitiers et ses contemporains: Aux origines de la logica modernorum*, ed. Jean Jolivet and Alain de Libera, 377–400. Naples: Bibliopolis (History of Logic, 5).

———. 1990. 'Bradwardine and the use of positio as a test of possibility'. In *Knowledge and the Sciences in Medieval Philosophy II*, ed. Simo Knuuttila, Reijo Työrinoja and Sten Ebbesen, 574–85. Helsinki: Luther-Agricola Society (Publications of the Luther-Agricola Society B, 19).

———. 1997. 'Impossible positio as the foundation of metaphysics or, logic on the Scotist Plan?' In *Vestigia, imagines, verba: Semiotics and Logic in Medieval Theological Texts (XIIth–XIVth Century)*, ed. Costantino Marmo, 255–76. Turnhout, Belgium: Brepols (Semiotic and Cognitive Studies, 4).

———. 1999. Thinking the Impossible: Non-Reductive Arguments from Impossible Hypotheses in Boethius and Philoponus, *Oxford Studies in Ancient Philosophy* 19:279–301.

———. 2001. 'Abaelard on modality: Some possibilities and some puzzles'. In *Potentialität und Possibilität: Modalaussagen in der Geschichte der Metaphysik*, ed. Thomas Buchheim, Corneille H. Kneepkens and Kuno Lorenz, 97–124. Stuttgart, Germany: Frommann-Holzbook.

———. 2001. 'Obligations and liars'. In Mikko Yrjönsuuri, ed., 2001, 63–94; reprinted from *Sophisms in Medieval Logic and Grammar*, ed. Stephen Read, 357–81. Dordrecht, the Netherlands: Kluwer, 1993 (Nijhoff International Philosophy Series, 48).

———. 2003. 'An amputee is bipedal. The role of the categories in the development of Abelard's theory of possibility'. In *La Tradition médiévale des Categories (XIIe–XIVe siècles)*, ed. Joel Biard and Irène Rosier-Catach, 225–42. Louvain-la-Neuve, Belgium: Éditions de l'Institut Supérieur de Philosophie; Louvain and Paris: Peeters (Philosophes médiévaux, 45).

Moody, Ernst. A. 1975. *Studies in Medieval Philosophy, Science, and Logic: Collected Papers 1933–1969*. Berkeley, Los Angeles and London: University of California Press.

Moonan, Lawrence. 1994. *Divine Power: The Medieval Power Distinction up to Its Adoption by Albert, Bonaventure, and Aquinas*. Oxford: Clarendon Press.

Normore, Calvin. 1982. 'Future contingents'. In *The Cambridge History of Later Medieval Philosophy*, ed. Norman Kretzmann, Anthony Kenny and Jan Pinborg, 358–81. Cambridge: Cambridge University Press.

———. 1985. 'Divine omniscience, omnipotence and future contingents: An overview'. In *Divine Omniscience and Omnipotence in Medieval Philosophy*, ed. Tamar Rudavsky, 3–22. Dordrecht, the Netherlands: Reidel (Synthese Historical Library, 25).

———. 2003. 'Duns Scotus's modal theory'. In *The Cambridge Companion to Duns Scotus*, ed. Thomas Williams, 129–60. Cambridge: Cambridge University Press.

———. 2006. 'Necessity, immutability and Descartes'. In *Mind and Modality*, ed. Vesa Hirvonen, Toivo Holopainen, and Miira Tuominen, 257–83. Leiden, the Netherlands: Brill.

Parsons, Terence. 1995. 'Ruth Barcan Marcus and the Barcan formula'. In *Modality, Morality, and Belief: Essays in Honor of Ruth Barcan Marcus*, ed. Walter Sinnott-Armstrong, Diana Raffman, and Nicholas Asher, 3–11. Cambridge: Cambridge University Press.

Peter Abelard, 1919–27. *Philosophische Schriften I. Die Logica 'Ingredientibus'*, ed. Bernhard Geyer. Münster, Germany: Aschendorff (Beiträge zur Geschichte der Philosophie und Theologie des Mittelalters, 21,1–3).

———. 1956. *Dialectica*, ed. Lambert M. de Rijk. Assen, the Netherlands: van Gorcum (Wijsgerige teksten en studies, 1).

———. 1958. *Super Periermenias XII–XIV*, ed. Lorenzo Minio-Paluello. In *Twelfth Century Logic: Texts and Studies II: Abaelardiana inedita*. Rome: Edizioni di Storia e Letteratura.

Peter Lombard. 1971. *Sententiae in IV libris distinctae, I–II*. Grottaferrata, Italy: Collegium S. Bonaventurae ad Claras Aquas.

Peter of Poitiers. 1961. *Sententiae*, ed. Philip S. Moore and Marthe Dulong. Notre Dame, IN: The University of Notre Dame Press (Publications in Mediaeval Studies, 7).

Pinzani, Roberto. 2003. *The Logical Grammar of Abelard*. Dordrecht, the Netherlands: Kluwer (The New Synthese Historical Library, 51).

Plantinga, Alvin. 1974. *The Nature of Necessity*. Oxford: Clarendon Press.

Prior, Arthur. 1957. *Time and Modality*. Oxford: Clarendon Press.

Putnam, Hilary. 1973. Meaning and Reference. *Journal of Philosophy* 70:699–711.

———. 1975. *Mind, Language and Reality: Philosophical Papers*, vol. 2. Cambridge: Cambridge University Press.

———. 1990. *Realism with a Human Face*, ed. James Conant. Cambridge, MA: Harvard University Press.

Richard Campsall. 1968. *Questiones super librum Priorum Analeticorum*, ed. Edward A. Synan in *The Works of Richard of Campsall*, vol. 1. Toronto: Pontifical Institute of Mediaeval Studies.

Richard Kilvington. 1990a. *The Sophismata of Richard Kilvington*, ed. Norman Kretzmann and Barbara E. Kretzmann. Oxford: Oxford University Press.

———. 1990b. *The Sophismata of Richard Kilvington*, introduction, translation, and commentary by Norman Kretzmann and Barbara E. Kretzmann. Cambridge: Cambridge University Press.

Robert Grosseteste. 1912. *De libero arbitrio*, ed. in Ludwig Baur, *Die philosophischen Werke des Robert Grosseteste*. Münster, Germany: Aschendorff (Beiträge zur Geschichte der Philosophie des Mittelalters, 9).

———. 1991. *De libero arbitrio*, ed. in Neil Lewis, The First Recension of Robert Grosseteste's *De libero arbitrio*. *Mediaeval Studies* 53:1–88.

Robert Kilwardby. 1516. *In libros Priorum Analyticorum expositio,* Venice (under the name of Giles of Rome). Reprint Frankfurt am Main, Germany: Minerva, 1968.

Schmutz, Jacob. 2006. 'Qui a inventé les mondes possibles?' In *Les mondes possibles*, ed. Jean-Christophe Bardout and Vincent Juillien, 9–45. Caen, France: Presses universitaires de Caen (Cahiers de philosophie de l'Universite de Caen).

Siger of Brabant. 1954. *De necessitate et contingentia causarum*, ed. J. J. Duin in *La doctrine de la providence dans les écrits de Siger de Brabant*, 14–50. Louvain, Belgium: Editions de l'Institut Supérieur de Philosophie (Philosophes médiévaux, 3).

Spade, Paul Vincent. 1982. Three Theories of Obligationes: Burley, Kilvington and Swyneshed on Counterfactual Reasoning. *History and Philosophy of Logic* 3:1–32.

Stalnaker, Robert. 2003. *Ways a World Might Be: Metaphysical and Anti-Metaphysical Essays*. Oxford: Oxford University Press.

Street, Tony. 2005. 'Fahraddīn Ar-Rāzī's critique of Avicennan logic'. In *Logic und Theologie. Das Organon im arabischen und lateinischen Mittelalter*, ed. Dominik Perler and Ulrich Rudolph, 99–116. Leiden, the Netherlands: Brill (Studien und Texte zur Geistesgeschichte des Mittelalters, 84).

Sylla, Edith D. 2001. 'Ideo quasi mendicare oportet intellectum humanum: the role of theology in John Buridan's natural philosophy'. In *The Metaphysics and Natural Philosophy of John Buridan*, ed. Hans Thijssen and Jack Zupko, 238–45. Leiden, the Netherlands: Brill (Medieval and Early Modern Science, 2).

Thom, Paul. 2003. *Medieval Modal Systems: Problems and Concepts*. Aldershot, UK: Ashgate.

———. 2007. *Logic and Ontology in the Syllogistic of Robert Kilwardby*. Leiden, the Netherlands: Brill (Studien und Texte zur Geistesgeschichte des Mittelalters, 92).

Thomas Aquinas. 1948–50. *Summa theologiae*, ed. P. Caramello. Turin: Marietti.

———. 1952. *In Aristotelis libros De caelo et mundo, De generatione et corruptione, Meteorologicorum expositio*, ed. Raymundi Spiazzi. Turin: Marietti.

———. 1964. *In Aristotelis libros Peri Hermeneias et Posteriorum analyticorum expositio*, ed. Raymundi Spiazzi. Turin: Marietti.

———. 1965. *In octo libros Physicorum Aristotelis expositio*, ed. M. Maggiòlo. Turin: Marietti.

———. 1977. *In duodecim libros Metaphysicorum Aristotelis expositio*, ed. M.-R. Cathala and Raymundi Spiazzi. Turin: Marietti.

Uckelman, Sara. 2009. *Modalities in Medieval Logic*. ILLC Dissertation Series DS-2009-02, Ph.D. diss., University of Amsterdam, the Netherlands.

Vos, Antonie. 2006. *The Philosophy of John Duns Scotus*. Edinburgh: Edinburgh University Press.

Vos, Antonie, Henri Veldhuis, Aline H. Looman-Graaskamp, Eef Dekker and Nico W. den Bok. 1994. *John Duns Scotus: Contingency and Freedom: Lectura I 39*. Dordrecht, the Netherlands, Boston and London: Kluwer (The New Synthese Historical Library, 4).

Walter Burley. 1963. *De obligationibus*, ed. R. Green in *The Logical Treatise 'De obligationibus': An Introduction with Critical Texts of William of Sherwood (?) and Walter Burley*. Ph.D. diss., University of Louvain, Belgium.

William Ockham, 1974. *Summa logicae*, ed. Philoteus Boehner, Gedeon Gàl and Stephen Brown. St Bonaventure, NY: St Bonaventure University (Guillelmi de Ockham Opera philosophica, 1).

Wyatt, Nicole, 2000. Did Duns Scotus Invent Possible Worlds Semantics? *Australian Journal of Philosophy* 78:196–212.

Yrjönsuuri, Mikko. 1994. *Obligationes: 14th Century Logic of Disputational Duties*. Helsinki: Societas Philosophica Fennica (Acta Philosophica Fennica, 55).

———. 1998. The Compossibility of Impossibilities and *Ars Obligatoria*. *History and Philosophy of Logic* 19:235–48.

———, ed. 2001. *Medieval Formal Logic: Obligations, Insolubles and Consequences*. Dordrecht, the Netherlands: Kluwer (The New Synthese Historical Library, 49).

CHAPTER 15

MEANING: FOUNDATIONAL AND SEMANTIC THEORIES

MARGARET CAMERON

Is there a theory of meaning in the Middle Ages? If 'meaning', or 'linguistic meaning', is just shorthand for that which connects linguistic expressions to things in the world or to our thoughts, then it is trivially true that there were theories of meaning in the Middle Ages, just as there are in every philosophical age from the pre-Socratics to today. But if the question is supposed to mean, 'Is there a theory of meaning in the Middle Ages in the way that contemporary philosophers of language intend that expression?', then the answer is not at all straightforward. Indexing contemporary terms of art from the philosophy of language to any historical tradition turns out to be an unavoidably contentious, difficult project, not least because there is no consensus amongst contemporary philosophers over what theories of meaning are, or what they ought to do. Worse yet, even the basic theoretical terminology is inconsistently used. At the least, however, contemporary philosophers of language ordinarily recognise that the phrase 'theory of meaning' can be disambiguated in the following way. According to David Lewis (1970, 19; see also Stalnaker 1997),

> I distinguish two topics: first, the description of possible languages or grammars as abstract semantic systems whereby symbols are associated with aspects of the world; and, second, the description of psychological and sociological facts whereby a particular one of these abstract systems is the one used by a person or population. Only confusion comes of mixing these two topics.

First, there are *semantic theories*, which are concerned with *what* the semantic value of a linguistic expression is. These are most basically characterised as theories of reference and/or semantic theories. Second, there are *foundational theories of meaning*, which are concerned with *how* the linguistic expressions we use came to have their semantic values. Although the distinction is often blurred,[1] it needs to be kept sharp since each type of theory of meaning asks a different question: the first asks *what* the semantic value of an expression is; the second asks *how, or in virtue of which facts*, linguistic expressions have their semantic values.

With this distinction between types of theories of meaning, we can now ask: Was there a theory of meaning in the Middle Ages? Medieval philosophers, of course, did not explicitly recognise the distinction as it is drawn today between semantic and foundational theories. Nor did they speak in terms of an expression's 'semantic content'. Nonetheless, we can use this basic distinction—the distinction between how an expression comes to signify, versus what an expression signifies— as a means to sort out and clarify some of the medieval linguistic doctrines and debates. Medieval philosophers were committed to a doctrine of the imposition of names, which provided them with a foundational theory of meaning. According to most medieval theories, once a word was imposed to signify, its *significatio* became a permanent property of that word. But not all words are used by speakers as they were originally imposed to signify. Semantic theories, accordingly, were generated in order to account for the meanings of words used *other* than as they were imposed to signify. For this reason, we will begin with an outline of medieval foundational semantics and then examine the various semantic theories that were devised. We will be primarily concerned here with one variety of linguistic expression, namely, names (or common nouns).

FOUNDATIONAL THEORIES OF MEANING

Historians of medieval philosophy have been wary of tracking medieval philosophy of language along contemporary lines, especially when it comes to characterising the core medieval semantic notion, *significatio*. For a while some scholars treated it as akin to Frege's notion of 'meaning' or 'sense' (Sinn). At the same time, it was characterised as being hopelessly confused: 'From the beginning of the theory of meaning the word *significatio* (c.q. *significare*) was used in an ambiguous manner, both for the connotation of a universal nature . . . and for the denotation of an individual thing' (De Rijk 1967 II/1, 597–98). Some attributed the confusion to the influence of the debates over universals. Others seemed to suggest it is a result of theoretical naïveté. It was even suggested that medieval philosophers 'would have done a better job . . . if they had abandoned their notion of signification itself' (De Rijk 1982, 173). Moreover, the sheer variety of theories of meaning put forward in the last 120 years only makes it more confusing to gloss *significatio* as 'meaning' (cf. Spade 2002, 63).

Medieval philosophers themselves defined *significare* as 'to generate or constitute an understanding (*intellectus*)'. Accordingly, *significatio* ought to be characterised as a 'psycho-causal property of a term' (Ashworth 2003; Spade 1982). In this sense, the *significatio* of a linguistic expression is not an entity, as meaning is for many contemporary theories. Rather, an expression's *significatio* is what it does, namely, it gives rise to an understanding.

Medieval theories of *significatio* are built up on the basis of Aristotle's linguistic triad, which is outlined at the start of *On interpretation*. According to Aristotle (*De int.* 16a3–9; translation Ackrill 1963, 43), the relationship between names and things named is not direct since it is mediated by understandings, or the 'affections in the soul':

> Now spoken sounds are symbols (*notae*) of affections in the soul, and written marks symbols of spoken sounds. And just as written marks are not the same for all, neither are spoken sounds. But what these are in the first place signs of—affections in the soul—are the same for all; and what these affections are likenesses (*similitudines*) of—actual things—are also the same.

In Boethius's commentary on this passage, 'affections in the soul' is glossed as 'understandings' (*intellectus*), and as a result, what is primarily signified by a spoken utterance is an understanding. Given that Aristotle speaks of the relation between spoken words and understanding as a likeness, often the understanding itself was glossed as 'likeness' (*similitudo*). Medieval philosophers also inherited the idea that there are three types of word: that which is written, that which is spoken and that which is understood (Boethius, 1880, 29, 16–21). As a result, the understanding was sometimes called a mental word (*verbum mentis* or *cordis*).[2] Many agreed with Aristotle that generating a complete (*perfectus*) thought upon hearing an utterance was criterial for signification: the hearer's mind rests upon hearing a complete expression (*De int.* 16b19–21), although (as we will see below), some philosophers allowed for signification in cases where the corresponding understanding was somehow incomplete. Medieval philosophers also relied on a definition of the sign from Augustine (1995, 2): a sign is that which, upon hearing it, makes the hearer think of something beyond the sign. Thus, the *significatio* of a spoken expression *gives rise to* an understanding, or (for some medieval philosophers) is a 'presentation of some form to the understanding'.[3] Via this understanding, according to Aristotle and Boethius, the utterance signifies a thing, and it is for this reason that *significatio* is transitive.[4]

Medieval philosophers were alike in holding the view that *significatio* is conventional, and they explicitly recognised the importance of the role of the name-giver and the subsequent chain of speakers whose use of terms connects back to the original imposition. That spoken language is conventional is taught by Aristotle, according to whom written and spoken expressions vary (while the understanding (*intellectus*) and the thing (*res*) talked about are 'the same for all'; Aristotle (*De int.* 16a3–9)). This conventionalist doctrine was given some content by Boethius who, borrowing from Porphyry, distinguished between two types of imposition: primary and secondary imposition. According to Boethius (following Porphyry 1887, 33, 20), names were first imposed on things in order to designate what fell under the senses or thought: 'this substance will be called "gold", that "stone", that "water"' (Boethius 1880, 46). These are names of primary imposition. Once names began to be distinguished into types according to syntactic criteria, they were secondarily imposed: those names inflected by case are nouns, those with the distribution of time (or the consignification of time) are verbs (Boethius 1860, 159B–C). These words, which are names of names, are words of secondary imposition. Boethius does not say anything at all about what is in the mind of the impositor when names are first given, nor whether there is some conceptual content associated by the name-giver with the name. Medieval philosophers were sharply aware of the role of the impositor in naming and, as we will see in the next section, what is important is how this recognition played a role in the development of various semantic and hermeneutic doctrines.

Contemporary foundational semantic theorists divide the facts that explain how an expression acquired its semantic value into two types: internalist (or mentalist) and externalist (or non-mentalist). An internalist takes mental content to be sufficient to explain how linguistic expressions acquired their meaning, whereas an externalist contends that there is (at least) some non-mental contribution.[5] It is easiest to see what linguistic externalists have in common by seeing what they all reject, namely, the view that how linguistic expressions came to have their semantic value can be *sufficiently* explained in terms of mental or psychological facts about the speaker.[6] A well-known externalist theory is the causal (or historical) theory: something in the presence of the name-giver is named, and the name is transmitted via a chain of speakers who intend to use the name in the same way, thereby 'borrowing' reference from the name-giver himself. According to Saul Kripke (1980, 91), subsequent speakers must intend to use a name in the way originally imposed, just as happens in the naming of a baby: the name is passed along to friends and acquaintances 'from link to link as if by a chain'. The causal theory of reference explains how the content of linguistic expressions is first specified, namely, without reference to a name-giver's mental content but by the *historical linkage of name usage.*[7] Here we are not concerned with the use of the causal theory in determining the semantic values of linguistic expressions (which is a question for semantic theory), but only with its role in answering *how* linguistic expressions came to have the values that they do (the question of foundational semantics).

On what are names imposed, according to medieval thinkers? A few thought that words were imposed only on things individually present. The anonymous author of the twelfth-century logical treatise called *Ars meliduna* (f. 213rb; De Rijk 1967, II/2, 294) claimed that utterances were imposed in order to pick out individual referents (*nominare* or *appellare*), rather than to signify them (where signification is construed as picking out some nature or property of the thing named). The author compares the imposition to that of assigning a proper name: we don't ask by what name a baby boy will be signified, but by what name he will be called (*appellare*). For the Melidunenses, impositions function as labels for individuals. Since the cause of the imposition of a term is the impositor's understanding, they concede, vocal expressions do signify, but this signification is reducible to the term's appellation—the relation between a term and an individual existent.[8]

Another well-known example is that of Roger Bacon (1978, V-163, 132–33), who took an extensionalist theory of imposition to an extreme: contrary to the

Aristotelian-Boethian view, utterances are imposed directly on extra-mental things.[9] Bacon emphasised that words are constantly, and in a variety of languages, undergoing both tacit and explicit reimpositions, of which we ought to be constantly aware. Bacon's theory, which drew on Augustine's semiotics from *De doctrina christiana*, de-emphasised the role of understanding in imposition since linguistic expressions are signs of their referents (as smoke is a sign of fire). Philosophers after Bacon did not adopt his radical semiotics,[10] although (as has been well documented by historians of philosophy) his fusion of Augustinian sign theory with debates about imposition and signification had deep effects on medieval philosophy of language, most notably for his emphasis on speaker-relation (that is, signs are only actually signs *for speakers*, and if there are no speakers/interpreters of signs, they are signs only potentially).[11] This facet of Bacon's view ought to be contrasted with the predominant one commonly found in twelfth- and thirteenth-century logical textbooks: an utterance (*vox*) is not potentially a meaningful word but becomes one *simply* by way of an initial (i.e., historical) imposition.[12]

Most medieval thinkers, however, held that the impositor's understanding of a thing's nature or properties explained how the linguistic expression acquired its meaning. It is important to recognise that they differed on the question of whether the original name-giver had either a perfect or an imperfect understanding of what is named. Unlike some contemporary foundational theories, medieval philosophers did not hold the view that the name-giver's understanding of what is named can be *empty*.[13] What role, then, did the name-giver's understanding play in medieval explanations of how linguistic expressions acquired their semantic values?

Some medieval philosophers thought that a name's impositor would have a perfect understanding of the thing named. Of these, some thought the impositor to be Adam, who was proximate to God and so had privileged access to the essences of the things named. Aquinas addressed this question directly and held that Adam did know the natures of all the things he named (*ST* I, q. 94, ad 3). Others portrayed the impositor as a qualified metaphysician, intellectually equipped to pick out essences correctly. For example, modistic thinkers in the thirteenth century held the view that imposition secures signification since the name thereby acquires the properties of the thing named.[14] Consider the view of Albertus Magnus, who explicitly asked how it is that signification is united to a spoken utterance upon imposition.[15] He recognised the act of imposition as a voluntary, intentional act that brings together a vocal sound with a present object by way of gesture (*nutus*). But there is a second step that is necessary for securing signification. As Rosier-Catach (1994, 125) explains,

> Due to his expressive faculty (*potentia interpretativa*), the name-giver can create, in the vocal sound that he pronounces, a *species* or an image of the thing, identical to that which he has in his soul, as a function of his intention to signify. This faculty in effect governs the speech organs, and thus [it governs] the vocal production of the utterance, which is the percussed air; it 'impresses' on the spoken utterance the image contained in the intellect.[16]

The act of uttering some vocal sound aloud in the presence of some object(s), along with the impression that the species in the soul makes on the spoken utterance (odd as this sounds), are necessary and sufficient, according to Albert, for securing permanent signification.[17]

For these thinkers, imposition was a rich affair since on its basis the expression acquired a myriad of properties and modes of the things named. According to the early-fourteenth-century modistic grammarian Thomas of Erfurt (1972, 2.4; translated by Zupko 2011, §3, slightly modified):

> *Every mode of signifying is from some property of the thing* . . . since such notions or modes of signifying are not fictions, it must be that every mode of signifying radically originates from some property of the thing. This is plain thus: since the intellect, in order to signify, imposes the spoken utterance [*vox*] under some mode of signifying, it considers the property itself of the thing from which it originally drew the mode of signifying; this is because the intellect, since it is a passive power indeterminate of itself, does not advance to a determinate act unless it is determined from another source. Whence since it imposes the spoken utterance in order to signify under the determinate mode of signifying, it is necessarily moved by a determinate property of the thing; therefore some property of a thing, or mode of being of a thing, corresponds to any mode of signifying.

Upon imposition, spoken utterances acquired all of the modes of the thing named, and these modes of signifying are: active and passive; of active, essential and accidental; absolute and syntactical. Thomas notes that some might object to the theory since (for example) '*deitas* has feminine gender, which is a passive mode of signifying, but the property does not correspond to the thing signified, because it is a property of being acted upon, and feminine gender arises from this.' Other problems arise: 'negations and fictions fall under no properties whatsoever since they are not entities, and yet the significative expressions of negations and fictions have active modes of signifying (e.g., blindness, chimera, etc.)' (1972, 2.5; translated by Bursill-Hall 1972, 139, slightly modified). The modistic grammarian explains these oddities away, however, to preserve the doctrine: 'although *in Deo* is in reality not a passive property, we nonetheless imagine Him, as it were, being acted upon in our prayers' (ibid.), and so on. For the modists, imposition plays the crucial role in explaining how words came to have the meanings they do, but it also (as we will see in the following section) provided the basis for their semantic theory. The resulting inflexibility of meaning was characteristic of their doctrine. Given the tight (isomorphic) relationship between what is signified and what is understood, these philosophers held the view that 'something is named insofar as it is understood' (*sic intelligitur, sic et nominatur*; see, for example, Aquinas *ST* I, q. 13, a. 2, ad 3). This principle has recently been dubbed by Panaccio (forthcoming) the 'Modistic'[18] principle.

Not all medieval thinkers characterised what is known by the name-giver in such an idealised, epistemically optimistic way. That the perfect knowledge of the impositor was not always considered to be a requirement for successful naming was first noticed by Peter Abelard.[19] According to Abelard (1919, 23.20–24; translated by Spade 1994, 46), the impositor's knowledge of the object(s) named might be imperfect, but what secures reference is the impositor's *intention* to pick out something's nature:

> Yet any names of any existing things, insofar as is in their power, generate understanding rather than opinion, since their inventor [impositor] meant to impose them in accordance with certain natures or characteristics of things, even if he did not know how to think out the nature or characteristic of the thing.

Thus, for Abelard, the name-giver imposes names according to natures or properties of things. The correct interpretation of Abelard's point here has been an issue of recent debate. On a purely causal theory, naming is secured regardless of whatever descriptions or beliefs the name-giver associates with the thing named. What is Abelard's view?

According to Peter King (2010, §4),[20] Abelard anticipates the causal theory. What has raised controversy is King's claim (2010, §4) that Abelard's theory takes reference to be direct, and that the name-giver's understanding associated with a name can be completely wrong and yet reference is secured. If King is correct, then Peter Abelard's doctrine is a theory of direct reference, explained by the causal theory of names. However, the case for Abelard's semantics turns on whether or not Abelard did, in fact, hold that the original impositor can be 'completely ignorant' of the proper conceptual content that should be associated with a term' that is, whether mental content is empty.

According to Christopher Martin (2009, 203), Abelard did not endorse a direct reference theory of names, either for the name-giver or for subsequent speakers: '[Abelard] nowhere suggests that we can have a sound understanding that attends to the thing or to that which the image represents, as something which it is not'. According to Abelard (1933, 567), the original name-giver (Adam) 'followed the nature of things' when assigning names to things. At the same time, however, the name-giver was not in a position to provide an account of the nature or property of the thing named. If an object on which a name is to be imposed is present, then the understanding attends to the sense perceptions and abstracts from them what is needed for imposition to occur.[21] As Martin (2009, 208) explains,

> what the impositor has in his mind is an act of attention with which he focuses only on things of that kind, that is to say, for example, that he is able to recognise and demarcate the collection of things in the world which consists of all and only human beings. These are the things in the world that have in common the *status*[22] of being human, and it is to them that the new name 'human being' is applied by the impositor.

Note that for Abelard, as for Boethius, understandings are always accompanied by mental images.[23] Confusion over the question about whether the impositor can have an empty understanding of what he is naming arises in part because Abelard suggests that acts of attention can be directed at an image *differently* so as to constitute different understandings (2010, 3.01, 329; translation by Martin 2009, 193):

> Different acts of attention directed at the same image often constitute different understandings, as, for example, when I employ <the same> image to think of the nature of quality or the nature of whiteness. For seeing a piece of wood I attend to different features of it by employing the power of reason. For example, I now think of it in so far as it's wood, now simply in that it's a body, now in that it's a piece of oak, or a piece of fig wood.

But, as Martin (2009, 200–205) clearly shows, nowhere does Abelard suggest that the impositor can attend to some thing completely *otherwise* than it is. In other words, in seeing a piece of wood one cannot attend to it as a turnip (Martin's example), but only as conceived under different understandings of that thing (either sensed or imagined): as it is, as a body, as a particular type of wood, and so on.[24] The imperfection of the name-giver's understanding is recognised in virtue of the fact that it is rather difficult to know whether or not we do, in fact, have perfect understandings of what we talk about. According to Abelard (2001, 206–7; translation by Martin 2009, 210–11),

> In using speech we have learnt to what very many names apply, but we are not able, however, to state their sense or meaning. . . . Consider how all of us in our ordinary use of language know which things are called 'stones'. What the proper *differentiae* of stones are, however, and what the properties of this species are we are still unable, I believe, to assign a word with which we might complete (*perficere*) the definition or description of a stone.

This same sort of recognition of the name-giver's imperfect understanding is noted by John Duns Scotus, who remarked that there are four kinds of naming, ordered by degree of corresponding understanding. At one extreme, the namer knows nothing about what is named but merely utters some sounds; at the other, the namer has a perfect understanding of what is named (*Ordinatio* I, d. 22, q. un., Appendix A). The former case would not, however, result in successful naming. Although recent historians of philosophy have suggested that Scotus's name-giver might not know anything whatsoever about what he names,[25] this seems to be an exaggeration. In his question commentary on *On interpretation*, Scotus considers the question whether a name, once imposed, can lose its signification (in response to a view held by some of his contemporaries that if a thing no longer exists, it is thereby no longer understood, and thus its name no longer signifies). Scotus responds by reinterpreting the '*sicut intelligitur, sic et nominatur*' principle, which he indexes strictly to the impositor and not to subsequent users of names. According to Scotus (2004, q. 3, ad 4),

> signifying presupposes understanding in the sense that everything signified has already been understood, without which a spoken utterance would not have been imposed on it. But after it is imposed, an utterance can signify that to which it was imposed, even though it is [subsequently] understood by no one.

Scotus does not here specify what type of understanding the name-giver must have of what he names in order to produce a significant utterance, but it is clear that he believes that *some* degree of understanding is required. The *significatio* of a name as it was imposed is secured for subsequent speakers since, according to Scotus (2004,

I, q. 3, ad 4.2), even in the absence of things signified by an expression, the name can generate an understanding of *what the impositor* had in mind. Perhaps this is what Scotus (*Ordinatio* I, d. 22, q. un., n.4*)* means when he says that 'something can be signified more distinctly than it is understood', a comment taken by historians of philosophy to indicate Scotus's rejection of the Modistic principle that things are signified *insofar as* they are understood. As has been pointed out, while Scotus recognises this consequence of imposition, he neglects to develop the idea into a theory.

William of Ockham goes further than Scotus in his rejection of the Modistic principle '*sicut intelligitur, sic et nominatur*'. As Claude Panaccio (2004, forthcoming) has shown, the increasing tendency to characterise the intellective component of signification in terms of mental words or signs shifted the account of what occurs during imposition for signification.[26] According to Ockham (1974, I, 1; *OPh* I, 7–8; translated by Loux 1974, 50),

> I say that spoken words are signs subordinated to concepts or intentions of the soul not because in the strict sense of 'signify' they always signify the concepts of the soul primarily and properly. The point is rather that spoken words are imposed (*imponuntur*)[27] to signify the very things that are signified by concepts of the mind, so that a concept primarily and naturally signifies something and a spoken word signifies the same thing secondarily.

The important terminological change, as Panaccio (2004, 166) points out, is from spoken words *signifying* the concepts of the soul to their *being subordinated to* concepts (i.e., mental words) in the mind of the original impositor. Against other interpretations of Ockham's doctrine of subordination, according to which this subordination takes place *whenever* a speaker utters some word, Panaccio (2004, 170) argues that Ockham intends here to describe what occurs upon the *first imposition* of a word by the name-giver: 'the meanings of words, for Ockham, depend not upon what is going in the head of the speaker at the moment of utterance, but upon what they were originally subordinated to by the impositor'. This original subordination is explained by means of Ockham's theory of simple cognition.[28] To support this interpretation, Panaccio points to Ockham's own illustration (1974, III-2, 20; *OPh* I, 559) of his use of the absolute (i.e., non-connotative) term 'lion': Ockham himself has never seen a lion and so fails to have a corresponding absolute simple concept corresponding to 'lion', but he can nevertheless use the word meaningfully. Panaccio also points to this passage (1974, III-2, 29; *OPh* I, 558, emphasis by Panaccio) for support: 'since spoken words are conventional, absolute spoken names can be imposed upon the very same things of which we have—*or others have*—such absolute concepts'.

Recently, Panaccio (forthcoming) has developed this interpretation into a powerful case for William of Ockham's linguistic externalism: 'what we arrive at in the end is a clear form of linguistic externalism, quite similar to that proposed by Hilary Putnam in the 1970s'.[29] According to his interpretation, Ockham espouses a 'full-fledged' externalism, to the extent that even the name-giver can be ignorant of what he names and yet naming is successful. As evidence, Panaccio cites this passage from Ockham's *Ordinatio* (1967, I, d. 22, *q. un.*; *OTh* IV, 56; translated by Panaccio 2004, 171):

> Moreover, it is possible for somebody to impose this name 'a' to signify whatever
> animal will appear to him tomorrow. This being done, the word 'a' distinctly
> signifies this animal, and it will signify it for all those who are willing to use a
> word as it was imposed, even though the impositor does not have a distinct
> intellection of this animal, and maybe will not have one when it appears to him.

In this passage, Ockham explicitly notes that the name-giver of 'a' may fail to have
a distinct conception of a even when it appears before him. Recall that name-giving
on the causal theory requires the baptism of some object(s), as well as uptake by a
community of speakers, who then successively borrow the name's reference from
the name-giver himself. We can easily imagine that the dubbing ceremony was a
success, and that the causal-historical chain linking the naming of a to the next
speaker's use of the name 'a' to pick out a was sufficient to account for how 'a' comes
to be significant.[30]

It is important to notice that, for all these medieval thinkers, the name-giver's
understanding, whether perfect or imperfect, of the thing on which he imposes a
name plays some role in establishing and securing signification, and thereby in the
explanation of how a name came to have the signification it does.

With regard to the imposition of proper names, a number of remarkable passages
in John Buridan's writings have been flagged by Jennifer Ashworth and Gyula Klima
for their similarity to the contemporary causal theory of names.[31] Like Kripke, who
models his entire programme around the way in which proper names are assigned to
individuals, Buridan, too, seems to recognise that it is the causal chain connecting a
speaker's use of a name to its original imposition that is sufficient for securing reference. According to Buridan (1986, 9, 159–62; translated by G. Klima 2009, 86):

> concerning the terms 'Socrates' and 'Plato' I say that they are truly and properly
> individual terms, for the name 'Socrates' was imposed on this man by means of
> pointing [to him], as for example [by saying that] let this boy be named by the
> proper name 'Socrates'. For that name imposed in this way cannot apply to anybody
> else, except as a result of a new imposition, but then there will be equivocation.

Buridan thought that if the signification of 'Plato' or 'Aristotle' were due to descriptions associated with either Plato or Aristotle, signification would fail in case these
descriptions applied to some other men (e.g., 'the teacher of Aristotle', or 'the author
of *Metaphysics*'). Ostensive naming is sufficient to secure reference for proper
names. But Buridan did not extend the theory to account for the signification of
other types of names.[32]

Medieval philosophers were highly aware of the role that imposition plays in
signification, but they differed on the question of whether the original impositor
had either perfect or imperfect knowledge of what is named. In contrast, contemporary causal theorists are interested in cases where the impositor's understanding
is either imperfect or empty. Considered in this way, in a rather trivial sense, *all*
medieval philosophers held an externalist doctrine of foundational semantics
insofar as they are all committed to the conventional theory of signification according to which a word acquires its signification by way of being imposed by a name-
giver, and this signification can be preserved by means of name-users' intentions to

use the word as it was originally imposed. What prevents this observation from being trivial, however, is that philosophers widely disagreed about what it was on which names are imposed, and to what extent imposition secures signification considered as a permanent property of a term.[33] And medieval thinkers *also* explained how names came to have their signification in terms of some psychological facts, namely, the (perfect or imperfect) understanding of the thing(s) named by the name-giver, that is, the processes by which things named by the name-giver were cognised. The naïve, or perhaps simply optimistic, view expressed by some medieval philosophers—that name-givers, for one reason or another, had a perfect understanding of the things they named—would hardly be recognised as a version of 'internalism' by any contemporary philosophers of language, although it may be how we ought to characterise one version of internalism in the medieval tradition.

The recognition of the imperfect understanding of the impositor was one issue. A related issue was the question of the imperfect understanding associated with terms used by speakers. *Significatio*, as we have seen, was characterised in terms of the understanding that is generated by a name. However, some medieval philosophers recognised that we (often) fail to have perfect understanding, and yet the names we use still signify. Proper natures or substantial forms, which common nouns are said to signify, were recognised to be unknowable by humans, according to Thomas Aquinas, Duns Scotus and others. *How* we are 'led towards knowledge of the essential [principles]' became a topic of great debate after Aquinas (1968, I.1, 14–15).[34] This was an important realisation, one that expresses scepticism about our cognitive grasp of the things we experience and talk about.[35] Philosophers such as Ockham and John Buridan explicitly worried about how to avoid scepticism about our substantial concepts given our imperfect cognitive grasp of them.[36] The extent to which philosophers in this period employed linguistic strategies to answer these sceptical worries is a focus of current scholarship.

SEMANTIC THEORIES

Theories of meaning of this type investigate *what* the semantic content of a given linguistic expression is. Given the avid interest in issues in the philosophy of language in the Middle Ages, there are countless doctrines, topics and issues that concern the topic of medieval semantics. Since language was recognised to be conventional, imposition played a necessary role in securing a term's *significatio*. But the fact of imposition was not a sufficient explanation of a term's semantic value in its various contexts of use. There was widespread recognition that words can be used *either* as they were imposed *or* in another sense. Using words in the second way, however, does not eliminate the signification that they acquired upon being originally imposed. Rather, it requires the development of semantic theories or,

more properly, hermeneutic theories that can be used to ascertain *what* the semantic value of an expression is on a given occasion of its use. What follows is a *very*
brief overview of some of the major developments in semantic and hermeneutic
theory, focusing especially on the issue of using names other than as they were
imposed to signify.

One of the first efforts to account for this phenomenon can be seen in the early
twelfth century during Peter Abelard's milieu, during which they refined a notion of
linguistic translation (*translatio*). As Rosier-Catach (1997, 1999) has shown in detail,
signification by way of translation or semantic transference (not from one language
into another, but from one sense into another) was introduced in order to handle
cases of metaphorical language. For example, if one poetically says, 'The fields laugh',
the word 'laugh' cannot be taken in the sense for which it was originally imposed; but
by virtue of its lexical position next to 'the fields', it undergoes a transference of signification (1921, 121, 18). Any utterance of a term being used in a transferred way is not
a new imposition, that is, 'laugh' does not thereby become an equivocal term (1927,
399, 16–400, 2; 2010, 199, 422–200, 438). Importantly, however, it does not thereby
lose the signification it acquired upon being originally imposed. As Abelard notes,
there is only a conflict of meaning (*oppositio vocis*) if the expression is interpreted
according to the way the terms were originally imposed, but not according to the way
it is accepted in a given context of use (1927, 478, 28–479, 2). The doctrine of semantic
transference was of great use for hermeneutics, specifically for the interpretation of
theological language: given that imposition is a human act, names were 'instituted in
order to designate the creatures that humans were able to conceive' (Abelard, 1983, II
§70–78). Accordingly, when human words are used to talk about God and God's
nature, they 'necessarily exceed their proper institution (or imposition)' (ibid.).[37]

As we saw above, Modistic grammarians devised a semantic theory that was a
direct consequence of their foundational semantics: words are imposed and signify
insofar as they are understood, and they are understood insofar as they are in reality.
According to Jan Pinborg (1976, 258), 'sense [for the modistics] is static in so far as it is
established through imposition and cannot be changed through the influence of context
nor through changes in the extralinguistic world'. Modistic grammar was eventually
criticised on several fronts and was soon abandoned, most especially for its inflexibility.
It was thoroughly criticised (see Johannes Aurifaber in Pinborg 1967, 215–32) for its failure to account for the role of the will or intention of speakers when signifying. Moreover, as William of Ockham (1974, III, 4.10) charged, speaking in terms of 'modes of
signifying' was merely metaphorical, and to say that these modes are 'attached' or 'superadded' to the spoken sound upon imposition is metaphysically superfluous.[38]

Another type of medieval semantic theory has frequently been characterised as
a theory of reference, namely, the theory of supposition, or the doctrine of the properties of terms. Peter King (1985, 35, italics added) characterises the difference
between signification and supposition as follows:

> *Supposition* is a semantic relation, holding between term(s) and thing(s). The
> relation of signification, however, is also a relation of term(s) and thing(s). Yet it is
> one matter to assign certain terms to things, *so that a language may be set up in*

the first place; this is the contribution of signification. It is quite another matter to actually use that language to talk about things; this is explained by supposition.

According to this doctrine, which emerged in the mid-to-late twelfth century, terms are each endowed with the property of signifying. But when they are used in various contexts (e.g., sentences), they exhibit additional properties. These properties reveal the ways in which a given term can stand for, or supposit for, different things. A term has material supposition when it supposits not for what it signifies, but for itself (e.g., 'foot' has material supposition in this sentence: '"Foot" has four letters'). A term has simple supposition when it supposits for what it signifies (e.g., 'Man is a species'). Of course, debates over what the ontological status of the significate is motivated philosophers to adopt varying theories of simple supposition. A term has personal supposition insofar as it refers to an individual (e.g., 'Some man is present'). Different types of personal supposition were elaborated.[39]

It is common to find supposition theories glossed as 'reference theories' (see, for example, Spade 1988, 190). Again, however, we need to take care not to misunderstand the purpose of supposition doctrines when glossing them as theories of reference. As Catarina Dutilh-Novaes (2006) has shown, there is no such thing as 'a theory of reference' (unless the expression is taken in its most general sense to mean: What connects words and things?) to which supposition theory can be compared or assimilated. Moreover, supposition theories do not manage to do what modern theories of reference all aim to accomplish, namely, to *determine* the *unique* referent of a term. As Dutilh-Novaes has rather convincingly argued, suppositional theory can indicate only the variety of things for which a given term can (and cannot) be taken to stand in a proposition. The determination of reference, however, is something that an interpreter must do, and for this reason she characterises supposition theories as a species of hermeneutics.[40]

Dutilh-Novaes's characterisation of suppositional theory as a hermeneutic theory, providing for an interpreter a range of possible 'values' for a term found in a proposition from which he can decide which value is correct, is given further support by looking at a closely related area of medieval interest. Whether expressions (taken singly or in contexts) ought to be construed according to their literal sense (i.e., as they were imposed to signify), or in some other way, continued to be an issue of tremendous importance for medieval philosophers. This can be explained in part because of the role that interpretation of authoritative texts (in philosophy, such as the writings of Aristotle or the commentators, and in theology, such as the Bible or the writings of the Church Fathers) played during the period. A distinction was set up between interpreting an expression according to the literal sense of the words (*de virtute sermonis*), according to common usage (*usus communis*) or according to authorial intention. According to Ockham (1974, 237; translation by William Courtenay 2008, 218),

> it is important to determine when a term and a proposition are being taken *de virtute sermonis* and when *secundum usum loquentium* or according to the intention of the author. The reason is because there is hardly a word which is not in some way employed equivocally in various places in the books of the philosophers, saints, and authors. And therefore those wishing to take a word univocally

and in just one sense frequently err about the intentions of the authors and in the inquiry after truth, since almost all words are employed equivocally.

This dispute had theological and political implications, with some parties aiming to protect the truth of Scriptural language by defending the use of its metaphorical language, others arguing (often implausibly) that its truth can only be defended *de virtute sermonis*.[41] The distinction was set up to account for the fact that many names are equivocal—either accidentally or purposely. Tremendous debate took place, beginning especially in the thirteenth century, regarding whether names ought to be construed equivocally, analogically, or metaphorically, and whether their proper interpretation ought to be according to their original imposition, or as constrained by the context of their use, or by the intentions of the speaker or writer.[42]

CONCLUSION

It is important to keep the distinction between *how* things come to mean what they do, and *what* they mean. While the former question can be used to provide an answer to the latter, it doesn't do so necessarily. Medieval philosophers carefully considered how words came to mean what they do: they upheld a conventionalist doctrine of signification according to which names acquire their signification by means of imposition. They held various views on the role played by the name-giver's understanding in securing signification. Given that a word, once imposed, did not lose its signification, semantic (or hermeneutic) theories needed to be developed to account for the meaning of expressions used in various contexts where the meaning as originally imposed was to be resisted.

Whether it is useful or simply misleading to label medieval theories of foundational semantics, or medieval semantic theories, in terms of contemporary developments in the philosophy of language, has yet to be fully decided. Recent theories, such as those in foundational semantics known as 'externalist' or 'internalist', arose due to very different sorts of logical and philosophical pressures from those faced by medieval philosophers. Also, there is less consistency within contemporary philosophy of language over these technical terms and theories (as is the case with 'meaning' and 'reference') than we might like. Moreover, even those theories that have been characterised as 'internalist' turn out in many cases to be caricatures. Like many contemporary philosophers of language, historians of medieval philosophy seem to have John Locke's putative internalism in mind when thinking about ways to contrast the externalist features of medieval theories. Panaccio makes the contrast between Ockham's externalism and Locke's internalism (2003, 2004), citing the well-known passage from Locke's *Essay Concerning Human Understanding* III, 2, 2:

> words, in their primary or immediate signification, stand for nothing but *the ideas in the mind of him that uses them*. . . That then which words are the marks of

are the ideas of the speaker: nor can any one apply them as marks, immediately, to anything else but the ideas that he himself hath.

Locke's linguistic theory is often held up as the example of internalism at its extreme, so much so that on the basis of this passage, it is as if Locke defends a view of meaning assignment as wholly private, and meaning as solipsistic (see Panaccio 2006, 171). Giorgio Pini (2009, 261) seems to have a similar idea in mind when he suggests that *neither* linguistic internalism *nor* externalism could have been upheld until philosophers in the seventeenth century recognised the distinction between primary and secondary qualities, that is, 'only once sensible qualities have been moved from the world to our minds'. Although the topic cannot be pursued here, it ought to be mentioned that this characterisation of Locke is surely exaggerated and, on the face of things, implausible.[43] But internalism when read as a wholly private, solipsistic theory of meaning is not what is at issue in contemporary philosophy of language, and it shouldn't be the way to understand the distinctions when applied to the medieval context. The debate in foundational semantics between externalists and internalists concerns the *types of facts* that are used to explain how linguistic expressions acquired their contents (whatever those contents may be).

To answer the question whether medieval philosophers had a theory of meaning—insofar as 'theory of meaning' is variously interpreted today—turns out to be an extraordinarily difficult task.

NOTES

1. For example, some proponents of the new theory of reference used a foundational theory of meaning to account for *what* names mean. But a foundational theory need not entail any commitments for one's semantic theory.

2. See Panaccio (1999) for the development of the doctrine of mental words to doctrines of mental language.

3. From *Introductiones in logicam* (ed. De Rijk 1967, I, 565).

4. According to Jennifer Ashworth (2003, 81), a theory about *significatio* and any contemporary theory of meaning differ in that *significatio* is transitive, whereas meaning is not. Still, there are countless theories of meaning in contemporary philosophy, some of which could be characterised as 'transitive'.

5. See Speaks (2010, §3) for a brief summary. The slipperiness of technical terms in the philosophy of language is a point of great frustration. Even 'externalism' and 'internalism' are ambiguous since they are sometimes used to describe both foundational and semantic theories. See, for example, Wikforss and Häggqvist (2007, 375).

6. See Putnam (1978, 58): 'We [Kripke 1972 and Putnam 1975] were attacking the idea that speakers pick out referents in the following way: each term T is "associated" by each speaker with a property P_T (the "intension" of T). The term applies to whatever has the property P_T.' Their foundational semantics introduced the externalist factors that explain how words come to have their semantic values, although Kripke and Putnam differed on what the semantic values of those expressions are: see Hacking (2007).

7. There are other varieties of linguistic externalism held by contemporary philosophers of language, but we will focus on the version associated with the causal theory since it is most often alluded to by historians of medieval philosophy in their studies of medieval philosophy of language: see, for example, King (2010), Panaccio (forthcoming), Perler (2003) and Pini (2009). I am very grateful to Claude Panaccio for having sent me a copy of his paper in advance of its publication.

8. See Biard (1987, 2004).

9. See also Roger Bacon (1986, 280–83; 1988, §4, 54).

10. But see the controversies provoked by his theory (Ebbesen 1970).

11. See Biard (2006), De Libera (1991), Maloney (1983, 1984), Rosier-Catach (1994) and Tachau (1988).

12. For example, in the *Introductiones Montanae Minores* in De Rijk (1967 2/2, 21–24).

13. Externalist theories argue that mental content is 'wide', in other words, that the meaning of our words is determined by facts external to the name-giver. At the extreme, an externalist holds that the beliefs a speaker associates with things named can be entirely wrong (that is, empty), and yet the speaker's utterance is meaningful.

14. As has been shown by Rosier-Catach and others, there was no unified 'modistic school', but rather a collection of like-minded grammarians and philosophers who can be grouped together by similar approach. See Bursill-Hall (1972), Marmo (1999), Pinborg (1976, 1982) and Rosier-Catach (1994, 2010).

15. For this information I am gratefully reliant on Rosier-Catach (1994, 124–31).

16. For the views of those, such as Henry of Ghent, who criticised semantic contents in terms of impressions, see Spruit (1994, 205–12).

17. See Rosier-Catach (1994, 128–29).

18. Panaccio also glosses this as the 'Internalist' principle. But this is potentially misleading since contemporary versions of internalism in foundational semantics are quite unlike anything put forward by Modistic thinkers.

19. Abelard's realisation was not, it seems, historically influential.

20. King's account runs together the two types of theory of meaning (i.e., semantic theory and foundational semantics), and takes the causal theory of names to provide the basis for Abelard's semantic theory.

21. On Abelard's use of *attendere*, and so on, see King (1982), Martin (2009) and Rosier-Catach (2004).

22. On Abelard's notion of *status*, see King (2010, §2), Marenbon (1997) and Tweedale (1976).

23. Boethius draws this lesson from Aristotle's *De Anima* II.

24. This interpretive controversy was recently the subject of a talk by John Marenbon (Toronto 2010), commented upon by Andrew Arlig. Marenbon plans to publish his interpretation of this dispute.

25. See, for example, Perler (2003).

26. On the tendency to view concepts as signs in medieval philosophy of language, see Biard (2006).

27. Loux's translation is 'are used', but here we follow Panaccio's translation of 'imponuntur' as 'are imposed', which greatly changes the sense of the passage.

28. See Panaccio (2004).

29. I am grateful to Claude Panaccio for sending me his forthcoming paper on Ockham's externalism(s).

30. This passage in Ockham deserves further analysis. As Stalnaker (1997, 543) rightly emphasises, 'a proper Causal Theory of reference would have to specify just what sort of

causal connection is necessary and sufficient for reference, and that is a notoriously difficult demand'. Moreover, depending on whether we interpret the name of Ockham's animal *a* as a name of an individual or a kind, Ockham's account might be faced with the *qua problem* (see Devitt and Sterelny 1999, especially chapter 4).

31. See Ashworth (2004, 141–43) and Klima (2009, 69–76).

32. See Klima (2009, chapter 4).

33. But this is not so different from recent debates in the philosophy of language: according to Wikforss (2010, 65): 'a serious problem with the contemporary discussion is the assumption that the semantics of natural kind terms can be conducted independently of the metaphysical and scientific issues surrounding those kinds'.

34. There was also an awareness of problems with theological language. Many philosophers in the thirteenth century and after explicitly realised that theological language outstrips the speaker's understanding of what he talks about. According to Aquinas (*ST* 1.13.5), when we make predications of God, such as when we say, 'God is wise', 'it leaves the thing signified as incomprehended, and as exceeding the signification of the name'. See Ashworth (1980).

35. As Pasnau (2004) has shown, the medieval recognition that our grasp of substances is imperfect gives the lie to some rather well-known, but mistaken, early-modern characterisations of medieval thought. According to Pasnau (2004, 46), 'scholastic authors were the first to [i.e., keen to] stress that they had no idea of what substantial forms actually are'.

36. It is for these reasons that historians of philosophy have noted some parallels between certain contemporary externalist theories of meaning and the direction taken by some fourteenth-century philosophers. See Klima (2009, especially chapter 4), and Panaccio (2004, forthcoming).

37. For the study of *translatio* theories in the twelfth century, see Rosier-Catach (1997, 1999) and Valente (1995, 2007). See also the preface to Abelard's *Sic et non* (1976, 88–89) for his awareness of distinguishing between the literal meaning (*proprietas*) of an expression and its common usage (*usus*).

38. On the demise of modistic grammar, see Ashworth (1988) and Pinborg (1982), but see Kneepkens (2004).

39. See Ashworth (1974, 2010) and De Rijk (1967).

40. Dutilh-Novaes remarks that it is hardly fair to characterise supposition theories in terms of reference, and then—when they fail at this task—turn around and call them *bad* theories of reference.

41. The issue famously arose in a Parisian Statute in 1340 (*CUP* II, n. 1042). See Courtenay (2008, chapter 10) on the controversy and its relation to Ockham and his followers.

42. For texts on equivocation, see Ebbesen (1993, 1997, 1998). On analogy, see Ashworth (2008 and bibliography given there).

43. See Lenz (2010), which offers a defence of Locke as a social externalist about meaning.

BIBLIOGRAPHY

Aristotle. 1963. *Categories and De interpretatione*, translated with notes and glossary by J. L. Ackrill. Oxford: Clarendon.

Ashworth, Jennifer. 1974. *Language and Logic in the Post-Medieval Period*. Dordrecht, the Netherlands: D. Reidel.

———. 1980. *Can I Speak More Clearly Than I Understand? A Problem of Religious Language in Henry of Ghent, Duns Scotus and Ockham. Historiographia linguistica* 7:29–38.

———. 1988. 'Traditional logic'. In *The Cambridge History of Renaissance Philosophy*, ed. C. Schmitt, Q. Skinner and E. Kessler, 143–72. Cambridge: Cambridge University Press.

———. 2003. 'Language and logic'. In *The Cambridge Companion to Medieval Philosophy*, ed. S. McGrade, 73–96. Cambridge: Cambridge University Press.

———. 2004. 'Singular terms and singular concepts'. In *John Buridan and Beyond: Topics in the Language Sciences 1300–700*, ed. R. Friedmann, S. Ebbesen, 121–51. Copenhagen: The Royal Danish Academy of Sciences and Letters.

———. 2008. *Les théories de l'analogie du XIIᵉ au XVIᵉ siècle*. Paris: Vrin.

———. 2010. 'Terminist logic'. In *The Cambridge History of Medieval Philosophy. Vol. I*, ed. R. Pasnau, 146–58. Cambridge: Cambridge University Press.

Augustine. 1995. *De doctrina christiana*, ed. and trans. R. P. H. Green. Oxford: Oxford University Press.

Biard, Joël. 1987. 'Sémantique et ontologie dans l'Ars meliduna'. In *Gilbert de Poitiers et ses contemporains*, ed. J. Jolivet and A. de Libera, 121–44. Naples: Bibliopolis.

———. 2004. 'Le langage et l'incorporéal: quelques réflexions à partir de l'*Ars meliduna*'. In *Langage, sciences, philosophie au XIIe siècle*, ed. J. Biard, 217–34. Paris: Vrin.

———. 2006. *Logique et théorie du signe au XIVe siècle*. 2nd ed. Paris: Vrin.

Boethius. 1860. *In Categorias Aristotelis libri quattuor. PL* 64.

———. 1880. *Commentarii in librum Aristotelis Peri Hermeneias pars posterior secundam editionem et indices continens*, ed. C. Meiser. Leipzig, Germany: Teubner.

Bursill-Hall, G. L. 1972. *Thomas of Erfurt: Grammatica Speculativa*. An edition with translation and commentary. London: Longman.

Courtenay, William. 2008. *Ockham and Ockhamism: Studies in the Dissemination and Impact of His Thought*. Leiden, the Netherlands: Brill.

De Libera, Alain. 1991. 'Roger Bacon et la référence vide. Sur quelques antécédents médiévaux du paradoxe de Meinong'. In *Lectionum varietates, Hommage à Paul Vignaux*, ed. J. Jolivet and Z. Kaluza, 85–120. Paris: Vrin.

De Rijk, Lambertus. 1967. *Logica modernorum: A Contribution to the History of Early Terminist Logic. Vol. II/1. The Origin and Early Development of the Theory of Supposition; Vol. II/2. Texts and Indices*. Assen, the Netherlands: Van Gorcum.

———. 1982. 'On the origins of the theory of the properties of terms'. In *The Cambridge History of Later Medieval Philosophy*, ed. N. Kretzmann, A. Kenny and J. Pinborg, 161–73. Cambridge: Cambridge University Press.

Devitt, Michael and Kim Sterelny. 1999. *Language and Reality: An Introduction to the Philosophy of Language*. 2nd, enlarged edition. (1st edition 1987). Oxford: Blackwell.

Dutilh-Novaes, Catarina. 2006. *Formalizations après la lettre—Studies in Medieval Logic and Semantics*. Ph.D. diss., Leiden University, the Netherlands.

Ebbesen, Sten. 1970. Roger Bacon and the Fools of His Times. *Cahiers de l'Institut du Moyen-Âge grec et latin* 3:40–44.

———. 1993. Animal est omnis homo. Questions and Sophismata by Peter of Auvergne, Radulphus Brito, William Bonkes, and Others. *Cahiers de l'Institut du Moyen-Âge grec et latin* 63:145–208.

———. 1997. Texts on Equivocation. Part I. Ca. 1130–ca. 1270. *Cahiers de l'Institut du Moyen-Âge grec et latin* 67:127–99.

———. 1998. Texts on Equivocation. Part II. Ca. 1250–310. *Cahiers de l'Institut du Moyen-Âge grec et latin* 68:99–307.

Hacking, Ian. 2007. Putnam's theory of natural kinds and their names is not the same as Kripke's. *Principia* 11(1):1–24.

John Buridan. 1986. *Quaestiones in Porphyrii Isagogen*, in Jan Buridan, *Kommentarz do Isagogi Porfiriusza*, ed. R. Tatarzynski. *Przeglad Tomistyczny* 2:111–95.

John Duns Scotus. 2004. *Quaestiones in libros Perihermenias Aristotelis*, ed. R. Andrews, G. Etzkorn, G. Gál, R. Green, T. Noone, R. Plevano, A. Traven and R. Wood. Washington DC: Franciscan Institute.

King, Peter. 1982. *Peter Abailard and the Problem of Universals in the Twelfth Century.* Ph.D. diss. in Philosophy, Princeton University, Princeton, NJ.

———. 1985. *John Buridan's Logic: The Treatise on Supposition; The Treatise on Consequences.* Dordrecht, the Netherlands: Reidel.

———. 2010. 'Peter Abelard'. In *Stanford Encyclopedia of Philosophy*. http://plato.stanford. edu/entries/abelard/ (accessed 15 March 2011).

Klima, Gyula. 2009. *John Buridan.* Oxford: Oxford University Press.

Kneepkens, C. H. 2004. 'Some notes on the revival of modistic linguistics in the 15th century'. In *John Buridan and Beyond: Topics in the Language Sciences, 1300–700*, ed. R. L. Friedman and S. Ebbesen, 69–120. Copenhagen: Royal Danish Academy of Sciences and Letters.

Kripke, Saul. 1972. 'Identity and necessity'. In *Identity and Individuation*, ed. M. Munitz, 135–64. New York: New York University Press.

———. 1980. *Naming and Necessity.* Oxford: Blackwell.

Lenz, Martin. 2010. *Lockes Sprachkonzeption.* Berlin and New York: De Gruyter.

Lewis, David. 1970. General Semantics. *Synthese* 22:18–67.

Maloney, Thomas. 1983. The Semiotics of Roger Bacon. *Mediaeval Studies* 45:120–54.

———. 1984. Roger Bacon on Equivocation. *Vivarium* 22(2):85–112.

Marenbon, John. 1997. *The Philosophy of Peter Abelard.* Cambridge: Cambridge University Press.

Marmo, Costantino. 1994. *Semiotica e linguaggio nella scolastica: Parigi, Bologna, Erfurt, 1270–1330. La semiotica dei Modisti.* Rome: Istituto Storico Italiano per il Medioevo.

Martin, Christopher. 2009. 'Imposition and essence: What's new in Abaelard's theory of meaning?' In *The Word in Medieval Logic, Theology and Psychology*, ed. T. Shimizu and C. Burnett, 173–214. Turnhout, Belgium: Brepols.

Panaccio, Claude. 1999. *Le discours intérieur: de Platon à Guillaume d'Ockham.* Paris: Seuil.

———. 2003. 'Ockham and Locke on mental language'. In *The Medieval Heritage in Early Modern Metaphysics and Modal Theory, 1400–700*, 37–74. Springer.

———. 2004. *Ockham on Concepts.* Aldershot, UK: Ashgate.

———. (Forthcoming). 'Ockham's externalism'. In *Intentionality, Cognition and Mental Representation in Medieval Philosophy*, ed. G. Klima. New York: Fordham University Press.

Pasnau, Robert. 2004. Form, Substance, and Mechanism. *The Philosophical Review* 113(1):31–88.

Perler, Dominik. 2003. 'Duns Scotus's philosophy of language'. In *The Cambridge Companion to Duns Scotus*, ed. T. Williams, 161–92. Cambridge: Cambridge University Press.

Peter Abelard. 1919. *Glossae super Porphyrium*, ed. B. Geyer. Vol. 1 of *Peter Abaelards philosophische Schriften: Die Logica 'Ingredientibus'.* Münster, Germany: Aschendorff (Beiträge zur Geschichte der Philosophie und Theologie des Mittelalters 21.1).

———. 1921. *Glossae super Praedicamenta Aristotelis*, ed. B. Geyer. Vol. 2 of *Peter Abaelards philosophische Schriften: Die Logica 'Ingredientibus'.* Münster: Aschendorff (Beiträge zur Geschichte der Philosophie und Theologie des Mittelalters 21.2).

———. 1927. *Glossae super Periermeneias Aristotelis*, ed. B. Geyer. Vol. 3 of *Peter Abaelards philosophische Schriften: Die Logica 'Ingredientibus'*. Münster, Germany: Aschendorff (Beiträge zur Geschichte der Philosophie und Theologie des Mittelalters 21.3).

———. 1933. *Logica nostrorum petitioni sociorum*, ed. B. Geyer. Vol. 4 of *Peter Abaelards philosophische Schriften: Die Logica 'Nostrorum Petitioni Sociorum', Die Glossen zu Porphyrius*. Münster, Germany: Aschendorff (Beiträge zur Geschichte der Philosophie und Theologie des Mittelalters 21.4).

———. 1976/7. *Sic et non*, ed. B. Boyer and R. McKeon. Chicago: Chicago University Press.

———. 1983. *Opera theologica* III, ed. E.M. Buytaert and C. Mews. Turnhout, Belgium: Brepols (Corpus christianorum continuatio mediaevalis 13).

———. 2001. *Collationes*, ed. G. Orlandi and J. Marenbon. Oxford: Oxford University Press.

———. 2010. *Glossae super Peri hermeneias*, ed. K. Jacobi and C. Strub. Turnhout, Belgium: Brepols (Corpus christianorum continuatio mediaevalis 206).

Pinborg, Jan. 1967. *Die Entwicklung der Sprachtheorie im Mittelalter*. Münster/Copenhagen: Aschendorff (Beiträge zur Geschichte der Philosophie und Theologie des Mittelalters 42.4).

———. 1976. 'Some problems of semantic representation in medieval logic'. In *History of Linguistic Thought and Contemporary Linguistics*, ed. H. Parret, 254–78. London: Variorum. Berlin: de Gruyter; reprinted in *Medieval Semantics: Selected Studies on Medieval Logic and Grammar*, ed. S. Ebbesen.

———. 1982. 'Speculative grammar'. In *The Cambridge History of Later Medieval Philosophy*, ed. N. Kretzmann, A. Kenny and J. Pinborg, 254–69. Cambridge: Cambridge University Press.

Pini, Giorgio. 2009. Scotus on Knowing and Naming Natural Kinds. *History of Philosophy Quarterly* 26(3):255–72.

Porphyry. 1887. *Isagoge et in Aristotelis Categorias commentarium*, ed. A. Busse. Berlin: Reimer (Commentaria in Aristotelem Graeca IV.1).

Putnam, Hilary. 1975. *Mind, Language and Reality.* Cambridge: Cambridge University Press (*Philosophical Papers*. Volume 2).

———. 1978. *Meaning and the Moral Sciences.* London: Routledge and Kegan Paul.

Roger Bacon. 1978. An Unedited Part of Roger Bacon's *'Opus maius': 'De signis'*, ed. K. M. Fredborg, L. Nielsen and J. Pinborg. *Traditio* 34:75–136.

———. 1986/1987. *Summulae dialectices*, in Les *Summulae dialectices* de Roger Bacon, ed. Alain de Libera. *Archives d'histoire doctrinale et littéraire du moyen âge* 53:139–289; 54:171–278.

———. 1988. *Compendium studii theologiae*, ed. Thomas S. Maloney. Leiden, the Netherlands.

Rosier-Catach, Irène. 1994. *La parole comme acte: sur la grammaire et la sémantique au XIIIe siècle*. Paris: Vrin.

———. 1997. 'Prata rident'. In *Langages et philosophie: hommage à Jean Jolivet*, ed. A. De Libera, A. Elamrani-Jamal and A. Galonnier, 155–76. Paris: Vrin.

———. 1999. 'La notion de translation, le principe de compositionalité, et l'analyse de la prédication accidentelle chez Abélard'. In *Langage, science et philosophie au XIIᵉ siècle*, ed. J. Biard, 125–64. Paris: Vrin.

———. 2004. 'Les discussions sur la signifié des propositions chez Abélard et ses contemporains'. In *Medieval Theories on Assertive and Non-Assertive Language*, ed. A. Maierú and L. Valente, 1–34. Florence: Olschki.

———. 2010. 'Grammar'. In *The Cambridge History of Medieval Philosophy*, vol. I, ed. R. Pasnau, 196–216. Cambridge: Cambridge University Press.

Spade, Paul. 1982. 'The semantics of terms'. In *The Cambridge History of Later Medieval Philosophy*, ed. N. Kretzmann, A. Kenny and J. Pinborg, 188–96. Cambridge: Cambridge University Press.

———. 1988. 'The logic of the categorical: The medieval theory of descent and ascent'. In *Meaning and Inference in Medieval Philosophy: Studies in Memory of Jan Pinborg*, ed. Norman Kretzmann, 187–224. Dordrecht, the Netherlands: Kluwer.

———. 1994. *Five Texts on the Mediaeval Problem of Universals: Porphyry, Boethius, Abelard, Duns Scotus, Ockham*. Indianapolis, IN: Hackett.

———. 2002. *Words, Thoughts and Things: An Introduction to Late Medieval Logic and Semantic Theory*. pvspade.com/Logic/docs/thoughts1_1a.pdf (accessed 15 May 2008).

Speaks, Jeff. 2010. 'Theories of meaning'. In *The Stanford Encyclopedia of Philosophy*. http://plato.stanford.edu/entries/meaning/ (accessed 14 February 2011).

Spruit, Leen. 1994. *Species intelligibilis: From Perception to Knowledge. Vol. I. Classical roots and medieval discussions*. Leiden, the Netherlands: Brill.

Stalnaker, Robert. 1997. 'Reference and necessity'. In *A Companion to the Philosophy of Language*, ed. B. Hale and C. Wright, 534–54. Oxford: Blackwell.

Tachau, Katherine. 1988. *Vision and Certitude in the Age of Ockham: Optics, Epistemology and the Foundations of Semantics 1250–345*. Leiden, the Netherlands: Brill.

Thomas Aquinas. 1968. *St. Thomas Aquinas Quaestiones De Anima: A Newly Established Edition of the Latin Text with an Introduction and Notes*, ed. J. Robb. Toronto: Pontifical Institute of Mediaeval Studies.

Thomas of Erfurt. 1972. *Thomas of Erfurt: Grammatica Speculativa. An edition with Translation and Commentary*, ed. G. L. Bursill-Hall. London: Longman.

Tweedale, Martin. 1976. *Abailard on Universals*. Amsterdam: North-Holland.

Valente, Luisa. 1995. 'Langage et théologie pendant la seconde moitié du XIIe siècle'. In *Sprachtheorien in Spätantike und Mittelalter*, ed. S. Ebbesen, 33–54. Tübingen, Germany: Gunter Narr Verlag.

———. 2007. *Logique et théologie: les écoles parisiennes entre 1150 et 1220*. Paris: Vrin.

Wikforss, Asa and Soren Häggqvist. 2007. Externalism and a posteriori semantics. *Erkenntnis* 67(3):373–86.

———. 2010. 'Are natural kind terms special?' In *The Semantics and Metaphysics of Natural Kinds*, ed. H. Beebee and N. Sabbarton-Leary, 64–83. New York: Routledge.

William of Ockham. 1967. *Guillelmi de Ockham Opera Theologica*, vol. I, ed. G. Gál. St Bonaventure, NY: The Franciscan Institute.

———. 1974. *Guillelmi de Ockham Opera Philosophica* I, ed. P. Boehner, G. Gál and S. Brown. St Bonaventure, NY: The Franciscan Institute.

Zupko, Jack. 2011. 'Thomas of Erfurt'. In *The Stanford Encyclopedia of Philosophy* (Spring 2011 edition), ed. Edward N. Zalta. http://plato.stanford.edu/archives/spr2011/entries/erfurt/ (accessed 30 March 2011).

CHAPTER 16

....

MENTAL LANGUAGE

....

MARTIN LENZ

1. INTRODUCTION: TWO MODELS OF THOUGHT

What happens when you think? Are you thinking right now? I suppose you are at least processing sentences now. Is that thinking or part of it? Even if one looks up from a text and even if nobody is talking, episodes of thought appear to progress in our familiar internalised language, that is, internal 'images' of the written and spoken language that surrounds us. Is this internalised language the vehicle of thought? Or is there something else going on that constitutes 'real' thinking? Does it perhaps consist in a progression of 'sentences' that cannot be uttered since they do not pertain to any particular language we have learned? In brief: do we think in English or in some sort of Mentalese? It is difficult to tell. As Ruth Millikan recently reminds us on a Sellarsian note, we do not know anything about the mind just by having one.[1] Thinking about thought, about the nature of beliefs and concepts, clearly requires study and theorising. But both accounts of inner language, the one resorting to internalised language and the other one resorting to a mental language, are less ad hoc than they might at first appear to be.

On a first approximation, these two views display a radical rivalry on the structural nature of thought: while the first takes the structural features of thought to be something that humans acquire through learning language, the second approach sees thought's quasi-linguistic structure as essential. In other words: the first view is compatible with considering thought to be unstructured (or at least unstructured in any sense of 'quasi-linguistic structure' as we know it) and considering mainly human thought as shaped through language acquisition, whereas the second takes thought in general to have some sort of syntactic structure. Despite the host of intricate questions that ensue, these opposing views might be said to reflect the main models driving the medieval debates on mental language.

Both models seem to take their cue from the semantic triangle sketched in Aristotle's *Peri hermeneias*, according to which words signify concepts that, in turn, are taken to be resemblances of things in the world. But they differ crucially with regard to the level of thought, the first model allowing for two levels, the second for only one level of mental language. The first model—let's call it the *speech model*—has its roots in Augustine's *De trinitate* where Augustine distinguishes between two kinds of 'inner speech', namely, between proper mental words and internal images of conventional words. The second model—let's call it the *sentence model*—dates back to Boethius's second commentary on the *Peri hermeneias* where Boethius discusses only one kind of mental discourse. This mental discourse is supposed to be the prior and proper medium in which we think, and it is also considered structurally analogous to conventional language.

In spite of the ancient origin of these models, the debate between their different adherents did not really gain full force before the fourteenth century, when authors such as John Duns Scotus, William of Ockham and Gregory of Rimini confronted worries about the possible structure of the supposedly immaterial realm of thought and the limits of the proposed analogies between thought and language. These worries were prompted mainly by a *priority question*: according to the Aristotelian semantic triangle, the semantics of spoken sounds depend on mental concepts, to which the sounds are subordinated. Consequently, concepts are prior to conventional words in the order of semantic explanation. Now the question arises whether this priority can be extended to whole sentences. Even if mental concepts are semantically prior to words, it does not necessarily follow that mental sentences are prior to conventional sentences, unless one claims that thought is not solely semantically but also syntactically prior to conventional language.

Over the last three decades, the increasing scholarship dealing with medieval theories of mental language has clearly recognised the philosophical impact especially of Ockham's so-called mature account, in which he subtly joins and transforms both models into a theory that depicts mental language as the prior medium of thought common to all humans. The terms of this mental language are not conventionally significative words but naturally significative concepts composed into structured mental sentences that exhibit only semantically necessary syntactic features, that is to say, features devoid of any parts that render terms ornamental, equivocal or synonymous. Although Ockham draws on both models, his insistence that thought is syntactically structured clearly commits him to the Boethian camp; yet it ought to be noted that Ockham, unlike Boethius, avoids many problems arising from a straight structural analogy between language and thought by reducing mental language's syntax to semantically necessary features. Along with recent shifts in the philosophy of mind and cognitive science, the scholarly interpretations gradually shifted from taking Ockham's account as delineating a logically ideal language to viewing it rather as a way of explaining thought and cognition, crediting it with the status of a 'standard theory' to some extent even comparable to Jerry Fodor's Language of Thought Hypothesis.[2] As more recent research brings out, Ockham's theory of mental language wasn't the only game in town. Apart from a number of refinements by authors such as Walter Chatton, Robert Holcot and John Buridan, conceptions emerged that clearly favour the Augustinian speech model, most notably in the accounts of William Crathorn and Gregory of Rimini.[3] What has been unduly neglected in looking to Ockham for the standard theory, however, are the theoretical resources offered by these competing varieties of theories of thought. What is at stake here? Roughly speaking, the medieval mental language theorists face one central problem (that I would like to call the *Structure Problem*): from where do mental sentences get their structural elements? In a nutshell, unlike concepts that are taken to be caused by the things that they are concepts of, grammatical features or logical connectives do not seem to be caused by any particular things in the world. In other words, although we may claim to have, say, the concept of man, we will hardly say that this concept appears in the accusative or genitive case. So where do these features come from? Unless one argues that the mind employs equivalents of such features naturally (whatever that might mean), it seems that the Augustinian model has a clear advantage in claiming that proper mental sentences are unstructured, whereas the linguistic and logical features we seem to employ in thought appear only in improper mental language, that is, internalised language, and are thus derived from conventional language.

In the following paragraphs, then, I would like to show how this structural problem takes shape in the medieval debates on mental language (debates in which Ockham still deserves a prominent role, not as the inventor of a 'standard theory' but rather as someone who successfully imparted deep and fruitful worries). I shall argue that the variants of the received 'standard theory' face quite powerful competitors in medieval adherents of the Augustinian model, which compelled later theorists to rethink the relation between thought and language. Before looking at the discussion of structure, I (1) introduce the main ingredients of the rival theories and (2) show how they lead to competing views on the priority question. After setting out the 'standard theory' as an answer to this question, (3) I will take a look at competing solutions of the structure problem in more detail, while hinting at parallels in contemporary discussions.

2. TRADITIONAL INGREDIENTS: SEMANTICS AND THE TWO MODELS OF THOUGHT

While the idea of depicting thought as a kind of inner speech already appears in Plato, the most influential source for most medieval theories of mental language is Aristotle's *Peri hermeneias* (16a3–9), which is opened by a sketch of what might now be called the 'semantic triangle', depicting basic relations between the level of conventional linguistic units, the mental level of thought and the ontic level of things. One central question this model is designed to settle could be phrased as follows: how is it possible for written or spoken units to relate to things?

2.1 The *ordo orandi*

Brushing off early naturalist speculations about a 'natural resemblance' between words and things,[4] Aristotle confronts the problem of how mere sounds or written marks can bear any relation to anything at all. The well-known answer is: by convention (*kata syntheken, ad placitum*).[5] But conventionalism as such does not settle the ensuing question with regard to what the agreement (on a certain sound as signifying a certain thing) is stabilised and rendered translatable across different conventional languages. The stabilising element is not the elusive spoken sound or written mark, but the mental concept that is caused in us by the thing in question and thus is said to bear a resemblance to the thing. Roughly speaking, then, conventional linguistic units can be related to things only in virtue of their connection to mental concepts or passions of the soul, which, in turn, are taken to be similitudes of things. Written signs signify spoken sounds that signify the concepts or passions of the soul. Inspired by this semantic sketch and Boethius's interpretation of it, the scholastic tradition defended four main claims:

1. Linguistic units such as spoken sounds (*voces*) signify according to convention or voluntary imposition (*institutio, impositio ad placitum*).
2. Spoken sounds are signs (*notae*) of concepts (*passiones animae, conceptus, intellectus*).
3. Concepts are similitudes (*similitudines*) of things (*res*).
4. Concepts are—like the things they are concepts of—the same for all (*eadem apud omnes*).

Taken in conjunction, these tenets establish the so-called *ordo orandi* or *ordo significationis*:[6] they are considered fundamental in the explanation of the workings of language and of the relation between conventional linguistic units on the one hand and the invariable concepts and things on the other. If asked how the word 'apple' is semantically related to apples, a proponent of this model can tell the following story. The bare spoken sound 'apple' as such doesn't relate to anything else. But given that there are apples in the world and given your capacity to abstract the concept APPLE, you can learn to connect this concept to the word, such that the utterance of the word *evokes* the concept. It is, then, this 'psycho-causal' property of words—namely to evoke concepts—that ties words to concepts of things. Just as the apple causes the cogniser to form the concept of apple, the utterance 'apple' causes the concept in the hearer. Signification is thus an indirect relation between words and the world in that it is *mediated* by concepts.[7]

The *ordo orandi* is clearly designed to explain the semantic identity of conventional expressions (across different languages) and the connected concepts in relation to the things signified. The order of semantic explanation from thesis (1) to (4) seems to follow from an *inverse natural order* according to which there can be no (meaningful) sounds without concepts and no concepts without things that cause them. Accordingly, it is impossible to have (meaningful) language without concepts, while it seems certainly possible to have stable concepts without language. Thus, concepts are naturally prior to words. But in what sense are concepts prior? As we will see, the individual theses will be refined in many ways, but since we are interested mainly in mental language, we should concentrate on thesis (3) for now. As mental similitudes of things, concepts may be claimed to have some of the properties of the things grasped through those very concepts. If I stood in a garden in front of a tree and formed the concept 'tree', I can think about the tree by means of the concept even if I am no longer in the garden. My capacity for doing so can be explained by appealing to the concept's properties, which include—depending on the metaphysical theory—the formal features of trees or at least some sort of similitude to trees. By contrast, if I hear the utterance 'tree' I can also think of trees, but there is nothing in that very utterance that would explain my capacity to do so; the word itself has no properties relevant to explaining my capacity of thinking about trees, unless, of course, we add the claim that the word evokes the concept 'tree', which then enables me to think about trees. Accordingly, the word's functioning as a placeholder—as Aristotle claimed in the *Sophistical Refutations* (165a6–8)—is granted by its subordination to a concept. If the word 'tree' were subordinated to a different concept, say the concept 'cat', then your utterance of 'tree' would evoke the concept 'cat'. So concepts have *epistemic priority* over words.[8] Whatever else we make of the description of concepts as similitudes, as such they do not seem to qualify as constituents of a mental language since, rather than *having* semantic properties, they primarily seem to be introduced to explain the semantics of spoken sounds. It was not before 1250 that a crucial refinement occurred with regard to thesis (3). From the mid–thirteenth century onwards, concepts were not only taken to be similitudes but also natural *signs* (*signa naturalia*), signifying naturally those things that words signify conventionally.[9] Thus, concepts were credited not only with epistemic but also with *semantic priority* over words.

2.2 The Speech Model and the Sentence Model

Although we might say that the *ordo orandi* accounts for concepts as elements in a kind of mental lexicon, we don't yet have a 'grammar' for these concepts. In addition to the *ordo orandi*, we need at least a story about the structural dimension and the semantic evaluability of concepts. In other words: just as we do not utter isolated words such as 'apple' and 'red' but form whole sentences, we do not seem to think in isolated concepts but form whole judgements. With regard to such questions, medieval authors could resort at least to two different sources, namely, Augustine's doctrine of the *verbum nullius linguae* and Boethius's doctrine of the *tres orationes*.

(a) *The Speech Model:* Augustine's discussion of the 'word pertaining to no language' might at first seem to draw on the Aristotelian semantic triangle, except that he clearly differentiates between *two kinds of inner 'words'*: besides emphasising the (i) proper mental concepts as true graspings of things signified by spoken sounds, he also points out that our minds entertain (ii) images of words (pertaining to our respective languages), the so-called *imagines corpora-lium vocum*.[10] An important point is Augustine's assertion that the spatio-temporal structure of linguistic expressions and their internalised images are only an accidental feature of speech in that it only pertains to humans bound to the physical realm; proper speech is mental speech and thus prior to the vocal and written signs. This means that the semantic evaluability of (inner) speech does not depend on structural features, and so Augustine's talk of mental 'words' (*verba*) does not preclude the semantic evaluability of these units: proper mental words are units of knowledge; they are not 'sub-sentential' units in any modern sense but seen as *acts* of thought with an inherently true content. What makes these thoughts complete thoughts is not any sort of structure but the fact that they are assertive acts.[11]

(b) *The Sentence Model:* A somewhat different account is provided by Boethius's doctrine of the *tres orationes* suggesting a *structural analogy* between written, spoken and mental sentences. Referring to Aristotle's *De anima*, Boethius clearly points out that truth and falsity pertain to the 'combination of concepts'. He does not only speak of mental concepts but of 'mental nouns' and 'verbs' as well as of semantically evaluable thoughts, thus allowing for a semantic as well as a 'grammatical' description of the units of thought.[12]

While both models have in common that they invoke the crucial elements (spoken sounds on the one hand, concepts and things on the other hand) involved in the semantic triangle and stress their difference as one between conventional diversity and natural uniformity, they provide entirely different perspectives on the structural dimension of thought, the first relegating structure to human linguistic expressions and their images, the second assuming a structural analogy.

In the course of numerous medieval debates ranging from angelic communication, divine versus human thought and knowledge to logic and grammar, the *ordo orandi* and the two models have been married and divorced in various ways. Anselm of Canterbury's famous proof in the *Proslogion* and a passage from the *Monologion* are an early testimony of combining the Augustinian speech model with the *ordo orandi*: the fool's thought that there is no God can only occur in internalised language, not in proper thought.[13] A mixture of various traditions was then transmitted and subtly transformed by authors such as Avicenna, Albert the Great and Thomas Aquinas as well as by authors adhering to versions of the so-called *grammatica speculativa*.[14]

Despite their similarities it is important to bear in mind that the two models rest on different perspectives. Some recent criticisms suggest that Augustine's view is deficient in that it underestimates the role of structure.[15] But this is somewhat beside the point. Roughly speaking, given its focus on grasping the true mental word (a mental process in which the difference between seeing and saying is taken to be irrelevant), the speech model, rather, seems to stress the aspect of *action* in thought; crucial is the *act of judging* something to be thus and so. By contrast, the sentence model puts more weight on the elements that are *represented* and *related* to one another in thought. Of course, this is no more than an indication of different tendencies, but if a close analogy with contemporary views is sought, one could—with all due reservations—say that the speech model focuses on the propositional attitudes, while the sentence model takes its lead from the propositional contents and the required vehicles of representation.

3. PRIORITY QUESTIONS

With the semantic priority of concepts and these models in place, various sorts of theories of mental language with different explanatory purposes seem to suggest themselves. Especially in the commentaries and treatises on logic from 1300 onwards, we encounter a sharpened awareness of the theoretical tensions that led to more detailed theoretical designs. While logicians in the early thirteenth century, most notably William of Sherwood and Peter of Spain, still introduce their analyses with reference to the units of conventional language, Thomas Aquinas and John Duns Scotus describe the three standardised units of logic (term, sentence and syllogism) in psychological terminology, namely, by differentiating three related operations of the mind (*tres operationes intellectus*): the first operation (*simplex apprehensio*) results in concept formation, the second operation (*iudicium*) is the joining of concepts or judgement and the third amounts to joining judgements to an argument or syllogism.[16] The appeal to psychological rather than linguistic units can be seen as a response to the common demand that all logicians should study the logic, which is the same everywhere, rather than deal with the peculiarities of conventional languages.[17] Combined with the description of concepts (and later even the acts of concept formation) as natural signs, the psychological terminology provided a new means for a unified account of the proper subject of logic. Accordingly, Aquinas and Scotus both claim the priority of mental over the linguistic realm. As Aquinas puts it, if it were not for the social nature of humans, the mental operations would be entirely sufficient for thought *and cognition.*[18]

   Although both expositions of the mental operations are based on similar premises, the treatment in Scotus is striking in that he has to confront strong objections as to whether there can be sentences in the mind (*enuntiationes in mente*) at all. According to the unnamed opponent, there cannot be sentences in the mind since sentences have parts such as nouns and verbs, but the mental realm does not admit of parts. This line of argument clearly rests on the speech model, which confines structural elements to the physical realm. Scotus, however, seems unimpressed and responds by resorting to a different aspect of the speech model, when he claims that the parts and properties of the sentences of conventional spoken or written language pertain to them not in themselves but only secondarily, namely, in that they are signs of mental sentences. Thus, Scotus combines the claim of the priority of the mental with the Boethian sentence model according to which mental operations are structured.[19]

Yet, the claim that mental sentences are both prior and structured rests uneasily not only with the speech model. The question is: can the priority of mental concepts really be extended to mental sentences? Even if we grant that mental operations—despite their supposed immateriality—might be structured in some sense, there remain serious problems: first, it is unclear how the structure is acquired; second, it is doubtful in what sense it can be prior to the structure of conventional sentences. The common recourse to the *ordo orandi* is not very helpful since the *ordo orandi* only accounts for epistemic and semantic and not for the syntactic priority of mental language. Worse still, the objection cited holds not only for sentences but has repercussions on the theory of concepts, too. For concepts qua constituent parts of sentences seem to require different properties from concepts qua similitudes or signs of things.

Thus, the wish to make the priority claim leads straight to the structure problem noted above, as is testified by the intense debates in authors such as Walter Burley and Richard Campsall. The seemingly simple idea that mental sentences are sentences in the proper sense, while the semantic and syntactic features of conventional languages are parasitic on mental language, obviously had to be defended from scratch. What are the parts, it is asked, that a sentence consists of: are they spoken sounds, concepts or perhaps even things?[20] All these candidates received serious attention. Whereas bare, spoken sounds are ruled out for the reason that a sentence cannot be reduced to a mobile entity flying from one place to another, the idea is refined by resorting to images (or even concepts) of spoken sounds; images or concepts of sounds, it is argued, do not simply cease to exist—that is, the implausible token view is refined to a conception of linguistic types allowing for a 'more fundamental level of linguistic representation', as Panaccio puts it.[21] On this view, the parts of sentences do not simply consist of our fleeting utterances but of storable images of words. This internalised language approach gains even more momentum when merged with the view—already established by grammarians in the mid–thirteenth century—that images or *concepts of sounds* can be associated with *concepts* of things such that they can evoke each other. In this case the psycho-causal property of words to evoke concepts of things is no longer restricted to matters between the speaker and the hearer; rather, it is taken as an intrapersonal mechanism of reciprocal association of internalised language and thoughts of things. According to Burley, however, not even concepts of things—the most traditional candidates—can be taken to be the primary parts of mental sentences: since concepts are signs of something else, there must be still a more fundamental level, namely, that which is ultimately signified. Consequently, he takes the things themselves (signified by conventional terms) to be the basic units of the mental sentence (later appropriately called *propositio in re*) 'joined' by a mental act. In the following years, Burley and others increasingly refined their respective views, paying particular attention to the structure of mental language.[22]

4. The Structure Problem

The structure problem is dealt with repeatedly in Ockham's work. Ockham tried to provide a solution by assigning two different roles to concepts: they are the basic units of semantics as well as constituents of structured thought. According to his so-called mature theory, conceptual content is acquired by a causal relation between the world and the mind, but since our mind is endowed with the capacity to form structured sentences, these concepts can function as constituent parts of mental sentences.[23] The latter aspect especially seems to make Ockham's notion of mental language comparable to Jerry Fodor's Language of Thought Hypothesis.[24] According to both Ockham and Fodor, mental language is semantically and syntactically prior to spoken language.

This approach can be read, indeed, as a response to many of the difficulties that have been mentioned. Combining the Augustinian doctrine of the word that belongs to no language with the Boethian sentence model, he accepts only semantically necessary structural features, that is, features rendering sentences true or false. While, for example, 'Some sheep are white' is true, 'All sheep are white' is false; consequently, the different quantifiers must be mirrored in mental language. This move has a clear advantage over the mere claim of a structural analogy: in claiming that syncategorematic terms such as 'is' and 'all', as well as features such as case, number and verbal modes are semantically necessary, Ockham seems to have found a way to ground the desired syntactic priority of mental language in the semantic priority established in the *ordo orandi*.

What does this amount to? In attributing quasi-syntactic features to concepts, Ockham's approach can be said to capture one of the crucial characteristics that any theory of thought should take into account, namely, what Fodor called the systematicity of thought. Someone who is able to think, for instance, that Mary loves John, is certainly able to think that John loves Mary.[25] Yet, this systematicity ascribed to thought does not seem to be a feature of the world. However appealing the ascription of structural features to concepts might be, then, it leaves us with the problem of accounting for the origin of such features.

While it is, at least in principle, easy to see that, independently of the mastery of any conventional language, cognitive contact with the world endows our minds with concepts of things, no unproblematic story seems to be available for the mental correlates of 'all', 'is', 'and' or cases such as 'of man' (as opposed to 'man') and different modes of verbs. A difficulty related to the origin of these features is to account for the mental correlation of grammatical and logical functions expressed, for example, by different cases or positions in word order: 'Cats love dogs' superficially seems to contain the same components as 'Dogs love cats', but a story accounting for the acquisition of the concepts DOG, CAT, LOVE, seems to give us no indication of how these concepts are determined to function as subjects, objects or predicates, as it were. Among the various mental language theorists, Ockham is one of the first who not only explicitly addressed this problem but also suggested different solutions to it.

Looking at the course of the debates, this issue appears to be one of the 'hard' problems that kept recurring even among the late scholastics in the seventeenth century.

Generally speaking, three sources of structural features seem to be conceivable: (1) things or states of affairs, (2) the mind and (3) conventional language. Each of these options (or combinations of these) comes with different burdens. While option (3) clearly threatens the alleged syntactic primacy of mental language, options (1) and (2) seem to require strong metaphysical or psycho-semantic premises. So let's take a closer look at each of these options.

4.1 Option (1): Things as a Structural Source for Mental Sentences

As we have already noted, it appears that logicians committed to realism and defending a *propositio in re* theory, such as Walter Burley and Richard Brinkley, went, in some sense, for option (1). The basic idea of this account is that the subject and predicate of a given proposition such as 'a is F' are things in the world, whereas the structurally binding element—the correlate of the copula 'is'—is taken to be an act in the mind. This view already puzzled their contemporaries. Do these sentences consist in real compositions of things? Burley immediately made it clear that such sentences are not real conjunctions of things in the same way as, say, a house is a composition of stones and wood; such a sentence is, rather, an intellectual composition occurring if the intellect grasps that things are the same and yet different.[26] Another worry both Burley and Brinkley had to confront concerns the actual location and unity of the sentence: if subject and predicate are things in the world, while the combining copula is in the mind, then where is the actual sentence, and how are we to account for its unity? As is already clear from the former answer, the location of such a sentence cannot be determined simply by confining it either to the mind or the world; however, since the actual composition takes place in the mind, the sentence can be said to be in the mind.[27]

In depicting mental sentences as consisting of units belonging at once to the mind and the world, Burley and Brinkley force us to reconsider the deep-rooted idea that a thought or mental sentence has a definite place. But despite the strong realism this view is committed to, it has some immediate benefits. For it offers a means not only for bridging but also for avoiding the supposed gap between the realm of the mind and the world. Just like some versions of content externalism defended in contemporary debates, it takes external things and states of affairs not as something that thoughts solely 'conform to' or 'differ from', but rather, as something that our mind is related to or interacts with. Thought, then, is not a wheel that is threatened to spin freely in its own realm of the mental but something that is tied to the world it is about.[28]

It is rarely noted that the *propositio in re* theory held also attractions for the most well-known nominalist opponent of Burley, namely William of Ockham. Long before he came to defend his so-called mature theory, he at least toyed with the idea that the subject, predicate and even the copula are outside the mind. A conventional sentence such as 'Whiteness is in Socrates' is supposed to signify the whiteness, Socrates and the actual relation of inherence such that the 'whole sentence will have being outside the soul'.[29] Besides the obvious limitations of this remarkable idea, Ockham soon devised a conception more in line with his nominalism. Arguing from the general premise that everything existing outside the mind is particular, he concedes that things might be elements of a proposition so long as they are singular things, whereas general terms are conceptual units abstracted from things. The mental copula, however, is to be taken as an act uniting the terms (consisting of concepts or singular things).[30] Yet, although things might be seen as parts and thus as structural elements of sentences, the structuring or composing device is located in the mind in all of the accounts. Thus, the explanatory burden seems to rest on option (2).

4.2 Option (2): The Mind as the Structural Source for Mental Sentences

All theories of mental language seem to take it for granted that our mind performs mental acts in order to form or combine concepts. Yet, while in concept formation these acts are a world-directed or cognitive affair, judging or combining concepts does not seem to be restrictable to world-directed cognition; it must also account for the structure of mental sentences. Thus, it seems that it must have some sort of syntactic dimension. Of course, we can simply stipulate that the mind 'does this somehow' (and go for an inference to the best explanation or even a transcendental argument). But a satisfactory account will at least try to address the difficulties that threaten this assumption.

Although Ockham's 'mature' theory attributes to thought a carefully devised syntactic dimension, he also sets the agenda for the ensuing debate on the structure problem with regard to option (2). Let us now have a look at the problem he sets out in his commentary on the *Peri hermeneias*. Take a conventional sentence such as 'Every whiteness is an entity' (*omne albedo est entitas*). If we ignore the indefinite article ('an'), the sentence seems to consist of a syncategorematic quantifier ('every'), two categorematic terms ('whiteness', 'entity') and the copula ('is'). Now, what is the corresponding mental sentence like? Let's assume—as many authors in the fourteenth century did—that, on analysis, the mental token or tokens corresponding to this sentence can be seen as one or more mental acts.[31] Ockham now asks what the act(s) of knowing such a sentence might be like, but that need not detain us for the moment. The vital question is: how many and what kind of acts do we have to assume? With regard to the questions of how many acts, he distinguishes two options: (a) there is either just one act that is not a real composition but equals such a composition, (b) or there is more than one act. Both options are problematic: if we assume that (a) there is just one act, we certainly ensure the unity of the mental sentence, but

we gain nothing to explain the structure that differentiates it from the mere formation of world-directed concepts. However, if the sentence consists of (b) as many acts
as the conventional proposition has parts, then it seems to follow that the mental
correlates of the sentences 'Every whiteness is an entity' and 'Every entity is a whiteness' are indistinguishable since we have no good reason to assume that mental acts
obey a successive word order rendering them distinguishable.[32]

If we accept this argument, we are back to option (a). Now one could perhaps
interpret the equivalence thesis in the following way: metaphysically speaking, there
is just one mental act that equals a judgement that can be said to consists of different
parts *only on analysis*, such that we should speak of different conceptual and quasi-
syntactic parts in mental judgements only in a derived but not in a metaphysical
sense. Such an argument could gain some ground by recourse to the (Fregean) idea
of the primacy of sentences over sub-sentential units, but Ockham neither expresses
such an idea nor explains the relation of equivalence any further. Instead, he offers
a refinement of option (2). The assumed indistinguishability of the two mental sentences obviously rests on the thesis that the acts could only render the sentences
distinguishable if they were ordered in sequence. But there is another possibility:
the acts could differ in that one of them is tied to a quantifier ('every'), such that the
acts corresponding to 'every whiteness' and 'whiteness' (and those corresponding to
'every entity' and 'entity') would be different and would, in turn, allow for differently
structured sentences. Although Ockham's mature position in the *Summa logicae*
seems to be more in line with the latter solution and the Boethian sentence model,
he ends the discussion in quite a tentative manner, and even in his later *Quodlibeta*
he doubts again whether structural features can really be part of our mental make-
up prior to any conventional imposition or contact with conventional language. To
the question, however, as to *what* we grasp through such a sentence, he replies that
what is grasped is neither something composed nor something simple since what is
grasped is not something in the mind but something in the extra-mental world. The
same problem is taken up again by later medieval mental language theorists. While
Robert Holcot would defend an Ockhamite version of a structured mental language,
Hugo Lawton (fl. 1325–1330) denied the existence of structured mental sentences in
the mind and pointed out that the Ockhamite recourse to *what* is grasped does not
settle the issue of structure at all.[33]

One of the most prominent opponents of Ockham's mature theory is Gregory
of Rimini, who discusses the example considered here at length.[34] He treats option
(b) as a mere *reductio* (if two mental sentences were to contain the same parts as the
conventional sentences, then the mental sentences would be indistinguishable) and
claims that mental sentences are unstructured simple acts of the mind. But what,
then, we might ask, is the difference between a simple world-related cognitive act
and a simple act that supposedly captures what is expressed by a whole sentence?
Gregory's answer is that the crucial difference does not lie in the structure but in the
fact that the proper mental sentence is an *assertive judgement*, whereas the cognitive
act carries no assertive force whatsoever. His point is that the whole idea of composing a sentence out of simple parts does not lead to a story about assertions or

judgements. It is not clear, he says, how someone who cognises without asserting and *then* (*deinde*) forms a mental sentence out of such simple cognitive acts could be said to cause any variation. The move from mere cognitive acts to an assertion is not rendered plausible by invoking more acts or structure. Following the Augustinian speech model, Gregory rests his argument on the distinction of two kinds of mental sentences. On the one hand, there are internalised conventional sentences; as such they neither have assertive force nor do they constitute any sort of knowledge. On the other hand, there are proper mental sentences or, rather, assertions, which he divides into two sorts: first, there are some that are caused in us *immediately* from direct cognitions or from former cognitions or even naturally without our knowing when or whence or in what way they have been caused. Such assertions—some of which could even be called more or less 'subpersonal'—can occur in us without us having learned a language; yet, because they rest on immediate cognitions (even if unknowingly so), all of these assertions can be said to be proper assertions and constitute knowledge. Second, there are (again, non-linguistic) assertions in the sense of beliefs that things are thus and so; they are assertions but do not constitute knowledge since they do not rest on immediate or direct cognitions in the aforementioned sense. Proper mental language is, then, unstructured; the key element that distinguishes it from structured (internalised) language is its assertive force.

The arguments Gregory invokes against the idea of structured proper mental language suggest that he was well aware of the difficulties of a so-called 'building-block' or 'bottom-up' model according to which the mind builds judgements out of prior simple cognitions. This is not to say, of course, that his opponents—if pressed on the matter—would have defended such a bottom-up model. Rather, it counters the historiographical prejudice that, before Kant or Frege, everyone took this kind of model for granted.[35] In any case, what Gregory assigns to thought on top of semantic priority is not some sort of syntactic priority but, instead, an *assertive priority*.

In giving priority to assertion over syntax, Gregory of Rimini seems to have hit a decisive mark. The crucial line is drawn, not through the propositionally structured vehicle of content as such, but by the propositional attitude. Comparable arguments for this content–attitude distinction can be found, for instance, in Peter of Ailly, who additionally urged the point that the semantic complexity does not require syntactic complexity and thereby sheds some light on Ockham's idea that a mental proposition might be ontologically simple but at the same time 'equivalent' to a complexion of acts. You might suppose, for example, that the conventional term 'white' corresponds to a simple cognitive act of grasping whiteness. But, on reflection, the mental term might turn out to be, in fact, a complex of acts corresponding to whatever nominal definition we are apt to give: so the acts might, in fact, signify something that corresponds to the complex nominal definition 'a thing in which whiteness inheres'. In other words, Peter calls attention to the vehicle–content confusion: the complexity of semantic content should not mislead us into assuming that the vehicle of that content ought to be complexly structured.[36]

4.3 Option (3): Language as a Structural Source for Mental Sentences?

Is it the vehicle/content confusion, then, that underlies the whole issue called the structure problem? If yes, there is a fast conclusion at hand. The supposed structure of mental language is, in fact, nothing but internalised conventional language. Conventional language as such neither carries assertive force nor constitutes knowledge. It is, of course, a medium we cannot dispense with because, on the one hand, we communicate and, on the other hand, we sometimes—perhaps quite often— entertain sentences that we neither assent to nor dismiss. But neither, it seems on Gregory's and Peter's model at least, do we need conventional language nor, indeed, any kind of linguistic structure for proper assertive thought.

But, we might ask, is it really feasible to defend the priority of assertion and deny the idea of structured vehicles in thought? Let's consider the structure problem once again. Although the points Gregory and Peter made certainly sharpen the focus, we should not underestimate the epistemic role of structural vehicles. Remember: Gregory did not only claim that we may have many beliefs unknowingly—'subpersonal' beliefs I called them thus—but he also maintained that it is this kind of immediate belief that constitutes knowledge. It is the second claim that Ockham would take issue with. The reason he gives is that my belief, say, that a donkey is not a stone, is, of course, an assertive mental sentence, but it does not constitute knowledge, which would require that I assent, not only that things are thus and so, but to the (mental) sentence. Ockham would concede that having such immediate beliefs is, indeed, prior to knowledge but does not constitute knowledge. Proper assent (as, for instance, in syllogistic reasoning) requires the availability of the (mental) sentence or meta-beliefs. Why? The reason is that, for proper assent, I need to access not only the underdetermined state of affairs that a donkey is not a stone, but also to the sentence itself.[37] How else would I be able, for instance, to infer the sentence as a conclusion from a chain of sentences, which requires—inter alia— assessing the middle term?

If this interpretation of Ockham's argument is correct, it is completely against the grain of Fodor, whose 'language of thought' is supposed to be sub personal. A look-alike of Ockham's idea is, rather, the well-known thesis among contemporary Davidsonians and higher-order theorists of thought, according to whom we need (internalised) sentences of public language in order to access the required structural elements for having beliefs. The basic idea is that, without access to the linguistic vehicles of thought, I could not form beliefs about beliefs and, thus, could not establish whether a given belief were true or false, or determine its relation to other beliefs.[38] To be sure, Ockham is neither a semantic inferentialist, nor does he claim that we necessarily need public (in the sense of a socially established) language to have beliefs at all. But what proper assertive thought does require, according to him, is access to structured (mental) sentences with, as it were, transportable parts. So while Gregory's and Peter's positions seem to relegate the requirement of structure to a content–vehicle confusion, Ockham's position seems to labour the fact that thought's structure, in order to be properly assertible, must be accessible and, therefore, cannot not be sub personal.

Looking back at the medieval models considered so far, we seem to find ourselves in a jam: either thought has assertive priority but no structure (this is Gregory's version of the speech model), or thought ought to be structured in order to permit the proper assent required for acts of knowing (Ockham's version of the sentence model). Can language come to the rescue?

As Ockham himself clearly admits in his early and even in his later work following his so-called mature theory, it seems that there are many concepts that we do impose at will (that is, in the same way as we conventionally impose words) and that we have to abstract the structural features of mental language from conventional language. This would, of course, undermine the supposed syntactic priority of mental language. Rather, internalised conventional language would in some cases be prior to thought. As we have noted in passing, this idea was dismissed by Burley but embraced already by Richard Campsall and fiercely defended by Ockham's opponent William Crathorn, who denied the common notion of mental sentences altogether and held that they are solely the species of conventional sentences.[39] Not surprisingly, perhaps, this kind of vehicle internalism concurs in both Ockham and Crathorn with a partial semantic externalism. It is the use of conventional signs that allows us to think distinctly about things that we cannot grasp or have distinct natural signs of. As is well known, it is this idea amongst others that will eventually lead to abolishing even the semantic priority of mental language.[40]

5. CONCLUSION

The irony is perhaps that with the growing depth of the dispute over the structure problem, the gap between the speech model and the sentence model gradually seems to have disappeared. While even fierce Augustinians would have to admit that we engage in structured thought where we lack immediate cognitive access, Boethians were forced to acknowledge that structure is mostly a feature deriving from internalised language. As I see it, the philosophically rewarding issue is not whether we need structure in thought or not (we do), but how fruitfully to circumvent a single-minded insistence on priority. Although medieval and contemporary views differ significantly in explanatory scope and goals, at least some general characteristics of these two models of thought are clearly defended in current debates among philosophers of mind. Since Jerry Fodor's launch of *The Language of Thought* in 1975, serious, if controversial, attention has again been given especially to the idea of a mental language taken as prior to and different from any acquired conventional language. A quick argument for assuming such a prior mental language is that learning one's first language seems to require some (subpersonal) inferential processes that already amount to some sort of systematic thinking, so that any account of thought in internalised conventional language would seem to be circular in that it explains thought through a language whose acquisition already requires thought.

From Fodor's point of view, then, any alternative account of thought as internalised conventional language amounts to no more than the 'silly theory that thinking is talking to oneself'.[41] The immediate worry posed by the competing internalised language accounts seems to lie in the ensuing conceptual relativity, infamously proposed by Whorf and Sapir. If we give up the Aristotelian idea of a stable conceptual realm and, rather, say that the development of human thought depends on the linguistic conventions of the community we are part of, it might seem that the realm of thought is not common to all humans but shaped by a variety of different and perhaps non-translatable conventions.[42]

But as Peter Carruthers, José Bermúdez and others have recently claimed, there are serious arguments for reviving the internalised language account without having to embrace conceptual relativism.[43] The renewed attention to conventional language as a way into shaping thought is not so much concerned with culturally relative 'conceptual schemes' but with the structural vehicles of thought provided by conventional languages. One basic move is to show that the alleged circularity is not vicious at all; rather, language acquisition is considered a process during which our minds acquire the structural resources that gradually shape and fine-tune our thought. Thus, our early encounters with structured items such as conventional language sentences do not necessarily require the systematic thinking that is displayed in someone with a perfect command of that language; rather, we might assume that it is precisely the early cognitive contact with such structured items whose very acquisition endows our minds with the growing systematicity required in explicit inferences.[44] Accordingly, conventional languages are not mere communicative devices to express mental sentences, but cognitive devices allowing for structured thought. Cutting a long story very short, perhaps we encounter a similar irony in the current debate in which the initially harsh oppositions seem to have brought about increasingly integrating views: once we admit that this conflict seems to come down to the question of whether to tie (the rationality of) thought to internal items in the mind or to external items in the (partly linguistic) world, there only remains the question of spelling out what it means for the mind to be located in the world.

NOTES

An earlier draft was presented at the conference on Medieval and Contemporary Philosophy, organised by John Marenbon at the Faculty of Philosophy, Cambridge, in July 2010. I owe special thanks to Tim Crane and John Marenbon for their instructive comments on my paper. I would also like to thank Stephan Meier-Oeser and Simone Ungerer for many helpful suggestions.

1. See Millikan (2010).

2. See especially Panaccio (1999b).

3. See Biard (2009) for the current state of research. On Augustine's influence see Meier-Oeser (forthcoming).

4. See Robins (1997).

5. See Aristotle, *De interpretatione* cap. 1 (16a3–8) and cap. 2 (16a26–29) as well as Boethius (1880, 20).

6. Boethius's treatment of the *ordo orandi* is treated extensively in Magee (1989, esp. 64–92). Cf. on the later developments up to the early-modern period, Lenz (2010, ch. II.2.1).

7. See Spade (1982, 188).

8. For the priorities according to the *ordo orandi*, I draw on Lenz (2008, esp. 107–15).

9. See Meier-Oeser (2003).

10. See Augustine, *De trinitate* XIV, 16, 22 (CCSL 50A, 452) and *De trinitate* XV (1968), 10–12 (CCSL 50A, S. 486–94).

11. Although Augustine's theory is often cited along with the Aristotelico-Boethian model, we should bear in mind that it is based on an entirely different epistemological foundation. Whereas Aristotle's account founds concept formation in our cognitive contact with things in the world, Augustine sees the proper origin of true 'words' in the 'knowledge of the mind'.

12. See Boethius (1880, 29 and 36).

13. See Anselm (1968), *Proslogion*, cap. 4 (Opera omnia I, 103).

14. See Panaccio (1999a, 397–413).

15. See Kahnert (2000).

16. See Aquinas (1989) (*Expositio libri Peryermenias* I.2) and Scotus (1891, 581).

17. See Knudsen (1982, 479–95).

18. See Aquinas (1989) (*Expositio libri Peryermenias* I.2, n. 2).

19. See Scotus (1891, 539–40).

20. See especially Walter Burley (1974, 238–59); cf. for the following, Lenz (2003, 53 ff.).

21. See Panaccio (1999a) and Meier-Oeser (forthcoming).

22. See Karger (1996) on these developments.

23. See Panaccio (2004).

24. See the appendix of Fodor's 1987 work as well as his 2008.

25. See Lenz (2004).

26. See Burley (1974, 247).

27. See Burley (1974, 252), and Brinkley (2004, 230–36). On Burley and Brinkley, see Cesalli (2007, esp. 264 ff.).

28. Contemporary content externalism famously draws on Putnam's Twin Earth Cases. See Pessin and Goldberg (1996, esp. 115 ff.) on the ensuing debates; cf. Lau and Deutsch (2010). Unlike contemporary versions of content externalism, however, the position defended here is meant to imply that we have cognitive access to the contents of our thoughts.

29. See Karger (1996).

30. See William of Ockham, *In II Sent. (Rep.)*, qq. 12–13 (1967-88: Opera Theologica V, 280). Cf. Lenz (2003, 88 f.).

31. Cf. Meier-Oeser (2004).

32. See Ockham, *In Periherm.* I, prooemium, §6 (1967-88: Opera Philosophica II, 354). Cf. Spade (1996, 123 ff.).

33. See Robert Holcot (1993, 80–81); Hugh of Lawton's arguments are quoted in Crathorn (1988, 172–75).

34. See Gregory of Rimini (1981, 30–35).

35. See, for example, Brandom (1994, 79).

36. See Peter of Ailly (1980, p. 37).

37. See Ockham, *Quodlibeta* III, q. 8 (1967-88: Opera Theologica IX, 233–34).

38. See Davidson (1982, 95–106), and Bermúdez (2010).

39. See Burley (1974, 241–42), Richard Campsall (1968, 50–68) and Crathorn (1988, 154–60).

40. See Lenz (2008 and 2010, ch. II.2.4 and II.2.5), for the development up to Locke.

41. Fodor (1998, 10).

42. The principle of relativity and the related tenet of conceptual incommensurability have been convincingly challenged by Davidson (1974), who claims that one needs a common rational ground to make the failure of translatability intelligible in the first place.

43. See Carruthers (1996), Cole (1997) and Bermúdez (2010).

44. See, for example, Dennett (1993, esp. 542).

BIBLIOGRAPHY

Anselm of Canterbury. 1968. *Proslogion*. In *Opera omnia* I, ed. F. S. Schmitt. Stuttgart-Bad Cannstatt, Germany: Frommann-Holzboog.

Aristotle. 1966. *Categoriae et Liber de interpretatione*, ed. L. Minio-Paluello. Oxford: Oxford University Press.

Augustine. 1968. *De trinitate libri XV*, ed. W. J. Mountain and Fr. Glorie. Turnhout, Belgium: Brepols (Corpus Christianorum series latina 50A).

Bermúdez, José Luis. 2010. Two Arguments for the Language-Dependence of Thought. *Grazer Philosophische Studien* 81:37–54.

Biard, Joel. 2009. *Le langage mental du Moyen Âge à l'âge classique*. Paris: Vrin.

Boethius. 1880. *Commentarii in librum Aristotelis Peri hermeneias, pars posterior*, ed. C. Meiser. Leibzig, Germany: Teubner.

Brandom, Robert B. 1994. *Making It Explicit: Reasoning, Representing and Discursive Commitment*. Cambridge, MA: Harvard University Press.

Carruthers, Peter. 1996. *Language, Thought and Consciousness: An Essay in Philosophical Psychology*. Cambridge: Cambridge University Press.

Cesalli, Laurent. 2007. *Le réalisme propositionnel: sémantique et ontologie des propositions chez Jean Duns Scot, Gauthier Burley, Richard Brinkley et Jean Wyclif*, Paris: Vrin.

Cole, David. 1997. *Hearing Yourself Think: Natural Language, Inner Speech and Thought*. http://www.d.umn.edu/~dcole/hearthot.htm (accessed 8 January 2011).

Crathorn. 1988. *Quästionen zum ersten Sentenzenbuch: Einführung und Text*, ed. F. Hoffmann. Münster, Germany: Aschendorff.

Davidson, Donald. 1974. 'On the very idea of a conceptual scheme'. In Donald Davidson, *Inquiries into Truth and Interpretation*. Oxford: Clarendon, 2001.

———. 1982. 'Rational animals'. In *Subjective, Intersubjective, Objective*. Oxford: Clarendon, 2001.

Dennett, Daniel. 1993. Learning and Labeling. *Mind and Language* 8(4):540–47.

Fodor, Jerry A. 1987. *Psychosemantics: The Problem of Meaning in the Philosophy of Mind*. Cambridge, MA: MIT Press.

———. 1998. *Concepts: Where Cognitive Science Went Wrong*. Oxford: Oxford University Press.

———. 2008. *LOT II: The Language of Thought Revisited*. Oxford: Oxford University Press.

Gregory of Rimini. 1981. *Lectura super primum et secundum Sententiarum. Tomus I: super primum prologus et distinction 1–6*, ed. W. Eckermann. Berlin and New York: De Gruyter.

John Duns Scotus. 1639/1891. *Opera omnia I*. Paris: Vivès. (Reprint.)

Kahnert, Klaus. 2000. *Entmachtung der Zeichen? Augustin über Sprache*. Amsterdam and Philadelphia: John Benjamins.

Karger, Elizabeth. 1996. Mental Sentences According to Burley and to the Early Ockham. *Vivarium* 34(2):192–230.

Knudsen, Christian. 1982. 'Intentions and impositions'. In *The Cambridge History of Later Medieval Philosophy*, ed. N. Kretzmann, A. Kenny and J. Pinborg, 479–95. Cambridge: Cambridge University Press.

Lau, Joe and Max Deutsch. 2010. 'Externalism about mental content'. In *The Stanford Encyclopedia of Philosophy*, ed. E. N. Zalta. http://plato.stanford.edu/entries/content-externalism (accessed 8 January 2011).

Lenz, Martin. 2003. *Mentale Sätze. Wilhelm von Ockhams Thesen zur Sprachlichkeit des Denkens*, Stuttgart, Germany: Steiner.

———. 2004. 'Oratio mentalis und Mentalesisch: Ein spätmittelalterlicher Blick auf die gegenwärtige Philosophie des Geistes'. In *Herbst des Mittelalters? Fragen zur Bewertung des 14. und 15. Jahrhunderts*, ed. J. Aertsen and M. Pickavé, 105–30. Berlin and New York: De Gruyter (Miscellanea Mediaevalia 31).

———. 2008. Why Is Thought Linguistic? Ockham's Two Conceptions of the Intellect. *Vivarium* 46(3):203–17.

———. 2010. *Lockes Sprachkonzeption*. Berlin and New York: De Gruyter (Quellen und Studien zur Philosophie 96).

Magee, John. 1989. *Boethius on Signification and Mind*. Leiden, the Netherlands: Brill.

Meier-Oeser, Stephan. 2003. 'Medieval semiotics'. In *The Stanford Encyclopedia of Philosophy*, ed. E. N. Zalta. http://plato.stanford.edu/entries/semiotics-medieval (accessed 8 January 2011).

———. 2004. 'Mental language and representation in late scholastic logic'. In *John Buridan and Beyond: Topics in the Language Sciences 1300–700*, ed. R. Friedman and S. Ebbesen, 237–65. Copenhagen: Reitzel.

———. (forthcoming). Die zwei Formen innerer Rede nach Augustinus: Zum historischen Ursprung der These der sprachlichen Verfasstheit des Denkens.

Millikan, Ruth G. 2010. Gedacht wird in der Welt, nicht im Kopf (Interview with Markus Wild and Martin Lenz). *Deutsche Zeitschrift für Philosophie* 58(6):982–1000.

Panaccio, Claude. 1999a. 'Grammar and Mental Language in the Pseudo-Kilwardby'. In *Medieval Analyses in Language and Cognition*, ed. S. Ebbesen and R. Friedman, 397–413. Copenhagen: Reitzel.

———. 1999b. *Le discours intérieur de Platon à Guillaume d'Ockham*, Paris: Éditions du Seuil.

———. 2004. *Ockham on Concepts*. Aldershot, UK: Ashgate.

Pessin, Andrew, and Sanford Goldberg, eds. 1996. *The Twin Earth Chronicles*. Armonk, NY: Sharpe.

Peter of Ailly. 1980. *Concepts and Insolubles*, trans. P. V. Spade. Dordrecht, the Netherlands: Reidel.

Pinborg, Jan. 1967. *Die Entwicklung der Sprachtheorie im Mittelalter*. Münster, Germany: Aschendorff.

Richard Brinkley. 2004. De propositione (Summa logicae V.1–5), ed. L. Cesalli. *Archives d'histoire doctrinale et littéraire du Moyen Age* 71:203–54.

Richard Campsall. 1968. *Quaestiones super librum Priorum analeticorum*, ed. E. A. Synan. Toronto: Pontifical Institute of Mediaeval Studies.

Robert Holcot. 1993. *Conferentiae*, ed. F. Hoffmann. Münster, Germany: Aschendorff.

Robins, Robert H. 1997. *A Short History of Linguistics*. London and New York: Longman.

Spade, Paul V. 1982. 'The semantics of terms'. In *The Cambridge History of Later Medieval Philosophy*, ed. N. Kretzmann, A. Kenny and J. Pinborg, 188–96. Cambridge: Cambridge University Press.

———. 1996. *Thoughts, Words and Things: An Introduction to Late Medieval Logic and Semantic Theory*. http://pvspade.com/Logic/docs/thoughts.pdf (accessed 8 January 2011).

Thomas Aquinas. 1989. *Expositio libri Peryermenias*, ed. R.-A. Gauthier. Rome and Paris: Commissio Leonina and Vrin.

Walter Burley. 1974. *Quaestiones in librum Perihermeneias*, ed. S. F. Brown. *Franciscan Studies* 34:200–295.

William of Ockham. 1967–88. *Opera philosophica et theologica*, cura Instituti Franciscani. St Bonaventure, NY: The Franciscan Institute.

Metaphysics and
Epistemology

....

CHAPTER 17

UNIVERSALS

....

CLAUDE PANACCIO

In his introduction to a recent collection of essays on universals, Arindam Chakrabarti writes that 'the problem of universals, threatened from time to time by oblivion but never by death, once again has come near the centre of the field' (Chakrabarti 2006, 3). The reference, there, is to the spectacular revival of metaphysics within analytical philosophy since the 1970s and to the preponderant place occupied in it by a lively controversy over something called 'universals'. By mentioning periods of quasi 'oblivion', Chakrabarti's remark is intended to evoke the logical positivist dismissal of metaphysics and its Wittgensteinian sequel in the mid–twentieth century, but it can also be taken to refer to the openly scornful attitude displayed by early-modern philosophers such as Descartes and Locke towards the great scholastic quarrel over genera and species. And by saying that the problem of universals *once again* has become central in philosophy, Chakrabarti no doubt implicitly refers his reader to the prevalence of this controversy in medieval philosophy, as well, maybe, as to the crucial disagreement between Plato and Aristotle over the former's so-called 'Theory of Ideas'. In the opening statement of his own introductory study on 'universals', J. P. Moreland goes even so far as to affirm that 'along with the metaphysics of substance, the problem of universals is the paradigm case of a perennial issue in the history of philosophy' (Moreland 2001, 1).

All of this presupposes that the issue discussed under this label by analytical philosophers is the very 'same' problem that William of Champeaux, Peter Abelard, John Duns Scotus and William of Ockham were quarrelling over between the twelfth and the fourteenth century. But is it? Some historians of medieval philosophy doubt it. The medieval problematic, according to them, is so intimately rooted in the intellectual world of the period that it cannot plausibly be seen as 'identical' with anything that the analytical philosophers of the last few decades have been occupied with: to think otherwise leads, according to this view, to anachronistic misunderstandings about what the medieval thinkers were up to. From which it would follow—rather unfortunately!—that the medieval debate has no direct relevance for current philosophical interests and that it must be seen, at best, as an intriguing patchwork of pre-modern curiosities.

My intention here is to re-examine the matter and to defend the moderately 'continuistic' idea that the appellation 'the problem of universals' is not equivocal when applied to the set of questions at issue under that name in medieval and in contemporary analytical philosophy,[1] and that at least some of the medieval developments and arguments on the topic are *directly* relevant for today's discussions.[2] I will first present the—prima facie plausible—case for discontinuism. I will then explain what I take to be at the root of both the medieval and the contemporary 'problem of universals', and in the following section I will claim, in a most traditional fashion, that the main dividing line with respect to this problem, in medieval as well as in contemporary philosophy, runs between realism and nominalism, taken in today's sense. Finally, I will outline one of the most salient medieval approaches to the problem of universals, which is, by and large, still relevant today: William of Ockham's nominalism.

1. The Case for Discontinuity

The best survey of the medieval dispute on universals ever is that of Alain de Libera (1996). The book, moreover, is not a mere presentation of doctrines; it also offers challenging theses about the place of the medieval discussion in the history of philosophy: the whole debate as it was then pursued, according to de Libera, belongs to an intellectual universe that is not ours anymore, that of what he calls the '*translatio studiorum*'. This he thinks of as a very long period extending from the ancient Greek philosophical schools up to the late fourteenth century, including Neoplatonism (Porphyry, Syrianus, Proclus, etc.) and Islamic philosophy (Al-Fârâbi, Avicenna, Averroes . . .) as well as Latin medieval thought, and ending very precisely with John Wyclif (c. 1325–1384), himself the author of a treatise *On Universals* (John Wyclif 1985). This '*translatio studiorum*' according to de Libera, is characterised by the constant 'recurrence' of a crucial opposition between two great metaphysics: Platonism and Aristotelism, and by the fact that *all* of philosophy during that period was developed in direct or indirect reference to the founding texts of Plato and, above all, Aristotle. A textual *tradition* was thus built up, which *entirely* accounts for what the philosophical problems were for the authors of the time. In the case under consideration here, in particular, de Libera holds that 'the origin of the *medieval* problem of universals is not in *our* world, it is in the philosophical systems and the network of statements that were available at the time when it precipitated into a *problem*' (Libera 1996, 63; my translation with the author's italics).

What *was* available in Latin in the twelfth, thirteenth and fourteenth centuries, basically, was the Aristotelian corpus along with some of its ancient and Arabic commentators: Porphyry, Boethius, Avicenna and Averroes mainly, with the later addition of Themistius, Ammonius, Simplicius and a few others (see Pasnau 2010, Appendix B, 793–801). From Plato, only a handful of dialogues were translated: the *Phaedo* and the *Meno* in the twelfth century, the *Parmenides* in the thirteenth and part of the *Timaeus* in the old Calcidius version; and they were not very widely circulated either. The opposition between Platonism and Aristotelism over universals became problematic for the medieval thinkers, according to de Libera, through the writings of Aristotle himself and of his commentators: not only did Aristotle explicitly summarise and criticise Plato's theory of Forms (most saliently in *Metaphysics* Z), but he also uncritically incorporated some disturbing Platonic elements in his own doctrine. This is what de Libera calls 'Aristotle's residual Platonism' (Libera 1996, 29), a striking manifestation of which is to be found in the last chapter of the *Posterior Analytics* (II, 19, 100b5–17), where Aristotle refers to a special 'intuition' by which the human mind correctly grasps the intelligible principles underlying all sciences. This cognitive capacity for a priori intellectual knowledge, de Libera remarks, was at odds with Aristotle's theory of abstraction as it seemed to require the position of purely intelligible objects of a Platonic sort. Most of de Libera's book is intended to show that the whole debate on universals until the end of the fourteenth century comes down to a series of sophisticated attempts at reconciling authoritative statements of this sort with each other. The medieval problem of universals in this context was a matter of working out a coherent fit within a definite (mostly Aristotelian) *textual* tradition.

De Libera is right to a very large extent, of course: much of the medieval debate revolved around the interpretation of Aristotle, Boethius, Avicenna and Averroes, which is not, obviously, what primarily interests today's analytical philosophers. The very formulation of the medieval problem of universals, for one thing, was directly dependent upon three questions raised by Porphyry in his introduction to Aristotle's theory of categories, the celebrated *Isagoge*, originally written in Greek:

> (a) whether genera and species are real or are situated in bare thoughts alone, (b) whether as real they are bodies or incorporeals, and (c) whether they are separated or in sensibles and have their reality in connection with them. (Porphyry 1994, 1)

Porphyry himself refrained from providing answers to these questions, which he deemed too 'profound' for a mere introductory manual, but his wording of them, as rendered in Latin by Boethius in the sixth century, decisively oriented the entire medieval discussion and defined its contours by delimiting the range of possible answers. Boethius, moreover, discussed the passage in his own commentary on it and submitted a stock of arguments and theses, coined from an Aristotelian perspective, that became, along with Porphyry's text, unavoidable references for the subsequent debate up to the fourteenth century. Porphyry, admittedly, never used the word 'universal' in his *Isagoge* himself, wondering only about 'genera' and 'species', but Boethius did, and the term was accepted by the Latin tradition as the covering label for the discussion of Porphyry's three questions, on the basis of the (once more textual) fact that Aristotle had characterised genera and species as being 'predicated of many' in the *Categories* (e.g. 3b16–18) and that he defined a 'universal' as what can be predicated of many in the treatise *On Interpretation* (17a39–40). Everything about the very position of the medieval problem of universals thus seems to be directly rooted, as de Libera suggests, in a restricted group of 'founding' texts, which, to put it mildly, are not 'authoritative' anymore.

And not only the problem, but also the solutions that were given to it—or at least some of them—are hardly intelligible apart from this textual tradition. A salient example—one that actually played a determinant role in de Libera's general approach—is that of the thirteenth-century Dominican Albert the Great (ca. 1200–80), whose theory of universals was widely influential until the fifteenth century.[3] De Libera himself has very usefully identified the main components of this theory—the three states of the universal, the indifference of essence and exemplarist causality—and he has shown for each of them how it is linked with both the Neoplatonist and the Aristotelian textual networks (Libera 1990, 179–213; 1996, 245–62). This is worth looking at in some detail in the present context.

First, Albert takes on a distinction that was common among the Neoplatonist commentators of Aristotle since Ammonius in the fourth century, between the universal *ante rem*, the universal *in re*, and the universal *post rem* (Libera 1990, 180–95). The point of the distinction among the Neoplatonists was to pave the way for the reconciliation of Plato and Aristotle, which was a major piece of their big scheme: [4] Aristotle, they would claim, since he was first and foremost a natural philosopher, cared only about universals *in re* (the common natures within singular things) and universals *post rem* (the concepts in the mind), while Plato, the real master of First philosophy, was interested in universals *ante rem* (the separate Forms). Albert probably got the distinction from Eustratios of Nicaea, a Greek philosopher of the late twelfth century whose commentary on Aristotle's *Nicomachean Ethics* was partly translated in Latin by Robert Grosseteste in 1247, but he attributes it to Plato himself, whom he accuses of mistakenly accepting the independent existence of the universals *ante rem*. Albert's own position, however, does not amount to a mere rejection of such metaphysically prior universals: it is to locate them within the First Principle—God himself—and to identify them with the Divine Ideas, which, he thinks, 'precontain' (*precontinere*) the essential natures of all created things.

The second main component of Albert's theory is the doctrine of the 'indifference of essence', which he borrows from Avicenna (Libera 1990, 204–19). In the *Metaphysics* of his great philosophical encyclopedia *al-Shifa*, or *The Healing*, Avicenna held that an essence or nature such as horseness is *in itself* indifferent with respect to universality and singularity, or with respect to being in the mind or in external things: 'Horseness', he famously wrote, 'is in itself only horseness' (Avicenna 2005, V, 1, 149).[5] Albert accepts the idea as a way of accounting for the fact that the very *same* nature or essence can be considered in itself, or as it is exemplified in singular things, or again as it is present in human minds under the guise of a concept. As de Libera insists, though, the 'essence in itself' is not to be identified for

Albert with the universal *ante rem*. The essence in this view is not an additional thing in the world; it is that which can exist in different ways—or have various 'modes of being' (*modi essendi*)—according to whether it is in God, in singular substances or in thinking minds.

The third component—and the most important one in de Libera's convincing interpretation of Albert—is the Neoplatonist notion of 'exemplary causality'. Albert presumably got it from the *Book of Causes*, which he believed to have been written by Aristotle himself, but which was, in fact, a collection of Neoplatonist developments, mostly from Proclus's *Elements of Theology*, assembled in the ninth-century Baghdad school. The original idea here is that there is a metaphysical hierarchy of 'Intelligences' ultimately stemming from the One by some sort of 'emanation', the intrinsic nature of each new inferior reality being the result of the exemplary 'influence' of the former. The point of Albert's reappropriation of the theme is to account for the metaphysical connection between universals *ante rem*—the Divine ideas— and their exemplifications in the world and in created minds. This gives the Albertinian conception of universals its unity and coherence: universals *in re* and universals *post rem* are emanations from the universals *ante rem* in God, which themselves emanate from God's own unity, and the idea of the indifference of essence allows us in this scheme to see the three levels of universals as a descending hierarchy of 'modes of being' of the *same* natures or essences.

Albert's theory of universals, then, comes out as an ingenious weaving together of Aristotelian and Neoplatonist themes with an eye to reconciling the two great ancient philosophies within a Christian context. This whole project, of course, is very much alien to the predominantly naturalistic preoccupations of contemporary analytical philosophy, and emanation, in particular—which is at the heart of Albert's view—seems unintelligible today apart from its historical rooting in those 'authoritative' texts that constrained the medieval philosophical outlook. De Libera's thesis is that this is not peculiar to Albert but that it is true as well of the whole medieval discussion on universals.

2. THE PROBLEM OF UNIVERSALS NOW AND THEN

De Libera's approach draws the attention on a number of important historical features, the neglect of which, admittedly, would prevent us from understanding much of what was going on in the medieval debates. It remains, however, that the authors of the time certainly thought of themselves as discussing issues that had to do with reality and not merely with matters of textual interpretation. They were aware that those very 'authoritative' texts that inspired them so profoundly referred to *extramental* phenomena, and not only to each other, and they took it for granted that the evaluation of their mentors' doctrines—and of their own—ultimately depended on how well they could account for these phenomena. The debate on universals was no exception: much of the theses, arguments and examples adduced in it by the medieval protagonists refer to features of the world and of our relation to it that we are still puzzled by independently of Aristotle, Plato and Porphyry. When Albert the Great speaks of 'universals *post rem*', for example, he is referring to human mental conceptualisation, which is, of course, something that still interests philosophers of mind and cognitive scientists. Once this is realised, it can readily be gathered that the medieval and the contemporary debates on universals are ultimately *about* pretty much the same extra-textual phenomena.

Exactly what phenomena would that be? There are various sorts, obviously, and it is a somewhat controversial issue to decide which ones are the most relevant. What I want to suggest is that the basic feature a good theory of universals is supposed to account for, in the medieval as well as in the contemporary discussions, is the fact that *general terms* occur in sentences we deem to be true. A recent entry on 'Universals: the contemporary debate', for example, introduces the problem in the following way:

> Hold up your hands. Say, as you gesture with the right hand, 'Here is a hand', adding, as you gesture with the left, 'Here is another hand'. Have you not thereby proved *ipso facto* the existence of something common to both, viz. the existence of the property *being a hand*? (MacBride 2009, 276)

The recognizable phenomenon that is thought to require an explanation here is that we apply tokens of the same general word 'hand' to different singular objects in sentences we unhesitantly take to be true. This is, I claim, what gives rise to the problem of universals, both today and in the Middle Ages.

Several contemporary authors, admittedly, have insisted that the problem is not fundamentally linguistic: 'The issue', Keith Campbell says, for example, 'is entirely ontological. It concerns objects in the world and the properties they share with one another' (Campbell 1990, 28). This is something I do not wish to deny in a sense: it *is* expected from a good solution to the problem—and it was so expected in the Middle Ages as well—that it should rest on an acceptable theory of the basic sorts of entities that the world is *really* composed of and of how they are tied with each other. The question of universals, however, is not the whole of ontology. The puzzling phenomenon that *specifically* gives rise to it is precisely our use of general linguistic terms. Consider Bertrand Russell's classical approach in *Problems of Philosophy*: he starts with the commonly accepted fact that certain *words* are applicable to a large number of particular things and that virtually no *statement* can be made without including such general words, and he argues on this basis for the necessity of accepting universals in the ontology as *denotata* for these general terms (Russell 1912, Chapter 9).

According to Moreland (2001, 4), three phenomena are especially relevant for the ongoing discussion on universals: predication, abstract reference and exact similarity. But why should similarity be a problem in the first place? As Rodriguez-Pereyra (2002, 21) remarks: 'Why should the fact that different particulars resemble each other be more puzzling than the fact that different particulars, say, move towards each other?' Linguistic predication, by contrast, cries for an ontological explanation: are special referents needed for general words in addition to those of the singular terms they are predicated of? The answer is by no means obvious and until the question is elucidated; there is something crucial that we don't understand, not only about language but also about reality. As to abstract reference, it is equally puzzling, no doubt: what do singular abstract terms such as 'justice', 'whiteness' or 'animality' refer to in the world? But the reason why *this* question is related to the problem of universals—and not merely a separate problem for ontology—is that abstract terms such as these are usually connected in language with certain corresponding general predicates like 'just', 'white' and 'animal'. The upshot of it all is that the commonly recognizable puzzling phenomenon that gives rise to the contemporary problem of universals is that of *linguistic generality*.

This is true as well of the medieval problem. Recent research has made it clear, for example, that the first round of discussion on it that we know of in the Latin Middle Ages very much revolved around semantical questions. Rosier-Catch (2008) insists that this is what emerges in the *Glosulae super Priscianum*, an important survey of grammatical and philosophical issues from the early twelfth century, which provides a background for Peter Abelard's better-known doctrines. One central question, Rosier says, was 'whether common nouns can be seen as proper names for species' (Rosier-Catch 2008, 126; my translation). The realistic acceptance of universals *in re* in the *Glosulae* is precisely formulated in this linguistic fashion: 'this noun "man" is a word common to all men [. . .]. Yet it is also proper, it is like the proper name of this incorporeal species' (quoted by Rosier-Catch 2008, 151; my translation). And the same thing is found in a short early-twelfth-century *Treatise on Universals* edited by Dijs (1990):

> This same spoken word 'man' can be taken as proper. And then it signifies it [the universal nature] in its simplicity [. . .]; it names it and refers to it pretty much singularly. (Dijs 1990, 114, my translation)

Peter Abelard, at the same period, goes so far as to reformulate Porphyry's questions in a straightforwardly semantical way (see King 2007, 263–68). 'Are genera and species real or in bare thoughts alone?' is reinterpreted as asking about genus and species *terms* like the words 'animal' and 'man' if they 'signify any truly existing things' (Peter Abelard 1994, 51). 'Are genus and species bodies or incorporeals?' becomes: 'Do they [genus and species terms] signify subsistents that are corporeal or that are incorporeal?' (ibid.). And 'Are they separated or in sensibles?' is understood as a way of asking if these terms 'signify an intrinsic substance existing in a sensible thing' or something separate? (ibid., 53). These questions, Abelard adds, 'rightly arose about universal words' (ibid., 54), making it clear that Porphyry's questionnaire, in his interpretation, is about the 'modes of signifying' of general terms.

Abelard's reinterpretation, of course, is motivated to a large extent by his 'nominalist' conviction that generality is to be ascribed 'only to words' (Peter Abelard

1994, 37). His rephrasals, however, remain neutral between nominalist and realist solutions. A realist could answer Abelard's questions without qualms by saying that genus and species terms signify incorporeal common natures really existing within sensible things; and this is, in fact, a good way of presenting immanent realism as it was widely defended at the time: realists themselves strongly tended in the early twelfth century to phrase their position in semantical terms (Dijs 1990; Erismann 2007; Rosier-Catach 2008).

Even in the thirteenth century, as Abelard was almost entirely forgotten and immanent realism went virtually uncontested, the Porphyrian questions were standardly understood as arising from *predication*. And predication surely, whether this was explicitly acknowledged or not, primarily appeared to the medieval authors—as it still does our contemporaries—under the guise of a linguistic phenomenon: sentences are uttered in which a general term is truly predicated of a singular one as in 'this is a man', or of another general term as in 'man is an animal'. Take Robertus Anglicus's mid–thirteenth-century commentary on the *Isagoge* as edited by Piché (2005). The salient feature of a universal, for this author as for most of his contemporaries, is that it is supposed to be truly *predicated* of singular entities: in the relevant sense a universal is 'a common form predicated of many' (Robertus Anglicus 2005, 304, my translation). This is formulated, admittedly, as an ontological feature: the universal here is not a mere word or concept, it is a 'common form' that is taken to be 'something in reality, and not nothing' (ibid., 306). This, however, is the author's *solution* to Porphyry's first question. My point is that Robertus Anglicus reaches it by—quite typically—focusing on predication as a linguistic phenomenon, which he then accounts for by postulating an ontological analogue for it. This might or might not be legitimate, but in either case, if I am right, what the *problem* originally refers to and arises from, in the thirteenth as in the twelfth century, is the very same sort of commonly observable linguistic fact that gives rise to the contemporary debate.

The medieval solutions, for sure, were forcefully constrained by the accepted 'authorities'. Their fine-grained wording preferably had to be compatible with what Aristotle said, and their formulations would standardly resort to concepts, distinctions and arguments found in Boethius, Avicenna or Averroes. This was by no means irrational in the context: Aristotelian science had resisted the critical scrutiny of generations of philosophers, and it was reasonably thought to provide—if well interpreted—a secure basis for further enquiry and developments. This is why, as de Libera rightly stressed, the discussion on universals often revolved around questions of textual interpretation and around particular puzzles arising from the clash between apparently incompatible authoritative texts. Yet one must carefully distinguish such local constraints and puzzles from the basic philosophical problems. Those, I want to claim, usually arise from the need to account for commonly observable phenomena. In the case of the problem of universals, these primarily have to do with the use of general terms within linguistic sentential units, a phenomenon that was as puzzling for medieval philosophers as it is today.

3. Realism versus Nominalism

Another aspect by which the medieval and the contemporary debates on universals strikingly meet with each other is that the main dividing line among doctrines in both cases runs between those that accept the extra-mental and non-linguistic reality of universals and those that don't. In recent philosophical literature, the standard labels for these are 'realism' and 'nominalism'. Volume I of David Armstrong's 1975 landmark work on universals, for example, is entitled *Nominalism and Realism*: 'all Nominalists', he writes, 'agree that all things that exist are only particulars' (Armstrong 1978, I, 12); and realists, in his vocabulary, are those who deny that. MacBride (2009, 276) similarly characterises nominalism as 'the family of doctrines according to which reality consists *solely* of particulars' and realism as 'the family of doctrines according to which reality consists, in significant part at least, of universals'. Loux (2006) centrally opposes 'Metaphysical realism' and 'nominalism' in his discussion of the problem of universals, and virtually everybody in recent analytical philosophy who is interested in the problem does so as well.

It is agreed, of course, that each group admits of a number of varieties. Armstrong (1978) distinguishes at least four sorts of nominalisms—predicate nominalism, concept nominalism, class nominalism and resemblance nominalism—and two sorts of realisms—those that countenance 'transcendent' universals and those that do only with 'immanent' universals. In the last couple of decades, the main division among nominalists has been between 'resemblance nominalists' (e.g., Rodriguez-Pereyra 2002), who base their ontological accounts on mere resemblances, as their name indicates, and 'trope theorists', who hold that familiar concrete objects are bundles of singular properties called 'tropes' (e.g., Bacon 1995; Campbell 1990). On the realist side, the most salient opposition is still between some sort of Platonism, which posits universals in themselves apart from and independently of their exemplifications (e.g., Bealer 1982), and moderate or immanent realism, which allows only for universals that are exemplified and which tends to locate them (in some sense) within particular things or states of affairs (e.g., Armstrong 1989, 1997). It remains widely accepted, however, that the big parting of the ways in the recent debate is between those who accept universals in their ontology in one way or another—the realists—and those who don't—the nominalists.[6]

The same may be said of the medieval debate. There were, on one side, those who thought that a good account of general terms requires the admission of special realities in addition to the familiar *denotata* of concrete singular terms and, on the other side, those who held that such an enrichment of the ontology is neither necessary nor desirable.

The point can most readily be made in connection with how the discussion went on in the second half of the twelfth century, as schools of thought began to be distinctively identified by their positions with respect to universals. The central division, strikingly enough, was between the *reales* and the *nominales*. Announcing his intention to review the main trends among the philosophers of his time, Godfrey of Saint-Victor in *The Source of Philosophy* (dated 1178), for instance, attends primarily to this opposition (Iwakuma and Ebbesen 1992, 179–80). The mere resemblance of labels is not enough, of course, to warrant the identification of the medieval positions with the contemporary ones, and it has sometimes been suggested that the twelfth-century controversy between the two schools might not be so centrally related with the problem of universals (Courtenay 1991; Normore 1987). Recent research, however, has confirmed the traditional view: the *nominales* were the followers of Peter Abelard, and their most distinctive thesis was that universals are but names (*nomina*) rather than external realities, while the *reales* held that they are things (*res*) (Ebbesen 1992; Iwakuma 1992a; Marenbon 1992; Martin 1992; Panaccio 1999c). The latter were standardly sub-divided into several 'sects': the *Porretani*, who followed Gilbert of Porreta; the *Albricani*, who followed Alberic of Paris; the *Robertini*, who followed Robert of Melun; and the *Parvipontani*, who followed Adam Parvipontanus (Iwakuma and Ebbesen 1992, 173–74). But the main dividing line was taken to be between all of them on the one hand, and Abelard's followers, the *nominales*, on the other hand, as comes out from the impressive collection of passages from the late twelfth and early thirteenth century brought together by Iwakuma and Ebbesen (1992): in addition to Godfrey of Saint-Victor referred to earlier, Ralph of Beauvais, John of Salisbury, Stephen Langton, Peter the Chanter, Peter of Capua and William of Auxerre all routinely—and centrally—contrast the *nominales* and the *reales*, with the status of genera and species as the main bone of contention between the two groups.

I do not want to claim that the term '*nominales*', in particular, had *exactly* the same sense in the twelfth century as 'nominalism' does in today's analytical philosophy. It has been suggested by Iwakuma (1992b) that another label, that of '*vocales*', namely, was in use during the twelfth century to designate those who held, like Abelard's master Roscelin of Compiègne, that genera and species are mere vocal sounds (*voces*). The *nominales*, by contrast, identified universals with names (*nomina*), and they took the conditions of identity of a name to be significantly different from that of a mere vocal sound: distinct vocal sounds, they insisted, can be seen as instances of the same name, just as the nominative '*homo*' and its genitive '*hominis*', for example, are cases of the same name. This is the thesis of 'the unity of the name' (*unitas nominis*), which was sometimes attributed to the *nominales* (Courtenay 1991; Normore 1992; Panaccio 1999c). The label '*nominales*', then, was reserved for a particular variant of the tenet that universals are but linguistic units, and it cannot be seen in its twelfth-century use as precisely coextensive with today's 'nominalism'. The *vocales* and the *nominales*, however, even though they might have disagreed as to which linguistic units universals should be identified with, were clearly closer to each other on the status of universals than to any of the realist groups. The position of the *vocales*, in fact, seems to have appeared in the late eleventh century (Iwakuma 1992b) and to have quickly evolved into that of the *nominales*. Abelard himself, according to Shimizu (1995), first adopted it and moved from there to the thesis that universals are names. The point I want to stress is that, whatever the labels were, the main demarcation line among twelfth-century philosophers ran, in their own eyes, between those who accepted extra-linguistic universals in their ontology and those who did not.

In the thirteenth century—especially from the 1240s on—most of those who wrote on universals tended to agree on some form or other of Aristotelian immanent realism with the Christian addition of Divine ideas, as we saw earlier in the case of Albert the Great. Aquinas, for instance, holds that universals—in the technical sense of 'what is predicated of many'—'do not subsist outside the soul' (*Summa contra Gentiles* II, 75), but he accepts common natures *in re* as the ontological foundations for abstract conceptualisation (see, e.g., Pasnau 2002, 296–302).[7] And this is more or less what we find in John Duns Scotus (Boulnois 1992; Noone 2003) as well as in the mid-century masters studied by Piché (2005): Robert Kilwardby, John Pagus, Nicholas of Paris and Robertus Anglicus, among others. From the early fourteenth century, however, as the matter of universals became hotly debated again, the main controversy once more was between nominalists such as William of Ockham, John Buridan and their followers, and realists such as Walter Burley, John Wyclif and in general all the followers of Scotus, Aquinas and Albert the Great. The twelfth-century labels were not in use anymore— neither Ockham nor Buridan ever called themselves '*nominales*'—but the central issue still was whether universals should be accepted in extra-mental reality or not.

Ockham's lengthy discussion of the topic around 1317 in his *Ordinatio*, for example, is directed first and foremost against the 'common opinion' that a universal is something real outside the soul in some way or other (William of Ockham 1970, 99–226). And John Buridan's *Treatise on the Difference between the Universal and the Individual*, in the 1330s, is likewise principally aimed at refuting the realist thesis that universals exist outside the mind as distinct from individuals (John Buridan 1987). These nominalist positions, in turn, aroused quite a stir and were at the heart of the discussions on universals in the following decades. Francis de Prato's treatise *On Universals* and Stephanus of Reati's work of the same title, both written in Italy in the 1340s, explicitly take Ockham's nominalism as their polemical target (Amerini 2003, 2007). And the whole point of the Englishman John Wyclif's influential *On Universals* in the 1370s, to take just one more salient example, is to explain his realist theory that universals are non-linguistic entities and to defend it against nominalist objections (see Conti 2006, 2010, 654–9; Spade 1985).

By the fifteenth century, the practice was back again of labelling the various philosophical schools, and this was done primarily on the basis of their positions on universals (Kaluza 1988). William Evrie, for example, distinguishes in 1403 between the *nominales*, explicitly associated with Ockham, the *formalizantes*, who can be identified with the followers of Scotus, and the *peripatetici*, among which he ranges Albert the Great and Thomas Aquinas (Kaluza 1988, 15–17). And John of Nova Domus, who wrote a treatise *On the Real Universal* around the same period, considers as his archenemies certain 'modern' doctors whom Kaluza identifies with Buridanian nominalists (Kaluza 1988, 92–105).

I do not mean to suggest that the medieval theses on universals are not significantly different from those of today's philosophers. But recent research, I want to claim, tends to confirm that the medieval problem of universals was, as Klima (2004, §10) puts it, '*recognizably the same* problem' as the contemporary one, and that the main split in both historical situations with respect to *this* problem is between those who account for our use of general terms by positing universals in external reality in one way or another—the realists—and those who countenance only individuals in the ontology—the nominalists.[8]

4. OCKHAM'S CONTRIBUTION

Given these convergences between the medieval and the contemporary discussions on universals, it would be surprising that the former should have nothing to contribute to the latter. The medievals systematically explored a wide array of relevant theoretical strategies, lines of argumentation and conceptual distinctions, some of which, at least, still deserve to be seriously taken into consideration, even though they were originally coined in the context of a textual tradition that is not ours anymore. One salient medieval doctrine that is still philosophically relevant, in my view, is William of Ockham's specific brand of nominalism. I have tried to drive the point home on several occasions (e.g., Panaccio 1992, 2008); let me now briefly outline the case again before closing, as a privileged illustration of my main contention in the present paper.

A complete nominalist programme should include at least four components: (1) a criticism of the realist alternatives, (2) a detailed ontology, (3) a semantics for general terms, and (4) an account of cognition (Panaccio 2012). Ockham's approach, I would like to submit, provides interesting proposals on all four counts, as well as an appealing way of knitting them together.

Since general terms loom large in our assertive discourse, the prima facie presumption is that there must be something specifically corresponding to them in reality. Any attempt at promoting nominalism, then, must first explain what it takes to be unsatisfactory about realism. Ockham does it with a wealth of arguments. Some are based on Aristotle's authority or on Christian faith, as was customary in his time, but the most forceful ones are still of philosophical interest. Against the doctrine that universals are extra-mental substances of their own, he points out, for example, that they would then have to be merely additional units in the world. If such extra items are posited as separate from the individuals, there is no reason why the latter could not exist without them, and the universals, consequently, would be superfluous. If they are posited as intrinsic components of the individuals, on the other hand, it would follow that 'an individual would be composed of universals, so that the individual would not be any more a particular than a universal', which is absurd (William of Ockham 1974, I, ch. 15, 80).

Ockham's most elaborate criticism, however, is directed against Duns Scotus's notion that common natures are not really, but only *formally* distinct from the individuals that exemplify them. Socrates's human nature, on Scotus's view, is not a real additional thing within Socrates: it is Socrates's very nature as 'contracted' in him by his 'individual difference'. Scotus's strategy—which became widespread in the late medieval realist tradition (see Conti 2010) and which still sounds attractive to some—was to revise the very notions of identity and difference so as to make room for a more nuanced grade of ontological distinction. Ockham's main weapon against this rests on what we call today the Principle of the Indiscernibility of Identicals: if *a* is identical with *b*, then whatever is true of *a* is true of *b*. If Socrates's human nature is really identical with Socrates himself or with Socrates's individual difference, Ockham argues, then 'this nature is proper and not common' since neither Socrates nor his individual difference is a common entity (William of Ockham 1974, I, ch. 16, 83). Since the individual difference is certainly not formally distinct from itself, moreover, it follows, by a standard substitution of identicals, that 'the nature is not formally distinct from the individual difference' (ibid.), and Scotus is thus caught up in a straightforward contradiction. The whole string of arguments raises a genuine challenge for realism in all its variants: If the universal is really distinct from the individual, how can it account for the latter's intrinsic nature? If it is really identical with it, how can it be 'common' to anything else?

With respect to ontology, secondly, a nominalist cannot rest content with simply saying that only individuals exist. He or she must at least tell us if there are basic sorts of individuals and how they are connected with each other. Ockham in this regard has several intriguing theses to offer. For one thing, he distinguishes between singular substances such as horses, flowers or water, and singular accidental qualities such as particular patches of colour or degrees of heat. The latter, he holds, are distinct individual things themselves (*res*)—they are 'tropes', in today's parlance—but in the natural order each single quality is associated with, and dependent upon, a particular substance. Substances, on the other hand, can gain or lose accidental qualities without ceasing to exist. What essentially constitutes each one of them in its distinctive identity is not its qualities, but its 'essential parts': a number of singular substantial forms on the one hand, and a particular chunk of prime matter on the other hand (see, e.g., Book One of the *Summula philosophiae naturalis*; William of Ockham 1984, 155–213). Since a given substance can be made out of *several* substantial forms—e.g., a singular corporality, a singular sensitivity and a singular intellect in the case of a human being—each one of these Ockhamistic substantial forms can also be seen as a singular 'trope' in today's terminology, and the same is true of chunks of matter (Panaccio 2008). Ockham's ontology thus turns out to be a variety of trope theory in the modern sense, with a central distinction between accidental tropes (qualities) and essential tropes (substantial forms and chunks of matter). This is precisely the sort of 'nuclear theory of tropes' that Peter Simons (1994) advocates as a promising path for today's discussion on universals. What is interesting is that the approach has been explored by Ockham in great detail within the context of his own brand of Aristotelian hylomorphism.

The problem of universals being at its root, as I claim, a matter of correctly accounting for our use of general predicates, any nominalistic attempt at dispensing with general entities in the external world must face the challenge of providing an acceptable semantics for general terms. This is the third component of nominalism listed above, and it is probably where Ockham's input is the richest (Biard 1989; Klima 2010; Panaccio 1999b). He distinguishes between two sorts of general terms: the absolute and the connotative (William of Ockham 1974, I, ch. 10, 69–71). The former roughly correspond to what we call today 'natural kind terms': 'man', 'animal', 'stone', 'fire' and 'earth', for example. Ockham's strategy in their case is to have each one of them signify several individuals rather than a single universal: 'man' simultaneously signifies all men, and 'animal' simultaneously signifies all animals. Their sole semantical feature, in other words, is their extension. They have no nominal definition, in particular, and consequently, no inherent descriptive content, only 'multiple denotation' in today's philosophical jargon (Martin 1958). This presupposes that some singular things are *essentially* similar with each other—a position Ockham heartily endorses (Panaccio 1992, 258–67)—but it does not require that their common species or genera be extra entities in the outside world: essential similarity suffices, and this similarity itself is no extra 'little thing' in between the individuals in question.

Connotative terms, on the other hand, are more complex: in addition to their extension (which can be null in some cases), they 'obliquely' call to mind certain other individuals in the world. 'Father', for example, primarily signifies all fathers, just as 'man' primarily signifies all men, but it *connotes*, in addition, all those fathers' children: 'white' primarily signifies all white substances while connoting their singular whitenesses, and 'horseman' primarily signifies all horsemen while connoting horses. Ockhamistic connotation thus accounts for the semantics of all general predicates other than natural kind terms—especially relational predicates—without requiring anything but individuals in the ontology. The suggestion, it seems to me, still deserves to be exploited by today's nominalists.

Another useful semantical doctrine that Ockham adapts to his nominalist purposes is the medieval theory of *supposition*. The gist of it is that the extension of any general term, whether absolute or connotative, varies when it occurs within a proposition (William of Ockham 1974, I, ch. 63–77, 188–221). A term like 'cherry tree', for example, has a pre-contextual meaning for Ockham: taken in itself so to say, it signifies all past, present, future—and even possible—cherry trees. When it occurs within a given propositional context, however, it can stand for—or supposit for—only some of these pre-contextual *significata*: in 'all the cherry trees are in blossom', for example, the phrase 'cherry tree' is 'restricted' by the present-tense verb *to supposit* only for the presently existing cherry trees. In other contexts, it might even supposit for something it does not primarily signify, as in 'cherry tree is a general term' (this is called material supposition), or 'cherry tree is a natural kind concept' (this is called simple supposition). Ockham provides detailed rules for such extensional variations and uses the doctrine, in particular, to account for the truth of such statements as 'man is a species', where the term 'man', he claims, is taken in simple supposition and stands for the corresponding concept rather than for an extra-mental universal. This is exactly the move that the American nominalist Wilfrid Sellars has praised as 'the first major breakthrough in the theory of categories' (Sellars 1970, 62).

The fourth *desideratum* of a nominalist approach, finally, is to explain generality in human thought and knowledge. Ockham does it, basically, by extending his semantics into a theory of mental language (see Panaccio 1999a, ch. 9, 253–78; 1999b). Atomic concepts, in his view, are natural signs implemented in the mind by an innate mechanism of 'abstraction' causally triggered by 'intuitive' encounters with external singular things. Such concepts can then be combined with each other into true or false propositions governed by a syntax very similar to that of conventional spoken language. I have studied this theory at length elsewhere (Panaccio 2004) and tried to show that it provides a promising framework for addressing a number of riddles about concepts that plague contemporary philosophy of cognitive sciences. Combined with Ockham's ontology and semantics, it rounds out a nominalistic approach to mind, language and reality, which is still philosophically appealing both in its general outline and in some of its details. This is true as well, it seems to me, of the best contributions to the great medieval debate on universals, such as those of Abelard, Scotus or Buridan.

NOTES

1. The limitation to *analytical* philosophy in this context stems from the fact that there is no lively discussion of anything called 'the problem of universals' in contemporary non-analytical philosophy.

2. The position defended here will thus be very close to that of Galluzzo (2008).

3. Albert's way with universals decisively influenced, for example, the late-thirteenth- and fourteenth-century German Dominican school of Dietrich of Freiberg, Master Eckhart, Bertold of Moosburg and others (see Hoenen and de Libera 1995; de Libera 1994), as well as the early-fifteenth-century realist doctrine of John of Novus Domus (Jean de Maisonneuve) and his followers (see Kaluza 1988, 87–120).

4. The same distinction worked in pretty much the same way in the Baghdad school of the ninth century, especially in its leader Al-Fârâbi (see Vallat 2004).

5. See above, Chapter 5.3, for the context of this theory in Avicenna.

6. What is often called 'conceptualism'—the doctrine that universals are mere concepts in the mind—thus comes out as a variety of nominalism in today's most usual sense, since it does not countenance extra-mental universals. It is to be identified with what Armstrong (1978, 25) calls 'Concept Nominalism'.

7. Pasnau actually refuses to categorise Aquinas's doctrine as 'immanent realism' (Pasnau 2002, 301), but this is because he then focuses on universals in the technical sense, which, as I said, are merely in the mind for Aquinas. Since he immediately adds, however, that 'common natures are not constructed by the mind' for Aquinas and that 'they exist in reality' within singulars themselves, the doctrine still comes out as a paradigm case of what today's philosophers call 'immanent realism'.

8. Loux (2007) proposes that the main partition with respect to universals across the whole history of philosophy is not between realism and nominalism, but between 'constituent' and 'relational' strategies, the former wanting to solve the problem by an internal analysis of singular things (e.g., immanent realism and trope theories), and the latter by the

identification of some relation or other between singular things and something else (e.g., Platonism). This is quite idiosyncratic, though. And it is also somewhat artificial, since the idea of 'constituency' remains utterly unexplained in this context (Loux insists that it should not be understood as pointing towards ordinary part–whole relations, but he does not give much in terms of positive indications). Moreover, Loux sub-divides each of the two groups into those doctrines that do countenance universals in extra-mental reality and those that do not, which comes down to reintroducing the division between realism and nominalism as all embracing after all.

BIBLIOGRAPHY

Amerini, Fabrizio. 2003. *I trattati* De universalibus *di Francesco da Prato e Stefano da Rieti*. Spoleto, Italy: Centro italiano di studi sull' alto medioevo.

———. 2007. *De natura generis*: William Ockham and Some Italian Dominicans. *Documenti e studi sulla tradizione filosofica medievale* 18:453–82.

Armstrong, David M. 1978. *Universals and Scientific Realism*. 2 vols. Cambridge: Cambridge University Press.

———. 1989. *Universals. An Opinionated Introduction*. Boulder, CO: Westview Press.

———. 1997. *A World of States of Affairs*. Cambridge: Cambridge University Press.

Avicenna. 2005. *The Metaphysics of The Healing*. Trans. M. E. Marmura. Provo, UT: Brigham Young University Press.

Bacon, John. 1995. *Universals and Property Instances*. Oxford: Blackwell.

Bealer, George. 1982. *Quality and Concept*. Oxford: Clarendon Press.

Biard, Joël. 1989. *Logique et théorie du signe au xive siècle*. Paris: Vrin.

Boulnois, Olivier. 1992. Réelles intentions: Nature commune et universaux selon Duns Scot. *Revue de Métaphysique et de Morale* 97(1): 3–33.

Campbell, Keith. 1990. *Abstract Particulars*. Oxford: Blackwell.

Chakrabarti, Arindam. 2006. 'Introduction'. In *Universals, Concepts and Qualities*, ed. Peter Strawson and Arindam Chakrabarti, 1–15. Aldershot, UK: Ashgate.

Conti, Alessandro. 2006. 'Wyclif's logic and metaphysics'. In *A Companion to John Wyclif*, ed. I. C. Levy, 67–125. Leiden, the Netherlands: Brill.

———. 2010. 'Realism'. In Pasnau 2010, 647–60.

Courtenay, William. 1991. '"Nominales" and nominalism in the twelfth century'. In *Lectionum varietates*, ed. Jean Jolivet, Zenon Kaluza and Alain de Libera, 11–48. Paris: Vrin.

Dijs, Judith. 1990. Two Anonymous 12th-Century Tracts on Universals. *Vivarium* 28:85–117.

Ebbesen, Sten. 1992. What Must One Have an Opinion About? *Vivarium* 30:62–79.

Erismann. Christophe. 2007. Immanent Realism: A Reconstruction of an Early Medieval Solution to the Problem of Universals. *Documenti e studi sulla tradizione filosofica medievale* 18:211–29.

Galluzzo, Gabriele. 2008. The Problem of Universals and Its History. Some General Considerations. *Documenti e studi sulla tradizione filosofica medievale* 19:335–70.

Hoenen, Martin and Alain de Libera. 1995. *Albertus Magnus und der Albertismus*. Leiden, the Netherlands: Brill.

Iwakuma, Yukio. 1992a. Twelfth-Century Nominales: The Posthumous School of Peter Abelard. *Vivarium* 30:97–109.

———. 1992b. 'Vocales', or Early Nominalists. *Traditio* 47:37–111.

Iwakuma, Yukio and Sten Ebbesen. 1992. Logico-Theological Schools from the Second Half of the 12th Century: A List of Sources. *Vivarium* 30:173–210.

John Buridan. 1987. *Tractatus de differentia universalis ad individuum*, ed. Slawomir Szyller. *Przeglad Tomistyczny* 3:137–78.

John Wyclif. 1985. *Tractatus de universalibus*, ed. Ivan Mueller. Oxford: Clarendon Press.

Kaluza, Zenon. 1988. *Les querelles doctrinales à Paris*. Bergamo, Italy: Pierluigi Lubrina.

King, Peter. 2007. Abelard's Answers to Porphyry. *Documenti e studi sulla tradizione filosofica medievale* 18:249–70.

Klima, Gyula. 2004. 'The medieval problem of universals'. In *The Stanford Encyclopedia of Philosophy*, ed. E. N. Zalta. http://plato.stanford.edu

———. 2010. 'Nominalist semantics'. In Pasnau 2010, 159–72.

Libera, Alain de. 1990. *Albert le Grand et la philosophie*. Paris: Vrin.

———. 1994. *La mystique rhénane. D'Albert le Grand à Maître Eckhart*. Paris: Seuil.

———. 1996. *La querelle des universaux. De Platon à la fin du Moyen Âge*. Paris: Seuil.

Loux, Michael J. 2006. *Metaphysics. A Contemporary Introduction*, 3rd ed. London: Routledge.

———. 2007. Perspectives on the Problem of Universals. *Documenti e studi sulla tradizione filosofica medievale* 18:601–22.

MacBride, Fraser. 2009. 'Universals: The contemporary debate'. In *The Routledge Companion to Metaphysics*, ed. Robin Le Poidevin et al., 276–85. London: Routledge.

Marenbon, John. 1992. Vocalism, Nominalism and the Commentaries on the *Categories* from the Earlier Twelfth Century. *Vivarium* 30:51–61.

Martin, Christopher. 1992. The Logic of the *Nominales. Vivarium* 30:111–26.

Martin, Richard M. 1958. *Truth and Denotation*. Chicago: University of Chicago Press.

Moreland, J. P. 2001. *Universals*. Montreal: McGill-Queen's University Press.

Noone, Timothy. 2003. 'Universals and individuation'. In *The Cambridge Companion to Duns Scotus*, ed. Thomas Williams, 100–28. Cambridge: Cambridge University Press.

Normore, Calvin. 1987. 'The tradition of medieval nominalism'. In *Studies in Medieval Philosophy*, ed. John F. Wippel, 201–17. Washington, DC: The CUA Press.

———. 1992. Abelard and the School of the Nominales. *Vivarium* 30:80–96.

Panaccio, Claude. 1992. *Les mots, les concepts et les choses. La sémantique de Guillaume d'Occam et le nominalisme d'aujourd'hui*. Montreal/Paris: Bellarmin/Vrin.

———. 1999a. *Le discours intérieur. De Platon à Guillaume d'Ockham*. Paris: Seuil.

———. 1999b. 'Semantics and mental language'. In *The Cambridge Companion to Ockham*, ed. Paul V. Spade, 53–75. Cambridge: Cambridge University Press.

———. 1999c. 'Le nominalisme au xiie siècle'. In *Signs and Signification*, ed. H. S. Gill and Giovanni Manetti, Vol. 1, 17–33. New Delhi: Bahri Publications.

———. 2004. *Ockham on Concepts*. Aldershot, UK: Ashgate.

———. 2008. 'L' ontologie d'Ockham et la théorie des tropes'. In *Compléments de substance*, ed. Christophe Erismann and A. Schniewind, 167–81. Paris: Vrin.

———. 2012. *Le nominalisme*. Paris: Vrin.

Pasnau, Robert. 2002. *Thomas Aquinas on Human Nature*. Cambridge: Cambridge University Press.

———, ed. 2010. *The Cambridge History of Medieval Philosophy*. 2 vols. Cambridge: Cambridge University Press.

Peter Abelard. 1994. 'From the "Glosses on Porphyry" in his *Logica ingredientibus*'. In Spade 1994, 26–56.

Piché, David. 2005. *Le problème des universaux à la Faculté des Arts de Paris entre 1230 et 1260*. Paris: Vrin.

Porphyry. 1994. 'Isagoge'. In *Spade* 1994, 1–19.

Robertus Anglicus. 2005. 'Scriptum super libro Porphyrii' (with French translation). In
    Piché 2005, 263–333.
Rodriguez-Pereyra, Gonzalo. 2002. *Resemblance Nominalism*. Oxford: Clarendon.
Rosier-Catach, Irène. 2008. Les *Glosulae super Priscianum:* sémantique et universaux.
    Documenti e studi sulla tradizione filosofica medievale 19:123–77.
Russell, Bertrand. 1912. *Problems of Philosophy*. Oxford: Oxford University Press.
Sellars, Wilfrid. 1970. 'Toward a theory of the categories'. In *Experience and Theory*, ed.
    Lawrence Foster and J. W. Swanson, 55–78. London: Duckworth.
Shimizu, Tetsuro. 1995. From Vocalism to Nominalism: Progression in Abaelard's Theory
    of Signification. *Didascalia* 1:15–46.
Simons, Peter. 1994. Particulars in Particular Clothing: Three Trope Theories of Substance.
    Philosophy and Phenomenological Research 54:553–75.
Spade, Paul V. 1985. 'Introduction'. In *John Wyclif: On Universals*, trans. Anthony Kenny,
    vii–l. Oxford: Clarendon Press.
———. 1994. *Five Texts on the Medieval Problem of Universals*. Indianapolis, IN: Hackett.
Vallat, Philippe. 2004. *Farabi et l'École d'Alexandrie*. Paris: Vrin.
William of Ockham. 1970. *Scriptum in librum primum Sententiarum: Ordinatio*, ed. S.
    Brown and G. Gál. In *G. de Ockham Opera Theologica II*. St Bonaventure, NY: The
    Franciscan Institute.
———. 1974. *Ockham's Theory of Terms: Part I of the Summa Logicae*, trans. M. J. Loux.
    Notre Dame, IN: University of Notre Dame Press.
———. 1984. *Summula philosophiae naturalis*, ed. S. Brown. In *G. de Ockham Opera
    philosophica VI*, 137–94. St Bonaventure, NY: The Franciscan Institute.

CHAPTER 18

BEING

GYULA KLIMA

1. BEING THEN VERSUS BEING NOW

Perhaps the most difficult conceptual hurdle in the way of a contemporary analytical philosopher trying to approach medieval philosophy would be the notion of being or existence. For even with the fading of the once deafening war cry (*existence is not a predicate!!!*) of analytical philosophers of yore raiding the fortresses of traditional metaphysics (by then mostly abandoned and in ruins, offering an easy victory), the recent 'comeback' of metaphysics in its new, shiny, analytical armour did not bring with itself the recovery of the most fundamental notion of traditional metaphysics, which used to define itself as the science of being qua being. In any case, here I am trying to address those contemporary analytical philosophers who come with an open mind, with a willingness to learn, an aptitude to immerse in a genuinely different conceptual scheme, and the desire to shed the conceptual provincialism necessarily implied by exclusive reliance on intuitions shaped by the analytical literature of the past couple of decades.

In addressing this intended audience, I find it both useful and justifiable to begin this discussion with reference to a recent criticism of an eminent analytical philosopher, Sir Anthony Kenny, of the doctrine of being of an equally eminent medieval philosopher-theologian, Thomas Aquinas, and to develop a reconstruction of the doctrine of Aquinas that is just as exact and accessible as the Fregean doctrine that serves as Kenny's background, and is able to provide adequate replies to Kenny's main objections.

I find this strategy *useful* in the first place because it shows how easy it is, even for an eminent analytical philosopher specialised in Aquinas's thought, to miss Aquinas's point, if he tries to understand Aquinas's concepts by fitting them into the straitjacket of an 'alien' conceptual framework. In the second place, this strategy will also give me an opportunity to show 'in practice' what I take to be methodologically the most fruitful way to overcome the inherent drawbacks of Kenny's approach, indeed, in general, to handle argumentation across different conceptual schemes, namely, semantic analysis. For given that in this sort of argumentation we need to rely on intuitions based on fundamentally different, simple (and so, undefinable) concepts, in the context of an argument of this sort especially, we should be able to provide some means of identifying the relevant concepts with exactitude, in no matter what linguistic guise they show up in the course of the argument. But this is precisely what we have in a semantic reconstruction, in which any concept is exactly represented by means of its semantic function, characterised in a metaphysically neutral, abstract model simply in terms of its input and output, namely, argument(s) and value. For no matter what linguistic form expresses, for instance, the concept of propositional negation as we understand it in contemporary propositional logic, the concept is exactly characterised by means of a one-place function that takes the truth value of the proposition on which it operates as its argument (input), for which it yields the opposite truth value for the negated proposition as its value (output). But without going into an abstract discussion of the merits and demerits of this sort of methodological tool, I hope the subsequent discussion will justify its use at least for our present purposes.

As for the *justifiability* of the present attempt to approach 'the medieval notion of being' from an 'analytical background', I should note in the first place that my singling out Aquinas and Kenny for the purposes of this discussion should not be taken to imply that I believe Aquinas's doctrine was universally endorsed or even prevalent or typical in his own age, or that I would take it that whatever Kenny says about existence is the last word about it among contemporary analytical philosophers. After all, I count myself among contemporary analytical philosophers, while I am just about to argue that Kenny's claims should definitely not be taken to provide the last word on what *we* have to say about existence, especially if we manage to see what may be genuinely valuable *to us* in Aquinas's doctrine. Furthermore, I am quite aware of the fact that Aquinas's doctrine was definitely *not* the only or even the prevailing doctrine of his own time.[1]

Nevertheless, Aquinas's doctrine *became* immensely influential, well beyond his own era, which is precisely why he is the most influential medieval philosopher *today*; indeed, so much so that most contemporary philosophy students would get exposed to medieval philosophy first through Aquinas (if at all, and most would even stop there). But this is not due to a mere historical accident (let alone 'Church policy', which is usually no mere historical accident either). Although Aquinas's Avicennian doctrine of being was not generally endorsed and was severely criticised both by Augustinian theologians (such as Henry of Ghent), and by Averroist philosophers (such as Siger of Brabant), and later on by Scotists as well as nominalists, each for their own reasons, nevertheless, it certainly presents a stimulating, challenging, comprehensive, and, as I hope to show, intrinsically coherent way of thinking about the notion of being as the most basic notion (or rather cluster of analogical notions) involved in all human thought, ranging from the mundane and commonplace to the sublime and divine. But to make good sense of these high-flown claims, we need to start with the basics.

2. Kenny on Aquinas on Being

In sharp contrast to the judgement of admirers of Aquinas's thought, according to the verdict of Anthony Kenny in his book *Aquinas on Being*, Aquinas is 'thoroughly confused' on the notion of being (p. v), and thus his doctrine is 'one of the least admirable of his contributions to philosophy' (p. viii). In a critical review of Kenny's book (Klima 2004), I have argued that Kenny is wrong, and his criticisms of Aquinas simply miss their target: trying to judge Aquinas's claims in terms of the conceptual framework of Fregean logic, Kenny misconstrues those claims, and then he blames Aquinas for the resulting absurdities. Indeed, I have argued to the effect that in these criticisms Kenny sometimes behaves like someone who, having less than perfect command of English, would express shock at the barbarity of British *mores* when he is asked by native speakers 'to keep his eyes peeled' or to allow them 'to pick his brain'. But in such a situation we should certainly not blame the native speakers for the misunderstanding. Rather, we should blame the foreigner for delivering judgement before understanding the native speakers' point, simply for failing to master their idiom. Likewise, if we can show that it is simply Kenny's failure to master Aquinas's conceptual idiom that accounts for the absurdities he claims to derive from Aquinas's theses, then we should immediately see where the blame lies. In my critical review, I did so by directly engaging Kenny's arguments, pointing out exactly where they failed to grasp Aquinas's original points.

But that negative, critical approach did not allow me to provide a systematic, positive account of Aquinas's theory itself. Therefore, in this chapter, I will take the reverse course: I will first provide a systematic reconstruction of Aquinas's theory of being, and then, in possession of this reconstruction, I will show how Kenny's most fundamental objections to this theory result simply from his failure to grasp it.

3. Aquinas's Theories of Signification, Predication and Being

In the context of contemporary philosophical discourse, the best way to approach Aquinas's theory of being is by contrasting his analysis of a simple, singular predication, such as 'Socrates is wise', with some common modern analyses of the same. According to the standard modern logical analysis of this predication (first 'canonised' in a formal semantic system by Alfred Tarski), the function of the subject term is to pick out the individual named 'Socrates', the function of the predicate is to denote the set of all wise things, and the predication is true just in case the thing picked out by the subject is an element of the set denoted by the predicate. On this analysis, therefore, it seems plausible to assume that the function of the copula is to express the relation of elementhood between the referent of the subject and the set denoted by the predicate. Accordingly, this analysis would identify one sense of 'being' in addition to several others distinguished by Gottlob Frege, namely, the 'class inclusion sense', expressed by the copula of a universal sentence, the 'identity sense' expressed by the copula of an identity claim, the 'existential sense' expressed by the 'there is' construction, representable by means of the existential quantifier, and the 'actuality sense' (*Wirklichkeit*) expressible by the absolute use of 'is', indicating actual existence.[2] (Incidentally, at this point one might wonder why there is not a 'conjunctive sense' expressed by the copula of an existentially quantified statement, and what sense is expressed by the copula of a 'most'-sentence, which cannot be expressed by any standard first-order formula—but I should let this issue pass here.)

To be sure, on Frege's own analysis of the same simple predication, 'the "is" of predication' in it, in contrast to the 'is' of class inclusion, identity, and existence, should be regarded as a mere syntactical marker of the application of the predicate to the subject, but without any semantic content of its own. For on Frege's view, the predicate of this predication is an 'unsaturated' expression, demanding in itself completion by a subject term. As such, it denotes a function, namely, a function from individuals to the two truth values: the True and the False. Accordingly, the predication is true just in case the function denoted by the predicate yields the True as its value for the individual referred to by the subject as its argument. So, on this analysis, the copula of a singular predication should be regarded as a merely accidental 'surface feature' of the syntax of Indo-European languages (for which reason it is not even represented in standard predicate logic), and it is indeed missing in the syntax of several other, otherwise unrelated languages, such as Arabic, Russian, or Hungarian. (Actually, it should be remarked here that even in these languages, in different tenses, persons and moods, the addition of the relevant form of some equivalent of 'is' *is* required, so apparently it is rather the *lack* of a copula that should be counted as an accidental surface feature in these languages; but this is again an issue that cannot be pursued here.)

Aquinas's analysis of 'Socrates is wise' would be at odds with these modern analyses on almost every point, except for the observation that the function of the subject term in this predication is to pick out the individual named 'Socrates'.[3] For on Aquinas's analysis, the function of the predicate is not to denote a set, and the function of the copula is not to express the relation of elementhood in this set. And, of course, for Aquinas the predicate does not denote a function from individuals to truth values either. However, as in his seminal paper titled 'Form and Existence' Peter Geach has argued,[4] Aquinas's conception can faithfully be reconstructed in terms of assigning the predicate another semantic function, namely, a function yielding individualised forms for individuals. Accordingly, the predicate of 'Socrates is wise' has the function of signifying individualised forms, the individualised wisdom of each and every thing that can be wise, and the predication is true just in case the form signified by the predicate in the thing referred to by the subject is actual. Since the truth of the predication is thus dependent on the actual existence of the significate of the predicate in the referent of the subject, it is natural to think of the function of the copula as to assert precisely the actual existence of this significate. Indeed, as Aquinas explains in his commentary on Aristotle's *On Interpretation*, this is why the copulative function of linking predicate to subject is exerted by the verb that primarily signifies existence:

> The reason why [Aristotle] says that the verb 'is' co-signifies composition is that it does not principally signify composition, but secondarily; for it primarily signifies what occurs to the mind in the way of actuality absolutely: for 'is', uttered absolutely, signifies being in act, and hence it signifies as a verb. But since actuality, which the verb 'is' principally signifies, is in general the actuality of every form, whether it is a substantial or an accidental actuality, this is why when we want to signify any form or act to actually inhere [*inesse*] in a subject, we signify this by means of the verb 'is', either absolutely [*simpliciter*] or with some qualification [*secundum quid*] . . .[5]

This theory of predication (often referred to in the secondary literature as 'the inherence theory' on account of the central idea of the *actual inherence* of forms in their subjects) has a number of important, both logically and metaphysically relevant, implications: (1) In the first place, it must be clear that the notion of signification it attributes to predicate terms immediately yields a more fine-grained semantics for these terms than what either the Fregean or the Tarskian conception could provide. For in the latter, modern conceptions, the intensions of necessarily coextensive terms, such as 'triangular' and 'trilateral', are indistinguishable. But on the Thomistic conception, these terms have to have distinct significations, provided the trilaterality and the triangularity of any triangle are distinct (as they should be). (2) In the second place, the general form of the theory itself demands some distinction between several senses of being. According to this theory, for every true singular affirmative predication, there has to be some individualised form signified by the predicate in the subject. However, the forms signified by these predicates cannot all be regarded as beings in the same sense (indeed, they cannot all be regarded as *forms* in the strict metaphysical sense, let alone beings in the same sense as the substances they inform).[6] Consider the predication 'Homer is blind'. According to the inherence theory, this predication is true if and only if Homer's blindness exists. But for Homer's blindness to exist is nothing but for his sight not to exist. So the existence of Homer's blindness is nothing but the non-existence of his sight, and so, since nothing can be existence and non-existence in the same sense, this blindness cannot exist in the same sense as the opposite sight; therefore, this blindness cannot be an existent or being in the same sense as the opposite sight is. (3) Finally, the inherence theory clearly establishes a close connection between the notions of existence and truth, insofar as it grounds the truth of a singular predication in the actual existence of the significate of the predicate in the referent of the subject.

However, the last two points, the one concerning the need to distinguish various senses in which the *significata* of various predicates can be said to exist and the other concerning the connection between the notions of existence and truth, immediately give rise to a problem concerning Aquinas's theory. For Aquinas does indeed claim that the *significata* of various predicates exist in different senses of existence determined by the nature of the *significata* in question, and yet he also claims that the copula of affirmative predications signifies existence always in the same sense: in the sense in which it signifies the truth of a proposition.[7] How can we reconcile these two claims? Does the copula express various senses of existence, depending on the signification of the predicate it joins to the subject, or does it express uniformly the same sense in all predications? As we shall see, the simple answer is: both. But how is *that* possible?

4. The Multiplicity of the Semantic Functions of *Being* in Aquinas

A consistent solution to this problem can easily be provided if we consider the multiple semantic functions of the verb 'est' (or any of its equivalents) both in its role as the copula and as an absolute predicate, or '*est' tertium vel secundum adiacens*, according to common medieval terminology. The verb in itself as an absolute predicate ('*est' secundum adiacens*) simply signifies the actual existence of its subject (just as any ordinary predicate, such as 'wise', would signify its significate in the subject, i.e., the wisdom of the subject in question). The same verb as a copula ('*est' tertium adiacens*), however, signifies the actuality of its subject with respect to what is signified in it by the predicate, as well as the actuality of what is signified by the proposition that results from its joining the subject to the predicate as a whole, the so-called *enuntiabile*.

So, the simple solution to the foregoing problem is that in any given predication the copula signifies the existence of the significate of the predicate in the subject in the sense of existence determined by the nature of this significate, and yet it uniformly signifies the existence of the *enuntiabile* in the same sense in all predications. That is to say, it signifies existence in various senses with respect to the *significata* of various predicates, yet it signifies existence in one sense with respect to the *enuntiabile* signified by any proposition as a whole, containing any of these predicates. So, it signifies multiply in some respect (i.e., with respect to the significata of various predicates) and uniformly in some other respect (i.e., with respect to the significate of the whole proposition resulting from any predication). But this is quite possible, whence there is clearly no inconsistency involved in this position.

Yet, this solution still leaves a number of questions open. For even if it may provide a consistent interpretation for Aquinas's claims about the multiplicity of the senses of existence expressed in various predications and the uniform signification of the copula in all predications, it is still quite unclear how any of the senses of existence expressed by the copula are related to the senses of existence expressed by 'est' as an absolute predicate. Furthermore, it is quite unclear how any of these senses are related to the sense of identity Aquinas also attributes to the copula,[8] and in general, how the various senses of existence expressed by any absolute or copulative uses of the verb are supposed to be related to each other in Aquinas's celebrated theory of *the analogy of being.*

5. Predication and the Analogy of Being

The primary sense of 'est' or its English equivalent 'is' is obviously expressed by its use as an absolute predicate of primary beings, that is, primary substances, signifying their actuality absolutely, namely, the actuality of their substantial act of being, as in 'Socrates est' or 'Socrates is', which is to say that Socrates exists or, given that if he exists, then he is a living being, Socrates is alive. By contrast, in its function as the copula of the predication of an accident of such a substance, as in 'Socrates est videns', that is, 'Socrates is sighted', the verb has the function of signifying the actuality of the subject not absolutely, but with respect to the accident signified by the predicate, namely, the accidental act of being of Socrates's sight. In these two cases, therefore, the verb has the function of signifying real acts of being of primary substances, namely, their substantial and accidental acts of being (existence, *esse*), respectively. However, in the case of the predication of a privation, as we could see, the verb cannot have the function of signifying any real act of being, for the being of a privation is precisely the non-being of the opposite habit that would have real being, if it existed. Therefore, in the predication 'Socrates est caecus', that is, 'Socrates is blind', the verb can signify only the actuality of the *lack* of a real act of being: for the presence of blindness is the absence of sight. Still, this absence itself is present; this lack of real being is really actual, so it *is* there in some further sense of 'is'. But obviously the presence of this absence can only be expressed or conceived by means of conceiving the non-presence of the opposite real being. So, the presence of a privation hinges not only on the lack of real being, but also on the human mind's ability to conceive of the situation by applying its concept of negation necessarily involved in the concept of any privation (i.e., lack of some positive property that the subject could, or indeed naturally ought to, have). This is the reason why Aquinas would identify the being of privations as a sort of being of reason, *esse rationis*: not that he regarded their being as somehow fictional, or made up by reason, but as something the presence of which hinges both on the ways things are in reality and on the way this reality is conceived by human reason. The same type of consideration applies to the being of the *enuntiabile* signified by the whole proposition: when a proposition is true, then of course it signifies a situation that is really actual; but what the proposition as a whole signifies, which can be referred to by a corresponding sentential nominalisation, is also a being of reason, insofar as its presence is conditioned not only on the ways real beings are, but also on the activity of human reason capable of conceiving of this real situation by means of forming the proposition in question.[9]

As can be seen from the foregoing, on this conception, there *is* a systematic connection between the various absolute and copulative uses of the verb 'est' and its equivalents, which clearly accounts for the analogical relationship between the primary and secondary senses of the verb and the corresponding participle 'ens' or 'being'. The primary sense of the verb is expressed by its use as it is truly predicated of primary substances, as in

(0) x is.

Its various secondary senses are expressed by its use in variously qualified predications, where the qualification may be expressed either (1) by a predicate added to the verb functioning as a copula, or (2) as an explicit determination added to the verb used as an absolute predicate, or (3) by the nature of the subject of which the verb is predicated without any explicit qualification, as illustrated by the following three equivalent propositional forms, respectively:

(1) x is F
(2) x is-with-respect-to-its-F-ness
(3) The F-ness of x is

Here, x is some primary substance, and F is some *non-essential* predicate of x, signifying in it a real accident or a privation or even a relation of reason as in 'Socrates is admired by Plato'. What is important to realise about these propositional schemata is that the occurrences of 'is' in all of them signify the same act of being determined by the significate of the term 'F' (referred to by the corresponding abstract term 'F-ness' in the last two).[10]

Now where does identity fit into this scheme? It should be noticed here that in the foregoing schemata what provided the qualification of the sense of 'is' was the *significate* of the predicate in the thing referred to by the subject. The predicate, however, according to many medieval logicians (actually, a notable exception would be Peter of Spain)[11] functions there also with another one of its semantic values, namely, its (personal) *suppositum*,[12] that is, a thing that actually has its significate. Therefore, the sense of the copula in which it expresses the sense of identity may be regarded as the result of simply adding another qualification to the absolute form of the verb, namely, one that refers to the *suppositum*, rather than the significate of the predicate, as in

(4) x is-(actual)-with-respect-to-a-thing-that-is-F,

which is true just in case x is an F, that is, if x is identical with a thing that is F, namely, itself, provided it is F. So, in this sense the qualified sense of 'is' clearly expresses the actual identity of x with itself under the designation of being an F.[13]

Indeed, we can also explain along the same lines why the *enuntiabile* signified by the whole proposition has to be signified to be a being by the copula in the same sense in which it would signify the being of a privation or any other being of reason. For the primary semantic value of the predicate F is neither its *suppositum* (a thing that is actually F), nor its *ultimate significate* (the thing's individualised F-ness), but its *immediate significate*, namely, F-ness in general, as it is conceived by the abstractive mind forming the abstract concept expressed by the term F.[14] So, what the proposition as a whole signifies, namely, that x is F, is actual in the same sense in which we can say that

(5) x is-(actual)-with-respect-to-F-ness-(in-general).

Here the qualified predicate obviously has to express the actuality of the subject with respect to a being of reason, given that the qualification itself refers to something that is the direct object of reason, namely, the nature of the thing conceived in abstraction from its individuating conditions.

To be sure, Aquinas never spells out the idea expressed in the propositional schemata listed here in exactly such terms. However, several of his remarks made in various contexts about the primary and secondary senses of being relating to each other as unqualified (*simpliciter*) and qualified (*secundum quid*), as well as his remarks about how the different semantic values of the same term added to the copula may provide different qualifications on its primary sense (thereby determining different secondary senses of the verb), may well justify the connections expressed by the foregoing propositional schemata.[15]

Indeed, further justification may be gleaned from the fact that once we realise these connections, it is easy to see how Aquinas's claims about the analogical predication of being of substances, especially of God and his creatures, can also receive a consistent interpretation in the same framework.

6. The Analogy of Being between God and Creatures

Consider the absolute predication of being of some primary substance x, as in

(6) x is (or exists),

the predication of a substantial predicate S (i.e., one of the genera, species and specific differences on the tree of Porphyry in the category of substance) of the same, as in

(7) x is S

and the predication of being explicitly qualified by the significate of this predicate, namely, the essence of x, as in

(8) x is-with-respect-to-its-S-ness.

According to Aquinas's doctrine of the real distinction between essence and existence in creatures and the real identity of the same in God, if the variable 'x' in these schemata stands for a creature, then the significate of this qualified predicate and the significate of the predicate 'S' in x are distinct items of reality. However, if the variable 'x' stands for God, then these significates are the same, namely, the absolutely simple, indivisible divine nature, which is nothing but divine existence.

Clearly, the predicates of the two equivalent claims in (6) and in (8) signify the same single act of substantial being of x. However, if x is God, then, and only then, the determination referred to in the qualified predicate, namely, divine essence is not distinct from what is signified by the absolute predicate, namely, divine existence. Therefore, in this case and *only* in this case, the qualification does not impose any determination or limitation on the sense of the absolute predicate: God is the only entity that absolutely IS without any limitation whatsoever. By contrast, if x is a creature, then the determination referred to in the qualified predicate, a creaturely essence, is distinct from the significate of the absolute predicate, some creaturely existence. In this case, therefore, the determination does impose some limitation on the mode of being signified by the qualified predicate, in the sense that the nature of the creature delimits what the creature can or cannot be, have, do or suffer. Therefore, since the qualified predicate signifies the same act of being that is signified by the absolute predicate, the qualification imposes a determination also on the sense of the absolute predicate: a creature can only exist in the way determined by its limited nature. That is to say, the nature of a creature, being distinct from its existence, imposes an implicit determination on the sense in which the creature can be. For example, since for a man to be is for him to be a man, a man can only be in the way a man can be, which is an essentially limited form of existence. By contrast, even if also for God to be is for him to be God, for God to be is not a limited form of existence, since for God to-be-with-respect-to-his-divinity is the same as for God to-be-with-respect-to-his-existence, and an act of existence does not delimit itself.[16] So, it is only God whose existence is absolute BEING, whereas any creaturely existence is only being somehow, in a creaturely way. As Aquinas says:

> A created spiritual substance has to contain two [principles], one of which is related to the other as potency to act. And this is clear from the following. It is obvious that the first being, which is God, is infinite act, namely, having in Himself the whole plenitude of being not contracted to the nature of some genus or species. Therefore it is necessary that His being itself should not be an act of being that is, as it were, put into a nature which is not its own being, for in this way it would be confined to that nature. Hence we say that God is His own being. But this cannot be said about anything else; just as it is impossible to think that there should be several separate whitenesses, but if a whiteness were separate from any subject and recipient, then it would be only one, so it is impossible that there should be a subsistent act of being, except only one. Therefore, everything else after the first being, since it is not its own being, has being received in something, by which its being is contracted; and thus in any created being the nature of the thing that participates being is other than the act of being itself that is participated.[17]

The analogical character of the predication of being in this case is obvious, if we consider the following: just as the predication of being of an accident is diminished relative to the predication of being of a substance, so the predication of being of a created substance is diminished relative to the predication of being of God.[18] To be sure, this does not render the absolute predication of being of created substances diminished in and of itself; it is diminished merely relative to the 'absolutely absolute' predication of being of God.

In fact, the predication of being of created substances is epistemologically prior to the predication of being of God. But in the process of forming our concept of the being of God, we have to realise that even if creaturely being is better known, and thus epistemologically *prior to us*, creaturely being cannot be what is primarily signified by 'being' absolutely speaking, since creaturely being is, of course, ontologically secondary to divine being. It is precisely this disparity between the ontological order and the epistemological order that is reflected in the disparity between the *signification* and *mode of signifying* of the names we can properly apply to God on account of *what* they signify, although not according to *how* they signify:

> We should consider, therefore, that because names are imposed by us, and we do not know God except from creatures, [the names of God] are always defective in their representation with respect to their mode of signifying [*quantum ad modum significandi*], for they signify divine perfections in the way in which they are participated by the creatures. But if we consider the thing signified [*res significata*] by the name, which is that which the name is imposed to signify, we find that some names are imposed to signify primarily the perfection itself exemplified by God absolutely, without implying a certain mode in their signification, while others [are imposed] to signify a perfection in accordance with a certain mode of participation. For example, all cognition is exemplified by divine cognition, and all knowledge by divine knowledge. The name 'sense', however, is imposed to signify cognition in the manner in which it is received materially by a power of an organ. But the name 'cognition' does not signify a mode of participation in its principal signification. Therefore, we have to say that all those names which are imposed to signify some perfection absolutely are properly said of God, and they apply to Him primarily as far as the thing signified is concerned, although not as far as the mode of signifying is concerned, such as 'wisdom', 'goodness', 'essence' and the like.[19]

Thus, since according to Aquinas we gain our primary concept of being from created substances, we need to understand divine being by analogically 'stretching' our mundane concept. We first need to grasp the analogy between the being of created substances and accidents, thereby understanding that accidents exist in a diminished sense relative to substance. Then we can grasp the analogy between the being of created substances and God, whereby we understand that just as accidental being is diminished relative to substantial being on account of the limitation imposed on the accident's act of being by its nature, so creaturely being is diminished relative to divine being on account of the limitation imposed on a creaturely act of being by a creaturely nature. Thus, the primary significate of the term 'being' in the ontological order has to be divine being. But this is cognised by us only secondarily, on the basis of a primary concept we first acquire from creaturely being.[20] To be sure, if we gained our primary concept of being directly from God, that is, if the *primum cognitum* of our minds were divine being, and not created being in general, then we could understand created being directly as a sort of diminished being, delimited and specified by the limited nature it realises, and then the cognitive order would match the ontological order (and Plato/Augustine would be right against Aristotle/Aquinas). However, since our mind is first confronted with the being of created substances, it has to arrive at the cognition of divine being in this more circuitous way, at least in accordance with Aquinas's doctrine. But pursuing the implications of *this* observation would already lead our discussion into the *arcana* of late-medieval disputes concerning the primum cognitum, which is beyond the scope of this chapter.[21]

So, to keep this discussion within its pre-determined limits, let us return in closing to Anthony Kenny's qualms about Aquinas's doctrine, especially in connection with the thesis of real distinction, and the so-called *intellectus essentiae* argument for it in his *De Ente et Essentia*.

7. KENNY VERSUS AQUINAS ON THE REAL DISTINCTION

In his book, Kenny launched a two-pronged attack against Aquinas's doctrine. He tried to establish that Aquinas in his *intellectus essentiae* argument either was talking about existence in the sense of 'specific existence', in which case he was either talking nonsense, or essence and existence are distinct both in God and in creatures, or he was talking about existence in the sense of 'individual being', in which case essence and existence are identical both in God and in creatures. This argument fails on many counts.

In the first place, as I have argued in my review of Kenny's book, pace Geach et al., Aquinas simply does not have a notion equivalent to the notion of the Fregean 'specific existence', that is, the notion of an existential quantifier. In fact, a notion that would come closest to this notion in Aquinas's conceptual arsenal would be regarded by him not a concept of existence, but a *signum quantitatis*, namely, a *signum particulare*. In any case, Kenny's reason for holding that Aquinas would have to use in his argument the notion of specific existence is his unjustified assumption that Aquinas would take a phoenix to be by definition a fictitious bird as we do. However, from his argument, as well as from the parallel text of Aquinas's *Commentary on the Sentences*,[22] it is quite clear that Aquinas uses this example as the illustration of a real, but ephemeral natural phenomenon, like a lunar eclipse or a rainbow, the essence of which we could know perfectly well in terms of a scientific definition, yet we may not know whether this kind of thing actually exists at the present time. So, Kenny's objection definitely fails for this interpretation of Aquinas's argument, which intends to show the real distinction between the real essences of real things of nature, and their present act of existence.

But Kenny's objection fails for his second interpretation as well, even if that interpretation is somewhat closer to the truth (although it entirely fails to take into account the analogical character of 'is' and its equivalents as an absolute predicate of created substances and God). For Kenny bases his objection on the false assumption that the distinctness of essence and existence would have to mean that it is possible to have one without the other. (And so, he argues, since it is impossible to have a dog's existence without its essence, for a dog cannot be without being a dog, essence and existence would have to be the same also in the case of this creature.) However, this assumption is obviously false: for it is clearly possible to have distinct, yet necessarily concurrent, items in reality. For example, it is clear that the triangularity of any particular triangle is not the same as its trilaterality (unless sides and angles are the same items). But it is also clear that one cannot have a particular triangularity without a particular trilaterality. So, we have two really distinct items here, clearly distinguishable in Aquinas's fine-grained semantics (even if not distinguishable in the more coarse-grained modern conceptions), which are nevertheless inseparable in reality. Therefore, pace Kenny, real distinction does not have to mean real separability, which takes care of the other prong of his attack.

As far as Kenny's objections are concerned, therefore, there is nothing in them that would show that Aquinas is 'confused about being'. Indeed, if the foregoing considerations are helpful in any way to clarify the systematic aspect of Aquinas's doctrine as can be gathered from his several scattered remarks, then they may also prompt a better appreciation of the judgement of those admirers of Aquinas who find in his doctrine some of the profoundest metaphysical insights in the history of human thought.

But this is not even the most important lesson we may glean from the foregoing, again, with the assumption that I managed to make *some* coherent sense of Aquinas's doctrine with the help of the sort of semantic analysis that I promised to show 'in practice' at the beginning of this chapter. For what I think we may learn most importantly on the negative side from this 'exercise' is that the sort of conceptual analysis, often practised by analytical philosophers, that takes for granted the unquestionable status of their post-Fregean intuitions as the only acceptable measure of intelligibility is radically flawed and only paves the way to *ignoratio elenchi* when it is applied in engaging radically different conceptual frameworks (as is the case with engaging the history of philosophy or contemporary thinkers of different background, as in talking 'across the analytical-continental divide'). On the positive side, however, we can say that the most important lesson is that even such radical conceptual differences do not have to pose absolutely insurmountable barriers of communication across these different 'paradigms' (to use another fashionable term applied, quite enthusiastically, despite its 'analytical' origin, mostly on the other side of the analytical-continental divide, to such relatively isolated conceptual schemes or frameworks). For the semantic reconstruction I am proposing is not a mere literal rebuilding of the other party's concepts from the ready-made building blocks of our own conceptual framework, since that approach is doomed to failure especially in dealing with the most basic, simple concepts by which philosophers are most intrigued. Rather, this approach involves the semantic modelling of these simple concepts, based on a careful analysis of the language of the thinkers we are dealing with, and, especially, taking seriously their own reflections on their own usage and linguistic intuitions, that is, learning and accessibly modelling without prejudice what they meant by their own words and, accordingly, what we are supposed to understand by those words. For one thing is certain: without at least trying to do so, we are just going to talk past them in our (no matter how brilliant-looking) criticisms of their substantial doctrines.

NOTES

1. For a detailed, more historically oriented account of medieval theories of being and Aquinas's theory among them, please consult Klima (2011).

2. Cf. Haaparanta (1985, 13–14) and Geach (1968). For an entire volume of essays devoted to Frege's 'ambiguity thesis' and its pre-history, see Hintikka and Knuuttila (1986).

3. And this is actually the source of a rather tricky problem for Aquinas's theory of intellectual cognition, in which he insists that the intellect can *only* form universal concepts. For his treatment of the problem, see *Summa Theologiae* (henceforth ST) 1 q. 86, a. 1.

4. P. T. Geach, 'Form and Existence', *Proceedings of the Aristotelian Society*, 55 (1955), pp. 251–72, reprinted in his *God and the Soul* (London: Routledge & Kegan Paul, 1969), pp. 42–64.

5. 'Ideo autem dicit quod hoc verbum est consignificat compositionem, quia non eam principaliter significat, sed ex consequenti; significat enim primo illud quod cadit in intellectu per modum actualitatis absolute: nam est, simpliciter dictum, significat in actu esse; et ideo significat per modum verbi. Quia vero actualitas, quam principaliter significat hoc verbum est, est communiter actualitas omnis formae, vel actus substantialis vel accidentalis, inde est quod cum volumus significare quamcumque formam vel actum actualiter inesse alicui subiecto, significamus illud per hoc verbum est, vel simpliciter vel secundum quid . . . ' *In Perihermeneias* 1.5, n.22. The account of Aquinas's semantics of being provided in the following three sections is also published, with slight variations, in my contribution to Davies and Stump (2011). A formal semantics of the theory presented here informally can be found in the *Appendix* of Klima (2002).

6. As St Thomas wrote: ' . . . dicendum est quod illud a quo aliquid denominatur non oportet quod sit semper forma secundum rei naturam, sed sufficit quod significetur per modum formae, grammatice loquendo. Denominatur enim homo ab actione et ab indumento, et ab aliis huiusmodi, quae realiter non sunt formae'. *Quaestiones de potentia*, q. 7, a. 10, ad 8. Cf. also, e.g., Cajetan: 'Verum ne fallaris cum audis denominativum a forma denominante oriri, et credas propter formae vocabulum quod res denominans debet esse forma eius quod denominatur, scito quod formae nomine in hac materia intelligimus omne illud a quo aliquid dicitur tale, sive illud sit secundum rem accidens, sive substantia, sive materia, sive forma'. Cajetan 1939, 18.

7. Cf. *In Metaphysica*, lb. 6, lc. 4; lb. 5, lc. 9, n. 895.

8. Cf. *Commentary on the Sentences* [*Super Sent*] 3, d. 5, q. 3, a. 3; *In Meta* lb. 9, lc. 11; ST1, q. 13, a. 12; ST1, q. 85, a. 5, ad 3-um; ST3 q. 16, a. 7, ad 4-um, a. 9, ad 3-um.

9. For a more comprehensive treatment of Aquinas's conception of beings of reason along these lines, see Klima (1993).

10. For a technical, model-theoretical account of exactly how this secondary significa-tion of 'is' can be compositionally obtained from its primary signification, see Klima (2002).

11. See Klima (2003, esp. 529–30).

12. For a brief, up-to-date survey of the medieval theories of supposition, see Read (2006).

13. Cf. *Super Sent.*, lib. 3 d. 5 q. 3 a. 3 expos. 'Dicendum, quod differentia est inter nomina substantiva et adjectiva. Substantiva enim significant non tantum formam, sed etiam suppositum formae, unde possunt praedicari ratione utriusque; et quando praedi-cantur ratione suppositi, dicitur praedicatio per identitatem; quando autem ratione formae, dicitur per denominationem, sive informationem: et haec est magis propria praedicatio, quia termini in praedicato tenentur formaliter. Adjectiva autem tantum significant formam; et ideo non possunt praedicari, nisi per informationem: unde haec est falsa: essentia est generans; quamvis haec sit vera: essentia est pater. Cum igitur dicitur, filius Dei est homo, est praedicatio per informationem et identitatem; cum vero dicitur: essentia divina est homo, est praedicatio per identitatem, quia est idem secundum rem cum supposito hominis; non autem per informationem, quia natura divina non significatur ut suppositum subsistens in humana natura'.—'We have to say that there is a difference between substantive and adjective names. For substantives signify not only a form, but also the suppositum of a form and can be predicated on account of both. And when they are predicated on account of the suppositum, then the predication is said to be *predication by identity*; and when on account of the form, then it is said to be *predication by denomination* or *by information*. And the latter is a more appropriate predication, because terms as predicates are taken formally. Adjectives, however, only signify a form, and so they can be predicated only by information. Therefore, this is false: "the essence is generating", although this is true: "the essence is the Father". Thus, when it is said that the Son of God is a man, then the predication is by information and identity; but when it is said that the divine essence is a man, then it is by identity, for [the divine essence] is really identical with a suppositum of *man*, but not by information, for divine nature is not signified as a suppositum subsisting in human nature'. See also *Super Sent.*, lib. 3, d. 7 q. 1, a. 1, co; *Summa Theologiae* I, q. 39, a. 6, ad 2; *Summa Theologiae* I, q. 13, a. 12; *Contra errores Graecorum*, pars 1 cap. 18 co.

14. See Cajetan's astute discussion of this issue in Cajetan's *In De Ente et Essentia D. Thomae Aquinatis, Quaestio 7: Utrum natura absolute sumpta sit illa quae praedicetur de individuis*; Cajetan (1934, 100–101).

15. See again text quoted at note 5. See also *In Metaphysicam* 5.9, n. 5; *In Sent.* 2, d. 42, q. 1, a. 3, in corp.; *In Perihermeneias* 2.2, n. 3.

16. That an act of existence (a significate of the verb 'is' or 'exists') does not delimit itself is not some arcane metaphysical principle that only 'the initiated' could grasp: in general, a qualification added to a predicate referring to the significate of the predicate itself is non-diminishing, and so it can be dropped *salva veritate*. For example, saying 'This sheet of paper is white with respect to its whiteness (or with respect to its colour)' amounts to the same as saying absolutely, 'This sheet of paper is white'. By contrast, if the qualifica-tion refers to something else, say, the quantity informed by this whiteness, as in 'This sheet is white with respect to its one side,' then it is diminishing, for this claim can be true of a

sheet that is not totally white but only on one side, and in that case the qualification cannot be dropped *salva veritate*. For more about the issue of diminishing versus non-diminishing qualifications and their relation to analogical predication and the medieval treatment of the fallacy *secundum quid et simpliciter*, see Klima (1996).

17. 'Oportet enim in substantia spirituali creata esse duo, quorum unum comparatur ad alterum ut potentia ad actum. Quod sic patet. Manifestum est enim quod primum ens, quod Deus est, est actus infinitus, utpote habens in se totam essendi plenitudinem non contractam ad aliquam naturam generis vel speciei. Unde oportet quod ipsum esse eius non sit esse quasi inditum alicui naturae quae non sit suum esse; quia sic finiretur ad illam naturam. Unde dicimus, quod Deus est ipsum suum esse. Hoc autem non potest dici de aliquo alio: sicut impossibile est intelligere quod sint plures albedines separatae; sed si esset albedo separata ab omni subiecto et recipiente, esset una tantum; ita impossibile est quod sit ipsum esse subsistens nisi unum tantum. Omne igitur quod est post primum ens, cum non sit suum esse, habet esse in aliquo receptum, per quod ipsum esse contrahitur; et sic in quolibet creato aliud est natura rei quae participat esse, et aliud ipsum esse participatum'. *De spiritualibus creaturis.* q. un., a. 1.

18. It should be noted here, however, that this is not 'the criterion' on account of which 'being' ought to be regarded as predicated analogically of God and creatures. Throughout this paper, a predicate is regarded as analogical if and only if it has a primary sense and some secondary sense(s) somehow related to, and therefore derivable from, the primary sense by means of some diminishing qualification. This 'semantical derivability' need not reflect at all the actual process of the formation of an analogical concept. For the finer details of this issue in the context of thirteenth-century logic, see Ashworth (1991, 2004).

19. 'Considerandum est igitur, quod cum nomina sint imposita a nobis, qui deum non nisi ex creaturis cognoscimus, semper deficiunt a divina repraesentatione quantum ad modum significandi: quia significant divinas perfectiones per modum quo participantur in creaturis. Si autem consideremus rem significatam in nomine, quae est id ad quod significandum imponitur nomen, invenimus, quaedam nomina esse imposita ad significandum principaliter ipsam perfectionem exemplatam a deo simpliciter, non concernendo aliquem modum in sua significatione; et quaedam ad significandum perfectionem receptam secundum talem modum participandi; verbi gratia, omnis cognitio est exemplata a divina cognitione, et omnis scientia a divina scientia. Hoc igitur nomen sensus est impositum ad significandum cognitionem per modum illum quo recipitur materialiter secundum virtutem conjunctam organo. Sed hoc nomen cognitio non significat aliquem modum participandi in principali sua significatione. Unde dicendum est, quod omnia illa nomina quae imponuntur ad significandum perfectionem aliquam absolute, proprie dicuntur de deo, et per prius sunt in ipso quantum ad rem significatam, licet non quantum ad modum significandi, ut sapientia, bonitas, essentia et omnia hujusmodi; et haec sunt de quibus dicit Anselmus, quod simpliciter et omnino melius est esse quam non esse. Illa autem quae imponuntur ad significandum perfectionem aliquam exemplatam a deo, ita quod includant in sua significatione imperfectum modum participandi, nullo modo dicuntur de deo proprie; sed tamen ratione illius perfectionis possunt dici de deo metaphorice, sicut sentire, videre et hujusmodi. Et similiter est de omnibus aliis formis corporalibus, ut lapis, leo et hujusmodi: omnia enim imponuntur ad significandum formas corporales secundum modum determinatum participandi esse vel vivere vel aliquam divinarum perfectionum'. *In Sent.* 1 d. 22, q. 1, a. 2 co.

20. Cf. 'Quamvis enim secundum naturalem ordinem cognoscendi Deus sit primum cognitum, tamen quoad nos prius sunt cogniti effectus sensibiles eius'. *In De Hebdomadibus,* lc. 4. 'Respondeo dicendum quod, cum intellectus humanus, secundum statum

praesentis vitae, non possit intelligere substantias immateriales creatas, ut dictum est; multo minus potest intelligere essentiam substantiae increatae. Unde simpliciter dicendum est quod Deus non est primum quod a nobis cognoscitur; sed magis per creaturas in Dei cognitionem pervenimus, secundum illud apostoli ad Rom. I, *invisibilia Dei per ea quae facta sunt, intellecta, conspiciuntur*. Primum autem quod intelligitur a nobis secundum statum praesentis vitae, est quidditas rei materialis, quae est nostri intellectus obiectum, ut multoties supra dictum est'. ST1 q. 88, a. 3 co. 'Ad primum ergo dicendum quod in luce primae veritatis omnia intelligimus et iudicamus, inquantum ipsum lumen intellectus nostri, sive naturale sive gratuitum, nihil aliud est quam quaedam impressio veritatis primae, ut supra dictum est. Unde cum ipsum lumen intellectus nostri non se habeat ad intellectum nostrum sicut quod intelligitur, sed sicut quo intelligitur; multo minus Deus est id quod primo a nostro intellectu intelligitur'. Ibid. ad 1.

    21. A difficult, but very illuminating discussion of the problem can be found in the first question of Cajetan's commentary on Aquinas's *De Ente et Essentia, Quaestio 1: Utrum ens sit primum cognitum ordine et via originis*; Cajetan (1934, 2–19). See Cajetan, Thomas de Vio, *Commentary on Being and Essence*, translated from the Latin with an Introduction by L. H. Kendzierski and F. C. Wade, Milwaukee, Wis., Marquette University Press, 1964, pp. 40–61.

    22. Cf. *In Sent.* 2, d. 3, q. 1, a. 1, co.

BIBLIOGRAPHY

Ashworth, E. Jennifer. 1991. Analogy and Equivocation in Thirteenth-Century Logic. Aquinas in Context. *Mediaeval Studies* 54:94–135.

———. 2004. 'Medieval theories of analogy'. In *The Stanford Encyclopedia of Philosophy* (Winter 2004 edition), ed. Edward N. Zalta. http://plato.stanford.edu/archives/win2004/entries/analogy-medieval/

Cajetan, Thomas de Vio. 1934. *In De Ente et Essentia D. Thomae Aquinatis.* Turin, Italy: Marietti.

———. 1939. *Scripta Philosophica: Commentaria in Praedicamenta Aristotelis*, ed. M.H. Laurent. Rome: Angelicum

Davies, Brian and Eleonore Stump, eds. 2011. *The Oxford Handbook of Aquinas*, Oxford: Oxford University Press.

Geach, Peter T. 1955. Form and Existence, *Proceedings of the Aristotelian Society*, 55:251–72, reprinted in Geach (1969, 42–64).

———. 1968. What Actually Exists, *Proceedings of the Aristotelian Society* Suppl. Vol. 42:7–16, reprinted in Geach (1969, 65–74).

———. 1969. *God and the Soul.* London: Routledge & Kegan Paul.

Haaparanta, Leila. 1985. Frege's Doctrine of Being, Helsinki. *Acta Philosophica Fennica* 39:13–14.

Hintikka, Jaako and Simo Knuuttila. (1986). *The Logic of Being.* Dordrecht, the Netherlands: Reidel.

Klima, Gyula. 1993. The Changing Role of *Entia Rationis* in Medieval Philosophy: A Comparative Study with a Reconstruction. *Synthese* 96:25–59.

———. 1996. The Semantic Principles Underlying Saint Thomas Aquinas's Metaphysics of Being. *Medieval Philosophy and Theology* 5:87–141.

———. 2002. Aquinas' Theory of the Copula and the Analogy of Being. *Logical Analysis and History of Philosophy* 5:159–76.

———. 2003. 'Peter of Spain, the Author of the *Summulae*'. In J. Gracia and T. Noone (eds.), *Blackwell's Companion to Philosophy in the Middle Ages*, 526–31. Oxford: Blackwell.

———. 2004. On Kenny on Aquinas on Being: A Critical Review of *Aquinas on Being* by Anthony Kenny, Oxford: Oxford University Press, 2002. Feature review. *International Philosophical Quarterly* 44:567–80.

———. 2011. 'Being' and 'Substance, accident, modes'. In *The Encyclopedia of Medieval Philosophy*, H. Lagerlund, ed. Dordrecht, the Netherlands: Springer.

Read, Stephen. 2006. 'Medieval Theories: Properties of Terms'. In *The Stanford Encyclopedia of Philosophy* (Spring 2006 edition), ed. Edward N. Zalta. http://plato.stanford.edu/archives/spr2006/entries/medieval-terms/

CHAPTER 19

STATES OF AFFAIRS

LAURENT CESALLI

THE philosophical problem of the correspondence between what we think, what we say and 'what there is' is a perennial one. At the beginning of the *Sophistical Refutations* (1, 165a7–9), for example, Aristotle gives a synthetic formulation of it: since 'it is impossible in a discussion to bring in the actual things discussed: we use their names as symbols instead of them; and we suppose that what follows in the names, follows in the things as well' (Aristotle 1984, I, 278). But whereas this difficulty pertains to language (or thought) *in general*, it becomes remarkably acute when the linguistic expressions at stake are not simple names, but *bearers of truth and falsity*, namely, statements or, to use the medieval word for it, propositions.

This chapter addresses the following question: did medieval authors consider that just as names signify things, propositions, too, are semantically related to special objects—and if so, what kind of things did they think those special objects are? I shall begin with two short introductory remarks about the notion of state of affairs (SOA) as well as the identification criteria for the theories describing them *before* the technical category of SOA was coined (Sections 1 and 2); I shall then give a survey of the five main types of medieval answers given to the question of the nature of SOAs (Section 3); finally, I shall briefly compare the medieval conceptions with (some) later, that is late-nineteenth- and early-twentieth-century, as well as contemporary theories of SOAs (Section 4).[1]

1. THE NOTION (AND THE PROBLEM) OF SOAs

Talking about 'medieval theories of SOAs' is a bit like talking about 'medieval theories of intentionality' or of 'medieval ontology'—it requires one to specify carefully in what sense such an anachronistic expression will be used. In the following, I shall take the expression 'SOA' in its original sense, namely, as it was introduced at the turn of the twentieth century by thinkers such as Julius Bergmann (1879, I, 2–5), Carl Stumpf (1888) and Bertrand Russell (1956, 182),[2] in their firm and decisive reaction against idealism. Here is, for example, what Carl Stumpf writes in his *Leitfaden der Logik*: 'From the matter of a judgement we distinguish its *content* or the *state of affairs* expressed in the judgement. For example "God is" has God as its matter, "the being of God", as its content' (Stumpf 1888, 4). Roughly speaking, Bergmann, Stumpf and Russell see SOAs as *objective counterparts of acts of judging*. But those three philosophers diverge in their conception of the very nature of SOAs. Bergmann considers them as transcendent, abstract objects; by contrast, Stumpf wants them to be immanent contents of judgements;[3] and Russell, for his part, sees them as mere facts.[4]

Let us begin by sketching what can be labelled as 'the problem of SOAs'. There seem to be for philosophers equally good reasons to accept or reject SOAs as part of their ontologies. The main reason to accept SOAs consists in their high explanatory value. Indeed, they are introduced as objective counterparts of propositional attitudes such as judging, knowing or believing. Furthermore, SOAs can assume different semantic roles, such as being the meanings, or being the truth-makers of declarative sentences.[5] On the level of linguistic expressions, SOAs are essentially linked to declarative sentences. Grammatically, they are referred to by infinitive sentences or sentence nominalisations ('that-clauses'). Consider, for example, sentence *p*:

The Earth is round.

The different functions of SOAs can be illustrated by observing that:

— *p* means *that the Earth is round* (propositional meaning);
— if *p* is true, it is because it is the case, or it is a fact, *that the Earth is round* (truthmaking);
— if Jeff expresses his knowledge or belief by means of *p*, then he knows or believes *that the Earth is round* (object of knowledge and belief).

Not all philosophers, though, accept SOAs. They can be rejected because they are judged to be superfluous. So, for example, one can consider that propositional attitudes must have objects without also requiring that these objects are peculiar to them. On such a view, the object of Jeff's belief is identical with the object referred to by the noun 'Earth', and one would then say that the same object is referred to by the expressions 'Earth' and 'that the Earth is round' (but somehow differently). Another reason to reject SOAs consists in the difficulty of providing them with a well-defined status within one's ontology. More precisely, the difficulty lies in the fact that SOAs can neither be reduced to mental entities, nor to mere things, nor (obviously) to sentences themselves:

— If Jeff believes that *p*, he does so by means of some mental acts or states, but what he believes is distinct from his own mental acts or states.

— If Jeff says p, he is referring not just to the thing Earth, but to something
more: the expression 'Earth' does refer just to the thing Earth but, by
contrast with p, it lacks any truth value.
— What Jeff is stating by saying p is not p itself: what Jeff is stating has nothing
to do with a linguistic expression (although it can only be expressed by
means of a linguistic expression).

In short, then, the problem of SOAs arises from the tension between the good,
functional reasons for accepting them and the serious, ontological problems they
essentially involve.

2. IDENTIFICATION CRITERIA FOR
MEDIEVAL THEORIES

Both medieval and later philosophers faced and recognised the problem of
SOAs. Of course, in this as in the majority of cases, there is no terminological
uniformity between medieval and post-medieval philosophy. Nonetheless, there
are—as we shall see—medieval *and* post-medieval theories of SOAs. But how are
the medieval theories to be identified? On the basis of what has been said so far,
and in the absence of any terminological criterion, the medieval theories of
SOAs have to be identified by other, 'functional' criteria. Independently of its
location in the history of philosophy, a theory is to be counted as a theory of
SOAs if it describes:

a. special objectual correlates of propositional attitudes, or
b. special propositional meanings, or
c. what we would call facts or truth-makers.

Since not every medieval theory satisfies one or both of these 'functional' conditions, further, 'material' identification criteria have to be introduced, which will
allow us to identify not the theories as such, but entities that legitimately fall under
the notion of SOA. Such entities must be

d. the objects of theories of the types mentioned above under a, b or c
e. distinct from mental acts and states, and
f. distinct from linguistic expressions.

Medieval theories of SOAs—or the relevant elements from which such theories
can be reconstructed—pop up in many different fields of investigation, as well as in
unexpected textual environments. One finds them not only in logical, but also in
metaphysical and, most significantly, in theological works.[6]

3. WHAT KINDS OF ENTITIES ARE SOAs?— FIVE MEDIEVAL ANSWERS

We shall first consider the most intuitive position, namely, the one saying that since propositions are *about* things, the correlates of propositional attitudes must also be found within the realm of things (Section 3.1, 'Reism'); then we shall turn to the more sophisticated idea that not mere things *simpliciter* but certain modes of things are the correlates at stake (Section 3.2, 'Adverbialism'); third, an immanentist position will be presented (Section 3.3, 'Mentalism'); fourth, we shall consider solutions positing that the correlates of propositional attitudes are entities belonging to a sui generis realm of being (Section 3.4, 'Suigenerism); finally, we will examine the solution of those who simply deny the existence of correlates of propositional attitudes (Section 3.5, 'Eliminativism').

3.1. Reism

Reism comes in two basic kinds. One can posit that the counterparts of propositions are nothing but ordinary things (such is the opinion of Walter Chatton); or one can hold that those counterparts are *complexes of* ordinary things, thereby committing oneself to a richer (or heavier) ontology (such are the opinions of William Crathorn, Walter Burley and Richard Brinkley). As we shall see, John Wyclif has a complex theory in which both kinds of reism coexist.

Walter Chatton (d. 1343)[7] defends the idea that the object of an act of knowing or believing is a thing (or several things) and not, as Ockham had maintained, a mental proposition or *complexum* (*Ordinatio*, prol. q. 9; William of Ockham 1967, 266). More precisely, the objects of propositional attitudes are the thing (or the things) signified by a mental proposition.[8] There are two differences between a basic reist like Chatton and an eliminativist like Ockham. The first is a difference in their respective semantics: whereas eliminativists reduce the semantics of propositions to the semantics of *terms*, Chatton speaks of the thing (or things) that are signified by the *proposition* itself. The second difference pertains to ontology and explains why the first difference is more than a mere matter of terminology: while Chatton is prepared to say that a proposition like '*Sortes est homo*' signifies just the ordinary thing that is Socrates, he does not agree with Ockham's more specific claim that subject and predicate stand exactly for one and the same thing. According to Chatton, an ordinary thing like Socrates has a metaphysical structure involving a particular and a universal part, and such a composition is reflected by the two extremes of the proposition (*Reportatio*, I, d. 2, q. 3, a. 2; Walter Chatton 2002, 144–45).

Three authors—William Crathorn, Walter Burley[9] and Richard Brinkley—defend a position that can be labelled as 'complex reism'. They all think that the semantic counterparts of propositions are ontologically distinct from isolated ordinary things. According to his most virulent opponent—Robert Holkot (d. 1349)—William Crathorn (fl. 1330)[10] holds that what a proposition signifies is a thing (*res*) distinct from a written, spoken and mental proposition.[11] Reading Crathorn himself, one finds a more detailed explanation: when one knows, for example, that every composed thing is corruptible, one knows the 'thing' that is signified by the proposition '*omne mixtum est corrupti-bile*'.[12] Such a 'thing', however, is not a simple, ordinary thing, but a unitary complex that is the total significate of the proposition, and—contrary to the things signified by its terms—cannot be grasped by a natural concept (William Crathorn 1988, 270–71). In his last commentary on the *Categories*, Walter Burley (d. after 1344)[13] describes what he calls the total and adequate significate of a proposition as a 'complex thing' (*res complexa*) or a 'coupled being' (*ens copulatum*) and insists on its non-reducible character: it is neither the thing signified by the subject, nor the one signified by the predicate, but an aggregate made of both.[14] Richard Brinkley (fl. 1360),[15] for his part, considers that the total and adequate significate of a proposition is the ordered, integral whole constituted by the significates of its parts. For example, the significate of the proposition '*Sor videt Platonem*' consists in the things Socrates, Plato and Socrates's act of seeing, rightly ordered (*debite ordinatis*).[16]

Against the background of his strong metaphysical realism, John Wyclif (d. 1384)[17] elaborates a remarkably complex theory of the proposition involving, besides written, spoken and mental propositions, two further types of propositions whose parts are neither words nor concepts, namely, what he calls a real proposition (*propositio realis*), and what we would call a fact or a situation (*sic esse sicut propositio significat*).[18] Wyclif's theory has two major presuppositions: the first is the idea of a strict isomorphism between thoughts, words and things, which yields a metaphysical theory of predication: predication is not a matter of relations between words, but between things (John Wyclif 1985, 21–22). The second is the view that propositional structure is ubiquitous: according to Wyclif, whatever exists *is* a proposition (John Wyclif 1893, 14). Thus, on one hand, a particular man such as Socrates is a *propositio realis* because it has a subject (*ista persona*), a predicate (*natura humana*) and a copula (*essentia istius hominis*). On the other hand, a complex of ordinary things (a fact or situation) is a proposition as well because it is the ontological truth signified by a true (linguistic or mental) proposition (*veritas significata a parte rei*).

3.2. Adverbialism

Central to the adverbialist theories is the idea that things possess 'a mode', a kind of entity that 'accompanies' (or supervenes on[19]) ordinary things—the *modi rerum* (modes of things)—and that assumes the function of propositional significate. Such an opinion is defended, for example, by Richard Billingham, Nicole Oresme and Albert of Saxony. Unlike certain tenants of eliminativist adverbialism (Buridan and Peter of Ailly, see below, Section 3.5), Billingham's and Albert's position are not ontologically neutral: without situating propositional significates in the realm of things (simple or complex), they nonetheless accept the idea that a *modus rei* is 'something' (i.e., not a mere *nihil*).

According to Richard Billingham (fl. 1350), whose opinion on that matter is only known via Richard Brinkley's own tract on the significate of propositions, a proposition does not signify any thing or things, but only a 'mode of a thing' (*modus rei*).[20] Therefore, just as an adverb does not signify any being or action but only a way of being or acting, a proposition does not signify any thing, but only the thing's way of being.

We do not know of a full-fledged theory of the proposition by Nicole Oresme (d. 1382), but one finds relevant elements in his questions on the *Physics* and more precisely in his discussion of the nature of movement. Movement, according to Oresme, is neither a substance, nor an accident, but a kind of temporal extended 'collective'[21] (*res successiva*)—that is, a thing whose parts do not all exist at the same time—which he calls a mode or condition of the moved thing itself (Nicole Oresme 1994, 379). This mode has an ontological status distinct from that of substantial or inherent forms, which is comparable to that of certain relations and 'ways of behaving' (*taliter se habere*; Nicole Oresme 1994, 373). Although Oresme's *modus rei* is introduced in his definition of physical movement—in natural philosophy and not in logic or metaphysics—the justification he gives for accepting such an entity directly derives from propositional, truth-theoretic considerations: if one cannot account for the truth of a proposition like 'this is moving' ('*hoc movetur*') by only two things, the object moved and space, one *has to* acknowledge a third entity.[22] The significate of a proposition like '*hoc movetur*', then, is an extra-mental composition involving space, the thing moved, and a mode of this thing (here, its movement; Nicole Oresme 1994, 341).

In spite of his clear sympathy for Ockhamism, Albert of Saxony (d. 1390)[23] makes a significant concession to a form of realism by positing that there are entities that are neither substances nor accidents, but modes of things. They are what syncategorematic expressions signify.[24] The link between syncategorematic expressions and propositions is provided, on one hand, by Albert's identification of *modi rerum* and *complexe significabilia*, and, on the other, by his remark concerning the significates of the two expressions '*figura*' and '*esse figuratum*' ('figure', 'being figured'), the former being a simple name, and the second a propositional *dictum* (*Quaestiones super Physicam*, II, q. 3; Albert of Saxony 1999, 317). So, according to Albert, there are propositional significates, but they do not belong to the realm of categorical beings (substances, accidents); furthermore, those modes are not distinct from the things they modify in the way accidents are distinct from the things they qualify. This suggests that the ontological dependence of a mode on a thing is stronger than the one of an accident on a substance.

3.3. Mentalism

According to our typological scheme, the distinctive feature of mentalism is that it locates the semantic correlates of propositions within the mind. As many non-mentalist authors, mentalists accept that there are propositions in the mind (mental propositions), but contrary to the former, the latter posit that mental propositions have their counterparts in the mind as well. We shall now have a look at three cases of mentalism, namely, Thomas Aquinas, John Duns Scotus and Walter Burley.

Thomas Aquinas (d. 1274)[25] holds that objects of cognition have to be conceived as related to the cognitive faculty of a subject. This is not just to say that *obiectum* and *subiectum* are correlative notions, but that objects of cognition existentially depend on the cognitive activity of subjects: in a way, according to Thomas, the act of knowing produces the known object. This is most clearly set out in the theory of the mental word (*verbum mentis*), which is a mental object distinct from both the mental acts of the knowing subject and the *species intelligibilis* (*De Potentia*, q. 8, a. 1, resp.; Thomas Aquinas 1965, 66). Whereas *species* and acts have real, categorical existence in the mind (they are real qualities), concepts—that is, according to Aquinas, mental words—have a distinct mode of being: they possess a purely intelligible being (*Summa contra gentiles*, IV, c. 11; Thomas Aquinas 1930, 32). Now, our intellect yields mental words not only in the case of simple cognitive acts, but also when we produce mental propositions by composition or division.[26] This position leads to the conclusion that objects of knowledge are mental objects, products of mental propositional acts. Contrary to what one might fear, though, Aquinas's position is not a form of idealism. Indeed, the *verbum mentis* is itself essentially linked to the things in the external world: it is produced on the base of the *species intelligibilis*, which is itself a similitude of the external thing (*De potentia*, q. 8, a. 1). Furthermore, this essential link holds for non-propositional and for propositional knowledge as well. In fact, Aquinas says, extra-mental compositions correspond to mental, predicative compositions, so that the correlates of propositions have a *fundamentum in re.*[27]

In his first set of questions on Aristotle's *De interpretatione*, John Duns Scotus (d. 1308)[28] addresses the question of the ultimate significate of propositions, a question that suggests that a linguistic expression has (or can have) several, ordered significates. Thus, as Scotus points out, a written proposition signifies first a vocal one (*Quaestiones in primum librum Perihermeneias*, q. 2, n. 32; John Duns Scotus 2004a, 54), and a vocal proposition signifies a mental one, which, in turn, signifies the ultimate propositional significate that Scotus calls a composition of things.[29] This composition, however, is not to be understood as an extra-mental complex of things (*composition rerum ut existunt*)—Scotus does not defend a reist position, but rather as a composition of things as cognised (*compositio rerum ut intelliguntur*; *Quaestiones in primum librum Perihermeneias*, q. 2, n. 41; John Duns Scotus 2004a, 56–57). Scotus's position will be taken over and developed by Burley, the third and last tenant of mentalism I shall consider here.

We know at least five formulations of Walter Burley's theory of the proposition, and there are convincing arguments for both the claims that Burley defends just one, or several, distinct theories. Regardless of this particular issue, the formulation of the theory found in the so-called middle commentary on Aristotle's *De interpretatione* is clearly mentalist. Answering a relativistic objection saying that if a true mental proposition is a composition or division produced by the mind, then there will be as many truths as there are minds composing or dividing, Burley distinguishes two kinds of mental propositions: one that exists subjectively in the mind— it is the mental proposition in the standard sense of the expression—and one existing only objectively in the mind, an 'objective' proposition that he also calls a 'real proposition' (*propositio in re*)[30] and that terminates the chain of propositional signs and significates involving written, spoken and mental propositions.

3.4. Suigenerism

The 'suigenerist' answers given by medieval thinkers to the question of the ontological status of the correlates of propositional attitudes are characterised by their commitment to a specific realm to which such entities belong, and that does not depend on, nor is reducible to the realms of mental entities or things (substances and accidents) in the standard Aristotelian sense. We shall now briefly consider three examples: Peter Abelard, the anonymous authors of two logic textbooks from the late twelfth century—the *Ars Meliduna* and the *Ars Burana*—and the most famous exponent of the theory of the so called *complexe significabile*, namely, Gregory of Rimini.

In his *Logica Ingredientibus*, Peter Abelard (d. 1142)[31] says about propositions that they are semantically related to two types of entities: concepts (*intellectus*) on one side, and what is said or propounded by propositions (*dicta propositionum*) on the other side, the latter not being any of the existing things (*essentiae*).[32] The *dicta* are said to be the *quasi res* of propositions, not in the sense that they are 'pseudo-things' or are somehow dependent on things, but merely in a functional sense: within the semantics of propositions, *dicta* play the role things play in the semantics of names, namely, the role of non-linguistic and non-conceptual correlates. Abelard provides an elegant argument to show that *dicta* cannot be either things or concepts. Let us consider a necessary proposition—his example is: 'if it is a rose, it is a flower'—and ask ourselves what grounds its necessary character. Now, Abelard argues, (i) since the necessity of a proposition must lie in what it says or signifies, and (ii) because of the contingent nature of linguistic expressions, thoughts and things, therefore, the *dictum* of a necessary proposition has to be ontologically distinct from words, thoughts and things (*Glossae super Perihermeneias*, IV; Peter Abelard 2010, 133).

The fourth chapter of the *Ars Meliduma* (written around 1180) is devoted to the question of the nature of the *enuntiabilia*—that is, 'what can be said or stated'—a topic that is closely related to the discussions of the *dicta* by Abelard. Addressing the question of the ontological status of *enuntiabilia*, the author of the *Ars* lists (and rejects) three main opinions: (i) they are concepts produced by the pronunciation of words, that is, properties or accidents of the mind; (ii) they are compositions or divisions of a predicate and a subject, and thereby properties as well since every composition or division is a property; (iii) they are nothing properly speaking, but adverbial determinations. The author of the *Ars meliduna* goes on to say that all this tells us not what *enuntiabilia* are, but rather what they are not, and confesses that, at the end of the day, he does not know anything about *enuntiabilia*: '*Et generaliter, de nullo enuntiabili aliquid scio*' (*Ars meliduna*; Anonymous 1967b, 359). The author of another logical tract, the *Ars Burana* (written around 1200), goes beyond this pessimistic statement and gives a series of positive and negative qualifications for *enuntiabilia*: they are the significates of propositions, they are that which is understood when a proposition is understood, they cannot be sensed but only grasped by the intellect.[33] And if one asks to which ontological category they belong, the answer is that they are neither substances nor accidents, but belong to an 'eleventh' category, the '*predicamentum enuntiabilium*' (*Ars Burana*; Anonymous 1967a, 208).

Discussing (and rejecting) the opinions of Scotus, Ockham and Chatton on the nature of the object of knowledge, the English theologian Adam Wodeham (d. 1358)[34] introduces the notion of 'what is signifiable by a proposition' ('*significabile per complexum*'), which he calls the 'total significate of a proposition' ('*significatum totale propositionis*').[35] As for its ontological status—*quid est?*—he considers the question to be simply inappropriate (*inepta*): what a proposition signifies is not a 'what' (*quid*), but a 'to be something' (*esse quid*).[36] Gregory of Rimini (d. 1358)[37] famously takes up Wodeham's intuition but does not seem to consider the ontological question as inappropriate, for he devotes some pages of the prologue of his commentary on the *Sentences* to explain in what sense the propositional significate (or the object of knowledge)—which he (also) calls a *complexe significabile*—is indeed nothing, and in what sense it is not. Gregory starts from an apparently paradoxical situation: he concedes that the object of knowledge is nothing (*nihil*) but denies that science doesn't have any object (*nullum obiectum*; *Lectura*; Gregory of Rimini 1978, 9–10). The way out consists in showing that the word '*aliquid*' has several senses so that a given entity can be said to be *aliquid* in one sense and *non aliquid* in another. The three senses of '*aliquid*' distinguished by Gregory are, respectively: (i) whatever can be signified, in a complex or non-complex way, truly or falsely; (ii) whatever can be signified, in a complex or non-complex way, but only truly; (iii) an existing thing.[38] Now, according to Gregory, a *complexe significabile* is *aliquid* in senses (i) and (ii), and *non aliquid* only in the sense (iii).[39] The resulting (negative) picture is that the semantic correlates of true as well as of false propositions are entities that do not belong to the realm of what is commonly understood as a thing (*essentia, entitas existens*)—one would want to say: entities that *are*, but do not exist.

3.5. Eliminativism

The central idea of eliminativists is that propositional semantics does not require the existence of special counterparts for acts of judging. On this view, whatever is signified by a proposition can be signified by one of its parts. In that sense, eliminativism is a kind of reductionism (propositional semantics is reducible to the semantics of terms). For the sake of brevity, we will only consider the case of Ockham.[40]

In chapter 2 of the second part of his *Summa logicae*, Ockham (d. ca. 1348)[41] raises the question of the necessary and sufficient conditions for the truth of a singular, non-modal proposition. In his answer, he insists, first, on what *is not* required, namely: first, that subject and predicate are really the same; second, that what corresponds to the predicate in reality (= Pr) inheres in what corresponds to the subject in reality (= Sr); third, that Pr and Sr are united in reality. By contrast, what is necessary and sufficient for the truth of a proposition like '*iste est angelus*' is that subject and predicate supposit for the same thing (*Summa logicae*, II, 2; William of Ockham 1974, 249–50). In other words, what a proposition signifies is exactly the thing for which (if it is true) its subject and predicate terms stand, and this, according to Ockham's ontology, can only be a perfectly standard singular thing (substance or quality). To take another example, the proposition '*Sortes est animal*' ('Socrates is an animal') does not

signify that Socrates is (also) the thing that is signified by the predicate '*animal*'—
there is no such 'complex' thing—but only that the thing for which '*Sortes*' stands is
exactly the one for which '*animal*' stands.[42] It is noteworthy that Ockham accepts the
principle of truthmaking—namely, that a true proposition is made true by something
distinct from itself[43]—but does not conclude that what makes a proposition true
must be an entity distinct from what the terms of the proposition signify. There is no
complex, SOA-like entity that would account for the truth of a mental proposition: a
truth is nothing but a true proposition; a falsity, nothing but a false proposition.[44]

4. (SOME) LATER CONCEPTIONS OF SOAS: A COMPARATIVE FRAME

Provided that our criteria of identification of medieval theories of SOAs are accepted, and that our reading of the authors considered so far is correct, we have
gathered examples of medieval authors . . .

> . . . either accepting that there are SOAs and conceiving them as

(i) things, either in isolation ('simple' reists such as Chatton, and Wyclif) or
composing real extra-mental complexes of things ('complex' reists such as
Crathorn, Burley, Brinkley and Wyclif again)

(ii) supervenient entities accompanying ordinary things ('adverbialists' such
as Billingham, Oresme and Albert of Saxony)

(iii) immanent (i.e., mental) complex objects ('mentalists' such as Aquinas,
Scotus and Burley)

(iv) entities belonging to a specific ontological realm ('suigenerists' such as
Abelard, the author of the *Ars Burana* and Gregory of Rimini)

> . . . or:

(v) denying that there are SOAs at all ('eliminativists' such as Ockham,
Buridan, Ferribridge and Peter of Ailly)

In this last section of the chapter, we shall sketch a comparative frame by considering some late-nineteenth- and early-twentieth-century, as well as contemporary
theories of SOAs that, at least in our view, can meaningfully be compared with the five
types of solutions listed above. We shall choose only one or two exemplary theories
for each class of opinions although many more would deserve to be mentioned.[45]

4.1. Reism

Just as two kinds of reism ('simple' and 'complex') can be distinguished within medieval philosophy, one finds modern authors identifying SOAs with isolated, ordinary
things—such as, for example, one of the opinions defended by David Armstrong—
or with complexes of things—one would say, with facts—as Bertrand Russell does.

Those two approaches are not incompatible (Armstrong's position is a refinement of Russell's; Armstrong 1997, 19).

According to Armstrong, a basic SOA is nothing but an instantiated universal. But every ordinary thing in the world is correctly describable as being an instantiated universal ('bare particulars' exist only as intellectual abstractions). Thus, Armstrong's response to an eliminativist would not be that there are, besides ordinary things, entities of a particular kind that are SOAs, but that whatever exists is an SOA, so that the distinction between ordinary objects and SOAs collapses.[46] The reason why Armstrong generalises the existence of SOAs in this way is closely linked to his metaphysical realism: it is because there are universals, and because neither uninstantiated universals nor bare particulars exist, that whatever exists must be an SOA.[47]

Recalling the 'simple' reist theories exposed above (see above, Section 3.1)—the significates of (linguistic and mental) propositions are ordinary objects whose metaphysical structure involves particular and universal constituents—Armstrong's notion of 'thick' particular seems to be quite close to what Wyclif calls a *propositio realis*. Both authors maintain that this particular man (*iste homo*, in Wyclif's terms) considered without any relational properties (Armstrong's thick particular) is an SOAs. But Armstrong would reject Wyclif's terminology on the ground that the linguistic and the metaphysical levels should be sharply distinguished—even if every SOA is a truth-maker, it would be misleading to associate SOAs and propositions (Armstrong 2009, 39).

As for the 'complex' reist theories defended by Crathorn, Burley and Brinkley— the counterparts of propositions are complexes of ordinary things—an obvious candidate for comparative purposes is what the early Russell calls a proposition. Reacting against Frege's distinction between the sense (*Sinn*) of a statement as being an abstract meaning (*Gedanke*) and its reference (*Bedeutung*) as being one of only two remarkable objects (*das Wahre, das Falsche*), Russell, in a famous letter of December 1904, explains that when one asserts something—for example, *that the Mont Blanc is more than 4000 meters high*—what is asserted is not an abstract meaning, but a certain complex object of which Mont Blanc itself is a part (what is asserted is not the thought, but the object of the thought). Russell calls such an object a complex or an objective proposition.[48] Burley's or Brinkley's claim, for example, that the ultimate significates of a proposition (Russell would say: of a statement) is a complex whole whose integral parts are the things signified by the subject and the predicate terms comes quite close to a Russellian proposition in the sense just described.

4.2. Adverbialism

Adverbialism understood as an ontologically non-neutral position—that is, not in the way of Peter of Ailly's eliminativist adverbialism (see above, Section 3.5), but in the way of Billingham's or Oresme's position (see above, Section 3.2)—amounts to allowing for supervenient entities—'modes' of things—which do not belong to the realm of categorical being (they are neither substances, nor accidents) but are nonetheless concrete constituents of ordinary things.

A modern author who defends a kind of adverbialism is Anton Marty (1847–1914),[49] one of the first pupils of Brentano. Roughly, Marty's position is the following: as psychic phenomena, acts of judging are related to certain objects. For example, my judging that Socrates is white is an intentional act related to the object Socrates. But unlike presentations (*Vorstellungen*), judgings have also a content (*Urteilsinhalt*), as in the example just given: *Socrates's being white*.[50] Marty calls such a judgement content a *Sachverhalt*. Martyian SOAs belong to the ontological domain of what exists without being real. What exists and *is* real are corporeal or spiritual substances and their accidents (i.e., bodies and their properties, minds and their acts and states); what exists and *is not* real are, besides SOA, relations, collectives, space and time (Marty 1908, 317).

As non-real entities, SOAs are existentially dependent on real entities—as in our example: *Socrates's being white* is a non-real entity (a SOA), which depends on a real entity (Socrates). More precisely, Socrates's being white is said to be a non-real consequence (*nicht reale Folge*) of Socrates (Marty 1908, 320). A metaphorical way to express the relation between a non-real entity and its real base would consist in saying that the non-real entity is like an ontological shadow of its real base. It is crucial to note, however, that SOAs are absolutely mind independent: it is true that we only can grasp them through (subjective) acts of judging, but their existence is perfectly indifferent to our mental acts and states (Marty 1908, 295). Further, Martyian SOAs are temporal (but non-spatial) objects, they are causally inert and, as correlates of true acts of judging, they are truth-makers of true statements.

4.3. Mentalism

Marty developed his ontology of *irrealia* in a critical and constructive discussion with his master Brentano (1838–1917)[51] who, in his so-called middle period (i.e., from the *Psychologie* of 1874 to about 1904), came to the conclusion that every psychic phenomenon (presentation, judgement, emotion) has a non-real, immanent intentional object (*immanente Gegenständlichkeit*—Brentano 2008, 106). Around the turn of the century, however, both Marty and Brentano came to see that this is an untenable position, for it seems plainly false (and quite threatening for the very notion of objectivity) that the target of, say, any representation (*Vorstellung*), is an immanent object.

Brentano's middle theory is spelled out most extensively in two unedited texts from the years 1885–90, recently thoroughly studied in Chrudzimski (2004). Talking about the meaning of statements (*Aussagen*), Brentano says that just like names, statements have two sorts of semantic counterparts: on one hand, they are related to (immanent) contents; on the other, they are related to (transcendent) objects—that is, provided there are such transcendent objects. In other words, a psychic phenomenon, for example, an act of judging, has *in any case* an immanent correlate that is its content and its significate (*Inhalt, Bedeutung*).[52] The advantages of such a theory are obvious: it provides psychic phenomena with objects regardless of the actual state of the external world. A mentalist account of intentional objects is the most efficient way to solve the problem of terms deprived of reference and of statements about non-existents. But such a theory has also the major drawback that it locates the target of intentional acts within the mind—something that is rather counter-intuitive and epistemologically problematic.

Besides their immanent character, the SOAs of the middle Brentano share another distinctive feature with the propositional correlates of medieval mentalists such as Aquinas, Scotus or Burley (see Section 3.3 above): their being existentially dependent on mental acts. Modern and medieval mentalists endorse the principle that there are no SOAs without mental acts. However, the distinction between mental acts (medievals would say: what is subjectively in the mind) and their immanent contents (they would say: what is objectively in the mind) provides those immanent correlates with a certain degree of objectivity. In that respect, another Brentanian of the first generation, Carl Stumpf (1848–1936),[53] develops a remarkable theory of objective, immanent judgement contents (*Sachverhalte*) he also calls psychic formations (*Gebilde*), which are existentially dependent on mental acts (*Funktionen*).[54] Just as, for example, Aquinas's *verbum mentis* is produced by the mind and is to be distinguished from the extra-mental thing, the intelligible species and the acts of the intellect, Stumpf's SOAs (*Gebilde*) are distinct from extra-mental objects (*Gegenstände*), phenomena (*Erscheinungen*) and mental acts (*Funktionen*).[55]

4.4. Suigenerism

In 1936, the French scholar Hubert Élie published a study that is probably the first attempt to compare medieval and modern theories of states of affairs (Élie 2000). The book is mainly devoted to a comparison of Gregory of Rimini's theory of the *complexe significabile* with Meinong's conception of SOAs (or *Objektive*). Besides Meinong, however, another figure of the so-called 'Austrian philosophy' deserves to be mentioned when modern and medieval suigenerist approaches are compared: Adolf Reinach, certainly Husserl's most brilliant pupil. Modern and medieval suigenerists share the claim that SOAs belong to an ontological domain distinct from the one of thoughts (in a non-Fregean sense) and ordinary things. Just like Bolzanian *Sätze an sich* and Fregean *Gedanke*, Meinong's and Reinach's SOAs have a distinctive Platonic flavour. Both authors accept this heavy ontological cost in order to reject psychologism: logic does not describe the way we think; rather, it describes relations existing among purely mind-independent propositional correlates.

In the first years of the twentieth century, Alexius Meinong (1853–1920)[56] developed a theory of meanings (*Bedeutungen*) as objects (*Gegenstände*), which means that the theory of propositional significates will ultimately be a theory of objects (Meinong 1977, 42). It is well known that Meinong endorses an ontology comprising (among others) objects that exist (such as real objects) and objects that only subsist (such as ideal objects—Meinong 1971, 486–87). According to Meinong, acts of judging and of assuming (*Annahmen*)—which are themselves real objects—have special, necessarily ideal objects that are called *Objektive*.[57] Subsisting *Objektive* are the correlates of true judgements (and are themselves truths), non-subsisting ones correspond to false judgements (and are themselves falsities—Meinong 1977, 81). Furthermore, there are positive as well as negative *Objektive*, *Seins-* and *Soseinsobjektive* (i.e., existential and attributive *Objektive*), so that the whole range of possible statements is provided with ideal correlates belonging to a remarkable domain of non-existent (but possibly subsistent) objects.

Contrary to Husserl, who conceives of SOAs as ideal objects (partly) constituted of ordinary things,[58] Adolf Reinach (1883–1917)[59] locates SOAs in a separate ontological domain. Reinach argues as follows: it is a fact that we perform acts of judging and that these acts are subject to an a priori constraint such that a simple, ordinary object cannot be the object of judgement—it does not make any sense to say, for example, 'I believe, or I judge *a rose*'. Therefore, acts of judging must have special correlates, the *Sachverhalte*. They have to be distinguished from all the objects, be they real (like things or thoughts) or ideal (like numbers or propositions), for they are what is believed or asserted in an act of judging.[60] SOAs are ontologically distinct from real objects, but not from ideal objects such as numbers and propositions. What distinguishes SOAs from propositions—and this is a point about which Reinach criticises Meinong's theory of *Objektive* (Reinach 1989, 114, note 1)—is that the latter are bearers of truth values, while the former are the entities that make propositions true or false (Reinach 1989, 138, note 1). Accordingly, the realm of Reinachian SOAs is complete: to each possible act of judging (true or false, positive or negative), there corresponds an SOA. It follows that logic is ultimately nothing but the science of SOAs (Reinach 1989, 115).

Whereas the peculiar ontological status of Meinong's and Reinach's SOAs certainly allows one to compare them to the *enuntiabilia* described by the author of the *Ars Burana*—they belong to an 'eleventh category'—as well as with Gregory of Rimini's *complexe significabilia*—they are something (*aliquid*), but nothing existing—it is less obvious that they can be compared to Abelard's *dicta*, for he did not leave any explicit and positive development on their ontological status. However, their qualification as *quasi res* of propositions provides a plausible ground for comparison: just as SOAs are introduced by Meinong and Reinach as entities that, with respect to acts of judging, play a role analogous to the one played by things with respect to acts of presenting, *dicta* are, within the semantics of propositions, the functional analogues of *res*.

4.5 Eliminativism

In a paper published recently, Peter Simons defends the thesis that there are no SOAs at all (Simons 2009). Simons's strategy is clear and efficient: he starts by listing the functions SOAs are supposed to assume—truth-making, being objects of propositional attitudes and being the significates of sentences, just to name a few—and shows that these functions can be fulfilled without appealing to SOAs.

Before explaining how this is to be achieved, Simons mentions two inherent problems with SOAs. The first is the difficulty of providing them with an ontological status. Taking an SOA to be a whole composed of (at least) one concrete particular and one abstract universal—for example, the SOA *that John is tall* is composed of the concrete substance John and the abstract property of being tall—Simons shows that such a 'transcategorial' whole cannot be accounted for in mereology (against Russell), neither by conceiving of it as an abstract entity (against Meinong), nor by considering that it is a concrete entity (against Armstrong). The second problem is that Bradley's regress is indeed harmful.[61] The explanation of how the constituents of an SOA are related to form a whole involves an infinite regress: a relation R is needed to connect the particular and the universal constituents; then two further relations to relate R to its terms, and thus, a pair of relations is needed for each new relation . . .

But how are the three essential functions mentioned above to be fulfilled without SOAs? Here are Simon's suggestions: (i) The job of making true is done better by tropes (individual accidents, including events) than by SOAs. Thus, if John loves Mary, the proposition 'John loves Mary' is made true by *John's loving Mary*, which is a 'dependent, unique individual'. This trope, and not the SOA *that John loves Mary*, makes the proposition true. (ii) Propositional attitudes require only special *contents*, but no special objects (i.e., objects distinct from the things they simply are about). If John believes that Mary loves him, his belief has a content (namely, *that Mary loves John*) and is about Mary. True or false, the belief has the same content, and if it is true, then what makes it such is nothing but the trope *Mary's loving John*. (iii) The significates of sentences aren't SOAs, but propositions (which, if I understood Simons correctly, are also the contents of propositional attitudes). Therefore, the semantics of sentences does not require SOAs either.

Simons's reductionist argumentation in favour of an SOA-free world comes quite close to the eliminativist positions considered above in Section 3.5, at least in the sense that the fulfilment of the functions that are supposed to force one to accept SOAs does not require the acceptance of entities different from particular substances and particular accidents. And Simons's talking about propositions as meanings of sentences (or contents of propositional attitudes) does not entail his being a realist *à la* Bolzano, Frege or Husserl, for while he takes it for granted that meanings exist, he adds that they exist 'only insofar as meaningful acts of understanding exist in a community of speakers' (Simons 2007, 76). Since acts of understanding are concrete entities, if meanings existentially depend on such acts, meanings cannot possibly be abstract entities.

5. Concluding Remark

It is relatively easy to show that philosophers from different times share analogous *questions*. It is more difficult to demonstrate that they also share *answers*—or at least types of answers. The choice to set up a frame of comparison based on five purely systematic categories—reism, adverbialism, mentalism, suigenerism and eliminativism—without reference to their (possible) previous use in the historiography or in philosophical debates[62] was meant to provide a neutral and useable *tertium comparationis* between past and present theories. Medieval and modern philosophical reflections about the necessity to admit counterparts to propositional attitudes show comparable ranges of positive and negative solutions with comparable ontological commitments: the notion of state of affairs or *Sachverhalt* has a history that reaches far beyond its terminological introduction into the philosophical vocabulary at the end of the nineteenth century. Even at best, though, comparison cannot possibly mean identification: each of the theories briefly presented above conserves its irreducible specificity. But such a comparative collection of opinions—which one could perhaps rightly consider as a typical product of *historians*—might also turn out to be beneficial for today's so-called 'pure' *philosophers*.[63]

NOTES

1. Concerning the non-medieval theories, one may wonder why authors from the late nineteenth and early twentieth century are predominantly dealt with in the second part of this chapter (the only two strictly contemporary philosophers taken into account are D. Armstrong and P. Simons). There are two reasons for adding this third group of thinkers between contemporary and medieval theorists of SOAs. First, the technical notion of *Sachverhalt* originated at the end of the nineteenth century within the Austro-German tradition; second, the heritage of the medieval and post-medieval scholastic plays a crucial role in the thought of Brentano and his immediate heirs.

2. See also Wittgenstein, *Tractatus logico philosophicus*, proposition 2 (Wittgenstein 1961, 7), as well as below, Section 4.2.

3. In that sense, SOAs are immanent (mental) entities—what he calls *Gebilde* or formations—that are the contents of acts of judging.

4. In that sense, SOAs are concrete, actual situations. Other authors like Wittgenstein, for example, see facts as obtaining SOAs and non-obtaining SOAs as possible facts.

5. This list of roles and functions is merely meant to illustrate the high explanatory value of SOAs. The idea is not to say that in every SOA theory, SOAs assume *all* these roles. So, for example, if one identifies SOAs with truth-makers, one cannot also characterise SOAs as propositional meanings, since false propositions, too, have a meaning.

6. The general topic of propositional semantics has been dealt with in a number of works of the last eighty years. The main contributions are Ashworth (1978); Berger (1999); Biard (2004); Brower-Toland (2006); Cesalli (2007); Élie (2000); Karger (1995, 1996); Kretzmann (1970); de Libera (2002); Nuchelmans (1973); Perler (1990, 1992, 1994, 2006); Perez-Ilzarbe (1999); Rode (2005); Weidemann (1991). Although not focusing exclusively on the topic, Biard (1989), Spade (1996) and, above all, Tachau (1988) contain a lot of precious material.

7. On Chatton's position, see Nuchelmans (1973, 210–12) and Perler (1990, 147–57).

8. Walter Chatton, *Reportatio*, prol. q. 1, a. 1 (Walter Chatton 1989, 20–21).

9. As we shall see, Burley's theory can be interpreted in different ways, so that these authors will also be discussed under the mentalists (see below, Section 3.4).

10. On William Crathorn's position, see Nuchelmans (1973, 212–19); Perler (1992, 304–8); Schepers (1972); Tachau (1988, 255–74, esp. 269–70).

11. Robert Holkot, *Sex artiucli*, a. 1 (Robert Holkot 1993, 72–73).

12. William Crathorn, *Quaestiones in primum librum Sententiarum* (William Crathorn 1988, 269).

13. On Burley's position, see Cesalli (2007, 166–240); Conti (2000); Karger (1996); Müller (1997); as well as Cesalli (2011), which gives a complete list of the vast literature on Burley's theory.

14. Walter Burley, *Liber Praedicamentorum*, c. 12 (Walter Burley 1497, f. g6^{ra-b}). The notion of *propositio in re* is subject to different interpretations. In this passage, it clearly looks like a complex of extra-mental things. For another passage pointing to a different understanding of the notion—namely, a complex immament object—see below, Section 3.4.

15. On Brinkley's position, see the introduction of Fitzgerald in Brinkley (1987) and Gaskin (1997) as well as Cesalli (2007, 241–309).

16. Richard Brinkley, *De significato propositionis*, c. 1 (Richard Brinkley 1987, 34).

17. On Wyclif's position, see Conti (2006) as well as Cesalli (2007, 309–89).

18. John Wyclif, *Tractatus de logica*, c. 5 (John Wyclif 1893, 14–15).

19. Since any change in a given thing will affect the truth value of a proposition about it, the relation between a thing and its mode seems to fit with the definition of supervenience, according to which A supervenes on B iff there cannot be an A-difference without a B-difference.

20. Richard Billingham, in Richard Brinkley, *De significato propositionis* (Richard Brinkley 1987, 52).

21. In the technical sense, a 'collective' is an entity whose ontological status isn't reducible to that of its parts. For example, a forest is a 'collective' because, although it is exclusively composed of substances, it is not itself a substance.

22. Nicole Oresme, *Quaestiones super Physicam*, III.6 (Nicole Oresme 1994, 374).

23. On Albert's position, see de Libera (2002, 305–6).

24. Albert of Saxony, *Quaestiones super artem veterem* (Albert of Saxony 1988, 500).

25. On Thomas's position, see Klima (1993) as well as Panaccio (1999, 179–86).

26. Thomas Aquinas, *Summa theologiae*, I^a, q. 85, a. 2, ad 3 (1952).

27. Thomas Aquinas, *Summa theologiae*, I^a, q. 85, a. 5, ad 3 (1952). See also Thomas Aquinas, *In duodecim libros Metaphysicorum expositio*, lib. 9, lect. 11, n. 4 (1964).

28. On Duns Scotus's position, see Bos (1987); Cesalli (2007, 94–166); Marmo (1989); Pini (2002).

29. John Duns Scotus, *Quaestiones in duos libros Perihermeneias: in librum primum*, q. 1, n. 25 (John Duns Scotus 2004b, 143). See also *Quaestiones in primum librum Perihermeneias*, q. 2, n. 33 (John Duns Scotus 2004a, 54).

30. Walter Burley, *Commentarius in librum Perihermeneias*, § 1.26 (Walter Burley 1973, 61). As we saw in Section 3.1 above, the notion of *propositio in re* can also be interpreted as a transcendent complex object.

31. On Abelard's position, see Marenbon (1997, 202–9); Jacobi (2004); Rosier-Catach (2004).

32. Peter Abelard, *Glossae super Perihermeneias*, IV (Peter Abelard 2010, 135).

33. Anonymous, *Ars Burana* (Anonymous 1967a, 208).

34. On Wodeham's position, see Bermon (2007, 169–71, 311–19); Biard (2004); Brower Toland (2006); Karger (1995); Nuchelmans (1980); Perler (1994); Tachau (1988, 303–10).

35. Adam Wodeham, *Lectura secunda*, d. 1, q. 1 (Adam Wodeham 1990, 188 and 190).

36. Adam of Wodeham, *Lectura secunda*, d. 1, q. 1 (Adam Wodeham 1990, 195).

37. On Gregory's position, see Bermon (2007), 105–61; Biard (2004); Élie (2000); Gaskin (2003); Nuchelmans (1973), 227–42; Perler (1992, 317–26); Perler (1994); Spade (1996, 168–75); Weidemann (1991).

38. Gregory of Rimini, *Lectura*, prol., q. 1 (Gregory of Rimini 1978, 8–9).

39. Gregory of Rimini, *Lectura*, prol., q. 1 (Gregory of Rimini 1978, 9).

40. For other eliminativists, see, for example, John Buridan (d. after 1358), who decidedly fights against *complexe significabilia*. Not without irony, he says that the proposition '*complexe significabilia sunt chimaerae*' is false since according to him, every ordinary thing *is* a *complexe significabile*, for it can be signified by a proposition (*Sophismata*, I, 5; John Buridan 1977, 33). Another example is Peter of Ailly (d. 1420), who insists on the reducibility of propositional semantics to the semantics of terms (*Insolubilia*; Peter of Ailly 1495, Ciiiiʳ) Richard Ferribridge (fl. 1360) defends a similar opinion (*Logica seu Tractatus de veritate propositionum*; Ferribridge 1978, 223).

41. On Ockham's position, see Karger (1996); Lenz (2003, 73–138); Müller (1997); Panaccio (1999, 253–78); Robert (2004).

42. William of Ockham, *Summa logicae*, II, 2 (William of Ockham 1974, 250).

43. William of Ockham, *Expositio in librum Praedicamentorum Aristotelis*, c. 9, § 13 (William of Ockham 1978, 201).

44. William of Ockham, *Quodlibeta septem*, V, 24 (William of Ockham 1980, 578).

45. On modern theories of SOA, see Chrudzimski (2007, 2009); Morscher & Neumaier (2001); Mulligan (1987); Reicher (2009); Rojszczak (2005); Salice (2009); Smith (1996); Süssbauer (1995).

46. An argumentation that bears some affinities with Buridan's ironic remark about *complexe significabilia* (see above, n. 40) even if the philosophical consequence drawn by Armstrong is quite different.

47. David Armstrong (1989, 88–89). Note that, according to Armstrong, even if one conceives of properties as tropes (non-universal constituents), one is committed to something like SOAs. The only configuration where SOAs wouldn't be required would be a world where tropes would all be non-transferable (Socrates's whiteness would belong to Socrates's essence), but then, the very notion of contingency would be threatened (Armstrong 1997, 117).

48. Russell in Gabriel et al. (1980, 98–99).

49. On Marty's position, see Cesalli (2009); Chrudzimski (1999, 2009); Mulligan (ed., 1990); Rollinger (2010).

50. Marty (1908, 423–25).

51. On Brentano's position, see Chrudzimski (2004, 2009).

52. Franz Brentano, *Logik*, 36 (quoted in Chrudzimski 2004, 129).

53. On Stumpf's position, see Fisette (2006).

54. Stumpf (1907, 34).

55. Stumpf (1997, 130).

56. On Meinong's position, see Albertazzi et al. (2001); Chrudzimski (2007); Sierszulska (2005).

57. Meinong (1971, 487).

58. On Husserl's position, see Mulligan (1985).

59. On Reinach's position, see Künne (1987); Smith (1987).

60. Reinach (1989, 114).

61. Bradley's regress as exposed in Bradley (1916, 19–24) is not developed in the context of an explicit theory of SOAs (but within the general problem of inherence). However, the objection can be raised against mereological approaches of SOAs. Just as the

regress appears when one accounts for the unity of a substance and its qualities by positing relational ties between them, it also appears when one accounts for the unity of SOAs as being complex objects composed of different objects.

 62. As a matter of fact—and with the possible exception of suigenerism—all of these categories have their own 'past' in historiography and philosophy.

 63. I am grateful to Andrew Arlig, John Marenbon and Alexander Oliver for commenting on an earlier version of this chapter.

BIBLIOGRAPHY

Adam Wodeham. 1990. *Lectura secunda in librum primum Sententiarum,* ed. G. Gál and R. Wood. St Bonaventure, NY: The Franciscan Institute.

Albert of Saxony. 1988. *Quaestiones super Artem veterem*, ed. A. Munoz GarciaMaracaibo, Venezuela: Universidad del Zulia.

———. 1999. *Expositio et Quaestiones in Aristotelis Physicam ad Albertum de Saxonia attributae,* ed. B. Patar. Vol. II. Louvain, Belgium: Peeters.

Albertazzi, Liliana et al., eds. 2001. *The School of Alexius Meinong.* Aldershot, UK: Ashgate.

Anonymous. 1967a. *Ars Burana.* In L. M. de Rijk, *Logica modernorum.* Vol. II.2, 175–213. Assen: Van Gorcum.

———. 1967b. *Ars meliduna.* In L. M. de Rijk, *Logica modernorum.* Vol. II.1, 292–390. Assen: Van Gorcum.

Aristotle. 1984. 'Sophistical refutations'. In *The Complete Works of Aristotle,* Jonathan Barnes, ed. Vol. 1., 278–314. Princeton NJ: Princeton University Press.

Armstrong, David. 1989. *Universals: An Opinionated Introduction.* Boulder, CO: Westview Press.

———. 1997. *A World of States of Affairs.* Cambridge: Cambridge University Press.

———. 2009. 'Questions sbout states of affairs'. In *States of Affairs,* ed. M. E. Reicher, 39–50. Frankfurt am Main, Germany: Ontos.

Ashworth, Jennifer E. 1978. Theories of the Proposition: Some Early Sixteenth Century Discussions. *Franciscan Studies* 38:81–121.

Berger, Harald. 1999. 'Über Entstehen und Vergehen der Sachverhaltsontologie im Spätmittelalter'. In *Entwicklungslinien mittelalterlicher Philosophie,* ed. G. Leibold and W. Löffler, 208–21. Vienna: Hölder-Pichler-Tempsky.

Bergmann, Julius. 1879. *Allgemeine Logik. I. Reine Logik.* Berlin: Mittler.

Bermon, Pascale. 2007. *L'assentiment et son objet chez Grégoire de Rimini.* Paris: Vrin.

Biard, Joël. 1989. *Logique et théorie du signe au XIVe siècle.* Paris: Vrin.

———. 2004. 'Les controverses sur l'objet du savoir et les complexe significabilia à Paris au XIVe siècle'. In *Quia inter doctores est magna dissensio. Les débats de philosophie naturelle à paris au XIVe siècle,* ed. S. Caroti, 21–31. Florence: Olschki.

Bos, Egbert P. 1987. 'The theory of the proposition according to John Duns Scotus in his two commentaries on Aristotle's Perihermeneias'. In *Logos and Pragma. Essays on the Philosophy of Language in Honour of Prof. Gabriel Nuchelmans,* 121–39. Nijmegen, the Netherlands: Ingenium Publishers.

Bradley, Francis Herbert. 1916. *Appearance and Reality. A Metaphysical Essay.* London: Allen & Unwin.

Brentano, Franz. 2008 [1874, 1911]. *Psychologie vom empirischen Standpunkte. Von der Klassifikation der psychischen Phänomene*. Mit einem Vorwort der Herausgeber zur Ausgabe der veröffentlichten Schriften und einer Einleitung von Mauro Antonelli. Frankfurt am Main, Germany: Ontos.

Brower-Toland, Susan. 2006. Facts vs. Things. Adam Wodeham and the Later Medieval Debate about Objects of Judgment. *The Review of Metaphysics* 60(3):597–642.

Cesalli, Laurent. 2007. *Le réalisme propositionnel. Sémantique et ontologie des propositions chez Jean Duns Scot, Gauthier Burley, Richard Brinkley et Jean Wyclif*. Paris: Vrin.

———. 2009. Martys philosophische Position innerhalb der österreichischen Tradition. *Brentano Studien* 12:121–81.

———. 2011. 'Propositio in re'. In *Mots médiévaux offerts à Ruedi Imbach*, ed. I. Attucha, D. Calma, C. Koenig-Pralong and I. Zavattero, 523–36. Porto, Portugal: Fédération Internationale des Instituts d' Études Médiévales.

Chrudzimski, Arkadiusz. 1999. Die Intentionalitätstheorie Anton Martys. *Grazer Philosophische Studien* 57:175–214.

———. 2004. *Die Ontologie Franz Brentanos*. Dordrecht, the Netherlands: Kluwer.

———. 2007. *Gegenstandstheorie und Theorie der Intentionalität bei Alexius Meinong*. Dordrecht, the Netherlands: Springer.

———. 2009. Sachverhalte, Objekte und Supervenienz. Brentano, Marty und Meinong. *Brentano Studien* 12:99–119.

Conti, Alessandro. 2000. Significato e verità in Walter Burley. *Documenti e studi sulla tradizione filosofica medievale* 11:317–50.

———. 2006. 'Wyclif's logic and metaphysics'. In *A Companion to John Wyclif*, ed. I. C. Levy, 67–125. Leiden, the Netherlands: Brill.

Élie, Hubert. [1936] 2000. *Le signifiable par complexe. La proposition et son objet. Grégoire de Rimini, Meinong, Russell*. Paris: Vrin. [Original title: Le signifiable par complexe].

Fisette, Denis. 2006. *Renaissance de la philosophie. Quatre articles de Carl Stumpf*. Paris: Vrin.

Gabriel, G. et al., eds. 1980. *Gottlob Freges Briefwechsel mit D. Hilbert, E. Husserl, B. Russell, sowie ausgewählte Einzelbriefe Freges*. Hamburg, Germany: Meiner.

Gaskin Richard. 1997. Russell and Richard Brinkley on the Unity of the Proposition. *History and Philosophy of Logic* 18:139–50.

———. 2003. '*Complexe significabilia* and Aristotle's categories'. In *La tradition médiévale des Catégories (xiie–xve siècles)*, ed. J. Biard and I. Rosier-Catach, 187–205. Louvain, Belgium: Peeters.

Gregory of Rimini. 1978. *Lectura super primum et secundum Sententiarum*, ed. D. Trapp and V. Marcolino, Vol. 1. Berlin: W. de Gruyter.

Jacobi, Klaus. 2004. 'Philosophy of language'. In *The Cambridge Companion to Abelard*, ed. J. E. Brower and K. Guilfoy, 126–56. Cambridge: Cambridge University Press.

John Buridan. 1977. *Sophismata*, ed. T. K. Scott, Stuttgart, Germany: Frommann Holzboog.

John Duns Scotus. 2004a. 'Quaestiones in primum librum Perihermeneias'. In Johannes Duns Scotus, *Quaestiones in libros Perihermenias Aristotelis; Quaestiones Super Librum Elenchorum Aristotelis*, ed. Robert R. Andrews et al., 43–132. St Bonaventure, NY: The Franciscan Institute (Opera Philosophica 2).

———. 2004b. 'Quaestiones in duos libros Perihermeneias: Primum et secundum'. In Johannes Duns Scotus, *Quaestiones in libros Perihermenias Aristotelis; Quaestiones Super Librum Elenchorum Aristotelis*, ed. Robert R. Andrews et al., 135–221. St Bonaventure, NY: The Franciscan Institute (Opera Philosophica 2).

John Wyclif. 1893. *Tractatus de logica*. Vol. 1, ed. M. Dziewicki London: Trübner.

———. 1985. *Tractatus de universalibus*, ed. I. Mueller. Oxford: Clarendon.

Karger, Elisabeth. 1995. William of Ockham, Walter Chatton and Adam Wodeham on the Objects of Knowledge and Belief. *Vivarium* 33(2):171–96.

———. 1996. Mental Sentences according to Burley and the Early Ockham. *Vivarium* 34(2):192–230.

Klima, Gyula. 1993. The Changing Role of *Entia Rationis* in Medieval Semantics and Ontology: A Comparative study with a Reconstruction. *Synthese* 96:25–58.

Kretzmann, Norman. 1970. Medieval Logicians on the Meaning of the *Propositio*. *The Journal of Philosophy* 67:767–87.

Künne, Wolfgang. 1987. 'The intentionality of thinking: The difference between state of affairs and propositional matter'. In Mulligan 1987, 175–88.

Lenz, Martin. 2003. *Mentale Sätze. Wilhelm von Ockhams Thesen zur Sprachlichkeit des Denkens*. Stuttgart, Germany: Franz Steiner Verlag.

Libera, Alain de. 2002. *La référence vide. Théories de la proposition*. Paris: Presses Universitaires de France.

Marenbon, John. 1997. *The Philosophy of Peter Abelard*. Cambridge: Cambridge University Press.

Marmo, Costantino. 1989. 'Ontology and semantics in the logic of Duns Scotus'. In *On the Medieval Theory of Signs*, ed. U. Eco, C. Marmo, 143–93. Amsterdam: John Benjamins.

Marty, Anton. 1908. *Untersuchungen zur Grundlegung der allgemeinen Grammatik und Sprachphilosophie*. Halle, Germany: Niemeyer.

Meinong, Alexius. 1971 [1904]. 'Über Gegenstandstheorie'. In *Alexius Meinong. Gesamtausgabe*, Vol. II, ed. R. Haller and R. Kindinger, 481–535. Graz, Austria: Akademischer Druck-und Verlagsanstalt.

Meinong, Alexius. 1977 [1910]. 'Über Annahmen'. In *Alexius Meinong. Gesamtausgabe*, Bd IV, ed. R. Haller and R. Kindinger, 1–384. Graz, Austria: Akademischer Druck-und Verlagsanstalt.

Morscher, Edgar and Otto Neumaier, eds. 2001. *Satz und Sachverhalt*. Sankt Augustin, Germany: Akademia Verlag.

Müller, Paola. 1997. Utrum propositio mentalis componitur ex rebus vel ex conceptibus. Un dibattito tra Ockham e Burleigh. *Veritas* 42(3):659–69.

Mulligan, Kevin. 1985. Wie die Sachen sich zueinander verhalten: Inside and Outside the Tractatus. *Theoria* 2:145–74.

———, ed. 1987. *Speech Act and Sachverhalt. Reinach and the Foundations of Realist Phenomenology*. Dordrecht, the Netherlands: Kluwer.

———, ed. 1990. *Mind, Meaning, and Metaphysics. Anton Marty's Philosophy and Theory of Language*. Dordrecht, the Netherlands: Kluwer.

Nicole Oresme. 1994. *Quaestiones super Physicam, III, 1–8*. In S. Caroti, La position de Nicole Oresme sur la nature du movement: Problèmes gnoséologiques, ontologiques, sémantiques. *Archives d'histoire doctrinale et littéraire du moyen âge* 61:303–85.

Nuchelmans, Gabriel. 1973. *Theories of the Proposition. Ancient and Medieval Conceptions of the Bearers of Truth and Falsity*. Amsterdam: North Holland Publishing Company.

———. 1980. Adam Wodeham on the Meaning of Declarative Sentences. *Historiographia Linguistica* 7:177–87.

Panaccio, Claude. 1999. *Le discours intérieur. De Platon à Guillaume d'Ockham*. Paris: Seuil.

Pérez-Ilzarbe, Paloma. 1999. *El significado de las proposiciones. Jerónimo Pardo (+1502) y las teorías medievales de la proposición*. Pamplona, Spain: Ediciones Universidad de Navarra.

Perler, Dominik. 1990. *Satztheorien. Texte zur Sprachphilosophie und Wissenschaftstheorie.* Darmstadt, Germany: Wissenschaftliche Buchgesellschaft.

———. 1992. *Der propositionale Wahrheitsbegriff im 14. Jahrhundert.* Berlin: Walter de Gruyter.

———. 1994. Late Medieval Ontologies of Facts. *The Monist* 77:149–69.

———. 2006. 'Satz, Seele und Sachverhalt. Der propositionale Wahrheitsbegriff im Spätmittelalter'. In *Die Geschichte des philosophischen Begriffs der Wahrheit,* ed. M. Enders and J. Szaif, 191–210. Berlin: Walter de Gruyter.

Peter Abelard. 2010. *Glossae super Peri hermeneias,* ed. K. Jacobi and C. Strub. Turnhout, Belgium: Brepols (Corpus Christianorum continuatio mediaevalis 206).

Peter of Ailly. 1495. *Insolubilia.* Paris: D. Roce.

Pini, Giorgio. 2002. *Categories and Logic in Duns Scotus. An Interpretation of Aristotle's Categories in Late Thirteenth Century.* Leiden, the Netherlands: Brill.

Reicher, Maria-Elisabeth, ed. 2009. *States of Affairs.* Frankfurt am Main, Germany: Ontos.

Reinach, Adolf. 1989 [1911]. 'Zur Theorie des negativen Urteils'. In *Adolf Reinach. Sämtliche Werke,* Bd. 1, ed. K. Schuhmann and B. Smith, 95–140. Munich: Philosophia Verlag.

Richard Brinkley. 1987. *Richard Brinkley's Theory of Sentential Reference.* 'De significato propositionis' *from Part V of His* 'Summa logicae', ed. M. J. Fitzgerald. Leiden, the Netherlands: Brill.

Richard Ferribridge. 1978. 'Logica seu Tractatus de veritate propositionum'. In *Pauli Veneti Logica magna. Secunda pars. Tractatus de veritate et falsitate propositionis et Tractatus de significato propositionis,* ed. F. Del Punta, 223–28. Oxford: Oxford University Press.

Robert, Aurélien. 2004. 'Les propositions singulières chez Guillaume d'Ockham'. In *Medieval Theories on Assertive and Non-Assertive Language,* ed. A. Maierù and L. Valente, 377–99. Florence: Olschki.

Robert Holkot. 1993. 'Sex articuli (Conferentiae)'. In Fritz Hoffmann, *Die 'Conferentiae' des Robert Holcot O.P. und die akademischen Auseinandersetzungen an der Universität Oxford 1330–1332,* 65–127. Münster, Germany: Aschendorff.

Rode, Christian. 2005. Sätze und Dinge. Die propositio in re bei Walter Burley und anderen. *Bochumer Philosophisches Jahrbuch für Antike und Mittelalter* 10:67–90.

Rojszczak, Artur. 2005. *From the Act of Judging to the Sentence. The Problem of Truth Bearers from Bolzano to Tarski,* ed. J. Wolenski. Dordrecht, the Netherlands: Springer.

Rollinger, Robin. 2010. *Philosophy of Language and Other Matters in the Philosophy of Anton Marty.* Amsterdam: Rodopi.

Rosier-Catach, Irène. 2004. 'Les discussions sur le signifié des propositions chez Abélard et ses contemporains'. In *Medieval Theories on Assertive and Non-Assertive Language,* ed. A. Maierú and L. Valente, 1–34. Florence: Olschki.

Russell, Bertrand. 1956. 'The philosophy of logical atomism'. In Bertrand Russell, *Logic and Knowledge,* 177–281. London: Allen and Unwin.

Salice, Alessandro. 2009. *Urteile und Sachverhalte. Ein Vergleich zwischen Alexius Meinong und Adolf Reinach.* Munich: Philosophia Verlag.

Schepers, Heinrich. 1970. Holcot contra dicta Crathorn I: Quellen, Kritik und biographische Auswertung der Bakkalareatschriften zweier Oxforder Dominikaner des XIV. Jahrhunderts. *Philosophisches Jahrbuch* 77:320–54.

———. 1972. Holcot contra dicta Crathorn II: Das significatum per propositionem: Aufbau und Kritik einer nominalistischen Theorie über den Gegenstand des Wissens. *Philosophisches Jahrbuch* 79:106–36.

Sierszulska, Anna. 2005. *Meinong on Meaning and Truth.* Frankfurt, Germany: Ontos Verlag.

Simons, Peter. 2007. 'Truth in virtue of meaning'. In *Metaphysics and Truthmakers*, ed. J. M. Monnoyer, 67–78. Frankfurt am Main, Germany: Ontos.

———. 2009. 'Why there are no states of affairs'. In *States of Affairs*, ed. M.-E. Reicher, 111–28. Frankfurt am Main: Ontos.

Smith, Barry. 1987. 'On the cognition of states of affairs'. In Mulligan 1987, 189–226.

———. 1996. 'Logic and the *Sachverhalt*'. In *The School of Franz Brentano*, ed. L. Albertazzi, M. Libardi and R. Poli, 323–41. Dordrecht, the Netherlands: Kluwer.

Spade, Paul Vincent. 1996. *Thoughts, Words and Things. An Introduction to Late Medieval Logic and Semantic Theory*. http://pvspade.com/Logic/docs/thoughts1_1a.pdf (accessed January 2011).

Stumpf, Carl. 1888. *Leitfaden der Logik*. Manuscript preserved in Leuven, Belgium, Husserl Archive Ms Q13.

———. 1907. *Zur Einteilung der Wissenschaften*, Berlin: Verlag der königlichen Akademie der Wissenschaften.

———. 1997 [1906]. 'Erscheinungen und psychische Funktionen'. In *Schriften zur Psychologie*, dir. H. Sprung and L. Sprung, 101–42. Frankfurt am Main: Peter Lang.

Süssbauer, Alfons. 1995. *Intentionalität. Sachverhalt. Noema. Eine Studie zu Edmund Husserl*. Freiburg im Breisgau, Germany: Kurt Alber.

Tachau, Katherine. 1988. *Vision and Certitude in the Age of Ockham. Optics, Epistemology and the Foundations of Semantics 1250–345*. Leiden, the Netherlands: Brill.

Thomas Aquinas. 1930. *Summa contra gentiles. Liber quartus*. Rome: Ad sedem commissionis Leoninae (Editio Leonina, vol. XV).

———. 1952. *Summa theologiae. Pars prima et Prima secundae*, ed. P. Caramelo. Turin: Marietti.

———. 1964. *In duodecim libros Metaphysicorum expositio*, ed. M.-R. Cathala and R. M. Spiazzi. Turin: Marietti.

———. 1965. *De potentia*. In *Quaestiones disputatae*. Vol. 2. ed. P. M. Pession, 7–276. Turin: Marietti.

Walter Burley. 1497. *Super artem veterem Porphyrii et Aristotelis*. Venice [contains, among other commentaries, the *Liber Praedicamentorum* and the *Liber Perihermeneias*].

———. 1973. 'Commentarius in librum Perihermeneias', ed. S. F. Brown. Walter Burley's Middle Commentary on Aristotle's Perihermeneias (Commentarius medius). *Franciscan Studies* 33:45–134.

Walter Chatton. 1989. *Reportatio et Lectura super Sententias. Collatio ad librum primum et prologus*, ed. Joseph C. Wey. Toronto: Pontifical Institute of Mediaeval Studies.

———. 2002. *Reportatio super Sententias. Liber I, distinctions 1–9*, ed. Joseph C. Wey. Toronto: Pontifical Institute of Mediaeval Studies.

Weidemann, Hermann. 1991. Sache, Satz und Sachverhalt: Zur Diskussion über das Objekt des Wissens im Spätmittelalter. *Vivarium* 39(2):129–47.

William Crathorn. 1988. *Quästionen zum ersten Sentenzenbuch*, ed. C. Hoffmann. Münster, Germany: Aschendorff.

William of Ockham. 1967. *Scriptum in librum primum Sententiarum. Ordinatio. Prologus et Distinctio Prima*, ed. G. Gál and S. Brown. St Bonaventure, NY: The Franciscan Institute (Opera theologica I).

———. 1974. *Summa logicae*, ed. Ph. Boehner et al. St Bonaventure, NY: The Franciscan Institute (Opera philosophica I).

————. 1978. *Expositio in librum Praedicamentorum Aristotelis*, ed. G. Gál. St Bonaventure, NY: The Franciscan Institute (Opera philosophica II).

————. 1980. *Quodlibeta septem*, ed. J. C. Wey. St Bonaventure, NY: The Franciscan Institute (Opera philosophica IX).

Wittgenstein, Ludwig. 1961. *Tractatus Logico-Philosophicus*, trans. D. F. Pears and B. F. McGuiness. London: Routledge.

CHAPTER 20

PARTS, WHOLES AND IDENTITY

ANDREW ARLIG

MEDIEVAL philosophers appreciate the fact that in order to account for the individuality and identity of things, one must often take into account the parts of these things. For example, in order for a house to exist, there must be some things that are not only potentially but actually parts of a house, and to be actual parts of a house, these parts must be placed in close proximity to one another and arranged in the right way. More controversially, one might think that some house is *this* house and not *that* house in virtue of the fact that it is composed out of *these* parts and not some others. And even more controversial still is the thought that this house would cease to exist if it were to lose any of these parts. It can take some work to sort through the many ways in which mereology informs and is informed by theorizing about identity and individuality. As we will see shortly, if one's theory of sameness and difference is not adequately subtle, confusions and unnecessary difficulties can flourish. And, indeed, some puzzles that seem to have vexed medieval thinkers will appear to our eyes to be sophisms. But there are other medieval puzzles that we will not need to be encouraged to appreciate.

1. IS EACH PART THE SAME AS ITS WHOLE?[1]

Many medieval puzzles concerning mereology and identity can be traced back to ancient Greek philosophical discussions.[2] We will begin with this ancient question: Is the whole the same or different from *any one of* its parts?[3] This question will probably strike the modern reader as odd, for surely a part, such as my hand, is not the same as the whole, my body. Of course, it is also false to say that my hand is utterly distinct from my body—after all, my hand is a part of my body. But if my hand is not distinct from my body, then it is not entirely different from my body. And if my hand is not entirely different from my body, then in some sense, my hand is the same as my body. Clearly, we are in danger of succumbing to sophistry if we do not take care to elucidate the precise manner in which a single part is different from, and yet not entirely distinct from, its whole. Medieval philosophers understood this need clearly, and they came up with numerous solutions. I will provide two examples.

In a question on Aristotle's *Physics*, which was once attributed to Siger of Brabant, our author queries whether the whole and the part are the same. As is standard practice in the thirteenth century, our author first outlines some prima facie reasons to believe that the whole is the same as any one of its parts and some prima facie reasons to believe that the whole is different from each of its parts. Here are the reasons to think that the whole and any one of the parts of the whole are the same:

> It seems that it is so [i.e. that the whole is the same as any one of its parts]. Those things are one whose substance is one. But the substance of the whole and of the part is one. For the parts do not possess a substance in act apart from the substance of the whole; otherwise, they would be substantially distinct entities. Nor would the whole be one substantial being. Therefore, [the whole and the part are the same]. Moreover, according to the reasoning of the Commentator [viz. Averroes], if the whole is other than this part, for the same reason [the whole] is other from this part and from that part and so for forth for all the [remaining parts]. Therefore, all the parts will be other than the whole (*aliae a toto*). But there is no whole except all its parts (*nisi omnes eius partes*). Therefore, the whole will be other than the whole.[4]

Hence, it seems that the whole is the same as any one of its parts. Our author then presents some reasons to assert the opposite. Here is the most interesting argument:

> Moreover, suppose this part is the same as the whole and that part is the same as the whole. Since each of [these parts] is the same with respect to one and the same [whole], they are the same with respect to one another. It follows that all the parts in relation to themselves will be the same and, thus, the whole will be something indivisible, possessing no sort of diversity.[5]

If a part P_1 were the same as the whole, and a part P_2 were also the same as the whole, then it would follow that two distinct parts, P_1 and P_2, are the same. Worse, still, if there is no difference between P_1 and P_2, and P_1 and P_2 are the parts of the whole, then it follows that the whole has no real parts. 'P_1' is just another name for the whole; it does not name something less than the whole. Hence, given the generality of the discussion, all wholes *really* will be indivisible things. (I say 'really' because the argument does not preclude the possibility that the whole is divisible in some conventional manner.) But surely my left hand is not the same as my right hand, nor can it be the case that really my body is not a composite.

On the one hand, the part cannot be different from its whole; otherwise, the whole would fail to be one (and for that matter, the part would fail to be a part of that whole). On the other hand, the part cannot be the same as the whole since that would entail that the hand and the foot are the same, and worse, that the whole has no parts. The author proposes to solve the puzzle by utilizing a distinction that he finds in Aristotle's *Sophistical Refutations*, namely, the distinction between predication *per se*, or *simpliciter*, and predication with respect to something (*secundum quid*):

> Hence, I say that the whole is not the same as this part in the primary sense, but that it is the same as this part with respect to this part (*secundum hanc partem*), and thus, with respect to something (*secundum quid*). Furthermore, the whole is the same as a different part with respect to a different part (e.g. a man is the same as the foot with respect to the foot), and with respect to this part [the whole] is different from another part. Accordingly, the whole is the same as this part with respect to something, and it is also different from that part with respect to something, and hence, this part is different from another part. Thus, the whole in one manner is the same as the part, and in another manner different. And, thus, it is not different from a part unless on account of the difference of a part to a part. Therefore, since the whole does not differ from a part unless on account of the difference of another part, it follows that [the whole] is the same as the part essentially, yet different with respect to something.[6]

A part P_1 is not utterly distinct from the whole since if the whole were utterly distinct from P_1, then that whole would not be the whole that consists of P_1 and the other parts. But P_1 is not identical to the whole since the whole contains parts that are not identical with P_1. Hence, P_1 is the same as the whole in a qualified way, namely, with respect to P_1. Accordingly, P_1 is the same as the whole with respect to P_1, and another part P_2 is the same as the whole with respect to P_2. But P_1 is not the same as P_2 with respect to P_1. Nor is P_1 the same as P_2 with respect to P_2. Hence, P_1 and P_2 are different. This is precisely what we would hope for. Socrates's hand is the same as Socrates in a respect, and hence, Socrates's hand and Socrates are not distinct. But Socrates's hand is not the same, even in a qualified way, as his foot. The hand and the foot are absolutely different.

The distinction between *per se* predications and predications *secundum quid* can be quite useful. Consider Aristotle's well-worn example: It is false to say that an Ethiopian whose teeth are white is white *simpliciter*; nevertheless, an Ethiopian is white *with respect to his teeth* (*secundum dentes*).[7] In the case of the Ethiopian, the distinction between predication *simpliciter* and predication *secundum quid* has some measure of plausibility, but that is because the distinction is based on the way that the properties of a thing inhere in the parts of that thing. The Ethiopian is not white *simpliciter* because many of his exterior parts are not white. He is white with respect to his teeth because some of his parts—namely, the teeth—are white. (Notice as well that it is false to say that the Ethiopian has no share in whiteness—again, since some of his parts do participate in whiteness.) In short, the *simpliciter/secundum quid* distinction is plausible insofar as it is explained in terms of the properties of the parts of the subject. But given that this is true, it is not illuminating to claim that a part P_1 is the same as the whole with respect to being the part P_2, or that that P_1 is not the same as P_2 with respect to being the part P_1. In order to apply the distinction between predication of sameness *simpliciter* and sameness *secundum quid* to the whole as such and its parts as such, it seems that we need to find yet another fact that grounds the distinction.

What might help would be the notion of mereological overlap. If our author had that notion, he could separate cases where A and B do not overlap from cases where A and B are merely different because they do not coincide.[8] It is unclear why the author of the question on the *Physics* does not draw this distinction. But the phenomenon of mereological overlap was not unknown to medieval thinkers. When the twelfth-century philosopher Peter Abelard turns his attention to rationalising the relations between the Persons of the Trinity, he pushes to one side the framework of sameness and difference that he finds in Boethius's treatment of the Trinity, and he develops his own elaborate and unique theory of sameness and difference.[9] Items can be the same or different (1) in number or *essentia*, (2) in definition, (3) in 'property', (4) in likeness (*similitudine*) and (5) with respect to change.[10] Much could be said about these different modes, and indeed, much has already been said about the notion of something being different from another in property, since this mode of difference seems to offer us an insight into the relation between a statue and the clay out of which it is made.[11] But for our purposes, the key mode of sameness and difference is the first.

Abelard's ingenious solution to the problem of whether a whole is numerically the same as its part is to ground numerical sameness and difference in the more basic relations of sameness and difference in *essentia*. In this part of Abelard's works, a thing's *essentia* should not be thought of as that thing's quiddity, but rather its concrete being.[12] Thus, in Abelard's view, my *essentia* just is the composite of all my material bits and some forms. Given that my *essentia* is a composite, Abelard insists that we must keep track of these parts when we are determining whether some things are the same or different in *essentia*. Specifically, according to Abelard, A is the same in *essentia* as B if and only if the *essentia* of A coincides with the *essentia* of B.[13] Discrete things, such as Socrates and Plato, clearly fail to coincide mereologically, and hence, they are different in *essentia*. Yet, given that mereological coincidence is necessary for essential sameness, A and B can differ in *essentia* even if some parts are shared. For example, Socrates's hand is different in *essentia* from Socrates. This is true because, while Socrates's hand is included along with the other parts 'in the quantity of the whole', the quantity of Socrates's hand's *essentia* does not exhaust the quantity of Socrates's *essentia*.

Using this understanding of the *essentia* of composite things, Abelard develops the following account of numerical sameness and numerical difference:[14]

> A is numerically the same as B if and only if A is the same in *essentia* as B.
> A is different in *essentia* from B if and only if the *essentia* of A does not coincide with the *essentia* of B.

> *A* is numerically different from *B* if and only if the *essentia* of *A* does not overlap with the *essentia* of *B*.

An important implication of Abelard's theory is that Socrates's hand and Socrates are neither numerically the same nor numerically distinct.

> This should be noted: in every case, if one is the same in *essentia* as another, then the one is numerically the same as the other, and vice versa. Nevertheless, it is not always true that, if one is different in *essentia* from another, they are numerically diverse from one another (as we had already said). For example, a part is different in *essentia* from its whole, but it is not numerically different. *But perhaps it is not the case [that the part is] numerically the same, unless someone says 'numerically the same' in a negative manner—i.e. 'not numerically distinct'.*[15]

Socrates's hand is different in *essentia* from Socrates, since the *essentia* of his hand does not coincide with his *essentia*. Nevertheless, the *essentia* of his hand overlaps with his *essentia* since every part of his hand overlaps with a part of him. Hence, Socrates's hand is not numerically distinct from Socrates, and yet Socrates's hand is not numerically the same as Socrates.

According to Abelard the proposition that *A* is not numerically the same as *B* does not entail the proposition that *A* and *B* are numerically different. This might at first seem to be an outlandish result. It is true that Abelard is using the words 'numerically the same' and 'numerically different' in unfamiliar ways. But if we reflect for a moment, the theory is not incoherent, and as it happens, Abelard's theory of identity anticipates a contemporary proposal by David Armstrong, who claims that mereology 'may be thought of as an extended logic of identity, extended to deal with such cases of partial identity'.[16] What Armstrong means is that strict numerical identity and strict numerical difference are the endpoints of a spectrum of cases. Between these endpoints, we find cases of more or less extensive overlap. The case of Socrates and his hand is one of many of these in-between cases.

For that matter, there are good reasons why medieval thinkers should have considered speaking of numerical sameness and difference in Abelard's funny way. With Abelard's mereological characterisation of numerical sameness and difference, we are better equipped to describe the complex set of relations that hold between a thing and its parts. For example, it is true on Abelard's account that any two non-overlapping parts of a whole are numerically different from one another. My right hand is numerically different from my left hand. At the same time, my right hand is not numerically different from me, and my left hand is not numerically different from me. Nevertheless, it does not turn out that my left hand is numerically the same as my right hand because being not numerically different does not entail numerical sameness. Hands, like all parts of wholes, are not numerically different from their bodies and they are not numerically the same. The observation that my hand is not numerically the same as my body prevents the sophistical conclusion that the right hand is numerically the same as the left hand.

2. The Whole Is Nothing Other than Its Parts

We have seen that medieval thinkers were very much attuned to the special link between a part and its whole. Medieval philosophers were also aware of the special link between a whole and all the parts taken together. Indeed, some medieval thinkers were inclined to think that the whole just is its parts and that they are it. Abelard, as it happens, claims that a whole is 'nothing other than' its parts taken together.[17] As we will see in the final section of this chapter, Abelard does not mean that there is no new fact about the world when the parts are brought together. Nevertheless, it is a striking and substantive claim about the whole and its parts, for Abelard is asserting that the whole is no new *thing* in addition to the things that are its parts.

Abelard never to my knowledge defends this proposition, but we could perhaps motivate it on his behalf. Consider some composite, such as a pile of stones. What is this pile? Abelard reasonably would reply that it is a specific collection of stones that are more or less located in the same place and at the same time. Take away a stone, and strictly speaking, you have a different pile since the original group of stones that was located here is not identical to the group of stones that is now here.

Now consider a house. To make a house, we need some materials—say, some bricks, boards, nails and cement. We also need to arrange these materials. Medieval thinkers would say that we must add a house *form* to the materials. So what is the house? It seems that the only plausible answer is that the house is the materials plus the house form. Account for all the particular materials—that is, identify the sum of the material parts—and account for the form, and you will thereby account for this house. One might even think it is the house form that will account for the identity and individuality of the house. Specifically, unlike the pile that loses a stone, one might think that if a house loses a stone, the house form guarantees that the remaining materials will continue to be this house. Yet, Abelard thinks that the house form does not guarantee that the materials will remain this house. Rather, *this* particular house form depends upon *these* particular parts for its existence. For Abelard, the house form is merely the way in which the things that constitute the house are disposed.

> For as it has been said, matter now actually conjoined to form is nothing other than this material thing (*materiatum*)—for example, this golden ring is nothing other than gold manipulated into a round shape, and this house is [nothing other] than these timbers and these stones to which this arrangement is superadded.[18]

The arrangement of the house is not a *thing* (*res/essentia*), and only things can be parts of the house. Moreover, the identity of the arrangement of these parts depends upon these parts. Hence, the right sort of arrangement will make a specific sum of parts a house, but it will not make different sums of parts the same house. This means that the loss of even one stone will compromise the existence of *this* house, which is only these parts arranged in such-and-such manner.

We should note that Abelard is not committed to the view that when one removes a stone, the remaining parts automatically will be bereft of the sort of arrangement that is needed in order to have a house.

> We do [not] say that if this little stone is removed, that *a* house would not remain in the rest of the parts; rather, that *this* [house], namely, the one that is constituted out of this little stone and the additional parts, would not remain.[19]

When we remove a stone from this house, *a* house might still exist since the remaining timbers and stones may still be arranged in such-and-such manner. But the collection of the remaining stones and timbers arranged housewise is not the same thing as the collection of this stone and all the remaining stones and timbers arranged housewise.[20] If there is any difference in the set of parts, one has a different house.

Piles, aggregates in general and artefacts are, hence, no things other than their parts. But like most medieval thinkers, Abelard conceded that there is a difference between, on the one hand, aggregates and artefacts, and on the other hand, substances. The difference is due to the difference between accidental forms and substantial forms. Almost every medieval philosopher believed that there was a difference between artefact construction and substantial generation. Indeed, Abelard believed that all substantial generation comes about through God's agency. No human could ever create a substance; humans could merely place substances close together.[21] When a substantial form combines with some things, a new thing is created. And in this sense, a substance is some thing other than that out of which it is created. But, interestingly, Abelard distinguishes between parts and ingredients.[22] 'Ingredients' is the label that I give for Abelard's notion of that out of which something comes to be. The parts are in a sense some of that out of which a thing is, and hence, all parts are ingredients. But not all ingredients are parts, since in order for *A* to be a part of *B*, *A* must still be present in *B* after composition. For example, the flour, water and eggs are ingredients of the bread, and the tree is an ingredient of the house, but none of these are parts. So, a substance is something other than its ingredients. But it is not clear whether a substance is something other than its parts. All that Abelard tells us is that 'the matter of a cadaver is not a man, but these limbs which when they were ensouled had been a man'.[23] This is ambiguous. Are there limbs present only when the soul is imbuing the body—which is the classic Aristotelian thesis of homonymy—or is Abelard merely claiming that a man exists only when there are some limbs, there is a soul, and this soul actually enlivens the limbs?

In general, Abelard wonders whether the whole is nothing other than its 'integral' parts. In later medieval discussions, philosophers often distinguish the substantial form and the matter from the other parts of a substance, designating them as 'essential' or 'substantial' parts. Let us compare substantial parts to one other category of part identified by Walter Burley, namely, the parts derived from the form (*partes secundum formam*).[24] Parts derived from the form are usually found in living things, and they are defined in terms of the functions of the animal; hence, for convenience, we can call them functional parts. Functional parts are derivative parts for which the principle of homonymy holds. Once removed from the eye socket, this fleshy orb is no longer an eye other than in name. Once the animal is dead, the remaining material thing is a body only in name. In contrast to the functional parts, the essential parts are the parts that make a whole substance what it is, and it is upon the substantial form (or, for many thinkers, forms[25]) and the matter that this sort of whole depends for its existence. One might think that the proper account of the composition of a whole should make mention only of its essential parts since all other kinds of parts are either derivative of these or superfluous. Hence, is it the case that the whole is nothing other than its essential parts?

As it turns out, even if we restrict our attention to substances and their essential parts, there is no medieval consensus as to whether the whole is nothing other than its parts. Duns Scotus, for example, argues that a composite substance must be some absolute thing that is really distinct from its matter, its substantial forms, its relational forms and any collection of two or more of these parts.[26] The arguments that Scotus uses to support this claim are complicated.[27] But Scotus's basic strategy relies upon the common Aristotelian principle that there are different degrees of unity, and in particular, that the unity of an aggregate is weaker than the unity of a substance.[28] Scotus takes the claim that a composite substance is no other thing than all the essential parts taken together to be equivalent to the thesis that an individual composite substance is merely the aggregate of all its individual essential parts. But surely that cannot be correct since if a substance were nothing other than its forms and its matter, then there would be no way to distinguish the unity of a substance from the unity of an aggregate.[29]

While Scotus's basic strategy relies upon an Aristotelian assumption about unity, Scotus also offers an argument that should have a general appeal since it is a specific application of a compelling challenge to any view that understands all mereological composition in terms of aggregation or compounds. Consider a simple ham sandwich.[30] The sandwich consists of one slice of ham, one slice of cheese and two slices of bread. But surely if I were to scatter the ham, cheese and bread across my room, the ham sandwich would not exist, even though the ham, the cheese, and the bread still do. Using more or less the same line of reasoning, Scotus insists that if a composite substance is nothing other than its essential parts, then it should not be possible that the composite be destroyed while both its parts exist. But, in Scotus's view, matter and substantial forms can exist independently of each other, and so, it is possible that the composite can be destroyed while its substantial parts still exist. A natural answer to this sort of challenge is to claim that the composite is not merely the substantial forms and the matter, it is the forms and the matter standing in the right relation R to one another.[31] Unfortunately, this will not help. The relation R is itself a separable thing, which means that it, too, could exist independently of the whole. So, the proposition that the composite substance is nothing other than its substantial forms, the matter and a relation is equivalent to the proposition that the substance is an aggregate of these three elements. The revised analysis of composition will fall afoul of the same arguments that Scotus used against the original position. Therefore, Scotus reasons, the composite substance is some third, absolute being, which is not only different from the parts taken singularly, but also other than both of the parts when taken together.[32]

William of Ockham rejects Scotus's position. The forms and the matter are by their nature such that, unless impeded, they would create the appropriate sort of unity, a unity greater than that of an aggregate.[33] There is, hence, no pressure to posit a new thing that is really distinct from the essential parts of the substance.

There is, of course, much more that could be said about this debate between Scotus and Ockham, but I will not pursue the arguments any further, in part because I believe that this has been adequately done elsewhere.[34] Instead, I wish to take a different path and investigate some of the consequences of the position that the whole is nothing other than its parts. In particular, it appears that the idea that a whole is nothing other than its parts prompted some medieval thinkers to also assert that a whole depends upon all of its parts for its persistence.

3. PERSISTENCE

Abelard asserts that a whole is 'nothing other than' its parts, by which he means that a whole is no *thing* other than its parts. Add his belief that many of the forms of things are results of the configuration of a specific set of parts, and it is easy to see why Abelard would be tempted by the thought that wholes are not only individuated by their parts, but that they also existentially depend upon their parts.

The thesis that a whole existentially depends upon its parts is commonly called the doctrine of mereological essentialism. James Van Cleve has helpfully noted that, in fact, there are three grades of mereological essentialism:[35]

1. A whole cannot survive the destruction of a part.
2. A whole cannot survive the removal of a part.
3. A whole cannot survive the rearrangement of its parts.

Abelard explicitly considers endorsing grades 1 and 2. For example, in one discussion in his *Dialectica*, Abelard argues that the position that a whole is nothing other than its parts taken together entails the further position that if a specific whole W consists of parts $P_1, P_2, \ldots P_n$, then for every time t, W exists at t only if $P_1, P_2, \ldots P_n$ all exist at t.

> Therefore, anyone who attributes existence (*existentiam*) to this house thereby concedes the same to this little stone and all the other parts taken together, because this house is nothing other than this stone and all the additional parts taken together. Thus, when this house exists, it must be the case that this little stone and all the additional parts taken together [exist].[36]

But if it is the case that, for every time t, W exists at t only if $P_1, P_2, \ldots P_n$ all exist at t, it would seem to follow that W ceases to exist at some particular moment t_n when P_1 is destroyed at t_n.

But if this collection of all [these parts] exists all at once, it necessarily follows that this little stone exists. For if this little stone is not, the collection of all [these parts]—that is, the [collection] of this little stone and the rest taken together—is not. Therefore, if this house is, this little stone is. Thus, if this little stone is not, this house is not.[37]

Abelard's understanding of the claim that the whole is nothing other than its parts is remarkable since his starting assumption entails a dramatic thesis, namely, that if any little stone in the wall of this house is destroyed, then this house is destroyed—and we mean that it is destroyed 'in substance', not merely altered cosmetically. Moreover, for reasons too complicated to elaborate here, Abelard has argued that even if a stone is removed (but not destroyed), this house ceases to exist.[38]

To many a modern thinker, Abelard's claim about houses will seem remarkable enough. But for medieval Aristotelians, this claim about houses, or any other arte-fact, would be less than shocking. Artefacts are accidental unities; the kind of unity they possess is only slightly stronger than that of heaps and certainly much weaker than that of substances. So, it would not be too great of a shock for an Aristotelian to learn that artefacts are mereologically unstable. But after Abelard discusses the instability of houses, he explores the possibility that human beings are also similarly unstable. Here, however, his remarks are terse and hard to interpret.[39] Moreover, Abelard says next to nothing about non-human substances. Hence, it is unclear whether Abelard thinks that mereological essentialism holds for aggregates and artefacts alone, or whether he is willing to say that mereological essentialism holds for substances as well.

We have evidence that Abelard embraces a version of mereological essen-tialism of at least grade 2. Given what Abelard thinks about the forms of artefacts—namely, that they depend upon the configuration of a specific set of parts—it seems that Abelard should also endorse a version of grade 3 mereological essen-tialism for artefacts. Abelard never explicitly endorses grade 3 mereological essen-tialism. Yet, Abelard's basic premises do seem to be at the root of some positions endorsed by some of his followers, namely, the so-called Nominales. For example, in an anonymous commentary on the *Categories*, which is most likely from the later twelfth century (or perhaps the earliest part of the thirteenth), its author states the following position:

[. . .] we say that every removal and every addition of a part, and every transpo-sition of parts alters the *essentia* of the whole. But that which is sick cannot cease to be sick unless either some part is subtracted from or added to it or some of [the parts] have been transposed. Therefore, it cannot cease to be sick unless it ceases to be. And, thus, it cannot be healthy.[40]

These remarks are consistent with other evidence that the Nominales defended a strong version of mereological essentialism, or as they put it, that 'nothing grows' (*nihil crescit*).[41]

So, Abelard claims that 'no thing possesses more parts at one time than at an-other'.[42] This appears to be an assertion that grade 2 mereological essentialism holds for a significant range of objects—certainly, aggregates and artefacts, perhaps other wholes as well. There is also reason to believe that Abelard is logically committed to a version of grade 3 mereological essentialism. But I should mention two important caveats.

First, as Van Cleve points out, the three grades as stated are 'merely temporal versions of essentialism'. A 'full-blooded' version of mereological essentialism should tell us what mereological changes are compatible with the survival of a whole through various possible worlds. The following are full-blooded statements of grades 1 and 2:[43]

1. If *P* is part of *W*, then *P* exists in every possible world in which *W* exists.
2. If *P* is part of *W*, then *P* is part of *W* in every possible world in which *W* exists.

It is not clear that Abelard had a clear enough understanding of synchronic alternative possibilities to make sense of the distinction between the temporal claims and the full-blooded modal claims.[44] Given that it is not clear that Abelard has the resources to distinguish between temporal and modal claims, one might want to avoid saying that, strictly speaking, Abelard is a mereological *essentialist*. To satisfy those who have this worry, from this point forward I will say that Abelard and his followers are committed to various grades of the doctrine of *mereological rigidity*.

The second caveat is that Abelard might have changed his mind. In Abelard's commentary on the *Categories*, he seems to offer a different analysis of survival:

> However, perhaps [the problem of increase] can easily be solved this way, namely, if we say that the thing that increases is that which transforms by means of the addition of something else into the sort of composite which does not retreat from its nature or property, just as if some water is added to water, the water to which there has been an addition transforms into some specific composition which is also called water.[45]

Abelard might be saying that a whole can gain or lose parts and yet survive, provided that it retains its distinctive property or nature.[46] This passage does not need to be understood in this manner, and in fact, I think the solution offered in this passage is consistent with the thesis of mereological rigidity.[47] The proper interpretation of this passage from the *Categories* commentary cannot be determined here, but no matter how we end up reading this passage, this seems true: At some stage in his career, Abelard seriously considered the doctrine of mereological rigidity, and in these moments he countenanced applying the doctrine to not only artefacts, but also human beings.

Abelard is not the only medieval philosopher who entertained the thesis of mereological rigidity. Medieval logicians routinely considered a 'maximal proposition'—that is, roughly, a proposition that warrants inferences—which can be rendered as follows:

> For any *P* such that *P* is a part of an integral whole *W*, if *P* is not, then *W* is not.

On its face, this proposition seems to imply mereological rigidity, and some medieval logicians at least flirted with this implication. For instance, here is what the thirteenth-century logician Radulphus Brito has to say about the maximal proposition:

> But, on the contrary, from the parts to the whole [the proposition] holds destruc-
> tively, because when even one part is destroyed, the form of the whole does not
> remain. But because each part is required for the being of the whole, it follows
> that [the maximal proposition from part to whole holds destructively].[48]

At first, it might seem that Radulphus is endorsing universal mereological rigidity, but in fact, it is unclear what specific metaphysical conclusions we should infer. The example of an *integral* whole that Radulphus gives is a house. But trees, cats and human beings may be substantial or essential wholes, and not integral wholes. Another possibility is that my cat may be considered either insofar as it is a material whole or insofar as it is a 'formal' whole (*totum secundum formam*).[49] A material whole is a specific aggregate of matter, and it is subject to mereological rigidity. A formal whole is a thing delimited by a substantial form, and according to some, a cat insofar as it is a formal whole can gain and lose parts. Finally, Radulphus may be contrasting a thing's wholeness with its being incomplete, or 'mutilated'. One of the senses of 'whole' that Aristotle identifies is the sense in which a thing has everything that it should have.[50] If this is the idea behind Radulphus's notion of a thing having a 'form of the whole', then a thing can fail to have all the parts it should have and yet still persist.

Whereas many of these logicians' treatments are intriguing yet ambiguous, we do find some later medieval philosophers explicitly working out the metaphysics of persistence, and the results are often surprising. John Buridan, for example, distinguishes between three senses of 'being numerically the same'.[51] In order for A to be 'totally' the same in number as B, it must be the case that A is B, and 'nothing is of the integrity of this [A] which is not of the integrity of that [B] and vice versa'. But even if A and B do not meet this strict criterion, A can be 'partially' the same as B if A is a part of B or if the major or principal part of B is preserved in A. And, finally, A and B can be the same in a 'less proper' sense provided that there is a continuous succession of different parts proceeding from one to the other.

With this distinction in place, Buridan is able to identify the precise manner in which one thing is numerically the same as something else. Careful reflection on the definition of total numerical sameness reveals that only incorruptible things can be numerically identical over time in this sense of numerical sameness. Corruptible things, by contrast, are constantly gaining and losing material bits, and this constant flow of bits in and bits out prevents these things from being totally numerically identical:

> The second conclusion is this: the precise thing which is Socrates today is not
> totally the same as that which precisely was Socrates yesterday, because some
> parts have flowed out from that which precisely was Socrates yesterday, and some
> parts have flowed in from the outside. In this manner [he] is not totally the same
> before and after, if anything has been removed and anything has been added. And
> this is justified just as it was argued above: That which precisely was Socrates
> yesterday is A, and let us call that which accrues to him, due to the fact that it has
> been added, B. It stands that now Socrates is the composite of A and B. Therefore,

> Socrates is not totally the same as *A*, and yet yesterday he was totally the same as that which is *A*. Thus, it remains that Socrates now is not totally the same as that which was Socrates yesterday.[52]

Note Buridan's assumption that a whole is nothing other than its parts. When I use the name 'Socrates' today to refer to a whole (*A and B*), I cannot be using it to name the very same whole that I was referring to yesterday (namely, *A*) since *A and B* is not *A*. *A* can never be anything other than *A*, *B* can never be anything other than *B* and *A and B* can never be anything other than *A and B*.

Three-year-old Socrates is not totally the same in number as the thirty-year-old Socrates. But this does not trouble Buridan. Socrates has a different set of persistence conditions. Three-year-old Socrates and thirty-year-old Socrates are partially the same in number since the most principal part of three-year-old Socrates, namely, his intellective soul, is the most principal part of thirty-year-old Socrates.[53] While matter has flowed in and flowed away, Socrates's intellective soul has remained the same. Hence, we are entitled to claim that three-year-old Socrates is numerically the same as thirty-year-old Socrates in the sense that three-year-old Socrates is partially the same as thirty-year-old Socrates.

Other things are said to be the same in number in the third, less proper sense. For example, the river at t_1 and the river at t_2 are neither totally nor even partially the same in number. We, instead, must say that this river is the same as that river in the sense that the river at t_2 is connected to the river at t_1 through a continuous succession of watery parts.

Perhaps it is no shock to learn that the river at t_1 and the river at t_2 (both of which we call the Seine) are not even partially the same river. But it probably is a surprise to learn that in Buridan's view the horse born in 2000 and the one that is in the stable in 2010 are the same merely in virtue of a succession of parts.

> Therefore, the name 'Browny' [viz. the name of a horse] is a discrete name of a proper quality, just as that the name 'Seine' is. And it must be conceded on account of this that in some manner [something], for which the name supposits, remains the same in number. But I believe that this 'numerical' identity should be understood in terms of a continuous succession of parts accruing to a new thing, while the previous parts go away, so that if I say 'The Seine has lasted for a thousand years', the sense is this: Some parts have continuously replaced other parts for a thousand years. And the same applies as well to a horse and a dog, given that [a horse, for example] remains always the same, or similar in appearance, throughout this sort of succession [of parts].[54]

If throughout the succession of parts that occurs from year zero to year ten there is a horse, then we are entitled to say that the horse has remained the same. However, the horse now in the stable is only causally related by a continuous series of inflowing and, then, out-flowing bits to the horse born in 2000.

At this point, one might have the impression that Buridan is distinguishing between a 'strict' sense of identity, which we must use when speaking as philosophers, and a 'loose' sense of identity, which we may use when speaking with the vulgar. But it is far from clear that this is Buridan's intention, and it is fairly certain that he did not want to appear to his contemporaries to be someone expressing such a view. In 1277 a list of prohibited propositions was imposed at the University of Paris. Among the theses explicitly condemned was the following:

> That a man through nourishment can become someone else, both numerically and individually.[55]

Like all subsequent masters of arts, Buridan would have taken great care to not endorse a condemned proposition. Thus, it should not be surprising to learn that in his commentary on Aristotle's *Physics*, Buridan presents the three senses of numerical sameness in order to 'easily solve' the problem of whether 'Socrates is today the same that he was yesterday'. He notes that *if* the only criterion available were the one used to determine whether *A* is totally the same as *B*, then the old and the new Socrateses would not be numerically the same man, but in fact, there is another perfectly legitimate sense of being numerically the same, one that allows us to say truthfully that the child Socrates is numerically the same as the elder Socrates. In short, Buridan insists that different criteria for persistence apply to different kinds of beings. He is not claiming that the only legitimate sense of numerical sameness is the sense in which changeless objects are numerically the same.[56]

Notice, however, how close someone like Buridan is to making the conceptual leap to the position that not only rivers but also humans and horses 'persist' merely in a loose and popular sense of the word, and hence, a leap to a radically new way of conceiving of substances.[57] Buridan's definition of total numerical sameness is the closest analogue to our contemporary notion of identity. If one were to think that 'numerical sameness' must be interpreted as total numerical sameness, and if one assumed that total numerical sameness is transitive (as our notion of identity is), then it is easy to see how one would be led to the conclusion that the three-year-old human being that we name 'Socrates' is 'really' not the same man as the thirty-year-old human being, and that the cat on the mat in 2000 is 'really' not the same cat as the cat on the mat in 2010. Viewed in this light, one could see Buridan as yet another medieval who was unwilling to take the radical conceptual leap that was eventually taken by philosophers in the seventeenth century (or as someone who was too afraid of the Church to say what he really thought). But perhaps, instead, we should see this as a case where Enlightenment and contemporary metaphysicians have largely ignored a promising way to defuse problems of material constitution and persistence over time.

4. COMPOSITION AND IDENTITY

A significant group of medieval thinkers held that a whole is 'nothing other than' its parts, and some of these thinkers understood that this commitment might entail some rather remarkable propositions, ones that we have compared to mereological essentialism. But at this point, we need to clarify precisely what medieval philosophers mean when they assert that a whole is nothing other than its parts, or that the whole just is its parts and that they are it.

One way to understand this claim would be to interpret it as the assertion that 'composition is identity'—that is, that the whole is numerically identical (in the strictest of senses) to the sum of its parts.[58] But it is not clear that every whole is a sum. Let $P_1, P_2, \ldots P_n$ be the nails, boards, bricks and so forth that could make up a house. $P_1, P_2, \ldots P_n$ taken altogether are a mereological sum, but they might not be a house. Indeed, 'taken altogether' need not even imply that, for example, P_1 and P_2 are in the same location, let alone touching one another. $P_1, P_2, \ldots P_n$ may be scattered throughout the universe. All that needs to be true in order for the sum of P_1, $P_2, \ldots P_n$ to exist is that P_1 exists, P_2 exists and $\ldots P_n$ exists. If we combine this understanding of sums with the thesis that composition is identity, we get a very strong position, namely, that there is *no difference at all* between a thing and the sum of that thing's parts.

Yet, we have already seen that when someone like Abelard or Ockham says that the house is nothing other than its parts, he is not asserting that the sum of all the parts or even the act of aggregating these parts is sufficient to create a whole in all cases. Sometimes composition requires something more. In other words, in many cases, philosophers like Abelard and Ockham must offer a moderate answer to what contemporary metaphysicians refer to as the 'special composition question'.

The special composition question asks not for an explanation of what composition is, but rather for a specification of precisely when composition occurs.[59] Put somewhat more rigorously, the question is this:

> What necessary and jointly sufficient conditions must any Xs satisfy in order for it to be the case that there is an object composed of those Xs?[60]

The answer is expected to take the following form:

> Necessarily, for any non-overlapping Xs, there is an object composed of the Xs if and only if . . .

Universalism and Nihilism are the extremes of a range of answers that one might provide to the question.[61] The Universalist asserts that there is an object composed of the Xs whenever there are some Xs. The Nihilist answer to the special composition question is that the Xs never compose something.

As it happens, if the special composition question had been posed to medieval thinkers, some of them might have given responses that echo Universalism and Nihilism. For example, the infamous but elusive eleventh-century thinker Roscelin of Compiègne might have been a Nihilist, since we are told that he held the 'insane' view that 'no thing is composed of parts' and that all talk of parts is really talk about 'utterances', not things.[62] In some *sententiae* attributed to Abelard, some arguments (also possibly derived from Roscelin) are reported that attempt to prove that 'whole' is merely a word.[63] A careful inspection of the arguments reveals that their realist opponents believe that any plurality of things is a whole thing. The Roscelinians attempt to exploit this belief to show that no whole is a thing.[64] On the face of it, the proposition that every plurality of things is a whole is equivalent to Universalism, and interestingly enough, Abelard holds that every plurality of things is a whole.[65]

So, at first blush, Abelard is a Universalist. Yet, Abelard's position is importantly nuanced. Universalism, as it is usually conceived, is in a sense conservative. Specifically, it presumes that there is only one mode of composition.[66] Yet, like most medieval mereologists, Abelard claims that there are different kinds of wholes, and hence, he does not think that there is only one mode of composition.[67] For Abelard, if there are some Xs, the Xs compose a 'plurality'. If the Xs are close together in space, then the Xs also compose an aggregate. In the case of pluralities and aggregates, the Xs not only compose the whole, they are the whole. That is, for wholes of these types, composition is identity. But under certain other conditions, the Xs can compose something that is more than a mere collection or aggregate, namely, a whole with structure. And it is in these cases that Abelard—and as we will see shortly, also Ockham—will concede that while the Xs compose the structured whole, the Xs are not identical to this whole.

Now it might seem that medieval philosophers in general would answer the special composition question in much the same way that Peter Van Inwagen has answered the question:

> Necessarily, for any non-overlapping X's, there is an object composed of the X's if and only if either (1) the activities of the X's constitute a life or (2) there is only one of the X's.[68]

There is an affinity between Van Inwagen and Aristotelians because, like Van Inwagen, the Aristotelian asserts that there is a dog composed of the Xs only if the Xs together function in the way that dogs distinctively function. But Van Inwagen's answer is much more stringent than medieval Aristotelian views of composition, even those held by anti-realists like Abelard and Ockham. Van Inwagen is committed to the view that there are ('really') no artefacts or non-living composite things. That is, with respect to putatively composite non-living things, Van Inwagen is an *eliminativist*: strictly speaking the boards, bricks, nails and so forth do not compose a house since these items do not constitute a life. Nevertheless, when the boards, bricks, nails and so forth are arranged 'housewise', we are entitled to say in our everyday discourse that 'There is a house'.

I find no evidence in the writings of Abelard or Ockham which shows that they think that 'really' there are no houses.[69] Rather, they will admit that houses are real wholes that happen to have a lesser grade of unity than substances such as trees and cats. Hence, at least in the case of artefacts, Ockham and Abelard answer the special composition question in more or less this manner:

> For any non-overlapping X's, there is an object composed of the X's if and only if the Xs exist and the Xs stand in the appropriate relations with respect to one another.[70]

For instance, Ockham claims that the whole is the matter and the form 'conjoined all at once and united' (*simul iunctis et unitis*). Notice how Ockham continues:

> And concerning composites which are one *per se*, it is true without restriction
> (*simpliciter*) that everyone of these are their parts all at once and conjoined, so
> that this whole is not unless its parts exist all at once. But concerning artifacts it is
> different, since one part can remain and be distinguished from the others, so that
> the parts can be all at once in the natural course of things even though they are
> not united. And thus this whole is not always and necessarily these parts when
> they exist, but rather it is only these parts when they exist when the parts are in
> the required manner united and arranged locally and suitably. However, when
> they are separated or locally arranged in an unsuitable manner, then the whole
> (for example a house) is not these parts.[71]

For substances, the whole is identical to the sum of the essential parts. A substance
is nothing other than its essential parts since if these two parts exist, they will immediately (barring a supernatural act) conjoin and be the composite substance.[72] In
other words, Ockham can (if he wants) assert the stronger thesis that composition
is identity for composites of essential parts since there will not be a case in the natural course of things that mirrors the problem of a house in relation to its house
parts—that is, where one will find a substantial form and matter collected together
'in a pile' and yet not composing a substance. Artefacts like houses, however, are
different. In addition to the materials, there must be the right sort of arrangement.
That is, the right sort of relations between the materials must obtain.

Abelard, too, asserts that one needs more than an aggregate of parts to make a
house, and like Ockham, he identifies the same difference maker:

> Those things from which the arrangement (*compositio*)[73] of a house has been
> removed cannot be called this house; nor is the existence of the matter sufficient for
> this house to be. For, now, before its fabrication the stones and boards can<not> be
> called a house.[74] Rather, for form an arrangement is necessary. Thus, it does not
> follow that if these stones and boards exist, then this house exists, unless they
> remain in accord with an arrangement which is in the disposition of the parts.[75]

In order for a house to exist, the materials must exist. But the existence of the materials is not sufficient. The materials must be positioned and arranged in the appropriate manner. Once these things are arranged, the collection of the stones and the
boards possess the form of a house.

Abelard and Ockham, therefore, deny that composition is identity, and they
refuse to endorse eliminativism. At the same time, they insist that the whole is
nothing other than its parts. To many of their critics, both medieval and modern,
it seems that Abelard and Ockham are trying to do too much with too few ontological resources.[76] Walter Chatton, for example, challenged many of Ockham's
reductivist positions by defending and then appealing to a rule that states that if
three things do not suffice to verify a proposition, then one must add a fourth.[77]
Using Chatton's rule, the following challenge could be put to Abelard and Ockham. Abelard denies that the relations between parts that make some things a
house are themselves things. Ockham also seems committed to this position.[78]
Thus, when Abelard and Ockham claim that the whole is nothing other than the
parts, they are taking a much harder path. They are claiming that if one considers

the things present in a whole and the things present in the parts that compose the whole, there is no difference in the tally of things that are present. The whole possesses no *thing* that the mere aggregation of its parts lacks. But if there is nothing that the whole possesses that the parts taken together do not also possess, then what is it that makes it true that the parts actually compose a whole?[79] For both Abelard and Ockham, the answer to Chatton must be that no extra thing is required. In Abelard's case, the fact that some things have been arranged is sufficient for composition. And we have already seen, Ockham claims that the truthmaker for composition is that the form exists and the matter exists and there is nothing impeding their natural inclination to combine.[80] These answers reveal that the dispute between medieval anti-realists and their opponents is often ultimately a disagreement about what can be a truthmaker. But exploring this dispute, let alone adjudicating it, is the task for another paper.[81]

NOTES

1. I assume throughout this chapter that all parts are what contemporary mereologists call 'proper' parts. A is an 'improper' part of B if and only if A is either a proper part of B or A is B (see Simons 1987, 9–11, and ch. 2, passim). We can safely ignore improper parts. I know of no medieval thinker who appeals to any notion of 'part' that is plausibly construed as the relation of being an improper part of something.

2. See Sedley (1982), Barnes (1988) and Harte (2002).

3. See Sextus Empiricus, *Adversus Dogmaticos* III (*Adv. Math.* IX), §§ 335–7 (1914, 282), with discussion by Barnes (1988, 259–68).

4. *Quaestiones in Phys.*, q. 19 (Siger de Brabant 1941, 47). Cf. Aquinas *in Phys.* 1, lectio 3.

5. Idem.

6. *Quaestiones* q. 19 (1941, 47–48).

7. *Soph. El.* 167a10–14.

8. *A coincides* with B if and only if every part of A is a part of B and every part of B is a part of A. *A overlaps* with B if and only if there is at least one thing that is both a part of A and a part of B.

9. *Theologia Christiana* III, §§ 138–63 (Abelard 1969, 247–55). Compare to Boethius's theory of identity in *De Trin.* 1 and *In Isag. 2nd ed.* 2.6.

10. This is the framework offered in the second of three versions of the *Theology*. For discussion of the divergences between the frameworks offered in the different versions of Abelard's *Theologies*, see Marenbon (2007).

11. Brower (2004, 226–34). For more on how problems pertaining to the Trinity served as a catalyst for medieval reflections on identity and individuation, see Chapter 33 (this volume).

12. In Abelard's works 'essentia' has a number of meanings. See De Rijk (1981, 19–24).

13. *Theologia Christiana* IV, § 12 (Abelard 1969, 271).

14. For a more elaborate exposition, including a presentation of all the key texts, consult Arlig (2005, 165–80).

15. *Theologia Christiana* III, § 153 (Abelard 1969, 252.1862–68), *my emphasis.*

16. Armstrong (1997, 18).

17. For example, Abelard (1970, 550.6–7), and (Abelard 1970, 344.34–35).

18. Abelard (1970, 560.34–561.2.) See also Abelard (1970, 551.4–10).

19. Abelard (1970, 550.18–20). I accept Henry's reading of this passage, which requires that we add a 'non' in line 18 of the edited text (1991, 83).

20. For more on this point, see Arlig (2007, 214–17).

21. Abelard (1970, 419–20).

22. Abelard (1970, 575.18–32).

23. Abelard (1970, 575.31–32).

24. Walter Burley (1966, 301–2). Sometimes functional parts are thought to be a type of integral part; sometimes they are distinguished from integral parts. On the different kinds of parts at work in medieval mereological systems, see Arlig (2006) and Arlig (2011, 163–67).

25. In the Middle Ages, there was debate over the unity of the substantial form. The minority view, defended by most notably Aquinas, was that a substance could only have one substantial form (Pasnau 2002, 126–30). The dominant position was that a single hylomorphic composite consists of prime matter plus many substantial forms.

26. Cross (1995, 158).

27. For a helpful guide through the arguments, see Cross (1995), and Cross (1999, 145–49).

28. Cross (1995, 141–44).

29. Cross (1995, 145); Cross (1999, 147).

30. The example and argument comes from Kit Fine (1999, 62–64).

31. Fine (1999, 63–64).

32. *Ordinatio* 3.2.2; cf. Cross (1995, 158).

33. *Summula Philosophiae Naturalis* I.19; *Quaestiones variae* 6.2; cf. Cross (1999, 149–60).

34. In addition to Cross (1995, 1999), see Normore (2006, 744–47).

35. Van Cleve (1986, 141).

36. Abelard (1970, 550.9–13).

37. Abelard (1970, 550.13–17).

38. See Arlig (2007, 210–14); and Henry (1972, 120–29).

39. See Arlig (2007, 224–27), and Henry (1991, 105–7).

40. Ebbesen (1999, 397).

41. For the Nominales see Courtenay (1991), Ebbesen (1992), Normore (1992), and Martin (1998).

42. Abelard (1921, 300.20–21; 1970, 423.29–30).

43. Van Cleve (1986, 141); cf. Chisholm (1973, 581–82).

44. On Abelard's understanding of possibility, see Martin (2001). Later medieval thinkers did develop a model of modality that clearly allowed for synchronic alternative possibilities (see Chapter 14, this volume).

45. Abelard (1921, 299.30–34).

46. Martin (1998, 5–6).

47. Arlig (2007, 219–20 and 224–27).

48. *Quaestiones super Top.* 2.9 (Radulphus Brito 1978, 45). A rule is taken 'destructively' when the denial of the antecedent term implies the denial of the consequent. Hence, if the *part* is not, the *whole* is not. The same rule taken 'constructively' states that if the *part* is, the *whole* is. Radulphus asserts that this constructive inference is false since parts can exist even though the house does not exist. For example, the parts that will make up my house might sit on the lot for many days before the builders come and construct the house.

49. Walter Burley (1966, 301).

50. Aristotle *Metaph.* 5.26, 1023b26–27. On being mutilated (*kolobon*), see *Metaph.* 5.27.

51. The key texts are Buridan's *Quaestiones super libros De generatione et corruptione* 1.13 (2010) and the final redaction of his *Quaestiones super libros Physicorum* 1.10. The Latin text for the later is most accessible in Pluta's helpful study (2001, 52–59). Buridan also touches upon these issues in a much more cursory fashion in his questions on the *Metaphysics* (*In Metaphys.* 7.12). For discussion of Buridan's theory of persistence, see King (1994) and Normore (2006, 751–52).

52. *In De gen.* 1.13 (Buridan 2010, 112–13).

53. *Quaes. super Phys.* 1.10 (see Pluta 2001, 57), and *In Metaphys.* 7.12 (1518, 48va).

54. *In De gen.* 1.13 (Buridan 2010, 113).

55. Prop. 87: *Quod homo per nutritionem potest fieri alius numeraliter et individualiter.* (Hissette 1977).

56. Many thanks to Claude Panaccio and Peter King, as well as other members of the audience at Toronto, for making this point clear to me.

57. See Normore (2006, esp. pp. 753–54) and Pasnau (2011, ch. 29, esp. pp. 695–710).

58. For a defence of the thesis that composition is identity, see Lewis (1991, 81–87).

59. Van Inwagen (1990, 30–31).

60. Here I use the formulation of the question presented by Markosian (2008, 342). For those unfamiliar with the locution 'the *X*s', see Peter Van Inwagen's explanation (1990, 21–30).

61. Van Inwagen (1990, 72–90).

62. Abelard (1970, 554.37–555.2). This is Kluge's (1976) reading of Roscelin's fragments and the doxographical reports. For arguments in favour of nihilism, see Rosen and Dorr (2002), and Schaffer (2007, 175–78).

63. Minio-Palluelo (1958, 114–15).

64. Henry (1990, 100, 109–10).

65. Abelard (1970, 422.4–5). Abelard's generous thesis concerning composition was ridiculed by many of his contemporaries. See the report of a debate between Abelard and Alberic in *Introductiones Montane maiores* 69rb (quoted in De Rijk 1966, 16; English translation in Tweedale 1976, 151).

66. I owe this point to Alex Oliver.

67. Abelard (1970, 546–48). For more on the 'liberalism' of medieval mereology, see Arlig (2006) and Arlig (2011).

68. Van Inwagen (1990, 82).

69. Interestingly, Abelard does suggest that some wholes are 'fictions', that is, useful fabrications of our minds. For example, there are, strictly speaking, no wholes consisting of moments of time. However, while Abelard might be comfortable saying that 'my house' names a fictional object—since it is a logical construction out of a series of different houses—it does not follow that Abelard believes there are no houses at all. On 'temporal wholes' and the possible extension of his thesis to other objects, see Arlig (2007, 220–23).

70. Notice that this *seems* to be Ockham's answer even for the composite of a substantial form with matter, for through divine intervention a substantial form and some matter could be placed together and yet fail to form a hylomorphic composite.

71. *Summula philosophiae naturalis* 1.19 (Ockham 1974–88, vol. 6, 206.35–45).

72. See Cross (1999, 154–56).

73. At least in this and related passages, the Latin term '*compositio*' should not be rendered as 'composition'. A *compositio* is not merely the cobbling together of parts, as 'composition' might suggest to the modern reader; these parts, once cobbled together, must take on a structure or form.

74. The emendation is mine. The argument requires the addition of a 'non'. On the necessity of arrangement in order to have an artefact, see also Abelard (1921, 171).

75. Abelard (1970, 550.38–551.4).

76. See Spade (1999). For a sympathetic appraisal of Abelard, see King (2004). For Ockham, see Adams (1987, vol. 1, 287–313).

77. *Reportatio* 1.30.1 a. 4; quoted in Maurer (1984, 464).

78. Ockham must concede that these relational properties are not things, for he famously reduced the categories to Substance and Quality. Terms corresponding to the latter eight categories were merely indirect ways of speaking of the two kinds of items that are real, individual substances and individual qualities. On relations, see Adams (1987), vol. 1, ch. 7.

79. There is a similar argument that Scotus uses to justify the claim that relations are things (*Ordinatio* 2.1.5; cf. Adams 1987, vol. 1, 219; Henninger 1989, 76).

80. See the end of Section 2 and the references there.

81. The following individuals graciously read and commented extensively on drafts of this article: Samir Chopra, Catarina Dutilh-Novaes, Catherine Kemp, Robert Pasnau, Graham Priest, Justin Steinberg and Rega Wood. Presentations based on this material were given at Cornell, Cambridge and the University of Toronto. In particular, I must thank my commentators Alex Oliver and Alisa Koonce (both at Cambridge), and Claude Panaccio (Toronto). I thank every one of them for the questions, criticisms and advice that I received.

BIBLIOGRAPHY

Abelard, see Peter Abelard.

Adams, M. M. 1987. *William Ockham*. 2 vols. Notre Dame, IN: University of Notre Dame Press.

Arlig, A. 2005. *A Study in Early Medieval Mereology: Boethius, Abelard, and Pseudo-Joscelin.* Unpublished Ph.D. dissertation, The Ohio State University, Columbus. Available as a PDF document through OhioLink Electronic Theses and Dissertations Center (http://www.ohiolink.edu/etd).

———. 2006. 'Medieval mereology'. In *The Stanford Encyclopedia of Philosophy*, ed. Edward N. Zalta. Originally published 2006, substantially revised 2011 (http://plato.stanford.edu/).

———. 2007. Abelard's Assault on Everyday Objects. *American Catholic Philosophical Quarterly* 81:209–27.

———. 2011. 'Is there a medieval mereology?' In *Methods and Methodologies: Aristotelian Logic East and West, 500–1500*, ed. M. Cameron and J. Marenbon, 161–89. Leiden, the Netherlands: Brill.

Armstrong, D. M. 1997. *A World of States of Affairs*. Cambridge: Cambridge University Press.

Barnes, J. 1988. 'Bits and pieces'. In *Matter and Metaphysics*, ed. Jonathan Barnes and Mario Mignucci, 224–94. Naples: Bibliopolis.

Brower, J. 2004. 'Trinity'. In *The Cambridge Companion to Abelard*, eds. J. Brower and K. Guilfoy, 223–57. Cambridge: Cambridge University Press.

Buridan, see John Buridan.

Chisholm, R. 1973. Parts as Essential to Their Wholes. *Review of Metaphysics* 26:581–603.

Courtenay, W. J. 1991. 'Nominales and nominalism in the twelfth century'. In *Lectionum Varietates: Hommage a Paul Vignaux (1904–1987)*, ed. J. Jolivet, Z. Kaluza and A. de Libera, 11–48. Paris: J. Vrin (Études de Philosophie Médiévale 65).

Cross, R. 1995. Duns Scotus's Anti-Reductionistic Account of Material Substance. *Vivarium* 33:137–70.

———. 1999. Ockham on Part and Whole. *Vivarium* 37:143–67.

De Rijk, L. M. 1966. Some New Evidence on Twelfth-Century Logic: Alberic and the School of Mont Ste Geneviève (Montani). *Vivarium* 4:1–57.

———. 1981. 'Abailard's semantic views in the light of later developments'. In *English Logic and Semantics: From the End of the 12th Century to the Time of Ockham and Burleigh*, ed. H. A. G. Braakhuis, C. H. Kneepkens and L. M. de Rijk, 1–58. Nijmegen, the Netherlands: Ingenium Publishers.

Ebbesen, S. 1992. What One Should Have an Opinion About. *Vivarium* 30:62–79.

———. 1999. Anonymous D'Orvillensis' Commentary on Aristotle's Categories. *Cahiers de l'Institut du Moyen-Âge Grec et Latin* 70:229–423.

Fine, K. 1999. Things and Their Parts. *Midwest Studies in Philosophy* 23:61–74.

Harte, V. 2002. *Plato on Parts and Wholes: The Metaphysics of Structure*. Oxford: Clarendon Press.

Henninger, M. G. 1989. *Relations: Medieval Theories 1250–325*. Oxford: Clarendon Press.

Henry, D. P. 1972. *Medieval Logic and Metaphysics: A Modern Introduction*, London: Hutchinson & Co.

———. 1990. 'Master Peter's mereology'. In *De Ortu Grammaticae: Studies in Medieval Grammar and Linguistic Theory in Memory of Jan Pinborg*, ed. G. L. Bursill-Hall, S. Ebbesen and K. Koerner, 99–115. Philadelphia: John Benjamins Publishing.

———. 1991. *Medieval Mereology*. Amsterdam and Philadelphia: B.R. Grüner Publishing (Bochumer Studien zur Philosophie vol. 16).

Hissette, R. 1977. *Enquête sur les 219 articles condamnés à Paris le 7 mars 1277*. Louvain, Belgium: Publications Universitaires.

John Buridan 2010. *Quaestiones super libro De generatione et corruptione Aristotelis*, ed. M. Steijger, P. J. J. M. Bakker and J. M. M. H. Thijssen. Leiden, the Netherlands: Brill (History of Science and Medicine Library vol. 17).

King, P. 1994. 'John Buridan's theory of individuation'. In *Individuation in Scholasticism: The Later Middle Ages and the Counter-Reformation, 1150–650*, ed. Jorge E. Gracia, 397–430., Binghamton, NY: SUNY Press.

———. 2004. 'Metaphysics'. In *The Cambridge Companion to Abelard*, ed. Jeffrey E. Brower and Kevin Guilfoy, 65–125. Cambridge: Cambridge University Press.

Kluge, E.-H. W. 1976. Roscelin and the Medieval Problem of Universals. *Journal of the History of Philosophy* 14:405–14.

Lewis, D. 1991. *Parts of Classes*. Oxford: Basil Blackwell.

Marenbon, J. 2007. Abelard's Changing Thoughts on Sameness and Difference in Logic and Theology. *American Catholic Philosophical Quarterly* 81:229–50.

Markosian, N. 2008. 'Restricted composition'. In *Contemporary Debates in Metaphysics*, ed. Theodore Sider, John Hawthorne and Dean W. Zimmerman, 341–63. Malden, MA, and Oxford: Blackwell Publishing.

Martin, C. J. 1998. The Logic of Growth: Twelfth-Century Nominalists and the Development of Theories of the Incarnation. *Medieval Philosophy and Theology* 7:1–15.

———. 2001. 'Abaelard on modality: Some possibilities and some puzzles'. In *Potentialität und Possibilität*, ed. Thomas Buchheim, Corneille Henri Kneepkens and Kuno Lorenz, 97–124. Stuttgart, Germany: Frommann-Holzboog.

Maurer, A. 1984. Ockham's Razor and Chatton's Anti-razor. *Mediaeval Studies* 46:463–75.

Minio-Paluello, L. 1958. *Twelfth Century Logic, Texts and Studies, vol. II: Abaelardiana Inedita*. Rome: Edizioni di Storia e Letteratura.

Normore, C. G. 1992. Abelard and the School of the Nominales. *Vivarium* 30:80–96.

———. 2006. Ockham's Metaphysics of Parts. *Journal of Philosophy* 103:737–54.

Ockham, see William of Ockham.

Pasnau, R. 2002. *Thomas Aquinas on Human Nature: A Philosophical Study of Summa theologiae Ia 75–89*. Cambridge: Cambridge University Press.

———. 2011. *Metaphysical Themes 1274–1671*. Oxford: Clarendon Press.

Peter Abelard. 1919. *Logica 'ingredientibus', pt. 1: Glossae super Porphyrium*. In *Peter Abaelards Philosophische Schriften*. I. *Die Logica 'Ingredientibus*. 1: die Glossen zu Porphyrius*, ed. Bernhard Geyer, 1–109. Münster, Germany: Aschendorffshen Buchhandlung (Beiträge zur Geschichte der Philosophie des Mittelalters 21, pt. 1).

———. 1921. *Logica 'ingredientibus', pt. 2: Glossae super Praedicamenta Aristotelis*. In *Peter Abaelards Philosophische Schriften*. I. *Die Logica 'Ingredientibus'. 2: die Glossen zu den Kategorien*, ed. Bernhard Geyer, 111–305. Münster, Germany: Aschendorffshen Buchhandlung (Beiträge zur Geschichte der Philosophie des Mittelalters 21, pt. 2).

———. 1969. *Theologia Christiana*, ed. E. M. Buytaert. Turnhout, Belgium: Brepols (Corpus Christianorum Continuatio Mediaevalis, no. 12).

———. 1970. *Dialectica*, 2nd ed., ed. L. M. de Rijk. Assen, the Netherlands: Van Gorcum.

Pluta, O. 2001. 'Buridan's theory of identity'. In *Metaphysics and Natural Philosophy of John Buridan*, ed. J. M. M. H. Thijssen and J. Zupko, 49–64. Leiden, the Netherlands: E.J. Brill.

Radulphus Brito. 1978. *Quaestiones super libro Topicorum*, ed. N.J. Green-Pedersen. *Cahiers de l'Institut du Moyen-Âge Grec et Latin* 26:1–92.

Rosen, G. and C. Dorr. 2002. 'Composition as a fiction'. In *The Blackwell Guide to Metaphysics*, ed. Richard M. Gale, 151–74. Oxford: Blackwell.

Schaffer, J. 2007. From Nihilism to Monism. *Australasian Journal of Philosophy* 85:175–91.

Sedley, D. 1982. The Stoic Criterion of Identity. *Phronesis* 27:255–75.

Sextus Empiricus. 1914. *Sexti Empirici Opera*, vol. 2, ed. Hermann Mutschmann. Leipzig, Germany: Teubner [reprinted 1984].

[pseudo] Siger of Brabant. 1941. *Questions sur la physique d'Aristote*, ed. Philippe Delhaye. Louvain, Belgium: Éditions de l'Institut Supérieur de Philosophie (Les Philosophes Belges: Textes et Études 15).

Simons, P. 1987. *Parts: a Study in Ontology*. Oxford: The Clarendon Press.

Spade, P. V. 1999. 'Ockham's nominalist metaphysics: some main themes'. In *The Cambridge Companion to Ockham*, ed. Paul V. Spade, 100–17. Cambridge: Cambridge University Press.

Tweedale, M. M. 1976. *Abailard on Universals*. Amsterdam, New York and Oxford: North-Holland Publishing.

Van Cleve, J. 1986. Mereological Essentialism, Mereological Conjunctivism, and Identity Through Time. *Midwest Studies in Philosophy* 11:141–56.

Van Inwagen, P. 1990. *Material Beings*. Ithaca, NY: Cornell University Press.

Walter Burley. 1966. *De toto et parte*, ed. H. Shapiro and F. Scott. *Archives d'histoire doctrinale et littéraire du Moyen Age* 33:299–303.

William of Ockham. 1967–86. *Opera Theologica*, 10 vol., numerous editors. St Bonaventure, NY: Franciscan Institute of St Bonaventure University.

———. 1974–1988. *Opera Philosophica*, 7 vol., ed. by Philotheus Boehner, revised and completed by Gideon Gál and Stephen Brown. St Bonaventure, NY: Franciscan Institute of St Bonaventure University.

CHAPTER 21

MATERIAL SUBSTANCE

HENRIK LAGERLUND

1. INTRODUCTION

Although the notion of substance lies at the very heart of the Western and Middle Eastern philosophical traditions, it is not much talked about in contemporary philosophy. A reason for this might be that substance is so much associated with Aristotelian philosophy that if you invoke the term you almost immediately commit to a view where individuals like you and me, as well as animals and plants, are substances or what is ontologically basic. Most contemporary thinkers instead talk about what they call concrete particulars. According to such a view, you and I are not ontologically basic but made up of more basic entities—be it atoms or impressions.[1]

When substance is discussed in contemporary philosophy, it is often discussed in terms of language and in terms of what so-called substance terms or natural kind terms pick out. Most contemporary philosophers treat these general terms as predicates, that is, to talk about something as a 'human' or as 'water' is to be saying or thinking that it bears a certain description. In this sense, when I understand something as being a human or water, I am said to represent these as having certain sets of properties, or as having certain relations to other things, or as having a certain inner nature, or as being an origin or a cause. Aristotle and the medieval philosophers dealt with in this article, on the other hand, treat kinds as subject terms in the same way as individuals like 'Socrates'. Differences like these make comparison with contemporary views difficult.[2]

For Aristotle, however, substances are the cornerstone of his metaphysics. In the *Categories*, he draws a distinction between primary and secondary substances. Primary substances are individuals like you and me, while secondary substances are universals like being or animal, that is, kinds or, in his language, species and genus.

This early view goes through some changes in his later works. These changes do not make substance less important. On the contrary, in the *Metaphysics* he treats substance as the principal case of being, and since metaphysics is about being qua being it is correct to say that metaphysics is foremost about the causes and principles of substances. The most radical divergence from the view in the *Categories* comes in *Metaphysics* Z, which asks the question: What is a substance? Although the answer to this question turns out to be very complicated, it is form that comes out on top in the end. This has a profound influence on medieval philosophy and is the source of the doctrine of substantial form.

Aristotle's emphasis on substance introduced many problems into Western metaphysics. Three of these remain pressing issues throughout the Middle Ages: (i) What accounts for the unity of a substance through accidental change? (ii) What gives a substance its nature or essence? (iii) What happens to a substance after a process of generation and corruption? The first of these persisted as perhaps the main problem in relation to substance throughout medieval and early-modern times. The answers to the second and third questions changed as the notion of substance changed during this time. I will not consider the two latter questions in this article.

I will outline four different views of material substance. They were all discussed throughout the Middle Ages, and they form the basis for the discussion of substance well into early-modern times. They are:

(1) The unity account
(2) The plurality of forms account
(3) The mereological account
(4) The atomistic account

(1) and (2) are related in the sense that they are both hylomorphic accounts of material substances. I will treat them under one heading. The other two are less known, and I will in particular deal with (3) since it is the most important later non-hylomorphic account of substance, and as we shall see, it is hugely important for later more modern discussions of substance.[3]

2. HYLOMORPHIC ACCOUNTS OF MATERIAL SUBSTANCES

I will divide this section into two and deal with two related but separate hylomorphic accounts of material substances. The first account is the unity account of substance developed foremost by Thomas Aquinas. It is extraordinary influential, but, at the time it was developed, it was not popular at all. The standard account in the thirteenth century was instead the plurality of forms account, which is here represented by John Duns Scotus.

The reason I sort these two accounts under one heading is that the defenders of these views generally agreed that a material substance is a composite of matter and substantial form. The dominant concern or, rather, the view that had to be upheld was the identity or unity of a substance, or, put in a different way, the assumption that a substance is one thing (*unum per se*). Natural substances, plants and animals, are such kinds of things while artefacts, houses and chairs, are not. They are instead accidentally one (*unum per accidens*). This assumption explains why these thinkers rejected atomism, for example. They argued that an atomistic account of substance cannot explain in what way a substance is a unit, since it is made up of parts, that is, atoms. As will be clear, this was also the primary concern for many atomists. The two assumptions mentioned above will also underlie the debate about substance well into the seventeenth century.

The difference between these two accounts instead lies in the structure they attribute to substances. Aquinas stresses the unity of substantial form and the complete passivity of matter, while by contrast Scotus argues that matter cannot be purely passive and that a substance is made up of several substantial forms.

2.1. The Unity Account of Material Substances

One of the main differences between the two hylomorphic accounts of material substances outlined here is their view of matter. Aquinas thinks that all sub-lunary substances are composed of prime matter and substantial form. Spiritual substances like angels are pure immaterial forms, he claims. Without form and matter, there would be no generation and corruption and no change.

Prime matter cannot be directly known, however, Aquinas thinks, since it is purely passive. It can only be known by analogy. We know that matter must exist because there must be something underlying change, that is, something must be the subject of change, since form accounts for what kind of change it is, but it is not what changes. He says in his commentary on Aristotle's *Physics* that we recognise wood to be something besides the form of the bench or the bed (*In I Physics*, lect. 13, n. 118; Thomas Aquinas 1965, 59). Whatever persists through change must be matter. This matter is, however, always in potentiality to all forms (*In I Physics*, lect. 15, n. 138, 68), and all actuality that prime matter has it gets it from the substantial form in it. In fact, prime matter cannot exist without a form inhering in it. Aquinas thinks that not even God could create prime matter without form.

The most important conclusion Aquinas draws, however, is that there can be only one substantial form in a single being. If this was not the case, then a substance would not be one thing (*ST*, I, q. 73, a. 3; Thomas Aquinas 1970). Although a material substance looks as if it has parts, there are no parts that are prior to the existence of the substance, that is, it is not made out of parts. The single substantial form instead 'virtually contains' the forms of the elements (*ST*, I, q. 76, a. 4). The substantial form of an animal dominates the matter to such a high degree that all the properties of the animal are due to the substantial form. An animal body, for example, exhibits features that are attributed to it because it contains water, but, according to Aquinas, there is no water in the body. Instead, there are flesh and bones that have, in the process of being made out of water, acquired some of the powers and features water has.

Substantial form is, for Aquinas, the key to answering all the three questions mentioned in the introduction above. The unity or identity of the substance is due to its substantial form. The nature is also due to the form, and the generation and corruption of a substance is explained by the coming and going of the substantial form. This is for the most part straightforward in material substances, but the case of the human soul and its alleged immortality provides a particular challenge for him.

There is a hierarchy among forms. The forms of lower bodies are closest to matter and possess no operations other than activity and passivity. Above these forms are the forms of compounds, which have operations derived from the celestial bodies. Above these are plants, and then come the souls of animals and humans. Aquinas writes in the first question of his *Quaestiones de anima* (Thomas Aquinas 1984, q. 1, 48):

> Higher still than these [that is, animal souls] are human souls, which bear a likeness to higher substances [for example, angels] even in the genus of knowledge, since they are able to know immaterial things through the operation of understanding. However, human souls differ from these higher substances in this, namely, that they possess the nature of acquiring the immaterial knowledge of the intellect from that knowledge which comes from sensing material things.

The peculiar ontological status Aquinas wants to attribute to the human soul becomes even clearer if we read further in *Quaestiones de anima* (q. 1, 48). He writes:

> For insofar as a soul possesses an operation which transcends material things, its very existence is raised above and does not depend on its body. But insofar as a soul by nature acquires its immaterial knowledge from what is material, it is clear that the fulfillment of its nature cannot be achieved apart from union with a body. For a thing is not complete in nature unless it possesses those things which are demanded for the proper operations of its nature. In this way, therefore, a human soul insofar as it is united to its body as its form still possesses an act of existence which is elevated above the body and does not depend on it; clearly then this soul is constituted on the boundary line between corporeal and separate substances.

To clarify this argument, it is important to look a bit earlier in the same question where Aquinas lays down two conditions something has to fulfil in order to be called a *hoc aliquid*, that is, a 'thing' or a substance. First of all, it has to subsist per se, that is, be self-subsistent, and, second, it has to have a complete nature, that is, be located in a genus–species structure. The human intellective soul exists *per se* separate from matter, but since it also is a substantial form, it is only part of a substance and does not have a complete essence. The human soul is, therefore, not *simpliciter* a *hoc aliquid* (*Quaestiones de anima*, q. 1, 46–47; Bazan 1997, 115–16).

Being a substantial form and not a complete thing, the soul has a natural inclination to complete its essence and be unified with a body. In *Summa Theologiae* (I, q. 76, a 6; Thomas Aquinas, 1970), he writes:

> It belongs to the very essence of the soul to be united to the body, just as it belongs to a light body to float upwards. And just as a light body remains light when forcibly displaced, and thus retains its aptitude and tendency for the location proper to it, in the same way the human soul, remaining in its own existence after separation from the body, has a natural aptitude and a natural tendency to embodiment.

The substantial or essential union of the body and the soul is explained in this way by Aquinas; that is, the soul has this natural inclination to be united to a body or to some matter in order to complete or fulfil its nature. All this seems straightforward, but despite what he himself claims, the soul's union with the body cannot be essential. If the soul can exist apart from the body, the union seems to be accidental. The possibility of separation without destruction destroys the essential connection between soul and body. It seems, therefore, not possible to hold onto Aquinas's view that the soul is self-subsistent and essentially inherent in matter. It is, therefore, not clear in what sense the soul and the body or the informed matter are one or *unum per se* (Bazan 1997; Lagerlund 2004; Rozemond 1998).

2.2. The Plurality of Forms Account of Material Substance

Scotus argues explicitly against Aquinas's view of matter. Prime matter cannot be pure potentiality since it would not be able to fulfil its role as a subject of inherence for substantial forms or as the substratum underlying change. The main argument Scotus produces against Aquinas is based on a distinction between two types of potentiality, namely objective and subjective potentiality. Something has objective potentiality if it does not exist, but can. Scotus's example is the standard example of a possible object, namely the Antichrist. He is objectively potential because he does not exist now but will. Something has subjective potentiality, on the other hand, if it exists and can be something that it is not at present (Cross 1998, 17–19).

With this distinction at hand, Scotus points out that Aquinas's prime matter is objectively potential and hence does not exist. If prime matter does not exist, then obviously it cannot be the subject of change and of inherence of substantial forms. It seems that on Aquinas's view matter only exists when united to a form, which in a sense Aquinas does think, but given what has been said above it looks as if matter has been reduced to form.

Scotus instead thinks that prime matter has subjective potentiality. As such, it exists as a positive being independent of being informed by a substantial form. It also follows from this that matter has an essence. God can know this essence, but we can only know it in relation to some form. The idea that matter has an essence independent of form will come to have an enormous influence on philosophy. It is easy to see that it threatens to collapse Aristotle's distinctions between potentiality and actuality and analogously between matter and form. These distinctions do not look so straightforward anymore, once it is supposed that matter has some actuality. Scotus does not claim that one of the properties of matter independently of form is quantity; that is, matter does not have extension prior to the inherence of some quantity. As we will see, Ockham rejects this and identifies quantity with the material substance itself.[4]

Matter and form are the essential parts of a substance, according to Scotus. Unlike Aquinas, Scotus also holds that a substantial form is an individual item just by itself. Aquinas had argued that although a substantial form exists only as part of a composite of form and matter, it is an individual only because it is united to matter, and matter, he thinks, is the individuating principle. For Scotus it is an individual independently of the matter it inheres in (Ord. 2.3.1.5–6; John Duns Scotus 1950–, vii, 489).

The view defended by Aquinas that substances have only one substantial form was not a very popular view in the thirteenth and fourteenth centuries. The Archbishop of Canterbury, Robert Kilwardby, in fact, condemned Aquinas' view of human nature in England in 1277, and the condemnation was reiterated by his successor, John Pecham, in 1284 (Zavalloni 1951, 216–19).

The main arguments against Aquinas were also primarily theological. When Christ died on the cross, his soul was separated from his body, but during the three days before the Resurrection, the body was laying in the tomb, and during that time it retained its identity. If there is only one substantial form, which is the intellectual soul, then it seems as if the body cannot retain its identity since it needs a new substantial form. A new substantial form implies a new substance. This is a very counter-intuitive view and, more importantly, against religious belief (Zavaloni 1951, 317–19; Cross 1998, 55).

Scotus also generalises this argument to an argument claiming that a body remains the same through death. It can only do this if it is a unit of substantial form and matter. The specific intellectual and immortal human soul leaves the body composite in death; hence, a living human being is a composite of matter and at least two substantial forms. Many pluralists, however, thought that there was a substantial form for each of the main powers of the living creature so that a human being was made up of at least three substantial forms, one corresponding to the nutritive and reproductive powers, one to the sensitive powers and a third for the intellective powers.

Ockham nicely summarises the philosophical arguments for the plurality of substantial forms in his *Quodlibeta*. He gives three arguments for a real distinction between the sensitive soul and the intellective soul. The first argument focuses on the impossibility of contrary appetites in a soul. He writes (William of Ockham 1991, II, q. 10, 132–33):

> It is impossible that contraries should exist simultaneously in the same subject. But an act of desiring something and an act of spurning that same thing are contraries in the same subject. Therefore, if they exist simultaneously in reality, they do not exist in the same subject. But it is manifest that they exist simultaneously in a human being, since a human being spurns by his intellective appetite the very same thing he desires by his sentient appetite.

Since there can be contrary appetites in a human being, these appetites must be in separate souls.

The second argument has to do with sensation. He argues that sensations exist subjectively in the soul, but no sensation can exist subjectively in the intellective soul, since a separate soul would then, by God's absolute power, be able to sense, and this is absurd, according to Ockham. In the third argument, he points to the problem that what is numerically the same cannot be both extended and non-extended, both material and immaterial. The sensitive soul is extended and material, since it exists as whole in the whole body and as part in each part of the body, while the intellective soul is non-extended and immaterial, since it exists as whole in the whole body and as whole in each part of the body, and from this it follows that they must be really distinct (William of Ockham 1991, II, q. 10, 133–34).

To claim that there is a real distinction between the sensitive and intellective souls means for Ockham that they can exist apart from each other. This poses the same problem for him as it did for Aquinas: namely, the union seems to be accidental, and furthermore, how do we know that the intellect is a form at all and not a universal intellect as Averroes argues in his long commentary on Aristotle's *De anima*?[5] Ockham is well aware of this problem and addresses it in q. 10 of the first quodlibet. He there poses the question whether it can be demonstrated that the intellective soul is the form of the body and writes the following (William of Ockham 1991, I, q. 10, 56):

> The other [difficulty] is whether one can know evidently through reason or through experience that we do understand, taken 'understand' to mean an act proper to an immaterial substance of the sort the intellective soul is claimed to be, i.e., a substance that is ingenerable and incorruptible and that exists as a whole in the whole body and as a whole in each part of the body. / . . . /As regards the second difficulty, I claim that if by 'intellective soul' one means an immaterial and incorruptible form that exists as a whole in the whole body and as a whole in each part, then one cannot evidently know either through reason or through experience that (i) such a form exists in us, or that (ii) an act of understanding proper to such a substance exists in us, or that (iii) such a soul is the form of the body. / . . . /Rather, we merely believe these three things [by faith].

Although he recognises the problem and tries to discuss it to some extent, he also realises that he cannot solve it satisfactorily using natural reason alone. The problem of the intellective soul's union with the body, therefore, becomes something we must believe by faith (Lagerlund 2004).

3. THE MEREOLOGICAL ACCOUNT OF MATERIAL SUBSTANCE

The fourteenth century saw a remarkable change in the way substance, particularly material substance, was conceptualised. It was a change away from an Aristotelian concept towards a modern concept. The change is foremost motivated by certain metaphysical principles, but it threatened to completely undermine the form/matter hylomorphism, and it ploughed the way for corpuscularianism as well as atomism.

Even though thirteenth- as well as fourteenth-century thinkers agreed that a composite substance was composed of matter and substantial form(s), the way some fourteenth-century thinkers spelled this out radically differed from the traditional more Aristotelian ways outlined above. William Ockham was foremost responsible for these changes. He challenged previous thinking by systematically rethinking metaphysics (Normore 2006).

Ockham's ontology includes individual substantial forms, individual accidental forms and individual matters. A composite substance is composed of its essential parts, namely, its matter and form. Besides its essential parts, a substance also has integral parts, like flesh bones, hands, and so forth. Anything with integral parts is extended and material. All things with essential parts are composed of matter and hence also have integral parts and are extended, according to Ockham. Everything extended is a quantity, and every quantity is divisible into quanta, hence there are no indivisible matters and substances.

Ockham insists that a substance is nothing but the parts that make it up. This is contrary to Aquinas and Scotus, who held that although substances have integral parts, these parts depend ontologically on the whole of which they are parts. Each part of a substance is actual and not dependent on anything to make them actual, Ockham argues, again contrary to Aquinas and Scotus.

All the forms in all material substances are also extended. In a piece of wood, all the forms are extended just as the matter they inform. The only non-extended forms are the human intellectual soul, angels and God on Ockham's view. Angels and God are, however, outside nature, and hence the only non-extended or immaterial form in nature is the human soul.

Two metaphysical theses are of crucial importance for understanding the changes in the concept of a substance that takes place with Ockham:

i.   A whole is nothing but its parts.[6]
ii. All parts of an actual substance are themselves actual, and their actuality is not derived from the whole.

As all material substances change and since change in Ockham's view means that some part is replaced, the problem of unity or identity over time and change becomes particularly problematic. Given his view of substance, it is not clear what constitutes the unity or identity over time of a substance. On Aquinas's or Scotus's views, this is not an issue since a substance will be the same as long as it has the same substantial form, and if the substantial form goes, so does the substance. This is what substantial change means on their view, but for Ockham there are no privileged parts like that. A substance is a substance due to its parts, and all parts are individual parts of the substance. No substance on this view is after a process of growth, for example, numerically the same as before. Ockham does not explicitly address this problem, but Buridan does (Lagerlund 2011; Normore 2006; Pluta 2001).

To determine the issue, Buridan outlines three ways in which something can be numerically the same over time, namely, totally, partially and successively. Something that never gains or loses a part is totally the same over time. Something is

numerically the same in its entirety, as he puts it, if its integrity is completely preserved. He writes in the *Physics* (John Buridan 1509, I, q. 10, f. xiii^va-b):

> In this sense, I am not the same that I was yesterday, because something was
> part of my integrity yesterday, which has already been used up, and something
> was not part of my integrity yesterday, which has meanwhile been added
> through nourishment. In this sense, Seneca says in one of his letters to
> Lucilius: no one is the same in youth and old age, not even the same yesterday
> and today, because our bodies are swept away as are the rivers. And in this
> sense, Heraclitus is also perfectly right in saying that we are continually
> changed in such a way that we cannot step twice into the same river as entirely
> the same each time.

On this view only indivisible substances are totally the same over time. There
are only three such things, according to both Ockham and Buridan, namely, God,
Angels and the human soul.

Things that are partially the same over time are such things that have a principal
part that is totally the same over time. In nature, it is only humans that are partially
the same over time since our principal part, the intellective soul, remains totally the
same. Buridan explains (John Buridan 1509, I, q. 10, f. xiii^vb):

> And in this sense, it is true that you are the same who has been baptise nearly
> forty years ago, especially so as this act primarily benefit the soul and not the
> body. And in this sense, it is possible for me to peruse you for some unjust
> treatment of my person or to feel beholden to reward you, because also the unjust
> or meritorious actions primarily stem from the soul and not from the body.

As it turns out, the only natural substances that are partially the same over time are
humans. All other substances have a weaker form of sameness.

Buridan never explicitly tells us what is required for something to be successively the same over time. He gives an example of the river Seine that is said to be
the same river over a millennium because the water parts succeed each other continuously (John Buridan 1509, I, q. 10, f. xiii^vb):

> Thus, the same river is called 'Seine' for nearly one thousand years, in spite of the
> fact that, strictly speaking, just now nothing whatsoever is part of the Seine that
> was part of it ten years ago. In this sense, both the sea and the sublunary sphere
> are called eternal, and a horse is the same through its whole life, and similarly the
> body of a human is the same. [. . .] It is not properly true, that the Seine, which I
> see, is the same as what I saw ten years ago. This way of talking is conceded
> because the water which we now see is called 'Seine', and the water which I saw
> ten years ago was also called 'Seine', and all the water which made up this river in
> between was at every single moment called 'Seine'. And it is because of this
> continuous succession that we can say that the name 'Seine' is a discrete and
> singular name, although it is not discrete in the same strict sense as it would be if
> the river Seine remained totally the same all the time.

This is not sameness, properly speaking, Buridan seems to think, since there is
nothing of the whole that is the same over time, but rather there is a succession of
entities, related enough so that the same name can be applied.

Although no composite substance in nature, except humans, remains the same after growth or decay, one can say on Buridan's view that a horse or a river is the same over time because of the continuity of its parts, and this sort of sameness does not require that any given part remain through the change.

On this view, then, nothing except a human in nature has an identity or unity stronger than a heap or a river. An animal, for example, is the same over time in the same way as the river Seine is the same over time. From birth to death, the animal is the same because there is a succession of parts succeeding each other occupying the same spatiotemporal location. This is true of a heap as well, and there is no other unity to an animal. This succession of entities over time allows for the appearance that the name picks out the same entity over time, although it in reality picks out several entities continuously succeeding each other. There will be limit problems, of course, questions like: when does a horse stop being a horse, and when does it begin to be a horse? There is no end to such a substance by death, but as the body of the horse decays over time it eventually stops being a horse. This view will have a problem accounting for substantial change. In fact, all change seems to be a form of alteration.[7]

In his discussion of the doctrine of the plurality of substantial forms, which he does not subscribe to in its traditional form, in Book VII, q. 14, of his *Metaphysics*, Buridan writes (John Buridan 1588):

> One can imagine many ways in which there are a plurality of substantial forms. In one way through a quantitative division of forms. In this way a part of a form is a form, and therefore it follows that in every composite substance there are infinite partial substantial forms as well as infinite parts of matter, unless of course we are talking about a human being whose form is not extended and not divisible.

Again we see him emphasising the difference of the human soul, which is a simple and an indivisible substantial form. All other form and matters are infinitely divisible.

The discussion of this view of substance became even more detailed in the generation of thinkers that came after Buridan. I will here be looking at Albert of Saxony and John Marsilius of Inghen. Albert develops the view of the metaphysical composition of substance in Questions 7, 8 and 9 of book I of his *Physics* commentary (Albert of Saxony 1999, 94–142). Question 7 is about whether a whole is its parts, Question 8 is about whether by adding some part to a whole, or similarly by removing some part from the whole, a new whole is made, and 9 asks the epistemological question whether a cognition of a whole depends on its parts. In Question 8, he restates Buridan's three criteria for numerical identity of a substance. Based on this he draws a number of conclusions. These are the third and the fourth (130):

> The third conclusion is about numerical identity in the second sense. A human being remains the same at the beginning of its life as well as at its end. This is proved because its principal part remains the same, that is, it's intellective soul. . . .
> The fourth conclusion is about the same kind of identity. A horse is not the same at the end of its life as in the beginning. This is held to be the case because its matter as well as its form does not remain the same.

His view here does not deviate from Buridan's at all (131):

> The fifth conclusion is about the third kind of numerical identity. It is correct to
> say that the horse is the same in number in the beginning of its life as well as at its
> end, and Seine or a river is the same now as it has been for hundreds of years.
> This is proved because of a certain succession of parts that mutually holds the
> same figure or disposition because of which something can be said to be the same
> over time, in accordance with the description of the third mode of numerical
> identity.

It is due to the succession of parts that we can refer to a thing as the same thing, although strictly speaking, it is continuously changing. Albert's view seems not exactly like Buridan's, but I will not comment here on what 'figure or disposition' could mean.

In Question 10, however, he comments on generation and successive development of a material substance (152):

> Forms of donkeys or some other heterogeneous [body] other than a human being
> are generated successively. . . . One part of the form of a donkey is first educed
> from one part of the matter and after that another part of the form from another
> part of the matter. It follows that the form of a donkey is generated successively,
> and this goes for any other heterogeneous body other than a human being.

According to this view, forms of non-human substances are educed (*educere*) from matter. As the text explains, this is a successive process, so parts of the form are educed from parts of the matter, and another from another part of the matter and so on. Related to this is a well-known discussion about *minima materia*. Both Albert and John Marsilius of Inghen comment on this (John Marsilius of Inghen 1518, I, q. 13, f. Xiii^va):

> I posit this conclusion that a minimal matter is granted under which a heteroge-
> neous mixed body can be generated.

Albert also says (Albert of Saxony 1999, I, q. 10, 153):

> The third conclusion is that a minimal matter is granted by which power the
> whole form of a donkey can be educed or a form sufficient for which the compo-
> sition of the form and the matter is said to be a donkey.

As I mentioned before in relation to Ockham, every bit of extended matter is a quantity, and what these authors are insisting is that there is a minimal boundary of the quantity of matter that can generate, that is, develop, into something with a certain form. A *minima materia* is a minimal quantity of matter below which it cannot generate. These are not atoms or indivisibles, since they are divisible, but perhaps they are best likened to corpuscles. They are the units of physical interaction and change. It is also worth noticing that a mere mechanical cutting out of some adequate quantity of matter ought to be able to generate a substance.

By accepting Ockham's metaphysics, Buridan and his followers are led to a very particular view of material substances. Form and matter have become more and more alike on this view, and a view of substance very similar to a corpuscularian view of substance seems to emerge. Form has also lost its ability to solve the problem of change—the very problem it was partially introduced to solve in the first place.

There are many parallels between the mereological view of substance and later Cartesian views. To see this, consider a puzzle in Descartes's scholarship about a couple of phrases in the *Principles*, which seems to imply a view of material substance slightly different than the more famous view in the *Meditations*. Descartes writes 'each and every part of [a material substance], as delimited by us in our thought, is really distinct from the other parts of the same substance'. As he also tells us in the *Principles* that a real distinction 'exists only between two or more substances', these two claims together imply that every part of a substance is also a substance. This is similar to Buridan's claim seen above that all parts of a form are themselves forms. The problem is to understand what relationship he is here assuming between substances. Vere Chappell has argued that this view can be interpreted in several ways. In one way it implies a view that some contemporary metaphysicians call mereological essentialism. He writes that 'if the parts of a substance are substances, then substance x would depend on substance y, if y is a part of x, and if every substance has to have, in order to exist, just the parts it does have' (Chappell 2008, 260). On another interpretation the relationship might be the reverse, namely, that 'if the parts of a substance x are substances, then they depend on x in the sense that they would not exist if x did not exist'. On the view here outlined, whatever the relationship is between substances, there is a concern as to what accounts for the unity or identity over time and change of a substance since a substance is nothing but the parts that at a given time make it up. Descartes never adequately answers this question.

By promoting the view that the parts of a substance are also substances, Descartes goes against the hylomorphic account of substance, but he seems to align himself to the mereological account. As we have already seen, this view also undermines the notion of substantial form, at least as it was understood by Aquinas and Scotus. The mereological account of material substance implies a fundamental rejection of some central Aristotelian concepts. It is not in the seventeenth century that a break with an Aristotelian conception of material substance is first seen, but in the mid–fourteenth century.

4. The Atomistic Accounts of Material Substance

One of the major targets of criticism in Aristotle's *Physics* was Democritus's atomistic account of substance. It has been traditional to say that for this reason atomistic accounts of substance were not very popular, if they existed at all, in the Middle Ages. The traditional view of history also has it that it was through the rediscovery of Lucretius's *De rerum natura* in the early fifteenth century that atomism again became a viable theory, and it was subsequent to this that atomism was taken up by some of the mechanical philosophers of the seventeenth century. Recent research has shown that not only were atomistic accounts of substance discussed throughout the Middle Ages, but *De rerum natura* was read and copied throughout this time period as well (Grellard and Robert 2009, 3–4).

It is still true that the canonical thinkers of the time were not atomists, but there was nevertheless a substantial and sustained discussion of atomism. This is particularly true of the fourteenth century, which, as we have seen, saw major changes in the notion of substance. I will here deal with two of the foremost atomists, namely Nicholas of Autrecourt and John Wyclif.

Nicholas of Autrecourt's atomism is motivated by his general criticism of Aristotle. Accepting an atomistic view of substance entails for him a rejection of matter and form, potentiality and actuality. On his view there is no prime matter, unless prime matter means a collection of atoms, and there are no substantial forms. There are, however, very few actual arguments for atomism given by Nicholas. Instead, he seems to think that it gives the best explanation of natural phenomena. It is from that starting point that he begins to develop his position.

Instead of talking about atoms, he often refers to *minima naturalia*. As we have seen, thinkers adhering to the mereological view of material substance do this as well, but they mean something different with this term. Something that is still divisible. Nicholas means atoms that are indivisible. In the *Universal Treatise*, he writes (Nicholas of Autrecourt 1971, 60):

> For natural forms are divisible into their smallest units in such a way that these, when divided off from the whole, could not perform their proper action. And so, though they are visible when existing in the whole, they are not visible when dispersed and divided or separated. For this is true even according to the mind of Aristotle when he says that natural beings have maximum and minimum limits.

A substance is hence a collection of atoms arranged in a certain way.

Anyone defending this kind of view of substance has to address the problem of the unity of an atomic compound. Nicholas does this explicitly. His suggested solution involves the introduction of a distinction between different kinds of atoms. Some atoms are essential to the whole while others are accidental (Nicholas of Autrecourt 1971, 68–69). Now, this distinction does not by itself, of course, solve the problem of the unity of a substance, but he combines it with an idea of a force that attracts the essential atoms together (Nicholas of Autrecourt 1971, 63):

> Perhaps there is something there which connects and retains the indivisibles in this union, as a magnet does with iron. The stronger the force of this thing, the longer the subject survives as a subject. If there were a force of this kind, it would be called a quasi-formal principle of the thing.

This 'quasi-formal principle' binds the essential atoms together. The substance retains its identity as long as it has all its essential atoms. Losing one of them means the destruction of the substance.

On the one hand, Nicholas rejects the distinction between substantial and accidental change and reduces generation and corruption to local motion, but the distinction he draws between essential and accidental atoms seems to bring it back. The force he is talking about also looks very much like a substantial form—at least in function. In a sense one can thus say that the unity problem of material substances forces him to revert to what looks like an Aristotelian view. It was, however, very common to combine atomism with a form/matter hylomorphism. An example of this can be found in the works of John Wyclif.

Unlike Nicholas, Wyclif did not motivate his atomism by criticism of Aristotle. His motivations were primarily theological (Michael 2009, 220). Like many later atomists, Wyclif combined a form/matter ontology with the idea that matter is made up of indivisible atoms. The idea is that atoms constitute prime matter, but that in all natural substances there is a substantial form that unites them into one thing. Wyclif argues, following Aristotle, that everything is made up of the four elements, that is, of earth, air, fire and water, but he thinks they are composed of atoms bound together into elements by substantial forms. He hence agrees with Scotus and Ockham that prime matter is actual and extended, but it is only a thing, that is, a unit with an essence once there is a composite of atoms and form.

The elements combine into so-called *minima naturalia*,[8] which are the fundamental compounds of natural bodies. These are similar to Buridan's *minima naturalia*, and given the atomism, they also remind us of Gassendi's molecules. These minimal parts of nature generate further complex structures that can be parts of natural bodies. Bodies of plants and animals are formed from these structures, and they are united into one thing by a substantial form. For living things this substantial form is a soul. It is obvious from this that each material substance has several substantial forms in it. Wyclif's view of substance is hence a fascinating mix of Aristotelian natural philosophy and metaphysics and atomism.[9] The main reason for this odd combination is the unity problem.

5. CONCLUDING REMARKS AND AN EXCURSION INTO THE SEVENTEENTH CENTURY

Out of the four accounts of substance discussed in this article, the first two are well known, but the other two, developed in the fourteenth century, are much less known and much closer to what we like to think of as more modern or mechanistic accounts of material substance. I have already indicated this, but I would like to put the mereological view, in particular, into perspective by relating it to the famous discussion of substance in the Arnauld-Leibniz correspondence (Leibniz 1967).

The latter half of this correspondence is devoted to substance and substantial form. It deals with problems that come out of the Cartesian view of material substance or out of what I have labelled the mereological account of substance. Leibniz is very critical of the mechanical view of substance he finds in Descartes, and he objects that on such an account of substance only humans are real substances since only humans are united by an immaterial, indivisible substantial form. He argues that only a true unit can be a substance. In the draft of the letter of 8 December 1682, he writes that 'bodily substance does not consist of extension and divisibility, for it will be conceded that two bodies set apart from one another . . . are not really one substance' (Leibniz 1875–90, II, 72). If matter is extended and divisible, he continues, then 'one will never find a body of which it may be said that it is truly one substance'. The argument that is lurking in the background is often called the unity argument and can be summarised in the following way:[10]

  (i)   Every substance is a true (substantial) unit.
  (ii) Everything whose essence is extended is divisible.
  (iii) Everything that is divisible is a being by aggregation.
  (iv) Nothing that is a being by aggregation is a true (substantial) unit.
  (v)   Hence, everything whose essence is extension is not a true unit.
  (vi) Therefore, nothing whose essence is extension is a substance.

The consequence of this argument is that only an immaterial, that is, non-extended, and hence simple, entity is a substance. To justify his first premise, he draws a distinction between substantial or true unity and accidental or phenomenal unity (Leibniz 1875–90, II, 100–101):

> I agree that there are degrees of accidental unity, that an ordered society has more unity than a chaotic mob, and that an organic body or a machine has more unity than a society; that is to say it is more appropriate to conceive of them as a single thing, . . . Our mind notices or conceives of certain genuine substances which have various modes; these modes embrace relationships with other substances, from which the mind takes the opportunity to link them together in thought and to enter into the account one name for all these things together, which makes for convenience in reasoning.[11]

All accidental unity is hence unity by convention. The point he is trying to make is, of course, that on a Cartesian view of material substance everything except a human mind is an accidental unity. Arnauld has no problem accepting this conclusion, that is, that there exist 'only "machines" or "aggregates" of substances' (87) in nature. For Leibniz this is unacceptable. A substantial form that is indivisible and indestructible must hence unite all natural substances.

The debate between Arnauld and Leibniz could be recast as a debate between a mereological account and a hylomorphic account of substance. As we have seen, Buridan tries to account for the numerical identity of material substances, but that account will always be vulnerable to Leibniz's argument. In order to get his strong view of what counts as a substance, Leibniz, on the other hand, ends up with a view where only simple souls or minds are substances. The debate about material substance set up in this article is, as indicated, a continuous debate from the thirteenth to the seventeenth century. It centres on the problem of unity, but it underlies and determines the developments in philosophy and science during this time period.

NOTES

....

1. See Loux (2006) for a good introduction to some contemporary views on concrete particulars including an Aristotelian.

2. There are views similar to Aristotle's in the literature. Millikan (2000) argues for a view close to Aristotle's, but her view is foremost an epistemological view of substance and not so much metaphysical or ontological. There is a similar epistemological discussion in the fourteenth century, Lagerlund (2010), but this is not the topic of this article.

An exception to this is D. Wiggins' view presented in the book *Sameness and Substance* from 1980 and in a substantially revised version in 2001. He takes his starting point in the Aristotelian question: What is it? The answer to this question picks out a substance and is given by what Wiggins calls a sortal concept, which is very similar to what Aristotle calls a secondary substance. A sortal concept delineates a substance over time in the sense that if something is a substance, it satisfies the same sortal concept throughout its existence. Most of Wiggins's book is then devoted to explaining how this can be the case and how something can be the same over time without making identity relative.

3. Many of the theories discussed in this chapter are dealt with in much more detail in Pasnau (2011). A reliable overview can be found in McCord Adams (1987, Chapter 15).

4. In *Summula philosophiae naturalis*, he writes, 'it is impossible that matter should lack extension' (William of Ockham 1984, 191).

5. *Commentarium magnum in Aristotelis De anima libros*, II, 7, p. 138, and II, 32, p. 178, in Averroes Cordubensis (1997).

6. Scotus rejected this principle; Cross (1998, Chapter 5).

7. The problem of identity over time is well known in both the history of philosophy and in contemporary philosophy (for a summary, see Gallois 2011). Both Plato and Aristotle can be interpreted as facing up to Parmenides's challenge that nothing changes. Aristotle solves this by the distinction between substantial and accidental change and the distinction between form and matter. Ockham and Buridan, on the other hand, need another explanation since they seem to reject Aristotle's solution. In contemporary philosophy, this problem has been at the forefront of metaphysics for some time (Geach 1967; Wiggins 2001). Particularly, views of things or substances as mereological wholes have struggled with Ockham's and Buridan's problem. One of the more famous solutions to this is D. Lewis's four-dimensional view of things (Lewis 1986). On this view, an object O1 is at time t1 not strictly identical to an object O2 at time t2, but defined over time in four dimensions, O1 and O2 are the same object. It is quite consistent to interpret Buridan's view of successive identity in this way, although he, of course, never explicitly talks in this way.

The problem of identity has since ancient times been discussed in terms of Thesu's ship. The parts of the ship are over the years replaced until there are no original parts left any more, and then the original parts, having been saved, are put together into another ship. The problem is now, of course: which ship is the original ship or are they the same ship? Buridan's notion of successive identity would give the answer that the first ship is still the original one, and the other ship is a new ship built of old parts. This seems to me to be the right answer.

8. As can be seen from what I have said so far, there are two uses of *minima naturalis* at this time. On one use it simply means an atom, but on another it means a minimal generating unit, that is, a set of atoms or a set of extended parts, depending on whether you are an indivisibilist or a divisibilist about matter. See Murdoch (2001).

9. As E. Michael has shown, there are substantial similarities between Wyclif and the seventeenth-century atomist Daniel Sennert (Michael 2009).

10. For this formulation see Sleigh (1990, 119).

11. Leibniz is here referring to the forming of substance concepts. His account is similar to Buridan's. See Lagerlund (2010).

BIBLIOGRAPHY

Albert of Saxony. 1999. *Expositio et quaestiones in Aristotelis Physicam*, ed. B. Patar. 3 vols. Louvain, Belgium: Edition Peeters (Philosophes Medievaux XXXIX–XLI).

Averroes Cordubensis. 1997. *Commentarium magnum in Aristotelis De anima libros*, ed. F. S. Crawford. Cambridge, MA: The Mediaeval Academy of America.

Bazán, Carlos. 1997. The Human Soul: Form and Substance? Thomas Aquinas' Critique of Eclectic Aristotelianism. *Archives d'histoire doctrinale et littéraire du moyen âge* 64:95–126.

Chappell, Vere. 2008. 'Descartes on substance'. In *A Companion to Descartes*, ed. Janet Broughton and John Carriero. Oxford: Blackwell, 251–70.

Cross, Richard. 1998. *The Physics of Duns Scotus*. Oxford: Clarendon Press.

Gallois, André. 2011. 'Identity over time'. In *The Stanford Encyclopedia of Philosophy* (Spring 2011 Edition), ed. Edward N. Zalta. http://plato.stanford.edu/archives/spr2011/entries/identity-time/ (accessed March 2011).

Geach, Peter. 1967. 'Identity'. *Review of Metaphysics* 21:3–12.

Grellard, Christophe. 2009. 'Nicholas of Autrecourt's Atomistic Physics'. In Grellard and Robert, 2009.

Grellard, Christophe and Aurélien Robert, eds. 2009. *Atomism in Late Medieval Philosophy and Theology*, Leiden, the Netherlands: Brill.

John Buridan. 1509. *Quaestiones super octo Physicorum libros Aristotelis*. Paris.

———. 1588. *In Metaphysicam Aristotelis quaestiones*. Paris. (Reprint Frankfurt: Minerva, 1964.)

John Duns Scotus. 1950–. *Opera Omnia*, ed. C. Balic et al. Vatican City: Vatican Polyglot Press.

John Marsilius of Inghen. 1518. *Questiones subtilissime Johannis Marcilii Inguen super octo libros Physicosum*. Lugduni.

Lagerlund, Henrik. 2004. John Buridan and the Problem of Dualism in Early Fourteenth Century Philosophy. *Journal of the History of Philosophy* 42(4): 369–88.

———. 2011. The Changing Face of Aristotelian Empiricism in the Fourteenth Century. *Quaestio* 10 : 315–27.

Leibniz, Gottfried F. W. 1875–90. *Die philosophischen Schriften von Gottfried Wilhelm Leibniz*, ed. C. I. Gerhardt. Berlin: Weidmannsche Buchhandlund.

———. 1967. *The Leibniz-Arnauld Correspondence*, ed. and trans. H.T. Mason. New York: Manchester University Press.

Lewis, David. 1986. *The Plurality of Worlds*, Oxford: Blackwell.

Loux, Michael. 2006. *Metaphysics: A Contemporary Introduction*. London: Routledge.

McCord Adams, Marilyn. 1987. *William Ockham*, Notre Dame, IN: University of Notre Dame Press.

Michael, Emily. 2009. 'John Wyclif's Atomism'. In Grellard and Robert, 2009.

Millikan, Ruth. 2000. *On Clear and Confused Ideas: An Essay About Substance Concepts*. Cambridge: Cambridge University Press.

Murdoch, John E. 2001. 'The Medieval and Renaissance Tradition of Minima Naturalia'. In *Late Medieval and Early Modern Corpuscular Matter Theories*, ed. C. Lüthy, J. Murdoch and W. Newman, 91–132. Leiden, the Netherlands: Brill.

Nicholas of Autrecourt. 1971. *Universal Treatise*, trans. L. Kennedy, R. Arnold and A. Millward with an introduction by L. Kennedy. Milwaulkee, WI: Marquette University Press.

Normore, Calvin. 2006. Ockham's Metaphysics of Parts. *Journal of Philosophy* 103(12):737–54.

Pasnau, Robert. 2011. *Metaphysical Themes 1274–1671*. Oxford: Oxford University Press.

Pluta, Olaf. 2001. 'Buridan's Theory of Identity'. In *The Metaphysics and Natural Philosophy of John Buridan*, ed. J. M. M. H. Thijssen and J. Zupko, 49–64. Leiden, the Netherlands: Brill.

Rozemond, Marleen. 1998. *Descartes's Dualism*. Cambridge, MA: Harvard University Press.

Sleigh, Robert. 1990. *Leibniz and Arnauld: A Commentary on Their Correspondence*. New Haven, CT: Yale University Press.

Thomas Aquinas. 1954. *In octo lobros Physicorum Aristotelis expositio*, ed. P. M. Maggiolo. Turin: Marietti.

———. 1970. *Summa Theologiae*, trans. Timothy Sutton. London: Blackfriars.

———. 1984. *Questions on the Soul*, trans. J. H. Robb. Milwaukee, WI: Marquette University Press.

Wiggins, David. 2001. *Sameness and Substance Renewed*. Cambridge: Cambridge University Press.

William of Ockham. 1984. *Brevis Summa libri Physicorum, Summa philosophiae naturalis, et Quaestiones in libros Physicorum Aristotelis*. (Opera philosophica VI), ed. S. Brown. St Bonaventure, NY: St Bonaventure.

———. 1991. *Quodlibetal Questions*, trans. A. J. Freddoso and F. E. Kelley. New Haven, CT: Yale University Press.

Zavalloni, Roberto. 1951. *Richard de Mediavilla et la controverse sur la pluralité des formes*. Louvain, Belgium: Éditions de l'Institut Supérieur de Philosophie.

CHAPTER 22

MIND AND HYLOMORPHISM

ROBERT PASNAU

FOR later medieval philosophers, writing under the influence of Aristotle's natural philosophy and metaphysics, the human soul plays two quite different roles, serving as both a substantial form and a mind. To ask the natural question of why we need a soul at all—why we might not instead simply be a body, a material thing—therefore requires considering two very different sets of issues. The first set of issues is metaphysical and revolves around the central question of why a human being needs a substantial form. The second set of issues is psychological and turns on the question of why we should suppose that our mind is aptly characterised as a soul. This chapter takes up these two questions in turn and then turns to whether we should suppose that one and the same thing—a soul—is both substantial form and mind. This dual-function thesis is the most distinctive feature of later medieval psychology and is one reason that work from this era remains well worth reading today. Whereas modern thought furnishes many sophisticated discussions of the immateriality of mind, and the metaphysics of body, philosophers since Descartes have rarely considered that it might be one thing, the soul, that accounts for both thought and substantial unity.

1. SOUL AS FORM

In a seminal recent paper, Judith Jarvis Thomson remarks that 'surely a Tinkertoy house is made only of Tinkertoys; surely it has no additional ingredients, over and above the Tinkertoys it is made of' (Thomson 1983, 201). For Thomson, the Tinkertoys are simply a particularly vivid illustration of a point she wants to make about material substances in general. Big bodies are made from smaller bodies, and they contain nothing other than bodies. The appeal of this way of viewing the situation is easy to see, since it is hard to imagine what other sorts of parts a body could have, and hard to see what might motivate our seeking to find any other kinds of parts. Even so, medieval philosophers almost without exception reject Thomson's claim and suppose instead that material substances, in addition to whatever smaller bodies they might be composed of—their *integral* parts—are also composed of various non-bodily parts of a more *metaphysical* sort. For authors writing under the influence of Aristotle, such metaphysical parts are characterised as either form or matter, and the formal parts are further divided into those that are accidental and those that are substantial.

A full defence of this Aristotelian metaphysical programme would require a separate defence of these three kinds of metaphysical parts—prime matter, accidents and substantial forms—each of which admits of its own rationale. Here our focus is on only the last of these, and especially on those substantial forms, rational souls, that are found in human beings. From the medieval perspective, however, the case for postulating a rational soul rests in large part on arguments that extend much farther than the human case, applying not just to living things but to material substances in general. This is to say that the heart of the medieval case for postulating a rational soul rests on the fact that we are material substances, and that in general material substances cannot be understood on the model of Tinkertoys, as simply collections of smaller bodies assembled in a certain way. Beyond the familiar flesh, blood, bones and other integral parts that compose us in Tinkertoy fashion, we are made up of some further sort of entity, a substantial form.

It is, admittedly, not usual to view the medieval doctrine of soul from this perspective, from the bottom up rather than the top down, so that one postulates the rational soul as a consequence of broader metaphysical doctrines rather than as a special case that may or may not apply outside of the human domain. This first kind of perspective is hard for us to recognize because the word 'soul' itself seems properly at home only in the human case and fits awkwardly into a broader metaphysics of substance. Moreover, we have been taught by Descartes and others to regard the spread of soul talk beyond the human case as a disastrous bit of scholastic overreaching, taking an idea that has its place within us and putting it to work in places where it has no business at all. Descartes's perspective is, however, fundamentally alien to the medieval tradition. That tradition sees Aristotle's *De anima* not as a treatise on human nature, but as the first, foundational work in a longer cycle of biological works. A soul, accordingly, in the Aristotelian tradition, is simply the first internal principle of life, in anything that is alive (cf. *De an.* II.1, 412a28). Whatever it is within a thing that most basically explains its being a living substance, that is what the thing's soul is. This thesis, in turn, is seen as simply a particularly vivid instance of Aristotle's broader metaphysics, according to which, what distinguishes substances from non-substances is that they are not just a heap of integral parts but are the parts somehow unified, by a substantial form. Viewed from this perspective, all living things, of course, have a soul, and the only question in the human case concerns what that soul is like.

The distinctive features of the rational soul will emerge once we turn our attention from metaphysics to psychology. What first needs discussion, however, are the
metaphysical reasons that led medieval authors to insist on a soul as something over
and above the integral, Tinkertoy parts. Here we might consider three lines of
thought, two of which were developed in considerable detail by medieval authors,
and a third that is suggested by recent work in metaphysics.

First, there is the argument from change. If bodies are simply aggregates of
smaller bodies, with their only parts being integral parts, then any kind of change to
such a body will wreak havoc on our conception of what that body is. In particular,
we will have no grounds to distinguish between, in medieval terms, accidental and
substantial change—or, in other words, between cases of change to a substance that
are identity preserving (accidental change, or alteration) and cases of change that
are identity destroying (substantial change, or generation and corruption). John
Buridan, for instance, writing in the mid-fourteenth century, considers the view
that 'matter disposed in one way is fire, disposed in another way it is water, air, or
stone' (Buridan 1989, *In De an.* III.11). This is to say that there are no substantial
forms within substances, and that the difference between one substance and another
rests simply on matter's being arranged in one way or another. The view is an old
one, Buridan says, and was rejected by Aristotle for good reason:

> This was the view of Democritus, Melissus, and those who claimed that every-
> thing is one in substance. For they were not so foolish as to believe that this
> human being is the same in number as that one, but [they did make this claim]
> for things that appear to be generated from one another: for instance, if from
> earth A comes water B, and from water B comes grass C, and from grass C comes
> horse D, and so on for all species of generable and corruptible things, then horse
> D is the same as what was grass, water, and earth, since the same matter that they
> claimed to be the whole substance of the thing was first earth, then water, grass,
> and horse, disposed in one way and then another. These claims are extremely
> obscure and dangerous, however, for in the same way a donkey was a stone, and a
> stone has always existed, and no horse or human being has ever been generated,
> although matter has been made a human being or a horse. These things have been
> sufficiently condemned by Aristotle and others, and in no way would I want to
> assent to them. (Ibid.)

If the difference between earth, water, grass and horse is just a difference in their
material parts and how those parts are arranged, then Buridan thinks we will be
pulled towards a view on which nothing ever undergoes substantial change. The
very same thing—call it a stone if you like, though the choice of nomenclature is
arbitrary—'has always existed', at some times looking more like a horse or a donkey,
but never becoming anything different from what it has always been.

A similar statement of this same kind of argument for substantial form can be
found a few years later in Marsilius of Inghen. Marsilius takes up the question of
whether there is any need for a mixed body to have a substantial form that is something more than the four elements and their primary qualities (hot, cold, wet, dry),
mixed according to a certain proportion. The first in his series of seven arguments

for the affirmative makes a point much like Buridan's, that without substantial form the distinction between alteration and generation collapses. But whereas Buridan imagines the opponent of substantial form eliminating generation entirely, and treating all change as mere alteration, Marsilius supposes to the contrary that 'if in the mixed body there is no other form beyond the forms of the elements, it would follow that alteration would be generation' (Marsilius of Inghen 1505, *In Gen. et cor.* I.22). This is to say, in effect, that with no further resources beyond the elements and their qualities, any case of alteration might be counted as a case of generation. This is the opposite of the result Buridan describes, but really these are two sides of the same coin. For if the distinction between alteration and generation collapses, one could say either that all alteration is generation, or that no alteration is generation. Either substances never endure through change but instead always become something new, or they always endure through change and never become something new. The plausible middle ground that respects our intuitions about the individuation of material objects cannot hold. That sort of principled distinction between generation and alteration requires substantial form.

To be sure, neither Buridan's nor Marsilius's argument is decisive. For one thing, it could just be that one or the other of the radically revisionary metaphysical results described is true. Maybe nothing does go out of existence, or maybe nothing endures through change. More palatably, there are doubtless other ways in which a more commonsensical metaphysics might be preserved. Perhaps, for instance, it is just a brute fact that a donkey exists if and only if material stuff is arranged in one or another of various ways, and that as soon as the arrangement strays beyond those limits, that substance ceases to exist, and something else begins to exist. But if this is supposed to be just a brute fact, then it is hard to resist the suspicion that the boundaries of what counts as a donkey are just conventional. Without some further element—something beyond the integral parts arranged in Tinkertoy fashion—it is hard to see what would ground any sort of objective limits in the sort of change consistent with a thing's preserving its identity. Anyone moved by such considerations should find later medieval thought particularly interesting because never before or since have philosophers devoted such intensive efforts to developing a theory of what such further elements might be.

A second, related kind of metaphysical argument for substantial form targets synchronic unity—that is, the apparent fact that certain aggregates of material stuff have a special sort of togetherness that justifies our thinking of them as substances rather than as mere heaps. It is interesting that Buridan, at the start of the long passage quoted earlier, lets the pre-Socratics off the hook in this regard, allowing them the difference between one human being and another. Even so, such distinctions are highly problematic on this sort of reductive view. If all there are are corpuscles of various shapes and sizes, variously arranged, then it is not easy to see how we might draw the boundary lines, at any given moment, between one substance and another. Scholastic authors appeal to substantial form to explain such facts. The sixth of Marsilius's arguments for substantial form, for instance, runs as follows:

Sixth, [if there are no substantial forms, then] no mixed body would be one. The consequent is false, and the inference holds because there will be four elements so proportioned, and they will not be some further one thing. (Marsius of Inghen 1505, *In Gen. et cor.* I.22)

This is supposed to be so obvious as to need no further explanation. For if a body is simply 'four elements so proportioned', then what makes it one thing rather than a collection of uncountably many particles coming in four basic kinds? We would have no basis for regarding the parts of a tree as parts of a single substance, and no basis for regarding an individual donkey as a single substance, rather than as many distinct substances or, alternatively, as part of a larger substance such as the whole medina, or indeed the whole material universe. Again, substantial forms are not the only way to proceed, but without *something* to determine these boundary lines, the ontology of common sense appears to be alarmingly conventional.

A third kind of consideration in support of substantial form comes from the role it might play in avoiding the threat of vagueness. Vagueness is a threat because it seems as if things in the world cannot be vague, but yet at the same time it seems that the sorts of boundaries described above must be vague. How can there be a sharp cutoff, for instance, between what counts as a mere heap and what counts as a genuinely unified substance? Some things, such as a donkey, are clearly not heaps; other things, such as a pile of stones, clearly are heaps; some things appear to be just hopelessly poised in between. At what point, for instance, is the grain consumed by the donkey a part of the donkey, rather than being a foreign element inside the donkey's alimentary canal? Similar questions arise about the precise point at which things come into existence and go out of existence. All of this seems vague, which suggests that there seems to be no good answer to the question of what is and is not a unified substance. Many modern metaphysicians have found such questions so worrisome as to be driven towards postulating that nothing composite counts as a single entity, or that everything, no mattered how scattered, counts as a single entity. Obviously, it would preferable to have some less radical solution to these problems.

Later medieval authors have such a solution ready to hand. For any given region of material stuff, there will be a non-vague fact about whether the bodies in that region are informed by a given substantial form, and whether they continue to be so informed over time. To be sure, we will not be in a position to know the truth about such fine-grained details, and so facts about the unity and identity of substances will look vague to us. The vagueness, however, is purely epistemic; the world is determinate. This kind of epistemic solution is a well-known modern answer to the problem of vagueness. To many it seems incredible, however, that the natural world could contain such hidden facts about the exact boundaries of things. Again, the later medieval era recommends itself as the period when such a conception of the world, as made determinate by Aristotelian forms, has been worked out in the most complete detail.

Here then are three kinds of work that the doctrine of substantial form might do, both in our own case and in the case of other substances. Admittedly, clearly identifying this work is a double-edged sword. On one side, a clear sense of what substantial forms are supposed to do helps to make the doctrine less obscure. But it may at the same time serve to make it seem wholly incredible. Can we really suppose that, beyond the Tinkertoys, there is also a form of Tinkertoy, or some such thing, that grounds our familiar ontology of persisting, unified substances? Even if—worst-case scenario—postulating such a form is the only way to save common sense, it is not clear that the gain is worth the cost. Perhaps we are better off giving up on common sense. This, in effect, is what the great anti-scholastic figures of the seventeenth and eighteenth century all concluded, in one way or another, and the resultant proliferation of wild metaphysics is the price they paid.

The exact cost of substantial form depends, however, on how the theory is spelled out. One question concerns how widely to postulate such forms. Medieval authors generally deny, for instance, that artefacts have substantial forms. Hence, they can grant the case of Tinkertoys: convention rules in such questions of unity and identity because an assembly of Tinkertoys is never a real substance at all. The view can be made still more readily defensible if masses of non-living stuff (pools of water, stones) are likewise excluded, so that the only aggregate material substances will be living things. Here, unfortunately, medieval authors tend to be less clear about their position.[1]

A second, all-important question regarding the cost of substantial form concerns what sort of thing these substantial forms are supposed to be. The theory can be given at least a patina of respectability if one insists that substantial forms are simply *abstracta*. Modern philosophers are accustomed to deploy abstract entities in all sorts of respectable domains, from mathematics to ethics, and so one might find their use here to be equally palatable. To be sure, it is quite unclear what it even means to characterize a thing as abstract rather than concrete. But it is far from clear, on any construal, that substantial forms on the medieval conception could fall on the abstract side of that divide. They are, for one thing, very much located in time and space. The substantial form of this donkey exists right here, where the donkey exists, and inheres in all and only those integral parts that compose the donkey. Moreover, medieval authors understand substantial forms to be causally efficacious. Far from being mere abstract characterisations of an essence or a function, the medieval substantial form is a causal agent in the most straightforward way. Thus, when Marsilius of Inghen considers the possibility that a substance such as a donkey might be generated and later corrupted entirely as a result of the varying mixtures of elements within it, he objects not just on the grounds that there would be no non-arbitrary boundaries, but also on the grounds that varying mixtures of elements simply could not—as a physical matter—give rise to something with the properties of a donkey:

> Nor does it help to say that [different substances] are of distinct most specific species because of the distinct disposition of the proportions in their elemental qualities. For they are not said to differ in species through the distinct proportion and disposition in their material qualities. For if the whole substance of these mixed bodies were the elements, without any new form added on, then it would

follow that their elements would not differ in species, and [so] neither would the mixed bodies that are those elements differ in virtue of their distinct qualitative dispositions or proportions. (Marsius of Inghen 1505, *In Gen. et cor.* I.22)

Causes at the micro-level simply could not produce a wholly new macro-level entity such as a donkey, 'without any new form added on'. One needs that substantial form not just to do metaphysical work, but also to do physical, biological work.

It is hard to see how we, today, could accept the existence of anything like a substantial form, when viewed in this sort of concretely causal sort of way. Our physics and biology have developed in ways that do not tolerate any such central, organising principle. So if we are to embrace substantial forms, they will have to be somehow more abstract in character. But if we try to take this general metaphysical picture and apply it to the human case, we run into trouble. For whatever we might want to say about substantial forms in general, the human substantial form—the rational soul—is not supposed to be merely a bit of metaphysical *abstracta*. On the contrary, the rational soul, if it is anything at all, is at least in part the human mind. But the human mind, though it may be immaterial, seems indisputably a causal agent. Hence, a full appreciation of the medieval theory of soul requires us to go beyond metaphysics, into psychology, and consider what needs to be said about the soul when viewed as the human mind.

2. SOUL AS MIND

Put in terms of high scholastic metaphysical jargon, a substantial form is the actuality of a substance, conferring on matter the substantial existence (*esse*) in virtue of which it is actually what it is. In Thomas Aquinas's terms, whereas an accidental form makes a thing be such (e.g., hot or coloured), a substantial form *dat esse simpliciter*—'gives existence unconditionally' (*Summa theol.* 1a 76.4c). But this is not to say that the substantial form merely accounts for the difference between existing and not existing, as if it were the task of accidental forms to fill in all of the details of what the thing is like. Rather, the accidental forms are responsible only for a thing's non-essential properties, leaving the substantial form to account for what the thing essentially is. The substantial form of a donkey, then—the donkey soul—gives rise to all the features of the thing in virtue of which it is a donkey, whatever those defining features may be. Indeed, for the soul of a donkey to account for the *esse simpliciter* of a donkey just is for it to make a certain aggregate of matter such as to have all the biological characteristics of a donkey. To have these characteristics just is what it is for a donkey to exist. As Aristotle had remarked, 'for living things, living *is* existing' (*De an.* II 4, 415b13). The implication is that there is no such thing as existence beyond the specific ways of functioning manifested by specific kinds of things.

When we apply these remarks to the human case, the result is that the human soul will be responsible for what makes us essentially human. Here we face a choice.

On one picture of human nature, we are simply minds, incidentally attached, for a certain period of time, to a certain sort of body. On another sort of picture, we are essentially biological organisms, coming into existence through certain biological processes and existing for as long as the living organism exists. On this view, we are not essentially minds at all. These two perspectives point towards two very different directions along which one might develop a theory of the human soul. Medieval authors, however, almost without exception, refuse to choose one option to the exclusion of the other. Instead, they treat it as essential to human nature both to be essentially minds and to be essentially biological organisms. This is the point of the familiar definition of human beings as *rational animals*. To have it both ways requires viewing the human soul as fulfilling two quite different functions, one biological and the other psychological. The soul must be, in short, both a mind and the form of a body. For later medieval Christian authors, such a double function was, in fact, an ecclesiastical mandate. The Condemnations of 1277 at the University of Paris forbade denying that the intellect is the actuality of the body, or treating the intellect–body relationship as like that of sailor to ship. In 1312, the Council of Vienne declared it heretical to hold that 'the rational or intellective soul is not *per se* and essentially the form of the human body'. These statements guaranteed that the later medieval Christian theory of soul would be required to do double duty as both a theory of mind and a theory of the biological organism.[2]

As we will see below, this dual conception of the human soul gave rise to a lively scholastic dispute regarding whether some sort of distinction needs to be drawn between the mental and the biological aspect of soul. Is there a distinction of powers here, or perhaps even distinct substantial forms? There was general agreement, however, on the underlying assumption that the operations of mind are fundamentally distinct from the operations of body. This is not a verdict required by anything said so far. For even if human beings are essentially both minds and bodies, it could well be that the human soul actualizes the mind by actualising our bodies—presumably, our brains—in a certain way. To say this would be to treat the mind as something wholly biological and corporeal, a special feature of human beings, perhaps, but special in something like the way that having opposable thumbs is special—a special feature of our bodies.

We have now arrived, of course, at the old and vexed dispute between materialists and dualists. Medieval authors, almost without exception, reject materialism. But although that much is clear, it is difficult to characterize where the thesis of hylomorphism stands relative to the more straightforward dualism of Plato or Descartes. As should already be clear, later medieval authors do not fall into the camp of the dualists rather than the materialists simply because they ascribe souls to human beings. This by itself decides absolutely nothing in that debate because to postulate a soul is simply to postulate a substantial form and as such arises out of general metaphysical considerations that have nothing to do with the question of how mind stands to body. The characteristic medieval duality between mind and body arises from their denial that the soul accounts for mental phenomena in the way it accounts for other features of living organisms, by informing the body.

Instead, according to most medieval authors, the soul gives rise to the human mind without actualising matter at all. This is to say that the human soul by itself, quite independently of the body, is responsible for the thinking and willing that are the characteristic operations of mind. Although there are many things one might mean by 'dualism', this is the most common and widely accepted medieval formulation: that the operations of mind are performed by the soul independently of the body.

Even though dualism, so conceived, was almost universally embraced, there was considerable controversy over whether the thesis could be proved. The most prominent advocate of such proofs was Aquinas, who put particular weight on the following argument (with numbers supplied for the premises):

> It is necessary to say that the principle of intellectual operation, which we call the soul of a human being, is a non-bodily and subsistent principle. For [1] it is clear that through the intellect a human being can cognize the natures of all bodies. But [2a] that which can cognize certain things must have none of those things in its own nature, because that which exists in it naturally would impede its cognition of other things. In this way we see that a sick person's tongue, infected with a jaundiced and bitter humor, cannot perceive anything sweet; rather, all things seem bitter to that person. Therefore if the intellectual principle were to contain within itself the nature of any body, it could not cognize all bodies. But every body has some determinate nature. Therefore [3a] it is impossible for the intellectual principle to be a body. [3b] It is likewise impossible for it to operate *through* a bodily organ, because [2b] the determinate nature even of that bodily organ would prevent the cognition of all bodies. Analogously, a determinate colour not just in the pupil, but even in a glass vase, makes liquid poured into that vase seem to be of the same colour. Therefore [4] this intellectual principle, which is called mind or intellect, has an operation of its own that the body does not share in (*Summa theol.* 1a 75.2c).³

What drives this argument is the idea that the intellect displays a startling plasticity in its cognitive range. Our other cognitive capacities—sight, hearing and so on—are each rigidly limited to a certain domain, that of colour, sound and so forth. But the intellect, according to the first premise of the argument, can think about anything (or at any rate anything in the material realm, which is as strong a claim as Aquinas takes himself to need). The second premise of the argument then asserts that such plasticity would be impossible if the intellect either (a) were a body or (b) were to operate through a body. From these two premises the sub-conclusions of (3a) and (3b) immediately follow, and they together yield dualism in the sense defined above: that the mind operates independently of the body.

If the human soul is responsible for the operations of the mind, and if the mind operates independently of the body, then the human soul is certainly a very special kind of form. Every other form with which we are familiar, substantial or accidental, performs its function in virtue of actualising matter in a certain way. The accidental form of blue, for instance, is a certain sort of actualisation of a body, and accordingly, colour is inconceivable apart from a body. Similarly, the substantial form of a donkey actualizes matter in such a way as to produce the complex biological systems characteristic of donkeys. All of those systems are corporeal, in the sense that they are bodies so-and-so constituted and would not be the systems they are if they were, somehow, incorporeal. What Aquinas is arguing for, in the case of mind, is that here the soul is responsible for a feature of human beings that (3a) is not a body and (3b) does not rely on any body for its operation. It is in this precise sense that Aquinas, and other medieval Aristotelians, contend that the human soul is immaterial. It is not immaterial because it is a form. There are, after all, forms everywhere in nature, and they are perfectly ordinary parts of material substances. Nor is the human soul immaterial because it fails to inform a body or lacks location. The human soul does inform a body, just as every form does by nature, and so is located where that body is located. What makes the human soul immaterial is that it does something more— it has an operation that it carries out independently of the body, inasmuch as the human soul, all by itself, thinks.

But even if this is a conclusion that medieval authors generally accepted, still they disagreed over whether it could be proved. One who thought it could not was William Ockham. With Aquinas's arguments evidently in mind, Ockham takes up the question of whether 'one can know evidently through reason or through experience that we think, taking "thinking" to mean an act proper to an immaterial substance of the sort the intellective soul is claimed to be' (William Ockham 1991, *Quodlibet* I.10). Ockham certainly does not seek to deny that we are aware of our own thinking. The question is whether we can know through reason or experience that thought is the operation of an immaterial substance, the soul alone. That this thesis is *true* Ockham does not deny. But he thinks that it is something one must take on faith, as a Christian. So he responds to the question as follows:

> If by 'intellective soul' one means an immaterial and incorruptible form that exists as a whole in the whole body and as a whole in each part,[4] then one cannot evidently know either (a) through reason or (b) through experience that such a form exists in us, or that an act of thinking proper to such a substance exists in us, or that such a soul is the form of the body. . . . Now (a) it is evident that these things cannot be demonstrated, since every argument meant to prove them presupposes things that are doubtful to a human being who is following natural reason. Nor (b) are they proved through experience. For we experience only acts of thinking and acts of willing and similar such things. But one who follows reason along with experience would maintain that these are all operations and passions that are caused in and received in that form that he would claim distinguishes a human being from a brute animal. And even though, according to the faith and according to the truth, this form is an intellective soul that is an incorruptible form, the person in question would nonetheless maintain that this form is extended, generable, and corruptible. And it does not seem that experience would establish a different sort of form. (Ibid.)

An argument for dualism, Ockham contends, would be grounded in either (a) reason or (b) experience. Dismissing each in turn, he concludes that the soul's immateriality can be accepted only as a matter of faith.

With respect to arguments from reason, Ockham dismisses them all with a wave of his hand, remarking that 'every argument . . . presupposes things that are doubtful to a human being who is following natural reason'. It would have been nice, at this point, if Ockham had offered us a few examples of failed arguments. Still, it is easy enough to see what he means, if we go back to the argument from Aquinas quoted above. Although the logical form of Aquinas's argument is valid, none of the premises are self-evident in the way they would have to be to yield what Ockham calls 'evident knowledge'. It is not perfectly clear, for instance, as the first premise has it, that the intellect *can* 'cognize the natures of all bodies'. Even more doubtful is the second premise (2a, 2b): that the determinate nature of a bodily organ restricts the scope of what such an organ can cognize. Although the comparisons to taste and sight are suggestive, it is far from clear that they generalize. There is no reason at all to be confident that the intellect, if it relied on the brain, would similarly be limited in the scope of what it could grasp. This is, of course, just one argument, albeit a particularly well-known one. Still, the intervening centuries have not made it seem any more likely that a demonstrative argument for the mind's immateriality is forthcoming.

What about experience? Ockham contends that all we experience are the acts themselves of mind—acts of thinking, willing and so on. There is nothing in these experiences that points towards any sort of distinctive, non-physical origin. The usual sort of biological explanations, in terms of a substantial form actualising the body, would seem to serve perfectly well. This part of Ockham's case would meet with no dispute from Aquinas, who thinks that the truth of dualism can be established only using reason. In recent years, however, this second path has taken on a certain sort of appeal among some dualists. For it is sometimes suggested that simple introspective reflection on the character of mental experience provides reason for thinking that such a thing cannot be explained in ordinary biological terms. A simple question—How could the brain account for *that?*—is in some quarters taken seriously as a powerful argument. Ockham, for his part, sees nothing in the experience of thought or volition that points towards a non-biological, immaterial explanation.

It is interesting, in this connection, that the kinds of mental phenomena at issue for Ockham and his contemporaries are different from what they are for us. We now think of perceptual states—seeing a colour, say—as paradigmatic examples of the sort of mental phenomena that resist physical explanation. But for Ockham, as for other medievals, sensation is indisputably a biological process. We sense as other animals sense, using physical organs, and though those organs are capable of sensation only in virtue of being actualised by the soul, the story here is not fundamentally different from the story for our locomotive or digestive powers. The cases that are supposed to be special, then, are cognitive and volitional acts at the intellectual level—the level of abstract, universal thought. When Ockham claims that the introspective experience of our own mental states does not point towards any sort of special cause, he is saying that abstract thoughts and volitions seem, on their face, to require no more special explanation than does sensation or nutrition. In every case, if we followed reason alone, we would expect their cause to be a form that is 'extended, generable, and corruptible'.

For Ockham, then, it must be a matter of faith that the human soul is of a fundamentally different kind from the souls of other animals. At this point one might wonder why such a claim *had* to be held on faith. Could one not be a devout Christian and still think that the human soul is a physical, biological form just like other substantial forms? Certainly, there have been and there continue to be theists of all kinds, including Christians, who think just this. The difficulty arises when one comes to the question of the soul's immortality, which is clearly a non-negotiable tenet of at least the Christian faith. For the human soul to be immortal, it must evidently be capable of existence apart from the body, inasmuch as the human body does not ordinarily survive death. Aquinas, however, insists—and his contemporaries largely agree—that the human soul can exist apart from the body only if it can function apart from the body.[5] This puts tremendous weight on the thesis of dualism, in the precise sense defined earlier. For if even the operation of thought requires a body, then it is hard to see what else the rational soul might be capable of doing apart from the body. Accordingly, if dualism cannot be proved, it looks as if the soul's immortality cannot be proved.

Supposing dualism can be proved, one might still have doubts regarding immortality. After all, even if it is true that the soul thinks and wills on its own, this does not guarantee that the soul will continue to do so when separated from the body. The further step required here is particularly evident for medieval Aristotelians because of their insistence that human beings are essentially corporeal—not just souls, but soul–body composites. Insisting on our essentially corporeal nature entails that although *our souls* may survive death, apart from the body, *we ourselves, as human beings*, do not survive death. Of course, for the Christian, that cannot be the end of the story, and so what theologians like Aquinas argue is that we are able to exist after death only once our bodies are resurrected. Until that happens, your separated soul does not count as a person, or as a human being, or even as you:

> Abraham's soul is not, strictly speaking, Abraham himself; it is rather a part of
> him (and so too for others). So Abraham's soul's having life would not suffice for
> Abraham's being alive. . . . The life of the whole compound is required: soul and
> body. (Thomas Aquinas 1882–; IV *Sent.* 43.1.1.1 ad 2.)[6]

In as much as no one thinks the resurrection of human bodies can be proved philosophically, this doctrine precludes establishing the immortality of human beings. Aquinas thus thinks that although the *soul's* immortality can be proved, human immortality must be taken on faith.

The entanglement of soul and body makes still more trouble than this, however, with respect to immortality. Part of the reason Aquinas and other medieval Aristotelians insist on the essential bodily component of human beings is that they think the body—in particular, the five external senses plus imagination, memory and the other internal senses of the brain—play an essential role in thought and volition. Indeed, Aquinas, John Duns Scotus and others insist that the human mind can think nothing at all without a phantasm—that is, without some kind of accompanying sensory image, which the brain produces a steady stream of, in order to give concrete shape to the abstract thoughts of intellect.[7] How can this doctrine be squared with dualism's insistence on the mind's separate function? For Aquinas, the answer turns on a distinction in senses of 'can'. The human soul can think and will without the body, in the sense that this is metaphysically possible. But as things are, in this life, when the soul is entwined with the body, it is not naturally possible to think without sensory images. So what then will happen after death? Aquinas insists that there will then be room for other possibilities. In particular, he insists that 'once separated from its body, the soul will have a different mode of cognition, like that of other substances that are separate from body' (*Summa theol.* 1a 75.6 ad 3). The other substances to which he refers are the angels. Aquinas's position, therefore, is that the human soul, in the period of time between death and the resurrection, will shift to a different mode of cognising, one not dependent on sensory experience, but rather attuned to divine illumination. Thus, 'a separated soul uses intellect just like the angels do, through species that it receives from the influence of the divine light' (*Summa theol.* 1a 89.3c).

All of this maneuvering is meant to bridge the gap between the soul's immateriality and its immortality. Unsurprisingly, it met with considerable scepticism. Pietro Pomponazzi (1462–1525) devoted an entire treatise to challenging various arguments for the soul's immortality and characterised this part of Aquinas's account as a tale worthy of Ovid's *Metamorphoses* (Pietro Pomponazzi 1948, ch. 9). It is, indeed, quite hard to see how philosophical reflection alone can get us all the way to the thesis that human beings live forever. Too much would seem to rest on contingencies concerning the divine will. A lesser task is to establish that the character of the human soul is fundamentally different from other souls, and in general from other substantial forms. But although this was generally believed to be so, its susceptibility to philosophical demonstration was less clear.[8]

3. MIND AS FORM

For most later medieval authors, the soul is both the form of the body and the immaterial principle of thought. In virtue of the first, soul and body are said to make a single, unified substance. In virtue of the second, the soul is said to be immaterial and immortal. It is, however, not easy to see how these two doctrines can co-exist, and many of the leading philosophical debates of the medieval era engaged with this issue.

The most radical proposal in this domain treated the intellect not only as distinct from the human soul, but even as outside the human substance—as a single immaterial entity, shared by all human beings. This was a natural way to read Aristotle's remarks about the *nous poietikos*, which the *De anima* had described, in remarks notorious for their obscurity, as 'separable, unaffected, and unmixed . . . immortal and eternal' (*De an.* III.5, 430a17–23). Even many orthodox Christian authors were prepared to equate this 'agent intellect' with something beyond human nature, usually understood as God himself.[9] But this seemed tenable in the case of agent intellect because it left another intellectual power, Aristotle's *nous pathetikos* or 'possible intellect,' within the human soul, distinct for each individual. A more radical idea was that even this possible intellect might be something outside human nature, so that while each of us would have an individual soul, no one would have an individual mind. We think by somehow sharing in the thought of a centralised mastermind. This idea was popularised by Averroes and became very influential among Latin authors such as Siger of Brabant and Paul of Venice.[10] Although today the view is likely to seem too bizarre to be taken seriously, it can be seen as simply one way of understanding what it means to insist on the intellect's immateriality. For if we are persuaded that the mind is immaterial, and that human beings in contrast are corporeal, then one solution is to treat the mind as something outside of us, something whose operations we somehow manage to participate in, as it were, at a distance.

Such a view could scarcely be squared with orthodox religion. In Islam, Averroes's views were generally scorned. Among Christian authors, though various philosophers were tempted by Averroism, the theologians were united in their opposition. Aquinas and Ockham, for instance, for all they differed, both thought it flatly incoherent to suppose that the human power of thought is shared among all human beings. According to Ockham, the same intellect cannot know a thing and, at the same time, be ignorant of it—hence, according to the Averroist doctrine it would be impossible for one person to know something that another person does not know (*Quodlibet* I.11). Aquinas's argument is similar. Imagine that Socrates and Plato share a single eye. Then there would be two people seeing, but one act of vision. (Imagine, better, that Socrates and Plato share the same visual power all the way up into the brain. How could they be seeing different things?) This would be so in the case of intellect, too, which is bad enough, but Aquinas thinks that case is still worse because he thinks, not implausibly, that the intellect is constitutive of our individual identities. Hence, in contrast to the case of the shared eye, 'if there is a single intellect, then no matter how different all the other things are that the intellect uses as instruments, there is no way in which Socrates and Plato could be said to be anything other than a single thinker' (*Summa theol.* 1a 76.2c).

Setting the Averroistic hypothesis aside, and supposing that each human being has its own intellect, there is still a further question of how that intellect stands to the soul. As we saw already, Church authority from the early fourteenth century forward mandated treating the intellect as the form of the body. This goes beyond saying that the *soul* is the form of the body. One might embrace that view, for the sort of metaphysical reasons described earlier, and yet think that the *mind* or *intellect*, as something immaterial, cannot possibly inhere in the body as its form. Aquinas was the leading proponent of the orthodox Church view, offering philosophical arguments not just for the thesis that a human being requires a substantial form, a soul, but also for the thesis that this substantial form must be the principle of thought. For if mind and body were not united as form to matter, but simply as mover to moved, then there would be no way to account for the evident fact 'that it is oneself who thinks' (*Summa theol.* 1a 76.1c). The most we could say, Aquinas argued, is that there is thinking going on within us. Ockham, in contrast, thought that no philosophical arguments were available here. Just as we say that someone is an oarsman because of his oar, so we might say that I am a rational animal because of my intellect (*Quodlibet* I.10). Now one obvious difference, which Aquinas makes much of, is that we think of human beings as *essentially* rational, not essentially oarsmen. Part of what is at issue here is whether that itself can be proved. As before, however, it is not implausible to think that having an intellect is part of what defines us as the individuals we are. Aquinas by no means demonstrates that the hylomorphic theory of substantial form is the only way to capture the notion of an essential attribute, but he challenges his opponents to produce some other coherent account of the situation. It is not adequate, Aquinas urges, simply to treat human beings as a composite of two distinct substances, mind and body, even if those substances are tied together by quite extensive causal connections.

Although the appeal of Aquinas's hylomorphism is clear enough, there was considerable scepticism among later medieval authors regarding whether the view is ultimately coherent. The intellect's immateriality, as we have seen, consists in a certain sort of independence from the body. How is this compatible with its being the form of the body? Aquinas's arguments notwithstanding, many accepted Church orthodoxy on this point only as a kind of unintelligible mystery. John of Jandun, a leading Latin proponent of Averroism, was not so rash, in the censorious atmosphere of fourteenth-century Paris, to defend the Averroistic unicity thesis. Instead, he simply recites the orthodox line that the intellect is the form of the body and then adds, with more than a hint of animus towards the intellectual restrictions under which he worked: 'Everything that the Catholic faithful say, I say to be unconditionally true, without any doubt, even if I do not know how to show it. Let those who know how to do this rejoice. For my part, I hold and profess these things on faith alone' (John of Jandun 1587, III.12, col. 291).[11]

For authors seeking to maintain some commitment to a hylomorphic account of soul–body unity, but doubtful of how soul could be both form and mind, it was common to postulate the existence of multiple substantial forms.[12] Scotus, for instance, postulated that human beings have both a rational soul, responsible for thought, volition and perception, and a further substantial form that actualizes the body, the *forma corporeitatis*. Ockham maintained that human beings contain three substantial forms: the rational soul, the sensory soul and a substantial form of the body. This does not quite remove the sense of paradox that comes from treating the soul as both a form of the body and an immaterial power. For the pluralists, the intellect is *still* a form of the body. But the approach at least distinguishes between the kind of form that the rational soul is and the kind of form that actualizes an ordinary corporeal substance. By drawing this distinction, the pluralists were able to account for the intuition that a living thing has, as it were, two axes of identity, on the one hand as a living thing, and on the other hand as a body. The living thing may cease to exist, on this picture, while the body yet endures, as a corpse. Aquinas, in contrast, insisted that every substance has only a single substantial form, which required him to maintain that when the living thing goes out of existence, every part of that thing goes out of existence, all the way down to the level of prime matter, which is the only enduring substratum for substantial change. This does not on its face seem very plausible—it looks like a person's body can survive death, at least for a short time—but Aquinas contended that such tightly bound identity conditions are precisely what distinguish substances as unified entities. Anything that is less tightly bound is a mere heap.[13]

Aquinas's unitarianism is extremely austere in its insistence that the human substance, like any material substance, is nothing more than a composition of prime matter with a single substantial form. (Accidental forms are then added to that substantial composite to yield the *per accidens* unities that we are familiar with—the white dog, the musical Socrates, etc.) An important part of what makes this theory coherent, however, is that Aquinas regards substantial forms as themselves having structure. In the case of souls, he distinguishes between the essence of the soul and its powers, so that in the human case, for instance, he can speak of the soul itself, which informs prime matter, and the various powers—agent and possible intellect, will, internal and external senses, and so on—which are themselves accidents of the soul. This is how Aquinas squares the soul's status as form with its status as immaterial intellect. It is the soul, strictly speaking, and not the intellect, that is the form of body. The pluralists, with other distinctions in place, generally felt no need to distinguish between the soul and its powers. They generally treat the rational soul as simple, a conclusion they held to befit its immaterial status.[14]

This debate between unitarians and pluralists continued throughout the scholastic era, without any consensus ever emerging. The unitarian position of the Thomists offered a beautifully clear account of what substantial forms are but imposed a degree of substantial unity that struck many as incredible. The pluralist account fitted better with common sense. But in distinguishing the rational soul from the form of the body, pluralists made it hard to understand the sense in which the rational soul is itself a form. Inasmuch as we understand the notion of a substantial form at all, we understand it in the paradigmatic case where the form gives a body its defining characteristics. Although the pluralists were compelled by their Christian faith to maintain that even the rational soul is the form of the body, it is often hard to see what force other than verbal can be ascribed to such pronouncements. Such tendencies culminated in the case of René Descartes. He proposed simply to jettison all talk of souls, and speak in the human case only of the simple, extensionless, immaterial mind. Is the mind the form of the body? Of course it is, says Descartes, ever eager to be a good Catholic, but knowing full well just how little such claims had come to mean within the scholastic tradition.[15]

NOTES

1. I have argued that Thomas Aquinas accepts as material substances only living things and the smallest bits of each kind of non-living stuff—see Pasnau (2002a, ch. 3). This reading of Aquinas is, however, controversial, and it is no more clear what position other later medieval authors would take.

2. For 1277, see Piché (1999, n. 7). For the Council of Vienne, see Denzinger (1967, n. 902).

3. For another version of this argument, see Thomas Aquinas (1999, 345,131–59); *In De an.* III.7, sec. 680, which elaborates on a sketch along these lines that Aristotle had put forth at *De anima* (III.4, 429a18–24).

4. Ockham here stresses the standard medieval doctrine that the human soul, rather than being spatially extended in the usual way, exists throughout the whole body, and wholly in each part of the body. Following Henry More, the seventeenth-century critic of the doctrine, we can label this 'holenmerism'. Ockham mentions this here because he takes it to be an important aspect of what makes the human soul distinctively immaterial. Aquinas, in contrast, thinks that all complex substances have holenmeric substantial forms (see, e.g., *Summa theol.*, 1a 76.8). On the relationship between holenmerism and immateriality, see Pasnau (2011, ch. 16). On Ockham's theory of soul more generally, see Adams (2001).

5. See, for example, Thomas Aquinas (1961–67; *Summa contra gentiles* II.80, sec. 1618): 'It is impossible for a substance to exist that has no operation'.

6. For other texts from Aquinas that make the same point, see *Summa theol.* (1a 29.1 ad 5), *Summa theol.* (2a2ae 83.11 obj. 5 & ad 5), *Quaest. de potentia* (9.2 ad 14) and *In Primam Corinth.* (15.2.924). For further discussion of this difficult doctrine, see Pasnau (2002a, ch. 12). For a different reading of Aquinas here, which seeks to find room to treat the separated soul as the same human person, see Stump (2003, ch. 1).

7. See, for example, John Duns Scotus (1950-; *Lectura* II.3.2.1 n. 255) and Aquinas (*Summa theol.* 1a 84.7).

8. Other critical discussions of Aquinas's account of human immortality can be found in John Duns Scotus (1962, *Ordinatio* IV.43.2), and even in the great Thomist Cajetan (1965, III.2). Blasius of Parma (1974) is very unusual among medieval authors in denying even that the rational soul is immaterial. But Parma, appealing to divine contingencies in the opposite direction, remarks that even if our souls are material, still there is surely a way in which God can preserve our existence after death.

9. See Alexander of Aphrodisias (1990), Avicenna (1968–72, V.5), Averroes (2009), III.18–19 and William of Auvergne (2000), VII.3–4.

10. See Averroes (2009), Siger of Brabant (1972) and Paul of Venice (1503, *De an.* ch. 37). See, too, the anonymous Parisian questions on *De anima* I–II in Pasnau (2002b).

11. For similar remarks see Henry of Harclay (2008), IX.59 and Peter Auriol (1605), II:224b; *Sent.* II.16.1.2.

12. For the general question of unicity or multiplicity of substantial forms, see above, Chapter 21.

13. Aquinas, *Summa theol.* 1a 76.3–4; John Duns Scotus 1639; *Ordinatio* IV.11.3; Ockham, *Quodlibet* II.10–11. For further discussion of the scholastic debate over the plurality of substantial forms, see Adams (1987, ch. 15) and Pasnau (2011, ch. 25).

14. The thesis that the soul is identical with its powers was standard in the twelfth century, particularly among Cistercian authors (see McGinn 1977), and in the early thirteenth century (see Lottin 1948–60, I:483–90) and would be taken up again by Ockham (1967-1989; *Sent.* II.20) and the later nominalist tradition. For Aquinas's real distinction, see *Summa theol.* (1a q. 77). Strictly speaking, Scotus invokes a formal distinction between the rational soul and its powers (John Duns Scotus 1639, *Reportatio* II.16), but the subtleties of that less-than-real distinction need not concern us here. For recent discussions of the relationship between the soul and its powers, see King (2008) and Pasnau (2002a, ch. 5).

15. For further discussion of Descartes's views in this domain, in comparison to the scholastics, see Rozemond (1998) and Pasnau (2011, chs. 24–25).

For valuable feedback on this chapter, I am indebted to Martin Lenz and John Marenbon.

BIBLIOGRAPHY

Adams, Marilyn McCord. 1987. *William Ockham*. Notre Dame, IN: University of Notre Dame Press.

———. 2001. Ockham on the Soul: Elusive Proof, Pialectical Persuasions. *American Catholic Philosophical Quarterly* 75:43–77.

Alexander of Aphrodisias. 1990. 'De intellectu'. In *Two Greek Aristotelian Commentators on the Intellect*, trans. F. Schroeder. Toronto: Pontifical Institute of Mediaeval Studies.

Averroes. 2009. *Long Commentary on the De anima of Aristotle*, tr. R. C. Taylor. New Haven, CT: Yale University Press.

Avicenna. 1968–1972. *Liber de anima seu Sextus de naturalibus*, ed. S. Van Riet. Leiden, the Netherlands: Brill (Avicenna Latinus).

Blasius of Parma. 1974. *Les quaestiones de anima*, ed. G. Federici Vescovini. Florence: Olschki.

Cajetan (Tommaso de Vio). 1965. *Commentaria in libros Aristotelis De anima liber III*, ed. G. Picard and G. Pelland. Bruges, Belgium: Desclée de Brouwer.

Denzinger, Heinrich, ed. 1967. *Enchiridion symbolorum*, 34th ed. Freiburg, Germany: Herder.

Henry of Harclay. 2008. *Ordinary Questions*, ed. M. G. Henninger. Oxford: The British Academy.

John Buridan. 1989. 'John Buridan's philosophy of mind: An edition and translation of book III of his "Questions on Aristotle's De anima" (third redaction), with commentary and critical and interpretative essays', ed. J. Zupko. Ph.D. diss., Cornell University.

John Duns Scotus. 1639. *Opera omnia*, ed. L. Wadding. Lyons. (Reprinted 1968, Hildesheim, Germany: Olms.)

———. 1950–. *Opera omnia*, ed. C. Balić et al. Vatican City: Typis Polyglottis Vaticanis.

———. 1962. *Philosophical Writings*, trans. A. B. Wolter. Edinburgh: Nelson. (Reprinted Indianapolis: Hackett, 1987.)

John of Jandun. 1587. *Super libros Aristotelis de anima subtilissimae quaestiones*. Venice. (Reprinted Frankfurt: Minerva, 1966.)

King, Peter. 2008. The Inner Cathedral: Mental Architecture in High Scholasticism. *Vivarium* 46:253–74.

Lottin, Odon. 1948–60. *Psychologie et morale aux XIIe et XIIIe siècles*. Gembloux, Belgium: Duculot.

Marsilius of Inghen. 1505. *Quaestiones de generatione et corruption*. Venice. (Reprinted 1970, Frankfurt: Minerva.)

McGinn, Bernard, ed. and trans. 1977. *Three Treatises on Man: A Cistercian Anthropology*. Kalamazoo, MI: Cistercian Publications.

Pasnau, Robert, trans. 2002a. *Cambridge Translations of Medieval Philosophical Texts, vol. III: Mind and Knowledge*. Cambridge: Cambridge University Press.

———. 2002b. *Thomas Aquinas on Human Nature: A Philosophical Study of* Summa theologiae *I.75–89*. Cambridge: Cambridge University Press.

———. 2011. *Metaphysical Themes 1274–1671*. Oxford: Clarendon Press.

Paul of Venice. 1503. *Summa philosophiae naturalis*. Venice. (Reprinted Hildesheim, Germany: Olms, 1974.)

Peter Auriol. 1605. *Commentariorum in secundum, tertium et quartum Sententiarum et Quodlibeti*. Rome.

Piché, David, ed. 1999. *La condamnation parisienne de 1277*. Paris: Vrin.

Pietro Pomponazzi. 1948. 'On the immortality of the soul'. In *The Renaissance Philosophy of Man*, ed. E. Cassirer et al., 280–381. Chicago: University of Chicago Press.

Rozemond, Marleen. 1998. *Descartes's Dualism*. Cambridge, MA: Harvard University Press.

Siger of Brabant. 1972. *Quaestiones in tertium De anima; De anima intellectiva; De aeternitate mundi*, ed. B. C. Bazán (Leuven, Belgium: Publications universitaires).

Stump, Eleonore. 2003. *Aquinas*. London: Routledge (Arguments of the Philosophers).

Thomas Aquinas. 1999. *Commentary on Aristotle's* De anima, trans. R. Pasnau. New Haven, CT: Yale University Press.

———. 1882–. *Opera omnia*, ed. Leonine Commission. Rome: Commissio Leonina.

———. 1961–7. *Liber de veritate Catholicae fidei contra errores infidelium, seu Summa contra gentiles*, ed. C. Pera, P. Marc and P. Carmello. Rome: Mariett.

Thomson, Judith Jarvis. 1983. Parthood and Identity across Time. *Journal of Philosophy* 80:201–20.

William of Auvergne. 2000. *The soul*, trans. R. J. Teske. Milwaukee, WI: Marquette University Press.

William Ockham. 1967–89. *Opera philosophica et theologica*. St Bonaventure, NY: Franciscan Institute.

———. 1991. *Quodlibetal questions*, trans. A. Freddoso and F. Kelley. 2 vols. New Haven, CT: Yale University Press.

CHAPTER 23

....

BODY AND SOUL

....

PETER KING

MODERN philosophy is haunted by the spectre of Cartesian dualism: the view that a human being is a composite of two fundamentally different substances, one material (the body) and the other immaterial (the mind or soul). Medieval philosophers usually do not go so far. While they recognise immaterial living beings, such as angels and God, they do not think souls are necessarily immaterial, much less intrinsically subsistent, entities. Human souls are a special case, being partly immaterial (in a limited way) but non-subsistent, and strictly speaking, not substances at all. This philosophical position—similar to contemporary property dualism or non-reductive materialism—was the widespread, though not universal, consensus in the Latin Christian West throughout the Middle Ages. Despite the obvious connection of these issues with religious dogma, medieval philosophers were largely undogmatic in their approaches to them, perhaps because their doctrinal commitments pulled in opposite directions: on the one hand, to personal post-mortem survival, on the other hand, to the resurrection of the flesh. In consequence, they carefully distinguished what ought to be believed as a matter of faith from what could be established by argument. Their consensus view was thought to be the most philosophically defensible view in its own right, and not the least of its attractions was that it avoided the pitfalls we now recognise in Cartesian dualism.

Medieval philosophers did not know about Descartes, of course. Yet they were well aware of a 'Platonic dualism' that has most of the features of Cartesian substance dualism: Plato was taken to hold that the human soul and the human body are distinct substances, the former immaterial and the latter material, and that sensing, like thinking, is properly a function of the soul rather than the body. So wrote Aquinas in *Summa theologiae* (1a q. 75 art. 3):

> Ancient philosophers did not draw any distinction between sense and intellect,
> and attributed both as being up to a bodily principle. Plato, however, did draw a

distinction between intellect and sense, but he attributed each one to a non-bodily principle, maintaining that sensing, like thinking, holds of the soul in its own right.

The claim that sensing stems from an immaterial principle was rejected in the Middle Ages, on the grounds that sensing is intrinsically bound up with the body.[1] But the notion that thinking might somehow be immaterial and independent called for subtle consideration. Even assuming that the mind can be identified as part of the individual soul,[2] there are still puzzling questions that need to be addressed. Is it part of the nature of the intellect or the intellective soul to be immaterial? Is it capable of existence apart from the body? If so, is such separated existence natural to it? If not, why not? These questions were usually addressed in a more general fashion: what is the soul, and what kind of relation does it have to the body?

1. MEDIEVAL PLATONISM

If any medieval philosopher were to have endorsed some version of the 'Platonic dualism' sketched briefly above, it would be the one with whom the Middle Ages has its beginning: Augustine. He certainly gives this impression in several of his earlier writings. In *De immortalitate animae* 9.16 (ca. 387), for example, Augustine argues that the mind (*animus*) as a principle of life cannot 'lack itself' and so must always be alive, hence surviving the dissolution of the body—and in 10.17 he attacks the view that the mind might be no more than a particular organisation (*temperatio*) of the body, arguing that such a view cannot account for the (supposed) fact that we exercise our minds to their fullest when they are withdrawn from the body. Thus, it seems that for Augustine the mind is not material and has features, including life itself, independently of the body. So, too, in *De quantiate animae* 13.22 (ca. 388), where Augustine explicitly declares that 'the mind is not a body nor anything like a body', on the grounds that it could then not understand anything immaterial, leading Augustine to formulate a definition of the mind as 'a certain substance that shares in reason and suited to rule over the body'.[3] This seems to be borne out in the definition he offers in his contemporaneous *De moribus ecclesiae catholicae* 1.27.52 (ca. 388): a human being is 'a rational soul (*rationalis anima*) using a mortal and earthly body'. Augustine, therefore, seems to be a Cartesian dualist *avant la lettre*: he recognises the mind or rational soul as immaterial in its nature and a substance distinct from the body, which makes use of the body but naturally continues to live even after the dissolution of the body. This should not surprise us given the degree to which Descartes was indebted to Augustine.

Matters are not as they seem at first glance, however. Take Augustine's declaration that the soul is 'a certain substance'. In the context of *De quantitate animae* 13.22, this follows immediately upon Augustine's claim that the mind is not one of the four elements—earth, air, fire or water—but, rather, has 'a nature that is proper to it'. Hence, when he says that the mind is a certain substance, he is not using the term 'substance' in the technical sense of a subject capable of existence in its own right; he means only that the soul is some sort of stuff or other, though not the same as the mundane elements. Immediately after giving his definition, Augustine raises the question whether the mind has quantity or local extension even though it is not a body, that is, even though it is not ordinary material stuff (14.23). And while it is true that the rational soul shares in reason, is suited to rule the body and makes use of the body, none of these features entail that it is a substance independent of the body (or even that it is intrinsically immaterial).

Similarly, Augustine's description of the rational soul as 'using the body' in *De moribus ecclesiae catholicae* (1.27.52) refers to an earlier discussion (1.4.6) in which he points out that we are composites of body and soul (*ex anima et corpore nos esse compositos*) and, acknowledging that human beings are thereby two—he carefully does not say 'two *things*'—he states unequivocally that we are human beings only when body and soul are conjoined, 'for the body would not be a human being if there were no soul, nor again would the soul be a human being if a body were not animated by it'.[4] Augustine asks whether one of the two factors is the more principal: are human beings composed of body and soul equally, like 'two horses harnessed together'? Or is the body more principal, as when we call the vessel alone a 'lamp' on account of the flame it supports? Or is the soul more principal, as we say that a horse rider is not the horse and the rider, but the rider alone in virtue of guiding the horse? He endorses the last alternative when he asserts that the rational soul makes use of the body, as a horse rider makes use of a horse. But that is not to say that the soul is a substance independent of the body; a horse rider without a horse is no horse rider at all, and, as noted, Augustine insists that human beings are made up of body and soul taken together. This is the position he explicitly endorses in his mature works. In *De trinitate* (15.7.11), Augustine tells us that soul and body combine to produce a human being, 'a rational substance made up of soul and body'.[5] Here the word 'substance' is used technically, for a unified being capable of independent existence. Likewise, in *De cura pro mortuis gerenda* (3.5, ca. 422), Augustine maintains that bodies are not mere external ornaments or aids to the soul, but instead, are integral to human nature.[6] The soul itself has a 'certain natural impulse to look after the body' (*naturalis quidam appetitus corpus administrandi*), as Augustine puts it in *De Genesi ad literam* (12.35.68, ca. 415) while discussing the resurrection of the flesh and the glorified body we receive after the Last Judgement,[7] which keeps it conjoined to the body and renders it incomplete when it is not so conjoined. A separated soul is in an unnatural state, though not necessarily an impossible one.

Augustine's denial of substancehood to the human mind/soul, and his reluctance to allow it existence in its own right, is compatible with his claims that (a) the human mind/soul is in some sense non-bodily, and (b) it may exist in separation from the body. Augustine can support (a) by taking the human mind/soul to have some ontological standing in its own right, without being a substance. Accidents, for instance, are non-substantial existent individuals. So, too, if the human mind/soul were a strongly supervenient or emergent feature of living human beings. (Strong supervenience is plausible for the human mind/soul because it is not physical in its nature.) Furthermore, Augustine can endorse (b) on analogy with the status of accidents in the miracle of the Eucharist. The physical accidents of the bread and wine, which depend of their nature on physical substances in order to exist, are miraculously kept in existence by God while their underlying substances are destroyed. (They are replaced by the substance of the body and the blood of Christ, respectively.) Now the existence of these physical accidents—their colour, shape, flavour, position and the like—in the absence of their underlying substances is certainly unnatural, and perhaps impossible, since it takes God's miraculous intervention; the existence of the human mind/soul is perhaps only unnatural, since, unlike the physical accidents involved in the Eucharist, the human mind/soul need not be intrinsically material. On this score, post-mortem survival would be logically possible though not by natural means. This seems to be Augustine's mature philosophical view, and arguably his view from the earliest days of his conversion, and it is a version of the consensus position described above. Furthermore, since post-mortem survival depends on direct divine assistance, whether miraculous because it is impossible or merely because it is not attainable through natural means, then the view that the human mind/soul can exist apart from the body is not capable of proof but is held as a matter of faith alone.

Augustine, therefore, rejected Platonic dualism, and a fortiori Cartesian dualism, in the case of human beings. Nor did Platonic dualism fare any better in the later Middle Ages—a fate due in no small measure to Augustine's rejection, buttressed by what they took to be a decisive refutation by Aristotle (*De anima*, 1.3 (406b25–28).[8] Thomas Aquinas puts it succinctly (*Summa theologiae*, 1a q. 76, art. 1): If soul and body are distinct substances, they must be related as mover and moved, on the straightforward grounds that they do interact although they are distinct; but if they are mover and moved, they cannot then form a unity since features we normally attribute to the whole person (such as motion) would be attributed only *per accidens*, on Plato's view, to one or the other of the two substances—or, in contemporary terms, mental causation would always be indirect. Put simply, a composite of two distinct substances will never add up to a unified 'third' substance and, hence, be no more than an accidental unity. This is the core of several objections Aquinas puts forth against platonic dualism, and it captures Augustine's uneasiness about the ontological independence of the human soul. For all that, it is important that the human soul, the intellective soul, is at stake here; neither Augustine nor Aquinas took seriously the idea that the souls of brute animals might be subsistent. Furthermore, they each recognised the existence of immaterial intellective substances, namely, angels, so they were well aware of the metaphysical possibility that there be non-physical minds. The difficulty is trying to have it both ways, to maintain that the human mind/soul is a substance and, simultaneously, the substantial form of the body, in such a way that it is each of these in virtue of its very nature. Even Aquinas (*Summa contra gentiles* 2.56) is driven to admit that such a view has no rational foundation:

> Something that is one in its account does not result from two permanent beings, unless they are related as substantial form and matter . . . Hence it remains for us

> to ask whether an intellectual substance could be the substantial form of some
> body. Well, to those who consider it rationally, it seems that this is impossible.
> Something one cannot result from two actually existing substances, for the act of
> each is that by which it is distinguished from the other. Now an intellectual
> substance is an actually existing substance, as is apparent from what has been
> said. Likewise for a body as well. Hence we see that something that is one cannot
> result from an intellectual substance and a body.

Aquinas is careful to say that it seems impossible, at least 'to those who consider it rationally [*rationabiliter*]' since faith requires him to leave open the possibility of post-mortem existence for the human soul, despite the fact that such a belief flies in the face of (natural) reason.

John Duns Scotus is more forthright in his rejection of Platonic dualism. In his late *Quodlibeta* (9.5), Scotus asks whether God could bring it about that an angel, that is, an intellectual substance, could inform matter qua informing substantial form. He replies that it is not possible (9.6) and offers several arguments to that effect, the first of which holds for cases beyond that of the angel—for the human mind/soul, clearly—and is the strongest. Scotus begins by distinguishing three senses in which something can be a per se being (9.7), namely, when it: (a) exists in isolation or apart from a subject, the way an accident is a being per se when not inhering in a subject; (b) neither actually inheres, nor has an aptitude to inhere, in another; (c) is simply unable to be ordered per se to any further actualisation belonging to it per se beyond the one it has. Substances and substantial forms can be beings per se according to (b), the latter because it does not, strictly speaking, inhere in a subject but, instead, informs its subject. But the most proper sense in which something is capable of existence per se is (c), according to which something is not only actual but complete. Scotus argues that something like the human mind/soul is not a being per se according to (c) if it is a substance according to (b):

> A substantial form is ordered *per se* to the being (*esse*) of the whole composite.
> This being, however, is simply the act of the composite primarily and that of the
> form participatively, because a part is only said 'to be *per se*' incidentally (that is
> *per se* participatively), whereas the whole is said 'to be' primarily. Therefore, what
> subsists of itself and is unable to be ordered *per se* to some being cannot be a form
> *per se*. (Duns Scotus, Quodlibeta 9.8 [Alluntis 345].)

Scotus's technical jargon is forbidding but clear: an intellectual substance cannot be one in itself and also become one (or worse yet, be the principle of unity) in combination with something further. Since the human mind/soul clearly exists in combination with the body to produce something that is one, the position that it is in itself a substance, capable of full independent existence, has to be given up—as Scotus explicitly does, arguing for it in the remainder of his *Quodlibeta* 9. He takes Aquinas to task for not being sufficiently clear in his account, in particular for not distinguishing (b) and (c). The human mind/soul is such as not to require anything else to exist, in particular, a human body, but in that condition it is not of its nature complete, which is why there is a resurrection of the flesh in the end.

Despite their several differences, Augustine and Aquinas and Scotus agree that Platonic dualism should be rejected, and they even agree on the general shape of the grounds for its rejection, namely, the insuperable difficulty of the human mind/soul being at once independent and also capable of engendering a distinct complete unity in combination with something else. It should, however, be noted that in the first half of the thirteenth century some philosophers, apparently inspired by Avicenna, opted to deny instead the claim that the human mind/soul could engender such a unity in combination with the body: John Blund and Philip the Chancellor, for instance, denied that the soul could be a form (and hence, a principle of unity) on the grounds that forms were necessarily bound up with their matter and perishable with it, and hence the soul was an independent substance only accidentally united to the body—a dualist view deemed too radical by the next generation of thinkers, such as William of Auxerre and Hugh of St-Cher, who argue that the human soul must somehow incorporate the power of 'substantial unification' (*unibilitas substantialis*) in combination with the body.[9] In the end, the loser in the contest was the position that the human mind/soul could be a substance. It therefore must be some sort of (substantial) form. But how can any sort of form inform the body and yet persist in its absence? This is the question that dominated the other mainstream of medieval philosophy, which took its inspiration from the texts of Aristotle rather than from the platonic tradition.

2. MEDIEVAL ARISTOTELIANISM

With the translation and assimilation of Aristotle's philosophical corpus, a process that took roughly the century from 1150 to 1250, the way was cleared for a new understanding of psychology through his *De anima*. According to Aristotle, 'psychology' is the branch of natural philosophy that deals with things whose nature involves being alive. The first order of business, therefore, is to clarify what is meant by 'life'. After working through several definitions, Aristotle concludes that the soul is a principle of life, in that it is 'the first actuality of a natural body structured with organs' (*De anima*, 2.1, 412a27–28). Here 'organ' is taken generally, so that even parts of plants, such as leaves, qualify as organs (412b2–3).[10] Aristotle then goes on to point out that the powers and capacities of the soul form three natural clusters: nutrition and growth are associated with the vegetative soul as found in all living things; perception and movement with the sensitive soul found in all animals; and thought with the intellective soul in human beings. Broadly speaking, these souls are ordered hierarchically, distinguished by the kinds of things to which they belong. Whether they are really distinct from one another was the subject of much dispute throughout the Middle Ages.[11] Aristotle said almost nothing about the prospect of non-organic life, other than his infamously obscure comments about possible separability of the intellect, but he did say a great deal about organic life, and his medieval disciples followed him in this regard, beginning their discussion of soul with plant and animal life and only gradually building up to the complicated issue of human (intellective) life. In the first half of the thirteenth century, a consensus was formed on at least the correct way to understand the vegetative and sensitive souls, the springboard for the analysis of the human soul.[12]

According to Aristotle, in plants and extremely simple animals the soul is divisible and extended, and thereby material. The life of a plant, for instance, is generally diffused throughout the plant. If shoots are cut from one plant and then nurtured on their own, the result will be a new plant, with a new life of its own (the death of either will not affect the life of the other). The life of each is no more than the actualisation of the nutritive capacities of each, which seems to be a purely material phenomenon. Hence, the vegetative soul is material. The case is similar for the sensitive souls of extremely simple animals: sponges, worms and bivalves. Much like a plant, a worm can be cut in half, and each half can continue to live its own separate life; since a worm is capable of self-movement and has at least some powers of sensation (touch), it must have a sensitive soul. In medieval terminology, these simple animals have an 'incomplete' sensitive soul, as divisible and extended as the vegetative soul in plants. Matters are different in other animals, whose sensitive souls are complete; their bodies, unlike the bodies of sponges or worms or shellfish, are articulated into organs, and their souls, while they are extended in their bodies, are not divisible— separated parts of higher animals do not continue to live independently. Instead, the soul is present in such animals 'as a whole in the whole and as a whole in every part':[13] each part of the animal's body is vivified by the (complete) sensitive soul, but there is no particular place in which that soul is located, and it is present as a whole in each part of the animal's body. That is, life of the sort possessed by anything but the simplest kinds of animals—hereafter I drop the reminder—is a non-localised property of the living animal. Hence, the sensitive soul in animals is indivisible, in that no part of the sensitive soul can be isolated from any other part of the sensitive soul.[14] Now the bodies of animals are complex because they are made up of organs, that is, local physiological structures that carry out specific bodily functions: heart, stomach, lungs, kidneys, liver. Some organs will be sense organs, responsive to a range of changes in external stimulus and the proximate bodily vehicle for its associated sense faculty: eyes for vision, ears for hearing, and the like. According to the standard medieval reading of Aristotle, a given sense faculty is associated with a particular bodily organ. What makes an organ fit to be a sense organ is its differential response to different external material causes: the eyes to colour and shape, the nose to odours and so on. This differential response is a matter of the sense organ's being put into some determinate physiological configuration in response to an external cause. The ability of the sense organ to take on a determinate configuration— that is, the organ's responsiveness—simply is the actualisation of the sense faculty and applies only to the sense organs of bodies vivified by the sensitive soul. The sense faculty is reduced from potency to act as the sense organ is put into its new determinate configuration: what it is for the cat to see the mouse is for the cat's eye to 'take on' the typical grey colour shape in its eye. Seeing the mouse or, more exactly, seeing the grey shape, is something that happens in the cat through the reduction of the sense organ associated with vision from potency to act.

The life of an animal, at least of a complex animal, is a holistic feature of the animal. It is therefore not identifiable with some matter or some material part belonging to the animal—or, put in medieval terms: the (sensitive) soul is not a body. That is to say, the life of a complex organic system consists at least partially in the appropriate interaction of its constituent organic sub-systems, and the proper functional relation among the parts is not itself a part, and a fortiori not a material part. Rather, the sensitive soul is (weakly) supervenient on the material constituents that make up the animal's body and wholly dependent upon them. But this does not give the sensitive soul any independent ontological weight, for such things can be 'reduced' or 'eliminated' in favour of the arrangement and disposition of the material parts upon which they supervene. And what is true for the sensitive soul as a whole also holds for the activity of sensing.[15] Sense perception is consequent upon the physiological changes in the sense organ without being itself a material phenomenon. The sense organ is the proximate subject of the sensing, as noted, but the act of sensing is properly received in the ensouled composite as a whole: we do not say that the eyes see, but rather that the cat sees.[16] Sensing is therefore an activity that can take place only through a bodily organ, much as dancing requires a dancer. This is true of all operations of the sensitive soul. As Aquinas puts it (*Summa theologiae*, 1a q. 75, art. 3), 'Hence, it is clear that the sensitive soul does not have any operation on its own; rather, every operation of the sensitive soul belongs to the composite, and so it follows that since the souls of non-human animals do not operate on their own, they are not subsistent'.

In addition to the external senses, animals also have an inner sense that integrates the deliverances of the external senses. This was thought to have exactly the same ontological status as the external senses, on the grounds that it worked in the same way: the inner sense is an organic power, and the organ in question is commonly identified as the heart (or less commonly, as part of the brain). The upshot is that the sensitive soul, common to non-human animals and to human beings, was understood to be a thoroughly material affair: since all its activities are defined in reference to matter, it must existentially depend on matter.[17] The materiality of the sensitive soul, therefore, has two aspects: dependence upon bodily organs and dependence upon the whole composite. Hence, there need not be anything more to a live animal than its material parts and their interconnected functioning.

3. PHILOSOPHICAL MATERIALISM

As with the sensitive soul, so, too, with the intellective soul—or so argued several philosophers at the beginning of the fourteenth century. They held that the immateriality and substantiality of the intellective soul could not be proved; some went so far as to hold that natural reason dictates the conclusion that the intellective soul is as material as the sensitive soul, and that the opposite is held only through faith, in the teeth of reason. This position was historically associated with Alexander of Aphrodisias, as reported by Averroes, who is said to have thought that thinking is the highest perfection that can be 'educed' from matter. I refer to the philosophers who adopt these positions as 'philosophical materialists', since philosophical reasoning alone, apart from revealed truth, would lead them to be materialists.

Philosophical materialism seems to have gotten off the ground with the movement known as 'the new philosophy', that is, nominalism.[18] William of Ockham states philosophical materialism as follows:

> If we understand 'intellective soul' to mean an immaterial and incorruptible form that is whole in the whole body and whole in every part, then it cannot be evidently known through reason or through experience that there is such a form in us ... It is clear that this cannot be demonstrated, since every argument proving these things accepts points that are doubtful to one who follows natural reason. (*Quodlibeta* 1.10 [*OTh* 9 63:39–64:49])

Here Ockham says only that immateriality is one of a set of features that are not demonstrable since the arguments put forward rely on dubious claims, but shortly later he clarifies his view:

> Someone following natural reason would grant that we do experience thinking in ourselves, which is the act of a material and corruptible form; and he would consequently declare that such a form is received in an extended form. Nor do we experience the thinking that is the proper operation of an immaterial substance. (*Quodlibeta* 1.10 [*OTh* 9 65:88–93])

Ockham treads carefully, but he clearly endorses the strong claim that natural reason alone leads one to conclude that the intellective soul is no more immaterial than the sensitive soul.

Where Ockham is cautious, Buridan is bold. In his third series of lectures on the *De anima*, Buridan declares that natural reason leads to philosophical materialism:

> I shall firstly list the conclusions that someone would hold if he were to use only natural reasons, without the catholic faith, through principles having evidentness from appearances by the nature of sense and intellect, without any special supernatural revelation ... The seventh such conclusion (which was the view of Alexander of Aphrodisias) is that [the human intellect] is generable and corruptible, extended, drawn forth [from matter], inherent, and multiplied. Yet we should nevertheless hold firmly that not all these conclusions are true, since they are contrary to the catholic faith. But I believe that conclusions opposed to them are not demonstrable without special supernatural revelation. (*Quaestiones in De anima* [henceforth *QA*], 3.6, John Buridan 1989, 48:48–52 and 51:99–105—subsequent references are to this edition.)[19]

Alexander's position, which Buridan endorses, is that the human intellective soul, like the animal sensitive soul, is a supervenient feature of the arrangement of its material constituent parts:

> Alexander of Aphrodisias declared that the human intellect is a generable and
> corruptible material form, drawn forth out of a potentiality belonging to matter,
> and it is extended by the extension of matter, just like the soul of a cow or the soul
> of a dog, and it does not remain after death. (*QA*, 3.3; 22:59–62)

Philosophers who follow natural reason alone, Buridan maintains, would come to
hold Alexander's position: the human intellective soul is just as material as 'the soul
of a cow or the soul of a dog', with no special ontological status.

Buridan criticises arguments that try to establish that the human intellect is in
any way a substance in its own right, and he also offers four positive arguments for
philosophical materialism (*QA*, 3.4; 32:83–34:130). First, if the intellective soul were
separable, then it would either (a) not belong to the essence of the human being
since it would be by nature independent of it; or (b) the human being would not
have the sort of unity characteristic of a primary substance, an objection we have
seen in nascent form in Augustine and later developed by Aquinas and Scotus (§1).
Second, a non-material intellective soul would be no 'closer' (*proximior*) by its
nature to any one human body rather than to another, since as a semi-independent
substance it does not, strictly speaking, inhere in any; hence, natural reason would
not identify an intellect as belonging to any one person rather than to another.
Third, Socrates's soul moves from place to place with him, or it does not; but if the
mind/soul were immaterial it would not be localizable, in which case the preceding
argument applies. Fourth, by natural reason we would not hold that the mind/soul
exists prior to our birth, and the situation is symmetric for death. The upshot, Buridan concludes, is that 'setting aside the catholic faith and supernatural infusion of
the truth into us, our natural reason would dictate that the human intellect is drawn
forth out of power belonging to matter, and that it is generable and corruptible' (*QA*,
3.5; 42:91–95).

If the intellective soul merely supervenes on the body, like the sensitive soul,
then it is simply impossible for it to exist apart from the body—it would be like
preserving the watch's working without the watch, a contradiction in terms. Buridan likens it to the articles of faith: the separate existence of the mind/soul is not
evident, 'unless God were to produce that evidentness for us by His special grace
and beyond the common course of nature, just as He could make evident to anyone
the article of the Trinity or of the Incarnation' (*QA*, 3.3; 25:148–26:151). These articles
of faith are simply beyond human comprehension, as is the post-mortem existence
of the human mind/soul. No wonder Buridan earlier called the intellective soul
'miraculous' (*QA*, 2.9, John Buridan 1984, 138).

Buridan's view—or perhaps just his example—seems to have been adopted by
many of his students. Marsilius of Inghen, for example, inserts what Olaf Pluta has
called a 'hidden question'—a question embedded in another question—into his
own questions on the *De anima*, namely, whether the intellect uses a bodily organ
to think; Marsilius argues that the brain is literally the organ associated with
thinking. Later nominalists are even more bold: Nicholas of Amsterdam, for
instance, argues that according to natural reason the mind is purely material.[20] By
the time of the Renaissance, the common wisdom had it that the intellective soul

was purely material—at least, according to natural reason. But the disclaimers about natural reason became fewer and farther between while the physiological evidence for the materiality of thinking was piled higher and higher, until a philosopher such as Giacomo Zabarella could devote literally hundreds of pages to the 'purely natural' (materialist) investigation of the mind, in his massive *De rebus naturalibus in libros Aristotelis de anima* (1590). Psychology was well on the track to being a purely natural science at that point, having no need of any kind of dualism to explain cognitive phenomena.

4. THE METAPHYSICS OF HYLOMORPHIC COMPOUNDS

The philosophical materialists were committed to the strong view that the human mind/soul is supervenient on the human body, much like the sensitive soul (as described in §2). While their view seems to follow logically, being no more than an extension of the logic regarding the sensitive soul to the case of the intellective soul, it did not follow directly upon it historically. For although philosophical materialism became dominant at the end of the Middle Ages, as noted, it was not the mainstream view earlier. Instead, the consensus in the High Middle Ages was that some version of the Augustinian solution canvassed in §1 above had to be correct, a version of property dualism that granted the human mind/soul to be a form with some kind of ontological standing independent of its combination with matter—a status with sufficient ontological independence to allow the form to be the locus of emergent non-material properties (namely, the mental properties of thinking and willing). In the second half of the thirteenth century, the effort to clarify the Augustinian solution and make it precise in an Aristotelian framework was carried out as part of the larger project of getting clear about the metaphysics of hylomorphic compounds, that is, of form/matter composites. The context in which debates over the metaphysical nature of such hylomorphic compounds took place had to do with whether a substance had only a single substantial form (the 'unitarian' position) or more than one (the 'pluralist' position). The central point at issue was the unity of the form/matter composite, which is the worry at the heart of the Augustinian solution.

The case of Henry of Ghent is instructive. Initially hesitant in his *Quodlibeta* 1.4 (1276), he developed a full theory of the plurality of substantial forms in human beings in his *Quodlibeta* 2.2 (1277), 3.6 (1278) and 4.13 (1279).[21] The restriction is important. Henry accepts Aristotle's dictum (*Metaphysics* 7.13 1039a3–5) that a being that is per se one cannot be produced by two beings that are each already in act, at least in the normal course of events. Unity is possible, however, when the constituent elements of a hylomorphic compound are related as act and potency. Henry therefore maintains that in each non-human form/matter composite there is but a single form, which actualises prime matter and so brings about a unified composite substance. Human beings have to be treated differently, though, because of the non-material character of the human mind/soul; since thinking is an activity independent of the body, Henry reasons, its actualisation (accomplished via a form) cannot be drawn forth from the power of matter. Hence, there must be two distinct forms at work in the hylomorphic compound that is a human being. On the one hand, there is the form of the body (*forma corporeitatis*), which is the counterpart to the sensitive soul: it 'prepares' the body by organising it in human-like ways so that there is a body that is properly disposed to become animated, that is, to be a living human body, when vivified by the sensitive soul. Here the sensitive soul may be said to be drawn forth from the power of matter, as described in §2 above. But in the case of human beings, it does something more, namely, prepare the body to be capable of receiving the intellective soul. This is not a natural process. Rather, God directly creates and infuses the intellective soul in each human being—a way of recognising the point that mental properties as emergent cannot be explained, or not fully explained, by the material features of the hylomorphic compound.[22] Now both the form of the body and that of the intellective soul inform the single subject at once; there is no temporal separation in their metaphysical action. But how do they combine to produce a unity?

According to Henry, each of the forms acts in concert to provide a single subsistence to the hylomorphic compound that is the human being. The form of the body imparts life and structure and organisation to the human body, 'perfecting' it as a kind of animate existence, whereas the form that is the intellective soul 'perfects' the human being as a partially spiritual creature capable of non-material acts. Neither form is sufficient without the other: the form of the body alone would not produce a complete and unified concrete being (*suppositum*) on its own, and neither would the intellective soul. For the perfection imparted by the intellective soul is realised in a material composite and hence requires that there be an appropriately disposed body receptive to its activity; the perfection imparted by the form of the body produces an animal that is capable of and fit for a certain kind of life, namely, a life characterised by intelligent thought and choice, but cannot on its own provide that life. Since they are each suited to inform the same (prime) matter, they are coordinate forms, although the action of the intellective soul is 'higher'—rather as though two people were to lift a piano that neither can lift alone, though one of them is far stronger than the other and hence more important. Technically, each form is said to provide its own natural being (*esse*) to the composite, and conjointly they have a single action of making it be a concrete object: a single unified substance that has its distinctive existence, which Henry calls the *esse suppositi* (the being that characterises the supposit). As forms, each gives being to the composite; as a non-material form, the intellective soul has a supernatural rather than a natural origin and is its own separate ontological principle.[23] Not surprisingly, Henry refrained from giving any philosophical arguments for the post-mortem survival of the human mind/soul, which is so bound

up with the material form of the body that it is hard to see how it could be separated. Since faith teaches that it is created and infused from without, we may also
have faith that it survives the dissolution of the material composite of which it is a
part. But this is not a conclusion at which we can arrive through natural reason, as
Henry is careful to underline. Presumably, the intellective soul qua form does not
have sufficient ontological independence to make it clear that it survives the dissolution of the composite; Henry's position seems to be that it cannot do so of its
own accord, and that direct divine intervention is required for it to continue in
existence once the composite is no more.

   Henry's view is complex and subtle.[24] Yet despite the lengths to which Henry
went to describe the conjoint action of the two substantial forms in human beings,
some philosophers objected that he still did not provide a satisfactory account of the
unity of the concrete individual. Godfrey of Fontaines, for example, considers Henry's theory at length in his *Quodlibeta* 2.7 (*PhB*, 2, 95–133) and 3.5 (*PhB*, 2, 194–211),
both from 1286, and begins (114–15) with the objection that two substantial forms
cannot combine to produce something that is essentially one.[25] Yet for all his objections to Henry, Godfrey does not in the end take a stand on the ontological status of
the composite. He ranks several theories in order of what he takes to be their plausibility and, indeed, declares that his hesitation stems from the difficulty in squaring
the non-physical nature of thought with its role as the substantial form of a material
composite. There must be some kind of unity in human beings, but Godfrey cannot
explain how it comes about, and so does not commit himself to any particular account of the metaphysics of hylomorphic compounds. Thus, Godfrey accepts the
mainstream consensus on property dualism but is dissatisfied with the current
attempts to make it more precise.

   Godfrey's insistence on the unity of the concrete individual human being is in
keeping with the medieval consensus. It is sometimes taken as evidence that he
endorses the unicity of substantial form—Thomas Aquinas's position. Yet, as we
have seen, the challenge for the Augustinian solution from the very beginning has
been to give an adequate account of how the human mind/soul could have some
ontological independence from the body and, nevertheless, be the substantial form
of the composite. Aquinas's view, though a minority position, was at one with the
consensus on this point. What put his view out of the mainstream was his claim that
unity of a substantial composite was entirely due to its having only a single simple
substantial form. This may have given a principle of unity at a stroke, but it denied
one of the key intuitions of the Augustinian solution, namely, that some constituent
principles of a concrete individual could have an ontological standing that was partially the same as that of the composite as a whole and partially different from it. By
countenancing only a single form, Aquinas rendered any such talk at best metaphorical and at worse simply incorrect.[26] Even those philosophers like Godfrey who
insisted on unity as fundamental were more than willing to speak as though there
were a plurality of forms in the individual, and to think that the interrelation of
these forms had to be the foundation of whatever unity the composite had; the
debate centred on how this could be possible.

The most sophisticated exponent of the mainstream consensus was John Duns Scotus. In the generation after Henry and Godfrey, he began his analysis from the nature of unity, arguing that a composite could be made up of a series of other entities as long as they were ordered to a single form.[27] In brief, Scotus recognises in a concrete living being the following entities, each of which has some claim to existence in its own right: prime matter, the form of the body, local forms of bodily organs, and the soul. How all these disparate individual entities constitute a unified object that has some claim to be treated as ontologically basic will take some delicate handling.

Form plays two distinct roles in the constitution of material particulars according to Scotus: (a) it informs matter, and (b) it is an essential part of the whole composite. Yet these features of form, when it is in a composite, are not essential to form, Scotus holds, since we can see that form lacks these 'imperfections' in the case of the divine (*Ordinatio* 1 d. 8 p. 1 q. 4 nn. 213–14, Vat. 4 271:1–272:9), where it neither informs anything nor is a constituent principle of anything further. Form can therefore be self-sustaining: it is prior to matter, and prior to the composite as well, since each is in act through the form and not conversely (*Quaestiones super Metaphysicorum libros Aristotelis* 7 q. 6 n. 9, OPh 4 143:1–10) and thus has some being of its own (n. 12). But if form need not inform matter and has being of its own, then it is possible for a bodily form to exist independently of matter—a conclusion Scotus draws explicitly (*Reportatio* 2 d. 12 q. 2 n. 12 (WV 23 20a)). In a living being, Scotus argues that there must be at least two distinct forms: the form of the body, which structures the organic body as a whole and also explains the numerical identity of a corpse with the living body it previously was (*Ordinatio,* 4 d. 11 p. 1 a. 2 q.1 nn. 278–284, Vat. 12 265:964–267:41); and the animating soul. Scotus argues further on the grounds of human generation that if God, and not the human parents, provides the soul in generation, the parents seem left with contributing only the matter to their progeny, which seems to underestimate their role. Scotus therefore proposes that human parents contibute a substantial form, namely, the form of the body, which is further informed by the human soul (*Ordinatio,* 3 d. 2 q. 3 nn. 111–112, Vat. 9 165:849–166:861) contributed by God. However, the matter is not first organised by the form of the body and then by the human soul at different times, but both inform the matter at once, a point he takes over from Henry of Ghent.

Scotus is careful to distinguish the existence (*esse*) that each component element of a particular living being has. For example, the soul has existence *per se* and this existence is separate from the existence of the composite of which the soul is a constituent element, even though when combined with the body the soul has existence through the composite (*Quaestiones in Metaphysicorum libros Aristotelis,* 7 q. 6 nn. 12–13, OPh 4 143:16–144:8). The point here is subtle. Scotus is maintaining that although the constituent elements of a unified whole have their own individual existences, the whole, nevertheless, may have only one existence, and the existences of the constituent elements be somehow dependent upon the existence of the whole. In replying to the sort of objection mooted by Godfrey of Fontaines and Thomas of Sutton, which tries to infer the uniqueness of substantial form from the fact that the composite is a single existence, Scotus writes:

> I grant the first claim, that there is only one existence that belongs to one being. But the second proposition, that one existence requires exactly one form, should be denied . . . For just as 'being' and 'one' are divided into simple and composite, so too are 'existence' and 'one existence'. Therefore, existence that is essentially one is not precisely restricted to simple existence, just as nothing divided is precisely restricted to one of the divisions that divide it. In this way there is one existence of the whole composite, which nevertheless includes many partial existences, just as the whole is one being and nevertheless contains many partial beingnesses. For I know nothing about this fiction that the existence supervening on the essence is not composite if the essence is composite. The existence of the whole composite includes the existence of all the parts in this way, and it includes many partial existences belonging to the many parts or forms, just as the whole being made up of many forms includes those partial actualities. (*Ordinatio*, 4 d. 11 p. 1 art. 2 q. 1 nn. 250–51 [Vat. 12 255:722–37])

The existences of the constituent parts of the composite are not simply added or aggregated; they have, instead, an essential order to one another, and overall an essential order to the 'topmost' substantial form that gives existence to the whole composite, as Scotus goes on to say. In this way the whole composite can be divided into act and potency, namely, the final 'completive' (*completiua*) form and the remainder of the composite. And as with existences, so with the beings themselves, the unity of the composite is to be found in the union of its constituent elements through an internal essential order. The beings that are the matter and the form are distinct (*Quaestiones in Metaphysicorum libros Aristotelis*, 8 q. 4 n. 41, *OPh* 4 501:9–13), but they are essentially ordered to one another (Ibid. nn. 31–3, *OPh* 4 498:13–499:8).

Scotus takes the ordering of forms to be pervasive, and the inability of certain forms to be so ordered is a special feature of per se beings. Recall from §1 above that Scotus distinguished three types of per se beings: those that can exist in isolation from a subject; those that do not inhere, whether actually or aptitudinally, in a subject; and those that are simply unable to be ordered per se to any further actualisation belonging to it in its own right beyond the one it has. As noted, the last is crucial, because that is the sort of being that is had by something that is ontologically basic, the suppositum (i.e., the fully actual concrete particular). Being unable to be per se ordered to any further act is the mark of the concrete. That is why the individual has a privileged place in Scotus's ontology. But recognising this is compatible with granting the independent ontological status of the substantial form that may inform the composite, as the human mind/soul does.

The essential ordering of the constituent parts of a composite substance is therefore a description of the unity of the composite. Scotus is clear that his account describes the unity but does not strictly speaking explain it since the principle of the essential ordering has to do with the act–potency relations among these elements, which are given immediately and not susceptible of further analysis.[28] Furthermore, the essence of the composite is something distinct from any of its constituent elements: it is a composite of form as such and matter as such. It cannot be identified simply with the substantial form since that is only one of the constituents of the composite and has its own proper essence and existence, as we have seen. However, the substantial form does give further actuality to the remainder of the elements that make up the composite, and, on this score, it can be called the 'partial form' of the composite (*Ordinatio*, 3 d. 2 q. 2 nn. 81–83, *Vat.* 9 152:626–153:646). It should not be confused with the 'form of the whole' (viz. the whole composite), which is 'not an informing form' but, rather, that in virtue of which the composite as a whole has a nature or quiddity.[29] In short, the essence of the composite is something over and above the parts of the composite, not reducible to them. What it is to be this composite (or this kind of composite) is itself an emergent feature. The essence of the composite, then, is tightly linked to all of the constituent elements of the composite, as they are essentially ordered to one another. Indeed, it seems as though an individual composite can have an essence only if all its constituents are properly aligned. Finally, the metaphysical glue that holds together an individual as a unity is the tightest available in the Aristotelian universe: the unity that comes with potency and act.

The upshot is that, for Scotus, the unity of the composite is preserved by the correct ordering obtaining among its component entities, which allows for essential and existential (in)dependence. In the particular case of the human mind/soul, it is not essentially dependent upon the composite of which it is a constituent part; whether it depends on the composite for its existence is a matter that has to be left to faith—natural reason cannot show that it continues in existence after death. Yet even if it does, it does not have the full actuality proper to a suppositum since in that state it cannot discharge what appears to be one of its essential functions, namely, its aptitude to inform a body and make it human. (To inform a subject is not an essential feature of form qua form, but it does appear to be an essential feature of the human mind/soul.) It may continue to have this essential aptitude even when it is in no position to exercise it, but it cannot be or be a part of a fully actual concrete being unless it is realised. Not for nothing was Scotus known as the subtle doctor.

5. CONCLUSION

With Scotus's account of the unity of the composite substance, the medieval elaboration of the Augustinian solution reached its apex. One or another version of it held sway as the mainstream consensus for the remainder of the Middle Ages, until philosophical materialism came into its own. The careful analysis of the ontological status of the constituent principles of a hylomorphic compound was one of the great achievements of the medieval thought, one that owed nothing to dogma but everything to subtle philosophical thinking at its best. Its replacement by philosophical materialism can be seen as the continuation of a naturalistic trend in scholastic thought that was only displaced by the less sophisticated Cartesian dualism that ushered in modern philosophy. We will only be the richer for a proper appreciation of medieval thought on this score.

NOTES

....

    * All translations are mine.

    1. See the discussion in King (2007).

    2. Pasnau 2007 calls this the 'mind–soul' problem. It was posed in stark fashion by Averroes, who held that thinking is a function not of the individual soul but, rather, of a single separate intellect that is common to all human beings, with which individual minds are in touch when they appear to think.

    3. That is: *substantia quaedam rationis particeps, regendo corpori accomodatur*.

    4. Augustine, *De moribus ecclesiae catholicae* (1.4.6). There is an approving reference to this view in *De ciuitate Dei* (19.3).

    5. Augustine, *De trinitate* (15.7.11): *substantia rationalis constans ex anima et corpore*. Augustine never decides how best to describe the soul–body union, but he usually uses words like 'mixture' or 'blend' or 'fusion', which certainly cut against the grain of Cartesian substance dualism: see O'Daly (1987, 42–44) and Rist (1994, 97–104).

    6. Augustine, *De cura pro mortuis gerenda* (3.5).

    7. See Bynum (1995, 94–104) for Augustine's positive account of the Resurrection.

    8. See Plato, *Theaetetus* (34C–37C), and the discussion in Bazàn (1997).

    9. See John Blund, *Tractatus de anima* (2.1.15). Philip the Chancellor adopts the same view (*Summa de bono*, 281) and holds that the human mind/soul, like a form, acts to perfect the human body when it is combined with matter but is separate from matter as a substance (281:54–282:60). Bieniak (2010) canvasses the debates and their historical development.

    10. It was not lost on medieval philosophers that Aristotle's definition seems to exclude non-organic life (angels), to say nothing of non-temporal entities (God); they sidestepped the issue by holding that in the *De anima* Aristotle was engaged in natural philosophy and so quite properly did not take account of supernatural beings.

    11. For convenience I will speak as though they are really distinct, but their metaphysical status is a question that can for the most part be addressed separately: philosophers who accept a plurality of substantial forms will hold that the human intellect is literally separable from the body-bound sensitive and vegetative souls, while philosophers who insist on the unicity of substantial form will hold that the whole soul is separable from the body (at which point its sensitive and vegetative powers have no outlet for their exercise). The issue is taken up with reference to the intellective soul in §4 below.

    12. See Dales (1995) for a sketch of philosophical psychology in the thirteenth century.

    13. This common tag was taken from Augustine, *De trinitate* (6.6.8), who derives it from late Platonism.

    14. The sense faculties can be altered or damaged by interference with their associated sense organs, and hence, the sensitive soul depends to some extent on the proper configuration of the body.

    15. Many contemporary philosophers think that the existence of sensory qualia, at least in humans, does argue for a more robust ontological status for the subject of such qualia—although they are reticent as to whether animals have such sensory qualia. See King (2007) for a discussion of qualia in medieval philosophy.

    16. See, for instance, Duns Scotus, *Ordinatio* (4 d. 44 q. 2 n. 6 [WV 20 217a–b]).

    17. Defenders of the unicity of substantial form argue that the sensitive soul is immaterial in virtue of being a set of powers lodged in the complete human soul (which includes both intellective and sensitive powers); there need not be a contradiction between existing in an immaterial state and not being able to exercise sensitive powers while in that state.

18. See Pluta (2007b) for a sketch of how widely held philosophical materialism was at the turn of the fourteenth century, particularly in Paris.

19. See Zupko (1993) for Buridan's view of the soul.

20. See Pluta (2000) and (2007a) for the views of Marsilius and Nicholas, respectively.

21. Henry seems to have put forward his theory in the face of ecclesiastical pressure: see Porro (2006) for this point and a discussion of the 'suppressed' passage (omitted from the final redaction), in which Henry describes the sorts of pressure brought to bear against him, in his *Quodlibeta* (10.5).

22. See Macken (1979) and Wilson (1982) for an account of Henry's theory of the human composite.

23. Henry's claim that the intellective soul must be combined with the form of the body in order to exist led some philosophers to charge him with holding that the intellective soul is (at least partly) material. This is the essence of one of the objections raised by Thomas of Sutton to Henry's account: see Klima (2001) for a full discussion.

24. It is more subtle than can be explored here. For one thing, Henry's claim that there is only an intentional distinction between essence and existence in the form/matter composite is a key part of his analysis of its metaphysical structure.

25. See also Wippel (1981, 332–36).

26. Aquinas's discussion of the dual nature of the human mind/soul, as both substantial form and independent substance, is most famously put forward in *Summa theologiae* (1a q. 75 art. 1): see Bazàn (1997). Aquinas's insistence on the unicity of substantial form made it difficult, if not impossible, for him to give a coherent account of the post-mortem survival of the human mind/soul—to say nothing of how a corpse could be numerically the same as a human body. Cross (2002) and Klima (2009) are recent attempts to show how Aquinas's theory holds together; Pasnau (2002) is more sceptical. There was another respect in which Aquinas was apart from the mainstream: he seems to have held that the post-mortem survival of the human mind/soul is natural, not requiring any direct divine intervention: see his argument in *Summa theologiae* (1a q. 75 art. 6) and *Quaestiones disputatae de anima* (14), which argue that the immaterial form that is the human mind/soul cannot be destroyed by the destruction of the composite it informs and, hence, perdures; see Novak (1987).

27. See the careful and insightful discussion in Cross (1995), which begins with this point.

28. Scotus explicitly denies that his account provides an explanation: *Quaestiones super Metaphysicorum libros Aristotelis* (8 q. 4 n. 11 and n. 54; *OPh* 4 492:8–13 and 504:13–20, respectively); *Ordinatio* (3 d. 2 q. 2 n. 84; *Vat.* 9 153:647–154:665); *Lectura* (2 d. 12 q. un. nn. 49–51; *Vat.* 19 88:11–89:21); see Cross (1995). The further inexplicability of act–potency relations is a consequence of the fact that they transcendentally divide being, and hence, there is nothing higher in terms of which an explanation could be provided.

29. Cross (1995) argues at length for this thesis.

BIBLIOGRAPHY

Bakker, Paul and Johannes Thijssen, eds. 2007. *Mind, Cognition, and Representation: The Tradition of Commentaries on Aristotle's 'De anima'*. Franham and Burlington, Vermont: Ashgate (Ashgate Studies in Medieval Philosophy).

Bazàn, Bernardo. 1997. The Human Soul: Form and Substance? Thomas Aquinas's Critique of Eclectic Aristotelianism. *Archives d'histoire doctrinale et littéraire du Moyen Âge* 64:95–126.

Bieniak, Magdalena. 2010. *The Soul-Body Problem at Paris, ca. 1200–250.* Leuven, Belgium: Leuven University Press.

Bynum, Caroline Walker. 1995. *The Resurrection of the Body in Western Christianity, 200–1336.* New York: Columbia University Press.

Cross, Richard. 1995. Duns Scotus's Anti-Reductionistic Account of Material Substance. *Vivarium* 33:137–70.

———. 2002. 'Aquinas and the mind-body problem'. In *Mind, Metaphysics, and Value in the Thomistic and Analytical Traditions*, ed. John Haldane, 36–53. Notre Dame, IN: University of Notre Dame Press.

Dales, Richard. 1995. *The Problem of the Rational Soul in the Thirteenth Century.* Leiden, the Netherlands, New York, and Cologne, Germany: Brill (Brill's Studies in Intellectual History 65).

Godfrey of Fontaines. 1904. *Les quatre premiers Quodlibets de Godefroid de Fontaines*, eds., M. de Wulf and A. Pelzer. Louvain, Belgium (*Les philosophes Belges tom.* 2). Abbreviated 'PhB'.

Henry of Ghent. 1518. *Quodlibeta III and IV.* Paris: Badius.

———. 1979–. *Henrici de Gandauo opera omnia.* Leuven, Belgium: Leuven University Press. His *Quodlibeta* I was edited by R. Macken in Vol. 5 (1979), *Quodlibeta* II edited by R. Wielockx in Vol. 6 (1983) and *Quodlibeta* X edited by R. Macken in Vol. 14 (1981).

John Blund. 1970. *Tractatus de anima*, ed. D. Callus and R. Hunt. Oxford: Oxford University Press (British Academy, Auctores Britannici Medii Aevi 2).

John Buridan. 1984. *Quaestiones in De anima 2.* In *John Buridan on the Soul and Sensation*, ed. P. Sobol. Ph.D. dissertation, Indiana University.

———. 1989. *Quaestiones in De anima 3.* In *John Buridan's Philosophy of Mind*, ed. J. Zupko. Ph.D. dissertation, Cornell University.

John Duns Scotus. 1891–95. *Reportatio.* In *Joannis Duns Scoti Doctoris Subtilis Ordinis Minorum opera omnia*, ed. L. Wadding. Lyons 1639; republished, with slight alterations, by L. Vivès, Paris 1891–5. Abbreviated 'WV'.

———. 1950–. *Lectura and Ordinatio in Iohannis Duns Scoti Doctoris Subtilis et Mariani opera omnia*, ed. C. Balić et al. Rome: Typis Polyglottis Vaticanae. Abbreviated 'Vat.'

———. 1968. *Obras del Doctor Sutil Juan Duns Escoto: Cuestiones Cuodlibetales*, ed. Felix Alluntis. Madrid: Biblioteca de autores cristianos [edition of *Quodlibeta*].

———. 1997. *Opera philosophica* III–IV, ed. G. Etzkorn et al. St Bonaventure, NY: The Franciscan Institute Press 1. Abbreviated 'OPh'. [edition of *Quaestiones super libros Metaphysicorum Aristotelis*].

King, Peter. 2007. 'Why Isn't the Mind-Body Problem Medieval?' In Lagerlund, Yrjönsuuri and Alanen (2007, 187–205).

Klima, Gyula. 2001. 'Thomas of Sutton on the Nature of the Intellective Soul and the Thomistic Theory of Being'. In *Nach der Verurteilung von 1277. Philosophie und Theologie an der Universität von Paris im letzten Viertel des 13. Jahrhunderts. Studien und Texte*, ed. Jan Aertsen et al., 436–55. Berlin and New York: Walter de Gruyter (Miscellanea Mediaevalia 28).

———. 2009. Aquinas on the Materiality of the Human Soul and the Immateriality of the Human Intellect. *Philosophical Investigations* 32:163–82.

Lagerlund, Henrik, Mikko Yrjönsuuri, and Lilli Alanen, eds. 2007. *Forming the Mind: Essays on the Internal Senses and the Mind/Body Problem from Avicenna to the Enlightenment.* Dordrecht, the Netherlands: Springer Verlag.

Macken, Raymond. 1979. 'Unité et dimorphisme de l'homme selon Henri de Gand'. In *Teoria e prassi: Atti del VI Congresso del Centro Internazionale de Studi e Relazioni Culturali e della Fonazaione Balmesiana*, ed. B. D'Amore and A. Giordano, 177–82. Genoa/Barcelona 8–15 September, 1976. Naples.

Novak, Joseph. 1987. 'Aquinas and the incorruptibility of the soul'. In *History of Philosophy Quarterly* 4:405–21.

O'Daly, Gerard. 1987. *Augustine's Philosophy of Mind*. London: Duckworth Publishers.

Pasnau, Robert. 2002. *Aquinas on Human Nature*. Cambridge: Cambridge University Press 2002.

———. 2007. 'The mind-soul problem'. In Bakker and Thijssen (2007, 3–19).

Pluta, Olaf. 2000. 'Utrum intellectus utitur organo corporeo in intelligendo: Eine verborgene Frage in den De anima-Quaestionen des Marsilius von Inghen'. In *Philosophie und Theologie des ausgehenden Mittelalters*, ed. M. Hoenen and P. Bakker, 159–74. Leiden, the Netherlands, Boston and Cologne, Germany: Brill.

———. 2007a. 'Materialism in the philosophy of mind: Nicholas of Amsterdam's *Quaestiones de anima*'. In Bakker and Thijssen (2007, 109–26).

———. 2007b. 'How matter becomes mind: late-medieval theories of emergence'. In Lagerlund, Yrjönsuuri and Alanen (2007, 149–68).

Porro, Pasquale. 2006. 'Doing theology (and philosophy) in the first person: Henry of Ghent's *Quodlibeta*'. In *Theological Quodlibeta in the Middle Ages: the Thirteenth Century*, ed. C. Schabel, 171–231. Leiden, the Netherlands: Brill.

Rist, John. 1994. *Augustine: Ancient Thought Baptized*. Cambridge: Cambridge University Press.

Thomas Aquinas. 1888–9. *Summa theologiae, pars prima*. Rome: Commissio Leonina (*Opera omnia* 4–5).

William of Ockham. 1980. *Opera theologica* 9, ed. J. Wey. St Bonaventure, NY: St Bonaventure University. Abbreviated 'OTh'. [Edition of *Quodlibeta*]

Wilson, Gordon. 1982. Henry of Ghent and René Descartes on the Unity of Man. *Franziskanische Studien* 64:97–110.

Wippel, John. 1981. *The Metaphysical Thought of Godfrey of Fontaines: A Study in Late Thirteenth-Century Philosophy*. Washington DC: Catholic University of America Press.

Zabarella, Iacobus. 1966. *De rebus naturalibus in libros Aristotelis de anima libri XXX (1590)*. Reprint, Frankfurt-am-Main: Minerva GMBH.

Zupko, Jack. 1993. How Are Souls Related to Bodies? A Study of John Buridan. *The Review of Metaphysics* 46:575–601.

CHAPTER 24

....

ETERNITY

....

TANELI KUKKONEN

AT first blush, eternity looks to be almost an ideal candidate when it comes to demonstrating the continued relevance of medieval materials for present-day philosophical discussions. Whether eternity denotes timelessness or everlastingness, after all, remains as much an open question today as it was in the Middle Ages (see, e.g., Ganssle 2001; Ganssle and Woodruff 2002). Contemporary philosophers also refer to medieval authors as a matter of course in their contributions to the topic—Boethius and Anselm are standard ports of call, with Augustine and Aquinas following closely behind—and, what is more, they appear to do so with more than an antiquarian interest in mind. The medieval authors are ostensibly introduced into the debates as authentic discussion partners.

Unfortunately, upon closer inspection the reasons for this congruence show themselves to be rather less encouraging. For one thing, we are dealing here with a fairly insular field of study. Medieval debates on eternity mostly revolved around the mode of being attributable to God, and in this regard things have not changed by much. Few contemporary philosophers outside the fields of philosophy of religion and philosophical theology have expressed an interest in debating eternity, and so the paradigm case for eternity remains the eternity of God.[1] By contrast, the cognate issue of time has attracted ample attention from non-religious philosophers, and so the discussion has moved well past theological concerns and into territory that medieval philosophers would scarcely recognise. Corresponding to this, contemporary philosophers who discuss time may pause briefly to consider Aristotle and Newton, but they rarely venture beyond this in terms of historical materials and almost never claim to be presenting an authoritative reading of the ancient authorities, let alone one that is supposed to enjoy continued contemporary relevance. Philosophical treatments of eternity seem curiously deferential by comparison: almost invariably there is an attempt to line up at least some of the relevant authorities behind one's preferred point of view. An uncharitable reader might be led to conclude that contemporary philosophers defer to their medieval predecessors not because the latter have anything particularly interesting to contribute, but because the former are beholden to traditions of arguing *ex auctoritate*.

The full picture, thankfully, is much brighter. We possess several studies that are both philosophically acute and that show a serious level of engagement with medieval and modern sources alike—a rare and altogether welcome state of affairs. For all that, it does seem as though those same studies circle around a fairly limited set of issues and interpretive controversies. This is regrettable even if one accepts that issues related to eternity are unlikely ever to prove a top-drawer attraction for philosophers of a non-religious persuasion. What I would like to do in this essay is point to some of the ways in which future research into medieval philosophy might help the discussion of eternity break out of its present confines.

1. Boethius *Modernorum*

It is useful to begin from some modern takes on Boethius. With the jury still out as to whether any of the big 'P's in ancient philosophy (Parmenides, Plato, Philo, Plotinus) developed a notion of eternity clearly distinct from temporal everlastingness, it has become customary to cite Boethius as the first star witness when it comes to establishing what the 'Western', 'late classical', 'medieval' or, indeed, 'Christian' view of eternity as timelessness might be. There are good reasons for this: in his short work *On the Trinity* and above all in the *Consolation of Philosophy*, Boethius presents in poetic terms a threefold distinction between eternal Being, infinite duration such as the Aristotelian universe enjoys and temporal becoming. And because Boethius's remarks were cited by countless scholastic authors through the Middle Ages, it is easy to see how his views would be held up as being authoritative as well. Yet it is by no means obvious what, precisely, Boethius wishes to say about eternity, over and above the fact that it is very unlike our own evanescent and temporally limited existence. Boethius famously defines eternity as 'the unending and perfect possession all at once of interminable life' (*interminabilis vitae tota simul et perfecta possessio: Consolation* V, prose 6), but several mutually exclusive interpretations of these pregnant words have been put forward over the past couple of decades alone.

The most influential contemporary interpretation of Boethius comes from Eleonore Stump and Norman Kretzmann, two philosophers who at the same time are respected scholars in medieval philosophy. In an article entitled simply 'Eternity', Stump and Kretzmann (1981) argue for an understanding of eternity that involves duration as an essential component. According to Stump and Kretzmann, this is the most natural way to understand the interminable nature of eternal life to which Boethius's definition testifies; besides, they claim, the weight of the tradition in which Boethius stands (Parmenides, Plato and Plotinus for earlier, Aquinas for later) inclines in this direction as well. Notwithstanding this durational concept of eternity, Stump and Kretzmann, again on the basis of Boethius, claim that an eternal life is atemporal, that is, without succession: being 'all at once' (*tota simul*), as Boethius's phrase has it, entails that there can be no passage of any sort within the eternal and so no time as conventionally understood.[2] The need to account for the way in which such an entity—one that enjoys infinite atemporal duration and that has all of its existence at once—may still have every temporal event present to it leads Stump and Kretzmann, furthermore, to postulate a special type of simultaneity, which they call ET-simultaneity.

Stump's and Kretzmann's understanding of eternity as atemporal duration has come in for criticism from both sides. Some thinkers have questioned the very coherence of the notion of eternal duration and doubted on historical grounds whether Boethius subscribed to it (Rogers 1994), while others have questioned whether Boethius in fact wished to profess divine timelessness (Marenbon 2003, 135–38). Stump and Kretzmann, in turn, have dug in their heels: in their defence of their position, Boethius's definition is cited as a succinct expression of 'paradigmatic, genuine duration' (1987, 219). More recently, Brian Leftow (1991, 112–46) has, with some modifications, defended this characterisation both as a viable interpretation of Boethius and as the most intelligible construction of what eternity might mean. Thus, the notion of atemporal duration, stretched out alongside the entire length of time (whether finite or finite), has come to enter the philosophical vocabulary as an image of what the medieval and Christian view of eternity was supposed to be like. Specifically, it is supposed to respond to certain perceived tensions in how eternity is described in medieval philosophy, insofar as infinity, omnipresence and atemporality are all routinely ascribed to God in the texts.

What is striking in all this, certainly from a historian's point of view, is how superficial the attempts at contextualising Boethius can sometimes seem. For example, Leftow (1991, 118–19) attempts to ground his notion of eternity as (atemporal) duration in the Platonic model provided by the *Timaeus*, a text on which Boethius explicitly relies. The majority interpretation among late ancient Platonists was that the sensible universe enjoys infinite temporal extension and that it does so in imitation of the perfection of its source (Baltes 1976–78). From this, Leftow contends, it naturally follows that that source should include infinity, and thus infinite extension, among its attributes as well. In a similar vein, Stump and Kretzmann (1981, 431) mention Plotinus's treatise on eternity and time, where we find a close analogue to Boethius's definition at *Enneads* 3.7.3, only to emphasise Boethius's substitution of 'interminable' where Plotinus has 'without extension or interval' (*adiastatos pantakhē*). For Stump and Kretzmann, this counts as evidence that Boethius is willing to attribute duration to divine eternity, whereas Plotinus is not. But all these claims are dubious since to most post-classical authors the infinity of God—for Boethius, the interminability of divine life—signifies primarily completeness and perfection, not extension.[3] What this means for the imitation relation, as Katherin Rogers has already pointed out (1994, 3–6), is that infinite extension, seen precisely as imitation, must fall well short of whatever true infinity and its attendant perfection looks like. Otherwise, what would the difference be between the two? And this is a much less forced reading anyhow of the distinction between sempiternity and eternity that Boethius wants to sketch out. The *spatium* of infinite time acts as an imperfect counterpart to the *plenitudo* of divine eternity.[4]

All of the above are still examples of legitimate disagreements regarding matters of historical interpretation. What is more disconcerting is that in modern analytical uses of Boethius, ad hoc definitions of terms are sometimes allowed to substitute for any historical work at all. The results can border on the comical, as in the following, offered with a straight face as an interpretation of the Old Testament custom of calling Yahweh a living God:

> If God is living, he has a life. Lives consist of events. There could not be an event with no TTPs [*scil.* typically temporal properties]: an event which is never present is just an event which never occurs . . . So a God with a life must have a present, and so some TTPs. (Leftow, in Ganssle and Woodruff 2002, 24)

Never mind for the moment the exotic TTPs that supposedly infuse the world of the Psalmist, Samuel and Hosea. What is more remarkable from our point of view is that all this forms part of an attempt to give an account of Boethius's divine present or permanent now (*nunc permanens*). Boethius's words in *On the Trinity* are here stretched to fit a decidedly Procrustean bed of TTPs and instantaneous events, while what Boethius himself may have understood by the dual notions of life and presence is left altogether by the wayside. Stump and Kretzmann (1981, 431–32) are scarcely better when they bluntly claim that because Boethius defines eternity in terms of life, this must mean that such items as, for instance, number, truth and the world (taken as a whole) will necessarily be denied eternity in the relevant sense. Such a decree can only be issued if one is prepared to ignore all of the historical dimensions of Boethius's words: by the sixth century, Plotinus's way of equating being, life and intelligence had become common currency in Patristic circles, and it is quite possible that Boethius was also aware of the more complex metaphysical schemes of the later Neoplatonists, especially the school of Athens (Syrianus and Proclus). Any one of these might bring a good many entities besides God into the ambit of eternally living beings; the custom of calling the cosmos itself a living creature, meanwhile, goes all the way back to Plato's *Timaeus* (*Tim.* 30b–33b). Whether Boethius subscribed to the full Neoplatonic picture of reality is open to question, but whether that picture provides a tighter correspondence to his outlook than talk of TTPs and ET-simultaneities is, I think, not.

2. THE VIEW FROM THE MOUNTAINTOP

Neoplatonic influences enter medieval philosophy from another direction as well. One may trace a direct line of influence from Hilary of Poitiers's (d. 368) and Augustine's treatises *On the Trinity* to the commentaries on Peter Lombard's *Sentences* that evoke the triad being–life–intelligence when explaining the Son's co-eternality with the Father.[5] From here the notion finds its way to scholastic texts everywhere, and from Augustine's treatment the further inference could be drawn that providential history rests in the Word of God somehow in a present manner. For the latter idea, Boethius's famous simile could also be evoked of God as being akin to the person standing on a mountaintop, taking in the underlying surroundings at a glance.

In modern terms, all this is easily accommodated if one reads it as an expression of the tenseless or B-theory of time. Here, foreknowledge turns out not to be fore-knowledge at all: rather, the whole of time is open to a simple and simultaneous cognitive act that stand outside the ambit of time altogether and more closely resembles direct perception.[6] The view has resurfaced in recent years (Ganssle in Ganssle and Woodruff 2002, 165–81); its perhaps most famous formulation is in Anselm of Canterbury's treatise *On the Harmony of God's Foreknowledge, Predestination, and Grace with Free Choice* 1.5: 'Just as every place, and those things that are in any place, are contained in the present time, so too every time, and those things that are at any time, are enclosed all at once in the eternal present' (tr. T. Williams). Commenting on John 8:58, 'Before Abraham was, I am', Aquinas similarly notes with Gregory the Great the incongruence between the tenses and explains that this is because God's eternity means that there is no past and future for him, only present. God's eternality accordingly encompasses all time in one indivisible present.[7]

Remarkably, neither Augustine nor Anselm seem to regard such a B-series view of divine knowledge as being incompatible with absolute passage in the life of generated creatures, and hence, a tensed or A-series manner of relating facts about created existence. This may appear inconsistent or even incoherent to the modern reader, who is accustomed to seeing a clear line drawn between the two. In recent years, for instance, William Lane Craig, in line with Paul Helm and Alan Padgett earlier (Helm 1988, Padgett 1992), has argued that only a tenseless or B-theory of time is compatible with the timeless interpretation of divine eternity. As to the implications, where Helm sees a compelling reason to accept the B-theory view of time, Craig sees an invitation to weigh the merits of the B-theory against the A-theory (Craig in Le Poidevin 1998, 221–50), and Padgett straightforwardly concludes that the problems associated with the B-theory—what Padgett calls the stasis view—rob the timeless interpretation of divine eternity of any attraction it may have. Craig has since come out in favour of the A-theory or tensed interpretation of time as well, which is unsurprising given his conviction that only a God who enters time can interact with creation in meaningful ways. However, what Augustine's and Anselm's mix of eternalist and presentist, tenseless and tensed language tells is that medieval philosophers saw no need to choose sides in such a clear-cut manner. This mirrors Visser's and Williams's (2009, 99–105) finding that neither one of the contemporary categories of endurance and perdurance adequately captures Anselm's metaphysical intuitions. Nor will it do to label Anselm a four-dimensionalist, as Rogers (2007) has done, without taking into account the way Anselm occasionally resorts to presentist language. If there is a tension here, as seems undeniable, it may yet prove fertile philosophically. Then again, it may not: whatever the case may be, the way to find out is to work through the implications of the actual medieval texts.[8]

What this also means, in my estimation, is that both Plotinus's and Boethius's favourite metaphor regarding eternity, the one that has eternity as the point at the centre of an imaginary circle and time as its circumference, cannot so easily be swept aside as Stump and Kretzmann seem to want when they advance their pre-ferred metaphor of two lines extended side by side.[9] Whatever our intuitions as temporal creatures might say regarding time as an arrow proceeding in a rectilinear manner, with the past no longer existing while the future does not do so yet, none of these need reflect reality; rather, our intellectual efforts may force a re-evaluation of such commonplace notions. And this, in turn, occasions a more general observa-tion: for medieval philosophers, as for Boethius and the ancient Platonists, the line from *explanandum* to *explanans,* from imitation to reality or from metaphor to true *logos* generally flows in the opposite direction from what Stump, Kretzmann, Leftow and other analytically minded contemporary philosophers of religion are accus-tomed to. This may indeed be one area where the Continental tradition offers some useful insights: Boethius is indeed heir to an entire tradition that privileges a 'meta-physics of presence', the point here being that the primary mode of being and pres-ence is the intelligible or divine one. In line with the two-level model proposed by Plato in the *Timaeus*, Plotinus, Proclus and all who came after sought to show how the life of intellect (*nous*) stands at a fathomless remove from that enjoyed by sen-sible existence. It is the former and not the latter that truly deserves to be called 'being', and as a consequence any model that seeks to understand eternity in terms of time should be treated with caution. In other words, while we might be inclined to liken time to an arrow and, similarly to this, to treat eternity in a linear fashion, the reality of eternity according to the Platonist will in fact be quite different, and even our understanding of time may be twisted into an unfamiliar shape once we assess the matter intellectually (witness the cyclical picture of time that emerges from the metaphor of the centre and the circumference).[10]

Paul Helm's remarks regarding this point are, I think, revealing. When discuss-ing Boethius, Helm writes, 'the idea of God as the center of a circle with time being represented by the circumference is also defective, because *of course* the temporal order is linear and not circular' (Helm in Ganssle 2002, 38; my emphasis). But I submit that to the late ancient Neoplatonist this would not have been so self-evident at all. Even Aristotle, the most consistent A-theorist in all of ancient philosophy and the one most committed to the inexorable passage of time, may have subscribed to a cyclical view when it comes to the overarching celestial clock (see White 1992, 95). And although again the depth of Boethius's Neoplatonic commitments may right-fully be questioned, the mere fact that he adopts this particular metaphor in an in-tellectual environment that is suffused with notions of cyclical time should give us pause.

The question of what is to be taken metaphorically and what literally extends to our understanding of Boethian divine presence. Leftow sensibly advocates the lit-eral approach: presence being a perfection, one would expect Boethius's God to enjoy it more than created entities. Leftow, furthermore, astutely posits that Aristotelian categorical theory might be relevant here, specifically the category of 'the when' (*pote*), since it is in the context of discussing the categories and their applicability to God-talk that Boethius presents his remarks in *On the Trinity* (Leftow, in Ganssle and Woodruff 2002, 24–25). Yet it is doubtful whether historical concerns in any way motivate his preference since there is no further attempt in Leftow to situate Boethius within the late ancient discussions. This is a pity, given that the latter were particularly rich when it comes to just this question. To be precise, Iamblichus (d. 325 AD) had advanced an intellective theory (*noēra theoria*) regarding Aristotle's *Categories,* one that asserted that for each of Aristotle's ten categories an underlying and primary reading could be given that relates it to intelligible reality.[11] This resulted in an intellectual time—in McTaggart's terms, a tenseless B-series of 'before' and 'after' rather than 'past' and 'future'—being posited to match the phenomenological (A-series) time of passage experienced by ensouled creatures, with the notion of the present serving as the principle that binds together the two with the primary presence enjoyed by eternal Being.[12]

Whether or not Boethius took in any of Iamblichus's views is again debatable. But what should scarcely need defending is the observation that a more informed historical understanding of Boethius's intellectual climate has the potential to yield better results than the haphazard application of modern intuitions to ancient texts. After all, wherever the Platonic influence is strong in the medieval period, we do find these metaphors seized upon in their full strength. John Scot Eriugena, for instance, not only maintains that 'the universe of creatures is eternal in the Word of God' but illustrates this through the twin examples of all numbers already being contained in the monad and an infinity of radii proceeding from a single central point in a circle (*Periphyseon* 3.8 in John Scot 1981, 72–75). The implication is that the radii unfold eternally and infinitely from the point, with the circle of time a delimiting instantiation of this ideal manifold. There is scarcely reason to deny that this is a difficult philosophical idea, but then again one should not dismiss out of the hand the idea that Eriugena had something definite in mind, and perhaps something worth pursuing.[13]

I am not the first to make these observations. Herbert Nelson (1987, 11–12), for instance, criticises Stump and Kretzmann for applying terms such as 'presentness', 'duration' and 'simultaneity' univocally across mundane (temporal) and divine (timeless) reality as well as for privileging the contemporary connotations of these terms. Nelson additionally points out that temporal distance for Stump and Kretzmann equals ontic distance (1987, 14): I would only add that such a view would have appeared quite alien to most pre-modern thinkers. Starting from an ontology of being and beings, time would appear to any post-Plotinian philosopher (except, perhaps, for al-Rāzī) as a concomitant of either motion, soul or sheer diversity, depending on the strength of one's Aristotelian or Platonic commitments. But time certainly would not assume the position of an overarching reality that would in any sense map out divine and created existence: time is explicable through eternity, not the other way around.

3. In Defence of Historicity

Why does any of this matter? Why should we trouble ourselves with the Boethius of history when the modern Boethius, strange Franken-creature that he may be (that is to say: composed in equal parts of historical and analytical components), very clearly has managed to stir up quite a bit of attention on his own? Or, to put the question in a more pointed way, why should we bother with trying to discern the minute nuances hidden in Boethius's remarks, when those remarks by most every-one's agreement are vague and allusive? If Stump's, Kretzmann's and Leftow's Boethius (or Paul Helm's, or Nelson Pike's or William Lane Craig's) promises a more fully developed and tightly argued (in modern analytical terms) account of eternity than Boethius's Boethius ever did, can we not simply declare ourselves done with the latter?

Well, a first answer would be that greater historical accuracy is to be valued for its own sake. But that scholarly line of defence, however right-minded, may not con-vince the contemporary reader. Historical research is hard work; for it to feel worth-while, the rewards have to be commensurate. A second line of argument accordingly takes its start from the observation that for all his fame, Boethius only provides one episode in the long history of discussing eternity in Western philosophy. Assuredly, his obscure roots and complex legacy should provide further resources for reflecting on whether all options have been exhausted in the modern discussions concerning eternity. The very opaqueness of Boethius's remarks, this is to say, may turn out to be a strength, insofar as his medieval reception can be used to turn the spotlight on the various problems associated with the various interpretations of eternity doing the rounds today.

To pick but one illustrative example, Albert the Great analyses Boethius's char-acterisation of eternity as life in the light of Aristotle's *On the Soul* (2.1–4). On the face of it, this might be deemed anachronistic as well, as Boethius is unlikely to have had the technical Aristotelian understanding of life at the back of his mind when writing the *Consolation*. For his part, Aristotle certainly did not share any of Boethi-us's theological concerns when he spoke about the conditions and characteristics of life. And yet Albert's analysis—in brief, that life has to do with an activity of the soul that is conducive to its ultimate actuality and specific mode of perfection—plainly has more historical warrant than Stump's, Kretzmann's and Leftow's ad hoc defini-tions. What is more, Albert's elucidations are given in the context of defining eter-nity as a measure and as a duration: thus, acquaintance with his views through, say, Henryk Anzulewicz's study of them might enrich contemporary treatments of the 'atemporal duration' thesis (just as awareness on the historians' part of the Stump-Kretzmann-Leftow thesis assuredly would enliven the systematic dimension of their work).[14]

Third, a picture of Boethius that does not make him into a stand-in for the me-dieval tradition entire but that instead sees him as occupying a distinctive position at the threshold between ancient and medieval thought can help us to steer clear of some of the pitfalls associated with lumping all 'timeless' interpretations of eternity together in a single compound view. For neither are those philosophers critical of the atemporal view innocent of casting their own anachronistic projections onto the historical materials. For instance, William Hasker (1989, 177–85) among contemporary philosophers seems unusually attuned to the deep metaphysical roots of the doctrine of divine timelessness as grounded in the equation between immutability, simplicity and fullness of being. He has, moreover, the good sense to treat this not merely as Hellenic confusion but as a powerful and attractive worldview in its own right. And yet when Hasker (in Ganssle and Woodruff 2002, 201–2) issues an impassioned plea to set aside 'Greek speculation' as exemplified by Boethius in favour of the 'biblical God', who is not only intimately involved in human history but actually becomes incarnate within it, it is plain that he is not speaking about just any biblical God, but specifically the Christian one, and perhaps the Christian God as circumscribed by the creed of Chalcedon (it is not clear to me that either an Arian or a Sabellian would be tied up in the same kinds of knots regarding the issue of eternity as professing Chalcedonians are). A Jewish or Muslim thinker or pagan monotheist (a figure still very much on Boethius's mind when he wrote the *Consolation*) may have had a partly or wholly different range of issues and problems in mind.[15] On the whole it is useful to distinguish between the philosophy of religion as an academic exercise, religiously oriented philosophy in its various guises (pagan, Eastern, Abrahamic, to name but a few) and specifically Christian philosophy, and even the latter is not a monolithic entity, certainly not in its historical dimensions. A careful examination of the various ways in which classical and medieval authors dissect arguments for and against different types of eternity can serve to sort out some of the intuitions and conceptual presuppositions that are regarded as commonplaces in the contemporary debate.

This connects with the broader issue of Hellenisation and de-Hellenisation; once more, a sense of historical perspective may help to curb any tendencies towards needless simplification. Hasker's polemical moves, for instance, are in line with certain de-Hellenising trends in twentieth-century Christian theology, trends to which other thinkers criticising timeless eternity have pledged explicit allegiance (e.g., Kneale 1961; Pike 1970; Swinburne 1993; Wolterstorff 1982). And yet if we recognise the Hellenic component already in the wisdom literature of the Hebrew Bible, in Philo and in every Christian thinker who took inspiration from these sources, then any attempt to extricate Hellenism from 'biblical' Christianity will begin to look more and more like an abstract exercise (see Ramelli and Konstan 2007). Hellenism was there all along: its various strands, along with biblical materials such as the stories of the Yahwist and the poetry of the Psalmist, form the core around which every theological piece of writing turned, whether wittingly or unwittingly. As a consequence, what we encounter in the Middle Ages is a blend of ideas swirling around in various constellations, some of which resist any easy reduction into either Hellenic or anti-Hellenic, atemporalist or temporalist thinking.

One example of this is the way extension and duration become terms used to describe eternity in the Latin scholastic materials from the late twelfth century onwards. Even if the ascription of duration to Boethian eternity rests on shaky grounds, without a question such language is littered through scholastic texts (not all of them: Albert the Great unblinkingly endorses talk of duration, while Aquinas in the *Summa theologiae* 1.10.1 gingerly, and I think quite deliberately, employs *duratio* only in the *videtur quod* arguments).[16] One may regard this simply as signalling the seriousness with which scholastic authors approached the biblical texts and their interpretation in the early Fathers of the Church, but this hardly suffices as an explanation, seeing as the mixing of pointillist (or non-extended) and durational (or extended) language produced all manner of philosophical trouble for the authors in question, trouble of which they were quite cognisant. Albert, for instance, in his *De quattuor coaequaevis* expends a great deal of energy neutralising the more troublesome implications of the notion of a divine *spatium* or *duratio,* indicating that it is only the mind's inability to imagine the infinity of God except in terms of extended parts that forces such language upon us. An analysis more faithful to Augustine's puzzling approach will, rather, draw a connection between the now of the present and the non-flowing eternity of the divine presence (see *Conf.* 11.14).

This is enlightening enough in itself, but Albert's comments additionally point towards the most plausible historical explanation for the prevalence of explaining eternity as duration in the scholastic materials. This is the way that *spatium*, or extension, figures in the definitions of both eternity and time in the influential Latin translation of the *Book of Definitions* by the tenth-century Jewish author Isḥāq Isrā'īlī.[17] Several late ancient authors assign to at least some Platonists the Stoic notion, much derided by the Peripatetics, that time would be a simple extension (*diastēma*) of some sort rather than the number of motion. This idea seems to have reached the scholastics through Isḥāq in a technical formulation, and through Patristic texts less formally. A similar analysis could then be applied to aeviternity, on which more will be said in what follows, and even eternity proper. Reinforcing this was the existing characterisation of both eternity and time as measures (*mensurae*), a turn of phrase that in the case of eternity produced much trouble for theologians keen on preserving God's absolute illimitability.

It seems to me that it is this widespread adoption of durations and measures in scholastic texts that has prompted modern philosophers like Leftow to read a similar view into thinkers like Boethius and Anselm, authors in whose works the language is absent and in whose thought their presence is debatable. The elision is still not justified textually: Boethius, far from equating the *spatium* of infinite time with the *plenitudo* more properly predicated of eternity, deliberately keeps the two apart, while Anselm never once evokes *duratio* or any other extensional term as far as I can tell. But again my real point is that if one were to explore the philosophical force of Leftow's, Stump's and Kretzmann's 'Boethian eternity', the medieval reception of Boethius might prove a better starting point than Boethius's own brief and inconclusive words. More in general, reaching beyond Augustine, Boethius and Anselm and into the complex way in which these figures and others (Eriugena; Plato via Calcidius; and yes, Aristotle) were received may yet throw light on the contradictory interpretations of Boethius currently doing the rounds, for instance, and much that is of independent interest besides. Much valuable work has already been done in this vein (see Fox 2006; Porro 2001); a prospective defence of Leftow's interpretation might take its start, say, from Albert's remarks on the intellectual distension of eternal being in his *De causis et processu universitatis* 2.1.8 (Albertus 1993, 69–71).

Another lead to follow, as the above example from Isḥāq shows, would be the development of medieval Arabic thought. This involves the *kalām* tradition of speculative theology as much as the more familiar (relatively speaking) brand of Aristotelianism found in Avicenna and Averroes. Islamic analyses of eternity as a whole are a crucially understudied resource whose significance has yet to be assessed, let alone digested.[18] By way of illustration, let me simply begin by quoting 'Alī Ibn Muḥammad al-Jurjānī's (d. 1413) characterisation of eternity in his *Book of Definitions*: 'Eternity is the permanent present, which is equal to the extension of the divine presence. It is the concealed [aspect] of time; through it, that which has no beginning and that which has no end become one'.[19] The reference to what has no beginning and what has no end (*al-azal wa al-abad*) finds elucidation in the corresponding definitions much earlier in the book: these state that pre-eternity denotes infinite duration of existence on the side of the past, while post-eternity stretches similarly into the future (Jurjānī 1845, 16). In other words, there is a presumption of an infinite stretch of time that extends both ways, *a parte ante* as well as *a parte post*; notwithstanding this, each point in the time line finds unity in the permanent present in a manner that is not immediately obvious to us (hence its concealment).

I would submit that this provides a tighter fit for Stump and Kretzmann's atemporal duration—ET-simultaneity and all—than does anything found in Boethius. At the same time, it is plainly obvious that al-Jurjānī knows nothing of the Boethian tradition; instead, he arrives at a late stage of an independent line of philosophical reasoning that stretches from the earliest days of Islamic thought and through Avicenna's transformative labours to its blossoming in subsequent centuries. If there are similarities here, then they are due to philosophers in different environments working through the implications of certain classical notions in parallel.

4. THE NECESSARY AND THE ETERNAL

Another noticeable parallel is found in the threefold classification of beings Jurjânî puts forward when defining *azal* and *abad*. On opposing ends of the scale, we have that being which lacks both beginning and end (God) and that which has both (sublunary individuals); in between lie beings that, while having begun to exist, may be spared the fate of ever perishing. This third group, the *abadî*, of which souls form an example, is called 'perpetual' in several late-twelfth- and early-thirteenth-century Latin texts (or, just to make things more confusing, also on occasion 'sempiternal' or 'aeviternal'). Jurjānī goes on to rule out the possibility of anything being pre- but not post-eternal on the grounds that whatever is pre-eternal in the sense of *qadīm* cannot become non-existent. This, too, accords with an established line of thought in Latin scholasticism.[20]

The asymmetry between the latter two cases—it is possible for something with a beginning to have no end, whereas the converse does not apply—is marked and calls for explanation. Historically, it has to do with the reception of Plato's and Aristotle's respective cosmologies: the former had claimed that God may bestow immortality on creatures (*Timaeus* 41b–c) while the latter, in an argument explicitly directed at Plato, had maintained that the very notion of something having a beginning but no end is incoherent just because the converse case of a beginningless existent meeting an end is impossible (*De caelo* 1.12). What lends the ensuing debate interest in the present context is the way in which it mixes modal notions with intuitions regarding the eternal and the infinite: though it is not possible to do the long and complex story any kind of justice within the confines of this essay, the following section will point out some of the implications for the topic of eternity.

As a starting point, we may consider al-ʿĀmirī (d. 992), a Muslim philosopher working from a version of the pseudo-Aristotelian *Liber de causis* when construct-ing his own *Kitāb al-fuṣūl* (see Wakelnig 2006). ʿĀmirī takes Proclus's notion of there being one level of reality 'above', one level 'with' and one level 'after' eternity from the *Elements of Theology* (prop. 88 = *De causis* 2), then supplements this with a level that is 'with' time and one that is 'in' time. The crucial move here is the one that pushes God beyond eternity: similarly influenced by t he *Liber de causis*, Latin authors in the thirteenth century variously assert that God is either above (*supra*) or outside (*ultra*) eternity because of his ontological priority to both. In an ontology of participation, this could be spelled out by saying that God, as the first principle and as the source of all being, is the author of eternity, which in turn could be used to explain Boethius's stray statement in his *On the Trinity* to the effect that God's permanent now (*nunc permanens*) somehow makes eternity.[21]

Now, what ʿĀmirī takes to be beyond eternity the late ancient Platonists would describe as lying beyond being (*epekeina tēs ousias*). However, similarly to Christian medieval authors, ʿĀmirī prefers to regard God as pure being or Being itself (*ipsum esse, mawjūd bi-l-dhāt*). Through Avicenna's works this reinterpretation of God's place in the great chain of being passed on to medieval Latin learning (the common denominator here is the Arabic *Theology of Aristotle*), but it leaves a structural prob-lem. Whereas with late Neoplatonism, eternity could be associated with Being and Intellect and God raised, consequently, above both, in any system where God is placed on the level of Being and Intellect it becomes difficult to distinguish between things that are co-eternal.

The standard response was to fall back on the Platonist notion of causal depen-dency in the absence of temporal procession. In the Latin domain, Augustine's example of the footprint in the dust (*Civ.* 10.31) could be adduced: in the *City of God*, Augustine, though he holds to a beginning of time when it comes to the material universe, pleads ignorance when it comes to whether spiritual creatures might have existed from eternity that would nonetheless not be fully co-eternal with God (*Civ.* 12.15). This is the standard way of framing the issue from Eriugena onwards. Though other principles besides God may be eternal, none of them are co-eternal with Him. Still, the question remains whether this puts enough distance between the different ranks of beings, especially if it is the case that angels and the like do not enter temporality the same way that, for example, the eternally rotating heavens do. The various conflicting descriptions of whether God lies beyond *aeternitas* or merely beyond *aeviternitas* testify to the difficulties experienced by the scholastics in hitting upon a satisfactory formula.

An analogous problem arose in Islamic thought. Robert Wisnovsky (2004) has shown that the central question facing early Muslim theologians was how to characterise effectively the difference between God and the world, Creator and creature. The formulation they hit upon was that God is eternal (*qadīm*—originally just 'ancient', comparable to *antiquum* in Dionysius), while everything in the world is originated (*muḥdath*).[22] The temporal beginning of the world having become an unassailable point of dogma as well as the first step in *kalām* proofs for God's existence (see Davidson 1987, 117–212) was all well and fine, until the time came to establish what the mode of being of God's attributes was, among them God's speech or the Qur'ān. The emerging consensus was that since any change in God was inadmissible, the attributes had to be co-eternal with God. However, that then produced a new problem: if the attributes are eternal, then are they eternal in themselves (*qadīm bi-nafsihi*) or through a reified eternality (*qadīm bi-qidam*)? If the former, then the force of setting apart God's essence through attributing eternity to Him seems to be lost; if the latter, then the eternality of eternality has to be accounted for, which would seem to threaten to set up an infinite regress (see Juwaynī 1950, 139). What the latter scenario suggests is that the Muslim philosophers were struggling with the implications of a metaphysics of participation without, however, having available to them the full toolkit of the late Neoplatonists. The latter could simply have said that eternity itself (which the Platonists did reify) is not itself eternal in any standard sense.[23]

The Muslim solution was to underline the contingency of every existent except for God, even the putatively eternal ones. The solution is known to us primarily through Avicenna's metaphysical works; indeed, via Aquinas's Third Way it has become part of our common philosophical vocabulary. But it was hit upon first independently by *kalām* authors. Al-Isfarā'īnī (d. 1027), for instance, puts it that what is really meant by God's eternality (*qidam*) is his absolute self-subsistence: the lack of temporality that the divine attributes enjoy does not yet guarantee their priority in this privileged way.[24] Eventually the fusing of Avicennian and *kalām* perspectives led to an ontological reconfiguration where the eternal/temporal divide ceased to matter. Not only did this open the door to regarding the physical universe as eternal yet created (the doctrine of eternal creation, or *ḥudūth azalī*), but also it even became possible for a thinker such as the Jewish Peripatetic Ibn Kammūna (d. 1284) to suggest that there is nothing wrong in regarding the human soul pre-eternal since its contingency does not suffer therefrom. Avicennian metaphysical contingency remained a contested notion both in Arabic and in Latin philosophy,[25] but what resulted from the widespread adoption of Avicenna's frame-work was that mere temporal markers were no longer regarded as either a necessary or a sufficient condition for separating Creator from created.

Modal metaphysics could interact with conceptions of eternity in other unex-pected ways. John Duns Scotus, through embracing synchronic contingency in his celebrated *Lectura* 1.39, effectively commits himself to a dynamic interpretation of time and a non-existent future. Though Duns Scotus's retention of atemporalist language when describing God makes it difficult to assess how clearly he foresaw the implications for time in his conception,[26] William Ockham, with his penchant for streamlining matters, draws the inevitable conclusion. Since any given state of affairs remains contingent until its actualisation, new items enter God's knowledge with the passage of time. Gregory of Rimini proceeds further along the Ockhamist path.[27] This opens up to a picture of eternity that is, finally, fully in the A-theorist, presentist and sempiternal vein.

5. SEMPITERNITY

In fact, the interpretation of eternity as sempiternity—that is, everlasting temporal succession—constitutes a whole other field of study where we have barely begun to assess the possible contribution of medieval philosophy to contemporary discus-sions. With the contemporary debates centred squarely on whether the notion of timeless eternity is coherent, eternity as everlastingness has received much less crit-ical scrutiny. This is all the more surprising if, as some have claimed, divine sempi-ternity is now close to being the new orthodoxy (Ganssle and Woodruff 2002, 1; Leftow 1991, 3; contrast Wolterstorff 1982, 77). Quite aside from discussions re-garding divine foreknowledge and eternal action, the medieval materials are helpful inasmuch as they do not focus exclusively on the sempiternity of *God*. The medieval worldview included other candidates for everlastingness, ranging from the angels and the celestial spheres down to cyclically recurring worldly processes.[28] The hotly disputed issue of the eternity of the world, in particular, emerges as a kind of coun-terpoint to the aforementioned discussion of timeless divine eternity. (Dales 1990; Dales and Argerami 1991; Davidson 1987).

To begin with, we may remark that the notion of God's reality 'running along-side' time, which we find in contemporary philosophy in the likes of Stump, Kretzmann and Leftow, is more commonly attached to Aristotelian analyses of re-ality within medieval philosophy. This is natural inasmuch as Aristotelian eternity does not connote standing outside of time; it means only that a wholly changeless substance is neither preceded nor followed by anything else. Eternal things, then, exist together *with*, rather than *in*, the eternal motion and time of the cosmos. The notion of running alongside is accordingly used in an uncomplicated manner in Averroes, and Aquinas attaches it to the *aevum* of the angels and the rotations of the heavenly bodies on the grounds that changes in either, whether potential or actual, can be mapped onto the temporal order of the sub-lunary world.

What is remarkable about Averroes is the straightforward way in which he conjoins a sempiternal model of eternity with a strictly apersonal view of God. This should serve as a reminder to those who, like William Lane Craig, would insist that only a temporally involved God can enter into personal relations with the universe or initiate one that has a beginning in time.[29] At best this turns out to be a necessary but not sufficient condition: despite having time running constantly alongside him, it is not at all clear that Averroes's God is so involved, and it is, furthermore, clear that his effect is just as eternal as He is himself:

> The two existences are as different as possible, while their connection is a necessary thing; for if they were not connected in perpetuity (I mean, if one of the two existences existed first, separately, and then was converted to the second existence) the impossible could become possible. For the existence capable of motion to exist without the eternal existence is clearly absurd, unless the effect can exist without the cause; while from the separate existence of the eternal existence, without the existence subject to motion, it would follow that the existence of the latter is impossible, unless it is possible for the nature of the eternal to be converted to the nature of time and motion. (Ibn Rushd 1991, 10–11)

The argument here is the traditional one: to explain a limited creation issuing or coming to be from a supreme being of unlimited extension, some change must be postulated in the latter, but to do such a thing is to compromise divine simplicity and immutability and to introduce potentiality to that which has none. Thus, for an Aristotelian like Averroes, the everlastingness of the world follows necessarily from the everlasting nature of God.

This contention, of course, did not go uncontested in the Middle Ages; indeed, strenuous claims were made to the contrary, to the effect that reason necessarily demands a temporally limited creation. Crucial to the creationist position was a set of arguments, first advanced by John Philoponus (d. 574), issuing from the impossibility of an actual infinite.[30] Philoponus's arguments enjoyed an extraordinary afterlife first in Islamic theology and then, following Bonaventure, in Franciscan thought (Davidson 1987, 86–116; Sorabji 1983, 210–13). In the wake of these debates, there arose in the works of Henry of Harclay, Gregory of Rimini and others analyses, for example, of unequal infinites and of discrete time (Cross 1998; Kretzmann 1982). In recent years, William Lane Craig has defended the philosophical cogency of the argument from the impossibility of an infinite past in the form that he dubs the *kalām* cosmological argument (Craig 1979). Craig has also pointedly maintained that mathematical speculation has little to do with what can take place in the actual physical world, thus seeking to fend off any appeal to post-Cantorian set theory in defending the possibility of an infinite past. Nevertheless, when, for example, Quentin Smith on the basis of 'orthodox quantum mechanics, the Special Theory of Relativity, and the General Theory of Relativity' calls for a realist metaphysics that incorporates 'an infinite sequence of infinitely long temporal intervals' (Smith in Le Poidevin 1998, 181), it seems plain that the issue remains stubbornly unresolved.

Remarkably, the creationist view comes coupled with a notion of discrete time in the mainstream of Islamic theology prior to Avicenna and for a long time after. Due to the general Occasionalist framework of *kalām*, this leads to a worldview that in some ways shows a remarkable affinity with the space–time manifold as described by philosophers such as David Lewis, J. J. C. Smart and D. C. Williams. Most notably, the notion that simultaneity denotes simply 'togetherness' crops up in *kalām* texts with some frequency. Despite this, we do not find in *kalām* a metaphysics of perdurance; rather, God's everlastingness is of the enduring kind.

As we may have come to expect by now, the results thus resist easy classification. I will pick only three representative examples, each of which would deserve a more detailed treatment than is possible here. Abū al-Barakāt al-Baghdādī (1077–1164) holds time to be a concomitant of existence, its measure and duration: not even God escapes time since to say that he is eternal is simply to say that he is the changelessly Enduring (*bāqī*). As time assumes a position of considerable priority on the existential ladder—it is not associated with change but instead is a general metric for the length of existence—it becomes a subject of metaphysics and, in the strict sense, indefinable. But since time is a concomitant of existence rather than part of its definition, God and, more generally, all existents do not depend on time for their existence but, rather, time depends on their existence (Baghdādī 1357, 3:35–49).

The notion that time depends not only on existents but also on their co-existence is put to inventive use by Abū al-Maʿālī al-Juwaynī (1028–85) in his *Book of Guidance*. Here Juwaynī considers the objection that affirming an eternal (*qadīm*) God makes time into something infinite and without beginning. Juwaynī counters that since before the creation of the world God was alone in His existence, there is no reason to postulate any kind of passage in this primordial state (Juwaynī 1950, 32–33). God's pre-eternity on this picture is a single moment, whereas his existence following creation 'speeds up' in the sense of passing through a sequence of events or collections of moments. Notwithstanding this, his mode of existence remains firm and unchanged throughout. (The same model had been used by earlier Muʿtazilite thinkers to make sense of eternal damnation: a single new creation at the Last Judgement is enough, as the world thereafter can be regarded as it were frozen in place.)

A discussion of God's eternity (that is, *qidam*) is conspicuously missing from Abū Ḥāmid al-Ghazālī's (1056–1111) treatment of the divine attributes in his dogmatic treatises. Neither does Abū Hurayra's authoritative list of the so-called beautiful names of God, of which there are ninety-nine, include *qadīm* (or for that matter, *abad* or *azal*), so that the occasion to discuss these disputed terms does not arise in Ghazālī's commentary on these so-called *Beautiful Names*. Yet the designation 'the Enduring' (*al-Bāqī*) does occur in Abū Hurayra's list. This provides Ghazālī with the occasion to discuss eternity and all that goes with it.

Ghazālī points out first of all that only an existent essentially necessary of existence (*al-mawjūd al-wājib wujūdu-hū bi-dhāti-hi*) is enduring in the requisite sense. Next comes an interesting formulation: Ghazālī says that when the *mind* relates such an existence to the future, it comes to be called the enduring, while when the mind relates it to the past, it is called the ancient (*al-qadīm*). In addition, when the existence of that which endures is determined not to terminate in a last member, it is said to be 'everlasting' or post-eternal (*abadī*), while if it is determined not to terminate in a first in the past it is said to be pre-eternal (*azalī*). Ghazālī further underlines the point that all these temporal expressions arise only when the mind relates necessary existence to the past and to the future; such an existence in itself lies comprehensively outside of the temporal order:

> Only mutable things enter into the past and the future, since these are temporal expressions and only change and motion enter time . . . what is too exalted for change and motion is not in time, so that in it there is neither past nor future: moreover, in it antiquity and endurance do not differ. [. . .] It is necessary for things to be generated, one after another, for there to be a division into a past which has gone and expired, a current [moment which is] present, and that whose renewal is expected afterwards. So to the extent that there is no renewal and no expiration, there is no time either. (Ghazālī 1971, 159–60)

All of this is quite Avicennian; moreover, most of it finds close correspondence in Augustine. Augustine in the *Confessions* (11.13) says that God precedes all past time, just as he will survive all future time; also, citing the Psalms (102:27), he says that God's years have no end, only to hastily add that God's years neither come nor go, whereas our existence is marked precisely by the passage of time. Augustine is, furthermore, reasonably clear in that the past is no longer and the future not yet. All that actually exists is the present, with the mind projecting itself into the past through the act of recollection and into the future by way of expectation (*Conf.* 11.28). At a minimum this goes to show how in post-Avicennian Islamic thought, many classical ideas recur in unexpected shapes.

6. Concluding Remarks

The sheer richness of the medieval materials points to the futility of labelling any one conception of eternity the 'classical' or 'medieval' view, let alone the 'Orthodox' one. Instead, what emerges from these discussions is that the criteria for orthodoxy as well as for philosophical cogency were as fluid and contested in the Middle Ages as they are today. A few observations nonetheless present themselves.

The first is that in the Middle Ages enquiries into the nature of eternity were invariably and intimately intertwined with ontological concerns. This is to say that eternity in medieval philosophy is treated not as an abstract concept, but as an aspect of that which is eternal: in modern parlance, what is at issue is eternality as an attribute of one or another existent thing. The importance of this must not be overlooked, as it helps to explain the shape that many of the discussions take. With God, the aim is to show how his eternity entails no entanglement with any aspect of creation; with other possibly eternal beings, to show how their eternity still does not make them equal to God. It is this that is the driving force in adding to the distinctions one finds in medieval texts. Accordingly, the extensional interpretation as a rule finds more favour with those authors who do not envision other entities besides that which would be similarly infinitely extended, while the notion that true eternity is comparable to an instant functions as a fallback for those who have more cause to worry about setting up a distinction between God and other eternal entities.

Another observation that arises from a comparison of the historical and contemporary readings is that at the heart of the controversy regarding the temporal and atemporal interpretations of eternity is a fundamental difference in philosophical intuitions regarding questions of time and knowledge (or time and explanation). For those who prefer an interpretation of eternity that is modelled on everlastingness, the ordinary passage of time and the notion of temporally keyed facts appear reasonably straightforward; we know what these things are and what they mean, whereas what is mysterious and obscure is the notion of an atemporal entity and mode of knowing. By contrast, advocates for the timeless or eternalist view appear to regard timeless truths as the primary object of knowledge and cognition, with the line of explanation accordingly flowing from the top down, as it were. To call these the perennial Aristotelian and Platonist camps is perhaps too much, yet it is remarkable how persistent contending intuitions of these sorts can be.

NOTES

1. Sorabji (1983, 98–136) forms an exception although he, too, circles back to the question of God's timelessness (253–67).

2. Here Stump and Kretzmann certainly have the tradition on their side: innumerable medieval texts underline how the eternal life of God is without succession (*sine successione*), with most elaborating that this is because in the divine everything is present all at once. For an early example, see Thierry of Chartres (d. ca. 1150), *In Boethii librum De Trinitate* 4.72 (Thierry of Chartres 1971, 209).

3. See Sweeney (1992) and for a compact medieval presentation, for example, Aquinas, *Summa theologiae* 1.10.1; similarly Aquinas, *In Sent.* 1.8.2.1–2 (Thomas 1980, 1:22b–23c).

4. See Plotinus, *Enneads* 6.5.11 and 6.8.18 (both cited by Rogers): another relevant comparison is found in Proclus's *Elements of Theology*, see propositions 48–9, 52 (where it is explicitly stated that eternity is 'not strung out', *anepitatos*), and 55. For the purposes of comparing Plotinus and Boethius, Beierwaltes (1967) remains helpful.

5. See Hilary, *De Trin.* 1.4–13, 8.43 (Hilary 1979–80, 3–15, 355–56); Augustine, *De Trin.* 6.10; *Sent.* 1.8 (Peter Lombard 1971, 95–103).

6. On the problem of foreknowledge and free will in the Middle Ages, see Rudavsky (1985).

7. *In uno indivisibili includit omne tempus*: Super Ioannem 8.8 (Thomas 1980, 6:294c). Notice also how Deut. 32:40 (*vivo ego in aeternum*) is used to temper the claim that God's immutable life is everlasting (*vita Dei est sempiterna*): Aquinas, *Summa contra Gentiles* (1.99.5). For Anselm's views on divine eternality, see *Monologion* (18–24) and *Proslogion* (13, 18–21).

8. One reason why Anselm is favourably viewed by analytical philosophers is that his writings share many features with theirs: Anselm did not write very much, he did not work from a tremendous amount of sources and he does not appear especially beholden to tradition.

9. Stump and Kretzmann (1981, 441, n. 18); see Boethius, *Consolation* IV, prose 6, and for comments, for example, Aquinas, *Summa contra Gentiles* 1.66.7. Leftow (1991, 147–58) considers the circle and line metaphors to be complementary.

10. Proclus and Ibn Rushd (the Latin Averroës), fairly unalloyed representatives of the Platonic and Peripatetic philosophical poles, each draw the added inference that time as a circle will be infinite, as will the lifespan of the physical universe: see Kukkonen (2000, 123–26) and Ibn Rushd, *Questions in Physics*, q. 3 (Ibn Rushd 1991, 4–7). The contrast with modern intuitions is again marked—and again this is coming from two thinkers who assuredly thought of themselves as pious and theologically high minded.

11. On the category of 'when' according to Iamblichus see Simplicius (1907, 354–57).

12. Sambursky and Pines (1971, 12–17) lay out Iamblichus's theory alongside the relevant texts (26–47); see also Plass (1977). In the interest of completeness, one should point out that in late Athenian Platonism, eternal beings, too, participate in the higher principle of Eternity, which is consequently pushed beyond the intelligible realm. For comments see Steel in Porro (2001, 9–10); because the Neoplatonic passages that push Eternity (the hypostasis) beyond things eternal did not receive much play in the Middle Ages, the theme will be passed on here.

13. As regards the dialectic of infinity and finitude, many Sufi texts exhibit similar characteristics: for materials see Böwering (1999).

14. For appeals to the Boethian definition, see Albertus Magnus, *De quattuor coae-quaevis* 2.3.2 (Albertus 1895, 340–50); *Super Dionysium de divinis nominibus* 6.2 (Albertus 1972, 328); cf. Anzulewicz in Porro (2001), 83–129.

15. It is well documented that late ancient pagans, as well as Muslims and Jews in the Middle Ages, heaped scorn on the eternal-yet-incarnate God of the Chalcedonians, and that one of their central criticisms was precisely that the Incarnation implicates God in the passage of time. Yet these critics surely thought themselves pious precisely while doing so. Thus, each of the three claims that a 'theist', a 'monotheist' or a 'biblical theist' cannot advocate timeless divinity fails on historical grounds.

16. See similarly Aquinas, *In Sent.* 1.8.2.1 (Thomas 1980, 1:22b–23a); *In Phys.* 8.2.20 has it that 'aeternitas Dei . . . non habet extensionem aut prius et posterius' (Thomas 1980, 4:127b). Other texts are less careful: the *Summa contra Gentiles* (2.35) has *Dei autem duratio, quae est aeternitas*. For more examples culled from Bonaventure and Aquinas, see Fox (2006, 284, n. 4); Fox (2006, 298, n. 46) convincingly disputes Leftow's (1991, 118–19) contention that one could detect a chronological development from non-extensional to extensional language in Aquinas.

17. *Liber de definicionibus* 49–50: the Arabic original will have had *mudda*, also extension, see Altmann and Stern (1958, 74–76).

18. An indication of this is the fact that whereas I have thus far in this essay been able to refer to Latin texts by standardised practices of annotation, all Arabic references must be keyed to specific printed editions, many of which leave much to be desired.

19. al-dahr huwa al-ān al-dāʾim alladhī huwa imtidād al-ḥaḍra al-ilāhiyya wa-huwa bāṭin al-zamān wa bi-hi yattaḥidu al-azal wa al-abad: Jurjānī (1845, 111).

20. Jurjānī (1845, 16–17); similarly, for example, Robert Kilwardby, *De tempore*, q. 23 (Kilwardby 1987, 44).

21. For example, Aquinas, *In De nom. div.* 10 (Thomas 1980, 4:578a–579a); Albert, *De causis* 2.1.9 (Albertus 1993, 71–72); cf. Fox (2006), 236–39.

22. See *De nom. div.* 10 (Dionysius 1990, 214–17).

23. Walker (1978, 361–62) suggests that Ismâ'îlî thinkers may have had a grasp of these conceptual tools; cp. also Aquinas, *In Sent.* 1.19.2 (Thomas 1980, 1:52a–53a).

24. 'Aqîda, IV.2 and fragments 21–22 in Frank (1989).

25. For example, Henry of Ghent maintains that it is simply not possible for something to be created from eternity without thereby assigning both being and non-being to a single thing: *Quodlibet* I, qq. 7–8 (Henry 1613, 1:7–9) and *Quodlibet* VIII, q. 9 (op. cit. 2:20–25). In effect, this reverts to the Aristotelian position that eternity is tantamount to necessity (*De gen. et corr.* 2.10.338a1–3). Averroes says much the same, although he draws the opposite conclusion, namely, that the eternal universe is indeed necessary in every respect: see *Tahâfut al-tahâfut* I, IV, X and especially *Questions in Physics*, q. 9 (Ibn Rushd 1991, 33–36).

26. Cross (1997) accordingly paints a more traditional picture of Scotus.

27. DeWeese (2004, 186–200) offers a useful overview.

28. Aquinas, for instance (*Summa theologiae* 1.61.2 ad. 2), maintains that the angels' operations, even if standing outside of the motion of the sphere and thus conventional physical time, would still be successive and thus susceptible to some kind of temporality in the metaphysical sense.

29. Leftow (1991, 78–80), unlike Helm (1988, 90) does not see anything logically problematic about a truly immutable God sustaining a world throughout infinite time and therefore regards immutability and timelessness as separable concepts. In this he follows a precedent set earlier not only by Aquinas (which Leftow might recognise), but also by Averroes (which seems less likely).

30. See also Chapter 2, p. 32.

BIBLIOGRAPHY

Albertus Magnus. 1895. *De quatuor coaequaevis*, ed. A. Borgnet. Paris: L. Vives (*Opera omnia* 34).

———. 1972. *Super Dionysium De divinis nominibus*, ed. P. Simon. Aschendorff, Germany: Monasterii Westfalorum (*Opera omnia* 37.1).

———. 1993. *De causis et processu universitatis a prima causa*, ed. W. Fauser. Aschendorff, Germany: Monasterii Westfalorum (*Opera omnia* 17.2).

Altmann, Alexander and Samuel M. Stern. 1958. *Isaac Israeli. A Neoplatonic Philosopher of the Early Tenth Century*. Oxford: Oxford University Press.

Baghdādī, Abū al-Barakāt al-. 1357. AH. *Kitāb al-mu'tabar*, ed. S. Yaltkaya. 3 vols. Hyderabad.

Baltes, Matthias. 1976–78. *Die Weltentstehung des platonischen Timaios nach den Antiken Interpreten*. 2 vols. Leiden, the Netherlands: E.J. Brill (Philosophia Antiqua 30, 35).

Beierwaltes, Werner. 1967. *Plotin über Ewigkeit und Zeit*. Enneade III 7. Frankfurt, Germany: Klostermann (Quellen der Philosophie, Texte und Probleme 3).

Böwering, Gerhard. 1999. 'Ideas of time in Persian Sufism'. In *The Heritage of Sufism*, Vol I, ed. Leonard Lewisohn, 199–233. Oxford: Oneworld.

Craig, William Lane. 1979. *The Kalām Cosmological Argument*. London: MacMillan.

Cross, Richard. 1997. Duns Scotus on Eternity and Timelessness. *Faith and Philosophy* 14:3–25.

——. 1998. Infinity, Continuity, and Composition: The Contribution of Gregory of Rimini. *Medieval Philosophy and Theology* 7:89–110.

Dales, Richard C. 1990. *Medieval Discussions of the Eternity of the World*. Leiden, the Netherlands: E.J. Brill.

Dales, Richard C. and Omar Argerami, eds. 1991. *Medieval Latin Texts on the Eternity of the World*. Leiden, the Netherlands: E.J. Brill.

Davidson, Herbert Alan. 1987. *Proofs for Eternity, Creation, and the Existence of God in Medieval Islamic and Jewish Philosophy*. Oxford: Oxford University Press.

DeWeese, Garrett J. 2004. *God and the Nature of Time*. Aldershot, UK: Ashgate.

Dionysius. 1990. *Corpus Dionysiacum I. De Divinis Nominibus*, ed. Beata Regina Suchla. Berlin: Walter de Gruyter.

Fox, Rory. 2006. *Time and Eternity in Mid-Thirteenth-Century Thought*. Oxford: Oxford University Press.

Frank, Richard M. 1989. Al-Ustādh Abū Isḥāk: An ʿAḳīda together with Selected Fragments. *Mélanges de l'Institut Dominicain d'Études Orientales du Caire* 19:129–202.

Ganssle, Gregory A., ed. 2001. *God and Time. Four Views*. Downers Grove, IL: InterVarsity Press.

Ganssle, Gregory A. and David M. Woodruff, eds. 2002. *God and Time. Essays on the Divine Nature*. Oxford: Oxford University Press.

Ghazālī, Abū Ḥāmid Muḥammad al-. 1971. *Al-Maqṣad al-asnā fī sharḥ maʿānī asmāʾ Allāh al-ḥusnā [The Pinnacle in Explaining the Meaning of God's Beautiful Names]*, ed. Fadlou Shehadi. Beirut: Dār al-mashriq.

Hasker, William. 1989. *God, Time, and Knowledge*. Ithaca, NY: Cornell University Press.

Helm, Paul. 1988. *Eternal God. A Study of God without Time*. Oxford: Oxford University Press.

Henry of Ghent. 1613. *Quodlibeta*. 2 vols. Venice.

Hilary of Poitiers. 1979–80. *De trinitate*, ed. P. Smulders. 2 vols. Turnhout, Belgium: Brepols (Corpus Christianorum series latina 62).

Ibn Rushd, Abū al-Walīd Muḥammad [Averroes]. 1991. *Averroes' Questions in Physics*, trans. Helen Tunik Goldstein. Dordrecht, the Netherlands: Kluwer (The New Synthese Historical Library 39).

John Scot Eriugena. 1981. *Periphyseon (De Divisione Naturae) liber tertius*, ed. I. P. Sheldon-Williams. Dublin: The Dublin Institute for Advanced Studies (Scriptores Latini Hiberniae 11).

Jurjānī, ʿAlī Ibn Muḥammad al-. 1845. *Kitāb al-taʿrīfāt [Book of Definitions]*, ed. G. Flügel. Leipzig, Germany: G. Vogel.

Juwaynī, ʿAbd al-Malik Abū al-Maʿālī. 1950. *Kitāb al-irshād ilā qawāṭiʿ al-adilla fī uṣūl al-iʿtiqād [The Guide to Conclusive Proofs Regarding the Foundations of Belief]*, ed. Muḥammad Yūsuf Mūsā & ʿAlī ʿAbd al-Ḥāmid. Cairo.

Kilwardby, Robert. 1987. *On Time and Imagination. De Tempore. De Spiritu Fantastico*, ed. P. O. Lewry. Oxford: The British Academy (Auctores Britannici Medii Aevi 9).

Kneale, William. 1961. Time and Eternity in Theology. *Proceedings of the Aristotelian Society* 61:87–108.

Kretzmann, Norman, ed. 1982. *Infinity and Continuity in Ancient and Medieval Thought*. Ithaca, NY: Cornell University Press.

Kukkonen, Taneli. 2000. Proclus on Plenitude. *Dionysius* 18:103–28.

Le Poidevin, Robin, ed. 1998. *Questions of Time and Tense*. Oxford: Oxford University Press.

Leftow, Brian. 1991. *Time and Eternity*. Ithaca, NY: Cornell University Press.

Marenbon, John. 2003. *Boethius*. Oxford: Oxford University Press.

Nelson, Herbert J. 1987. Time(s), Eternity, and Duration. *Philosophy of Religion* 22:3–19.

Padgett, Alan G. 1992. *God, Eternity, and the Nature of Time*. New York: St. Martin's Press.

Peter Lombard. 1971. *Sententiae in IV libris distinctae*, 3rd ed. Rome: Grottaferrata (Spicilegium Bonaventurianum 4).

Pike, Nelson. 1970. *God and Timelessness*. London: Routledge and Kegan Paul.

Plass, Paul. 1977. *Timeless Time in NeoPlatonism*. *Modern Schoolman* 55:1–19.

Porro, Pasquale, ed. 2001. *The Medieval Concept of Time*. Leiden, the Netherlands: E.J. Brill (Studien und Texte zur Geistesgeschichte des Mittelalters 75).

Ramelli, Ilaria and David Konstan. 2007. *Terms for Eternity. Aiōnios and Aïdios in Classical and Christian Texts*. Piscataway, NJ: Gorgias Press.

Rogers, Katherin A. 1994. Eternity Has No Duration. *Religious Studies* 30:1–16.

———. 2007. Anselmian Eternalism. *Faith and Philosophy* 24:3–27.

Rudavsky, Tamar, ed. 1985. *Divine Omniscience and Omnipotence in Medieval Philosophy*. Dordrecht, the Netherlands: D. Reidel.

Sambursky, Samuel and Shlomo Pines. 1971. *The Concept of Time in Late Neoplatonism*. Jerusalem: The Israel Academy of Sciences and Humanities.

Simplicius of Cilicia. 1907. In *Aristotelis Categorias Commentarium*, ed. C. Kalbfleisch. Berlin: G. Reimer.

Sorabji, Richard. 1983. *Time, Creation, and the Continuum*. London: Duckworth.

Stump, Eleonore and Norman Kretzmann. 1981. Eternity. *The Journal of Philosophy* 78:429–58.

———. 1987. Atemporal Duration: A Reply to Fitzgerald. *The Journal of Philosophy* 84:214–19.

Sweeney, Leo. 1992. *Divine Infinity in Greek and Medieval Thought*. New York: Peter Lang.

Swinburne, Richard. 1993. 'God and time'. In *Reasoned Faith*, ed. Eleonore Stump, 204–22. Ithaca, NY: Cornell University Press.

Thierry of Chartres. 1971. *Commentaries on Boethius*, ed. Nikolaus M. Häring. Toronto: Pontifical Institute of Mediaeval Studies.

Thomas Aquinas. 1980. *Opera Omnia*, ed. R. Busa. 7 vols. Stuttgart-Bad Cannstatt, Germany: Frommann-Holzboog.

Visser, Sandra and Thomas Williams. 2009. *Anselm*. Oxford: Oxford University Press.

Wakelnig, Elvira. 2006. *Feder, Tafel, Mensch: Al-ʿĀmirīs Kitāb al-fuṣūl fī l-maʿālim al-ilāhīya und die arabische Proklos-Rezeption im 10 Jh*. Leiden, the Netherlands: E.J. Brill (*Islamic Philosophy, Theology, and Science* 67).

Walker, Paul. 1978. Eternal Cosmos and the Womb of History: Time in Early Ismaili Thought. *International Journal of Middle East Studies* 9:355–66.

White, Michael J. 1992. *The Continuous and the Discrete. Ancient Physical Theories from a Contemporary Perspective*. Oxford: Clarendon Press.

Wisnovsky, Robert. 2004. One Aspect of the Avicennian Turn in Sunnī Theology. *Arabic Sciences and Philosophy* 14:65–100.

Wolterstorff, Nicholas. 1982. 'God everlasting'. In *Contemporary Philosophy of Religion*, ed. S. M. Cahn and D. Shatz, 77–98. Oxford: Oxford University Press.

CHAPTER 25

SCEPTICISM AND METAPHYSICS

DOMINIK PERLER

1. MEDIEVAL SCEPTICISM AND ITS LIMITS

When we engage in philosophical debates, it seems quite easy to present sceptical arguments that cast doubt on our entire body of knowledge. We simply need to put forward a hypothesis according to which we might be wrong about all the things we think we know. Since the time of Descartes, philosophers have been quite familiar—some would even say, obsessed—with this kind of reasoning. Could it not be that a malicious demon is constantly deceiving us, causing all kinds of beliefs about an external world, while no such world exists? Given that this hypothesis looks so simple, it is surprising that pre-Cartesian authors do not seem to have worried about it. Medieval philosophers committed to the Aristotelian tradition do not seem to have asked the fundamental question whether or not we can have knowledge of an external world. Their main concern was not to establish *that* we can have knowledge but to explain *how* we acquire it. They entered into lengthy discussions about the following problems: What kind of cognitive processes are required for the acquisition of knowledge? What kind of knowledge do we gain by means of these processes? And what are the objects of our knowledge? In all these debates, they seem to have taken for granted that we are able to have knowledge and even a solid theory of knowledge.

Why did they not radically question our knowledge claims? There are at least three apparently simple answers to this question. First, until the sixteenth century, medieval philosophers had only little knowledge of ancient sceptical sources that could have inspired them to formulate sceptical hypotheses. In particular, it is said that they were not familiar with Sextus Empiricus's *Outlines of Scepticism*, translated into Latin in 1562, which sparked what R. Popkin famously called a 'sceptical crisis' in the early-modern period.[1] Second, one might refer to the all-embracing theological culture in which medieval philosophy was practised. Given the dominant Christian belief that God is a benevolent creator who endows all human beings with reliable cognitive capacities, it would have been odd to ask whether or not knowledge is possible. The appropriate question to pose was how human beings can make best use of their natural cognitive capacities and thereby acquire knowledge. Third, one might mention the institutional framework that excluded radical sceptical debates from the outset. Medieval philosophers were supposed to comment on authoritative texts, especially on Aristotle's writings, and therefore dealt with sources that were inspired by epistemological optimism.

Given these arguments, which have often been mentioned in the scholarly literature, it seems clear that radical scepticism could not be an issue for medieval philosophers.[2] Yet a closer look at these arguments shows that they are far from being convincing. First, it is necessary to acknowledge the simple fact that ancient sceptical sources were available in the Middle Ages. Sextus Empiricus's *Outlines of Scepticism* were translated into Latin in the late thirteenth century already; three manuscripts from this time have been transmitted.[3] Thanks to this work, scholastic authors were familiar not only with a number of sceptical arguments, but also with Agrippa's famous trilemma that seems to exclude successful justification of knowledge claims: justification leads to an infinite regress, is circular or ends with a dogmatic assumption. Even more influential was the Academic tradition, which was well known thanks to Cicero's *Academica* and Augustine's *Contra Academicos*.[4] In these works medieval interpreters could find a number of sceptical hypotheses that appealed to illusions, dreams and deceptions.

Second, the all-embracing theological culture did not prevent medieval philosophers from taking sceptical arguments seriously. On the contrary, this culture gave rise to radical hypotheses that went beyond the arguments formulated by pagan philosophers. The most influential hypothesis was what might be called 'the argument from divine omnipotence'. Theologians from the twelfth century onwards claimed that God can use his potency not only by acting according to the 'ordained power' (*potestas ordinata*), which respects the natural laws, but also by making use of the 'absolute power' (*potestas absoluta*), which is only bound to the law of non-contradiction and does not need to respect the natural laws.[5] Thus, using his absolute power, God could cause in me a cognitive state presenting a tree and make me believe right now that I am standing in front of a tree even though no tree is present. He could do it in such a perfect way that I would not be able to distinguish the naturally caused belief from the supranaturally induced one. A number of medieval authors (especially Duns Scotus and his followers) took this possibility very seriously, thus pondering the possibility of radical deception.[6] In addition, they were familiar with Christian demonology, according to which 'fallen angels' can use their supranatural power and intervene in natural cognitive processes in order to deceive human beings. It would therefore be erroneous to assume that the Christian context somehow blocked all attempts to formulate sceptical hypotheses.

Third, the Aristotelian tradition was not as dismissive with regard to sceptical arguments as it might seem at first sight because interpreters did not uncritically repeat Aristotle's epistemological claims.[7] A number of late-medieval Aristotelians did not begin their commentaries on the *Posterior Analytics* with the question of what knowledge is, but with the more fundamental question of why we are entitled to attribute knowledge both to ourselves and to other human beings. For instance, John Buridan opened his extensive commentary with the question whether knowledge of a demonstration is possible. This led him to the more fundamental question whether human knowledge is possible at all.[8] Only after discussing this question and evaluating a long list of sceptical arguments, ranging from cases of sensory illusion to dreams and divine deception, did he tackle the classical Aristotelian problem of explaining the structure of demonstrative knowledge. This procedure clearly shows that he was not only interested in the questions of what knowledge is and how it can be acquired, but also in the genuinely sceptical problem whether or not we are justified in making knowledge claims.

Given these replies to the traditional interpretation, it would be misleading to claim that medieval philosophers simply ignored sceptical problems or that they dismissed challenges to knowledge claims as irrelevant. They clearly saw that sceptical arguments need to be taken seriously and paid close attention to their consequences. Yet, they also realised that these arguments are to be discussed in a metaphysical context, and they attempted to dissolve sceptical arguments by showing that they are in conflict with a number of basic metaphysical principles. I intend to elucidate this close connection between epistemological and metaphysical issues by presenting two case studies, namely Thomas Aquinas's analysis of the demon hypothesis and John Buridan's reaction to the argument appealing to divine omnipotence. I hope that an examination of these two cases will make clear that one cannot understand how and why radical doubts were rejected or neutralised by medieval authors unless one pays attention to their explicit and implicit assumptions about the nature of knowledge claims and the methods for evaluating them.

2. THOMAS AQUINAS

Like every Christian author, Thomas Aquinas assumes that there are not only good angels who protect and support human beings, but also bad ones who attempt to hurt them.[9] He ascribes supernatural powers to these demons, arguing that the use of their powers enables them to have access to human thoughts. In fact, Aquinas contends that they can grasp these thoughts in two ways: either by directly seeing them in each human intellect, or by apprehending external signs that indicate the presence of internal thoughts.[10] A demon can therefore read, as it were, all the thoughts in my intellect right now, or he can listen to my words, as other human beings are doing, and understand that these spoken sounds express certain thoughts. But what exactly does a demon read? In Aquinas's view, he grasps so-called 'intelligible species', which are produced on the basis of phantasms and present the essence of material things to the intellect.[11]

Let me explain this scholastic jargon by means of an example. Suppose that I am standing in a garden and admiring a tree covered with fresh snow. Being in this situation, I receive a number of visual and other sensory impressions that enable me to form a sensory image, which presents the tree with a certain shape, size and colour. This image, the so-called 'phantasm', is produced in the inner senses and changes as soon as I get new sensory information. On this basis my intellect is able to abstract a special cognitive entity, the 'intelligible species', which presents the essence of a tree—not just the essence of the particular tree in front of me, but of every tree. Thanks to this species, the essence comes to exist in my intellect and can be inspected by an angel that scrutinises my intellect.

This inspection, taken as such, does not have sceptical implications. As long as the demon merely watches the way I am thinking without intervening, I do not need to worry about the reliability of my cognitive process. The fact, however, that Aquinas takes an inspection to be possible is far from being trivial. It shows that he subscribes to what is nowadays called 'the transparency thesis'. The human intellect is conceived of as some kind of glassy thing in which inner objects can be perceived—not only by the thinking person who is using that thing, but also by an external observer who can look at it and detect various objects, namely, the essences of external things. But Aquinas does not confine himself to the transparency thesis. He adds what may be called 'the manipulation thesis', for he unmistakably holds that a demon can intervene in the cognitive process and make a person apprehend things that do not actually exist. Thus, a demon may act upon me right now and make me believe that a tree covered with snow is standing in front of me. How can he do that? In Aquinas's view, a demon is able to manipulate the material basis of a thought, that is, he can rearrange the sensory impressions I have stored in my brain (according to his physiology, these are 'spirits and humours'), thereby creating a phantasm that does not correspond to anything real in the material world.[12] Since the phantasm always provides the basis for intellectual activity, an erroneous phantasm will inevitably give rise to an erroneous thought.

This is a genuine sceptical hypothesis. How does Aquinas deal with it? First of all, one should note that he is not claiming that a demon directly acts upon the intellect. He does not ponder the possibility that Lucifer or some other bad angel can tamper with my intellect and implant an intelligible species that presents the essence of something that is not actually the case. Why not? The problem is not, as one may suspect, that the intellect as something immaterial is immune to external manipulation. An angel is an immaterial being that can very well stand in a causal relation to another immaterial being. The problem is more complex. If a demon were manipulating the human intellect, it would act against a principle of perfection that regulates every intellectual activity. Aquinas describes this principle as follows:

> One should note that the intellectual activity of a human being is brought to
> perfection in accordance with two things: the intelligible light and the intelligible
> species. This happens in such a way that the apprehension of things occurs
> according to the species. But the judgement about apprehended things is brought
> to perfection in accordance with the intelligible light. This natural intelligible light
> is intrinsic to the human soul . . .[13]

Obviously, the problem is not that a demon would lack the power to bring about
a species in the intellect, say a species that presents the essence of a tree. The real
problem is rather that this action alone would not cause a judgement about a tree.
The so-called natural light would prevent such a judgement. (To use a computer
analogy, one could say that it would be like receiving a computer virus. The consequences of this action would be blocked by the antivirus firewall, and no damage
would be done.) But why, one may ask, should we assume that there is a natural
light that brings the intellect to perfection and therefore neutralises demonic actions? Why could it not be the other way round, namely, that the demon somehow neutralises the natural light? (After all, there could be a new virus that passes
the firewall and produces all kinds of strange transactions.) It is in his answer to
questions on this line that Aquinas makes clear how strongly he is committed to
a metaphysical principle. He claims:

> In corporeal things, the higher power supports and strengthens the lower one. In
> the same way, the intellectual light of a human being can be strengthened by the
> angelic light so that it makes better judgements. This is what a good angel intends
> to do, but not a bad one. Therefore, good angels, but not demons, can set a soul in
> motion so that it has an understanding.[14]

It is clear that Aquinas appeals to a certain hierarchy of beings, which is given in
nature and cannot be violated, not even by demons. According to this hierarchy, a
higher being like an angel can help a lower being like a human being in its natural
actions. In particular, it can support humans in their natural striving for cognition.
But it cannot annihilate this striving or act against it by radically deceiving the
intellect and causing in him false judgements. That is why only good angels, but not
bad ones, can have an impact on the intellect and set it in motion. And even good
angels cannot intervene unless there is some sensory material; they cannot act out
of nothing.

Two aspects in this argument deserve attention. First, it is noteworthy that
Aquinas does not adduce an epistemological argument in order to block the sceptical hypothesis. He is not saying, for instance, that a demon could bring about an
intelligible species but that this species would be qualitatively different from a natu
rally produced one so that the intellect could always distinguish them. Instead,
Aquinas appeals to a genuinely metaphysical argument, claiming that there is a
hierarchy of beings and that higher beings must support lower ones. This is, of
course, a disputable argument. Why should there be a hierarchy? And why should
it be impossible for higher beings to deceive lower ones? The answer to these questions is to be sought in Aquinas's metaphysics of creation, which relies on the crucial
thesis that one cannot understand the world of created things unless one sees them

as being part of an all-embracing order in which each thing has a certain function that cannot arbitrarily be destroyed by other things.[15] Without such an order, the world would be completely unintelligible. Admitting radical demonic deception would amount to giving up the intelligibility of a well-ordered world.

There is yet another aspect in Aquinas's argument that deserves attention. Claiming that the intellect is perfected by the so-called 'intelligible light', he takes for granted that there is a state of perfection for the human intellect, as there is one for every natural thing. More precisely, he subscribes to a principle of natural tele-ology according to which the intellect naturally develops its cognitive capacity and thus produces an increasing number of true judgements. Any restriction or imped-iment on this natural development is corrected by the 'intelligible light'.

Taking into account these two points, one can easily see that Aquinas's use of the demon hypothesis is strikingly different from the later Cartesian use. While he uses a number of metaphysical principles, Descartes does not appeal to such principles, neither to a hierarchy principle nor to natural teleology. In the First Meditation, *everything* is cast into doubt, including the seemingly harmless theses that our intel-lect is part of an overall order and that it is meant to be used in a correct way so that it produces true judgements. Given an all-embracing metaphysics of creation that assigns a natural perfection to human intellects, this is not an option for Aquinas. He introduces the demon hypothesis as a radical challenge to our knowledge claims but then neutralises it by means of metaphysical principles, which, in turn, are not questioned.

However, even if demons are not able to manipulate the intellect, they can inter-vene on the level of the inner senses. As we have seen, they can rearrange spirits and humours in the brain, thereby producing new phantasms. We have also seen that phantasms are the indispensable basis for intellectual activity. This line of reasoning can easily lead to a radical sceptical argument: If it is possible that *every* phantasm is supernaturally produced and deceptive, *every* thought can be deceptive as well. Since we lack a neutral criterion that would enable us to distinguish deceptive phan-tasms from nondeceptive ones, we can never tell whether our thoughts are based on erroneous phantasms or not. Consequently, all of our thoughts are exposed to doubt.

A closer look at Aquinas's texts reveals, however, that he does not draw this conclusion. Why not? Does he simply overlook the sceptical potential in his own remark about the possible manipulation of phantasms? Let me explain why I do not think that this is the case by returning to the tree example. Suppose that a demon is tampering with my brain and producing a phantasm that presents a tree that, sur-prisingly, has wings and is flying through the air. The presence of this phantasm triggers my intellect and makes me have the strange and obviously false belief that there is a flying tree. However, having a thought amounts to grasping the essence of a thing. In Aquinas's view, the object of the intellect is not the individual material thing, but its essence.[16] Grasping the essence amounts to understanding the consti-tutive features of a thing. Of course, one might not understand in detail what these features are, but one has at least a dim understanding. Thus, when I am grasping the essence of a tree, I roughly understand that a tree is a plant, that it has a trunk and that it is blooming in spring, even though I may not understand all of its bio-chemical features. As dim and vague as my grasp of the essence may be, I realise that a tree cannot have wings. Consequently, I understand that the essence of a tree excludes the property of being a flying thing. So, I may have a deceptive phantasm that makes me spontaneously have the thought of a flying tree, but my grasp of the essence makes me immediately realise that this is the thought of something that is not the case and cannot even be the case. The crucial point is that it is not some special phenomenal quality of this thought that makes me dismiss it as a false one. The reason why I am not deceived is that I realise that the thought includes incompatible features.

Now one might object that this line of reasoning relies on the strong assumption that I am able to understand what belongs to the essence of a tree and what is contrary to this very essence. But why should that be so? Could it not be that I am utterly incapable of having the slightest idea of what is constitutive of a tree? Could it, therefore, not be that I have no clue whether or not a tree can have wings? If a demon were making me have the phantasm of a flying tree, I would immediately think that there is a flying tree in this room, without realising that this is impossible. Why should that be ruled out?

Here, Aquinas once more makes use of a metaphysical principle. He assumes that the human intellect is built in such a way that it cannot but correctly grasp the essence of a thing. In fact, he claims:

> The intellect's proper object is the quiddity of a thing. So the intellect makes no mistakes, strictly speaking, with respect to the quiddity of a thing. But the intellect can be mistaken with respect to what surrounds the thing's essence or quiddity, namely when it orders one thing to another, either through composition or division or else through a process of reasoning.[17]

Applied to the tree example, this means that I cannot be mistaken when I think that a tree is a plant, that it has a trunk and that it can grow and die. These features belong, as it were, to its metaphysical make-up and are constitutive of its essence. But I can be mistaken when I think that a particular tree has one thousand leaves or that it has a height of eight meters. When I proceed in this way 'through composition or division', I predicate accidental features of a tree—features that do not belong to its essence. The crucial point is, of course, that Aquinas clearly distinguishes thoughts about accidental features from thoughts about the essence of a thing, assuming that the latter ones are never mistaken. This enables him to counter the objection that one may never know whether or not there can be a flying tree. Since we correctly grasp the essence of a tree, we immediately realise that this essence excludes the property of having wings.

I hope this makes clear what kind of argumentative strategy Aquinas chooses when dealing with the demon hypothesis. He first accepts it as a possible scenario but then rules it out by appealing to an essentialist principle according to which the cognitive structure of the human intellect and the structure of cognizable objects match perfectly. The intellect is, as it were, by nature designed to grasp the essence of a thing.[18] Does this mean that error and deception are completely ruled out? Not at all. At least two types of error are still possible. First, I may make a false existential judgement due to demonic intervention. For instance, Lucifer may cause in me a phantasm of a tree when no tree is present. Then, I will come up with the false judgement that there is right now a tree in front of me. This type of judgement does not violate the essentialist principle because even when my judgement about the existence is wrong, my grasping of the essence is correct. Second, the demon may also alter my phantasm and add some features to it so that I think, for instance, that the tree has red flowers although it, in fact, has blue ones. This, once more, would not violate the essentialist principle because false judgements about accidental features are always possible. As we have seen, Aquinas concedes that there may be a so-called false 'composition or division', that is, a judgement in which an accidental property is mistakenly attributed to a thing exhibiting a certain essence. But this judgement can be compared to other ones and eventually be corrected. I can, for instance, compare my actual judgement about the tree to judgements I have made yesterday and last week, and I can evaluate whether or not I have collected a consistent bundle of judgements. Should it turn out that one of them does not fit into this bundle, it can be eliminated. That is why a false judgement caused by demonic intervention is not more threatening than a judgement that is based on a sensory deception. Such a deception (for instance, when I see a stick partly submerged in water and judge that it is broken) only occurs under special circumstances and can be corrected when judgements made under other circumstances are taken into account.[19] Likewise, demonic deception only occurs under special circumstances and can be corrected when assessed against the background of judgements made under other circumstances.

Of course, this line of reasoning is far from being innocent. It may give rise to worries about the famous criterion problem. How can we distinguish normal circumstances from exceptional ones? What criterion can we use in order to tell which judgements are correct and which ones should be discarded? Aquinas never addresses these problems, presumably because he subscribes to some form of reliabilism, as Eleonore Stump convincingly argued.[20] That is, he takes it for granted that the cognitive apparatus, including both senses and intellect, is built in such a way that it reliably produces correct cognitions when working under normal circumstances. Given this reliability, we do not need to evaluate each and every judgement. Only judgements that do not fit into the coherent net of our judgements ought to be evaluated and eventually excluded.

It might help to compare Aquinas's position to contemporary reliabilism in order to understand its specific point. Nowadays, there are many forms of reliabilism, but all of them assume that beliefs and other kinds of cognitive states are like well-constructed instruments that are designed to produce the right kind of result. David Armstrong compared beliefs to a thermometer that reliably indicates the temperature in a room.[21] Of course, a thermometer may make mistakes, but only if it is broken. A well-functioning thermometer is designed to indicate the temperature as it really is. Likewise, beliefs are somehow designed to indicate what is really the case. Only 'broken beliefs', that is, beliefs occurring in a dysfunctional mind, are false and lead us astray. And these beliefs only make sense if they are understood against the background of a large number of true beliefs. They are, as it were, the exception to the rule. It is precisely this idea that can also be found in Aquinas when he emphasises that our judgements are in principle correct because they are formed by an intellect that is designed to function correctly. We have an intellect in the image of God, as Aquinas repeatedly says,[22] and therefore all the cognitive means we need to cognise things as they really are. Of course, our intellect is not as infinite and perfect as the divine one. That is why we incidentally make mistakes. But given that our intellect is built in the image of God, mistakes can only be exceptional cases. It would be absurd to assume that all of them are wrong.

Here again, it is an underlying metaphysical assumption that enables Aquinas to deal with cases of local deception. Given that our cognitive apparatus has a natural function that it fulfils correctly under normal circumstances, errors and deceptions are exceptional cases that can be detected and corrected. That is why Aquinas never worries about demonic intervention, even though he acknowledges that this kind of manipulation is possible. The important point is that this antisceptical stance is not due to an ignorance or a dismissal of sceptical arguments. Instead, it is based on a number of metaphysical principles that serve as an overall antisceptical framework. This framework allows for *local* doubts about the correctness of this or that judgement, but not for a *global* doubt.

3. John Buridan

Aquinas is well aware of the fact that God, unlike an angel, can manipulate every cognitive process. In principle, God could arbitrarily implant an intelligible species in my intellect and make me have a false belief. Should he do so, he would clearly deceive me, which is bad, and a bad action is always a deficient action. But God is a perfect being, as Aquinas points out, and therefore always brings about perfect actions that are in no way deficient.[23] That is why Aquinas never considers the possibility that God might deceive human beings.

This argument, later repeated by Descartes in the *Meditations*,[24] is not as evident as it may look at first sight. Why should deceiving necessarily be something bad? Perhaps God implants false thoughts in human beings in order to support and protect them, like a good father who lies to his children in order to protect them from brutal truths. In the fourteenth century, Robert Holkot already made this objection, pointing out that deceiving is only a bad action when it is done with a bad intention. But who knows—perhaps God is having the best intentions when implanting false thoughts in our intellect.[25] This kind of reasoning made a number of fourteenth-century philosophers reconsider the possibility that God may use his 'absolute power' and directly intervene in cognitive processes. John Buridan was familiar with this hypothesis and reported it as follows:

> . . . the intellect could be deceived by a supernatural cause with respect to evident
> propositions, because God could make a fire without heat, and he could create as
> well as maintain in your sense a sensory species without there being an object.
> Based on this evidence, you would judge as if an object were present. And so you
> would make a false judgement.[26]

How does Buridan react to this hypothesis? Unlike Aquinas, he does not dismiss it
by claiming that this would contradict God's perfection; he takes it to be a real possibility. Moreover, he does not try to refute it by appealing to a criterion that would
allow us to distinguish the supernaturally produced species from the naturally produced one. He concedes that God could cause a cognitive act that is qualitatively
indistinguishable from a naturally produced one. Nevertheless, he does not draw
the conclusion that we can never trust our acts and that we therefore need to give up
all our knowledge claims. He rather states that we still have so-called 'natural
evidence' that is not threatened by a possible divine intervention:

> This natural evidence is still aptly called natural, because on the basis of this
> evidence a human being cannot be deceived in the common course of nature,
> even though one may be deceived by a supernatural cause. This evidence is
> sufficient for natural knowledge.[27]

Obviously, Buridan does not claim that natural evidence, which is the kind of evidence provided by the senses, is insufficient and that it needs to be supplemented by
another form of evidence. He, rather, contends that this evidence is sufficient for a
certain domain of knowledge, namely, natural knowledge, and that it would be
erroneous to look for another evidence that is more robust and that enables us to
eliminate cases of divine deception. In the context of daily life and scientific investigations, natural evidence is all the evidence we need and can strive for. Let me
explain this point with a modern example.

Suppose that a friend is asking you how old you are. You indicate your age and
seem to have fully answered the question. But then your friend is replying: 'Are you
sure? Could it not be that you were misinformed about the date of your birth?' So
you contact your parents and other people who were present at your birth, get a
confirmation about the date and tell your friend that you are certain. But your friend
is still not satisfied. 'Could it not be that your parents lied to you or that they simply
mixed up the dates?' So you go to the hospital you were born at and ask for official
documents. But your friend is still not satisfied and asks: 'Could it not be that the
authorities in the hospital mixed up the documents?' So you go to the town hall and
ask for a copy of the birth certificate that confirms the hospital documents. 'But
could it not be', your friend then says, 'that the authorities in the hospital and in the
town hall want to deceive you? Could it not be that they all lie to you?' At this point
you may lose your temper and reply that this crazy hypothesis simply does not
make sense. A friend who suggests that the entire world conspires to deceive you
does not need an argument, but psychological help. Trying to stay calm and friendly,
you respond: 'Theoretically, it may be possible that everybody is lying to me. However, in this situation it does not make sense to take this possibility seriously. Having

checked all the documents, I have all the natural evidence I need to be sure about my date of birth. This kind of evidence suffices as a justification for my everyday belief. It does not need to be supplemented or strengthened by another kind of evidence that rules out every deception. It would be inappropriate to raise the standard of justification up to a point where I need to have a knock-down argument against every possible objection'.

It is on this line that we can understand Buridan's appeal to natural evidence. He does not make the dogmatic claim that natural evidence guarantees infallibility and that it rules out any possible deception. Nor does he simply deny that, theoretically speaking, there could be divine manipulation. But he chooses what might be called a contextualist strategy: In the context of everyday life and natural science, it is perfectly legitimate to make knowledge claims that are based on sensory information. The standards of justification should not be raised to a point where just any absurd hypothesis must be refuted. That is why natural evidence is perfectly sufficient for natural knowledge. It is not the person having and using natural evidence who needs to present a further justification, but the objector who presents a bizarre and artificially constructed hypothesis. He should be urged to explain why his hypothesis is relevant in an everyday situation and why we must take it seriously.[28]

If we understand Buridan's reply on this line, we can see that he rejects an assumption implicitly made by his contemporaries who refer to God's possible intervention in order to weaken or reject everyday knowledge claims. They assume that one should start with the most bizarre scenario and look for the most general justification, thereby ignoring the fact that justification is always required in a certain context and that it should be relevant in that context. In the situation of everyday life and of scientific investigations, nothing but natural evidence is relevant and nothing else is to be sought.

This contextualist strategy gives rise to at least two objections. First, one may ask if natural evidence is, in fact, sufficient for everyday life. Given that this kind of evidence is based on sensory experience, there can be many illusions and deceptions due to the imperfection of our senses, even without there being divine intervention. Why is Buridan so confident that sceptical worries disappear in the light of natural evidence? Second, one may point out that it hardly helps to refer to the context of everyday life because this context can always be changed. One can always move to the context of theoretical discussions, in which the possibility of divine intervention ought to be taken seriously. So how can Buridan be content with natural evidence that is adduced in a context that can always be challenged, namely, when one leaves the situation of everyday discussions and engages in philosophical debates?

Let me look at Buridan's reply to these objections. As to the first, he concedes that our senses are fallible and that they sometimes give rise to false judgements; in his *Commentary on the Posterior Analytics* he mentions fourteen cases of possible deception.[29] But the fact that sensory information can *sometimes* be misleading should not give rise to the worry that it might *always* be deceptive. For this type of information causes an entire net of judgements that can be compared and tested. If it turns out that a particular judgement does not fit into this net because it has a special cause, it can be corrected. Buridan illustrates this with the famous example of a person travelling on a ship who sees the trees on the shore and falsely thinks that they are moving.[30] This error occurs because this person is moving and therefore receives visual inputs that go up and down on his eyes. Consequently, he forms images of moving trees, which give rise to the judgement that the trees are moving. As soon as this person realises that it is this special situation that makes him have images of moving trees, he can compare the judgement made in this situation with judgements made in other situations, namely, when he was standing on the shore. He then notices that there is a certain reason for his judgement made on the ship and that it does not cohere with all the other judgements about the very same trees. The decisive point is, of course, that the person's intellect can detect the reason for his erroneous judgement and correct it. Admittedly, it may not be able to do this in every situation, and it may take some time to compare and evaluate different types of information, say, about the location of the trees as well as of oneself. But in principle the intellect is able to correct an error by locating a single judgement in a net of judgements and by testing the coherence of the entire net. In any case, there can only be particular judgements that turn out to be false, but it cannot be the case that the entire net of judgements is mistaken.

Why not? What makes Buridan so confident that our senses are in principle reliable and that they cause judgements that, for the most part, are true even if some of them may turn out to be false? Buridan is not at a loss for an answer. Responding to the sceptic who suggests that the senses are never to be trusted, he firmly holds:

> For nature, taken as such, always acts in a correct and perfect way. But sometimes, due to an impediment, a deficiency occurs in nature or in the way it is operating.[31]

Buridan obviously assumes that there can only be local error because only a local impediment can prevent nature from bringing about a perfect action, that is, a true judgement. As soon as the impediment is removed (say, one leaves the ship and looks at the trees while standing on a firm ground), the error can be corrected. What is striking here is that Buridan does not doubt that the senses as part of nature are in principle designed to provide correct information. Consequently, he is convinced that the senses yield natural evidence that is sufficient for natural knowledge. Justification is not required for sensory information as a whole, but only for this or that particular sensory judgement made in a special situation.

Lurking in the background of this reasoning is the teleological assumption that all the capacities in nature have a natural goal, namely, to be actualised correctly. If they are triggered in the right way, they achieve their goal. Senses and intellect as natural capacities are designed to produce true judgements unless there are external obstacles that prevent them from actualising their potential. In Buridan's view, the reliability of our cognitive processes is nothing more than an example for the reliability that is somehow built into all natural processes. He explicitly holds that the intellect has a 'natural inclination' to form true judgements:

> The intellect, which by its natural inclination is ordered toward the true, gives its
> assent to a universal principle on the basis of experiences.[32]

Here, again, we see that the antisceptical strategy relies upon a metaphysical principle: The application of a teleological principle leads Buridan to the conclusion that global error is excluded and that natural evidence can therefore be trusted.

What about the second objection I have mentioned? Could a sceptic not respond that appealing to natural evidence may suffice in everyday life but that it is questionable in philosophical debates where stronger justification is needed? Buridan grants that one could leave the context of everyday life and introduce the hypothesis of divine manipulation. But as far as he is concerned, this hypothesis is nothing but the product of theological speculation and has no relevance whatsoever for the assessment of our knowledge. At one point he disparagingly refers to 'these very bad people who want to destroy the natural and the moral sciences' and talk about a deceiving God.[33] These people are not only bad because they ascribe to God a malicious intention, but also because they transfer the standard of justification that may be appropriate for the rather artificial context of theological speculation to the context of everyday life and natural science. Even if it is conceivable that God could intervene and deceive us in a special situation, the natural capacities still preserve their function of producing judgements that are in principle true. The natural order is not annihilated by a punctual intervention. Therefore, there may only be a *local* doubt about the correctness of this or that judgement, a doubt that can be refuted when the entire net of judgements is evaluated. But there cannot be a *global* doubt that puts all our judgements on trial. This kind of doubt would simply ignore our 'natural inclination' towards cognitive perfection.

4. METAPHYSICS AND MEDIEVAL SCEPTICISM

This brings me back to my initial remarks about the reasons why medieval philosophers did not discuss radical scepticism. The main reason was not that ancient sceptical sources were not available to them. Thanks to Cicero's *Academica* and Augustine's *Contra Academicos*, they were familiar with a number of sceptical strategies, including arguments about sensory illusion, dreams and supernatural deception. Nor was the main reason that Christian dogmas ruled out radical scepticism. On the contrary, a number of genuinely Christian assumptions—among them the assumption that demons and the omnipotent God can intervene in cognitive processes—stimulated sceptical thoughts and provided the material for sceptical hypotheses. Finally, the main reason was not that Aquinas, Buridan and many other medieval philosophers were so much in the grip of Aristotelianism that they were only interested in the question of how knowledge is acquired without raising the basic question if knowledge is possible at all. The main reason is, rather, to be sought in the metaphysical principles that formed the framework for their epistemological debates. If one operates within Aquinas's principles, namely, that there is a hierarchy of beings, that higher beings have the function of supporting lower ones and that human beings occupy a special place in this hierarchy, a place that guarantees reliable capacities, radical scepticism cannot be an issue. And if one uses Buridan's principles, claiming that there is natural teleology and that our senses are designed to provide us with natural evidence, global doubts cannot arise either. The metaphysical system sets limits to sceptical worries.

But why then, one may ask, did the metaphysical system not become the object of sceptical attacks? Why did medieval philosophers not radically question the principle of natural teleology or the idea that there is a hierarchically ordered world? The obvious answer would be that philosophers committed to Aristotelianism could not raise radical doubts because it is precisely the principle of teleology and the idea of a cosmological structure that are at the bottom of Aristotelian metaphysics. Yet this answer would be too simple because the commitment to Aristotelianism was itself motivated by at least two fundamental reasons. The first one appealed to the principle of intelligibility, which I already mentioned when quickly explaining Aquinas's dismissal of radical demonic deception. If one were conceding that there is no order in the world and that supernatural beings can suspend or destroy all natural cognitive mechanisms, one would admit that there are no metaphysical structures that govern the relationship between different types of beings in the world—anything could be. But if this were the case, we could never make sense of the world, that is, we could never explain certain facts and events by referring to certain structures. For instance, we could not say that someone knows what a tree is because he or she has seen trees and learned about their typical features. We could never refer to the use of natural capacities but would be condemned to describe a mere fact by saying: 'There is no explanation for this knowledge. Perhaps this person knows what a tree is because she has been in contact with trees, perhaps because a demon has intervened, perhaps because of something else. We cannot say why'. It is precisely in order to avoid this kind of collapse of all explanations that medieval philosophers were committed to the principle of intelligibility. Only a world in which certain structures regulate the behaviour and development of various things is an intelligible world. And only in such a world can we provide explanations for facts, including epistemic facts.

There is still another reason for the appeal to basic Aristotelian principles. As I repeatedly pointed out, both Aquinas and Buridan take it to be of crucial importance that we have natural cognitive capacities that are correctly actualised under normal circumstances. Now these capacities are important not only for the acquisition of knowledge. They are also required for the evaluation of knowledge and for the reflection on the possibility of knowledge. We could not engage in philosophical debates about the range and possibility of knowledge if we were not equipped with cognitive capacities that enable us to develop sceptical and antisceptical arguments. And we would not be able to put forward coherent and sound arguments if we did not have reliable capacities that make it possible to develop a well-ordered series of premises and conclusions. Should we have no such capacities, we could always ask:

'But why should I trust my own way of arguing for or against the possibility of knowledge? If I lack reliable cognitive capacities, nothing can be taken for granted, not even my reflection upon sceptical arguments'. It is precisely to refute this kind of self-destruction of philosophical debates that medieval philosophers subscribed to the metaphysical principle that human beings are endowed with more or less reliable cognitive capacities. Every rational debate presupposes the use of these capacities.

It is important to pay attention to these metaphysical principles that formed, as it were, the framework for sceptical debates, not only when looking at epistemological discussions in the later Middle Ages, but also when studying the evolution of sceptical debates from the thirteenth to the seventeenth century. What made radical scepticism in the early-modern period possible was not so much the invention of new arguments. All the relevant arguments, ranging from sensory illusions to dreams, hallucinations and demonic as well as divine deception, were already present in the medieval period. What made a radicalisation possible was the use of these arguments in a new theoretical setting. This is most obvious in Descartes, who introduced the famous radical doubt by bracketing seemingly uncontroversial metaphysical principles concerning the structure of a well-ordered world and the general reliability of our cognitive capacities. What is so radical in the First Meditation is not the appeal to an omnipotent demon but the fact that Descartes discusses this hypothesis without neutralising it by invoking the principle that a demon cannot destroy the natural capacities of subordinated beings.

This leads me to a final methodological remark concerning the study of the history of scepticism. When examining the rise of radical sceptical arguments, we should not simply concentrate on isolated arguments or on texts that transmitted these arguments from Antiquity to the early-modern period. Nor should we look for so-called medieval precursors of Cartesian arguments. It is of crucial importance to evaluate the metaphysical framework in which these arguments were situated—a framework that dramatically changed in the early-modern period due to the decline of Aristotelianism. As soon as Descartes and other seventeenth-century authors no longer accepted the claims that there are natural substances in the world, endowed with capacities that are meant to be correctly actualised, the entire picture of the natural world changed—not only the picture of the objects to be investigated, but also the picture of the investigating human subjects. It was no longer possible to assume that human beings are endowed with natural cognitive capacities and that they can correctly actualise them under normal circumstances, thus acquiring knowledge. The first questions to ask were why we are entitled to ascribe reliable cognitive capacities to human subjects and why we are justified in assuming that the use of these capacities yields knowledge. This means, of course, that philosophical enquiries were inevitably driven by a sceptical motivation—a motivation alien to medieval authors inspired by epistemological optimism. It is, therefore, not surprising that Mersenne, Gassendi, Descartes and many other modern anti-Aristotelians did not only ask what the appropriate objects of scientific investigation are and how these objects ought to be studied. They also (and even primarily) raised the sceptical question whether such an investigation is possible at all. The rejection of metaphysical principles that had been at the basis of Aristotelian optimism inevitably led them to formulate this question. I emphasise this point because it is sometimes argued that radical scepticism is a natural attitude that every philosopher adopts once he or she reflects upon the possibility and limits of knowledge, no matter what his or her metaphysical commitments are. When we look at the way medieval Aristotelians and early-modern anti-Aristotelians dealt with sceptical hypotheses, we see that such an attitude is far from being metaphysically neutral. It was precisely their metaphysical position that motivated them to accept or to question the thesis that knowledge is possible.

NOTES

1. Popkin (2003, 35) claims that 'prior to the publication of Sextus Empiricus, there does not seem to be very much serious philosophical consideration of scepticism'.
2. Pasnau (2003, 214) neatly summarises the main thesis of this research tradition: 'Skepticism simply ceased to be a prominent topic of discussion until the end of the Middle Ages. Instead, attention was focused on how knowledge is acquired. Here the issue was not how to define knowledge—the question that Plato originally posed and that dominated later twentieth-century epistemology—but how to understand the cognitive operations that generate it.'
3. See Wittwer (2002). However, there is no sign of a wide reception in the later Middle Ages. It would therefore be misleading to speak about a Pyrrhonian tradition in the Middle Ages. Nevertheless, the simple fact that the text was translated and that manuscripts have been transmitted in three important intellectual centres (Paris, Venice, Madrid) testifies to the interest in sceptical sources.
4. See Schmitt (1972, 18–42). In the second half of the thirteenth century, Henry of Ghent made explicit use of both Cicero's and Augustine's texts. For an analysis of this background, see Perler (2006, 33–85).
5. On the origin and development of this theory of twofold power, see Courtenay (1985, 1990).
6. On debates in the Scotist tradition, see Randi (1987). This tradition shaped theological as well as philosophical debates far beyond the medieval period, as Funkenstein (1986, 117–201) convincingly showed.
7. Even when repeating his claims, they did not simply present antisceptical arguments but critically discussed and evaluated them. On the variety of Aristotelian arguments that paved the way for sceptical debates, see Barnes (1987).
8. See *Quaestiones in Analytica Posteriora* (= *In Anal. Post.,* q. 2): 'Utrum possibile sit nos aliquid scire'.
9. On the classification of angels and the role bad ones, the demons, play in Aquinas's metaphysics of creation, see *Summa theologiae* (= *STh*) I, q. 63–64. For a comprehensive analysis of Aquinas's angelology, see Suarez-Nani (2002). On the philosophical impact of angelology, see Irribaren and Lenz (2008).
10. See *Quaestiones disputatae de malo* (= *De malo*, q. 16, art. 8, corp., Opera omnia XXIII, 320–1); *STh* (I, q. 57, art. 4, corp).

11. Aquinas presents the core idea of this cognitive theory in *STh* (I, q. 84–86). For a detailed exposition, see Pasnau (2002, 267–329), and Perler (2002, 61–89).

12. See *De malo* (q. 16, art. 11, corp., Opera omnia XXIII, 330).

13. *De malo* (q. 16, art. 12, corp., Opera omnia XXIII, 333): 'Est autem considerandum quod intellectualis hominis operatio secundum duo perficitur, scilicet secundum lumen intelligibile et secundum species intelligibiles, ita tamen quod secundum species fit apprehensio rerum, secundum lumen intelligibile perficitur iudicium de apprehensis. Inest autem animae humanae naturale lumen intelligibile . . .'

14. *De malo* (q. 16, art. 12, corp., Opera omnia XXIII, 333): '. . . et ideo, sicut in rebus corporalibus superior uirtus adiuuat et confortat inferiorem uirtutem, ita per lumen angelicum confortari potest lumen intellectus humani ad perfectius iudicandum. Quod angelus bonus intendit, non autem angelus malus; unde hoc modo angeli boni mouent animam ad intelligendum, non autem demones.'

15. That Aquinas attributes a key role to this thesis becomes clear in the fifth of the so-called 'Five Ways' he adduces in order to demonstrate God's existence. In *STh* (I, q. 2, art. 3, corp.), he argues that all natural things are ordered towards an end ('ordinantur ad finem') and that, consequently, there must be a being that establishes this order. It is the premise of this argument that expresses a commitment to a metaphysical principle: Things do not arbitrarily or randomly exhibit certain properties, nor do they randomly actualise certain capacities and thereby fulfil certain functions. What properties and capacities they have and how they can use them is fixed by a certain order—an order that is given in nature and that cannot be changed.

16. He emphasises this point in *STh* (I, q. 86, art. 1).

17. *STh* I (q. 85, art. 6, corp.): 'Objectum autem proprium intellectus est quidditas rei. Unde circa quidditatem rei, per se loquendo, intellectus non fallitur. Sed circa ea quae circumstant rei essentiam vel quuidditatem, intellectus potest falli, dum unum ordinat ad aliud, vel componendo vel dividendo vel etiam ratiocinando.'

18. This does not amount to the claim that the intellect immediately grasps the entire essence when it comes in contact with an object. There can be (and, in fact, often is) a transition from a first stage of partial and inadequate understanding of an essence to later stages of more complete and more adequate understanding. The crucial point is not that there is right from the start a full understanding, but that the intellect is, as it were, from the start on the right track: Even the most incomplete grasping includes some aspects of the essence. On this epistemological optimism that is at the bottom of Aquinas's theory of intellect, see Kretzmann (1991) and Perler (2002, 65–70).

19. Not only external circumstances, but also internal ones (e.g., dysfunctional sense organs), are to be taken into account, as Aquinas explains in *STh* (I, q. 17, art. 2, corp.). But he hastens to add that dysfunctions are exceptional cases. In principle, the organs function correctly and therefore provide correct sensory information—what happens in *some* cases should not be conflated with what happens in *most* cases.

20. See Stump (2003, 217–43).

21. See Armstrong (1973, 166–75).

22. See *STh* (I, q. 93, art. 2, 4 and 6).

23. See *STh* (I, q. 25, art. 3, ad 2); *Summa contra Gentiles* (= *ScG*; I, cap. 39, n. 316–23, pp. 48–49).

24. See *Meditationes* I and IV (ed. Adam and Tannery, VII, 21 and 53).

25. See Robert Holkot, *In quatuor libros Sententiarum quaestiones* (lib. III, q. 1, p. CCC). For a detailed analysis of this argument, see Perler (2010).

26. *In Anal. Post.* (I, q. 2, corp.): '... circa tales propositiones euidentes intellectus posset decipi per causam supernaturalem; quia deus posset facere ignem sine caliditate, et posset facere in sensu tuo et conseruare speciem sensitivam sine obiecto, et ita per istam euidentiam tu iudicares ac si obiectum esset praesens, et iudicares falsum'.

27. *In Anal. Post.* (I, q. 2, corp.): 'Tamen illa euidentia naturalis bene dicitur naturalis, quia secundum illam non potest homo decipi stante communi cursu naturae, licet deciper-etur per causam supernaturalem; et haec euidentia sufficit ad naturalem scientiam'.

28. To use Williams's terminology (see Williams 2001, 151), one may say that the person who claims to have knowledge based on natural evidence is in a 'default position'. It is the objector challenging these knowledge claims who is in charge of justifying his sceptical position.

29. See *In Anal. Post.* (I, q. 2). A similar list can be found in *In Metaphysicen Aristotelis Quaestiones* (= *In Met.*; I, q. 2). All the examples Buridan mentions can be traced back to Diogenes Laertios and to other ancient authors who reported sceptical arguments, as Borbély (2005) showed.

30. See *In Anal. Post.* (I, q. 2, ad 3).

31. *In Met.* (II, q. 2, f. 10ra): 'Natura enim quantum est de se semper agit recte et perfecte, sed aliquando per impedimentum accidit peccatum in natura siue eius operatione'.

32. *In Met.* (II, q. 1, f. 9rb): '... intellectus per naturalem inclinationem suam ad verum predispositus per experientias assentit universali principio'. On the role natural inclination plays in Buridan's epistemology, see Zupko (1993, 211–221).

33. See *In Met.* (II, q. 1, f. 9ra).

BIBLIOGRAPHY

Armstrong, David M. 1973. *Belief, Truth and Knowledge.* Cambridge: Cambridge University Press.

Barnes, Jonathan. 1987. 'An Aristotelian way with scepticism'. In *Aristotle Today. Essays on Aristotle's Ideal of Science*, ed. Mohan Matthen, 51–76. Edmonton, Alberta, Canada: Academic Print.

Borbély, Gábor. 2005. 'Sceptical arguments in later medieval philosophy, their sources and their impact upon Descartes'. In *Der Einfluss des Hellenismus auf die Philosophie der frühen Neuzeit*, ed. Gábor Boros, 35–52. Wiesbaden, Germany: Harrassowitz.

Courtenay, William J. 1985. 'The dialectic of omnipotence in the high and late middle ages'. In *Divine Omniscience and Omnipotence in Medieval Philosophy*, ed. Tamar Rudavsky, 243–69. Dordrecht, the Netherlands, Boston and Lancaster, UK: Reidel.

————. 1990. *Capacity and Volition. A History of the Distinction of Absolute and Ordained Power.* Bergamo, Italy: P. Lubrina Editore.

Descartes, René. 1983. *Meditationes de prima philosophia*, ed. Charles Adam and Paul Tannery. Oeuvres VII. Paris: Vrin.

Funkenstein, Amos. 1986. *Theology and the Scientific Imagination from the Middle Ages to the Seventeenth Century.* Princeton, NJ: Princeton University Press.

Irribaren, Isabel and Martin Lenz, eds. 2008. *Angels in Medieval Philosophical Inquiry. Their Function and Significance.* Aldershot, UK: Ashgate.

John Buridan. 1588/(reprint 1964). *In Metaphysicen Aristotelis Quaestiones*. Frankfurt am Main: Minerva.

———. *Quaestiones in Analytica Posteriora*. Undated preliminary edition by Hubert Hubien. http://individual.utoronto.ca/pking/resources/buridan (accessed 1 August 2011).

Kretzmann, Norman. 1991. Infallibility, error, and ignorance. *Canadian Journal of Philosophy*. 17(Suppl.):159–94.

Pasnau, Robert. 2002. *Thomas Aquinas on Human Nature. A Philosophical Study of Summa theologiae Ia 75–89*. Cambridge and New York: Cambridge University Press.

———. 2003. 'Human nature'. In *The Cambridge Companion to Medieval Philosophy*, ed. A. S. McGrade, 208–30. Cambridge and New York: Cambridge University Press.

Perler, Dominik. 2002. *Theorien der Intentionalität im Mittelalter*. Frankfurt am Main: Klostermann.

———. 2006. *Zweifel und Gewissheit. Skeptische Debatten im Mittelalter*. Frankfurt am Main: Klostermann.

———. 2010. 'Does God Deceive Us? Skeptical Hypotheses in Late Medieval Epistemology'. In *Rethinking the History of Skepticism. The Missing Medieval Background*, ed. Henrik Lagerlund, 171–92. Leiden, the Netherlands: Brill.

Popkin, Richard. 2003. *The History of Scepticism. From Savonarola to Bayle*. Oxford and New York: Oxford University Press.

Randi, Eugenio. 1987. *Il sovrano e l'orologiaio. Due immagini di Dio nel dibattito sulla 'potentia absoluta' fra XIII e XIV secolo*. Florence: La Nuova Italia.

Robert Holkot. 1518/(reprint 1967). *In quatuor libros Sententiarum quaestiones*. Frankfurt am Main: Minerva.

Schmitt, Charles. 1972. *Cicero Scepticus. A Study of the Influence of the Academica in the Renaissance*. The Hague, the Netherlands: M. Nijhoff.

Stump, Eleonore. 2003. *Aquinas*. London and New York: Routledge.

Suarez-Nani, Tiziana. 2002. *Les anges et la philosophie. Subjectivité et fonction cosmologique des substances séparées à la fin du XIIIe siècle*. Paris: Vrin.

Thomas Aquinas. 1952. *Summa theologiae*, ed. P. Caramello, Turin and Rome: Marietti.

———. 1961. *Summa contra Gentiles*, ed. C. Pera. Turin and Rome: Marietti.

———. 1982. *Quaestiones disputatae de malo*. Opera omnia XXIII, ed. P.-M. Gils. Rome and Paris: Commissio Leonina & Vrin.

Williams, Michael. 2001. *Problems of Knowledge. A Critical Introduction to Epistemology*. Oxford and New York: Oxford University Press.

Wittwer, Roland. 2002. Zur lateinischen Überlieferung von Sextus Empiricus. *Pyrrhoneioi Hypotyposeis. Rheinisches Museum für Philologie* 145:366–73.

Zupko, Jack. 1993. Buridan and Skepticism. *Journal of the History of Philosophy* 31:191–221.

Moral Psychology, Ethics, Political Philosophy and Aesthetics

CHAPTER 26

FREEDOM OF THE WILL

THOMAS PINK

1. INTRODUCTION

Freedom was a central notion within medieval psychological and ethical theory. It mattered as a metaphysical power, as a right and as a desirable goal or condition. But the fundamental notion was of freedom as a metaphysical power to determine for ourselves how we acted, a power that was seen as primarily enjoyed and exercised within the rational or intellectual mind, on most views at the point of the will, our capacity for choice and decision. Thanks to the dominant model of human action in the Middle Ages, freedom as a metaphysical power was characteristically seen as a freedom specifically of the will.

The will was a faculty for choice or decision that came to us with the intellect, the faculty for knowledge and cognition, and it was at the point of the will that the human capacity for action and so for freedom was immediately exercised. Will and intellect differentiated us from the lower, non-rational animals and left it true that we were made in the image of God. Like the intellect, the will was a faculty that operated without any bodily organ and, with the intellect, could survive bodily death.

Because the will was metaphysically free, it could be governed by and answerable to a moral law and so bound by moral obligation. This meant that our exercise of the will was the basis of merit or desert of reward or punishment, and it determined our ultimate destiny after bodily death.

The will's metaphysical freedom could be used to explain and provide a basis for freedom as a value within ethical theory. Freedom as a right could be understood as a normative recognition of the metaphysical power in the form of a right to its unimpeded exercise. And freedom as a desirable goal or condition of liberation could be understood as a state in which the metaphysical power was perfected.

In modern philosophy the metaphysics and ethics of freedom are understood very differently and are linked to very different theories of the mind and of human action. There is scepticism regarding freedom as a metaphysical power; or if the existence of such a power is admitted, it is often given a reductive treatment in terms of other kinds of power found in wider nature. The primary locus of the power of freedom, as of action, is no longer the will, but what Hobbes termed voluntary or willed action—something that medieval philosophers regarded as a merely secondary form of action. And ideas of freedom as a right and as a desirable state of liberation are generally explained other than by reference to freedom as a metaphysical power— usually by reference to a conception of reason as a locus of autonomy.

2. THE WILL AND HUMAN ACTION

Medieval theories of human decision making and action assimilated a rich body of theory from Antiquity. In particular, from the thirteenth century on these theories were shaped by reflection on the newly reappropriated work of Aristotle, albeit an Aristotle read through a Latin philosophical vocabulary already embodying conceptions from Augustine and the Stoics.

The will was a motivational or appetitive faculty or capacity distinguished by its relation to reason and the intellect. Whereas our passions were shared with the lower animals, the motivations of the will were peculiar to rational or intellectual beings such as ourselves and the angels. Motivations of the will were directly responsive to cognitions of the intellect involving general concepts and, in particular, a general concept of the good, whereas passions, by contrast, were non-intellectual motivations responsive only to the senses and the imagination and their presentations of particulars—presentations that involved no conceptual generality. As befitting its intellectual grasp of general concepts, the will's operation was non-corporeal, whereas passions were corporeal states.

As a capacity for intellectual motivation, the will also constituted our capacity for action in fully intentional or deliberate form. Action primarily occurred in actions of the will—such as in acts of choice or *electio*. What general conception of action lay behind this location of action in the will?

Intentional action occurs as the deliberately purposive; it involves goal directed ness—the deliberate use of means to attain ends. So a central feature of any theory of action will be its account of purposiveness. And it was through its understanding of purposiveness in fully intentional or deliberate form—purposiveness as it was found in adult human agency—that the scholastic tradition located action primarily in the will.

In the Middle Ages, there was a widespread consensus about how such purposiveness was to be understood—a consensus that went back to Augustine and the Stoics and that, though less clearly present in Aristotle himself, was naturally read into his texts by medieval philosophers. Purposiveness, and with it intentional action, was understood to consist in a distinctively practice- or agency-constitutive mode of exercising reason. In exercising reason we respond in various ways to an object of thought. In exercising the intellect, we respond to truth, that is, to objects of thought—things believed—as true. In exercising the will, we respond to objects of thought—things willed or favoured—as good. More specifically, in willing outcomes we respond to objects of thought as goals to be attained—not only as goods, but as goods to be attained through our willing of them. We have then a model of the purposiveness constitutive of action that is *practical reason based*—as consisting in a distinctively practice-constitutive exercise of our capacity for rationality, to direct ourselves towards objects of thought as goals.[1] The primary locus of action so understood was in decisions or choices of the will, which were termed *actus eliciti*—*elicited* actions of the will itself.

In some cases the action of the agent ended with these—as when the immediate object of the will was not a further willed action of the agent, but an object beyond the agent.[2] For the will was a locus of emotion in intellectual form, as in the case of the intellectual love of God and neighbour, where the will's object was another person. And such emotion was itself seen as a form of free action. But in other cases, the object of the will was further willed action—the operation of other capacities outside the will. Thus, I might will or decide to give alms, alms giving involving the extending of the hand, and so the exercise beyond the will of a corporeal capacity for motion. These further willed actions were generally termed *actus imperati*—*commanded* or *imperated* actions, or external actions, by contrast to the internal or elicited actions of the will itself. Externality here meant externality to the will, but not necessarily externally observable behaviour. For external or imperated action might also involve something that, though external to the will itself, was still mental or 'inner', such as the willed formation of a belief within the intellect, as in the occurrence of a meritorious and saving act of faith. Together elicited and imperated actions made up the category of the *voluntarium*, elicited acts constituting direct cases of agency, imperated acts only indirect cases, through their relation to the elicited acts that motivated them.

Why were elicited actions the only direct case of agency? That was because it was in the will that the defining case of agency—intellectual direction towards an object of thought as a goal—was immediately to be found. In imperated action considered in itself, there was, in the case of belief, only intellectual direction towards an object of thought as true, or else there was only the non-intellectual operation of a merely corporeal capacity. Goal-directed action could still be found in these imperated cases, but only derivatively, insofar as the imperated action was willed and motivated by a prior elicited action, inheriting the goal of that elicited action. Thus, I might choose to cross the road as a means to reaching the market, and my resultant willed road crossing would be an imperated action aimed at the same object of reaching the market through crossing the road.

Fundamental to the explanation of action in terms of its goal or purpose was formal causation. For the purpose of an elicited action of the will was given by the object of thought that informed it as its goal—an object of thought that then derivatively informed the further imperated act motivated by that elicited act. Aquinas described the completed human action as a form–matter complex, with the imperated act of a capacity external to the will standing as matter to the form provided by the elicited action of the will itself.[3]

This theory of action is a theory of purposiveness—of the relation of an action to its goal or object. It is to be distinguished from a theory of freedom, which is a theory of the capacity or power of an agent to determine for himself how he acts. For that second kind of theory is concerned with the importantly different relation of an agent to his action. And the relation of an action to its object is not obviously the same as that of an agent to the action he determines. The object of an action is an object of thought that, like an object of belief or of desire, may or may not be actual, whereas the relation of a free agent to his action is a relation between the exerciser of a power and an outcome that the power determines, where both entities must be actual. And it is far from obvious that each of these two very different relations involving, besides the action, two very different relata, should be constituted in the same way or explained by one and the same theory. Nevertheless, a fundamental difference between medieval and modern conceptions of freedom lies in a change in the relation between the theory of purposiveness and the theory of freedom.

Medieval theories of freedom certainly built on and presupposed the dominant practical reason-based theory of action, but they did not generally try to explain freedom in terms of the account that had been given of purposiveness. Whereas we shall find, especially in British philosophy following Hobbes, a tendency to use a radically new account of purposiveness that appealed exclusively to efficient causation also to provide a new account of freedom as a metaphysical power. A new theory of the relation of an action to its object was used also to explain the relation of an agent to the action he determined.

In medieval theories of freedom, there was a wide consensus about the constitution of action. But as we are about to see, because the account given of freedom was not straightforwardly adapted from the account of purposiveness, there was much less consensus about the constitution of freedom. It is true that the competing medieval accounts of freedom often involved disagreement about psychological questions, such as about the precise relation of the will to the intellect. Was the operation of the will closely tied to the intellect, as intellectualists such as Aquinas supposed? Or could the will operate to varying degrees independently of the intellect as voluntarists such as Scotus and Ockham supposed? But these differences involved no disagreement about the fundamental model of agency, which remained in all cases practical reason based.

3. Freedom as a Metaphysical Power

Medieval conceptions of freedom combined two elements in tension. The first element was the idea of a multi-way power, that is, a power that by its nature left it up to us which actions we performed, one and the same power being exercisable to determine one action or another. Peter Lombard referred to free will [*liberi arbitrii*], which the philosophers have defined as the 'free judgement of the will' [*liberum de voluntate iudicium*], because the very power and ability of the will and reason, which we said above was free will, is free regarding whichever alternative it pleases because it can be moved freely to this or to that.[4]

This multi-way nature was often characterised as involving liberty of exercise—a freedom to do A or to refrain, and in many but not all cases, a further liberty of specification—a freedom to do A or to do some specific alternative B.

But this power was also conceived in aretaic terms as being diminished by the ethical corruption of the agent, and as enhanced by his ethical perfection. Freedom was enjoyed in its perfect or most complete form by God, the infinitely good being, union with whom, though only as a divine gift and only through the help of divine grace, was the ultimate goal of the ethical life and so, too, the ultimate goal of human action. So the theory of freedom was part of a general account of creation, fall and redemption—a process of corruption and recovery both ethical and metaphysical in which freedom took correspondingly reduced and recovered forms.

Adam's fall was a fall from an original state of created innocence into a state of ethical degradation—a state that was described as one of servitude to sin. And Christ's redemption was described as a release from the same servitude, bringing ultimate ethical perfection in heaven, a state that was described as one of perfect liberty or freedom, a supernatural condition transcending our original created condition and approaching, as far as the retention of our created human nature could permit, the condition of God. These descriptions of various kinds of ethical condition obviously used a vocabulary of freedom and unfreedom. But more than that, the conditions were characterised by specific reference to variations in freedom considered as a metaphysical power.[5] As we were originally created, the metaphysical power of freedom was a *libertas minor*—a power both to do good and also to do bad. Whereas the servitude of fallen humanity to sin involved a reduction in the power to do good—a weakened power to do good that became dependent on divine assistance through grace—the final liberation of heaven would involve our enjoyment of the *libertas maior* enjoyed eternally by God, then perfection of our power of freedom through the complete removal of any power to do bad or to sin.

Central to this moralisation of the power of freedom was the relation of freedom to reason. With some exceptions, most theorists held that any enjoyment of the power of freedom presupposed the possession of intellect or reason. On most views, human freedom was not to any substantial degree also shared by the lower animals. And in its perfect form, the exercise of freedom would always and infallibly follow the direction of reason. Indeed, it seemed that the *libertas maior* of heaven might, in effect, coincide with a perfected human capacity for reason.

Hence, in a writer such as Anselm we see a tendency to characterise freedom proper as really a capacity to do right. Thus, Anselm defined freedom of choice or will as 'the power to preserve rectitude of will for its own sake'.[6] The moralisation of freedom thus involved a certain tendency to rationalism about freedom—an assimilation of freedom to rationality.

But the assimilation could not be complete, as it was in considerable tension with the conception of freedom as a multi-way power. For the capacity for reason is not obviously by nature a multi-way power. In those cases where reason requires that we do one specific thing, it is not at all clear that the capacity for reason need involve any capacity to do otherwise at all, doing otherwise being something that reason actually excludes. Indeed, there was an obvious paradox arising from freedom's being by nature both a multi-way power and a mode of excellence coincident, in perfected form, with reason. For the perfection of the power, as a *libertas maior*, appeared to involve the removal of one crucial kind of alternative—the removal of the power to sin. The perfection of freedom seemed then to involve, in one respect, its diminution as a power over alternatives. But this diminution was rarely admitted to be truly a diminution in freedom itself. What appeared to be a reduction in freedom was generally explained and celebrated as, correctly understood, its increase. As Lombard observed, relying on the authority of Augustine:

> Indeed a choice [*arbitrium*] that is quite unable to sin will be the freer . . . after the confirmation of beatitude there is to be a free will in man by which he will not be able to sin; and this free will is now in the Angels and in the Saints, who are with the Lord; and certainly it is the more free, as it is the more immune from sin and the more prone to good. For one is the further from that servitude of sin, of which it is written: *He who works sin is the slave of sin*, as one's judgment is freer in choosing the good.[7]

So freedom was a power that by its very nature made alternatives available. But it was also a power that was enhanced by ethical perfection, so that in its most complete form it had to exclude unethical and unreasonable alternatives, thus ruling out any possibility of its being exercised defectively.

This tension raised theological problems. It was difficult for freedom to remain a mode of excellence while still playing its normal role in ethical theory—a role that very much depended on its nature as a power to do more than one thing. Take, for example, the theory of the incarnation and redemption. Christ, as the perfect man, in his human life already fully enjoyed freedom in perfected form. But precisely because freedom in perfected form precluded any power to sin, in his case the power of freedom could no longer easily do the work its imperfect form could do for ordinary humans—which is serve as a basis of merit for doing right. Merit for doing right in this life depended on one having freedom in the form of power or control over whether or not one did right, and so merit for doing right depended on the power to do wrong. Now Christ's human obedience to the command of the Father to sacrifice himself on the cross was redemptive only on the assumption that it was meritorious. But as a perfect human, Christ lacked, or so it seemed, the power to disobey that command.[8]

God not only served as the pattern of freedom, exemplifying freedom in perfect form. He was also its source in us as our creator. That could affect the theory of freedom as a metaphysical power in another way. For medieval philosophers had to devise a theory not only of how the power might be perfected and increased, but also of how far the power's possession and exercise by the agent was consistent with the impact on the agent of power exercised from without, by other beings. Now the determination of an agent's choice by some created object, such as an angel or a planet, were it possible, was widely viewed as something that would impose necessity and remove freedom. But since God was creator and the source of freedom, determination by God was not universally viewed as having the same implication. Even in this life, God's determining, through grace, the agent to do good was held by Aquinas to be consistent with the agent's retention of the power to do otherwise. On Aquinas's view, such divine determination in the direction of the good by the very creator of our freedom preserved freedom and contingency, and it did not impose necessity.[9]

Not everyone accepted Aquinas's doctrine. For example, in early-modern Jesuit writers such as Molina we find a clear sense that determination of the agent's action by any external cause, even by God, is a threat to freedom—and so a kind of determination that any acceptable theory of the operation of divine grace must clearly reject.[10] But this Molinist view was not yet uncontroversial. So the free will debate in its modern form did not yet clearly exist. Nowadays the debate between incompatibilists and compatibilists is assumed to be about the implications of causal determination from without just considered in itself, irrespective of the metaphysical and ethical dignity of the external cause. Thus, determination of the agent by causation from without is taken by modern incompatibilists to be an automatic threat to freedom in every case, whether the external cause be creator or created. But this assumption has only become general in modern times.

If freedom was based on reason, what explained its apparent limitation to the practical sphere? For reason extends to the theoretical, and indeed, it might appear that it is the cognitive or immediately theoretical faculty of the intellect that underpins our capacity for reason generally. So what explains why freedom is a freedom primarily of the will rather than of the intellect, if that, indeed, is how freedom is to be understood?

In Aquinas, freedom was explained in terms of an aspect of our theoretical grasp of the good. The good is the object of reason in its practical form. But the good is also the subject of cognitive or intellectual enquiry: the good falls within the truth at which the intellect is directed. And it was as such a subject that Aquinas used the good to explain the basis of our freedom. For the good was seen by him as attaching in this world to a variety of options—options that realised it in incomplete or finite form. So, in an enquiry about what it is best to do, that left the practical intellect free to judge any one of a variety of options as the best to pursue. And this freedom at the point of the intellect explained why the will was free to choose one option rather than another. And, indeed, the freedom of the will had to be related to a corresponding freedom of the intellect. For Aquinas was an intellectualist about the operation of the will. *Electio* at the point of the will was a function of the agent's intellectual judgement about which option was best.

So while freedom was a characteristic of the will as its subject, Aquinas taught that its cause was to be found in reason, freedom of choice or *liberum arbitrium* being described by him as the free judgement of reason.[11] And the will's status as an intellectual or rational faculty was derivative, owing to its acts being informed by those of the intellect. The liberating state of *beatitudo* or happiness, which was the destiny of the saved in heaven, was primarily a state of the intellect as involved in the beatific vision or contemplation of God.

For Scotus, however, the will's freedom depended on a duality in the good that was its object—as consisting both in the good that lay in the happiness of the agent and in justice, where the good was pursued for its own sake. But the nature of freedom was not exhausted by the nature of the will's intellectually presented object. Freedom was understood by Scotus to consist in a power of the will to determine itself, and the presence of this power was only revealed to us in our experience of our own choices.[12] Moreover, the will determined its actions as an efficient cause of them, judgements of the intellect serving only as secondary, partial or non-determining efficient causes. The will could operate to a degree independently of judgements made by the intellect. Indeed, appealing to the characterisation of rational power by Aristotle in *Metaphysics* Book IX as involving a potential to opposites, in Scotus's view, thanks to the possibility of freedom, it was the will rather than the intellect that was the truly rational power. For Scotus, reason did, after all, involve by its very nature a capacity for alternatives, and it was not the intellect but the will itself that, thanks to its freedom, could constitute the primarily and properly rational faculty.[13] Again, it was the will rather than the intellect that was the primary source of the liberating happiness of heaven, as the faculty by which we direct ourselves to God in love of him.

Besides freedom as a power over alternatives, there is also voluntariness in the sense in which the term would exclusively be used by Hobbes. This is the property of occurring as and through being willed. Voluntariness and freedom have often been identified, but they involve, on the face of it, quite distinct powers. Freedom is a multi-way power over alternatives, whereas voluntariness is not similarly multi-way. Certainly one may both be able to do A on the basis of willing to do A and able to refrain on the basis of willing to refrain. But these are distinct one-way powers, not a single two-way power. One power may be possessed without the other: someone may be able to stay in a room on the basis of willing so to do but, because unbeknown to them the room is locked, be unable to leave on the basis of willing so to do.[14] And certainly only one of these distinct powers can ever be exercised at a given time.

And though an agent may have the capacity to act as he wills, he may lack freedom of will; he may not be able to determine for himself what he wills. In which case, if freedom of action depends on a freedom of will, there may for this reason be voluntariness without any accompanying freedom. On the other hand, there seems nothing in the idea of freedom that immediately implies voluntariness. For it may be up to me what I decide or will, so that I have freedom of will. But it may not be possible for me to take specific decisions on the basis of decisions so to decide; I may not be able to will as I will. Even if there is freedom of will, there may not be such a thing as a voluntariness specifically of the will.

It was widely held by many in the medieval tradition that voluntariness did not suffice for freedom. But was it necessary for freedom? This question about voluntariness arose from within the theory of action. Voluntariness was a feature of imperated actions, which by their very nature occurred on the basis of a prior willing of them. But was it in any form a feature of elicited acts of the will themselves, and if so, a feature of action and so of free action generally? One view that had supporters from Augustine and Anselm through Scotus and down to Suarez was that elicited actions of the will, and so also free actions of the will, must by their very nature be willed. But this characteristic of being willed did not involve any relation to a prior act of will distinct from and motivating of it—which would involve a vicious regress—but was a reflexive feature of the act of will itself and something internal to it: as Suarez put it, citing Anselm: 'omnis volens ipse suum velle necessario vult'—anyone who wills necessarily wills his own willing.[15]

Other thinkers objected that the appeal to voluntariness did no work in the theory of how elicited acts constituted purposive doings—that work was done by the practical reason–based model—nor, given the differences mentioned above between freedom and voluntariness, in any account of their freedom. In any case, it was obvious that elicited acts of the will were not reflexively and internally self-willed. Acts of will no more willed themselves than acts of seeing saw themselves.[16]

A further question concerned the nature of freedom itself. Freedom seemed to involve a kind of power to determine. But what kind of power, and how was it related to other powers in nature? It was natural to think that its exercise involved efficient causation, certainly at the point of imperated actions, which were widely seen as efficiently caused by the elicited acts that motivated them. But it was also natural to see efficient causation as involved in the free performance of the elicited acts themselves. The free agent could be seen as an efficient cause of his own decisions and choices. The Scotist tradition put emphasis on this conception of freedom as an efficient causal power of agents, and it was under the influence of that tradition that Suarez gave this view its most sophisticated expression in the *Metaphysical Disputations*. Suarez distinguished between necessary and free or contingent causes. Necessary causes were non-rational substances, such as stones, which under any given condition could produce but one effect, as when a stone once thrown at a window with a given force would only break it. Free causes were rational substances, such as humans or angels, and these operated contingently, with efficient causal power taking multi-way form. Under a given set of conditions, a free cause was sufficient for a variety of possible effects, and which effect it produced was up to the cause. Our knowledge of our possession of this distinctive causal power was based on our experience of our own agency, which revealed its existence to us.[17]

4. THE ETHICAL SIGNIFICANCE
OF FREEDOM

In medieval ethical theory, freedom was a central ethical notion along with law, and the two phenomena were treated as existing in a complex harmony. By contrast the early-modern period saw the development of a very different kind of ethical theory.

In attempting to rid ethical theory of any dependence on freedom as a metaphysical power, Hobbes was to argue that freedom and law are quite opposed notions, freedom properly understood requiring the absence of law and law serving simply to limit freedom.

In scholastic moral theory, law provided humans with direction towards the good that carried the force of obligation—a direction that freedom in the form that we enjoy it in this life, as a power to do evil as well as good, especially required. Moreover, insofar as law imposed obligations, it presupposed the very power of freedom that it directed. This presupposition operated through what was often seen as a constitutive connection between obligation and desert of punishment for its breach. For desert or *meritum* required the agent to have had control over whether or not he breached the obligation.

The same dependence of law and obligation on freedom also came from the relation of obligation to blame. Obligation was a standard to breach which was to be blameworthy for doing wrong. But blame was often held to be a criticism that presupposed a power of freedom on the agent's part. Consider Aquinas's characterisation of blame:

> Hence a human action is worthy of praise or blame in so far as it is good or bad. For praise and blame is nothing other than for the goodness or badness of his action to be imputed to someone. Now an action is imputed to an agent when it is within his power, so that he has dominion [*dominium*] over the act. But this is the case with all actions involving the will: for it is through the will that man has dominion over his action . . . Hence it follows that good or bad in actions of the will alone justifies praise and blame; for in such actions badness, fault and blame come to one and the same.[18]

Blame was understood by Aquinas as a criticism in which the badness of an agent's action was imputed to the agent, so that the agent counted as bad to have done what he did. And what warranted this imputation was the agent's control or *dominium* over his action—his freedom to determine for himself which action he performed.

The primary form of law as it governed humans was the natural law. And natural law was reason itself in preceptive form—a form in which it did not merely recommend through *consilia* but imposed obligations through *praecepta*. In other words, the natural law was a directive form of reason—reason that with the binding force of obligation served to direct the proper use of freedom. Now any directive force of reason must directly address and apply to the will. For it is at the point of the will— the point at which we choose or decide to perform this action rather than that—that we immediately respond to directives of practical reason. So it was the will that the binding directives of reason in its obligatory or preceptive form had immediately to address. That meant that the natural law had immediately to bind the will. Obligations of the natural law were immediately obligations on the will. As Aquinas made clear, under natural law we were bound to will obligatory external actions, and bound not to will prohibited ones, so that the existence of an obligation to give alms implied a corresponding obligation to decide and intend to give alms.[19] Behind this lay a conception of obligation, not simply as a kind of command—though obligations might be imposed through commands—but as a demanding mode of justificatory support or, to use a term from Suarez, a demandingly preceptive *vis directiva* or justificatory force.[20]

If natural law involved a directive force of practical reason that, like any such, had directly to address the will, and this particular justificatory force, as obligatory and preceptive, was by its nature freedom-directive, then that had an obvious implication. The will would have to be a locus of free action; freedom would have to be exercised at the point of the will. So the location of the metaphysical power of freedom in the will followed both from the dominant practical reason–based model of action, but it was also something required by the dominant model of natural law and obligation as involving a distinctively obligatory or preceptive justificatory force.

Not only did the general conception of natural law as a demanding justificatory force of reason presuppose a freedom and agency of the will; such a freedom of the will was also presupposed by the view taken of what the natural law specifically required. It was the content as well as the general nature of the natural law that dictated the location of freedom. For the natural law primarily required love of God and of neighbour as bearing the image of God. And love was, as we have seen, conceived as involving a free action of the will that had God or our neighbour as its object.

Law not only presupposed freedom as a metaphysical power. It also constituted freedom as a right and in its highest form, as the law of grace of the new covenant, directed us towards the perfect freedom of heaven—towards freedom as a state of liberation.

The term *dominium* could pick out both the metaphysical power of freedom—as we saw in Aquinas's account of the conditions for fair blame—but was also used to refer to a right of control or possession, which involved a right to exercise the metaphysical power. A phrase used by an author such as Suarez was *dominium libertatis*, or dominion over one's freedom. Nature not only gives us a power of freedom; through the law of nature it also gave us the right to exercise it:

> If, however, we are speaking of the natural law of dominion, it is then true that liberty is a matter of natural law, in a positive, not merely a negative sense, since nature itself confers upon man the true dominion of his liberty . . . For liberty rather than slavery is a precept of the natural law, for this reason, namely, that nature has made men free in a positive sense (so to speak) with an intrinsic right to liberty, whereas it has not made them slaves in this positive sense, strictly speaking.[21]

5. Towards a New Metaphysics of Freedom

Modern theories of freedom are in various ways the legacy of Hobbes's attack on the very reality of freedom as a metaphysical power of self-determination. This attack was deeply influential. If freedom remained as any kind of power thereafter, it often did so reduced to a complex case of some other power of a kind that Hobbes did admit into his metaphysics, such as voluntariness. Hobbes's attack on freedom as a metaphysical power was part of a wider attack on the scholastic understanding of freedom's ethical significance. And this had an equal effect on subsequent philosophy. It led ethical theory generally to begin to detach itself from commitment to freedom as a metaphysical power, and it also led, especially within the Anglo-Saxon tradition, to conceptions of that metaphysical power that were increasingly detached from ethical theory. In particular, there was an abandonment of the aretaic model that tied the perfection of the metaphysical power to ethical excellence.

Central to Hobbes's scepticism is his reduction of action in general to what had previously been the special and secondary case of willed or imperated action—what Hobbes was now to term 'voluntary action'. Hobbes completely abandoned any theory of purposiveness as consisting in a distinctively practical mode of exercising reason located in the will as a special intellectual or rational appetite. Indeed, he found the idea of intellectual or rational appetites distinct from the passions unintelligible:

> For I do not fear it will be thought too hot for my fingers, to shew the vanity of words such as these, Intellectual appetite, conformity of the appetite to the object, rational will, elective power of the rational will; nor understand I how reason can be the root of true liberty, if the Bishop (as he saith in the beginning) had the liberty to write this discourse. I understand how objects, and the conveniences and inconveniences of them, may be represented to a man by the help of his senses; but how reason representeth anything to the will, I [do not] understand . . .[22]

Instead, Hobbes introduced a new model of purposiveness that could only apply to the case of what had previously been called imperated action. To act purposively was always to do something voluntarily, on the basis of a prior will to do it—a will that, in line with much medieval action theory, Hobbes conceived to be an efficient cause of the action it motivated. But now this motivating will was no longer itself a prior case of action, but passive. This was because, as Hobbes insisted, the will itself is not voluntary as are the actions willed that it motivates:

> I acknowledge this liberty, that I can do if I will, but to say, I can will if I will, I take to be an absurd speech.[23]

Given Hobbes's view that the will is not itself voluntary, his new model of action as nothing more than voluntariness just could not apply to willings or motivations.

Hobbes also denied the status of actions to willings because of his particular conception of voluntariness. For Hobbes voluntariness was never an internal or reflexive phenomenon. Rather, it always involved efficient causation of the action willed by a prior willing distinct from it. That meant that if actions were by nature voluntary, the willings of them could not be actions too, on pain of a vicious causal regress.

The object or content of the motivating will to act still provided the goal at which the action willed was directed. But since the motivating will was not itself a purposive action, but merely a passion or passive desire, purposiveness—being a response made to a goal in order to attain it—was restricted to the action willed. It followed that all explanation in terms of purposes now involved reference to a motivating efficient cause. So Hobbes could afford to claim that all explanation of action in terms of the purposes for which it was performed had to be in terms of efficient causes. In fact, Hobbes claimed to find the idea of motivation by causes other than efficient ones, such as by formal causes, completely unintelligible:

> Moved not by an efficient, is non-sense.[24]

That meant that it was the very nature of action to involve the exercise of efficient causal power—a kind of power that, as we have seen, had already been appealed to in order to characterise the power of freedom. On Hobbes's account of action, though, the immediate bearer of this power was no longer the agent, but rather a passive motion of the will within the agent. And that motivation as passive was not the product of any free causation on the agent's part, but rather, the determined effect of a chain of necessary causes for which the agent had no responsibility.

Hobbes did not even begin to claim that the operation of this passive willing involved the agent's determining for himself how he acted. Indeed, Hobbes regarded the very idea of self-determining freedom as unintelligible because it was inherently and viciously regressive:

> And if a man determine himself, the question will still remain what determined him to determine himself in that manner.[25]

He also regarded as unintelligible the Suarezian attempt to model freedom as a special kind of contingent or multi-way efficient causal power. That was because any power that was genuinely sufficient to produce an effect must, in his view, when present actually produce it, so that a cause sufficient for a range of contrary effects—a cause involving indetermination, as Hobbes put it—must simultaneously produce them all, which was impossible:

> But that the indetermination can make it happen or not happen is absurd; for indetermination maketh it equally to happen or not to happen; and therefore both; which is a contradiction. Therefore indetermination doth nothing, and whatsoever causes do, is necessary.[26]

So all efficient causation was in terms of necessary causes; every cause could produce but one effect, and there was no contingency about how it would operate.

Freedom was no longer a kind of contingent power since all power operated through necessity. That meant that far from being itself a kind of power, freedom could only amount to an absence of obstacles to other kinds of power:

> Liberty is the absence of all impediments to action, that are not contained in the nature, and in the intrinsecal quality of the agent.[27]

As such, freedom was not restricted to rational creation, nor was its perfection tied to ethical excellence:

> how reason representeth anything to the will, I understand no more than the Bishop understands there may be liberty in children, in beasts, and inanimate

creatures. For he seemeth to wonder how children may be left at liberty; how
beasts imprisoned may be set at liberty; and how a river may have a free course.[28]

Moreover, in involving obligations law was not harmonious with freedom, but
its essential opposite. Law in imposing obligations imposed a kind of block to the
power of appetites. And as with Hobbesian liberty generally, there was nothing
more to liberty as a right than the absence of such a block—in this case through the
absence of some restricting law. Just as there was no metaphysical power of freedom, there was no room for a normativity of law of the kind that natural law was
understood to constitute by the scholastic tradition: there was no room for law as a
special directive force of reason that gave normative recognition to the power of
freedom both by imposing obligations to direct its exercise (*lex* or *ius*) and by
affording rights to protect its exercise (*ius*):

> For though they that speak of this subject, use to confound *Ius*, and *Lex*, *Right*
> and *Law*; yet they ought to be distinguished; because Right, consisteth in liberty
> to do, or to forbeare; Whereas Law determineth, and bindeth to one of them; so
> that Law, and Right, differ as much, as Obligation and Liberty; which in one and
> the same matter are inconsistent.[29]

But although Hobbes himself denied that freedom could be a metaphysical
power, this denial was not maintained so obstinately by his successors. For the
power that was used by Hobbes to characterise purposiveness—the efficient causal
power of motivations—was used by Locke and many successors also to give a positive account of freedom as a power. The Hobbesian theory of an action's relation to
the object at which it was directed was turned into a theory of the agent's relation to
the action he determines. The agent was identified with the motivations of his will—
even though these were now passive motivations that preceded his agency and were
no longer his deliberate doing. The actions efficiently caused by those passive motivations were, nevertheless, to count as determined by the agent.

In effect, a reductive account was given of freedom as a complex, two- or multi-
way case of voluntariness. The theory of freedom familiar from classical English-
language compatibilism was born. The power of freedom to do A or not is now a
complex, composed of the power to do A as an effect of wanting or willing to do A,
and of the distinct power to refrain from doing A as an effect of wanting or willing
to refrain.

Even those theorists of freedom who opposed this compatibilist theory, perhaps in the cause of some form of libertarianism, often did so to some degree or
other within the metaphysical framework that Hobbes imposed.

Thus, conceptions of the metaphysical power of freedom were increasingly
detached from any theory of the agent's metaphysical and ethical perfection. Conceptions of freedom were increasingly neutral on what would constitute the ethical
improvement of the agent. And the operation on the agent of the infinitely good
creator whose image they bore no longer was treated as having distinctive implications for human freedom. Determination of one's action by God was as much (or as
little) a threat to freedom as its determination by any other created being.

6. THE TRANSFORMATION OF ETHICS

Just as ethical theory ceased to shape and condition accounts of freedom as a metaphysical power, so at the same time that metaphysical power ceased to play a role in ethical theory. Either the ethical life ceased to be directed at the liberation of the agent, or the condition of liberation increasingly ceased to be understood by reference to freedom as a metaphysical power. And notions of responsibility, of obligation and of liberty as a right were similarly detached from the theory of freedom as a power.

We may see two tendencies within ethical theory following Hobbes. One is a naturalism very much in the spirit of Hobbes himself, and the other a rationalism in the spirit of Kant. Both traditions, naturalist and rationalist alike, eventually detached ethical theory from any commitment to freedom as a multi-way metaphysical power, and this is true even of the post-Kantian rationalist tradition despite Kant's own commitment to the noumenal existence of freedom as a power. Unlike the naturalist tradition, though, the rationalist tradition continued to conceive of the ethical life as involving and aiming at a condition of liberation, this time involving not a perfection of metaphysical freedom, but rather, the perfection of reason in the form of autonomy.

The post-Hobbesian reduction of freedom to a complex case of voluntariness had one especially important consequence for ethical theory. Freedom as a multi-way power ceased to be a condition of moral responsibility. And that is because on the reductive account of freedom as a complex case of voluntariness, a power to act otherwise is no longer being exercised to determine action. Freedom is no longer a single power that if possessed at all must be a power to do more than one thing. It is now a combination of distinct powers each to do but one thing—a power to do A on the basis of a will or desire to do A and a distinct power or will to refrain from doing A on the basis of a will or desire to refrain—each power being exercised without the other, and each being capable of being possessed without the other. So now when an agent does A, no multi-way power of freedom—no power to act otherwise—is ever actually exercised by him. The only power to act being exercised is the one-way power to do A as an effect of willing to do A. The power to refrain is the quite distinct power to refrain as an effect of willing to refrain, and this power is obviously not being exercised at all. But how can the responsibility of the agent depend on a power to do otherwise that is never actually exercised? It is voluntariness—doing what one does because one wills or wants to do it—on which moral responsibility now comes to depend; the presence of a freedom to do otherwise becomes irrelevant.[30]

The conception of self-determination as involving multi-way freedom came under pressure within the medieval tradition primarily from rationalism about freedom linked to an aretaic conception of freedom as something perfected by growth in virtue. The perfection of freedom involved an assimilation of freedom to reason and so the exclusion of some power over alternatives. By contrast we can now see that the conception of self-determination as inherently multi-way was coming under pressure within post-Hobbesian philosophy from quite another direction. This was a divorce of self-determination from any aretaic conception of it and, instead, a naturalistic reduction of freedom to a complex case of voluntariness—an inherently one-way efficient causal power also to be found in non-rational nature and in particular in the actions of lower animals.

But it is also true that the determination of willed action by passive motivations is not a particularly plausible model for understanding self-determination. For why should we identify the agent with motivations within him that are not within his control and not of his own doing?

The long-term effect would be to detach the ethical significance of action conceived as voluntariness from any connection with genuine self-determination. A modern example of this is the Hartian project of understanding responsibility for the voluntary not in terms of any theory of desert based on self-determination, but rather, in terms of a fair choosing system. On this model, which Hart intended for legal responsibility within a legal system, responsibility for doing wrong is understood by reference to the liability it brings to pressure and sanction.[31] But the fairness of a sanction is not explained in terms of its being the deserved response to the misexercise of some metaphysical power of self-determination. Instead, the fairness of the sanctions is understood both in terms of their general deterrent and reformative utility, but also in terms of the fairness of their application. And they will be fairly applied if those subject to them are given a fair chance of avoiding them. Hence, their application is restricted to the voluntary, since voluntary action—action subject to the will—is action that we can perform or refrain from at will, as a means to avoiding sanctions.

Obligation, the standard we are responsible for meeting, is no longer being conceived on this Hartian approach as a special force of reason directive of a metaphysical power of freedom, and it is instead understood simply as a sanction-backed standard on the voluntary. And with this reconstruction of the idea of obligation comes a thinning out of the very theory of reason or rationality. Within medieval ethics the directives of reason in practical form were tied to a rich metaphysics of the self, of which the power of freedom was a central feature. Practical reason could take the distinctive form of obligatory law precisely because it directed not just a bare capacity for reason, but a genuine capacity for self-determination. But once that capacity was lost from ethical theory, or disregarded by it, the theory of practical reason would have to be correspondingly simplified.

And so we arrive at modern theories of ethical rationality that see ethical standards as no more than general standards of reason, with the blame that asserts them as no more than a general form of rational criticism. On such views blame is no longer what Aquinas conceived it to be—a condemnatory criticism that presupposed a personal metaphysical *dominium* over one's actions and that was specifically directed at free action. It becomes, instead, on some views a mere assertion of unreasonableness that can apply equally to voluntary actions and to passive desires and emotions.[32]

How then are rights to liberty and ideas of liberation to be understood, if not by appeal to some theory of freedom as a metaphysical power? A crucial concept here is that of autonomy. The idea of autonomy in modern philosophy derives from Kant's conception of rational self-legislation, but in a form detached from his metaphysics of noumenal freedom—which was already a withdrawal from a serious theoretical metaphysics of freedom, the theoretically knowable phenomenal world having already been surrendered by Kant to universal causal determinism.

The post-Kantian rationalist tradition has much in common with the rationalising trend in medieval theories of freedom, insofar as freedom is assimilated to a certain excellence in one's capacity for rationality. But the idea of a power to determine action for oneself has been abandoned. Instead of the idea of a power of self-determination that operates independently of other powers, we have the idea of a capacity for rationality that operates independently of external standards. This can take a number of forms. There is the Kantian idea of rational or ethical standards as the legislated or constructed product of human reason.[33] Or there is the Millian idea of a capacity to live according to values of one's own, developed apart from the standards of one's culture.[34]

Autonomy so understood can involve a kind of liberation, insofar as one's reason develops to a level that liberates one from dependence on standards or values external to one. And liberty as a right can be explained in terms of a right to freedom from kinds of pressure or coercion that would obstruct the attainment of autonomy.

What is unclear is how desirable the enjoyment of such a form of rationality might be. Certainly there is nothing in rationality that generally demands or requires the preservation of alternative options. Indeed, in theoretical reason, removal of all options but one—through evidence or proof—when available, is highly desirable. If within the practical sphere there is an intuitive right not to be coerced, that may turn out to be precisely because we have, in metaphysical freedom, a genuine multiway capacity to determine for ourselves how we act—a capacity that would be obstructed by coercive pressure in one particular direction, no matter how favoured by reason that one direction might be.

NOTES

1. For discussion of the practical reason-based model, see Pink (2004)
2. For discussion of this possibility, see Suarez (1856–70, volume 4, 308).
3. See Aquinas *Summa Theologiae* (1a2ae, q.17, a. 4).
4. *Sententiae* II, d. 25, cap. 1§2; Peter the Lombard (1981, 461).
5. For a classic discussion, see Peter the Lombard (*Sententiae* II, d. 25; 1981, 461–69).
6. Anselm (1968, volume 1, 212).
7. Peter the Lombard (*Sententiae* II, d. 25, cap. 4; 1981, 463).
8. For the difficulty, and a lucid and comprehensive discussion of attempted solutions within the scholastic tradition, see Suarez (1856–70, volume 18, 282–92).

9. See Aquinas (*Summa contra Gentiles* III, 94; Aquinas 1961, 138–41); Aquinas (*Summa theologiae* I, q.19 a. 8, and q. 22–23, especially q. 23 a. 6) and Thomas Aquinas (1950, 114–33). For a classic discussion from a neo-Thomist Dominican perspective, see Garrigou-Lagrange (1936).

10. See, for example, Molina (*Liberi arbitrii . . . concordia*, Part 7, q. 23, a. 4–5, disputatio 1, membrum 7; 1953, 501–10).

11. *Summa Theologiae* 1a2ae, q. 17, a. 1, ad 2; Aquinas (1950, 81).

12. *Quaestiones super libros Metaphysicorum* (q.15); John Duns Scotus (1997, 682–83).

13. *Quaestiones super libros Metaphysicorum* (q.15); John Duns Scotus (1997, 675–99).

14. See John Locke, *An Essay Concerning Human Understanding* (II, 21 §10), and Locke (1973, 238).

15. For defence of this view and discussion of prior support for it, see Suarez (1856–70, volume 4, 196).

16. 'And in like manner a willing is produced from the will, but is not itself willed through its own production; just as a seeing . . . is not itself seen through its own production.' Vasquez (*In primam secundae Sancti Thomae*, disputation 23, chapter 2; 1611, 165).

17. See metaphysical disputation 19 'On necessary and free causes', section 2, §13, in Suarez (1856–70, volume 25, 697), and in Suarez (1994, 291).

18. *Summa Theologiae* (1a2ae, q. 21, a. 2); Thomas Aquinas (1950, 112).

19. *Summa Theologiae* (1a2ae, q.100, a.9); Aquinas (1950, 463).

20. For discussion of this Force model of moral obligation, its history and its implications, see Pink (2005, 2009a).

21. *De legibus* (book 2, chapter 14, §16); Suarez (1856–70, volume 5, 141).

22. Hobbes (1656, 35–36).

23. Hobbes (1656, 29).

24. Hobbes (1656, 59).

25. Hobbes (1656, 26).

26. Hobbes (1656, 184).

27. Hobbes (1656, 285).

28. Hobbes (1656, 35–36).

29. Thomas Hobbes (1996, chapter 14), 'Of the first and second Naturall Lawes, and of Contracts'.

30. For a discussion of the effect on modern ethical theory of this transformation in the understanding of moral responsibility and its basis in self-determination, see Pink (2009b).

31. Hart (1968).

32. See Scanlon (1998, 22).

33. See Kant (1996).

34. See Mill (1989).

BIBLIOGRAPHY

Anselm. 1968. *S. Anselmi Cantuariensis Archiepiscopi Opera Omnia*, ed. F. S. Schmitt. Stuttgart-Bad Cannstatt, Germany: Friedrich Fromann Verlag.

Garrigou-Lagrange, Reginald. 1936. 'Prémotion physique'. In *Dictionnaire de Theologie Catholique*, volume 13, 31–77. Paris: Letouzey et Ané.

Hart, Herbert. 1968. *Punishment and Responsibility*. Oxford: Clarendon Press.

Hobbes, Thomas. 1656. *The Questions Concerning Liberty, Necessity and Chance, Clearly Stated between Dr Bramhall Bishop of Derry, and Thomas Hobbes of Malmesbury*, London.

———. 1996. *Leviathan*, ed. Richard Tuck, Cambridge: Cambridge University Press.

John Duns Scotus. 1997. *Quaestiones super libros metaphysicorum Aristotelis libri VI–IX*. New York: St Bonaventure University.

Kant, Immanuel. 1996. '*Groundwork* of the metaphysics of morals'. In *Practical Philosophy*, ed. Mary Gregor. Cambridge: Cambridge University Press.

Locke, John. 1973. *An Essay Concerning Human Understanding*, ed. P. H. Nidditch. Oxford: Clarendon Press.

Mill, John Stuart. 1989. *On Liberty*, ed. Stefan Collini. Cambridge: Cambridge University Press.

Molina, Luis de. 1953. *Liberi arbitrii cum gratiae donis, divina praescientia, providentia, praedestinatione et reprobatione concordia*, ed. J. Rabeneck. Madrid: Sapientia.

Peter the Lombard. 1981. *Sententiae in IV Libris Distinctae*. Grottaferrata, Italy: Collegii S. Bonaventurae ad Claras Aquas.

Pink, Thomas. 2004. 'Suarez, Hobbes and the Scholastic Tradition in Action Theory'. In *The Will and Human Action: From Antiquity to the Present Day*, ed. Martin Stone and Thomas Pink, 127–53. London: Routledge.

———. 2005. 'Action, will and law in late scholasticism' In *Moral Philosophy on the Threshold of Modernity*, ed. Jill Kraye and Risto Saarinen, 31–50. Dordrecht, the Netherlands: Springer (The New Synthese Historical Library 57).

———. 2009a. 'Natural law and the theory of obligation'. In *Psychology and Philosophy*, ed. Sara Heinämaa and Martina Reuter, 97–114. Dordrecht, the Netherlands: Springer (Studies in the History of Philosophy of Mind 8).

———. 2009b. Power and Moral Responsibility. *Philosophical Explorations* 12:127–51.

Scanlon, Thomas. 1998. *What We Owe to Each Other*. Cambridge, MA: Harvard University Press.

Suarez, Francisco. 1856–70. *Opera Omnia*, ed. C. Berton. Paris: Vives.

———. 1994. *On Efficient Causality: Metaphysical Disputations 17, 18 and 19*. New Haven, CT: Yale University Press.

Thomas Aquinas. 1961. *Summa contra gentiles*. Turin: Marietti.

———. 1950. *Summa theologiae*. Turin: Marietti.

Vasquez, Gabriel. 1611. *In primam secundae Sancti Thomae* I. Ingolstadt, Germany.

CHAPTER 27

....

MORAL INTENTION

....

IAN WILKS

WHAT sort of intention should inform properly virtuous action? Are we to be judged on the basis of both action and intention, or only on the basis of the latter? Ancient sources are not silent on the role reasoning and decision play in the process of enacting a virtue. But medieval philosophers seem to have, from the outset, motive for giving these matters much closer attention.

Two figures of that era achieve centrality in the history of this matter: Peter Abelard and William of Ockham, who alike adopt the strong position of claiming that only moral intention, not ensuing action, is a suitable basis for moral judgement. This shared thesis is pivotal in their respective moral theories and produces between them what deserves to be considered a fairly distinctive strand of moral theory within the larger setting of medieval thought. When centuries later Immanuel Kant famously claims that 'a good will is not good because of what it effects or accomplishes, because of its fitness to attain some proposed end, but only because of its volition' (Kant 1996, 50), he is revisiting this kind of Abelardian and Ockhamist outlook. This outlook seems to belong neither to virtue theory nor natural law theory—the two staples of medieval moral speculation—and, in a Kantian setting, is not necessarily associated with either. It will be the business of this chapter to consider the early evidence of this strand of moral theory in the writings of St Augustine and St Anselm, and then to observe it as it achieves full expression in the writings of Abelard and Ockham.[1]

1. TWO PRECURSORS

....

In an extended passage from Augustine's polemical tract *Against Julian* (*Contra Julianum*), we find a good example of how the problem of moral intention can be posed as a general challenge to classical moral theory.[2] If the pagan understanding of virtue were fully adequate, it would make pagans just as able to excel morally as Christians. This cannot be because there must be some element specifically added by the Christian outlook that allows greater achievement of virtue to adherents of the faith. That element, suggests Augustine, is emphasis on the character of moral intention.

Pagan understanding, he believes, construes virtues and vices too much in terms of the actions to which they give rise, and not enough in terms of underlying motivation. The problem with this is that virtues and vices can start to blend into each other if referenced only to behaviour. After all, the sort of thing one does in displaying constancy is often very like the sort of thing one does in displaying stubbornness. The same holds for prudence and cunning, which call upon the same abilities of the mind. What is the real difference between virtue and vice? It seems to lie in the motive underlying behaviour. The avaricious may well enact the cardinal virtues out of avarice, showing courage in submitting to many challenging pursuits, temperance in refraining from expensive pleasures, prudence in accumulating wealth, and justice by not committing theft (thereby avoiding reprisals). However, each such case of seeming virtue is in fact a vice, and what makes it so is the kind of motive at work (Augustine 1998, 391; 1865, 747).

Now, as Augustine acknowledges, the pagan tradition does not wholly overlook these points. He approvingly cites Cicero's suggestion that virtues operate under the constraint of reason—'Virtue is a habit of the mind suitable to the limit of nature and to reason' (Augustine 1998, 391; 1865, 747)[3]—and hence are not merely to be understood in terms of external behaviour. So have some pagans achieved the correct understanding of virtue after all? Not so, claims Augustine. What they lack is insight into the very nature and reason cited in the definition: 'They spoke the truth, but they did not know what was suitable for setting free and making happy the nature of moral beings' (ibid.). Our nature seeks freedom and happiness, which have been revealed by Christian teaching to be attained in fullest form in eternal life with God. In his critique of pagan morality, Augustine has in mind a specific non-God-oriented purpose in the enactment of supposed virtue: personal glorification through attainment of excellence. The motive at work in striving to be virtuous may simply be, at core, just an exercise in pride. Helping a person in danger is good, 'but those who do this do not do this good deed in a good way, if they act more out of love for human glory than the glory of God' (Augustine 1998, 393; 1865, 749). Pagan morality is a product of loving oneself. Morality in the truest sense is a product of loving God. When the behaviour associated with the seeming virtue is a product of self-love then the semblance deceives; the seeming virtue is real only when that behaviour is a product of loving God.

The character of the motivation underlying action emerges as paramount in moral evaluation. In particular it is the character of the will that is decisive. Many of the 'things which are seen to receive praise from human beings' fail to arise from a good will and therefore do not deserve a reputation as 'true virtues, as good works, and as done without any sin' (Augustine 1998, 400; 1865, 755). A good will—marked by purposes that tend towards God and away from the self—is the locus of moral achievement, not the acts that arise from it.

In general we can say that the need to distinguish Christian from pagan morality creates a focus on the interior properties of moral life and directs attention to the role an account of moral intention must play in a Christianised theory of virtues. Augustine cannot be said to have achieved a systematic account of this sort himself, but he leaves to posterity, in this and other writings, a compelling expression of the utility of such an account.[4]

From its outset the medieval tradition is receptive to this concern, even when the problem of distinguishing Christian from pagan virtue loses some of its urgency with the cultural ascendency of Christianity. We find a manifestation of this in the moral theory of St Anselm, who is both representative of his era and a lasting influence on his successors. His moral theory emerges indirectly in *On Truth* (*De veritate*), a by-product of his discussion of truth; the account of truth developed here is given an ethical aspect, which, at least to a modern reader, appears at the outset quite foreign.

The starting point is the familiar claim that the truth of a statement is its correspondence to what it represents; when it 'signifies that what is is, then truth is in it and it is true' (Anselm 1998b, 153). Anselm gives two quick transitional characterisations of what is involved in being a true statement: such a statement, he says, does what it 'ought to do', what it 'should' do (Anselm 1998b, 153). A true statement achieves the purpose set for statements and on this basis is described as having *rectitudo*. This word admits various translations but here means 'rightness'—a word that in English likewise carries the dual suggestion of being true, and also, in some deeper sense, even an ethical sense, being appropriate.[5] A statement when true achieves rightness in the deeper sense of doing what is appropriate for a statement— doing what it is supposed to do.

Importing the idea of purpose into an account of truth may seem odd, but it is not too remote from some of our own idiomatic usage. If we describe someone as 'a true friend', we suggest full realisation of the qualities of friendship. We sometimes describe things as true to type, where the phrase 'true to' suggests proximity to a standard or norm. Statements can be true *of* whatever they signify, but they can also be true *to* their nature as statements by signifying that what is is. That is the sense in which their truth is a state of rightness. Indeed, anything can be described as being true in this way and achieve rightness because of that truth because anything can be true to its own nature. Anselm accordingly speaks of the truth of an action (1998b, 156; 1968b, 181), the truth of the senses (1998b, 158; 1968b, 183) and the truth of the essence of things (1998b, 160; 1968b, 185). Of fire, for example, we can say that 'when it heats, it does what it ought' and therefore 'exhibits truth and rightness' (1998b, 157; 1968b, 182). On this account truth is a pervasive concept, which reaches into all aspects of being and is not limited to service as a specialised category of statements. The same ubiquity applies to rightness.

The question is whether it also applies to a third concept that appears for discussion: justice. It is easy to think of justice and rightness as being very alike, if not the same. So can justice be included in this sweeping alignment of rightness and truth? If so, then we could appropriately say that it 'seems right and just that fire should be hot' just as we can say that it seems right and just that 'each man should love those who love him' (Anselm 1998b, 166; 1968b, 191–92). But in Anselm's view, we cannot say this, at least not on the normal understanding of justice. Justice is not simply a matter of developing the nature that is intrinsic to us, as is the case with rightness and truth. Considerations of process intrude; what matters is also the *way* in which that nature is realised.

Justice is the province of those with rational natures, those who are capable of understanding what rightness is (Anselm 1998b, 167; 1968b, 192). But it is not just a matter of understanding rightly. It is also not just a matter of acting rightly, because the internal process leading up to the action is all important. Justice is a matter of willing rightly, Anselm says (1998b, 167; 1968b, 193). The question is then what constitutes right willing, and the answer fastens on the reason or purpose to which the will is directed in making its determination. Like anything else, a will can achieve rightness, can be true to type. It does this when it wills as it ought. But someone who has this rightness of will, whose will wills as it ought, needs something extra in order to manifest justice in that act of will. What is needed is a specific motive for such willing. And the motive is this: rightness of will must be aimed for as an end in itself. If it is coerced or induced by material advantage, there may still be rightness of will—the will may still be operating true to type—but the person exercising this will is not demonstrating justice. These are the insights that yield up the key definition: 'Justice is rightness of will preserved for its own sake' (1998b, 169; 1968b, 194).

So the virtue of justice is achieved by someone whose will does not merely will as it ought but wills as it ought *because* it ought. 'What it ought' is not further specified in Anselm's discussion here; presumably the will is willing as it ought when it is willing in accordance with moral law. We are given some examples of this: willing to bar entry to a murderer, willing to return stolen goods and willing to feed the hungry (Anselm 1998b, 168; 1968b, 193). All of these acts of willing involve the will's being true to type and achieving rightness—in other words, being the sort of thing that a human will is by nature supposed to be. But to achieve justice requires another step. Feeding the hungry is doing what one ought. Willing to feed the hungry is willing what one ought—but this is still not justice. Justice in this case is willing to feed the hungry *because that is what one ought to will*. In other words, it is cultivating a good will *for its own sake*.

The virtue of being just is presented here as being chiefly a matter of how one wills, not how one acts. Indeed, the willed action need not even be forthcoming; there can be rightness of will 'even if it is impossible that what we rightly will come about' (Anselm 1998b, 169; 1968b, 194). The will must be motivated by a very specific reason—the motivation to will as one ought to will—and as with Augustine it is the achievement of this reasoned act of will that underlies the virtue.[6] The emphasis on willing rightly, the identification of a certain kind of reason as a formal property of right-willing, the detachment of this right-willing from considerations of outcome—all of these features of Anselm's analysis represent a decided move towards the completely intention-based moral theories to be found in Abelard and Ockham. Witness this comment from his *Virgin Conception and Original Sin* (*De conceptu virginali et de originali peccato*):

> My argument that an action is called unjust not in itself, but rather through an unjust will, is clearly demonstrated by those things that on occasion are done not entirely without justice, such as killing a man, as Phineas did [Numbers 25:6–12]; or sexual intercourse between married couples or between animals. (Anselm 1998c, 363; 1968c, 144)

Taken by itself this passage seems to express the uncompromising emphasis on moral intention, supported by provocative examples, which is the hallmark of Abelard's approach. Having said that, it must be admitted this appearance is clouded somewhat by lines that immediately ensue: 'However, it is less obvious in things which can never be done without injustice, such as perjury, and other actions which perhaps we will not name here' (Anselm 1998c, 363; 1968c, 144). Some actions will always be accompanied by bad intention, so in effect they will always occasion sin in the agent. Even though it is the will that is actually sinful, one can still claim that the action cannot be performed without sin. Anselm seems in this way willing to blunt the edge of his position. But not so Abelard, who shows no hesitancy in taking it to its logical extreme.

2. ABELARD AND THE DEBATE OVER MORAL INTENTION

In the historical situation immediately prior to Abelard, the emphasis on moral intention as the key element of moral assessment continues. Texts from the schools of William of Champeaux and Anselm of Laon suggest an essentially theological interest in this view as a means of emphasising that evil is entirely the product of a will capable of forming intention, and by implication not a product of the creative activities of God (Lottin 1942–60, V.221, 302). But there seems to be no protracted investigation of the full ethical implications of this doctrine until Abelard's *Ethics* (*Ethica*), a work noteworthy in medieval culture for being a very early attempt at providing a systematic treatise of moral theory.

In this treatise the emphasis on moral intention is paramount. Abelard takes its role in constituting sin as given and considers whether any other aspect of the agent plays a similar role. Are vices, desires, pleasures or actions relevant to sin? He provides a series of non-concomitance arguments to answer 'no' in each case: any vice can be present without sin, any desire for what is sinful can be present without sin, any pleasure associated with sin can be present without sin and any action condemned as sinful can take place without sin. Only moral intention is relevant; when it is informed by scorn (*contemptus*) for God it is never present without sin. Abelard uses the term 'intention' (*intentio*) as opposed to 'will' (*voluntas*), deploying that latter term to denote an agent's prevailing desire (Mann 2004, 284).[7] The whole basis of moral assessment, he accordingly argues, is to be regarded as lying in the quality of the intention and consent (*consensus*) to be found in the agent.[8] It is scorn that is chiefly objectionable to God, just as its opposite, obedience, is chiefly acceptable (Abelard, 1971, 129).

How can vice be present without sin? Even though one is disposed to sin by the vice, one can still operate contrary to disposition by not sinning. In fact, doing so represents an elevated achievement of not sinning because 'victory is so much more brilliant for being more difficult' (Abelard 1971, 5). Consenting in such a way as to maintain an attitude of obedience to God, not scorn, is given a certain authenticity by unfolding in adverse circumstances where reasoned considerations must hold their own against vice. So the presence of vice is clearly consistent with the absence of sin, and this, Abelard suggests, shows that vice is simply not the same thing as sin.

Neither, and for the same reason, is will (in other words, desire). The presence of bad will is consistent with the absence of sin—and indeed, like vice, provides the 'material for a struggle' (Abelard 1971, 7). It can therefore represent an elevated moral achievement. The non-concomitance argument works the other way around, too; the absence of bad will is consistent with the presence of sin. Abelard uses the example of a servant killing a murderous master in self-defence. The servant has consented to this disruption of social order and therefore committed a sin (as Abelard understands the situation) but is presented as doing this unwillingly. There is no bad will, but sin is present, nonetheless. So for both reasons, we can say that will (desire) is not the same thing as sin.[9]

This is the form the argument takes about actions. The presence of bad action is consistent with the absence of sin, and the presence of sin is consistent with the absence of the bad action. These two points are presented thus:

> Moreover, I think everyone knows how often things that should not be done are done without sin, when, that is, they are committed under coercion or through ignorance, as for example if a woman is forced to lie with another woman's husband or if a man who has been tricked in some way or other sleeps with a woman whom he thought to be his wife or kills in error a man whom he believed he, as a judge, should kill. . . . What the Lord said has similarly to be understood: 'Whosoever shall look on a woman to lust after her,' that is, whosoever shall look in such a way as to fall into consent to lust, 'hath already committed adultery in his heart' [Matthew 5:28], although he had not committed the deed of adultery, that is, he is already guilty of sin although he is still without its outcome. (Abelard 1971, 25)

This first part of this passage claims that an act of adultery can be present without the sin (as can an act of killing) when performed unconsentingly, through coercion or ignorance. The second part claims that the sin of adultery can be present without the act, when a de facto consent is formed but not enacted. So a bad act is not the same thing as sin.

Vice and bad desire/will may actually enhance the moral quality of consents, but not bad actions. Actions are without exception morally neutral—even good actions, such as charitable giving. Someone might form the intention to give and yet be robbed, removing any opportunity to carry the intention through. Such a person is not to be viewed as less worthy in this regard than another who forms the same intention but is actually able to carry it out. Bad actions do not increase the sin, and good actions do not increase the worthiness. Abelard compares this neutrality of moral value in actions to the neutrality of truth value in a statement like 'Socrates is sitting'; the statement varies in truth and falsity depending on whether Socrates is actually sitting or not (Abelard 1971, 53). An action likewise varies in moral value depending on the quality of the accompanying intention and is labelled 'good' or 'bad' only derivatively from that intention (Abelard 1971, 47). The essentials of moral life are wholly internal to the experience of the agent.

Abelard's advocacy of this view carries forward, and indeed completes, the trend of emphasising moral intention seen in earlier figures. This advocacy goes hand in hand with his acceptance of a rigorous distinction between body and soul. The separation of the two is such that a bodily defect cannot be taken by extension to constitute a defect of the soul. He claims that 'nothing pollutes the soul except what is of the soul' (Abelard 1971, 23), and in the same vein argues that the control we exercise is over our consents, not our actions, so it is the consents that should be judged, for 'what is less within our power is less worthy of being commanded' (Abelard 1971, 23, 25). The goodness achievable in the operation of the soul is distinct from that achievable by physical action, and whatever sort of goodness is involved in the latter adds nothing to the former. The two are incommensurable, and 'the name "good" does not keep the same meaning' (Abelard 1971, 53). At a metaphysical level that shows why the action is irrelevant to moral worth.[10]

Consenting to something happens when 'we in no way draw back from its accomplishment and are inwardly ready, if given the chance, to do it' (Abelard 1971, 15). Since the chance need not arise, the physical act has only a counterfactual status in reckoning sin; it is only relevant as something that would happen, given the consent, should conditions permit. This detachment of moral acts from physical happenings has seemed to many to imply a problem. If acts do not matter, only consents, then how do we tell what an acceptable consent is? Exterior acts generally have pretty discernible properties by which they can be described, and by which morally appropriate ones can be distinguished from morally inappropriate ones. Are there similarly discernible properties by which such distinctions can be made in the domain of consents? One can imagine a theory in which the onus is on moral agents to consent only to what they *believe* should be consented to, with no further provision for the objective truth or falsity of those beliefs. Such a theory would indeed be subjectivist in nature. And some have taxed Abelard with exactly that kind of approach.[11]

But the charge is false. The Decalogue and other moral precepts still hold, on his view; they must simply be reconceptualised to transfer moral status from exterior act to consent:

> Behold, the Lord says: 'Thou shall not kill,' 'Thou shall not bear false witness.' If, following the sound of the words, we take these to refer only to the deed, guilt is by no means forbidden nor is fault thereby, but the action of a fault is prohibited.

> Truly, it is not a sin to kill a man nor to lie with another's wife; these sometimes
> can be committed without sin. If a prohibition of this kind is understood,
> according to the sound of the words, to refer to the deed, he who wants to bear
> false witness or even consents to speaking it, as long as he does not speak it,
> whatever the reason for his silence, does not become guilty according to the Law.
> For it was not said that we should not want to bear false witness or that we should
> not consent to speaking it. (Abelard 1971, 27)[12]

A non-literal interpretation of scripture is advocated here, one that takes the simple step of glossing references to actions as references to consents. The Decalogue is not telling us what not to do. It is telling us what not to consent to do. Note that the consent is still specified by its object, by what is consented to, by the physical act cited in the precept. Bad consents (sins) are consents to acts prohibited by edict of God—just as bad desires are desires for such acts, bad pleasures are pleasures taken in such acts, and morally relevant bad dispositions of mind (vices) are dispositions for such acts. There is no radical departure here from usual moral intuitions, just an initiative to understand their moral content in a very specific way.

Christians need only execute this simple step of translation to achieve moral clarity. But what about non-Christians, who do not have access to the Decalogue and other scripture-based precepts? For them there is a more general recourse: insight into what is morally appropriate through innate grasp of natural law. 'Natural law', says Abelard, 'is what the reason naturally innate in all people urges should be put into effect, and therefore remains the same among all people' (Abelard 2001, 145). As examples of this law, he cites injunctions to worship God, to love one's parents and to punish the wicked, examples that suggest that essential content of Christian teaching is available to Christian and non-Christian alike. So the latter may simply take the content of this and, as above, reconceptualise it as a morality of intention and consent. The result will be a coherent expression of morals.

The distinction of Christian and pagan moral outlooks is not erased by this. A key difference is preserved in Abelard's account of the virtues of charity and justice. From a pagan perspective, as Abelard recounts it, justice is the most important virtue of all. It is not just one of the four cardinals—the others being prudence, temperance and courage—but in fact the chief of those four. He actually regards prudence as serving the epistemic basis for virtues—'the mother or origin of the virtues' (Abelard 2001, 131)—rather than being one itself properly speaking. That leaves three cardinals, of which courage and temperance operate in subordinate roles as shielding the virtue of justice from the destructive effects of desire and fear, respectively (Abelard 2001, 135). That then leaves justice standing alone as the centrepiece of pagan virtue, and Abelard defines it as 'the virtue that bestows on everyone his due while preserving the common benefit' (Abelard 2001, 135). Justice is altruistic in character, but it involves an altruism detached from any reference to God. By contrast, when Abelard describes charity—following in the Augustinian tradition—it differs from justice in having this reference to God built into its very operation. As such it is the centrepiece of Christian virtue: 'If virtue is understood in its proper sense, as that which obtains merit from God, charity alone should be called virtue.

On account of the fact that it makes people just, brave and temperate, it is rightly called "justice", "courage" and "temperance" ' (Abelard 2001, 119). Elsewhere Abelard characterises charity as 'right love, which is directed towards that to which it ought to be: love of God for his own sake or of one's neighbour for the sake of God' (Marenbon 1997, 288).[13] What does this tell us about the difference between justice and charity? The justice of giving everyone their due while preserving the common benefit does not seem as if it would be, in effect, that far removed from the charity of loving God and one's neighbour for the sake of God. But, of course, the character of the underlying motivation differs by being referenced to God in the case of charity but not so (or at least not necessarily so) in the case of justice. In any theory that reduces everything to moral intention, of course, a difference of underlying motivation makes all the difference in the world.

This viewpoint is of a piece with the Augustinian emphasis on love of God. It is, more generally, a reflection of Anselm's emphasis on not just the content of one's willing but having the right reason for willing. Abelard inherits a practice of understanding the special moral achievement open to the Christian believer in terms of the internal process in which moral events unfold. But with Abelard that understanding becomes controversial in its exclusive appeal to internal process. Here we finally have a full-fledged ethics of moral intention. But because of its controversial nature, there now appears in medieval thought a recognizable *problem* of moral intention.

This problem is definitely recognised as such by Abelard's contemporaries. Among the heresies charged against him in the Council of Sens (1140), we find his ethical views presented in broadest outline; only the identity of sin with consent and contempt for God, and its distinction from desire, are cited (Abelard 1969b, 480). While the brief summary supplied in this source is not a measured attempt to encapsulate his doctrine, it bears witness at least to the element of controversy present therein. This controversy casts a long shadow. What with the condemnation of Abelard's view and the general neglect of early-twelfth-century philosophical writings in the rush to incorporate newly-uncovered Greek and Islamic texts into the canon, one might expect the aftereffect of Abelard's moral theory to be short lived. But, in fact, it manages to leave a rather important trace in a rather visible source: the *Sentences* of Peter Lombard.[14] This work is an extensive pastiche of philosophical viewpoints from contemporary and prior eras, seeing wide use as a training text in the philosophical curriculum. Abelardian claims about intention and act make an appearance in the second book:

> But it is asked whether all acts of men are good or bad from affective disposition (*affectus*) and end. . . . This seems to be the case to some, who say that all actions are indifferent, so that they are neither good nor evil in themselves, but that every action is good from a good intention and evil from an evil intention. According to them, any action can be good, if done with a good intention. (Lombard 2008, 199; 1971–81, I.2.557)

Against this Lombard endorses the safe opinion that bodily acts have some relevance to moral assessment; this safe opinion is widely adopted and is subject in the ensuing decades to various elaborations. In general the medieval tradition emphasises the importance of intention as a key facet of its Christian orientation, but it is leery of doing this in a way that entirely excludes the properties of the act itself as morally relevant. The thirteenth century yields many commentators on the problem of moral intention, but it does not appear to be until Ockham's work in the fourteenth that an intention-based theory is again as explicitly upheld as Abelard's.[15]

3. WILLIAM OF OCKHAM

'Does the exterior act have its own proper moral goodness and evilness?', asks Ockham in his *Quodlibetal questions* (*Quodlibeta septem*) (Ockham 1991, I.85; 1980, 100)—referring thus to physical behaviour, as distinct from the underlying interior act.[16] No, he says. The very same exterior act can be considered good on one occasion, evil on another. Given that it is the same act, there appears to be no basis for that variance within the act itself. So whence arises the variance? One can walk to church for the sake of worshipping God, or do the same for the sake of appearing pious to onlookers. The act appears good in the first case and evil in the second, and the difference seems pretty obviously to lie in that for the sake of which the act is done, in other words the intention (Ockham 1991, I.87; 1980, 101). So the act seems to inherit its moral quality from its relation to underlying intention. Does this relation actually make a real difference in the physical act itself? Not at all, answers Ockham—no more than when 'the will commands that a fire light a candle in a church' or 'commands a donkey to defecate in a church'; the fire and donkey may, indeed, with no impediment, carry out the command, but they inherit no interior moral quality in consequence of doing so (Ockham 1991, I.87–88; 1980, 102). It is the commanding will that bears the moral quality, not the thing operating as its instrument, whether it be the fire, the donkey—or the act.[17]

When the same exterior act is initiated by a good interior act, and then sustained by a bad interior act, we have a case where the changing moral quality evident in this registers no change in the exterior act itself, among whose physical properties none is gained or lost. So the moral quality, Ockham argues, can only be imputed to the underlying interior act (Ockham 1991, I.88; 1980, 102). Imagine a person who voluntarily chooses suicide by jumping off a cliff. But on descent his convictions suddenly change, and he finds himself regretful of the act and would reverse it if he could. Obviously he cannot, and the descent continues. From that point in the descent to its finish, the 'act of willing against the fall is virtuous and meritorious' (Ockham 1991, I.88; 1980, 103); but if the act of falling was itself at the outset vicious, and none of its defining physical properties change, then it must continue to be so throughout. So we would have a vicious exterior act and a virtuous interior act, 'and the man would be vicious and virtuous at the same time' (ibid.). This thought experiment suggests to Ockham that, since the same moral status cannot always be unambiguously attributed to both interior and exterior acts, it should be considered applicable only to the interior. In general these arguments all play the same role for Ockham as non-concomitance arguments play for Abelard, leading him likewise to espouse an intention-based moral theory.

The next question is whether Ockham's version of this can answer a charge of subjectivism. Is there a constraint in place on what counts as a good action? As noted, Abelard has a response to this worry. But does Ockham have one, too, if likewise challenged? In fact, it is easy enough to find materials for such a defence. First among these would be his conception of moral science as containing two kinds of universal propositions: those that are known on the basis of 'self-evident propositions' (Ockham 1997, 75), and those that are derived as empirical generalisations, and that 'we can only know evidently in virtue of experience' (ibid.). From these generalities, attained both conceptually and empirically, are derived further propositions, particular in nature, having bearing on this or that individual action. So moral science gives us a self-evident generality like 'Everyone who acts generously should be treated generously', and then, in application to a particular situation where someone acts generously, derives a claim like 'This man should be treated generously' (ibid.).

This notion of moral science is then subject to refinements that make it a sturdy ground for moral life. If it is only acts of willing that carry moral worth, not exterior acts, we need to know what the sort of willing is that carries positive moral worth. There is, says Ockham, 'an act so virtuous that it cannot be rendered vicious; willing to do something because it is divinely commanded is such an act' (Ockham, 1997, 71). Willing something because it is divinely commanded—because it *is* divinely commanded, not just because it is *thought* to be so—will not vary in moral quality from one occurrence to the next. Regardless of circumstances, such an act of will can only be virtuous (that is, can only be the sort of act that instils a virtue or flows from one). Now the act as so described—'willing to do something because it is divinely commanded'—can undergo many specifications, depending on how 'to do something' is understood. It can, for example, be an act of willing to go to church. Going to church is, like any physical act, morally neutral. But when construed as a specifying part of this more complex act—willing to go to church because it is divinely commanded—we can say with confidence that that larger act it is part of is, taken as a whole, a virtuous one. A range of physical and mental acts, construed as likewise substituted, yield the same result: they become a specifying part of the more complex act of willing to do them because it is divinely commanded. Morally indifferent themselves, they become, in that context, part of a more complex act that is necessarily virtuous. As Ockham puts it, they are 'contingently virtuous' (Ockham, 1997, 69) and could never become 'determinately virtuous' if they could only exist in association with other contingently virtuous acts. It takes association with a necessarily virtuous act to bring them to the point of being determinately virtuous, and the act of willing to do something because it is divinely commanded is precisely that necessarily virtuous one. As such it plays the pivotal role in moral life.

Moral science will have at its core principles that express the sorts of acts we should will to do because of divine command. These principles constitute objective reference points for interior acts, as natural law does on Abelard's account—and so we see how Ockham and Abelard alike furnish a response for the worry about moral subjectivism. On the other hand, Ockham's interpretation of the Decalogue (and by implication, other moral precepts) differs somewhat from Abelard's. On Ockham's view, all of the commandments cite interior acts, but some additionally cite the corresponding exterior acts as well. So (to supply an example—which he does not do) the edict against adultery is to be taken as proscribing both the act and intention, while the one against coveting proscribes only the intention. The act and intention in combination constitute a different sin than the intention alone, Ockham argues, but only in the sense that the act 'intensifies' (Ockham 1991, I.89; 1980, 104) the intention. The addition of the act, in other words, makes the intention more pronounced and therefore makes a difference—but the difference so made is not one that implies a special moral status for the act itself. But immediately on the heels of this response, Ockham suggests another: some precepts apply to the acts as well as the intention 'in order that an occasion for erring not be given to simple people, who believe that there is no sin except in the exterior act' (Ockham 1991, I.90; 1980, 105).

Ockham also operates in parallel with Abelard by accounting for the highest achievement of moral intention in terms of the operation of the virtues. While Abelard does this in his discussion of charity and justice, Ockham's approach is to distinguish five different degrees of virtue according to the quality of motivation at work. The first, and lowest, degree involves motivation that looks only to the character of the act itself and its result; one acts 'in conformity with right reason, as it dictates that such acts should be performed, according to the proper circumstances respecting precisely this work, on account of the worthiness of this work itself as an end' (Ockham, 1997, 81). The second degree maintains this sort of motivation except with heightened resolve, such that no obstacle deters it from acting, even one as severe as the threat of death (Ockham, 1997, 83). So far the virtuous conduct achieved in these degrees is consistent with an over-arching goal of attaining happiness, in this life or the next. But when the third degree of virtue is achieved, happiness is ruled out as such a goal. This degree repeats the requirements of the first but adds that the act be willed 'precisely and solely because it is dictated by right reason' (Ockham, 1997, 83). In that case the pursuit of happiness cannot be the over-arching goal, since what is dictated by right reason is pursued as an end valuable in itself. The fourth degree of virtue builds on the third. Those who achieve it will an act because it is dictated by right reason and do this 'precisely on account of love of God' (Ockham, 1997, 83). At this point the willing corresponds to the necessarily virtuous act described above and proceeds perfectly in accordance with moral science. A personal agenda of happiness is out of the picture; the agenda that replaces it is one of following the dictates of reason by way of loving God. The fifth degree makes the kind of addition seen in the second, by maintaining this sort of motivation in the most adverse possible circumstances. The heroic soul that achieves this fifth degree sacrifices all, but for right reason on account of love of God, not for a personal agenda of being happy. This characterisation seems to play the same kind of role in Ockham's moral theory that Abelard's discussion of the virtue of charity plays in his—and has the additional merit, less evident in Abelard's presentation, of emphasising how steep the moral challenge is of realising in full the highest achievement of moral intention.[18]

4. Concluding Remarks

The above conspectus of medieval views on the role of moral intention is intended to throw into relief an issue that recurs throughout this era: how far to weight the motives behind actions in rendering moral judgement. How far do the actions themselves matter? It is presumed by all parties that motives are to be weighted heavily. The point of difference is whether they should be weighted exclusively. The perceived radicals in this discussion—Abelard, Ockham—argue for exclusivity. There is a certain irony in their status as radicals: what they are doing is upholding an element of moral theory that is from the outset a characteristic preoccupation of Christian moral theorists, and yet proceeding with an uncompromising emphasis that puts them at odds with many of those same theorists. They are doing too much of what their own tradition regards as a good thing, so what they are doing is seen by some as a bad thing.

The problem of moral intention is but one of a constellation of debating topics around which medieval moral theory organises itself. Nonetheless, the outlook that it furnishes has a special place in the wider history of moral theory, and a reach well beyond the medieval setting in which it appears. Alisdair MacIntyre has broadly characterised this outlook as 'the interiorization of the moral life with its stress on will and law', explaining the idea of interiorisation thus: 'Everything turns on the character of the interior act of the will. Character therefore, the arena of the virtues and the vices, simply becomes one more circumstance, external to will. The true arena of morality is that of the will and of the will alone' (MacIntyre 1984, 168). The great historical embodiment of this outlook is, of course, Immanual Kant, in whose 'writings . . . we have reached a point at which the notion that morality is anything other than obedience to rules has almost, if not quite, disappeared from sight' (MacIntryre 1984, 236). This Kantian focus on the will, the law, and the will's adherence to the law is an outcome already pointed to in various degrees by the medieval figures considered above. Among these figures we find emphasis on the activity of a free will in moral choice; the pursuit of a good will as the objective of this activity; adherence to moral law as the form to be taken in the pursuit; and, in consequence, the merely derivative worth of actions on this moral accounting. These themes of Kantian moral theory clearly have a prior life in medieval sources. Of course, in this early context, the outlook is intertwined with virtue theory, and that may help obscure the fact that what emerges here is a strand of moral theory fairly distinct in its own right. Medieval moral theory is dominated by questions about virtues and vices, but in this instance we see how such questions draw their investigators into areas well removed from the understood preserve of virtue theory itself.[19]

NOTES

1. Primary texts will be cited from published translations. Cross-references will be provided to the original Latin text, except in cases where the translation is accompanied by that text on facing pages: Abelard (1971), Abelard (2001) and Ockham (1997).

2. For discussion of this point, and its place in the wider context of Augustinian moral theory, see Kent (1995, 25–27), and Kent (2003, 232–34).

3. This definition is found in *De inventione* 2.53 (Cicero 1968, 327).

4. The historical influence of this account is one question. Whether it is entirely fair to pagan morality is another; for an attempt to address this latter issue (somewhat in favour of the pagan tradition), see Irwin (2007, 1:422–33).

5. I am following the suggestion of Katherin A. Rogers for translation of this term; see 2005, 251. For a different approach to rendering this term, see Williams and Visser (2001, 223, note 5) (pp. 222–25 of this article provide brief but useful commentary on *De veritate*. Also helpful for commentary is Rogers (2008, 63–66), and Brower (2004, 234–49)). Ralph McInerny uses 'rectitude' for *rectitudo*, so in citations where the word appears I have taken the liberty of altering that translation to read 'rightness'.

6. This Anselmian viewpoint, with its obvious Kantian overtones, is presented in Brower (2004) as a deontological theory. See Sønnesyn (2008) for debate over the application of the label 'deontological'.

7. Abelard's understanding of *voluntas* is complex and shifts from earlier works to later. For an account of this change, and the resulting relationship between *voluntas* and *consensus*, see Marenbon (1997, 258–64).

8. It is generally assumed that *intentio* and *consensus* denote essentially the same element of Abelard's moral theory. For a dissenting view on this, see Cameron (2007, 335–36, especially note 49). See also King (1995, 214, note 4). This exegetical problem has no implications for the theme I am pursuing in this study, so I will employ the terms 'intention' and 'consensus' without concern to distinguish them.

9. Abelard (1971, 19) addresses the point about pleasure chiefly with the examples of marital sex and the pleasing flavours present in natural food items; these, he argues, provide cases where the presence of pleasure is consistent with the absence of sin.

10. As with Anselm, there are obvious Kantian overtones to this view. The best-known discussion of this likeness is found in King (1995).

11. McInerny (1992, 100–101), provides a good example of the disregard to which Abelard's moral theory has been subjected on this basis.

12. Note the close association of wanting with consenting in this passage. Abelard risks seeming to coalesce the two notions here, even though he argues forcefully for their distinctness in other places. This seems attributable more to loose presentation than doctrinal complexity. For the biblical reference, see Deuteronomy 5:17, 20.

13. This citation is Marenbon's rendering of a passage from an early version of the *Theologia scholarium* (Abelard 1969a, 405), which expresses a view echoed elsewhere in Abelard's writings (Marenbon 1997, 288, note 10; 299, note 15).

14. Hoffmann (2003, 77–80), provides a helpful account of Lombard's role in transitioning the debate over moral intention from Abelard to his successors.

15. The Thomistic approach to these questions—centred on the distinction between internal and external acts—is to be found in Aquinas *Summa theologiae* I–II, q. 18, aa.2–11, and *De malo* q. 2. For helpful discussion of these doctrines, see Gallagher (1990) (and Pilsner 2006, 76–91, for an account of the internal/external distinction). Hoffmann (2003) provides an account of the historical transition from Abelard through Lombard to Aquinas (and Scotus). The respective positions of Abelard and Aquinas are compared in Gallagher (1995) and, more polemically, in Sokolowski (1985, 208–14). Osborne (2007) provides a survey from mid-thirteenth-century figures to Ockham, with, in particular, coverage of approaches found in the Franciscan tradition prior to Scotus. The Scotistic approach must be understood against the background of his distinction between primary and secondary goodness—for which see Williams (2003, 335–42) and Ingham and Dreyer (2004, 180–85).

16. This is a key theme of Osborne (2007), especially 129–30. See also Holopainen (1991, 20–22).

17. On the moral neutrality of acts in Ockham, see King (1999, 229–31) and Freppert (1988, 40–42).

18. For a discussion of Ockham's arguments, which gives some account of the reactions of his own contemporaries, see Adams (1981, 10–30).

19. Many thanks to the participants of *The Oxford Handbook of Medieval Philosophy* Colloquium, Nov. 12–14, 2010, at the University of Toronto, for helpful comments on this chapter—especially Brad Inwood and John Marenbon.

BIBLIOGRAPHY

Abelard, see Peter Abelard.

Adams, Marilyn McCord and Rega Wood. 1981. Is to Will It as Bad as to Do It? *Franciscan Studies* 41:5–60.

Anselm. 1968a. *S. Anselmi opera omnia*, ed. F. S. Schmitt. 6 vols. Stuttgart-Bad Cannstatt, Germany: Friedrich Frommann Verlag.

——. 1968b. *De veritate*. In Anselm 1968a, I.173–99.

——. 1968c. *De conceptu virginali et de originali peccato*. In Anselm 1968a, II.137–73.

——. 1998a. *Anselm of Canterbury: The Major Works*, Brian Davies and G. R. Evans, trans. Oxford and New York: Oxford University Press.

——. 1998b. *On Truth*, trans. R. McInerny. In Anselm 1998a, I.153–74.

——. 1998c. *Virgin Conception and Original Sin*, trans. Camilla McNab. In Anselm 1998a, II.357–89.

Augustine. 1865. *Contra Julianum*. In *Patrologia latina* 44, ed. J. P. Migne, 641–874. Paris: Garnier.

——. 1998. 'Answer to Julian'. In *Answer to the Pelagians* 2, trans. Roland J. Teske, 221–536. *The Works of Saint Augustine* 24, ed. John E. Rotelle. Hyde Park, NY: New City Press.

Brower, Jeffrey E. 2004. 'Anselm on ethics'. In *The Cambridge Companion to Anselm*, ed. Brian Davies, 222–56. New York: Cambridge University Press.

Cameron, Margaret. 2007. Abelard (and Heloise?) on Intention. *American Catholic Philosophical Quarterly* 81:323–28.

Cicero. 1968. *De inventione. De optimo genere oratorum. Topica*, ed. E. H. Warmington, trans. H. M. Hubbell. Cambridge, MA, and London: Harvard University Press and William Heinemann.

Freppert, Lucan. 1988. *The Basis of Morality According to William Ockham*. Chicago: Franciscan Herald Press.

Gallagher, David. 1990. Aquinas on Moral Action: Interior and Exterior Act. *Proceedings of the American Catholic Philosophical Association* 64:118–29.

———. 1995. 'Will and deed in Abelard and Aquinas'. In *Moral and Political Philosophies in the Middle Ages*. Proceedings of the Ninth International Congress of Medieval Philosophy, Ottawa, Ontario, Canada, 17–22 August 1992, ed. B. Carlos Bazán, Eduardo Andújar and Léonard G. Sbrocchi, 676–86. New York, Ottawa and Toronto: Legas.

Hoffmann, Tobias. 2003. Moral Action as Human Action: End and Object in Aquinas in Comparison with Abelard, Lombard, Albert, and Duns Scotus. *The Thomist* 67:73–94.

Holopainen, Taina. 1991. *William Ockham's Theory of the Foundations of Ethics*. Helsinki: Luther-Agricola-Society.

Ingham, Mary Beth and Dreyer, Mechthild. 2004. *The Philosophical Vision of John Duns Scotus: An Introduction*. Washington, DC: The Catholic University of America Press.

Irwin, Terence. 2007. *The Development of Ethics: A Historical and Critical Study*. 2 vols. Oxford: Oxford University Press.

Kant, Immanuel. 1996. 'Groundwork of the metaphysics of morals', trans. and ed. Mary J. Gregor. In *Practical Philosophy*, ed. Allan Wood. Cambridge: Cambridge University Press.

Kent, Bonnie. 1995. *Virtues of the Will: The Transformation of Ethics in the Late Thirteenth Century*. Washington, DC: Catholic University of America Press.

———. 2003. 'The moral life'. In *The Cambridge Companion to Medieval Philosophy*, ed. A. S. McGrade, 231–53. Cambridge: Cambridge University Press.

King, Peter. 1995. Abelard's Intentionalist Ethics. *The Modern Schoolman* 72:213–31.

———. 1999. 'Ockham's ethical theory'. In *The Cambridge Companion to Ockham*, ed. Paul Vincent Spade, 227–44. Cambridge: Cambridge University Press.

Lombard, see Peter Lombard.

Lottin, Odon. 1942–60. *Psychologie et morale aux XIIe et XIIIe siècles*. 6 vols. Gembloux, Belgium: J. Duculot.

MacIntyre, Alasdair. 1984. *After Virtue*, 2nd ed. Notre Dame, IN: University of Notre Dame Press.

Mann, William E. 2004. 'Ethics'. In *The Cambridge Companion to Abelard*, ed. Jeffrey E. Brower and Kevin Guilfoy, 279–304. Cambridge: Cambridge University Press.

Marenbon, John. 1997. *The Philosophy of Peter Abelard*. Cambridge: Cambridge University Press.

McInerny, Ralph. 1992. *Aquinas on Human Action: A Theory of Practice*. Washington DC: Catholic University of America Press.

Ockham, see William of Ockham.

Osborne, Thomas M., Jr. 2007. The Separation of the Interior and Exterior Acts in Scotus and Ockham. *Medieval Studies* 69:111–39.

Peter Abelard. 1969–87. *Petri Abaelardi opera theologica*, ed. E. M. Buytaert and C. J. Mews. 3 vols. Turnhout, Belgium: Brepols (Corpus Christianorum continuatio mediaevalis 11–13).

———. 1969a. *Theologia scholarium, recensiones breviores*. In Abelard 1969–87, II.373–451.

———. 1969b. *Capitula haeresum Petri Abaelardi*. In Abelard 1969–87, II.453–80.

————. 1971. *Ethics*, trans. D. E. Luscombe. Oxford: Clarendon Press.

————. 2001. *Collationes*, trans. John Marenbon and Giovanni Orlandi. Oxford: Clarendon Press.

Peter Lombard, 1971–81. *Sententiae in IV libris distinctae.* 2 vols. Grottaferrata, Italy: Editiones Collegii S. Bonaventurae ad Claras Aquas.

————. 2008. *The Sentences. Book 2: On Creation*, trans. Giulio Silano. Toronto: Pontifical Institute of Mediaeval Studies.

Pilsner, Joseph. 2006. *The Specification of Human Actions in St Thomas Aquinas.* Oxford: Oxford University Press.

Rogers, Katherin A. 2005. Anselm on Eudaemonism and the Hierarchical Structure of Moral Choice. *Religious Studies* 41:249–68.

————. 2008. *Anselm on Freedom.* Oxford: Oxford University Press.

Sokolowski, Robert. 1985. *Moral Action: A Phenomenological Study.* Bloomington: Indiana University Press.

Sønnesyn, Sigbjørn Olsen. 2008. 'Ut sine fine amet summan essentiam': The Eudaemonist Ethics of St Anselm. *Medieval Studies* 70:1–28.

William of Ockham. 1967–86. *Opera theologica*, ed. Gedeon Gál et al., 10 vols. St Bonaventure, NY: Franciscan Institute Press.

————. 1980. *Quodlibeta septem* ed. J. Wey. In Ockham 1967–86, IX.

————. 1984. *De connexione virtutum*, ed. J. Wey. In Ockham 1967–86, VIII.323–407.

————. 1991. 'Quodlibetal questions', trans. Alfred J. Freddoso and Francis E. Kelley. 2 vols. New Haven and London: Yale University Press.

————. 1997. *On the connection of the virtues*, trans. Rega Wood. West Lafayette, IN: Purdue University Press.

Williams, Thomas. 2003. 'From metaethics to action theory'. In *The Cambridge Companion to Duns Scotus*, ed. Thomas Williams. Cambridge: Cambridge University Press.

Williams, Thomas and Sandra Visser. 2001. Anselm's Account of Freedom. *Canadian Journal of Philosophy* 31: 221–44.

CHAPTER 28

VIRTUE AND LAW

TERENCE IRWIN

1. VIRTUES OR LAWS?

Recent writers have commended Aristotle to the attention of contemporary moral philosophers on the ground that he is a virtue theorist. Some have advocated virtue ethics as a third way in moral theory that releases us from the unattractive choice between Kantian and utilitarian (or between deontological and consequentialist) theories.[1] Moral philosophers who welcome virtue ethics on this ground have drawn some of their inspiration from Aristotle. Their enthusiasm for him is intelligible; for he has quite a lot to say about the virtues, but he says very little that fits easily into a Kantian or a utilitarian framework. We may readily infer that he offers a non-Kantian and non-utilitarian account of morality that gives the central place to the virtues; and hence, we may regard him as a virtue theorist, or at least as an ancestor of virtue theory.

If we commend Aristotle as a virtue theorist, we may be inclined to commend some medieval moralists for the same reason. Like Aristotle, they discuss the virtues and take them to be central in a correct account of morality. To this extent, they seem to be virtue theorists, and we may suppose that they belong to the history of virtue ethics. We may even suppose that virtue ethics is somehow characteristic of pre-modern moral philosophy, and that the rejection of virtue ethics is a mark of a specifically modern (seventeenth century or later) tendency in moral philosophy.[2] One might regard Kant, or one of his modern predecessors, as the paradigmatic contrast with virtue ethics. This may be why Anscombe's thoroughly misguided paper 'Modern Moral Philosophy' has been a source of revived interest in virtue ethics.[3] If we place the medieval moralists in the tradition of virtue ethics, we might expect them to share the theoretical ambitions of virtue ethics and to be open to the objections that face this tradition.[4]

But medieval moralists also raise difficulties for critics who seek to place them in a tradition of virtue theory. For they also connect morality with the requirements of natural law. In this respect they seem to introduce claims that are unwelcome to many virtue theorists. If we introduce laws, we seem to introduce general rules and principles. If we think morality is basically determined by general rules, we seem to abandon the priority of virtue. A natural law theorist, therefore, does not seem to be an unqualified virtue theorist.[5]

If we are to make some progress beyond this expression of puzzlement about the relation between Aristotle and medieval virtue theorists—real or alleged—we need to be more careful about the terms of our comparisons and contrasts. If a virtue theorist is simply someone who recognises virtues, and a natural law theorist is someone who believes in natural law, historical examples make it obvious that someone can be both a virtue theorist and a natural law theorist. But if 'virtue theory' refers to something more specific than a belief in virtues, we need to look more closely at what a virtue theory might say, and why it might appear to conflict with a conception of morality as natural law.

2. VERSIONS OF VIRTUE THEORY

The moralists who commend virtue theory as a third way take virtue theory to claim more than that there are virtues of character.[6] They also believe that a virtue theory attributes a role to the virtues that they would not have if either deontological or consequentialist theories were true. Different possible roles mark different versions of a virtue theory.[7]

Virtue theory introduces a contrast between being and doing. Virtues, as Aristotle understands them, are traits of character, marking different sorts of persons, and hence different ways of being good or bad. If we treat virtue as the central element in morality, we treat morality as a way of being, rather than a set of things to be done. Certainly, a virtuous person sees reasons to act in appropriate ways, but the actions are appropriate because they belong to the virtues. Both deontological and consequentialist theories, by contrast, are theories of morality that define the rightness of right action. Since they take right action as their object of study, they assume that actions are fundamental in morality. These action-oriented theories offer general rule, principles, and laws that prescribe ways of doing rather than ways of being.

According to this division, a theory of natural law seems to offer an account of right action. Laws prescribe types of actions by prescribing the observance of general rules. If we take morality to consist in the observance of the natural law, we seem to agree with deontological and consequentialist views insofar as we take right action to be fundamental, and states of character to be at best secondary. Hence, a moralist who appears to be both a virtue theorist and a natural law theorist seems to give us conflicting answers to our question about whether being or doing is fundamental.

If we make being prior to doing, or make character prior to action, we might understand priority as an epistemological or as a metaphysical thesis.

We claim epistemological priority for virtue over action if we claim that we cannot know what actions are right except by reference to the judgement of the virtuous person. This judgement is guided not by general rules about right action, but by perception of what is right in particular cases. Even if we are unsure what the right general rule is, we may be confident about the right thing to do in particular cases. General rules are inductive generalisations from the perceptions of the virtuous person. This doctrine about knowledge of right action is sometimes called 'particularism'.[8]

We claim metaphysical priority for virtue if we maintain that actions are right insofar as they manifest a virtue and wrong insofar as they manifest a vice, whereas virtue and vice do not essentially involve right or wrong action.[9] We have a thesis about priority only if we can define virtue and vice apart from any tendency to action. 'Insofar as' indicates a claim about explanatory priority, and so it gives us a non-circular account of what the rightness and wrongness of action consists in.[10]

A stronger thesis about metaphysical priority affirms that the rightness of an action consists not simply in its being a manifestation of virtue, but in its being thought right by a virtuous person. This thesis goes beyond the claim about epistemological priority. The epistemological thesis is consistent with the objectivist view that the rightness of action is distinct from its being thought right by the virtuous person. According to the strong metaphysical thesis, the objectivist view is mistaken because rightness is not distinct from the virtuous person's judgement but is constituted by it.

This strong metaphysical thesis might be taken to give the fundamental ground for the explanatory thesis and the epistemological thesis. We might argue that these other two theses are true because the strong metaphysical thesis is true. The constitutive claim about rightness and the virtuous person's judgement explains why actions are right because they manifest virtue, and why we have to rely on the virtuous person's judgement; we have no other reliable rule to the recognition of right action because rightness consists in a relation to the virtuous person's judgement.

Since 'virtue theory' is a quasi-technical expression, but without any precise sense, it is a waste of our time to ask whether a real virtue theorist has to maintain all the theses we have mentioned, or only one of them, or some other thesis altogether. It is enough to observe that virtue theory is often taken to involve at least some of these theses. We may describe them as moderate and extreme versions of a virtue theory. They all imply that reference to the virtues is primary in the determination of rightness of actions, and that theorists who try to describe rightness of actions without reference to the virtues are mistaken.

If we choose to restrict the range of virtue theories in this way, we make it clear that a moralist who recognises virtues and takes them to be morally important does not thereby become a virtue theorist. One might well believe they are important without also believing that they provide a third way distinct from deontological and consequentialist accounts of right action. For present purposes, then, I propose to use 'virtue theory' and 'virtue theorist' to refer to the belief in a third way.

3. Is Aristotle a Virtue Theorist?

Though we are not at present concerned with Aristotle in his own right, it is useful to indicate briefly why virtue theorists might suppose that he is—explicitly or implicitly—one of them.

It is easy to show that Aristotle takes virtues to matter in ways that fall short of a virtue theory. In the *Nicomachean Ethics,* he does not simply assert that there are virtues, and that they are states of character that dispose us to right actions. In his view, virtues are not simply tendencies to right action, and their value is not wholly exhausted by the right actions they produce. The virtues are non-instrumental goods in their own right. Their value helps to explain the value of acting virtuously. While virtuous people and others can perform virtuous (just, temperate, etc.) actions, only the virtuous person can act virtuously, because acting virtuously requires the exercise of a virtuous character (1105a28–b9).

To show that Aristotle accepts the epistemological thesis of virtue theory, we may appeal to his assertion that general rules do not always allow us to identify virtuous actions in particular situations without the exercise of moral judgement. We can only find rules that are usually correct (1094b19, 1103b34, 1164b27). If we cannot give a general definition that will tell us what to do in particular situations, the discrimination depends on perception (1109b20, 1126a31). This is why the prudent person needs perception (1142a23). Such remarks may appear to commit Aristotle to particularism.[11]

He accepts the explanatory priority of virtue if he believes that the virtue of agents explains the rightness actions, and that the converse is false. Perhaps this is what he means by saying that actions are just (etc.) when they are such as the just person would do (1105b5). According to this explanatory claim, the relation of just actions to the virtue of justice explains their being just, and the converse does not hold. In that case Aristotle accepts a metaphysical thesis about the priority of virtue to action.

How strong a metaphysical thesis does he accept? We might argue that he accepts the strong metaphysical thesis we mentioned earlier, insofar as he asserts that things are good if they seem good to a virtuous person, and the virtuous person is the measure of good and bad (1176a15; 1113a29). Perhaps he means that the judgement of the prudent person constitutes, and does not detect, the rightness of an action. There is nothing more to being right than being judged right by the prudent person.[12]

If Aristotle accepts all these claims, he asserts a strong version of a virtue theory. He is an extreme virtue theorist since he holds that an attempt to find a general account of right actions apart from the judgement of the virtuous person is misguided. Since Aristotle is not my primary concern in this essay, I will not discuss the case for attributing all these views to him, but I will simply take them to give the content of an Aristotelian virtue theory. I do not mean to assert the historical accuracy of the label 'Aristotelian'.[13]

This short description of an Aristotelian virtue theory may give us some idea of what to look for when we turn to medieval Aristotelians, and especially to Aquinas. They will be Aristotelian virtue theorists to the extent that they take virtue to be prior, in one or another of these different ways, to principles of right action. Since Aquinas takes over and expounds Aristotle's description of the virtues of character, we might expect that he will also take over Aristotelian virtue theory.

4. IS AQUINAS A VIRTUE THEORIST?

If, however, medieval moralists are virtue theorists, we may wonder how they can also be natural law theorists. For natural law theory seems to commit them to the recognition of general principles that give specific directions for action, quite apart from the judgement of the virtuous person. Contrary to the epistemological claim of virtue theory, natural law seems to present principles that are not mere generalisations from the judgement of virtuous people. Contrary to the explanatory claim, natural law seems to make the rightness of actions prior to, or at any rate not posterior to, the goodness of persons. Contrary to the strong metaphysical claim, natural law seems to make actions right independently of how things appear to the virtuous person.

This apparent conflict between natural law theory and virtue theory is even clearer in the case of moralists who take natural law to include the Ten Commandments, or a similar body of precepts about right and wrong action. Such a conception of natural law seems to incorporate the legal outlook of the Hebrew Scriptures in an account of morality.

We can now suggest a range of options for the interpretation and evaluation of the views of a moralist who discusses both the virtues and the natural law:

1. He takes both virtue and natural law to be fundamental; hence, he tries to be both a virtue theorist and a natural law theorist. But since he gives two incompatible accounts of what is fundamental in morality, he cannot consistently hold both views.
2. He takes one of these elements in morality to be fundamental, and the other to be subordinate, so that he is really a law theorist or a virtue theorist.
3. He takes neither element to be more fundamental than the other, but he takes them to provide answers to different and logically independent questions.
4. He takes them to support each other. Neither element is more fundamental than the other, but the account of natural law makes the account of virtue more credible, and the converse is also true.

To decide among these options, we would need to consider each medieval philosopher separately. Different views about the character and status of natural law, and of its relation to the will of God, may lead to different answers to the questions we have raised.[14] In the rest of my discussion, I will stick to Aquinas. His discussions of the virtues and of natural law are full enough to allow us to answer our questions. Moreover, his account of the virtues is close enough to Aristotle's to allow us a clear view of the relation between an Aristotelian theory of the virtues and a doctrine of natural law. What does an account of natural law add to an account of the virtues?[15] Does it add anything that Aristotle or an Aristotelian ought to welcome?

5. Is Virtue Prior to Law?

A reason to suppose that virtue is prior to law is the simple fact that in the *Summa Theologiae* Aquinas introduces his discussion of the virtues, sins and vices before he introduces law. We might infer that he takes the understanding of virtue to be independent of, and even prior to, the understanding of laws and general principles in morality. But we have reason to question this inference if we find that the discussion of virtue refers to and presupposes a grasp of laws and general principles.

We may be able to see what Aquinas believes on this point if we look at the remarks on law that precede the Treatise on Law. He agrees with Augustine's view that the goodness of the will depends on the eternal law.[16] He rejects the suggestion that because the rule of the human will is right reason, the goodness of the human will does not depend on the eternal law. For since right reason depends on the eternal law, the goodness of the human will also depends on the eternal law. We become aware of the eternal law either through our own reason or through some further revelation (1–2 q19 a4).

These remarks do not imply that the virtues require any explicit awareness of laws. When our reason is correct, we in fact grasp part of the eternal law, but Aquinas does not say that we have to be aware of the eternal law as such, or that we have to try to discover the content of any general rules. Insofar as the virtues of character restrict themselves to natural reason, they do not seem to mention law or rules. As Aquinas says, the proximate guide (*regula*) for the human will is natural reason, while the ultimate guide is the eternal law (1–2 q21 a1). We may need a more explicit grasp of the eternal law if we want to fill the gaps in human reason by appeal to legislation, but we do not seem to need any explicit grasp of it to acquire the virtues of character. The virtues that arise from nature and natural reason concern the moral philosopher, whereas the virtues that conform explicitly to the eternal law concern the theologian (1–2 q71 a5 ad5). The virtues that concern the moral philosopher, therefore, do not seem to require explicit reference to law. Similarly, Aquinas's frequent references to sin as a violation of the eternal law do not imply that virtue explicitly refers to law.

These remarks about the eternal law do not mention the natural law, which is relevant to the virtues considered by the moral philosopher. Aquinas does not say that the virtuous person has to reflect consciously on the general principles contained in the natural law in order to acquire or to exercise the virtues of character.

This degree of independence from law makes it easier to understand the place of the virtues of character in the structure of the *Prima Secundae*. Since these virtues are about human actions insofar as they proceed from will and passion, Aquinas discusses the virtues after his treatment of human acts and of passions. Virtues result from the exercise of free will (1–2 q55 a1 ad2), and hence an understanding of the virtues requires a grasp of the free will.[17] Since virtue uses free will well, we need to understand what constitutes a good use of free will. The will, according to Aquinas, is necessarily directed towards happiness as its ultimate end. Hence, a good use of free will directs the will towards a correct conception of the ultimate end. This connection between virtue and happiness explains why Aquinas introduces the whole discussion of will, action and virtue, with his treatise on the ultimate end.

So far, then, we have no reason to question our initial tentative inference from the structure of the *Prima Secundae*, that virtue is prior to law. To this extent, then, Aquinas appears to accept one element of a virtue theory. Does the Treatise on Law give us any reason to change our minds?

6. Natural Law and Its Precepts[18]

Aquinas begins the Treatise on Law without any specific reference to the virtues. The connection between laws, commands and reason requires a discussion of law in a discussion of human rational action. The task of law is to command and to forbid, and this is also the task of practical reason; that is why law belongs to reason. Law is a rule and measure of human acts, and so the application of practical reason to action introduces law (1–2 q90 a1). Morality is a set of principles that state the requirements of natural law.[19]

Aquinas traces his doctrine to Aristotle's division between natural and legal justice. He takes natural law to embody natural justice. The nature of a human being 'in so far as he discerns wrong (*turpe*) and right (*honestum*) in accordance with reason' is the basis for natural justice and for natural law.[20]

Law and virtue are both directed towards the final good. Since the ultimate end is the first principle of practical reason, law, as a manifestation of practical reason, is directed towards the ultimate end, and hence towards happiness (1–2 q90 a2). The natural law includes principles of practical reason that apply to us because of our human nature; hence, the first of these principles states that good is to be done and pursued and evil is to be avoided (1–2 q94 a2). Since the natural law is a rational principle, it is guided by the first principle of practical reason, which directs us towards the ultimate good.[21] Since the pursuit of this good is the first principle of natural law, the other principles embody the rational structure of the ultimate good.

The natural law prescribes the actions of all the virtues, insofar as it prescribes actions in accordance with nature (1–2 q94 a3). The actions that are natural for human beings are those that accord with their nature as rational beings. Their natural judgement gives them a natural inclination towards these actions.[22] The highest precepts that guide this natural judgement are immediately derived from the first principle, in accordance with the order of natural inclinations. Some concern self-preservation, others concern the satisfaction and control of bodily appetites and others concern social life.[23] These common principles require us to act in accordance with reason, but further enquiry is needed to decide what is involved in acting in accordance with reason.[24] Specific precepts are derived from reflexion on the naturally social character of human beings (1–2 q95 a4).

This reflexion on rational and social nature results in precepts such as the Decalogue (1–2 q100 a1). The precept against killing is derived from the precept against harming (1–2 q95 a2). The basis of specific precepts is the principle about human nature and especially about the naturally social character of human beings. The needs of a human community explain the provisions that are found in different forms in different human societies for property, exchange and so on. Hence, the law of nations—that is, the laws and institutions found universally in different nations—is derived from the law of nature by a conclusion that is close to the principles (1–2 q95 a4).

The precepts of the Decalogue are not the highest common principles of natural law, but they are the most general guides to action that can be derived from the common principles. They contain the common principles in the sense in which an immediate conclusion contains its premises. The precepts of the law of nations are less obvious than the precept against killing, but they are more obvious than those that 'by the diligent inquiry of wise people are found to accord with reason' (1–2 q100 a3). Reflexion on the needs of a human community tells us that (e.g.) every community needs to assure some protection, security and support for human social life, but it does not tell us how to fulfil these aims in different circumstances.

7. THE ROLE OF PRUDENCE

What kind of enquiry, then, is needed to reach definite moral conclusions from the higher precepts of the natural law? Aquinas may appear to set out the precepts of natural law deontologically, without reference to the outlook of the virtues. In his view, universal conscience (synderesis) grasps the ends of human life, which are 'fixed' or 'definite'; the means to these ends are not fixed and hence are subject to prudence (ST 2–2 q47 a15). Universal conscience is infallible and inextinguishable. If Aquinas supposes that we can begin from an infallible grasp of ends that are already fixed apart from deliberation, he appears to assume cognitive resources beyond those recognised by Aristotle.

This appearance, however, is misleading. Acceptance of the very first principle, that good is to be done and evil avoided, is not a distinctive mark of the virtuous agent, but a defining feature of a rational agent. Someone who did not accept it would not be capable of virtue or vice, since he would be unwilling to refer a proposed action to what is good, all things considered, and therefore would not be a rational agent at all. Since every rational agent grasps the basic principle of natural law, virtuous and vicious people all grasp it.

Something must mediate, therefore, between universal conscience and the virtuous person's conception of the end.[25] Mediating principles are more definite than the principles grasped by synderesis, and more detailed than the very general precepts that include the Decalogue. The prescription of universal conscience commits us to the further principle: 'It is reasonable to impose whatever control over appetite is needed for action in accordance with reason'. This principle does not identify a specific and determinate type of control over appetite. To find the more specific principles that identify the right kinds of actions, we need rational inquiry. And so we need prudence, to inquire correctly.[26]

The specific good pursued by a virtue is its proximate end, and prudence discovers this by reference to the ultimate end.[27] To find what promotes the ultimate end, prudence deliberates about different possible conceptions of happiness. The right conception of happiness identifies the ways in which the different virtues achieve the mean that consists in acting in accord with reason.[28] These ways of acting in accord with reason are the distinctive end of the virtuous person.[29]

Since prudence discovers the virtuous end, it is needed for the correct election that results in acting virtuously. Prudence ensures the right motive for the action because its deliberation about happiness forms the end of the virtuous person's actions. Prudence requires the moral virtues, and they require prudence.[30] Virtuous people act rightly insofar they act on correct election, and hence on the appropriate motive.[31] If we are guided by prudence, we do the generous action, say, for the right reason, and not simply on impulse.[32] Since prudence is necessary for the perfection of the reason that is involved in election, it is necessary for moral virtue.[33]

8. PRINCIPLES, RULES AND EXCEPTIONS

Can we say anything more definite about how prudent deliberation works, or about how a prudent person can show that a given conclusion is correct? If we cannot, we may conclude that, after all, Aquinas is really an extreme virtue theorist because he leaves it to the judgement of the prudent person to decide what is right in each particular case, and being right consists simply in being what the prudent person judges in particular cases.

To evaluate this conclusion, we should look more closely at how the prudent person deliberates, to see what considerations and what standards are to be followed.[34]

Do these details of the precepts of natural law tend to show that Aquinas is or is not a virtue theorist?

We might argue that he is a virtue theorist because he takes virtue prior to law. For he allows that when the precepts become more detailed, they also cease to be universal rules without exceptions. If we are to tell in a particular case whether we ought to follow the rule or recognise a legitimate exception to it, must we not rely on the judgement of the virtuous person, without reference to any general rule?

This question directs our attention to the general rules that belong to the subordinate precepts of the natural law. Attempts to describe appropriate general rules face two apparently reasonable but apparently conflicting demands: (1) Principles should be epistemically accessible and reliable, so that we can see both that and why they are a reasonable basis for decisions. (2) They should be applicable to specific situations, so that we can recognise when they apply and what they require. If they are not applicable, they cannot guide choices and actions.

Aquinas's discussion of the subordinate precepts raises questions about accessibility and applicability. He believes that after the first level (the common principles grasped by synderesis) and the second level (including the Decalogue) we can find two subordinate levels of precepts. Precepts at the third level are derivations from natural law; those at the fourth level are determinations rather than derivations. Precepts at the second level, including the Decalogue, do not require detailed enquiry because they are obvious consequences of the common principles. But precepts at the third level can be derived from the common principles only by further reflection (q100 a1, 3).

The Decalogue, for instance, includes duties to God and to one's neighbour because everyone easily recognises such duties. It omits our duties to ourselves because these are not so easily recognised.[35] Prudence is needed to find the less obvious precepts that are outside the Decalogue. Precepts at the fourth level are not derived from the first principles as conclusions from premises. They are 'determinations' rather than 'derivations' because they specify one among a number of possible ways of fulfilling a requirement of natural law. The natural law requires, for instance, that wrongdoers should be punished, but it does not require that they should receive this or that punishment. A specific law of punishment prescribes a specific way, not itself required by natural law, of fulfilling the generic requirement of natural law (1–2 q95 a2; a4 ad1).

Precepts at the fourth level have exceptions because they depend on a particular act of legislation. We should, for instance, drive on the left except where there is a different rule of the road. Precepts at the third level also have exceptions; Aquinas picks Plato's example of returning a deposit. This precept follows from the common first principles insofar as it is valid for most cases, but it has some exceptions. Hence, we need to reason about the cases in which it ought not to be followed (q94 a4). The fact that the precept has exceptions gives an opening for the self-serving and dishonest arguments that question the precept even on the occasions when it should be observed.[36] To answer self-serving arguments, we need prudent deliberation that separates genuine from spurious exceptions.

9. Precepts without Exceptions

It may also seem clear that the precepts of the Decalogue, and other precepts at the second level, have exceptions. The Decalogue seems to consist of general rules that can be readily applied to particular situations. Since they can be so readily applied, they seem to have obvious exceptions. Though the Decalogue forbids killing, it is sometimes right to kill evildoers and enemies. Are these not exceptions to the precept against killing?[37]

Aquinas answers 'No'. The precept states a principle about wrongful killing, not a general rule that prohibits all killing (1–2 q100 a8 ad3) If, therefore, we recognise justifiable killing, we have found not an exception to the precept, but a way to state it more accurately. To state the precept accurately and completely, we would need to identify all the circumstances that justify killing. The general rule 'Do not kill anyone' corresponds to 'Give back what you have borrowed', if we understand 'kill' in the ordinary way. Aquinas acknowledges that this general rule has exceptions, but he denies that they are exceptions to the principle about killing. His interpretation of 'Do not kill' as 'Do not kill unjustifiably' is parallel to 'Render to people what is owed to them'. The Decalogue, in his view, consists of principles that have no exceptions and are accessible and reliable, when properly understood.

But if Aquinas is right, the precepts of the Decalogue do not seem to be applicable. We cannot apply the precept against killing until we can identify unjustifiable killing. Similarly, we might think the precept against coveting what belongs to our neighbour has obvious counter-examples. If I want to buy my neighbour's car and offer a fair price for it, I seem to have coveted it, but quite legitimately. But if the precept really refers to inordinate desire, the attempted counter-example fails. The applicability of the precept now depends on judgements about which desires are inordinate.

If Aquinas explains the Decalogue correctly, he needs to distinguish the precepts of natural law from specific formulations of them.[38] 'Do not kill' is an inadequate formulation of the precept about homicide because it does not make it clear that the precept prohibits only unjustified killing, and because it does not say what makes a killing unjustified. The precept that we capture only partially in our brief formulation is too complicated to state.

Why should we agree with Aquinas's view that the precept is a complex principle, without exceptions, and beyond our capacity to formulate? Why not prefer the apparently more straightforward view that the precept is a simple rule, easy to formulate and with many exceptions? If he is right, we ought never to violate the precept. But we may think this is not an advantage of his position. Why not just recognise frankly that we sometimes ought to violate the precept? One might perhaps accuse Aquinas of making the precept inviolable at the cost of making it inapplicable.

Aquinas, however, has a good reason for his treatment of the precepts. They are precepts of practical reason about what is suitable to human nature. Practical reason and prudence take account of the systematic character of the precepts of natural law. Since natural law expresses what is suitable to human nature, the different precepts do not express separate moral requirements. On the contrary, a given precept requires a specific action only if that action is right and appropriate for human nature in these circumstances. Reflexion on killing, on wanting something that belongs to one's neighbour and on returning deposits, shows us that these types of actions are not wrong in all circumstances. A prudent person appeals to other precepts and virtues. If the precepts of natural law are the products of prudent reflexion on what is appropriate for human nature, they have to be complex enough to capture the considerations that matter to a prudent person. Since the precepts of the Decalogue belong to the natural law, they have to be as complex as the natural law requires.

Is this enough to justify Aquinas's treatment of the Decalogue? We might prefer to treat it as a series of simple rules with exceptions, on the ground that this treatment makes the precepts more readily applicable. If we can identify instances of killing without further moral controversy, we can then specify the exceptions to the general rule. This procedure may seem more straightforward than Aquinas's treatment of the precepts as complex principles.

But even if we speak of rules and exceptions, we have to face the questions that arise for Aquinas. For in order to see what justifies the exceptions, we have to appeal to the principles that Aquinas appeals to. Some exceptions to the simple rule about killing might rely on the principle of not harming the innocent. Exceptions to the rule about returning deposits rely on reasons for keeping a deposit. These reasons rely on more general principles (e.g., about not helping someone to harm innocent people, if the owner of the gun is demanding it back in order to kill other people or himself). These principles will be complex; they cannot be reduced to simple rules unless we allow exceptions to these rules on the basis of still further principles.

If, then, we treat the precepts of the Decalogue as simple rules, we have to identify exceptions on the basis of complex principles. Hence, we need to recognise complex principles. Aquinas has a good reason to build complex principles directly into the Decalogue.

10. THE CONNECTION BETWEEN LAW AND VIRTUE

What should we conclude, therefore, about the relation between natural law and the virtues? Though the Treatise on the Virtues does not affirm that the virtues depend on laws or general principles, the Treatise on Law affirms that the precepts of natural law include the actions corresponding to all the virtues. We need to discover the precepts of natural law in order to find the actions that are required by the virtues.

We could not have all the virtues and still lack the knowledge that we gain by discovering the precepts of the natural law. For we discover these precepts by reflexion on the actions that, given our nature as rational beings, promote our final good. Deliberation discovers the actions that promote our final good. Good deliberation is the function of the intellectual virtue of prudence, which also requires the virtues of character.

According to Aquinas, then, the understanding of natural law tells us about the right direction of prudent deliberation. If we simply knew that prudence deliberates about the human good, we might reasonably suppose that its starting point is too indefinite for any useful deliberation. Aquinas, however, believes that the human good that concerns prudence is the good for human nature, and that we deliberate prudently insofar as we consider what is appropriate for human nature, understood as rational and social. The virtues of a human being are those that are suitable for human nature and for the actions that promote the good of human beings with their nature.

Reflexion on human nature does not yield a body of general principles that constitute a purely deontological theory of the right. Aquinas's teleological conception is not only consistent with his doctrine of natural law, but it is actually built into that doctrine. He does not subordinate the virtues to rules or principles that are external to them. Nor, however, does he subordinate rules and principles to virtues. He does not try to fix the character of the different virtues without an account of the actions that they aim at. On the contrary, reflexion on the requirements of natural law determines the appropriate actions; the virtues are the states of character that aim at the appropriate actions, as determined by this reflexion.

Aquinas's claims about prudence and virtue support this conclusion. The mark of a genuine virtue is the correct grasp of the virtuous person's distinctive end. Prudence reaches this grasp by deliberation. The prudent person's deliberation is correct insofar as it discovers the actions and states that are suitable for the rational and social nature of human beings. The relevant facts about this rational and social nature constitute a standard of correctness that is external to the outlook of the virtuous person and is not constituted by that outlook; hence, the correctness of correct deliberation does not consist wholly in its being the deliberation of the virtuous person.

Aquinas, therefore, does not believe that the judgement of the virtuous person is primary in determining what is right or wrong in a particular case. Admittedly, the right action cannot always be fixed by simple rules that can be applied without the exercise of moral judgement. We can accept principles of the form 'Do not kill unjustly' or rules of the form 'Do not kill unless . . .', but both the principles and the rules need further moral judgement, to decide whether (e.g.) this is unjust killing or this is one of the cases to be included in 'unless . . .' In some cases the correct moral judgement will need the special insight of the prudent person; for only the prudent person can bring all the virtues to bear insofar as they are relevant to a particular situation. But this role for the virtuous person does not imply that the rightness of an action or a rule consists entirely in being judged right by the virtuous person.

Some reflexion on Aquinas's claims about the principles and precepts of natural law helps us to appreciate some of the possibilities that we obscure if we suppose that the trichotomy between deontology, consequentialism and virtue ethics identifies the only plausible theories of the right. He does not accept a deontological position because he does not recognise basic principles of right that are independent of the good. He does not accept a consequentialist position because he does not take rightness to consist wholly in good consequences. He is not a virtue theorist because he does not take virtuous characters to be prior, in any of the ways I have discussed, to right action.

The fact that Aquinas does not fit into this trichotomy of views implies nothing about the merits of his view. We have no reason to suppose that the trichotomy captures all the views that deserve attention. Though he is not a virtue theorist, his discussion of the precepts of natural law gives us a good reason to value the virtues and to cultivate them in ourselves and in other people. If we cannot capture the precepts of the natural law in simple rules that can be readily applied by someone who lacks virtue and prudence, we are more likely to fulfil these precepts if we cultivate the virtues than if we simply try to learn simple rules. The complex principles need sound moral judgement to apply them correctly. We will do better if we cultivate the virtues that are the source of this sound moral judgement.

Aquinas's discussion of natural law, therefore, makes it clear why it is reasonable to cultivate the virtues, and what difference they make to the right application of complex moral principles to specific situations. He gives an appropriately prominent place to the virtues in his account of the agents who can fulfil the precepts of the natural law. But it is nonetheless worth our while to observe that he is not a virtue theorist. The role that he ascribes to the virtues is distinct from the role that the virtue theorist ascribes to them. We can endorse the role of the virtues in Aquinas's theory without endorsing the dubious claims of virtue ethics.

NOTES

1. I do not mean to endorse the position of virtue theorists who take these to be the relevant options. See the last section.

2. Hence, Kent (1995) describes her book as a contribution to the 'investigation of virtue ethics' (3) and speaks of 'scholastic virtue theory' (3), and she speaks of 'the transformation of classical virtue ethics that eventually produced the Kantian good will' (254); in Kant 'virtue ethics is, if not entirely absent, at least changed beyond recognition' (1). Similarly, Lisska (1996, 46–47, 139–40, 249) speaks of virtue ethics, or 'Aristotelian "virtue ethics"' (which he finds in the work of Alasdair MacIntyre) without further specification.

3. On Anscombe and virtue ethics, see Crisp (1996, 2). I have discussed her views in Irwin (2007–9, vol. 2, ch. 32).

4. Schneewind (1990) discusses some criticisms of virtue ethics, which he takes to be an Aristotelian position, though he notices that Aquinas is not an unambiguous representative of this tradition.

5. According to Schneewind (1997, 20, 287), Aquinas subordinates the virtues to laws.

6. Different statements of virtue theory may be found in Prichard (1949, 11–12); Watson 1997.

7. On the various types and degrees of virtue theory, see Crisp (1996, 7): 'A pure virtue ethics, then, will suggest that the only reasons we ever have for acting or living in any way are grounded in the virtues. The fact that some way of life instantiates the virtues of justice, honesty, generosity, and so on, constitutes the sole reason for pursuing it; and there is no reason to pursue any other kind of life'. This description of pure virtue ethics makes it clear how virtue theories can come in degrees.

8. On particularism see the essays in Hooker and Little (2000).

9. Hursthouse (1999, 39) contains a careful discussion of the specific commitments of a virtue theory. She understands the explanatory priority of virtues to right actions as follows: 'The theoretical distinction between the two [sc. virtue ethics and deontology] is that the familiar rules, and their applications in particular cases, are given entirely different backings. According to deontology, I must not tell this lie because, applying the (correct) rule "Do not lie" to this case, I find that lying is prohibited. According to virtue ethics, I must not tell this lie because it would be dishonest to do so, and dishonesty is a vice'.

10. Slote (1995, 240) discusses 'agent-based views, which, unlike Aristotle, treat the moral or ethical status of actions as entirely derivative from independent and fundamental ethical/aretaic facts (or claims) about the motives, dispositions or inner life of the individuals who perform them'. Slote denies that Aristotle accepts holds an agent-based position of this sort. He takes Hursthouse (plausibly) to attribute such a view to Aristotle and to endorse it herself.

11. I have argued that Aristotle is not a particularist, in Irwin (2000).

12. One might take Cooper (1999, 276n) to hold that Aristotle accepts the strong metaphysical thesis: 'The *spoudaios* himself is the final measure or standard of this sort of value'. Whether Cooper has the strong metaphysical thesis in mind depends on how 'final' is to be understood.

13. I believe that, in fact, the label is inaccurate.

14. Different views on natural law and the virtues among medieval philosophers are discussed by, for example, Irwin (2007–9, vol. 1, chs. 21, 26, 27), Adams (1999) and Williams (2003).

15. On natural law and the virtues in Aquinas, see Williams (2003, 334 and n.5).

16. Aquinas, *Summa Theologiae* (hereinafter *ST*) 1–2 q19 a4 sc. References beginning '*ST* 1–2' refer to *ST Prima Secundae.*,

17. I pass over some details about the connection between free will (liberum arbitrium) and will (voluntas).

18. Further details on the natural law may be found in Finnis (1980, chs. 1–2) and Lisska (this volume).

19. *De Veritate*, q16 a1.

20. *In Ethica Aristotelis*, v 12, §1019; *ST* 1–2 q91 a2 sc.

21. *ST* 1–2 q90 a2; q94 a2. This treatment of the first principle may be contrasted with the account offered by Grisez (1970, 353–8).

22. At *Summa contra Gentiles* iii 129, Aquinas speaks of a 'natural criterion of reason'. Cf. *Scriptum super Sententiis* (hereinafter *Sent.*), iv d33 q1 a1.

23. *ST* 1–2 q94 a2, a4; q95 a4.

24. *ST* 1–2 q94 a4; 2–2 q47 a7.

25. *Sent.* ii d24 q2 a3; *ST* 2–2 q47 a7.

26. *ST* 1–2 q94 a3; 2–2 q56 a1.

27. *ST* 2–2 q123 a7.

28. *In Epistulam Pauli ad Romanos*, on 8:1; *Sent.* iii d33 q2 a3.

29. *ST* 2–2 q47 a6 ad3; a7; 1–2 q66 a3 ad3; *Sent.* iii d33 q2 a5 sol.

30. *ST* 1–2 q57 a4–5; q58 a3–5.

31. *ST* 1–2 q57 a5; q59 a1.

32. *ST* 1–2 q24 a3 ad1; q77 a6 ad2.

33. *ST* 1–2 q19 a7 ad2; q58 a4 ad1; q65 a1.

34. I have also relied on Suárez's discussion of the precepts of the natural law. See Irwin (2007–9, vol. 2, §444–45).

35. *ST* q100 a3; a5 ad1; 2–2 q56 a1; q122 a1.

36. Passions or bad habits or a bad natural condition may distort one's grasp of a secondary precept (1–2 q94 a4; cf. q94 a6; q99 a2 ad2.)

37. See Scanlon (1998, 199).

38. See Suarez, *De Legibus* ii 13.6.

BIBLIOGRAPHY

Adams, M. M. 1999. 'Ockham on will, nature, and morality'. In *Cambridge Companion to Ockham*, ed. P. V. Spade, ch. 11. Cambridge: Cambridge University Press.

Cooper, J. M. 1999. 'Reason, moral virtue, and moral value'. In *Reason and Emotion*, ch. 11. Princeton, NJ: Princeton University Press.

Crisp, R. C. 1996. 'Modern moral philosophy and the virtues' In *How Should One Live?* ed. R.C. Crisp, ch. 1. Oxford: Oxford University Press.

Finnis, J. M. 1980. *Natural Law and Natural Rights*. Oxford: Oxford University Press.

Grisez, G. G. 1970. 'The first principle of practical reason'. In *Aquinas: A Collection of Critical Essays*, ed. A. J. P. Kenny, 340–82. Garden City, NY: Doubleday.

Hooker, B. W. and M. Little, eds. 2000. *Moral Particularism*. Oxford: Oxford University Press.

Hursthouse, R. 1999. *On Virtue Ethics*. Oxford: Oxford University Press.

Irwin, T. H. 2000. 'Ethics as an inexact science: Aristotle on the ambitions of moral theory'. In Hooker and Little 2000.

——. 2007–9. *The Development of Ethics*, 3 vols. Oxford: Oxford University Press.

Kent, B. D. 1995. *Virtues of the Will*. Washington, DC: Catholic University of America Press.

Lisska, A. J. 1996. *Aquinas' Theory of Natural Law*. Oxford: Oxford University Press.

Prichard, H. A. 1949/2002. 'Does moral philosophy rest on a mistake?' In *Moral Obligation* (Oxford: Oxford University Press), and in *Moral Writings*, ed. J. MacAdam (Oxford: Oxford University Press).

Scanlon, T. M. 1998. *What We Owe to Each Other*. Cambridge, MA: Harvard University Press.

Schneewind, J. B. 1990. The misfortunes of virtue. *Ethics* 101:42–63.

——. 1997. *The Invention of Autonomy*. Cambridge: Cambridge University Press.

Slote, M. A. 1995/1997. Agent-Based Virtue Ethics. *Midwest Studies in Philosophy* 20(1995):83–101. Reprinted in *Virtue Ethics*, ed. R. C. Crispand and M. A. Slote, ch. 12. Oxford: Oxford University Press, 1997.

Suarez, F. 1971–81. *Tractatus de Legibus ac Deo Legislatore*, ed. L. Perena et al., 8 vols. Madrid: Consejo Superior de Investigaciones Cientificas.

Watson, G. L. 1997. 'On the primacy of character' in *Virtue Ethics*, ed. D. Statman, ch. 3, 56–81. Washington, DC: Georgetown University Press.

Williams, T. 2003. 'From metaethics to action theory'. In *Cambridge Companion to Duns Scotus*, ed. T. Williams, ch. 11. Cambridge: Cambridge University Press.

CHAPTER 29

NATURAL LAW

ANTHONY J. LISSKA

CONTEMPORARY analytical philosophers, Elizabeth Anscombe (1958), Alasdair MacIntyre (1999), Henry Veatch (1971) and Martha Nussbaum (2006), criticise English language moral theory for expressing overly Kantian or utilitarian directions. Rather than pose the 'obligation question' first—a common Kantian and teleological approach—these contemporary critics suggest asking the Aristotelian question: 'What kind of lives should we live?' These philosophers argue that Aristotelian moral theory, with the natural law theory developed by Thomas Aquinas a direct descendant, provides a corrective to the dominance of Kantian or deontological moral theory on the one hand and utilitarian/consequentialist approaches on the other. Through most of the twentieth century, ethical naturalism rooted in Aristotle did not contribute significantly to moral discussions in analytical philosophy. The heritage of natural law theory found in medieval philosophy, however, has been rediscovered by analytical moral and political philosophers and philosophers of law. Several important issues formulated recently are aligned structurally with positions posed by philosophers in the central tradition of medieval natural law theory. These metaphysical and moral queries reflect a tradition of moral realism that is important for normative ethical and political theory and for jurisprudence. This essay discusses the meta-ethical presuppositions necessary for understanding the ethical naturalism common to several contemporary natural law arguments. The architectonic of this analysis, while conscious of the historical antecedents in medieval Aristotelianism with special reference to Thomas Aquinas, concentrates on the contemporary thrust of natural law discussions.

Natural law theory at its best has a realist foundation based on human persons; this moral theory has rationality articulated as a necessary condition and is cognizant thoroughly of the common good or the public interest. Natural law theory, once placed with antiquated theories of ethical naturalism, now provides substantive analysis in contemporary moral theory, social and political theory, and jurisprudence. However, ethical naturalism, in order to be grounded in an order of nature, demands a realist ontology of natural kinds. This essay attempts to spell out the set of conditions necessary for natural law moral and legal theory through an analysis of the writings of several contemporary analytical philosophers and the role these central metaphysical concepts play in the respective theories.

1. Thomas Aquinas and the Classical Canon for Natural Law

The classical canon for natural law theory is often cited as Questions 90–97 in the *Prima Secundae* of the *Summa Theologiae*, where Aquinas develops a fourfold division of law: eternal law, natural law, human law and divine law. In discussing Aquinas, this essay concerns principally the first two—namely, eternal law and natural law. Aquinas distinguishes between eternal law and divine law. Divine law, for Aquinas, is a set of biblical propositions. Eternal law is the set of divine archetypes contained in the divine mind. Natural law is the set of moral principles based on human nature, which is an instantiation of the archetype of human nature in the divine mind. Positive law is the set of laws in agreement with the principles of natural law that are found in any given society promulgated by those in charge who have care of the community. While recent scholarship suggests that there is no singular canonical reading of Aquinas on natural law, nonetheless, this essay will emphasise ontological foundationalism—rooted in Aquinas's ontological and epistemological realism—in providing an analysis of natural law theory exemplified in the writings of several contemporary philosophers yet congruent with the texts of Aquinas.

In line with Aristotle, Aquinas's natural law theory is a second-order enquiry in which Aquinas builds his moral theory upon his philosophical anthropology of the human person. An ethical naturalist, Aquinas constructs a realist 'metaphysics of morals' but not a Kantian transcendental version. He builds his human nature ontology first, and from this philosophical anthropology flows moral principles and norms, indicating that his meta-philosophy is ontologically realist without being foundationalist. Scott MacDonald (1993) articulated this meta-philosophical theme: 'Aquinas does not build his philosophical system around a theory of knowledge. In fact, the reverse is true: he builds his epistemology on the basis provided by other parts of his system, in particular, his metaphysics and psychology'. This same meta-theory holds for Aquinas's natural law theory dependent upon an order of nature. As a second-order activity, moral theory is based on the metaphysical foundation, which is the essence or natural kind of the person. Aquinas avoids adopting what Henry Veatch (1971) once called 'the transcendental turn', central to Kantian moral theory and independent of any realist order of nature. Aquinas's ethical naturalism rooted in his ontology and philosophy of mind is never anti-realist and internalist but explicitly realist and externalist.

Aquinas argues that a human person is, by definition, a synthetic necessary unity grounding a set of potentialities, capacities, or dispositions, which is a dispositional analysis of a natural kind. A disposition, which translates '*inclinatio*' in Aquinas's texts—is a structured causal set of properties that leads towards the development of the property in a specific way. In his hylomorphic metaphysics, the substantial form is the ontological ground for dispositional properties. The proponents of the 'new natural law theory' reject this ontological foundationalism. However, more than several philosophers studying the structure of Aquinas on natural law theory—several of whom will be discussed later in this essay—accept this ontological foundationalism as a necessary condition for and a propaedeutic to understanding Aquinas on natural law. For instance, in their essay, 'Being and Goodness', Stump and Kretzmann (99) suggested that 'Aquinas's ethics is embedded in his metaphysics . . .' Furthermore, they (98) argued that 'in contemporary discussions, the unusual ethical naturalism that underlies all of (Aquinas's) moral philosophy has been neglected; consequently . . . its basis in his metaphysics (is) not as well known . . .' They (98) go on to write that 'Aquinas's naturalism is a kind of moral realism that deserves serious reconsideration. It supplies for his virtue-centred morality the sort of meta-ethical foundation that recent virtue-centred morality has been criticized for lacking'. In addition, John Haldane (2004, 136) referred to Aquinas's moral theory as 'objectivist naturalism'. This essay is in general agreement with the principal tenor of the Stump/Kretzmann analysis and Haldane's ascription of 'objectivist naturalism'.

2. CONTEMPORARY POSITIONS ON NATURAL LAW MORAL AND LEGAL THEORY

The surprising renewal of natural law jurisprudence rising like the phoenix in mid–twentieth century began with the jurisprudential writings of H. L. A. Hart (1961, 194 ff.) and Lon Fuller (1964, 84–86); following the Second World War, Hart and Fuller focused attention on the Nuremberg trials and the corresponding criminal charges of 'Crimes against Humanity'. In the context of a pervasive legal positivism, Hart and Fuller asked how the concept of 'Crimes against Humanity' could be justified philosophically. Central to this revival were Hart's 'core of good sense' in classical natural law theory and Fuller's account of 'substantive' and 'procedural natural law'. The contributions of Hart and Fuller, utilizing references to medieval natural law theory, to the contemporary revival of natural law theory are never to be underestimated. The Italian philosopher of law, Alessandro P. d'Entrèves (1970, 153–54), working at Oxford with Hart, published a seminal text developing a secular version of natural law that could speak to diverse peoples with differing religious commitments. D'Entrèves was much impressed with the work of Hart, who he suggested owed much to Hobbes. While d'Entrèves referred to medieval and early-modern natural law theories often, nonetheless, he believed that Aquinas, for one, could not separate his natural law theory from divine or religious presuppositions. Hence, d'Entrèves argued that only a modified medieval theory, if such were possible, would be acceptable for twentieth-century natural law discussions.[1] D'Entrèves was not alone in suggesting that natural law theory is always co-extensive with theological presuppositions. This theological emphasis continues to be a conundrum haunting philosophical theories of natural law.

Twenty years after the initial writings of Hart and Fuller, moral theory in English-speaking philosophy charted a new course with the 1981 publication of Alasdair MacIntyre's remarkable *After Virtue* (1981), with roots deeply planted in Aristotle and his medieval followers, especially Aquinas. Nonetheless, Elizabeth Anscombe's 'Modern Moral Philosophy' (1958, 1–19) served as an earlier wake-up call to analytical philosophers. Anscombe suggested the theoretical and practical bankruptcy of much analytical moral theory based either on emotivism or consequentialism. Furthermore, using natural law theoretical claims, she called for a re-working of philosophical psychology, a reinterpretation of practical reason and a return to moral virtue, which were necessary conditions for a constructive renewal of ethical theory in analytical philosophy. Structurally, MacIntyre's philosophical writing followed Anscombe's general schema discussing issues central to Aristotelian ethical naturalism. Philosophers beyond neo-Thomism or neo-scholasticism, however, have undertaken much of the recent creative work in natural law theory.

In discussing contemporary natural law theory, the following four claims, which are congruent with Aquinas's theory, are central to this analysis, which is termed 'ontological foundationalism':

1. The ontological possibility of essence or natural kinds
2. A dispositional view of essential properties determining the content of a natural kind
3. An adequate epistemological/philosophy of mind apparatus providing an awareness of essences or natural kinds in the individual
4. A theory of practical reason undertaking the ends to be pursued in terms of human nature

3. MacIntyre's Return to Ontological Foundationalism

MacIntyre's moral treatises exerted significant influence in the resurgence of interest in natural law moral philosophy; his monumental moral manuscripts are clarion calls for renewed work in Aristotelian ethical naturalism. What Russell Hittinger (1989, 449) proposed twenty-five years ago still holds: 'If nothing else, MacIntyre has made this [Aristotelian] recoverist project professionally respectable. Less than a decade [now over two decades] has passed since its publication, yet many are already prepared to admit that *After Virtue* represents something pivotal'. *After Virtue* produced a cottage industry centring on virtue ethics, akin structurally to issues on virtue articulated in many medieval natural law treatises (Adkins and Williams 2005). Anscombe and MacIntyre, among others, have argued against placing the virtue ethics of Aristotle and the natural law theory of Aquinas into the meta-ethical dustbin with those theories of ethical naturalism judged, often too quickly, of succumbing to Moore's naturalistic fallacy. In *After Virtue*, however, MacIntyre was chary about committing his theory to an ontological foundation. Nonetheless, in *Three Rival Versions of Moral Enquiry*, MacIntyre (1990, 58) wrote: 'The concept of good has application only for beings insofar as they are members of some species or kind'.

In *Dependent Rational Animals*, MacIntyre returned to Aristotle's long-neglected 'metaphysical biology' and he discussed the philosophical importance of his return to this once-rejected ontological position. The query MacIntyre put forward is: Does one need an ontological foundation for an Aristotelian theory of the human person? Haldane (2000, 154) argued that in *Dependent Rational Animals*, MacIntyre 'retracts this criticism and argues that an idea of the good for an agent cannot be formed independently of having a conception of the kind of being it is'. This metaphysical turn proposed a significant move towards ontological realism since MacIntyre now rejected his earlier almost post-modernist abhorrence of questions leaning towards ontological foundationalism. MacIntyre (1999, x) himself explained this significant change:

> In *After Virtue* I had attempted to give an account of the place of the virtues,
> understood as Aristotle had understood them, within social practices, the lives of
> individuals and the lives of communities, while making that account independent
> of what I called Aristotle's 'metaphysical biology'. . . . I now judge that I was in
> error in supposing an ethics independent of biology to be possible. . . . No
> account of the goods, rules and virtues that are definitive of our moral life can be
> adequate that *does not explain*—or at least point us towards an explanation—how
> that form of life is possible for beings who are biologically constituted as we are,
> by providing us with an account of our development towards and into that form
> of life. (Italics not in the original.)

Commenting on his early work, MacIntyre (Knight 1998, 263) remarked: 'This . . . connection between virtue and metaphysics I had not understood when I wrote *After Virtue*'.

In reflecting upon a naturalism necessary for moral theory, MacIntyre is not a lone voice crying in the wilderness. Philippa Foot (2000, 123) once argued: 'My thesis . . . is that the grounding of a moral argument is ultimately facts about human life . . .; the evaluation of the human will should be determined by facts about the nature of human beings and the life of our own species. . . .'. Foot's claim is aligned ontologically with MacIntyre's return to a metaphysical biology. In principle, these positions are reducible to a philosophical anthropology, and both suggest the importance of a metaphysically grounded theory of an 'order of nature'. This ontology is a necessary condition for explicating consistently a realist natural law theory. Contemporary moral philosophers will note immediately that these positions are opposed to the purportedly specious claims of 'speciesism' articulated by Peter Singer (Sunstein and Nussbaum 2004, 78–92) and other post-modernists. Singer's charge of speciesism is more a rhetorical moniker than it is a justified argument. In any event, contemporary analytical philosophers like MacIntyre, Anscombe and Foot argue that without an ontological foundationalism, a moral theory purportedly rooted in the species-specific sortal properties of human nature is shredded and vacuous. MacIntyre (Knight 1998, 157) once wrote: 'These stories . . . have genuine application to human lives only if and because metaphysics as well as moral claims can be sustained within philosophy'.

4. VEATCH'S ONTOLOGICAL FOUNDATIONALISM

Henry B. Veatch (1986, 1990) is another non-Thomist twentieth-century philosopher who considered natural law theory as a conceptual response to non-cognitivism and intuitionism and who addressed the importance of natural law in developing an adequate account of human rights. Acknowledging the importance of Aquinas on his own philosophical work, Veatch (1986, 13) once wrote: 'May I simply say that my own program ought perhaps to be regarded as amounting to little more than exercises in dialectic, and in a dialectic directed to the overall purpose of trying to rehabilitate Aristotle and Aquinas as contemporary philosophers'. The thrust of Veatch's meta-philosophy was to engage classical ethical naturalism into a dialectical discussion with non-cognitivism and intuitionism then prevalent in mid-century analytical philosophy. Veatch's *For an Ontology of Morals* began this significant dialectical discussion with modern and contemporary analytical moral philosophy. Like MacIntyre, Anscombe and Nussbaum, Veatch (1971, 3) ponders the following issue: 'Could it be that contemporary ethics has just about reached a dead end?'

As an Aristotelian realist, Veatch criticised the presuppositions of Kantian philosophy that had made serious inroads into contemporary philosophy. With Kant, what Veatch called 'the transcendental turn' is dominant. In using the transcendental turn, Veatch brought to the forefront of philosophical discussion the radical nature of conceptual dependency that characterizes Kantian philosophy and, according to Veatch, much mid-twentieth-century moral philosophy. This conceptual dependency marked by the transcendental turn entails a denial of both metaphysical and moral realism and depicts the foundationalist nature of many philosophical issues common to modern philosophy from the time of Descartes onwards.[2] One consequence of the transcendental turn is the abandonment of philosophical realism, and, *a fortiori*, of natural law theory rooted in any 'order of nature'. Gilson once noted in discussing realism in medieval philosophy: '*Ab esse ad nosse valet consequentia*', which is in opposition to the transcendental turn; the transcendental turn is the meta-philosophical principle against which Veatch marshalled much of his argument. This meta-philosophy explains the almost absence of serious work in as well as entrenched philosophical opposition to natural law theory in the predominant secular writers in Western philosophy during the first half of the twentieth century. Veatch sought to reinstate ontology as a necessary condition for undertaking moral theory. Veatch used what he called 'The *Euthyphro* Question' to justify foundational claims. Ralph McInerny's (1992) natural law account is similar structurally to Veatch's analysis. MacIntyre (Knight 1998, 38), too, suggested that ' . . . the salient feature of contemporary politics marks the frustration of the political hopes of the Enlightenment and especially of Kant'.

In discussing how natural law might embrace a theory of obligation, Veatch (1990, 116) adopted what he called a 'metaphysics of finality', which he gleaned from the insights of René-Antoine Gauthier. The ends to be attained are determined by the content of the natural kind of the human person. Veatch and Gauthier argue that this differs radically from ordinary teleological or consequentialist theories like utilitarianism. Therefore, the dispositional view of human nature rooted in Aristotelian potentialities enables Veatch's version of natural law theory not to succumb to the charges of the naturalistic fallacy and provides a justification for a theory of obligation. In other words, these ends ought to be obtained because of the very dispositional structure of human nature. The ends are not arbitrary but are determined by the natural kind of human nature itself. Obligation is rooted in the ends themselves. This is an important claim necessary to explicate conceptually the theory of teleology necessary for natural law theory. This teleology grounded in the concept of a natural kind comprised of dispositional properties provides an alternative account of teleology to that found in modern and contemporary consequentialist moral theories. In effect, this renders Bentham's (Schofield 2003) charge that natural rights were nothing but 'rhetorical nonsense—nonsense on stilts', vacuous conceptually.

5. FINNIS AND THE 'NEW NATURAL LAW' THEORY

John Finnis's (1982, 1983, 1998) work is almost singularly important in bringing medieval theories of natural law into mainstream discussions within twentieth-century analytical jurisprudence. His *Natural Law and Natural Rights* developed a contemporary reconstruction of classical natural law. Finnis, however, while claiming that his moral and legal theory is in the stable with other contemporary natural law authors, nonetheless rejects the ontological foundationalism that MacIntyre, Veatch, Anscombe, McInerny and Foot adopt. In constructing his natural law theory, Finnis appropriated the early insights of the American neo-Thomist, Germain Grisez;

Grisez's (1965) seminal article on practical reason was an important hallmark for what has become known as 'the new natural law' theory. In articulating and defending this revisionist natural law theory, Finnis (1982, 22) puts forward what he takes to be a list of basic human goods: life, knowledge, play, aesthetic experience, friendship, practical reasonableness and religion. Finnis, however, argues that this set of basic goods, which are *per se nota* propositions, is known directly by practical reason. This determination is what Finnis refers to as the concept of 'objectivity', rather than the concept of 'nature'. These basic goods, however, are not grounded in a philosophical anthropology, which Finnis calls 'reductivism'. In *Fundamentals of Ethics*, Finnis (1983, 22) wrote: 'Ethics is not deduced or inferred from metaphysics or anthropology', and that '. . . the first principles of natural law . . . are not inferred from metaphysical propositions about human nature'. Accordingly, Finnis rejects endorsing any reductive form of moral theory rooted in any form of natural kind anthropology. Thus, Finnis is opposed in principle to the ontological foundationalism found in much classical and contemporary natural law theory, especially in Veatch, MacIntyre and McInerny.

What drives Grisez, Finnis and their ally, Robert George (1993), is developing a natural law theory capable of sidestepping Moore's naturalistic fallacy. If the basic goods are not reducible to natural properties, this non-reductivism purportedly avoids the naturalistic fallacy and any form of the 'is/ought' problem. Because the basic goods are not derived from an ontology of the human person, they are 'stand-alone' moral properties known directly by practical reason. Haldane (2000, 154) and this author (Lisska 1984, 288–90) have suggested that the awareness of the basic goods appears reducible to intuition similar to Sir David Ross's (1930, 19–20) account in *The Right and the Good*. George, it should be noted, has published profusely defending Finnis's account of natural law theory. His *Making Men Moral* proposes to reconcile natural law theory with human rights theories in the American liberal tradition.

In offering a critique of Finnis's revised theory of natural law, Veatch and McInerny, among others, argue that Finnis has removed the metaphysical foundation for natural law (Lisska 1991, 55–71). McInerny (1998) once argued that Finnis's theory is reducible to 'Natural law without nature'. MacIntyre's later writings illustrating his rediscovery of Aristotle's metaphysical biology respond in principle to the new natural law philosophers. It appears, moreover, that the shadow of Kant hovers more heavily on this so-called 'new theory of natural law' than Grisez, Finnis or George are wont to admit. Furthermore, if the new natural law theory is similar to Ross's 'intuitionism', then the awareness of the basic human goods is dependent upon a direct intuitive awareness of these goods, through which Finnis incorporates a cognitive dimension into practical reason. This approach renders practical reason more cognitive than what most medieval Aristotelians, especially Aquinas, would accept. Aristotelians classically divided reason into two functions: theoretical reason, which is the 'knowing' aspect of reason, and practical reason, which is the 'choosing' or 'undertaking' aspect of reason. Moreover, choosing or undertaking depends on prior knowledge; one can only choose or undertake that which is a 'good' after knowing that it is a good. The new natural law theory account appears to conflate the Aristotelian distinction between theoretical and practice reason. MacIntyre, Veatch and McInerny, in elucidating natural law, adopt ontological realism of human nature as a necessary condition for elucidating the fundamental human goods.

In defending Finnis, George (1993, 35) argued that Finnis adopted an epistemological principle first, in which analysis points to the ontological structure of the human person; this is what Gilson would refer to as '*a nosse ad esse valet consequentia*'. Hence, in some way there is a 'pointing' back to the human nature by an analysis of the basic goods first. The worry here is that it would seem that, insofar as MacIntyre and Veatch adopt a form of metaphysical realism, there is a structure of reality prior to the epistemological issues. George appears to have adopted the transcendental turn that Veatch indicates is incompatible theoretically with metaphysical realism and natural law theory. In *De Veritate* (q. 21 a. 3 arg. 1), as Veatch (1990, 256) noted, Aquinas wrote: 'secundum Philosophum . . . bonum est in rebus'; this passage is translated: 'Good is found in things, as the Philosopher (Aristotle) indicates'. How practical reason points back to human nature is unclear in the new natural law theory.

6. Nussbaum's 'Capabilities Approach' and 'Aristotelian Ethical Naturalism'

Martha Nussbaum, never one to travel far from her original Aristotelian efforts, suggested the importance of Aristotelian insights for government and politics. In this regard, Nussbaum is aligned conceptually with the political and legal goals of natural law theory proposed by Hart, Fuller and d'Entreves. Nussbaum (1993, 265) once wrote:

> I discuss an Aristotelian conception of the proper function of government, according to which its task is to make available to each and every member of the community the basic necessary conditions of the capability to choose and live a fully good human life, with respect to each of the major human functions included in that fully good life. I examine sympathetically Aristotle's argument that . . . that task of government cannot be well performed, or its aim well understood, without an understanding of these functionings—[i.e.], the major human functions included in that fully good life.

In discussing the 'major human functions' necessary for justified human law, Nussbaum is connected closely with several concepts central to a natural law position. In addition, Nussbaum (Magee 1998, 53) once wrote: '. . . among the good things [in Aristotle's political theory], is an account of the proper function of government or politics as the provision to each citizen of all the necessary conditions for the living of a rich good human life'. The 'Capabilities Approach' is central to determining the content for a 'rich good human life'.

Nussbaum's work illustrates important themes long associated with natural law moral and political theory. Medieval and renaissance natural law philosophers in principle adopted these meta-ethical principles on the nature of society and the role of good government, which are significant in terms of their non-enlightenment structure. Interesting similarities exist between Aquinas's set of dispositional properties defining human nature and Nussbaum's 'capabilities approach'. Nussbaum (2006, 21), in *Frontiers of Justice*, suggests that her capabilities approach 'revives the Grotian natural law tradition . . . ' and argues (2006, 285) that the basic capabilities are not based on any particular human person but are 'the basic capacities characteristic of the human species'. Nussbaum argues that the capabilities represent the 'necessary conditions of a life worthy of human dignity'. She (2006, 76–78) lists ten 'central human functional capabilities', which are: 'life, bodily health, bodily integrity, imagination, emotions, practical reason, affiliation, compassion for other species, play, and control over one's environment in both the material and political senses'. In 'Non-Relative Virtue', Nussbaum (1993, 263–64) developed an earlier and mildly modified list of these capabilities.

In contrast to contractarian rights theory—what Christine Korsgaard (2003) refers to as the 'constructivist' position exemplified by John Rawls and Bernard Williams—Nussbaum (2006, 87) argues: '. . . the capabilities approach is . . . an outcome-oriented theory and not a procedural theory'. She continues: 'the capabilities approach goes straight to the content of the outcome, looks at it, and asks whether it seems compatible with a life in accordance with human . . . dignity'. In providing only what one might call a 'thin theory of the good', modern and contemporary contractarian political theories attempt to dismiss any connection with natural rights and natural law. Contractarian theory separated the right from the good, whereas the Aristotelians affirm a relational dependence between the two. Nussbaum's texts mirror Martin Golding's (1975, 31) natural law suggestions that political and legal theory must be attentive to 'human needs, human purposes, and the human good'.

In *Frontiers of Justice*, Nussbaum (2006, 86) argues that 'the Aristotelian account insists that the good of a human being is both social and political', which resonates with classical natural law theory. Yet Nussbaum, like Finnis, rejects any dependence on an ontological foundation for moral and political claims; she does not adhere to the 'reductive thesis' against which Finnis railed. Aligning her position with the Stoics, Nussbaum (2006, 36) argues: 'We may, however (with Cicero, who was agnostic in metaphysics), view these claims as freestanding ethical claims out of which one might build a political conception of the person that can be accepted by people who hold different views in metaphysics and in religion'.

Prima facie, Nussbaum's analysis appears foundationally to resemble Finnis's non-reductivism. What needs to be discussed is how Finnis's direct awareness of the basic human goods through practical reason is similar to or differs from Nussbaum's awareness of the fundamental human capabilities. Nussbaum (2007, 15) appears to postulate the 'free-standing' human capabilities as a theoretical means by which she can develop a workable social and political theory bypassing the formalism of Rawls and Dworkin. Finnis appeals to a direct cognitive relation in order to be aware of the basic human goods. Nonetheless, both philosophers appear to be theoretically cozy with some form of intuitive awareness that is non-reductive and self-evident. Veatch, MacIntyre and McInerny all demand more ontological justification.

In addition, Nussbaum argues that the ethical naturalism of Aristotle must be modified with a second natural law insight of the Stoics. In developing her capabilities approach to value theory, Nussbaum chides Aristotle for missing the concept of significant moral equality that, she suggests, is found in the seminal natural law writings of the Stoics. Nussbaum argues that Aristotle granted citizenship in the polis only to male Greek citizens, entailing that slaves, women and children were placed in an inferior status. Accordingly, Nussbaum modifies her Aristotelianism by accepting 'human equality' that she insists is found in the Stoics. Most historians of philosophy agree that the Stoics condemned slavery since each human person is part of the universal 'brotherhood of mankind', implying that all persons need to share in and profit from the largess of the polis. For Nussbaum, Aristotle provides the content for the political theory—the historical roots of her capabilities approach—while the Stoic concept of 'universal brotherhood' entails in a preliminary way what later modern and contemporary philosophers call human rights.

That there are significant similarities to medieval theories of the human person articulated in Nussbaum's capabilities approach is not to be gainsaid; however, the scope of the foundational applicability differs. What is needed is an ontological foundation in the human person on which a theory of the human good is rooted. Here medieval philosophers like Aquinas and Nussbaum part company. In addition, for Aquinas, this set of human properties is not known solely by intuition—mental awareness of which both Finnis and Nussbaum appear to adopt; an intuitive awareness of basic goods or human capabilities, it would seem, is not a sufficient condition to ground a moral theory of the human person. Nussbaum (2006, 305) noted: 'The capabilities approach . . . starts from the notion of human dignity and a life worthy of it'. Medieval philosophical realists would argue that ontological questions— especially the natural kind of a human person—are necessary conditions for ethical naturalism. Grotius (1625), too, it appears, connected his theory of human rights to a metaphysical theory of human nature, when he wrote that dignity and sociability are the two polls around which a moral theory must be built. Sociability he characterised as 'an impelling desire for fellowship, that is for common life, not just any kind but a peaceful life, and organized according to the measure of his intelligence, with those who are of his kind'. Nussbaum, however, appears foundationally to be aligned more closely with Finnis's new natural law theory than with the ontological foundationalism articulated by MacIntyre and Veatch.

7. DWORKIN AND 'NATURAL LAW REVISITED'

Several commentators on contemporary natural law have suggested that Ronald Dworkin's jurisprudential theory is a significant contribution to natural law jurisprudence, with reference to his *Taking Rights Seriously* (1978), *Law's Empire* (1986) and '"Natural" Law Revisited' (1982) as illustrations. These arguments elucidate Dworkin's analysis of judicial decision making, where the moral principles of a society are necessary conditions for justified legal decisions in the courtroom.

Dworkin is widely regarded as a creative jurisprudential voice articulating what he calls 'naturalism'. Dworkin argues that the validity of a legal system depends upon the moral norms common to the fundamental governing principles of a society. Furthermore, the moral principles of freedom, due process and equality are essential to the United States's Constitution. Given this structure, it was inconsistent theoretically that the United States adopted slavery. Human rights are, Dworkin suggests, the political 'trumps' that protect the individual person against what he calls 'majoritarian preference'. In demanding that the laws of a society be congruent with the basic political morality of that society, his legal positivist critics suggest that Dworkin has entrenched natural law leanings. How entrenched and accurate this natural law leaning really is, however, is an important philosophical question that must be addressed.

In his '"Natural" Law Revisited', Dworkin (1982, 165) discusses moral principles necessary for judicial decision making in the following way:

> According to naturalism, judges should decide hard cases by interpreting the political structure of their community in the following, perhaps special way: by trying to find the best justification they can find, *in principles of political morality*, for the structure as a whole, from the most profound constitutional rules and arrangements to the details of, for example, the private law of tort or contract. In the past several years, I have tried to defend a theory about how judges should decide cases that some critics . . . say is natural law theory and should be rejected for that reason. If . . . any theory of law sometimes depends on the correct answer to some moral question is a natural law theory, then I am guilty of natural law. . . . Suppose this is natural law. What in the world is wrong with it? [Italics not in original.]

Here one observes an influential English-speaking analytical philosopher of law considering the principles of political morality as necessary conditions for adequate judicial decisions. Furthermore, Dworkin provides a specific reference to natural law theory. That this is at least a prima facie connection with some of the issues in classical natural law theory should be apparent. However, by naturalism Dworkin means the process of determining from the principles of political morality the best justification for a legal decision. Dworkin's naturalism is neither equivalent to nor co-extensive with natural law theory, either 'classical' or 'new'.

Insofar as Dworkin remains agnostic about the role human nature or any theoretical claims about an order in nature might play as foundational for his moral and political principles, he does not fit under the umbrella of natural law as discussed in this essay. Natural law philosophers respond to the contractarianism of Dworkin—and to Rawls and Nozick—by proposing a 'thick' as opposed to a 'thin' theory of the human good. This natural law account based on a metaphysics of natural kinds poses a foundational query for contemporary rights philosophers adopting a 'thin theory' of the human good. Natural law philosophers argue that this lacuna is a theoretical problem with most theories of liberal jurisprudence.

The natural law account articulated in this essay based on a metaphysics of natural kinds suggests a moral and a jurisprudential limit for contemporary rights philosophers like Dworkin—and his contemporaries, Nozick and Rawls—who adopt 'thin theories' of the human good. These theories lack any substantive content based on the foundational principles of human nature. Liberalism in jurisprudence, by its very definition, denies any role for substantive content to the fabric of lawmaking. Dworkin (1984, 191) once wrote that '. . . government must be neutral on what might be called the question of the good life'. Without the content that a theory of a human person provides, jurisprudence is limited in its attempt at achieving a substantive theory of human rights. Rawls's person who has a passion for counting blades of grass in city squares or Dworkin's beer-drinking TV addict both may be leading a good life—one of 'integral human fulfilment', to appropriate a Finnis term—provided they have chosen these ends after mature reflection. This appears similar to Finnis's 'objectivity'. A thick theory of human nature espoused by the ethical naturalism put forward in this essay requires more than what Rawls, Nozick and Dworkin's thin theories permit.

In his *Making Men Moral*, from the perspective of the new natural law theory, George (1993) addresses the set of issues that contemporary philosophers refer to as 'moral perfectionism'. Moral perfectionism is consistent, it would appear, only within the context of a theory of the human person grounded on a theory of the natural kind of human nature. This natural law schema provides a set of properties that determine the content of the human good to be attained. Without this content, one falls quickly into the vacuum of formalism. Such formalism is, in many ways, the hallmark of Kantian moral theory, most 'good-reasons' moral theories, all legal positivism, much legal realism, and most liberal jurisprudence. One might ask: what justifies a morally right action for Kant or a set of human rights for Dworkin, Nozick or Rawls? In the end, it is the exercise of reason itself—what contemporary moral philosophers often refer to as a 'good-reasons approach' to moral reasoning. Dworkin often refers to this 'good-reasons' method of rational justification in legal matters. What the natural law position offers, if only in a broad and general way, is a set of human properties or qualities—human nature—without which a justification of a moral theory or a legal system—including a set of human rights—does not respond to Veatch's *Euthyphro* question. Since human nature or essence depends upon the foundational structure of a natural kind, a set of metaphysical claims is a necessary condition towards explicating natural law theory. In commenting on Rawls's formalist—or 'good-reasons'—theory of moral justification, Nussbaum (1986, 311) once noted: 'Aristotle's view of *phronesis* cannot avail itself of this strategy . . . [of] value neutral abilities such as imagination, empa-thy, factual knowledge'. Hence, Nussbaum (1986, 311) argues that the person of prac-tical reason utilizes more reasoning abilities than 'an enumeration of intellectual abilities. . .' Nussbaum seeks more in her account of human rights theory than Rawls's procedural formalism; this is where her capabilities approach enters the discussion. Nussbaum, however, considers the postulation of the stand-alone capacities as suffi-cient; MacIntyre, Veatch and McInerny require an ontological justification for the postulation.

8. THE ROLE OF NATURAL-KIND ONTOLOGY

In order to grasp the import of medieval ethical naturalism as developed in the texts of Aquinas and its impact on contemporary natural law theories, one needs to under-stand the concept of a natural kind as an essence necessary for ontological justifica-tion; this suggests an interesting realist connection with recent analytical philosophy. Michael Ayers (1981, 248) observed that late-twentieth-century philosophical work illustrated similarities with the Aristotelian elucidation of natural kinds: '. . . there is some awareness that the [Kripke/Putnam] view [on natural kinds] is not so new as all that, since it is not at all unlike Aristotelian Doctrine'. Ayers (1981, 267) also wrote that the evidence of modern biology suggests that a species, as a natural kind, '. . . is a far cry from the radical arbitrariness that Locke (and most Empiricists) took to infect all classifications'. In the last two decades of the twentieth century, serious discussions about the concepts of essence and essential properties—especially as generated through the means of modal logic—returned to vibrancy in several writ-ings by analytical philosophers.[3] This account of natural kind as an essence is analo-gous with the 'metaphysically necessary' that Kripke discussed in *Naming and Necessity* (Kripke 1971: 144–46). MacIntyre's later defence of his once-rejected 'meta-physical biology' illustrates the realism resonating in recent renditions of natural law. This is what Finnis rejects as a necessary condition for natural law theory.

Accordingly, a necessary condition for moral naturalism is a metaphysical theory of a natural kind of the human person. Unlike modern and contemporary empiricists and nominalists, Aristotle grounded his moral theory in the essential properties central to the structure of a human person. In his *Categories* (Barnes 1984, 3), Aristotle distinguished between properties 'said of' an individual or pri-mary substance and properties 'found in' an individual or primary substance. This distinction grounds the important ontological difference between essential or sor-tal predication and accidental or incidental predication. Natural law moral theory depends on the development of the sortal dispositional properties determining the human essence. If properties 'said of' an individual refer to an empty class, then natural law theory will be moribund from the beginning. In opposition to current anti-realism common to contemporary philosophy following Kant, most contemporary natural-law philosophers work within the context of ontological realism and epistemological realism. As MacIntyre was forced to admit eventually, natural-law moral theory is impossible theoretically without philosophical realism as a necessary condition. In principle, natural-law theory requires as a necessary condition a form of externalism justified by at least a modified reliabilism in the philosophy of mind. Dworkin and Finnis would absent their theories from these ontological and epistemological requirements.

Moreover, moral theory, and a fortiori a theory of human or positive law and a derivative but not an explicit theory of human rights, is rooted in the foundation of the human person as an instance of a natural kind. A human person is, by definition, a substantial unity grounding a set of capacities, which is a dispositional analysis of a natural kind. A disposition is a structured causal set of properties that leads towards the development of the property in a specific way. The structure of a tulip bulb is organised biologically to produce a tulip flower and not a geranium. And so forth. In Aristotelian metaphysics, the substantial form is the ontological ground for this set of dispositional properties. Aristotle divides these capacities into three generic headings, which serve as the basis of this theory of a natural kind for human persons. This account of human nature—the human natural kind and 'order of nature'—is based upon the insights of Aristotle's *Nicomachean Ethics* and *De anima*. Following the suggestion Plato (Wedberg 1971, 49) offered in the *Phaedrus*, natural-law philosophy uses ontological essences to categorize nature—to 'divide nature at its joints'. To appropriate medieval terminology, human nature is the *quidditas* determined by *materia prima* and *forma substantialis*. Formal cause is a necessary condition for explaining the structure of the external world. In responding to Putnam's apparent lack of an ontological realism from an Aristotelian perspective, Haldane (2002, 97) referred to 'the metaphysical skull' of reality. Using the terminology of Everett J. Nelson (1967, 19–33), a natural-kind essence might best be referred to as a realist set of 'synthetic necessary properties'. This discussion of essence comprised of dispositional properties required as an ontological foundation for natural-law theory differs from that held by most modern and contemporary philosophers; an essence is not a set of fixed, static, simple properties. The Aristotelian biological paradigm for philosophical explanation rejects the mathematical model so common to Plato and later to Descartes, and also to Russell and Moore. An essence composed of dispositional properties is 'directed towards' a certain developmental end, which is where the teleological enters a natural-law account. A set of dispositions reaches its 'end' when the set has developed as it should according to its very nature or being—which refers to its internal causal structure. To function well is to develop the dispositions or capacities according to the nature or structure one has, which is a *de re* and not a *de dicto* account. In the essentialist language of the hylomorphism common in Aristotelian studies, the development of the dispositional properties of the substantial form, which is the formal cause, is to attain the final cause. Often in their accounts of natural law, MacIntyre, McInerny and Veatch resort to these Aristotelian philosophical categories. In an analogical fashion, Nussbaum used the capabilities of the human person.

The final cause as a teleological goal is built into the very structure of the human essence, which is what Veatch and Gauthier called 'The Metaphysics of Finality'. The development of the human dispositional properties leads to what Aristotle called *eudaimonia*. The virtues common to MacIntyre's *After Virtue* are the acquired means that enable each human agent to exercise those actions that determine *eudaimonia*—or *felicitas* and *beatitudo*, as Aquinas referred to 'functioning well' and contemporary Aristotelians 'flourishing'. This is the foundation in human nature for what natural law philosophers call the natural moral laws, which is the structure of ethical naturalism as developed by MacIntyre, Veatch and McInerny.

Hence, the natural-law theory of MacIntyre, Veatch and McInerny requires, as an obligation, for each human agent to act in such a way that one's natural, human ends are fulfilled, which leads to *flourishing* of a human person. Moreover, like Aquinas, MacIntyre, Veatch and McInerny emphasize the prominence of reason as opposed to will. To the contrary, Scotus and Ockham alter the direction of the discussion emphasizing the role of the will and the ensuing voluntarism as central to natural law. Throughout his discussion of lawmaking and moral theory, Veatch following Aristotle argues that reason, both speculative and practical, is to be employed. Harkening back to a medieval text, law is, as Aquinas states, 'an ordinance of reason'. A purely voluntarist account of either moral theory or jurisprudence is inadequate conceptually. In contemporary jurisprudence, Hart, Fuller and Golding defend versions of reason and are opposed to a voluntarist account. MacIntyre (Knight 1998, 265) once wrote: 'Unlike Rorty, I believe that there are strong and substantive conceptions of truth and rational justification'.

9. THE GOD QUESTION IN CONTEMPORARY NATURAL LAW

One issue that contemporary students of natural law confront right from the beginning is the role God plays in any general theory of natural law. Aquinas (Lisska 1996, 264), for instance, writes that the natural law in some way participates in the eternal law: 'Hence, it is obvious that the natural law is nothing other than the participation of the eternal law in the rational creature or human being'. Many commentators assume that it follows that God must be a necessary condition for understanding contemporary natural law. D'Entrèves (1970, 153–54), for example, in discussing Aquinas on natural law, wrote the following:

> Now it seems to me that in our divided world the first and most serious stumbling block to the Thomist conception of natural law lies precisely in its premise . . . of a divine order of the world, which St. Thomas recalls at the very beginning of his theory of law, and from which he infers, with unimpeachable logic, the most detailed and specific consequences: *supposito quod mundus divina providentia*

regatur, ut in primo habitum est. Once that premise is granted, the whole majestic edifice of laws can be established on it: eternal law, the natural law, human law, and divine law. All are ultimately based on and justified through the existence of a supreme benevolent being.

Commenting on this issue, D. J. O'Connor (1967, 60) wrote that '. . . the nature of law depends upon establishing the existence of a provident God who planned and guides the universe', while Alan Ryan (1985, 180) argued that 'a secular natural law theory is simply incoherent'.

An important question is, of course, where does God fit into an analysis of natural law rooted in the *Summa Theologiae* texts in which Aquinas explicitly distinguished eternal law from the divine law. Briefly put, divine law as revelation does not apply to a philosophical analysis of ethical naturalism. Eternal law, on the other hand, is reducible to the divine archetypes in the mind of God. A consistent account of natural law requires a metaphysical theory of natural kinds, which is the first question to be addressed. Like Kripke and Putnam, knowledge of a natural kind is possible without knowledge of God or the eternal law. Once natural kinds are justified, a contemporary natural theologian might pose a second ontological question: is the individual instance of a natural kind itself ontologically self-explanatory and totally independent, or is it a dependent being?

Natural theologians like Brian Davies (2002, 239) and Norman Kretzmann (2001, 3–22), accordingly, would ask a further, second-order metaphysical question: 'How come any universe at all?' or simply put, 'Why is there something rather than nothing?' The natural theologian challenges the naturalist to find a place on 'the metaphysical chessboard', arguing that the analysis of human nature—even as an instance of a natural kind—entails that a human person is a dependent being. This requires some form of the 'essence/existence' distinction, an ontological distinction that a naturalist metaphysician like Aristotle is not keen about affirming (Owens 1993, 38–59). The natural theologian must convince the naturalist that a dependent being—or 'contingent being' in cosmological argument circles—demands a real relation with an independent, Necessary Being. God as the '*Actus Purus*'—existence itself—is what provides a response to the question about ontological dependency. In his *Aquinas on Being*, Anthony Kenny (2002) questions the philosophical soundness of this analysis of Aquinas. This author is less pessimistic about this ontology in Aquinas.

For the philosophical, natural theologian, God, as Necessary Being, responds to this second-order metaphysical question about the dependent character of individuals of natural kinds. However, one could construct a theory of natural law rooted only in a natural-kind ontology with an essence composed of dispositional properties. What the natural theologian provides additionally is an explanation in terms of ontological dependency. The ethical naturalist, so the natural theologian would suggest, has not developed a false moral theory but rather an incomplete metaphysical theory. Veatch and MacIntyre, for example, can develop a theory of ethical naturalism from their accounts of a human essence as a natural kind. It is only when ontological dependency is raised by a natural theologian that God as a Source of Existence becomes significant philosophically. Without a divine being, nonetheless,

Veatch and MacIntyre can develop a consistent metaphysics of natural kinds, which is a sufficient condition for an ontological ground underpinning natural law. In responding to d'Entrèves, O'Connor and Ryan, this is a compelling reason that God is not a necessary condition for explicating natural-law theory.

In *Natural Law and Natural Rights*, Finnis (1982, 400) articulated a similar position on the relation of God to understanding the first principles of natural law: 'For Aquinas, there is nothing extraordinary about man's grasp of the natural law; it is simply one application of man's ordinary power of understanding'. Knowing human goods is, in principle, a human activity undertaken in normal human ways of knowing. In commenting on Finnis's work, Charles Covell (1992, 222–23) wrote: 'In *Natural Law and Natural Rights*, (Finnis) claimed that the principles of natural law admitted of an entirely secular derivation, which involved no metaphysical assumptions regarding the existence, nature or will of God'. While Finnis would not endorse natural-kind anthropology and is opposed in principle to ontological foundationalism in natural law, nonetheless, his position is independent of Theological Definism or Divine Prescriptivism. Covell (1992, 223) further notes: 'Indeed, (Finnis) emphasised that it had been an essential feature of the Thomist system that, for Aquinas, the first principles of natural law were self-evident to human reason, whereas the knowledge that union with God ranked as the final human end could be acquired only through revelation'.

10. CONCLUDING OBSERVATIONS

This concludes a somewhat rapid sojourn down the highways of several contemporary reiterations of natural-law theory. The historical connections of natural law are important aspects of this narrative, which are in accord with classical ontological and epistemological realism; both are necessary conditions for a consistent theory of natural-law moral, political and legal theory. Furthermore, this essay suggests how a concept of teleology might be incorporated into contemporary natural-law theory. What the natural law position offers, if only in broad brushstrokes, is a set of human qualities—human nature—without which a justification of a moral theory or a legal system—including a set of human rights—is sought in vain. Since human nature or essence depends upon the foundational structure of a natural kind, a set of metaphysical claims is a necessary condition towards explicating natural law theory.

In concluding this analysis of late-medieval natural-law theory as developed by Aquinas and its connections with modern and contemporary philosophy, one might consider Golding's (1975, 31) suggestions, noted earlier, about the philosophical significance of natural-law jurisprudence:

> The lesson of the natural law tradition is that both [legal effectiveness and legal obligation] involve attention to human needs, human purposes and the human good. Whatever the problems of this tradition, we cannot ignore its lesson in trying to understand the law that is.

While Golding appeals to Fuller's procedural natural law and appears worried about the ontological demands required for a full development of natural-law theory, nonetheless, he has offered important insights about the philosophical import of natural law. A theory of dispositional natural kinds conjoined with a metaphysics of finality may transcend the conventional worries about the ontology required for natural-law theory. In opposition to Bentham's empiricist worries about natural-law theory, contemporary philosophers provide an 'unstilted' version of natural law and offer the opportunity for continued discussion with empiricists on one hand and Kantians on the other, resolving the difficult yet fascinating philosophical issues in natural-law moral and political theory and in jurisprudence.

NOTES

1. I have argued elsewhere that d'Entrèves is mistaken conceptually on this interpretation of Aquinas, which is essentially a form of Divine Command Prescriptivism. See Lisska (1996, ch. 5).

2. One might argue that the seeds of Descartes's philosophy of mind and the demise of realism are found in the philosophy, especially the theory of perception, of Francisco Suarez, the great Jesuit scholastic philosopher of the sixteenth century. However, that is a point for another essay in the structural history of philosophy.

3. This renewed interest in essence as a substantive metaphysical question is common to both Anglo-American and European analytical philosophers. One needs but consider the 'Metaphysical Project' currently being undertaken at the University of Geneva under the auspices of Kevin Mulligan and Fabrice Correia.

BIBLIOGRAPHY

Adkins, E. M. and Thomas Williams, eds. 2005. *Thomas Aquinas, Disputed Questions on Virtues*. Cambridge: Cambridge University Press.

Anscombe, Elizabeth. 1958. Modern Moral Philosophy. *Philosophy* 33(124, January):1–19.

Ayers, Michael. 1981. Locke versus Aristotle on Natural Kinds. *Journal of Philosophy*. 78(5): 247–72.

Barnes, Jonathan. 1984. *The Complete Works of Aristotle*. Princeton, NJ: Princeton University Press.

Covell, Charles. 1992. *The Defence of Natural Law*. New York: St Martin's Press.

Davies, Brian. 2002. 'Aquinas on What God Is Not.' In *Thomas Aquinas: Contemporary Philosophical Perspectives*, ed. Brian Davies, 227–42. New York: Oxford University Press.

d'Entrèves, A. P. 1970. *Natural Law*. Second revised edition. London: Hutcheson University Library.

Dworkin, Ronald. 1978. *Taking Rights Seriously*. Cambridge, MA: Harvard University Press.

———. 1982. 'Natural' Law Revisited. *The University of Florida Law Review*. 34(2):165–88.

———. 1984. 'Liberalism'. In *A Matter of Principle*, 181–204. Cambridge, MA: Harvard University Press.

———. 1986. *Law's Empire*. Cambridge, MA: Belknap Press of Harvard University Press.

Finnis, John. 1982. *Natural Law and Natural Rights*. Oxford: Clarendon Press.

———. 1983. *Fundamentals of Ethics*. Oxford: Oxford University Press.

———. 1998. *Aquinas: Moral, Political and Legal Theory*. Oxford: Oxford University Press.

Foot, Philippa. 2000. 'Does moral subjectivism rest on a mistake?' In *Logic, Cause and Action*, ed. Roger Teichmann, 107–24. Cambridge: Cambridge University Press.

Fuller, Lon. 1964. *The Morality of Law*. New Haven, CT: Yale University Press.

George, Robert. 1993. *Making Men Moral*. Oxford: Oxford University Press.

Golding, Martin. 1975. *The Philosophy of Law*. Englewood Cliffs, NJ: Prentice-Hall.

Grisez, Germain. 1965. The First Principle of Practical Reason. *Natural Law Forum*. 10:168–96.

Grotius, Hugo. 1625. 'The law of war and peace'. In Nussbaum 2006.

Haldane, John. 2000. Thomistic Ethics in America. *Logos* 3(4):150–68.

———. 2002. 'Realism with a metaphysical skull' (with response by Putnam). In *Hilary Putnam: Pragmatism and Realism*, ed. J. Conant and Urszula Zeglen, 97–104. London: Routledge.

———. 2004. 'Natural law and ethical pluralism'. In *Faithful Reason*, ed. John Haldane, 129–51. London: Routledge.

Hart, H. L. A. 1961. *The Concept of Law*. Oxford: Oxford University Press.

Hittinger, Russell. 1989. After MacIntyre: Natural Law Theory, Virtue Ethics and *Eudaimonia*. *International Philosophical Quarterly* 29(4):449–61.

Kenny Anthony. 2002. *Aquinas on Being*. Oxford: Oxford University Press.

Knight, Kelvin, ed. 1998. 'MacIntyre: an interview with Giovanna Borradori'. In *The MacIntyre Reader*, 255–66. Notre Dame, IN: University of Notre Dame Press.

Korsgaard, Christine. 2003. 'Realism and constructivism in twentieth century moral philosophy'. In *Philosophy in America at the Turn of the Century*, 199–222. Charlottesville, VA: The Philosophy Documentation Center.

Kretzmann, Norman. 2001. *The Metaphysics of Theism*. Oxford: The Clarendon Press.

Kretzmann, Norman and Eleonore Stump. 1991. 'Being and goodness'. In *Being and Goodness: The Concept of the Good in Metaphysics and Philosophical Theology*, ed. Scott MacDonald, 98–128. London: Routledge.

Kripke, Saul. 1971. 'Identity and necessity'. In *Identity and Individuation*, ed. Milton K. Muniz, 135–64. New York: New York University Press.

Lisska, Anthony J. 1984. Review of *Fundamentals of Ethics*, by John Finnis. *New Blackfriars* 65(768):288–90.

———. 1991. Finnis and Veatch on Natural Law in Aristotle and Aquinas. *The American Journal of Jurisprudence* 36:55–71.

———. 1996; 1998. *Aquinas's Theory of Natural Law: An Analytic Reconstruction*. Oxford: The Clarendon Press.

MacDonald, Scott. 1993. 'Theory of knowledge'. In *The Cambridge Companion to Aquinas*, eds. Norman Kretzmann and Eleonore Stump, 160–95. Cambridge: Cambridge University Press.

MacIntyre, Alasdair. 1981. *After Virtue*. South Bend, IN: University of Notre Dame Press.

———. 1990. *Three Rival Versions of Moral Enquiry*. London: Duckworth.

———. 1998. 'Politics, philosophy and the common good'. In Knight 1998, 235–53.

———. 1998. 'Plain persons and moral philosophy: Rules, virtues and goods'. In Knight 1998, 136–53.

———. 1999. *Dependent Rational Animals: Why Human Beings Need the Virtues*. Chicago, IL: Open Court.

Magee, Bryan. 1998. *The Great Philosophers*. Oxford: Oxford University Press.

McInerny, Ralph. 1992. *Aquinas on Human Action*. Washington, DC: Catholic University of America Press.

———. 1998. On-line Review of *Aquinas's Theory of Natural Law*. *The Medieval Review*. http://hdl.handle.net/2027/spo.baj9928.9801.010

Nelson, Everett J. 1967. 'Metaphysical Presuppositions of Induction'. Presidential Address, 1967 meetings of the Western Division of the American Philosophical Association. *Proceedings and Addresses of the American Philosophical Association, 1966–68*, 19–33. Yellow Springs, OH: American Philosophical Association.

Nussbaum, Martha C. 1986. *The Fragility of Goodness*. Cambridge: Cambridge University Press.

———. 1993. 'Non-Relative Virtues'. In *The Quality of Life*, eds. Martha Nussbaum and Amartya Sen, 242–69. Oxford: Clarendon Press.

———. 2006. *Frontiers of Justice*. Cambridge, MA: The Belknap Press of Harvard University Press.

———. 2007. Constitutions and Capabilities: 'Perception' Against Lofty Formalism. *The Harvard Law Review: The Supreme Court Edition* 10–97.

O'Connor, D. J. 1967. *Aquinas and Natural Law*. London: Macmillan.

Owens, Joseph. 1993. 'Aristotle and Aquinas'. In *The Cambridge Companion to Aquinas*, eds. Norman Kretzmann and Eleonore Stump, 38–59. Cambridge: Cambridge University Press.

Ross, W. D. 1930. *The Right and the Good*. Oxford: The Clarendon Press.

Ryan, Alan. 1985. 'Utility and ownership'. In *Utility and Rights*, ed. R. G. Frey, 175–95. Minneapolis, MN: University of Minnesota Press.

Schofield, P., C. Pease-Watkin and C. Blares. 2003. *Jeremy Bentham: Rights, Representation and Reform*. Oxford: Clarendon Press (*The Collected Works of Jeremy Bentham*).

Singer, Peter. 2004. 'Ethics beyond species and beyond instincts'. In *Animal Rights*, ed. Cass R. Sunstein and Martha C. Nussbaum, 78–92. New York: Oxford University Press.

Veatch, Henry B. 1971. *For an Ontology of Morals*. Evanston, IL: Northwestern University Press.

———. 1986. *Human Rights: Fact or Fancy?* Baton Rouge, LA: Louisiana State University Press.

———. 1990. *Swimming Against the Current in Contemporary Philosophy*. Washington, DC: Catholic University of America Press.

Wedberg, A. 1971. 'The theory of ideas'. In *Plato: I: Metaphysics and Epistemology*, ed. Gregory Vlastos, 28–52. Garden City, NY: Doubleday and Company.

CHAPTER 30

RIGHTS

CARY J. NEDERMAN

DURING the Latin Middle Ages, the language of 'right' (*ius*) and 'rights' (*jura*) along with a host of related terminology was on wide display—in law books and public decrees (clerical as well as secular), in philosophical treatises as well as political polemics. Although medieval culture had inherited some of this rights orientation from ancient Rome, especially its law and its leading schools of philosophy, the concept of *ius* had special applicability to the legal and political conflicts endemic to the Latin Middle Ages. Both in the church and in the secular sphere, fundamental questions were rife about which persons or offices possessed legitimate power (*potestas*) or jurisdiction (*jurisdictio*) to govern over which subjects or possessions and in what ways. Authority over people and property overlapped in a confusing and cross-cutting fashion, a heritage not only of so-called 'feudalism' but also of the vital role played by ecclesiastical officials in temporal affairs and the often unclear boundaries between the clerical and the secular realms. Little wonder that, once Roman Law was rediscovered during the course of the eleventh and twelfth centuries, and the great system of European *ius commune* (civilian and canon law) began to emerge, a preponderance of legal dispute turned on the correct assignment of rights to their just claimants.

So, in a literal and technical sense, there were plenty of concepts of rights during the Middle Ages. But this begs underlying questions about whether the widespread medieval use of rights language, first of all, had any strong philosophical foundations and whether, moreover, the way(s) in which medieval thinkers conceived of rights has any significant relation to more recent ideas of rights. In other words, the truly important issues arise from the theoretical underpinnings of medieval discussions of *ius* and their connection with more recent applications of rights. In this regard, it may be useful to distinguish between three categories of rights: legal rights, natural rights and human rights (compare this classification with Vincent 2010, 23–27). The first connotes the sorts of rights that are positively granted by statutory law or code, or at least by the force of custom. The validity of such rights derives from the legitimacy of the grantor, hence posing the key conceptual dilemma of the right of the office or official to confer a given legal benefit in the first place. The right of a tenant to use a piece of real estate that has been ceded to him depends upon the validity of the grant by which he possesses the land; the right of a judge to render judgement upon a litigant assumes that his jurisdiction licitly extends to the person in question. During the Middle Ages, such rights were constantly in dispute, for example, the continuing issue of whether and in what ways clerics were susceptible to secular courts and laws, and laity were subject to ecclesiastical statutes and judges.

The second category, natural rights, denotes the doctrine that human beings possess a set of powers, freedoms, and/or competencies to the extent that they enjoy complete and exclusive dominion over their mental and bodily facilities—and the fruits thereof—in the form of personal property. Thus, a natural rights theory entails a conception of private ownership grounded on the status of the individual human subject. The rights arising from nature (which, during the Middle Ages, meant from the consequences of divine creation) are both inalienable and imprescriptible, in the sense that any attempt to renounce or extinguish them would constitute at the same time the cessation of one's personhood. An important feature of the fully developed idea of natural rights is its direct and immediate political bearing. Given that natural rights may not be curtailed or eliminated without the denial to a person of his or her very humanity, any government that attempts to suppress them without due process has no claim on the obedience of its citizens. Natural rights always take precedence over artificial communal or public rights that might be imposed by political institutions.

Finally, human rights are both the most universal and the most concrete of the three categories. A 'human' right is one that pertains to a person, regardless of circumstance (nationality, class, religion) or physical condition (race, gender, age, disability), on the basis of a fundamental and absolute dignity inhering in humanity. According to Samuel Moyn (2010), a concept of human rights in a full and proper sense involves several components. First, a human right is entirely general, in the sense that it does not depend upon legal, political, religious, cultural or institutional factors in order to stake a claim on its respect; its bearer does not need to be a citizen or subject of a particular state or a member of some other group. Second, a human right must be specifiable in a positive and definite sense—it involves a right 'to' something, say a basic income or clean drinking water, in addition to formal assurance of freedom 'from' external domination. Third, human rights place a moral obligation on every person towards his or her fellows to defend and uphold those rights wherever and whenever they are violated; human rights, therefore, have an international, indeed a global, purchase, demanding the extension of duties beyond sovereign borders.

Historically speaking, positing the existence of the legal concept of rights during the Middle Ages seems the least controversial claim. Here the documentary and contextual evidence strongly indicates a coherent framework for the articulation of rights. The question of whether or not medieval thinkers articulated some version of a natural rights theory has been more contentious and is by no means settled. There remain many scholars committed to the view that the 'discovery' of natural rights is a modern event, occasioned by the Enlightenment, and even among those who endorse the medieval 'origins' of natural rights, there is considerable disagreement about the sources (see Mills 1997, 16; Pagden 2003). Finally, it would seem most open to debate whether the Middle Ages was capable of generating any notion of human rights in the sense of a cross-territorial duty to protect one's fellow human beings when their basic conditions of life are in jeopardy. After all, only the Roman Church during the Middle Ages possessed the moral and political wherewithal to pursue claims of injustice on an international scale. Yet however much it adhered in principle to a moral theology that espoused fundamental human equality based on divine creation, in practice the Church introduced and enforced many invidious distinctions between believers and non-believers, not to mention between various groups within the body of the faithful itself (such as orthodox versus heterodox, clerics versus laity), that override the practical implications of a concept of human rights.

In this chapter, I wish to examine some dimensions of these three concepts of rights as they resonated in the political and legal philosophy of the Middle Ages. In particular, I propose, first of all, to unravel some of the complexities involved in the 'overlapping' of systems of legal rights with reference to one medieval author—John of Paris—who rejected simplistic or reductionistic accounts of supreme authority over persons and goods. Recognising that different sorts of legal rights pertained to different kinds of political and legal institutions and offices, he attempted with considerable theoretical ingenuity to untangle and distinguish multiple varieties of *ius*. Second, I shall evaluate the strengths and limitations of recent scholarship's efforts to identify the origins of natural rights theory in various ideas of *ius naturale* propounded by medieval legal, philosophical and theological thinkers. Specifically, I will address the work of the main competing lines of interpretation concerning this topic found in the work of Michel Villey and Brian Tierney, with an eye to evaluating the extent to which medieval concepts of *ius naturale* can be said to presage modern natural rights. Finally, I intend to take up the question of whether the medieval worldview was capable of generating any conception of human rights as described above. In this connection, I shall argue that the spirit, and some of the substance, of contemporary human rights discourse may indeed be found in the thought of Marsilius of Padua and Bartholomé de Las Casas. In sum, I hope to show that several languages of rights found during the Middle Ages can be shown to possess coherence and cogency.

1. LEGAL RIGHTS

Disputes concerning who possessed what sorts of rights over whom and what were endemic to the medieval period. The Investiture Controversy (actually a series of engagements between clerical and lay lords, the best known of which occurred in the late eleventh century between Pope Gregory VII and German Emperor Henry IV), the conflict between King Henry II of England and Archbishop Thomas Becket of Canterbury over the Constitutions of Clarendon (1164) and the polemical battles between French King Philip IV (the Fair) and Pope Boniface VIII at the turn of the fourteenth century all reflected facets of this profound dilemma. Without recourse to a modern conception of sovereignty, all sides claimed legitimate grounds for the possession of final and supreme legal rights, based on competing conceptions of the nature of political power. The result was not so much a reasoned dialogue as a pitched war of words in which the participants seemed incapable of finding any common ground whatsoever that might lead to a mutually acceptable resolution. Conflicting and incommensurable ideas of the basis of legal rights afforded contending parties sticks with which to beat their opponents into submission.

In marked contrast, one figure of the time stands out for proposing a way of sorting divergent claims concerning legal rights: the Dominican Master John (Quidort) of Paris, who in 1302–3 composed a treatise that has come down to us with the title *De potestate regia et papali* (see Nederman 2009, 222–30). This tract is useful in the present discussion for its attempt to sort out the complex differences between distinct types of legal rights attributable to various institutions and offices depending upon their nature and condition. While there is no indication that John's work had any practical effect, *De potestate* illustrates concisely the many complications posed by contending conceptions of legal rights and strives to sort them out in a manner that assigns each to its appropriate sphere. John is a self-described moderate. He explicitly opposes two contrasting positions that he views as erroneous: the so-called 'error of the Waldensians' (presumably referring to the heretical movement founded by Peter Waldo), which holds that ecclesiastical officials have no rightful role to play in temporal affairs, and the 'error of the Herodians', that is, those who view the church as a this-worldly kingdom (John of Paris 1969, 69–71; 1974, 1–3). John seeks to chart a middle course between the two in such a way as to accommodate what would seem to be otherwise incompatible rights claims. In so doing, he reveals the many different ways in which medieval thinkers could and did conceive of legal rights, and he thus presents a useful guide to the topic.

The conceptual key to John's unravelling of the complexities of overlapping and competing systems of legal rights is the careful and strict distinction he draws between jurisdiction (*jurisdictio*) and dominion or lordship (*dominium*). Jurisdiction refers to 'the right (*ius*) of determining what is just and unjust with respect to . . . property rights and dominion over external goods' (John of Paris 1969, 98; 1974, 30). By contrast, dominion denotes the primary power or capacity to 'order, dispose, keep or transfer' possessions 'without injury to anyone else', what we might call the legal right of ownership (96; 28). The heart of *De potestate* addresses three central questions arising from this distinction. First, who is lord of the goods of the Church? Second, who enjoys dominion over the property of laypeople? And third, what is the proper relationship between the Church and the possessions of the laity? In a series of chapters that comprise the main body of the text, John first offers his own answers to these questions, then proposes a set of potential objections to his positions and finally provides detailed response to supposed counter-arguments. The over-arching result of his enquiry is that various legal rights can and must be classified analytically according to the different types of persons and offices exercising them.

The era in which John lived had seen numerous attempts to centralise legal authority over temporal as well as ecclesiastical property in the hands of the pope, reflected in papal decrees as well as in polemical treatises by scholastic authors such as Giles of Rome and James of Viterbo. Much of the force of John's argument is directed against such efforts. In the case of the goods possessed by the Church, he asserts that 'no individual person has property rights and dominion over them'; rather, since 'ecclesiastical goods, as ecclesiastical, are used for communities and not for individual persons', ownership of them can only be said to reside in the community itself (John of Paris 1969, 91; 1974, 22). In other words, the property rights of the Church are entirely communal in nature. This is true in a double sense. First, all local ecclesiastical communities are said to enjoy dominion over the lands, buildings and moveable objects that they have acquired. Membership in such a community confers upon 'an individual person . . . a right of use over such things to sustain him according to his need . . . [He] does not have this right as an individual but as a part and member of the community' (91; 23). Different members of the community, depending upon their ranks (say, a bishop as distinct from a canon), may have differential claims to Church goods, but membership within the community remains the only grounds for the rights that each possesses. Second, because the Church is also a universal entity, whole in and of itself, what pertains to particular communities is true also of the Catholic community: 'Only the community of the universal Church is lord and proprietor over all goods generally, while communities and churches individually have dominion over the goods appropriate to them' (91; 23). The conclusion to be derived from this analogy is obvious: Just as bishops or other heads of ecclesiastical communities are not owners of the goods held commonly by them, so the pope is not lord of the property of the universal Church.

What, then, is the rightful role of the pope (or, for that matter, other spiritual leaders)? In John's view, the head of any ecclesiastical unit, including the pope, is a 'dispenser' and 'administrator' of the property shared by his community, in accordance with the principles of justice and for the sake of the common good. If the pope were indeed lord of the goods of the Church, he could use them howsoever he wishes without any reference to the needs of his fellow clerics; however, this would violate the very purpose for which property is donated to religious organisations. Thus, it must be that 'the pope alone is not lord. Rather, he is the general dispenser; and the bishop or abbot is a special or immediate dispenser, while the community has true dominion over goods' (93; 25). John goes so far as to declare that the head of an ecclesiastical community (whether abbot, bishop or even the pope), if he appears to be 'disposing of goods unfaithfully and for the private and not for the common good', may rightfully be deposed from office (95; 26). Nor can such officials retaliate against those, whether clerics or laymen, who 'are protesting in possible and legitimate ways against him for an unwarranted disposition', since neither the pope nor anyone else has been granted the legal right to do so as a result of his spiritual station and power (95–96; 26–27).

Neither does the pope enjoy legal rights over the temporal property of the laity. The earthly goods of non-clerics are rightfully apportioned by a means other than assignment by clergy. Specifically, John explains that the external goods of the laity are not granted to the community, as is ecclesiastical property, but

> are acquired by individual people through their own art, labor, or industry, and individual persons, insofar as they are individuals, have right (*ius*) and power and true lordship over them. And each person is able to order, dispose, dispense, retain, and alienate his own according to his will (*pro libito*) without injury to others, since he is lord. And therefore such goods do not have order and connection amongst themselves nor towards one common head who has them to dispose and dispense, since each one may order his things according to his will. (John of Paris 1969, 96–97; 1974, 28 [translation modified])

John holds that lay lordship over temporalities owes nothing whatsoever to an interlocking system of property relations created artificially by a 'just' division of the common. Private goods enter into some social setting only by an act of volition on the part of their proprietors, as through acts of exchange or concession.

Yet what happens in instances when 'injury to others' does occur or when public needs arise that transcend the capacity of individuals or groups thereof to redress them? John is no anarchist. Instead, he invokes the concept of jurisdiction, which he specifically ascribes to secular rulers to determine the just and unjust uses of temporal goods. John is very precise in his construction of his explanation of the connection between individual property and the authority possessed by earthly governors. Jurisdiction, he says, is rendered necessary by the entry of private proprietors into voluntary mutual relations with one another.

> For the reason that it sometimes happens that the common peace is disturbed on account of such external goods, as when someone takes that which is another's, and also at times because some people, who are excessively fond of their own, do not convey it according to what the needs and utility of the country require, therefore a ruler is instituted by the people to restrain such acts, in the manner of a judge discerning the just and the unjust, a vindicator of injuries, and a measurer of the just proportion owed to each for the common needs and utility. (John of Paris 1969, 97; 1974, 28–29 [translation modified])

According to John, the temptation on the part of some to override the rights of others, in conjunction with the need for individuals to attend the common interest, comprise the only justifications for the jurisdiction of rulers. Hence, those who antecedently exercise private property rights must and do authorise the appointment of a judge and executor over themselves and their goods. Yet note that 'a ruler has the power of judging and ascertaining with respect to the goods of those under his authority without, however, having dominion over them . . .' (98; 30). The distinction between lordship and jurisdiction is clear-cut and firm.

Two further important points about the correct relationship between the rights of the church and those of the laity follow from John's conception of dominion in the secular sphere. First, the pope's spiritual rights as head of the Church and ultimate dispenser of its goods do not entitle him to any jurisdiction over the property of laymen. Citing the example of Christ, and the 'error of the Herodians', John asserts that the Redeemer's 'kingship' did not extend to temporal affairs and thus that jurisdiction has not been conceded to the pope or any other priest (John of Paris 1969, 98–100; 1974, 30–33). Second, in cases of 'extreme necessity', when Christians—lay and clerical alike—are imperiled by threats such as 'an invasion of pagans', John contends that 'all the goods of the faithful, even the chalices, belonging to churches are common and to be shared . . .' Hence, the ruler 'has the power to dispense and determine what is to be turned over for the common needs of the faith' (John of Paris 1969, 97–98; 1974, 29). In other words, the imposition of emergency taxes on the Church pertains to the authority of secular government, and the pope is duty bound to provide aid from the community property under his dispensation as 'a declaration of right'. By insisting upon these two points, John consequently delimits precisely where the rights of the priesthood and its leaders end concerning the conduct of public business that falls squarely into the temporal realm. In doing so, he evidently hoped to disentangle the knotty dilemmas posed by the overlapping legal rights that so often confounded secular-spiritual relations during the Middle Ages.

2. Natural Rights

Far and away the greatest recent attention surrounding concepts of rights in the Middle Ages has been devoted to the issue of whether (or how) medieval thinkers pioneered the idea of natural rights. The past fifty years or so have witnessed a series of efforts to establish that natural rights, in the sense that we continue to use that phrase today, were not an invention of modern, liberal, political philosophy (Locke) and practice (the American and French Revolutions) but of medieval philosophy, theology and law. This poses a serious challenge to the conceit of many scholars that 'rights talk' arose as one of the seventeenth-century innovations associated with modernity and/or capitalism. Specifically, two main (and somewhat incongruous) lines of interpretation have been proffered. Michel Villey pioneered the thesis that the idea of natural rights emerged in the early fourteenth century during the conflict between Pope John XXII and members of the Franciscan Order over the doctrine of voluntary absolute poverty, and in particular crystallised in the writings of William of Ockham. By contrast, Brian Tierney has proposed that the development of natural rights should be traced even further back in time to legal and scholastic authors of the twelfth and thirteenth centuries, especially to the great canon lawyers.

The terminology associated with *ius naturale* was, of course, in wide usage throughout the Latin Middle Ages; about this there is no dispute. A pertinent question about its connotation arises from an important conceptual distinction between so-called 'objective' and 'subjective' interpretations of *ius naturale*—natural 'right' versus natural 'rights'. The former reflects the sense of 'natural law' as a set of moral duties imposed by God and incumbent upon human beings as part of divinely cre- ated order, whereas the latter suggests that rights pertain to persons as free individ- uals who thereby enjoy full control over their bodies and property. The proper judge of violations of 'objective' *ius naturale* could only be God Himself (or some autho- rised human deputy), while the appropriate judge in cases in which 'subjective' rights are trampled upon would be the injured individual.

In a series of articles and books produced over a period of several decades, Michel Villey proposed that the origin of the subjective interpretation of *ius naturale* could be traced to the writings of William of Ockham composed during the 1330s and 1340s in response to the efforts of Pope John XXII and his successors to sup- press the Franciscan doctrine of the sanctity of absolute poverty. One faction within the Franciscan Order asserted that in order to imitate Jesus to the greatest extent possible, mendicants forgo ownership of property in their own right, and that they could use such goods as were necessary for their survival (nourishment, shelter) without owning them. In other words, individuals were free to renounce personal property rights in the name of the pursuit of holiness. Thus, to the extent that it was necessary to identify the 'owner' of property possessed by the Order, such goods pertained to the stewardship of an external office, specifically, the pope. While this position was initially accepted by the Church, John XXII determined it to be flawed and denied that voluntary renunciation of ownership rights as distinct from mere usage was possible; for him, instead, use necessarily conferred a non-renounceable right of ownership.

In Villey's view, William of Ockham's involvement in the dispute led to the statement of a wholly novel understanding of natural rights, according to which the liberty to exercise or to renounce one's *ius* was a power (*potestas*) inhering in the human will. Once this bridge was crossed, Villey says, the entire edifice of clas- sical 'objective' natural right was doomed (a development that utterly appalled and disgusted him, as he makes clear). Now right, rather than being conceived as an objectively binding moral duty to God, mediated through nature, was simply a power that reflected whatever a particular human being chose. How did Ockham achieve such a profound transformation? Villey attributes Ockham's status as 'the father of subjective rights' to his embrace of the metaphysical doctrine for which he is best known, namely, 'nominalism, an individualist philosophy' (Villey 1964, 98). By bringing his nominalist principles to bear on legal and moral problems, Ock- ham introduced the idea that individuals by nature possessed rights in the form of sovereign power over themselves and their external goods, something like self- proprietorship or autonomy.

While Villey's account of the genesis of subjective natural rights has been chal- lenged in various ways (see Tuck 1979), the most sustained attack has been mounted by Brian Tierney, who proposes an alternative interpretation of the historical record. From Tierney's perspective, the emergence of subjective rights represented not a fundamental break with the medieval worldview, but one of the greatest bequests of the Middle Ages to humanity: 'The idea of natural rights grew up—perhaps could only have grown up in the first place—in a religious culture that supplemented rational argumentation about human nature with a faith in which humans were seen as children of a caring God', that is, the distinctively Christian, Occidental circumstances of the High and Late Middle Ages (Tierney 1997, 343; cf. 346–88). Tierney carefully demolishes the two central prongs of Villey's thesis: first, that Ockham's nominalism shaped his conception of rights; and second, that Ockham's equation of *ius* with *potestas* was a wholly new and startling development that only took root because of the Franciscan controversy (Tierney 1997, 30–42). As Tierney amply demonstrates, ideas quite similar to Ockham's in conception and language were found far and wide from at least the twelfth century onwards and were especially abundant within the works of medieval canon lawyers from whom scholastic authors likely inherited them. To take just one salient example from the late thirteenth-century Parisian schoolman Godfrey of Fontaines:

> On account of this, that each one is bound by the law of nature to sustain his life, which cannot be done without exterior goods, therefore also by the law of nature each has dominion (*dominium*) and a certain right (*ius*) in the common exterior goods of this world which right also cannot be renounced. (quoted in Tierney 1997, 38)

Of this passage Tierney remarks, 'Here the meaning of the word *ius* shifted from objective natural law to subjective natural right in the course of a single sentence' (Tierney 1997, 38). Certainly, Godfrey, who was no friend of the Franciscan cause, seems to be endorsing central features of an individualistic conception of property ownership that we associate with modern natural rights theory. Over the course of his scholarship, Tierney has been able to cite similar passages from a plethora of texts to support the assertion that subjective natural rights discourse possessed a long and venerable lineage in medieval thought.

Although Tierney is surely correct that medieval authors from Gratian forward expressed the inviolable freedom of individual human beings in the language of *ius naturale*, this claim in itself does nothing to upset fundamentally the conventional view that part and parcel of modern natural rights theory is a concomitant political teaching. As Quentin Skinner has shown, 'subjective' rights mattered in early-modern thought insofar as they had direct political consequences for the powers enjoyed by government over individuals (Skinner 1978, vol. 2, 302–48). More recently, Moyn has asserted essentially the same point, although to different effect (Moyn 2010, 20–23). The issue was not that persons per se are bearers of rights or can assert moral claims as a result thereof, but that such rights constitute the basis of a system of political rule that must not only recognise them but, perhaps more importantly, must be legitimised entirely in relation to them. The modern appeal to rights conveys the absolute priority of the individual in relation to all other, particularly political, considerations. If, *à la* Burke, the only rights that properly enjoy political force are socially derived, then possessing a natural right is not relevant to our evaluation of political institutions, although it may be important in other spheres of human life.

Tierney's work fails to demonstrate that medieval natural rights had such political overtones. For the most part, he evinces no recognition that such a connection between natural rights and politics must explicitly be drawn at all. On the few occasions on which Tierney does engage in an extensive investigation of the political dimensions of medieval natural rights, the results are decidedly mixed. His test case seems to be William of Ockham. On the one hand, Tierney suggests that Ockham's deployment of natural rights language outside of the context of the Franciscan debate was hazy and perhaps wholly polemical (Tierney 1997, 174). On the other hand, he asserts that 'one could make a good case for regarding the *Breviloquium* [*de principatu tyrannico* by Ockham] as the first essentially rights-based treatise on political theory' (Tierney 1997, 185). But the evidence (even as presented by Tierney) seems to contradict this claim. Ockham's recurrent references in *Breviloquium* and elsewhere to 'the rights and liberties granted by God and nature' do nothing whatsoever to protect the individual from the unilateral intrusions of the secular ruler (or even, if more rarely, the ecclesiastical lord) into the lives of subjects. Ockham evidently placed no rights-based limits upon the exercise of political power whenever the common good might be endangered. It was left up to the ruler alone to determine what constituted a clear and present danger to the public welfare. In sum, only a very skewed reading of Ockham permits one to find within his writings anything resembling a 'rights-based political theory', at least in some meaningful modern sense.

3. HUMAN RIGHTS

The idea of human rights requires a commitment to a belief in 'duties beyond borders', that is, the position that rights are to be defended without regard for sovereign power or national self-determination. As Moyn (2010) has emphasised, human rights can be distinguished historically from natural rights by the claims of the former to universality without recourse to specific, territorially fixed forms of political order against which they are asserted by citizen or subject populations. In this sense, human rights are deeply cosmopolitan in a way that natural rights are not. Whereas Moyn and others believe that the doctrine of human rights arises only in the late twentieth century, there are inklings of such a view already during the Middle Ages, rooted in a Stoic-inflected but essentially Ciceronian conception of a unitary humanity that binds all people to respect a fundamental principle of justice, regardless of political (or even religious) identities, grounded in the constitution of human reason.

One illustration of this may be found in the early-fourteenth-century anti-papalist Marsilius of Padua, whose *Defensor pacis* (completed in 1324) teaches an explicit lesson about the responsibility that follows from the recognition of a common bond of humanity (see Nederman 1995). The overt 'purpose' of the *Defensor pacis*, which is divided into three discourses, is 'to expose the singular cause of strife' that currently infects parts of Europe (in particular, the *Regnum Italicum*, by which is meant Northern Italy) 'so that it may henceforth be readily excluded from all kingdoms and cities, and informed rulers and subjects can live more securely and tranquilly' (Marsilius of Padua 1932/1956, I.1.7). At the end of its first discourse, Marsilius renews his contention that 'there has occurred the separation of citizens and finally the degeneration of the Italian cities or polities', and he fears that 'this pernicious pestilence, which is completely opposed to all human quietude and happiness, could readily infect other kingdoms of faithful Christians throughout the world with the same corrupt root of vice' (I.19.12, I.19.13). And in the third discourse, he declares that 'in the preceding, we have assigned the singular cause by means of which civil discord or intranquility now exists in certain kingdoms and communities, and will exist in all the remaining ones (unless prohibited) in the future' (III.1). The *Defensor pacis* identifies this cause of political disruption as the pope, or more specifically, the papacy's attempts to regulate temporal affairs.

One of the most distinctive features of the *Defensor pacis'* argument is the manner in which it addresses the specific conditions of the *Regnum Italicum* in relation to the rest of European society. On the one hand, Marsilius clearly concentrates on the actual circumstances of Italian politics. But, on the other hand, he manifests concern that the threat he identifies is at least potentially posed in equal measure to every territory that recognises the spiritual authority of the pope. The reason that Italy has proven more susceptible to papal intervention, Marsilius claims, is its relative disorganisation. The *Defensor pacis* accuses the Roman pontiff of behaving 'more harshly towards those who can least ably resist, such as Italian individuals and communities, whose kingdom is divided and wounded in virtually all its parts and can easily be oppressed' (Marsilius of Padua 1932/1956, I.19.11). By contrast, popes have been more circumspect regarding those 'such as kings and princes whose capacity of resistance and coercion is more formidable. Towards the latter, they gradually creep and continue creeping in the attempt to usurp jurisdictions which they dare not invade all at the same time' (I.19.11). While in Italy the machinations of the papacy are most overt and destructive, Marsilius believes that a similar programme of encroachment stands behind all papal policies towards temporal governments. Hence, the Marsiglian plan of opposition is meant to have general appeal. The *Defensor pacis* seeks to stem Rome's incursions into 'all kingdoms' and to remedy 'that singular cause of quarrels which threatens no small injury to all kingdoms and communities' (I.19.12, I.1.4). In other words, Marsilius hopes that those temporal authorities who are still fit to act will halt and reverse the spread of the papacy's earthly powers before the papal plan of global dominion is realised.

Marsilius was certainly aware of the risks anyone undertook in resisting papal government. Consequently, he resolves to demonstrate why rulers and communities— especially those in locales where the papacy's threat had not yet penetrated—ought to wager their salvation and temporal safety against the renunciation of the pope's right to intercede in earthly affairs. Obviously, there was little ground for appeal to self-interest in this regard; prudence would suggest that those territories where the papacy had not yet been a source of intranquility should remain uninvolved, rather than gamble with the souls of their princes and inhabitants. But Marsilius insists that, beyond claims of self-interest, a dual responsibility to aid one's fellows by opposing the papal regime overrides all other considerations:

> We ought to wish for peace, to seek it if we do not already have it, to conserve it once it is attained, and to repel with all our strength the strife opposed to it. To this end individual brethren, and in even greater degree groups and communities, are obliged to help one another, both from the feeling of heavenly love and from the bond or right (*ius*) of human society. (Marsilius of Padua 1932/1956, I.1.4)

In part, then, our duty to aid fellow human beings derives from the Christian virtue of charity. Yet he is not satisfied with a purely religious foundation upon which to construct opposition to the papacy. Instead, he reinforces the Christian duty to reject papal infringement upon earthly jurisdiction with a parallel objection arising from rights derived from the sociable nature of human beings. Marsilius invokes the thought of Cicero to support his account of society. In the introductory remarks to the first discourse, the *Defensor pacis* quotes at length from *De officiis* to the effect that human beings exist, according to their natures, in order to serve their fellows rather than merely to satisfy themselves. Nature instils in man the duty to act for the public benefit above all else: 'Whoever desires to and is capable of discerning the common utility is obliged to give . . . his vigilant care and diligent efforts' to whatever threatens 'harm to all states and communities' (I.1.4). Human sociability forms a universal bond, not confined to one's own community but extending beyond fixed political units to all peoples. This doctrine generates the naturalistic foundations of a generalised human responsibility to discover and to stamp out anti-social beliefs and practices wherever they occur.

The doctrine of extra-political human rights is developed to a far greater degree in the conclusion to Discourse I. Marsilius again authorises a broadly based, purely temporal responsibility to oppose interference with human 'peace and happiness'. The resistance advocated by the *Defensor pacis* is of two sorts. First, one must repel enemies of earthly tranquility by revealing their identities to all who will listen. Instruction can be a powerful tool in the war against those who seek to disturb the social order. But, second, one must move beyond education to direct action: whoever takes up the banner of discord and temporal misery must be halted by any means available to knowledgeable antagonists. Marsilius insists once more that the rationale for his position is found in the properties of human nature: 'Every person is bound to do this for another by a certain quasi-natural law (*ius quasi naturale*), the duty of friendship and human society' (Marsilius of Padua 1932/1956, I.19.13). In other words, one is subject to the natural requirement to seek the good of one's fellows without regard for one's personal welfare. Marsilius indicates that any other mode of conduct would be unjust, a position in defence of which he explicitly cites Cicero:

> To these [namely, the tasks of identifying and fighting the enemies of human happiness] all are bound who have the knowledge and ability to take action: and

those who neglect or omit them on whatever grounds are unjust, as Tully testified in *De officiis*, Book I, Chapter V, when he said, 'There are two kinds of injustice: one, of those people who inflict it; the other, of those who do not drive away the injury from those upon whom it is inflicted, if they can.' See, then, according to this notable statement of Tully, that not only those are unjust who inflict injury on others, but also those who have the knowledge and ability to prevent injury being inflicted on others, yet do not prevent it. (I.19.13)

Marsilius comments that it is for fear of incurring the accusation of injustice himself that he took up the cause against the papacy. But his statements have a force that transcends mere personal application. They suggest that a necessary corollary of the natural bond of human association is a duty to perform justice in both its aspects: not only to refrain from doing injury, but also to protect others from harm when it is imminent. The clear implication is that society itself is impossible without the acknowledgement of this obligation arising from the principle of justice proposed by Cicero. Otherwise, individuals would care more for their own circumstances than for the good of all members of the community—a view self-evidently incongruent with a stable society, for Marsilius. Failure to act when one might do so is a vicious affront to one's social nature, to one's humanity.

Marsilius consequently affirms the existence of rigorous standards of responsibility binding on all persons and communities claiming to be included within the civilised fraternity. If one knows of any injury in the process of commission and yet declines to repulse it when one can, one is culpable just as surely as if one were the source of the harm. Marsilius imputes to this Ciceronian dictum a decisive meaning: those who live in polities untouched by civil strife are not thereby absolved of regard for the occurrence of intranquility in other places. Rather, should one be aware of some cause of human misery while failing to stem it as much as one can, one is equally at fault and blameworthy for the unhappiness that occurs. Transposed into modern terms, the *Defensor pacis* promotes a strong and comprehensive version of the notion of duties beyond borders based on a conception of rights that pertain to all human beings.

Even more compelling as a theorist of human rights is the Spanish Dominican and Bishop of Chiapas, Bartolomé de Las Casas, who, although writing in the first half of the sixteenth century, remains firmly ensconced in the legal, moral and political discourses of the Middle Ages (Nederman 2000, 99–115). Las Casas produced a large volume of polemical, philosophical, historical and anthropological treatises in support of the rights of the native population of the Americas. One feature shared by this diverse array of writing is its reliance upon a Ciceronian principle of fundamental human equality. Las Casas follows Cicero in arguing that human beings are distinguished by an ability to reason, as well as to perceive divinity and to associate in an organised fashion; these functions define them as members of the human race and accord them basic individual and cultural rights. Las Casas insists that the use of force in order to 'civilise' so-called 'barbarians' (or alternatively, to destroy them) is not only self-defeating, but also both inhumane and uncivilised. To employ coercion is inhumane because it fails to take into account that humanity is defined by possession of certain inborn, but imperfectly realised, potentialities; it is uncivilised because it mistakes Occidental cultural development for a singular process that no other people is capable of recapitulating, except perhaps at sword's point.

Las Casas has been hailed for his declaration that 'all the nations of the world are human beings' (Las Casas 1951, 2.96). More rarely noticed is that he ordinarily asserts this claim in the context of a discussion of Ciceronian principles of human nature. Indeed, Las Casas's most extensive defence of the doctrine of equality, in the *Apologética Historia*, ascribes the idea expressly to Cicero himself: 'Tully posited in Book 1 of *De legibus* [that] . . . all the nations of the world are human beings, and all human beings and each one of them form no less the definition [of humanity] than any other, and this is that they are rational' (Las Casas 1967, 1.257). Las Casas then enumerates the psychological qualities on the basis of which human beings are deemed to possess reason. The passage underscores the Ciceronian provenance of human reason by advancing an extensive series of quotations from *De legibus*. The precise phrase 'all the nations of the world are human beings' is Las Casas's own invention. Yet it follows directly from his appropriation of Cicero: the powers of the human mind being identical in all cases, and the faculty of reason being therefore universal, 'all the lineage of humanity is one, and all human beings as regards their creation and natural existence are alike' (Las Casas 1967, 1.258) The ascription of human equality Las Casas finds in Cicero's writings becomes the cornerstone of his defence of Indian peoples against European oppression.

This egalitarian precept effectively undercuts any attempt to withhold the status of humanness from certain peoples on the grounds that their conditions of life are barbarous. Hence, Las Casas denies that any people as a whole could be barbarian in the strict Aristotelian sense of 'slaves by nature' who lack the facility for self-governance. As he concludes in the *Apologética Historia*, 'It is an impossibility of all impossibilities that an entire nation may be incapable or so barbaric and of little judgment or lesser or diminished reason that it does not know how to govern itself' (Las Casas 1967, 1.260). But is Las Casas simply addressing the condition of entire populations rather than of discrete individuals? The wording of his treatises sometimes suggests a concern with the equality of groups, not of each of their particular members. On other occasions, however, Las Casas does explicitly specify that his claim about the equal powers of reason applies to persons as individuals:

> Human beings are more rational than other creatures and are conferred in their souls, upon their creation, with the seeds and beginnings and natural inclinations of the senses and the virtues, and they are by no means deficient in the exercise of these qualities . . .; and the entire human race and every individual member of it [possesses] . . . all these characteristics, dispositions and natural human inclinations [that] are natural and universally the same in all human beings, as was affirmed above by the declared judgment of Tully. (Las Casas 1967, 1.362)

The essentially invariant presence of a rational faculty among individual human beings is confirmed for Las Casas by the extreme rarity of persons who are impeded in their use of reason. He maintains that those few persons whose souls do not equip them to exercise reason are to be counted among the monstrosities of nature, comparable to people born with extra limbs or organs, whose existence is commonly explained by reference to divine (extranatural) causes (1.259). That such deformities—whether of the body or the soul—occur so infrequently simply provides further proof that nature is consistent in granting the same properties—psychological as well as physiological—to each and every human being.

Two related tokens of human equality for Las Casas, arising from the inherent powers of human reason, are the universal acknowledgement of the existence of a divine being or supernatural power and the capacity to form societies. Again, his arguments are based on theoretical principles derived explicitly from Cicero. These doctrines can only be addressed briefly in the present context. In the first instance, Las Casas quotes lavishly from *De natura deorum* as well as from *Disputationes Tusculanae* and *De legibus* in support of the claim that 'all the nations in the world, no matter how barbarous and wild they may be, can and may be moved to know and understand that some Lord exists, a creator, mover and consecrator of all things, who is more excellent than humanity, whom all human beings call God' (Las Casas 1967, 1.374). Such awareness of divinity, in turn, depends upon 'the light of reason and the agency of understanding', that is, natural properties of 'all human beings of the world, no matter how barbarous, uncivilized and wild and isolated on lands or islands or far-flung places they may be' (1.375). To the extent that human reason is universal, so knowledge of the divine manifests itself without exception.

Likewise, throughout his treatises, Las Casas employs Cicero's account in *De inventione* (and recapitulated in other of his writings) of the origins of communal life founded on human reason. For instance, *Historia de las Indias*, a work that primarily chronicles the early Occidental voyages of discovery, prefaces its detailed recounting of European contact with the Indians by reminding its audience of the historical experience common to all peoples. 'No generation or nation of the past, neither before nor after the deluge', he observes, was so advanced 'that at its beginnings it did not suffer from very many flaws of wildness and irrationality, such that it lived without politics (*policia*)' (Las Casas 1951, 1.16). Although all the peoples of the earth first 'lived without houses and without cities and as brute animals', still 'they came together by the use of reason and took hold of those things pertaining to human capacity' (1.16). As authority for these assertions, Las Casas quotes but a single source—the preface to *De inventione*—and proceeds to expand upon and extrapolate from it at length:

> And thus it appears that although human beings at the beginning were totally uncultivated, and, as they did not work the land, ferocious and bestial, but by the natural discretion and talent that was innate in their souls, since God created them rational creatures, being ordered and persuaded by reason and love and good industry, which is the proper way for rational creatures to be attracted to the exercise of virtue, there is no nation whatsoever, nor could there be, regardless of how barbarous, wild and depraved its customs may be, that cannot be attracted and ordered to all the political virtues and all the humanity of domesticated, political and rational human beings . . . (1.16)

As illustration of this point, Las Casas reports that no less a nation than Spain itself originated out of a 'barbaric' people whose ferocity rivaled that ascribed to the Indians. If the Spanish could arrive at a mature culture, he implies, then so surely can the indigenous inhabitants of America. Following Cicero, he maintains that human beings are united—across all geographic and cultural divides—by reason. Equality of reason thus entails for Las Casas that every nation experiences an identical process leading to full human association, including political institutions.

It is clear that Las Casas believed that this doctrine of universal human rights had practical ramifications. He explicitly denies that Spain and other nations enjoy the *ius* to make war on and dispossess the peoples of the New World. Conquest, he says in *De unico modo*, is

> contrary to that which is established for naturally moving and guiding rational beings toward goodness. It is contrary to the natural art of inducing such beings to goodness, which natural reason dictates that all doctors or other teachers ought to possess. It is contrary to the methods used by the wise philosophers, taught and illuminated by the natural light, for winning over the most barbarous people to the way of living humanly. (Las Casas 1942, 502)

The prosecution of such unjust warfare is indeed so unnatural, Las Casas declares on the authority of Cicero's *De officiis*, that even one's own death is to be preferred to the violent injury of the life, limb and estate of innocent persons (506). For to dispossess or otherwise harm our fellow human beings is to 'violate the *ius* of human society', the essential bond that links human beings together through their common reason (see 504, 542, 544). In fact, Las Casas maintains that the Indians are owed recompense for the misery and deprivation that have already been inflicted by the violent conduct of war upon them. 'The observance of justice', he declares, 'necessarily requires compensation to be made, therefore they [Europeans] are obligated to make restitution' (544). The right of society will not be restored until the material consequences of manifest injuries have been reversed and that which has been unjustly appropriated is returned to its legitimate possessors.

Nor does Las Casas stop there. He, furthermore, occasionally proposes a legitimate right of resistance to conquest on the part of the Native Americans. Given the universality of human reason, religion and society, those who would oppress a populace with violence are, in effect, enemies of humanity who have renounced the right to be treated peacefully. The connection between a Ciceronian conception of human solidarity and the propriety of resistance to those acting inhumanely is explicitly drawn, for instance, in *Historia de las Indias*. Las Casas asks whether there exists 'any reasonable people or nation in the world that, through the authority of natural law and reason, would not' respond with force to the violence of the Spanish conquest. He then immediately proclaims the universality of human nature with reference to *De legibus* and concludes that no nation is unjustified in responding to oppression because all people naturally 'hate evil and shun the painful and the harmful' (Las Casas 1951, 2.396–97). Elsewhere, Las Casas remarks with approval that 'Tully understands that all human beings are obligated by natural *ius* to defend their God, or gods taken for the true God' (Las Casas 1965a, 1.408). In still another

work, he observes, 'When some people, kingdom or city suffers oppression or mo-
lestation from some tyrant, it can justly contest him who tyrannizes over it, and be
freed from its weighty yoke by killing him, according to Tully, *De officiis*, Book 3',
from which he then quotes (Las Casas 1965b, 1008–10). In sum, Las Casas conveys
that human rights extend so completely to all of mankind that even non-Christian
peoples may legitimately repulse oppression by Christians; no one may cloak himself in religious rectitude as an excuse for violating the duties stemming from the
universal bond of humanity. The evidence of Las Casas reveals just how inaccurate
it is to assert that when Europeans encountered 'the disconcerting novelty of American native peoples, . . . they could make no simple breakthrough to "humanity" . . .
because they relied on the categories of classical philosophy and medieval religion
to interpret the radical difference of indigenous cultures abroad' (Moyn 2010, 16).
Rather, as we have seen, it was precisely those preceding traditions that brought Las
Casas to defend 'humanity' and the rights pertaining thereto with such vigor.

4. CONCLUSION

The aim of the foregoing chapter was to demonstrate not only that rights were a
much-debated part of the legal and political scene of the Middle Ages, but also
that considerable conceptual energy was devoted to understanding and applying
them. This survey is by no means comprehensive; the authors and texts surveyed
here are intended merely to illustrate the many ways in which concepts of rights
were analysed and deployed in the medieval period. Any scholar interested in the
history of rights must, therefore, take cognizance of the Middle Ages in order to
form a complete image of the topic.

BIBLIOGRAPHY

John of Paris. 1969. *De potestate regia et papali*. Stuttgart: Klett Verlag.
———. 1974. *On Royal and Papal Power*. Trans. A. P. Monahan. New York: Columbia
        University Press.
Las Casas, Bartolomé de. 1942. *De unico vocationis modo omnium gentium*. Ed. Agustín
        Millares Carlo. México City: Fondo de Cultura Economica.
———. 1951. *Historia de las Indias*. 3 vols. Ed. Agustín Millares Carlo. México City: Fondo
        de Cultura Economica.
———. 1965a. *Una disputa o controversaria*. In Bartolomé de Las Casas, *Tratados*. 2 vols.
        México City: Fondo de Cultura Economica.
———. 1965b. *Tratado comprobotorio del imperio soberano*. In Bartolomé de Las Casas,
        Tratados. 2 vols. México City: Fondo de Cultura Economica.

———. 1967. *Apologética Historia Sumaria*. 2 vols. Ed. Edmundo O'Gorman. México City: Universidad Nacional Autónomia de México.

Marsilius of Padua. 1932/33. *Defensor Pacis*. 2 vols. Ed. Richard Scholz. Hannover, Germany: Hahnsche Buchhandlung.

———. 1932/56. *The Defender of Peace*. Trans. Alan Gewirth. New York: Columbia University Press.

Mills, Charles. 1997. *The Racial Contract*. Ithaca, NY: Cornell University Press.

Moyn, Samuel. 2010. *The Last Utopia: Human Rights in History*. Cambridge, MA: Harvard University Press.

Nederman, Cary J. 1995. *Community and Consent: The Secular Political Theory of Marsiglio of Padua's Defensor Pacis*. Lanham, MD: Rowman & Littlefield.

———. 2000. *Worlds of Difference: European Discourses of Toleration, c.1100–c.1550*. University Park: Pennsylvania State University Press.

———. 2009. *Lineages of European Political Thought: Explorations along the Medieval/Modern Divide from John of Salisbury to Hegel*. Washington, DC: Catholic University of America Press.

Pagden, Anthony. 2003. Human Rights, Natural Rights, and Europe's Imperial Legacy. *Political Theory* 31: 171–99.

Skinner, Quentin. 1978. *The Foundations of Modern Political Thought*. 2 vols. Cambridge: Cambridge University Press.

Tierney, Brian. 1997. *The Idea of Natural Rights*. Atlanta: Scholars Press.

Tuck, Richard. 1979. *Natural Rights Theories: Their Origin and Development*. Cambridge: Cambridge University Press.

Villey, Michel. 1964. La genèse du droit subjectif chez Guillaume d'Occam. *Archives de philosophie du droit* 9:97–127.

Vincent, Andrew. 2010. *The Politics of Human Rights*. Oxford: Oxford University Press.

CHAPTER 31

AESTHETICS

ANDREAS SPEER

1. WHAT IS IN QUESTION

The question of whether there was a medieval aesthetics involves more than one historical and philosophical abstraction. Can we really speak of an aesthetics specific for a millennium, which was called 'medieval' not by the people living in this period themselves, but because of the invention of Petrarch and his humanist friends?[1] It was in the very same period that the first steps to conceptualise art in a stricter sense as visual art took place in the context of the Latin Renaissance culture—and only there.[2] This conceptualisation finally led to the powerful master narrative of a philosophical aesthetics related to a concept of the 'fine arts'. Although one can discover the first attempts to found a philosophical aesthetics in Baumgarten and Kant, it was mainly Hegel who restricted the proper object of the 'aesthetica'—defined by Baumgarten as *'scientia cognitionis sensitivae'*[3]—to the *'schöne Künste'*, the 'fine arts', and established aesthetics as an autonomous philosophical discipline, as we can read in the introduction of Hegel's lectures on the philosophy of art, delivered in Berlin in 1828. 'For this science treats not of beauty in general, but purely of the beauty of art', Hegel concludes; 'the proper expression for our science is "philosophy of art", and more specifically, "philosophy of fine art"'.[4]

But can any universal aesthetic paradigm that invokes trans-historical categories of beauty and art improve our understanding of medieval art? It is revealing that more or less all histories of medieval aesthetics like those of Edgar de Bruyne[5] or Umberto Eco[6] are based on equating *'pulchrum'* and 'beautiful', *'ars'* and 'art', *artifex* and 'artist'. Taken in a trans-historical sense, 'art' and 'beauty' became the key categories of a master narrative, which was driven by the idea that there is a kind of trans-historical essence in art, everywhere and always the same, but which discloses itself through history. This means that, for Hegel, to speak about art is to speak about something that is, by definition, something in the past. This master narrative was the starting point and the basis for art history as an autonomous discipline, and it can also be seen as a kind of 'metaphysical' justification for the classic art museum, where we nowadays find most of the objects of medieval art.[7] Furthermore, it is not surprising that this narrative also directs the entries under aesthetic keywords in standard dictionaries and compendia.

It is certainly not possible to redefine the whole question of whether there was a medieval aesthetics in this article. But I will try to draw some lines that might indicate the direction in which we have to rethink this question. For this purpose I have chosen three examples, which have been always at the centre of the history of medieval aesthetics and the various attempts of its conceptualisation. They also indicate the difficulty in relating the question of aesthetics exclusively to philosophy or even to address it as a philosophical question.

2. ABBOT SUGER'S WRITINGS ON THE ABBEY CHURCH OF SAINT-DENIS

2.1. Panofsky's Paradigm

The writings of Suger on the abbey church of Saint-Denis reflect the abbot's building campaign and the festivities surrounding the celebrating of the laying of the cornerstone for the chevet until the solemn consecration of the rebuilt choir of the abbey church, north of Paris, on 11 June 1144, which up to the present times is considered the birth of Gothic architecture, or in Erwin Panofsky's own words, 'the parent monument of all Gothic cathedrals'.[8] Its construction was overseen by Abbot Suger himself, who recorded this historical landmark in his own writings, with their precise descriptions of how things proceeded from the laying of the cornerstone to the consecration of the finished choir, and with reflections on the goals of the medieval *architectus* and the place of a Pseudo-Dionysian light metaphysics within them. This influential picture, which even today provides the dominant paradigm for the understanding of medieval art, was mainly Panofsky's creation, established, in particular, in his highly suggestive introduction to the edition.[9]

Panofsky's stylisation of Suger as a humanistic figure rests upon the placing of him within a timelessly relevant intellectual tradition, which he found in the continuity and the transformation of Platonic philosophy. In his famous early treatise, *Idea*, written in 1924, Panofsky already mentioned Neoplatonic light metaphysics as a leitmotif in Western thought, which reflects—following the Warburg approach—the continuity of the ancient world from Augustine to Dante, Ficino, Bruno and even to quantum mechanics, which seems to function according to measure, number and weight—the famous saying from the Book of Wisdom

(11,20).[10] From this perspective Gothic architecture became the transformation of a metaphysical system. The 'architecture of light' gives expression to an intellectual experience, a creative process within an artist's mind; it enables us to experience the supernatural divine light in worldly materiality, leading the human intellect to a knowledge of God.

The idea, however, that Gothic architecture is to be understood as a transformation of a metaphysical or theological system is commonly related to Pseudo-Dionysius the Areopagite, who, in a legend originating in Saint-Denis and propagated by Abbot Hilduin in order to establish the Royal Abbey as the *altera Roma*, became identified with St Denis, Paris's first bishop-martyr, whose relics are preserved in the abbey church of Saint-Denis. But in fact, this idea of an overall connection between historical data and speculation is based on the trans-historical assumption of a congruity between modern and medieval notions of aesthetics[11].

This same problem remains with attempts to use, for example, Hugh of St Victor rather than Pseudo-Dionysius to provide a contemporary theological and philosophical background. Conrad Rudolph's attempt to establish Hugh as the true creative theological genius responsible for the fundamental 'artistic change' at Saint-Denis is also driven by the conviction that a leading creative idea (metaphysical or theological) must inform the architectural principles of an artwork—in this case, the Gothic cathedral.[12] Otto von Simson tried to do the same in his book *The Gothic Cathedral*, where he aims to demonstrate that Neoplatonic-Dionysian philosophy was the efficient cause of Gothic architecture, whereas Panofsky had attempted to relate philosophical and theological speculations on light to the lustre of the art treasure and the radiating stained glass windows merely by a weak analogy.[13] But von Simson's enterprise failed as did Panofsky's later effort to unite the system of Gothic architecture with the intellectual character of the High Middle Ages—his ambitious attempt to elucidate the 'genuine cause-and-effect-relation' between the scholastic method (above all, that of Thomas Aquinas) and the architectural principles of the Gothic cathedral.[14]

In any case, most of the various endeavours to criticise Panofsky, or even to replace his vision, while nevertheless speaking of, for example, the 'birth of the Gothic', have not, in fact, overcome his paradigm, which is guided by the Hegelian understanding of aesthetics as the leading master narrative. What is needed, and what, moreover, may not be avoided, is a careful reconstruction of how a medieval figure like Suger experienced art, and what expression he has given to these experiences. Following this appoach, Suger's new choir, which was part of his building campaign and the restoration of the dynastic cult tradition of the *monasterium ter beati Dionysii sociorumque ejus,*[15] might be seen as part of an ongoing architectonical change that finally led to the vision of an integrated church: the idea of the Gothic cathedral.[16]

2.2. Liturgy and Aesthetic Experience

In the prooemium to his treatise *De consecratione*, Suger himself clearly reveals his method and his intentions. 'We have endeavored'—Suger writes—'to commit to writing, for the attention of our successors, the glorious and worthy consecration of this church sacred to God and the most solemn translation of the most precious martyrs Denis, Rusticus and Eleutherius, our Patrons and Apostles, as well as of the other saints upon whose ready tutelage we rely. We have put down why, in what order, how solemnly and also by what persons this was performed, in order to give thanks as worthy as we can to Divine grace for so great a gift, and to obtain, both for the care expended on so great an enterprise and for the description of so great a celebration, the favorable intercession of our Holy Protectors with God'.[17]

On a cursory glance, our primary source, the *accessus* to Suger's *De consecratione*, gives a first idea: that liturgy is the main topic and also the key to what Suger expresses, what we commonly conceptualise in terms of medieval art. What a modern historian of architecture like Otto von Simson finds 'disappointing', namely, Suger's way of reporting and describing architectural structures,[18] echoes the same lack of understanding regarding context that we have noticed in Panofsky. Both historians seem to overlook the central importance for Suger of liturgy and worship. Contrary to Panofsky's insinuations, Abbot Suger did not behave like a modern movie producer.[19] As von Simson rightly maintains, he is not actually interested in aesthetics as such, he is much more guided by liturgical needs. There can be no doubt about this, as the structure of his treatise shows. It is articulated according to the liturgical order of the three famous liturgical events reported by Suger: the consecration of the renewed western part on 9 June 1140, the laying of the cornerstone for the renovation of the eastern part on 14 July 1140, and finally the consecration on 11 June 1144 of the rebuilt choir, the most central part and pinnacle of Suger's enterprise.[20]

As Suger himself states, liturgy serves as a key concept for the understanding of his 'creative' enterprise. This is true if one searches for the reasons for rebuilding the abbey church. These are, in the first place, to be found in a detailed and urgent report concerning dangerous overcrowding, particularly on feast days. On these days, because of the narrowness in the area of the transept crossing, the place where pilgrims entered the crypt, 'the brethren partaking of the most holy Eucharist could not stay' and 'oftentimes they were unable to withstand the unruly crowd of visiting pilgrims without great danger'.[21] Evidently, the leading motive for the rebuilding campaign was liturgical. It was for the sake of the liturgy that Suger tried to restore the damaged parts of the abbey church, to enlarge and reconstruct others, and to revive forgotten elements of the ancient tradition of worship, especially those linked to the Merovingian and Carolingian kings Dagobert, Pippin and Charles the Bald. Suger connects the consecration of the rebuilt part of the abbey church with the *translatio* of the relics of its holy patrons St Denis and his companions Eleutherius and Rusticus and with the consecration of the new altar.[22] Thus, the consecration of only one part of the abbey church assumes the character of an initial consecration of the entire church. In this context, it becomes significant that Suger interprets the consecration of the central eastern area by analogy with the legendary consecration of the old basilica performed by Christ himself, the so-called *consécration légendaire*.[23]

Furthermore, as we can see in the introductory part of *De consecratione*, Suger links the tradition of worship of the holy patrons both to the legendary founding of Saint-Denis by King Dagobert as well as to the cult of Dagobert.[24] By doing so, he renews and strengthens the ecclesiastical and dynastic connection between the French kingdom and the French Royal Abbey. The new upper church and the new altar with the relics of the holy patrons become the pre-eminent place for the *summi pontifices* (the bishops) and for the *persone authentice* (persons of authority).[25] The lower church, for its part, retains the relics of Christ's Passion, the principal object of popular cult.[26] Suger himself reflects upon this ordering in his allegorical explanation of the liturgy. It is thus in the liturgy where, to quote Suger's epilogue, 'the material conjoins with the immaterial, the corporeal with the spiritual, the human with the Divine'.[27] Here lies the real foundation of the interconnection between the different parts of the abbey church.

The sources reveal the clearly performative character of what we might call Suger's aesthetic experience and reflections on it according to the model and function of liturgy. Similarly, the value of his descriptions of construction lies in the descriptive purpose, and this was determined by the liturgical context. Though, without exception, all the passages could be read as simple descriptions of construction, they are, in fact, connected to a specific liturgical function. Because of this, any architectural analysis made independently of the building's liturgical uses becomes meaningless. It is only in their liturgical context that the descriptions can be understood according to the rhetorical model of *ekphrasis*. Therefore, Suger highlights the liturgical processions, the order of the altars and of the patron saints, the order of all items of furniture and treasures, of the *ornamenta* and *thesauri*, as well as that of the verses and *tituli*. These elements should be read as a reference system by which Suger guides his reader through his basilica—as he does in the first part of his *De administratione*, when he guides the reader on an imaginative journey through the abbey's possessions.[28]

2.3. Light and Beauty

The inscriptions on the stained-glass windows and various epitaphs, composed by Suger himself and carefully reported in his own writings, were, in particular, taken by Panofsky as arguments for his thesis that Neoplatonic, in particular, Dionysian, speculation about light had a strong influence on Suger's creative enterprise. For Panofsky, Suger's poetry gives evidence of a purely aesthetic experience of the new architecture expressed in Neoplatonic language.[29] But a careful analysis discloses a quite different background that consists of the epigrams of Prosper of Aquitaine, which belonged to the reading matter of the schools at this time, along with the poetry of Venantius Fortunatus and the sequence of the consecration of a church by Notker of St Gall, and not least the verses of the Irish monk Dungal and the *Carmina* of Paulinus of Nola, which reflect on the enlargement of the basilica of St Felix.[30]

By contrast, there is no evidence that Suger has ever read the works of Pseudo-Dionysius, or of one of his great commentators like Eriugena or Hugh of St Victor.[31] This is even more striking since Suger cites Abbot Hilduin's historical sources *in extenso*, especially his *Gesta Dagoberti*.[32] Moreover, these sources are at the very centre of his various attempts to justify his enterprise.[33] It is not, therefore, surprising that he nowhere speaks of beauty in the Dionysian idiom, lauding its *claritas, splendor* and *consonantia*. Neither does he speak of beauty with reference to the Augustinian model in which 'beauty' is defined by *proportio, harmonia* and *consonantia*.[34] And we should note that the passage in Suger's *De consecratione* in which one can find a certain accumulation of 'aesthetic' terminology is linked to his description of the old Carolingian basilica founded by King Dagobert, which 'was shining with every terrestrial beauty and with inestimable splendor'.[35]

The fascination for what one calls medieval aesthetics—or shall I say, the prejudice—has led to a methodological circle: one finds what one is looking for. By closely following the criteria of the historico-critical method, we are able to gain new insights into Suger's library—and by doing so in his way of conceptualising his aesthetic experiences. We have to turn our view to those theological sources that come from the 'living liturgy': from the liturgical offices and the celebration of the Eucharist, or from the scriptures and religious poetry. All the motifs concerning light metaphors can indeed be found in the liturgy and within the prayers of the liturgy of the church's consecration contained within the twelfth-century *Ordinarium* that embodies the *ordo missae*.[36]

Consider again the question of Suger's guiding principle, in the light of these results and evidence. Let us look once more at the *locus classicus* for Sugerian light aesthetics, his description of the enlarged stained-glass windows. It must be read within its context. From a grammatical point of view, the phrase in which Suger speaks about the 'elegant and praiseworthy extension of the radiating chapels (*in circuitu oratoriorum*), by virtue of which the whole church would shine by the wonderful and uninterrupted light of the most luminous, radiant windows passing through the beauty of the inside'[37] is a simple addition or appendix to the description of the complex space, where the transept crossing meets the choir. The radiating chapels are not part of Suger's crucial effort to balance the 'medium' by geometrical and arithmetical means, by relating the axis of the old basilica and of the new enlargement (*medio novi augmenti*) to the dimensions of the new side aisles.[38] Suger does indeed mention them because of their enlarged stained-glass windows. But let us compare the description of the old Carolingian church and its liturgical background, and let us remember that Suger tried to re-establish the old traditions of the Merovingian and Carolingian kings, including the *laus perennis*, the perennial praise before the tombs of the Holy Patrons and Martyrs.[39] Then, one can imagine a monk who experienced, year after year, the liturgical offices:[40] light passing through the sanctuary might have impressed him in the same way that it does a modern visitor. But here is the hermeutical difference: our medieval monk at Saint-Denis would *never* have celebrated a 'creative artistic event' with which the history of Gothic glass may be said to have begun.[41] Suger certainly never did. Perhaps he would have perceived the light streaming through the window as a symbol of the perennial liturgical order within the changing hours of the office,[42] as a representation of God's own beauty and goodness to which all creatures are called and in which all are able to participate.

The theology we have here to recognise, is not a speculative one, which serves according to a Hegelian paradigm of aesthetics as the leading creative idea behind the artistic enterprise, and which has inspired a new architecture. Suger's theological approach is deeply rooted within the daily life of a medieval monk, and within a tradition that might be called 'living theology': a combination of schooling, of liturgy-rooted, monastic piety and of personal lecture interest of a learned monk.[43] This living theology in Suger's time lasted, mainly in the monasteries, already more than a millennium. Thus, a careful re-reading of Suger's writings reveals that liturgy and worship history are the key in which Suger expresses what we commonly conceptualise in terms of medieval art.

3. Thomas Aquinas

3.1. Aesthetics

I have already mentioned Thomas Aquinas, whose writings figure prominently in almost all scholarly discussions of medieval aesthetics. In his *Gothic Architecture and Scholasticism*, Erwin Panofsky invokes Thomas to ground the 'genuine cause and effect relation' between the scholastic method and the architectural principles of the Gothic cathedral by linking Gothic architecture to certain features of Aquinas's argumentative style.[44] Compared with the emphasis on the formal style, a more philosophical approach to aesthetics was taken by Umberto Eco and Francis F. Kovach, who were looking in Aquinas's writings for a coherent aesthetic theory.[45] Both were convinced that one can speak meaningfully of Aquinas's 'writings in aesthetics' and that they constitute a discrete and important unit of his thought. Thus, in the foreword to the new edition of *The Aesthetics of Thomas Aquinas*, Eco describes his goal as the presentation of the aesthetic theory of Thomas Aquinas as a constitutive, coherent and self-contained element of his larger philosophical system.[46] Moreover, all these writers presuppose the modern conviction that the proper object of Aquinas's aesthetics will be found in the intersection of two key concepts, beauty and *ars*.

3.2. Beauty—*Pulchrum*

Looking at the texts gathered by these and other authors, one notices immediately that beauty is nowhere neatly thematised in Aquinas's work. It is treated only in passing, if at all, and strictly bound to a specific context, as we will see straightaway. Only Chapter 4 of Aquinas's commentary on Pseudo-Dionysius's *De divinis nominibus* constitutes an exception.[47] Of all of Thomas's writings, his commentary of this treatise by an enormously influential anonymous Neoplatonist of the sixth century[48] contains his most extensive remarks on the beautiful. But surprisingly, his commentary on the *De divinis nominibus* is generally not invoked in attempts to reconstruct his philosophical aesthetics; rather, it is treated as something of a special case.

Instead, theoreticians of Aquinas's aesthetics make much out of his so-called 'formal definition of the beautiful', his effort to characterise beauty in its 'objectivity', with reference to its 'autonomous appearance'.[49] Things are called beautiful, according to Thomas Aquinas, because they are pleasing to look at (*pulchra enim dicuntur quae visa placent*).[50] A glance at the larger hermeneutical context of this description—that is, Aquinas's teaching about the nature of God and of the good (*bonum*) in his *Summa theologiae*—points to the shaky character of this definition, and thereby calls into question certain standard approaches to his aesthetics. Following the view of Pseudo-Dionysius that the good, on account of its relation to the beautiful, has the character of a formal cause, Aquinas speaks of good in its proper sense as an object of the appetitive power of the soul. The beautiful, however, is an object of the rational power, when one considers its attractiveness *qua* object of knowledge. It is in this context that one finds Aquinas's remarks about the things that are called beautiful because they are pleasing to look at. Thomas is clearly defining the concept of beauty in a very special sense. The beautiful is, to a certain extent, defined a posteriori, through an analogy to the good, 'since they are grounded in the same reality, viz., the form, and it is for this reason that the good is praised as beautiful'.[51] Just as it belongs to the notion of the good, that in it all desire finds rest, so it belongs to the notion of the beautiful, that in being regarded or thought, intellectual desire finds rest.

Aquinas begins by asking what, at the level of the senses (*sensus*)—at the level of being struck and attracted in an initial and unmediated way by an object of knowledge—draws the cognitive power (*vis cognoscitiva*) to an object of knowledge. Being 'struck' and 'attracted' by a thing is seen as constituting the initial form of knowledge (*cognitio*) of that thing. The senses are drawn by the well-proportioned character (*debita proportio*) of an object of knowledge, for in this *debita proportio*, a kind of likeness (*similitudo*) is recognised.[52] Aquinas thus first speaks of the beautiful and its modes of expression at the level of sense perception, that is, well before it acquires the character of judgement, much less of an aesthetic judgement. In effect, he expands the cognitive power in general, by incorporating both the cognitive (*visa*) and the appetitive (*placent*) elements of the definition into his own account. Every act of knowledge occurs by means of assimilation (*per assimilationem*). Every similiarity, however, is in reference to form. By means of this analysis, Aquinas confirms the Dionysian claim that the beautiful is related in a certain way to the formal cause, that they are in this respect the same in the subject, although they differ conceptually.[53]

Pseudo-Dionysius's claims about the beautiful also figure prominently in a second classic text traditionally invoked in reconstructions of Aquinas's aesthetics. Again in the *Summa theologiae*, in the middle of his discussion of the Trinity, Thomas lists three sets of 'notes of the beautiful': first, 'integrity' (*integritas*) or 'perfection' (*perfectio*); second, 'right proportion' (*debita proportio*) or 'harmony' (*consonantia*)—both terms are taken from Pseudo-Dionysius, as are their parallels, 'commensurate character' (*commensuratio*) and 'convenience' (*convenientia*)—and third, 'clarity' (*claritas*).[54] Clarity (*claritas*) and harmony (*consonantia*), which come together in the notions of the beautiful (*pulchrum*) and the honourable (*honestum*), are traced by Aquinas, with reference to Book 4 of *De divinis nominibus*, to the notion of God as cause of the beautiful.[55] God is called beautiful insofar as God is the cause of the harmony and clarity of all being. A body is called beautiful when it has well-proportioned members and a 'clear', that is, healthy, colour. A soul is called beautiful that makes well-ordered use of its spiritual gifts, in accord with the spiritual clarity of reason. In the very same context, Aquinas undertakes to expound the two definitions of 'likeness of beauty' (*species sive pulchritudo*)—attributed to the Son by Hilary of Poitiers—and of 'beauty or perfection' (*pulchritudo sive perfectio*) to illustrate how the Son truly and perfectly possesses the nature of the Father. Both definitions express Hilary's intention to affirm, by means of the concept of image (*species sive imago sive pulchritudo*), the perfect agreement in essence shared by Father and Son.[56] Hence—and Thomas emphasises what he has said before by invoking Augustine's saying 'where there is agreement, and first equality'—we see that an image is said to be beautiful if it represents a thing perfectly, even an ugly thing.[57] And this—Thomas continues—agrees with what is proper to the Son insofar as he is the Word, which 'is the light and splendor of the intellect', as John Damascene puts it, 'the perfect Word to whom nothing is lacking' and 'the art of the omnipotent God', as we can read in Augustine.[58]

There is no good reason to separate this 'aesthetic' language and its concepts from the systematic context of Aquinas's teaching on the divine nature. Their close association with its systematic background, which itself finds confirmation in similar associations within the tradition, makes suspect the claim that this definition can be treated as a 'material' definition of beauty divorced from its larger context.

Another option as a starting point for the reconstruction of a medieval aesthetics was beauty as one of the transcendentals—attributes shared by all existing things. But can the transcendental dimension serve for a systematic comparison—on a metaphysical level—of beauty with other goods? Jan Aertsen has convincingly shown that beauty is missing even from Aquinas's most complete enumeration of the transcendentals, that is, his list of the most common attributes of being in the opening article of his *Quaestiones disputatae de veritate*, and holds no special place among the transcendentals.[59] As we can see from the most systematic context where Thomas treats the beauty within the context of the good, namely, in his commentary to the fourth book of Pseudo-Dionysius's *De divinis nominibus*, it is only in connection with his teaching about the divine nature and the divine attributes that Thomas speaks of the beautiful alongside the good. The beautiful adds something to the notion of the good—a certain orderedness to the intellectual powers. But it adds nothing to the concept of being, which means that it has no primary relation to being. In fact, the good and the beautiful are really identical because both are grounded on the form qua common subject of predication. On this point, Thomas upholds the Dionysian formula of their identity: 'the good is praised as beauty' (*bonum laudatur ut pulchrum*), although he modifies it in the sense mentioned above, through his extension of the good to the true, reiterating that the beautiful adds to the good a certain orderedness to the intellectual powers.[60]

3.3. Art—*Ars*

In a similar vein, we may question the assumption that beauty related to an artwork (*Kunstschönheit*), art and artist correspond neatly in meaning to the Latin terms *pulchrum/pulchritudo*, *ars* and *artifex*, respectively. The argument for a tidy parallelism between both conceptual fields assumes that the same sorts of objects as the medievals spoke about using their terms 'ars' and 'pulchrum' can be characterised as 'art' and as 'beautiful' and that we find the specific object of aesthetics in the intersection of both terminologies. But, in fact, the differences between modern and medieval aesthetics manifest themselves with particular acuteness over the understanding of *ars* and *artifex*. In the modern terminology, both of the corresponding terms ('art' and 'artist') are normally related to an individual creative subjectivity, which is conscious of itself as such, expresses itself as such and which understands artistic beauty as autonomous.

In order to see this difference in background, let us consider Aquinas's conception of *ars* and *artifex*. Should one seek an equivalent for the creative and autonomous kind of production, one would find that such activity is reserved for God alone; only the divine will is capable of creation out of nothing (*creatio ex nihilo*). On Aquinas's view, this unique way of 'bringing forth' is to be distinguished from two other ways of creativity, which, unlike the absolute creativity of the divine power, are subject to many conditions: (i) the work of nature, which, in a way, is bound to matter and generates substantial forms; and (ii) bringing forth as making in general: '*facere*'.[61] Thomas explicates this second notion by appealing to the example of the *artifex* who is constrained by the limits both of matter and of substantial form in general. He is constrained, one might say, by the limits of nature: by the matter and form of the thing to be made, which for the *artifex*—the artist as well as the craftsman—assume the character of principles.[62] Therefore, the artist's and the craftsman's creativity is contingent and limited by its ontological conditions, which in essence narrow down the creativity of the *artifex* to a kind of rearranging things and bringing forth their undeveloped potential.

This is the context of ideas in which Thomas Aquinas makes his well-known remarks about *ars* as the imitation of nature (*imitatio naturae*). The *artifex*—no matter whether we understand by this term a craftsman or an artist—remains bound to the conditions of creaturely being: it is in this sense that he 'imitates' nature. Stated more precisely, *ars*—which again covers both craftsmanship or artistry—is the application of right reason to something makeable (*applicatio rationis rectae ad aliquid factibile*).[63] Consequently, as a habit of action (*habitus operativus*), it applies its powers, in conformity with its design and with the laws of production, to the task to be accomplished alone, and not to the uses of the thing produced or the intentions of its users. For this reason, in accordance with the Aristotelian distinction between *praxis* and *poiesis*, *ars* encompasses a knowledge of making distinct from use or doing. *Ars* is thus, for Thomas, primarily of a productive and technical nature, as in building or producing something.[64] It is, then, of a necessarily particular nature, ordered to a certain defined and thus particular end, the work to be realised, and employs certain limited means (*determinata media*) to reach this end. *Ars* rises above its concrete, technical domain only through its association with the wider horizon of human goal setting.[65]

This understanding of *ars* derives, as I have already mentioned, from Aristotle and is itself an expression of that epochal turn in medieval intellectual history, which is to a great extent occasioned by the thirteenth-century reception of the Aristotelian corpus in its entirety. Influenced by Aristotle, Aquinas determines the understanding of *ars* quite differently from the traditional concept of the highly complex notion of *ars* stemming from the ancient concept of the seven liberal arts and its educational programme, which encompasses the entire spectrum of human knowledge and human skills. In the thirteenth century, under the influence of Aristotelian philosophy, the concept of *ars* became more differentiated. *Ars* (or *techne*) was understood as mediating, on the theoretical plain, between experience (*experientia* or *empeiria*) and knowledge or understanding (*scientia* or *episteme*). Consequently, an *artifex* became distinguished by his field-specific expertise, directed towards particular subjects. The differentiation of meanings within the concept of *ars* known to Aquinas followed on another epochal change: the loss of the notion of a theory of the sciences encompassing all human knowledge and activity, and of the speculative certainty, affirmed well into the twelfth century—most tellingly in the *Didascalicon* of Hugh of St Victor—of the deep unity of the technico-productive, scientifico-philosophical and theological bodies of knowledge.[66]

The relative independence of artistic knowledge (*ars*) and scientific knowledge (*scientia*), as it is articulated by Thomas, led on the one hand, to the loss of the conception of beauty in the sense of an 'anagogical way' *(mos anagogicus)* uplifting the mind from the material towards the immaterial. Nevertheless, a more restricted concept of *ars* is one of the presuppositions of theoretical reflection within the specific domain of a particular art. As a result of this reflection, the meanings of aesthetic notions associated with individual arts began to grow. This development led finally to the modern scheme of the fine arts, which itself saw further theoretical elaboration in the Renaissance.[67] Such an understanding of aesthetics is not to be found in the Middle Ages; the statements of Thomas Aquinas about 'art' and 'beauty' must not be taken in this sense. Paul Oskar Kristeller rightly suggests that the attempt to conceptualise an aesthetics in accord with scholastic principles is a modern projection.[68]

Nevertheless, there is a connection between the medieval and the Renaissance conceptualisation of art. One path is the conceptual parallelism between painting and poetry expressed in the famous dictum *ut pictura poesis*.[69] Another important step towards the modern conception of the fine arts in the intersection of the aesthetic categories *ars* and *pulchrum* is the canonisation of the three visual arts: painting, sculpture and architecture. They now gain within the order of the mechanical arts an increase of aesthetic meaning, as we can see from the writings of those Renaissance artists who reflected on their artistic development. In trying to underpin theoretically the process of canonisation, they took into consideration not only the ancient, but also the medieval discussions, as we can see, for instance, in the so-called third commentary of Lorenzo Ghiberti, who cites extensively, beside Vitruvius, medieval sources like Alhazen, Averroes, Avicenna, Witelo, Roger Bacon and John Peckham.[70]

4. The *Schedula diversarum artium*

4.1. An Anonymous Treatise and the Theophilus-Rogerus Legend

One of the most striking models for the medieval understanding of art and craft is an anonymous untitled treatise known as *De diversis artibus*, or the *Schedula diversarum artium*.[71] The title is taken from a remark at the end of the first prologue, and its attribution to 'Theophilus' or 'Theophilus presbyter' is taken from the first line of this prologue. Probably written in the first quarter of the twelfth century, the treatise is one of the most important, and certainly the most cited and most discussed, of all medieval craft treatises, and it was copied widely until the time of printing.

In art and craft history, the *Schedula* is known as the most famous and most complete craft manual of the Middle Ages. The treatise consists of three books: the first describes the craft of painting, the second book deals with glass and the third with metalwork, especially with precious materials like gold and silver, but also with the founding of bells and the construction of organs. All three books have longer introductions, which legitimise in a spiritual manner the meaning of the techniques described in the following chapters and recipes.

It was, in particular, the first book that attracted the attention of Gotthold Ephraim Lessing in 1774, when he was librarian of the Herzog August Bibliothek at Wolfenbüttel. When he published a notice and extracts from *Cod. Guelf. 69 Gudianus latinus* in his *Vom Alter der Ölmalerei aus dem Theophilus Presbyter*,[72] the *Schedula* was immediately considered the first concrete and irrefutable evidence for the use of oil paint, centuries before its supposed invention in the early fifteenth century, which over a century later (1550) had been attributed to the van Eycks by Giorgio Vasari in his famous *Le Vite de' più eccellenti architetti, pittori, et scultori Italiani*.

The discovery of an additional name 'Rugerus' in a Vienna manuscript (MS 2527) and its identification with the anonymous presbyter 'Theophilus', along with the provenance of the major manuscripts, and regional peculiarities of the craft practices described, led to the ascription of this treatise to Roger of Helmershausen, who is considered an artist monk, whose manufactory has substantially contributed to the treasure of the Paderborn cathedral.[73] This identification led to the literary fiction of a talented craftsman monk who set out in the *Schedula* his ideas about artistic creation and brought to its final conclusion the artistic impulse of the entire Romanesque period. In fact, the past two centuries have produced an untold quantity of art-historical, art-technological and conservation–restoration scholarship that is based wholly or in part on Theophilus, to the extent that it has become impossible to refer to Romanesque art, or to any medieval painting, glass or metalwork, without reference to the *Schedula*.

Again we can recognise the guiding idea that creative departures and renewals require a theoretically demonstrable motive, an innovative guiding principle that destroys ingrained habits, and that has an individuality that cannot be derived from underlying historical patterns of perception and behaviour. But this long unquestioned picture, based on evidence of style, and on author and period, is now being criticised. Both the identification of Theophilus with Roger of Helmarshausen and the connection of the *Schedula* with goldsmiths associated with the art treasure of Paderborn have both been questioned. While the Theophilus of the prologue may indeed have been a monk and priest, it has become unclear or even improbable that he was also a practising craftsman.[74] Moreover, there is a major disagreement in contemporary scholarship on why the text was written and to which genre the text belongs: whether the author was principally concerned to transmit and promote certain standards and techniques in craft, or whether he was primarily concerned to contribute to the theological debate on the *artes mechanicae* and church ornament. These questions become even more complicated by the variation in the treatise's reception and use, which seem to have been in some cases scholarly and in other cases practical.[75]

4.2. An Encyclopedic Treatise on the Various Arts

The collapse of the hypotheses about author and workshop has led to a new interest in the nature of the treatise, which is called *Schedula diversarum artium*, into its genre, structure, transmission and reception. The picture is highly complex, but enlightening for the question of medieval aesthetics.

First of all, we have to acknowledge that the *Schedula* is a composite text that embodies diverse traditions, rather than a coherent text by a single author. We have to take into consideration that different parts might have been composed by different individuals with different objectives, writing in different locations and environments, and at different times. Therefore, different parts reflect different practices and interpretations: recipes for making colours, for example, the variations of blue (lib. I, cap. 14; lib. II, cap. 12); mere technical instructions, for example, the detailed description of the making of chalices and founding of bells (lib. III, cap. 42–44, 50, 85), the separation of gold and silver (lib. III, cap. 70) or the production of Spanish gold (lib. III, cap. 48); or those related to a certain liturgical practice, as we can see, for example, in the chapters on the censers (lib. III, cap. 60, 61).[76] Some of those descriptions are detailed and reflect a precise knowledge about the craft process of production; others are pretty general and not even understandable without an expertise in the very subject.

Hence, it is unclear for what purpose the *Schedula* was composed. It has long been assumed that its intention and use was practical. But none of the surviving copies show traces of its direct use in a workshop. The first prologue reveals a wide encyclopedic interest, when it promises the reader to examine 'whatever kinds and blends of various colours Greece possesses; whatever Russia knows of workmanship in enamels or variety of niello; whatever Arabia adorns with repoussé or cast-work, or engravings in relief: whatever gold embellishments Italy applies to various vessels or to the carving of gems and ivories; whatever France esteems in her precious variety of windows; whatever skilled Germany praises in subtle work in gold, silver, copper, iron, wood and stone'.[77] Here one can clearly find hermeneutical elements for what Arthur C. Danto has called the 'transfiguration of the commonplace'.[78] What makes the objects and techniques of craft and art special stems either from the value of the material or from the skilfulness of the craftsman or artist or from an increase of meaning and representationality of that object within its mainly liturgical context.

The author of the prologues, who calls himself Theophilus, was probably the compiler who brought together and edited texts that already existed in some form. This most likely occurred in the first quarter of the twelfth century, most probably in Germany.[79] The material was taken from other recipe collections, some of them known like the *Mappae Clavicula*, the *Compositiones ad tingenda musiva*, or the *Eraclius*, but most unknown.[80] In the same way, the *Schedula* itself was excerpted in the so-called *Lumen animae*.[81]

A further indication of how the text has to be read and for what purpose it was written is given by the context of transmission of each manuscript. In the *Gudianus* 69, the oldest manuscript from Wolfenbüttel, as in other manuscripts, the *Schedula* follows the famous treatise *De architectura* of Vitruvius—a treatise that never served as a practical book for architects during the Middle Ages but, rather, was part of the encyclopedic tradition of learning in the *longue durée* of the ancient seven liberal arts. The richness of this tradition and how it has to be understood are documented in the famous *Didascalicon* written by Hugh of St Victor, who had his earliest schooling in Hamersleben near Halberstadt.[82]

4.3. Art and Artist

Like Hugh of St Victor, the author of the prologues of *Schedula diversarum artium*, 'Theophilus', provides us with a highly complex theological and spiritual vision about the understanding of art. The three prologues form a tricolon: a great introduction at the beginning takes its programmatic output *in exordio* and presents the human creativity in the context of the order of creation, followed by a shorter prologue to the second and again a great prologue to the third book, which parallels the seven *artes* with the seven gifts of the Holy Spirit.[83]

Although the author Theophilus portrays himself as a humble priest and emphasises that all the things he is talking about are offered freely by God himself, the prologues present us with a praise of *ingenium* and *ars* as the expression of the true likeness of God. Full of self-consciousness, the author speaks of the participation in divine prudence, the divine decree and of the *ingenium* via the *libertas arbitrii* and the resulting free will. Although man was 'wretchedly deceived by the guile of the devil' and lost the privilege of immortality through the sin of disobedience, God had implanted wisdom and intelligence in him, so 'that whoever will contribute both care and concern is able to attain a capacity for all arts and skills, as if by hereditary right'.[84] Thus, man has a right to his creativity; it is his duty to his inventiveness and to participate in this way in the *opus restaurationis*. We receive all this freely, to administer in true humility. Therefore, the reader should also eagerly look at this record of the various arts, 'read it through with a retentive memory and cherish it with a warm affection'.[85] The praise of work and the warning against idleness fits into this picture, as do the exemplary figures of David, Solomon and Moses, to which the prologues to the second and the third prologue prominently refer, and also the elevation of the seven liberal arts by attributing them to the seven Gifts of the Holy Spirit. For 'through the spirit of wisdom, you may know that all created things proceed from God and nothing without him'.[86]

The author who is speaking here is certainly not a *magister operis*—no foreman, who as a practising craftsmen (and certainly not an idealised Renaissance artist) would have been actively involved in the making of craft or art, but an *architectus*, who like the captain of a ship is not the person who has mastered best all the trades of shipbuilding, but who is more aware than anyone else of the purpose and goal of the whole and compiles for this purpose the requisite knowledge in the style of an encyclopedia, a study book like that of Hugh of St Victor.[87]

Here again the question arises as to the exact understanding of the underlying concept of 'art', which should not be understood in the disciplinary terms of the 'fine arts'. Although, like Hugh of St Victor in his *Disdascalicon*, the Theophilus of the *Schedula* elevates the mechanical arts to the rank of that creative activity by which man's intellect shines by what it invents—namely, by the many types of painting, weaving, sculpturing and casting, which is why we admire the artists together with nature[88]—there is no indication of a unity of theoretical and speculative on the one hand and practical and technical problem solving on the other—as happens with regard to Renaissance art, as we can see in Alberti. The *Schedula* is a good example of this separation. Neither the regulatory framework of an '*ars artium*' nor the allegorical or anagogical interpretation of the building or of the architect in accordance with 1 Cor 3.10 as 'wise architect' can be understood in terms of specific design conditions for the craft activity itself, nor in terms of aesthetic parameters.[89]

The absence of those aesthetic categories or concepts that we usually look for as the subject of aesthetics does not mean, however, that the specific nature of an excellent work of art or craft and how it is distinct from its daily counterpart have not been reflected. Unlike 'simple things', art shows its character of representation. Art is based on anything, about anything, is susceptible to a reciprocal manner, is the subject of self-esteem and has an intrinsic value. Arthur C. Danto has spoken of the 'transfiguration of the commonplace'. This 'transfiguration' to a large extent results from an interpretation, which identifies and defines what parts and properties of the object belong to the work of art.[90] In this way the reflection on material value and on necessary skills, on use and performance within a mainly liturgical context and finally on the goal of art as a participation in the *opus restaurationis* points to the new understanding of medieval aesthetics that takes its point of departure in a reconstructive hermeneutics for the experience of medieval art.[91]

5. INSTEAD OF A CONCLUSION

Let us pose again the question of whether there was a medieval aesthetics. The three cases we have discussed show the complexity of this question and of the possible answer:

(i)   Certainly, there can be no doubt that there was an aesthetics in this period we usually still call the Middle Ages. But the re-reading of Suger's writings on the abbey church of Saint-Denis of Aquinas's mainly theological questions concerning beauty and art, and of the *Schedula diversarum artium* clearly indicates that we should not lightly apply any universal aesthetic paradigm or invoke trans-historical categories of beauty and art in order to improve our understanding of what we are accustomed to call 'medieval art'.

(ii) The multiple meanings of artistic activity in the Middle Ages, some of them related to particular conceptions of beauty, can only be understood when read with a general hermeneutical reservation. This does not amount to a general denial of the category of the aesthetic, the function of which certainly does not consist in the manifestation of supra-temporal properties of being but is, rather, heuristic; it consists in an encounter across diverse horizons of understanding, which themselves are located in this diversity of interests.

(iii) We have to call into question the idea that creative departures and renewals require a theoretically demonstrable motive, an innovative guiding principle that destroys ingrained habits, the individuality of which—as Pierre Bourdieu has put it—cannot be derived from underlying historical patterns of perception and behaviour.[92] The alleged unity of the technico-productive, scientifico-philosophical and theological bodies of knowledge cannot even be found in those texts most closely related to craft and artistry. In fact, we have to acknowledge a relative independence of artistic knowledge (*ars*) and scientific understanding (*scientia*), as it is articulated by Aquinas, which makes the anagogical reading of beauty less fitting.

(iv) We have also to question the assumption of most of the histories of medieval aesthetics that beauty related to an artwork (according to the Hegelian meaning of *Kunstschönheit*) corresponds neatly in meaning to the Latin terms *pulchrum* or *pulchritudo*; the same is true of the supposed parallelism of *ars* and *artifex*. This is even truer with regard to the assumption that the specific object of aesthetics is characterised by the intersection of both terminologies as 'art' and as 'beautiful'.

(v)   Even if we have to make our contemporary understanding the point of departure, the hermeneutic circle does, however, have another side. We are obviously not merely interested in understanding our own perceptions, but also in understanding that which is unknown, that which is unfamiliar and that which is foreign. What is needed is a careful reconstruction of how medieval figures like Abbot Suger or Thomas Aquinas or Theophilus, the humble priest, experienced art, and what expression they have given to these experiences. What I have introduced for the purpose of Saint-Denis as 'a reconstructive hermeneutics for the experience of medieval art' may also serve as a hermeneutic working model for the more general question of how philosophical or theological aesthetics can proceed with regard to an art world unstructured by any master narrative.[93]

(vi) Finally, we might consider that the question of a medieval aesthetics goes beyond the distinction between philosophy and theology. The examples we have discussed point to different theological contexts mainly concerned with liturgy and speculative theology, which lead to the growth of meaning regarding objects of art and craft.[94] Theoretical reflection on this growth of meaning as well goes beyond an understanding of philosophy in a narrow sense, especially if philosophy is characterised merely by its independence from theology. Most of the aesthetic patterns allude to theological features, as we have seen in Thomas Aquinas, when he speaks about aesthetic perception on the sense level in analogy to Trinitarian relations. This is even truer with regard to the anagogical dimension, when the visual object is understood as a symbol for an invisible reality because it lifts the material upwards to the immaterial. But the true object of the culminating act of vision (*visio*) is no longer a visible concrete one, but the ineffable God.[95] Hence, aesthetics must be understood in a comprehensive and expanded manner, which goes beyond the borders defined by a concept of philosophical aesthetics that tries to find its object in the intersection of art and beauty.

NOTES

1. See Petrarch's *Epistolae de rebus familiaribus et variae*, liber I, epistula 6; Petrarch (1859–64, 53), and also Petrarch's polemical treatise *De sui ipsius et multorum ignorantia*; Petrarch (1906) and Mommsen (1942).

2. Perpeet (1987). On the canonisation of the fine arts by Giorgio Vasari, see Roggenkamp (1996).

3. *Aesthetica* § 1 (Baumgarten 1750).

4. *Vorlesungen über die Ästhetik* I; Hegel (1970, 25).

5. De Bruyne (1946; 1947) (transl. 1969).

6. Eco 1956 (rev. transl. 1988), 1959 (transl. 1985), 2004 (transl. 2004).

7. Belting (1995, 138); see Hegel (1970, 25). See further Danto (1997, esp. ch. 3, 'Master Narratives and Critical Principles', 41–58).

8. See the preface to the first edition of Panofsky (1946, VII). Cf. (1994a, esp. 109–10).

9. Panofsky (1979).

10. See Panofsky's letter to Harry Bober of 18 September 1945, cited in Reudenbach (1994, 118, n. 39) from: *A Commemorative Gathering for Erwin Panofsky at the Institute of Fine Arts in Association with The Institute for Advanced Studies, March the Twenty-First*. Princeton (1968, 19).

11. For a survey see Paschovsky, Binding and Meinhardt (1986); also Jeauneau (1997).

12. Rudolph (1990, 32–47 and 69–75); for critical remarks, Speer (2001, esp. 62–64).

13. Von Simson (1956, esp. 21–58, part I, ch. 2); see the critical discussion of von Simson's thesis in Binding (1995) and Panofsky (1979, 18–26).

14. Panofsky (1951, esp. 27–35).

15. See Dufour (1992–94), vol. II, 338, n. 163 and 465, n. 220, and also *Ordinatio* (Suger 2000) 4.14.

16. Binding (1995, 227–35). See further Binding (1999).

17. *De consecratione* (Suger 2000) 7.48–58 (transl. Panofsky 1979, 85). The Latin text used throughout is of Suger (2000), as also for references to *De ordinatione* and *De administratione*. The translation by Panofsky is of the old, pre-critical text.

18. Von Simson (1956, 123–24).

19. Panofsky (1979, 14–15).

20. On these dates see Pickavé (2000, in particular 157–58).

21. *Ordinatio* 36.199–204 (transl. Panofsky 1979, 135). See also *De consecratione* 10.81–12.100 and *De administratione* 164.714–18.

22. *De consecratione* 87. 537–95. 580.

23. *De administratione* 183. 835–37. See also *De consecratione* 47. 283–86 and 93. 567–68. The treatise *De dedicatione ecclesie beatissimi ariopagite Dyonisii sociorumque eius* is edited in Liebman (1945).

24. *De consecratione*, 8–9 and 88–90.

25. *De consecratione*, 61.382–83.

26. *De consecratione*, 10–13 and 51; see Speer in Suger (2000, 41–43).

27. *De consecratione*, 98.615–16 (transl. Panofsky 1979, 121).

28. *De adminstratione*, 3–159, see Speer in Suger (2000, 27–29 and 37). See Speer (2009).

29. Panofsky (1979, 22).

30. See the sophisticated analysis by S. Linscheid-Burdich, 'Beobachtungen zu Sugers Versinschriften in *De administratione*' in Suger (2000, 112–46, esp. 114–20).

31. Dominic Poirel has recently tried to give some new evidence for Dionysian influence on Suger, especially through the Victorine school: see Poirel (2001b).

32. The *Gesta Dagoberti* are part of the same part of MS Vatican Reg. lat. 571 (which contains Suger's *De consecratione* as well as other pieces belonging to the Saint-Denis tradition, for example, the *Miracula Sancti Dionysii*: see Pickavé (2000, 147–49).

33. See for, example, the emphasis which Suger lays on the *conuenientia et coherentia antiqui et noui operis* (*De consecratione* 20.137).

34. See Aertsen (1991a and 1992), and Speer (1995).

35. *De consecratione* 9.67–78, esp. 67–74; (transl. Panofsky 1979, 87).

36. See Andrieu (1938, 176–95) for the *Ordo ad benedicandam ecclesiam* of the twelfth-century Pontificale Romanum. See Speer (1998).

37. *De consecratione* 49.295–302 (transl. Panofsky 1979, 101). The understanding of this description is highly controversial; see Speer (2005a).

38. On the phrase 'in medio ecclesiae', see Neuheuser (1993, at 146–52).

39. See Robertson (1991, 13–23, 37–38, 220, 224–25); Van der Meulen and Speer (1988, 137–38 and nn. 375–77).

40. A good example is an annotated breviary from the early twelfth century, MS Vendôme, Bibliothèque Municipale 17C; see Robertson (1991, 435–36).

41. Von Simson (1956, 100).

42. See Speer (2005b, esp. 93–97).

43. See Speer, 'Abt Sugers Schriften zur fränkischen Königsabtei Saint-Denis', in Suger (2000, 34–35, 38, 62–65).

44. Panofsky (1951).

45. Kovach (1961); Eco (1956, transl. Eco 1988).

46. See Eco (1988, VII–VIII).

47. Cf. see Speer (1990, at 325–33 and 339ff.); see also Aertsen (1991 at 78–84).

48. See above, Chapter 1, p. 20; Chapter 2, p. 31.

49. See Eckert (1974, 232); Assunto (1982, 64 ff.).

50. *Summa theologiae* Ia, q. 5, a. 4, ad 1. Henceforth, all references to Aquinas are to the first book of the *Summa theologiae* unless otherwise noted.

51. Ibid., cf. the first argument (q. 5, a. 4, arg. 1), which is taken from the fourth chapter (§ 7) of *De divinis nominibus* (*Patrologia Graeca* 3, 704A).

52. Q. 5, a. 4, ad 1; cf. *Summa theologiae* IIaIIae, q. 145, a. 2; see Speer (1990, 326–30).

53. Q. 5, a. 4, arg. 1 and ad 1.

54. Q. 39, a. 8, c. See Eco (1988, 98–121).

55. *Summa theologiae* IIaIIae, q. 145, a. 2, c, and Thomas Aquinas (1950); *In De divinis nominibus* IV, lect. 5, n. 339.

56. Q. 39, a. 8, c; cf. Hilary of Poitiers (1979, 1980) *De Trinitate*, II; Augustine, *De Trinitate* VI, 10.

57. Q. 39, a. 8: Unde videmus quod aliqua imago dicitur esse pulchra, si perfecte repraesentat rem, quamvis turpem'.

58. Q. 39, a. 8, c with reference to Johannes Damascenus (1995), *De fide orthodoxa* I, 13 and Augustine (1968), *De Trinitate* VI, 10.

59. Thomas Aquinas (1975-1970-1972-1976); *De veritate*, q. 1, a. 1, c. Concerning Aquinas's general account on the transcendentals, see Aertsen (1996 and 1991b); see further Eco (1988).

60. Q. 5, a. 4, ad 1; cf. Thomas Aquinas (1950); *In De divinis nominibus* c. 4, lect. 5, 356. See Aertsen (1996).

61. Q. 45, a. 2.

62. Q. 45, a. 2, c.; cf. Thomas Aquinas (1954); *In II Physicorum.*, lect. I, n. 145.

63. Q. 45, a. 2, ad 3.

64. *Summa Theologiae* IaIIae, q. 57, a. 4, c.

65. *Summa Theologiae* IIaIIae q. 47 a. 4 ad 2. Cf. Wieland (1983).

66. See, in comparison, Hugh of St Victor, *Didascalicon*, II, 1 (Hugh of St Victor 1939, 23–5; cf. also Hugh of St Victor 1997)) and Aristotle, *Metaphysics* I,1–2 (980 a 21–983 a 23); *Nicomachean Ethics* VI.3–6 (1139 b 14–1141 a 8). Cf. Thomas Aquinas (1971); *In libros Metaphysicorum*, lib. I, cap. 1 and Thomas Aquinas (1969); *Super Ethica*, lib. VI, cap. 3–4. See Senger (1993, esp. 219–23). Concerning the change in understanding art and sciences, see Craemer-Ruegenberg and Speer (1994).

67. See Speer (1995, esp. pp. 192–95).

68. Kristeller (1976, esp. 175).

69. Kristeller (1976, at 183–84).

70. Ghiberti (1947); see further the extensive introduction and commentary Bergdoldt (1988, XL–LXIII).

71. *Schedula*, lib. I, prol. 1 and 3. References to the *Schedula* are to Theophilus (1961). See also the edition in Theophilus (1874). For a *status quaestionis*, see Speer and Westermann-Angerhausen (2006, esp. 253–55).

72. Lessing (1781).

73. See Theophilus (1874, xliii). This attribution was attacked in Degering (1928). See Speer and Westermann-Angerhausen (2006).

74. See Brepohl (1999) and Wolter (2006, 222–42).

75. See the contributions in Stiegemann and Westermann-Angerhausen (2006).

76. See Theophilus (1961, 10–13, 44–45, 93–99, 111–19, 128, 150–59).

77. *Schedula*, lib. I, prol. 4.

78. Danto (1981).

79. See note 75.

80. *Mappae Clavicula* (1974).

81. Theophilus (1874, 360–74); see also the introduction (XXIII–XLVII).

82. Ehlers (1991).

83. *Schedula*, lib. I, prol., 1–4; lib. II, prol., 36–7; lib. III, prol., 61–4.

84. *Schedula*, lib. I, prol., 1; see Reudenbach (1994b).

85. *Schedula*, lib. I, prol., 4.

86. *Schedula*, lib. III, prol., 62.

87. Concerning the differentiation between 'architectus' and 'magister operis', see Binding (2004) and Senger (1993).

88. Hugh of St Victor (1939, 16–17); Reudenbach (2003).

89. See Binding (1998).

90. See note 78.

91. I developed this hermeneutic approach for the first time in 'Vom Verstehen mittelalterlicher Kunst' in Speer (1993); see also Speer (2000).

92. See Bourdieu (1967).

93. See note 91.

94. See Hamburger (2005a); Speer (2005c).

95. See Hamburger (2005b, 374–412); Kessler (2005, 413–39).

BIBLIOGRAPHY

Aertsen, Jan A. 1991a. Beauty in the Middle Ages: A Forgotten Transcendental. *Medieval Philosophy and Theology* 1:68–97.

———. 1991b. 'Die Frage nach der Transzendentalität der Schönheit im Mittelalter'. In *Historia Philosophiae Medii Aevi. Studien zur Geschichte der Philosophie des Mittelalters*, ed. B. Mojsisch and O. Pluta, 1–22. Amsterdam: Grüner.

———. 1992. 'Schöne (das), II. Mittelalter'. In *Historisches Wörterbuch der Philosophie* VIII, 1351–356. Basel, Switzerland: Schwabe.

———. 1996. *Medieval Philosophy and the Transcendentals. The Case of Thomas Aquinas.* Leiden, the Netherlands, New York, and Cologne, Germany: Brill (Studien und Texte zur Geistesgeschichte des Mittelalters 52).

Andrieu, Michel. 1938. *Le Pontifical Romain au Moyen Âge I: Le Pontifical Romain du XIIe siècle*. Vatican City: Biblioteca Apostolica Vaticana (Studi e Testi 86).

Assunto, Rosario. 1982. *Die Theorie des Schönen im Mittelalter*. Cologne, Germany: DuMont (first published 1963).

Augustinus, Aurelius. 1968. *De Trinitate*, ed. W. J. Mountain and Fr. Glorie. Turnhout, Belgium: Brepols (Corpus Christianorum series latina 50 and 50a).

Baumgarten, Alexander Gottlieb. 1750. *Aesthetica*. Frankfurt; reprinted 1961, Hildesheim, Germany: W. Olms.

Belting, Hans. 1995. *Das Ende der Kunstgeschichte. Eine Revision nach zehn Jahren*. Munich, Germany: Beck.

Bergdoldt, Klaus. 1988. *Der dritte Kommentar Lorenzo Ghibertis. Naturwissenschaft und Medizin in der Kunsttheorie der Frührenaissance*. Weinheim, Germany: VCH.

Binding, Günther. 1995. 'Die neue Kathedrale. Rationalität und Illusion'. In *Aufbruch—Wandel—Erneuerung. Beiträge zur 'Renaissance' des 12. Jahrhunderts*, ed. Georg Wieland, 211–35. Stuttgart, Germany: Frommann-holzboog.

———. 1998. *Der Früh-und hochmittelalterliche Bauherr als sapiens architectus*, 2. überarb. und erg. Auflage. Darmstadt, Germany: Wissenschaftliche Buchgesellschaft.

———. 1999. *High Gothic. The Age of the Great Cathedrals*. Cologn, Germany: Taschen.

———. 2004. *Meister der Baukunst. Geschichte des Architekten-und Ingenieurberufes*. Darmstadt, Germany: Wissenschaftliche Buchgesellschaft.

Binding, Günther and Andreas Speer eds. 1993. *Mittelalterliches Kunsterleben nach Quellen des 11. bis 13. Jahrhunderts*. Stuttgart, Germany: Frommann-Holzboog (2nd edn 1994).

Bouché, Anne-Marie and Jeffrey F. Hamburger, eds. 2005. *The Mind's Eye: Art and Theological Argument in the Medieval West*. Princeton, NJ: Princeton University Press.

Bourdieu, Pierre. 1967. Postface to E. Panofsky *Architecture gothique et pensée scholastique*, 133–67. Paris: les Editions de Minuit.

Brepohl, Erhard. 1999. *Theophilus Presbyter und das mittelalterliche Kunsthandwerk*. 2 vols. Cologne and Weimar, Germany, and Vienna: Böhlau.

de Bruyne, Édgar. 1946. *Études d'esthétique médiévale*. Vol. 1: *De Boèce a Jean Scot Erigène*; Vol. 2: *L'époque romane*; Vol. 3: *Le 13e siècle*. Bruges, Belgium: De Tempel.

———. 1947. *L' esthétique du moyen âge*. Louvain, Belgium, and Paris: Institut Supérieur de Philosophie (Essais philosophiques 3).

———. 1969. *The Aesthetics of the Middle Ages*. Trans. Eileen B. Hennessy. New York: Ungar.

Craemer-Ruegenberg, Ingrid and Andreas Speer, eds. 1994. *Scientia und ars im Hoch-und Spätmittelalter*. Berlin and New York: W. de Gruyter (Miscellanea Mediaevalia 22).

Danto, Arthur C. 1981. *The Transfiguration of the Commonplace: A Philosophy of Art*. Cambridge MA: Cambridge University Press.

———. 1997. *After the End of Art. Contemporary Art and the Pale of History*. Princeton, NJ: Princeton University Press.

Degering, Hermann. 1928. 'Theophilus Presbyter qui et Rugerus'. In *Westfälische Studien. Alois Böhmer zum 60. Geburtstag gewidmet*, 248–62. Leipzig, Germany: Hiersemann.

Dionysius the Areopagite. 1990. *De divinis nominibus*, ed. Beate Regina Suchla. Berlin: W. de Gruyter (Patristische Texte und Studien; 33).

Dufour, Jean, ed. 1992–94. *Recueil des actes de Louis VI*. 4 vols., Paris: Boccard.

Eckert, Willehad-Paul. 1974. 'Der Glanz des Schönen und seine Unerfülltheit im Bilde. Gedanken zu einer Theologie der Kunst des heiligen Thomas von Aquin'. In *Thomas von Aquino. Interpretation und Rezeption*, ed. W. P. Eckhert, 229–44. Mainz, Germany: Grünewald.

Eco, Umberto. 1956, 1970. *Il problema estetico in San Tommaso*. Milan: Bompiani.

———. 1959. *Sviluppo dell'estetica medievale* [*Art and Beauty in the Middle Ages*, 1985]. Milan: Marzorati.

———. 1988. *The Aesthetics of Thomas Aquinas*. Cambridge, MA: Harvard University Press.

———. 2004. *Storia della bellezza* [*History of Beauty/On Beauty*]. Milan: Bompiani.

Ehlers, Joachim. 1991. 'Hugo v. St. Viktor'. In *Lexikon des Mittelalters* V, 177–78. Munich and Zurich: Artemis.

Eraclius. 1842. *Deutsches und französisches Gedicht des 12. Jahrhunderts (jenes von Otte, dieses von Gauthier von Arras)*, nebst mittelhochdeutschen, griechischen, lateinischen Anhängen und geschichtlicher Untersuchung, ed. Hans Ferdinand Massmann. Quedlingburg and Leipzig: Basse.

Ghiberti, Lorenzo. 1947. *I commentari*, ed. Ottavio Morisani. Naples: Ricciardi.

Hamburger, Jeffrey F. 2005a. 'The place of theology in medieval art history: Problems positions, possibilities'. In Bouché and Hamburger 2005, 11–31.

———. 2005b. 'The medieval work of art: Wherein the "work"? Wherein the "art"?'. In Bouché and Hamburger (2005, 374–412).

Hegel, Georg Friedrich Wilhelm. 1970. *Vorlesungen über die Ästhetik* I. Frankfurt am Main, Germany: Suhrkamp (Theorie-Werkausgabe 13).

Hilary of Poitiers. 1979, 1980. *De Trinitate*, ed. Pieter F. Smulders. Turnhout, Belgium: Brepols (Corpus Christianorum series latina 62.1/2).

Hugh of St Victor. 1939. *Didascalicon. De Studio Legendi*, ed. C. H. Buttimer. Washington, DC: The Catholic University Press.

———. 1997. *Didascalicon de studio legendi (Studienbuch)*, translation and introduction by T. Offergeld. Freiburg im Breisgau, Germany: Herder (Fontes Christiani 27).

Jeauneau, Édouard. 1997. 'L' abbaye de Saint-Denis introductrice de Denys en occident'. In *Denys l'Aréopagite et sa postérité en orient et en occident*, ed. Ysabel de Andia, 361–78. Paris: Institut d'Études Augustiniennes (Collection des Études Augustiniennes—Série Antiquité 151).

John Damascene. 1955. *De fide orthodoxa. Versions of Burgundio and Cerbanus*, ed. Eligius M. Buytaert. St Bonaventure, NY: Franciscan Institute.

Kessler, Herbert L. 2005. 'Turning a blind eye: Medieval art and the dynamics of contemplation'. In Bouché and Hamburger 2005, 413–39.

Kovach, Francis J. 1961. *Die Ästhetik des Thomas von Aquin. Eine genetische und systematische Analyse*. Berlin: W. de Gruyter.

Kristeller, Paul Oskar. 1976. 'Das System der modernen Künste'. In P.O. Kristeller, *Humanismus und Renaissance II: Philosophie, Bildung und Kunst*, 164–206. Munich, Germany: W. Fink.

Lessing, Gotthold Ephraim. 1781. 'Theophilus Presbyter, Diversarum artium schedula'. In *Zur Geschichte und Literatur aus den Schätzen der herzoglichen Bibliothek zu Wolfenbüttel*, VI. Beitrag, 291–24. Braunschweig, Germany: in der Buchhandlung des Fürstlichen Waysenhauses.

Liebman, Jr., Charles J. 1945. La consécration légendaire de la basilique de Saint-Denis. *Le Moyen Age* 45:252–64.

Linscheid-Burdich, Susanne. 2000. 'Beobachtungen zu Sugers Versinschriften in De administratione'. In Suger 2000, 112–46.

Meulen, Jan van der and Andreas Speer. 1988. *Die fränkische Königsabtei Saint-Denis. Ostanlage und Kultgeschichte*. Darmstadt, Germany: Wissenschaftliche Buchgesellschaft.

Mommsen, Theodor E. 1942. Petrarch's Conception of the Dark Ages. *Speculum* 17:226–42.

Neuheuser, Hanns Peter. 1993. 'Die Kirchweihbeschreibungen von Saint-Denis und ihre Aussagefähigkeit für das Schönheitsempfinden des Abtes Suger'. In Binding and Speer 1993, 116–83.

Panofsky, Erwin. 1946. *Abbot Suger on the Abbey Church of St.-Denis and Its Art Treasures*. Princeton, NJ: Princeton University Press.

———. 1951. *Gothic Architecture and Scholasticism*. Latrobe, PA: Archabbey Press.

———. 1979. *Abbot Suger on the Abbey Church of Saint-Denis and Its Art Treasures*, 2nd. ed. by G. Panofsky-Soergel. Princeton, NJ: Princeton University Press.

Paschovsky, A., G. Binding and H. Meinhardt. 1986. 'Dionysius'. In *Lexikon des Mittelalters* III, 1076–83. Munich and Zurich: Artemis.

Perpeet, Wilhelm. 1987. *Das Kunstschöne. Sein Ursprung in der italienischen Renaissance.* Freiburg and Munich, Germany: Alber.

Petrarca, Francesco. 1859–1864. *Epistolae de Rebus Familiaribus et Variae*, ed. Giuseppe Fracassetti. Florence: Le Monnier.

———. 1906. *De sui ipsius et multorum ignorantia*, ed. Luigi M. Capelli. Paris: Champion.

Pickavé, Martin. 2000. 'Zur Überlieferung der drei Schriften des Suger von Saint-Denis'. In Suger 2000, 147–62.

Poirel, Dominique, ed. 2001a. *L'abbé Suger, le manifeste gothique de Saint-Denis et la pensée victorine.* Actes du Colloque international à la Fondation Singer-Polignac (Paris) le mardi 21 novembre 2000. Turnhout, Belgium: Brepols (Rencontres médiévales européennes, 1).

———. 2001b. 'Symbolice et anagogice: L'école de Saint-Victor et la naissance du style gothique'. In Poirel 2001a, 141–70.

Reudenbach, Bruno. 1994a. 'Panofsky und Suger von St. Denis'. In *Erwin Panofsky. Beiträge des Symposions Hamburg 1992*, ed. B. Reudenbach, 109–22. Berlin: Akademie-Verlag (Schriften des Warburg-Archivs im Kunstgeschichtlichen Seminar der Universität Hamburg, Band 3).

———. 1994b. '"Ornatus materialis domus Dei". Die theologische Legitimation handwerklicher Künste bei Theophilus'. In *Studien zur Geschichte der europäische Skulptur im 12. bis 13. Jahrhundert*, ed. Herbert Beck and Kerstin Hengevoss-Dürrkopp, 1–16. Frankfurt am Main, Germany: Schriften des Liebighauses.

———. 2003. 'Praxisorientierung und Theologie. Die Neubewertung der Werkkünste in De diversis artibus des Theophilus Presbyter'. In *Helmarshausen. Buchkultur und Goldschmiedekunst im Hochmittelalter*, ed. Ingrid Baumgärtner, 199–218. Kassel, Germany: Euregioverlag.

Robertson, Anne W. 1991. *The Service-Books of the Royal Abbey of Saint-Denis. Images of Ritual and Music in the Middle Ages.* Oxford: Oxford University Press.

Roggenkamp, Bernd. 1996. *Die Töchter des 'Disegno'. Zur Kanonisierung der Drei bildenden Künste durch Giorgio Vasari.* Münster, Germany: LIT.

Rudolph, Conrad. 1990. *Artistic Change at St-Denis. Abbot Suger's Program and the Early Twelfth-Century Controversy over Art.* Princeton, NJ: Princeton University Press.

Senger, Nicola. 1993. 'Der Begriff "architector" bei Thomas von Aquin'. In Binding and Speer 1993, 208–33.

von Simson, Otto. 1956, 1988. *The Gothic Cathedral. Origins of Gothic Architecture and the Medieval Concept of Order.* Princeton, NJ: Princeton University Press.

Speer, Andreas. 1990. Thomas von Aquin und die Kunst. Eine hermeneutische Anfrage zur mittelalterlichen Ästhetik. *Archiv für Kulturgeschichte* 72(2): 323–45.

———. 'Vom Verstehen mittelalterlicher Kunst'. In Binding and Speer 1993, 13–52.

———. 1995a. Jenseits von Kunst und Schönheit? Auf der Suche nach dem Gegenstand einer philosophischen Ästhetik. *Allgemeine Zeitschrift für Philosophie* 20(3):181–97.

———. 1995b. 'Schöne (das)'. In *Lexikon des Mittelalters* VII: 1531–4. München, Germany, and Zürich: Artemis.

———. 1998. 'Art as liturgy. Abbot Suger of Saint-Denis and the question of medieval aesthetics'. In *Roma, magistra mundi. Intineraria culturae mediaevalis.* Mélanges offerts au Père L.E. Boyle à l'occasion de son 75e anniversaire, ed. J. Hamesse, 855–75. Louvain-la-Neuve and Turnhout, Belgium: Brepols (FIDEM Textes et Études du Moyen Âge, 10.2).

———. 2000. Beyond Art and Beauty. In Search of the Object of Philosophical Aesthetics. *International Journal of Philosophical Studies* 8:73–88.

———. 2000, 2008. 'Abt Sugers Schriften zur fränkischen Königsabtei Saint-Denis'. In Suger 2000, 13–53.

————. 2001. 'L'abbé Suger et le trésor de Saint-Denis: une approche de l'expérience artistique au Moyen Âge'. In *L'abbé Suger, le manifeste gothique de Saint-Denis*, ed. D. Poirel, 59–82. Turnhout, Belgium: Brepols.

————. 2005a. 'Suger et le chantier de Saint-Denis: Pour une nouvelle lecture de ses écrits sur l'abbaye'. In *Textes et archéologie monumentale. Approches de l'architecture médiévale*, P. Bernardi, A. Hartmann-Virnich and D. Vingtain, 41–50. Montagnac, France: éditions monique mergoil (Europe médiévale 6).

————. 2005b. 'Lux mirabilis et continua. Remarques sur les rapports entre la spéculation médiévale sur la lumière et l'art du vitrail'. In *Le vitrail roman et les arts de la couleur. Nouvelles approches sur le vitrail du XIIe siècle*, ed. J.-F. Luneau, 85–97. Clermont-Ferrand, France.

————. 2005c. 'Is there a theology of the gothic cathedral? A re-reading of Abbot Suger's writings on the abbey church of Saint-Denis'. In *The Mind's Eye: Art and Theological Argument in the Medieval West*, ed. A. M. Bouché and J. F. Hamburger, 65–83. Princeton: Princeton University Press.

————. 2009. Kunst ohne Kunst? Interartifizialität in Sugers Schriften zur Abteikirche von Saint-Denis. *Zeitschrift für deutsche Philologie*, Sonderheft Interartifizialität 128:203–20.

Speer, Andreas and Hiltrud Westermann-Angerhausen. 2006. 'Ein Handbuch mittelalterlicher Kunst? Zu einer relecture der, Schedula diversarum artium'. In *Schatzkunst am Aufgang der Romanik. Der Paderborner Dom-Tragaltar und sein Umkreis*, ed. Christoph Stiegemann and Hiltrud Westermann-Angerhausen, 249–58. Munich, Germany: Hirmer.

Stiegemann, Christophe and Hiltrud Westermann-Angerhausen, eds. 2006. *Schatzkunst am Aufgang der Romanik. Der Paderborner Dom-Tragaltar und sein Umkreis*, Munich, Germany: Hirmer.

Suger. 2000. *Abt Suger von Saint-Denis. Ausgewählte Schriften: Ordinatio, De consecratione, De administratione*, ed. A. Speer and G. Binding. Darmstadt, Germany: Wissenschaftliche Buchgesellschaft (2nd ed. 2008).

Theophilus. 1874. *Schedula Diversarum Artium. Revidierter Text, Übersetzung und Appendix,* ed. A. Ilg. Vienna: Braunmüller (Quellenschriften für Kunstgeschichte und Kunsttechnik des Mittelalters und der Renaissance 7).

————. 1961. *The Various Arts*. Translated from the Latin with Introduction and Notes by C.R. Dodwell. London and New York: Oxford University Press.

Thomas Aquinas. 1950. *In librum Beati Dionysii De divinis nominibus expositio,* ed. C. Pera. Turino: Marietti.

————. 1954. *In octo libros Physicorum Aristotelis expositio,* ed. M. Maggiòlo. Turin: Marietti.

————. 1969. *Sententia libri Ethicorum*, Rome: ad Sanctae Sabinae (Opera omnia 47 [Leonine edition]).

————. 1975, 1970, 1972, 1976. *Quaestiones disputatae de veritate.* Rome: editori di San Tommaso (Opera omnia 22, 1–3 [Leonine edition]).

————. 1971. *In XII libros Metaphysicorum Aristoteles expositio*, ed. R. M. Cathala and R. M. Spiazzi. Turin: Marietti.

Wieland, Georg. 1983. Zwischen Naturnachahmung und Kreativität. Zum mittelalterlichen Verständnis der Technik. *Philosophisches Jahrbuch* 90:258–76.

Wolter, Jochem. 2006. 'Schriftquellen zur Geschichte der Goldschmiedekunst bis zur Rogerzeit'. In *Schatzkunst am Aufgang der Romanik. Der Paderborner Dom-Tragaltar und sein Umkreis*, ed. Christoph Stiegemann and Hiltrud Westermann-Angerhausen, 222–42. Munich, Germany: Hirmer.

Philosophy of Religion

CHAPTER 32

ARGUMENTS FOR THE EXISTENCE OF GOD

GRAHAM OPPY

Some suppose that medieval philosophers developed successful *proofs* of the existence of God: consider, for example, the espousal of the *kalām* cosmological syllogism by William Lane Craig (in Craig 1979; Craig and Smith 1993; Craig and Sinclair 2009; and numerous other works). Others suppose that medieval philosophers discovered materials that can be fashioned into successful *proofs* of the existence of God: consider, for example, the refurbishing of Scotus's causal argument by Timothy O'Connor (in O'Connor 1993, 2008; and elsewhere). However, we need not join company with those who offer these kinds of estimations in order to defend the view that contemporary philosophers can learn valuable lessons from *some* medieval discussions of arguments about the existence of God.

For the purposes of the following discussion, and in accordance with the scope of this volume, I shall adopt a fairly relaxed view about the extent of the medieval period. The philosophers whom I shall consider below—Philoponus, Anselm, Maimonides, Aquinas and Scotus—can all plausibly be supposed to have produced arguments that are proper deservers of the label 'medieval arguments for the existence of God'. In the first part of my discussion, I shall consider recent enthusiasm, for arguments for the existence of God in the works of these medieval philosophers, in the writings of Craig, Robert Maydole, Robert Koons, David Oderberg and O'Connor. After that, I shall turn to some more general reflections on the role of argument and proof in medieval thought about the existence of God.

1. PHILOPONUS (AND CRAIG)

Simplicius's commentaries on Aristotle's *De Caelo* and *Physics* attribute the following three proofs of the generation of the universe to John Philoponus (490–570 CE), locating them in Philoponus's now lost work *Contra Aristotelem*:[1]

Argument 1

1. If the universe were eternal, then the generation of any non-eternal object would be preceded by an infinite series of generations of non-eternal objects.
2. An infinite series cannot be traversed.
3. (Hence) The universe is not eternal.

Argument 2

1. If the universe is eternal, then there has been an infinite number of past generations.
2. The number of generations is increasing.
3. An infinite number cannot be added to.
4. (Hence) The universe is not eternal.

Argument 3

1. The numbers of the revolutions of the planets and fixed stars are multiples of one another.
2. (Hence) If the universe were eternal, there would be infinite numbers of past revolutions in varying multiples.
3. Infinite numbers cannot be multiplied.
4. (Hence) The universe is not eternal.

As Davidson (1969) notes, these arguments were taken up by medieval Islamic and Jewish philosophers; they became mainstays of the philosophers of the *kalām*. Moreover, these arguments—or variants thereof—are endorsed by Craig (1979) as 'supports' for the *kalām* cosmological syllogism:

1. Everything that begins to exist has a cause.
2. The universe began to exist.
3. (Hence) The universe has a cause.

I think that it is quite implausible to suppose that the three arguments from Philoponus are successful proofs of their (shared) conclusion; and no more plausible to suppose either that the *kalām* cosmological syllogism is a successful proof of its conclusion or that the three arguments from Philoponus are somehow capable of providing 'support' for the second premise of the *kalām* cosmological syllogism.

The major problem that I find for each of the three arguments from Philoponus is the falsity of the premises about infinite numbers, infinite collections and infinite series.

Against Philoponus's claim that an infinite number cannot be added to, I would make the following observations. Suppose we have a collection of infinitely many apples, with cardinality $\aleph_0$. If we add an orange to our collection of apples, then we shall have a collection of infinitely many pieces of fruit, with cardinality $\aleph_0$. Because it is a defining feature of infinite collections that the cardinality of some proper parts is the same as the cardinality of the whole, it is no surprise that adding the orange to the collection of apples does not increase the *cardinality* of the collection of fruit. Nonetheless, there is a perfectly good sense in which adding the orange does increase our holding: there is now a kind that is exemplified in our holding that was not previously exemplified therein. There is nothing to stop addition to an infinite collection; however, in the kind of case that Philoponus envisages, addition to an infinite collection will not increase the *cardinality* of that collection (even though there may be other, perfectly good senses in which our collection will be enlarged).

Similar considerations apply to Philoponus's claim that infinite numbers cannot be multiplied. Because it is a defining feature of infinite collections that the cardinality of some proper parts is the same as the cardinality of the whole, it is no surprise that the *cardinality* of the rotations of the heavenly bodies in infinite time is the same, even though the heavenly bodies complete rotations at different rates. There is no impossibility in the multiplication of infinite numbers; however, as Philoponus in effect discerns, the result of multiplying $\aleph_0$ by q, where q is any non-zero rational number, always yields $\aleph_0$. Moreover, there is *also* a perfectly good sense in which, if one body rotates twice as fast as another, then it completes twice as many rotations in infinite time: for the limit, as n tends to ∞, of the ratio of the number of rotations performed by the faster body in n years to the number of rotations performed by the slower body in n years, is exactly two. As in the first case, we *can* make sense of the idea that one collection of cardinality $\aleph_0$ is greater than another collection of the same cardinality: there is not always a unique unambiguous answer to the question 'Is A larger than B?' when A and B are both infinite in size.

The claim that an infinite series cannot be traversed requires more extended discussion. The falsity of the third premises in the second and third arguments is, I think, manifest only because of developments in our understanding of the infinite in the centuries since Philoponus produced his arguments. (Cantor's investigations put transfinite set theory on secure foundations; Weierstrass laid similarly secure foundations for real analysis.) What I take to be the falsity of the second premise in the first argument is, I think, not quite so readily demonstrated.

If we set aside the possibility of 'infinity machines'—that is, of processes in which an infinite series is realised in a finite interval because the sub-intervals occupied by successive steps in the series stand in an appropriately decreasing geometric ratio— then it seems to me to be true that an infinite series cannot be traversed, in the following sense: it cannot be that there is an infinite series of things that has both predecessors and successors. If there is an infinite series of things, then it must be open in one direction: and, in the direction in which it is open, there is nothing that is 'beyond' *all* of the things that belong to the series. If, for example, you start counting from 0, and consider forever adding 1's at a constant rate: 0, 1, 2, 3, . . ., then you will never finish in the following sense: you will never reach a point at which you are doing something other than counting, with all of the numbers having been counted. However, if you keep counting forever, there is no number that remains forever unenumerated: the infinite series of numbers is traversed because every number is counted. Since, if the universe were eternal, there would be an infinite series open in the past, Argument 1 will only go through if the second premise is interpreted to mean that an infinite series that is open in one direction cannot be traversed—and that isn't so.

If what I have argued here is correct, then no one should now suppose that Philoponus's three arguments are proofs of their conclusions, nor should anyone now suppose that Philoponus's three arguments somehow lend support to the *kalām* syllogism. (For an argument for the more ambitious conclusion that no one should now suppose that the *kalām* cosmological syllogism is a proof, see, for example, Oppy [2006a].) If we can learn anything from *these* three arguments offered by Philoponus, it can only be something about the advances that we have made in our understanding of the infinite since the time at which he wrote.

Perhaps reflection upon these arguments might also prompt some modesty or caution in our evaluations of the merits of our own a priori arguments. I certainly do not think that it was *silly* of Philoponus to have supposed that he had here good objections to the hypothesis of the eternity of the world. Moreover, if by 'our world' we mean 'our universe', as that expression is typically used in contemporary cosmology, then I take it that the conclusion for which Philoponus argues is actually true. However—and here I would part company with Philoponus—I take it to be an open question whether we should suppose that the 'natural' past is eternal, or 'infinite', because it is an open question whether we should suppose that the 'natural' past is more extensive than the past of 'our universe'. (For extended discussion of these matters, see Oppy [2006b]. For conflicting opinion, see, for example, Craig and Sinclair [2009]. Many other contributions to recent discussion of these matters are listed in the bibliography of Nowacki [2007].)

2. ANSELM (AND MAYDOLE)

In Chapter 2 of his *Proslogion*, Anselm of Canterbury (c. 1033–1109) gives one of the most famous arguments in all of philosophy:

> Even the fool is convinced that something than which nothing greater can be conceived is in the understanding, since when he hears this, he understands it;

and whatever is understood is in the understanding. And certainly that than which a greater cannot be conceived cannot be in the understanding alone. For if it is even in the understanding alone, it can be conceived to exist in reality also, which is greater. Thus if that than which a greater cannot be conceived is in the understanding alone, then that than which a greater cannot be conceived is itself a thing than which a greater can be conceived. But surely this cannot be. Thus without doubt something than which a greater cannot be conceived exists, both in the understanding and in reality.

Opinion of this argument has always been largely negative: most who have ventured to comment upon it have taken the view that it is not a successful proof of the existence of God. Moreover, this negative opinion extends to the class of arguments to which Anselm's argument has come to belong: most who have pronounced upon the matter have declared that there are no successful a priori proofs of the existence of God. Indeed, many commentators have gone further still and insisted that there *cannot* be successful a priori proofs of the existence of God. (For further discussion of the history of ontological arguments, see Oppy [1996, 2006a], Dombrowski [2006], and Harrelson [2009].)

There are, however, some contemporary philosophers who give a more positive estimation of Anselm's *Proslogion* 2 argument. For example, Leftow (2005) claims that it is valid, and that there is a strong case for one of its premises. About the other premise, all he says is: 'I will not try to settle whether it is true'. Perhaps this suggests that he is not sanguine about the prospects for a non-question-begging defence of the other premise. Be that as it may, there are others who give a yet more positive estimation of the argument. According to Maydole (2009), the argument is valid, all of its premises are true, none of its premises are question begging, and there is no successful parody that can be made of the argument, that is, no Gaunilo-style adaptation of the line of reasoning in support of, say, an 'island than which no greater island can be conceived'.

I think that Maydole's position is quite implausible.

The strength of Gaunilo's objection to Anselm's argument is obvious upon inspection of the proper parody:

Even the fool is convinced that some island than which no greater island can be conceived is in the understanding, since when he hears this, he understands it; and whatever is understood is in the understanding. And certainly that island than which a greater island cannot be conceived cannot be in the understanding alone. For if it is even in the understanding alone, it can be conceived to exist in reality also, which is greater. Thus if that island than which a greater island cannot be conceived is in the understanding alone, then that island than which a greater island cannot be conceived is itself an island than which a greater island can be conceived. But surely this cannot be. Thus without doubt some island than which a greater island cannot be conceived exists, both in the understanding and in reality.

It is perfectly clear that the one argument is valid just in case the other is. Moreover, it is equally clear that the premises of the one argument are no less acceptable than the premises of the other. ('Being than which no greater being can be conceived' has the same degree of 'understandability' as 'Island than which no greater island can be conceived'; and there just are no grounds for insisting that it is greater for a being than which no greater being can be conceived to exist in reality (than it is for it to exist in the understanding alone) that are not equally good grounds for insisting that it is greater for an island than which no greater island can be conceived to exist in reality (than it is for it to exist in the understanding alone).) When we observe that Maydole's formalisation of the two arguments does not deliver this verdict, the proper conclusion for us to draw is that there is clearly something wrong with his formalisation of the arguments. (For a much more detailed critique of Maydole's discussion, including identification of points at which, as I see it, his formalisations do not do justice to Anselm's text, see Oppy [forthcoming b].)

If we agree—as we should—that the conclusion of Gaunilo's parody is unacceptable, then, given the evident strength of Gaunilo's parody of Anselm's argument, we can certainly conclude that either Anselm's argument is invalid, or else it possesses at least one unacceptable premise. However—and this is, according to taste, either the charm or the frustration of Anselm's *Proslogion* 2 argument—there is no straightforward way to decide whether we should say that the argument is invalid, or that exactly one of the premises is false, or that both of the premises are false, or that more than one of these claims are correct.

There have been many attempts in the recent literature to give formal and semi-formal renderings of Anselm's *Proslogion* 2 argument, and there have been numerous recent attempts to set out a theoretical framework that makes sense of his talk of 'existence in the understanding', and of his distinction between existence in the understanding and existence in reality. (For discussion of the literature up until 1994, see Oppy [1996]. For discussion of some of the more recent literature, see Oppy [2007a, 2007b].) The most striking feature of this recent literature is how vastly these many renditions and theoretical frameworks differ from one another. Perhaps unsurprisingly, the next most striking feature of this recent literature is how unsatisfying most of these renditions and theoretical frameworks are as attempted *interpretations* of the text that Anselm bequeathed to us. (In this context, it is interesting to note that Maydole accuses Anselm of having been mistranslated, or of having misspoken, because our text has it that 'the fool is convinced that something than which no greater can be conceived is in the understanding' when it should say that 'the fool is convinced that the *concept* of something than which no greater can be conceived is in the understanding'. According to Maydole, Anselm supposes that it is inconceivable that one and the same thing could exist both in the understanding and in reality. Yet the evidence of the text surely says otherwise; consider, for example, the repeated use that is made of the word 'alone'.)

In the light of the considerations advanced here, it seems to me to be pretty evident that no one should now suppose that Anselm's *Proslogion* 2 argument is a proof of its conclusion. Of course, that's not to say that it is inconceivable that Anselm's text might inspire the production of a proof of the existence of God; all I have suggested here is that we have good reason to suppose that plausible interpretations of Anselm's text have not yielded cogent arguments for its conclusion. (Elsewhere—in Oppy [1996,

2006a]—I have argued that no one has yet produced a cogent a priori argument for the existence of God. While that claim—if correct—may provide some inductive support for the claim that we are unlikely ever to have a cogent a priori argument for the existence of God, it is also consistent with the claim that someone may someday discover such a proof.) However, even if the text itself has no direct lesson for us, there is clearly much to be learned about the argument, and much to be learned from the nearly millennial discussion that has followed the initial production of the text. Consider, for example, the extensive discussion of (a) questions concerning the analysis of existence claims, precipitated by Kant's insistence that existence is not a real predicate; (b) questions concerning the general theory of intentional items, as pursued by Meinong and countless subsequent philosophers; and (c) questions concerning the proper understanding of the charge that an argument is question begging. In the case of questions about existence and intentional items, there is good reason to think that considerations about ontological arguments played a central role in motivating further investigation of these concerns (and there is no doubt that Kant and Meinong were deeply interested in the application of their analyses and theories to the discussion of ontological arguments).

3. Maimonides (and Koons)

In his *Guide for the Perplexed*, Maimonides (1135–1204) sets out a number of arguments for the existence of God. There is some debate about exactly what attitude he had towards these proofs, and about how he might have reconciled these proofs with his apophatic theological views. Nonetheless, many have supposed that Maimonides intended to defend the standing of the arguments that he sets out as proofs, and some have supposed that we can more or less follow Maimonides in supposing that the arguments that he sets out are successful proofs. So, for example, Koons (1997) sets out and defends an argument from contingency that he says 'closely resembles Maimonides' fourth proof' (194).

The argument that Maimonides gives goes like this:

1. We see things pass from states of potentiality to states of actuality.
2. Whenever we see things pass from states of potentiality to states of actuality, we see agents for those transitions that are separate and distinct from those transitions.
3. Whenever agents for transitions from states of potentiality to states of actuality themselves pass from states of potentiality to states of actuality, those further transitions of those agents from states of potentiality to states of actuality themselves require agents that are separate and distinct from the initial agents and their transitions.
4. An infinite regress of agents of transition from states of potentiality to states of actuality is impossible.

5. (Hence) There must be an agent of transitions from states of potentiality to states of actuality in which there is no potentiality.

The argument that Koons gives goes like this:

1. For any x and y, x is a part of y iff everything that overlaps x overlaps y.
2. If there are some ϕ's, then there exists a sum of all of the ϕ's; for any x, x overlaps this sum iff x overlaps all of the ϕ's.
3. For any x and y, x = y iff x is a part of y and y is a part of x.
4. Situations necessitate the actual existence of their parts.
5. The actual existence of all of the members of a sum necessitates the actual existence of the sum.
6. Causation is a binary relation between actually existing situations.
7. Causes and effects do not overlap, in other words, they have no parts in common.
8. For any given wholly contingent situation x, there is a (defeasible) presumption that x has a cause.
9. (Therefore) If there are any contingently existing situations, then there is a necessarily existing situation that is the cause of the Cosmos, that is, of the sum of all wholly contingent situations.

Clearly, there is room to argue about the extent to which Koons's argument really does closely resemble Maimonides's fourth proof. Moreover, the fact that there is such room points to some problematic features of contemporary discussions of arguments about the existence of God. I think that the only useful way to individuate arguments is in terms of the premises and conclusions: argument A is the same as argument B just in case (i) argument A and argument B have exactly the same premises; and (ii) argument A and argument B have exactly the same conclusion. After all, even the very smallest changes in the formulation of premises and the conclusion of an argument can make an enormous difference to the standing of an argument: changing one word at one point in an argument can render a valid argument invalid (and vice versa), a true premise false (or vice versa), a non-question-begging argument question begging (and vice versa) and so on. Moreover, I think, the only useful way to sort arguments into families is in terms of commonality of premises and/or conclusions: so, for example, there is the family of arguments that share the conclusion 'God exists', and, within that family, there is the sub-family of arguments that share the premise 'All wholly contingent situations have causes', and so on. One consequence of the application of these standards is that labels like 'the ontological argument' and 'the cosmological argument' are poorly formed, since there is no premise that is common to all ontological arguments, and no premise that is common to all cosmological arguments. And, of course, another consequence is that it isn't true that Maimonides's fourth proof and Koons's argument from contingency belong to even one common family: the conclusions of these arguments are distinct, and there is no premise that is shared between them.

Even if I am right to think that we should not be too keen to follow Koons in thinking that his argument 'closely resembles' Maimonides's fourth proof, we can still ask ourselves whether either the argument of Maimonides's fourth proof or the argument that Koons develops—which is, perhaps, in some sense, inspired by Maimonides's fourth proof—is a successful argument. If scrutiny of medieval arguments for the existence of God inspires contemporary authors to produce successful arguments for the existence of God, then, one might think, that, in itself, would be good reason to prompt further consideration of those medieval arguments. So we turn, albeit briefly, to a consideration of the merits of the arguments developed by Maimonides and Koons.

On the one hand, it seems to me that no one should be keen to claim that the argument that we have attributed to Maimonides is such that contemporary naturalists ought to be persuaded by it. Naturalists are committed to something like the following view: causal reality is exhausted by natural reality; natural reality decomposes into (maximal) parts under the causal relation. Now, plausibly, if one part of natural reality under the causal relation ('A') is causally downstream from another part of natural reality under the causal relation ('B'), then the causing of A by B involves a transition from a state of potentiality to a state of actuality. But, of course, ex hypothesi, on the naturalist view, there is no agent for this transition: there is nothing beyond, or apart from, the states of natural reality and the causal relationships that hold between them. To insist on the truth of the third premise in the argument that Maimonides gives is simply to beg the question against naturalism. (Of course, we don't 'see' transitions between global states of natural reality, so naturalists are not automatically committed to the denial of the second premise in Maimonides's argument. Perhaps naturalists might want to deny that second premise as well, but it would take us well beyond the confines of the present discussion to explore this suggestion properly.) The proper conclusion to draw is that, at least for us in the twenty-first century, it is perfectly clear that Maimonides's argument is not a successful proof of its conclusion.

On the other hand, it is, at the very least, controversial whether we should suppose that Koons's argument is a successful proof of the existence of God. No doubt unsurprisingly, it seems to me that there is no reason for contemporary naturalists to suppose that Koons's argument provides them with good reason to revise their beliefs in the non-existence of God. The key question to ask is what naturalists might think about the global shape of natural reality. Is there an initial state of natural reality and, if there is an initial state of natural reality, what is the modal status of that initial state? If naturalists suppose that there is no initial state, or if they suppose that there is a contingently obtaining initial state, then, at the very least, they will insist that the causal principle upon which Koons relies requires modification:

8'. For any given contingently existing *non-initial* situation, there is a (defeasible) presumption that x has a cause.

(If there is no initial state of natural reality, then an initial situation is any situation that overlaps with an infinite initial segment of natural reality.) And, of course, from this revised principle, you cannot get out the conclusion that there is a cause of the Cosmos. On the other hand, if naturalists suppose that there is a necessarily obtaining initial state of natural reality, then naturalists will insist that what Koons

calls 'the Cosmos' is not quite the whole of natural causal reality—since, by definition, 'the Cosmos' is wholly contingent—and will accept with equanimity the conclusion that 'the Cosmos' has a necessarily obtaining cause (taking it that this necessarily
obtaining cause is just the necessarily obtaining initial state of natural reality).

As in the preceding discussions, I must, of course, note that the views that I have
stated here are controversial. For further considerations on the one side of the debate
about the standing of Koons's argument, see Koons (1996, 2000, 2001, 2008); for
considerations on the other side of this debate, see Oppy (1999, 2004, 2006a, 2010).

4. AQUINAS (AND ODERBERG)

The treatment of arguments for the existence of God in the *Summa Theologiae* of
Thomas Aquinas (c. 1225–74) has become one of the staple topics in introductory
philosophy. Generations of students have been invited to engage in detailed critical
analyses of the Five Ways (*Summa Theologiae*, I, q. 2, a. 3). Here, I shall just make
some brief observations about the First Way (an argument that has some obvious
affinities with Maimonides's fourth proof, discussed in the section above):

1. Some things change.
2. Whatever changes is changed by something else.
3. There is no infinite regress of changing things.
4. (Hence) There is something that changes other things but that is not itself
   changed (which all call 'God').

(Note that, in this formulation of the argument, I omit the sub-argument that Aquinas gives on behalf of the third premise. What I have given here is the overall logical
skeleton for the argument of the First Way; the details of Aquinas's defence of the
various 'major' premises is not something that I can hope to take up in this brief
overview.)

While estimation of this argument has not been as consistently negative as estimation of Anselm's *Proslogion* 2 argument, nonetheless, it has long been majority
philosophical opinion that the argument fails. And, in recent times, the view has got
about that this argument has been killed by Kenny. (Kenny [1969] claims that all of
the Five Ways are marred both by argumentative errors—equivocations, fallacies
and so forth—and by reliance on outdated physics and cosmology.)

There are, however, some contemporary philosophers who give a much more
positive estimation of the First Way. For example, Davies (2004) gives a very sympathetic exposition of a 'causal argument' that has affinities with each of the first
three ways; while he does not explicitly claim that the First Way is a successful argument for its conclusion, it seems plausible to conjecture that he is sympathetic to
that opinion. Other contemporary philosophers are even more forthright. Oderberg (2010) claims that the First Way has far more going for it than is commonly

supposed: it is not tied to outdated cosmology, nor is it vitiated by the fallacies that Kenny levels at it. Indeed, in Oderberg's estimation, the First Way is a very strong argument, ripe for reinvestigation and reappraisal. He argues in detail that the second premise of the argument is 'plausible, defensible, and immune to the many . . . criticisms fired at it by Kenny', and he at least implicates that he also thinks that the same can be argued for the third premise, and for the claim that the First Way is a valid argument.

I think that it is quite implausible to suppose that the First Way is a cogent argument for the existence of God. If it were a cogent argument, it would have to defeat naturalism: the view that causal reality is exhausted by natural reality. Naturalists suppose that there is a fundamental causal relation that applies to the global states of natural reality: global states of natural reality are caused by antecedent global states of natural reality (except in the case of the initial global state of natural reality, if there is such a state). Naturalists suppose that the global state of natural reality changes—but, of course, they do not suppose that it is changed by something else. Does this mean that naturalists must deny Premise 2 of the First Way? Not necessarily. Naturalists might suppose that change in the global state of natural reality is constituted by changes in states of local parts of natural reality—and so it remains open to them to insist that all changes in states of local parts of natural reality are changes in things that are brought about by changes in other things.

Here is a simple—non-quantum, non-relativistic—model that may help to fix ideas. Suppose that a global state of natural reality consists of a collection of massive particles—that is, particles that possess mass—distributed over a spatial manifold. Each of the massive particles is both a contributor to the gravitational field over the manifold, and something that is acted on by the gravitational field over the manifold. The evolution of the gravitational field over the manifold depends upon the evolution of the positions of the particles, and the evolution of the positions of the particles depends upon the evolution of the gravitational field. But the gravitational field has no existence independently of the existence of the massive particles: in the absence of the particles, there is no gravitational field over the spatial manifold.

In this simple model, there are only two things that change: the positions of the particles and the local values of the gravitational field. Moreover, in this model, it is true that the local values of the gravitational field entirely depend upon the positions of the massive particles; and in this model, it is also true, for each of the massive particles, that the evolution of its position depends upon the evolution of the positions of all of the other particles—change in position of any one of the particles is brought about by the gravitational field (which, at the location of the particle in question can be thought of as the net gravitational effect that the other particles exert on it). So, in the model, Premise 2 of the First Way is true.

We can add to our simple model a specification of an initial state—an initial distribution of massive particles over the manifold. If we do this, then, in our simple model, Premise 3 of the First Way will also be true. And, of course, in our simple model, Premise 1 of the First Way is true. Yet, in our simple model, it is not obviously true that there is something that changes other things but that is not itself changed (never mind something that deserves to be called 'God').

Of course, so far, we have only considered a simple model. But it is easy to see that a fully developed naturalist view will preserve all of the essential features of the simple model. Naturalists may well be undecided about the question of infinite regress. Naturalists may well be undecided whether, if there is an initial natural state, that initial natural state is then necessary (and/or involving things that exist of necessity). However, naturalists will insist that there is no need to postulate an external 'changer' for natural reality: instead, we need only suppose that the evolution of natural reality is mutually interactive, in the manner of the massive particles and the gravitational field in our simple model. (Perhaps it might be said that mass is an unchanging changer in the simple model. Even if that is right—and even if it is also said that, in reality, there are certain 'conserved quantities' that are unchanging changers—it will remain the case that there are no grounds for identifying this unchanging changer—or those unchanging changers—with God.)

Kenny (1969) includes a discussion of a two-body universe that has some affinity to the simple model discussed above. Against Kenny, Oderberg (2010, 152–53) argues that Premises 2 and 3 of the First Way are false in Kenny's two-body universe because either it is, in principle, impossible to say whether either body is really being moved by something distinct from itself, or else there is an infinite loop of causal influence (since the influence of one body on the other influences the influence that the other body has on the one). Setting aside any consideration of the justice of these claims as criticisms of Kenny, it is clear that these criticisms get no purchase against our simple model (and hence, also, that these criticisms get no purchase against the kind of naturalism that I have sketched). At the very least, we would need to be given very much more in order to defeat the suspicion that the First Way is actually undermined by its reliance on outdated physics and cosmology.

Of course, there is much more to be said about the Five Ways. (For some of that further discussion, see Oppy [2006a] and, of course, Kenny [1969].) However, I think that no one should now suppose that the First Way—or, indeed, any of the Five Ways—is a proof of its conclusion. Moreover, while, for all that I have argued here, it remains possible that the First Way might inspire a proof of the existence of God, I think that there are very good grounds for supposing that there are no extant successful causal cosmological arguments for the existence of God. (I argue for this conclusion in Oppy [2006a]. Meyer [1989] provides an example of an interesting argument inspired by the Five Ways.) As before, I must add that I do not think that Aquinas's arguments are silly: if we have reason to think that the First Way is not a successful argument, this is in large part because of subsequent developments in our understanding of physics and cosmology, and because of very recent advances in the construction of purely naturalistic theories of the world in which we live.

5. SCOTUS (AND O'CONNOR)

John Duns Scotus (1266–1308) provides a very complicated proof of the existence of God in his *De Primo Principio* (and elsewhere). In outline, the overall proof goes something like this:

1. There is exactly one first efficient cause.
2. There is exactly one first final cause, that is, an ultimate goal of all activity.
3. There is exactly one first 'pre-eminent' being, that is, a maximally excellent being.
4. Anything that is a first efficient cause is also a first final cause, anything that is a first final cause is also a first 'pre-eminent' being and anything that is a first 'pre-eminent' being is also a first efficient cause.
5. (Hence) There is exactly one being that is a first efficient cause, a first final cause, and a first 'pre-eminent' cause. (From 1–4)
6. Anything that is a first efficient cause, a first final cause, and a first 'pre-eminent' cause is infinite and endowed with will and intellect.
7. There is at most one being that is a first efficient cause, a first final cause and a first 'pre-eminent' cause, infinite and endowed with will and intellect.
8. (Hence) There is exactly one being that is a first efficient cause, a first final cause and a first 'pre-eminent' cause, infinite and endowed with will and intellect. (From 5–7)
9. (Hence) God exists. (From 8)

Each of the premises in this overall argument is supported by detailed sub-proofs. So, for example, the outline of the argument in support of the first premise goes something like this:

1. Some nature among beings can produce an effect.
2. Something able to produce an effect is simply first, that is, it neither can be produced by an efficient cause nor does it exercise efficient causality in virtue of anything other than itself.
3. If what is able to cause effectively is simply first, then it is itself incapable of being caused since it cannot be produced and is independently able to produce its effects.
4. A being able to exercise efficient causality that is simply first actually exists, and some nature actually existing is capable of exercising such causality.
5. A being unable to be caused is of itself necessarily existent.
6. It is the characteristic of but one nature to have necessary being of itself.
7. (Hence) There is exactly one first efficient cause. (From 1–6)

And, of course, each of the premises in this sub-argument—and in all of the other sub-arguments—is supported by detailed sub-proofs. (I shall not exhibit further details of Scotus's argument here.)

I think that Scotus's proof is magisterial. I also think that it is pretty clear that no one should now regard it as a successful proof of the existence of God. As I indicated in my discussion in the previous section of this paper, it is not clear that naturalists need to object to the first premise in Scotus's overall argument, nor is it clear that naturalists need to object to any of the details in the sub-proof set out above. However, naturalists will certainly object to the second and third premises in Scotus's argument, and I think—though I cannot argue for this here—that the arguments that Scotus offers for his second and third premises are quite evidently not cogent. (There is, for example, no reason at all for naturalists to grant that there are final causes in nature.)

O'Connor (2008) defends an argument for the existence of God that has interesting affinities with Scotus's derivation. O'Connor divides his proof into two stages: the 'Existence' stage and the 'Identification' stage. The 'Existence' stage is quite similar to the sub-argument that Scotus gives for his first premise. However, in the 'Identification'—the stage that is meant to do the work of identifying the first efficient cause with God—O'Connor appeals, instead, to considerations about the apparent fine-tuning of the universe for life: at least roughly speaking, he claims that the apparent fine-tuning of the universe for life is best explained by the activity of a being endowed with will and intellect.

As I have argued in detail elsewhere—Oppy (2011a, forthcoming a)—O'Connor's argument is no more cogent than Scotus's derivation: naturalists can plausibly and reasonably claim that, on any view that one might take about the *scope* of the fine-tuning for life of causal reality, the naturalist hypothesis affords at least as good an explanation of that apparent fine-tuning at no greater theoretical cost. (Very crudely: If the fine-tuning is present throughout the whole of causal reality, then it might be necessary or it might be brutely contingent, but, either way, there is no theoretical advantage that accrues to theism but not to naturalism. And, if the fine-tuning is present only in part of causal reality, then, on any account, it is ultimately a matter of objective chance—and so, again, there is no theoretical advantage that accrues to theism but not to naturalism.)

Of course, even if I am right about the standing of O'Connor's argument, it remains open that there might be some *other* way of forging an identification between a first efficient cause and God. Perhaps, for example, considerations about the presence of consciousness and the presence of reason in the universe might be thought to do the trick. However, as things now stand, it seems to me that it is quite clear that no one has yet produced a cogent argument of this kind. (For detailed defence of this claim, see Oppy [2006a].) While the derivation of *De Primo Principio* is clearly a major intellectual achievement, no one has found a way to update it to make it a compelling argument for twenty-first-century (naturalistic) philosophers.

6. STANDARDS

Here is a natural thought that one might have about the standards that an argument must achieve if it is to be counted as *cogent*: the argument must be such that it ought to convince anyone who does not already accept the conclusion of the argument to embrace that conclusion. So, for example, a cogent argument for the existence of God must be such that it ought to convince any atheist to accept the conclusion that God exists.

Some might suppose that this standard sets the bar too high. Perhaps it is too much to expect that a cogent argument ought to convince those who are already firmly of the opinion that the conclusion of the argument is false. Perhaps, instead, we should insist only that a cogent argument must be such that it ought to convince anyone who is undecided about the conclusion of the argument. On this apparently weaker standard, a cogent argument for the existence of God must only be such that it ought to convince any agnostic to accept the conclusion that God exists. (For a detailed discussion of these standards, see Oppy [2011b]. For a contrasting view, see, for example, Davis [1997].)

On either view about the standards that an argument must achieve if it is to be counted as cogent, it is clear that the standard directs us to consider the views of those who do not already accept the conclusion of the argument: in order to determine whether we have a cogent argument for the existence of God, we need to consider whether that argument rules out worldviews that deny the existence of God, and we need to consider whether that argument establishes that worldviews that deny the existence of God are less probable or credible than worldviews that affirm the existence of God. But, in order to do either of these things, we need to give detailed consideration to the nature of the competing worldviews: we can't determine whether an argument rules out worldviews that deny the existence of God unless we have a clear view of the commitments of those worldviews, and we can't determine whether an argument establishes that worldviews that deny the existence of God are less probable or credible than worldviews that affirm the existence of God unless we have a clear view of the commitments of those worldviews.

For us, in the twenty-first century, naturalism—the view that causal reality is exhausted by natural reality—is one of the significant competitors to theism. If an argument neither rules out naturalism nor establishes that naturalism is less probable or credible than theism, then that argument simply cannot be a cogent argument for the existence of God. Because naturalism is a leaner theory than theism, that is, a theory with fewer ontological and theoretical commitments, a cogent argument for theism needs either to show that naturalism is incoherent, or else to point to explanatory deficiencies in naturalism: explanatory gaps that both need to be filled and are filled by theism, and the like. However, when we consider medieval arguments for the existence of God, they are not plausible candidates to fit this bill: they are not plausible demonstrations that naturalism is incoherent, nor are they plausible demonstrations that naturalism suffers from explanatory deficiencies that theism can remedy. The above discussions of arguments from Philoponus, Anselm, Maimonides, Aquinas and Scotus are illustrations of this point, but I do not think that there are any arguments from the period that point to a different conclusion.

Doubtless it will be said that this result is hardly surprising: our authors did not frame their arguments in the light of a clear understanding of twenty-first-century naturalism. Indeed, it is a plausible conjecture that our authors did not even entertain the possibility of coherent and comprehensive naturalistic conceptions of the world (let alone proceed to attempts to try to figure out the details of such conceptions). When we try to think seriously about the range of theories that our authors did take seriously, and about the conceptual resources that were available to them for the evaluation of that range of theories, then perhaps it should not seem so strange to us that they supposed that the arguments that they presented really were proofs of, or demonstrations of, or cogent arguments for, the existence of God. It is, I think, not too hard to see how Scotus's argument could seem quite compelling against a background in which, for example, the full schedule of Aristotelian causes is simply taken for granted. (Of course, there is more to say about the full range of things that need to be taken for granted in order to find Scotus's argument compelling. However, for the purposes of the current discussion, it is sufficient to have one example of an unargued assumption that is reasonably rejected by twenty-first-century naturalists.)

If there is something to the considerations that I have just rehearsed, then I think that we are driven to the conclusion that no one should now expect to be able to take over the argumentative component of natural theology from medieval authorities. No one should now think that we can prove the existence of God by using the same arguments—or modified versions of the same arguments—that were current in medieval times. We cannot learn how to prove the existence of God from medieval arguments for the existence of God. However, as I have already insisted, this does not mean that we cannot learn anything from an examination of medieval arguments for the existence of God. Apart from learning something about things that we have ceased to take for granted since medieval times, we might also be encouraged to recognise and acknowledge limitations in our own abilities to construct proofs and cogent arguments in connection with perennially disputed philosophical questions.

NOTE

1. For further details on Philoponus, see above, Chapter 2, p. 32.

BIBLIOGRAPHY

Craig, William Lane. 1979. *The Kalām Cosmological Argument*. London: Macmillan.
Craig, William Lane and Quentin Smith. 1993. *Theism, Atheism and Big Bang Cosmology*. Oxford: Clarendon.
Craig, William Lane and James D. Sinclair, 2009. 'The Kalām cosmological argument'. In *The Blackwell Companion to Natural Theology*, ed. W. Craig and J. Moreland, 101–201. Oxford: Blackwell.
Davidson, H. 1969. John Philoponus as a Source of Medieval Islamic and Jewish Proofs of Creation. *Journal of the American Oriental Society* 89:357–91.

Davies, Brian. 2004. *An Introduction to Philosophy of Religion*, 3rd edition. Oxford: Oxford University Press.

Davis, Stephen. 1997. *God, Reason and Theistic Proofs*. Edinburgh: Edinburgh University Press.

Dombrowski, Daniel. 2006. *Rethinking the Ontological Argument: A Neoclassical Theistic Response*. Cambridge: Cambridge University Press.

Harrelson, Kevin. 2009. *The Ontological Argument from Descartes to Hegel*. Amherst, NY: Humanity Books.

Kenny, Anthony. 1969. *The Five Ways: St. Thomas Aquinas' Proofs of God's Existence*. London: Routledge & Kegan Paul.

Koons, Robert C. 1997. A New Look at the Cosmological Argument. *American Philosophical Quarterly* 34(2):193–211.

Koons, Robert C. 2000. *Realism Regained: An Exact Theory of Causation, Teleology and the Mind*. New York: Oxford University Press.

———. 2001. Defeasible Reasoning, Special Pleading and the Cosmological Argument: A Reply to Oppy. *Faith and Philosophy* 18:192–203.

———. 2008. Epistemological Foundations for the Cosmological Argument. *Oxford Studies in Philosophy of Religion* 1:105–33.

Leftow, Brian. 2005. 'The ontological argument'. In *The Oxford Handbook of Philosophy of Religion*, ed. W. Wainwright, 80–115. Oxford: Oxford University Press.

Maydole, Robert. 2009. 'The ontological argument'. In *The Blackwell Companion to Natural Theology*, ed. W. Craig and J. Moreland, 553–92. Oxford: Blackwell.

Meyer, Robert. 1987. 'God Exists!' *Noûs* 21:345–61.

Nowacki, Mark. 2007. *The Kalam Cosmological Argument for God*. Amherst, NY: Prometheus.

O'Connor, Timothy. 1993. Scotus on the Existence of a First Efficient Cause. *International Journal for Philosophy of Religion* 33:17–32.

———. 2008. *Theism and Ultimate Explanation: The Necessary Shape of Contingency*. Oxford: Blackwell.

Oderberg, David. 2010. '"Whatever is changing is being changed by something else": A reappraisal of Premise One of the First Way'. In *Mind, Method and Morality: Essays in Honour of Anthony Kenny*, ed. J. Cottingham and P. Hacker, 140–64. Oxford: Oxford University Press.

Oppy, Graham. 1996. *Ontological Arguments and Belief in God*. Cambridge: Cambridge University Press.

———. 1999. Koons' Cosmological Argument. *Faith and Philosophy* 16:378–89.

———. 2004. Faulty Reasoning about Default Principles in Cosmological Arguments. *Faith and Philosophy* 21:242–9.

———. 2006a. *Arguing about Gods*. Cambridge: Cambridge University Press.

———. 2006b. *Philosophical Perspectives on Infinity*. Cambridge: Cambridge University Press.

———. 2007a. 'Ontological Arguments'. In *Stanford Encyclopedia of Philosophy*. http://plato.stanford.edu/entries/ontological-arguments/ (accessed 6 October 2010).

———. 2007b. 'Ontological arguments'. In *Philosophy of Religion: Classic and Contemporary Issues*, ed. P. Copan and C. Meister, 112–26. Oxford: Blackwell.

———. 2010. Epistemological Foundations for Koons' Cosmological Argument? *European Journal for Philosophy of Religion* 2(1):107–25.

———. 2011a. O'Connor's Cosmological Argument. *Oxford Studies in Philosophy of Religion* 3:166–86.

————. 2011 b. 'Prospects for successful proofs of theism and atheism'. In *Gottesbeweise von Anselm bis Gödel*, ed. J. Bromand and G. Kreis, 599–642. Frankfurt am Main: Suhrkamp Verlag.

————. Forthcoming a. 'God'. In *Continuum Companion to Metaphysics*, ed. B. Barnard and N. Manson. London: Continuum.

————. Forthcoming b. 'Maydole on Ontological Arguments'. In *Ontological Arguments Today*, ed. M. Szathkowski.

CHAPTER 33

PHILOSOPHY AND THE TRINITY

RICHARD CROSS

THE Christian doctrine of the Trinity raises some formidable philosophical problems. The most well-known can be expressed in the following mysterious bit of theological arithmetic: there are three divine persons, Father, Son and Spirit; each person is God; but there is only one God. Or, more or less equivalently, each divine person is the one God, but each divine person is non-identical with any other divine person. These claims are supposed to render certain more technical claims theologically impermissible: for example, that there is more than one divine essence or nature, or that the divine essence/nature is in any sense divisible. (The divine essence is numerically identical in all three persons, even though the persons are not identical with each other.)

Equally, the distinctions between the persons—and their being the same as the divine essence—are supposed to be necessary features of God. We might capture this by claiming that there is no possible world in which God fails to be a Trinity of persons. But it is held that there are origination relations between the divine persons: the Father is something like the causal origin of the Son, and Father and Son together (according to the theologians I consider) are something like the causal origin of the Spirit (the so-called '*filioque*': the Spirit proceeds from the Father *and the Son*). In the technical language of the medieval theologians, the Father *generates* the Son, and Father and Son together *spirate* the Holy Spirit. And it seems to make little sense to think of something whose existence is necessary in the way outlined having a causal explanation (other, perhaps, than itself).

It is in their discussions of all of these issues that the ablest minds of the Middle Ages tested some of their most significant theses about identity, sameness, individuality and causation, and in what follows I present some of the solutions they proposed, attempting to show that at least some of the answers are not merely ad hoc. Meta-physical analyses that have their primary application in the natural world turn out to be equally applicable in the case of the Trinity, too. Paradoxically, the aim of maximum theoretical generality permits the theologians to sharpen their analyses of the material world in interesting ways, while not driving these analyses. So in the first section, I begin to consider a cluster of issues related to kinds of *sameness*: same-ness with, and without, identity. I use the notion of material constitution to illustrate this, and give reasons to show that, while some theologians developed sophisticated accounts of sameness, they nevertheless reject the applicability to the Trinity of con-stitution models. The ways in which they reject them rely on the thought that the divine essence is supposed to be common to more than one person in a way that the relevant kinds of material constituent cannot be. So in the second section, I consider the issues of sameness and identity in relation to theories of universals (since univer-sals are paradigm relevant cases of commonality to more than one thing). In the third section, I examine the relation between the doctrine of the Trinity and divine simplicity. God is supposed to be wholly simple, including neither distinct parts nor (according to some thinkers) distinct properties, and on the face of it a strong doc-trine of divine simplicity seems to require that the divine essence is the only ground for claims about the three distinct persons. Theologians disagreed sharply on the adequacy of such a view, but the theologian who develops most fully a theory of sameness with and without identity holds that the application of this to the doctrine of the Trinity requires rejecting a strong account of divine simplicity. Finally, in the fourth section, I consider the relation between necessity and causation, given that two of the divine persons (the Son and the Spirit) are both necessary and (appar-ently) causally dependent. In all of this, I discuss a number of thinkers but focus on Duns Scotus since he is responsible for the systematic development of the relevant notions of sameness, and their application both to the material world and to the Trinity.

There are some further issues, too, which I will not have space to discuss here. I mention them now to give a sense of the range of Trinitarian discussion in the Middle Ages. For example, it seems intelligible to consider what might be entailed on the supposition—easily conceived, after all—that the doctrine is false. So some simple thought experiments seem to raise problems of a more general nature for the logic of counterfactuals, given that the falsehood of the doctrine is supposed to be an *impossibility*. The theology of the Trinity is the main context for the discussion of this issue (see, e.g., Martin 2004). Furthermore, the doctrine of the Trinity was a *locus*—perhaps the most important *locus*—of a further very important discussion in medieval philosophy: namely, theories of cognition and (to a lesser extent) action. The reason for this is that Augustine made use of analogies from human psychology—the soul and its cognitive and appetitive acts—to help provide some kind of way of understanding Trinitarian doctrine. I do not look at these topics here, not because they are not of considerable interest, but because they seem largely extrinsic to the doctrine of the Trinity itself—albeit that some theologians, perhaps somewhat strangely, thought that talk of the Son's procession in the manner of a concept produced from the memory, and of the Spirit's procession in the manner of an appetitive act produced by the will, should be understood somehow literally and not merely metaphorically (see Duns Scotus 1959, 75; *Ordinatio*, l.1, d.13, q.un., n.23).[1] In any case, all of my discussions here will be highly selective and make no pretensions towards completeness.

1. SAMENESS AND IDENTITY (1): CONSTITUTION AND COUNTING

One very significant recent account of the Trinity, proposed by Jeffrey E. Brower and Michael C. Rea (2005), claims that we can give some purchase to the doctrine by considering a kind of numerical sameness that falls short of identity: the divine essence and any divine person are the same as each other, but not identical with each other. (Both identity and sameness-without-identity are transitive: hence, on this view the persons are the same as each other, too, but not identical with each other.) Rea exploits what he takes to be the Aristotelian doctrine of accidental sameness as a way of introducing the relevant kind of relation. Socrates and seated-Socrates (Socrates along with the form of seatedness, existent for just as long as Socrates is sitting) are accidentally the same, and accidental sameness is

> (i) ... the relation that holds between an accidental unity [e.g. seated-Socrates] and its parent substance [e.g. Socrates]; (ii) it is neither necessary identity nor contingent identity (because Aristotle tells us that if *a* and *b* are accidentally the same, they are in a way the same and in a way different; but if *a* and *b* are identical—either necessarily or contingently so—there is no way in which they are different); and (iii) it is a species of numerical sameness: if *a* and *b* are accidentally the same, then they are 'one in number', though, according to Aristotle, they are not 'one in being'.
> ... I take it that (roughly speaking), for any *a* and *b*, *a* and *b* are numerically the same just in case *a* and *b* are to be *counted* as one thing. (Rea 1998, 320)

Brower and Rea hold that this notion of sameness can solve not only elevated heavenly problems such as the Trinity, but also everyday earthly ones such as material constitution. Thus, it is held, constitution is not identity: a statue of Athena, for example, is constituted by its bronze and is numerically the same material object as its bronze, without being identical with its bronze (after all, it clearly has some modal properties that the lump of bronze lacks, and vice versa). So we should construe 'Athena is bronze' as 'Athena is constituted by a lump of bronze': the 'is' of constitution is to be distinguished from the 'is' of identity (Brower and Rea 2005, 71). In the account offered by Brower and Rea, Athena is the same as the bronze, but not identical with it. Similarly, the divine essence is the same as each divine person, but not identical with it, and this is because the divine essence is something like the sole *constituent* of each divine person. The divine essence constitutes each divine person in a way analogous to that in which the bronze constitutes Athena. But the analogy is not ungrounded or empty since the constitution relation, while applied in the context of an immaterial being, has all the same formal characteristics of the same relation applied in cases such as Athena.

Construing the relation between the divine essence and each divine person along the lines of a constitution relation has a long theological history, all the way back to the early Church. Most importantly, Augustine sees that there is some kind of analogy between gold and a gold statue, on the one hand, and the divine essence and a divine person, on the other. His reason for this is that he holds that three statues might all equally be gold without there being three golds (see Augustine 1968, 264:74–76, 90–97; *De trinitate*, l.7, ch.VI.11:74–76, 90–97):[2] 'gold', of course, is a mass noun, not a count noun. But this by itself does not get us very far, precisely because 'God' is a count noun, not a mass noun. What Augustine would need is three gold statues made (simultaneously, I suppose) of one *lump* of gold.

Among the scholastics, Henry of Ghent—while probably unaware of the precedent in Abelard (covered later)—is the most conspicuous explicit user of a constitution model, in the sense that Henry argues that thinking of the divine essence as something like matter (as 'quasi matter', in Henry's terminology) is the only way of avoiding the view that the Son is created: the Son is made 'from the divine substance' (generated), not 'from nothing' (created), and this suggests some sense in which we might think of the divine substance as the *substrate* of the persons (Henry of Ghent 1520, II, fo. 83vD; *Summa quaestionum ordinariarum*, a.54, q.3).[3] The essence is like a material constituent of an object that is non-identical with its constituent, and the non-identity is grounded in a difference of form or predicate between the constituent and the object constituted. In the case of a divine person, the relevant 'form' is the personal property: a property unique to each person that distinguishes that person from the other two. Standardly, such properties were thought to be origination relations.[4]

All of these points are made in the following quotation:

> Three things, in some sense really distinct [from each other] are to be considered in a production, namely, the material subject which is in potency to form, the form itself which the agent educes into act from the potency of the matter, and the composite constituted in being from both, which is the *per se* end term of a natural production. To these three, really distinct [from each other] in the production of a creature, there can be found three corresponding things in a divine production, distinct [from each other] merely according to reason, namely, the divine essence, the personal property, and the *suppositum* or person containing both of them in itself. . . . A person in God is something constituted from the essence with a property, though without composition . . .
>
> Just as matter in a natural production is the subject of generation (to the extent that it is in potency to the form, and through this to the composite that is to be generated from it), so in a divine production—for example, in the generation of the Son, and likewise in the spiration of the Holy Spirit—the essence is as it were the subject of generation, as something in potency; . . . 'being born' names

the property had through the generation, by which the Son is constituted in generated being and is distinguished from the Father. (Henry of Ghent 1520, II, fo. 84rE; *Summa quaestionum ordinariarum*, a.54, q.3)

Admittedly, Henry is interested here merely in clarifying the origination of the Son and the metaphysical conditions required for such origination. But Henry's proposal has some further metaphysical consequences: namely, that the divine essence and a personal property are in some sense the constituents of a divine person, and that they can be so without entering into any kind of composition. How does Henry understand this non-composition claim? The idea is not very fully worked out, but Henry seems to hold that the divine essence is 'one and the same singular thing', and that the personal properties 'differ merely rationally from it' (Henry of Ghent 1520, II, fo. 84vH; *Summa quaestionum ordinariarum*, a.54, q.3).[5] That is to say, the only item grounding Trinitarian claims is the divine essence, but, nevertheless, non-synonymous predications can be made of the persons, such that Father, Son and Spirit are distinct from each other. Claiming that the personal properties differ 'merely rationally' from the divine essence means that Henry is open to the worry that there are not sufficient forms in God to account for the differences in predication between the three persons. I return to this in Section 3.

Henry's way of spelling out the constitution model is open to the philosophical objection that there is no even moderately close analogy from the material world to the Trinitarian case. On Henry's view, the same essence can constitute three distinct persons. But just as in Augustine's gold statue example, the same gold would need to be simultaneously three distinct statues. And this does not seem readily intelligible. Scotus raises exactly this objection—the same matter cannot be simultaneously the subject of more than one distinct composite (Duns Scotus 1956b, 58–59; *Ordinatio*, l.1, d.5, p.2, q.un., nn.88–89). If, Scotus claims, we need to identify something that can be common to more than one composite, we need to think not of matter, but of form and universals (Duns Scotus 1956, 76–77; *Ordinatio*, l.1, d.5, p.2, q.un., nn.135–36; see, too, Duns Scotus 1950, 348; *Ordinatio*, l.1, d.2, p.2, qq.1–4, n.386). He does not reject Henry's question as illegitimate—he could hardly have done so since the claim that the Son is from the substance of the Father was canonised at the Council of Nicaea in 325. Scotus claims that the Son is indeed 'from the substance of the Father', and not (like a creature) 'from nothing': but the sense of 'from' is that of causality or dependence: and 'from the substance of the Father' is just another way of claiming both that the Son is generated by the Father and that the Son is of the same essence as the Father (Duns Scotus 1956, 62–63; *Ordinatio*, l.1, d.5, p.2, q.un., n.99).

The notion of sameness-without-identity was systematically applied in a Trinitarian context first of all by Abelard some 150 years before Henry, using the notion of material constitution as an illustration of the kind of relation he has in mind. (Clearly the two relations are different: sameness-without-identity is symmetrical; constitution is not.) Abelard argues that there are cases in which two things can be numerically the same—say, a lump of wax and a waxen image—but nevertheless differ 'in property':

> [The wax: viz. the] matter of the waxen image and what is made from it do not
> share all their properties in common, since the matter of the waxen image is not
> made from matter (that is, the wax itself is not made from wax), just as what is
> made from the matter in this case is not the matter (that is, the waxen image is
> not the matter of the waxen image). (Abelard 1969, 248; *Theologia Christiana*, l.3,
> c.140; translation from Brower 2004, 227)

In creaturely cases such as these, Abelard associates the difference in predicate with
a difference in *form*: the different predications are grounded in different forms in
the waxen image (wax form, image form). We can count different items on the basis
of these different forms—different hylomorphic compounds, for example—without
counting (say) different material objects. The crucial thing for Abelard, however, is
not the constitution model—which he simply uses to illustrate the notion of sameness-without-identity—but this very account of sameness.[6] The persons are the
same as, but non-identical to, the essence, and we can count different persons without counting different essences.

In Abelard's application of the notion of sameness-without-identity to the doctrine of the Trinity, there is a crucial difference between the divine case and cases of
material constitution. According to Abelard there are no forms in God other than
the divine essence; so while there are differences in predication (we can make claims
about the Father—for example, that he generates the Son—that are false of the Son),
these differences are not grounded in any real difference of form (Abelard 1969,
256–7; *Theologia christiana*, l.3, c.166).[7] The differences in predication are grounded
simply 'by the nature of the divine essence' (Brower 2004, 251).[8] Brower offers the
following helpful critical assessment:

> The coherence of Abelard's account, and hence his solution to the logical problem
> of the Trinity, ultimately depends on the coherence of his assumption that the
> simple divine substance can ground the applicability of predicates such as 'father'
> and 'son'. For once we grant this assumption, it would appear that Abelard is
> justified in concluding that there is a disjunction among the persons that is both
> real and numerical. Now as far as I can tell, Abelard does not himself give us any
> compelling reason to accept this assumption, or even to think it is coherent.
> (Brower 2004, 251)

This problem does not seem to be unique to Abelard—indeed, we have already seen
it in Henry of Ghent. As I will show in Section 3, most thinkers accept the strong
account of divine simplicity, according to which the only entity available to ground
predications *in divinis* is the divine essence. And I will return then to the question
of the coherence of this view.

Duns Scotus, as I noted above, disagrees with the constitution model, at least as
presented by Henry. But he nevertheless makes the notion of sameness-without-
identity central to his account of the Trinity. And he holds that the notion has wide
metaphysical application: hence the ease with which he can apply it to the Trinitarian case. Indeed, Scotus is, as far as I know, the first philosopher to provide both
an ontology and a corresponding technical terminology that allow for pervasive use
of the distinction between sameness with and without identity, and for this reason

he forms the main focus of my chapter. His theological achievement is to show how what he takes to be common or garden distinctions map exactly onto the Trinity. Scotus thus offers a metaphysics of substance that aims at maximal generality. I consider the relevant features of Scotus's account of material substance in the next section. Here, I want to focus on an initial account of sameness-without-identity that Scotus uses as the basis of some claims that he makes about how to *count* in God. The claim is that each divine person is the same as the divine essence, but not identical to it. Scotus makes the point as follows:

> The person . . . is unqualifiedly the same as the essence by a most perfect same-ness. But they are nevertheless distinguished in some way, because [they are distinguished] qualifiedly, from the nature of things, because they are not formally and adequately the same. . . . Not formally, because, to the extent that the same-ness is grounded in the essence and has the person as its end term, it is not true that the essence is the person, formally, because an absolute does not include anything relational in its formal notion. . . . Nor are the essence and the person adequately the same, whether according to predication and coextension, or according to excellence and perfection . . . for the essence is formally infinite in perfection whereas the person is not; and 'person' is said of three [things], whereas 'essence' is not. (Scotus 2004–8, II, 343–44; *Reportatio*, l.1A, d.34, p.1, q.1, n.4)

Talk of being 'formally' the same and 'adequately' the same are (roughly) ways of talking about Leibniz-style identity: if two items are identical, they share all the same properties. The argument here is supposed to show that a divine person cannot be identical in this sense with the divine essence, even though it is numerically the same as the divine essence, since a divine person and the divine essence do not sat-isfy the relevant condition. First, persons are, or include, relations: and such a rela-tion cannot be a feature of the divine essence. Equally, the essence has a property—intrinsic infinite perfection—not had by every feature of a divine person (according to Scotus, for reasons we need not concern ourselves with here, the fea-tures that distinguish the persons from each other lack this property: their perfec-tion is parasitic on the intrinsic perfection of the divine essence). Finally, the extension of (divine) *person* is wider than the extension of (divine) *essence*: there are three divine persons, but only one divine essence.[9] Still, why think that the divine persons and the divine essence are the same at all? Scotus maintains that insepa-rable things are the same. And the persons and the essence are inseparable (see Duns Scotus 1639, XII, 81; *Quodlibetum*, q.3, n.15).

Now, part of the recent discussion of constitution models for the Trinity focuses on the questions of counting with which I began this essay. We count by *identity* under some sortals, and by *sameness* under others. Brower and Rea put the point as follows:

> Likely candidates [for sortals that allow us to count by identity] are technical philosophical sortals like 'hylomorphic compound', or maximally general sortals, like 'thing' or 'being'. . . . Although cases of material constitution will never, on the view we are proposing, present us with two material objects in the same place at the same time, they will present us with (at least) two *hylomorphic compounds* or

things in the same place at the same time. But we deny that this commitment is problematic. By our lights, it is a conceptual truth that material objects cannot be co-located; but it is not a conceptual truth that hylomorphic compounds (e.g., a statue and a lump, a fist and a hand, etc.) or things (e.g., a material object and an event) cannot be co-located. (Brower and Rea 2005, 63)

So in the case of the statue of Athena, we might claim that there are two things (the lump of bronze and Athena, counting by identity) and one material object (counting by sameness). In the divine case, we could count four things by identity (the essence and the three divine persons), and one God by sameness—'God' is, after all, treated by theologians as something analogous to a natural-kind sortal (hence, talk of the divine *nature*), and Brower and Rea's commonsense intuition is that we count by sameness under such sortals.

Scotus makes similar claims about counting in Trinitarian cases, and he makes these claims explicit in the context of a treatment of the *filioque*. Scotus holds that the divine persons share intellect and will, and he holds that this shared mentality entails shared agency (Duns Scotus 1639, XII, 205; *Quodlibetum*, q.8, n.6).[10] The Father and the Son produce the Holy Spirit by common agency—specifically, *spirating*—and so are treated as one agent.[11] Each one is, in our terminology, the same as, but not identical to, the divine essence. How are we to count in such a case? Scotus holds that different sortals provide for counting in different ways, and specifically he holds that very general sortals provide for counting by identity in a way that kind-sortals do not. The issue is this: how many *spirators* should we count: one or two? The idea is that Father and Son are one substance—the same as the divine essence, but non-identical with it—and Scotus holds that in such cases we do not count by identity (i.e., in this case, by identity of person):

> When a numerical term is added to a substantive, as if we say 'two spirators', the adjectival numerical term [viz. 'two'] immediately has a substantive on which it depends, since an adjective determines that on which it depends. Therefore the significate of its substantive is denoted to be [plurally] numbered. (Duns Scotus 1959, 51; *Ordinatio*, l.1, d.12, q.1, n.46)

Father and Son are the same, so we count just one spirator: the point of the passage is that if there were two spirators there would be two items that would fail to be the same as each other. 'Spirator' is a sortal under which we count by sameness, not identity. Still, there are two persons, and Scotus thinks that we can ask the same question about 'spirating ones (*spirantes*)': how many *spirantes* are there? Now, Latin allows the substantival use of participles in a way that English tends not to. But Scotus treats the participle grammatically here simply as an adjective that lacks a substantive for it to modify. He takes there to be an implied substantive, but this substantive to be wholly unspecified—'ones', or 'somethings', or 'persons' ('person' is not the name of a natural kind in medieval Aristotelian metaphysics). And Scotus's view is that it is exactly such very general sortals—for example, 'ones', 'somethings', 'persons'—that allow for counting by identity. Hence, '*spirans*' is a term under which we count by identity:

> The [plural] enumeration of a determinable form [in the case of a determinable adjectival term and not of a substantival one is] on account of [the adjectival term's] association with a *suppositum* [i.e., person]. When [an adjective numerical term—e.g., 'two'] is added to a [determinable] adjective, as when we say 'two *spirantes*', both [terms] . . . are dependent on a third on which they depend and which is determined by them. In the case at hand, this is 'someones' or 'persons', as if we were to say 'Three creating someones', or 'three [creating] persons'. (Duns Scotus 1959, 51; *Ordinatio*, l.1, d.12, q.1, nn.45–46)

So according to Scotus, there are two divine persons spirating the Holy Spirit, and in such cases we count by identity, and count two *spirantes*. It seems that the default position here (e.g., counting under 'natural kind' sortals such as 'spirator') is counting by sameness; it is only certain very general sortals that license counting by identity.

2. Sameness and Identity (2): Constituents and Universals

As I suggested above, Scotus's views on sameness-without-identity were formulated in part in the context of his theory of universals. Many—not all—of the most significant theologians of the High Middle Ages are realists on the question of what we would label 'universals' and they would label 'common natures'. But they understand their realism in a very distinctive way, claiming—in line with an Aristotelian tradition that can be traced to Alexander of Aphrodisias, if not to Aristotle himself—that common natures are somehow *divisible*: instantiation amounts to the division of a nature into numerically discrete particulars (particulars that fail to be really the same as each other) (on this, see Tweedale 1984). As Scotus sees it, such common natures have some kind of reality since they are supposed to do some explanatory work: namely, to account for the fact that a number of individuals resemble each other in kind-relevant ways. And he maintains that every real entity exhibits some kind of unity. But the unity of the common nature cannot be numerical sameness because in that case the common nature would be numerically the same as all of its instances, and the instances would thus be numerically the same as each other. (I return to Scotus's discussion of this point below.) So the common nature, Scotus reasons, must have some kind of non-numerical sameness since the nature is in itself neither numerically one nor numerically many (thus, we now have three kinds of sameness: identity; sameness-without-identity; non-numerical sameness).[12] This nature receives the accidental modification of numerical unity/plurality—it becomes really one or many—on instantiation (Duns Scotus 1973, 403; *Ordinatio*, l.2, d.3, p.1, q.1, n.32). But this numerical unity/plurality requires explanation, too, over and above the nature itself. So Scotus reasons that any complete individual of a given kind (substance or accident) includes some intrinsic feature—a nature—in virtue of which it is the same in species as any other instance of the same kind, and that any complete individual of a given kind also includes some intrinsic feature—a thisness or haecceity—in virtue of which it is distinct from any other instance of the same kind (see, e.g., Duns Scotus, 1973, 474–75; *Ordinatio*, l.2, d.3, p.1, qq.5–6, nn.168–70). These features cannot fail to be really the same as each other since according to Scotus such failure requires separability: inseparable properties must be really the same as each other. And each feature must itself be individual since Scotus accepts the scholastic (Aristotelian) commonplace that anything existing in an individual is itself individual. This, indeed, is the point of thinking of common natures as divisible. Natures exist only as instantiated (as numerically one or many), even though they need some intrinsic reality (and non-numerical sameness) to be the subject of this sort of instantiation/division (see again Duns Scotus 1973, 403; *Ordinatio*, l.2, d.3, p.1, q.1, n.32). So Scotus maintains that a complete individual substance (or a complete individual accident or accident-trope) includes two individual constituents. One is an individuator, and the other—a particular nature, the feature responsible for explaining how the substance (or accident trope) belongs to the kind it does—is something that does not intrinsically include whatever it is that makes it the individual it is. This second item is something whose individuality is '"borrowed" from the subject to which it belongs' (Tweedale 1999, II, 402), and the individuality of the subject itself is explained by its intrinsic thisness.[13] The particular nature and the substance are really the same, but non-identical (since the substance includes a thisness not included by the particular nature), and the particular nature and thisness are together constituents of the complete substance.

Scotus picks out two features of such particular natures that are relevant to his discussion of the Trinity. He labels them communibility 'by identity' and communicability 'by informing':

> Something is said to be communicable either by sameness (such that that to which it is communicated *is* it), or by informing (such that that to which it is communicated is *in virtue of* it, but is not it). In the first sense, a universal is said to be communicated to a singular; in the second sense, form [is communicated] to matter. Therefore any nature, as it exists in itself and as a nature, is communicable in either way: viz. to many *supposita*, each of which is it, and also as *that in virtue of*, as a form in virtue of which the singular or *suppositum* is a being with a quiddity, or one having a nature. And a *suppositum* is incommunicable with the opposed two-fold incommunicability. (Duns Scotus 1950, 346; *Ordinatio*, l.1, d.2, p.2, qq.1–4, nn.379–80)

Talk of communicability 'by sameness' is supposed to be in part a way of talking of the real sameness of a complete substance—here labelled a '*suppositum*'—and its particular nature, even though the substance and the nature are not identical. This sort of communicability includes real sameness, but it is not the case that all real sameness is communicability: quite the reverse, as Scotus makes clear in the last sentence; a whole substance and its individual nature are really the same, but the whole substance is not communicable. So the relevant kind of sameness is something akin to that which would hold between a whole and a proper part: inseparable from each other, but with an asymmetrical inclusion relation. Talk of the relation between a universal and a particular in this context draws attention to the further implication of the passage, that *individuators* (thisnesses; personal properties) are not thus communicable: the notion of a nature's being *shared* in some way or another is relevant since it is precisely the ways in which natures can be shared that Scotus is attempting to clarify in the passage.

But the nature is also supposed to be able to explain how it is that the particular substances are the kinds of things that they are; hence, it cannot be (in our Leibnizian sense) identical with any of the substances: it is that 'in virtue of which the singular or *suppositum* is a being with a quiddity, or one having a nature'. Again, the terminology is confusing, but the point is that being 'that in virtue of which . . .' is supposed to be a way of picking out Aristotelian forms: things structuring or configuring the substances of which they are forms. Natures are configurers, and they are the same as, but not identical with, the substances they configure. (Note that Scotus holds, as this passage makes clear, that identity and distinction relations can obtain between things and their properties [substance and particular natures, for example], and, as we shall see below, between properties, too. In all cases, the tests for non-identity are those spelled out in the Trinitarian discussion in Section 1 above: being subjects of distinct predicates; being non-co-extensive; differing in perfection. Indeed, it is in the Trinitarian discussion that Scotus works out his fullest account of these issues.)

The divine essence clearly has some features in common with such particular natures. As Scotus notes in the passage just quoted, a nature—whether a created nature or the divine essence—'is communicable . . . to many *supposita* . . . as *that in virtue of*, as a form in virtue of which the singular or *suppositum* is a being with a quiddity, or one having a nature'. He makes the same point about the divine nature elsewhere:

> Deity of itself is that by which God is God, and also that by which a subsistent (to which [an 'individual' property] *a* belongs) is God: . . . being *that by which* is not an imperfection in a creature, but pertains to quiddity as quiddity. (Duns Scotus 1956, 67; *Ordinatio*, l.1, d.5, p.2, q.un., n.112)

The fact that each divine person has the divine essence explains each person's being divine. But the divine nature lacks the divisibility feature of created natures: there is only one God, or one divine essence/nature (see, e.g., Duns Scotus 1950, 346; *Ordinatio*, l.1, d.2, p.2, qq.1–4, n.381).

Equally, the divine essence is communicable 'by sameness': really the same as three persons, really shared by exemplified by, we might say—three complete substances. Why suppose that the divine essence is indivisible: the same as three distinct persons? Scotus develops his reasoning in the context of a discussion of the necessity for division in created cases. Now, on the face of it, the divisibility claims— tied in as they are with the notion of non-numerical sameness—are hard to understand, and I begin with Scotus's arguments in favour of the necessity for division in creaturely cases. For example, on the notion of non-numerical sameness, David Armstrong comments as follows:

For myself, I cannot understand what this second, lesser, sort of identity is. Partial identity, as when two things overlap but do no more than overlap, or when two things have some but not all the same properties so that their nature 'overlaps', can be understood readily enough. But identity is just identity. . . . I take it that the Realist [on the question of universals] ought to allow that two 'numerically diverse' particulars which have the same property are *not* wholly diverse. They are partially identical in nature and so are partially identical. (Armstrong 1978, 112)

On Armstrong's view, a universal is simply numerically identical in each particular thing that instantiates it. But Scotus has—he believes—strong reasons for making the divisibility claim. He objects to a position—such as Armstrong's—that universals could be identical in each particular:

This position is more irrational than Plato's one on ideas (which Aristotle ascribed to him), which was to posit one substance, existent *per se* and being the whole substance of this and that, and thus neither to be proper to one, nor to be its existence *in* it. But this opinion posits that one substance under many accidents, while being sensible, will be the whole substance of all individuals, and this substance of that thing [x], and in something [y] other than that thing [x]. And it will also follow that the same substance will simultaneously have many quantitative dimensions of the same kind, and do so naturally, because this substance is under this quantity, and the same [substance] under another [quantity].[14]

Scotus objects to Plato's view that a form is not proper to an individual, and to his view that the form is extrinsic, rather than a constituent. But he objects even more strongly to the idea that such a form—with numerical identity and common to many, *à la* Armstrong—could be a constituent of many things.

What should we make of this? The first of the two arguments is that one self-identical nature would be numerically the same as a number of things that lack numerical sameness amongst themselves, which violates the transitivity of numerical sameness. The second argument claims that, if the nature in Socrates were numerically identical to the nature in Plato (in something like the way that Armstrong suggests), then Socrates and Plato would have the same accidents, which is clearly false. A key assumption of this second argument is that accidents inhere in (indivisible) natures—rather than, say, the whole substance constituted by the individual nature and individuating feature. Why accept this? I think what Scotus has in mind is that the nature determines the kinds of accident that can inhere, and to do this it needs itself to be the subject of inherence.[15] It might be thought that making this assumption entails too many subjects: the individual nature and the complete substance—since we want Socrates, as much as his individual nature, to be the subject of (say) wisdom. But this depends on how we count: we usually, other than in technical philosophical and theological contexts, count by sameness, not identity, and Socrates, while not identical with his nature, is certainly numerically the same as it. There are not two subjects of inherence—two human beings—but just one.

Scotus holds that the divine essence is such an individual nature, numerically the same as, but non-identical with, the three divine persons. Each person is the same as the essence, but non-identical with it, just as a material substance is the same as the particular nature that is a constituent of its, but non-identical with it. The difference is that the divine essence can be shared by three persons in a way that a particular creaturely nature is not: it can be numerically the same as three persons, given that the persons are numerically the same as (but, in our sense, non-identical with) each other. Equally, divine activities *ad extra* are numerically identical in each person, and the divine attributes likewise; hence, analogous to Scotus's claims about accidents in the passage just quoted, there is no objection to one and the same divine essence being the same as each person: Scotus makes this point in relation to divine activity (Duns Scotus 1959, 54–55; *Ordinatio*, l.1, d.12, q.1, n.51). Just like an Armstrong-style universal, the divine essence is shareable, and the persons that have it are partially identical. Scotus associates this kind of shareability with limitlessness: it is only a limitless or infinite particular essence that can be identically the same in more than one substance, or the same as (but non-identical to) more than one substance (presumably, the thought is that limited particular natures are somehow tied to—limited to—just one substance) (see Duns Scotus 1950, 348; *Ordinatio*, l.1, d.2, p.2, qq.1–4, n.385). Equally, an infinite essence is indivisible: there cannot be more than one infinite essence (see Duns Scotus 1950, 339; *Ordinatio*, l.1, d.2, p.2, qq.1–4, n.367). None of this gives us reason to believe that the doctrine is true: it is merely supposed to show that the doctrine is coherent—that such-and-such an essence could be identical in more than one person, or really the same as more than one person.

So thinking of the divine essence as a (shared) form seems to put us in the neighbourhood of Armstrong-style universals, rather than, say, that of material constitution: putting it a different way, the sameness-without-identity is the sameness of a form and its substance, not that of matter and its substance. The relevant asymmetrical relation is one of configuring, not of constitution: Scotus notes, for example, that the Trinity involves Armstrong-style universals at *Ord.* 2.3.1.1, nn.36 and 39 (Vatican, II, 405–6, 408, quoting John of Damascus 1973, 28; *Expositio fidei*, 8, ll. 223–28, 231–33, 238–40; Latin translation at John of Damascus 1955, 42–44), and Henry of Ghent goes so far as to say that there is a sense of 'universal' in which the divine essence is straightforwardly a universal (see Henry of Ghent 1520, II, fo. 310rN; *Summa quaestionum ordinarium*, 75.6 ad 1). (For a similar claim, see, too, Aquinas 1929–47, I, 483–84; *Scriptum super libros sententiarum*, l.1, d.19, q.4, a.2 ad 1.) Scotus, in effect, accepts two kinds of common natures: those communicable by being divided, and those communicated without division (since indivisible). And this acceptance gives us, too, two kinds of particulars: *individuals*, the instantiations of a divisible nature, themselves indivisible (and the divine essence, itself indivisible, though not an instantiation of anything); and (for want of a better term) *incommunicables*, those exemplifying, or somehow constituted by, an indivisible or particular nature. Persons are those incommunicables that have intellect and will. Talk of 'communicability' in this context can, incidentally, most likely be traced to the twelfth-century theologian Richard of St Victor, confronted with Boethius's definition of a person as 'an individual substance of rational nature' (Boethius 2000, 214; *Contra Eutychen et Nestorium* 3:171–72). As Richard noticed, the divine essence is numerically identical in each divine person, and this suggests that it is indivisible. And if it is indivisible, it seems to satisfy Boethius's definition of 'person'. And this would entail four persons in God—four indivisible items (Richard of St Victor 1958, 187; *De trinitate* l.4, c.21:221–30). Rather, persons are incommunicable on Richard's account (Richard of St Victor 1958, 188; *De trinitate*, l.4, c.22:21–23), such that they 'cannot belong to more than one thing' (Richard of St Victor 1958, 119; *De trinitate*, l.2, c.12:27–28). So the divine essence is not a person, and quaternitism is not entailed.

3. Sameness and Identity (3): Forms, Relations and Divine Simplicity

One problem, identified by Brower (as I noted above), that emerges from the positions of both Abelard and Henry is that the divine essence is supposed to be sufficient to ground non-synonymous predications of the different divine persons. We might call this, very loosely, the problem of truthmaking: the divine essence is wholly simple and undifferentiated, and it is not clear how such an entity could be the sole ground for different claims made about three distinct persons. In fact, many theologians deny that there are any forms in God other than the divine essence. For example, Aquinas, like Henry, holds that the personal properties are 'really the same' as the divine essence, and merely rationally distinct (Aquinas 1952–56, 193a; *Summa theologiae*, p.1, q.39, a.1 c), and what this amounts to is the claim that the divine essence is the only ground for every Trinitarian predication. The opposing view would be to multiply forms in God: in addition to the divine essence, we would need to posit personal properties as items somehow distinct from the essence, but somehow tied to it. Both views are supposed to be consistent with the application of sameness-without-identity in this context: the difference is whether the lack of identity is grounded in some additional form or not. Claiming that the personal properties are forms is the move made by Brower and Rea (2005, 68), and in this they are anticipated by Scotus. Scotus defends this view precisely to deal with worries such as that expressed by Brower in relation to Abelard's position. But there is no doubt that it is a minority position in the Middle Ages.

What would motivate a view such as Scotus's, requiring, as it does, different *grounds* for some of the different predications *in divinis*? After all, Trinitarian claims are supposed to be necessary, and we might think that such claims need no grounding. But this would be a mistake, and in any case the medievals would not have seen the issue in just this way. Even those supporting strong accounts of divine simplicity maintain at least one ground for Trinitarian predications: namely, the divine essence. And it might be hard to convince anyone—even if we wanted to— that Trinitarian claims are analytic. Now, it is important to grasp that underlying Scotus's views are some distinctive *metaphysical* claims. The medievals by and large agree that accidental properties are what we would call *tropes*: particular properties tied to particular individual substances: the wisdom of Socrates, for example, distinct from the wisdom of Plato. Scotus holds that God's attributes, while not accidents, are sufficiently similar to creaturely ones that, if an attribute is a trope in the creaturely case, then it will be in the divine case, too—albeit a trope from which its substance is inseparable (unlike an accident trope). In the following quotation, Scotus refers to God's wisdom and goodness as infinite wisdom and infinite goodness:

> There is a distinction [between essential divine perfections] preceding the intellect in every way, and it is this: that wisdom really exists in reality, and goodness really exists in reality, but real wisdom is not real goodness. Which is proved, for if infinite wisdom were formally infinite goodness, then wisdom in general would be formally goodness in general. For infinity does not destroy the formal notion of the thing to which it is added. (Duns Scotus 1956, 261; *Ordinatio*, l.1, d.8, p.1, q.4, n.192)

(Scotus does not, of course, hold that there are tropes grounding every true predication about God or creatures, and a significant portion of his metaphysics is devoted to working out what the explanatory bedrock for various different predications might be: where we might need to posit a distinct trope, and where we can do without one.)

The Trinitarian issue is nicely focused by thinking about a simple real-world case: that of merely relational change. According to Aristotle, spatial location is wholly relational (*Physica* 3.1, 209a31–b1), and (as Scotus noticed) this entails that changes in location are merely relational changes (Duns Scotus 2006, 29; *Ordinatio*, l.3, d.1, p.1, q.1, n.61). Aristotle's account is aporetic, since he claims that there can be no merely relational changes (Duns Scotus 2006, 25; *Ordinatio*, l.3, d.1, p.1, q.1, n.54, referring to Aristotle, *Physica* 5.1, 225b11–13).[16] Scotus rejects this Aristotelian view and maintains instead that relational changes can be basic. Scotus argues that the basicality of certain relational changes can be explained only if relations are in some sense *things*, or (in another way of talking that Scotus also uses), that every relation involves something inherent in the things related, yet distinct from every intrinsic property—every property not requiring the existence of something extrinsic to it (Duns Scotus 1973, 101–2; *Ordinatio*, l.2, d.1, q.5, n.200).[17] What distinguishes relations—in the spirit though not the letter of Scotus, we might label them 'relation tropes'—from monadic properties is that relations intrinsically involve some reference to something else. Scotus buttresses his defence of merely relational changes by appealing to cases of composition from parts. If it is true that there cannot be merely relational changes, then there cannot be such changes between the parts or properties of a thing. But it seems that there are since previously disjoint parts can be united, and conjoint parts disunited (Duns Scotus 1973, 105; *Ordinatio*, l.2, d.1, q.5, n.209).

This discussion of relation tropes helps—I hope—to let us see what is at stake in the truthmaking requirement. But talk of relations turns out to be central to medieval understandings of the Trinity since it was universally held that the personal properties—the properties that distinguish the divine persons from each other—are the relations of origin that I mentioned above. And one reason for this is the belief, held by some theologians, that relations are *not* things, and that they can thus serve to distinguish the divine persons without compromising divine simplicity (on this, see, e.g., Aquinas 1952–56, 193; *Summa theologiae*, p.1, q.39, a.1 c). For Scotus, this way of thinking is completely misguided. He maintains that if there are to be real distinctions between the divine persons, then there must be forms in God over and above the divine essence—in this context, he calls them 'formalities', to draw attention not to a limited degree of reality but to a degree of abstractness: unlike forms, formalities are not concrete agents (items that interact in with the world in [efficiently] causal ways), but constituents of such agents.[18] Equally, talk of forms suggests some kind of hylomorphic analysis in terms of composition from actuality and potentiality, and Scotus holds that such composition really would be incompatible with divine simplicity (Duns Scotus 1956, 271; *Ordinatio*, l.1, d.8, p.1, q.4, n.213). But in line with his affirmation of formalities, Scotus holds that if relations are to distinguish the divine persons, they must have some kind of reality over and above the divine essence:

> [The Father] formally possesses communicable entity, otherwise he could not communicate it; and he really possesses incommunicable entity too, otherwise he could not positively be a *suppositum* in real entity. (Duns Scotus 1950, 350; *Ordinatio*, l.1, d.2, p.2, qq.1–4, n.390)

The communicable entity is the divine essence, and the incommunicable entity the Father's personal property—his relation to the other persons. Although the personal property is the same as both the essence and the divine person, it is incommunicable in the sense that it is not a particularised nature, but something more akin to a thisness or individuator. And both property and essence are equally real, and as real as the person that they constitute:

> The relation constitutes the person only as compared to the essence. But it does not constitute a person other than as a thing, otherwise the person, as formally constituted, would not be a thing. Therefore the relation, as compared to the essence, is a thing. (Duns Scotus 1639, XII, 70; *Quodlibetum*, q.3, n.4. For further discussion of the whole issue, see Cross 2005a, 240–44)

Given that Scotus thinks of relations, as much as monadic properties, as *things*, it is perhaps no surprise that Scotus holds it to be equally possible—at least on conceptual grounds—that the personal properties are non-relational tropes, though he accepts the relation view fundamentally on the grounds of the weight of tradition (on this, see Cross 2005a, 195–202).

Now, something's having an essence as a constituent can—but need not—involve composition from parts, and Scotus holds that, in the case of a divine person, it does not. He claims, rather, that there is a formal distinction between the essence and the personal property (two 'formalities', which fail to be Leibniz-style identical) in a divine person, and that such a distinction does not entail composition:

> How it obtains that the notion of a relation in a thing is not formally the same as the notion of essence, and that they nevertheless do not constitute a composite

when they co-occur in the same thing, is in this way: that notion [i.e. the notion of the essence] is perfectly the same as this [one: i.e. the notion of the relation]: for on account of the infinity of the one notion [i.e. of the notion of the essence], whatever can be with it is perfectly the same as it. Therefore the perfection of sameness excludes all composition and quasi-composition, which sameness is on account of infinity. Nevertheless, infinity does not destroy the formal notions, such that it would not be the case that this is formally not that.

Therefore, there is no quasi-composition from these. And for this reason, there is nothing from them like a composite from act and potency, but there is from them one completely simple thing, because the one notion is perfectly— indeed most perfectly—the same as the other, and nevertheless they are not formally the same. For this does not follow: 'they are perfectly the same by the sameness of simplicity, therefore they are formally the same.' . . . And the same perfect sameness excludes all aggregation, because the same thing is not aggregated with itself. (Duns Scotus 1956, 69–70; *Ordinatio*, l.1, d.5, p.2, q.un., nn.117–18)

Relation and essence are non-identical because they are the subjects of different predicates. But they are inseparable from each other because they are necessary features of a divine person. So they are really the same as each other. Infinity is significant because Scotus believes it possible to show that there can be only one infinite being, as I noted above. And given this, the divine attributes, and the divine essence and personal properties, must all be inseparable, and thus really the same. But of course, infinity does not explain the nature of the tie between them—so to this extent the account is curiously non-explanatory. At any rate, the gist of this passage is that numerical sameness does not entail identity. Essence and relation are numerically the same, but non-identical, just as the item that they constitute is numerically the same as them, but non-identical with either of them. When Scotus talks about the real sameness of two or more *properties*, he means to pick out some non-relational ties between them, and it is the fact that the tie is non-relational that secures lack of composition (on this, see Cross 2005a, 104–14). The language is confusing. In terms of the material I discussed above, Scotus's real sameness is sameness-without-identity, his formal sameness is (roughly) identity in our Leibnizian sense (see n.9 above) and his formal distinction is a way of spelling out (among other things) how two items can be the same without being identical (in our sense). Divine wisdom and goodness are the same but not identical: they are part of a collection of properties or forms united by a non-relational tie into a substance that has self-identity (the divine essence), and that is numerically the same as, but non-identical with, any divine person. And, of course, not all really the same things are tied non-relationally: the persons are really the same (really the same, in our terminology), but there are real relations between each of them. The domain of items really the same and tied non-relationally is that of properties (essence and relation, in the divine case), rather than property and complete item (essence and person).

Note that Scotus is happy to talk of these properties, the essence and the relation, as 'things': thus, he talks of essence and relation as 'thing and thing' (Duns Scotus 2004–8, II, 328; *Reportatio*, l.1A, d.33, q.2, n.59). So it turns out that we can count at least seven things in God: the essence, the three personal properties and the three persons—counting by identity; of course, these things are all one and the same counting by sameness. But just as in the constitution view, in addition to symmetrical relations of real sameness between these things, there are asymmetrical relations between them, too. Relation and essence are, as we have seen, analogous to forms or properties of the persons—just as, on the constitution view, the essence constitutes the persons. The essence and relations *explain* features of the persons:

> This is the order of unities in God. First, there is the unity of the essence, which is both real and according to reason. After this unity there follows the formal distinction of essence and property. . . . Thirdly, after the qualified [i.e., formal] distinction of essence and property, there follows the distinction of the persons, which necessarily presupposes the real distinction [i.e., non-identity] of essence and property, because, since the essence and property constitute a real person, unless they were distinguished in some way really, the person would be nothing other than an *ens rationis*. (Duns Scotus 2004–8, II, 333–34; *Reportatio*, I.1A, d.33, q.2, nn.73–75)

It is these asymmetrical relations that explain the different statuses of the various things in God: essence and property as *forms* (formalities, more properly) of a divine person, the essence communicable in the two ways outlined in Section 2 (i.e., by identity and by informing), and the persons incommunicable in the same two ways. So persons and essence are non-identically the same as each other, such that the essence is numerically identical in each person without each person's being identical with the essence or with each other person.

One final observation: on the Trinitarian question, there is perhaps something to be said for the view of divine simplicity that Scotus rejects. After all, the divine essence is more or less unknown: perhaps it is just a sort of conceptual simple that is such that it can ground all sorts of different predictions of the divine person. That this is mysterious need not surprise, given divine ineffability. After all, what account are we entitled to expect Abelard, Aquinas or Henry to offer? Provided their view does not generate an obvious contradiction, it seems that it may be not unreasonably held. Scotus, of course, expects something more from a philosophical theory than this, and he feels entitled to use the whole apparatus of his formal distinction to provide what is required, since he has other reasons for thinking that this sort of distinction is unproblematic: namely, that it is required to explain certain features of the material world. And it is this that makes his view philosophically interesting, and the theology philosophically principled.

4. THE MODAL STATUS OF DEPENDENT DIVINE PERSONS

So it seems compatible with talk of divine necessity that there are forms in God other than the divine essence. But this does not solve another closely related modal issue, one that I mentioned at the beginning of this chapter. Suppose that anything constituted by the divine essence is a necessary existent. The Son and the Holy Spirit are constituted by the divine essence. Given this, what sense can be made of the claim that the Son and Holy Spirit *proceed from* the Father? On the face of it, procession seems to be some kind of causal relationship, such that the Son and the Holy Spirit *depend* on the Father (or, given the *filioque*, that the Son depends on the Father, and the Holy Spirit on the Father and the Son). One obvious way that we have of spelling out the nature of a dependence relation is counterfactually: x depends on y if and only if, if y did not exist, x would not exist. This account of dependence raises a nice problem for the dependence of one necessary existent on another—as in the Christian doctrine of the Trinity. The problem is this. If each divine person is a necessary existent, we cannot readily make use of a counterfactual analysis of dependence since such an analysis would require positing an impossibility—namely, the non-existence of the cause, something that is supposed to be a necessary existent. And underlying this is an even more basic problem: how to avoid the thought that the existence of the Son and Holy Spirit is overdetermined, since their existence is sufficiently explained by their exemplification of the divine essence, and sufficiently explained by their necessary causal relation to the Father.

Again, the most extensive and sophisticated discussion of these issues can be found in Scotus, and, as we shall see, Scotus ultimately comes to the view that we simply cannot think of the relevant relation as causal at all—despite some of the shorthand ways in which he speaks of it in texts I discuss in this paragraph. Thus, on the overdetermination question, Scotus simply asserts that there is no formal contradiction in supposing that existence is overdetermined in this way. As he sees it, the explanations are of two different kinds, and this is sufficient to block any putative contradiction. He argues that talk of exemplifying an essence—or being constituted by it—falls under the general category of formal causality, and talk of being 'from another' roughly under the general category of efficient causality. So something can be formally 'from itself' (i.e., be a necessary existent) and be efficiently 'from another' (i.e., have some kind of origination relation to another person). Contradiction would arise only in the cases that the same thing was formally from itself (i.e., was a necessary existent) and from another (i.e., was not a necessary existent), or that it was efficiently from itself (i.e., was a self-cause) and from another (i.e., was totally caused by something other than itself) (Duns Scotus 1950, 280; *Ordinatio*, l.1, d.2, p.2, qq.1–4, n.259). This concedes the overdetermination, but denies that such overdetermination is incoherent.

What about the counterfactual analysis of dependence? Scotus considers this at some length and comes to the conclusion that, whatever the relation between Son and Father, it cannot, strictly speaking, count as an example of dependence. He holds that there is a counterfactual component in any full analysis of causal dependence—strictly speaking, the kind of dependence that he would label *efficient* causal dependence, not formal. (He does not believe that the counterfactual analysis is a complete analysis of efficient causation since he wants to be able to include some account of properly causal *powers*, too, but considering this would take me too far away from the task at hand.) Now, the relation between Son and

Father fails to satisfy the counterfactual requirement. But Scotus does not argue for this on the basis of the impossibility of a counterfactual analysis of causation in any divine case. On the contrary, he is strongly wedded to counterfactual components in an analysis of causation and thinks that such components are required in the analysis of God's causal relations, too. He supposes God to be the primary cause of everything else, and he thinks this can be coherently explicated on a counterfactual analysis of dependence. He has other reasons for thinking the analysis fails in the case of the second and third persons of the Trinity.

He argues for this by considering the case of a God who necessarily produces whatever he produces. Even in such a case, Scotus avers, the counterfactual analysis is applicable. Suppose the non-existence of everything other than creatures. In such a case, creatures would lack a necessary condition for their existence (namely, God), and so the supposition entails that there are no creatures either. Although Scotus does not say so, he presumably holds that the opposite implication is not sound: if there were no creatures, there would be no God—even in the case that the production of creatures is necessary. Indeed, Scotus's argument requires this assumption because the conjunction of these two claims is required for the counterfactual analysis of dependence that Scotus proposes (see Duns Scotus 1950, 282; *Ordinatio*, l.1, d.2, p.2, qq.1–4, n.261, part of which I quote in a moment). So, whatever the modal status of such creatures, God's modal status is somehow 'greater', as Scotus puts it (Duns Scotus 1950, 282; *Ordinatio*, l.1, d.2, p.2, qq.1–4, n.261). Clearly, this commits Scotus to the view that there are meaningful cases in which there are conditionals with counter-possible antecedents that are true, and cases in which such conditionals are false (on this, see Martin 2004). The relevant contrasting case is the existence of the Son: we cannot coherently posit the existence of the Son but the non-existence of the Father, or the existence of the Father but the non-existence of the Son since Father and Son are not wholly disjoint—indeed, they are the same, though non-identical:

> The Son cannot not be even if we circumscribe everything other than himself in entity, because he cannot not be unless we circumscribe the producing person [viz. the Father], and the producer is not other in entity than the product [viz. the Son]. (Duns Scotus 1950, 281; *Ordinatio*, l.1, d.2, p.2, qq.1–4, n.261)

And if we do posit that there is a Son but no Father, we posit a genuine contradiction—an incompossibility, not just an impossibility—explicitly maintaining of the *same* thing both that it is and that it is not, and from such a contradiction anything does, indeed, follow:

> That which is formally necessary from itself cannot not be if we circumscribe anything else whose circumscription does not include incompossibility (by positing another to exist); but if we circumscribe anything else by incompossibility, what is formally necessary of itself can not-be, just as when one incompossible is posited, another incompossible follows. (Duns Scotus 1950, 280; *Ordinatio*, l.1, d.2, p.2, qq.1–4, n.260)

So Scotus is fully committed to a counterfactual account of causal dependence as a necessary component of his analysis of causality—indeed, his acceptance of some counterpossible consequences allows him to include a counterfactual account in that analysis of all kinds of dependence, including that of creatures on God.

The discussion shows that Scotus does not regard the origination relations between Father, Son and Spirit as genuine cases of efficient causal dependence. He claims that causal dependence can only obtain between wholly disjoint items, or items that are not really the same:

> Dependence follows the formal entity of what is dependent on that on which it depends. Therefore when they have the same entity, there is no dependence, even though there can be a precondition (*praeexigentia*) [for one *suppositum* and not for the other], if one *suppositum* has [the entity] from another. (Duns Scotus 1950, 286; *Ordinatio*, l.1, d.2, p.2, qq.1–4, n.267)

So there is some kind of ontological, but not causal, dependence. Again, there seems to be a curious lack of explanatory power in Scotus's solution: he seems to merely have found a new way of labelling the problem. But in an early text, Scotus gives an example (though admittedly one that he does not appeal to later):

> A conclusion is formally necessary from itself, such that it has necessary formal truth, and nevertheless it is necessary from another, as from the principles on which it depends. Therefore, to a far greater extent, the Son of God, who depends on nothing, is formally necessary from himself, but nevertheless productively necessary from another. (Duns Scotus 1960, 175–6; *Lectura*, l.1, d.2, p.2, qq.1–4, n.186)

The principles and conclusions that Scotus is talking about are the premises and conclusions of syllogisms within an Aristotelian science. Any proposition in an Aristotelian science is supposed to be necessary (recall Aristotle's essentialism, shared by Scotus). But the structure of an Aristotelian science is supposed to be such that premises genuinely *explain* conclusions. The conclusions are, we might say, *grounded* necessary truths. Scotus's point is that, if such overdetermination is an integral part of Aristotelian science, the supposed problems that overdetermination raises will clearly be far greater than merely a threat to the coherence of the Christian doctrine of the Trinity: the whole structure of Aristotelian scientific endeavour will be undermined.

5. CONCLUSION

At least in their most refined versions, medieval views of the Trinity attempt to show how the tools of metaphysics can be imported to the world of theology with minimal need for adaptation and thus provide cases in which thinkers attempt to provide metaphysical theories of maximal generality. In the case of Scotus, some of the metaphysical distinctions are worked out most fully in the case of the Trinity, since this provides a paradigmatically hard case. But the same distinctions can be—and are—applied to the created world in ways no more problematic. There are other ways in which such views could be philosophically fruitful: perhaps in the case that the doctrine provided us with a radically new way of looking at the created world. I do not know of a thinker who pursued this line: in cases where the doctrine is thought to make metaphysical commitments that could not have been predicted from an analysis of the material world, the problem is that these commitments seem to be incompatible with such an analysis, and the solution is simply to appeal to mystery. This is the route taken, a little later than Scotus, by Ockham, for example, who denies any sort of sameness other than identity (on sameness in Ockham, see Adams 1987, I, 16–17; for the consequently mysterious nature of Trinitarian theology for Ockham, see Adams 1987, II, 999–1003). Ockham will, of course, need to offer a different account of material constitution from one that requires sameness-without-identity. But that is a different story.[19]

NOTES

1. For a discussion of this, see Friedman (2010, c. 2).

2. For a discussion of this, see Cross (2007).

3. Before Henry, Anselm uses the analogy of a river (see Anselm 1946–61, II, 31–32; *De incarnatione Verbi*, c.13), one that earlier appeared, more clearly as a constitution analogy, in Gregory of Nazianzus (1978, 338:6–10; *Oratio* 31, c.31). For the divine essence as a substrate for the persons, see, too, Basil of Caesarea (1886, 577C; *Contra Eunomium*, l.2, c.4). The notion that the divine essence might be a substrate for the persons replaced the view, probably held in the early fourth century, that the Father is the substrate for the (remaining two) persons: on this, see Wolfson (1970, 335).

4. On medieval debates surrounding such origination relations—whether they are to be construed as analogous to categorial relations, or to items in the categories of action and passion—see Friedman (2010, c. 1).

5. The situation in Henry may be more complicated given his view that the relations are *modes* of a monadic form: see Henry (*Summa quastionum ordinariarum*, a.55, q.6, ed. in Flores 2006, 214:241–47). But I do not have space to consider the details of Henry's view here. For preliminary discussion, see Cross (2005b).

6. For observations on the limits of the analogy, see Marenbon (2004).

7. The text is discussed in Brower (2004, 240), and the material in this paragraph largely derives from Brower's discussion.

8. I exclude from this claim, of course, contingent claims made on the basis of the Son's assumption of a human nature in the Incarnation.

9. Strictly speaking, only adequate sameness is Leibniz-style identity. Scotus uses his talk of formal sameness to capture the asymmetry involved in the notion of the relation between essence and person in this context: the person includes the essence along with a relation—hence, the essence does not include the person. So at the third ellipsis in the above passage, Scotus continues: 'But to the extent that sameness is understood to be grounded in the person, and to have the essence as its end term, they are the same formally, because person includes in its formal notion, as something belonging to it' (Duns Scotus 2004–8, II, 344; *Reportatio*, l.1A, d.34, q.1). Formal sameness/distinction is thus a way

of isolating containment relations between two things that are really the same: the person contains (is formally the same as) the relation; the relation does not contain (is not formally the same as) the person.

10. Given this, the scholastics made some rather complex proposals to show how shared mentality and agency do not entail that all *internal* divine activities—generation and spiration—are shared by all three persons. For some examples, see Cross (2005a, 203–22).

11. See, for example, Duns Scotus (1959, 6–7; *Ordinatio*, l.1, d.11, q.1, n.18, Duns Scotus 1959, 53–55; *Ordinatio*, l.1, d.12, q.1, nn.49–51, Duns Scotus 2006, 96–97; *Ordinatio*, l.3, d.1, p.2, q.un., n.216).

12. For both of these claims, see Duns Scotus (1973, 404; *Ordinatio*, l.2, d.3, p.1, q.1, n. 34). Scotus draws attention to the nature's explanatory role; see, for example, Duns Scotus (1973, 398; *Ordinatio*, l.2, d.3, p.1, q.1, n.18). Aquinas claims that the nature 'considered in itself' is 'neither one nor many': a claim clearly related to Scotus's thought that the nature has a non-numerical unity; see Aquinas (1976, 374a–b; *De ente et essentia* 3:37–45).

13. As Scotus puts it, the thisness is 'primarily' numerically one (it explains the numerical unity of anything united to it); the complete substance is *per se* numerically one (the explanation of its numerical unity is intrinsic to it, though non-identical with it); the particular nature is 'denominatively' numerically one (its unity is explained by some feature that is extrinsic to it, though really the same as it): see Duns Scotus (1973, 477–78; *Ordinatio*, l.2, d.3, p.1, qq.5–6, n.175).

14. 'Est haec positio magis irrationalis quam Platonis de ideis quam imponit sibi Aristoteles, quod esset ponere unam substantiam per se existentem, et esse totam substantiam huius et illius, et tunc non esset proprium huic, nec etiam esse eius in isto. Sed ista opinio ponit quod una substantia sub multis accidentibus erit tota substantia omnium individuorum et tunc erit haec substantia huius et in alio ab isto, et tamen sensibilis. Sequitur etiam quod eadem substantia simul habebit plures dimensiones quantitatis eiusdem rationis, et hoc per naturam, quia haec substantia sub illa quantiate et eadem sub alia' (MS Worcester Cathedral, F. 69, fo. 100v; MS Merton College, Oxford, 61, fo. 167r; Duns Scotus, *Reportatio*, l.2A, d.12, q.5 [the text published in Duns Scotus 1639, XI, 326b, is not the *Reportatio* but the *Additiones* of William of Alnwick]; see, too, e.g., Duns Scotus 1959, 54–55; *Ordinatio*, l.1, d.12, q.1, n.51, where Scotus applies the principle to activity: numerically one essence entails identity in agency, too). For unity of agency as a way of distinguishing Trinitarian activity from the activity of other individuals of the same kind who exemplify Armstrong-style universals, see the fourth-century theologian Gregory of Nyssa (1958, 44:7–53:3; *Ad Ablabium*). Scotus would not have been aware of this work, but Gregory's thought passed into the West through Augustine and John of Damascus. Stress on unity of activity is clearly found in Augustine: see, for example, Augustine (1968, 36; *De trinitate*, l.1, c.IV.7:22–24); see, too, Augustine (1968, 83; *De trinitate*, l.3, c.II.3:46–47), Augustine (1968, 223; *De trinitate*, l.5, c.XIV.15:35–37), the last of which Scotus cites: Duns Scotus (1639, XII, 205; *Quodlibetum*, q.8, n.3). For the position of John of Damascus, see below.

15. For a thought something like this, see Duns Scotus (1639, XII, 492; *Quodlibetum*, q.19, n.2).

16. Scotus notes Aristotle's difficulties: 'Where he says that there is no motion in relations, he says that there is motion in place, and nevertheless place implies no absolute form but merely a relation' (Duns Scotus 2006, 19; *Ordinatio*, l.3, d.1, p.1, q.1, n.61). The motion principle is usefully discussed in Henninger (1989, 8–10).

17. See also Duns Scotus (1973, 98, 117–18; *Ordinatio*, l.2, d.1, q.5, nn.195, 234–35); for the inherence of such relations, see the discussion in Henninger (1989, 89–92).

18. For something like this observation, see Dumont (2005, 8, n.3).

19. I would like to thank Andy Arlig, John Marenbon, Chris Shields and Tom Ward for extensive comments on an earlier draft of this paper, and the members of the Center for Philosophy Religion discussion group at the University of Notre Dame (in particular, Billy Abraham, Andy Chignell, Paul Draper, Tom Flint, Sam Newlands, Mike Rae, Peter van Inwagen and Jerry Walls), for making a different earlier draft the subject of two intensive discussion sessions. I learned a great deal from all of them, and much of what is good in the paper is owed to them; mistakes remain my own, of course. And finally, thanks to Stephen Dumont for kindly showing me his copy of the relevant folio of MS Worcester Cathedral, F. 69.

BIBLIOGRAPHY

Abelard, see Peter Abelard.

Adams, Marilyn McCord. 1987. *William Ockham*. 2 vols. Notre Dame: University of Notre Dame Press (Publications in Medieval Studies, 26).

Anselm. 1946–61. *Opera omnia*, ed. F. S. Schmitt. 6 vols. Edinburgh: Thomas Nelson.

Aquinas, see Thomas Aquinas.

Armstrong, D. M. 1978. *Nominalism and Realism*. Cambridge: Cambridge University Press.

Augustine. 1968. *De trinitate*, ed. W. J. Mountain. Turnhout, Belgium: Brepols (Corpus christianorum series latina, 50/50A).

Basil of Caesarea. 1886. *Opera omnia. Tomus primus*. Paris: J.-P. Migne (Patrologia graeca, 29).

Boethius. 2000. *De consolatione philosophiae. Opuscula theologica*, ed. Claudio Moreschini. Munich and Leipzig, Germany: K. G. Saur (Bibliotheca scriptorum Graecorum et Romanorum Teubneriana).

Brower, Jeffrey E. 2004. 'Trinity'. In *The Cambridge Companion to Abelard*, ed. Jeffrey E. Brower and Kevin Guilfoy, 223–57. Cambridge: Cambridge University Press.

Brower, Jeffrey E., and Michael C. Rea. 2005. Material Constitution and the Trinity. *Faith and Philosophy* 22:57–76.

Cross, Richard. 2005a. *Duns Scotus on God. Ashgate Studies in the History of Philosophical Theology*. Aldershot, UK, and Burlington, VT: Ashgate.

———. 2005b. Relations and the Trinity: The Case of Henry of Ghent and Duns Scotus. *Documenti e studi sulla tradizione filosofica medievale* 16:1–21.

———. 2007. *Quid tres?* On What Precisely Augustine Professes Not to Understand in *De Trinitate* V and VII. *Harvard Theological Review* 100:215–32.

Dumont, Stephen D. 2005. Duns Scotus's Parisian Question on the Formal Distinction. *Vivarium* 43:7–62.

Duns Scotus, see John Duns Scotus.

Flores, Juan Carlos. 2006. *Henry of Ghent: Metaphysics and the Trinity*. Leuven, Belgium: Leuven University Press (Ancient and Medieval Philosophy: De Wulf-Mansion Centre, Series 1, 36).

Friedman, Russell L. 2010. *Medieval Trinitarian Thought from Aquinas to Ockham*. Cambridge and New York: Cambridge University Press.

Gregory of Nazianzus. 1978. *Discours 27–31 (Discours théologiques)*, ed. Paul Gallay. Paris: Editions du Cerf (Sources Chrétiennes, 250).

Gregory of Nyssa. 1958. *Opera dogmatica minora. Pars I*, ed. F. Mueller. Leiden, the Netherlands: Brill (Gregorii Nyesseni opera, 3/1).

Henninger, Mark G. 1989. *Relations: Medieval Theories 1250–1325*. Oxford: Clarendon Press.

Henry of Ghent. 1520. *Summa quaestionum ordinariarum*. 2 vols. Paris.

John Duns Scotus. 1639. *Opera omnia*, ed. L. Wadding. 12 vols. Lyons.

———. 1950. *Ordinatio. Liber primus. Distinctio prima et secunda*, ed. C. Balić et al. Vatican City: Vatican Polyglot Press (Ioannis Duns Scoti opera omnia, 2).

———. 1956. *Ordinatio. Liber primus. A distinctione quarta ad decimam*, ed. C. Balić et al. Vatican City: Vatican Polyglot Press (Ioannis Duns Scotus opera omnia, 4).

———. 1959. *Ordinatio. Liber primus. A distinctione undecima ad vigesimam quintam*, ed. C. Balić et al. Vatican City: Vatican Polyglot Press (Ioannis Duns Scoti opera omnia, 5).

———. 1960. *Lectura in librum primum sententiarum. Prologus et distinctiones a prima ad septimam*, ed. C. Balić et al. Vatican City: Vatican Polyglot Press (Ioannis Duns Scoti opera omnia, 16).

———. 1973. *Ordinatio. Liber secundus. A distinctione prima ad tertiam*, ed. C. Balić et al. Vatican City: Vatican Polyglot Press (Ioannis Duns Scoti opera omnia, 7).

———. 2006. *Ordinatio. Liber tertius. A distinctione prima ad decimam septimam*, ed. B. Hechich et al. Vatican City: Vatican Press (Ioannis Duns Scoti opera omnia, 9).

———. 2004–8. *The Examined Report of the Paris Lecture: Reportatio I-A*, ed. Allan B. Wolter and Oleg V. Bychkov. 2 vols. St Bonaventure, NY: Franciscan Institute Publications.

John of Damascus. 1955. *De fide orthodoxa*, ed. E. M. Buytaert. St Bonaventure: Franciscan Institute; Louvain, Belgium: E. Nauwelaerts; Paderborn, Germany: F. Schöningh (Franciscan Institute Publications, Text Series, 8).

———. 1973. *Die Schriften des Johannes von Damaskos, II: Expositio fidei*, ed. B. Kotter. Berlin and New York: de Gruyter (Patristische Texte und Studien, 12).

Marenbon, John. 2004. Abelard's Changing Thoughts on Sameness and Difference in Logic and Theology. *American Catholic Philosophical Quarterly* 81:229–50.

Martin, Christopher J. 2004. 'Formal consequence in Scotus and Ockham: Towards an account of Scotus' Logic'. In *Duns Scot à Paris: Actes du colloque de Paris, 2–4 Septembre 2002*, ed. Olivier Boulnois, Elizabeth Karger, Jean-Luc Solère and Gérard Sondag, 115–50. Turnhout, Belgium: Brepols (Textes et études du Moyen Age, 26).

Peter Abelard. 1969. *Opera theologica*, II, ed. E. M. Buytaert. Turnhout, Belgium: Brepols (Corpus christianorum continuatio mediaevalis, 12).

Rea, Michael C. 1998. Sameness without Identity: An Aristotelian Solution to the Problem of Material Constitution. *Ratio* 11:316–28.

Richard of St Victor. 1958. *De trinitate*, ed. Jean Ribaillier. Paris: Vrin (Textes philosophiques du moyen âge, 6).

Thomas Aquinas. 1929–47. *Scriptum super libros sententiarum*, ed. P. Mandonnet and M. F. Moos. 4 vols. Paris: Lethielleux.

———. 1952–6. *Summa theologiae*, ed. P. Caramello. 5 vols in 3. Turin and Rome: Marietti.

———. 1976. *De ente et essentia*. Rome: Editori di San Tommaso (Opera omnia, 43).

Tweedale, Martin M. 1984. Alexander of Aphrodisias' Views on Universals. *Phronesis* 29:279–303.

———. 1999. *Scotus vs. Ockham: A Medieval Dispute over Universals*. 2 vols. Lampeter, UK: Edwin Mellen Press.

Wolfson, Harry Austryn. 1970. *The Philosophy of the Church Fathers: Vol. 1. Faith, Trinity, Incarnation*. 3rd edition. Cambridge, MA: Harvard University Press.

INDEX

....

This Index contains both subject and name entries. Arabic and Jewish names are indexed under the usual final element of their names (e.g. al-Baghdādī; Ibn Daud), except where a widely-used Latin name exists (e.g. Avicenna, Gersonides). Ancient Greek writers are indexed under their usual names in English; medieval Greek writers under their Christian names if they are known as 'X of Y' (e.g. George of Trebizond), but otherwise under their second names. Latin writers working before c. 1500 are indexed under their Christian names, but this criterion is applied flexibly, so that some earlier writers who are always known by their second names (e.g. Boccaccio, Ficino) or by a cognomen (e.g. Bonaventure) are indexed under them. Writers after 1500 are indexed under their second names.

Boethius of Dacia 152, 198, 212
Commentary on *Topics* 204
Bolzano, Bernard 246, 289, 435
Bonaventure 201, 208–10, 213, 247
Boniface VIII, Pope 646
books, production of 199
Book of Causes: see *Liber de causis*
Book on the Pure Good 27, 76, 132–33
Bourdieu, Pierre 676
Bracciolini, Poggio 227–28
Bradley, F. H. 439
Bradley's Regress 435
Brentano, Franz 432
Brower, Jeffrey and Michael C. Rea
'Material Constitution and the Trinity' 707,
711–12, 718
Bruno, Giordano 662
Bukhara 84
Burgundio of Pisa 167
Burke, Edmund 651
Busembaum, Hermann
Medulla 248

Cajetan, Cardinal (Thomas de Vio) 230, 232
Commentary on Aquinas, *Summa Theologiae* 234
Calcidius
Commentary on *Timaeus* 21, 183, 534
Calov, Abraham 251
Campbell, Keith 390
Cantor, Georg 246, 689
Capabilities Approach 630–32
Capreolus: see John Capreolus
Carmelites 200
Carnap, Rudolf 313
Carruthers, Peter 378
Cassiodorus
Institutiones 168
Cassmann, Otto 251
casuistry 252
Categoriae decem 168
categories 252
categorical ontology 166–67
eleventh category (*predicamentum enuntia-bilium*) 428
reduced to substance and quality 212
ten categories 24, 72, 166
division into rejected 228
see also: God, and the Aristotelian categories
cathedral schools 169
Caubraith, Robert
Quadrupertitum 226
cause 26
efficient 114, 156, 318, 577, 580–81, 699, 723
everything has a 37
exemplary causality 388–89
of existence 133
First Cause, the 113
see also: God
final 25, 37, 114, 628, 640, 699

first causes and principles 88–89
formal 571–72, 636, 668
free 577
material 156
mental causation 508
necessary 577, 581
occasionalist theories of causation 540
pre-eminent 699
Procession of Son and Holy Spirit as causal or
not 723–25
causal reality is limited to natural reality 697
causal theory of reference: see reference, causal
theory of
substantial forms as 491–92
see also: determinism, causal
eternity, as causal primacy
censorship 250
Chakrabati, Arindam 385
Chalcedonian Creed 532
Chaldaean Oracles 229
change
accidental: 488
and see substance, substantial change
Chappell, Vere 479
charity: see love
Charlemagne 169
Charles the Bald 169
Chartres 169
School of 170, 185–86
chimera 325
choice 60–61, 137, 156, 158–59, 163, 252, 569, 576,
629
Choumnos, Nikephoras 36, 42, 46–49
Christ, Jesus: see Trinity, the Son
Chrysoloras, Manuel 227
Church
relationship between Eastern and Western 35
227, 18, 21, 589, 652, 655–56
Academica 548, 559
De inventione 21, 657
De legibus 656–57
De natura deorum 657
De officiis 654–55, 658–59
Disputationes Tusculanae 657
Somnium Scipionis 35
Topica 21, 292–93
citizenship 644
Clauberg, Johannes 254
Cleomedes 48
clerical status 198
cognition 547–62, 668
abstractive 212
intuitive 212
transparency thesis 550
and the Trinity 706
collationes 202–3
Cologne, Dominican *studium* at 200
commentary, as a genre 167
types of 204

CPSIA information can be obtained at www.ICGtesting.com
Printed in the USA
BVOW09s0914231115

427831BV00026B/25/P

9 780190 246976